HANDBOOK
of
ETHNOGRAPHY

International Editorial Board

HANDBOOK
of
ETHNOGRAPHY

Edited by

Paul Atkinson, Amanda Coffey, Sara Delamont,
John Lofland and Lyn Lofland

SAGE Publications
London • Thousand Oaks • New Delhi

SAGE Publications Ltd
6 Bonhill Street
London EC2A 4PU

SAGE Publications Inc
2455 Teller Road
Thousand Oaks, California 91320

SAGE Publications India Pvt Ltd
32, M-Block Market
Greater Kailash - I
New Delhi 110 048

British Library Cataloguing in Publication data

A catalogue record for this book is available from the British Library

ISBN 0 7619 6480 0
ISBN 0 7619 6481 9 (pbk)

Library of Congress catalog record available

Typeset by SIVA Math Setters, Chennai, India
Printed in Great Britain by The Cromwell Press Ltd, Trowbridge, Wiltshire

Contents

Notes on Contributors

Paul Atkinson is Professor of Sociology at Cardiff University, UK. He has conducted and directed ethnographic research in medical, educational and cultural settings. His publications include *The Ethnographic Imagination* (1990), *Medical Talk and Medical Work* (1995), *Making Sense of Qualitative Data* (with Amanda Coffey, 1996) and *Ethnography: Principles in Practice* (with Martyn Hammersley, 2nd edition 1995).

Mike Ball is Senior Lecturer in Anthropology and Sociology at Staffordshire University, UK. His teaching and research interests are in interactional analysis, research methods and ethnomethodology. He has published extensively on the analysis of visual data. He is co-author of *Analyzing Visual Data* (1992), organizing editor for a special edition of the journal *Communication and Cognition* entitled 'Studies in Visual Analysis', and a contributor to Jon Prosser's edited collection, *Image-Based Research* (1998).

Michael Bloor has a personal chair in the School of Social Sciences at Cardiff University, UK. He is Director of the Health and Social Care Research Support Unit and has just begun a part-time secondment to Cardiff's Seafarers International Research Centre to plan and conduct a five-year programme of research on seafarers' occupational health and safety. His most recent books are *Selected Writings in Medical Sociological Research* (1997) and *Sociology of HIV Transmission* (1995). He has conducted ethnographic work in outpatient clinics, therapeutic communities and a common lodging house, and has undertaken a street ethnography of male prostitution.

Lodewijk Brunt is Professor of Urban Studies at the University of Amsterdam, The Netherlands. In recent years he has been conducting fieldwork both in India and Scotland and he is interested in matters of time – the use and meaning of public and private time schedules. He is the editor-in-chief of the Dutch *Sociologische Gids* and the European editor of the *Journal of Contemporary Ethnography*. He is preparing a book on the comparative analysis of Bombay, Glasgow and Amsterdam.

Kathy Charmaz is Professor of Sociology and Co-ordinator of the Faculty Writing Program at Sonoma State University, USA. She assists faculty in writing for publication and teaches in the areas of sociological theory, social psychology, qualitative methods, health and illness and ageing and dying. Her books include two recent co-edited volumes, *The Unknown Country: Death in Australia, Britain* *and the USA* (1997) and *Health, Illness, and Healing: Society, Social Context and Self* (1999). She is the author of *Good Days, Bad Days: The Self in Chronic Illness and Time* (1999), which won awards from the Society for the Study of Symbolic Interaction and the Pacific Sociological Association. Dr Charmaz currently serves as president of the Pacific Sociological Association and as editor of *Symbolic Interaction*.

Amanda Coffey is Lecturer in Sociology in the School of Social Sciences, Cardiff University, UK. Her doctoral research was an ethnographic study of occupational socialization among trainee accountants. Her publications include *The Ethnographic Self, Making Sense of Qualitative Data* (1999), and *Feminism and the Classroom Teacher* (2000). Her recent research includes work on young people and citizenship. She is one of the founding editors of the journal *Qualitative Research*.

Martin Cortazzi is Professor of Education at Brunel University, UK, where he supervises doctoral candidates and teaches on Teacher Education programmes. He specializes in Language Education and the Teaching of English to Speakers of Other Languages (TESOL). He is a Visiting Professor in China at Nankai, Renmin and Hubei Universities. His publications are in the areas of narrative analysis, discourse, cultural aspects of learning, and primary education. Recently his research has focused on language learning in East and Southeast Asia and in the Middle East.

Mary Jo Deegan is Professor of Sociology at the University of Nebraska-Lincoln, USA. She specializes in classical and contemporary theory, history of sociology and qualitative methods. She is the author of more than 100 articles and has written or edited twelve books, including *Jane Addams and the Men of the Chicago School, 1892–1918* (1988), *Women in Sociology* (1991), and introductions to edited books by Charlotte Perkins Gilman (*With Her in Ourland*, 1997 and by George Herbert Mead (*Play, School, and Society,* 1999, and *Essays on Social Psychology).*

Sara Delamont is Reader in Sociology at Cardiff University, UK. She has a first degree in Social Anthropology and a PhD in educational sociology. She is the author of ten books, including *Knowledgeable Women* (1989), *Fighting Familiarity* (1995) and *The Doctoral Experience* (2000), is the editor of ten others, and has published more than fifty papers. She was the first woman president of the British Education Research Association, and was the first European Associate Editor of *Teaching and Teacher Education*.

Robert Dingwall is Professor of Sociology in the School of Sociology and Social Policy and Director of the Institute for the Study of Biorisks and Society at the University of Nottingham, UK. His career has spanned both medical sociology, which was the field of his PhD from the University of Aberdeen, and sociology of law, through his work at Oxford University. These are united by a general interest in professions, work, organizations and interaction. He is currently completing a programme of work on divorce mediation and developing new research on genetics and society issues.

Robert M. Emerson is Professor of Sociology at the University of California, Los Angeles, USA. From 1983 to 1986 he served as editor of the ethnographic journal, *Urban Life*. His publications on ethnographic and field research methods include an edited collection of readings on ethnography, *Contemporary Field Research* (second edition, 2000), *Writing Ethnographic Fieldnotes* (1995), co-authored, with Rachel I. Fretz and Linda L. Shaw. Substantively his work uses qualitative methods to analyse both decision-making practices in institutions of social control, including juvenile courts, psychiatric emergency teams, public schools and prosecutors' offices, and the dynamics of interpersonal troubles and informal social control. He is currently engaged in a study of family caregiving for persons with Alzheimer's disease.

James D. Faubion is Associate Professor of Anthropology at Rice University in Houston, Texas, USA. His special interests include ancient and modern Greece, social thought, social and cultural movements, and millennialism. He is the author of *Modern Greek Lessons: A Primer in Historical Constructivism* (1993); and editor of *Rethinking the Subject: An Anthology of Contemporary European Social Thought* (1995), and *Essential Works of Michel Foucault, Volume 2: Aesthetics, Method, and Epistemology* (1998), and *Essential Works of Michel Foucault, Volume 3: Power* (2000).

Nigel Fielding is Professor of Sociology and co-Director of the Institute of Social Research at the University of Surrey, UK. His research interests are in qualitative methods, policing and new research technologies. Amongst his publications are *Using Computers in Qualitative Research* (1991, with R.M. Lee), and *Computer Analysis and Qualitative Research* (1998, with R.M. Lee), which draws on the first field research in the world on how researchers use qualitative software. He is a member of the editorial boards of *Qualitative Inquiry, The Howard Journal of Criminal Justice. Forum Qualitative Sozialforschung/Forum for Qualitative Social Research*, and the Sage/SRM-Database for Social Research Methodology. He is currently co-Director of the CAQDAS Networking Project, the UK's national centre for qualitative software, and co-editor of the New Technologies for Social Research book series (Sage).

Gary Alan Fine is Professor of Sociology at Northwestern University, USA. He received his PhD in Social Psychology at Harvard. He is author of several books grounded in ethnographic research, including *With the Boys: Little League Baseball and Preadolescent Culture* (1987), *Morel Tales: The Culture of Mushrooming* (1998), and *Kitchens: The Culture of Restaurant Work* (1996). His current research is a study of the development of the market in self-taught art.

Rachel I. Fretz is a folklorist who teaches qualitative research and writing in the Writing Programs at the University of California, Los Angeles, USA. She specializes in ethnographic research, narrative enquiry and the rhetoric of representation; her publications on African narrations draw on her extensive field research among the Chokwe peoples of the Congo (Zaire) and Zambia. She co-authored, along with Robert M. Emerson and Linda L. Shaw, *Writing Ethnographic Fieldnotes* (1995).

Tuula Gordon is Professor of Women's Studies and Social Sciences in the Department of Women's Studies, University of Tampere, Finland. With a team including Janet Holland and Elina Lahelma, she has conducted a collaborative, comparative, cross-cultural ethnographic study, which they have published with Macmillan as *Making Spaces: Citizenship and Difference in Schools*. Tuula is author of *Feminist Mothers* (1990): *Single Women on the Margins* (1994) and *Democracy in One School? Progressive Education and Restructuring* (1986), and co-editor of *Unresolved Dilemmas: Women, Work and the Family in the United States, Europe and the Former Soviet Union* (1997).

David Hess, is a cultural/medical anthropologist and Professor of Science and Technology Studies at Rensselaer Polytechnic Institute, USA. He is the author of ten books on science and the public, including theoretical books in the sociology and anthropology of science, technology and medicine, such as *Science and Technology in a Multicultural World*. His current research includes a book on the controversial research tradition on bacteria as possible agents in cancer causation (*Can Bacteria Cause Cancer?*), a book of interviews with women opinion leaders who used alternative/complementary cancer therapies (*Women Confront Cancer*, with Margaret Wooddell), and a book on the evaluation problem and the politics of methodology for alternative cancer therapies (*Evaluating Alternative Cancer Therapies*).

Barbara Sherman Heyl is Professor in the Department of Sociology and Anthropology at Illinois State University, USA. She was educated in Sociology at Stanford University (AB) and the University of Illinois, Urbana–Champaign (PhD). She has served as President of the Midwest Sociological Society. Her past research on prostitution utilized both life history and ethnographic interviewing and appeared as *The Madam as Entrepreneur* (1979); a new paperback edition is in preparation. Her recent research involves a longitudinal, qualitative study of special education in Germany, published both in Spain and the United Kingdom, and includes 'Parents, politics, and the public purse: activists in the special education arena in Germany' in *Disability and Society* (1988).

Dick Hobbs is Professor of Sociology at the University of Durham, UK. His research interests are deviance, working-class entrepreneurship, professional and organized crime, and crime and social order in the context of the night-time economy. His publications include *Doing the Business: Entrepreneurship, the Working Class and Detectives in the East End of London* (1988), and *Bad Business: Professional Crime in Modern Britain*. With Tim May he edited *Interpreting the Field: Accounts of Ethnography* (1993).

Janet Holland is Professor of Social Research and Director of the Social Sciences Research Centre, South Bank University, London, UK. With a team including Tuula Gordon and Elina Lahelma, she has conducted a collaborative, comparative, cross-cultural ethnographic study, which they have published with Macmillan as *Making Spaces: Citizenship and Difference in Schools* (2000). She is co-author of *The Male in the Head* (1998), and co-editor of *Sex, Sensibility and the Gendered Body* (1996);

Sexual Cultures: Debates and Issues in Feminist Research and Pedagogy (1995) and *Identity and Diversity: Gender and the Experience of Education* (1995).

Allison James is Reader in Applied Anthropology at the University of Hull, UK, where she is also currently Director of the Centre for the Social Study of Childhood. Her main research interests are in childhood, ageing, health and the life course. Her most recent publications are *Childhood Identities* (1993); *Growing Up and Growing Old* (with J. Hockey, 1993) and *Theorizing Childhood* (with C. Jenks and A. Prout, 1998). She is currently researching children's perception and understandings of time (with P. Christensen and C. Jenks) on a project funded under the ESRC Children 5–16 research programme.

Elizabeth Keating is Assistant Professor of Anthropology at the University of Texas at Austin, USA. She received her PhD from the University of California, Los Angeles. Her research interests include: the role of language and other semiotic systems in the construction of social hierarchies, specialized language registers, relationships between language and space, language and gender, and influences of technology on communicative practices. She has conducted fieldwork in Pohnpei, Micronesia, and has investigated computer-mediated videotelephonic communication between deaf and hearing callers in Texas. Her publications include *Power Sharing: Language, Rank, Gender and Social Space in Pohnpei, Micronesia* (1998), as well as articles on the uses of language in the construction of social stratification and gender categories.

Elina Lahelma is Lecturer in Education at the University of Helsinki, Finland. She is currently working as a Senior Fellow at the Academy of Finland. With a team including Tuula Gordon and Janet Holland, she has conducted a collaborative, comparative, cross-cultural ethnographic study, which they have published with Macmillan as *Making Spaces: Citizenship and Difference in School* (2000). She has written extensively on gender and education.

Patti Lather is a Professor in the School of Educational Policy and Leadership at Ohio State University, USA, where she teaches qualitative research in education and gender and education. Her work includes *Getting Smart: Feminist Research and Pedagogy with/in the Postmodern* (1991) and, with Chris Smithies, *Troubling the Angels: Women Living with HIV/AIDS* (1997). She is presently working on a manuscript, *Getting Lost: Feminist Efforts toward a Double(d) Science*. Her favourite academic achievements thus far are a 1995 sabbatical appointment, Humanities Research Institute, University of California-Irvine, seminar on feminist research methodology and a 1997 visiting appointment at Goteborg University in Sweden. Her hobby aspiration is to learn to play the accordion.

John Lofland is Professor Emeritus of Sociology at the University of California, Davis, USA. His book-length ethnographies include *Doomsday Cult* (1966, 1977), *Symbolic Sit-ins* (1985), *Polite Protesters* (1993) and *Old North Davis* (1999). Founding editor of *The Journal of Contemporary Ethnography*, he has served as

President of the Pacific Sociological Association and the Society for the Study of Symbolic Interaction and as Chair of the American Sociological Association's sections on Collective Behavior and Social Movements and the Sociology of War and Peace. He is a recipient of the Society for Symbolic Interaction's George Herbert Mead Award for outstanding career contributions to the study of human behaviour and social life. His most recent work focuses on the sociology of local history and historic preservation, one report of which is (with Phyllis Haig) *Davis, California, 1910s–1940s* (2000).

Lyn Lofland is Professor and former Chair of Sociology at the University of California, Davis, USA. Her publications include *A World of Strangers* (1973), *The Craft of Dying* (1978, with John Lofland), *Analyzing Social Settings* (1983, 1995) *The Community of the Streets* (edited with Spencer Cahill) (1994) and *The Public Realm* (1998). She has served as President of the Pacific Sociological Association and the Society for the Study of Symbolic Interaction and as Chair of the American Sociological Association's section on Community and Urban Sociology. In 1995 she received from that section the Robert & Helen Lynd Award for lifetime contributions to the study of human settlements. Her current research focuses on the occupational role and culture of the land developer.

Sharon Macdonald is Senior Lecturer in Social Anthropology and Sociology at the University of Sheffield, UK. She was trained as a Social Anthropologist at Oxford University; and has carried out ethnographic fieldwork in the Scottish Hebrides, the Science Museum, London, and currently in Bavaria, Germany. Her publications include *Inside European Identities: Ethnography in Western Europe* (ed. 1993), *Reimagining Culture: Histories, Identities and the Gaelic Renaissance* (1997) and *The Politics of Display: Museums, Science, Culture* (1998). She also edits *The Sociological Review*.

Peter K. Manning took his PhD from Duke University, USA. He is Professor of Sociology and Criminal Justice at Michigan State University, USA. He has been a Fellow of Wolfson and Balliol Colleges, Oxford and of the Oxford Centre for Socio-Legal Studies. Recent publications include a second edition of *Police Work* and (with Brian Forst) *Privatization of Policing: Two Views* (1999) and the forthcoming *Managing Contingencies: A Communicational Theory of Policing*. His current research includes fieldwork on community policing, the rationalization of policing with emphasis on the role of information technology, and legal decision-making.

Julie Marcus is Professor of Social Anthropology and a member of the Centre for Cultural Risk Research at the Bathurst campus of Charles Sturt University, Australia. Her doctoral research was carried out in Turkey and described the impact of Islam on daily life in a large Turkish city. Most recently she has carried out research into racism, policing and gender in Australian culture and for the past decade has worked in and around Alice Springs in central Australia. She is the author of *A World of Difference*: *Islam and Gender Hierarchy in Turkey* (1992), *First in Their Field: Women and Australian Anthropology* (1993), *A Dark Smudge Upon the Sand: Essays on Race, History and the National Consciousness* and

Yours Truly, Olive M. Pink. Professor Marcus is currently working on a history of anthropology and land ownership in Alice Springs, a full-length biography of the anthropologist Olive M. Pink, and is preparing a volume of essays on secrecy and surveillance in Australian culture today.

Ilja Maso is Professor of Philosophy of Science, Methodology and the Theory of Research at the University for Humanist Studies, Utrecht, The Netherlands, and Visiting Professor of Qualitative Research at the Catholic University of Leuven, Belgium. He has published books and articles on empirical phenomenology, ethnomethodology, qualitative research, everyday explanation, 'method and truth', scientific fundamentalism, meaningful research, dreaming, coincidence and panpsychism. His last three books, in Dutch, were *The Meaning of Coincidence* (1997), *Qualitative Research: Practice and Theory* (1998, with A. Smaling) and the texts of *The Atlas of the World of Experience* (1999, with S. Sombeek).

Jim Mienczakowski is Foundation Dean of the Faculty of Education and Creative Arts, Central Queensland University and Dean of the Central Queensland Conservatorium of Music, Australia. His construct of critical ethnodrama has evolved into a new and important form of ethnographic practice for arts and education practitioners. Current research focuses on the emotional trauma of cosmetic surgery, trajectories of recovery from sexual assault and includes submissions to State Government Social Impact reports affecting community change. As an invited expert witness, he provided testimony for the 1999 HCCC report into cosmetic surgery, and he currently serves on an advisory group which assesses health promotional theatre involving issues of youth suicide.

Richard G. Mitchell is a Professor of Sociology in his twentieth year of teaching at Oregon State University. He is an ethnographer with interests in avocational risk-adventure and professional ethics, and has written books in each of these areas. For the past decade he has been studying separatist, segregationist and millennial social movements. His PhD is from the University of Southern California, and his current avocations are sea kayaking and mountaineering.

Elizabeth Murphy is Senior Lecturer in the School of Sociology and Social Policy at the University of Nottingham, UK. Her major research interests are in medical sociology and the sociology of food. Her PhD, from the University of Southampton, related the health concepts of people with diabetes to their response to lifestyle advice. These interests have been further developed in relation to other clinical areas. More recently, she carried out a longitudinal study of mothers' choice about infant feeding, with particular reference to response to professional advice. She has also directed a review of the application of qualitative methods to health research.

Ken Plummer is Professor of Sociology at the University of Essex, UK. His main research interests focus upon story tellings, humanistic theory (especially symbolic interactionism), sexuality and the politics and morality of 'intimacies'. He has written numerous articles and authored or edited some ten books including

Sexual Stigma (1975), *The Making of the Modern Homosexual* (ed., 1981) and *Telling Sexual Stories* (1995). His book *Documents of Life* (1983) has recently been published by Sage in a second edition (2000). Currently he is working on a study provisionally called 'Intimate Citizenship'. He is the founder editor of the journal *Sexualities*.

Melvin Pollner is Professor in the Department of Sociology at the University of California, Los Angeles, USA. His research interests include the construction of the self and foundational issues in interpretive and qualitative sociology, especially ethnomethodology. He has conducted research on a variety of psychiatric and legal settings and is currently examining the construction of community on the Web and stock market investment decisions. His current research examines the interpenetration of the Web and financial markets. His publications include *Mundane Reason: Reality in Everyday and Sociological Discourse* (1987).

Deborah Reed-Danahay is Associate Professor of Anthropology and Director of the Anthropology Program at the University Texas at Arlington, USA. She is author of *Education and Identity in Rural France: The Politics of Schooling* (1996) and editor of *Auto Ethnography: Rewriting the Self and the Social* (1997). She is interested in education, childhood and youth, and constructions of agency and identity. Most of her fieldwork has been conducted in rural France, although she has also completed an ethnography of Alzheimer's care in the United States. Current projects include the study of rural French memoirs, and an ethnographic study of new constructions of identity in the educational policies and projects of the European Union.

Paul Rock is Professor of Social Institutions at the London School of Economics and Political Science, UK. He took his first degree at the LSE and then a DPhil at Nuffield College, University of Oxford. He has been a Visiting Professor at the University of California, San Diego; Simon Fraser University; the University of British Colombia and Princeton University; a Visiting Scholar at the Ministry of the Solicitor General of Canada; and a Fellow of the Center for the Advanced Study of the Behavioral Sciences in Stanford, California. His interests focus on the development of criminal justice policies, particularly for victims of crime, but he has also published articles on criminological theory and the history of crime. His most recent books include *The Social World of an English Crown Court* (1993); *Reconstructing a Women's Prison* (1996); *After Homicide: Practical and Political Responses to Bereavement* (1998) and (with David Downes) *Understanding Deviance* (fourth edition, 1998).

Linda L. Shaw is an Associate Professor of Sociology at California State University, San Marcos, USA. Her interests focus on the impact of social welfare policy on the everyday lives of the poor and marginalized groups. She has published in the area of community care for chronic mental patients and co-authored *Writing Fieldnotes* with Robert M. Emerson and Rachel I. Fretz (1995). She is currently using qualitative methods to analyse the impact of welfare reform on the everyday lives of recipients of public assistance.

Beverley Skeggs is Professor of Sociology at Manchester University, UK. She was Co-director of the Centre for Women's Studies at Lancaster University from 1993 to 1997. Her books include *Formations of Class and Gender, Issues in Sociology: The Media* (with J. Mundy) (1997) and she has edited *Feminist Cultural Theory* and *Transformations in Feminist Theory*. She has also written on issues of popular culture, 'race', postmodernism, education, cultural studies and space. She is presently working on an ESRC funded project on 'Violence, Sexuality and Space'.

Greg Smith is Senior Lecturer in Sociology at the University of Salford, UK. His teaching and research interests are in ethnographic and interaction sociology and sociological and cultural theory. He is co-author of *Analyzing Visual Data* (1992) and *Introducing Cultural Studies* (1999). He has published on the sociology of Erving Goffman, most recently as editor of *Goffman and Social Organization: Studies in a Sociological Legacy* (1999).

Vicki Smith is Professor of Sociology at the University of California, Davis, USA. She took her PhD from the University of California, Berkeley. Her dissertation research at Berkeley led to her first book *Managing in the Corporate Interest: Control and Resistance in an American Bank* (1990) about the impact of corporate restructuring at the Bank of America on middle managers' jobs and social relations. Her subsequent research has focused on published a number of journal articles based on that research. Her forthcoming book (Spring 2001), *Crossing The Great Divide: Worker Risk and Opportunity in The New Economy*, uses organizational case study research to compare the experiences and aspirations of American workers as they encounter new forms of work and employment.

Jonathan Spencer is Professor of the Anthropology of South Asia and Director of the Graduate School of Social and Political Studies at the University of Edinburgh, UK. He is the author of *A Sinhala Village in a Time of Trouble* (1990) and co-editor (with Alan Barnard) of the *Encyclopedia of Social and Cultural Anthropology* (1996).

Liz Stanley is Professor of Sociology and Director of Women's Studies at the University of Manchester, UK, and still thinks that 'Doctor' is the only academic title worth having. Her research and writing interests are concerned with 'auto/ biography', radical sociology and feminist epistemology; in the rest of her life, she enjoys the 'earthly pleasures' that Colette evokes so wonderfully.

Christopher Tilley is Professor of Material Culture in the Department of Anthropology and Institute of Archaeology, University College London, UK. Recent publications include *Metaphor and Material Culture* (1999), *An Ethnography of the Neolithic* (1996) and *A Phenomenology of Landscape* (1994). His current research interests are in landscape and representation in the UK and in material forms and the politics of identity in the South Pacific.

Joost Van Loon is a senior lecturer in Social Theory at the Department of English and Media Studies of the Nottingham Trent University, UK, where he is associated with the Theory Culture and Society Centre. He has published extensively in the areas of culture, post-structuralism, mass media, technology and risk, including *The Risk Society and Beyond: Critical Issues for Social Theory* (co-edited with Barbara Adam and Ulrich Beck) (2000). He is also co-editor of the journal *Space and Culture*. His current research interests are focused on newly emergent viruses and epidemic-risk management.

Christopher Wellin holds a PhD in Sociology from Northwestern University, USA where he also served as lecturer. Currently, he is a post-doctoral fellow at the Institute for Health and Aging, University of California, San Francisco, USA. Among his interests are the sociology of work/occupations, field methods and institutional care (particularly for the aged and chronically ill). His ethnographic studies of the organization of work, authority and careers range across multiple settings, including group homes for the aged, theatre and stage craft, and industrial work. He is revising his dissertation – a multi-year case study of shop floor knowledge and managerial rhetorics in the transition to computer-automation in a factory – for expected publication by Cornell University/ILR Press.

Editorial Introduction

MAPPING ETHNOGRAPHIC DIVERSITY

The chapters that follow this introduction are intended to provide the reader with a *tour d'horizon* of ethnographic methods and ethnographic research in the social sciences. As with any exercise of this scope, it is an ambitious undertaking. Attempts to generate a comprehensive and authoritative volume on most aspects of the social sciences are ultimately doomed to failure. The field is too broad and diffuse: it escapes the neat categorizations that are demanded by encyclopaedic treatments. Moreover, the intellectual terrain is normally contested: authority and tradition are constantly undermined. It is inevitable that the coverage will be incomplete, and that treatments of its subject matter will be matters of debate. Our topic – the conduct and conceptualization of ethnographic fieldwork – is especially subject to such constraints and contradictions. So the commission to edit a Handbook of Ethnography is a well-nigh impossible task. Although it has been a feature of social science research through most of the twentieth century, and has become pervasive across a wide range of disciplinary applications, ethnography escapes ready summary definitions. In recent years, indeed, it has become a site of debate and contestation within and across disciplinary boundaries.

This volume is not definitive in the sense of defining its subject matter, nor in the sense of excluding other interpretations. It is, however, *authoritative* in that we chose contributors who are leading scholars. We encouraged our contributors to interpret the topics we assigned to them with some degree of latitude. We certainly did not set them the task of mechanistically 'reviewing the literature'. A handbook such as this one cannot serve the long-term interests of the research community if it is little more than a series of annotated bibliographies. Such exercises become rapidly out of date and divert attention from the longer-term perspectives and intellectual antecedents of a field. There are few if any genres of scholarly writing that are less life-enhancing than the literature review. Of course, we have asked our authors to provide adequate guidance to our readers about the range of published literature, but we have

not judged authors or chapters, and do not want them to be judged by others, as if they were sterile exercises in reviewing *the* literature. Our intention was something much more intellectually engaging than that. The resultant contributions more than fulfil that expectation.

International excellence was our primary criterion in selecting our authors, and our plans for the volume were always international in scope. When they had written for us we gave their work to referees who are equally distinguished and also drawn from an international pool of expertise. The actual volume, therefore, is the result of the interactions between those authors and their peers. We did not seek to impose on those distinguished authors too tight a specification of how they were to write each chapter. Having identified for our own editorial purposes the desirable range of material a volume such as this ought to cover, and having sketched out a broad summary of contents, we have trusted the judgement of each author to interpret those themes. We have, therefore, granted licence to our contributing authors to exercise their own expertise in tackling the various chapter topics we laid before them. No treatment of such a complex and potentially contested set of topics can ever claim to be comprehensive. Each chapter could alone sustain a multiplicity of different interpretations, and we could multiply the examples, selections of literature to be reviewed, and so on more or less indefinitely. For these reasons we have not sought to impose our own prescriptive models and definitions in the editorial process. We do not think it a good idea to empanel an array of international experts, encourage them to exercise their own judgement, and then steal their thunder by editorial fiat. For these reasons, too, we have resisted any temptation to offer our own canonical definitions or justifications of ethnographic research. We ourselves have been suspicious of various attempts to tidy up the history of ethnographic research either through the imposition of 'traditions' or through the construction of historical schemas or periodizations. In particular, we have explicitly avoided any typology or developmental schema for ethnography which assumes a linear model of progress, or tries to erect 'pure' categories. That is, we explicitly eschew the five (six) moments model of Lincoln and Denzin (1994) or the typologies of authors like Jacob (1987) or Leininger (1992). They can serve useful pedagogical functions, but can ultimately do violence to the complexities of research and its historical development. Hence we see little point in trying to generate a definitive list of the core characteristics of ethnography as an approach to social research, or to tie it to restricted disciplinary allegiances. In compiling this collection, therefore, we have operated with a broad definition of ethnography. We have deliberately commissioned chapters that display its deep and diverse roots, its wide-ranging methods, and its many applications. We are not interested in trying to define a canon. Moreover, we have outlined many of our own views and perceptions elsewhere, and we do not recapitulate those contributions here (Atkinson, Coffey and Delamont, 1999; Coffey, 1999; Coffey and Atkinson, 1996; Delamont, 2001; Delamont, Coffey and Atkinson, 2000; Hammersley and Atkinson, 1995; Lofland and Lofland, 1995).

There are, of course, broad family resemblances between the various methods and applications that have characterized ethnographic research over the years. Its centrality to social or cultural anthropology is unquestionable. Indeed, when anthropologists seek the defining characteristic of their own discipline, they more often than not cite the centrality of ethnographic fieldwork. Likewise, they recognize that the conduct of ethnographic work provides a special biographical and intellectual experience that is the touchstone of being an anthropologist. Anthropologists no longer define their research sites or 'fields' exclusively in terms of exotic cultures and distant places. Anthropologists have been and are continuing to explore cultural settings closer to 'home'. One no longer has to travel a great physical distance in order to encounter cultural and social difference or to engage in the *rite de passage* that is anthropological fieldwork (Amit, 2000; Delamont, Atkinson and Parry, 2000). Although there are increasing convergences between the subject matter of anthropologists and sociologists, their commitments to ethnographic research are frequently celebrated in mutual isolation. Indeed, some anthropologists even manage to deny the existence of ethnographic field research outside their own disciplinary boundaries. Not only do they recognize its centrality to anthropology, they claim it as a unique attribute of that discipline. Despite all evidence to the contrary, some anthropologists will claim that sociologists and others all use surveys or other quantitative approaches, while they alone are committed to fieldwork (cf. Amit, 2000). Ironically, however, sociologists can lay claim to a heritage of ethnographic research that is just as venerable and just as central to some of its intellectual traditions. Urban sociology and the study of small communities in cities, towns and rural settings is almost a century old. The work that originated in and was inspired by the Chicago School of sociology in the United States can reasonably claim a pedigree of ethnographic research that is unbroken since the 1920s. Likewise, the closely related theoretical tradition of symbolic interactionism – again an American intellectual tendency – has a commitment to ethnographic work that spans the same period.

On these grounds, then, we cannot equate ethnography with only one disciplinary tradition. In this handbook we have deliberately and systematically placed anthropological and sociological perspectives alongside each other. We have commissioned chapters from both disciplines on historical and contextual issues, as well as on methodological topics. Chapters that focus on specific empirical areas also address disciplinary diversity. Too often ethnography is claimed by one or the other discipline, too often there is mutual ignorance and incomprehension. Here the 'two traditions' (Delamont and Atkinson, 1995) are irrevocably enmeshed and juxtaposed. Too often the history of ethnography is treated in rigid disciplinary and developmental frames. Ethnography, in our view, has never been the sole preserve of anthropology, nor of Chicago sociology, nor of symbolic interactionism, nor of any other interest group. Its various manifestations have always been marked by diversity. There has rarely been a single orthodoxy that has been so strongly dominant as to exclude all difference.

Contemporary ethnographic research is often characterized by fragmentation and diversity. There is certainly a carnivalesque profusion of methods, perspectives and theoretical justifications for ethnographic work. There are multiple methods of research, analysis and representation. It is tempting to see this profusion just as a symptom of a *fin de siècle* and of the postmodern condition. The narratives of contemporary metatheory (postmodern, post-structuralist, post-feminist, post-colonial and so on) all assume or describe one specific type of historical 'past' for ethnographic research methods. They outline a developmental trend that culminates in contemporary, fragmentary practices. Paradoxically, celebrations of the postmodern include their own grand narratives of intellectual history – while appearing to eschew such narrations. Moreover, such narratives can be unduly neglectful of past achievements that do not fit neatly into their developmental frameworks.

It is dangerously easy to assume that for a period of several decades, ethnographic research, notwithstanding subtle differences between disciplines and other intellectual contexts, was undertaken under the auspices of a stable orthodoxy. Ethnographies, in the dual sense of fieldwork and its textual products, can seem, in retrospect, to be governed by the assumptions of realist writing and an uncritical approach to data collection. Such a stable universe of methods and texts, gives way to a series of intellectual crises and a destabilization of the orthodoxy. Signalled by the publication of Clifford and Marcus' (1986) *Writing Culture*, the ethnographic text was perceived as undergoing a crisis of confidence. Previously the text, typically the monograph, recorded the central processes of fieldwork and was the most important product of qualitative research. After Clifford and Marcus, qualitative research took what is variously called the linguistic turn, or the interpretative turn, or the rhetorical turn or simply *the turn* – with its accompanying legitimation crisis. One consequence of the turn is an enhanced awareness of ethnographic writing (Atkinson, 1990, 1992, 1996; Atkinson and Coffey, 1995). Anthropologists, for instance, reflect upon fieldnotes: how they are constructed, used and managed. We come to understand that fieldnotes are not a closed, completed, final text: rather they are indeterminate, subject to reading, rereading, coding, recording, interpreting, reinterpreting. The literary turn has encouraged (or insisted) on the revisiting or reopening, of ethnographers' accounts and analyses of their fieldwork, notably in the work of Wolf (1992), Richardson (1990, 1992), Wolcott (1990) and the feminist responses to Clifford and Marcus such as the collections edited by Behar and Gordon (1995) and James et al. (1997). The representational crises of this period put in hazard not only the products of the ethnographer's work, but the moral and intellectual authority of ethnographers themselves. The 'crisis' was not founded merely in ethnographers' growing self-consciousness concerning their own literary work and its conventional forms. More fundamentally, it grew out of the growing contestation of ethnographers' (especially mainstream Western ethnographers') implicit claims to a privileged and totalizing gaze (Boon, 1982; Clifford, 1988). It led to increasingly urgent claims to legitimacy on the part of so-called indigenous ethnographers, and for increasingly complex relationships between ethnographers' selves, the selves of 'others' and the texts they both engage in (Coffey, 1999).

The dual crises of representation and legitimation form the new taken-for-granted. This is characterized by continuing diversity and a series of tensions. Lincoln and Denzin (1994: 581), for instance, characterize the present as 'a messy moment, multiple voices, experimental texts, breaks, ruptures, crises of legitimation and representation, self-critique, new moral discourses, and technologies'. They identify a field confronting a number of fundamental issues – a sustained critique of positivism and post-positivism, ongoing self-critique and self-appraisal, continuing crises of representation in our texts and authority we claim from them, an emergence of a 'cacophony of voices speaking with varying agendas' (Lincoln and Denzin, 1994: 409) and the growing influence of technology – which in turn are contributing to a constant redefinition of the field. This moment is also time for consolidation, and a sharpening of the critique of qualitative research, while attempting at the

same time to correct its excesses and to move on. As we have alluded to earlier, Denzin and Lincoln utilize their idea of moments or phases in the development of ethnography to speculate about the future (as they define it – the sixth moment(s)). They project a further multiplication of voices, styles, stories – and hence multiple futures for qualitative (ethnographic) research. The multiplicity of perspectives and practices in contemporary ethnography are not in doubt. Indeed, they are well rehearsed and documented (Atkinson and Silverman, 1997; Coffey and Atkinson, 1996; Ellis and Bochner, 1996). Ethnography can indeed be characterized in terms of its own cultural diversity. However, overly attributing this multiplicity to presents and futures glosses over the historical persistence of tension and differences. Contrasts between previous positivist, modernist and self-confident (but narrow) perspectives, and the contemporary carnivalesque diversity of standpoints, methods and representations, are often too sharply drawn. It both presents too orthodox a past and equally could be taken to imply that all contemporary qualitative research takes place from a position of an intellectual field teeming with contested ideas and experimental texts (see also Atkinson et al., 1988 for a critique of a different exercise in categorizing ethnographic research). We would suggest that a chronological, and linear view of development (such as the model offered by Lincoln and Denzin) is in danger of doing a disservice to earlier generations of ethnographers.

It is far from clear that there ever were monolithically 'positivist' and 'modernist' phases in the historical trajectory of qualitative research. It would be as wrong to assume that all ethnography in past generations was conducted under the auspices of a positivistic and totalizing gaze, as it is to imply that we are all 'postmodern' now. We would wish to take issue with the narrow view that there was ever a traditional, hegemonic ethnographic order – 'that order that insists on marginalizing the new, not treating it as a version of a new order of things, and always defining it as an aberrant variation on the traditional way of doing things' (Denzin, 1997: 251). Nor would we want to suggest that 'new', so-called experimental forms of ethnography or messy texts are wrong or irrelevant. Our point is much less profound. Over the development of ethnography there has been a repeated dialectic between what might be thought of as a dominant orthodoxy, and other, centrifugal forces that have promoted difference and diversity. There is, for instance, little need to appeal only to recent developments in ethnographic writing and commentary as evidence of 'blurred genres'. Relationships between the aesthetic and the scientific, or between the positive and interpretivist have been detectable for many years – indeed throughout the development of ethnographic research this century. (Admittedly, they have not been equally remarked on, nor have they taken the same form at all times.) It is a well-known aspect of the history of sociology – but it bears repetition in this context – that the early period of urban ethnography in Chicago drew on aesthetic and literary models as much as on models of 'scientific' research. The sociological perspective was fuelled by the textual conventions of realist fiction. The sociological exploration of the 'life' – through the life-history for instance – was influenced by the novel of development, such as Farrell's *Studs Lonigan* trilogy. Equally, some of the literary inspirations drew broadly speaking on a sociological perspective. More generally still, the ethnographic tradition and literary genres in the United States have displayed intertextual relationships over many decades. The styles of urban realism, the literary creation of characters and types in the city, and the narrative of modern fiction – these all contributed to the styles of ethnographic representation. The systematic *analysis* of these intertextual relations may be a fairly recent preoccupation, but the genres are more enduring *and* more blurred than the moments model suggested by Denzin and Lincoln.

The nature of those intertextual linkages deserves closer attention. It is clearly insufficient to deal with a monolithic 'ethnography' on the one hand and an equally undifferentiated 'literature' on the other. The specific relationships between American fiction and ethnographic reportage are but one set of possible homologies and influences. For example, there were significant parallels between Malinowski's ethnographic enterprise and Joseph Conrad's literary work. Likewise, there were multiple cultural and literary commitments that informed Edward Sapir's anthropology and his linguistics. In doing so he also reminds us that in the figure of Franz Boas himself – its founding hero – American cultural anthropology was born out of a complex mix of epistemological and aesthetic commitments. Equally, Ruth Benedict's particular development of one strand of Boasian anthropology was hardly conceived and reported in a narrowly scientistic manner. Zora Neale Hurston's experimental ethnographic writing is another example that has received some attention recently, but deserves wider recognition.

Our point here is not to review yet again fairly well-known commentaries on ethnography, literature and aesthetics. Rather, we emphasize the extent to which ethnography in sociology or anthropology – whether conceived in terms of method or its textual products – has never been a stable entity. It has been marked by contrasts and tensions that are not merely departures from an established orthodoxy. The conduct of ethnographic research has rarely, if ever, been established solely under the auspices of a positivist orthodoxy. American cultural anthropology, for instance, has displayed a repeated tension between the nomothetic search for law-like regularities, and the idiographic interpretation of cultures. In essence we take issue with Denzin's suggestion that the

'dividing lines between a secular science of the social world and sacred understandings of that world are *now* being challenged and, in some cases, erased' (Denzin, 1997: xviii; emphasis added). The point is that these dividing lines were never so starkly drawn in the first place. Given the highly personalized nature of anthropological fieldwork and authorship, it is far from clear that any major practitioner ever subscribed to a purely scientistic or positivist perspective. Indeed, although it is virtually impossible to demonstrate, one suspects that the social and academic elite members of the community of anthropologists never subscribed to anything quite as vulgar or artisan as a single scientific method or its equivalent. The sociology of scientific knowledge would strongly suggest that the elite core of the subject never espoused such crude oversimplifications as the subsequent historical accounts attribute to them. The emphasis on personal qualities and the uniquely biographical experience of fieldwork meant that the discipline of anthropology was often portrayed as an essentially 'indeterminate' mode of knowledge acquisition.

To summarize, ethnographic research has always contained within it a variety of perspectives. As a whole it has never been totally subsumed within a framework of orthodoxy and objectivism. There have been varieties of aesthetic and interpretative standpoints throughout nearly a century of development and change. The ethnographic approach to understanding cultural difference has itself incorporated a diversity of intellectual cultures. There have undoubtedly been changing intellectual fashions and emphases, and the pace of change has perhaps been especially rapid in recent years (although here again we would take issue with a model that has change moving ever-more quickly and developmental phases becoming increasingly truncated). These so-called trends actually reflect long-standing tensions, rather than constituting a new and unique moment in ethnographic research. They continue the centrifugal and centripetal tendencies that have been perceptible for many years, and represent the diverse and broad concerns of a past as well as a present (and future) ethnography (Delamont and Atkinson, 1995).

DEFINING ETHNOGRAPHY

Notwithstanding such differences and tensions, the ethnographic traditions do share many common features, as is evident in the chapters contained in this volume. They are grounded in a commitment to the first-hand experience and exploration of a particular social or cultural setting on the basis of (though not exclusively by) participant observation. Observation and participation (according to circumstance and the analytic purpose at hand) remain the characteristic features of the ethnographic approach. In many cases, of course, fieldwork entails the use of other research methods too. Participant observation alone would normally result in strange and unnatural behaviour were the observer not to talk with her or his hosts, so turning them into informants or 'co-researchers'. Hence, conversations and interviews are often indistinguishable from other forms of interaction and dialogue in field research settings. In literate societies the ethnographer may well draw on textual materials as sources of information and insight into how actors and institutions represent themselves and others. In principle, indeed, the ethnographer may find herself or himself drawing on a very diverse repertoire of research techniques – analysing spoken discourse and narratives, collecting and interpreting visual materials (including photography, film and video), collecting oral history and life history material and so on. In recent years, this array of methods and techniques has become widespread, and they have been documented and disseminated under the rubric of qualitative research methods. In that guise they have spread far beyond the disciplinary confines of anthropology and sociology. In so doing, the social settings in which they are used have also diversified. There are now flourishing traditions of qualitative research in nursing and health studies, in studies of work and organizations, in science and technology studies, in human geography, in social psychology, in educational research, cultural, media and theatre studies, and many other domains of empirical research. Indeed, it is one of the strengths of these methodological commitments and their concomitant disciplinary interests that they have sustained substantial volumes of empirical research. Anthropologists and symbolic interactionist sociologists, for instance, have consistently grounded their work in major pieces of empirical investigation, based on intensive field research. And it is just as well that they have done so over the decades, while other social and cultural specialists have gone in for rather less firmly rooted work, with far too much fashionable theory and intellectual faddism, and insufficient attention to the realities of everyday life.

We have not, however, developed this volume as a general handbook of qualitative research methods. There is one obvious pragmatic reason for that: it already exists (Denzin and Lincoln, 1994). Our reasons go beyond that, however. We believe that there remains a central place in the social disciplines for the intensive investigation of a research agenda that is characteristic of the ethnographic spirit, and that this is not necessarily captured by the connotations of a generalist qualitative methods label. Indeed, a good deal of what currently passes for qualitative research has little systematic grounding in the methods and commitments (intellectual and personal) that we associate with the term 'ethnography'. Close inspection of the relevant literatures and textbooks suggests that all too often authors and researchers are talking about the conduct of in-depth interviews – or focus groups – divorced from contexts of social action; or are amassing textual materials, diaries and biographies independently of the social contexts in which they are produced or used. These are often important ways of gaining principled understandings of social life and personal experience, but should not necessarily be equated with ethnographic research. Whatever the range of data collection techniques, we believe that ethnographic research remains firmly rooted in the first-hand exploration of research settings. It is this sense of social exploration and protracted investigation that gives ethnography its abiding and continuing character.

This does not mean that ethnography always means exactly the same to all social scientists at all times or under all circumstances. Clearly there have been and will continue to be differences. We have already alluded to the persistent difference between sociology and anthropology. They do not necessarily reflect profound differences in the actual conduct of field ethnography, but do reflect different mythological charters for the different subjects. There are, moreover, differences in national traditions. Even within anthropology there are national distinctions. American cultural anthropology and British social anthropology, for instance, have had quite distinctive intellectual histories. At a more finely grained level, there are – also within anthropology – distinctive regional differences: different global regions have been reflected in subtly but significantly different traditions of research and writing (Fardon, 1990). British and American sociologists have exerted mutual influence, but there are differences between their sociologies as well. There are, too, different constellations of research and writing that are characteristic of specific substantive domains. The conduct of ethnography is, moreover, no preserve of English-speaking academics. Its spread has been global. For those reasons, then, we have been at pains to include in this volume contributions from an international array of authors, as well as a cross-disciplinary one. Our board of editorial advisers also reflects an international and interdisciplinary relevance for contemporary ethnography. While the Anglophone international community predominates, we have included contributions from different continents. We have also had each chapter refereed by at least one referee from a country other than the author's. The overall volume is, therefore, interdisciplinary and international in scope.

ORGANIZATION OF THE HANDBOOK

The contents of this handbook are set out in three broad sections. Each is preceded by an editorial introduction that sets the scene for the individual chapters. We do not, therefore, recapitulate those more detailed discussions here, but provide a brief overview. In Part One are a series of chapters that explore various intellectual and substantive contexts of ethnographic work – both disciplinary and empirical. Collectively these enable an appreciation of some of the origins of ethnography in sociology and anthropology, community studies and elsewhere. It is important to recognize that there are distinctive differences in national orientation – for instance between British and American anthropologists – and these are addressed in the various contributions. Some of the key sources for ethnographic research are explored, and various strands of the ethnographic imagination are located in British and American sociology, in Chicago sociology and symbolic interactionism, in community studies and the documentary realism of Mass-Observation. Here we also include chapters about key ideas and concepts that inform ethnographic research. In principle this could again have been extended to a much larger catalogue of themes, topics and problems. We and our contributors have necessarily been selective. It is not our intention to provide a comprehensive review of absolutely all of the potentially vast range of issues here. Rather, the contributions lay out some of the most significant epistemological and methodological issues that inform varieties of contemporary ethnographic work. Some of the major theoretical movements that have impinged on the development and conduct of ethnography, such as symbolic interactionism, semiotics, phenomenology and ethnomethodology are addressed, together with the impact of movements such as feminism and postmodernism (these are further addressed in Part Three of the handbook). The contributions help to (re)establish the rich intellectual traditions that have informed ethnographic research and its epistemological underpinnings. The chapters help us to crystallize the variety of intellectual tendencies and key differences between them (as well as the family resemblances) that have contributed to the resilience of ethnographic methods in a world of changing ideas and emphases.

Equally, it is crucial to locate the use of ethnographic research in at least some of its key contexts of application. Part Two thus contains chapters focusing on distinctive domains of ethnographic research. These are not simply different locales in which field research just happens to have taken place. Rather, the ethnographic treatment constructs the various fields in particular intellectual ways. The ethnographic study of scientific laboratories, for instance, is part of a characteristic reconstruction of the laboratory as a particular kind of site. The ethnographic study of educational settings and processes equally constructs classrooms as the setting for particular kinds of processes and interactions. Ethnographic fieldwork, and the disciplinary

commitments that inform it, constructs the objects of research as well as providing ways of exploring them. Hence this series of chapters addresses the contribution that ethnography has made to the study of distinctive empirical areas *and* the contribution that the study of these distinctive arenas has made to the development of ethnography.

Part Three turns from the contexts and concepts that have informed ethnography to a consideration of its present and future conduct. These chapters explore a number of key aspects of data collection, analysis and representation. They are not intended to substitute for the many books of practical advice on the day-to-day performance of ethnographic work. Rather, some of the key domains and debates are addressed and explored. It is characteristic of ethnographic research that such strategies and methods are far from inert, transparent or mechanistic information-gathering exercises, or routine analytic procedures (Wolcott, 1994). We cannot divorce the methods and the analyses from broader disciplinary and conceptual frameworks. While all methods of data collection and analysis are imbued with theoretical ideas – however implicit – the qualitative methods of the ethnographer are especially contested and debated. Here, therefore, we have collected chapters that deal with some of the main strategies of data construction, such as fieldnotes and interviewing and the analysis of narratives and biographical materials. We also include a consideration of one of the most significant areas of innovation in recent years – the use of computer software for the organization, management and analysis of ethnographic data. Part Three also pays considerable attention to the consequences of *the turn* for ethnographic representation, and considers the possible futures of ethnographic work.

In essence, the *Handbook of Ethnography* celebrates a certain unity in diversity. We fully recognize the extent to which ethnographic research means different things in different intellectual fields, disciplines or national contexts. The contemporary conceptualization of ethnography – whether or not labelled as postmodern (post-structural, post-feminist, critical) – reflects a proliferation of theory, methodology and praxis. Equally, we seek to reclaim a tradition. Notwithstanding the manifest diversity, there remain the core achievements of ethnographic research over the best part of a century. It is all too easy to get caught up in the methodological or epistemological strife and to lose sight of the abiding commitment to the principled exploration and reconstruction of social worlds, our engagement with our fellow men and women, our commitment to the interpretation of local and situated cultures. While theoretical fashions can come and go, the products of ethnographic research remain extraordinarily durable. We continue to read and to encourage our students to read ethnographic monographs from across different specialist domains and across the decades. We do so because many of them are among the classics in their field. Here the metaphor of the classic is particularly apt. Classic design endures while fashion waxes and wanes. Classics have a double valency: they are of their time, yet are constantly available for subsequent generations. The ethnographic gift of the classic monograph is not, therefore, just a romantic device to suspend settings and cultures outside of history. It captures the essential tension at the heart of the ethnographic enterprise: the local has general significance, and the temporally specific has lasting value. The enduring value of the ethnographic tradition is grounded in its attention to the singular and the concrete. The chapters that follow are testimony to this endurance and excitement in the ethnographic approach and should be read in that spirit.

REFERENCES

Amit, V. (ed.) (2000) *Constructing the Field*. London: Routledge.
Atkinson, P.A. (1990) *The Ethnographic Imagination*. London: Routledge.
Atkinson, P.A. (1992) *Understanding Ethnographic Texts*. Thousand Oaks, CA: Sage.
Atkinson, P.A. (1996) *Sociological Readings and Re-readings*. Aldershot: Gower.
Atkinson, P.A. and Coffey, A. (1995) 'Realism and its discontents: the crisis of cultural representation in ethnographic texts', in B. Adam and S. Allen (eds), *Theorising Culture*. London: UCL Press. pp. 103–39.
Atkinson, P.A. and Silverman, D. (1997) 'Kundera's *Immortality*: the interview society and the invention of the self', *Qualitative Inquiry*, 3: 304–25.
Atkinson, P.A., Coffey, A.J. and Delamont, S. (1999) 'Ethnography: post, past and present', *Journal of Contemporary Ethnography*, 28 (5): 460–71.
Atkinson, P.A., Delamont, S. and Hammersley, M. (1988) 'Qualitative research traditions', *Review of Educational Research*, 38 (2): 231–50.
Behar, R. and Gordon, D. (eds) (1995) *Women Writing Culture*. Los Angeles: University of California Press.
Boon, J.A. (1982) *Other Tribes, Other Scribes: Symbolic Anthropology in the Comparative Study of Authors, Histories, Religions and Texts*. Cambridge: Cambridge University Press.
Clifford, J. (1988) *The Predicament of Culture*. Cambridge, MA: Harvard University Press.
Clifford, J. and Marcus, G.E. (eds) (1986) *Writing Culture*. Berkeley, CA: University of California Press.

Coffey, A. (1999) *The Ethnographic Self*. Thousand Oaks, CA: Sage.
Coffey, A. and Atkinson, P.A. (1996) *Making Sense of Qualitative Data*. Thousand Oaks, CA: Sage.
Delamont, S. (2001) *Fieldwork in Educational Settings*, 2nd edn. London: Falmer Press.
Delamont, S. and Atkinson, P.A. (1995) *Fighting Familiarity*. Cresskill, NJ: Hampton Press.
Delamont, S., Atkinson, P. and Parry, O. (2000) *The Doctoral Experience*. London: Falmer Press.
Delamont, S., Coffey, A. and Atkinson, P. (2000) 'The twilight years?', *International Journal of Qualitative Studies in Education*, 13 (3): 223–38.
Denzin, N. (1997) *Interpretive Ethnography: Ethnographic Practices for the 21st Century*. Thousand Oaks, CA: Sage.
Denzin, N. and Lincoln, Y. (eds) (1994) *Handbook of Qualitative Research*. Thousand Oaks, CA: Sage.
Ellis, C. and Bochner, A. (eds) (1996) *Composing Ethnography*. Walnut Creek, CA: Sage.
Fardon, R. (ed.) (1990) *Localizing Strategies*. Edinburgh: Scottish Academic Press.
Hammersley, M. and Atkinson, P.A. (1995) *Ethnography: Principles in Practice*, 2nd edn. London: Routledge.
Jacob, E. (1987) 'Qualitative research traditions', *Review of Educational Research*, 57 (1): 1–50.
James, A., Hockey, J. and Dawson, A. (eds) (1997) *After Writing Culture*. London: Routledge.
Leininger, M. (1992) 'Current issues, problems and trends to advance qualitative paradigmatic research methods for the future', *Qualitative Health Research*, 2 (4): 392–415.
Lincoln, Y.S. and Denzin, N.K. (1994) 'The fifth moment', in N.K. Denzin and Y.S. Lincoln (eds), *Handbook of Qualitative Research*. Thousand Oaks, CA: Sage. pp. 575–86.
Lofland, J. and Lofland, L. (1995) *Analyzing Social Settings*, 3rd edn. Belmont, CA: Wadsworth.
Richardson, L. (1990) *Writing Strategies: Reaching Diverse Audiences*. Newbury Park, CA: Sage.
Richardson, L. (1992) 'The consequences of poetic representation', in C. Ellis and M.G. Flaherty (eds), *Investigating Subjectivity*. Newbury Park, CA: Sage.
Wolcott, H.F. (1990) *Writing up Qualitative Research*. Newbury Park, CA: Sage.
Wolcott, H.F. (1994) *Transforming Qualitative Data*. Thousand Oaks, CA: Sage.
Wolf, M. (1992) *The Thrice Told Tale*. Berkeley, CA: University of California Press.

PART ONE

Introduction to Part One

In this first section we bring together a series of chapters that outline some of the intellectual contexts within which ethnographic research has been fostered, developed and debated. We make no attempt to cover every discipline and every period of ethnography's various trajectories over the course of the twentieth century. Our authors identify and describe some of the key sources and inspirations that have nurtured ethnographic research.

The development of ethnographic fieldwork in sociology is inextricably linked – in history and in mythology – with the rise of the discipline in Chicago. The University of Chicago was the matrix in which there developed a rich tradition of urban sociology, heavily dependent on the detailed investigation of local social settings and cultures. The empirical investigations of the Chicago School were significantly – but by no means exclusively – grounded in ethnographic fieldwork. In later manifestations the postwar Chicago School added renewed emphases on the ethnographic exploration of work, socialization and complex organizations. That tradition was by no means dependent on the theoretical concerns of symbolic interactionism, but a series of key figures brought the ethnographic and the interactionist strands together, promoting a potent combination of theory, method and empirical research. For those reasons, therefore, we include prominently among these introductory chapters treatments of the Chicago contribution (Deegan) and of symbolic interactionism (Rock). These complementary chapters provide a valuable background to the development of ethnography and intellectual traditions that have spread well beyond the United States and have exerted an influence beyond the disciplinary confines of sociology.

The conduct of ethnographic fieldwork – originally in 'exotic' settings and more recently in a more diverse range of social worlds – has been the most distinctive characteristic of anthropology as a discipline. In some respects the anthropological tradition has been characterized by a degree of stability and continuity over many decades. Equally, there have been intriguing differences, debates and disputes among anthropologists. There have been key differences between American cultural anthropology and British social anthropology. Two chapters explore those two traditions. Faubion traces some of the main strands of American anthropology while Macdonald deals with the history of anthropology and ethnographic fieldwork in the United Kingdom. Of course, those are not the only national schools or traditions and we do not intend to imply that they exhaust the entire field of scholarship, which has certainly not been confined to the Anglophone world. Indeed, a systematic exploration of the place of ethnography in different intellectual and national contexts deserves further treatment, but that would be another volume in its own right and beyond the scope of this handbook.

The distinctive tradition of community studies receives separate treatment in the chapter by Brunt. The ethnographic study of small-scale social settings in rural and urban locations has been a recurrent preoccupation for social scientists. Such inspirations were, of course, reflected in the earliest sociological and anthropological studies. Community studies have additionally generated their own characteristic preoccupations. Ethnographic fieldwork has in turn helped to define the connotations of 'community' in the social sciences. Again, the investigation of communities goes well beyond the English-speaking world of the social and cultural disciplines. Stanley, by contrast, deals with a rather different aspect of our intellectual background. Documentary reportage informed ethnographic representations from the early years of the twentieth century, including the influence of journalistic writing. Stanley discusses one particular tendency in the United Kingdom – Mass-Observation. While that was in many ways an idiosyncratic approach to the collection and reporting of observational data about everyday life, its influence and its style had wider resonances. Stanley offers a unique new interpretation of Mass-Observation.

All of these approaches in sociology, anthropology and community studies frequently inscribed a number of assumptions about the 'observed'. Much of ethnography was founded on the asymmetry between the observer and the observed – even the demotic style of Mass-Observation – sometimes in the context of a colonial asymmetry, or class, ethnic and gender differences. It is, therefore, appropriate to include the essay by Marcus on orientalism. Although it may dilute Edward Said's particular focus on Western constructions of the Near and Middle East (terms that only make sense from a West European vantage point), the general connotations of orientalist thinking and the accompanying critique are relevant to virtually all ethnographic undertakings. An awareness of the critique of orientalism is an inescapable feature of contemporary ethnographic work.

This introductory series of chapters continues to address a number of significant theoretical perspectives that have informed ethnographic research. They are dealt with here in separate chapters, and their respective authors do more than justice to the distinctive theoretical or methodological contributions. Such a treatment in a handbook of this sort should not be interpreted with undue literalness, however. These various perspectives are not exhaustive: they do not constitute a complete canon of philosophical or theoretical underpinnings. Equally,

they are not hermetically sealed and mutually exclusive 'paradigms'. We have referred already to Rock's chapter on symbolic interactionism; that is complemented by Pollner and Emerson on ethnomethodology and ethnography, Maso on phenomenology, Manning on semiotics, and Charmaz and Mitchell on grounded theorizing. These all furnish much of the 'interpretative' social science that informs and is informed by ethnographic research. There is, however, no simple one-to-one relationship between a method or a research strategy on the one hand and a specific philosophical stance on the other: there are family resemblances between theoretical approaches and methodological preferences. Likewise, although there are differences between theoretical positions – which may even be incompatible on some counts – it is often unhelpful to overemphasize theoretical differences and to police the symbolic boundaries between them too obsessively. The fact that we present them here as separate chapters does not mean that we or our authors wish to insist upon their exclusivity. Researchers need to be aware of the historical and theoretical traditions within which – or against which – their work is located. But they need to draw sustenance from them rather than experiencing them as straitjackets. Equally we need an informed awareness of these intellectual traditions if we are to avoid naive beliefs to the effect that ethnographic and other 'qualitative' research strategies are either novel (clearly they have a long heritage) or self-justifying (for they do not substitute for disciplinary and theoretical understanding). The chapters in this first section of the handbook, then, help us to set the right historical and intellectual context for a well-informed appreciation of ethnographic research in the social sciences.

1

The Chicago School of Ethnography

MARY JO DEEGAN

The University of Chicago towered over the intellectual and professional landscape of sociology from 1892 until 1942.[1] It reputedly trained over half of all sociologists in the world by 1930 (and it continues to graduate large cohorts, although in a much more diversified and international arena). This large group of scholars fundamentally shaped the discipline through its faculty and their doctorally trained students who produced thousands of books and articles (see, for example, Fine, 1995; Kurtz, 1984). A powerful and prolific subgroup of these sociologists created the Chicago School of ethnography,[2] the focus of this chapter. This vast enterprise is the subject of considerable, often conflicting, scholarship, and I offer one way to navigate through this sea of ideas.

First, I define a set of 'core Chicago ethnographies' (hereafter referred to as 'core ethnographies') conducted by sociologists affiliated with the University of Chicago. Each sociologist analysed the everyday life, communities and symbolic interactions characteristic of a specific group. The studies were self-consciously identifiable and were based on a shared vision of the discipline and society. They were produced between approximately 1917 and 1942 and usually by the doctoral students of Robert E. Park and Ernest W. Burgess. Secondly, I present a brief overview of the intellectual apparatus underlying these ethnographies that is now called 'social ecology', (and largely indebted to the work of Park and Burgess: for example Park and Burgess, 1921; Park, Burgess and McKenzie, 1925), and 'Chicago symbolic interactionism' (that emerges primarily from the ideas of W.I. Thomas, George H. Mead, and John Dewey).[3] These ideas were continued by their sociological students, especially by those who later became faculty at the University of Chicago. Thirdly, I analyse

the controversies over defining the 'Chicago School of sociology' and its stepchild, the 'Chicago School of ethnography'. Fourthly, I briefly examine some major scholars and books exploring the Chicago School ethnographic heritage between 1942 and 1970. Fifthly, I conclude with a few exemplars of this continuing tradition between 1970 and the present.

THE CORE CHICAGO SCHOOL ETHNOGRAPHIES, 1917–1942

Between approximately 1917 and 1942 Park and Burgess trained a remarkable group of students who wrote a series of now-famous ethnographies (see Tables 1.1 and 1.2). These books were often published in the University of Chicago Sociological Series and were introduced or discussed by Park or Burgess. In general, these ethnographies studied face-to-face everyday interactions in specific locations. The descriptive narratives portrayed 'social worlds' experienced in everyday life within a modern, often urban, context (Short, 1971). The investigator 'took the role of the other' (Mead, 1934) in these empirical investigations. A dynamic process incorporating social change, especially disorganizing and rapid changes in values and attitudes (Thomas and Znaniecki, 1918–1920), was emphasized. An openness to people, data, places and theory was intrinsic to the ethnographic process, so a strict set of criteria cannot and should not be applied.

The core ethnographies were significantly expanded and popularized by a related group of books I call 'the Chicago Sociology Studies' (see Table 1.3).[4] These studies were linked to the core

Table 1.1   *Robert Park's Prefaces and Introductions to Chicago Ethnographies*

1917	'Introduction', pp. vii–xvii in *The Japanese Invasion*, by Jessie F. Steiner (Chicago: McClurg)
1923	'Editor's Preface', pp. xxiii–xxvi in *The Hobo*, by Nels Anderson
1927a	'Editor's Preface', pp. ix–xii in *The Gang*, by Frederick M. Thrasher (rev. 1936)
1927b	'Introduction', pp. ix–xiii in *The Natural History of Revolution*, by Lyford P. Edwards
1928a	'Foreword', pp. vii–ix in *The Ghetto*, by Louis Wirth
1928b	'Introduction', pp. vii–x in *The Strike*, by Ernest T. Hiller
1929a	'Introduction', pp. vii–x in *The Gold Coast and the Slum*, by Harvey Warren Zorbaugh
1929b	'Introduction', pp. vii–ix in *The Saleslady*, by Frances R. Donovan
1932	'Introduction', pp. xi–xx in *The Pilgrims of Russian Town*, by Pauline V. Young
1934	'Introduction', pp. ix–xxii in *The Shadow of the Plantation*, by Charles S. Johnson
1935	'Introduction', pp. xiii–xxv in *Negro Politicians*, by Harold F. Gosnell
1937a	'Introduction', pp. xiii–xvii in *The Marginal Man*, by Everett V. Stonequist (New York: Charles Scribner's Sons)
1937b	'Introduction', pp. xxiii–xxxvi in *The Etiquette of Race Relations in the South*, by Bertram W. Doyle
1937c	'Introduction', pp. vii–xiv in *Interracial Marriage in Hawaii*, by Romanzo Adams (New York: Macmillan)
1938	'Introduction', pp. ix–xvi in *An Island Community*, by Andrew W. Lind
1940	'Introduction', pp. xi–xxiii in *News and the Human Interest Story*, by Helen MacGill Hughes
1942	'Introduction', pp. xi–xxi in *Negroes in Brazil*, by Donald Pierson

All titles published by the University of Chicago Press, unless otherwise noted.

Table 1.2   *Ernest Burgess' Prefaces and Introductions to Chicago Ethnographies*

1930	'Discussion', pp. 184–97 in *The Jack Roller*, by Clifford R. Shaw
1931	'Editor's Preface', pp. xi–xii in *The Natural History of a Delinquent Career*, by Clifford R. Shaw in collaboration with Maurice E. Moore
1932a	'Editor's Preface', pp. ix–xiv in *Small-Town Stuff*, by Albert Blumenthal
1932b	'Introduction', pp. iv–ix in *The Taxi-Dance Hall*, by Paul Goalby Cressey
1932c	'Editor's Preface', pp. ix–xii in *The Negro Family in Chicago*, by Edward Franklin Frazier
1939/1951	'Preface', pp. iii–ix in *The Negro Family in the United States*, by Edward Franklin Frazier

All titles published by the University of Chicago Press.

ethnographies in the following way. These studies generally used more statistical data, and these data were usually combined with a series of qualitative techniques such as interviews, face-to-face interactions and life histories. These studies shared the epistemological assumptions of the core ethnographies and combined them with macro-structural patterns, such as rates of suicides [Cavan, 1928] and incarceration [Reckless, 1933]. A dynamic process was emphasized that was receptive to people's language and triangulated data. The sociologists tended to be doctoral students at the University of Chicago, studying with Park and Burgess, but especially with Burgess.[5] Because of my focus here, I only refer to the related Chicago studies when they illustrate an important feature of the core ethnographies.

These slippery definitions of sociology and ethnography are exemplified in the core ethnography of Charles Johnson [1934], Park's student, who analysed Jim Crow segregation in the South.

This study enlarged the boundaries of 'Chicago' ethnographic sociology on important dimensions. Thus his work extended the urban focus of many Chicago ethnographies to a rural setting. More than any other book introduced by Park, Johnson's volume employed quantitative data and stressed an anthropological 'South/developing' world-view. In addition, Johnson analysed 'folk societies' within the 'natural history' framework. He emphasized marginal people' [Park, 1934: xii] and documented the plantation as a major institution in the lives of disenfranchised black farmers many years after the Civil War ended. Johnson interpreted the plantation system in an international context requiring ethnographic study and analysis. This ethnography is more political and macro in orientation than most of the core ethnographies, and it is more similar to the related Chicago sociology studies. Both sets of studies employ an analogous approach to using data and thinking about communities.

Table 1.3   *A Selective List of Chicago School Studies Related to the Core Chicago Ethnographies*

1927	E.R. Mowrer, *Family Disorganization*, with 'Foreword' by Ernest W. Burgess, pp. vii–xi
1928	Ruth Shonle Cavan, *Suicide*, with 'Introduction' by Ellsworth Faris, pp. xi–xvii
1928	Vivien M. Palmer, *Field Studies in Sociology: A Student's Manual*, with 'Introduction' by Ernest W. Burgess, pp. vii–viii
1929	Ernest W. Burgess (ed.), *Personality and the Social Group*, with 'Preface' by Ernest W. Burgess, pp. vii–ix
1931	Ackerson Luton, *Children's Behavior Problems*, with 'Editor's Preface' by Ernest W. Burgess, p. ix
1932	E.R. Mowrer and Harriet Mowrer, *Domestic Discord*
1932	E.R. Mowrer, *The Family*ᵃ
1933	Heinrich Kluver, *Behavior Mechanisms in Monkeys*, with 'Editor's Foreword' by Ernest W. Burgess, p. x
1933	Walter C. Reckless, *Vice In Chicago*
1938	Ruth S. Cavan and Katherine H. Ranck, *The Family and the Depression*, with 'Introduction' by Paul S. Schroeder and Ernest W. Burgess, pp. vii–xiii
1938	Clifford R. Shaw, Henry D. McKay and James F. McDonald with Special Chapters by Harold B. Hanson and Ernest W. Burgess, *Brothers in Crime*
1939	Robert E.L. Faris and H. Warren Dunham, *Mental Disorders in Urban Areas*, with 'Introduction' by Ernest W. Burgess, pp. ix–xx
1940	Nels Anderson, *Men on the Move*

All titles published by the University of Chicago Press.
ᵃDedicated to Ernest W. Burgess.

Robert E. Park and Ernest W. Burgess and the Weaving of Chicago Sociology as a Theoretical Tapestry

Robert E. Park and Ernest W. Burgess dramatically shaped and honed the skills of their students and colleagues who contributed collectively to the identifiable theory and style of scholarship known worldwide as 'Chicago sociology' (Faris, 1967). This chapter draws attention to a defining component of that process: the seventeen influential books that Park encouraged and for which he wrote prefaces and introductions from 1917 to 1942 (see Table 1.1) and the six influential books[6] that Burgess encouraged and for which he wrote prefaces and introductions from 1930 to 1939 (see Table 1.2). These works, and Park and Burgess' mentorship, emerged in a complex mix of intellectual trends in the city of Chicago and its leading academy: the University of Chicago. Park and Burgess were not, therefore, isolated 'great men', but worked squarely within a long, collective intellectual tradition beginning in 1892 (Deegan, 1988).

Park's and Burgess' questions, interests, criticism and support molded and enhanced the sociological labors of the authors of the core ethnographies. The works appear diverse, but Park and Burgess drew from each ethnography to generate a coherent and evolving theoretical vision. The result is a veritable tapestry of patterns that retain the individual style and distinctive interests of each sociologist while the prefaces and introductions realize the explicit aim to place each study in a larger, ever-expanding conceptual framework.

The Theoretical Tapestry of the Chicago Ethnographies

Park and Burgess, in the role of dissertation advisors, influenced the form and content of numerous sociological studies, including most of those noted in Tables 1.1, 1.2 and 1.3.[7] Doctoral professors hold powerful positions in a *rite de passage* wherein students become professional sociologists:

> The sociology dissertation process is a liminal journey, a passage characterized by ambiguity, uncertainty, and crisis in which the student self is abandoned and a new professional self claims a world of power, authority, maturity, and responsibility. (Deegan and Hill, 1991: 322)

Although each student's interests were unique, Park and Burgess held a common focus, generating a network of collegial friends who asked and answered interrelated questions. With Park and Burgess' guidance, their students wove a 'theoretical tapestry' in which patterns emerged and reinforced each other for more than four decades.[8]

Park's and Burgess' integrative style of theorizing involved numerous 'conversations'[9] with students and colleagues that collectively generated the mind, self and community characteristic of the Chicago School of sociology. They acted as stewards, shepherding and recommending manuscripts for publication by the University of Chicago Press.[10] This dynamic, interactive and collegial process resulted in a systematic theory and method that is misunderstood by many interpreters today.

Most sociological commentators employ a 'great man' model focusing on individually defined thinkers such as Max Weber, Emile Durkheim or Karl Marx. This authoritative, patriarchal model fits neither Park and Burgess' intellectual style nor their theory of society. The Chicago ethnographies vividly depicted everyday life and revealed communities 'with unity and charm' [Park, 1929a: vii]. The books were intended for undergraduate classrooms and (unlike formal, European theorists) spurned complex, abstract theoretical language. Park and Burgess' contribution to the theoretical tapestry of Chicago sociology, their conversational insight and sociological world-view were echoed and articulated in hundreds of subsequent books and articles. The volumes discussed below are vital to the Chicago project and to an adequate understanding of Park and Burgess' theoretical vision.

Curiously, although Park and Burgess co-authored major texts together, taught the same students, created a body of interrelated ethnographies, and influenced each other over a number of years, Park is surrounded by a veritable industry (such as Gubert and Tomasi, 1994; Lal, 1990; Lindner, 1996; Matthews, 1977; Rauschenbush, 1979; Shils, 1991) while Burgess (1973, 1974) has had only two anthologies posthumously collected. Although Park provided more prefaces and introductions to the ethnographies, they shared the training of the students. Considerably more information is available on Park, therefore, than on Burgess, and much of this information is seriously biased. Accordingly, although Burgess wrote prefaces for E. Franklin Frazier's The Negro Family in Chicago [1932] and The Negro Family in the United States [1939], Hughes ([1963] 1974) wrote only about Park's influence on Frazier in the latter's obituary. Similarly, Lindner (1996: 83–4, 139–45) included Clifford Shaw's The Jack Roller [1930] and Paul G. Cressey's The Taxi-Dance Hall [1932] as examples of Park's influence, but these books were introduced by Burgess. The latter, moreover, had a particularly long and close relationship to Shaw, discussed further below.

The pattern of overlooking Burgess' contribution disconnects the core Chicago ethnographies from the broad range of related Chicago studies. When Burgess is included within the analyses of core ethnographies, a new pattern appears, revealing a greater flexibility toward combining quantitative and qualitative data; a more careful footnoting of intellectual resources and debts; a more accurate picture of the collaborative role of producing core ethnographies; and a more careful study of individual influences. In other words, if Burgess is studied in greater depth, the analyses of the core ethnographies incorporate more 'Chicago style'

theory and practices within their methodological and intellectual apparatus.

This intellectual approach was systematically influenced by Mead, whose course in 'Advanced Social Psychology' was required for sociology students. After his death in 1931 Blumer continued the course and Mead's ideas. This formed a common background of assumptions about the self, the other, interactions, language and the human possibility to be rational and take the role of the other (Mead, 1934). The majority of the Chicago faculty that strongly influenced the core ethnographies, specifically Thomas, Faris and Burgess, were Mead's students. Although Park was not directly Mead's student, his work was permeated with Meadian roots. Thus both Park and Mead studied with William James; Park studied with Mead's life-long friend and colleague John Dewey; and Park was influenced by Thomas, Mead's student. The combination of this network yielded a theory stressing human flexibility, the importance of the genesis of the self, the definition of the situation, and the role of the community in the social process.

Park's modern supporters repeatedly assert that he lacked a systematic theory (e.g., Matthews, 1994: 36; Shils, 1991: 127). In contrast, I argue that Park and Burgess' system was emphatically collaborative and that their major theoretical conversations can be located in the twenty-two core ethnographies and this dense theoretical commonality. Unlike Shils (1994: 22), I do not claim Park as a 'co-author' of any of the books in Table 1.1, but as 'something of what the Victorians called a "rattle", a nonstop talker' (Matthews, 1994: 37) who helped shape them. Park's 'rattle' reflected the theoretical world-view of Chicago sociologists, and the students and colleagues of Park and Burgess provided concrete information to support or challenge their ideas from 1917 to 1942.

Park's and Burgess' introductory essays, moreover, trace their evolution through interrelated intellectual journeys as I demonstrate below. Every essay connects their overarching ideas with each author's particular study. Taken together, Park and Burgess' essays reveal the evolving continuity and complexity of their ideas – aspects of their work readily seen when evaluated as interrelated, ongoing theoretical conversations. The major themes uniting this corpus are summarized below.

Urban Society as a Locus for Social Change

Park wrote that 'human society and civilization are a consequence of the coming together of diverse races and peoples in intimate association and co-operation that we call society' [Park, 1937c: x]. Cities, he argued, emerge from ethnic and racial differences, but he held that the assimilation of these differences becomes a vital possibility when the differences are mixed in an urban 'melting pot' [Park, 1937c: vii]. Urban life, for Park, was an inevitable movement leading to the decline of differences and diversity. Park divided the world into 'two classes: those who reached the city and those not yet arrived' [Park, 1935: xiv]. His general theory articulates the steps in this global transformation.

The 'natural areas' of the city   Research on the 'natural areas' of Chicago was a hallmark of the core ethnographies. They were 'local studies' that documented unique parts of the midwestern metropolis. To Park and Burgess, 'natural areas' were transitional urban structures in which social differences maintained themselves as distinct patterns in a larger, undifferentiated society. Park and Burgess saw these careful, local studies within a comprehensive tapestry pointing from the specific to the general. Park wrote, for example: 'Every great city has its bohemias and its hobohemias; its gold coast and little Sicilies; its rooming-house area and its slums' [1929a: ix].

Chicago's 'gold coast and slum' [Zorbaugh, 1929] abutted each other physically, but created immense social distances such that the respective residents 'cannot, even with the best of good will, become neighbors' [Park, 1929a: ix]. Such 'natural areas' were ecological 'zones' sheltering different lifestyles and customs. Each subsequent ethnography refined Park and Burgess' understanding of Chicago's social mosaic. Zorbaugh's study, for example, linked 'hobos' [Anderson, 1923] who lived in 'the rialto of the Underworld' with gangs in 'little hell' [Thrasher, 1927]. Chicago's 'natural areas' were important pieces in an unfolding intellectual and empirical exploration in Park's and Burgess' analyses of the city as a social form.

Cressey repeated and extended this pattern in his study of *The Taxi-Dance Hall* [1932]. There he cited Zorbaugh's [1929] concept of 'the rialto of the Underworld' that was based on the work of Anderson [1923], as well as Anderson's study of 'the main stem' of the hobo district. Thrasher's 'social disorganization' in 'interstitial areas' was reflected in the spatial location of dance halls [Cressey, 1932: 231]. Thrasher also relied on the maps generated by the Local Community Research Committee (see Map II, p. 59 in [Cressey, 1932]).

Park pushed and coordinated these studies, yet he did not control or directly participate in them (Matthews, 1994: 37), and this was probably true for Burgess, too. This independence of thought appears, for example, in Nels Anderson's [1923] report on homeless men. Anderson (who was in fact a 'hobo' for more than a year before studying with Park and Burgess [Anderson interview with author, 1979]), was sympathetic with his population. Anderson was less judgemental than Park concerning

what constituted the 'inside' and 'outside' of urban society. To Park, however, the homeless man was an 'outcast' who lived in a 'natural area' where his lifestyle was acceptable [Park, 1923: xxv].

The intellectual distance between Park and his students was tangible and is reflected also in Louis Wirth's [1928] volume on the Jewish ghetto in Chicago. To Park, 'the ghetto' was simply another 'natural area'. It was 'a term which applied to any segregated racial or cultural group' [Park, 1928a: viii]. Wirth, however, depicted the Jewish ghetto in its unique historical, cultural, religious and political context. The transplantation of the ghetto from Europe to the United States was unlike other segregated groups, Wirth argued. Anderson's 'hobohemia' could never have been just another 'ghetto' to Wirth, as it was to Park.

The 'natural history' of collective behavior   Lyford Edwards' [1927] study of revolution and Ernest Hiller's [1928] analysis of strikes evidence Park's interest in the collective transformation of society. These violent forms of social change established tactics and 'natural patterns' that could be analysed and typified [Park, 1927b: x]. Labor 'strikes' were one step in a series of radical social changes [Park, 1928b: ix] that could result in more encompassing social change. In searching for mechanisms of collective change, Park pointed also to the 'natural history of the career of the African in Brazil', a course Donald Pierson [1942] saw resulting in assimilation within the larger society of the nation [Park, 1942: xxi].

Burgess [1932b: iii] also noted that one of the major goals of Cressey's analysis of taxi-dance halls 'was to trace the natural history of the taxi-dance hall as an urban institution, to discover those conditions in city life favorable to its rise and development, and to analyse its function in terms of the basic wishes[11] and needs of its patrons'. Thus Cressey used symbolic interaction, social ecology and triangulated data to determine the natural history and functions of an urban institution.

Juvenile delinquency   Clifford Shaw produced a series of remarkable studies on juvenile delinquency. *The Jack Roller* [1930] is acknowledged as a core ethnography, but Shaw's *The Natural History of a Delinquent Career* (written in collaboration with Maurice E. Moore, [1931]) is often not considered a core ethnography (it is considered a core ethnography here). The multi-authored [Shaw, McKay, McDonald, Hanson and Burgess, 1938] follow-up book is a longitudinal, familial, triangulated study continuing the analyses of the other books (the third book is considered a related Chicago school study here). In the latter book, *Brothers in Crime*, the original jack roller and his four felonious brothers comprised a familial group of criminals whose crimes began in their youth.

By 1938, Shaw had produced two books on the 'original' delinquent and had known this person for sixteen years [Shaw, 1938: x]. Multiple, longitudinal methods were used in the last, most complex study, and an array of Chicago institutions supported the work. Burgess wrote a separate chapter, instead of a preface, for this text.

Shaw is widely recognized for his central role in the 'life history' or 'biographical' (e.g., Lindner, 1996: 139–45) method, but most of these critiques are reductionistic. Lindner (1996: 144) exemplifies this type of view: 'Essentially, however, Shaw's findings boil down to sociological "translations" of psychological prejudices.' The use of 'case histories ... from the records of case-work agencies, courts, correctional institutions, schools, behavior clinics, from interviews with friends and relatives of the brothers, and from autobiographical documents and personal interviews with the boys themselves' [Shaw et al., 1938: x] are 'outside' ethnography or 'sociological theorizing' while other, similar works are 'inside' this circle. Here, Shaw's first two books are considered core ethnographies and are directly linked to the third, related volume. All were deeply influenced by Burgess.

Women and the changing division of labor Frances Donovan's [1929] study was the only Parkian monograph focused on social changes affecting women. *The Saleslady* (together with *The Woman Who Waits*: Donovan, 1920), examined the new woman who entered 'into the broader fields of economic life' [Park, 1929b: viii]. Donovan was not a doctoral student, but she earned a Bachelor's degree at the University of Chicago in 1918 and interacted with Chicago sociologists in the 1920s. Park judged *The Saleslady* was not an academic work, but surmised it would sell and, perhaps, inspire other 'insider' books by occupational practitioners.[12] Park's resistance to 'the new woman'[13] was consistent with his ambivalent response to Donovan's clearly excellent work (Deegan, 1988: 199). When a woman wrote on a topic more central to Park's interests, however, he could be enthusiastic, like he was with the work of Helen MacGill Hughes, discussed next.

Newspapers Information is crucial to modern society, and newspapers fascinated Park, a former reporter. He strongly supported Helen MacGill Hughes' [1940] attempt to define 'news' and distinguish it from other types of information, 'rumor and gossip, for example, and propaganda' [Park, 1940: xii]. Newspapers are part of popular culture, together with movies and popular literature, wrote Park [1940: xxiii]. Newspapers worldwide actively change how events are chronicled and remembered, a point Park [1940: xxii] found significant.

The 'human interest story' is an especially influential medium of change. Such stories reflect:

> ... a universal element in the news. It is what gives the news story its symbolic character. It is the ability to discover and interpret the human interest in the news that gives the reporter the character of a literary artist and the news story the character of literature. It is in the human interest story that the distinction between the news story and fiction story tends to disappear. [Park, 1940: xxi]

To Park, newspapers recorded – and sometimes fabricated – the life history of a person and people. Human interest stories present 'natural areas' to people who live outside their boundaries. Nonetheless, wrote Park, it is sociologists – not reporters – who write 'the big news' and have the time and privilege to thoroughly examine a social question or behavior.

Small town life Albert Blumenthal's study of *Small Town Stuff* [1932] is a fascinating contrast to the frequent urban emphasis of other core Chicago ethnographies. Blumenthal followed the participant observation model and lived in his small community for an extended period. Introduced by Burgess, Blumenthal's work is often overlooked in discussions of these ethnographies. Thus the books on Park (e.g. Lal, 1990; Rauschenbush, 1979) have ignored Blumenthal's work and even work intending to study the sociological methods of the ethnographies (e.g. J. Platt, 1996) have done so.

Race and the Nation-State

A major theme in Park's outlook was the race question. Social isolation and inbreeding created the worldwide diversity of people and culture [Park, 1937a: x]. Park held that segregation ends abruptly when faced with changing technology and new social customs. Patterns of difference combine and mingle in modernizing nations. The initial clash of peoples, exacerbated by visible physiological differences, could result in either 'a nation within a nation' (à la Booker T. Washington [Park, 1942: xx]), exemplified by the situation of African Americans; or in a 'melting pot,' as in Brazil [Park, 1942: xvi]. Harold Gosnell's [1935] study of 'Negro politicians' showed how African Americans were then entering the 'wider' civic domain. A new middle class created 'a transfer of political power' [Park, 1935: xxiv]. This was also a 'human interest story' that captured the popular imagination [Park, 1935: xxv; Park, 1940].

'Race relations have everywhere so largely determined the structure of human society,' wrote Park [1937a: viii], that race itself is an organizing rule for social order. Park thereby analysed race as a 'macro-level' process embodied in individuals who live in specific groups. Park's conception surpasses the limitations of a face-to-face, social psychology of race. His sociology of race relations contains important epistemological assumptions that deserve consideration in modern evaluations of his work. Frazier's series of studies of American race relations, especially his work on the Negro family [1932, 1939/1951], connected patterns of discrimination with family patterns, one of the most pressing areas of research in race relations. Burgess [1939/1951: iii] explicated Frazier's work as an important international landmark similar to Thomas and Znaniecki's (1918–1920) research on the Polish peasant.

Creating the urban melting pot   Park idealized homogenous cultures wherein differences between racial and cultural groups disappear. In Park's mind, this 'melting pot' has interim stages where differences are maintained, bounded and cherished. Everett Stonequist's [1937] 'marginal man', however, crosses cultures within his personal experience, becoming a micro-level force for macro-level change and 'advancement' of the differing groups he represents. The 'mulatto' is an exemplar of a person between two worlds who helps society move toward mutual understanding and more homogeneity [Park, 1937a].

Park conceived that understanding between the demarcated worlds within the melting pot would dissolve its internal boundaries. In this context, Hawai'i and Brazil were, for Park, models of assimilation, whereas the rural South in the United States was a backwater of prejudice and social stagnation. Hawai'i, to Park, was 'the most notable instance of a melting-pot of the modern world' [1938: xiv]. Andrew Lind [1938] traced the 'cycle' of social changes in Hawai'i as a function of changes in land use: a 'succession' in an ecological model of change. In Donald Pierson's [1942] study of Brazil, the African 'diaspora' [Park, 1942: xx] resulted in intermarriage and 'assimilation': 'the Aryanization of the African' [Park, 1942: xvii]. Both Hawai'i and Brazil, Park observed, exhibited a dramatically different acceptance of racial differences than was evidenced by racial patterns in the southern United States.

Barriers to the melting pot in the United States   E. Franklin Frazier's [1939] study of the Negro family was comparable to W.I. Thomas and Florian Znaniecki's *The Polish Peasant in Europe and America* (1918–1920), according to Ernest Burgess [1939/1951: iv]. The influence of neighborhood yielded family patterns that were 'not a matter so much of race as of geography' [Burgess, 1932c: xi]. Variations in behavior arose from the community situation, not from innate traits [p. xi]. Frazier [Burgess, 1939/1951: v] also documents the mother/child bond as the primary one in African American life and the family as a social product. Unlike Park, Burgess [1939/1951: vi, viii] emphasizes democracy and government policy, namely social security, as factors shaping the family and community.

In the rural South Jim Crow segregation obstructed the blending of black and white society. Johnson's [1934] study of the southern plantation, noted above, documented this regional difference from the North. Bertram Doyle [1937] described yet another regional barrier to the melting pot process: the legacy of Southern etiquette in the American South. Doyle showed the persistence of these demeaning rituals and the 'social distance' that they maintained [Park, 1937b: xxx]. Although society changed its formal laws, interpersonal segregation remained. The themes outlined above – social change, urbanization and the race question – were Park's forte, but not his individual creation. His evolving perspective was but part – an important part – of a large, community tapestry of midwestern design.

The Larger Theoretical Tapestry at the University and in the City

Park and Burgess were heirs to a stable tradition of empirical research, focused on the city, passed on by their predecessors (Schutz, 1967) at the University of Chicago. Albion W. Small, the first chair of the Department of Sociology, defined the city as a 'sociological laboratory' as early as 1896 (Deegan, 1988: 37). From Charles Zueblin, Park inherited established courses on the city. The Chicago mapping tradition was institutionalized in coursework by Charles Henderson, whose early students charted cities and villages in the field (Deegan, 1988). Burgess was a student of Small, Mead, Thomas and Henderson; while Thomas, who brought Park to the University of Chicago, profoundly influenced Park's thought.[14] Park, Burgess and Ellsworth Faris (the latter a 'silent' Chicago-trained partner/colleague) comprised the selection committee for the University of Chicago sociology series. Further, John Dewey (Park's professor at the University of Michigan) strongly influenced his former student (Matthews, 1977). As Dewey was central to 'Chicago pragmatism' (Rucker, 1969), his epistemological assumptions tied Park to a powerful line of social thought in which Burgess and Faris were trained.

Several University of Chicago departments also supported the work of Chicago ethnographers. For many decades, political scientists, such as Charles Merriam, social workers, such as Edith Abbott and Sophonisba Breckinridge, philosophers, such as George H. Mead, and geographers, such as Paul Goode, encouraged students and fostered the ideas associated today with 'Chicago sociology'. The massive interdisciplinary project at Chicago is at best only partially understood and documented today (Deegan, 1988; Rucker, 1969; Shils, 1994).

Outside the academy *per se*, Jane Addams and the numerous colleagues who shared her life at

Hull-House, the famous social settlement,[15] also shaped the intellectual and empirical traditions of the Chicago School of sociology (Deegan, 1988). For example, Mary McDowell, a former Hull-House resident, sponsored Anderson's initial work.[16] Organizations founded and maintained by Hull-House residents provided data for many authors (Wirth, Shaw, Anderson and Zorbaugh, among others). More broadly, Chicago ethnographers (with little or no acknowledgement) used records provided by entities with Hull-House ties: the Institute for Juvenile Research, the Juvenile Court, various Chicago social settlements, and myriad social welfare agencies. Hull-House and its residents contributed directly to the Chicago ethnographies sponsored by Park – albeit recognition of this fact is muted in most scholarship on the Chicago School (Deegan, 1988; Platt, 1996).

Other important influences on the core ethnographies must also be noted. These include the School of Social Service Administration and its faculty, especially Edith Abbott and Sophonisba Breckinridge (Deegan, 1988, 1991, 1996). Chicago philanthropists, especially Helen Culver and Ethel Sturgess Dummer (Platt, 1992), financed numerous research endeavors of Chicago sociologists. The Chicago Urban League was vital to Park's students who studied African Americans (Matthews, 1977: 176–7). Finally, the 'literary realism' movement gave energy and form to Chicago sociology (Cappetti, 1993). This broad conglomeration of cultural, social welfare, urban, and civic forces influenced the Chicago school of sociology in virtually countless and complex ways. Another dimension of the core ethnographies is found in the Chicago graduates who deliberately extended the original corpus, discussed next.

Core Chicago ethnographies and a selective group of related Chicago School studies A large, fascinating group of books and articles were generated by Park and Burgess and their students that were related to the core ethnographies. Only a few of these related studies are examined here, but they show the pattern of expanding the influence of the core ethnographies (Table 1.3;[17] see Kurtz, 1984 for a longer list). Burgess, for example, edited a collection of papers presented in 1928 at the American Sociological Society meetings. Thomas was then president of the society, and the papers continued his theoretical and methodological work. Many Chicago allies were included, for example, Thomas, Reuter, Park, Hughes, Hayner, R.E.L. Faris, Gosnell, Shaw and Reckless.

Similarly, Walter C. Reckless authored a complex and comprehensive book on *Vice In Chicago* [1933], extending the work of the Chicago ethnographers and, in particular, the 1911 report of the Chicago Vice Commission, *The Social Evil in Chicago*, submitted by Thomas among others (Deegan, 1988: 207). With five maps and seventy-eight tables, this quantitative, qualitative, historical study was a *tour de force*, drawing on more than twenty years of research on the city of notorious gangsters such as Al Capone and John Dillenger.

Robert E.L. Faris (son of Ellsworth Faris) and H. Warren Dunham conducted a massive ecological study of schizophrenia and other psychoses in their tome *Mental Disorders in Urban Areas* [1939]. Their first chapter summarizes and reviews many core ethnographies sponsored by their teachers (including the senior Faris), fellow students and colleagues. Faris and Dunham [1939] explicitly connect quantitative and qualitative analyses into a unit of analysis.

Ruth Shonle Cavan's study of *Suicide* [1928], with an introduction by Ellsworth Faris, also utilizes quantitative and qualitative analyses and sensitively reprints large selections from the diaries of two women who killed themselves. Although Cavan does not explicitly draw on gender, her perspective was gendered and supportive to women. Since Cavan could never have face-to-face interaction with the deceased subjects, technically she did not conduct an ethnography. Her style of analysis, however, closely followed that of the core ethnographies.

The family studies of Ernest Russell Mowrer and Harriet Mowrer – *Domestic Discord* [Mowrer and Mowrer, 1932] (the only volume to explicitly acknowledge her colleagial and substantial work),[18] *The Family* [E.R. Mowrer, 1932] and *Family Disorganization* [E.R. Mowrer, 1927] – provide a 'Chicago' analysis of a stable yet changing social relationship. Their work counterbalances the emphasis on delinquents, migrants and anonymous relations often found in the core ethnographies. These books emerge primarily from the influence of Burgess and Thomas.

By 1940 Anderson had critically and prematurely described his 1923 book on hoboes as dated. In 1931 he wrote a cynical satire about himself and his research: 'I cleansed my soul by transferring all the old emotions about *The Hobo* to one Dean Stiff, anonymous author of the parody' [Anderson, 1940: 2]. Rejuvenated by his disavowal of ideas and style, he once again began studying migrant men.

Most of the authors of the core Chicago ethnographies were prolific and critical. Their many volumes often directly extended or reflected on their earlier ethnographies. In general, other scholars were no more critical of their works, although many scholars act as if these doctoral students never wrote again or never changed and matured. The sample studies included here only hint at this vast, largely unexamined resource for studying Chicago ethnographies. Almost all were sponsored by Burgess through introductory essays.

The 'Chicago School' as a Continuing Theoretical Tapestry

Taken together, the authors listed in Tables 1.1 and 1.2 launched what became a substantial academic industry producing literally hundreds of honorifics, glosses, commentaries, explications, revisions and extensions. The dense, interconnected literature of Chicago scholarship created a powerful, integrated vision of sociology – its practice and concepts – that shaped the discipline from the 1920s to the present (Kurtz, 1984).

The corporate character of this enterprise is not always recognized. A few scholars give little weight to the intellectual skills of Park's students. Shils (1994: 33), for example, asserts that 'practically none of them wrote anything of any consequence after they passed out of the presence of Park'. Instead of this 'isolated great man' interpretation, I view Park's work as more collaborative and his teaching as more durable and effective. As an adviser and conversational partner to Chicago social scientists, particularly doctoral students, Park helped them take what was 'only the first liminal journey during a lifetime of full-fledged academic and scholarly adventures' (Deegan and Hill, 1991: 330). I posit that Park and Burgess' theoretical vision winds its way through the vast and often sophisticated work of the authors of the core ethnographies. Hence, these works, together with Park's and Burgess' introductory essays, are essential to an analysis of the Chicago ethnographic legacy.

THE THEORETICAL FOUNDATION OF THE CHICAGO ETHNOGRAPHIES

Although there are myriad explicit references to Park, Burgess and Thomas in the core ethnographies, the common world-view also emerges from Dewey and Mead, who worked within a large network of academicians, students, activists, family, friends and community and educational organizations in which they implemented their ideas. This vast interconnecting group and associated institutions were anchored at the University of Chicago but included other people, cities and academic institutions such as William James at Harvard University in Boston and Charles H. Cooley at the University of Michigan in Ann Arbor. I call this 'the world of Chicago pragmatism', and for our purposes, I focus on Mead here.

Mead's most important book, *Mind, Self and Society* (1934), establishes the social nature of the self, thought and community as a product of human meaning and interaction. Each person becomes human through interaction with others. Institutional patterns are learned in communities dependent on shared language and symbols. Human intelligence is vital for reflective behavior, and social scientists have a special responsibility to help create democratic decision-making and political action, especially in the city. The scientific model of observation, data collection and interpretation is fundamentally a human project. Sociologists can learn to take the role of others because this is how all humans learn to become part of society (Deegan, 1987, 1988; for a more extensive review of Mead's bibliography, see Mead, 1999).

This powerful and elaborate model of human behavior is usually implicit rather than explicit in the core Chicago ethnographies. Although the Meadian model permeates these writings and social thought, many scholars in this school claimed, or scholars studying their work claim, that the ethnographies were atheoretical. Almost all the authors of the core ethnographies, moreover, were students of Mead (see student list in Lewis and Smith, 1980).

Herbert Blumer called Mead's social psychology symbolic interaction or 'Chicago symbolic interactionism' (for example, Blumer, 1969; Manis and Meltzer, 1980), and it is now a significant specialty within the discipline. This group has a separate organization, journal and approach to training sociologists.[19] Other important theoretical resources were Thomas and Znaniecki's ground-breaking *The Polish Peasant in Europe and America* (5 vols, 1918–1920) as well as other work by Thomas on the definition of the situation (see Thomas, 1923; Thomas and Thomas, 1928; see also Blumer, 1939).

The Introduction to the Science of Sociology, nicknamed the 'Green Bible' for its near-sacred status, was edited by Park and Burgess and first published in 1921. This book guided all Chicago ethnographies, and most sociologists, between 1921 and 1941. This compendium of serious, scholarly writings bears little resemblance to today's slick, corporate product. Other central Park and Burgess writings included their analysis of the city (for example, Park, Burgess and McKenzie, 1925), the press, collective behavior (Park, 1950, 1955) and demographic patterns found in urban life (for example, Burgess 1973, 1974).

The combination of Mead, Dewey, Thomas, Park and Burgess, as well as the other Chicago scholars such as Small, Vincent and Henderson, created a vibrant and flexible theory of everyday life that undergirded the Chicago ethnographies. This theory interacted with the ethnographic methods, discussed next.

THE METHODOLOGICAL FOUNDATION OF THE CORE ETHNOGRAPHIES

Each core ethnography discusses its methods for data collection. Usually these involved multiple methods (now called 'triangulation') and drew on the methodological textbook of Vivien M. Palmer, *Field Studies in Sociology: A Student's Manual* [1928]. This text was developed under the guidance of Burgess who also wrote an introduction for it (see Table 1.3). Palmer [1928: ix] also thanked Park and the Hugheses, among others, for their help in its development.

Palmer's book complimented the Green Bible, but the centrality of her work is rarely acknowledged in print today. But the book flap for the 11th edition of the Green Bible described Palmer's work as a manual like a 'laboratory manual is to the physical sciences'. It was 'keyed to the principle textbooks in sociology – including *An Introduction to the Science of Sociology*'. Palmer drew frequently on the core ethnographies for her examples, showing the interconnectedness of students, faculty, quantitative and qualitative methods. Thus she presented Anderson's book on *The Hobo* [1923] as an example of mapping (a quantitative technique) that was done under Park's guidance [Palmer, 1928: 73–4]. Palmer [1928: 129–56] also stressed the importance of Thomas' 'life history method', the use of observation [pp. 161–7], diaries [pp. 106–7; 180–2], interviews [pp. 168–79], and case analyses [pp. 200–7].

Mapping had a central role in the core ethnographies as well as an important role in the theory of social ecology. The large maps plotted for the city of Chicago – the sociological laboratory – were stored with other data in a room where students learned about methods, used census data and coordinated their different interests and experiences. Creating a map was often a student assignment, and interpreting its data was stressed (for example, see Palmer [1928: 218–27]).

'The Methodological Note' in Thomas' and Znaniecki's *Polish Peasant* (1918–1920) was also frequently assigned as a way to learn about data collection, especially how to create cases to analyse and to generate a life history document. Blumer (1939) stated that this book and its note were the most central resource in sociology between 1917 and 1939, the peak era for the core ethnographies.

Finally, the student sociologists often lived in the settings studied, walked the streets, collected quantitative and qualitative data, worked for local agencies, and had autobiographical experience emerging from these locales or ones similar to them. Thus Chicago students and faculty employed triangulated methods.

THEORETICAL CONTROVERSIES: WHAT IS A SCHOOL? A METHOD? WHO IS IN A SCHOOL?

The Chicago School of sociology once dominated the discipline and continues to influence it, but this presence was clearly choreographed and dramaturgically

presented. Many contemporary scholars, especially in Britain, are confused by this sociological pattern and are trying to create order out of a method intended to be associated with literary metaphors, human understanding and a bit of flair (Carpetti, 1993) – or maybe 'hype' would be less respectful but more accurate.

Three of these British analyses are summarized here. First, Martin Bulmer (1984) discussed Burgess' place in a 'forgotten' quantitative tradition but neglected his role in a qualitative tradition while his collaborative stance with Park was downplayed. Bulmer's interpretation stresses a dichotomous view of Park as the leader and quantitative work as distinct from the overall project in Chicago sociology.[20] Jennifer Platt has a more careful series of critiques of Chicago school ethnologies and qualitative methods (see especially Platt, 1996). Despite her attempt to be exhaustive, however, she overlooked most of Burgess' writings on methods and undervalued the significance of Palmer's work. These crucial errors led her to assert that participant observation methods did not emerge at Chicago until the 1940s and 1950s, but Burgess [1932a: x] was training students in this technique, documented by Albert Blumenthal's ethnography of a small town [1932], that Platt did not examine. By adopting a quantitative framework that counted the number of studies rather than a comprehensive view analysing a person as an embodied researcher, Platt did not find a unique qualitative tradition at Chicago. But deciding if work is quantitative *or* qualitative is a distinction that fails in a number of cases. Thus John Landesco (1933) used quantitative methods in his study of crime, but he was also a convicted and incarcerated felon. Landesco had a deep understanding of the everyday life of criminals that made him an active participant and a longitudinal observer.

Lee Harvey (1987) tried to debunk the 'myths of the Chicago school' including the myth of 'Chicagoans as ethnographers' (pp. 74–108). Although Harvey is correct in pointing to an exaggeration of the single-minded qualitative approach and the contemporary form of participant observation, he repeats this type of error by denying the recognizable, substantive, unique characteristics of the Chicago ethnographers and suggests that they be called a 'unit' or some other diminutive term as an improvement (pp. 213–20). His reductionistic understatement muddies an already mixed pool of ideas and politics.[21]

Other scholars are engaged in re-cutting the historical pie in such a way that Columbia and their quantitative research methods get a bigger piece. Two examples of this revisionist thought are found in the writings of Dorothy Ross (1991), and Stephen Park Turner and Jonathan H. Turner (1990).

Most of the controversies noted in the section are hotly contested. Less attention is focused on the more important questions that concern the relation of the core ethnographies to the larger society and the validity of their depictions. In particular, the role of women in the ethnographies – as subjects, authors and colleagues – is problematic. Women as half the population in everyday life are severely understudied and underrepresented in the core Chicago ethnographies. The topic selections are also male-biased, focusing on populations in which men predominate: hoboes, juvenile delinquents, the male patrons of dance halls and gang members. Park and Burgess, moreover, had equivocal ideas about women and politics and actively separated themselves from women as sociologists (Deegan, 1988). The often ambivalent, if not conservative, politics of Park and Burgess is underexamined, as well.

In comparison to the era between 1890 and 1920, Park and Burgess, and their colleagues, ushered in a 'dark era of patriarchal ascendancy' in which the study of women was eclipsed. The critique of sexist ideas and practices in this school (summarized in Lengermann and Niebrugge-Brantley, 1998) has resulted in little internal analysis or critique. Some Chicago scholars vehemently deny that this pattern ever existed (Deegan, 1995).

Park's loyalty to Booker T. Washington profoundly shaped the political agenda of the race relations analyses, and Park's animosity toward the great sociologist W.E.B. Du Bois limited the application of the latter's more egalitarian and militant ideas within the discipline, especially in the core ethnographies. John Stanfield (1985) demonstrated that archival evidence denies the commonly held view that Park was a significant ghostwriter for Washington or an important advisor to him. The ostracism of African American critics from within the school is clearly documented in the response by the Chicago ethnographers, Park, and Everett C. Hughes to the work of Oliver C. Cox (Hunter, 2000; Hunter and Abraham, 1987). Finally, the legacy of Frazier's Victorian criticism of African American women has been profoundly negative. In particular, *The Moynihan Report* (reprinted in Rainwater and Yancy, 1967) used Frazier's writings to justify stereotyping African American mothers as too strong and independent to be endured by the African American father.[22]

The conservative, accommodationist position of the core Chicago ethnographies has been the subject of many debates in African American literature (e.g. Cox, 1944; Green and Driver, 1976; Stanfield, 1985). Despite this voluminous scholarship, largely condemnatory, many sociologists studying the Chicago school of race relations, including Park and his famous African American students, continue to unreflectively praise the Chicago literature and Park's role in it.

Finally, the methodological techniques of collecting and interpreting data are far more sophisticated today than they were prior to the Second World War. Major qualitative texts refined these procedures and a few are particularly notable. Most recently, and more frequently in disciplines other than sociology, unquestioned assumptions made by ethnographers are under critique. The white, male, middle-class perspective of many Chicago sociologists raises many obvious issues, but more subtle questions, often complex theoretical problems, need to be considered. Thus how does anyone understand the experience of another? How many ways can the same action be defined? Can a stranger ever understand an insider or an 'alien' culture? What is the role of observation and its distinctiveness from voyeurism or spying? What is reality? How important are differences between a sociologist and a subject if they vary by age, race, class, gender, sexual preference, able-bodiedness, or weight? Can anyone be objective? Why should an observer be objective? Each of these questions has been answered by different theorists and in different disciplines (as other chapters in this volume demonstrate).

Continuing the Core Ethnographic Tradition, 1942 to the Present

An easy way to refute the disputed and muddled claims over the existence of the Chicago School, its method and its theory is to read the hundreds of Chicago-style ethnographies. One could devote years to reading thousands of these studies in books and articles, but discovering the pattern, resources and contributions of the school can be garnered by reading the relatively small set of core ethnographies noted here. The tradition established by the early ethnographers was continued in various universities throughout the United States. This was particularly evident after Hughes left Chicago for Brandeis (Reinharz, 1995) and Blumer left Chicago for Berkeley.

An excellent summary of the legacy of the core ethnographies is found for various specialization in Gary A. Fine's (1995) book on the Chicago legacy between 1945 and 1960. Major figures such as William F. Whyte, Erving Goffman, Anselm Strauss, Gregory Stone, Howard S. Becker, and Fred Davis are all discussed there.

The University of Chicago Press institutionalized Chicago ethnographies originally, and it persists in this support through reprints with new introductions. Thus many of the books in Tables 1.1, 1.2 and 1.3 remain available to new readers and students. The introductions often provide an overview of the book's reception, audiences and role in sociology and occasionally the larger society. The late Morris Janowitz took an especially active role in this process by editing the *Heritage of Sociology* series. In many ways – in terms of its broad scope, support for Chicago graduates in the past and the then-present, and its stature within the discipline – Janowitz created a series modeled after the original sociological series sponsored by Park, Burgess and Faris. He continued to teach this tradition in his classes until his retirement in 1979, training new cohorts of Chicago sociologists in the process.

In addition to the *Heritage of Sociology* series, produced on a smaller scale and edited by Donald L. Levine in the 1980s and 1990s, Chicago ethnographies are flourishing in many universities and being published by many presses, especially by the University of California Press. John Van Maanen's qualitative sociology series for Sage Publications, for example, has published qualitative methods books every year, for many years. Not too surprisingly, Van Maanen (1988) is himself a product of the Chicago ethnographic tradition. Norman Denzin and Helen Znaniecka Lopata also edit annual book series often supporting the ethnographic tradition. Similarly, the *Journal of Contemporary Ethnography* (founded in 1971 as *Urban Life*) continues to support and publish new ethnographic literature that is produced at a steady and prolific rate.

New departments continue to emerge as institutional resources for ethnographies and these vary by personnel and eras. Thus the University of California–San Diego, the University of Georgia, the University of Nevada–Las Vegas, the University of New York–Syracuse, the University of California–San Francisco, the University of Texas–Austin, the University of California–Berkeley, and the University of California–Los Angeles have been home to such enterprises. The University of Trento in Italy, and sociologists in Poland are two international resources for the elaboration of core ethnographies, as well.

CONCLUSION

The Chicago ethnographers were central figures in the development of a unique Chicago School. They generated a vital picture of urban life grounded in local studies and a sympathetic eye on human behavior. Their contributions to scholarship and a reflexive society are now classics recognized by sociologists throughout the world.

As teachers, mentors, critics, faculty members and gatekeepers to the University of Chicago Press, Park and Burgess structured and abetted the formation of the Chicago ethnographers, their worldviews and their writings. Their students continued Park and Burgess' influence throughout their own careers and, in time, the next generation of students continued and augmented this tradition.

The theoretical tapestry undergirding the core ethnographies took form in a rich intellectual and social milieu that included other Chicago sociologists who were Park and Burgess' predecessors and contemporaries. Faculty and students from cognate departments and disciplines, especially philosophy and social work, were also part of this environment. In addition, social agencies and social settlements, principally Jane Addams and Hull-House, contributed fundamental ideas and data to this intellectual project and, importantly, also challenged the men of the University of Chicago.

Today's heirs to the Chicago sociological tradition continue to weave a tapestry in what is now a considerably more complex and diverse discipline. Contemporary sociology is a more national and international endeavor with multiple visions and actors. Within this vast enterprise, however, Park and Burgess and their vision of sociology remain catalysts for the study of human behavior and its embeddedness in specific people and places.

NOTES

1 These dates encompass the start of the Department of Sociology at the University of Chicago and end with the last publication date of the core Chicago ethnographies. Other dates for other topics could be selected and are the subject of considerable discussion. See Fine, 1995 and Harvey, 1987 for examples of this type of debate.

2 The group studied here did not formally call themselves 'Chicago school ethnographers' between 1892 and 1942. They did, nonetheless, consciously self-identify as a group with a specific method. They often called this a 'hands on' or 'getting one's hands dirty' method and contrasted this scornfully to merely quantitative methods or 'armchair philosophy' involving only library research. I asked Everett C. Hughes, a Chicago ethnographer as both a student and a faculty member, specific questions on self-identification and research methods in an oral history interview, April, 1972, held at the University of Chicago for students there. When I tried to get more specific information and probed on their ability to know these things at the time they were emerging as ideas and methods, he gruffly replied: 'Do you think we were a pack of idiots who didn't know what we were doing?' Herbert Blumer, another Chicago ethnographer as both a student and a faculty member, verified this information as well.

3 The effect of W.I. Thomas, George H. Mead and John Dewey is multidimensional and multigenerational. Thus Burgess studied with Mead and Thomas, and the latter studied with Dewey. Dewey trained Park, at the University of Michigan, and Thomas mentored Park at the University of Chicago. See a partial chart of these relationships in Deegan, 1988: 16 and a partial list of Mead's sociology students in Lewis and Smith, 1980: 192–3.

4 Throughout the text the use of square brackets denotes citations of references to be found in Table 1.1 (introductions by Park), Table 1.2 (introductions by Burgess) or Table 1.3 (studies related to the core ethnographies). The

works listed in the Tables are not subsequently included in the list of references at the chapter's end.

5 Burgess sponsored a study of two- and three-year-old children at play that was directed by Dorothy Van Alstyne (1932). Burgess wrote a preface to this fascinating analysis that combined participant observation and quantitative measurement of how small children play. This project was not called sociology and was sponsored by the Behavior Research Fund headed by Burgess. This book is not included in the Tables here but fits the pattern of Chicago school ethnographies.

6 Park's larger number of ethnographic books can be interpreted as an indicator of Park's greater power, the most common interpretation, or of a collegial division of labor between Park and Burgess. In the latter case, they divided the work into two parts with different, compatible emphases.

7 The confused published record makes it difficult – without further archival research – to state accurately which authors in Tables 1.1 and 1.2 were Park's or Burgess' doctoral advisees. There are errors even in the more public records, such as catalogs or lists of staff. I err on the side of caution and see both Park and Burgess as interacting colleagues in the production of the core ethnographies. For some, Park or Burgess may have been a doctoral committee member, a classroom instructor, or simply a like-minded colleague. In all cases, however, Park and Burgess' imprint and acknowledged influence is clear. Lists of doctoral degrees granted at the University of Chicago from 1893 to 1935 are found in Faris, 1967: 135–40 and from 1946 to 1965 in Fine, 1995: 387–403.

8 My theoretical analysis of the ritual collage across time and space is more fully drawn in Deegan, 1998: 151–67.

9 I am using the term 'conversations' as Mead (1934) used it. Conversations are part of the process of creating a self, in this case a professional self (see discussion in Deegan and Hill, 1991).

10 See numerous letters and documents to this effect in the University of Chicago Press Records, Department of Special Collections, University of Chicago.

11 The reference here is to Thomas' concept of 'wishes' as the inborn impulses to have new experiences, security, recognition and response. These wishes generated a large bibliography summarized and used in Park and Burgess, 1921 (e.g., definitions, pp. 488–90; bibliography, pp. 500–1).

12 Park to Laing, 22 November 1928, University of Chicago Press Records, box 154, folder 4.

13 Park's antipathy to women as equals and colleagues is analysed in Deegan, 1988 (discussion, pp. 213–16); Deegan, 1992 (distortion in concepts); Deegan, 1991 (role in generating the 'dark era of patriarchal ascendancy'), and summarized in Deegan, 1995.

14 See, for example, Park [1942].

15 More information on the theory and praxis of Hull-House can be found in Jane Addams' sociological autobiographies (1910, 1930). Charlene Haddock Seigfried (1996) and I (Deegan, 1999) link this work to the ideas of Mead and Dewey as well.

16 Anderson interview, 30 August 1979.

17 Some scholars might argue that some of these books are 'core' Chicago ethnographies, too. Again, I took a cautious definition where the core ethnographies are widely recognized by many scholars, although I have generated this particular term in this chapter.

18 E. Mowrer [1932: x] wrote in the preface of *The Family* that: 'For constant encouragement, stimulus, and assistance the author is under obligation to Harriet R. Mowrer.' The professional collegial status of his wife, who specialized in the same area and was trained at the same school, is not mentioned nor is her assistance specified. He [E. Mowrer, 1927: xv] wrote in the preface of *Family Disorganization* that: 'Harriet R. Mowrer, who contributed to the case-study section both in analysis and materials'. This is the substantive portion of the book, pp. 127–265. The total book is 308 pp. long.

19 Many Meadian scholars interpret Mead's thought very differently from Blumer's interpretation, and this is only one of many controversies in Chicago scholarship (e.g. Deegan, 1988; Lewis and Smith, 1980).

20 For a more detailed critique of Bulmer, see Deegan, 1985.

21 For a more detailed critique of Harvey, see Deegan, 1990.

22 Anthony Platt (1991) believes that Moynihan misinterpreted Frazier, but I do not (Deegan, 1992).

References and Further Reading

Unpublished Materials

University of Chicago Press Records. Department of Special Collections, University of Chicago, Chicago, Illinois.

Personal Interviews

Personal interview with Nels Anderson by Mary Jo Deegan. Boston, Massachusetts, 30 August 1979.

Personal interviews and conversations with Ruth Shonle Cavan by Mary Jo Deegan between 1976 and 1993.

Books and Articles

Park's and Burgess' prefaces and introductions, and bibliographic citations of the core ethnographies and related Chicago School studies, are found in Tables 1.1, 1.2 and 1.3 respectively.

Addams, Jane (1910) *Twenty Years at Hull-House*. New York: Macmillan.

Addams, Jane (1930) *The Second Twenty Years at Hull-House*. New York: Macmillan.

Blumer, Herbert (1939) *An Appraisal of Thomas and Znaniecki's The Polish Peasant*. New York: Social Science Research Council.

Blumer, Herbert (1969) *Symbolic Interactionism*. Englewood Cliffs, NJ: Prentice–Hall.

Bogue, Donald (1974) 'Introduction', in *The Basic Writings of Ernest W. Burgess* (ed. Donald J. Bogue). Chicago: Community and Family Study Center, the University of Chicago. pp. ix–xxiv.

Bulmer, Martin (1984) *The Chicago School of Sociology*. Chicago: University of Chicago Press.

Burgess, Ernest W. (ed.) (1929) *Personality and the Social Group*. Chicago: University of Chicago Press.

Burgess, Ernest W. (1973) *On Community, Family, and Delinquency* (ed. Leonard S. Cottrell, Jr, Albert Hunter and James F. Short). Chicago: University of Chicago Press.

Burgess, Ernest W. (1974) *The Basic Writings of Ernest W. Burgess* (ed. Donald J. Bogue). Chicago: Community and Family Study Center, the University of Chicago.

Burgess, Ernest W. and Bogue, Donald J. (eds) (1964) *Contributions to Urban Sociology*. Chicago: University of Chicago Press.

Cappetti, Carla (1993) *Writing Chicago*. New York: Columbia.

Cox, Oliver C. (1944) 'The racial theories of Robert E. Park and Ruth Benedict', *Journal of Negro Education*, 13 (Fall): 452–63.

Deegan, Mary Jo (1985) 'Book Review of Martin Bulmer, *The Chicago Tradition'*, *Contemporary Sociology*, 14 (May): 365–6.

Deegan, Mary Jo (1987) 'Symbolic interaction and the study of women', in Mary Jo Deegan and Michael R. Hill (eds), *Women and Symbolic Interaction*. Boston, MA: Allen and Unwin. pp. 3–15.

Deegan, Mary Jo (1988) *Jane Addams and the Men of the Chicago School, 1892–1920*. New Brunswick, NJ: Transaction Books.

Deegan, Mary Jo (1989) *American Ritual Dramas: Social Rules and Cultural Meanings*. Westport, CT: Greenwood Press.

Deegan, Mary Jo (1990) 'Book Review of *The Chicago School* and *Myths of the Chicago School of Sociology'*, *British Journal of Sociology*, 41 (December): 587–90.

Deegan, Mary Jo (ed.) (1991) *Women in Sociology: A Bio-Bibliographic Sourcebook*. Westport, CT: Greenwood Press.

Deegan, Mary Jo (1992) 'Professional life behind the veil', Keynote address at the Hawai'i Sociological Association meetings.

Deegan, Mary Jo (1994) '"The marginal man" as a gendered concept', in Renzo Gubert and Luigi Tomasi. (eds), *Robert E. Park and the 'Melting Pot' Theory*. Trento, Italy: Reverdito Editizioni. pp. 55–71.

Deegan, Mary Jo (1995) 'The second sex and the women of the Chicago School, women's accounts, knowledge, and work, 1945–1960', in Gary Fine (ed.), *A Second Chicago School?* Chicago: University of Chicago Press. pp. 322–64.

Deegan, Mary Jo (1996) 'Dear Love, Dear Love: feminist pragmatism and the Chicago female world of love and ritual', *Gender and Society*, 10 (October): 590–607.

Deegan, Mary Jo (ed.) (1998) *The American Ritual Tapestry: Social Rules and Cultural Meanings*. Westport, CT: Greenwood Press.

Deegan, Mary Jo (1999) 'Play from the perspective of George Herbert Mead', in George H. Mead, *Play, School and Society* (ed. and intro. by Mary Jo Deegan). New York: Peter Lang.

Deegan, Mary Jo and Hill, Michael R. (1991) 'Doctoral dissertations as liminal journeys of the self', *Teaching Sociology*, 19 (July): 322–32.

Donovan, Frances (1920) *The Woman Who Waits*. Boston, MA: Gorham.

Faris, Robert E.L. (1967) *Chicago Sociology: 1920–1932*. Chicago, IL: University of Chicago Press.

Fine, Gary A. (ed.) (1995) *A Second Chicago School?* Chicago: University of Chicago Press.

Goffman, Erving (1959) *The Presentation of Self in Everyday Life*. Garden City, NY: Anchor Books, Doubleday.

Green, Dan S. and Driver, Edwin D. (1976) 'W.E.B. Du Bois', *Phylon*, 38 (4): 308–33.

Gubert, Renzo and Tomasi, Luigi (eds) (1994) *Robert E. Park and the 'Melting Pot' Theory* (Sociologia, No. 9). Trento, Italy: Reverdito Editzioni.

Harvey, Lee (1987) *Myths of the Chicago School of Sociology*. Aldershot: Gower.

Hughes, Everett Cherrington ([1963] 1974) 'E. Franklin Frazier: a memoir by Everett C. Hughes', in E. Franklin Frazier, *The Negro Church in America*. New York: Schoken.

Hunter, Herbert (2000) *The Sociology of Oliver C. Cox: New Perspectives* (ed. Herbert Hunter). Greenwich, CT: JAI Press.

Hunter, Herbert and Abraham, Sameer V. (eds) (1987) *Race, Class, and the World System*, by Oliver C. Cox (intro. by Herbert M. Hunter and Sameer V. Abraham). New York: Monthly Review Press.

Kurtz, Richard (1984) *Evaluating Chicago Sociology*. Chicago, IL: University of Chicago Press.

Lal, Barbara Ballis (1990) *The Romance of Culture in an Urban Civilization*. London: Routledge.

Landesco, John (1933) 'Member of the 42 Gang', *Journal of Criminal Law and Criminology*, March: 967–80.

Lengermann, Patricia and Niebrugge-Brantley, Jill (1998) *The Women Founders of the Social Sciences*. New York: McGraw–Hill.

Lewis, J. David and Smith, Richard L. (1980) *American Sociology and Pragmatism*. Chicago: University of Chicago Press.

Lindner, Rolf (1996) *The Reportage of Urban Culture*. New York: Cambridge University Press.

Lyman, Stanford M. (1990) *Civilization*. Fayetteville, AR: University of Arkansas Press.

Manis, Jerome and Meltzer, Bernard (1980) *Symbolic Interactionism*, 3rd edn. Boston, MA: Beacon Press.

Matthews, Fred H. (1977) *Quest for an American Sociology*. Montreal: McGill–Queens University Press.

Matthews, Fred H. (1994) 'The roles of Robert E. Park in the Chicago School', in Renzo Gubert and Luigi Tomasi (eds), *Robert E. Park and the 'Melting Pot'*

Theory (Sociologia, No. 9). Trento, Italy: Reverdito Editzioni.

Mead, George H. (1934) *Mind, Self and Society* (ed. and intro. by Charles Morris). Chicago, IL: University of Chicago Press.

Mead, George H. (1999). *Play, School, and Society* (ed. and intro. by Mary Jo Deegan). New York: Peter Lang.

Park, Robert E. (1928) 'Human migration and the marginal man', *American Journal of Sociology*, 33 (May): 881–93.

Park, Robert E. (1931) 'Personality and cultural conflict', *Publications of the American Sociological Society*, 25 (May): 95–110.

Park, Robert E. (1937) 'Cultural conflict and the marginal man', introduction to *The Marginal Man*, by E.V. Stonequist. New York: Scribner's. pp. xiii–xviii.

Park, Robert E. (1941) 'Methods of teaching', *Social Forces*, 20 (October). Reprinted in *Militarism, Imperialism, and Racial Accommodation* by Stanford M. Lyman. Fayetteville, AR: University of Arkansas Press (1992). pp. 306–18.

Park, Robert E. (1950) *Race and Culture*. Glencoe, IL: The Free Press.

Park, Robert E. (1955) *Society*. Glencoe, IL: The Free Press.

Park, Robert E. and Burgess, Ernest W. (1921) *Introduction to the Science of Sociology*. Chicago: University of Chicago Press.

Park, Robert E., Burgess, Ernest W. and McKenzie, Robert D. (1925) *The City*. Chicago: University of Chicago Press.

Persons, Stow (1987) *Ethnic Studies at Chicago, 1905–1945*. Urbana, IL: University of Illinois Press.

Platt, Anthony (1991) *E. Franklin Frazier Reconsidered*. New Brunswick, NJ: Rutgers University Press.

Platt, Jennifer (1992) '"Acting as a switchboard": Mrs Ethel Sturgess Dummer's role in sociology', *American Sociologist*, 23 (Fall): 23–36.

Platt, Jennifer (1996) *A History of Sociological Research Methods in America, 1920–1960*. Cambridge: Cambridge University Press.

Rainwater, Lee and Yancy, William (eds) (1967) *The Moynihan Report and the Politics of Controversy*. Cambridge, MA: MIT Press.

Rauschenbush, Winifred (1979) *Robert E. Park*. Chapel Hill, NC: University of North Carolina Press.

Reinharz, Shulamit (1995) 'The Chicago School of sociology and the founding of Brandeis University graduate program in sociology', in Gary A. Fine (ed.), *A Second Chicago School?* Chicago: University of Chicago Press. pp. 273–321.

Ross, Dorothy (1991) *The Origins of American Social Sciences*. New York: Cambridge.

Rucker, Darnell (1969) *The Chicago Pragmatists*. Minneapolis, MN: University of Minnesota Press.

Schutz, Alfred (1967) *The Phenomenology of the Social World* (trans. G. Walsh and F. Lehnert, intro. by G. Walsh). Evanston, IL: Northwestern University Press.

Seigfried, Charlene Haddock (1996) *Pragmatism and Feminism*. Chicago: University of Chicago Press.

Shils, Edward (1991) 'Robert E. Park, 1864–1944', *American Scholar*, 60 (Winter): 120–7.

Shils, Edward (1994) 'The sociology of Robert E. Park', in Renzo Gubert and Luigi Tomasi (eds), *Robert E. Park and the 'Melting Pot' Theory* (Sociologia, No. 9). Trento, Italy: Reverdito Edizioni. pp. 15–34.

Short, James F., Jr (1971) *The Social Fabric of the Metropolis*. Chicago, IL: University of Chicago Press.

Smith, Dennis (1988) *The Chicago School: A Liberal Critique of Capitalism*. New York: Macmillan.

Stanfield, John (1985) *Philanthropy and Jim Crow in American Social Science*. Westport, CT: Greenwood Press.

Thomas, W.I. (1923) *The Unadjusted Girl: With Cases and Standpoint for Behavior Analysis*. Boston, MA: Little, Brown.

[Thomas, W.I.], Park, Robert E. [listed erroneously as first author] and Miller, Herbert A. (1921) *Old World Traits Transplanted*. New York: Harper and Brothers. [Reprint, with the authorship of 'W.I. Thomas together with Robert E. Park and Herbert A. Miller', and a new introduction by Donald R. Young. Montclair, NJ: Patterson Smith, 1971.]

Thomas, William I. and Swaine Thomas, Dorothy (1928) *The Child in America: Behavior Problems and Programs*. New York: Knopf.

Thomas, W.I. and Znaniecki, Florian (1918–1920) *The Polish Peasant in Europe and America*, 5 vols. Boston, MA: Richard G. Badger. (Vols. 1 and 2 originally published by University of Chicago Press, 1918.)

Turner, Ralph H. (1967) 'Introduction', *Robert E. Park: On Social Control and Collective Behavior*. Chicago: University of Chicago Press.

Turner, Stephen Park and Turner, Jonathan H. (1990) *The Impossible Science*. Newbury Park, CA: Sage.

Van Alstyne, Dorothy (1932) *Play Behavior and Choice of Play Materials of Pre-School Children*. Chicago: University of Chicago Press.

Van Maanen, John (1988) *Tales of the Field: On Writing Ethnography*. Chicago: University of Chicago Press.

Whyte, William Foote (1981) *Street Corner Society*, 3rd rev. edn. Chicago: University of Chicago Press.

2

Symbolic Interactionism and Ethnography

PAUL ROCK

This handbook makes it clear how very many different forms of ethnography there are. In this short chapter it would be best if I focused upon symbolic interactionism only as it bears upon ethnography, and ethnography only as it bears upon symbolic interactionism. In doing so, and mindful of the contested history of interactionism, I shall reconstruct a version of the theory which dwells upon the activities of people in face-to-face relations. That is a version which places interactionism on the borders between micro-sociology and social psychology where its ideas engender the fewest dilemmas and contradictions (see Rock, 1979). And I shall draw particularly heavily, but not exclusively, on work that was written in the theory's hey-day, the three decades of the 1950s, 1960s and 1970s.

'Symbolic interactionism' was the 'somewhat barbarous' name (Blumer, 1969: 1) belatedly awarded in 1937 to a distinctive style of sociological reasoning and methodology that had evolved in and about the Department of Sociology of the University of Chicago during the previous two decades. It was only one of the many interconnected intellectual currents that flowed out of the department at the time (others included functionalism, subcultural theory, social ecology, disorganization theory, social epidemiology and survey research; see Bulmer, 1985) but it is on interactionism alone that this chapter will dwell.

The department was an original, having been founded in 1892, at the same time as the new university and when sociology itself was only just beginning to take form. There had been no earlier generations of sociologists working professionally in institutional settings in America or anywhere else to establish what forms the discipline should take

(Robert Park, one of the pre-eminent early members of the department, declared that he had never heard the word 'sociology' whilst he was a student at the University of Michigan between 1883 and 1887; Rauschenbush, 1979: 78). A primal, large department, well funded by monies supplied by the Rockefeller family and by civic commissions preoccupied with the moral condition of a city undergoing rapid social change (see Reckless, 1933), it was set within a university that was not only driven by an insistence on the primacy of research (MacAloon, 1992: 3) but which also held no settled preconceptions about what sociology should be. Leonard Cottrell, one of those who had studied in the department at the beginning of the century, recollected that '[we were] rejecting all the traditional answers and institutions that were allegedly the stabilizers of society' (Carey, 1975: 154).

The emphasis was on improvization and openness, and, *inter alia*, the outcome was to be an investigative tradition that was disseminated in a bulky series of research monographs published by the University of Chicago Press (Fine supplies a near exhaustive list of those monographs, Fine, 1995); the founding in 1895 of what was to become a major journal, the *American Journal of Sociology*, that was unrivalled until the appearance of the *American Sociological Review* in 1936; and the editing of the standard American sociological textbook, the *Introduction to the Science of Sociology* (Park and Burgess, 1921), that became known colloquially as the 'Green Bible'.

Sociology cultivated at the University of Chicago bestrode the early history of the discipline in the United States. It was to be eclipsed only in the

1930s with the rise of social science at Harvard University (and especially the publication in 1937 of Talcott Parsons' *The Structure of Social Action*) and the flight of German and Austrian intellectuals to Columbia University and the New School for Social Research (Krohn, 1993). It is significant that it was precisely at that point, when it no longer held sway, that it was christened. It *was* sociology for many purposes (see Chapter 1 by Mary Jo Deegan). In the 1930s, 1940s and 1950s, the University of Chicago exported teachers and ideas to universities throughout the United States, and especially through the contiguous Midwest, to Northwestern University and the State Universities of Indiana, Iowa and Minnesota, and from thence to the West and the many branches of the University of California, where it thrived in the 1960s. Interactionism survives now, albeit in diminished form, being celebrated in its own eponymous journal, *Symbolic Interaction*, and learned society, the Society for the Study of Symbolic Interaction.

So central was interactionism in its hey-day, so intermeshed was it with the practical conduct of empirical enquiry, that for a long while its students professed not to be aware of contrasting ways of conducting sociology. Faris observed of the time of the inception of the theory, 'Students at Chicago in the 1920s never heard the term *symbolic interactionism* applied to their social psychology tradition and no member of the department either attempted to name it or encouraged such naming. Every consideration was given to open exploration, none to naming or defending doctrine' (Faris, 1967: 88). It was only when they ventured out and encountered others who did things differently that they became fully conscious that they did, in fact, embody a distinct intellectual stance. Of a later period, one of the department's most eminent students, Howard Becker, recalled that 'although we fought a lot with one another, without quite knowing it we all shared that basic point of view and became more aware of it as we got out into the world and met people from Columbia, Harvard and other places who didn't seem to understand things the right way' (in Debro, 1970: 162).

THE ORGANIZING ASSUMPTIONS OF SYMBOLIC INTERACTIONISM

Symbolic interactionism has always been an open, deceptively modest, loosely organized and self-consciously unreflective practice, and it has never been possible (or even deemed desirable) to lay down precisely what it comprises. Indeed, as I shall show, it is inclined to be theoretically self-silencing because it has resisted systematization on systematic grounds. Becker once told me that 'it's not an easy

position to understand ... partly, I think, because (like Zen) it's so simple'.

Perhaps the most forthright approximation to a definition was that propounded by Herbert Blumer, the man who had given it a name: 'The symbolic interactionist approach rests upon the premise that human action takes place always in a situation that confronts the actor and that the actor acts on the basis of *defining this situation* that confronts him' (Blumer, 1997: 4; emphasis in original).

Underpinning that seemingly straightforward description are a number of discursive themes that were current at the time when interactionism was conceived (for a rather different, more structural model of symbolic interactionism and the work of the Chicago sociologists, see Deegan, Chapter 1). There is *idealism*, which stresses the pervasive importance of consciousness as an organizing process in history, society and psychology. We do not react to 'facts' as they 'really are' (how could we ever do so?), but to our consciousness of those facts, and that consciousness is necessarily interpretive and *experiential*. Robert Park once reflected that 'the real world [is] the experience of actual men and women and not abbreviated and shorthand descriptions of it that we call knowledge' (Baker, 1973: 255). There is, by extension, an opposition to what might be called 'academicism', 'the idea that what is important is not messy experience but rather the true nature of the world underlying its appearances, as embodied in scientifically produced knowledge' (this statement is taken from the helpful observations of an anonymous referee of an earlier draft of this chapter).

Consciousness is not static. It is held to move dialectically, constituting itself synthetically stage by stage as ideas are objectified into seemingly external events and actions that confront a thinker as alienated phenomena and which elicit responses that can become alienated from their author in their turn. Ironically, symbolic interactionism was itself to become subject to just such a dialectical turn: at first it was little more than an understated way of pursuing enquiry; it was later to be reified as a 'school' which could be discussed, taught and practised; it became subject to criticism and then, in the eyes of some of its critics, it was displaced by later postmodernist (Denzin, 1997) or radical theories (Plummer, 1979).

The idealism underpinning interactionism was to be counterbalanced by an empiricism which maintained that people are not quite free, in Ernest Gellner's expression, to 'roll their own world'. Reality is not a mere projection of the individual imagination (Charles Peirce said 'some things are *forced* upon cognition ... there is the element of brute force existing whether you opine it not'; in Mills, 1964: 158). Neither is it infinitely malleable. It constrains and informs because, in Blumer's phrase, it 'can "talk back" to our pictures of it' (Blumer, 1969: 22). If facts do not imprint themselves photographically on a blank mind, and if mind cannot liberally invent its own environment, consciousness will unfold within a special process that transcends both polarities, the 'knowing–known transaction' that merges thinker, thought and things known into a single dialectic. Put concretely, people are held to confront problems in the world by acting upon it. In acting, they will learn about the world and so reformulate their ideas; and that reformulation, in its turn, may induce them to return to the world with new questions which can lead to yet newer ideas; and on and on until the problem has been solved for practical purposes, or until the questioner has retired because of boredom, satiation or distraction. At each step, not only will the world appear to change but so will those who question it as they learn more about their environment and their identity within it, their capacities and potentiality.

Descriptions of the structure of that process were to be elaborated by Simmel's neo-Kantian *formalism*, which argued that the proper business of sociology is not to attend to the unique and indescribable contents of experience but to the more general *forms* which consciousness employs to organize, interpret and name experience (Levine, 1971; Ray, 1991). We may never encounter the same situation twice, but, as conscious members of society, we do deploy a very general grammar, lexicon or logic of forms which enables us to ascertain what kind (or form) of situation lies before us and what kind (or form) of response we might appropriately make. Instances of such concepts are the career, hierarchy, conflict, succession and symbiosis, and their use may be discovered throughout interactionist writing.

Formalism echoes arguments about the dialectic of the knowing–known transaction. Simmel also held that, in their effort to break free from convention and constraint, people continually engender new ways of doing and seeing things that can become detached, fixed and constraining, only to excite new responses that can themselves become formalized. Each twist in that dialectical spiral will incorporate and re-arrange some part of what has gone before, the internal and the external, the subjective and the objective, and each will transcend its predecessor in a fashion that cannot be explained merely by summing its parts. In art, for example, one aesthetic school after another will surrender to its successor, each being championed for a while as a liberating new way of seeing the world, only subsequently to be dismissed as a formalistic restraint by the next generation. But, at the same time, each school may absorb some part of the style of its predecessors through borrowing and negation, through what Hegelians would call 'sublation'.

Those themes have a number of correlates. First, thought is interpreted almost wholly as *purposive*, practical and intentional: it is an *activity*, and a symbol is itself defined by interactionists as action towards an object which is rehearsed in the imagination. Secondly, thought is *emergent*: if it is considered to be part of a process of practical activity, if it is dialectical, moving stage by stage, constituted as it reacts to itself and to features of the world about it, it cannot be simply reduced down to its initial conditions. Neither, by extension, can it always be predicted in advance because each stage will incorporate and synthesize new elements in new ways. Thirdly, thought entails a constant interaction between mind and its environment in which each constitutes the other: the dualities of mind and matter were thought to have been quite superseded in the forms of the knowing–known transaction. Thinkers were no longer considered to be alienated observers contemplating an external world. On the contrary: facts, as Lafferty once said, 'are bits of biography' (Lafferty, 1932: 206). Fourthly, and by simple extrapolation, thought and action are *situated*: they are always and everywhere directed by identifiable thinkers towards specific problems located within a discrete historical, autobiographical and social context – and context is itself defined and recognized by purpose, thought and action:

> In actual experience, there is never any ... isolated singular object or event; an object or event is always a special part, phase or aspect, of an environing experienced world – a situation. The singular object stands out conspicuously because of its especially focal and crucial position at a given time in determination of some problem of use or enjoyment which the *total* environment presents. (Dewey, 1938: 67)

Fifthly, thought is *reflective*: it can turn back on itself, its acts and its setting. In so doing, it creates selves by bifurcating consciousness into subject and object, thinker and thing thought, namer and thing named, 'I' and 'me'. The 'I' in the language of George Herbert Mead is that which thinks, sees and names, and it can never be directly scrutinized because it would then instantly cease to be an 'I' and become a 'me' in its stead. It evades inspection and, by extrapolation, direct personal and social control. Yet the 'I' is manifestly in conversation or relation with its 'me', indeed with its many 'me's, and it is constituted socially as they are.

The 'me', by contrast, is the self made visible, audible and objective, and there are as many 'me's as there are situations in which it can be displayed. One is not quite the same with one's lover, employer, children, parents or strangers. Each of those others summons up a modified or edited performance which is considered appropriate to the situation. Yet there is no simple determinism operating in this scheme. People *interpret* the reality about them. They do not respond as if they were automata. If situations can elicit selves, it is held, selves can also shape situations, and, in that process, there may be variability, changefulness and ambiguity enough to permit opportunities for improvization and innovation (Turner, 1962).

Intrinsic to the workings of social action, then, is the very consciousness of the thinker as one who can think about himself or herself thinking. What makes human action distinctive is the capacity of people not only to understand the world symbolically but also to understand themselves and others as symbolic and symbol-using beings. People respond to themselves and others, and their responses are mediated in part by a vicarious imagination of the other and his or her responses, by what has come to be called taking the role of the other. In that process not only do gestures have a potential to bear meaning for others, becoming significant, but self and other can become synthesized in consciousness, and the social is born. That idea of the 'significant gesture' is at the very heart of interactionism because it is in the rehearsal of action that one anticipates the other's reaction and builds it into one's own imminent behaviour, becoming, as it were, symbolically both self and other in the emerging act. Mead put it that 'It is through the ability to be the other at the same time he is himself that the symbol becomes significant' (Mead, 1922: 161).

People thereby make sense of the world by attempting to interpret themselves and others as they are revealed through emerging, situated acts on the social scene. They are obliged to try to decipher the meanings and boundaries of gestures, selves and situations that are in continual interaction with one another. Interactionists would claim no sovereign powers for the intellects either of themselves as observing sociologists or of the people whom they describe. People, it should be repeated, do not and cannot fully know themselves and others 'as they really are'. To the contrary, selves and gestures are understood *inferentially* and *probabilistically*, and definitions may be subject continually to testing, revision and reversal as action unfolds. For the most part, of course, people do not have the time or curiosity diligently to check every display before them. Much must be taken on trust and much must be conventionalized. It is only when they discover that they cannot understand one another at all well or when encounters are particularly fateful that people may become aware of the indeterminate, tentative and fragile character of interpretive work (Glaser and Strauss, 1965). And interaction may then dissolve into an infinite regress where one cannot fully know what the other knows about what one knows about the other.

Those who count most in the formulation of the significant gesture are, prosaically enough, called 'significant others', because it is principally to them, through, with and before them that actions are symbolically constructed: 'the "other" forms the self as the self forms the "other". In all situations of social life, the "other" is manifest, concretely or abstractly. And as the "other" manifests itself, its character and content become causally significant to the emergence of the self and *its* nature and content' (Perinbanayagam, 1975: 502). Significant others define acts and selves, and they are themselves situated: who is important in the phrasing of one gesture (say, the writing of a book) may be unimportant in another (the passing of a driving test, buying a drink or completion of a tax return). And they themselves have the ability to define situations: the appearance of a lover, adversary, hero or employer on the social scene may not only transform its significance but also the very meaning of the people who populate it.

Being symbolically incorporated in the relations of the self, part of the inner conversation which phrases action, significant others are not required physically to be present to affect gestures. It is enough that some image of them plays a part, and those images may have only the most tangential connection with the embodied reality of another. Significant others are editings of knowledge, constituted for purposes of action, and they can be idealizations or, indeed, fictions. Remember Alexander who was under the spell of his ancestor, Achilles, Joan of Arc and her angels or David Berkowitz who believed himself to be possessed by a demon called Son of Sam. Significant others may not even be discrete others, but anonymized and universalized distillations that have been compressed into a 'generalized' other or symbolic community devised by the self, and instances would include the family, neighbours, the nation, 'people' at large or, indeed, humanity itself. Whenever someone wonders 'what will people say?', there is an invocation of the generalized other.

SYMBOLIC INTERACTIONISM AND ETHNOGRAPHY

It is evident that any research grounded in symbolic interactionism will be tentative, empirical and responsive to meaning. The social world is taken to be a place where little can be taken for granted *ab initio*, a place not of statics but of process, where acts, objects and people have evolving and intertwined local identities that may not be revealed at the outset or to an outsider. It does not do to presume too much in advance. Knowledge, it is held, is not won in the library but in the field, and it is for that very reason that ethnographers conduct fieldwork. In an important passage, Park and Burgess argued:

> It has been the dream of philosophers that theoretical and abstract sciences could and some day perhaps would succeed in putting into formulae and into general terms all that was significant in the concrete facts of life. It has been the tragic mistake of the so-called intellectuals, who have gained their knowledge from text-books

rather than from observation and research, to assume that science has already realized its dream. (Park and Burgess, 1921: 15)

'Ethnography' itself is a term that was somewhat loosely borrowed from social anthropology, and it alludes to the situated, empirical description of peoples and races. There are other terms which also cover the same procedure – fieldwork, qualitative sociology, participant observation, what Geertz called 'thick description' (Geertz, 1973) – and they all aim at a method that is imbued with many interpretive strands and layers, committed in some measure to reconstructing the actor's own world-view, not in a lordly way but faithful to the everyday life of the subject. The precise terminology is not especially important: in symbolic interactionism these words are worn lightly, not intended to signal very firm differences and barriers between approaches.

The practice of interactionist ethnography flows directly from the organizing assumptions of symbolic interactionism itself. In following interactionist epistemology, in what is inevitably a substantially personal account of the relationship between symbolic interactionism and fieldwork, my first presumption will be that useful social and sociological learning is not a state but a matter of practical exchange, a *process* (those who seek a more straightforward guide to practice could consult Lofland, 1971 or Hammersley and Atkinson, 1995). I would hold that knowledge is not a product of the scholar's intellect and reasoning alone because it addresses an external world that contains properties and patterns that may exceed the scholar's imagination, behave in ways other than those conceived by the imagination or behave in just *one* of the many ways that the imagination can conceive, a way that the imagination cannot justifiably single out above all others. So it was that Baszanger and Dodier summarized the methodological requirements of ethnography as the need for an empirical approach; the need to remain open to features that cannot be listed in advance of study; and the need to 'ground' phenomena observed in the field (Baszanger and Dodier, 1997: 8).

Of course one does not go presuppositionless into the social world each time, a complete innocent, with no foundation of expectations or knowledge. But it does not do to take existing writing and information on trust. It is not as if reports, analyses and data sets are wholly independent, objective sources of knowledge about the world. They are themselves social products, and the way in which they were assembled – the meanings and assumptions they incorporate, the patterns of activity that constituted them, the things that were seen and were not seen by those who compiled them – cannot be taken for granted. They require some explication, decoding or 'unpacking'. After all, another author or researcher may not have gone to research in the same way, at the same time and in the same place,

and for the same reasons, asking the same questions or using the same perspectives. And it will not do to assume that, just because another piece of research or data set uses familiar terms and classifications, it is dealing with issues identical to one's own. The standardization or comparability of social phenomena must always be in doubt. A university in Colorado or Calcutta is not necessarily the same as one in Cambridge, Massachusetts or Cambridge, England; delinquents in Boston, Massachusetts, are not necessarily the same as those in Boston, Lincolnshire; delinquents in 1958 are not necessarily the same as those in 1998. All that remains to be demonstrated. There is, remarked Peirce, a disease of language that presupposes quite unwarrantably that things with the same names are the same in essence. So the fact that books purport to touch on one's topic are no guarantee that they do so in ways that are directly applicable, and without independent enquiry one will never know how they might coincide with or differ from what one would find oneself. They provide at best no more than what Blumer called the 'sensitizing concepts' that point one in particular directions but cannot tell one what one will find when one arrives.

If valid knowledge does not reside simply in the intellect, it certainly does not reside wholly in the world to be examined. Interactionist ethnographers are not naive empiricists. Quite the reverse. They argue that they cannot but plan, choose and have purposes as they pick their way amongst the great mass of events around them, and they must do so in ways that will themselves change as they learn more about them. Research is not passive or neutral. It is interactive and creative, selective and interpretive, illuminating patches of the world around it, giving meaning and suggesting further paths of enquiry. In this sense, it is a process that does not start from fixed conditions and a clear vision of what lies ahead but changes with each stage of enquiry so that many important questions emerge only *in situ*. It is virtually impossible to anticipate what will be encountered, thought and conjectured as a finely textured piece of research unfolds, and it is not helpful to proceed as if one can do so. Fetterman remarked that 'ethnographic work is not always orderly. It involves serendipity, creativity, being in the right place at the right or wrong time, a lot of hard work, and old-fashioned luck' (Fetterman, 1989: 12). It is better only to make sure that one is heading in the right way. One may have a set of reasonable, informed anticipations, what William James called 'knowledge about' the world, but one will not be entitled to assume that one has an expert, intimate understanding (James' 'knowledge of' the world) until quite late in the history of any project. It follows that to hedge oneself in with firm hypotheses, research designs and instruments will do little more than blind oneself to the world, preventing oneself from responding effectively to what one might discover in what Agar has called a learning role (Agar, 1986: 12).

Questions must then be formulated as research advances, data collection and interpretation being treated as interlaced processes (see Okeley, 1994: 21). Indeed, strictly speaking, *data* – things which are given – is a most misleading term. Far better would be *capta*, things which are seized. Symbolic interactionist research itself is open-ended, provisional and uncertain of its final outcome. By the end, all being well, that process, that dialectic of interrogation, that moving backwards and forwards in a work of encountering negations and transcending them, only to produce new negations, will yield some useful answers, but it would be foolish to try to foreclose on them too soon. Indeed, premature analysis may merely edit out possibly rewarding lines of enquiry (see Silverman, 1993: 36).

The second presumption is this: by and large, ethnographers attach considerable importance to the practical knowledge that people on the social scene, the actors or the subjects, employ to guide their own actions. It is not only the ethnographer who goes to the world and interprets it, who engages in the knowing–known transaction, who synthesizes the symbolic materials of everyday life. Subjects do so too. They are importantly interpretive beings themselves and the social world they occupy is a world of meanings, symbols and motives. They also construct their lives purposefully and practically out of the meanings they bestow on what is around them and within an environment constituted by the meanings and purposes of others. The social world is in this manner preformed by the active intelligence of its participants. One descends as a researcher upon a society that is already interpretively at work, actively prestructured by its occupants. To neglect that is to neglect its proper character. But to heed it can be a source of strength because there may be at least some basic isomorphism or identity between the interpretive practices of the ethnographer and his or her subjects. One is not studying an alien entity, but a process that may (as it were) be grasped from within (see Hammersley and Atkinson, 1995: 2). That deference to the special constitution of social life, Blumer would maintain, is at the very centre of interactionist methodology (Blumer, 1969: 27–8).

At almost every stage, then, the ethnographer will seek to understand and reproduce the logic-in-use of the subjects on the social scene because *that* is the material of social life and of sociology, the motive power that drives social action. The ethnographer can only claim to have knowledge about others' knowledge, interpretations of others' interpretations, models of others' models. His or her secondary, mediated knowledge may be useful, public, accessible and illuminating, but it is also necessarily dependent and derivative. He or she may be obliged to argue that, for many practical purposes, the ultimate authority on a person's life and actions must be that

other person, that the ethnographer will have but a fleeting glimpse of matters known much more intimately, intensely and extensively by him or her, and that ethnography itself is a representation or imitation that is not, in many respects, quite authentic and certainly not the thing itself.

What ethnography *can* contribute is a disciplined unravelling of the breadth and complexity of relations: it can ask questions unasked by actors on the social scene; it can pursue problems of little interest to those on the social scene; it can compare and contrast in ways that insiders do not do; and it can be rigorous as others are not. It furnishes knowledge that is well worth having. But it is a consequence that judgements about the adequacy of the ethnographic account must be referred back whenever possible to the subject; that ethnographic knowledge does not claim to be immeasurably wiser or cleverer than the subject's knowledge; and that the sociologist cannot and should not talk confidently about manifest and latent functions, false consciousness or rationalization. Sociological knowledge is *different*, fit for different purposes, but it is not superior in every degree. In that difference, of course, there may lie the source of a possible difficulty for the ethnographer because his or her account may contradict that which would be given by a subject or subjects, and it is not easy for the interactionist to fall back on the defence that his or her position rests on a wider, better informed or more sophisticated appreciation of what is happening.

There are limits to what can be known. I have argued that knowledge is necessarily provisional, bound temporally and contextually, shaped both by the particular purposes and experiences of the observer, and by the encounters which he or she had with particular others in the field. It can lead to only the most modest extrapolation of forms, offered often without the assurance that the 'same' forms might not be combined in quite unexpected ways elsewhere, and it can certainly say little about what are called 'macro-structures', unless those macro-structures are approached only in their local manifestation.

It must be said in parenthesis that those who do *not* espouse such an epistemology tend to find such a formulation unsatisfactory. It makes difficult any attempt at replication or comparison of findings, any systematic accumulation of learning, any investigation of questions about substantial historical and social processes, or any significant advancement of theory. It does not lend itself to the construction of clear hypotheses or tests for assessing the adequacy of theory. It can lead interactionist ethnographers, in the eyes of their critics, to be almost wilful in their emphasis on the importance of the biographical and contingent in research (see Farberman, 1975). Becker, for example, would insist that there is no reason to suppose that different ethnographers (or indeed the same ethnographer) visiting the 'same' site with different questions at different times should see and report the same things (1971: 40–1). If a sociologist–ethnographer never steps into the same field twice, if not even the sociologist–ethnographer himself or herself is quite the same, there is no need to insist on consistency over time, and there is a companion risk not only that ethnography will lose discipline but that every criticism can be sidestepped.

PARTICIPANT OBSERVATION

A duality of approach leads to a duality of role. Powdermaker captured the distinction nicely by describing 'the way of an anthropologist' as that of 'stranger and friend' (Powdermaker, 1966: 115–19). Interactionist research hinges on participant observation: *participant* because it is only by attempting to enter the symbolic lifeworld of others that one can ascertain the subjective logic on which it is built and feel, hear and see a little of social life as one's subjects do (see Geer, 1964; Liebow, 1993), but *observer* because one's purposes are always ultimately distinct and objectifying. As an observer, one tries to stand back and analyse in a way possibly foreign to the subject, asking questions deemed eccentric or irrelevant for practical purposes by the subject, possibly, indeed, exceeding the bounds of common sense and decorum. The ethnographer must in this sense be sometimes a little naive by design – becoming the outsider who does not quite understand what is going on, asking for information which everyone either knows already or does not wish to probe. He or she may have to spend a very considerable time in the field, seeing what happens, doing what the subjects do, reading what the subjects read, eating what the subjects eat, noting, recording, thinking, learning and gaining trust, being able eventually to replicate some of the subjective knowledge of the world under view, but knowing always that that reproduction will never be wholly 'genuine' because it is an artifact produced by one who was not, after all, a complete insider with the insider's aims and understanding.

Experiential accounts (if not every methodological instruction manual) make it evident that there are risks attached to both phases of participant observation. The first is that one will not leave the academic world fully enough to see how one's subjects view the things they do and succeed in doing the things they do – one will remain alienated, seeming to oneself and others to be a stranger who does not fit and cannot understand. The second risk is that one will 'go native' and cease to think as an academic altogether. Sociologists of religion have been converted at evangelical crusades, and sociologists of the police have enlisted. The matter has been discussed in fictional form in Alison Lurie's *Imaginary Friends* (1978), where the sociologist-hero ends by leading the flying saucer cult he set off to study.

Much has been written about the balancing and blending of the two roles of participant – learning the experiential world from within – and observer – analysing it from without. Some advocate periods of withdrawal as an observer, withdrawal perhaps to the study, the library and the university so that one can clear one's head and regain perspective before returning as a participant. One can sometimes be candid with key informants, not concealing one's academic preoccupations although knowing that they cannot perhaps bring quite the same perspectives to bear on those preoccupations (if only because it is *their* lives and actions that are being explored and more likely, that they will not find them as interesting as one does oneself. One can try to remain private in the fastness of one's own head, seeking to be a little estranged, not wholly immersed, although much has been and can be made of the unauthentic performance and the problem of bad faith, and there are times when one is not allowed to be alone. Some groups play on invading the self, attempting to break down the divide between the private and the public, and research in that instance may not permit an internal retreat. I once had to comfort a distressed research student who had been investigating a new religious movement whose conversion technique consisted precisely of refusing the would-be convert any space or time in which to escape, badgering him publicly hour after hour.

A NATURAL HISTORY
OF ETHNOGRAPHIC WORK

Let me now try to recapitulate some of the main stages of research. One begins characteristically with a problem or the search for a problem. My experience is that *everything* is engaging or can be made so. There is no part of the social world that will remain boring after the application of a little curiosity. Sociologists have studied 'Moonies' (Barker, 1984) and Scientologists, environmental health officers (Hutter, 1988) and traffic wardens, civil servants (Rock, 1990) and homicide 'survivors' (Rock, 1998), crack cocaine dealers (Bourgois, 1995) and bartenders, *gigolos* and mistresses (Salamon, 1984), taxi-dancers and cabdrivers (Davis, 1959), card players and *coquettes*, janitors (Gold, 1952), and all to good effect, conveying the densely nuanced, intricate and artful character of social life. What chiefly renders a problem significant and interesting is the analytic capacity of the ethnographer rather than any 'intrinsic' merit of the phenomenon at hand (although some would criticize that catholicism of approach for its alleged propensity to trivialize; see Liazios, 1972).

Perhaps selection is best ruled by criteria of practicability. Ethnography is intense, lengthy and 'data-rich', and it cannot and probably should not embrace too many people and too wide a field of activity (see Fielding, 1993: 155). Many ethnographers will spend a considerable time studying the doings of only a handful of people. Secondly, it is prudent to search for a problem that is an extension of the known, a logical next step from territory that is familiar. Embarking on research is something of an adventure and it can be lonely, taxing and baffling. No one will ever be as interested in one's work as one is oneself. One will spend long periods living with problems in a condition of intellectual solitude, and it is a great comfort to know that one is, as it were, near land, not too far out, not out of one's depth. Yet it would not do to engage simply in repetition of an earlier piece of research (although strictly speaking, of course, one can never undertake the same research twice) because repetition is tedious and liable to be flawed by the inattentiveness that stems from the assumption that one has seen it all before, that one does not have to look too hard, that there is little to learn, that one knows it already. On the other hand, venturing into terrain that is too alien will be disconcerting because it offers no paths and little reassurance that one is looking around oneself with an intelligent and informed eye. The new and the strange which is not *too* new and strange may be the best compound, if only because ethnography demands a coming-together of the insider's understanding with the outsider's puzzlement, a state most often accomplished where the new is a little old, and the untoward familiar, where one may learn from perspective through incongruity. The sociologist of the civilian police might then look at private detectives or at the military police but he or she might be unwise to look at tin miners or priests.

The textbooks and colleagues sometimes give one a heroic image of the sociologist–ethnographer as a man or woman with clear eyes and penetrating vision who can, from the first, see ahead and understand what is to be seen, who can plan and act purposefully, striding out into the field like Indiana Jones (see Bryman, 1988: 8–9). One's own experience tends to be quite different. It is of an initial confusion and muddle, a lack of purpose and direction, no sense of one's bearings but a reluctance to say so. One begins with very little useful knowledge of the research problem and the research site, only a sense acquired at some point that there may be something interesting to be found. The prime ethnographic maxim is that one cannot know what one is exploring until it has been explored. Everyday knowledge, knowledge *about* the problem, is really not quite good enough for purposes of research.

One usually feels transparent at first, purporting to do research about something but actually knowing little about it, an authority without expertise, a fraud (Atkinson, 1996). And if one does not know what to do, why on earth did one embark on a career as a social scientist? Of course, those with some experience of research will know that this phase will come and that it will go, that it is an inevitable precursor of understanding, and that one should bear it with fortitude. But those without experience may find it frightening.

The usual thing to do at first is build up an initial, tentative appearance of intellectual command by immersing oneself in reading. Ethnography characteristically begins not in the field at all but in the library, although libraries may not really be of much help. There seems very often to be nothing of interest written about one's subject area, although one is mindful that there may always be a book covering everything that one proposes to research on the very next shelf, a book that is written in a masterly style that will render one's entire project nugatory.

One reads avidly in and around an area, alternating between believing that nothing of importance has been written and that there is absolutely nothing to add. Yet, little by little, one does find that one does begin to learn something, that one is no longer quite so fraudulent, that one knows a little of what to say. Little by little, too, the very business of being in a library tends to become autonomous and self-sustaining. It is something that one is doing quite well, one begins to feel comfortable there, one knows what one is doing, rewards become apparent, ideas emerge, and there are new intrinsic satisfactions and new beguiling problems. One becomes interested in the history of ideas and the history of the phenomenon, and in what others as yet unread may have to say (there is always another important book that one *must* read). Libraries are warm, familiar places, and there is a reluctance to quit them. It may, after all, be best to do a bookish study. Why not? That is what most scholars do. It is perfectly respectable, indeed more respectable than field research, and one's grasp of bibliography and the history of scholarship is much firmer. Why wander off into the as yet untried terrain of field research which may be less hospitable, where academics are not at home, where the world is not predigested for the academic's consumption, where there is no certainty that anything will be brought off, a world that is colder and wetter, where results are gained much more painfully, and where one might make a fool of oneself?

The choice of a social world is a matter of cardinal importance. Unlike the bookish researcher or the macho-economists with their big data sets, one has to spend long periods with one's subjects and one had better like them a little and they had better like one too (see Fielding, 1993: 158). One has to build up trust, confidence and friendship so that one sees and hears something of the inner life of a social group. One cannot do so with everyone. Not everyone would let one in. The white, middle-class, middle-aged male sociologist would have difficulty in finding acceptance in any number of worlds.

How does one begin? Cold calling is not easy. It is usually best to begin with those at hand, the people who may repose enough trust in one to allow access to their private lives. After all, unless a group is committed to allowing the free entry of strangers, there is usually no good reason why they *should* embrace an outsider. Choice may then be affected by a set of elementary questions. Is one a member of the group oneself? Does one know a member? Does one know someone who knows a member? Networks are important and much ethnography actually turns out to be the social anthropology of one's own kind (an eminent sociologist of deviance, summarizing his own research, was once heard to say *sotto voce*, 'after all, we were only talking about ourselves').

When one does eventually drag oneself into the field, a number of matters strike one immediately. First, an academic or a research student is not always a very important person. One may indeed have no situated identity or an imputed identity which obstructs the practice of research, being regarded perhaps as a plainclothes police officer in a world of drug dealers (Bourgois, 1995) or a management spy amongst employees. Besides, people are often very busy with their everyday affairs and one has very little in the way of a moral, practical or social claim on them; there is no reason why they *should* help one, and any assistance will look remarkably like charity, leading eventually to a sense of debt and an anxiety about betrayal when the writing begins. Secondly, the world is a buzzing confusion and one doubts one's capacities as a sociologist anew. The world is not laid out as an analytic landscape: to the contrary, it abounds with language and actions that seem at once mysterious and banal. In such a position, it is best to look and see what can be seen, to try to get some sense of the regularities of what is before one. It would be foolish to plunge in too soon with naive questions. Such a step might only expose the sociologist's lack of understanding, and exhaust whatever limited goodwill there may be. Busy people will not consent to be interviewed repeatedly by the manifestly inept.

It is better to remain on the margins at first, available, just about visible, but not too demanding. Show interest. See who the others about one are. Observe those whom they deal with. Be available. Observe and chart everyday routines. Listen to others: being prepared to listen is a rare enough asset in social life and it will be rewarded (La Rochefoucauld once defined a bore as someone who talks about himself when you want to talk about *your* self).

INFORMANTS

Very typically at this stage, someone will emerge, *deus ex machina*, like a fairy godmother, to help the forlorn ethnographer. Such a one will become an informant, a helpmeet, a source of introductions and commentary. The informant is often both sociable and knowledgeable but one should be beware of the consequences of the flood of relief that washes over one's dealings with such a guide. The informant cannot offer more than a single, embedded perspective on the complexities of the world, his or her account will be situated, limited and motivated, and it will always have to be qualified by conditions as yet unimagined. Why, one will come to wonder, are they telling you all this? Is theirs a self-serving narrative? One *must* search out others for qualifying perspectives, even if those others are not as friendly or accessible as the informant. One must observe as many parts of the social setting and as many participants as one can. One must sample the world theoretically for its systematic contrasts. One must engage in what Denzin called triangulation, checking everything, getting multiple documentation, getting multiple *kinds* of documentation, so that evidence does not rely on a single voice, so that data can become embedded in their contexts, so that data can be compared.

In pursuing this stage of data collection, and indeed every other stage, it is imperative to engage in a written conversation with oneself. Imagine yourself sitting at a desk in a year or so, actually beginning to write, more confident then than now, having a firmer sense of the patterning of things, perusing all the notes, transcripts and documents that you have gathered. Those materials are, in effect, messages to a future self, and they will lose some of their immediacy and context. What is clear *now* will not be so clear later on. Patiently explain to a future self what you are doing, why you think it is interesting, why you have chosen to record what you have, what relevance it will have. Later, much of that will appear strikingly commonplace, but it ensures that notes will retain their utility (Becker, 1986).

At this stage, too, it is advisable to be omnivorous (Becker, 1998). One is not in a position to judge what is useful and what is not, what will be used and what will not. How can one assess future meaning? One is building up a skein of materials whose import is emergent and changing, whose significance will be determined by things as yet unseen and unthought, which may form a critical mass whose significance will become clear, but one cannot now make much sense of them. One is so busy that one often does not have time properly to absorb or analyse them. Fieldwork cannot always be reflective. Indeed, it may be difficult enough to sustain a conversation without attending simultaneously and in alienated fashion to the forms of experience. Do not try, in consequence, to preclude or censor anything that might be germane. In my own work, on every occasion, without fail, it is only when I sit and write that I discover what I seem to have been seeing all along. It is only then, when ideas have been objectified on a screen, that one can begin to answer Graham Wallas' question, 'How do I know what I think until I see what I say?' (Weick, 1995: 12). I have never ever asked precisely the right questions *in situ* or followed exactly the right tracks. Instead, it was by asking the *wrong* questions that I came to see that the questions *were* wrong but only after the event and frequently too late to undertake adequate methodological repairs. Subsequent analysis is always in this sense something of a botch, a matter of making good with what one has at one's disposal. It never takes place in ideal circumstances. I have now resigned myself to the inevitability of that process. What earlier research does, in effect, is to establish the preconditions for a later understanding that could never have been anticipated at the time.

There is a further imperative that will then flow out of the research process. One must be prepared to live with uncertainty for long periods. One may have a dawning sense that things are becoming clear but the owl of Minerva, Hegel told us, flies at twilight. Resign oneself to living through a long Arctic day where nothing is clear and everything is distorted.

The process in these early and middle stages is not unlike trying to construct a jigsaw or mosaic whose overall design can only dimly be seen but whose configuration changes with each new piece found or offered. In effect, each new piece alters the picture and the emerging whole alters and directs the search for each succeeding piece. That is another guise assumed by the dialectic of research, a guise in which everything moves in response to everything else, in which multiple interpretations seem to abound, and in which each episode brings a new analysis, a new answer and a new question. Little words and phrases can trigger an avid curiosity: Blanche Geer and Howard Becker learned a lot from medical students' use of the word 'crock', for example. It pointed to the students' quest for clinical cases that would be educationally useful – a crock was one from whom nothing could be learned and was therefore worthless for purposes of medical training (Becker et al., 1961).

Sparks of understanding occur in the field or when the mind is allowed to mull over what it has seen and heard, when one is in the bath or shower or walking, sparks that will need instant enquiry, that clamour for attention because everything before will suddenly seem deficient and exposed until they have been investigated. William Foote Whyte wrote 'most of our learning in [the field] is not on a conscious level. We often have flashes of insight that come to us when we are not consciously thinking about a research problem at all' (Whyte, 1951: 510).

Those are the beginnings of theorizing and they cannot be forced or made methodical or systematic. Theorizing will come, and it comes out of the interplay between a receptive and curious mind and a world explored over time and with diligence.

A closer examination of those flashes, intuitions and insights will sometimes show them to be threadbare, but one can never be sure at the outset. It is only when one has mined a vein for what it will offer that uncertainty will give way to the rejection or acceptance of a once bright idea, and acceptance itself will often devalue inspiration. How could one have not seen what is now so apparent and banal, what anyone could have known, that is not really very interesting? The insight-turned-platitude will then be superseded by another insight that will demand exploration in its turn. It is as if one were making a series of intellectual forays into the terrain around one, and each foray will consist typically of a series of linked questions, a lattice of problems that lead into one another, that will be pursued until one is satisfied that one knows enough, that there are no remaining mysteries substantial enough to justify being detained further. And what emerges is the groundwork of a book or a report. It is a process that Howard Becker called 'sequential analysis' (Becker, 1971).

As that process attains a kind of pulse, as it gains pace and rhythm, so the most exciting period begins. Uncertainty alternates with certainty. One moves backwards and forwards between what is becoming an embryonic theory and the social world, asking new questions, returning to change the theory, going back to the world with new questions, and so on in a series of ricochets that build up one stage after another. In what Hammersely and Atkinson have likened to a funnel (Hammersley and Atkinson, 1995: 206), there is a progressive sharpening of focus and a growing sense of structure which dispel uncertainties and pare away irrelevances.

There is a point in research where a kind of intellectual monomania takes over. *Everything* seems to touch on the research at hand. Where once nothing was written, now *everything* has a bearing on one's interests. People's every conversation is rife with significance for one's work. One is forever scribbling little notes before one forgets what has been said or read. The whole universe becomes Ptolemaic, revolving around one's special problem. What could be more important than the moral career of the debtor or the rebuilding of Holloway Prison? Why do people waste their time writing or thinking about anything else? It is at that point that one starts drafting prefaces in the imagination, prefaces that one will almost certainly come to regret later, lamenting the blindness of others who could not see the overwhelming importance of debtors, of black women, or white women, of police sergeants or stipendiary magistrates, or of prison architecture. Decades have gone by and the fools have not appreciated how criminology *must* hinge around the crimes committed by farmworkers. The discipline is flawed and will not be whole until one's own research is published.

CONCLUDING PHASES

With that great surge of power one typically leaves the field. One is driven by a powerful, driving urge to write, to spread understanding, defuse the feeling of urgency and get on with analysis. No more is to be learned in the field. Indeed, quite often people in the field now come to one and seek advice, reversing the roles of subject and observer.

Quitting the field is not easy. The field may have become a second home, a place where exciting and pleasurable things happened, where one came alive, where people were helpful. People call Ottawa dull. For me, after an ethnographic study of the Ministry of the Solicitor General of Canada, it was and is a City of Light. Once, in an unguarded moment, I declared that I would not be seen dead in Wood Green, an unprepossessing suburb of north London. Wood Green may not be a City of Light but I certainly now regard it with affection. And there is another kind of problem. Recall that one invested a deal of oneself in cultivating people and building relations that are now about to be shed, exposing their instrumental and exploitative character. The ethnographer who courted others, who had seemingly limitless time to listen, is now revealed as a person who can no longer be bothered and is in a hurry to be off. And he or she is off to expose what has been learned to the world. It is patent that one has *used* people (although friendships can remain, and should remain, if only for research purposes that I shall explain). Some have become very vexed about the ethics of observation and of ethnography, worrying about their predatory character. The problem is probably best resolved, as Jack Douglas once suggested, by applying the morality and common sense of everyday life. But one should certainly be reluctant to describe or quote named or identifiable figures without obtaining their permission, and I have found that seeking comments on description and quotation can often be illuminating, forming the foundation of another stage in the research process.

The next phase should be appropriately chastening, a fall from *hubris*, consisting of long periods spent patiently editing all those materials so eagerly found. It is often boring, an apparent time out of play, an unwanted interval between the intoxication of fieldwork (what Jules Henry called passionate ethnography) and the mastery of writing. Editing will follow the pattern of the groundwork constructed in sequential analysis, and it will itself be an anticipation and early articulation of the writing process. The headings and subheadings under which one classifies materials, the headings that came increasingly to organize one's searches in the field, will then prestructure the final argument, the order of classification being itself the order of argument to come. In short, the manner in which one lays out data for report is itself an early mirror of that report. It is at that point that one begins to notice odd gaps, deficiencies, things not covered as well as they might have been, questions not asked, responses not made to answers by respondents. One begins to carp a little at the stupidity and myopia of that earlier incarnation of oneself, the person who had flattered himself or herself to be analytically in control of everything about him but was actually purblind. It may not be too late to return to the field to retrieve some of the losses, but it is inevitable that one will proceed to writing with a consciousness that one does not know quite everything, that there *was* neglect, that omissions will have either to be glossed over or, better, openly admitted.

At first, one is daunted by the sheer difficulty of reducing all that one has learned and seen to a unilinear argument that cuts a path through what is invariably sensed as a totality with parts that are not separate at all but features of a fused and simultaneously interacting whole. One will be all too conscious, too, that it is difficult to translate a vivid world of noises, sights and smells, a world of embodied people where the visual is as important as the oral, to writing which is confined to the oral alone. There is a sense of future betrayal, that what was so exciting and dramatic may become unfaithful, monochromatic and dull, very unlike the original.

Writing itself may not be so difficult, it is what academics are *supposed* to be able to do, and it has its dangers. Any competent and intelligent person will be able to concoct persuasive narratives that make sense of the edited data lying before him or her. The problem is that that analysis may become a little *too* much like story-telling, a kind of game which is detached and *sui generis*, and in which the imagination is allowed to become sovereign again. After all, the plausibility of a story concocted in the study, a story that elides some of the mistakes and gaps of fieldwork, is not necessarily the same as something one might very tentatively and diffidently call truthfulness. Verisimilitude is in part artfulness and one must be constantly beware of imagining that the first attempts to give coherence to data are the same as a reproduction of the social world itself. One is looking at partial reports, fragments and traces that are not at all (as Max Weber warned us) the same as society itself. Verisimilitude, too, is usually obtained by simplifying, forgetting, neglecting the difficult anomaly, and making everything coherent and orderly. The ability to write must be recognized also as an ability to deform and censor, and anomalies are best confronted rather than circumnavigated.

TESTS OF ADEQUACY

At some point one should return with one's analysis and present it to one's subjects because it is *their* lives that one is reporting and one may have got things 'wrong'. It is the case that one has only been a fleeting visitor to a world and that one will have remained something of a stranger. One can never have the insider's competence and it is useful and courteous to enlist that competence to peruse what one says. Of course, insiders may be too busy, bored, baffled or polite to give proper attention to what one has written, but they are, in a sense, existentially authoritative about their own lives, and I have always found it valuable to listen to them. Their comments are often helpful and one's text can now serve, in effect, as an accumulation of questions that one did not have the understanding to put when in the field. Sometimes, of course, insiders will be overly swayed or converted or too polite to contest what one says. Sometimes, they will deny the very right of an outsider to analyse their doings. Denzin observes that 'We do not have an undisputed warrant to study anyone or anything. Subjects now challenge how they have been written about ... Those we study have their own understandings of how they want to be represented' (Denzin, 1997: xiii). My most recent piece of work studied homicide 'survivors', the families of homicide victims, some of whom certainly took it that an outsider's cool analysis is little more than another form of revictimization.

At the same time, it would not do to accept those others as the final arbiter of an account. Theirs is only one voice, and the depth and length of their experience may have to be offset by the breadth of ethnography, by the different aims and interests of sociology, and by the capacity of analysis to contextualize, annotate, compare and contrast – to transcend – the particularities of any single perspective (Silverman, 1993: 199). At the very least, a consideration of contradictory responses may lead to a transcending sense of the structured and time-bound distribution of perspectives. And there is another test of analysis.

Each social world seems to have its own distinctive logic-in-use, aesthetic or pulse, and once one cultivates an ear for that pulse, once one knows the patterning of processes, analysis comes (see Becker, 1998; Vaughan, 1986). Indeed, the aesthetic structure of a world is what many seek chiefly to understand. It links together different acts, people and processes and gives them coherence and intelligibility, driving them on, generating events in a fashion that can seem simple, powerful and pleasurable. It is their principle of unity (Bittner, 1965: 252–3). It is a little like the quest for the line of beauty, the search for the aesthetic at the heart of things. Recall what Crick and Watson said about the double helix: they would know the structure of DNA because it would be beautiful (Watson, 1970). Poincaré said much the same about mathematics (Poincaré, 1913). Ultimately, it is probably an indefensible criterion but it is intuitively convincing, a Keatsian test. Knowing that aesthetic, that sense of the musicality of the social world, and being able to convey something of it to others is the end of research for many. And it does resonate with the symbolic interactionist quest for an understanding of the logic-in-use deployed by people as they define themselves and the situations that confront them.

Acknowledgement

I am grateful to Bridget Hutter for her help in preparing this chapter.

REFERENCES

Agar, M. (1986) *Speaking of Ethnography*. London: Sage.

Atkinson, P. (1996) *Sociological Readings and Re-readings*. Aldershot: Avebury.

Baker, P. (1973) 'The life histories of W.I. Thomas and Robert E. Park', *American Journal of Sociology*, 79 (2): 243–60.

Barker, E. (1984) *The Making of a Moonie*. Oxford: Blackwell.

Baszanger, I. and Dodier, N. (1997) 'Ethnography: relating the part to the whole', in D. Silverman (ed.), *Qualitative Research: Theory, Method and Practice*. London: Sage. pp. 8–23.

Becker, H. (1971) *Sociological Work*. London: Allen Lane.

Becker, H. (1986) *Writing for Social Scientists*. Chicago: University of Chicago Press.

Becker, H. (1998) *Tricks of the Trade; How To Think About Your Research While You're Doing It*. Chicago: University of Chicago Press.

Becker, H., Geer, B., Hughes, E. and Strauss, A. (1961) *Boys in White*. New Brunswick, NJ: Transaction Books.

Bittner, E. (1965) 'The concept of organization', *Social Research*, 32: 239–55.

Blumer, H. (1969) 'The methodological position of symbolic interactionism', in *Symbolic Interactionism*. Englewood Cliffs, NJ: Prentice–Hall. pp. 1–100.

Blumer, H. (1997) 'Foreword' to L. Athens, *Violent Criminal Acts and Actors Revisited*. Urbana, IL: University of Illinois Press.

Bourgois, P. (1995) *In Search of Respect: Selling Crack in El Barrio*. New York: Cambridge University Press.

Bryman, A. (ed.) (1988) *Doing Research in Organizations*. London: Routledge.

Bulmer, M. (1985) *The Chicago School*. Chicago: University of Chicago Press.

Carey, J. (1975) *Sociology and Public Affairs: The Chicago School*. Beverly Hills, CA: Sage.

Davis, F. (1959) 'The cabdriver and his fare', *American Journal of Sociology*, 64: 158–65.

Debro, J. (1970) 'Dialogue with Howard S. Becker', *Issues in Criminology*, V (2): 20–9.

Denzin, N. (1997) *Interpretive Ethnography*. Thousand Oaks, CA: Sage.

Dewey, J. (1938) *Logic*. New York: Henry Holt.

Farberman, H. (1975) Symposium on symbolic interaction, *The Sociological Quarterly*, 16 (4): 435–7.

Faris, R. (1967) *Chicago Sociology, 1920–1932*, San Francisco: Chandler Publishing.

Fetterman, D. (1989) *Ethnography Step by Step*. Newbury Park, CA: Sage.

Fielding, N. (1993) 'Ethnography', in N. Gilbert (ed.), *Researching Social Life*. London: Sage. pp. 154–71.

Fine, G. (ed.) (1995) *A Second Chicago School?* Chicago: University of Chicago Press.

Geer, B. (1964) 'First days in the field', in P. Hammond, *Sociologists at Work*. New York: Basic Books. pp. 322–44.

Geertz, C. (1973) *The Interpretation of Culture*. New York: Basic Books.

Glaser, B. and Strauss, A. (1965) *Awareness of Dying*. Chicago: Aldine.

Gold, R. (1952) 'Janitors vs tenants', *American Journal of Sociology*, 57: 486–93.

Hammersley, M. and Atkinson, P. (1995) *Ethnography: Principles in Practice*, 2nd edn. London: Routledge.

Hutter, B. (1988) *The Reasonable Arm of the Law*. Oxford: The Clarendon Press.

Krohn, C.-D. (1993) *Intellectuals in Exile: Refugee Scholars and the New School for Social Research*. Amherst, MA: University of Massachusetts Press.

Lafferty, T. (1932) 'Some metaphysical implications of the pragmatic theory of knowledge', *Journal of Philosophy*, 29 (8): 197–207.

Levine, D. (ed.) (1971) *On Individuality and Social Forms: Selected Writings of Georg Simmel*. Chicago: University of Chicago Press.

Liazios, A. (1972) 'The poverty of the sociology of deviance: nuts, sluts and perverts', *Social Problems*, 20 (1):

Liebow, E. (1993) *Tell Them Who I Am*. New York: Penguin.

Lofland, J. (1971) *Analyzing Social Settings*. Belmont, CA: Wadsworth.

Lurie, A. (1978) *Imaginary Friends*. Harmondsworth: Penguin.

MacAloon, J. (1992) *General Education in the Social Sciences: Centennial Reflections on the College of the University of Chicago*. Chicago: University of Chicago Press.

Mead, G. (1922) 'A behavioristic account of the significant symbol', *Journal of Philosophy*, 19 (6): 157–63.

Mills, C.W. (1964) *Sociology and Pragmatism*. New York: Paine–Whitman.

Okeley, J. (1994) 'Thinking through fieldwork', in A. Bryman and R. Burgess (eds), *Analyzing Qualitative Data*. London: Routledge. pp. 18–34.

Park, R. and Burgess, E. (eds) (1921) *Introduction to the Science of Sociology*. Chicago: University of Chicago Press.

Parsons, T. (1937) *The Structure of Social Action*. New York: McGraw–Hill.

Perinbanayagam, R. (1975) 'The significance of others in the thought of Alfred Schutz, G.H. Mead and C.H. Cooley', *Sociological Quarterly*, 16: 500–21.

Plummer, K. (1979) 'Misunderstanding labelling perspectives', in D. Downes and P. Rock (eds), *Deviant Interpretations*. Oxford: Martin Robertson. pp. 85–121.

Poincaré, J. (1913) *The Foundations of Science*. New York: Science Press.

Powdermaker, H. (1966) *Stranger and Friend*. New York: W.W. Norton.

Rauschenbush, W. (1979) *Robert Park: Biography of a Sociologist*. Durham, NC: University of North Carolina Press.

Ray, L. (1991) *Formal Sociology*. Aldershot: Edward Elgar.

Reckless, W. (1933) *Vice in Chicago*. Chicago: University of Chicago Press.

Rock, P. (1979) *The Making of Symbolic Interactionism*. London: Macmillan.

Rock, P. (1990) *Helping Victims of Crime*. Oxford: The Clarendon Press.

Rock, P. (1998) *After Homicide*. Oxford: The Clarendon Press.

Salamon, D. (1984) *Control and Observation of Neutral Systems*. London: Pitman.

Silverman, D. (1993) *Interpreting Qualitative Data: Methods for Analysing Talk, Text and Interaction*. London: Sage.

Turner, R. (1962) 'Role-taking: process versus conformity', in A. Rose (ed.), *Human Behaviour and Social Processes*. London: Routledge and Kegan Paul. pp. 20–40.

Vaughan, D. (1986) *Uncoupling: Turning Points in Intimate Relationships*. New York: Oxford University Press.

Watson, J. (1970) *The Double Helix*. Harmondsworth: Penguin.

Weick, K. (1995) *Sensemaking in Organizations*. Thousand Oaks, CA: Sage.

Whyte, W.F. (1951) 'Observational field-work methods', in M. Jahoda, M. Deutsch and S.W. Cook (eds), *Research Methods in Social Relations*, vol. 2. New York: Dryden Press. pp. 493–513.

3

Currents of Cultural Fieldwork

JAMES D. FAUBION

In *The Savage Mind*, Claude Lévi-Strauss declares the method of the historian a method 'with no distinct object' ([1962] 1966: 262). With only slight exaggeration, much the same might currently be said of fieldwork in cultural anthropology. At the very least, such fieldwork has an increasingly unstable object, or if not even quite that, an increasingly indefinite plurality of objects. The notorious, long-standing polysemy of 'culture' notwithstanding, matters have not always been so wrought with ambiguity. A heuristic 'oscillograph' of cultural anthropology might register three distinct methodological phases, three currents of methodological formation and reformation. The first of these – call it the 'constitutive' current – commences with the work of Franz Boas and his extraordinary coterie of students – Edward Sapir, Ruth Benedict (cf. Geertz, 1988; Caffrey, 1989; Modell, 1983), Elsie Clews Parsons (cf. Deacon, 1997; Rosenberg, 1982), Robert Lowie, Zora Neale Hurston (cf. Plant, 1995), and Alfred Kroeber, among many others. It culminates with Lévi-Strauss and such American cognitivists as Charles Frake, Harold Conklin, Ward Goodenough, and the young Stephen Tyler. It persists, but as only one of many other disciplinary alternatives. The second – call it the 'critical' current – commences roughly with the publication of *Rethinking Anthropology* (Hymes, 1972), and gains momentum with the publication of *Anthropology and the Colonial Encounter* (Asad, 1973), *Toward an Anthropology of Women* (Reiter, 1975), *Orientalism* (Said, 1978), *Writing Culture* (Clifford and Marcus, 1986) and *Women Writing Culture* (Behar and Gordon, 1995). It, too, persists, but is showing recent symptoms of exhaustion or, in any event, self-repetition. The third – once designated an 'experimental moment,' but by now a distinctive current in its own right – commences with the reflexive turn in the later 1970s

(see Rabinow, 1977; cf. Stocking, 1983), coalesces for a while into 'anthropology as cultural critique' (see Marcus and Fischer, 1986), and includes much of the most eye-catching (and controversial) research of the past decade. Summarily, if a bit reductively, one might characterize the general drift as follows: if previously, culture was the fieldworker's question, it has increasingly become his, or hers, to put into question.

CONSTITUTIVE MODELS: PATTERN, LANGUAGE, TEXT

It must be noted at the outset that 'cultural anthropology' is no less crisp or constant a category than 'culture' itself. Though institutionally more prominent in the United States than in either France or Great Britain, it is not the exclusive province of any one of them. In contrast, say, to prehistory or linguistics, it has very few procedural rules or technologies properly its own. The opening chapter of Malinowski's *Argonauts of the Western Pacific* (1922: 1–25) has become as central to its methodological tradition as to that of its 'social' counterpart. Both traditions have brandished the standard of 'participant observation,' however paradoxical that standard may be. Both have demanded that fieldworkers gain some measure of fluency in the languages which their interlocutors natively speak. Both have demanded that they spend time enough among their interlocutors to acquire a sense of what Malinowski called 'the imponderabilia of everyday life,' and both have demanded that they attend to what their interlocutors say, to what they profess to believe and value, and to what they actually do. Cultural anthropologists can hardly dare to be blind to institutional processes. Social anthropologists can hardly dare to be blind to symbols. More than a few cultural anthropologists have been ardently scientistic. At least a few social anthropologists have been resolutely idiographic. Indeed, many anthropologists are neither cultural nor social, but rather both at once.

If cultural anthropology is methodologically distinctive, it is so first of all because of what it grants topical or thematic pride of place, not because of what it defines fieldwork to be. Among such nineteenth-century anthropological pioneers as Edward Tylor and Henry Louis Morgan (and still, indeed, for Malinowski) 'culture' was, well, just everything, from hunting implements to chiefdoms; there was nothing yet to distinguish it from 'society'. Only when Boas' protégés began to notice that their professional lexicon and their professional interests were palpably at odds with the lexicon and the interests which A.R. Radcliffe-Brown was beginning to champion in England did a sub-disciplinary divide emerge (see Kroeber, 1935; cf. Radcliffe-Brown, [1940] 1952). Yet if that divide was, in one respect, an anthropological latecomer, it was, in another, anthropologically long overdue. The Boasians had a healthy respect for the natural sciences. Yet the thinkers and theorists from whom they derived their understanding of culture had preceded Tylor, and were almost all Germanic, historicist and (what one would now call) hermeneutical. Radcliffe-Brown, for his part, looked for theoretical inspiration not much farther back than to Emile Durkheim, but took from Durkheim a distillate of French positivism well suited to his own taste at once for formalism and 'hard data'. The Boasians and those who would join Radcliffe-Brown as properly social anthropologists predictably found themselves disagreeing over the causative weight to be assigned to such phenomena (or epiphenomena) as beliefs and values, but only derivatively. True to their theoretical precursors, they disagreed more fundamentally over the very nature of the suprapsychic, the supra-individual, or what they were alike inclined to designate the 'superorganic'. Though with many twists and turns, their disagreement has endured. So, too, has its methodological fallout.

Lowie is well known for having cast culture as 'a thing of shreds and patches'. Yet with the rest of his Boasian colleagues, he persisted in casting it also as a synergistic totality, an integral whole. Tylor had, of course, himself written of culture as a 'complex whole', but the Boasians were not simply reproducing his precedent. For the anthropologists of the nineteenth century, 'culture' was a near synonym of 'civilization', and civilization was itself a grand human unity, low or crude in its 'primitive' manifestations, high and refined in its modern ones. It evolved; and general principles governed its evolutionary development. For the Boasians, in contrast, 'culture' was more importantly plural, not one but instead many things, if sometimes more simple, sometimes more complex. Its manifestations were discrete. They could be counted. They were spatially distinct. For the social anthropologists, there were 'societies'. For the Boasians, analogously, there were 'cultures'. Yet if societies perhaps evolved, if they could be disposed into evolutionary 'types', cultures were another matter entirely. Above all, they were particular; they were diverse.

Was the presumption of the plurality of cultures brought to fieldwork, or rather a product of it? A difficult question. On the one hand, it is worth noting that the longitudinal and diffusionist research of the 'ethnologists' and the German Kulturkreis school, from which Boas and Lowie took their initial inspiration, was informed less by spatial than by temporal conceptions of culture. Nor did its primary aim lie in the explication of the integrity of one or another cultural whole. On the contrary, its aim – post-structuralist *avant l'heure*, as it were – lay in the tracing of the flow of artifacts and traits from a putative or actual cultural 'center' outward to its always shifting 'peripheries'. On the other hand, 'holism' had already become the methodological signature of research in the Germanic *Geisteswissenschaften* ('mental' or 'spiritual sciences', literally), with the most prominent examples of which Boas took pains to familiarize his students. In any event, only once the Boasians took to the field did holism cease to refer to the immanent coherence of distinct periods in the historical past and begin instead to refer to the coherence of 'cultures' subsisting in an effectively timeless 'ethnographic present'.

Holism in fact became the methodological byword of both social and cultural research, and has remained so until quite recently. The models of society which Radcliffe-Brown acquired from Durkheim, and which would prevail within social anthropology even after John Beattie's objections (1964: 56–60), came ultimately from zoology and biology; they cast society as an organism, or as 'organismic', a synergistic totality built of various parts which served, jointly and severally, to sustain the whole. Cultural anthropologists have, however, found little if any use for 'organismic analogies'. Seeking other models for the qualitative hallmarks of cultural integrity, or the integrity of cultures, they borrowed not from biology but instead from the *Geisteswissenschaften* themselves. Malinowski came to conceive of cultures as vast instrumental repertoires, a melange of institutions and techniques, beliefs and values, all of which served the satisfaction of what he thought were a universal set of primary, and a more variable set of secondary, human 'needs' (1939). Such 'pure functionalism' has had many methodological cousins, especially among 'cultural materialists' (see Harris, 1979) and among 'cultural ecologists' from Julian Steward (1955) to Roy Rappaport (1968) and the young Clifford Geertz (1959, 1963). For the majority of them, 'adaptation' is methodologically central, and the investigation of the relations among customs and given physical environments the regulative idea of fieldwork itself. Though vulnerable to the complaint that might be lodged against functionalisms of any other sort – that they encourage the telling of just-so stories rather than the discovery of genuine explanatory connections – they are hardly yet beyond the methodological pale. It is nevertheless somewhat paradoxical that Malinowski should himself have advocated a mode and program of research which leads no more often toward the 'native's point of view' than away from it, to customs about whose 'latent' or 'disguised' functions natives might not have any point of view at all (see, for example, Codere, [1956] 1967).

The Boasians were perhaps the more consistent cultural theorists, even if they were not the better fieldworkers, and even if they promulgated ambiguities of their own. Benedict probably deserves to be ranked first among them, though her thinking owed much to Boas and to Edward Sapir. Her *Patterns of Culture* (1934) is in any case the most systematic and intellectually the most sophisticated of the early Boasian manifestos, and its impact is still evident, some forty years later, in Geertz's theoretical and methodological writings (1973: 3–30; 1983: 55–70; cf. 1988). For Benedict, cultures were both logically and causally prior to individual personalities, but still 'psychic'. Their most telling and instructive analogues resided in psychic processes and psychic structures, and especially in those structures which certain German psychologists had designated *Gestalten* – 'patterns' or 'schemas' which organized and mediated human perception and human feeling, and without which human experience would be little more than a confusion of kaleidoscopic sensations (1934: 51–2). For Benedict, cultures were 'like that': patterns or schemas which organized and mediated on the collective or intersubjective plane what the psychologists' *Gestalten* did on the subjective plane. They were inherently selective: no culture could possibly accommodate every perception, every feeling; every culture had its experiential canon, its experiential marginalia, its experiential trash bin.

Benedict largely confined herself to research into 'personality' or 'character' (see also Benedict, 1946; cf. Mead, 1930; Gorer and Rickman, 1949; Hsu, 1953; Whiting and Child, 1953; DuBois, 1955; Gorer, 1955; Kluckhohn and Leighton, 1962; Lee, 1976) – to what later anthropologists would come to think of as 'ethos' (dispositions and motivations) and 'ethics' (codes of conduct). She would leave research into 'world-view' (the term is still used to designate understandings of reality or the nature of things) to other colleagues. Yet she recognized both character and world-view to be equally patterned, even if they sometimes manifested their boundaries in qualitatively distinct ways. Seeking their boundaries, she

put into practice those methodological directives which would guide cultural fieldwork throughout its constitutive phase, however many amendments they might have acquired. On the one hand, she looked to acts of disapproval, of punishment and rejection which would reveal the limits of the culturally permissible, the culturally established divide between the 'deviant' and the 'normal' (1934: 257–70). (Durkheim could approve.) On the other hand, as both the pretext and the on-going stimulus of research, she loooked to instances of incomprehension, of bafflement which would reveal the limits of culturally constituted 'common sense' (1934: 237).

Benedict's patterns were, however, analytically (and so methodologically) ill-defined in at least one crucial respect. Her distinction between 'Apollonian' and 'Dionysian' cultures is merely the best-known case in point (1934: 78–9). On the face of it, the distinction enframed what seemed to be straightforward descriptions of modalities of character which one people or another self-consciously embraced. So the Apollonian Hopi esteemed the pacific, introverted, retiring, withdrawn man (1934: 98–101). The Dionysian Kwakiutl, in contrast, esteemed the bellicose megalomaniac, acutely sensitive to insult and quick to defend his honor – if need be, by committing suicide (1934: 190–220). Yet the 'Apollonian' was hardly a part of the Hopi vocabulary, nor the 'Dionysian' even a remote gloss of any explicit Kwakiutl value. Benedict followed Schopenhauer and Nietzsche in what was in fact a technical usage of both, which not even the ancient Greeks would readily have comprehended, however dear Apollo and Dionysus might have been to them. Moreover, she employed psychologistic terminology with intentional irony. 'Withdrawal' was symptomatic of pathology for her Western readers – but the very height of virtue among the Southwest pueblos. 'Megalomania' was a neurosis – but not among the indigenes of the Northwest Coast. Was the interpreter sacrificing ethnographic accuracy in the name of object lessons? Was she imposing rather than 'discovering' her diagnostic categories?

Considering reports of Hopi elders frightening and thrashing the youth over whom they presided during ceremonies of initiation, John Bennett was led to ask how Benedict could ever have deemed the pueblos an Apollonia (Bennett, 1946). Nor is Benedict alone in having been taken to task for an alleged excess of interpretive license. Robert Redfield and Oscar Lewis famously disagreed over the character of the residents of the barrios of Tepoztlán (Redfield, 1930; Lewis, 1951). Derek Freeman raised doubts about Margaret Mead's suspiciously 'instructive' assessment of adolescence in Samoa (and continues to do so: see Mead, 1928; Freeman, 1983, 1999). Lévi-Strauss himself has been called to account for 'inventing' more than a few of the myths which he has so assiduously proceeded to decrypt (cf. Leach, 1970: 64–6). Geertz has been called to account for having extrapolated an iconic Balinese cockfight from the inconsistent proceedings of several particular cockfights (Dundes, 1994). And so on.

Virtually all cultural anthropologists would now agree that interpretations are inherently indeterminate, that two (or more) interpretations of the same evidence might be equally 'correct', that interpretive conflicts are thus practically unavoidable. Questions of what might control interpretive extravagance nevertheless remain. Benedict's answer was – as all such answers must be – hypothetical. It rested in the presumption that the cultural production of personality or character must always work with a common human store of psychological materials – perceptual faculties, emotional drives and responses, and a finite array of basic temperaments or temperamental proclivities (1934: 253–4). Cultural interpretation thus had the psychologies of perception and of motivation (or whatever their abiding facts would turn out to be – more Freudian than Gestaltist, for example) as its ultimate descriptive resource and its ultimate hermeneutical constraint. However hypothetical, Benedict's position was persuasive. But then again, she offered it to those who were, for the most part, already converted. At least until the 1950s, it would have been rare to find a cultural anthropologist who begged, au fond, to differ with it (cf. Geertz, 1973: 37–43).

Yet language was soon to have its day – suggestively at first, and then as a virtual culturological juggernaut. In 1936, Benjamin Whorf had hypothesized that languages played much the same role that Benedict had assigned to Gestalten ([1936] 1956a). In his later restatement of it, the hypothesis (if it can be called that) became even stronger: that the syntactic and semantic categories of any particular language in fact comprised the actual Gestalten through which its native speakers saw, felt and thought about the world ([1941] 1956b). The notion was in fact Romantic: Friedrich Schlegel had entertained it seriously more than a century before. Yet the 'Sapir–Whorf hypothesis', as it came to be known, was generally received not simply as novel but also as so radically relativistic as to be self-paradoxical. Lévi-Strauss would articulate a more rationalist and – during the constitutive phase of cultural anthropology, anyway – far more influential alternative. Enter 'structuralism' – a theory of culture which, in its inaugural formulation, owed something to Immanuel Kant, something to Jean-Jacques Rousseau, something to Karl Marx, even something to Boas, but most of all to the linguists Ferdinand de Saussure and Roman Jakobson. Lévi-Strauss conceived of structuralism as a psychological theory, but unlike Benedict, he sought not to borrow from psychology but rather to rectify it. What was culture? At least in its originary and uncorrupted modality, it was the immediate outcome of the human mind's spontaneous drive to render into

discrete quanta and qualia the unbroken continuum of raw sensation. Benedict's Gestalten were thus not entirely off the theoretical mark, but were nevertheless derivative of more primordial operations. The key to the logic of those operations lay with phonemes – the atomic elements out of which words and sentences of every spoken human language are composed. Phonemes are what white noise is not; they are communicatively functional units of sound. Every spoken language has its own phonemic system, and every phonemic system resolves into a matrix of binary oppositions between units of sound which do, and units of sound which do not, exhibit a particular sonic feature (voiced vs. voiceless, for example, or sibilant vs. non-sibilant). Phonemes can thus only be identified through their differences from one another, and within the larger matrix to which they belong.

The atomic elements of culture are 'signs' – words, but also whatever else that, upon being heard or seen or touched or tasted, 'makes sense' (Lévi-Strauss, [1962] 1966: 18). For Lévi-Strauss, the analysis of signs and the analysis of phonemes are closely parallel – or would be, were the matrices are which signs are situated not considerably more vulnerable to historical wear and tear than phonemic matrices, and were signs thus not considerably more likely than phonemes to drift into increasingly accidental, increasingly arbitrary, and increasingly unreadable relationships to one another. The contemporary world confronts the anthropologist with an insular sign system here and there, still more or less intact; but for the most part, it is a world of semiological ruins, of the scattered shards of systems long since fallen victim to the double assault of historical change and the insensate scrutiny of scientific and technical reason. The anthropologist's first task is for Lévi-Strauss thus one of salvage – as it was, indeed, for Boas. Among the extant remnants of the 'primitive', the fieldworker was first obliged to collect what he could of the surviving fragments and still accessible memories of an older language, an older cosmos, in which nature and culture, the physical and the spiritual, were still part of the same ultimate order. Boas himself had set a methodological standard in his supervision of the meticulous elicitation and recording of what was left of the mythologies of the native North Americans. Affirming much the same standard, a later generation of researchers, the cognitivists, had undertaken to retrieve the classificatory principles and lexical components of 'primitive science' – botany, zoology, physiology, and so on – in North and in South America, in Asia and the insular Pacific.

Yet for Lévi-Strauss (who famously preferred to leave fieldwork to others), the anthropologist was not yet done. Indeed, he had barely begun. What remained was the analytical reassembly or reconstruction of proper sign systems out of the significative bits and pieces which the fieldworker had brought home. In such monographs as *The Savage Mind* ([1962] 1966) and the four compendious volumes of *The Mythologiques* ([1964] 1969; [1966] 1973; [1968] 1978; [1971] 1981), Lévi-Strauss himself has provided the grandest examples of what the latter task would seem to demand. *The Mythologiques* especially have reminded more than a few readers of Frazer's *Golden Bough* (1922), an even grander compendium of 'primitive beliefs' now widely disparaged for its insensitivity to context and the impressionistic whimsy of so many of its comparisons. More aptly, and more fairly, however, the project of *The Mythologiques* might be compared to the hunt for 'proto-Indo-European', that ancient and lost language in which living languages from Hindi and Bengali to French and English putatively have their common source. Seeking not the prototypical myth but rather the prototypical grammar of myth, Lévi-Strauss begins as near as possible to the present. His data are such myths as fieldworkers (some of them not anthropologists but missionaries) have been able to gather from their primitive interlocutors in the past two centuries or so. Yet he insists that any particular myth demands an initial decryption in light of the specific community to which its teller belongs.

Hence, a minimal analytical unit which in fact looks very much like 'a culture', construed as a group of people who share, and mutually understand, the same systems of signs. Its boundaries are thus cybernetic; they mark those limits beyond which information cannot flow (without translation). Its rough linguistic analogue is that of the speakers of any particular living language. Yet like the linguist in the hunt after proto-Indo-European, Lévi-Strauss presumes a historical connection between any one culture and all the others in its region – and so, a connection between the myths of one and the myths of all the others. The linguist looks to cognate terms and cognate syntactic rules as evidence that different languages share a common origin. Lévi-Strauss looks to cognate characters and cognate stories as evidence that two myths derive from what was once the same sign system. Were evidence rich enough, the linguist might ultimately succeed in gleaning the basic grammar of proto-Indo-European from its various offspring. Were evidence rich enough, Lévi-Strauss might ultimately succeed in gleaning the basic grammar of myth – and with it, the basic and originary grammar of culture as such.

Alas, the evidence is not sufficiently rich, and Lévi-Strauss' project is consequently highly speculative. It is also highly formalistic. Much less the formalist – indeed, somewhat anti-formalist – Geertz would gradually assemble a third model of culture, in initial opposition not to Lévi-Strauss but to the Boasian legacy itself. His early point of attack is the search for substantive cultural universals (the substantive elements which every marriage, say, or every religion has in common), the misguidedness of which he locates in a long-standing failure to appreciate the evolutionary thrust of cultural dynamics (Geertz, 1973: 43–54). Against the view (which was Boas', though by no means his alone) that culture is the last of human acquisitions, sitting on top of or 'capping' a species already biologically, psychologically and socially 'complete,' Geertz asserted what the majority (though not all!) of contemporary cultural anthropologists could easily approve. His thesis was double: first, that human evolution had involved the influence of the cultural on our various other vital dimensions no less than the reverse; and second, that cultural capacities came not simply to replace an ever-diminishing store of instincts, but to transcend them, freeing us from having to find our particular environmental niche and enabling us instead to learn how to adapt to an indefinitely wide variety of niches, from the Arctic to the tropics. That the key to culture might subsist in what was substantively constant could thus not be farther from the truth. What was key about culture for Geertz was precisely the indefinite, perhaps endless, diversity of its substantive realizations.

So far, the Geertzian position is functionalist, and indeed, it owed much to the (more or less) Durkheimian functionalism of Talcott Parsons. Yet for all his respect for Parsons, Geertz would soon begin to have his doubts about the adequacy of conceiving culture simply, or primarily, as a sort of collective life support. In his celebrated essay on religion, he would lend far more intellectual weight to (Germanic, hermeneutical) Weberian than to (positivist) Durkheimian sociology (1973: 87–125). In his later work, he would increasingly favor interpretive diagnosis over functionalist analysis. There is more than a hint of the Boasian here, which the admiring portrait of Benedict in *Works and Lives* (Geertz, 1988) only underscores. Yet Geertz's mature model of culture is not psychologistic, and less Boasian than Parsonian in its emphasis on symbols in action, or symbolic action. It borrows two crucial presumptions from Ludwig Wittgenstein's *Philosophical Investigations* (1953): one, that words and other signs and symbols can have or convey meaning only if there is some intersubjectively available means for deciding upon their correct use (in short, that there can be no such thing as a 'private language'); and the other, that words and other signs and symbols have or convey meaning only within intersubjectively recognizable practical contexts (in short, that meaning is a matter of usage) (see Geertz, 1973: 12–13). It borrows its governing analogies from Paul Ricoeur (1971): cultural interpretation is like textual interpretation; cultures are like texts (see Geertz, 1973: 448; cf. Geertz, 1983: 68–70).

Texts, for their part, are of many kinds. Following Ricoeur, Geertz rejects the analogical merits of those 'radically symbolic', free-floating, inexhaustibly reinterpretable sorts of texts celebrated in the writings of such literary theorists as Roland Barthes (1977) and such philosophers as Jacques Derrida ([1967] 1974). Cultures aren't 'like that'. They resemble more such texts as Charles Dickens' *Tale of Two Cities* or Mark Twain's *Adventures of Tom Sawyer and Huckleberry Finn*: of convention-laden form, more or less tidily self-enclosed, susceptible to plural but not an infinite number of plausible interpretations, good reads. Yet even this analogy is imperfect, because cultures are not narratives. Their primary medium is not print but action. This aside, for Geertz as for 'symbolic anthropologists' from Victor Turner (e.g., 1974) and David Schneider (e.g., 1980) to Nancy Munn (1973), Sherry Ortner (1974b) and James Fernandez (1986), they are constituted of interwoven figures (of speech and of action); they have prevailing motifs ('sacred' and 'key' symbols); and they embody perspective – what Geertz repeats Malinowski in calling 'the native's point of view' (1983: 57–58).

What, then, of fieldwork? It rarely requires the ferreting out of the underlying logic or depth grammar which allegedly informs the ways in which people use whatever words or other signs and symbols they do. The fieldworker should attend first to the lineaments of the various contexts in which people say and do particular sorts of things – buy and sell, christen their children and bury their dead, place bets and fall into trances, and so on. The 'logic' of such action-contexts is typically messy, and with rare exceptions, largely informal; and the logic which ties one action-context to another more messy and informal still. Yet for Geertz, it is precisely such messiness that prevails in the less than ruly, everyday goings-on of a culture, and precisely what an excessively formalist approach to culture could only distort, if not positively misrepresent. The fieldworker hardly dare ignore the language of his or her native interlocutors, but should address it not as an autonomous system but rather as so much significative potential, not as a map or predictive 'rulebook' of cultural practice but rather as a repository of orientations which might as often be bent or broken as obeyed. Particularly telling are those words and other signs and symbols which frequently recur within or across action-contexts, and among such words and signs and symbols, those above all which have the greatest organizational effect, whether semiotic or practical. Such motifs are not, however, Benedict's patterns. They are not the fieldworker's but the natives' creation – hence, the Malinowskian restriction which Benedict did not (consistently) incorporate into her own program of research. How might the fieldworker know whether his or her determinations of context, of meaning, of subsidiary and key symbols is correct? There is no other proof but the ability to talk and to interact gracefully with the natives themselves. The proof is performative.

FROM PRACTICAL ONTOLOGY
TO THE PRACTICAL CRITIQUE OF ONTOLOGY

It would be a mistake to downplay the divergences among Benedict's, Lévi-Strauss' and Geertz's models of culture, or indeed to downplay the divergences of their methodological consequences. Yet it would be just as much of a mistake to downplay the ontological presumptions – presumptions about the very nature, the very being, of culture – on which they mutually depend. At the risk of running somewhat roughshod over more minute details, one might remark three hallmarks or properties which, disagreements aside, virtually all of the major contributors to the constitution of cultural anthropology would in fact have recognized as properties of culture as such. The first of these allows for the shift from talk of culture to talk of cultures. Call it the property of boundedness. It has its strongest – and least plausible – expression in the 'insular conceit': the presumption that each culture, if not literally confined to an island, could be approached as if it were. Yet very few researchers in fact embraced such a conceit as anything more than a methodological convenience, an artifice which, if not altogether innocent, served to endow fieldwork (and ethnographic writing) with manageable limits. For most, the boundaries which cultures possessed were at once permeable and 'fuzzy'. Even while they continued to write in the ethnographic present, most were perfectly well aware that cultures were historical formations (if not always historically in formation), that it was frequently difficult to determine precisely just where one culture ended and another began, and that among geographically proximate cultures, there was likely to be just as much evidence of intermixture as of isolation (cf. Firth, 1959). Hence, if cultural research had its specific site in one or another community or village or literal island, it had its broader locus in a 'culture area'. Exhibiting shared traits or cultural complexes, culture areas nevertheless had boundaries of their own, and boundaries no different in kind from geographically more restricted boundaries which they encompassed. What could be said of an individual culture could thus be said of a culture area as well. For Benedict, both revealed their edges at those (usually fuzzy) interfaces at which one complex of norms and values gave way to another. For Lévi-Strauss, both revealed their edges as precipitous drops in the level of the flow of information. For Geertz, both revealed their edges as the sometimes abrupt, sometimes gradual ebbing of conversational (and experiential) familiarity. But in every case, edges were presumed to 'be there'; no culture worthy of the name could exist without them.

The second presumptively natural property of any culture worthy of name was the property of integration. Benedict once again produced the foundational argument (1934: 45–56), and very little would be conceptually added to it, even if for each new model, a somewhat different vocabulary would need deploying. Consistently, Benedict's own terms were those of Gestalt psychology, and her basic claims distinctly Gestaltist in tenor. Even if a thing of shreds and patches, a culture had always also to be a thing of stitches and seams, a quilt or tapestry, however ragged or threadbare. It could perhaps absorb its share of paradoxes. Yet it could not be so blatantly rife with paradox, or inconsistency, or incoherence, that the people whose culture it was were left bereft of stable channels of experience or stable guidelines of action. Too much in the way of what would later come to be called 'cognitive' or 'affective dissonance' (Wallace, 1956) was humanly intolerable. Cultures were just those sorts of entities which – for most people, most of the time – kept such dissonance at an acceptable minimum. They were matrices of expectability. Without them, human beings would be forced to take up every experience, every practical option, as a novelty – which is to say, as Geertz would later have it, that they would simply be reduced to the condition of 'basket cases' (1973: 49). Lévi-Strauss was inclined to think integration a more palpable quality of the cultural past. Benedict, Geertz and most everyone else were very much inclined to think it a necessary quality of any variety of ethnographic presents, if a quality perhaps more evident outside than within the borders of the modern West. Lévi-Strauss conceived of integration as an 'aesthetic' property, or in any event as a property which resulted from the same sorts of digital and analogical mental operations as did the structural 'economy' of a Clouet oil ([1962] 1966) or Mozart symphony ([1964] 1969). Geertz (1973: 345–59) would be joined by Pierre Bourdieu ([1972] 1977) and many others in rejecting the putative intellectualist exaggerations of Lévi-Strauss' reconstructions of culture before the fall, though Geertz, too, would come increasingly to conceive of integration itself as aesthetic – if only more roughly so.

Neither quite the same as its boundedness nor quite the same as its integration was culture's presumptive systematicity. Unsurprisingly, Lévi-Strauss' formulation was the most exacting. Cultural systems were 'mechanical' – closed rather than open, of an only finite number of variables, and each variable of which stood in definable relation to every other (Lévi-Strauss, [1953] 1973: 378–82). That the fieldworker would virtually never encounter such systems face-to-face, that he or she would virtually always be sifting among shards, was neither here nor there. It was in their (lost) mechanicity that the only intelligibility of cultural systems as systems lay. A daunting formulation,

indeed – and it has had only a very occasional adherent beyond Lévi-Strauss himself. Yet the sort of holism which the Boasians imported to the study of culture was only slightly more modest, and no less methodologically suggestive. It, too, encouraged a program of both research and textual representation for which each symbol served as the interpretive 'context' for every other, and each cultural 'part' (from dietetics to religion) as the interpretive context at once for every other part and for the totality that comprised them. Poetically speaking, culture was a matter of metonyms and synecdoches. Methodologically and textually, it might thus be approached from two quite distinct vantages. One of these was an interpretive survey of a culture (or a cultural system) as a totality. Malinowski's *Argonauts* afforded one classic example; some half century later, the four volumes of Lévi-Strauss' *Mythologiques* would afford another, even more prodigious. Yet as totalistic surveys, the *Argonauts* and the *Mythologiques* are in fact methodological exceptions. Far more often, cultural (and for that matter, social) research would adopt not the whole of a culture but rather one or another of its parts as its primary object – from the potlatch of the native Northwest coast of America (Codere, [1956] 1967) to the 'dreamings' of the Australian desert (Stanner, 1958; cf. Clifford, 1988: 314; cf. also Geertz, 1973: 21–2). What separated such a strategy of research from its nineteenth-century forerunner – the collection and analysis of 'traits' – was precisely its poetical rationale. If, indeed, cultures were metonymic and synecdochic, the fieldworker could be reasonably confident that each cultural part would in fact reveal something of the cultural whole, if not as an epitome then at least as a refraction. In principle, only participant observation, only sustained empirical enquiry, could render such confidence legitimate; only empirical enquiry would enable the fieldworker further to select, among an array of potential analytical foci, those which were in fact most 'representative'. The quest for the representative animated Boas (who tended to seek out the ageing repositories of lore and mores, the wise men and wise women of a culture) as much as his students (who tended to seek out the interactive nexuses of cultural acquisition – parent and child, teacher and apprentice, and so on). In their aftermath, it continued to animate a cultural anthropology which, throughout its constitutive period, was increasingly likely to elevate to an axiomatics of research those sorts of partitive types or categories already comparatively established to be the most culturally dense – whether as epitomes, or as refractions, or as both.

These are, in short, the ontological postulates which reigned over what has been called cultural anthropology's 'golden age' – between the 1920s and the 1950s – and even beyond it, to the early 1960s. By the later 1960s, however, something of an interregnum had begun to have its day. Especially in the United States, cultural anthropologists of a younger generation would come together to voice collective worry over their disciplinary legacy, and to call for disciplinary reformation. The dominant tenor of their malaise was of the same pitch as that of the broader protests of the period; it was not 'metaphysical' but rather political and moral. Kathleen Gough may have been the first to level an accusation which many others would reiterate in the next decade: anthropology was a 'child of imperialism' which had failed utterly to come to terms with its parentage (Gough, 1968; cf. Asad, 1973). For Gough herself, as for many other neo-Marxists (see Caulfield, 1972; Wolff, 1972), the corrective lay first in the inauguration of an anthropology of imperialism, and more specifically, of an anthropology which would leave behind its pretensions to objectivity in favor of a normative enquiry into the relative benefits and vices of capitalist and socialist regimes. Only thus could anthropology attain contemporary 'relevance' (Gough, 1968). It would, however, only attain maturity when it had further come to take full reflexive account of its own situation within the past and present world-system. General critical consensus had it that anthropologists would thus have to pursue a four-fold *examen de conscience*. Politically, they needed to interrogate the role which anthropology had played, and continued to play, in sustaining and reinforcing domination, whether by providing 'useful information' to colonizing powers, lending legitimacy to inherently conservative and hierarchical models of social and cultural life, or cultivating professional ignorance of the dynamics and technologies of power (Nader, 1972; Willis, 1972; Wolf, 1982; Wolff, 1972). Morally, they would need to interrogate anthropology's professional values, and particularly to ask whether its polished relativism resulted less in the nourishment of cosmopolitan tolerance than in quiescence to injustice and violence (Clemmer, 1972; Diamond, 1972). Ethically, they would need to interrogate the quality and consequences of their own curiosity, the extent to which their ways and means of knowing and understanding less respected than exploited other human beings. Epistemologically, they would need to re-examine anthropological knowledge itself: its actual empirical basis; its actual subjects and objects; the actual scope and impartiality of its claims (Scholte, 1972). As Bob Scholte put it, anthropologists could no longer put off undertaking the 'ethnology of anthropology' (1972: 431; cf. Bennett, 1946; Berreman, 1966).

If in more roundabout fashion, a practically motivated critique thus arrived at much the same theoretical threshold at which Pierre Bourdieu ([1972] 1977) was arriving in France; and neither the ontological edifice nor the methodological apparatus of the culturological golden age would ever be quite the same again. Were cultures naturally bounded, after all? To repeat, even during the golden age, such a postulate had never been taken entirely for granted, and social anthropologists from Radcliffe-Brown forward (Radcliffe-Brown, [1940] 1952; cf. Leach, 1954: 17–18) had registered consistent suspicion of it. Moreover, many cultural researchers had studied such processes as 'acculturation', 'assimilation', and 'syncretization', which had as much to do with the breaching and shifting of cultural boundaries as with their endurance (e.g., Linton, 1940; cf. Spicer, 1961). The neo-Marxists of the 1960s wished, however, to press the issue much further. Mina Caulfield, for example, drew upon Fredrik Barth's analysis of ethnicity (1969) in arguing that the border between one culture and another might, sometimes at least, be the result of a strategy of resistance rather than of an intrinsic tendency toward the insular (Caulfield, 1972: 202). Richard Clemmer (1972) seconded her conclusion. Neither was quite prepared to execute the complete ontological erasure of the 'perimetric' culture. Yet both were harbingers of two theoretical trends. One of these has cast 'cultures' not as naturally bounded wholes but instead as artfully constructed differentia – sometimes found, sometimes invented, from one case to the next (cf. Hobsbawm and Ranger, 1983; Spooner, 1986). The other has increasingly cast the cultural not as spatial but rather as temporal and processual. In its neo-Marxist version, it has stressed a dissemination of 'ideology' from the centers to the peripheries of a world-system which no longer permits any neat division between one culture and another, between what is culturally 'inside' and what is culturally 'outside' (e.g., Comaroff, 1985; Nash, 1979; Ong, 1987, 1990; Schneider et al., 1972; Spindler, 1977; Taussig, 1980). In other versions – especially those 'post-colonialist' versions which, following Weber more than Marx, give as much weight to 'ideal' as to material motives and interests – the second trend has elevated the exilic, the diasporic and the hybrid to the status of culturological *primi inter pares* at which most of the anthropologists of the golden age would have scoffed. A certain diffusionism has consequently made a comeback – but an interpretivist and nominalist diffusionism, lacking any implication that it might uncover the universal laws of cultural dissemination, or of intercultural imporosity or osmosis (e.g., Appadurai, 1991; Basch et al., 1994; Hannerz, 1996; Ossman, 1994; Tsing, 1993).

If not naturally so bounded, then might cultures not naturally be quite so integrated, either? Few if any anthropologists have been tempted to board that impetuous (or as it is sometimes also known, 'postmodernist') bandwagon which would trumpet flux and incoherence as our true cultural lot. And sensibly enough: Benedict's position cannot plausibly be turned altogether on its head. Yet, before the 1970s, cultural complexity and cultural differentiation were relegated to something of a disciplinary side-line, and a sideline largely inscribed within the conceptual strictures of Robert Redfield's distinction between 'Little' and 'Great' traditions (Redfield, 1955; Srinivas, 1966) or the programmatic evolutionism of one or another grand theory of 'modernization' (Singer, 1972; cf. Geertz, 1973). Among the contributors to Hymes' volume, William Willis, Jr seems in retrospect to have been the most eloquent harbinger of a critical corrective which would rapidly transport the treatment of both complexity and differentiation to the very center of cultural research. An African American, Willis put together a full-scale assault on the racism which he detected in even the most generous-minded of the practitioners of a discipline that had, after all, specialized in the study of 'dominated colored peoples – and their ancestors – living outside the boundaries of modern white societies' from its earliest beginnings (Willis, 1972: 123; cf. Deloria, 1969). 'Color-blindness' was not a solution, but part of the problem; so, too, that 'liberal' relativism which granted the 'savage' his nobility but maintained a scrupulous 'neutrality' in the face of his 'distress and misery' (Willis, 1972: 126). If solution there was, it might come in some measure through the inauguration of a systematic ethnography of the urban ghetto and the poor (cf. Valentine and Valentine, 1970). It might come in even better measure through the systematic recruitment and training of 'black and other colored anthropologists' (Willis, 1972: 147). And liberalism had to go; 'political radicalism' would have to come to stand in its place (1972: 148).

Willis' vision is yet to be realized (to put it mildly). Yet, his voice was far from being lost in the wilderness, not least because it benefitted and has continued to benefit from the reinforcement of many others – 'colored', ethnic, international and transnational, gendered and sexed (or sexualized), whether alone or in combination. They continue to be too disharmonic to constitute a single chorus. Willis claimed allegiance to a 'nationalism' for which Franz Fanon was the proximate, but Marxism the ultimate, theoretical precedent (Fanon, 1968, 1969; Clark, 1991; Maddox, 1993; cf. Nkrumah, 1964). Feminists could – and in the 1970s often did – claim Marxism as their own precedent (Etienne and Leacock, 1980; Sacks, 1974; Siskind, 1973; cf. Engels, [1884] 1975). The primary object of their critical attention was, however, very much their own: 'patriarchy', or more generally, the suzerainty which men have long and – it would seem – everywhere enjoyed within the sexual division of labor and the division of sexual labor (Coward, 1983; Millett, 1971; cf. de Beauvoir, [1949] 1975). Unsurprisingly, feminist cultural anthropologists tended to focus at least as much upon the symbolic as upon the sheerly material

organization of patriarchy. Virtually none found the classic Marxist conception of ideology adequate to the phenomena they encountered. Most would consequently join anthropologists of nationalism and ethnicity in seeking a more serviceable critical and analytical apparatus among the symbologically most sophisticated of Marx's successors. Georg Lukács (e.g., 1964, 1970), Herbert Marcuse (e.g., 1968), Raymond Williams (1958, 1981), and the theorists of the later Frankfurt School, were the earliest of their discoveries, but none of these would prove to have quite so broad and enduring an influence as Antonio Gramsci, whose concept of 'hegemony' – the exercise of domination through purely 'civil' means – has become a contemporary byword not merely of the discourses of cultural (and sociocultural) anthropology but also of those of the rather broader discourses of 'ethnic studies', 'subaltern studies' and 'post-colonial studies' (Deloria, 1995; Agarwal, 1994; Alexander and Mohanty, 1997; de Angulo, 1990; Anzaldúa, 1987; Comaroff, 1985; Gandhi, 1998; Gregory, 1998; Guha, 1997; Gupta, 1998; Johnson, 1992; Kaplan and Grewal, 1994; Kaplan et al., 1999; Kondo, 1990, 1997; Limón, 1994, 1998; Loomba, 1998; Lowe, 1996; Spivak, 1987, 1990, 1999; Spivak and Guha, 1988; Turner, 1993; Vigil, 1997, 1998; cf. Gramsci, 1959, 1988).

There has been much life outside of Marxism as well. In the 1970s, the 'political' was becoming increasingly 'personal,' and such embodied diacritics as race, ethnicity, gender, sex and sexuality increasingly conceived as diacritics not of 'class' but rather of 'status' and 'identity'. The latter categories were already central to Barth's 'constructionist' account of ethnicity (1969), which has remained without any real culturological rival. They were central as well to both of the paths along which the feminist anthropology of patriarchy has continued to unfold. One of these paths is a cobblestone of ethnographic challenges to the presumptive uniformity and universality of male suzerainty (Dubisch, 1986; Fernea, 1969; Guttmann, 1997; di Leonardo, 1979; MacCormack and Strathern, 1980; Rogers, 1975; Seremetakis, 1991; Strathern, 1988; Visweswaran, 1994; Weiner, 1976; cf. di Leonardo, 1991: 10–19). The other has led toward the reformulation of such suzerainty as a matter of the control of 'prestige' or 'symbolic capital' (Douglas, 1966; Ortner, 1974a; Ortner and Whitehead, 1981; M. Rosaldo, 1974 (but cf. M. Rosaldo, 1980); Yanagisako and Collier, 1987; cf. Bourdieu, [1972] 1977, 1998). Status and identity have also been the prevailing rubrics of the culturological investigation of sexualities, from Gayle Rubin's extraordinary supplement to Lévi-Strauss' theorization of the prohibition of incest to more recent studies – much indebted to Michel Foucault, and beyond him, to Judith Butler – of the 'performance' and 'performativity' of masculine and feminine expressions of self (Carrier, 1995; Cohen, 1995; Epple, 1998; Herdt, 1991a, 1991b;

Herdt and Stoller, 1990; Herzfeld, 1985; Jacobs and Cromwell, 1992; Lancaster, 1992; Lancaster and di Leonardo, 1997; Murray, 1992, 1997; Parker et al., 1992; Roscoe, 1991; Rubin, 1975; Weston, 1991; cf. Foucault, [1976] 1978, [1984] 1985; and Butler, 1990, 1991, 1997).

No chorus: but it is precisely the multiplicity of this still growing serial which lends its repeated demonstration of the systematicity of the relationship between the embodied diacritics of cultural complexity and asymmetries of power such incontrovertible force. If Willis might regret that it is not consistently 'radical', he might still take heart that it can still drop, or be threatened with, the occasional bombshell. Two examples must suffice. Nancy Scheper-Hughes' *Death Without Weeping* (1992), a study of infant malnutrition among the Brazilian poor, has garnered several awards, but just as many vehement rebuttals, especially from those who have taken umbrage at its insinuation of the Brazilian state's role in promoting 'infanticide'. Anastasia Karakasidou's *Fields of Wheat, Hills of Blood* (1997), an enquiry into ethnic consciousness among Greek Macedonians, appears to have inspired a bomb threat which induced its prospective publisher, Cambridge University Press, to execute a cautionary reversal of plans. Two members of the editorial board of the Press temporarily resigned in protest. (For the record, the subsequent release of the monograph under the imprint of the University of Chicago did not meet with any violence.)

A note, finally, on systematicity itself. A glance at virtually any contemporary journal of cultural anthropology might foster the impression that the discipline is now split between 'modernists', who continue to believe in the systematicity of everything from cognition to consumption, and 'post-modernists', who allegedly believe only in semiotic 'play' and interactive 'virtuality'. In small measure, such a split is genuine, but less dramatic than it is often portrayed to be. Cultural anthropologists may not know it, but they are in broad accord about the basic nature of cultural systematicity, if not always about its secondary elaboration. Lévi-Strauss aside, the rest have arrived at a tacit unanimity: the cultural is not in fact 'mechanical'; it is not by nature a closed but rather an open system. For better or worse, it thus permits only of what Lévi-Strauss himself was happy to cede to historians (and sociologists): 'statistical' description, at a scale inevitably different from that of the thing itself, and whether quantitative or qualitative, inevitably incomplete (cf. Bourdieu, [1972] 1977: 3–9).

FIELDWORK AT LENGTH AND AT LARGE

Perhaps, however, disciplinary unanimity does end there. At the very least, the critical current in cultural anthropology has met with anything but a uniform response. Some reject its ontological skepticism and cleave to the old order. A considerable number have taken its skepticism to heart; yet no shared ontological alternative, no common replacement model of culture unites them. In its absence, a growing legion of cultural anthropologists have come to stake their claim to disciplinary distinction not on the object of their research but instead on their procedures – on fieldwork itself. Such an argument may keep such rivals as those who profess to specialize in 'cultural studies' at a convenient distance, but it is not without an air of paradox. Lacking secure ontological footing, cultural fieldwork seems fated to dissolve into one of several equally unsatisfactory self-caricatures. Executor of a method genuinely without object, or at least without a stable object, the researcher might, like Lévi-Strauss' historian, simply invent one, to each researcher her own; but then ethnography would simply be an aesthetic exercise, an 'art' in the strictest sense of the term. Or she might resort to the established ethnographic record, extracting the misplaced assumptions, undefended presumptions and hidden biases of one or another project of the past or near-present. The critical current in anthropology indeed continues in much this vein; but were it the sole disciplinary current, anthropology would simply have devolved into nothing more than the sort of deconstructive or destructive textual commentary for which cultural studies is often berated. Or, finally, she might turn entirely inward, offering herself up as a cultural object even without being able to specify where the cultural in her or about her begins or ends. Here, 'fieldwork' would run the risk of falling back into the armchair – or the psychoanalytic couch – and dragging the cultural along with it.

If the going state of disciplinary affairs is not yet so dire, that is in part because the thematics of cultural complexity are themselves still being developed, expanded and refined (see, e.g., Comaroff and Comaroff, 1991; Gupta and Ferguson, 1997b; Ortner, 1989; Savigliano, 1995; Tsing, 1993; Verdery, 1996). Moreover, among those anthropologists dissatisfied with the constitutive models of culture – as pattern, or as language, or as text – there are increasingly many for whom disciplinary critique has given way to experiments in renovation and reconstruction which at least try to avoid falling either into mere fiction or mere navelgazing. They remain 'experiments' because they lack any common methodological a priori. In other words, they manifest little if any agreement on what new and improved model of culture might serve better than past contenders. Or, to put it more positively, they suggest a turn toward an increasingly resolute methodological pluralism, toward the common conviction that cultural analysis demands not one but many different ways and means. They remain experiments as well because – like the avant-gardist art and writing of the first half of this century – they manifest as much willingness to violate the conventional limits of their discipline as to respect them.

For all this, the experimental current in cultural anthropology has limits of its own, which ultimately derive less from ontological than from epistemological criteria, less from a consideration of what culture definitively is than from a consideration of how we might begin to know or to understand anything about it at all (cf. Gupta and Ferguson, 1997a; Stewart, 1991, 1996; Strathern, 1991). Once again, the later 1960s are a watershed, and *Reinventing Anthropology* the programmatic commencement of more substantive things to come. Invoking an existentialist or neo-Marxist humanism, many of that volume's contributors castigated their anthropological predecessors for treating their informants and interlocutors as specimens or cases – a simultaneously epistemological and political gesture which in effect demoted fully fledged human subjects to the lowly status of 'preconscious' scientific objects (Diamond, 1972; cf. Fabian, 1983; Price, 1983; R. Rosaldo, 1980; Wolf, 1982). Its final contributor was left to pose a positive methodological reform. Relying closely upon Johannes Fabian's synopsis of the work of Habermas, Bob Scholte urged an anthropology that would at last adjust itself to what the intersubjectivity of the cultural fully implied (see Fabian, 1971). Such an anthropology could no longer present fieldwork as an encounter between subject and object, nor even between one subject and another. It would instead have to present it as the encounter between (at least) one intersubjective order and another – that which the anthropologist, as an enculturated being, brought to the field, and that (or those) with which her informants and interlocutors confronted her. Three corollaries followed. First, the generative 'site' of anthropological understanding was not 'a culture' but rather the dynamic interface between divergent intersubjectivities; its temporality not an eternal present but the inescapably historical 'here' and 'now' of the intersubjective encounter (or confrontation). Secondly, the basic data of anthropological understanding were not simple or absolute but rather relational – the 'differences' between one intersubjectivity in the light of or in contrast to another. Thirdly, a fully mature anthropological understanding would have to be grounded as much in self-analysis as in the analysis of the other, in a reciprocal elucidation of others in light of or in contrast to the self and of the self in light of or in contrast to others. Hence, Scholte's call for a 'critical and reflexive' reorientation of the discipline (1972).

The call would be repeated several times: from outside anthropology, in James Clifford's 'On ethnographic authority' (1983); and within it, most constructively in George Marcus and Michael Fischer's *Anthropology as Cultural Critique*

(1986). Marcus and Fischer still write as if the interregnum of the previous decade remained in force. The discipline they describe is 'between paradigms', in 'transition' from its functionalist and structuralist past to a future of paradigms regained and suffering a 'crisis of representation' along its way. In retrospect, however, *Anthropology as Cultural Critique* – which has become a standard textbook in the United States – seems less a perusal of the 'experimental moment' to which its subtitle refers than the disciplinary consecration of an experimental current which has since only grown in measure and force. Marcus and Fischer could already cite several exemplary monographs – not all of them 'cultural critiques', perhaps, but all textually and thematically against the constitutive grain (cf. Abu-Lughod, 1991, 1993b). A great many more such monographs could be cited at present.

Textuality and thematics aside, the experimental current has also been a confluence of methodological innovations, at least some half dozen of which seem likely to endure. The first of these might be called 'situation analysis', though it should not be confused with the only superficially similar analyses of such interactionists as Erving Goffman or such ethnomethodologists as Harold Garfinkel. Paul Rabinow's *Reflections on Fieldwork in Morocco* (1977) and Jean-Paul Dumont's *The Headman and I* (1978) are its pioneer texts, and of the two, *Reflections* brings most fully to fruition the principles of ethnographic practice which Scholte had earlier advocated. Within it, participant observation has a thoroughgoing translation into hermeneutical enquiry. Yet the outcome is neither a revival of Boas nor a reaffirmation of the classic hermeneutical engagement between a subject and a text. Rabinow's is a more Hegelian perspective, a vantage from which fieldwork appears as a series of encounters between subjectivities in contest, the transcendence of which demands the researcher's continuous reassessment of place, of self, of other, and of the structural background which enframes and, at least in part, determines them. Demurring from Hegel, however, Rabinow envisions no ultimate synthesis, no ultimate fusion of intersubjective horizons. Fieldwork cannot result in the erasure or overcoming of intersubjective difference. It must end rather in the reflexive recognition of the possibility of that always partial, always limited fusion of horizons which he calls 'friendship'.

Yet another vector of experimental situation analysis less lies between than intersects the former two. On the one hand, it acknowledges the political situation of research, but substitutes for the antagonism or agonism of dialectics an agenda which recalls Kurt Wolff's dictum that the ethnographer must surrender himself or herself to the sovereignty of the other (Wolff, 1964). On the other hand, though it resists appealing to the speaker's or writer's unique privilege (as kin, as a national, as sexed, as oppressed) to legitimate its claims to ethnographic or anthropological insight or authority, it forges what for all intents and purposes can only be a rapprochement with what the nineteenth-century founders of hermeneutics declared to be the a priori of cultural understanding: projective empathy; the capacity to put oneself into the emotionality or sentimentality, into the aesthetics – the structured feeling and experience – of the other. At least a few of the recent virtuosi of such empathy deserve mention: Marjorie Shostak (1981), Lila Abu-Lughod (1986, 1993a), Ruth Behar (1996), and Julie Taylor, whose *Paper Tangos* (1998) is among the most eloquent – and among the most successful – of attempts to forge an intimate textuality that brings the other and the self into microcosmic commensurability against the backdrop of a world-systemic macrocosm.

A second experimental branch leads, whether as an alternative hermeneutics or as an alternative to hermeneutics, to 'practice analysis'. In 1984, Sherry Ortner put forward 'practice' as the 'key symbol' of anthropology since the 1960s. She had both social and cultural anthropology, both Bourdieu and Geertz, equally in mind. Fifteen years later, her intentionally sweeping characterization of practice as just about anything that has a political twist seems to conflate more than it elucidates, and is far from delimiting the specificity of the theoretical role which the concept of practice was designated to fulfill. First for Bourdieu, then for de Certeau ([1974] 1984), and Sahlins (1985), and many others, practice was that which stood between, and mediated, individual agency and supraindividual structure (whether social, or cultural, or both). For Bourdieu especially, it has been the fulcrum of an account of the 'unwitting' but active reproduction of social and cultural structures of domination. For de Certeau, it brought into resolution the scope and the modalities of tactical resistance to social and cultural structures 'in place' (cf. [1974] 1984: xix–xx). For Sahlins, it has operated as a sort of switching-post for the dynamic interplay of the structural determination of 'interest' and the 'interested' (if still often unwitting) inducement of structural change (cf. Kirch and Sahlins, 1992). Yeoman's service, indeed: yet for all its diverse utility, the theoretical centralization of practice effects a planar shift: from selves and others to 'habitus', 'subject positions', heterogeneous 'apparatuses' and conflictual 'fields'; and from a hermeneutics of situation to an analytics of the logics of sociocultural process.

In cultural anthropology, 'practice' now looms as the banner of several methodologies, each prescribing somewhat different plans and foci of research. Sahlins highlights the referential use of signs, and the risks which such usage can occasionally pose to the integrity of an already constituted cultural order. Recovering Vico, Michael Herzfeld (1987; cf.

Herzfeld, 1991) highlights instead the rhetorical force of signs in circulation, and the double and antagonistic meanings they often acquire in the historical course of their embattled absorption into cultural politics and the politics of culture. Rhetorical force and rhetorical practices are at a methodological premium in several less Vichian agenda as well, from Jean Comaroff's (1985), Sherry Ortner's (1989), John Borneman's (1992) to my own (Faubion, 1993). As cultural anthropologist, Bourdieu himself scrutinizes the field of ostensibly trivial but symbolically portentous discriminations which preserve the sovereignty of an aristocracy of 'good taste' over the mass of 'cruder' commoners ([1979] 1984). De Certeau also urged scrutiny of apparent trivia, from channel-surfing to cooking, not for the stratification they sustain but rather for the structural interstices and structural hiatus they expose. In the United States, however, neither Bourdieu nor de Certeau has had as decisive an impact on methodologies of practice analysis as Michel Foucault, whose transverse scanning of the 'discursive' and the 'extradiscursive', of 'knowledge' and 'power', sets the standard for a host of recent ventures into everything from development in Latin America (Escobar, 1995) to the colonialist erotics of race (Stoler, 1995), from medical entrepreneurialism in China (Farquhar, 1994) to language revival and ethnic separatism in the Spanish Basque country (Urla, 1993), from pronatalism (Horn, 1994) to the architecture of colonization during the fascist administration of Italy (Fuller, 1988; cf. Lindenbaum and Lock, 1993; and cf. Foucault, [1961] 1965, [1963] 1973 and [1966] 1973, [1969] 1972).

Foucault's methodological impact is further evident in a small but noteworthy number of forays into 'genealogy,' the retrospective unraveling of the social and cultural ancestry of some contemporary artifact or artifactual complex (cf. Foucault, [1971] 1998, [1975] 1977, [1976] 1978 and [1984] 1985). Many practice analyses include a genealogical component; all acknowledge the historicity of practice. Yet genealogy leaves the fieldworker no option but to traverse the terrain of the past as well as the terrain of the present, to include the dead among her interlocutors. Moreover, though it must always address practices, discursive and extradiscursive, its methodological scope is broader. The artifacts which might serve as its point of departure belong to no restricted class. Once again, Rabinow has been a pioneer. His *French Modern: Norms and Forms of the Social Environment* (1989), a veritable sociocultural genomics of the blandly functional urban planning which transformed the landscape of Paris and many of its far-flung satellites in the wake of the Second World War, is still the most complex token of its type (cf. Asad, 1993; Born, 1995). Genealogical approaches have the heuristic virtue – though not everyone might regard it as such – of bringing to the forefront a conceptual 'deregulation' which practice analyses sometimes achieve, but often leave in the background. Often emphasizing disruption, crisis, accident, contradiction and problematization rather than 'order', virtually always emphasizing the diachronic over the synchronic, they effectively do without any of the models of culture on which the constitutive current of the discipline has so far relied.

Their lesson is not that tradition is always 'invented' (cf. Hobsbawm and Ranger, 1983; Wagner, 1980). Nor is it simply that tradition may just as often be the product of unintended consequences as of intentional design. It is further that the traditional, the cultural, the social – the domain of the artifactual in general – is multi-scalar, if not down to every last artifact, at least down to a great many of them. Grasping for familiar metaphors, one might be tempted to revive yet again Lowie's 'shreds and patches'. But such an image won't quite do; it misleadingly suggests a substance of common cloth. Lévi-Strauss' 'bricolage' is a somewhat closer approximation, though only once disburdened of the 'bricoleur' and the mythologic that thinks itself through him (Lévi-Strauss, [1962] 1966: 16–21; [1964] 1969: 4–15). Ruminating over the implications not of genealogy but of chaos theory, Marilyn Strathern has wondered whether Donna Haraway's (1991) 'cyborg' – multi-scalar by definition – might preserve the metaphorical trenchancy of bricolage without dragging along all its formalist trappings in train (Strathern, 1991). It might – but the cyborg still suggests a maker, a 'cyborgeur', a mind behind the machine. Genealogists from Foucault forward have demonstrated convincingly enough that this need not be so. The artifactual may be cyborgic; but the cyborgic may be authorless.

Three further methodological innovations flow from the same conclusion which Strathern has in any event herself reiterated: enquiry into the cyborgic is not mere wandering through fragmentary rubble; it is rather a scouting for 'partial' and often ad hoc connections, neither the form nor the substance of which can be known in advance. One of these latter innovations amounts to a sort of 'team effort'. The teams at issue, however, no longer count only anthropological experts among their members. They include 'lay observers' as well. Defended sometimes in the name of the empowerment of the native voice, sometimes in the name of 'dialogue', sometimes in the name of generating Bakhtinian 'polyphony' (cf. Clifford, 1983), the team effort has had variable success, but even (or perhaps particularly) at its most awkward – as with Kevin Dwyer's *Moroccan Dialogues* (1982) – has confirmed the typically multi-scalar texture of intersubjectivities in contact. At its most distilled, such teamwork continues to take shape in the unstructured interview, at the anthropologist's bidding though not always

under his control (see, for example, Marcus, 1993). Tools other than the tape recorder have, however, produced compelling and unexpected results of their own. So, for example, Faye Ginsburg has trained her Australian aboriginal companions in the use of film and video cameras, and has witnessed the production of 'documentaries' quite different in scale and editorial composition than those she might have produced herself (see Ginsburg, 1993, 1994). As team member, moreover, Ginsburg is one of many anthropologists who have found themselves in what Marcus has deemed the role of the 'circumstantial activist' (1998: 98–9), a role in which the canonical relation of 'rapport' between ethnographer and informant may be transmuted into something much more like 'complicity' (Marcus, 1998: 105–31). Andrew Shryock has written in just such terms of his research among rival Palestinian historians (1997: 30–3). Michael Fischer and Mehdi Abedi's *Debating Muslims* (1990) and William Smalley, Chia Koua Vang and Gnia Yee Yang's *Mother of Writing* (1990) express a similar complicity in the joint signature, the textuality of multiple authorship (cf. also Bulmer and Majnap, 1977).

Geertz's 'Ritual and social change: a Javanese example' (1973: 142–69) is an exquisite epitome of the constitutive ethnography of events; its experimental offshoot might be called the 'event-chronicle'. Though there is nothing to prevent such a chronicle from being a team effort, it might still be the enterprise of a sole investigator, and have its end in a (more or less) conventional monograph. Geertz's essay remains within the model-theoretical parameters of 'modernization'. In contrast, the event-chronicle lacks general parameters. It is nominalist, even if the structural horizons to which it attends are at times no less expansive than those of the world-system itself. It is inherently unfinished, since only hindsight would permit its decisive closure. Its monographic tense is appropriately past, but its field methodology less that of a genealogy of the multi-scalar present than that of a genealogy in it. Crapanzano's *Waiting* (1985), a report on White South Africa at the verge of the fall of Apartheid, reflects a chronicler's practical wisdom in its suspension of climax. Some of the best of recent work in political (Das, 1995; Gal, 1991) and economic anthropology (Offe, 1985, 1996), and in the burgeoning anthropology of science (Fujimura, 1996; Hess, 1995; Latour and Woolgar, 1979; Rabinow, 1996, 1999; Traweek, 1988; Zabusky, 1995), shows similar methodological restraint. Yet that *Waiting* was originally published serially in *The New Yorker* points to a certain slippage of genres in which even some event-chroniclers themselves detect a disturbing trace of methodological wantonness (cf. Hannerz, 1998; Malkki, 1997; Marcus, 1998, 1999). Margaret Mead might have delighted in the chance to write for *The Ladies' Home Journal*, but never doubted that her ethnographic authority was the superior of its journalistic counterpart. As for Mead, so, too, for her disciplinary successors: fieldwork lent ethnography an epistemic density, a 'thickness' which journalism – always under the pressures of newsworthiness and press deadlines – could never rival. Between such journalists as Joan Didion, however, and anthropological event-chroniclers, any hierarchy seems hair-splitting. Perhaps this is because Didion's journalism is especially dense. But might it rather be that the fieldwork of the chroniclers has become increasingly thin?

Suspicions of methodological wantonness, or anemia, or both, also plague the last – and the most popular – entry in the contemporary roster of field experiments. Its affinate topics include exile, the diasporic and the hybrid, but also reception and consumption (Douglas and Isherwood, 1996; Miller, 1994), also globalization and localization (Friedman, 1992; Miller, 1995). Its lexicon features 'flows' and 'scapes' (Appadurai, 1991), the 'international' (Lee, 1995) and the 'transnational' (Glick Schiller et al., 1992; Gopinath, 1997; Kaplan et al., 1999; Puar, forthcoming Verdery, 1996, 1998; Yang, 1999), 'pluralism' and 'post-pluralism' (Strathern, 1992). Its methodology is what Marcus, the most trenchant of our monitors of the experimental current, has christened 'multi-sited' (1998: 79–104), and its proceduralism one of artifactual 'following' or tracking. Too literalist a parsing of 'multi-sitedness' would do violence to the spirit of Marcus' coinage. The ethnographer in pursuit of the mobile career of an idea, an object, a sentiment, or a population need not actually retrace every step her analysandum has taken, or actually set up camp at each stop it has made. Yet she must still have command, direct or indirect, of the multiple points of reference of each of the scales which it has retained, or acquired, or lost, along its particular way. Though the justification for such research seems plain – after all, we live in a world of exiles and hybrids, transnational flows, post-pluralist partialities – the criteria of its adequacy would, at least at first sight, seem exhausting, if not simply beyond reach. One need consider the time (and funding) required in our busy contemporary economy to chart the course of even a single film or popular song, a single technological invention or blueprint, in order to understand why the majority of ethnographic monitoring and tracking remains multi-sited only in the abstract. Short of having to be in more than one place at the same time (impossible even for the ethnographer), fieldwork might proceed cross-sectionally and sequentially, as a 'sampling' of the valency of an artifact in selectively diverse arenas. Arjun Appadurai suggested such a methodological solution in *The Social Life of Things* (Appadurai, 1986). Emily Martin adopted it in addressing the topos of 'flexibility' in the contemporary United States (Martin, 1994). Ethnographers of *objets d'art* have adopted similar

solutions in addressing the circulation of luxuries transnationally (e.g. Myers, 1992; Price, 1989; Steiner, 1994). A bit of thinness might creep in here, but perhaps within the limits of constitutive tolerance. In principle at least, a team effort – perhaps only anthropological, perhaps anthropological and lay – might prove a feasible strategy, and its results more satisfyingly dense. So far, however, tracking teams are very few and far between, and very little published.

The constitutive current in cultural anthropology is still with us; the critical current still vigilant; and the experimental current still doing what it can to explore, describe and diagnose emergent and unfamiliar cultural territories and temporalities. Even within the latter current, fieldwork is certainly not just what anyone might make of it; the constitutive 'old guard' and the critical new guard continue to hold the would-be avant-gardist to an unnegotiable minimum of professional propriety (as those who, like Carlos Castaneda, have breached the minimum have had to learn – often the hard way). Indeed, they should do so. Yet for all that it might disappoint those shopping for a methodological organon, such a minimum must suffice. The further determination of good methodological behavior can only come through the nostalgic or dogmatic refusal to countenance the possibility that the cultural might permit – might even demand – not fewer but rather an ever-greater assemblage of models and theories and proceduralisms in order to do it justice. Disciplinary and methodological matters would perhaps – one must stress, perhaps – have remained simpler, and less divisive, were anthropology (cultural and social) still restricted to the provinces of the 'primitive'. But in that case – presuming for the sake of argument that the 'primitive' has any categorical cogency whatsoever – it would simply have had less and less to do. Though it can appeal to a few constitutive precedents (Powdermaker, [1939] 1968; Mead, 1942), the experimental current has taken up precisely where the constitutive current of cultural (and social) anthropology – dutifully reproducing the conventional parceling of investigative and intellectual labor between specialists in 'the Rest' and specialists in 'the West' – largely left off. It has increasingly taken up 'the West,' and 'the modern', if not as its only site, or complex of sites, then as one site or complex of sites among many others. Thus relocated, thus multiply re-sited, it has endowed with ever-more concrete substance the hypotheses, or proto-hypotheses, which such social theorists as Reinhard Bendix have pressed since the early 1970s. One might state such proto-hypotheses straightforwardly: modernity is not one but culturally (and socially) many things; and it is up to the cultural (and social) fieldworker to explore, describe and diagnose at once what such a multi-scalar assemblage of artifacts is, or what it might be.

REFERENCES

Abu-Lughod, Lila (1986) *Writing Women's Worlds: Bedouin Stories.* Berkeley, CA: University of California Press.

Abu-Lughod, Lila (1991) 'Writing against culture', in R. Fox (ed.), *Recapturing Anthropology: Working in the Present.* Santa Fe, NM: SAR Press. pp. 137–62.

Abu-Lughod, Lila (1993a) *Veiled Sentiments: Honor and Poetry in a Bedouin Society.* Berkeley, CA: University of California Press.

Abu-Lughod, Lila (1993b) *Writing Women's Worlds.* Berkeley, CA: University of California Press.

Agarwal, Bina (1994) *A Field of One's Own: Gender and Land Rights in South Asia.* Cambridge and New York: Cambridge University Press.

Alexander, M. Jacqui and Mohanty, Chandra T. (1997) *Feminist Genealogies, Colonial Legacies and Democratic Futures.* New York: Routledge.

de Angulo, Jaime (1990) *Indians in Overalls.* San Francisco: City Lights Books.

Anzaldúa, Gloria (1987) *Borderlands = La Frontera: The New Mestiza.* San Francisco: Spinsters/Aunt Lute.

Appadurai, Arjun (ed.) (1986) *The Social Life of Things: Commodities in Cultural Perspective.* New York: Cambridge University Press.

Appadurai, Arjun (1991) 'Global ethnoscapes: notes and queries for a transnational anthropology', in Richard Fox (ed.), *Recapturing Anthropology.* Santa Fe, NM: School for American Research. pp. 191–210.

Asad, Talal (ed.) (1973) *Anthropology and the Colonial Encounter.* London: Ithaca Press.

Asad, Talal (1993) *Genealogies of Religion: Discipline and Reasons of Power in Christianity and Islam.* Baltimore, MD: Johns Hopkins University Press.

Barth, Fredrik (1969) 'Introduction', in Fredrik Barth (ed.), *Ethnic Groups and Boundaries.* Boston, MA: Little and Brown. pp. 9–38.

Barthes, Roland (1977) *Image/Music/Text* (trans. Stephen Heath). New York: Hill and Wang.

Basch, Linda, Glick Schiller, Nina and Blanc-Szanton, Cristina (eds) (1994) *Nations Unbound.* Langhorne, PA: Gordon and Breach Publishers.

Beattie, John (1964) *Other Cultures: Aims, Methods, and Achievements in Social Anthropology.* New York: The Free Press.

de Beauvoir, Simone ([1949] 1975) *The Second Sex* (trans. H.M. Parshley). London: Pan Books.

Behar, Ruth (1996) *The Vulnerable Observer: Anthropology that Breaks Your Heart.* Boston, MA: Beacon Press.

Behar, Ruth and Gordon, Deborah (eds) (1995) *Women Writing Culture.* Berkeley, CA: University of California Press.

Benedict, Ruth (1934) *Patterns of Culture.* Boston, MA: Houghton–Mifflin.

Benedict, Ruth (1946) *The Chrysanthemum and the Sword: Patterns of Japanese Culture.* Boston, MA: Houghton–Mifflin.

Bennett, John W. (1946) 'The interpretation of pueblo values: a question of values', *Southwestern Journal of Anthropology,* 2 (4): 361–74.

Berreman, Gerald (1966) 'Anemic and emetic analyses in social anthropology', *American Anthropologist,* 68: 349–54.

Born, Georgina (1995) *Rationalizing Culture: IRCAM, Boulez, and the Institutionalization of the Avant-garde.* Berkeley, CA: University of California Press.

Borneman, John (1992) *Belonging in the Two Berlins: Kin, State, Nation.* Cambridge: Cambridge University Press.

Bourdieu, Pierre ([1972] 1977) *Outline of a Theory of Practice* (trans. Richard Nice). Cambridge: Cambridge University Press.

Bourdieu, Pierre ([1979] 1984) *Distinction: A Social Critique of the Judgement of Taste* (trans. Richard Nice). Cambridge: Cambridge University Press.

Bourdieu, Pierre (1998) *La Domination masculine.* Paris: Seuil.

Bulmer, Ralph and Majnep, Ian (1977) *Birds of My Kalam Country.* Aukland: University of Aukland Press.

Butler, Judith (1990) *Bodies that Matter: On the Discursive Limits of "Sex".* New York: Routledge.

Butler, Judith (1991) *Gender Trouble: Feminism and the Subversion of Identity.* New York: Routledge.

Butler, Judith (1997) *The Psychic Life of Power: Theories of Subjection.* Stanford, CA: Stanford University Press.

Caffrey, Margaret (1989) *Ruth Benedict: Stranger in this Land.* Austin, TX: University of Texas Press.

Carrier, Joseph M. (1995) *De Los Otros: Intimacy and Homosexuality among Mexican Men.* New York: Columbia University Press.

Caulfield, Mina D. (1972) 'Culture and imperialism: proposing a new dialectic', in Dell Hymes (ed.), *Reinventing Anthropology.* New York: Pantheon. pp. 182–212.

de Certeau, Michel ([1974] 1984) *The Practice of Everyday Life* (trans. Stephen Rendall). Berkeley, CA: University of California Press.

Clark, John H. (1991) *Africans at the Crossroads: Notes for an African Revolution.* Trenton, NJ: Africa World Press.

Clemmer, Richard (1972) 'Truth, duty, and the revitalization of anthropologists: a new perspective on cultural change and resistance', in Dell Hymes (ed.), *Reinventing Anthropology.* New York: Pantheon. pp. 213–47.

Clifford, James (1983) 'On ethnographic authority', *Representations,* 1: 118–46.

Clifford, James (1988) *The Predicament of Culture.* Cambridge, MA: Harvard University Press.

Clifford, James and Marcus, George (eds) (1986) *Writing Culture: The Poetics and Politics of Ethnography.* Berkeley, CA: University of California Press.

Codere, Helen ([1956] 1967) 'The potlatch in Kwakiutl life', in Roger C. Owen, James J.F. Deetz and Anthony D. Fisher (eds), *The North American Indians: A Sourcebook.* New York: Macmillan. pp. 324–45.

Cohen, Lawrence (1995) 'The pleasures of castration: the postoperative status of hijras, jankhas, and academics', in Paul Abramson and Steven Pinkerton (eds), *Sexual Nature, Sexual Culture.* Chicago: University of Chicago Press. pp. 267–304.

Comaroff, Jean (1985) *Body of Power, Spirit of Resistance: The Culture and History of a South African People.* Chicago: University of Chicago Press.

Comaroff, Jean and Comaroff, John (1991) *Of Revelation and Revolution: Christianity, Colonialism, and Consciousness in South Africa.* Chicago: University of Chicago Press.

Coward, Rosalind (1983) *Patriarchal Precedents: Sexuality and Social Relations.* London: Routledge and Kegan Paul.

Crapanzano, Vincent (1985) *Waiting: The Whites of South Africa.* New York: Random House.

Das, Veena (1995) *Critical Events: Anthropological Perspectives on Contemporary India.* Delhi: Oxford University Press.

Deacon, Desley (1997) *Elsie Clews Parsons: Inventing Modern Life.* Chicago: University of Chicago Press.

Deloria, Jr, Vine (1969) *Custer Died for Your Sins: An Indian Manifesto.* New York: Macmillan.

Deloria, Jr, Vine (1995) *Red Earth, White Lies: Native Americans and the Myth of Scientific Fact.* New York: Scribner.

Derrida, Jacques ([1967] 1974) *Of Grammatology* (trans. Gayatri Chakravorty Spivak). Baltimore, MD: Johns Hopkins University Press.

Diamond, Stanley (1972) 'Anthropology in question', in Dell Hymes (ed.), *Reinventing Anthropology.* New York: Pantheon. pp. 401–29.

Douglas, Mary (1966) *Purity and Danger: An Analysis of Concepts of Pollution and Taboo.* London: Routledge and Kegan Paul.

Douglas, Mary and Isherwood, Baron (1996) *The World of Goods: Towards an Anthropology of Consumption,* rev. edn. London and New York: Routledge.

Dubisch, Jill (1986) 'Introduction', in Jill Dubisch (ed.), *Gender and Power in Rural Greece.* Princeton, NJ: Princeton University Press. pp. 3–41.

DuBois, Cora (1955) 'The dominant value profile of American culture', *American Anthropologist,* 57 (1): 1232–9.

Dumont, Jean-Paul (1978) *The Headman and I.* Austin, TX: University of Texas Press.

Dundes, Alan (ed.) (1994) *The Cockfight: A Casebook.* Madison, WI: University of Wisconsin Press.

Dwyer, Kevin (1982) *Moroccan Dialogues.* Baltimore, MD: Johns Hopkins University Press.

Engels, Friedrich ([1884] 1975) *The Origin of the Family, Private Property and the State.* New York: International Publishers.

Epple, Carolyn (1998) 'Coming to terms with Navajo *nádleehí*: a critique of *berdache*, "gay," "alternative gender," and "two-spirit"', *American Ethnologist,* 25 (2): 267–90.

Escobar, Arturo (1995) *Encountering Development: The Making and Unmaking of the Third World.* Princeton, NJ: Princeton University Press.

Etienne, Mona and Leacock, Eleanor (eds) (1980) *Women and Colonization: Anthropological Perspectives.* New York: Praeger.

Fabian, Johannes (1971) 'Language, history, and anthropology', *Journal for the Philosophy of the Social Sciences,* 1 (1): 19–47.

Fabian, Johannes (1983) *Time and the Other: How Anthropology Makes Its Object.* New York: Columbia University Press.

Fanon, Franz (1968) *The Wretched of the Earth.* New York: Grove Press.

Fanon, Franz (1969) *Toward the African Revolution* (trans. Haakon Chevalier). Harmondsworth: Penguin.

Farquhar, Judith (1994) *Knowing Practice: The Clinical Encounter of Chinese Medicine.* Boulder, CO: Westview Press.

Faubion, James D. (1993) *Modern Greek Lessons: A Primer in Historical Constructivism.* Princeton, NJ: Princeton University Press.

Fernandez, James (1986) *Persuasions and Performances: The Play of Tropes in Culture.* Bloomington, IN: Indiana University Press.

Fernea, Elizabeth (1969) *Guests of the Sheik: An Ethnology of an Iraqi Village.* New York: Doubleday.

Firth, Raymond (1959) *Social Change in Tikopia: A Restudy of a Polynesian Community after a Generation.* London: Allen and Unwin.

Fischer, Michael M.J. and Abedi, Medhi (1990) *Debating Muslims: Cultural Dialogues in Postmodernity and Tradition.* Madison, WI: University of Wisconsin Press.

Foucault, Michel ([1961] 1965) *Madness and Civilization: A History of Insanity in the Age of Reason* (trans. Richard Howard). New York: Pantheon.

Foucault, Michel ([1963] 1973) *Birth of the Clinic: An Archaeology of Medical Perception* (trans. A.M. Sheridan Smith). New York: Pantheon.

Foucault, Michel ([1966] 1973) *The Order of Things: An Archaeology of the Human Sciences* (trans. Alan Sheridan). New York: Vintage Books.

Foucault, Michel ([1969] 1972) *The Archaeology of Knowledge* (trans. A.M. Sheridan Smith). New York: Pantheon.

Foucault, Michel ([1971] 1998) 'Nietzsche, genealogy, history', in James D. Faubion (ed.), *Essential Works of Michel Foucault,* vol. 2: *Aesthetics, Method, Epistemology.* New York: The New Press. pp. 369–91.

Foucault, Michel ([1975] 1977) *Discipline and Punish: The Birth of the Prison* (trans. Alan Sheridan). New York: Pantheon.

Foucault, Michel ([1976] 1978) *The History of Sexuality,* vol. 1: *The Will to Know* (trans. Robert Hurley). New York: Pantheon.

Foucault, Michel ([1984] 1985) *The History of Sexuality,* vol. 2: *The Use of Pleasure* (trans. Robert Hurley). New York: Pantheon.

Frazer, James (1922) *The Golden Bough: A Study in Magic and Religion,* vols 1–12. London: Macmillan.

Freeman, Derek (1983) *Margaret Mead and Samoa: The Making and Unmaking of an Anthropological Myth.* Cambridge, MA: Harvard University Press.

Freeman, Derek (1999) *The Fatal Hoaxing of Margaret Mead: A Historical Analysis of her Samoan Research*. Boulder, CO: Westview Press.

Friedman, J. (1992) 'The past in the future: history and the politics of identity', *American Anthropologist*, 94 (4): 837–59.

Fujimura, Joan (1996) *Crafting Science: A Sociohistory of the Quest for the Genetics of Cancer*. Cambridge, MA: Harvard University Press.

Fuller, Mia (1988) 'Building power: Italy's colonial architecture and urbanism, 1923–1940', *Cultural Anthropology*, 3 (4): 455–87.

Gal, Susan (1991) 'Bartok's funeral: representations of Europe in Hungarian political rhetoric', *American Ethnologist*, 18 (3): 440–58.

Gandhi, Leela (1998) *Postcolonial Theory: A Critical Introduction*. New York: Columbia University Press.

Geertz, Clifford (1959) 'Form and variation in Balinese village structure', *American Anthropologist*, 61: 991–1012.

Geertz, Clifford (1963) *Agricultural Involution: The Processes of Ecological Change in Indonesia*. Berkeley, CA: University of California Press.

Geertz, Clifford (1973) *The Interpretation of Cultures*. New York: Basic Books.

Geertz, Clifford (1983) *Local Knowledge: Further Essays in Interpretive Anthropology*. New York: Basic Books.

Geertz, Clifford (1988) *Works and Lives: The Anthropologist as Author*. Stanford, CA: Stanford University Press.

Ginsburg, Faye (1993) 'Aboriginal media and the Australian imaginary', *Public Culture*, 5: 557–78.

Ginsburg, Faye (1994) 'Embedded aesthetics: creating a discursive space for indigenous media', *Cultural Anthropology*, 9 (3): 365–82.

Glick Schiller, Nina, Basch, Linda and Blanc-Szanton, Cristina (1992) 'Transnationalism: a new analytic framework for understanding migration', in N. Glick Schiller, L. Basch and C. Blanc-Szanton (eds), *Towards a Transnational Perspective on Migration*. New York: Annals of the New York Academy of Science. vol. 645, pp. 1–24.

Gopinath, Gayatri (1997) 'Nostalgia, desire, diaspora: South Asian sexualities in motion', *Positions*, 5 (2): 455–77.

Gorer, G. (1955) *Exploring English Character*. London: Cresset.

Gorer, G. and Rickman, J. (1949) *The People of Great Russia*. London: Cresset.

Gough, Kathleen (1968) 'Anthropology: child of imperialism', *Monthly Review*, 19 (11): 12–27.

Gramsci, Antonio (1959) *The Modern Prince, and Other Writings* (trans. Louis Marks). New York: International Publishers.

Gramsci, Antonio (1988) *A Gramsci Reader, 1916–1935* (ed. David Forgacs). London: Lawrence and Wishart.

Gregory, Steven (1998) *Black Corona: Race and the Politics of Place in an Urban Community*. Princeton, NJ: Princeton University Press.

Guha, Ranajit (1997) *Dominance Without Hegemony: History and Power in Colonial India*. New York: Columbia University Press.

Gupta, Akhil (1998) *Postcolonial Developments: Agriculture in the Making of Modern India*. Durham, NC: Duke University Press.

Gupta, Akhil and Ferguson, James (eds) (1997a) *Anthropological Locations: Boundaries and Grounds of a Field Science*. Berkeley, CA: University of California Press.

Gupta, Akhil and Ferguson, James (eds) (1997b) *Culture, Power, Place: Explorations in Critical Anthropology*. Durham, NC: Duke University Press.

Guttmann, Matthew C. (1997) 'The ethnographic (g)ambit: women and the negotiation of masculinity in Mexico City', *American Ethnologist*, 24 (4): 833–55.

Hannerz, Ulf (1996) *Transnational Connections: Culture, People, Places*. London and New York: Routledge.

Hannerz, Ulf (1998) 'Reporting from Jerusalem', *Cultural Anthropology*, 13 (4): 548–74.

Haraway, Donna (1991) 'A cyborg manifesto: science, technology, and socialist-feminism in the late twentieth century', *Simians, Cyborgs, and Women: The Reinvention of Nature*. New York: Routledge. pp. 149–82.

Harris, Marvin (1979) *Cultural Materialism: The Struggle for a Science of Culture*. New York: Random House.

Herdt, Gilbert (1991a) 'Representations of homosexuality in traditional societies: an essay on cultural ontology and historical comparison, part 1', *Journal of the History of Sexuality*, 1 (3): 481–504.

Herdt, Gilbert (1991b) 'Representations of homosexuality in traditional societies: an essay on cultural ontology and historical comparison, part 2', *Journal of the History of Sexuality*, 1 (4): 603–32.

Herdt, Gilbert and Stoller, Robert J. (1990) *Intimate Communications: Erotics and the Study of Culture*. New York: Columbia University Press.

Herzfeld, Michael (1985) *The Poetics of Manhood: Contest and Identity in a Cretan Mountain Village*. Princeton, NJ: Princeton University Press.

Herzfeld, Michael (1987) *Anthropology through the Looking-Glass: Critical Ethnography in the Margins of Europe*. Cambridge: Cambridge University Press.

Herzfeld, Michael (1991) *A Place in History: Social and Monumental Time in a Cretan Town*. Princeton, NJ: Princeton University Press.

Hess, David (1995) *Science and Technology in a Multicultural World: The Cultural Politics of Facts and Artifacts*. New York: Columbia University Press.

Hobsbawm, Eric and Ranger, Terrence (eds) (1983) *The Invention of Tradition*. Cambridge: Cambridge University Press.

Horn, David (1994) *Social Bodies: Science, Reproduction, and Italian Modernity*. Princeton, NJ: Princeton University Press.

Hsu, Francis (1953) *Americans and Chinese: Two Ways of Life*. New York: Schuman.

Hymes, Dell (ed.) (1972) *Reinventing Anthropology.* New York: Pantheon.

Jacobs, Sue Ellen and Cromwell, Jason (1992) 'Visions and revisions of reality: reflections on sex, sexuality, gender, and gender variance', *Journal of Homosexuality*, 23 (4): 43–69.

Johnson, Patricia (ed.) (1992) *Balancing Act: Women and the Process of Social Change.* Boulder, CO: Westview Press.

Kaplan, Caren and Grewal, Inderpal (eds) (1994) *Scattered Hegemonies: Postmodernity and Transnational Feminist Practices.* Minneapolis, MN: University of Minnesota Press.

Kaplan, Caren, Alarcón, Norma and Moallem, Minoo (eds) (1999) *Between Woman and Nation: The State, Nationalisms, and Transnational Feminism.* Durham, NC: Duke University Press.

Karakasidou, Anastasia (1997) *Fields of Wheat, Hills of Blood: Passages to Nationhood in Greek Macedonia, 1870–1990.* Chicago: University of Chicago Press.

Kirch, Patrick and Sahlins, Marshall (1992) *Anahulu: The Anthropology of History in the Kingdom of Hawaii,* 2 vols. Chicago: University of Chicago Press.

Kluckhohn, C. and Leighton, D. (1962) *The Navaho.* Garden City, NY: Natural History Library.

Kondo, Dorrine (1990) *Crafting Selves: Power, Gender, and Discourses of Identity in a Japanese Workplace.* Chicago: University of Chicago Press.

Kondo, Dorrine (1997) *About Face: Performing Race in Fashion and Theater.* New York: Routledge.

Kroeber, Alfred (1935) 'History and science in anthropology', *American Anthropologist*, 37 (4): 539–69.

Lancaster, Roger (1992) *Life Is Hard: Machismo, Danger, and the Intimacy of Power in Nicaragua.* Berkeley, CA: University of California Press.

Lancaster, Roger and di Leonardo, Micaela (eds) (1997) *The Gender/Sexuality Reader: Culture, History, Political Economy.* New York: Routledge.

Latour, Bruno and Woolgar, Steve (1979) *Laboratory Life: The Social Construction of Scientific Facts.* Beverly Hills, CA: Sage.

Leach, Edmund (1954) *Political Systems of Highland Burma.* London: G. Bell and Son.

Leach, Edmund (1970) *Claude Lévi-Strauss.* Harmondsworth: Penguin.

Lee, Benjamin (1995) 'Critical internationalism', *Public Culture,* 7: 559–92.

Lee, Dorothy (1976) *Valuing the Self: What We Can Learn from Other Cultures.* Englewood Cliffs, NJ: Prentice-Hall.

di Leonardo, Micaela (1979) 'Methodology and the misinterpretation of women's status: a case study of Goodenough and the definition of marriage', *American Ethnologist,* 6 (4): 627–37.

di Leonardo, Micaela (1991) 'Gender, culture, and political economy: feminist anthropology in historical perspective', in di Leonard, Michaela (ed.), *Gender at the Crossroads of Knowledge: Feminist Anthropology in the Postmodern Era.* Berkeley, CA: University of California Press. pp. 1–48.

Lévi-Strauss, Claude ([1953] 1973) 'Social structure', in Paul Bohannon and Mark Glazer (eds), *High Points in Anthropology.* New York: Alfred A. Knopf. pp. 373–409.

Lévi-Strauss, Claude ([1962] 1966) *The Savage Mind.* Chicago: University of Chicago Press.

Lévi-Strauss, Claude ([1964] 1969) *Introduction to a Science of Mythology,* vol. 1: *The Raw and the Cooked* (trans. John and Doreen Weightman). New York: Harper and Row.

Lévi-Strauss, Claude ([1966] 1973) *Introduction to a Science of Mythology,* vol. 2: *From Honey to Ashes* (trans. John and Doreen Weightman). New York: Harper and Row.

Lévi-Strauss, Claude ([1968] 1978) *Introduction to a Science of Mythology,* vol. 3: *The Origin of Table Manners* (trans. John and Doreen Weightman). New York: Harper and Row.

Lévi-Strauss, Claude ([1971] 1981) *Introduction to a Science of Mythology,* vol. 4: *The Naked Man* (trans. John and Doreen Weightman). New York: Harper and Row.

Lewis, Oscar (1951) *Life in a Mexican Village: Tepoztlán Restudied.* Urbana, IL: University of Illinois Press.

Limón, José (1994) *Dancing with the Devil: Society and Cultural Poetics in Mexican-American South Texas.* Madison, WI: University of Wisconsin Press.

Limón, José (1998) *American Encounters: Greater Mexico, the United States, and the Erotics of Culture.* Boston, MA: Beacon Press.

Lindenbaum, Shirley and Lock, Margaret (eds) (1993) *Knowledge, Power and Practice.* Berkeley, CA: University of California Press.

Linton, Ralph (1940) *Acculturation in Seven American Indian Tribes.* New York: Appleton–Century–Crofts.

Loomba, Ania (1998) *Colonialism–Postcolonialism.* London and New York: Routledge.

Lowe, Lisa (1996) *Immigrant Acts: On Asian-American Cultural Politics.* Durham, NC: Duke University Press.

Lukács, Georg (1964) *Realism in Our Time: Literature and the Class Struggle* (trans. John and Necke Mander). New York: Harper and Row.

Lukács, Georg (1970) *Writer and Critic, and Other Essays* (trans. Arthur D. Kahn). London: Merlin Press.

MacCormack, Carol and Strathern, Marilyn (eds) (1980) *Nature, Culture and Gender.* Cambridge: Cambridge University Press.

Maddox, Gregory (ed.) (1993) *African Nationalism and Revolution.* New York: Garland.

Malinowski, Bronislaw (1922) *Argonauts of the Western Pacific.* New York: E.P. Dutton.

Malinowski, Bronislaw (1939) 'Group and individual in functional analysis', *American Journal of Sociology*, XLIV: 938–64.

Malkki, Liisa (1997) 'News and culture: transitory phenomena and the fieldwork tradition', in A. Gupta and J. Ferguson (eds), *Anthropological Locations: Boundaries and Grounds of a Field Science.* Berkeley, CA: University of California Press. pp. 86–101.

Marcus, George (ed.) (1993) *Late Editions,* vol. 1: *Perilous States: Conversations on Culture, Politics, and Nation.* Chicago: University of Chicago Press.

Marcus, George (1998) *Ethnography Through Thick and Thin*. Princeton, NJ: Princeton University Press.

Marcus, George (ed.) (1999) *Critical Anthropology Now*. Santa Fe, NM: School for American Research.

Marcus, George and Fischer, Michael M.J. (1986) *Anthropology as Cultural Critique: An Experimental Moment in the Social Sciences*. Chicago: University of Chicago Press.

Marcuse, Herbert (1968) *Negations: Essays in Critical Theory* (trans. Jeremy J. Shapiro). Boston, MA: Beacon Press.

Martin, Emily (1994) *Flexible Bodies: The Role of Immunity in American Culture from the Days of Polio to the Age of AIDS*. Boston, MA: Beacon Press.

Mead, Margaret (1928) *Coming of Age in Samoa: A Psychological Study of Primitive Youth for Western Civilization*. New York: William Morrow.

Mead, Margaret (1930) *Growing Up in New Guinea*. New York: William Morrow.

Mead, Margaret (1942) *And Keep Your Powder Dry: An Anthropologist Looks at America*. New York: William Morrow.

Miller, Daniel (1994) *Modernity – an Ethnographic Approach: Dualism and Mass Consumption in Trinidad*. London: Berg.

Miller, Daniel (ed.) (1995) *Worlds Apart: Modernity through the Prism of the Local*. London and New York: Routledge.

Millett, Kate (1971) *Sexual Politics*. New York: Avon/Equinox.

Modell, Judith (1983) *Ruth Benedict: Patterns of a Life*. Philadelphia: University of Pennsylvania Press.

Munn, Nancy (1973) *Walbiri Iconography: Graphic Representation and Cultural Symbolism in a Central Australian Society*. Ithaca, NY: Cornell University Press.

Murray, Stephen O. (1992) *Oceanic Homosexualities*. New York: Garland.

Murray, Stephen O. (1997) *Homosexualities*. Chicago: University of Chicago Press.

Myers, Fred (1992) 'Representing culture: the production of discourse(s) for aboriginal acrylic paintings', in George Marcus (ed.), *Rereading Cultural Anthropology*. Durham, NC: Duke University Press. pp. 319–55.

Nader, Laura (1972) 'Up the anthropologist – perspectives gained from studying up', in Dell Hymes (ed.), *Reinventing Anthropology*. New York: Pantheon. pp. 284–311.

Nash, June (1979) *We Eat the Mines and the Mines Eat Us: Dependency and Exploitation in Bolivian Tin Mines*. New York: Columbia University Press.

Nkrumah, Kwame (1964) *Consciencism: Philosophy and Ideology for Decolonization and Development with Particular Reference to the African Revolution*. New York: Monthly Review Press.

Offe, Claus (1985) *Disorganized Capitalism: Contemporary Transformations of Work and Politics* (ed. John Keane). Cambridge: Polity Press.

Offe, Claus (1996) *Modernity and the State: East, West*. Cambridge: Cambridge University Press.

Ong, Aihwa (1987) *Spirits of Resistance and Capitalist Discipline*. Albany, NY: SUNY Press.

Ortner, Sherry (1974a) 'Is female to male as nature is to culture?', in Michelle Zimbalist Rosaldo and Louise Lamphere (eds), *Women, Culture and Society*. Stanford, CA: Stanford University Press. pp. 67–88.

Ortner, Sherry (1974b) 'On key symbols', *American Anthropologist*, 75 (4): 1338–46.

Ortner, Sherry (1989) *High Religion: A Cultural and Political History of Sherpa Buddhism*. Princeton, NJ: Princeton University Press.

Ortner, Sherry and Whitehead, Harriet (1981) 'Introduction', in *Sexual Meanings: The Cultural Construction of Gender and Sexuality*. Cambridge: Cambridge University Press. pp. 1–28.

Ossman, Susan (1994) *Picturing Casablanca: Portraits of Power in a Modern City*. Berkeley, CA: University of California Press.

Parker, Andrew, Russo, Mary, Sommer, Doris and Yaeger, Patricia (eds) (1992) *Nationalisms and Sexualities*. New York: Routledge.

Plant, Deborah (1995) *Every Tub Must Sit on Its Own Bottom: The Philosophy and Politics of Zora Neale Hurston*. Urbana, IL: University of Illinois Press.

Powdermaker, Hortense ([1939] 1968) *After Freedom: A Cultural Study in the Deep South*. New York: Russell and Russell.

Price, Richard (1983) *First-Time: The Historical Vision of an Afro-American People*. Baltimore, MD: Johns Hopkins University Press.

Price, Sally (1989) *Primitive Art in Civilized Places*. Chicago: University of Chicago Press.

Puar, Jasib (forthcoming) 'Transnational configurations of desire: the nation and its white closets', in Matt Wray et al. (eds), *The Making and Unmaking of Whiteness*. Durham, NC: Duke University Press.

Rabinow, Paul (1977) *Reflexions on Fieldwork in Morocco*. Berkeley, CA: University of California Press.

Rabinow, Paul (1989) *French Modern: Norms and Forms of the Social Environment*. Cambridge, MA: MIT Press.

Rabinow, Paul (1996) *Making PCR*. Chicago: University of Chicago Press.

Rabinow, Paul (1999) *French DNA: Trouble in Purgatory*. Chicago: University of Chicago Press.

Radcliffe-Brown, A.R. ([1940] 1952) *Structure and Function in Primitive Societies*. New York: The Free Press. pp. 188–204.

Rappaport, Roy (1968) *Pigs for the Ancestors: Ritual in the Ecology of a Papua New Guinea People*. New Haven, CT: Yale University Press.

Redfield, Robert (1930) *Tepoztlán: A Mexican Village*. Chicago: University of Chicago Press.

Redfield, Robert (1955) *The Little Community: Viewpoints for the Study of a Human Whole*. Uppsala: Almqvist and Wiksells.

Reiter, Reyna (ed.) (1975) *Toward an Anthropology of Women*. New York: Monthly Review Press.

Ricoeur, Paul (1971) 'The model of the text: meaningful action considered as a text', *Social Research*, 38: 529–62.

Rogers, Susan Carol (1975) 'Female forms of power and the myth of male dominance: a model of female–male relations in peasant society', *American Ethnologist*, 2 (4): 727–56.

Rosaldo, Michelle Zimbalist (1974) 'Women, culture, and society: a theoretical overview', in Michelle Zimbalist Rosaldo and Louise Lamphere (eds), *Women, Culture and Society*. Stanford, CA: Stanford University Press. pp. 17–42.

Rosaldo, Michelle Zimbalist (1980) 'The use and abuse of anthropology: reflections on cross-cultural understanding', *Signs*, 5 (3): 389–417.

Rosaldo, Renato (1980) *Ilongot Headhunting, 1883–1974: A Study in Society and History*. Stanford, CA: Stanford University Press.

Roscoe, Will (1991) *The Zuni Man–Woman*. Albuquerque, NM: University of New Mexico Press.

Rosenberg, Rosalind (1982) *Beyond Separate Spheres: Intellectual Roots of Modern Feminism*. New Haven, CT: Yale University Press.

Rubin, Gayle (1975) 'The traffic in women: notes on a "political economy" of sex', in Rayna Rapp Reiter (ed.), *Toward an Anthropology of Women*. New York: Monthly Review Press. pp. 157–210.

Sacks, Karen (1974) 'Engels revisited: women, the organization of production, and private property', in Michelle Zimbalist Rosaldo and Louise Lamphere (eds), *Women, Culture, and Society*. Stanford, CA: Stanford University Press. pp. 207–22.

Sahlins, Marshall (1985) *Islands of History*. Chicago: University of Chicago Press.

Said, Edward (1978) *Orientalism*. New York: Pantheon Books.

Savigliano, Marta (1995) *Tango and the Political Economy of Passion*. Boulder, CO: Westview Press.

Scheper-Hughes, Nancy (1992) *Death Without Weeping: The Violence of Everyday Life in Brazil*. Berkeley, CA: University of California Press.

Schneider, David (1980) *American Kinship*. Chicago: University of Chicago Press.

Schneider, Peter, Schneider, Jane and Hansen, Edward (1972) 'Modernization and development: the role of regional elite and non-corporate groups in the European mediterranean', *Comparative Studies in Society and History*, 14: 328–50.

Scholte, Bob (1972) 'Toward a critical and reflexive anthropology', in Dell Hymes (ed.), *Reinventing Anthropology*. New York: Pantheon. pp. 430–57.

Seremetakis, C. Nadia (1991) *The Last Word: Women, Death, and Divination in Inner Mani*. Chicago: University of Chicago Press.

Shostak, Marjorie (1981) *Nisa: The Life and Words of a !Kung Woman*. Cambridge, MA: Harvard University Press.

Shryock, Andrew (1997) *Nationalism, and the Genealogical Imagination: Oral History and Textual Authority in Tribal Jordan*. Berkeley, CA: University of California Press.

Singer, Milton (1972) *When a Great Tradition Modernizes: An Anthropological Approach to Indian Civilization*. New York: Praeger.

Siskind, Janet (1973) *To Hunt in Morning*. London: Oxford University Press.

Smalley, William, Chia Koua Vang and Gnia Yee Yang (1990) *Mother of Writing: The Origin and Development of a Hmong Messianic Script* (Project trans. Mitt Moua). Chicago: University of Chicago Press.

Spicer, Edward (ed.) (1961) *Perspectives in American Indian Culture Change*. Chicago: University of Chicago Press.

Spindler, Louise (1977) *Culture Change and Modernization: Mini-models and Case Studies*. New York: Holt, Rinehart and Winston.

Spivak, Gayatri C. (1987) *In Other Worlds: Essays in Cultural Politics*. New York: Methuen.

Spivak, Gayatri C. (1990) *The Post-Colonial Critic: Interviews, Strategies and Dialogues* (ed. Sarah Harasym). New York and London: Routledge.

Spivak, Gayatri C. (1999) *A Critique of Postcolonial Reason: Toward a History of the Vanishing Present*. Cambridge, MA: Harvard University Press.

Spivak, Gayatri C. and Guha, Ranajit (eds) (1988) *Selected Subaltern Studies*. New York: Oxford University Press.

Spooner, Brian (1986) 'Weavers and dealers: the authenticity of an oriental carpet', in Arjun Appadurai (ed.), *The Social Life of Things: Commodities in Cultural Perspective*. Cambridge: Cambridge University Press.

Srinivas, Mysore N. (1966) *Social Change in Modern India*. Berkeley, CA: University of California Press.

Stanner, W.E.H. (1958) 'The dreaming', in William A. Lessa and Evon G. Vogt (eds), *Reader in Comparative Religion*. New York: Harper and Row. pp. 513–23.

Steiner, C.B. (1994) *African Art in Transit*. New York: Cambridge University Press.

Steward, Julian (1955) *Theory of Culture Change*. Urbana, IL: University of Illinois Press.

Stewart, Kathleen (1991) 'On the politics of cultural theory: a case for "contaminated" cultural critique', *Social Research*, 58 (2): 395–412.

Stewart, Kathleen (1996) *A Space on the Side of the Road: Cultural Poetics in an 'Other' America*. Princeton, Princeton, NJ: University Press.

Stocking, George (ed.) (1983) *Observers Observed: Essays on Ethnographic Fieldwork*, vol. 1. Madison, WI: University of Wisconsin Press.

Stoler, Ann L. (1995) *Race and the Education of Desire: Foucault's History of Sexuality and the Colonial Order of Things*. Durham, NC: Duke University Press.

Strathern, Marilyn (1988) *The Gender of the Gift: Problems with Women and Problems with Society in Melanesia*. Berkeley, CA: University of California Press.

Strathern, Marilyn (1991) *Partial Connections*. Sabage, MD: Rowman and Littlefield.

Strathern, Marilyn (1992) *After Nature: English Kinship in the Twentieth Century* (Lewis Henry Morgan Lectures, 1989). Cambridge: Cambridge University Press.

Taussig, Michael (1980) *The Devil̄ and Commodity Fetishism in South America*. Durham, NC: University of North Carolina Press.

Taylor, Julie (1998) *Paper Tangos*. Durham, NC: Duke University Press.

Traweek, Sharon (1988) *Beamtimes and Lifetimes: The World of High Energy Physicists*. Cambridge, MA: Harvard University Press.

Tsing, Anna (1993) *In the Realm of the Diamond Queen: Marginality in an Out-of-the-way Place*. Princeton, NJ: Princeton University Press.

Turner, Patricia (1993) *I Heard It through the Grapevine: Rumor in African-American Culture*. Berkeley, CA: University of California Press.

Turner, Victor (1974) *Dramas, Fields, and Metaphors: Symbolic Action in Human Society*. Ithaca, NY: Cornell University Press.

Urla, Jacqueline (1993) 'Cultural politics in an age of statistics', *American Ethnologist*, 20: 818–43.

Valentine, Charles A. and Valentine, Betty Lou (1970) 'Making the scene, digging the action, and telling it like it is: anthropologists at work in the dark ghetto', in Norman E. Whitten, Jr and John F. Szwed (eds), *Afro-American Anthropology: Contemporary Perspectives*. New York: The Free Press. pp. 403–18.

Verdery, Katherine (1996) *What Was Socialism, and What Comes Next?* Princeton, NJ: Princeton University Press.

Verdery, Katherine (1998) 'Transnationalism, nationalism, citizenship, and property: Eastern Europe since 1989', *American Ethnologist*, 25 (2): 291–306.

Vigil, James D. (1997) *Personas Mexicanas: Chicano High-schoolers in a Changing Los Angeles*. Fort Worth, TX: Harcourt Brace College Publishers.

Vigil, James D. (1998) *From Indians to Chicanos: The Dynamics of Mexican-American Culture*, 2nd edn. Prospect Heights, IL: Waveland Press.

Visweswaran, Kamala (1994) *Fictions of Feminist Ethnography*. Minneapolis, MN: University of Minnesota Press.

Wagner, Roy (1980) *The Invention of Culture*, rev. edn. Chicago: University of Chicago Press.

Wallace, Anthony (1956) 'Revitalization movements', *American Anthropologist*, 58: 264–81.

Weiner, Annette (1976) *Women of Value, Men of Renown*. Austin, TX: University of Texas Press.

Weston, Kath (1991) *Families We Choose: Lesbians, Gays, Kinship*. New York: Columbia University Press.

Whiting, J.W.M. and Child, I.L. (1953) *Child Training and Personality: A Cross Cultural Survey*. New Haven, CT: Yale University Press.

Whorf, Benjamin Lee ([1936] 1956a) 'An American Indian model of the universe', in John Carroll (ed.), *Language, Thought and Reality*. Cambridge, MA: Cambridge University Press. pp. 57–64.

Whorf, Benjamin Lee ([1941] 1956b) 'Language, mind and reality', in John Carroll (ed.), *Language, Thought and Reality*. Cambridge, MA: Cambridge University Press. pp. 246–70.

Williams, Raymond (1958) *Culture and Society*. London: Chatto and Windus.

Williams, Raymond (1981) *The Sociology of Culture*. London: Fontana.

Willis, William S. Jr (1972) 'Skeletons in the anthropological closet', in Dell Hymes (ed.), *Reinventing Anthropology*. New York: Pantheon. pp. 121–52.

Wittgenstein, Ludwig (1953) *Philosophical Investigations* (trans. G.E.M. Anscombe). New York: Macmillan.

Wolf, Eric (1982) *Europe and the People Without History*. Berkeley, CA: University of California Press.

Wolf, Margery (1992) *A Thrice-told Tale: Feminism, Postmodernism, and Ethnographic Responsibility*. Stanford, CA: Stanford University Press.

Wolff, Kurt (1964) 'Surrender and community study: the study of Loma', in Arthur A. Vidich, Joseph Bensman and Maurice R. Stein (eds), *Reflections on Community Studies*. New York: Wiley and Sons. pp. 233–63.

Wolff, Kurt (1972) 'This is the time for radical anthropology', in Dell Hymes (ed.), *Reinventing Anthropology*. New York: Pantheon. pp. 99–118.

Yanagisako, Sylvia and Collier, Jane Fishburne (1987) 'Toward a unified analysis of gender and kinship', in Jane Fishburne Collier and Sylvia Yanagisako (eds), *Gender and Kinship: Toward a Unified Analysis*. Stanford, CA: Stanford University Press. pp. 14–50.

Yang, Mayfair (ed.) (1999) *Spaces of Their Own: Women's Public Spheres in Transnational China*. Minneapolis, MN: University of Minnesota Press.

Zabusky, Stacia (1995) *Launching Europe: An Ethnography of European Cooperation in Space*. Princeton, NJ: Princeton University Press.

4

British Social Anthropology

SHARON MACDONALD

British social anthropology is generally said to have begun in the 1920s when the Polish-born, but British-claimed Bronislaw Malinowski (1884–1942) articulated its distinctiveness from the more general anthropological project which preceded it and set about establishing it in the academy. At the heart of Malinowski's definition of the 'new' discipline was 'ethnography' – detailed, first-hand, long-term, participant observation fieldwork written up as a monograph about a particular people.[1]

For Malinowski, and indeed for most social anthropologists today, ethnography is more than a 'method' or 'methodology' (cf. Miller, 1997: 16), and certainly more than 'participant observation' alone. The term 'ethnography' was then, and is now, used to describe both ethnography as practice – fieldwork in which participant observation is central but which may also include other approaches such as interviews and quantitative surveys (such as collecting genealogies or demographic data); and ethnography as product – the written text or ethnographic monograph. According to Daniel Miller, in a recent ethnographic study of capitalism (to which I return below), ethnography in social anthropology involves 'a series of commitments that together constitute a particular perspective' (1997: 16). And, of course, carrying out ethnographic fieldwork remains, as Malinowski established, a professional 'rite of passage' for British social anthropologists: in the 1998 Directory of the Association of Social Anthropologists (the professional association of British social anthropologists) only a handful out of nearly 600 members have no entry for 'fieldwork'.[2]

But why is ethnography so central to British social anthropology and what does it entail? *Is* the minimum year's ethnographic fieldwork more than an initiation trial for membership of what is widely seen as one of the most elite of social and cultural disciplines? Are charges of empiricism and colonial complicity, so often levelled at British social anthropology, legitimate? What *are* its 'ethnographic commitments', what 'particular perspective' do they enable and is this different from the perspective of those many other disciplines also conducting ethnography? And to what extent has this changed since the 1920s, especially in light of ramifying changes in anthropology's traditional subject matter (supposedly 'unchanging', 'distant' cultures) and in challenges both from within British social anthropology and from outside it?

A note here is necessary on what is meant by 'British social anthropology'. The term has come to be used for a particular 'intellectual tradition' beginning in the 1920s: 'a set of names, a limited range of ethnographic regional specialities, a list of central monographs, a characteristic mode of procedure, and a particular series of theoretical problems' (Kuper, [1973] 1975: 227). Not all members of this 'tradition' were British by birth – indeed only a minority were in its first two generations. The movement was never closed to international influences – for example, the French *Année Sociologique* school was a major source of theoretical inspiration. And while certain particularly (though not exclusively) 'British' obsessions – especially the 'two cultures' (science and arts) of which C.P. Snow wrote, and the related distinctions between 'intellectuals' and 'practical men', and 'the ideal' and 'the empirical' – have undoubtedly been played out in, and around, the discipline, it is not possible to identify a cardinal set of defining characteristics. Adam Kuper, anthropologist and historian of British social anthropology, says that as a distinctive intellectual movement, British social anthropology was over by the early 1970s (1996: 176). Certainly, anthropologists in Britain today are more diverse, both in the immediate anthropological ancestors they claim and in the range of anthropological research (theoretical and empirical) which they conduct – partly an outcome of their considerable expansion in number. Rather than stop my account in the 1970s, however, I have sought to press it up to the present, to look at those who are members of the anthropological association established by 'the British school' and of British university departments of social anthropology, to see what anthropologists in Britain are doing now, and, in particular, how the inheritance of the ethnographic project is bearing up.

This chapter, then, is a condensed account of the establishment, and later contest and partial reconfiguration, of the British social anthropological ethnographic project. My schematic story begins with Malinowski's contribution in order to highlight the legacy he provided for later generations in terms of a model of ethnographic practice and production, positioned within a set of tensions or ambivalences. I then follow this through to subsequent generations of British social anthropologists, examining various attempts to prise the ethnographic project away from its Malinowskian theoretical baggage, and from its original focus on 'simple societies'. This has entailed considerable challenge to that project – to the doing and writing of ethnography – and, in the process, to social anthropology. Not surprisingly, perhaps, the period since the 1970s has been one not just of expansion and diversification but also of considerable self-critique and 'introspection' (cf. Jackson, 1986). Yet despite the pronouncements of 'crisis' and even the 'end of social anthropology' (e.g. Banaji, 1970) that have been issued periodically since the 1970s, social anthropology and social anthropological ethnographic fieldwork continue in Britain today, and indeed do so, I suggest in the final part of this chapter, with renewed – though not unthreatened – vigour.

In this account, I orient my discussion around a small number of ethnographies which have (for the earlier periods at least) an iconic status in the discipline. Ethnographies, I should note, tend in social anthropology to be the vehicles through which major theoretical contributions are made or, perhaps more accurately, retrospectively attributed, and this is itself an indication of the centrality of the ethnographic monograph to the discipline. While selecting certain canonical texts risks reifying the status of heroes whose pedestals have come to seem wobbly, and of ignoring many other interesting contributions, I do so partly because this helps avoid crude caricatures of 'British social anthropology' and also because such texts continue to be a focus for debate about the nature of British social anthropology (as well as frequently being required reading for students) and, as such, are an important and continuing aspect of British social anthropologists' academic consciousness and self-definition – however they relate to them.

MALINOWSKI'S CHARTER

Malinowski's *Argonauts of the Western Pacific: An Account of Native Enterprise and Adventure in the Archipelagoes of Melanesian New Guinea* is one such canonical text (and Malinowski is a hero whose pedestal has probably been eroded more than that of any other British social anthropologist). Published in 1922, it is conventionally taken as marking the beginning of British social anthropology and, more specifically, of establishing it as a discipline based on what he called 'scientific ethnographic fieldwork'.[3] Although Malinowski exaggerated the extent of his innovation, and although the publication of his diaries in 1967 led some to question his credentials as a fieldworker, his remains one of the most important manifestos for the intellectual movement that was to become known as British social anthropology. Just as Malinowski argued that myth established a charter for social action, he attempted to create a charter for what anthropologists in the future would do ('scientific ethnographic fieldwork' written up in a characteristic format), and for putting this into practice by training, and campaigning for institutional recognition for, the next generation of social anthropologists.

While others had undertaken anthropological fieldwork previously, Malinowski's was at the time of unusual length (two years in the Trobriands) and intensity – not merely 'a sporadic plunging into the company of natives [but] being really in contact with them' (1922: 7) as he put it. Moreover, in *Argonauts* he presented this personal experience as a 'scientific' approach, capable of going beyond amateur accounts of 'native peoples' by providing 'concrete, statistical documentation' (1922: 24) of particular instances gathered together to illuminate 'general laws' invisible to a society's members themselves. Although Malinowski suggests in the conclusion of *Argonauts* that 'there is room for a new type of theory' (1922: 515) which will emphasize how 'aspects of culture functionally depend on one another' rather than explaining them in terms of their historical evolution or 'transmission' from other societies, this is not much developed in *Argonauts*, though it does, nevertheless, exemplify many of the ideas that he was later to present as his 'new functional theory'. As Stocking has remarked, this 'new theory' was 'less a reflection of theoretical reconsideration than a by-product of a new mode of ethnographic enquiry' (Stocking, 1984: 156). Nevertheless, and despite its shortcomings, Malinowskian functionalism helped to crystallize what was different about the kind of 'social anthropology' that he was trying to promote *vis-à-vis* earlier British anthropology.

First, his emphasis on the present, often today criticized as an unfortunate ahistoricism, was a counter to evolutionist and historical ways of understanding native life which sought explanations for contemporary social practices in the past. Malinowski's argument was that any social practice must have some social significance in the present and that it was the ethnographer's role to elucidate this through direct observation rather than to engage in historical speculation. Malinowski later expressed this as an attempt to elucidate the *function* of all social practices and argued that these were ultimately reflections of more basic biological and psychological needs (1944). Secondly, his insistence on 'holism' – that social practices be analysed within their overall social context ('in all [their] aspects'; 1922: 11) – challenged the common approach of his predecessors, such as James Frazer, to discuss cultural practices from diverse societies with little information given about the original social context. While Malinowskian 'holism' tended to lead to an unfortunate bounding of societies as islands unto themselves and to a proclivity to ramble from one thing to another in an almost 'stream of consciousness' fashion, it also meant that ethnographers had to try to understand societies 'in their own terms' and, as such, it helped question conventional analytical categories and distinctions. Thirdly, Malinowski maintained that a central goal of ethnography was 'to grasp the native's point of view, his relation to life, to realize *his* vision of *his* world' (1922: 25; emphasis in original). While not a formal aspect of his 'functional theory', and underestimated in its potential, this was crucially important in moving away from the predominant attempt to view native life 'from afar', and attempting not just to *see* those studied but to see *as* them.

The objectives of 'functional theory', as Malinowski defined it, then, could not be achieved without undertaking ethnographic fieldwork; and this made divisions between 'data', 'method' and 'theory' more seamless than in many disciplines. Moreover, Malinowski's *participant* observation' entailed not simply a particular methodological technique but a new way of relating to the object of anthropological study.[4] This direct first-hand engagement with the researched – this abolition of 'the gap between the library and life' (Grimshaw and Hart, 1993: 15) – opened up in new measure a potential to challenge orthodoxy and to throw the spotlight back onto the observers' cultural and disciplinary assumptions. In *Argonauts* this is evident, for example, in Malinowski's ridiculing of economists' fiction of 'Primitive Economic Man' which served as a counterpoint to 'Civilized Man' in various economic theories at the time.

However, the break with the broader anthropological approach which preceded, and to some extent coexisted with, *social* anthropology was not total. In particular, the new anthropology retained the subject focus on peoples who were still often termed 'primitive' (indeed, one of Malinowski's

later books was salaciously titled *The Sexual Life of Savages*, 1929); and no doubt some of the success of the fledgling discipline in becoming institutionally established was a continuing popular and academic thirst for accounts of 'others' which were, among other things, grist to the mill of both triumphant and nostalgic renditions of the allegory of 'Western' or 'European' 'civilization' (MacClancy, 1996).

As far as the anthropological monograph was concerned, there was already an established genre of books about 'exotic' peoples and Malinowski sought to marry this with his ethnographic perspective. This produced a form which claimed to be 'scientific' and was certainly full of 'concrete documentation' but which also, as Malinowski specifically comments in *Argonauts*, borrowed writing techniques from 'amateur' accounts in order to create a lively and readable description which would appeal to the general public as well as scholars (1922: 17). Techniques which he employs include 'the presentation of intimate touches of native life' (p. 17), analogies with examples that might be familiar to his readers (for example, the Crown jewels, *Hamlet*), commentary on his own feelings and responses, invocations to the reader to imagine themselves in his place, polemical calls for the 'understanding of other men's point of view' (p. 518) and, of course, a title which alludes to a popular classic. This set a model for the ethnographic monograph as a publicly accessible literary text rather than an abstruse scientific report.[5]

The calculated positioning between the literary and the scientific, and the academic and popular, and the play between depicting difference and illuminating humanist universalism (showing how Trobriand practices were not so strange as they might at first appear), was undoubtedly crucial to Malinowski's success in putting British social anthropology on the map. So too was his labour as an advocate for social anthropology. Here he sought to promote the discipline as both timely – the description of peoples whose ways of life would soon cease to exist ('Alas! The time is short ... '; p. 518) – and as timeless (like the classics), and as both 'impartial' and 'useful' (that is, with potential government application).[6] The seminar which he established at the London School of Economics (LSE) became the hub of the developing discipline and the majority of those who came to hold the new chairs of anthropology in Britain had been students of Malinowski's at the LSE or had attended his seminar. Moreover, Malinowski actively sought out research funding for social anthropology – vital if anthropologists were to be able to undertake fieldwork overseas – and successfully persuaded foundations, especially the US-based Laura Spelman Rockefeller Memorial – to provide funding for fellowships and for university posts (including Malinowski's own) in the new discipline and for an

International African Institute which became a base for much subsequent social anthropological Africanist research (established in 1926; Goody, 1995: 12–15; Kuklick, [1992] 1993: 56).

By the time of the outbreak of the Second World War, social anthropology remained, as Meyer Fortes, himself a member of Malinowski's seminar and later professor at Cambridge, put it, 'only a minority intellectual movement, almost, from some points of view, a lunatic fringe' (1978: 4). Nevertheless, it was a movement with a defined subject matter, approach and output, and, by then, an institutionalized position in the LSE, University College, London, Oxford and Cambridge. Given its size, a creditable body of ethnographic work had been produced, work with both scientific and literary aspirations, capable of capturing the public and academic imagination in its production of 'others' who could serve as an altar to the industrializing ego but who could also challenge some then popular fictions. Thus the framework of British social anthropology, and also some of the key ambivalences which were to fuel much of its continuing dynamic, were in place.

Consolidation and Consensus?

The period from the 1940s to the end of the 1960s is often regarded as one of 'consensus' (Ardener, 1989: 194) or 'routine' (Kuper, [1973] 1975: 150): ethnographic production settled into a standard pattern, and the discipline became more concerned with its own professionalization and internal academic debates and politics than some of the most striking realities about the worlds it was studying (Ahmed and Shore, 1995: 16). According to others, however, the period was part of a more fertile 'expansive moment', in which 'theoretical ... contributions became increasingly wider in scope' (Goody, 1995: 117), and in which British social anthropologists – many of whom were 'left-leaning' (1995: 155) – were more likely than not to support moves towards national independence in the countries they studied (1995: 155). Probably the two most common later criticisms of anthropologists in this period (criticisms often generalized to anthropologists *tout court*) are those of 'empiricism' and 'colonial complicity' (cf. Goody, 1995). I will deal with the first of these below, and turn to the second in the following section. First, however, I outline the growth of anthropology up to the 1960s.

Social anthropology expanded considerably in the post-war period, though it remained small compared with more established disciplines (and even with other relatively 'new' disciplines such as sociology).[7] In 1946 an organization of professional social anthropologists was established – the Association of Social Anthropologists[8] – and registered

twenty-one members. By 1961, the same organization listed 142 members who fulfilled its requirement that they 'hold[ing] or have held a teaching or research appointment ... in social anthropology, and either have a postgraduate degree in social anthropology or have published significant work in the field' (*ASA List of Members Rules*, 1961, quoted in Ardener and Ardener, 1965: 312, n. 7).[9] New departments of social anthropology were established: at the School of Oriental and African Studies and at Edinburgh in 1946, and at Manchester in 1949. Social anthropology found its way into other departments too: a 1953 survey listed twelve universities in which the subject was taught and thirty-eight teachers involved in doing so (Kuper, [1973] 1975: 151).

The 1961 Directory of Social Anthropologists provides an interesting overview of the discipline up to this point (only seven members listed in the 1946 directory had died by then). Fieldwork seems to be a *sine qua non* of membership; and the Directory analysis shows Africa to be overwhelmingly the most popular location for ethnographic study, with South Africa the most 'fieldworked' part of Africa prior to 1940, and East Africa from 1950.[10] The Pacific, the favoured fieldwork area in the early days, maintains the same numerical level of interest (which was by then considerably lower than the African total); and the Indian sub-continent, while less popular than the Pacific, shows a slow but steady increase in fieldwork presence. The most remarkable of the statistics on fieldwork area, however, is that of Europe, which shows virtually no fieldwork being carried out before the Second World War, but thereafter a steady climb to being outstripped only by Africa.

In terms of 'Chief Interests – Theoretical', the most popular entries to the Directory (as aggregated by Ardener and Ardener, 1965) are, listed in order of frequency of citation:

1 'politics, government';
2 'ritual, religion, mythology, belief, symbolism, witchcraft';
3 'social change';
4 'social structure, structure, social systems, social organization'; and then, crowding in at equal fifth
5 'methodology, theory'; 'social stratification, status, caste, class, age-groups'; 'jural relations, law'; and 'kinship'.[11]

Of course, such a list can only be a rough guide, and we might question the way in which the authors of the study have grouped certain topics (for example, separating 'prescriptive alliance', 'marriage stability' and 'family' from 'kinship'). Nevertheless, it is interesting in highlighting what some of the popular categorizations were; and it shows that anthropological interests at the time were fairly wide-ranging (though not nearly so extensive as in

1998, see below). The high ranking of 'social change', for example, illustrates that the synchronic focus of ethnography inherited from Malinowski had not prevented this becoming one of the main 'chief interests' of anthropologists in the period.[12] The list is also interesting for its omissions, as the authors of the study note. They draw particular attention to 'linguistics'. From the vantage point of the 1998 Directory, we might also note the absence of ethnicity and gender. Of course, these 'omissions' may be partly matters of nomenclature: in some cases, for example, what is now called 'gender' might have crept in under such categories as 'kinship'; though the changing terminology is itself a function of changing theoretical inflections.

The 'period of consensus' is identified with the theoretical stance known as structural functionalism. This theory, named so as to distinguish it from Malinowski's more easy-going, 'so-called' functionalism, was promoted particularly by Radcliffe-Brown (1881–1955), often regarded as the other 'founding father' of British social anthropology. Based on a somewhat impoverished reading of Durkheim, it casts societies as ordered systems whose constituent parts play a role in maintaining equilibrium. The task of the social anthropologist is to elucidate the 'social structure' – the pattern of 'real relations of connectedness' (Radcliffe-Brown, 1957: 45) – by which this occurs in a given society, something which Radcliffe-Brown hoped would lead to a comparative sociology of types of social structure. Instead, however, it often resulted in rather turgid ethnographies organized around a rather predictable set of chapters, each based on a different social institution – kinship, economics, politics, religion/magic, law/social control (a model which outlived the original theoretical framework and also found its way into standard British social anthropological textbooks). And while there were some gestures in the direction of the comparative project which Radcliffe-Brown had envisaged (for example, the collection on African political systems by Fortes and Evans-Pritchard, 1940), it never materialized in the form in which he had hoped.

If *Argonauts* had some literary affinities with Joyce's *Ulysses* (despite Malinowski's attempt to cast himself as Conrad), also published in 1922, the analogy for Radcliffe-Brown's approach was the anatomy textbook. Where Malinowski conceptualized society rather as one of the Kula necklaces he wrote about – a chain of one thing leading to another, which could potentially continue round in circles for ever – Radcliffe-Brown was clear that it was a rather mechanically conceived 'organism'. And where Malinowski had provided anthropology with a claim of a privileged vantage point derived from experience, Radcliffe-Brown added another key aspect of modern ways of seeing – a 'diagnostic' technique for analysing society into 'elements' which, the claim went, provided unique access not just to a 'way of life' but to an underlying orderly reality.[13]

This was a significant shift from the *veni, vidi, scripsi* empiricism of Malinowski. The transposition of experience into science was now seen to require more than orderly documentation. It needed a guiding diagnostic technique to get at what was *really* there beneath the surface. The route from experience to science, then, was problematized – and with it, the route from ethnographic observation to the construction of the monograph. As Evans-Pritchard put it in *The Nuer*: 'facts can only be selected and arranged in the light of theory' (1940: 261). However, what was neglected was attention to the epistemological status of observation, experience and the identification of 'facts' themselves. Empiricism, then, largely remained at the coming and seeing level; although at the same time the 'conquering' – both epistemologically and in terms of monograph-construction – of experience-derived facts was given much attention, at least among those who sought to move the discipline forward theoretically.

However, there was more sophisticated grappling with the question of what constituted a fact; and Pocock has argued that Evans-Pritchard's classic, *The Nuer. A Description of the Modes of Livelihood and Political Institutions of a Nilotic People* (1940), was original in precisely this way (1971: 75), though it is commonly regarded as archetypically structural functionalist. One of the most canonical of ethnographies, it has also been the subject of debate about the extent to which it illustrates complicity with colonial interests, and about the politics of its textual style. This makes it a useful monograph through which to examine some of these broader debates; and I will say more about it in the following section on colonial complicity.

Based on about a year's difficult fieldwork, carried out between 1930 and 1936, *The Nuer* is at one level oriented around the question of how a leaderless, apparently 'anarchical', group like the Nuer is socially ordered. At 266 pages, it is a relatively compact ethnography for the time and in addition to the chapters on the political, lineage and age-set systems, only includes a short introductory chapter (incorporating the drily witty account of the fieldwork which was enough to cause 'Nuerosis'), a chapter on Nuer interest in cattle, one on ecology, and one on time and space (that is, not your checklist chapter monograph). Despite the implied comprehensive portrait of the book's main title, Evans-Pritchard sets out specifically to include only material relevant to his thesis about Nuer political structure. This is not, however, to say that the book is primarily a theoretical account with description only brought in to make particular points. On the contrary, as in all his ethnographic work, 'theory was never spelled out' (Douglas, 1980: 24) but was left for the discerning reader to detect.[14] Stylistically, this is Hemingway: tautly crafted pretend reportage in which the 'bigger' messages are left implicit.[15]

Yet despite the 'Akobo realism', the appearance of transparency, as Geertz dubs it (1988: 61), Pocock argues that Evans-Pritchard's analysis is much more sophisticated than Radcliffe-Brown's X-ray technique. Instead of thinking that analysis can have direct access to 'structure', Evans-Pritchard's account recognizes 'that the words used and the things or behaviour to which they refer are to be understood in their relatedness' (Pocock, 1971: 75) – this is part of the broader metaphoric point of the otherwise surprising inclusion of a chapter on time and space. Moreover, these are themselves relative rather than fixed, as Evans-Pritchard emphasizes, for example, when he shows how the word 'home' can mean something different depending on whom you are talking to and where. 'The system' for Evans-Pritchard, then, is not so much like a *real* body as a set of abstract, dialectical principles: in other words, it is not just about 'masses and a supposed relation between these masses ... [but] relations, defined in terms of social situations, and relations between these relations' (Evans-Pritchard, 1940: 266). In relation to society, then, human meaning-making, and not just behaviour, becomes crucial; language – the mastery of which is already regarded as technically crucial to good ethnography (Ardener, 1971a: xiv) – is now shown to have 'deeper relevance' (Pocock, 1971: 79). Though only retrospectively, and only sometimes acknowledged, Evans-Pritchard's contribution can thus be claimed as the rolling pebble which would be followed by a stealthy landslide in British social anthropology which Pocock calls the 'shift from function to meaning' (1971: 72).[16]

There were others in the period who also addressed themselves in various ways to the implications of language for understanding society, though this often panned out less subtly as an either–or materialist versus idealist debate. One interesting case was Edmund Leach's unconventional and intellectually adventurous *Political Systems of Highland Burma* (1954). This described a number of very different social systems which he alternated between saying (a) really did swing from one to the other over a long period of time (150 years as he specified in one of his let's-get-real moments), (b) were 'fictions' conjured up by the Kachin themselves in language and ritual, or (c) – in a moment of unsustained daring – were just an 'as if' created by the anthropologist for presentational convenience. Perhaps Leach's willingness to even contemplate that 'it is' might only be 'as if' was partly a function of the loss of his own personal *veni, vidi* testimony: his fieldnotes. This was also part of the reason for his use of historical materials – materials which made an account of static equilibrium impossible to maintain. His struggle to create a fiction of some sort of regular system, though, is

an indication of the compulsion of the organistic model in anthropology at the time.

Some of the other relatively experimental ethnographies of the period showed the same ultimate caution. Various members of the Manchester School (the mainly Africanist group working with Max Gluckman), for example, attempted to put in the rich detail of individual presence that was typically eliminated in Radcliffe-Brown's clinical diagnoses of the body social. Victor Turner's use of 'social dramas' or 'extended case studies' – detailed narrative accounts of specific events with named individuals – in his *Schism and Continuity in an African Society* (1957) is the most famous example of this. However, even though this often focused on conflict rather than self-evident health, it was done within the broader medicalized project of elucidating the (ultimately functioning) 'system'. Individual agency seemed to be introduced but, as with stage actors, it was just a part in a bigger script. Talk of *process*, too, was also subsumed to the overriding project of illuminating the orderly principles ultimately at work. This was one way in which 'social change' was denied in 'non-modern' societies (cf. Wolf, 1982). The other, probably more common, approach entailed screening off *modern change from traditional* stability (cf. Asad, 1991: 318), thus making 'history' another European speciality.

Even the more adventurous of ethnographies in this period did not push such reflexivity as there was about what to put into an ethnography to more extensive questioning of the ethnographic enterprise itself. There was, throughout, the assumption of a privileged vantage point from which ordered reality could be perceived. And despite the fact that the claim to this privileged vantage point lay in having 'been there' (Geertz, 1988: Ch. 1), the 'certainty of representation' entailed a detachment of viewer and viewed (Mitchell, 1988: 7; after Heidegger). So while 'being there' could, and indeed should, be mentioned in the 'preface' or another inessential organ such as an 'appendix' (e.g. Evans-Pritchard, 1937), in order to establish the privileged vantage point, marks of the observer were eliminated from the main body of the text. This was called 'objectivity'. Despite all the sophisticated theorizing, observation itself, and the relationship between observer and observed, was left relatively untouched.

COLONIAL COMPLICITY?

The lack of attention to these aspects of ethnographic research created what came to be seen as a particularly glaring blind-spot over the colonial dimensions of anthropological ethnography in this period. The 'colonial critique' is generally said to have begun with Talal Asad's 1973 edited volume *Anthropology and the Colonial Encounter*,[17] though since then there has been further important scholarship and also a tendency, especially in some cultural studies commentary, to rather stereotype accounts of anthropology as a 'colonialist discipline'. There is not the space here to analyse this in detail but I hope to be able to indicate that the issues are more complex and subtle than they are sometimes presented as being. I do so by looking at the two main charges levelled against anthropologists of the 'consensus' period (charges often extended to anthropology in general): that they explicitly provided help to colonial regimes – that they were 'handmaidens' of colonialism; and that at a more implicit level they gave support to the colonial project through the silences, foci and style of their monographs.

Although many anthropologists of the consensus period worked in British colonies, colonialism was by no means an unquestioned political order. Britain's colonial empire had expanded massively in the late nineteenth and into the early twentieth centuries; but by the time the 'period of consensus' began, there were moves towards decolonization and independence. India and Burma became independent in 1947, and moves towards African independence were also under way – for example, the Sixth Pan-African Congress, held in Manchester in 1945, was a significant articulation of nationalist sentiment – though independence was not achieved for most African countries until the 1950s and 1960s. That many British anthropologists chose to work in British colonies is not surprising, given that this afforded easier access. Moreover, particularly after the Colonial Social Science Research Council was founded in 1946, funding was easier to gain for such areas; and the channelling of funding via the International African Institute had already helped make Africa a favoured fieldwork venue. In a minority of cases, there was funding to be had from colonial governments too – Evans-Pritchard's Nuer research, funded by the Anglo-Egyptian government of the Sudan, being an example.

But did these funding arrangements hold anthropologists in thrall to colonial demands? And how useful was anthropological research to colonial administrations? While there was a constant attempt by those (for example, Malinowski) involved in trying to garner funding for anthropology to argue that it was potentially useful, this was counterbalanced by many anthropologists' greater interest in the theoretical questions – especially the search for social structure – of the day, and a scientific model of 'pure' research which made many reluctant to get involved in the 'dirtier' business of 'applied'. (This distinction was sometimes expressed in terms of the 'scholar' versus the 'practical man', see James, 1973; university posts went to the former.)[18] Given that the most popular 'chief theoretical interest' listed in the 1961 Directory was 'politics, government' and that structural functionalism was concerned with questions of social ordering and conflict resolution, anthropologists were well placed for work of practical relevance to colonial administrations. In practice, however, most commentators seem to agree that they rarely made much impact. Asad, for example, concludes: 'the knowledge they [anthropologists] produced was often too esoteric for government use, and even where it was usable it was marginal in comparison to the vast body of information routinely accumulated by merchants, missionaries, and administrators' (1991: 315). In part, the unenthusiastic uptake of anthropological insight was due to the fact that post-Malinowskian anti-evolutionism ran counter to the world-view of most colonial administrators who had 'developed a distinctive variant of evolutionist anthropology to rationalize and guide their consistent managerialist practices', a world-view which allowed them to see themselves as 'merely the agents of inexorable historical forces, whose decisions constituted obedience to scientific laws of social evolution' (Kuklick, [1992] 1993: 183). The predilection of anthropologists for showing how 'native custom' 'made sense', and even that apparently 'mediaeval' practices such as witchcraft could be regarded as 'rational' (as Evans-Pritchard did in his study of Azande witchcraft, 1937), was fundamentally at variance with this.[19]

The complexity and ambiguity over anthropologists' roles can be usefully examined by turning back to *The Nuer*. As Pnina Werbner observes, Evans-Pritchard 'is singled out in anthropological cultural-studies discourse as the symbol of colonial oppression' (1997: 44);[20] and insofar as the Nuer research was specifically requested by the colonial government for defined ends, we might expect it to be an unequivocal example of anthropological 'complicity'. In the 1920s, the Nuer had been involved in a long war with the Anglo-Egyptian colonial government and the latter was clearly concerned that violence could easily erupt again in what seemed to it a particularly lawless and conflict-prone tribe. Evans-Pritchard's focus on political institutions and the maintenance of order was one which fitted the governmental remit aimed at finding ways to control the Nuer more effectively. However, the account he produced surely would not have assisted their task in any straightforward way. Contrary to prevailing imagery of the time, Evans-Pritchard depicts the Nuer as a relatively well-organized people despite their lack of identifiable political institutions. Moreover, he presents conflict as an integral, and rather well-regulated, part of this social organization. While some have argued that Evans-Pritchard's depiction of Dinka captured by the Nuer as willing subjects, or of the Nuer themselves maintaining human liberty in their colonial situation, might be seen as a metaphor for support for the colonial system (Kuklick, [1992] 1993: 276; Rosaldo, 1986: 96), others have suggested that Evans-Pritchard may have purposefully shaded his account of Nuer life in order to help prevent colonial intrusion (Arens, 1983). Minimizing status differences among the 'deeply democratic' (Evans-Pritchard, 1940: 181) Nuer and failing to identify even vestigial leaders would not have helped the Sudan Political Service's ambition of 'indirect rule'; and the lack of historical depth in his account may also have helped to play down what a later anthropologist described as the Nuer's 'insatiable appetite for conquest' (Sahlins, 1961, quoted in Kuklick, [1992] 1993: 275), an 'appetite' which could have been used to justify more thoroughgoing 'pacification'.

Obviously *The Nuer* is but one, albeit notorious, case in point but it illustrates ambiguity even in an instance where we might expect matters to be clear-cut. Recent scholarship has also emphasized that we should not reduce 'colonialism' to a single pattern but should recognize the variations and specificities in different contexts and for different players involved (for example, administrators, missionaries, different groups of 'colonized') (e.g. Thomas, 1994). But what of arguments that at more subtle levels the social anthropological ethnographic project helped to shore up colonial ways of seeing? Many of these, I suggest, are also more equivocal than they are generally presented as being. The structural functional representation of unchanging, stable societies, for example, while it fed into popular assumptions about fundamental differences between 'the West and the Rest' (Sahlins, 1976), also helped to show that such societies could and did work perfectly well in their own way without colonial 'assistance'. The use of the 'ethnographic present' (the convention of writing ethnographies in the present tense), on the one hand also contributed to an appearance of stasis, but on the other could help to caution readers against assuming such ways of life were over.[21] And distinguishing between a 'traditional' state of affairs and modern change, was more likely to depict the latter as disruptive than as a change for the better.

While I suggest that functionalist representations were more politically ambiguous than they tend to be depicted as being, this is not to say that they are unproblematic. The maintenance of a pristine observer–observed dichotomy and the neat identification of institutions were part of colonialist power-knowledge relations between 'the West' and 'its others' which rendered the latter passive to the former (Mitchell, 1988). This entailed considerable violence to the empirical – observation of which was supposed to be the ethnographic forte – as many kinds of participants (for example, colonial officials, missionaries), many aspects of life (such as change, dealings with government) and many complexities (sub-group differences, individual voices and relations with the ethnographer, for example) were blanked out. These exclusions were not a necessary consequence of the ethnographic approach – although it is sometimes blamed – but

were a function of the politically ambiguous (and then, of course, thought politically neutral) theoretical models employed. The empirical needed to be given more, not less, space to challenge a priori formulations. Theoretical perspectives needed to be expanded to allow anthropologists to tackle matters which, at ground level, they were well placed to tackle: for example, relations between colonial administrations and their subjects (cf. Feuchtwang, 1973). This was the challenge for ethnographers in the following decades.

CRISIS?

The colonial critique contributed to growing talk of 'crisis' and 'disintegration' in British social anthropology in the 1970s. So too did the more general sense of losing the tight-knit coherence of the consensus project. This latter was partly due to the fact that those who had formed the core group of British social anthropologists in the first generation reached retirement age between 1969 and 1972 (Kuper, [1973] 1975: 154). It was also, ironically, an outcome of an increase in the number of social anthropology staff and graduates as a result of the expansion of higher education in Britain in the 1960s. Although the 1960s universities were much more likely to open departments of sociology than social anthropology, quite a number of social anthropologists took up posts in sociology (something which itself contributed to the attention to questions of disciplinary identity). By 1968, when a survey of the discipline was undertaken, there were 240 members of the Association of Social Anthropologists, about a third of whom held teaching posts in Britain; and 'about 150 British postgraduate students in training, perhaps half of them proceeding to the doctorate' (Kuper, [1973] 1975: 152).

A number of new theoretical developments, beginning in the 1960s, inspired mainly by French anthropology, also seemed to offer some very different approaches to the subject and while on the one hand these suggested some revitalizing new directions, they also caused self-searching anxiety about the nature of social anthropology. Lévi-Straussian structuralism and structural Marxism both offered analytically powerful diagnostic techniques (the former setting itself up as a vantage point of vantage points) which addressed idealist–materialist concerns in what felt like innovative ways. Neither, however, seemed to necessarily demand ethnographic fieldwork – at least not the kind of detailed fieldwork that had become the hallmark of British social anthropology. As Ardener put it, they 'represented a consumption of anthropological texts, rather than a creation of them ... Anthropology not as life, but as genre' (1989: 205). As such, while on the one hand structuralism in particular gave anthropology a Left-Bank style intellectual kudos, the French influences also caused alarm among some British social anthropologists who saw in them a downgrading of fieldwork, a tendency towards abstract theorizing (very different from the 'say it through ethnography' British style), and a somewhat retrograde move towards a kind of evolutionism (Marxism) or cognitivism (structuralism). What developed in the more empirically oriented British context, however, were some very fruitful less-aggrandised uses of structural and Marxist techniques for exploring particular ethnographic cases and for suggesting comparative schemes rooted in specified sociological constellations or patterns within defined domains of life. In the case of structuralism, Victor Turner's analysis of Ndembu ritual (1967) and Mary Douglas' important corpus of work were notable examples.[22] More generally, structural techniques, largely divested of their universalizing dimensions, became part of the analytical armoury for dealing in particular, though not exclusively, with ritual and belief. Notable Marxist-influenced ethnographic works included those of Maurice Bloch (e.g. 1986); and Marxist insights came to articulate with (to use Althusser's term) the Manchester School's emphasis on conflict, a growing interest in history and political-economy and the colonial critique (Bloch, 1983).

Although French anthropological technique and insight was brought home to British social anthropology via ethnography, ethnography itself was not an unequivocally safe haven or unchallenged badge of disciplinary identity. Working in departments with sociologists, anthropologists become increasingly aware of the use of ethnographic methods by other disciplines. Moreover, the colonial critique had opened up a whole can of wormy questions about the politics of ethnographic fieldwork and the methodological editing out of history and 'the bigger picture'. At the same time, anthropology's traditional emphasis on fieldwork carried out in 'distant' locales was no longer a justifiable self-definition; and nor, increasingly, was it such a feasible possibility as formerly. Not only were 'distant' peoples increasingly hard to find as time–space compressed (Harvey, 1989); those who had been defined as 'distant' were increasingly vocal about refusing the appellation and also sometimes anthropological attention altogether. This, together with funding for fieldwork becoming harder to obtain, led still more anthropologists to turn their gaze towards Europe (see below). Moreover, the 1970s were a lean period financially in British academia and in search of new funding sources, new legitimacy and new job prospects, there were also concerted moves to promote anthropology as publicly and practically 'relevant' and 'useful' (leading most notably to the establishment in the early 1980s of the Group for Anthropology in Policy and Practice; Wright, 1995: 68).

The colonial critique, the increased attention to anthropology close to 'home', and the need to argue anthropology's 'relevance', all contributed to heightened levels of disciplinary introspection (Jackson, 1986) and self-critique. What *was* social anthropology and did it have any point in the contemporary world? Struggling with this inevitably also raised questions about ethnography. How could ethnography be 'sold' to agencies more comfortable with 'quick-fix', 'objective' quantitative research? Could anthropologists accept the time limits and specific remits that applied work outside the academy often entailed? And, indeed, was it possible to be an anthropologist without doing fieldwork at all? These questions also contributed to new attention to the power relations and ethics of ethnographic research as, among other things, anthropologists struggled with questions of to whom their work was to be 'useful' (governments or 'the people'?); and with different approaches to research in multidisciplinary teams.

Ethnography was also put under the spotlight by two other important and interrelated developments in the 1970s: the anthropology of women, and analytical and ethnographic reflexivity. In an article which did not mark the beginning of these movements but which inspired a good deal of debate, Edwin Ardener (1972) suggested that ethnographers, female as well as male, had tended to talk mainly to men and to take men's 'world-views' as the equivalent of the society's 'world-view'; and thus had ignored women's possibly different (and less directly expressed) perspectives. His own suggestive analysis of Bakweri women's ritual, which drew fruitfully on structural techniques, argued that 'society' could not be taken as singular and that ethnography was a potentially fertile means of reaching the voices of what came to be called 'muted groups' (Ardener, 1975). This had significant general implications for ethnography, both in its highlighting of past failure but also in its challenge to homogeneous models of society and its identification of ethnography – and detailed attention to *meaning* – as a way of getting at versions of experience that were not necessarily expressed directly and verbally. Ardener's approach was very much part of the broader movement that Pocock had referred to as the 'shift from function to meaning' (1971: 72) in its careful moving between indigenous classifications and experience and dissection of analytical categories. Interestingly, that approach – which can be seen in a good deal of stimulating anthropological work from the late 1970s on – never really acquired a name, though, perhaps too early or too audaciously, Ardener tried to call it 'the new anthropology' (1971b), an ASA volume edited by David Parkin used the term 'semantic anthropology' (Parkin, 1982a; after Crick, 1976), and later the term 'postmodern' was, controversially, suggested (see Ardener, 1985).[23] Central to it was an

attempt to consider both the 'subjects' of anthropological research and anthropologists themselves as
'active meaning-maker[s]' (Parkin, 1982b: xiii),
something which entailed 'extending the ethno-
graphical sensitivity to include the anthropologist
him/herself' (1982b: xiii). This was 'reflexivity' –
a term that gained much currency in the 1980s,
though it was often understood, and sometimes dismissed, as referring only to the influence of the personal identity of the ethnographer on the research,
rather than the wider business (of which attention to
the personal was an important part),[24] of 'anthro-
pologizing' every aspect of the anthropological-
ethnographic enterprise itself.

It was not coincidental that the 'semantic',
'reflexive' approach was gaining ground alongside
questions about how women had been studied, and
the contribution that women ethnographers had or
had not made, for both raised questions about the
'privileged vantage point' and the universality of
the ethnographic experience.[25] In an influential article published in 1975, 'The self and scientism'
(1975; reprinted in 1996: Ch. 2), Judith Okely drew
on her own gendered fieldwork experience among
traveller-gypsies in Britain and on issues raised by
the publication of Malinowski's diaries (in 1967),
to argue that the excision of the personal was based
on a 'false notion of scientific objectivity' ([1975]
1996: 27) and that subjectivity should be acknowledged and explored. Influenced by feminism,
Okely's perspective was part of a broader feminist
critique of objectivism in the social sciences (see,
for example, Harding, 1987 and Beverley Skeggs'
chapter (Chapter 29) in this volume). Less explicitly feminist, but nevertheless shaped by ethnographic attention to gender, is the work of Marilyn
Strathern, which exemplifies the semantic/reflexive
application of anthropological insight and meaning-
dissection to anthropological and what she sometimes calls 'Euro-American' categories and
practices.[26] This is illustrated, for example, in the
influential co-edited volume, *Nature, Culture and
Gender* (MacCormack and Strathern, 1980), and
especially her own contribution (Strathern, 1980),
which draws on ethnographic specificity to challenge Lévi-Straussian universalizing nature:culture
dichotomies.

By the early 1980s, then, the established anthropological project of 'scientific ethnography' was
under critical fire from many directions. ASA
Decennial conferences have become a venue for disciplinary stock-taking and the 1983 Decennial, held
in Cambridge (which was the first major anthropological conference that I, as a new graduate student
in anthropology, attended), was marked by a sense
of anxiety about the future, especially a concern
about the demographic maintenance of the discipline, its fragmentation into different specialisms,
and worry that auto-critique would dissolve it altogether (Rivière, 1989). At the same time, however,

especially among younger participants (and outside
the main plenary sessions), there was also a feeling
of excitement and potential generated by the challenge to redefine the discipline.

TOWARDS THE TWENTY-FIRST CENTURY

In the decade following the 1983 Decennial,
questions about anthropology's role and relevance
in a changing world, and the nature of the
anthropological-ethnographic endeavour – including the politics and ethics of fieldwork, the place of
the personal, and reflexivity – remained very much
on the agenda. The ASA volumes published in that
decade highlight both the wide range of interests
and also some of the predominant directions of the
discipline.[27] The concern with contemporary world
issues rather than conventional anthropological
categories is evident, with volumes on *Social
Anthropology and Development Policy* (Grillo and
Rew, 1985), *Migrants, Workers and the Social Order*
(Eades, 1987), *Contemporary Futures* (Wallman,
1992), *Socialism* (Hann, 1993) and *Environmentalism* (Milton, 1993). The semantic, reflexive current is exemplified in many of the contributions to
the other ASA volumes of the period: *Reason and
Morality* (Overing, 1985), *Anthropology at Home*
(Jackson, 1986), *History and Ethnicity* (Tonkin et al.,
1989), *Anthropology and the Riddle of the Sphinx*
(P. Spencer, 1990) and *Anthropology and Autobiography* (Okely and Callaway, 1992).

In the second half of the 1980s, the debates
which followed the publication of the *Writing
Culture* collection (Clifford and Marcus, 1986a)
in the United States (see Jonathan Spencer's
chapter (Chapter 30) in this volume) fuelled further
the expanding critique of ethnographic practice
and of objectivity in British social anthropology.
There were, however, some interesting differences
between the American position (as exemplified in
that volume and those associated with it) and much
of the British response. Asking, 'what is one of the
principal things ethnographers do?' and giving the
answer, 'they write' (Clifford and Marcus, 1986b:
vii), *Writing Culture* took up the metaphor of
culture as text current in American interpretivist
anthropology to provide a critique of writing styles
in ethnographic monographs (Malinowski and
Evans-Pritchard were two who came under the
lens). Contributors highlighted, among other things,
the ways in which many ethnographers made their
work appear authoritative through 'an ideology of
transparency of representation and immediacy of
experience' (Clifford, 1986: 2). 'Experimental'
writing strategies – such as personalized accounts
and the use of dialogue – were advocated (e.g.
Marcus and Fischer, 1986). Among the mixed
British responses were three main related claims:

1 that feminist anthropology, ignored in *Writing Culture*, had already made many of the same points as part of a more extensive epistemological critique;

2 that the writing culture approach narcissistically focused too much on the ethnographer and too little on those among whom ethnographers had worked; and

3 that an overemphasis on ethnographic writing deflected important concern from ethnographic *practice* and the wider politics of ethnographic production (e.g. Fardon, 1990; James et al., 1997; Moore, 1994; Okely and Callaway, 1992; Spencer, 1989). And while there have been experiments with more personalized and 'multivocal' ethnographies,[28] some British anthropologists have suggested journalism (Ahmed and Shore, 1995: 23) and popular writing (MacClancy, 1996) as appropriate models,[29] arguing that in their greater accessibility to non-academic audiences (increasingly likely to include those written about) these styles may encourage greater public engagement and thus more effectively challenge academic authority than esoteric experiments (cf. Grimshaw and Hart, 1993). Already engaged, then, in critical examination of itself in the wake of colonial and feminist criticism, and as a consequence of its own institutional and policy context, and the semantic turn, the tendency in British social anthropology was to cast the debate about representation more broadly to incorporate questions of ethnographic practice and the implicit politics of theorizing (Moore, 1996). This was to lead to a good deal of exciting new work and, by the time of the next ASA Decennial conference – 'The uses of knowledge: local and global relations' – in 1993, there seemed to be in British social anthropology a 'different ... tone from the earlier Decennial conferences ... a feeling of confidence, openness and enthusiasm' (Douglas, 1995: 16).

To some extent, however, this was against the grain of much of the institutional context for anthropology in Britain as swingeing financial cuts and a very narrow conception of 'value for money' continued to be applied throughout the public sector. Much research, including worthy social anthropological scholarship, was defined as 'irrelevant' by government;[30] and while the ASA campaigned hard to keep the number of teaching posts in social anthropology fairly steady, funding for research and postgraduate study fell markedly.[31] As part of the demand for 'value', a whole panoply of audit mechanisms was introduced, some of which particularly threatened anthropology's tradition of long-term ethnographic fieldwork, and especially overseas research.[32] Nevertheless, partly as a result of more open membership criteria, the ASA has continued to grow, the 1998 membership standing at nearly 600. A comparison with the 1961 Directory, discussed above, provides an interesting portrait of changes and continuities in the discipline across the intervening years.

By 1998, Europe has become the number one fieldwork area, though Africa comes a close second.[33] India is next, and the Pacific still attracts a sizeable interest. However, although Europe hosts the highest number of fieldworkers, nearly half of them have previously carried out fieldwork in another part of the world (a higher proportion than for any other area). Moreover, the category 'Europe' hides the fact that two-thirds of the European fieldwork has been carried out in Britain,[34] a consequence at least partly of the expansion of anthropological work, especially beyond PhD level, 'at home', and especially for UK-relevant policy research. In terms of 'Theoretical interests' (as the entry is now called), the most striking feature compared with 1961 is the enormous range of topics listed and the fact that many of these are not presented in terms of the fairly conventional set of categories evident in the 1961 Directory. However, while this makes creating a ranked list extremely difficult, it is possible to note some of the continuities with, and shifts from, 1961.[35] 'Politics, government', the most popular 'chief interest' in 1961, still attracts substantial attention but has slipped behind the second of the Ardeners' categories – 'ritual, religion, mythology, belief, symbolism, witchcraft' – which now probably enjoys more interest than any other; and behind two areas now receiving enormous attention, which were not mentioned in 1961: 'gender, women', and 'ethnicity, nationalism, identity'. Although some of what now counts as 'ethnicity' might previously have been studied as part of 'politics', it is worth noting that 'ethnicity, nationalism, identity' are foci which are much more likely to demand attention to 'indigenous' or 'local' semantic construction rather than 'objective' social organization.[36] Of the 1961 categories, 'kinship' and 'social change' have held up best, the latter receiving a particularly substantial amount of interest if we also include two related areas which are frequently listed in 1998: 'development' and 'history'. These more processual nominations are now considerably more popular than 'social structure, structure, social systems, social organization' which receive relatively little mention. 'Methodology, theory' is also rarely referred to, though this is perhaps because now specific approaches are more likely to be listed ('ethnography' itself, for example, is listed by about a dozen members).

Despite the expansion of the discipline in terms of numbers of people calling themselves 'anthropologists', and the geographical and theoretical range of interests, and despite the criticisms of ethnography over the intervening years, virtually all British anthropologists still carry out fieldwork – at least, almost all include at least one fieldwork entry in the 1998 Directory. Indeed, it seems to me that over the past decade, ethnography has been embraced in social anthropology with a renewed ardour. This, however, is an ethnography – as practice and product – which has, in some important respects, been reconfigured in light of the developments and critiques discussed above.

Problems with the earlier ethnographic model were its exclusions: of its own and its author's positionedness; of certain kinds of social constellations ('modern', 'familiar', 'fragmented', 'powerful'); and of 'bigger' subjects that stretched beyond 'communities'. Through these exclusions, social anthropological ethnography constructed a particular kind of ethnographic object – objectified, temporally and spatially sealed off from wider history and world systems, and frequently apparently 'simpler' than the kinds of worlds which anthropologists neglected. To be sure, there were exceptions to this; and indeed these have provided some of the inspiration for the reconfiguration. In the attempt to escape these problems, however, there has been some suggestion that ethnography itself should be abandoned; and a number of anthropologists have produced accounts entirely based on primary and secondary historical data, or on the analysis of discourse and imagery.[37] However, while these are certainly worthwhile forms in themselves to which anthropologists can and do bring a distinctive contribution, to abandon ethnography altogether would be to throw out the baby with the bathwater. The problems, after all, as I have noted above, were not so much with ethnography itself as with the screening out of certain topics, persons and domains of life which, far from being invisible, were often glaringly obvious.

So what approaches have anthropological-ethnographers adopted to deal with these problems? I should note that although I have restricted myself here (purely because of the remit to which I am writing) to anthropologists who might count as 'British' by either institutional training or workplace, many of the developments which I describe defy national boundaries – that, indeed, is perhaps an increasingly important current in academic life generally.[38] The first approach which can be identified is the shift of geographical emphasis towards Europe and especially Britain as noted above. Although this was partially fuelled by practical matters, it was also implicated in a significant reconfiguration of the discipline. Ethnographic research on Europe until well into the 1980s has been criticized for a tendency to 'tribalize' the continent by concentrating on small and rural locations (Boissevain, 1975; Chapman, 1982; Nadel-Klein, 1991). However, even the work of some of the earliest ethnographers of Europe based high in the mountains and well away from the metropoles, such as that of Julian Pitt-Rivers (1954) or John Campbell (1964), highlighted the impossibility of simply applying existing 'tribal' anthropological models. In doing so, they challenged simple 'us'/'them' dichotomies and thus began to reflexively undermine the characterization of anthropology as the study of the exotic (Fardon, 1990: 21–2; Herzfeld, 1987: 58–9). European ethnographic work showed itself capable of highlighting diversity within the continent (and within particular countries) – diversity which was often ignored by scholars from other disciplines (Cohen, 1982); and in the process, anthropology showed itself capable of coming at least 'part way home' (Cole, 1977).

Coming all the way home has, however, also meant tackling some areas which earlier ethnographers tended to neglect: in particular, documented history and nation-state relations. The challenge has been to do so without losing the rich 'on the ground' perspectives which ethnography could provide. While this is a dilemma that faced European ethnographers with a particular vengeance, it is not, of course, unique to Europe. Indeed, addressing the local *and* not just the national but the global, has come to be regarded as one of the major challenges facing an increasingly inter- and even transnational anthropology.

Ways in which social anthropologists from Britain and elsewhere have attempted to tackle these challenges have included providing greater historical depth and temporal situatedness to ethnographic accounts (e.g. Carsten, 1997; Dresch, 1993; Humphrey, 1996) and addressing subjects such as nationalism and modernity directly (e.g. Holy, 1996; Miller, 1994, 1997; J. Spencer, 1990). There has also been a new emphasis on those in positions of power and, alongside this, analysis of policy-making, national and even international cultural production (e.g. Born, 1995; Franklin, 1997; Harvey, 1996). Other ethnographic research has coupled analysis of national and international policies, products and developments (for example, new reproductive technologies, global media, state policies on education or culture) with research on the local experience and appropriation of them (e.g. Edwards, 2000; Gillespie, 1995; McDonald, 1990; Macdonald, 1997; Stafford, 1995; Stokes, 1992). Also entailing a shift in the kinds of people studied, has been a focus on mobile groups and individuals such as migrants (e.g. Gardner, 1995; Werbner, 1980) or tourists (see contributions to Abram, Waldren and McLeod, 1997; Crick, 1994). Such work is important in unsettling notions of bounded and homogeneous 'communities'. So too is research on 'mixed' and 'fragmented' 'communities', such as that by Baumann (1996) in Southall, London, or Jarman in Belfast (1997). Other anthropologists, building on earlier traditions but providing more nuanced reflexive accounts, have undertaken ethnography among groups whose particular perspective disrupts generalities about 'community' or 'society': for example, work on children (e.g. James, 1993; Toren, 1990), untouchables (Gellner and Quigley, 1995; Kapadia, 1995) degraded Brahmin funeral priests (Parry, 1994), or transvestites (Johnson, 1997).

In a somewhat different manner, there is also a significant strand of ethnographic work which develops an earlier critique of functionalism to highlight *individual* distinctiveness and negotiation. Particularly associated with the Manchester School, especially the transactionalist tradition,[39] this approach is exemplified in the ethnographic work of Anthony Cohen (1987) and Nigel Rapport (1993).[40] Individual voice has also been incorporated into multivocal and narrative accounts as a way not only of unsettling ethnographic authority but also, as in Pat Caplan's *Personal Narrative, Multiple Voices: The Worlds of a Swahili Peasant* (1997), of examining changing historical and gendered cultural formations both 'at home' and in this case in Tanzania. Furthermore, narrative and collage styles, perhaps employing poetry and polemic, have been used, as in Alan Campbell's impassioned *Getting to Know Waiwai* (1995), where the style directly contributes to Campbell's aim to convey to the reader the value of the Wayapí way of life and the awfulness of its destruction (see Campbell, 1996).

But what do we mean by ethnography here? As I noted at the beginning, social anthropologists do not just mean participant observation. Rather, as Daniel Miller (1997) has suggested, ethnography is a 'particular perspective' constituted by the following 'commitments':

1 'to be in the presence of the people one is studying, not just the texts or objects they produce' (p. 16);
2 'to evaluate people in terms of what they actually do, i.e. as material agents working with a material world, and not merely of what they say they do' (pp. 16–17);
3 'a long term commitment to an investigation that allows people to return to a daily life that one hopes goes beyond what is performed for the ethnographer' (p. 17);
4 'to holistic analysis, which insists that ... behaviours be considered within the larger framework of people's lives and cosmologies' (p. 17).

These commitments may well mean that anthropologist-ethnographers couple first-hand observation with interviews and with historical data and analysis of texts and imagery. Indeed, Miller himself does all of these in his own attempts to deal with the 'big topics' of 'modernity' and 'capitalism' through ethnography focused on Trinidad (1994, 1997).[41] As he argues, this kind of work – which can highlight cultural specificity and local meaning-making – is vital in the face of what are widely feared to be, and widely read off as, globally homogenizing forces.[42] And what an *anthropological* training also brings to this kind of ethnographic project is an awareness of cultural alternatives: of how things could be otherwise.[43]

To deal with multivocality and multiple agency, with fragmentation and movement, and with the complexities of positioning and identity in social worlds which are at once local *and* global has been the challenge. It is one which reconfigured social, and increasingly transnational, anthropology is well able to meet; and this is a central reason both for the growth of interest in ethnography across social and cultural studies (to which this volume is testament) and for the new anthropological, ethnographic confidence.

Epilogue: Personal Note

This is, of course, a particular positioned account of British social anthropology; and in order for the reader to situate it I provide the following (partial) biographical note. My own anthropological training was at Oxford University where my DPhil, on cultural and linguistic revival in the Scottish Highlands, was supervised by Edwin Ardener until his death in 1987. My anthropological work moved, in some respects, still closer to 'home' when I took up a research fellowship at Brunel University and carried out an ethnographic study of the Science Museum, London. There, and subsequently at the Universities of Keele and now Sheffield, I have worked in 'mixed' social anthropology and sociology departments, and have conducted work across disciplinary boundaries; something which I also do as editor of *The Sociological Review*. Next year I plan to carry out new anthropological-ethnographic research on cultural policy in Nuremberg, Germany.

Acknowledgements

I have been fortunate to have received some extremely helpful comments on this chapter and would like to thank Michael Beaney, Jeanette Edwards, David Gellner, Richard Jenkins, Adam Kuper, Jane Nadel-Klein, Peter Rivière and two anonymous referees. I also apologize that I was not able to take up all of the points made. Any errors or skewed perspectives are my own. I also extend thanks to those of the above who responded to my questions over what they thought were the most important ethnographies by British social anthropologists in the past ten years; and to Eric Hirsch and Pnina Werbner who were also kind enough to do so. Thanks are due too to Pat Caplan, John Eade, Wendy James and Nigel Rapport for help with information about the ASA.

NOTES

1 The extent of Malinowski's actual 'innovation' is debatable. Rivers had already established a fieldwork-based programme of which Malinowski was aware (Peter Rivière, personal communication; Grimshaw and Hart, 1993). However, it is Malinowski's articulation of an ethnographic project that has been particularly influential.

2 Most of these abstainers have failed to complete other sections too, suggesting that the lapse in some cases at least may be one of form completion rather than fieldwork.

3 The date is further cemented into anthropological history as this was the year in which the other 'founding father' of British social anthropology, Radcliffe-Brown, published his study of the Andaman islanders. Less often observed, but probably of equal significance for the development of the discipline, is the fact that Rivers died in 1922.

4 Ardener has noted that the beginning of 'modern' approaches 'in most areas of thought' (e.g. architecture and literary criticism) is marked by a '*perceived* change of technique, however trivial' (1989: 200). Whether it was fully innovatory or not, participant observation, like the use, say, of concrete and steel in architecture, was regarded as opening up dramatic new possibilities in ways of relating to its subject matter.

5 In some ways, it might have been expected that a more scientistic model of reporting would have been adopted in order to distinguish anthropological accounts more fully from amateur ones. That it was not, is probably due partly to Malinowski's personal literary inclinations and preferences, and to his attempt to harness popular interest in the discipline. More broadly, however, Malinowski's approach was also in keeping with a move in the legitimation of *scientific* research through making it public – an important strand in scientific truth claims since the eighteenth century and the decline of authorization through the individual nobility of the scientist (see Shapin, 1994). This *public* presentation of science was an important aspect of the establishment of public museums of science (see Macdonald, 1998); and much of Malinowski's talk in the first chapter of *Argonauts* about making evident scientific processes and results is part of this discourse. That Malinowski in fact made such processes more *obscure* by establishing a highly individual mode of field-work is a point made by Grimshaw and Hart (1993, 1995).

6 See, for example, James, 1973 for a discussion of the complexities of Malinowski's negotiation of these.

7 The British sociological directory for 1961 listed 669 members, compared with the 142 in the Association of Social Anthropologists (Ardener and Ardener, 1965: 312, n.10). Even though membership criteria were not identical, social anthropology would have been unable to summon up such a number by any criteria. Indeed, given that its figures were based on 'the Commonwealth', anthropology already had one factor boosting its numbers relative to the sociological organization.

8 The full title is 'Association of Social Anthropologists of the Commonwealth', though interestingly few historical accounts of the discipline even note this. In practice, it was an organization of those trained in British social anthropology; fourteen of the original members were based in the United Kingdom and seven overseas (Kuper, [1973] 1975: 151).

9 The *Rules* also state that membership is conferred by invitation and is 'restricted to persons of academic standing, who, in virtue of their published works and or [*sic*] posts held, can be recognized as professional social anthropologists' (*ASA List of Members*, 1961, quoted in Ardener and Ardener, 1965: 312, n. 7).

10 Members are asked to list all of the fieldwork visits that they have made: hence the retrospective dimension of the study. It should be noted that the Ardeners' calculations are based on visits rather than personnel, which means – especially given the fairly small numbers involved overall – that certain active fieldworkers can be responsible for augmenting the rates for particular areas.

11 Members can list as many areas of interest as they wish. The Ardeners caution against attaching too much significance to the actual numbers involved.

12 Asad notes, however, that interest of functionalist anthropologists in social change was generally restricted to 'modern' change and was closely allied with the simultaneous attempt to reconstruct 'traditional' cultures (Asad, 1991: 318).

13 My account draws on the work of historian of science and medicine John Pickstone (1994 here) and also on Mitchell, 1988.

14 Pocock suggests that this may have been partly a matter of academic diplomacy (1971: 79); though as Geertz points out, one of the main marks of 'the British school', particularly pre-1960s, is a particular tone of which 'a studied air of unstudiedness' (1988: 59) is key. It is worth noting that the politics of readability here are interestingly ambiguous. On the one hand, such theoretical understatement privileges the knowing reader who is sufficiently well versed in the ongoing debates to be able to read off its theoretical contribution, and as such creates a kind of exclusive clubbiness. Certainly, this was part of the 'Oxford style' (Evans-Pritchard was Professor of Social Anthropology at Oxford from 1946 to 1970) and a variant of it was still prevalent when I was a postgraduate in the 1980s. It was particularly manifested at Friday seminars when visiting speakers tried to exhibit their theoretical skill and would be flumoxed by some cryptic question (often from Godfrey Lienhardt), generally requiring broader scholarly erudition, which somehow – how was this? – the Oxford crew all understood. On the other hand, keeping ethnographic monographs relatively uncluttered of theoretical discussion made them more palatable to a non-anthropological audience. This non-anthropological audience, especially those with an interest in the particular people or place, was surely important even to anthropologists who did not wish to go quite as far down the road of popularization as Malinowski; and perhaps too, the College system at Oxbridge (where allegiance to a subject-mixed community of scholars was as important as was discipline speciality) encouraged a more ecumenical approach. The ambiguity of this particular ethnographic convention is not, I think, exclusive to it: indeed, it seems

to me that the 'politics' of what are rather militaristically called writing 'strategies' are frequently more fuzzy than they are usually described as being.

15 Hemingway's most famous work, *For Whom the Bell Tolls*, was also first published in 1940. For discussion of Hemingway's style in relation to ethnography, see Atkinson, 1990: 63–71.

16 It was not only *The Nuer* which played a part in this. Indeed, Evans-Pritchard's earlier work, *Witchcraft, Oracles and Magic among the Azande* (1937), has probably been more influential in exemplifying a semantic approach. Also important was his 1950 Marrett lecture (reprinted in Evans-Pritchard, 1962) in which he clearly positioned social anthropology as one of the humanities – most closely allied with history – rather than as a science.

17 This was based on a conference, though not an ASA conference. The topic had, in fact, been proposed by Talal Asad to the ASA but allegedly had been rejected on the grounds that 'we went through all this in the 1930s'. The conference was, then, something of a revolt against the ASA. I thank Wendy James for this information.

18 This distinction had a particular inflection in this period as many colonial administrators had gained knowledge of the kinds of places in which anthropologists typically worked and it has been suggested that anthropologists therefore felt a strong need to distinguish themselves from such 'practical men'. Edmund Leach is reported as having said that one of the main reasons for establishing the ASA was to 'prevent the Universities from employing unqualified refugees from the disappearing Colonial Service to teach "applied anthropology"' (Grillo, 1984: 310 as quoted in Wright, 1995: 67).

19 A nice example of this is the dismissal of the practical utility of an anthropological perspective by P.E. Mitchell, provincial commissioner in what was then Tanganyika: 'if an inhabitant of a South Sea Island feels obliged on some ceremonial occasion to eat his grandmother, the anthropologist is attracted to examine and explain the ancient custom which caused him to do so; the practical man, on the other hand, tends to take more interest in the grandmother' (1930; quoted in James, 1973: 53–4). Malinowski argued back against this, the pages of the journal *Africa* containing much debate in the 1930s about anthropological relevance or otherwise (see James, 1973).

20 Werbner provides an interesting account of the 'logic of encompassment' operating in cultural studies (and cultural studies' influenced anthropology) which propels Evans-Pritchard as 'an exemplary "pure" white, upper-class male' (1997: 44) to this role.

21 There are other issues involved too in the use of tense: see Davis, 1992.

22 See Douglas, 1966, 1970, 1975 for her earlier works; Fardon (1998) provides an insightful account of her work.

23 The term 'postmodern' is sometimes used to describe the growth of experimental styles in anthropology, though as in other areas of social and cultural studies there is debate about its suitability.

24 A paper given by David Pocock at the ASA Decennial conference in 1973 entitled 'The idea of a personal anthropology' was much talked about and cited, though it has never been published.

25 For discussion see, for example, Ardener, 1978; Bell et al., 1993; Caplan, 1992; and Moore, 1988.

26 See Strathern, 1994 for a brief academic autobiography; and 1988 and 1992a for substantial examples of her technique. Interestingly, Strathern has at one point suggested that her work might be termed 'deconstructive' (1992b: 73); and her use of the term 'auto-anthropology' (1986) has also been quite widely adopted to characterize at least one aspect of the semantic/reflexive strategy. More recently, she has developed some of the theoretical implications of her work in Strathern, 1994b.

27 Each year the ASA holds a conference, the theme for which is decided at the annual general meeting; and an edited collection is later produced. Although there is obviously a good deal of serendipity involved in the selection of themes, as these rely on individuals submitting proposals, there is an attempt to choose themes which are 'topical' and which will be likely to attract good participation. As such they act as a kind of indicator of predominant ongoing disciplinary interests.

28 These include the fairly tentative use of personal account and argument about 'versions' in Anthony Cohen's *Whalsay* (1987) and the extensive use of 'conversation' in Nigel Rapport's *Diverse World Views in an English Village* (1993), both of which came partly out of a Manchester School interest in individuals (which had earlier been manifested in transactionalism). Another Manchester example, in this case drawing on the recollection of particular informants, is Richard Werbner's *Tears of the Dead* (1991). Experimental forms influenced by feminist ideas and adopting more personalized styles include Katy Gardner's *Songs at the Rivers Edge* (1991), Helen Watson's *Women of the City of the Dead* (1991), Anna Grimshaw's *Servants of the Buddha* (1992), and Pat Caplan's *Personal Narrative, Multiple Voices: The Worlds of a Swahili Peasant* (1997); and earlier narrative accounts, such as Mary Smith's *Baba of Karo* (1954), were also 'reclaimed' (Callaway, 1992).

29 To some extent the argument for popular writing in particular draws on a longstanding current in anthropological writing, one especially evident in the 1980s in Nigel Barley's irreverent 'inside' accounts (1983, 1986, 1988).

30 At one point social anthropological research was singled out for ridicule as 'irrelevant' by the Public Accounts Committee (see Leach and Rivière, 1981). Interestingly, the original reference to a piece of research on Poland was later caricatured as 'Social anthropology in outer Ruritania' as events in Poland highlighted the value of the Polish work! The narrow conception of 'usefulness' continues to infect academia. It is institutionalized into, for example, the Economic and Social Research Council (the major source of social sciences funding in Britain) requirement that research applications contribute to its 'corporate objectives' of (1) 'UK economic competitiveness'; (2) 'Effectiveness of public services and public policy'; and (3) 'Quality of life'. Many of these developments are not, of course, exclusive to anthropology or to Britain: see, for example, Hill and Turpin, 1995.

31 By 1998 only 16 grants per year were available from the Economic and Social Research Council for postgraduate research in social anthropology. In 1973 the Institute of Social Anthropology in Oxford alone received 23 ESRC grants (Peter Rivière personal communication). This falling in PhDs is by marked contrast with the United States which has continued to expand: see Givens et al., 1998. At the same time, the requirement in Britain that PhDs be completed within four years (with the possibility of small extensions for dealing with a 'difficult language') – otherwise institutions risk being disqualified from receiving ESRC grants – is a serious threat to anthropological fieldwork. In many parts of the world, especially the United States, fledgling anthropologists now do more than the original ritual year. This relative constriction of the British social anthropology PhD puts British social anthropologists at an increasing disadvantage in the international jobs market.

32 In addition to the pressure to complete PhD research in four years, these include, with the Research Assessment Exercise (a periodic peer review of published work), an emphasis on a particular kind of temporally regular output. The RAE is widely believed (perhaps misguidedly) to discourage substantial in-depth scholarly work, interdisciplinary research, or writing that also attempts to reach non-academic audiences (and indeed review pieces such as this). Interestingly, some British social anthropologists have looked at these developments from an anthropological perspective (e.g. Davis, 1999; Strathern, 1995b).

33 The way in which I have calculated this differs from that of Ardener and Ardener (1965) in that I count the number of anthropologists carrying out fieldwork in a particular area rather than the number of instances of fieldwork. I have done this partly because in the 1998 Directory many members simply list areas rather than each instance of fieldwork. However, because researchers in Europe are presumably especially likely to make more frequent return visits than for more distant locations, my mode of calculating reduces the European instances relative to that used by Ardener and Ardener (1965), i.e. by their technique Europe would be even more dramatically the favoured fieldwork area.

34 Ardener and Ardener (1965) do not provide separate figures for Britain.

35 As a number of people have pointed out to me, many members probably never get round to changing their original entries. This, of course, may give a greater impression of continuity than would be the case if reviewing *current* interests (for which data are not, unfortunately, available).

36 For discussion of this distinction see Barth (1969), an article which has been very influential in shaping the anthropological study of ethnicity; see also Ardener, 1989: Ch. 3 and Jenkins, 1997.

37 For example, Goody, 1983, 1986, 1987, 1993, 1996 or Needham, 1985, 1987.

38 In social anthropology it is reflected in, among other things, the establishment of the European Association of Social Anthropologists in the late 1980s.

39 For an excellent account of the Manchester School see Werbner, 1990.

40 Cohen and Rapport set out their positions in Cohen, 1994; Rapport, 1997 and Cohen and Rapport, 1995.

41 See also his work on London: Miller, 1998.

42 These arguments are also made well in the volumes emerging from the 1993 Decennial: Fardon, 1995; James, 1995; Miller, 1995; Moore, 1996; and Strathern, 1995a.

43 See Howell, 1997 and Werbner, 1997 for some insightful commentary on the difference from cultural studies in this regard.

REFERENCES

Abram, S., Waldren, J. and McLeod, D. (eds) (1997) *Tourists and Tourism. Identifying with People and Places*. Oxford and New York: Berg.

Ahmed, Akbar and Shore, Cris (1995) 'Introduction: is anthropology relevant to the contemporary world?', in A. Ahmed and C. Shore (eds), *The Future of Social Anthropology. Its Relevance to the Contemporary World*. London and Atlantic Highlands, NJ: Athlone. pp. 12–45.

Ardener, Edwin (1971a) 'Introduction', in *Social Anthropology and Language* (ASA Monograph 10). London: Tavistock. pp. ix–cii. (Reprinted in Ardener, 1989.)

Ardener, Edwin (1971b) 'The new anthropology and its critics', *Man*, 6 (3): 449–67. (Reprinted in Ardener, 1989.)

Ardener, Edwin (1972) 'Belief and the problem of women', in J. La Fontaine (ed.), *The Interpretation of Ritual*. London: Tavistock. (Reprinted in Ardener, 1989.)

Ardener, Edwin (1985) 'Social anthropology and the decline of modernism', in J. Overing (ed.), *Reason and Morality* (ASA Monograph 24). London: Tavistock. (Reprinted in Ardener, 1989.)

Ardener, Edwin (1989) *The Voice of Prophecy and Other Essays* (ed. M. Chapman). Oxford: Blackwell.

Ardener, E. and Ardener, S. (1965) 'A directory study of social anthropologists', *British Journal of Sociology*, 16: 295–314.

Ardener, Shirley (1975) 'Introduction', in S. Ardener (ed.), *Perceiving Women*. London: Dent. pp. vii–xxiii.

Ardener, Shirley (ed.) (1978) *Defining Females: The Nature of Women in Society*. London: Croom Helm.

Arens, W. (1983) 'Evans-Pritchard and the prophets: comments on an ethnographic enigma', *Anthropos*, 78: 1–16.

Asad, Talal (ed.) (1973) *Anthropology and the Colonial Encounter*. London: Ithaca Press.

Asad, Talal (1991) 'Afterword. From the history of colonial anthropology to the anthropology of Western hegemony', in G. Stocking (ed.), *Colonial Situations: Essays on the Contextualisation of Ethnographic Knowledge*. Madison, WI: Wisconsin University Press. pp. 314–24.

Atkinson, Paul (1990) *The Ethnographic Imagination: Textual Constructions of Reality*. London and New York: Routledge.

Banaji, J. (1970) 'Anthropology in crisis', *New Left Review*, 64: 71–85.

Barley, Nigel (1983) *The Innocent Anthropologist. Notes from a Mud Hut*. London: British Museum.

Barley, Nigel (1986) *A Plague of Caterpillars. A Return to the African Bush*. London: Viking.

Barley, Nigel (1988) *Not a Hazardous Sport*. London: Viking.

Barth, Fredrik (1969) 'Introduction', in F. Barth (ed.), *Ethnic Groups and Boundaries: The Social Organisation of Culture Difference*. Oslo: Universitetsforlaget.

Baumann, Gerd (1996) *Contesting Culture: Discourses of Identity in Multi-Ethnic London*. Cambridge: Cambridge University Press.

Bell, D., Caplan, P. and Karim, W. (eds) (1993) *Gendered Fields*. London and New York: Routlege.

Bloch, Maurice (1983) *Marxism and Anthropology*. Oxford and New York: Oxford University Press.

Bloch, Maurice (1986) *From Blessing to Violence: History and Ideology in the Circumcision Ritual of the Merina of Madagascar*. Cambridge: Cambridge University Press.

Boissevain, Jeremy (1975) 'Introduction: towards a social anthropology of Europe', in J. Boissevain and J. Friedl (eds), *Beyond the Community: Social Process in Europe*. The Hague: University of Amsterdam.

Born, Georgina (1995) *Rationalizing Culture: IRCAM, Boulez, and the Institutionalization of the Musical Avant-Garde*. Berkeley and Los Angeles, CA: California University Press.

Callaway, Helen (1992) 'Ethnography and experience: gender implications in fieldwork and texts', in J. Okely and H. Callaway (eds), *Anthropology and Autobiography* (ASA 29). London and New York: Routledge.

Campbell, Alan (1995) *Getting to Know Waiwai: An Amazonian Ethnography*. London and New York: Routledge.

Campbell, Alan (1996) 'Tricky tropes: styles of the popular and the pompous', in J. MacClancy and C. McDonaugh (eds), *Popularizing Anthropology*. London and New York: Routledge. pp. 58–82.

Campbell, John K. (1964) *Honour, Family and Patronage: A Study of Institutions and Moral Values in a Greek Mountain Community*. Oxford: The Clarendon Press.

Caplan, Pat (1992) 'Engendering knowledge: the politics of ethnography', in S. Ardener (ed.), *Persons and Powers of Women in Diverse Cultures*. Oxford: Berg. pp. 65–88.

Caplan, Pat (1997) *Personal Narrative, Multiple Voices: The Worlds of a Swahili Peasant*. London and New York: Routledge.

Carsten, Janet (1997) *The Heat of the Hearth: The Process of Kinship in a Malay Fishing Community*. Oxford: Oxford University Press.

Chapman (1982) '"Semantics" and the "Celt"', in D. Parkin (ed.), *Semantic Anthropology*. London: Academic Press. pp. 123–43.

Clifford, James (1986) 'Introduction: partial truths', in J. Clifford and G.E. Marcus (eds), *Writing Culture. The Poetics and Politics of Ethnography*. Berkeley and Los Angeles, CA: California University Press. pp. 1–26.

Clifford, J. and Marcus, G.E. (eds) (1986a) *Writing Culture. The Poetics and Politics of Ethnography*. Berkeley and Los Angeles, CA: California University Press.

Clifford, J. and Marcus, G.E. (1986b) 'Preface', in *Writing Culture. The Poetics and Politics of Ethnography*. Berkeley and Los Angeles, CA: California University Press. pp. vii–ix.

Cohen, Anthony P. (1982) 'Belonging: the experience of culture', in A.P. Cohen (ed.), *Belonging. Identity and Social Organisation in British Rural Cultures*. Manchester: Manchester University Press. pp. 1–17.

Cohen, Anthony P. (1987) *Whalsay: Symbol, Segment and Boundary in a Shetland Island Community*. Manchester: Manchester University Press.

Cohen, Anthony P. (1994) *Self Consciousness: An Alternative Anthropology of Identity*. London: Routledge.

Cohen, A.P. and Rapport, N. (eds) (1995) *Questions of Consciousness* (ASA Monograph 33). London: Routledge.

Cole, John (1977) 'Anthropology comes part-way home: community studies in Europe', *Annual Review of Anthropology*, 6: 349–78.

Crick, Malcolm (1976) *Explorations in Language and Meaning: Towards a Semantic Anthropology*. London: Dent.

Crick, Malcolm (1994) *Resplendent Sites, Discordant Voices: Sri Lankans and International Tourism*. Chur, Switzerland: Harwood Academic Press.

Davis, John (1992) 'Tense in ethnography: some practical considerations', in J. Okely and H. Callaway (eds), *Anthropology and Autobiography* (ASA Monograph 29). London and New York: Routledge. pp. 205–20.

Davis, John (1999) 'Administering creativity', *Anthropology Today*, 15 (2): 4–9.

Douglas, Mary (1966) *Purity and Danger: An Analysis of the Concepts of Pollution and Taboo*. London: Routledge.

Douglas, Mary (1970) *Natural Symbols*. London: Barrie and Rockcliff.

Douglas, Mary (1975) *Implicit Meanings: Essays in Anthropology*. London: Routledge.

Douglas, Mary (1980) *Evans-Pritchard*. London: Fontana.

Douglas, Mary (1995) 'Forgotten knowledge', in M. Strathern (ed.), *Shifting Contexts. Transformations in Anthropological Knowledge*. London and New York: Routledge. pp. 13–30.

Dresch, Paul (1993) *Tribes, Government and History in Yemen*. Oxford: The Clarendon Press.

Eades, J.S. (1987) *Migrants, Workers and the Social Order* (ASA Monograph 26). London: Tavistock.

Edwards, Jeanette (2000) *Born and Bred: Idioms of Kinship and New Reproductive Technologies in England*. Oxford: Oxford University Press.

Evans-Pritchard, E.E. (1937) *Witchcraft, Oracles and Magic among the Azande*. Oxford: The Clarendon Press.

Evans-Pritchard, E.E. (1940) *The Nuer. A Description of the Modes of Livelihood and Political Institutions of a Nilotic People*. Oxford: The Clarendon Press.

Evans-Pritchard, E.E. (1962) *Essays in Social Anthropology*. Oxford: Oxford University Press.

Fardon, Richard (1990) 'Localizing strategies: the regionalization of ethnographic accounts', in R. Fardon (ed.),

Localizing Strategies: Regional Traditions of Ethnographic Writing, Edinburgh: Edinburgh University Press, pp. 1–35.

Fardon, Richard (ed.) (1995) *Counterworks: Managing the Diversity of Knowledge* (ASA Decennial Monograph). London and New York: Routledge.

Fardon, Richard (1998) *Mary Douglas: An Intellectual Biography*. London and New York: Routledge.

Feuchtwang, Stephan (1973) 'The colonial formation of British social anthropology', in T. Asad (ed.), *Anthropology and the Colonial Encounter*. London: Ithaca Press. pp. 71–100.

Fortes, Meyer (1978) 'An anthropologist's apprenticeship', *Annual Review of Anthropology*, 7: 1–30.

Fortes, M. and Evans-Pritchard, E.E. (eds) (1940) *African Political Systems*. London: Oxford University Press.

Franklin, Sarah (1997) *Embodied Progress. A Cultural Account of Assisted Conception*. London and New York: Routledge.

Gardner, Katy (1991) *Songs at the River's Edge. Stories from a Bangladeshi Village*. London: Virago.

Gardner, Katy (1995) *Global Migrants, Local Lives: Travel and Transformation in Rural Bangladesh*. Oxford: Oxford University Press.

Geertz, Clifford (1988) *Works and Lives. The Anthropologist as Author*. Cambridge: Polity Press.

Gellner, David N. and Quigley, Declan (eds) (1995) *Contested Hierarchies: A Collaborative Ethnography of Caste Among the Newers of the Kathmandu Valley, Nepal*. Oxford: The Clarendon Press.

Gillespie, Marie (1995) *Television, Ethnicity and Cultural Change*. London: Routledge.

Givens, D.B., Evans, P. and Jablonski, T. (1998) '1997 AAA survey of anthropology PhDs', http:www.amer-anthassn.org/97/SURVEY.HTM

Goody, Jack (1983) *The Development of Family and Marriage in Europe*. Cambridge: Cambridge University Press.

Goody, Jack (1986) *The Logic of Writing and the Organisation of Society*. Cambridge: Cambridge University Press.

Goody, Jack (1987) *The Interface between the Written and the Oral*. Cambridge: Cambridge University Press.

Goody, Jack (1993) *The Culture of Flowers*. Cambridge: Cambridge University Press.

Goody, Jack (1995) *The Expansive Moment. Anthropology in Britain and Africa, 1918–1970*. Cambridge: Cambridge University Press.

Goody, Jack (1996) *The East in the West*. Cambridge: Cambridge University Press.

Grillo, R. and Rew, A. (eds) (1985) *Social Anthropology and Development Policy* (ASA Monograph 23). London: Tavistock.

Grimshaw, Anna (1992) *Servants of the Buddha*. London: Open Letters.

Grimshaw, Anna and Hart, Keith (1993) *Anthropology and the Crisis of the Intellectuals*. Cambridge: Prickly Pear Press.

Grimshaw, Anna and Hart, Keith (1995) 'The rise and fall of scientific ethnography', in A. Ahmed and C. Shore

(eds), *The Future of Social Anthropology. Its Relevance to the Contemporary World*. London and Atlantic Highlands, NJ: Athlone. pp. 46–64.

Hann, C.M. (ed.) (1993) *Socialism: Ideals, Ideologies and Local Practice* (ASA Monograph 31). London: Routledge.

Harding, Sandra (ed.) (1987) *Feminism and Methodology*. Bloomington, IN: Indiana University Press.

Harvey, David (1989) *The Condition of Postmodernity*. Oxford: Blackwell.

Harvey, Penelope (1996) *Hybrids of Modernity. Anthropology, the Nation-State and the Universal Exhibition*. London and New York: Routledge.

Herzfeld, Michael (1987) *Anthropology through the Looking-Glass. Critical Ethnography in the Margins of Europe*. Cambridge: Cambridge University Press.

Hill, S. and Turpin, T. (1995) 'Cultures in collision: the emergence of a new localism in academic research', in M. Strathern (ed.), *Shifting Contexts*. London and New York: Routledge.

Holy, Ladislav (1996) *The Little Czech and the Great Czech Nation. National Identity and the Post-Communist Social Transformation*. Cambridge: Cambridge University Press.

Howell, Signe (1997) 'Cultural studies and social anthropology: contesting or complementary discourses?', in S. Nugent and C. Shore (eds), *Anthropology and Cultural Studies*. London and Chicago: Pluto Press.

Humphrey, Caroline (1996) *Shamans and Elders: Experience, Knowledge and Power Among the Daur Mongols*. Oxford: Clarendon Press.

Jackson, Anthony (ed.) (1986) *Anthropology at Home*. London and New York: Routledge.

James, Allison (1993) *Childhood Identities: Self and Social Relationships in the Experience of the Child*. Edinburgh: Edinburgh University Press.

James, A., Hockey, J. and Dawson, A. (eds) (1997) *After Writing Culture. Epistemology and Praxis in Contemporary Anthropology* (ASA Monograph 34). London and New York: Routledge.

James, Wendy (1973) 'The anthropologist as reluctant imperialist', in T. Asad (ed.), *Anthropology and the Colonial Encounter*. London: Ithaca Press.

James, Wendy (ed.) (1995) *The Pursuit of Certainty. Religious and Cultural Formations* (ASA Decennial Monograph). London and New York: Routledge.

Jarman, Neil (1997) *Material Conflicts: Parades and Visual Displays in Northern Ireland*. Oxford and New York: Berg.

Jenkins, Richard (1997) *Rethinking Ethnicity: Arguments and Explorations*. London: Sage.

Johnson, Mark (1997) *Beauty and Power. Transgendering and Cultural Transformation in the Southern Phillipines*. Oxford and New York: Berg.

Kapadia, Karin (1995) *Siva and her Sisters. Gender, Caste and Class in Rural South India*. Boulder, CO: Westview Press.

Kuklick, Henrika ([1992] 1993) *The Savage Within. The Social History of British Social Anthropology, 1885–1945*. Cambridge: Cambridge University Press.

Kuper, Adam ([1973] 1975) *Anthropology and Anthropologists: The British School, 1922–72.* Harmondsworth: Peregrine.

Kuper, Adam (1996) *Anthropology and Anthropologists: The Modern British School*, 3rd edn. London and New York: Routledge.

Leach, Edmund (1954) *Political Systems of Highland Burma: A Study of Kachin Social Structure.* London: London School of Economics.

Leach, Edmund and Rivière, Peter (1981) 'How daily life in Ruritania affects us all', *Times Higher Education Supplement*, 23 January, p. 11.

MacClancy, Jeremy (1996) 'Popularizing anthropology', in J. MacClancy and C. McDonaugh (eds), *Popularizing Anthropology.* London and New York: Routledge. pp. 1–57.

MacCormack, C. and Strathern M. (eds) (1980) *Nature, Culture and Gender.* Cambridge: Cambridge University Press.

McDonald, Maryon (1990) *'We are Not French!' Language, Culture and Identity in Brittany.* London: Routledge.

Macdonald, Sharon (1997) *Reimagining Culture: Histories, Identities and the Gaelic Renaissance.* Oxford and New York: Berg.

Macdonald, Sharon (1998) 'Exhibitions of power and powers of exhibition', in S. Macdonald (ed.), *The Politics of Display. Museums, Science, Culture.* London and New York: Routledge. pp. 1–24.

Malinowski, Bronislaw (1922) *Argonauts of the Western Pacific. An Account of Native Enterprise and Adventure in the Archipelagoes of Melanesian New Guinea.* London and New York: Routledge and Kegan Paul.

Malinowski, Bronislaw (1929) *The Sexual Life of Savages.* London: Routledge and Kegan Paul.

Malinowski, Bronislaw (1944) *A Scientific Theory of Culture*, Chapel Hill, NC: University of North Carolina.

Marcus, G.E. and Fischer, M.M.J. (1986) *Anthropology as Cultural Critique: An Experimental Moment in the Human Sciences.* Chicago and London: University of Chicago Press.

Miller, Daniel (1994) *Modernity – An Ethnographic Approach. Dualism and Mass Consumption in Trinidad.* Oxford and New York: Berg.

Miller, Daniel (ed.) (1995) *Worlds Apart: Modernity Through the Prism of the Local.* London and New York: Routledge.

Miller, Daniel (1997) *Capitalism: An Ethnographic Approach.* Oxford and New York: Berg.

Miller, Daniel (1998) *A Theory of Shopping.* Cambridge: Polity Press.

Milton, K. (ed.) (1993) *Environmentalism: The View from Anthropology* (ASA Monograph 32). London: Routledge.

Mitchell, Timothy (1988) *Colonising Egypt.* Berkeley, CA and Oxford: California University Press.

Moore, Henrietta (1988) *Feminism and Anthropology.* Cambridge: Polity Press.

Moore, Henrietta (1994) *A Passion for Difference. Essays in Anthropology and Gender.* Cambridge: Polity Press.

Moore, Henrietta (ed.) (1996) *The Future of Anthropological Knowledge.* London and New York: Routledge.

Nadel-Klein, Jane (1991) 'Reweaving the fringe. Localism and representation in British ethnography', *American Ethnologist*, 18 (3): 500–17.

Needham, Rodney (1985) *Exemplars.* Berkeley, CA: University of California Press.

Needham, Rodney (1987) *Counterpoints.* Berkeley, CA: University of California Press.

Okely, Judith ([1975] 1996) 'The self and scientism', in *Own and Other Culture.* London and New York: Routledge.

Okely, J. and Callaway, H. (eds) (1992) *Anthropology and Autobiography* (ASA Monograph 29). London: Routledge.

Overing, J. (ed.) (1985) *Reason and Morality* (ASA Monograph 24). London: Tavistock.

Parkin, David (ed.) (1982a) *Semantic Anthropology* (ASA Monograph 22). London and New York: Academic Press.

Parkin, David (1982b) 'Introduction', in D. Parkin (ed.), *Semantic Anthropology.* London: Academic Press. pp. xi–li.

Parry, Jonathan (1994) *Death in Banaras.* Cambridge: Cambridge University Press.

Pickstone, John (1994) 'Museological science? The place of the analytical/comparative in nineteenth-century science, technology and medicine', *History of Science*, 32 (2): 111–38.

Pitt-Rivers, Julian (1954) *The People of the Sierra.* London: Weidenfeld and Nicholson.

Pocock, David (1971) *Social Anthropology.* London: Sheed and Ward.

Radcliffe-Brown, A.R. (1922) *The Andaman Islanders.* Cambridge: Cambridge University Press.

Radcliffe-Brown, A.R. (1957) *A Natural Science of Society.* Chicago: The Free Press.

Rapport, Nigel (1993) *Diverse World Views in an English Village.* Edinburgh: Edinburgh University Press.

Rapport, Nigel (1997) *Transcendent Individual. Essays Towards a Literary and Liberal Anthropology.* London: Routledge.

Rivière, Peter (1989) 'New trends in British social anthropology', *Cadernos do Noreste*, II (2–3): 7–24.

Rosaldo, Renato (1986) 'From the door of his tent: the fieldworker and the inquisitor', in J. Clifford and G.E. Marcus (eds), *Writing Culture. The Poetics and Politics of Ethnography.* Berkeley, CA and London: California University Press. pp. 77–97.

Sahlins, Marshall (1961) 'The segmentary lineage: an organization of predatory expansion', *American Anthropologist*, 63: 323, 335, 343.

Sahlins, Marshall (1976) *Culture and Practical Reason.* Chicago and London: University of Chicago Press.

Shapin, Steven (1994) *A Social History of Truth. Civility and Science in Seventeenth-Century England.* Chicago and London: University of Chicago Press.

Smith, Mary (1954) *Baba of Caro.* London: Faber and Faber.

Spencer, Jonathan (1989) 'Anthropology as a kind of writing', *Man*, 24: 145–64.

Spencer, Jonathan (1990) *A Sinhala Village in a Time of Trouble. Politics and Change in Rural Sri Lanka*. Oxford: Oxford University Press.

Spencer, P. (ed.) (1990) *Anthropology and the Riddle of the Sphinx: Paradox and Change in the Life Course* (ASA Monograph 28). London: Routledge.

Stafford, Charles (1995) *The Roads of Chinese Childhood: Learning and Identification in Angang*. Cambridge: Cambridge University Press.

Stocking, George (1984) 'Radcliffe-Brown and British social anthropology', in G. Stocking (ed.), *Functionalism Historicised: Essays on British Social Anthropology*. Madison, WI: Wisconsin University Press. pp. 131–91.

Stokes, Martin (1992) *The Arabesk Debate: Music and Musicians in Modern Turkey*. Oxford: The Clarendon Press.

Strathern, Marilyn (1980) 'No nature, no culture: the Hagen case', in C. MacCormack and M. Strathern (eds), *Nature, Culture and Gender*. Cambridge: Cambridge University Press. pp. 174–222.

Strathern, Marilyn (1986) 'The limits of auto-anthropology', in A. Jackson (ed.), *Anthropology at Home* (ASA Monograph 25). London: Tavistock. pp. 16–37.

Strathern, Marilyn (1988) *The Gender of the Gift*. Berkeley, CA: University of California Press.

Strathern, Marilyn (1992a) *After Nature: English Kinship in the Late Twentieth Century*. Cambridge: Cambridge University Press.

Strathern, Marilyn (1992b) *Reproducing the Future: Anthropology, Kinship and the New Reproductive Technologies*. Manchester: Manchester University Press.

Strathern, Marilyn (1994a) 'Parts and wholes: refiguring relationships' and 'intellectual roots', in R. Borowsky (ed.), *Assessing Cultural Anthropology*. New York: McGraw–Hill. pp. 204–17.

Strathern, Marilyn (1994b) *Partial Connections*. London: Rowan and Littlefield.

Strathern, Marilyn (ed.) (1995a) *Shifting Contexts. Transformations in Anthropological Knowledge* (ASA Decennial Monograph). London and New York: Routledge.

Strathern, Marilyn (1995b) *The Relation. Issues in Complexity and Scale*. Cambridge: Prickly Pear Press.

Thomas, Nicholas (1994) *Colonialism's Culture: Anthropology, Travel and Government*. Cambridge: Polity Press.

Tonkin, E., McDonald, M. and Chapman, M. (eds) (1989) *History and Ethnicity* (ASA Monograph 27). London: Routledge.

Toren, Christina (1990) *Making Sense of Hierarchy: Cognition as Social Process in Fiji*. London: Athlone.

Turner, Victor (1957) *Schism and Continuity in an African Society: A Study of Ndembu Village Life*. Manchester: Manchester University Press.

Turner, Victor (1967) *The Forest of Symbols: Aspects of Ndembu Ritual*. Ithaca, NY: Cornell University Press.

Wallman, S. (ed.) (1992) *Contemporary Futures: Perspectives from Social Anthropology* (ASA Monograph 30). London: Routledge.

Watson, Helen (1991) *Women of the City of the Dead*. London: Hurst.

Werbner, Pnina (1980) *The Migration Process*. Oxford: Berg.

Werbner, Pnina (1997) '"The Lion of Lahore": anthropology, cultural performance and Imran Khan', in S. Nugent and C. Shore (eds), *Anthropology and Cultural Studies*. London and Chicago: Pluto Press. pp. 34–67.

Werbner, Richard (1990) 'The Manchester School in Central Africa', in R. Fardon (ed.), *Localizing Strategies*. Edinburgh: Edinburgh University Press.

Werbner, Richard (1991) *Tears of the Dead. The Social Biography of an African Family*. Edinburgh: Edinburgh University Press.

Wolf, Eric (1982) *Europe and the People without History*. Berkeley, CA and London: University of California Press.

Wright, Susan (1995) 'Anthropology: still the uncomfortable discipline?', in A. Ahmed and C. Shore (eds), *The Future of Social Anthropology. Its Relevance to the Contemporary World*. London and Atlantic Highlands, NJ: Athlone. pp. 65–93.

5

Into the Community

LODEWIJK BRUNT

The development and state of the social disciplines – especially anthropology and sociology – are inter-related intimately with ethnography and the study of communities (Hammersley, 1990: 3, 4). For many decades community studies have been practically the only way for students of social life to get some empirically based insight into human relationships and activities. For many people doing social research meant doing the study of a community. Some communities, like for instance the Trobrianders studied by Malinowski (1922) or the East Londoners described by Young and Willmott (1962), have become famous among social researchers and perhaps even the general public. In this chapter an attempt is made to get the genre of community studies into perspective. What different kinds of community studies might be distinguished and what have been their contributions to sociology and anthropology? Despite the fact that the genre has also been heavily criticized, empirical data are still being generated by the studying of communities. But the nature of these communities has changed radically, not only as a consequence of fundamental social change but also as a consequence of social researchers having different ideas about what constitutes a community.

The Nature of the Community

With respect to the importance of community studies in the development of academic anthropology and sociology, it may seem that there would be some consensus among the practitioners of these disciplines as to the nature of the community concept. For a substantial period this consensus appears indeed to have been present, mainly derived from the association between community and place. Two well-known pioneers in the tradition of community studies, Warner and Lunt (1941), stipulate that communities are collections of people sharing certain interests, sentiments, behaviour and objects by virtue of their membership of a social group. In primitive societies such communities are called 'tribes', 'bands' or 'clans', according to the authors, and in modern societies we speak of 'cities', 'towns' or 'neighbourhoods'. The common element of these different social groups is place. As Warner and Lunt (1941: 16, 17) explain: 'All are located in a given territory which they partly transform for the purpose of maintaining the physical and social life of the group, and all the individual members of these groups have social relations directly or indirectly with each other.' In looking for a suitable community to study, they went looking for an old New England community with an uninterrupted tradition and a large number of unique characteristics. 'Our search was for a community sufficiently autonomous to have a separate life of its own, not a mere satellite in the metropolitan area of a large city. Hence we hoped to find a place with a farming area around it, since this could be taken to imply that the community possessed a certain separation from other urban areas and a unity of its own,' say the authors (Warner and Lunt, 1941: 38, 39).

West (1945) undertook much the same enquiry in order to locate a 'pure' community, that had to be untouched by modern influences and that ought therefore to be situated at quite some distance from any highway. His 'Plainville, USA', where he eventually landed because his car had broken down in that very community, was supposed to be an almost self-sufficient agrarian settlement without recent immigrants, any amount of black inhabitants or even a native 'aristocracy'. The author had hoped 'to find a community where people were all living as nearly as possible on the same social and financial plane' (West, 1945: viii). In reality, however, there appeared to be outspoken social and hierarchical inequalities among the citizens of Plainville, mainly expressed by differences in ways of life or 'manners' as the locals themselves would have it (West, 1945: 120 ff).

The conception of a more or less autonomous and isolated human group is firmly rooted in biologically oriented nineteenth-century thinking. Human behaviour and human interaction could best be studied in their proper and original natural environment. Many of the founders of modern academic anthropology and sociology based their community studies on what Fletcher considers as the 'formula' of Frederic Le Play, that is, the close connection this French researcher declared to be existing between family, work and place (Fletcher, 1971: 833). When Dorothy and John Keur set out to study the Drents village of Anderen, in the eastern part of the Netherlands, they found this small and isolated community 'well suited to our research needs' (Keur and Keur, 1955: 13, 14). Work (agriculture), family and place (soil) play central parts in their study. The culture of a people, they argue, is greatly dependent on the soil and the climate in which it is rooted. 'Human culture is cut to fit nature's cloth', the authors say. 'While a large range of cultural manifestations may appear in the same environmental setting, as a variety of plants in botanical associations, not all will prove equally successful or even necessarily survive' (Keur and Keur 1955: 14). Not surprisingly they were interested in studying the connection between nature and culture. How far would the natural environment of the village determine the local cultural development? The title of their book – *The Deeply Rooted* – gives a clear clue of their findings. Even Elias, writing in the 1970s and pretending to be able to point out radical new ways of studying communities, conforms rather strictly to the association of social group and place. 'A community', the author argues (1974: xix), 'is a group of households situated in the same locality and linked to each other by functional interdependencies which are closer than interdependencies of the same kind with other groups of people within the wider social field to which a community belongs.' The author appears to be referring to exactly the kind of social group Warner and Lunt were looking for in New England, West was trying to find in the Mid West and the Keurs had expected to locate in the Netherlands.

With respect to locality or place there is no fundamental difference between an isolated agricultural village and the neighbourhood of a metropolis. 'The city is not [...] an artificial construction. It is involved in the vital processes of the people who compose it; it is a product of nature, and particularly of human nature,' states Park (1925: 1) in his classical blueprint for the analysis of the city. In this research programme, which has been a major source of inspiration for generations of academic urban explorers, the author exposes a sociological perspective on cities and urban life. The way inhabitants of cities are organized in groups and institutions, he argues, is not fundamentally different from any other form of human social life. The city and its inhabitants are organically related and might be considered as a corporate expression of both individual and social interests. The city is the 'natural habitat of civilized man', according to Park (1925: 2), and represents therefore a peculiar 'cultural type'. But as such the city constitutes an ideal location for sociological research. Civilized man is as interesting an object of investigation as primitive man, Park points out in a well-known passage. 'The same patient methods of observation which anthropologists [...] have expended on the study of the life and manners of the North American Indian might even be more fruitfully employed in the investigation of the customs, beliefs, social practices, and general conceptions of life prevalent in Little Italy on the lower North Side in Chicago, or in recording the more sophisticated folkways of the inhabitants of Greenwich Village and the neighborhood of Washington Square, New York' (Park, 1925: 3).

Just like the Keurs, who saw a strong relationship between the culture of Anderen and its natural environment, Park underlines the fact that 'the city is rooted in the habits and customs of the people who inhabit it. The consequence is that the city possesses a moral as well as a physical organization, and these two mutually interact in characteristic ways to mold and modify one another' (Park, 1925: 4). The most elementary forms of association one finds in the city, neighbourhoods, are based – as in the isolated villages of primitive man – on proximity and social contact. Each urban neighbourhood has its own special character, determined by interests and sentiments and the stability of the population, and together these neighbourhoods form the building blocks of the city. Although neighbourhoods sometimes are close in a physical sense, the social distance between them may be almost unbridgeable. This principle has been beautifully demonstrated by Zorbaugh (1929), one of Park's many talented pupils, and it has become the basis for the famous credo of the so-called Chicago School of urban sociology: the city as being 'a mosaic of little worlds which touch but do not interpenetrate' (Park, 1925: 40).

The seemingly universal character of the community, a social group based on place or a 'localized society' in the words of Anderson (1960: 24), has led some observers to conclude that the community is an integral part of the biological make-up of humankind. Without them, people would not be able to survive (Arensberg and Kimball, 1965: 97, 98; Scherer, 1972: xi, 2, 3). Apart from the notion of locality, however, there has not been much agreement among professional sociologists and anthropologists about the way communities are to be distinguished from other social phenomena. How can you recognize them? How can you be sure that communities still exist? Especially in the 1960s and 1970s when many things appeared to be changing rapidly, the concept of community was sometimes fiercely contested in anthropological and sociological circles. The atmosphere is aptly characterized by Warren (1969: 40), who ironically declares that 'the community is going to hell because I don't know the name of the man across the street in apartment 4B'. The reason for this crisis, according to this author, is the tendency to perceive communities primarily as localities. The existing notions about communities are too much oriented to the 'rural, sacred, primary-group-oriented, preindustrial society' (Warren, 1969: 42). In Warren's view communities have at least two dimensions: place and specific interests. Through these interests, according to the author, communities are linked with the wider world. The changes that have taken place amount to the increase of the importance of this dimension at the cost of the dimension of place.

However this may be, it does not enhance the visibility of communities. Even scholars who are convinced of the central place communities have in the life of human beings admit to the difficulty of this question. Scherer (1972: 2, 3) declares that human communities have always been in existence and will always be there, but she points out that modern communities have become less discernible than in earlier times. Social structures have become vague and flexible, according to this author, the best we can say is that communities are situated somewhere between the individual and the society. Hillery (1955) tried hard to find some common ground in the almost hundred definitions of community he had analysed but he did not succeed very convincingly, although there appeared to be some consensus about the nature of small, rural communities. Anderson (1960), who is citing Hillery's endeavour, seems to be quite pleased by the result. The fact that there are so many definitions to be analysed, he argues, is a clear indication of the importance of the community concept in the social disciplines (Anderson, 1960: 25). Others are rather sceptical. Many definitions were mutually exclusive, found Bell and Newby (1971: 29): 'A community cannot be an area and not be an area.' The only element all definitions appeared to have in common, the authors remark, is that they were dealing with people.

After a review of different attempts at all-encompassing definitions, Anderson (1960) sums up all the elements that seem to be of importance in connection to the community. 'The community, in short, may be thought of as a global social unity in which exist various types of social organization; it is also a location, and it is also a place where people find the means to live,' the author says. He continues: 'It is a place not only of economic activity and of human association, but it is also a place where memories are centered, both individual and "folk" memories. Moreover, the community has the quality of duration, representing an accumulation of group experiences which comes out of the past and extends through time, even though the individuals making up the community are forever coming and going' (Anderson, 1960: 26). We may conclude that according to this perspective there is little that does not belong to a community. No wonder, perhaps, that Anderson is pointing out that communities are dynamic and changing and could have many different qualities. 'In other words,' he remarks, 'the nature and extent of one's community is largely a matter of individual definition' (Anderson, 1960: 27).

IMAGINATION

Do communities exist in social reality or are they to be considered as some figment of the imagination? What about local identity? According to Lasch (1991), the concept of community, along with the whole discourse on the dichotomizing of 'folk' and 'urban' or '*Gemeinschaft*' and '*Gesellschaft*', etc. has led sociology and anthropology into a dead end street. The existence of a community, or even a separate family that is supposed to be characterized by such elements as intimacy, particularism, protection, solidarity and mutual care, has probably always been an illusion. 'The history of the modern family', exclaims the author (1991: 166) somewhat pathetically, 'shows the difficulty of making domestic life a haven in a heartless world. Not only has marriage become a contractual arrangement, revocable at will, but the pervasive influence of the market – the most obvious example of which is the inescapability of commercial television – makes it more and more difficult for parents to shelter their children from the world of glamour, money, and power.' In opposition to 'society', the concept of community has often been used as a device for generating nostalgic images of a harmonious, idyllic way of life.

Gusfield (1975) argued much the same some fifteen years earlier, but the outcome of his criticism is much more constructive. The dichotomous concepts of community and society, according to this author, are analytical by nature, not empirical. They refer to different types of human interaction and not necessarily to place (Gusfield, 1975: 33). Communities, by implication, should be perceived as entities consisting of people who consider themselves as being part of the same history or destiny, whether they are interacting with each other or not. A community is based on symbols or even attitudes, rather than concrete villages or urban neighbourhoods. In complex, pluralistic societies people have a multitude of identities that could generate the kinds of loyalties and motivations that constitute communities (Gusfield, 1975: 42). We should be very careful using the dichotomy of community and society, according to the same author, because we can easily be led to believe that there are no elements of communities to be found in anonymous cities, nor expressions of rational interests in small villages.

Gusfield's vision, however, had already been put into practice. In the 1968 Introduction to the revised edition of their 'classic' *Small Town in Mass Society* Vidich and Bensman point out the success they have had in abolishing the notion that there is a 'dichotomous difference between urban and rural, sacred and secular, mechanical and organic forms of social organization' (1968: vii). In their report they underline the relationship between Springdale, pseudonym for the New York community they studied, and the larger society of which it is part. They found overwhelming proof that 'even those local accomplishments of which the people were so proud were the results of operations of the large-scale, impersonal machinery of outside organizations whose policies in most cases were not even addressed to Springdale as a particular place but to Springdale as one of hundreds of similar towns which fell in a given category [...]. Springdale could only respond to these outside forces, but quite often took its own response to be a sign that the town was being original and creative' (Vidich and Bensman, 1968: 317, 318).

We have seen that there have been episodes in the development of the social disciplines in which communities were thought to have some definite local basis – a place – but anthropologists and sociologists have gradually realized the limitations of such a perception. In the course of the years it has become increasingly more difficult to find the 'pure' and 'untouched' villages that the first generation of community researchers have been looking for (assuming that such an endeavour has ever been possible). In the course of the twentieth century, however, it became progressively clear that such a condition had become exceptional rather than the usual or normal state of human affairs. Both social and geographical mobility did increase dramatically. Humankind had become 'foot-loose' on a global scale; a person will probably live and work in quite a number of different places during his or her lifetime, whereas his or her family, not to mention friends, colleagues or acquaintances, can be scattered all over the world. From the 1970s onwards many anthropologists have been redirecting their research interest from the countryside towards the cities, in most cases just following their informants

who were part of these processes of migration and urbanization. In their new fields of study they have been able to demonstrate that even as local communities are dispersed, for instance by migration, many people still retain a strong feeling of belonging and loyalty. These sentiments have sometimes appeared to constitute a strong force in uniting immigrant communities in the city. Anthropologists, however, have been able to show that the foundations of these communities are often invented or 'imagined'. But in a way, even Springdale is an invented community. Whereas its inhabitants proudly stress their local and cultural autonomy, in reality there is very little ground for this boosterism. Anderson (1991: 6) pertinently remarks: 'In fact, all communities larger than primordial villages of face-to-face contact (and perhaps even these) are imagined.' In the minds of all people you will find images of the communities – especially nations – they feel they belong to although they 'will never know their fellow-members, meet them, or even hear of them'. An important criterion used by Anderson to speak of a community is the existence of a 'deep, horizontal comradeship' that binds its members, regardless of any actual inequality or exploitation that may prevail (Anderson, 1991: 7).

And yet we have to be careful in concluding that the relationship between communities and place has come to a definite end. There is no need to assume that 'social areas' correspond necessarily to 'natural areas', according to Hunter (1974: 25), who studied the nature of communities in the city of Chicago. In his view communities are primarily symbolic by nature and are determined by names and other symbols, like flags, songs, frontiers or certain forms of behaviour. The content and meaning of these symbols are constructed through human interaction, which implies that communities like urban neighbourhoods are social products. As a consequence, in cities you are confronted with 'symbolic ambivalence' (Hunter, 1974: 192). Cities are not the neat mosaics Park was referring to, for some pieces do not fit and others are lost. Urban neighbourhoods often overlap and are sometimes completely ignored. The complexity of the urban landscape is much too intricate to be projected on 'city maps'. Does this mean that we should forget all about local communities? According to Hunter (1974: 70, 71) this would not be a wise decision. Even in a city like Chicago you could distinguish neighbourhoods which, after many decades, still function as 'meaningful symbolic communities' (Hunter, 1974: 25). The author refers to well-known strategies employed by urban designers and construction companies to mobilize people on the basis of community symbols (Hunter, 1974: 70, 71). The power of such symbols was clearly demonstrated in Amsterdam when the authorities tried to enhance the reputation of a notorious neighbourhood in the southeastern part of the city. When the place was known under its original name, the *Bijlmer*, many inhabitants left the area and it appeared to be practically impossible to get people interested in living there – even when spacious apartments were offered at extremely low rents. Recently the name of the neighbourhood has been officially changed to *Amsterdam Zuidoost*, and this symbolic action does seem to have helped considerably – in combination with large-scale rebuilding schemes – in increasing the attraction of living there.

WHAT COMMUNITY STUDIES DO

Looking back at the tradition of community studies – which for a substantial part overlaps with the history of ethnography – one could point out different specific contributions that have been made to the general fund of anthropological and sociological insights into the way human beings behave and relate to each other. I will try to highlight some of these contributions, realizing that my list cannot be anything but highly selective. I have been inspired by some remarks made some time ago by Den Hollander (1968: 66, 67), who has been one of the most ardent practitioners of community studies in the Netherlands. The first thing to be mentioned about community studies is perhaps that they remind us time and again of the subjectiveness and onesidedness of social perception. Some instances of differences in perspective have become almost classic. The most famous are the controversy between Redfield (1941) and Lewis (1951) on their respective widely differing interpretations of the same (Mexican) village and the fierce attack on Mead – after her death – by Freeman (1983) about the analysis of social life on Samoa, where both had conducted research. In the Netherlands the religious village of Staphorst has equally been studied several times by different researchers, and although their results have likewise been different, this circumstance has not been developed in a spectacular academic 'affair' (Groenman, 1947; Nooy-Palm, 1971). Quite recently a similar question arose concerning Whyte's famous study of North End, the Italian neigbourhood of Boston (Boelen, 1992; Whyte, 1992).

Intended or not, many such studies have directed our attention to the intimate interrelationship between institutions, elements of the social structure and the daily life of individual people all over the world. Through these studies one can get some feeling for the local or regional consequences of national political decisions. In general, I think, community studies are excellent devices for exploring the discrepancies between rule and reality. In every society there is some distance between the 'public face', the way things and arrangements are

being presented to the outside world and the 'private wisdom' (Bailey, 1969: 5): the pragmatic rules of daily – political – existence or how things really work. At their best, community studies lead us to this private wisdom. In the 1920s the world was led to believe that the Turkish nation was on its way to modernity. The charismatic Kemal Atatürk boasted about his succesful attempts to ban traditional practices and to bring the position of the Turkish people in line with the principles of Western civilization. One of the most spectacular features of his policy was the introduction of a completely new legal system, directly adopted from the Swiss Civil Code. On the basis of this code it could be declared that the position of men and women had become completely equal. Was it? No! Community studies, conducted in the countryside, have shown us that Atatürk's influence could never have been more than superficial outside the modernized capital of Turkey and a few other big cities (Stirling, 1966).

Local communities can normally be found in a situation of encapsulation by political entities of a higher order, often national states. Sometimes this relationship is no more than nominal, in cases where the agencies of the central power do not have the wish, the courage or the resources to interfere. Bailey (1969: 150) refers to the situation of the British empire in India, where enormous areas near the borders of Assam, China and Burma were simply 'unadministered'. Such a situation sometimes occurs within the boundaries of big cities as well. Not only the fast-growing metropolises in nineteenth-century Europe had their vast stretches of *terra incognita*, the same holds true for the megacities in Africa, Asia and Latin America as we know them today. It has been estimated that of the fifteen million or so inhabitants of Bombay, more than half are dwelling in slums or on pavements. These people, especially the pavement dwellers, are to all practical purposes as unadministered as the Konds under the British colonial regime or Acheh in the Dutch East Indies. Encapsulation can also imply some kind of predatory relationship: so long as the inhabitants of the encapsulated communities – sometimes enforced by military expeditions – pay their taxes or their harvests, they can do as they like. Sometimes this takes the character of a special transaction resembling a protection racket: '[t]he peasants paid up on the understanding that the ruling power would prevent other powers from sending out similar expeditions' (Bailey, 1969: 150).

Another version of this relationship is called 'indirect rule', referring to the situation where local communities manage their own affairs as long as they keep from violating certain important principles. At the other end of the scale you will find the situation in which local institutions are being replaced because they are supposed to be primitive, criminal, anachronistic or otherwise in conflict with the values of the central authorities. There, processes of integration or assimilation are taking place. Many community studies could find a place in this particular categorization, even if the authors may not have been aware of the relationship between their community and its social and political environment. The Dutch fishing community of Urk was subject to forced integration at the moment it was studied in the late 1930s by Meertens and Kaiser. As a consequence of the construction of the *afsluitdijk*, the wall that closes off the former Zuiderzee from the open seas, the Urkers had to find different ways of earning their money. This would bring radical changes in the community, although the researchers did not seem to have noticed (Bovenkerk and Brunt, 1977: 20, 21; curiously enough, though, the changes on Urk were clearly noticed by Plomp, 1940). The Jibaros, on the contrary, are an example of an unadministered community in Karsten's report on them, written in the same period (Karsten, 1935). In his monograph the author is well aware of the precarious situation of the Amazon hunters he studied. He dwells on the oppressive character of the Spanish colonial power which caused the seriously decimated Jibaros to free themselves from integration and administration by hiding in isolated, unpenetrable regions in Eastern Ecuador and Peru. In the meantime, however, most Jibaros have fallen victim to integration processes again, forced upon them by independent nation states trying to convince the world of their modern identities or by private entrepreneurs who are exploiting the riches of the natural environment where they were hiding.

Community studies have been an important source of inspiration not only because of their sensitivity for the interplay between different levels of integration. They have other qualities as well. More than other kinds of social research they have been conducive in focusing the attention on matters such as class, status and hierarchy. I realize the controversial nature of this statement, for Bell and Newby (1971) have singled out this very topic as probably one of the weakest elements of the genre. They grant that many community studies deal with social differences, but very few have anything to say about power that is worth reflecting upon. 'Power has not been defined as a significant problem area,' they say (Bell and Newby, 1971: 219). They explain this sorry state by referring to the fact that most of the communities studied are so small that there is simply not enough power around. It does seem somewhat strange, perhaps, to consider power as a certain kind of quantity or substance. Is there more power lying about in towns and cities than in villages? That is exactly what the authors seem to be thinking. Their view of power and politics appears to be rather formal, closely related to the 'official' political arena. In their view politics is a matter of formal governments and authorities. But

many students of communities have demonstrated the profits to be gained, that is, a better insight into the functioning of communities, by a more informal and relational perspective on power. According to Boissevain, for instance, power is not some object but the ability of a person to influence the behaviour of others independently of their wishes. There are many factors of potential importance to consider if we are discussing power, explains the author, including 'wealth and occupation or special relations which give access to strategic information, or resources such as jobs and licences that can be allocated' (Boissevain, 1974: 85). Referring to (small) communities, anthropologists have identified the nature and mechanisms of 'local-level politics'. This phenomenon refers to special kinds of political structures, namely 'those which are partly regulated by, and partly independent of, larger encapsulating political structures' (Bailey, 1968: 281). Local-level politics concerns the struggle for power and resources that is going on in villages, universities, laboratories, football clubs, trade unions, brothels, newspapers and families (Bailey, 1969, 1971, 1973, 1977; Swartz, 1968).

One of the most famous examples in this field of class, status, hierarchy and informal, local-level politics is undoubtedly the 'Yankee City Series', to which I have referred before. Typical for the kind of perception underlying this research project is the discovery of the 'clique', which is proudly presented by the authors of the first volume of the series (Warner and Lunt, 1941). During the fieldwork it had struck the research team that many inhabitants of Yankee City used to place themselves in the community by referring to notions as 'our crowd', 'the Jones's gang' or 'our circle' – a practice, by the way, which is quite familiar in other countries as well. In the Netherlands you may part seriously, part jokingly announce that you belong to 'OSM', which is a shorthand expression for '*ons soort mensen*', 'our kind of people', and which is completely different from 'DSM', meaning '*dat soort mensen*', or 'that kind of people'. The researchers realized only after a while that such statements were of prime importance in assigning people to their actual positions in the local hierarchy. Cliques were almost as important as families in placing people on the social scale. They are explicitly considered as informal associations by the authors, without written rules of entrance, of membership or the termination of membership. 'It has no elected officers nor any formally recognized hierarchy of leaders. It lacks specifically stated purposes, and its functions are less explicit than those of the family, the association, or the institution. The clique may or may not include biologically related persons; but all its members know each other intimately and participate in frequent face-to-face relations' (Warner and Lunt, 1941: 110, 111). There will hardly be a sociologist or anthropologist in the world who does not know about the Yankee City class structure. This order of six classes, varying from the 'upper upper class' to the 'lower lower class', is determined by economic considerations, especially money, but also by more informal criteria such as membership of associations, families and cliques. Warner and his collaborators show convincingly how people try to maintain, or even better their positions by strategic marriages and friendships.

Warner's enquiries constituted a rich source of inspiration for other studies into power and politics, eventually resulting in the fascinating, still ongoing debate on the distribution of power. Is political power concentrated in the hands of a few almighty persons who decide over our life and happiness from behind carefully guarded doors or is it scattered over a colourful multitude of persons, corporations and institutions? Depending on your answer you belong to the 'elitists' or the 'pluralists' and both parties are relying on an enormous body of studies and reports that prove their point. Hunter's *Community Power Structure* (1953), based on a study of 'Regional City' might be considered as the elitist bible, whereas the 'holy book' of the pluralists is most probably Dahl's *Who Governs?* (1961) about New Haven (Bell and Newby, 1971: 222 ff.).

A further aspect of community studies that has greatly stimulated the maturing of the social sciences is their ability to present general phenomena in a local social context. In the introduction to his intensive enquiry into the lives of five American families, Henry explains that the direct observation of these families in their own environments will produce new insights into the emotional disturbances that were haunting each of them. The study of human beings in their 'day-to-day surroundings' is the author's 'compelling goal of my scientific life'. Henry tells his readers that he is repelled by the artificiality of experimental studies of human behaviour 'because they strip the context from life'. In doing so this behaviour is deprived of its meaning. 'I have to see *that person* before me,' adds Henry (1973: xv; emphasis in original), 'and what I cannot see as *that actuality*, what I cannot hear as the sound of *that voice*, has little interest for me.' In many of the better community studies this context is exactly what is being put forward. Young and Willmott (1962) present the strong links between mothers and daughters in Bethnal Green within the framework of the neighbourhood, where more than half of all the inhabitants actually had been born and raised. As a consequence of the fundamental changes that were taking place in the London docks, the continuity of the father–son relationship had been seriously undermined. Many of the local affairs had fallen in to women's hands. Wallman (1982) shows that for the London authorities life in Battersea is clearly associated with 'colour' and 'ethnicity', whereas for the inhabitants themselves the importance of these associations depends on the practical everyday situations they find themselves in. Sometimes ethnicity is of importance in interaction, but most of the time other things carry more weight. Human life, even in 'problem areas' in the inner city, is too complicated for simplistic notions. Harrison's study of yet another neighbourhood in the city of London, however, seems to reduce the context to just that: in his view delapidated neighbourhoods like Hackney are to be considered as places 'where all our sins are paid for' (Harrison, 1983).

An excellent recent example of involving the context into the community is Liebow's study of a small group of homeless women connected to a shelter in Washington, DC (Liebow, 1993). People's identities, according to the author, are closely linked to their jobs. This is no different for people who depend on shelters for an occasional roof above their heads. On the contrary, for it is acutely realized by many of the homeless women Liebow dealt with that a job could mean a way out of their situation. Yet, from the outside it may seem that such people do not want to work hard, or do not want to better themselves or are just plain lazy because many find it extremely difficult to find ordinary jobs or to keep them. In Liebow's study it is shown how tricky it is for the homeless to get regular jobs. Seemingly simple things prove almost unsurmountable obstacles, like not having a telephone where prospective employers can reach you during the day. Moreover, even menial jobs demand a decent appearance. How can you keep your clothing clean and presentable when you are living out of bags and boxes? Liebow mentions the case of some women who did succeed in keeping jobs. Grace was one of them, but she was privileged for having a car she could make use of as a closet. 'She hangs her blouses, jackets, and skirts on a crossbar,' remarks Liebow (1993: 55). 'Underwear and accessories are piled neatly in a tattered suitcase on the front seat. Each item is tagged and coded so that she can pull out a matching outfit with relative ease.' Still, in this study it is shown how easy it is for chaos to take over and how much energy it takes to keep being organized. Negative experiences can easily deprive you of your self-confidence if you are completely on your own and being jobless often means being dependent and losing your self-respect even further. According to Liebow, some of the homeless women seem to try to fulfil an almost primitive need in continuous fruitless attempts to get work. 'Their needs are pre-social, elemental,' he writes (1993: 79). 'They know they are in deep trouble, in danger of losing their sanity and their humanity, and they are struggling to hold on. It is as if [they] believe with Freud that "work is man's principal tie to reality", and they feel that tie slipping away.' Without this context it would be practically impossible to understand the meaning of accounts on work and unemployment. Not only for homeless women, but perhaps for the working population in general as well. Den Hollander (1968: 67) rightly remarks how important it is to read community studies, for there are almost no other ways to make people realize how dangerous it is to attach an overwhelming importance to statistical data or easy generalizations.

COMMUNITY STUDIES AND ETHNOGRAPHY

In view of the many stimulating results of community studies, it is not surprising that they have for a considerable time been considered as the principal means to obtain the necessary empirical material for the construction of ethnological and sociological theories. Ethnographers were sent on expedition to faraway places to describe the daily lives of unknown tribes and primitive peoples or were busy probing communities in their own societies. This latter activity was sometimes called 'sociography' on the European continent and it was inspired by a strong tradition of journalistic and literary urban research that was developed in many nineteenth century metropolises (Brunt, 1990). Both ethnography and sociography were means of fact-finding, and for many years practically the only way to gather social facts has been through the method of studying communities.

Within the social disciplines a division of labour had taken place from the end of the nineteenth century onwards whereby at least formally one category of academicians provided the empirical information and the other category took care of the interpretation of this contribution and the generalizations that could be derived from it. Fletcher, in his overview of the development of modern sociology, deals with the 'fact finders' in an appendix, but underlines his conviction that their contribution was of equal worth with that of the 'grand theorists'. 'Their contribution lay in a different direction,' he puts forward (1971: 839), 'that of establishing techniques of investigation, and producing accurate descriptive knowledge of the contemporary conditions of society, which, in addition to other knowledge, could provide a vitally necessary basis for judgement, decision, and action.' In the same spirit, Kruijer, in his philosophical treatment of the social sciences, characterizes sociography (and, by implication, ethnography) as 'descriptive sociology' (1959: 18). It is an academic discipline with a definite function. Whereas sociology in general is directed to the formulation of social laws and universal propositions, sociography and ethnography (including community studies) aim at the 'singular propositions' which are the ingredients of generalizations.

Sociography and ethnography are of a very different nature, generally speaking (Kruijer, 1959: 23, 24): the first is 'individualizing', the second 'thematic'. Individualizing sociographies and ethnographies are directed to the study of a single group or system intending to increase the knowledge of that very object. The degree to which individualizing ways of social research are contributing to anthropology and sociology in general is determined rather by coincidence than by intent. Thematic studies, on the contrary, are directly of relevance to the development of general insights. According to Kruijer (1959: 216 ff.), ethnographers and sociographers employ different methods to present their 'thematic' results.

First, the phenomena actually studied can be portrayed as examples of a certain concept or social type: some ethnographers of the Surinamese communities of Bush Negroes, for instance, have argued that these are to be seen as variants of a West African type of society (Herskovits, 1958; Köbben, 1979; Thoden van Velzen and Van Wetering, 1988). Kruijer (1959: 218) also refers to sociographers' attempts to show that a particular category of people are constituting a social system or a social group. Just as Lewis (1966) has been trying to argue that the poor are not just some statistical entity but share a characteristic, world-wide culture, the Dutch sociographer Haveman (cited by Kruijer, 1959) pointed out that most of the unskilled labourers are not some anonymous *residu* of the Industrial Revolution but have their own specific ideals and way of life (in Valentine, 1968, the concept of a culture of poverty is critically discussed).

Secondly, sociographers and ethnographers have attempted to ascertain that the communities they have been studying could be placed on some continuum. This has been done by Loomis and Beegle, who compared five different types of community in order to rank them somewhere between a *Gemeinschaft* – the familistic kind of society – and a *Gesellschaft* – its contractual opposite (Loomis and Beegle, 1950; cited by Kruijer, 1959: 219). In Miner's study of the French-Canadian parish of St Denis (Miner, 1939; Freedman et al., 1961) it is shown that the modernization of the region to the south of the city of Quebec makes small communities like St Denis move from the '*folk*' end of the continuum to the '*urban*' end.

Thirdly, communities could be described on the basis of features that are considered 'central' or perhaps 'typical'. The Dutch anthropologist Köbben argued that the community of the Bete, in the West African nation of Ivory Coast, is driven by a 'women's complex'. The number of polygynous marriages is considerable among them, resulting in dazzling prices men have to pay to the families of their brides to be. Most emotions, conversations and activities, according to the author, circle around obtaining and maintaining women (Köbben, 1964: 188).

The most outspoken representative of the tradition in which communities are considered as complexes that are organized around one or more central values or thoughts has been Benedict. In her famous *Patterns of Culture*, she puts the 'Apollonian' Zuñi in contrast to the 'Dyonisian' Kwakiutl. 'The ideal man in Zuñi,' says the author, 'is a person of dignity and affability who has never tried to lead, and who has never called forth comment from his neighbours. Any conflict, even though all right is on his side, is held against him. Even in contests of skill like their foot races, if a man wins habitually he is debarred from running. They are interested in a game that a number can play with even chances, and an outstanding runner spoils the game: they will have none of him' (Benedict, 1934: 95). This is a far cry from the megalomaniac paranoia that characterized the communities that peopled the northwest coast of the United States.

In all these examples sociographers and ethnographers themselves have tried to interpret the significance of their findings, but there have been several attempts to build up collections of social descriptions to function as reservoirs, from which to dredge the empirical 'facts' constituting the foundation for generalizations and theoretical propositions. The most famous of these collections were the Human Relations Area Files and the Ethnographic Atlas. In the Netherlands Steinmetz started in the 1930s to collect information for his 'Archives'. Murdock's magisterial effort to analyse the principles of human descent, marriage and family was based on the Cross-Cultural Survey, compiled by the author himself from the early 1940s on. From this system Murdock used information on 70 communities from his native North America, 65 from Africa, 60 from Oceania, 34 from Eurasia and 21 from South America. Some communities were chosen because a good source was available, other communities were ignored because overrepresentation of particular areas had to be avoided (Murdock, 1949: viii, ix).

The process of reworking community studies into pieces of knowledge that can be used by general sociologists or ethnologists has been described by Stein (1960). For his 'theory of communities' he had to strip community studies of much of their content in order to develop 'a reliable body of knowledge'. 'In our effort to develop a somewhat more general theory', Stein continues, 'specific emphases in each of the sets of studies had to be extracted and conceptualized differently' (Stein, 1960: 97). This meant that the sociologist not only neglected much of the information gathered by the sociographers and ethnographers but also had to 'distort' facts that had been conceptualized differently by the original researchers. No wonder Stein confesses to his theoretical elaborations as being 'a challenging and even frightening task' (Stein, 1960: 98).

The typical attempts of the early days of ethnography at conducting encyclopedic research, in which all the aspects of local social life had to be covered, have been replaced by more realistic and sociologically refined endeavours to highlight a limited number of particular themes. My own study of the Dutch village of Stroomkerken in the early 1970s was directed at the conflicts between the local population and the 'Rotterdammers', recent immigrants from congested cities who were moving to the village looking for space and a more natural environment. The city people had no idea as to the intricate ways in which the local political system was organized, and time and again there were bitter clashes between the representatives of the different groups about positions of power and distribution of services and facilities (Brunt, 1974). In Merry's wonderful study (1981) of a neigbourhood in an Eastern American city, three different groups of inhabitants are compared concerning their attitudes toward public space. As a consequence of the black population being much more oriented towards the neighbourhood streets and parks than the Chinese – the population of East European stock balancing somewhere in between – she did find vastly differing patterns of 'urban fear' and feelings of safety. Duneier (1992), to mention just another example, studied a community of eldery (black) men gathering regularly in a certain cafe near the University of Chicago. Most of them only knew each other from hanging around there, looking at each other and having occasional conversations. The central theme of Duneier's study is masculinity and mutual respectability among elderly men.

CRITICISM AND BEYOND

Community studies have been the target of fierce criticism, especially during the 1960s and 1970s when all of the social disciplines appeared to have been drawn into a deep crisis (Gouldner, 1971). At the risk of being unfair to all the critics I only want to point out the most fundamental objections being raised against the community studies tradition. Although critical remarks have been directed at such issues as the lack of agreement in defining communities, and the bias towards studying small, isolated (and therefore 'exceptional') communities, many of these points have been raised by ethnographers themselves. And more often than not they have tried to find satisfactory solutions. More threatening to ethnography and community studies has been the growing conviction, especially in the restorative post-Second World War decades, that the genre of community studies in general ought to be considered as unscientific by its very nature. A community study, according to a well-known verdict by Glass, is 'the poor sociologist's substitute for the novel'. Not only do these studies lack decent numeracy by neglecting elementary population statistics, according to this authoritive source, they have also a penchant for a descriptive, narrative style. To the dismay of Bell and Newby, who cite Glass' remarks with obvious sympathy and understanding, this means 'that community studies can often be read *like* novels and some have, indeed, reached the best-sellers lists' (Bell and Newby, 1971: 13; emphasis in original). 'Real science', by implication, would be something else altogether.

It is not entirely clear what a scientific anthropology or sociology would look like in the minds of the critics. Bell and Newby repeatedly mention the non-cumulative nature of community studies and, among other points of criticism, the fact that most of them are completely useless for purposes of comparison (Bell and Newby, 1971: 13, 14; 32). They echo some of the central arguments put forward by Stacey in a more general account in which community studies are declared 'mythical' (Stacey, 1975). This author rejects the very idea of a community on the basis of her conviction that systems of social relations do not have geographical boundaries (except for global ones). As sociology is all about comparing, 'so-called community studies' have to be displaced by 'the study of social relations in localities' (Stacey, 1975: 239). It is striking that community studies have often been judged by external standards. A community study, as we have seen, is by definition aimed at the development of singular propositions, not at large-scale comparisons. Many critics seem to be directing their scorn at community studies in general but in actual fact they appear to be aware of only one particular genre of community studies. Much of what they are saying might be highly relevant, but only for the individualizing kind – but even in the 1950s and 1960s that kind of ethnography was rapidly disappearing from the domain of the social sciences.

However that may be, it must also be noted that the criticism – of which we have seen only the tip of the iceberg – has been mainly inspired by a perspective of the nature and purpose of science which is, again, not necessarily shared by every practitioner of ethnography and community studies. I am referring to positivism. This particular brand of philosophy is characterized by three elements. First, physical science dictates how social research should be conducted in terms of the logic of the experiment: quantitatively measured variables are manipulated in order to identify the relationships among them. Secondly, explanation of social phenomena and processes should be based on universal laws (or propositions) or statistical probability. Findings should be generalized. Thirdly, there is an overwhelming concern with a theoretically neutral observation language; procedures of observation have to be standardized (Hammersley and Atkinson, 1983: 4, 5). Although from the 1970s onwards

positivism gradually lost its dominant position in the social sciences, it does seem that community studies have become stigmatized forever. Some people, outside the field of social sciences as well as inside, are still thinking that these 'soft' ways of doing social research are primarily associated with a primitive, 'pre-scientific' stage in the development of the academic social disciplines. But how scientific and sophisticated would the social sciences have been without ethnography and community studies to explore social reality?

CONCLUSION

For a long time community studies and ethnography have been the most prominent ways for anthropology and sociology to understand social reality. It was assumed that local communities were microcosms of human culture (Arensberg and Kimball, 1965: 97): by studying a village or a small town one gained an intimate insight into local manifestations of the social world of which these settlements were a part. In the introduction to the PhD thesis of one of his students, Steinmetz, the first professor of sociology and ethnology at the University of Amsterdam, explained what this was all about: 'We Dutchmen want to understand our own people and its subdivisions as adequately as possible and the only means to that end is to start with the study of the parts, amounting to a series of monographs' (Steinmetz, 1929: vii). The enquiries Steinmetz and his successors promoted followed a fairly typical pattern. The first chapters often deal with matters of nature, the soil and the climate. Then we get some understanding of the physical characteristics of the population, demographical developments and material conditions. The climax consists of the attempts to enlighten the readers on the temperamental qualities of the local people; what are the psychological and historical grounds of their folklore, habits and costumes? Reading these studies you easily get the impression that the authors did their utmost to present full and rounded descriptions, as if they had been trying to reconstruct the 'original state' of the population studied (Bovenkerk and Brunt, 1977). Although this kind of individualizing research has disappeared almost completely from the fields of (Western) anthropology and sociology from the 1940s and 1950s onwards, many people still have such studies in mind when referring to ethnography or community studies. The thematic ethnographic research of today, however, has a totally different character. The seemingly iron link between community and place has been undermined and not many ethnographers will be thinking of the social phenomenon they have been studying as a microcosm of a whole cultural universe. Ethnographers have become wiser, and therefore more modest about their pretensions. Nevertheless, one thing has remained the same among ethnographers since the early beginning of the academic social disciplines: they are still convinced that social research has to be conducted within some context. The community is as good a context as any, even if imagined.

REFERENCES

Anderson, Benedict (1991) *Imagined Communities. Reflections on the Origin and Spread of Nationalism.* New York: Verso.

Anderson, Nels (1960) *The Urban Community: A World Perspective.* London: Routledge and Kegan Paul.

Arensberg, Conrad M. and Kimball, Solon T. (1965) *Culture and Community.* New York: Harcourt, Brace and World.

Bailey, F.G. (1968) 'Parapolitical systems', in Marc J. Swartz (ed.), *Local-Level Politics.* Chicago: Aldine. pp. 271–81.

Bailey, F.G. (1969) *Strategems and Spoils. A Social Anthropology of Politics.* Oxford: Blackwell.

Bailey, F.G. (ed.) (1971) *Gifts and Poison. The Politics of Reputation.* Oxford: Blackwell.

Bailey, F.G. (ed.) (1973) *Debate and Compromise. The Politics of Innovation.* Oxford: Blackwell.

Bailey, F.G. (1977) *Morality and Expediency. The Folklore of Academic Politics.* Oxford: Blackwell.

Bell, Colin and Newby, Howard (1971) *Community Studies. An Introduction to the Sociology of the Local Community.* London: George Allen and Unwin.

Benedict, Ruth (1934) *Patterns of Culture.* Boston, MA: Houghton–Mifflin.

Boelen, Marianne W.A. (1992) 'Street corner society: Cornerville revisited', *Journal of Contemporary Ethnography,* 21 (1): 11–52.

Boissevain, Jeremy (1974) *Friends of Friends. Networks, Manipulators and Coalitions.* Oxford: Blackwell.

Bovenkerk, Frank and Brunt, Lodewijk (1977) *De rafelrand van Amsterdam* [The Underside of Amsterdam]. Meppel, Amsterdam: Boom.

Brunt, Lodewijk (1974) *Stedeling op het platteland* [Urbanites in the countryside]. Meppel, Amsterdam: Boom.

Brunt, Lodewijk (1990) 'The ethnography of "Babylon": the rhetoric of fear and the study of London, 1850–1914', *City and Society,* 4 (1) 77–87.

Dahl, Robert A. (1961) *Who Governs? Democracy and Power in an American City.* New Haven, CT: Yale University Press.

Duneier, Mitchell (1992) *Slim's Table. Race, Respectability, and Masculinity.* Chicago and London: University of Chicago Press.

Elias, Norbert (1974) 'Towards a theory of communities', in Colin Bell and Howard Newby (eds), *The Sociology of Community. A Selection of Readings.* London: Frank Cass. pp. ix–xliii.

Fletcher, Ronald (1971) *The Making of Sociology. A Study of Sociological Theory,* vol. II: *Developments.* London: Michael Joseph.

Freedman, Ronald, Hawley, Amos H., Landecker, Werner S., Lenski, Gerhard E. and Miner, Horace M. (1961) *Principles of Sociology.* New York: Holt, Rinehart and Winston.

Freeman, Derek (1983) *Margaret Mead and Samoa. The Making and Unmaking of an Anthropological Myth.* Cambridge, MA: Harvard University Press.

Gouldner, Alvin W. (1971) *The Coming Crisis of Western Sociology.* London: Heinemann.

Groenman, S. (1947) *Staphorst. Sociografie van een gesloten gemeenschap* [Staphorst: The Sociography of a Closed Community]. Meppel, Amsterdam: M. Stenvert and Lom.

Gusfield, Joseph (1975) *Community: A Critical Response.* Oxford: Blackwell.

Hammersley, Martyn (1990) *Reading Ethnographic Research: A Critical Guide.* London: Longman.

Hammersley, Martyn and Atkinson, Paul (1983) *Ethnography. Principles in Practice.* London: Tavistock Publications.

Harrison, Paul (1983) *Inside the Inner City. Life Under the Cutting Edge.* Harmondsworth: Penguin.

Henry, Jules (1973) *Pathways to Madness.* New York: Vintage Books.

Herskovits, M.J. (1958) *The Myth of the Negro Past.* New York: Beacon Press.

Hillery, George A. (1955) 'Definitions of community. Areas of agreement', *Rural Sociology,* 20 (2): 111–23.

den Hollander, A.N.J. (1968) *Visie en verwoording. Sociologische essays over het eigene en het andere* [Vision and description. Sociological essays on the own and the otherness]. Assen: Van Gorcum, Prakke and Prakke.

Hunter, Albert (1974) *Symbolic Communities. The Persistence and Change of Chicago's Local Communities.* Chicago: University of Chicago Press.

Hunter, F. (1953) *Community Power Structure. A Study of Decision Makers.* Chapel Hill, NC: University of North Carolina Press.

Karsten, Raphael (1935) *The Head-Hunters of Western Amazonas. The Life and Culture of the Jibaro Indians of Eastern Ecuador and Peru.* Helsingfors: Societas Scientiarum Fennica.

Keur, John Y. and Keur, Dorothy L. (1955) *The Deeply Rooted. A Study of a Drents Community in the Netherlands.* Assen: Van Gorcum.

Köbben, A.J.F. (1964) 'Het systeem van ceremoniële betalingen bij de Bete [The system of ceremonial payments in Bete society]', in *Van primitieven tot medeburgers* [From Primitives into Co-Citizens]. Assen: Van Gorcum, Prakke and Prakke. pp. 154–93.

Köbben, A.J.F. (1979) *In vrijheid en gebondenheid. Samenleving en cultuur van de Djoeka aan de Cottica* [In Freedom and Detention, Society and Culture of the Cottica Djuka]. Utrecht: ICAU, University of Utrecht.

Kroeber, A.L. and Kluckhohn, Clyde (1952) *Culture. A Critical Review of Concepts and Definitions*. New York: Vintage Books.

Kruijer, G.J. (1959) *Observeren en redeneren. Een inleiding tot de kennisvorming in de sociologie* [Observations and Arguments. An Introduction to Knowledge in Sociology]. Meppel, Amsterdam: Boom.

Lasch, Christopher (1991) *The True and Only Heaven. Progress and its Critics*. New York: W.W. Norton.

Lewis, Oscar (1951) *Life in a Mexican Village: Tepoztlán Restudied*. Urbana, IL: University of Illinois Press.

Lewis, Oscar (1966) 'The culture of poverty', *Scientific American*, 215 (4): 19–25.

Liebow, Elliot (1993) *Tell Them Who I Am. The Lives of Homeless Women*. New York: The Free Press.

Loomis, Charles P. and Beegle, J. Allan (1950) *Rural Social Systems. A Textbook in Rural Sociology and Anthropology*. New York: Prentice–Hall.

Malinowski, Bronislaw (1922) *Argonauts of the Western Pacific*. London: Routledge and Kegan Paul.

Merry, Sally Engle (1981) *Urban Danger. Life in a Neighborhood of Strangers*. Philadelphia: Temple University Press.

Miner, Horace (1939) *St Denis, A French–Canadian Parish*. Chicago: University of Chicago Press.

Murdock, George Peter (1949) *Social Structure*. New York: The Free Press/Collier–Macmillan.

Nooy-Palm, Hetty (1971) *Staphorster volk. Cultureel-antropologische verkenning van een streekdorp* [Staphorst People: The Cultural Anthropological Exploration of a Stretched Village]. Meppel, Amsterdam: Boom.

Park, Robert E. (1925) 'The city: suggestions for the investigation of human behavior in the urban environment', in Robert E. Park, Ernest W. Burgess and Roderick D. McKenzie (eds), *The City*. Chicago: University of Chicago Press. pp. 1–47.

Plomp, C. (1940) *Urk. Sociografie van een eilandbevolking* [Urk. The Sociography of an Island Community]. Alphen aan den Rijn: Samsom.

Redfield, Robert (1941) *The Folk Culture of Yucatan*. Chicago: University of Chicago Press.

Scherer, Jacqueline (1972) *Contemporary Community. Sociological Illusion or Reality*. London: Tavistock.

Stacey, Margaret (1975) 'The myth of community studies', in, Camilla Lambert and David Weir (eds) *Cities in Modern Britain*. London: Fontana/Collins. pp. 237–47.

Stein, Maurice R. (1960) *The Eclipse of Community. An Interpretation of American Studies*. Princeton, NJ: Princeton University Press.

Steinmetz, S. Rudolf (1929) 'Voorrede [Introduction]', in A. Blonk, *Fabrieken en Menschen. Een sociografie van Enschede* [Factories and People]. Enschede: Twentsch Dagblad Tubantia. pp. vii–ix.

Stirling, Paul (1966) *Turkish Village*. New York: John Wiley.

Swartz, Marc J. (ed.) (1968) *Local-Level Politics. Social and Cultural Perspectives*. Chicago: Aldine.

Thoden van Velzen, H.U.E. and van Wetering, W. (1988) *The Great Father and the Danger. Religious Cults, Material Forces, and Collective Fantasies in the World of the Surinamese Maroons*. Dordrecht: Foris Publications.

Valentine, Charles A. (1968) *Culture and Poverty. Critique and Counter-Proposals*. Chicago and London: University of Chicago Press.

Vidich, Arthur J. and Bensman, Joseph (1968) *Small Town in Mass Society. Class, Power and Religion in a Rural Community*. Princeton, NJ: Princeton University Press.

Wallman, Sandra, and associates (1982) *Living in South London. Perspectives on Battersea 1871–1981*. Aldershot: Gower.

Warner, W. Lloyd and Lunt, Paul S. (1941) *The Social Life of a Modern Community*. New Haven, CT: Yale University Press.

Warren, Robert L. (1969) 'Toward a reformulation of community theory', in Robert Mills French (ed.), *The Community. A Comparative Perspective*. Itasca, IL: F.E. Peacock. pp. 39–48.

West, James (1945) *Plainville, USA*. New York: Columbia University Press.

Whyte, William Foote (1992) 'In defense of "street corner society"', *Journal of Contemporary Ethnography*, 21 (1): 52–69.

Young, Michael and Willmott, Peter (1962) *Family and Kinship in East London*. Harmondsworth: Penguin.

Zorbaugh, Harvey Warren (1929) *The Gold Coast and the Slum. A Sociological Study of Chicago's Near North Side*. Chicago: University of Chicago Press.

6

Mass-Observation's Fieldwork Methods

LIZ STANLEY

the subjectivity of the observer is one of the facts under observation ... Collective habits and social behaviour are our field of enquiry, and individuals are only of interest in so far as they are typical of groups ... Mass-Observation intends to make use not only of the trained scientific observer, but of the untrained observer, the man in the street. Ideally, it is the observation of everyone by everyone, including ourselves.

(Mass-Observation, 1937: 2, 30, 97)

surrealism is a science by virtue of its capacity for development and discovery and by virtue of the anonymity of its researches. Like science it is an apparatus which, in human hands, remains fallible.

(Madge, 1933: 14)

My chapter is concerned with exploring some aspects of the history of ethnographic fieldwork methods in the period immediately before, during and then after the Second World War. This history closely involves an independent research organization, Mass-Observation, which had an extremely high public profile in Britain over this period. Mass-Observation was a mass membership and politically radical alternative social science research organization which was active between 1937 and 1949 (useful introductions are provided by Calder and Sheridan, 1984; Cross, 1990; Sheridan, 1990, 1994; Stanley, 1995b).[1] Mass-Observation overall, as well as the three particular research projects I will be discussing later, has an interesting relationship to the development of ethnographic methods. Mass-Observation was active during the historical 'moment' in which, before the 1939–45 world war,

the academic disciplines in Britain were shifting and changing, seeking new alliances or even reconfigurations, and then after it, when new boundaries between the disciplines were being assembled and they were jockeying for place in anticipation of the expansion of higher education. In this context, Mass-Observation acted as a catalyst, a point of reference, and also a source of threat, for a number of the social sciences; and it was also, although more covertly, seen as a source of ideas as well.[2] The role of ethnographic fieldwork in Britain over this period was undergoing considerable development, developments which also occurred across the three Mass-Observation projects discussed later, as well as within academia. Indeed, fieldwork methods of investigation were of considerably wider academic interest at this time than just to sociology and anthropology. In particular, in Britain there was an enormous interest in developing an applied economic sociology as a 'synthetic social science' which would draw all the others under this umbrella within the expected expansion of higher education, and observational methods were seen as providing a potentially key approach within this. Beyond these historical significances, Mass-Observation is interesting in the history of fieldwork methods in another respect, because of the attempts made in a number of its research projects not only to use such methods but also to represent the results of this in innovative ways.

In the following discussion, I explore the complex and interesting relationship between Mass-Observation and the university-based social sciences in Britain, outlining what kind of 'alternative' to university-based social science Mass-Observation provided and also some of the divergent emphases within it. I then move on to examine some of the issues that arise in making generalizations about what 'it' as an organization was and did. Amongst its heteroglossia of methods, Mass-Observation used a range of fieldwork techniques, typically in distinctive ways in its different research projects. After outlining some of the non-obtrusive fieldwork methods it used, methodological aspects of three particular projects Mass-Observation carried out are discussed. These projects are known as *May the Twelfth*, the 'Economics of Everyday Life' and 'Little Kinsey'; they have been chosen for discussion here because, although they were carried out in different phases of the research 'life' of Mass-Observation between 1937 and 1949, they used related methodological strategies but had different degrees of success in bringing these to written and published conclusion.[3] The final section of the chapter looks at James Clifford's (1988) idea of 'surrealist ethnography' and considers to what extent and in what ways these three Mass-Observation projects exemplify the defining characteristics of this, and also why they experienced different degrees of success.

Mass-Observation and Social Science

The genesis of Mass-Observation as an organization was 'announced' in a variety of ways by its three founders, Tom Harrisson, Charles Madge and Humphrey Jennings, in newspaper letters and radio broadcasts, and in its earliest publications. Mass-Observation was variously portrayed by them as a new form of social science, an anthropology at home, a synthetic sociology, and as an alternative to the very different form that the university-based social sciences of the day had taken. Therefore, fundamental to the way that Mass-Observation was constructed and publicly presented were its apparently sharp differences from mainstream social science. However, outside of such public pronouncements, a much more complex relationship existed between Mass-Observation and social science. For instance, a number of well-known social scientists were associated with Mass-Observation; most notably, Malinowski was its treasurer during the earliest period of its existence, but the economists Philip Sargant Florence and John Jewkes, the sociologist Adolph Lowe, the psychologists T.H. Pear and Oscar Oeser and a good many others had a watching interest, sometimes supplied small sums of money for particular research projects and more often sent students to 'help out'. Malinowski's impact went further than this, and the continuing emphasis in Mass-Observation of the central necessity of practical fieldwork is in part due to the influence of Malinowski on Tom Harrisson and Charles Madge, although in part also due to two other influences on Harrisson:

the work of Chicago School sociology, and the 'penetrational' fieldwork methods used by Oscar Oeser, which I discuss later.

Neither then nor now was ethnographic fieldwork in Britain exclusively associated with anthropology or with only qualitative ways of working. The work of 'Chicago School' sociology and its emphasis on observation and the conduct of fieldwork-based research was of interest to many British social scientists as well as to Mass-Observation. In addition, the Survey Movement of the late 1930s (Bulmer et al., 1991) encompassed 'surveying' in the broad sense as well as the numerical one, and a number of people associated with it were on the fringes of Mass-Observation, including Alan Wells (1936) and Terence Young (1934). In addition to anthropology and sociology, applied psychology and economics in 1930s Britain were also interested in fieldwork methods, with members of these disciplines having a range of involvements with Mass-Observation. Oscar Oeser, a social psychologist at the University of St Andrews, for instance, took a considerable interest in Mass-Observation's research in Blackpool in the later 1930s and his methodological ideas about the uses of 'penetrational' fieldwork methods for community studies played an important part in underpinning Mass-Observation convictions about the importance of fieldwork for the work it was engaged in (Oeser, 1937, 1939; Stanley, 1992).

The idea of a complete separation between an 'oppositional' Mass-Observation and an 'institutionalized' social science was, then, more rhetorical than matched by strict practice. Instead, a wide variety of crossover points existed between Mass-Observation and social science, involving ideas about new topics and methodological innovations, as well as the movement of some researchers from Mass-Observation to academia or from academia to Mass-Observation (Stanley, 1990). Another indication of this complex interrelationship is provided by contemporary academic reviews of Mass-Observation publications, which expressed interest in it overall but commented on what were perceived as serious methodological problems (Bunn, 1943; Johoda, 1938, 1940; Malinowski, 1938; Marshall, 1937), although some discussions were more critical (Firth, 1938, 1939) or later even dismissive (Abrams, 1951).

Mass-Observation came into existence around the 'Abdication crisis' of 1936 as reacted to by three men, Harrisson, Madge and Jennings, who had rather different characters and interests. Consequently, at its inception the organization was not one but three rather different although related parts, focusing around, first, 'Worktown' (the covering term for Harrisson's various projects researching aspects of life 'from the inside' in the mill town of Bolton) and also 'Seatown' (the working-class holiday resort of Blackpool, also in the North of England);

secondly, modes of representation and particularly photography and film (Jennings' photographs and film-making of 'ordinary life' in Bolton and elsewhere, and his interest in using the techniques of documentary film-making in textual form); and, thirdly, involving 'ordinary people' in observing themselves as well as other people (Madge's interest in the observer as a 'subjective camera', with useful facts being seen as the result of many hundreds of such observations, and his organization of a 'National Panel' of mass observers to produce these). There were also shared concerns which drew Harrisson, Madge and Jennings together, including socialist politics and an engagement with surrealism; the practice as well as theory of Mass-Observation; and a political and ethical commitment to reworking the relationship between 'ordinary people' and science. The result was what Nick Hubble (1998: 10) has termed its 'politicizing of aesthetic techniques'.

Madge was a fairly well-known poet as well as a journalist, and during 1936 and 1937 he had experimented with both collective and found poetry. His discussions of this, both contemporaneously and with hindsight, emphasized the anti-elitist ideas about authorship and inspiration which underpinned both. In his found poetry in particular, Madge juxtaposed images and apparently discontinuous text to encourage the active involvement of readers, as Jennings was doing with photographic collages (Madge, 1933, 1937; Madge and Jennings, 1937). One of Harrisson's (1937) first publications was *Savage Civilisation*, an idiosyncratic account of the time he had spent in the New Hebrides (now Vanuatu) living with 'head hunters'. However, this text is more than idiosyncratic, for it is structured around discordancies of images and styles and uses a kind of 'montage' approach to writing an ethnographic account that demonstrates the extent to which Harrisson, sometimes depicted as uninterested in or even antipathetic to surrealism (McClancy, 1995), was in fact considerably influenced by its ideas about representation. Jennings, a friend of André Breton, a key figure in French surrealism, was co-organizer of the 1936 international surrealist exhibition which took place in London and closely involved in formulating styles of photography and documentary film-making which eschewed or undercut the realist claims more usually made for these representational means (M-L. Jennings, 1982; H. Jennings, 1986). By 1937, Jennings had carried out a number of photographic projects with Harrisson in 'Worktown', and had also worked with Madge on the production of one of Mass-Observation's earliest publications, *May the Twelfth*, a book about the Coronation Day of George VI using a textual version of montage combined with collage, to which I shall return later.

The interest of Harrisson, Madge and Jennings in the practice and theory of Mass-Observation is connected through their shared albeit rather different interest in surrealism, more particularly the theory 'beneath' surrealism which reworks the Freudian idea of the unconscious by casting this as impersonal and shared and giving rise to collective forms of expression in the image (that is, its exteriorized form), rather than seeing it as operating through the symbol (which represents an interiorized, psychologized and depoliticized notion of the unconscious). Harrisson was always self-consciously concerned with the 'mass' in Mass-Observation, something expressed not least through his close association with the publisher Victor Golancz, who was to have published a planned series of books from its work (only one of which materialized), and who was the key promoter of the Left Book Club in Britain.

Stuart Laing (1980) has proposed that there were five key meanings to the notion of 'mass': the new social conditions of the 1930s, the 'common man', the mass as observers of society and each other, the collection and organization of large amounts of documentation, and the public. While these were all involved in Mass-Observation, particularly when the research eye moves away from the triumvirate of Jennings, Madge and Harrisson towards the large numbers of other people who very quickly became involved in its work, its activities included other meanings of 'mass' as well. In particular, as the quotation from *Mass-Observation* at the start of my discussion indicates, 'mass' included both a recognition of the individual nature of observation and also a principled rejection of an individualized idea of the individual. What the 'mass' in Mass-Observation was concerned with was a focus on habits or repeated behaviours and the observation of these, and not on opinions or thoughts. It was from this that its research genesis around the investigation of public reactions to the Abdication crisis and the Coronation had derived, for these were seen by Harrisson, Jennings and Madge as two related events of resonant social importance in revealing the collective unconscious around the interplay of 'surface and image'.

Jennings left Mass-Observation after the production of *May the Twelfth*, partly in reaction to Harrisson's overbearing approach but also to concentrate on documentary film-making and specifically the short on 'Spare Time', filmed in Manchester, Salford and Bolton. It has been claimed that the change in style of Mass-Observation writings thereafter resulted from Harrisson's suppression of Madge's surrealist concerns (McClancy, 1995), although in fact this was due to something much more mundane: the huge amount of very diverse research data that the National Panel quickly produced, with Madge as its organizer needing to find ways of responding to and dealing with this (personal interview, Charles Madge with Liz Stanley, 23 June 1990).

Sociology and anthropology, the disciplines most obviously challenged by Mass-Observation, responded to it with a fascinated gaze which was coupled with criticizing its approach as that of a failed realist 'documentary' project and also one which rejected scientific expertise (e.g. Firth, 1938, 1939; Johoda, 1938, 1940; Malinowski, 1938). Certainly one impulse in Mass-Observation promoted non-elitist notions of authorship, eschewed certainty and disputed the conventional authority of science; however, at the same time it also promoted its own (better) version of science, and notions of authority, hierarchy and expertise were still very much a part of its approach. For instance, it was Madge as the organizer, compiler and interpreter of the National Panel's monthly responses to 'directives', as well as Harrisson as the orchestrator of the diverse range of activities that took place in 'Worktown', who looked for not only the surface information in documents of different kinds, but also the hidden patterns that existed across them. Again, the quotation from *Mass-Observation* which opens my discussion suggests that these twin but, as it turned out, contradictory impulses were consciously and deliberately part of Mass-Observation from the outset. Thus, although Mass-Observation involved 'the observation of everyone by everyone, including ourselves', it also involved 'trained scientific observers' as well (Mass-Observation, 1937: 97). These 'trained observers' were the more permanent Mass-Observation personnel who soon joined Harrisson and Madge and then worked on or organized various of its projects, some funded via commercial sponsors, some from money given by Victor Golancz, Ernest Simon, Lord Leverhulme and other charitable sources of sponsorship, as well as through 'Worktown' and the National Panel.

In spite of considerable overlaps of people, interests and approaches between Mass-Observation and the university-based social science disciplines, important differences remained. First, howsoever embedded in ideas about science, the idea of 'us observing ourselves', with this being done by observers without academic training, went against the grain of the 1930s professionalizing approach in the ascendant in the academic disciplines. Secondly, the notion of mass observers as 'subjective cameras', with analytical interest being directed towards the complexities of *how* observers saw and interpreted as well as *what*, was one which proposed that 'subjectivity' was not an optional extra, a 'bias' that could be removed by rigour, method and training. Perhaps more than any other aspect of Mass-Observation's approach, this idea challenged the increasingly scientific notion of professional expertise in mainstream social science, and indeed, as I shall go on to suggest, the version of it also contradictorily present in Mass-Observation itself. Thirdly, Mass-Observation promoted use of a heteroglossia of methods, particularly non-obtrusive methods such as counts, observations, follows and overheards, as well as day surveys and day diaries compiled by mass observers (Stanley, 1995a). For Mass-Observation, what made these methods effective was their use in a variety of different locations and then the analysis of the resultant data by examining the internal differences that resulted, rather than attempting to iron most of these out as irrelevant 'ends'. Very different ideas about method were being promoted in mainstream social science, with the result that, over time, Mass-Observation's approach to sampling came to be seen as deeply flawed, its methods as producing renegade data, and its analytic focus on differences within a dataset as illegitimate (as Stanley, 1995a discusses).

ORGANIZATIONAL COMPLEXITIES

So far, like many people who write about Mass-Observation, I have treated it as the product of three strands of intellectual and political interest which came together as a single organizational entity: 'it' stood for and did various things. Thus its objective was to study British life and find out what people really thought and did (Hubble, 1998); it conducted 'an anthropology at home' (Chaney and Pickering, 1985, 1986); it used a combination of straightforward reportage mixed with social science surveys, with the Worktown project being such a survey (Baxendale and Pawling, 1996); and I myself have characterized it as a mass radical alternative sociology (Stanley, 1990). Having worked on a wide range of the projects associated with Mass-Observation across its original period of active life (1937–49), however, I have become increasingly uncomfortable in making such generalizations, given the way the organization changed over time and the large number of internal fractures within and the loose structure of it. Mass-Observation was actually less of a unitary organization and more a set of interlinked practical, political and epistemological projects. Moving away from the level of public pronouncement and into the everyday conduct of the varied projects associated with Mass-Observation, what is revealed is an internally complex and highly differentiated kind of research organization, one marked by divergencies and internal fractures as well as some common features.

There was the simple and obvious distinction between the National Panel research organized from Blackheath in London initially by Charles Madge, and the 'Worktown' projects orchestrated in Bolton by Tom Harrisson working with a range of colleagues and volunteers. Thus the different approaches embedded within Worktown and the National Panel indicate the one line of internal separation and differentiation.

In addition, the relationship between Mass-Observation and university-based social science was not only complex but also changed markedly over the period of the original phase of Mass-Observation between 1937 and 1949 (Stanley, 1990, 1995b). Harrisson's approach was typically oppositional and combative, but also contradictorily combined with determinedly seeking academic support and academic contexts in which to promote Mass-Observation. Madge, however, was more conciliatory, more friendly with many academics, and more attracted to the apparatus of 'science' in imposing some kind of order on the mammoth amount of data that the National Panel had generated.[4] Indeed, the difference went further, for Harrisson was a keen proponent of the idea that Mass-Observation represented a new form of social science, inductively producing social laws concerning the workings of society which would be directly comparable to the laws which the Darwinian approach had produced for the natural sciences; while Madge's goals for its research activities were more modest and focused on small accretions of knowledge gained piecemeal. Consequently their different approaches to 'the mainstream' and to research and science constitutes a second line of internal difference.

Added to this, there was a distinction, first in Worktown and then in the activities which grew up around Mass-Observation's London headquarters, between those people who were volunteer mass observers whose involvement in Mass-Observation might consist only of sending written responses to National Panel directives, and the people who worked (often without much payment) over sometimes lengthy periods of time as 'hands on' researchers. Both mass observers and more involved volunteers might take part in various of the different activities of the organization, and a particular project could involve a distinct set of people who knew little or nothing about those who were involved on its other projects. Moreover, the various projects carried out proceeded from sometimes very different methodological bases, with some adopting entirely observational fieldwork-based methods and others using more direct methods of questioning, and with some focusing on behaviour while others were concerned more with opinion. And this was in spite of the very clear rhetorical insistence in its more public pronouncements that Mass-Observation eschewed direct methods, used only naturalistic observational methods, and was interested only in behaviour and not opinion.

Also over the period of its original 'life' between 1937 and 1949, all of these different internal differentiations and separations within Mass-Observation could and did change over time, the fourth line of internal difference. The most important disjunctures are represented by prewar, wartime and postwar phases in the 'life' of Mass-Observation, but other changes also brought about knock-on effects over time as well. A key example of this 'domino effect' concerns the organizational crossover between Harrisson and Madge which took place in November 1938. Madge felt increasingly swamped by the vast amount of material that came into Mass-Observation's headquarters from its National Panel members, and this, combined with interpersonal difficulties between him and Harrisson, resulted in them swapping organizational places, Harrisson taking charge of the National Panel and Madge moving to Bolton to conduct research on the 'Economics of Everyday Life'. This changeover seemed to the volunteers who had worked with Harrisson in Bolton as effectively the end of 'Worktown'. For them the Worktown project was composed by the activities established and flamboyantly managed by Harrisson, while Madge's approach was more methodical and conventional and concerned to carry out a specific piece of research. Harrisson indeed perceived the change as considerably more than one of emphasis; in an undated memo to Dennis Chapman, he explained the difference by criticizing the 'academic tendencies' of Madge and Gertrud Wagner, a sociologist Madge had recruited to the project (Mass-Observation Hist: TH to DC undated),[5] their painstaking conventionality in research terms at the expense of verve and innovation.

Some of the implications over time can be seen by looking briefly at the research careers of two members of Mass-Observation. One of the researchers working on the 'Economics of Everyday Life' project, Geoffrey Thomas, cut his research teeth on it; when war started he moved into the wartime Government Social Survey, then postwar he became the Director of the Government's Statistical Office and so in charge of the decennial Census. The career of Thomas thus represents an approach supposedly the antithesis of the observational and non-intrusive methods pioneered by Mass-Observation in the prewar period, although, as I have already noted, beneath the rhetorical surface methodological matters were always more complex. Similarly, Madge developed ideas about research very different from Harrisson's and, through contacts which he established with the economists Philip Sargant Florence and John Maynard Keynes around the 'Economics of Everyday Life' research, in 1940 he left Mass-Observation to carry out savings and spending research for the government; and this then underpinned his move into more institutionalized forms of social science, initially as director of Political and Economic Planning (PEP) and then, in 1950, as Professor of Sociology at the University of Birmingham.

I shall return to the Worktown 'Economics of Everyday Life' research later, and have introduced it here to point up the complexities and changes masked by treating Mass-Observation in unitary terms, by showing how an apparently simple change could have consequential implications for a number of aspects of the organization. In what follows I explore some of the ways in which fieldwork methods were used in three particular Mass-Observation projects: *May the Twelfth*, a book resulting from an investigation of Coronation Day and published soon afterwards in 1937; the 'Economics of Everyday Life' project carried out between November 1938 and early 1942; and the 'Little Kinsey' project carried out in 1949 at the cusp of the change from the old-style Mass-Observation to its transition into a commercial survey organization. These projects span Mass-Observation's organizational life, involved different sets of people, and occasioned different methodological and indeed epistemological responses around the changing use of fieldwork methods within Mass-Observation.

FIELDWORK METHODS IN THREE MASS-OBSERVATION PROJECTS

For many social scientists contemporaneously, and indeed until comparatively recently, Mass-Observation was known about mainly through swingeing criticisms made of it by Mark Abrams (1951), for it has been only from the 1980s on that archival research on Mass-Observation has been carried out. Abrams' critique derives from a very different kind of methodological position from Mass-Observation's; in part it reflects Abrams' role in a competitor market research organization, and anyway it also reduces the complexities of the research ideas and practices being used by Mass-Observation to some comforting and dismissable simplicities. In fact, at any one point in time between 1937 and 1949 Mass-Observation was dealing with a large number of research projects around the three main trajectories of its activities, in Worktown, through the National Panel, and in the commercially funded market research which was sometimes co-terminous with its other work, sometimes tangential, but always financially important. The research methods used across these projects were very diverse, although a fair degree of commonality was provided, first, by key researchers moving across projects, and, secondly, because much of the written output from Mass-Observation was produced by a small number of 'writers' who worked in its London headquarters and whose work imposed a common rhetorical style on its written outputs.

The National Panel research, coordinated initially by Charles Madge, included the regular use of day surveys and day diaries as well as asking its members to respond to the monthly 'directives' or interlinked sets of questions sent out from London (Stanley, 1995a). These data were written up in different ways, including as summary discussions in the regular 'Mass-Observation Bulletin' sent to Panel members, as reports to sponsors and funders where appropriate, and also within other kinds of Mass-Observation publications.[6] Research in Worktown under Tom Harrisson was equally diverse, and included paintings and poetry by friends of Harrisson, photographs from Humphrey Spender, as well as essays and reports which resulted from Harrisson's promotion of non-obtrusive methods and particularly observation. Harrisson had indeed, on occasion, suggested observers should put corks in their ears, the better to focus their observation on actual behaviour untrammelled by preconceptions derived from hearing talk (and 'observation' here also included 'counts' of behaviours and 'follows' of people whose behaviour was particularly interesting). Harrisson's central concern was with behaviour and not opinion, with what was public rather than private, although overall the Worktown research, including the 'Economics of Everyday Life' project which I discuss later, also included talk, particularly in the form of 'overheards' of naturally occurring conversation, within the social context in which it arose. The commercial research undertaken by Mass-Observation could be carried out via the National Panel, or through the Worktown project, or independently of these. It more often made use of formalized counts, or utilized Mass-Observation specific ideas about sampling populations, or involved formal interviews of 'key people' in relation to the topic investigated. In addition, all three sites of research used a form of covert or informal interviewing, in which a mass observer would engage someone in conversation and in effect carry out an interview, but without the 'respondent' being aware that this was the nature of the exchange.

Much of Mass-Observation's research was topic-based, including around, for instance, smoking behaviour, 'the suit' worn by men and its social significance, anti-semitic behaviour in connection with fascist marches in London, purchasing behaviour in shops, and sexual behaviour of different kinds of which the 'Little Kinsey' research was its apotheosis (Stanley, 1995b) and which I shall discuss later. The non-obtrusive methods associated with Worktown research under Harrisson were those also at the heart of the 'Economics of Everyday Life' project under Madge. These were well-established and distinctive methods promoted bullishly by Mass-Observation in its encounters with mainstream social science, although the original source was Harrisson's insistence on the importance of 'actual behaviour' rather than post-hoc formulated 'opinions' about behaviour. The key methods here were: first, 'counts' of behaviour of particular kinds, sometimes at a number of locations at exactly the same point in time (some of the research used in *May the Twelfth*, for instance, resulted from this); secondly, 'observations' of behaviour, focusing on exactly what was done how it was done and by whom (Mass-Observation's research on men's and women's smoking, for instance, derived from this); thirdly, 'overheards' of talk, often private conversations publicly engaged in, sometimes public talk of different kinds; and, fourthly, 'follows', situations in which mass observers followed people around, observing what they were doing, overhearing the talk they engaged in, sometimes also making counts of aspects of their behaviours. One early example of this is a report produced on a fascist 'Black Shirt' march in Bermondsey in London in 1937 by Herbert Howarth (Mass-Observation File Report 1937 A3), which contains a reported observation of people leaving a tube station, the group they formed and the position at different points in time of individuals within it noted graphically; their talk and conversation is recorded verbatim and assigned to particular people identified by age, sex and so on; and the reactions, including the spoken comments, of the crowds assembled to watch the march, are noted.

May the Twelfth: Day Surveys and an Ethnographic (Photo)montage[7]

Not long after Mass-Observation came into existence and its National Panel operational, a leaflet entitled 'Where were you on May 12th?' was widely distributed from February 1937 on, asking for people to respond to a set of questions about their behaviour on Coronation Day in May and to send these anonymously to Mass-Observation's London address, with seventy-seven such responses being received. In addition, National Panel responses were sought and were received from a further forty-three people; a 'Mobile Squad' of twelve Mass-Observation roving reporters in London and elsewhere were involved in reporting and commenting on the day's events around similar questions; and Humphrey Jennings took many photographs of Coronation Day, mainly of the crowds that assembled and the buildings they gathered outside of or occupied, as his photographic montages of the day show (e.g. M-L. Jennings, 1982: 16).

May the Twelfth: Mass-Observation Day Surveys 1937 by Jennings and Madge was published later in 1937. The structure of this book in one sense follows the course of Coronation Day and its events as these occurred in different parts of the country. Thus its opening chapter is concerned with preparations for the Coronation in the three months beforehand; the second and third chapters provide detailed accounts of the events as observed in London and elsewhere in Britain on the actual day of the Coronation; the fourth chapter provides many

individual reactions to its events and emotions; and the fifth and last chapter provides the results of the 'normal' Mass-Observation day survey for May 12th 1937. Jennings and Madge describe themselves, and appear on the book's cover, as its editors rather than as authors, in fact two editors among seven, and they write that they had arranged the material they were dealing with 'in a simple documentary manner' (1937: 347). However, the 'documentary manner' involved is by no means simple and considerably departs from the 'record the facts = the truth' notion of documentary, as even a cursory reading of the book suggests.

May the Twelfth is in fact not concerned with 'the Coronation' at all in the sense in which other documentary media of the time was concerned with it. That is, it is not concerned with the ritual events surrounding kingship itself, the actual consecration and coronation of George VI. Its focus is not on the apparently main events of the day at all, but rather on the side shows, those mundane necessary events which had been carried out beforehand to make it 'work' on the day, and the minutiae of the activities that 'ordinary people' in London and elsewhere in Britain engaged in. These events and behaviours of 'ordinary people' are presented in the form of both montage, each chapter composed by numbered segments containing press cuttings placed cheek by jowl with personal statements with editorial interventions; and also collage, because a multiplicity of agreeing and disagreeing people, points of view and geographical locations are included. The effect is to turn the gaze of the reader away from kingship and onto the mass of people, something which ironicizes the ritualistic aspects of the Coronation, or rather democratizes it as actually an event in which the responses of ordinary people are central rather than ancillary.

At the same time, *May the Twelfth* is concerned with more than the surface of behaviours, events and locations; and Chapter Four in particular deals with the often perverse or unexpected nature of people's responses to the Coronation, occurring almost 'in spite of themselves', while in one section the responses of particular people are presented on the same page with the reactions of their neighbours. This chapter is preceded by a quotation from Freud's *Totem and Taboo*, and is primarily concerned with the personally unexpected nature of people's 'beneath the surface' emotional responses to the day's events, but the social expectedness of these in relation to the symbolic and 'primitive' ritual of the consecration of kingship. Thus Jennings and Madge, for instance, comment about a report of people exchanging clothing with each other that similar activities are also a feature of the responses of 'savages' to the totemic rituals surrounding kingship.

May the Twelfth centres people 'speaking for themselves', with the role of the editors in constructing this being only minimally signalled, typically by implication through the artifices by which material is included and arranged rather than by direct statement of their editorial activities. The result is very much to emphasize that there was no single 'May 12th', but rather a large number of occasions composed by the specific experiences of many groups of people in their particular locations and with their particular vantage-points and, once brought together and assembled within the text, by the multiplicity of differences between these people even though apparently engaged in the 'same event'. Indeed, the representation of these actually constitutes the organizing framework of not only this chapter, but also the whole of *May the Twelfth*.

As well as the text itself, there are five separate indexes at the end of the book. The 'General' index is a conventional topic-based one, but which once more focuses upon 'the people' and their experiences, rather than on kingship and the Coronation itself. The four other indexes are of London streets and other places, the cuttings from newspapers and periodicals used in the book, popular songs, and the reports received from mass observers. The effect is not merely to enable the reader to chart their own routes through the text, but also to enable them to construct their own distinctive version of the day through what is a kind of 1930s text version of the hypertext linkages that can be written into web-based electronic documents. The result of this innovative approach to indexing is to encourage, by providing the means for, an active and non-linear reading of the text, and by so doing to undercut editorial authority through its overt dispersal of control over how readers might use the text.

For the book's editors, there was a point to this research venture which went well beyond the investigation of Coronation Day itself:

> From a scientific point of view, this book so far has no doubt been of interest in showing the kind of behaviour which Mass-Observation can observe. But it has been arranged mainly in a simple documentary way, without much attempt to suggest further possibilities of analysing the material. The unity of the material on May 12 is due to all the social life of that day being hinged on a single ceremony of national importance. On any other day, this unity will tend to disappear, and it is for social science to discover the unity, or lack of it, which is typical of a normal day ... But the purpose ... is to show another way in which the material ... can be analysed. (Jennings and Madge, 1937: 347)

This 'other way' was to analyse the day survey responses in relation to 'social areas', the term the editors use to indicate the three kinds of social networks a given observer is connected with: the people they know first-hand in all aspects of their lives; strangers and newcomers; and those public and/or mythical people and institutions that form the 'social horizon' known only abstractly and at third-hand. These were then used, in 'an experimental and try-out' way, to analyse reports from three different kinds of people with the possibility of reaching a 'scientific classification'; however, the editors also note that 'Other persons classifying the reports would almost certainly reach a different set of results' (pp. 370–1). This raises the twin but contradictory focuses on 'scientific classification' and 'different researchers, different results' that I noted earlier; and here they mark not only the same project, but also the same analytic strategy.

A Missing Voice: The 'Economics of Everyday Life' Project[8]

As noted earlier, in November 1938 Charles Madge and Tom Harrisson changed organizational places, with Harrisson taking charge of the National Panel in London and Madge's new involvement focusing on directing the 'Economics of Everyday Life' project in Worktown. Madge's particular interest was in its savings and spending component and his wider role in this project tailed off and then ended during 1940. However, the 'Economics of Everyday Life' project and the involvement of its other researchers remained active until early 1942, and it brought together Mass-Observation's concern with the minutiae of everyday life and the idea of using an applied economic sociology to investigate the dire economic straits daily experienced by many working-class people. An undated Worktown memo (Worktown/46, from other evidence probably written between late 1938 and late 1939) provides a list of the key researchers on the project (Charles Madge, Gertrud Wagner, Dennis Chapman, Geoffrey Thomas and Stanley Cramp), and also gives information about involvement from mainstream social scientists (Terence Young at the University of London was carrying out a shopping survey for Mass-Observation; Professors Ford at Southampton and Jewkes and others in the Economics Department at Manchester University were asking students to go to Worktown; and the importance of 'Dr Loewe' and his *Economics and Sociology* (Lowe, 1935) and the work of Bowley and Allen (Allen and Bowley, 1935) is commented on).[9]

Another internal memo (Worktown/46.B) describes the project as concerned with the 'factors influencing spending and saving at the income levels which include the great majority of the people of England'; and it states that Mass-Observation's planned fifth book on Bolton would be the 'Economics of Everyday Life', focusing on the actual observation of economic behaviour in everyday life. An important part of the planned research involved an investigation of savings and spending and was Madge's particular concern,[10] although much of the research was carried out by other 'Economics of Everyday Life' researchers as well as by him. This included what was at the time the unusual (both for Mass-Observation and for mainstream social science) method of carrying out detailed structured interviews with individual savers and also with representatives from savings organizations. Alongside this, a number of more specifically 'Mass-Observation' kinds of research took place, concerned with clothes, including the social function of the suit; the effects of Lent on retail sales; household budgets; the Worktown stomach, and the role of money; and also the role of work in Worktown. These different aspects of research were combined (again unusually both for Mass-Observation and for mainstream social science) with a 'special area study'.[11]

The idea of 'functional penetration', drawn from research concerned with unemployed Scottish jute workers in Dundee carried out by Oscar Oeser (1937, 1939) and colleagues, was an important influence on the 'Economics of Everyday Life' project. Oeser's research was an early kind of community study using ethnographic methods, in which members of the research team lived and in some cases worked in the area of study. Harrisson was particularly interested in Oeser's work; Oeser had visited Mass-Observation in Worktown and also Seatown, and the idea of 'functional penetration' influenced the 'Economics of Everyday Life' project, including through its researchers forming a team, members of which lived in Worktown and carried out a wide variety of linked research activities there.

Another innovative aspect of the research involved a 'special area study' which focused on a group of streets in the centre of working-class Bolton, a total of 630 adults (300 males and 330 females). As well as looking at the occupation, employment situation and household spending and saving patterns of these people, the special area study was also concerned with 'opinion forming'. The study was carried out using ethnographic and observational means, with Mass-Observation's researchers here too being influenced by the idea of 'functional penetration' of an area, with different members of the 'Economics of Everyday Life' research team becoming members of and investigating different aspects of the local community.

There are a number of differences between the research that was actually carried out and the contents of the planned book, first because various of the original features of the research were never completed, and secondly because some that were, and particularly here Madge's work on savings and spending, took on a trajectory of their own. There are also important continuities. First, the 'everyday' aspects of economic life remained central to the investigation, with the researchers looking at topics such as the social function of clothes and of food consumption. Secondly, the main method of carrying out the research was observation of public behaviour backed up by 'counts', 'overheards' and 'follows', with direct questioning of people about their private behaviour and opinions being analytically secondary to the general patterns built up through non-intrusive methods. And thirdly, work was seen as fundamental to social life, with 'work' conceptualized so as to include domestic labour as well as paid employment within the labour force. Overall, economic and social life were conceptualized as one and the same, or, rather, the economic was seen as a definitional component of 'the social'.

A number of aspects of the 'Economics of Everyday Life' project were highly innovative. The project combined investigating the everyday with an inductive theoretical analysis of this, and in both respects differed from 1930s mainstream social science, apart from the kind of economic sociology being promoted by Jewkes, Lowe and others. It was aware of gender, as well as of age, class, region and temporality as structural variables. It took gender seriously throughout its composing pieces of research, including by arguing that women made the economic system 'work' while receiving only a small proportion of its resources. In addition, it emphasized that in Worktown women worked throughout the economy as well as within the domestic sphere of the household. The project centred the role of money as an anonymous system of exchange binding together production and consumption; and it recognized that the use of money, if not necessarily its generation or its control, was largely the prerogative of women. Here again the project was highly innovative in refusing to separate consumption from production, seeing both as symbiotic and as fundamental to any understanding and theorization of everyday economics. And as well as these innovations with regard to method and theory, the 'Economics of Everyday Life' project was methodologically and epistemologically distinctive in some interesting ways.

Its particular utilization of the idea of 'functional penetration' was premised on the view that social life needed to be experienced in order to be understood, and that asking questions 'from the outside' was insufficient for proper understanding, which required actual participation in some kind of functional role in working and living in an area as the basis of fieldwork. It was for this reason that the project was based on its fieldwork researchers living in the area and knowing and observing it from the inside, and they participated in a wide range of activities in Worktown and took it as axiomatic that their research required this.

The work carried out within the 'Economics of Everyday Life' project shared with Mass-Observation more generally the view that the observer was central to research, not merely as a collector of information from other people, but rather as a 'subjective camera', someone who necessarily interpreted what was seen and heard and therefore what was recorded. Consequently, what was recorded was treated as contingent upon those who researched it as well as those who provided it. The 'Economics of Everyday Life' researchers worked closely together, gathered daily in the house Harrisson had rented and which was used communally. The specific research they were each engaged on was discussed by all members of the 'Economics of Everyday Life' team. Their broad approach was very different from the developing ideas of mainstream social science concerning objectivity and detachment, for they saw knowledge as collectively produced, necessarily interpretational and grounded in specific contexts, times and places, although related to more general themes and ideas.

The 'Economics of Everyday Life' project also put its particular spin on the more general Mass-Observation view of observation as its methodological cornerstone. The larger part of the project's research was based on a range of observational studies rather than direct questioning or other intrusive or semi-intrusive methods. Its concern was people's behaviour, what people actually did, rather than their post-hoc reports or interpretations of it. However, this is not to say that the project ignored interpretation and its role in mediating between the observation of behaviour and reporting this, as already indicated. It saw knowing about a community or an activity as an essentially collaborative activity, in the sense of bringing together and using different accounts from observations conducted from different viewpoints. In addition, it recognized that the informal aspects of research, gained by 'just living' in the area of study, were as important as those activities formerly defined as 'research' in the narrow sense.

The 'Economics of Everyday Life' project was not completed nor was any part of it published contemporaneously, although many fragments of writing and many recordings of data exist; and so it is impossible to say with any certainty how the completed research might have been presented in a published form. What remains are the large number of fragments, and the incomplete pieces of writing that would have formed the basis of a final text. These give a fascinating, indeed tantalizing, impression of what might have been, but in the form of a jigsaw puzzle for which at least half the pieces are missing. A number of factors were involved here.

First, Madge seems to have undertaken the project with a specific interest in savings and spending derived from his discussions with Maynard Keynes, and he left as soon as this took off. He was also more often than not absent from the 'Economics of Everyday Life' research, even during the period when he was its director, and certainly he failed to give it the kind of firm overall guidance that

might have brought it to a successful published conclusion. Secondly, after Madge left, Harrisson and other full-time Mass-Observation researchers in its London headquarters were called up for wartime military service, and then, as money ran out and/or as the 'phoney war' gave way to real war, so the project's key researchers necessarily moved on too. Thirdly, without clear direction, the remaining research became more diverse, as the researchers 'followed their noses' and interests emerged 'on the ground'. And fourthly, unlike a number of other Mass-Observation projects, there was no experienced 'writer' involved who took or was assigned responsibility for writing up the research and so imposing some kind of textual order on its diversity. However, as the discussion of 'Little Kinsey' which follows will suggest, even if there had been a Mass-Observation 'writer' involved, a final published text might still not have resulted. The contradictory methodological and epistemological positions I noted earlier remained unresolved, indeed unarticulated, in this project, and led to the development of a positivist numerically based approach to savings and spending being carried out, but with this being hand in hand with the development of an observational and 'penetrational' approach to economic life more generally.

Who Says and What Counts? From 'Churchtown' to 'Little Kinsey'[12]

The research team that carried out the 'Economics of Everyday Life' project was one in which, initially at least, there was a clear chain of command from its director, Charles Madge, to the researchers who worked to his direction. Similarly, behind the proclaimed democracy of the mass observers' involvement in the National Panel there was a national headquarters and a chain of command in which other people, directed by first Madge and then by Harrisson, drew together the myriad of observational responses to directives. Thus a hierarchical organizational structure existed around the National Panel as well as the 'Economics of Everyday Life' project: embedded in Mass-Observation as an organization was a contradiction between its publicly pronounced principle of Mass-Observation and 'speaking for yourself', and its increasingly 'professional' group of specialists who produced analytical knowledge from the descriptions provided by 'their' mass observers and wrote its public documents. This contradiction became crucial with regard to the 'Little Kinsey' research carried out in 1949.

In March 1949 Mass-Observation produced an internal memo headed 'Directive for penetrative work on sex survey' (TC12: Box 2, File 15p; Box 3, File 15), which sets out a programme for three closely linked kinds of research within a special area study of 'Churchtown', the city of Worcester.[13] The first and most important was for observational research of public courting and sexual behaviour, to include at least three dance halls to be visited on a number of occasions over a seven-day period, the 'worst' public houses, and some pornographic bookshops. The second component was the provision of back-up statistics, including arrest figures for eighteen sexual offences. The third component was for two types of interview to be conducted: formal interviews with 'executives', including clergy from the main religious denominations, and 'representative' officials, such as a probation officer, police officer, doctor and bar keeper; and a larger number of 'informal' interviews, where the person concerned did not know they were being interviewed but instead thought they were having a casual conversation with a stranger. The formal interviews were to focus on people's views about changes in sexual morality, and the informal ones on courtship, picking up, and kissing, cuddling and other kinds of public sexual behaviour.

At the point that the March 1949 memo was composed, the whole of the proposed study was to consist of 'penetrational' work around the three planned components of the project in 'Churchtown', with this then being compared with another contrasting local area study, of 'Steeltown', the city of Middlesborough. The different components of the research were to enable the research team to 'compare and contrast' their observational and non-obtrusive measures internally *within* each area study against its statistical and interview data, as well as *between* 'Churchtown' and 'Steeltown'. However, the main focus of the research changed rapidly and markedly: the observational components became subordinated to three major national surveys which were carried out only a few weeks after the memo was written but which are not even mentioned in it. The first was a national random representative survey of 200 people – known as the 'Street sample'; the second was a randomly selected postal survey of 1,000 each of clergy, doctors and teachers – the 'Opinion Leaders' survey; and the third was a postal survey of Mass-Observation's 1,000 strong National Panel.

This research, known within Mass-Observation as 'Little Kinsey' because it was conceived against the backcloth of the recent publication of the first Kinsey report in the United States, was paid for by the *Sunday Pictorial* and was in part published in a series of articles that appeared in the newspaper on 3, 17, 24 and 31 July 1949. As well as these short articles, written by *Pictorial* journalists from materials supplied by Mass-Observation, it was also intended to publish a Mass-Observation book, and a manuscript was produced and sent to the intended publisher, Allen and Unwin. However, the book on 'Little Kinsey' was not published at the time,[14] and precisely why remains a puzzle which in the last

resort is insoluble, not least because the writer on this project, Len England, in 1949 also the Office Manager of Mass-Observation, was unable to remember the details of why it failed to appear (personal interview, Len England with Liz Stanley, 22 August 1990). However, three overlapping factors seem to have been involved: organizational changes within Mass-Observation; external changes which affected what were seen as more and less acceptable research methods; and the ways in which the earlier observation material and the later survey material, when brought together within the draft manuscript, occasioned intellectual problematics which Len England as its writer was unable to solve.

In 1949, around a series of internal changes and in the wake of 'Little Kinsey' being carried out, the organization's old-guard and most importantly its remaining founder members surrendered their managerial and other interests in Mass-Observation, and a new guard took what then became 'Mass-Observation Ltd' into a new life dealing only with commercial market research. Behind these changes was the development and use of the computer and the postwar availability to research organizations not only of computer facilities but also of researchers skilled in their use. By 1949 Mass-Observation had its own computer and a number of research staff who were computer-experienced and, more importantly, had a very different attitude towards what was methodologically acceptable. For these newer members of staff, most of whom had been trained in the context of wartime research involving the quantified analysis of attitudinal research using representative sample data, 'scientific' styles of research were deemed to be the only acceptable ones. Pressure from them meant that what had been originally envisaged as a piece of qualitative research in the observational style pioneered by Mass-Observation, added to by the statistical and interview materials, instead became a large-scale national representative sample survey supported by two smaller surveys (see TC12: Box 2/A, letter 10 December 1938 from Len England to Brian Murtough, the Features Editor of the *Sunday Pictorial*). These and wider related developments about 'scientific' research in postwar Britain contributed to what became the 'Little Kinsey' emphasis on attitudes, and the move away from the originally planned observational and 'penetrational' studies of 'Churchtown' and 'Steeltown'. But other factors were involved as well, connected with the existence of both the 'new' survey data and the 'old' observational data and how these were brought together in the manuscript of 'Little Kinsey'.

The three related surveys are reported on in the text of 'Little Kinsey' in a tabular form (usually in whole percentage terms – 'out of every hundred X responded ... '). These numerical statements are then embedded in arguments developed around the topic that each chapter focuses on, and they are surrounded by extensive qualitative material which had been written verbatim by the interviewers as they worked through the questionnaire with members of the 'Street sample'. However, cutting across the material derived from the three surveys, there is also an earlier Mass-Observation observational and ethnographic presence in the text. This is formed by extensive quotation from reports by the Mass-Observation researchers who had worked in the initial 'Churchtown' and 'Steeltown' phase of the research (in the chapters dealing with prostitution and with sexual morality in particular); by Mass-Observation researchers who had written about public sexual behaviour in Seatown (Blackpool) in an earlier prewar project (in the chapter concerned with sexual morality); and by a Mass-Observation investigator writing about his involvement in a 'homosexual group'.

This ethnographic presence is clearly articulated within the text, and in effect if not in intent it subordinates the quantitative survey data and its analysis to the qualitative observational material. The dominant note is the existence of differences of opinion and points of view between British people on sexual matters, with the result that these competing rhetorical and methodological presences speak past each other about different kinds of data and 'facts' about sexual behaviour and sexual opinion. Thus, for instance, the survey data in 'Little Kinsey' is itself used in a very particular way. Categorical conclusions are only infrequently drawn about any aspect of 'people and sex', and instead the numerical data are presented around comparisons and differences between the three different survey groups, and through statements about differences within each survey group by age, education, income, sex, by whether people lived in villages, towns or cities and whether they were churchgoers or not. The result is that almost every statement has alongside it an alternative one, with both being presented as factual and true for different groups and individuals. Certainly the text of 'Little Kinsey' at a number of points indicates that the facts must be allowed to 'speak for themselves', but then it goes on to provide *alternative* facts, depending on people's social location, their class, age, sex and so on, and also whether they were surveyed, interviewed or observed.

Such textual complexity was in fact characteristic of Mass-Observation writings, for these typically encompass a polyphonous set of textual strategies which, through their diversity, signal that no one of these is to be seen as bearing the stamp of 'authority' within the text, which is rather authorially or editorially dispersed (as I have already noted regarding *May the Twelfth*). However, in some of Mass-Observation's published writings, different stances and points of view are brought together by the 'voice' of the writer articulating one particular point of view, so that the authorial stance is made consonant with one of the points of view represented within the text. An interesting and successful example of this is Mass-Observation's study of Britain's falling birth-rate, *Britain and her Birth-Rate* (Mass-Observation, 1945), which centres on women's dissatisfactions and their refusal to live lives like their mothers, and which relates this to their changing perceptions of relationships. In *Britain and her Birth-Rate* textual closure is achieved through centring one particular point of view, that of 'women' as a category group, a collectivity; however, the writer of 'Little Kinsey' took on a more difficult task, that of both representing the multiplicity of competing 'voices' made apparent by its methodologically contrastive data, and also producing a scientific text that made clear what 'the facts' were.

Although a manuscript in more or less final form was written, 'Little Kinsey' was not published contemporaneously. A number of attempts were made to wrestle with the dissatisfactions that were felt in-house about the draft manuscript, some of which were expressed to the external assessors of the project, who came from the voluntary bodies that Mass-Observation had consulted before the research began. However, precisely when and why, and by whom, the manuscript that reached Allen and Unwin was abandoned is not known. Certainly comparing the typescript with the earlier *Britain and her Birth-Rate*, some of the problems are clear. On the one hand, 'Little Kinsey' must have seemed sadly wanting in contemporary survey terms; and on the other, it offered neither precision in its numerical analysis nor even any clear statement as to 'what was going on' about sexual life in Britain. 'Little Kinsey' was written as a 'scientific' piece of work, rather than, as with *May the Twelfth*, a 'literary' one; and this produced constraints over the way its diverse facts could be represented, while the absence of either an internal ('the women') or an external ('science', 'surrealism') authorial point of view compounded these problems.

'SURREALIST ETHNOGRAPHY' AND THE FIELDWORK METHODS OF MASS-OBSERVATION

James Clifford (1988) has written on the idea of 'ethnographic surrealism' and in passing has invoked but not discussed the more radical possibility of 'surrealist ethnography'. Clifford's 'hypotheses' about surrealist ethnography are tantalizingly brief (1988: 146–7) and in fact focus on the notion of ethnographic surrealism, largely because in his view there are no pure types of surrealist ethnography to discuss, although for him Gregory Bateson's (1936) *Naven* comes perhaps closest. However, Clifford's brief comments suggest that surrealist ethnography should include five defining elements:

1 the central mechanism of the use of collage; that is, bringing things together that 'naturally' inhabit different times, places, contexts;
2 the use within this of 'moments' cut from their context of 'natural' occurrence and forced into a jarring proximity with each other;
3 the assumption both that there is a basis for comparison between these things at some deeper level, and also the sheer incongruity of such comparison on first sight;
4 the 'foreignness' of the elements assembled in the ethnographic collage in their context of presentation (and, although Clifford does not specifically note this, also of the means of their representation);
5 the resulting text leaves openly manifest the constructivist procedures involved in producing it.

Lying behind these is what seems to me an additional defining element of surrealist ethnography, which is that the text remains 'unfinished' in the sense of requiring an active engagement on the part of the reader to make sense of the collage of materials used, to make congruent, in diverse ways, what is incongruent or fractured within it, or indeed to resist doing so.

These ideas are interesting not least because of the resonance they have for thinking about Mass-Observation and its uses of fieldwork methods. And so in this conclusion I want to consider whether and to what extent these defining criteria of 'surrealist ethnography' are appropriate for thinking about the ways that Mass-Observation used fieldwork methods and attempted to produce written accounts of its research which reflected the complexities of everyday life thereby revealed. My discussion of *May the Twelfth*, the 'Economics of Everyday Life' and 'Little Kinsey' has focused on methodological aspects of these projects and how and in what ways these impacted upon the textual representation of the research. This provides a basis for thinking through the idea of surrealist ethnography.

Most obviously, of these projects, *May the Twelfth* consists of a collage of reports, sights and sounds assembled from different places which are represented and contained textually. In addition, the draft manuscript of 'Little Kinsey', both when examined through a close textual reading and also when this is compared against the many fragments of research records that survive from this project, demonstrates some of the same quality of collage and montage, for it assembles jarring elements in the co-presences brought together in its pages. In comparison with this, there is no certain way of knowing how the composing elements of the 'Economics of Everyday Life' project might have been brought together and what kind of text would have resulted. However, from the disparate fragments that remain, and the ways these 'come at' the notion of economic life from a wide variety of

different vantage points, it might have taken a similar textual form, but whether successfully as with *May the Twelfth*, or unsuccessfully as with 'Little Kinsey', cannot even be guessed at. If *May the Twelfth* is a completed jigsaw, and 'Little Kinsey' one missing only a few pieces, the 'Economics of Everyday Life' project has only a small number of its pieces joined together.

May the Twelfth reads, if not as a harmonious whole, then certainly as a fully completed project, with its discordancies, shifts and jumps clearly being fully intentional ones. This style of reading (and of writing) may be unfamiliar to present-day readers raised on more conventional academic writing; however, for many of its contemporary readers, who were likely to have been self-styled intellectuals or fellow-travellers for whom the names of Jennings and Madge would be already known, its credentials as a piece of experimental or surrealist writing would have been 'announced' by its authorship. In discussing 'Little Kinsey', I pointed out that the writer of this manuscript faced a probably impossible task, that of assimilating research data from different epistemological discourses and wielding them into a whole which needed to be articulated in the 'voice' of science. The result here is in fact ultimately disruptive, rather than there being merely discordant co-presences within the text. Compared with these other two projects, what final form the planned text of the 'Economics of Everyday Life' project might have taken remains unknown, but clearly it would have had to have wielded together the more positivist savings and spending material and the more interpretivist observational material on the other aspects of the economics of everyday life that the project generated.

While there are points at which the comparisons that the editors of *May the Twelfth* want readers to make are introduced in forced ways (of the 'savages do this too, you know' kind, for instance), generally the text is left considerably more open than this. By comparison, the draft manuscript of 'Little Kinsey' seems a failure, in the sense that the reader is neither given the firm guidance in how to read it that 'science' would have provided, nor are they enabled to read it in any other way. The result is that it is very difficult for the reader of 'Little Kinsey' to move from the forced co-presences within it, of fact and interpretation and abstracted numbers and grounded observations, to think about the comparisons, similarities and differences between them. Interestingly, the research fragments of the 'Economics of Everyday Life' project do permit these kinds of deeper comparisons, but only because there is no 'account' of what these are meant to add up to as a whole.

The 'exoticism' of *May the Twelfth* was achieved by subverting the apparently central nature of the ritual of kingship, and instead assembling an 'elsewhere' of the ordinary streets and people of Britain, engaged upon those other, more mundane and, the implication is, more important events that composed Coronation Day 1937. The 'Economics of Everyday Life' project achieved a similar effect in at least some of its composing pieces of research – the social significance of 'the suit' and the 'Worktown stomach', for instance – by exoticizing the quintessentially ordinary through focusing on it in detail and thereby assigning to it a significance not usually accorded. The text of 'Little Kinsey' could have achieved a similar effect to *May the Twelfth* by constraining the reader to note the comparisons between its more 'exotic' and potentially scandalous observational materials and the survey material it also contains; however, this did not happen and it is really only in the leftover observational material and the appendix containing an account of a 'homosexual group' (also leftover from earlier research) that this occurs.

May the Twelfth is an extremely 'open' piece of writing in the sense that there is little overt editorial control of the text. This begins, indeed, with the book's title, which does not include any reference to the Coronation; that it is 'about' this has to be read into the title by the reader. This is interestingly compared with the 'Economics of Everyday Life' materials, which exist in the form of research notes, drafts and fragments which are connected mainly through having been provided by researchers working on the same project rather than intellectual coherence or connectedness. Here there are *only* spaces around its fragments, which the reader necessarily fills to make any kind of sense of the project and what it was about, and no closure exists or can be made of these. In contrast with both, the draft manuscript of 'Little Kinsey' has a clear structure which derives from the apparent centrality of the survey material; and written drafts of chapters nearly all exist in what looks like final form and fit this structure closely. The degree of openness that exists here is provided in part by the unconventional emphasis on the 'ends' in its numerical data, and in part through the inclusion of observational materials from the earlier phase of the research. It is interesting to contemplate what the palimpsest text of the fieldwork studies of 'Churchtown' compared with 'Steeltown', only faintly observable in the text of 'Little Kinsey', might have been like if the earlier research strategy had not been superseded; given the memo outlining the earlier text and the fragments that remain, it might well have been a fully-realized observation- and fieldwork-based piece of writing.

May the Twelfth most certainly promotes, indeed in some respects requires, an active readership. I have noted its innovative use of indexing, which permits and indeed encourages the reader to move through the text in non-linear ways. In addition, the structure of the main text brings together through its use of collage and montage effects that are not fully realized, in the sense that it is the reader who has to make the links between these in order to make sense of its chapters and how these fit together. Again, the reader can approach the fragments of the 'Economics of Everyday Life' material in an open way because there is no encompassing text, no move towards any whole. The draft manuscript of 'Little Kinsey' has a relatively 'flat' way of using its different kinds of data, in which the reader is immersed in detail and provided with little indication of how to respond to what an analytical reading suggests are unresolvable tensions within it.

Overall, *May the Twelfth* was clearly an intentionally 'surrealist' project and one that exemplifies, indeed in some respects exceeds, the attributes attributed to 'surrealist ethnography'. It centrally uses collage and montage in the way the text is structured and presented, and these mechanisms represent in anti-referential ways the highly complex 'reality' of Coronation Day 1937. Clearly the two key editors structured the resultant text to be read on a number of different levels, the surface one of apparent description of the events on 12 May 1937, but also the 'beneath the surface' workings of the unconscious in underpinning people's often 'unexpected' and incongruently 'primitive' reactions. The text is a very 'rough' one that deliberately makes use of its 'report' character – paragraphs are numbered, reports are included and referenced to people by their age and sex, different kinds of text are brought together on the same page for the reader, rather than the editors, to unpack. Throughout the reader has to be an 'active reader' in working out the points of connection, the alluded to meanings, the intended conclusions to be drawn.

By contrast, the other two Mass-Observation projects I have discussed are not fully intentional examples of surrealist ethnography. Certainly they share some of its attributes, although sometimes these came into existence because problems that occurred prevented a more conventional kind of text from being produced, rather than having been deliberately chosen ways of writing and representing research materials. Also the 'Economics of Everyday life' project and 'Little Kinsey' both faced the same problematic as *May the Twelfth*, that of how best to represent the complexity of the research experience of everyday life, with its multiple points of view and shifting understandings and conclusions, within a single text. Indeed, as Clifford notes, this was the problem faced by Bateson's (1936) *Naven*. Here Bateson grappled with the interpretive hermeneutic issues involved by trying, and failing, to assimilate these within a functionalist, empiricist and realist generalized account, producing instead an ethnographic text which struggled to represent the epistemological issues, rather than the (failed) solution to these. But for these two Mass-Observation projects, the issues involved were compounded by trying to do this while also grappling with two sets of research data produced from different approaches and epistemological positions. Overall, the evidence here points in a different direction from that of *May the Twelfth*. This is that the complexity and the need to 'handle' the different kinds of research data was experienced as a problem, in the case of 'Little Kinsey' a largely insuperable problem, rather than as an opportunity. There is little sense that the researchers in the 'Economics of Everyday Life' project, and the writer of the text in the case of 'Little Kinsey', were able to call upon a well-articulated rationale and a set of intellectual principles for representing, even if not resolving, this which surrealist ideas provided and which, in my view, marks *May the Twelfth* as a fully realized surrealist ethnography.

What a discussion of these three projects brings into view is that the major contradiction embedded in the heart of Mass-Observation as a whole also impacted in consequential, although different, ways on these particular projects. Mass-Observation had a principled commitment to two equally foundational but mutually antagonistic principles: the idea of observers being 'subjective cameras' interpretively recording the world in their own ways; *and* the hierarchicalism of the 'new science' that Mass-Observation wanted to produce through the synthesizing role provided by its core researchers and writers, analysing and synthesizing the material that its mass observers merely collected. These produced not only different research approaches and different kinds of data, but also implied different ways of representing these, different styles of writing, different kinds of texts. It was only when one of these gained ascendancy over the other that a successful text resulted, in the way that surrealism enabled in the case of *May the Twelfth*. However, the 1949 changes which occurred in the wake of 'Little Kinsey' removed the contradiction thereby engendered by removing from the organization its commitment to observation and interpretation and firmly hitching 'Mass-Observation Limited' to the high positivism of contemporary market research. And here it was a clear commitment to conventional market research ways of operating that enabled another albeit very different resolution.

Although the use of fieldwork methods and approaches to research Britain survived and later flourished, what was lost sight of until fairly recently was this interesting and contentious past, in which political radicalism and methodological radicalism met through the activities and researches of Mass-Observation. The histories of the social sciences, market research, survey methods and fieldwork methods are closely intertwined in Britain over the period from 1937 to 1949. As I have endeavoured to show in the case of fieldwork methods, these complexities are shown in interesting ways through looking at Mass-Observation, its connections with and also separations from academia, and its attempts to use these methods in a number of its research projects.

Acknowledgements

This chapter was written while I was the Faculty of Arts Senior Research Fellow at the University of Auckland, New Zealand. During the period of the Fellowship I was based in Women's Studies, and I am grateful to Professor Maureen Molloy, Dr Heather Worth and Ms Hana Mata'u for making my time there so enjoyable, as well as to the Faculty of Arts for awarding me the Fellowship. I am as always extremely grateful to Dorothy Sheridan, Archivist at the Mass-Observation Archive at the University of Sussex, for help above and beyond the call of duty.

NOTES

1 See here some of the original early Mass-Observation publications and particularly Mass-Observation, 1937, 1939; Madge and Harrisson, 1938.

2 These come together and can be glimpsed in the pages of Bartlett et al., 1939, one of the compilations from a series of social science conferences convened to consider aspects of the likely expansion of higher education.

3 Inevitably this also means that some original materials are available only in archival sources. However, as my discussion indicates, a good deal of the relevant materials are widely available in published form in books and journal articles and can be accessed by interested readers in the usual way through libraries.

4 See here, for instance, the widely available microform set of papers from 'The Tom Harrisson Mass-Observation Archive', published by Harvester Press, which is both voluminous and contains only one part of Mass-Observation's records, that concerned with its internal file reports.

5 In a few cases it is not possible to provide references to secondary sources for readers of this chapter, as some of Mass-Observation's activities have not yet been published on. In these cases, I provide a reference to an archive source, which in all cases refer to collections held in the Mass-Observation Archive at the University of Sussex, UK.

6 In the first two years of its activities, these included not only responses to the monthly directives but also pieces of research concerned with the use of Persil washing powder, smoking behaviour, a fascist march in Bermondsey, the blackout and other air raid precautions, the West Fulham by-election, social attitudes to margarine, reactions to advertising, newspaper reading, the non-voter, the US diamond market, clothes, washing cloths, bad dreams and nightmares, personal appearance, a 'square deal' for railways, propaganda, the impact of railway posters and sport in wartime.

7 In addition to Jennings and Madge's (1937) *May the Twelfth*, see also Laing, 1980; M-L. Jennings, 1982; Chaney and Pickering, 1986; Hubble, 1998; and also Stanley, 1995a on Mass-Observation's day surveys more generally.

8 The 'Economics of Everyday Life' project not only has an extremely interesting topic of investigation, it is also interestingly bound up in this particularly crucial 'moment' in the development of fieldwork methods in Britain, and closely connected with a number of the 'methodological writings' that Mass-Observation staff were involved in producing at this time. See here Stanley, 1992 for a more detailed discussion.

9 The traffic between Mass-Observation and academia went in both directions. After the war Charles Madge moved into academia. Dennis Chapman joined the 'Economics of Everyday Life' project after working with Rowntree on his 1930s study of poverty in York; during and at the end of the war Chapman worked with David Glass and Ruth Glass on the reconstruction study of Middlesborough; while following the war he worked as an academic in the Business School at the University of Liverpool, as well as being involved in the formation of the Association of University Teachers (for an example of his sociological work, see Chapman, 1955). Similarly Gertrud Wagner had both a prewar, a wartime and a post-war track record as an academic in addition to her involvement in the 'Economics of Everyday Life' project. Initially she had been involved on the periphery of the Marienthal study carried out by Paul Lazarsfeld and Marie Johoda; later she was involved in carrying out a Liverpool-based university study of the evacuation of children from Manchester (Wagner, 1939), while after the war she returned to Austria and to an academic career there.

10 See here Mass-Observation Archive Topic Collection, archival references TC6.A-I; TC7.A-J; WT24.A-D.

11 See here respectively Mass-Observation Archive Topic and Worktown collections, archival references TC1.C; TC6.E; WT24.B,C; WT24.D; WT33D; and WT36.C, F, I.

12 As the last project carried out by 'old' Mass-Observation before it became a conventional market research organization, the sex research known within the organization as 'Little Kinsey' is of particular interest in tracing its final methodological shifts and changes. See Stanley, 1995b and 1996 for detailed discussions of this project.

13 Mass-Observation's involvement with this new piece of research came about because of its headquarters' links with voluntary agencies concerned with 'sexual' matters, including divorce, 'motherhood', under-age sexual activity, venereal disease and so on. The impetus was in part the forthcoming publication of the first part of the Kinsey Report in the United States, in part Mass-Observation wanting to investigate 'public opinion' about such matters; and accordingly it consulted key figures within the community of voluntary agencies that it frequently worked with.

14 However, the version which exists in typescript in the Mass-Observation archive was published in full in Stanley, 1995b.

REFERENCES

Abrams, Mark (1951) *Social Surveys and Social Action.* London: Heinemann.

Allen, Roy and Bowley, Arthur (1935) *Family Expenditure: A Study of its Variation.* London: Staples Press.

Bartlett, Frederick, Ginsberg, Morris, Lingren, Ethel and Thouless, Ralph (eds) (1939) *The Study of Society.* London: Routledge and Kegan Paul.

Bateson, Geoffrey (1936) *Naven: A Survey of the Problems Suggested by a Composite Picture of the Culture of a New Guinea Tribe Drawn from Three Points of View.* Cambridge: Cambridge University Press.

Baxendale, John and Pawling, Chris (1996) 'The documentary film and Mass-Observation', in *Narrating the Thirties: A Decade in the Making, 1930 to the Present.* Basingstoke: Macmillan. pp. 17–45.

Bulmer, Martin, Bales, Kevin and Sklar, Kathryn Kish (eds) (1991) *The Social Survey in Historical Perspective, 1880–1940.* Cambridge: Cambridge University Press.

Bunn, Margaret (1943) 'Mass-Observation: A comment on *People in Production*', *Manchester School*, No. 31: 24–37.

Calder, Angus and Sheridan, Dorothy (eds) (1984) *Speak for Yourself: A Mass-Observation Anthology.* London: Jonathon Cape.

Chaney, David and Pickering, Michael (1985) 'Democracy and communication: Mass-Observation 1937–1943', *Journal of Communication*, 36: 41–56.

Chaney, David and Pickering, Michael (1986) 'Authorship in documentary: sociology as an art form in Mass-Observation', in John Corner (ed.), *Documentary and the Mass Media.* London: Edward Arnold. pp. 29–44.

Chapman, Dennis (1955) *The Home and Social Status.* London: Routledge and Kegan Paul.

Clifford, James (1988) 'On ethnographic surrealism', in *The Predicament of Culture: Twentieth-Century Ethnography, Literature, and Art.* Cambridge, MA: Harvard University Press. pp. 117–51.

Cross, Gary (ed.) (1990) *Worktowners at Blackpool: Mass-Observation and Popular Leisure in the 1930s.* London: Routledge.

Firth, Raymond (1938) 'An anthropologist's view of Mass-Observation', *Sociological Review*, No. 31: 166–93.

Firth, Raymond (1939) 'Critique of Mass-Observation', unpublished lecture, Newcastle Literary and Philosophical Society, 30 January 1939.

Harrisson, Tom (1937) *Savage Civilisation.* London: Gollancz.

Hubble, Nick (1998) 'Walter Benjamin and the theory of Mass-Observation: surveillance contra surveillance at the first media coronation', unpublished paper, Surveillance Conference, Liverpool John Moores University, June 1998.

Jennings, Humphrey (1986) *Pandemonium*. Glencoe, IL: The Free Press.

Jennings, Humphrey and Madge, Charles (eds) (1937) *May the Twelfth: Mass-Observation Day Surveys 1937*. London: Faber and Faber.

Jennings, Mary-Lou (ed.) (1982) *Humphrey Jennings, Film-Maker/Painter/Poet*. London: British Film Institute in Association with Riverside Studios.

Johoda, Marie (1938) 'Review of *Mass-Observation* and of *May 12*', *Sociological Review*, No. 30: 208–9.

Johoda, Marie (1940) 'Review of *War Begins at Home*', *Sociological Review*, No. 32: 129–31.

Laing, Stuart (1980) 'Presenting "Things as They Are": John Summerfield's *May Day* and Mass-Observation', in Frank Glovership (ed.), *Class, Culture and Social Change*. Brighton: Harvester Press. pp. 142–60.

Loewe, Adolph (1935) *Economics and Sociology*. London: Allen and Unwin.

McClancy, Jeremy (1995) 'Brief encounter: the meeting, in Mass-Observation, of British surrealism and popular anthropology', *Journal of the Royal Anthropological Institute*, 1: 495–507.

Madge, Charles (1933) 'Surrealism for the English', *New Verse*, 6: 14–18.

Madge, Charles (1937) *The Disappearing Castle*. London: Faber and Faber.

Madge, Charles and Harrisson, Tom (1938) *First Year's Work, 1937–1938, by Mass-Observation*. London: Lindsay Drummond.

Madge, Charles and Jennings, Humphrey (1937) 'Poetic description and Mass-Observation', *New Verse*, No. 24.

Malinowski, Bronislaw (1938) 'A nation-wide intelligence service', in Charles Madge and Tom Harrisson (eds), *First Year's Work, 1937–1938, by Mass-Observation*. London: Lindsay Drummond. pp. 81–121.

Marshall, Thomas T.H. (1937) 'Is Mass-Observation moonshine?', *The Highway*, No. 30: 48–50.

Mass-Observation (1937) *Mass-Observation*. London: Muller.

Mass-Observation (1939) *Britain by Mass-Observation*. Harmondsworth: Penguin.

Mass-Observation (1945) *Britain and her Birth-Rate*. London: Advertising Standards Guild.

Oeser, Oscar (1937) 'Methods and assumptions of field work in social psychology', *British Journal of Psychology*, No. 27: 343–63.

Oeser, Oscar (1939) 'The value of team work and functional penetration as methods in social investigation', in Frederick Bartlett, Morris Ginsberg, Ethel Lindgren and Ralph Thouless (eds), *The Study of Society*. London: Routledge and Kegan Paul. pp. 402–17.

Sheridan, Dorothy (ed.) (1990) *Wartime Women: A Mass-Observation Anthology*. London: Heinemann.

Sheridan, Dorothy (1994) 'Using the Mass-Observation archive as a source for women's studies', *Women's History Review*, 3: 101–13.

Stanley, Liz (1990) 'The archaeology of a 1930 Mass-Observation project', *Sociology Occasional Paper* No. 27.

Stanley, Liz (1992) 'The "Economics of Everyday Life": A Mass-Observation project in Bolton', *North West Labour History Journal*, No. 17: 95–102.

Stanley, Liz (1995a) 'Women have servants and men never eat: Mass-Observation day diaries 1937', *Women's History Review*, 4: 85–102.

Stanley, Liz (1995b) *Sex Surveyed 1949–1994: From Mass-Observation's 'Little Kinsey' to the National Survey and the Hite Reports*. London: Taylor and Francis.

Stanley, Liz (1996) 'Mass-Observation's "Little Kinsey" and the British sex survey tradition', in Jeffrey Weeks and Janet Holland (eds), *Sexual Cultures: Communities, Values and Intimacy*. London: Macmillan. pp. 97–114.

Wagner, Gertrud (1939) *Preliminary Report on the Problem of Evacuation*. Liverpool: University of Liverpool Department of Social Sciences in association with the University Settlement.

Wells, Alan (1936) 'Social surveys and sociology', *Sociological Review*, No. 28: 274–94.

Young, Terence (1934) *Becontree and Dagenham: A Report for the Pilgrim Trust*. London: Becontree Social Survey Committee.

7

Orientalism

JULIE MARCUS

In 1986, the case of a former French diplomat jailed for spying for the Chinese government made news headlines around the world. 'M. Bouriscot was accused of passing information to China after he fell in love with Mr. Shi, whom he believed for twenty years to be a woman' reported the *New York Times*.[1] In his play, *M Butterfly*, written around this strange and remarkable story, David Hwang has the Frenchman choose between the reality of life as a European homosexual and the life of his dream, the illusion of himself loving a beautiful and exotic Chinese woman who, only incidentally, is a man. In a wrenching final scene Hwang's disgraced diplomat chooses the dream and its prison of illusions and loses himself.[2]

Readers of Edward Said's book *Orientalism* (1978) will not be surprised at the diplomat's choice, for in his study of novels, travellers' tales, music, political tracts and bureaucratic documents, Said delineates a discursive formation which he calls 'orientalism', a discourse which he shows to be the vehicle for representations of identity which are seriously deformed. Said proposes that in a broad and popular sense, texts discussing and describing the characteristics of the orient and its inhabitants utilize imagery which ensures that the world of the orient is always constructed as 'other' to 'the West'. In other words, 'the orient' and 'the West' are constructed in ways that mean that when speaking about the orient, one is also speaking about the identity and characteristics of the West. The comparison may be unspoken, but it is always there. According to Said, orientalism's representations of 'East' and 'West' are tied to each other in a relationship of power which is hierarchical; it is this relation which helps to shape the representations of the texts produced within it. In *M Butterfly*, David Hwang's dramatic rendering of the political scandal

which so fascinated the Western media in 1986 puts forward the proposal that 'Westerners' will always prefer their dream 'orient' because in the end, to forgo it involves severing a relationship of power which establishes a hierarchy of cultural differences which is embedded in a 'Western' psyche and embodied in the individual 'Western' persona. One cannot give it up and still remain the same; one cannot give it up and still retain superiority. The force of these cultural differences, the distinction between 'same' and 'other', 'we' and 'they', can be observed through the imperial language of race which is used to describe their transgression— 'going native', 'gone troppo', miscegenation, half-caste. Those unfamiliar with the pungency of the language of race and the ways in which it was embedded in the colonial psyche as a moral order will find them captured within George Orwell's first novel, *Burmese Days*, published in 1934. These are not cultural differences which can be lightly ignored, pushed aside easily, or stepped out of. *Orientalism* claims to show why this is so.

In Said's work, the orient is demonstrated to appear in many forms but tends always toward representations which rest upon sets of essentialized differences which mark out both a topography and a culture. The geography of Europe's 'orient' is marked into zones of near, far and middle, each with their special characteristics. In orientalist texts, the orient's culture appears as homogenized, static, anchored in a rigid traditionalism which most often is seen as breaking down through internal economic and moral decay. Orientals are elusive, given to perverse sexual and moral codes, languid and traditional. In the Middle East, the religion of Islam is necessarily implicated in these qualities. Said points out that these stereotypes stand in contrast to a 'West' that is energetic, inventive, progressing, and

'Westerners' who are open, honest, sexually normal, monogamous and Christian. While the 'West' is the home of rationality and science, the 'East' staggers under the yoke of irrationality, superstition and tradition. By distributing these qualities between the two domains, the moral universe of the orient comes to bear the characteristics which in Western culture are allocated to women while the rational 'West' is gendered as male. In this context a Western moral criticism of the ways in which Muslims treat their women is of central importance in legitimating economic and political domination. In it, too, the veil and the harem which guard the sexual and moral order of the generalized orient operate as sites of Western desire into which fantasies of perverse sexualities can be projected. These are the stereotypes and the relations of power which Said calls a discourse of *orientalism* in a critique which has had far-reaching consequences for European and American scholarship in general and for anthropology in particular.[3]

Said's delineation of the forms and operations of Western knowledge about its 'orient' was by no means the first critique of oriental studies, nor the first to use the term.[4] His particular achievement lay in using the theoretical potential of Michel Foucault's work on power and knowledge to delineate orientalism as a discourse that comprised a range of distinct disciplines. Said's orientalism became a field of knowledge, representation and political strategies of domination. It was a contribution that posed a major challenge to academic scholarship of the time. The history of responses to Edward Said's critical analysis of 'orientalism' shows that for many 'Westerners' the familiarities of the romanticized and feared domain of the orient can never be given up. Although often strongly resisted, his work has offered a challenge which has been productive and constructive and continuing. *Orientalism* was first published in 1978, and by 1984 one of my students was able to locate over four hundred critical academic references, responses and citations of the book. Over the years, the flood of commentary has broadened. The responses to *Orientalism* fracture along lines which indicate the significance of Said's analysis – its challenge to comfortable habits of thought and its continuing political significance.

A substantial block of initial responses to *Orientalism* came from those seats of oriental studies whose texts and scholars Said had thoroughly critiqued. These were defensive and sometimes pointed to inaccuracies of particular points which could be harnessed to the task of demolishing the general thrust of Said's critique. A number of responses to his work circulated around Said's identity as an expatriate Palestinian and his status as a skilled and effective American intellectual. While academics were quick to 'place' Said as a Palestinian refugee with an axe to grind, there were very few willing to place

themselves as equally racialized, political actors within an intellectual field which they dominated. In classical demonstrations of the power relations of otherness, the dominant grouping fought to retain its position of unmarked, undisclosed, objectivity.[5] If such responses displayed a dismaying degree of bad faith they also demonstrated the political salience of Said's analysis of the discourse of orientalism and the ways in which academic knowledge is indeed aligned with and inter-related to the practical politics of a Western diplomacy and economic policy in the 'middle' East.

A second early response questioned Said's understanding of Foucault's concepts of discourse, knowledge and power, and focused on both his understanding of the nature of representation and on his view of the relationship between representation and reality. In an extended essay, 'On *Orientalism*', James Clifford (1988) pointed to the unresolved conflict between Said's humanist perspectives and his use of concepts and methods developed by Foucault as part of an anti-humanist project. Clifford discusses the implications of the conflict arising from the attempt to bring together two such opposed political positions, both for Said's understandings of the nature of discourse and for his approach to questions of representation. Later, Homi Bhabha took up these issues in a different way. In his important essay, 'The other question', Bhabha (1994) discussed the difficulties of reconciling Foucault's notion of power/knowledge with Said's understanding of discourse. Despite the significant difficulties with Said's relationship to Foucault's work, the general thrust of Said's work is supported by each of these critics. Clifford (1988: 257) noted, too, that fundamentally *Orientalism* offers 'a series of important if tentative epistemological reflections on general styles and procedures of cultural discourse' and it is these which have been important for anthropologists.

Feminist responses to Said's work came a little later, perhaps because by the time of *Orientalism's* publication, feminist critiques of patriarchal knowledge drawing on Simone de Beauvoir's (1953) much earlier philosophical study of the ways in which woman became 'other' to man had already had an impact on the ways in which feminist anthropologists were conducting their research. In examining the scholarly practices of their own academic disciplines and in focusing on the lives and works of women, feminist scholars had been drawn to examine the structures of difference and the impact of power upon knowledge which were to become the focus of Said's study. Two very important collections of papers by feminist anthropologists, *Women, Culture and Society* (Rosaldo and Lamphere, 1974) and *Toward an Anthropology of Women* (Reiter, 1975) had already stimulated a widespread feminist interest in comparative studies of women's lives. They led also to a wave of new work being carried out on those societies in which women's lives were hidden from male investigators by local custom. Among them were the studies in Lois Beck and Nikki Keddie's influential collection, *Women in the Muslim World*, which was published in the same year as *Orientalism* and reflected earlier important work about Moroccan women's lives by Fatma Mernissi, published as *Beyond the Veil* in 1975.

When feminist responses to *Orientalism* did come, they did not focus directly on the discursive coupling of 'orient' and 'occident' in narrative and text with which male anthropologists engaged. More often they took as their starting point the intersections of gender and sexuality and the moral critique of 'oriental women' which Said's own analysis had laid bare but which he had not followed up. Nor had Said understood how crucial were gender and sexuality to the discourse of orientalism and the politics of representation which he had so clearly documented (Marcus, 1990, 1992). It is a point taken up and worked through by writers like Marianna Torgovnik, who, in *Gone Primitive*, noted that 'The best commentators in the general field of Western primitivism – Said, Miller, Clifford, all male – tend to treat in passing gender issues and related sexual issues that are enormously important and worthy of sustained attention' (1990: 17–18).[6] The initial lack of interest among male scholars in these elements of Said's work has to some extent circumscribed anthropological debates about the relationship of sexuality and race and these issues remain contested and fluid. Feminist interest in Said's work has developed in strength over the years, particularly among anthropologists interested in the place of sexuality, erotics and sexual identity. An important volume of papers on these themes collected by Lenore Manderson and Margaret Jolly (1997) focuses orientalist theory upon Asia (Thailand in particular) and the Pacific region and makes a substantial contribution to anthropological understandings of the impact of colonial regimes upon the sexual and gender orders of those subjected to them. This volume contains important discussions of the continuing assumptions of hegemony which inflect much anthropological analysis of colonialism and post-colonialism and of the ways in which the erotics of the gaze is understood. Most recently, in a study of Western fantasies of veiling, *Colonial Fantasies* (1998), Meyda Yegenoglu has offered a detailed and nuanced contribution to a feminist critique of Said's *Orientalism*.[7]

Said himself reviewed the commentary on *Orientalism* in 1985, concluding that his thesis had stood up reasonably well to sustained criticism. Since then the field has become more complex and also much broader. It sits now beside the critical perspectives which emerged with it – the post-colonialism of 'subaltern studies', the revived interest in imperialism and colonial regimes, the feminist

interest in the body and the continuing delineation of the power of race and racism within discourse. Both in terms of intellectual achievement and in terms of the productive power of Said's delineation of a field of study which has engaged some of the best minds of his era and produced a raft of critical books and articles, here is a work of profound and continuing significance right across the board of the humanities, the social sciences and the Enlightenment project on which they are based.

SAID, ORIENTALISM AND ANTHROPOLOGY

It is important to be clear about Said's contribution because it hinges neither on his precise understanding of particular aspects of Foucault's work, nor on how he articulates a distinction between representation and 'the real' world to which he would like to hold fast. Said attempted to delineate a discursive formation on the nature of the orient which he could demonstrate had governed and conditioned Western understandings of the societies and peoples who lived within it. He demonstrated how academic knowledge replicated and confirmed popular stereotypes which in fundamental ways were remarkably consistent over time, and he showed how the stereotypes and structures of the orient were crucial to Western fantasies of itself as the world of enlightenment, progress and evolutionary superiority. In carrying out his project, Said drew on a rich literature, one that spanned several centuries and national boundaries, one that included popular as well as academic texts and one that included the policy documents generated by the colonial bureaucracies of governments with imperial agendas. He captured the linkages between imperial power-brokers and their subjected populations, he explicated the personal politics of the greatest of orientalist scholars, he brought his critique to bear both on nineteenth century scholarship and on today's great American schools of oriental studies and linked their work to the American government's contemporary political projects in the Middle East. In sum, Said set out the relations between the categories of difference and the fields of power which created, polarized and represented them in texts.

His study pointed, too, to different regional and temporal modalities of Europe's orient, to the distinctions between the Far Eastern and Indian forms of orientalism and the discourses through which the 'Middle' Eastern societies and Islamic countries of Northern Africa were known. He delineated the moral hierarchies of oriental studies, the 'good' orient of classical Hindu India and the 'bad' orient of Islam everywhere (Said, 1978: 99). It is here that Said pointed to the very special relationship that Islam and the 'middle' East plays in European and

American orientalist discourse, a relationship which is particularly embedded in frontier wars and religious bigotry as well as in continuing Western imperialism. In his later works Said looked at this relationship in more detail, studying its narratives in *Culture and Imperialism* (1993) and the role of media representations of Islam and Arab societies in *Covering Islam* (1981).

Some scholars have remarked that Said's view of orientalism focuses most strongly on the Middle East and on Islamic studies, and that it fits there rather better than it does the oriental studies of east Asian societies and India. Indeed, Said believed that the political situation in the Middle East had created a particular intellectual environment which trafficked in forms of orientalism that were particularly strongly stereotyped. The common frontier, European political policies toward the Ottoman empire and Greece, the Israeli–Palestinian dispute, oil wars and continuing American expansion in the Middle East, created an environment which heightened the processes of stereotyping and in which it was particularly difficult for scholars to break away from orientalized stereotypes of Islam and Middle Eastern societies. The texts and scholarship he chose to analyse therefore relate mainly to the Middle East.

One might therefore expect that those anthropologists working in the Middle East, the home of the 'bad orient of Islam', would be most interested in, and most affected by, Said's delineation of how scholarly texts are constructed within orientalist discourse. That this is not always the case is illustrated by Michael Gilsenan's recent study *Lords of the Lebanese Marches. Violence and Narrative in an Arab Society* (1996). Gilsenan's detailed anthropological study of the beys and aghas of Akkar deals with issues of narrative, rhetoric, political violence, masculinity and texts, all of which are integral to Said's arguments about the replication of orientalized stereotypes. Yet at no stage does he engage with Said's arguments nor indeed, with those of Foucault, some of whose concepts of power underpin his narrative. Gilsenan's fascinating book has been written as if two decades of intellectual debate about orientalism in the Middle East, two decades in which anthropology has had to confront difficult theoretical, methodological, political and narrative problems about the nature of its texts, could safely be set aside. Perhaps this reflects a lingering faith in the power of empirical description and data to undo orientalism's fantasies. Certainly Gilsenan's work brings to the fore the faith in meticulous fieldwork that remains characteristic of the discipline. But it also might be an indication that the questions raised by Said's critique meet most resistance in the anthropology of the Islamic lands.

What of Said's critique, then, for those academic disciplines like anthropology which sought to juxtapose the orientalist world of the text with studies of the world as it was experienced by those who were known through them? What of those anthropologists who sought to use direct observation as a corrective to the stereotypes and tropes of texts? Can direct observation and lived experience ever act as a corrective to the discursive machinations and plays of power which are described as 'orientalism'? In *Orientalism*, the discipline of anthropology receives little direct mention. Scholars were nevertheless quick to see that Said's central questions were often those of traditional anthropology. Said asks them right at the end of his book, so that he is not simply justifying the task he has carried out but is in some sense throwing down the gauntlet. 'How does one *represent* other cultures?' 'What is *another* culture? Is the notion of a distinct culture (or race, or religion, or civilization) a useful one, or does it always get involved in self-congratulation ... or hostility and aggression. Do cultural, religious, and racial differences matter more than socio-economic categories, or politicohistorical ones?' (Said, 1978: 325). These are questions for anthropology.

In *Orientalism*, Said had some kindly words for Clifford Geertz, whose anthropology showed, he believed, an 'interest in Islam [which] is discrete and concrete enough to be animated by the specific societies and problems he studies and not by the rituals, preconceptions, and doctrines of Orientalism' (Said, 1978: 326). Although he was later to take a different view, at that time Said believed it possible for what he called the 'human sciences' to dispense with the stereotypes of orientalism, that the human failures of orientalist approaches could be remedied without resort to alternative dogmas which were equally debilitating. In Geertz's studies of Indonesian Islam he saw a way forward, just as he did with Maxime Rodinson's (1974) Marxist study of Islam and capitalism and Yves Lacoste's (1966) fascinating study of Ibn Khaldun which canvassed the 'birth of history and the past of the Third World'. These studies were based on texts rather than field research. Yet anthropology has been the discipline devoted to delineating cultural differences and it is anthropology which has been most involved with the European colonial endeavour. Anthropology has floated along the borders of empire and has been strongly criticized elsewhere as more often a servant of imperialism than its practical critic.

Anthropologists were rather quicker than he to place their discipline within the discourse Said described so clearly from literary and administrative texts. Initially, they understood more clearly than he, perhaps, that previous critical anthropological stances could not answer the questions which Said and Foucault (in a different context) were posing. They feared that orientalism's tropes could slip easily into empirical studies, a fear to be ably demonstrated in Deborah Reed-Danahy's (1995) perceptive account of Pierre Bourdieu's accounts of

Kabyle ethnography. The ability of anthropologists to challenge stereotyped views of other cultures and customs and their role as advocates for those disadvantaged and oppressed by colonial and neo-colonial regimes, indigenous despotism and national states of all kinds seemed to be at risk. How to distinguish the advocacy of anthropologists like Phyllis Kaberry in Africa and Paul Stirling in Turkey from those whose advocacy was colonial either in intent or in its realization? If a discourse on orientalism was so pervasive, what did it mean for disinterested scholarship, and what would happen to the outsider's privileged position of objectivity? Indeed, one of anthropology's most cherished fantasies, that of the eternal outsider, seemed under very serious threat indeed. For if Said were right, and anthropologists necessarily worked and wrote from within discursive formations, it was hard to see where that cherished outsideness could come from; and harder still to see what benefit it conferred. This is because of the ways in which an individually authored text was drawn into, and positioned within, a much broader stream of power/knowledge whose currents shaped it more fiercely than did its author. Said always reserved a role for authorship and always, too, a place for some form of material reality. And this is why I think that despite his own critique he was initially favourable to anthropology. He, like Ahmed (1991) who commented on the anthropological quietism of the Gulf War year, wanted to be able to do better and come closer to the reality which the objects of discourse lived within.[8] Even so, and while some anthropologists have not always grasped his approach on these matters, Said's work sent real shock waves through the discipline, provoking both shifts in focus and determined resistance to them.

By the time Said published *Culture and Imperialism* in 1993 he had developed a more critical approach to anthropology and to the processes by which it created its objective and scientific accounts of oriental societies. His faith in empirical studies as a means of redressing the narrative distortions of the texts of his analysis had been shaken. In *Culture and Imperialism* his study of Kipling's novel *Kim* is particularly detailed, partly because of the role of the central character, Creighton, as anthropologist; and partly in order to discuss Kim as colonial chameleon. Said points to the alliance between science and the administration and governance of populations which Creighton represents (Said, 1993: 184–5) and he gives a nuanced account of the ability of the outsider, Kim, to fade into the colonized 'other' without ever giving up or losing his 'self'. In these two characters Said seems to identify the two crucial elements of Foucault's notion of discourse: power/knowledge as constraint and power/knowledge as productive and constitutive. Said's understanding of Kim, Creighton and Kipling is such that it had to undermine his confidence in anthropology as an objective science

which might redeem the distortions of the past. And he refers here, too, to the frontier politics which has been so much a feature of the discipline, referring in particular to Claude Lévi-Strauss' characterization of anthropology as the 'handmaiden of colonialism' (Said, 1993: 184–5).

That anthropologists were not easily able to discard the tropes and metaphors of orientalist discourse can be seen in Lévi-Strauss' own encounter with Islam. Despite his clear understanding of the work of anthropology as a colonial technology and even a technique of governance, he remained comfortingly blind to his personal involvement in the tropes of orientalism. In his brief encounter with India and Islam in 1950 we see how one of the most important scholars of the century can falter when anthropology comes into contact with Islam. His essays 'Taxila' and 'The Kyong' come at the end of *Tristes Tropiques* (Lévi-Strauss, [1955] 1976). Into their elegant prose Lévi-Strauss introduces almost every trope of the traditional orientalist narrative. He begins with an unhappy encounter with a Muslim family in which he refuses to yield to gender sensitivities which were not his. Then, in his encounter with Delhi, the imperial dream collapses on the ramparts of reality. It is no accident, I suspect, that of all travellers' tales, arrival scenes set in Islamic cities are most likely to break with narrative conventions, most likely to appear insurmountably chaotic and irrational and most likely to occur at night. Gilsenan's arrival at a village two hours out of Beirut, for example, was at night (Gilsenan, 1996: xi). In Lévi-Strauss' description of his night arrival at Taxila and then at New Dehli he makes clear his uneasiness with Islam. As a prelude to examining the reasons for his hostile reaction to Islam he sets it in contrast to his clearer understanding of Hindu culture and its people whom he sees as 'our Indo-European brothers'. Lévi-Strauss' highly charged disparagement of the cultural practices and religious essences of Islam in Pakistan just after the political horrors of Partition is extraordinarily ill-considered. Whereas Buddhism can be described as a religion of universal kindliness and Christians as desiring dialogue with outsiders, Muslims are characterized as intolerant. '[T]hey are ... incapable of tolerating the existence of others as others' (Lévi-Strauss, [1955] 1976: 531). In thinking about this proposition it is difficult to believe that a scholar of such unchallengeable erudition could overlook the flight of persecuted Jews from Christian Europe to Muslim Spain, north Africa and the Ottoman lands of the eastern Mediterranean. It is difficult to understand the virulence of his confusion and stereotyping, his references to homosexuality and to the deadening aesthetic which characterizes the decadent Islamic art forms he observes.

'I am only too well aware of the reasons for the uneasiness I felt on coming into contact with Islam: I rediscovered in Islam the world I myself had come from; Islam is the West of the East. Or to be more precise, I had to have experience of Islam in order to appreciate the danger which today threatens French thought' (Lévi-Strauss, [1955] 1976: 531). Like Said's, Lévi-Strauss' political and intellectual project is an emancipatory one. What is fascinating is the way in which he brings a derisory, essentialized and orientalist approach to Islam in order to deal with the excesses and intellectual rigidity he sees flourishing in 'the West'. 'Now I can see, beyond Islam, to India, but it is the India of Buddhism, before Mohammed. For me as a European', he writes, 'and because I am a European, Mohammed intervenes, with uncouth clumsiness, between our thought and Indian doctrines that are very close to it, in such a way as to prevent East and West joining hands, as they might well have done, in harmonious collaborations' (Lévi-Strauss, [1955] 1976: 536). Lévi-Strauss' elegant and dreadful lament for a lost future which rests so firmly upon one of the most unexpected expressions of the orientalist tradition must cast a shadow over the emancipatory project of anthropology and is a gesture of recognition, perhaps, towards the approaching exhaustion of his form of structuralist sensitivity. Written in 1955, Lévi-Strauss' major works on mythology and totemism were still to come. Clifford Geertz places *Tristes Tropiques* into a tradition of nineteenth-century reformist writing represented by Flaubert in France, Nietzsche in Germany and Arnold, Ruskin and Pater in England (Geertz, 1988a: 40). Perhaps his response to Islam should also be set into a nineteenth-century intellectual tradition, one that in the twentieth century still found some difficulty in dealing with colonialism, one which preferred to deal with the postwar world through the subterranean excavations of the structures of thought rather than with the relations of power which governed those structures, one which retreated from the consideration of power relations comprehensively laid out by, for example, de Beauvoir in her 1949 explorations of the procedures of 'otherness' which made women 'the second sex'.

I mention Lévi-Strauss at this point for two reasons. First, because his uneasiness with Islam and the ease with which he slips into an unselfconscious use of the orientalist forms of narration so clearly delineated by Said should alert us to the special place of Islam and the Middle East within orientalist discourse. And second, because he is a crucially important anthropologist, a practitioner of the 'science' of other cultures – the humanist discipline most concerned with charting cultural difference and which is engaged in the task of comparing textual renderings of the societies with first-hand observations of their realities. The fact that Lévi-Strauss' liberal humanism foundered on the first rock of Islam he ever encountered brings out the special nature of orientalism and the special place of the 'middle' East in Westerners' sense of identity

and superiority. It points to the special problems it poses for anthropologists who research and write about the Middle East.

As I noted earlier, while Said was initially rather favourable about anthropology, anthropologists recognized the profound implications of *Orientalism* for the practice of their trade immediately. Said's favourable responses to Geertz's study of Indonesian Islam, however, led to a curiously muted response from anthropologists and other scholars working in the Middle East. To some degree they had been let off the hook and it was those with an interest in subordinated areas of the discipline, like gender studies, who were most interested in what he had to say. Anthropology's muted response came about because, in addition to anthropology receiving favourable mention, Said's *Orientalism* is, all in all, an analysis of texts and the representations they contain. Small wonder that the more provocative elements of *Orientalism* were often quietly set aside and that those who took its critique seriously found it was more compatible to deal with it from the point of narrative and text. Anthropological responses to *Orientalism* therefore came as a more general response to *Orientalism*'s implications for the narrative forms of anthropological writing rather than as a careful working through of the implications of his views for the contemporary anthropology of Islam and the nations of the Middle East and North Africa.

With hindsight, the textual shift in the discipline might be seen as predictable. In making this point I want to emphasize how much Said's framing of anthropology within orientalist discursive modes and practices shook the discipline and how deeply his commentary on the speaking about and for 'orientalized' peoples wounded the moral positioning of much of the best anthropological scholarship. One immediate effect of his critique was to thrust the more critical scholars into an engagement with the production and structuring of the literary forms of the ethnography, the forms of writing about other cultures made famous by social anthropology's founding fathers. Important work in this field was done by George Marcus, James Clifford and Michael M.J. Fischer although overall it was characterized by an unwillingness to deal with the ways in which individual authors were inextricably enmeshed with the authorial politics of their texts. Vincent Crapanzano's experimental ethnography, *Tuhami. Portrait of a Moroccan* (1980), created many debates about the voicing of texts and raised in poignant form the ways in which a discussion of a remarkable 'other' slipped so easily into a discussion, once again, of the Western 'self', the individual anthropologist as rational observer.

A second productive response to *Orientalism* was to bring into anthropology a new interest in other forms of representing the peoples traditionally studied by anthropologists. As 'visual anthropology' emerged as a field there was an efflorescence of work on the ethnographic photograph and the moving images of film, and a renewed interest in historical images, paintings, postcards and the diaries and unpublished notes of anthropologists. Among these, Elizabeth Edwards' collection of essays *Anthropology and Photography* (1992) gives a good overview of the direction of research. A third field of interest emerged around museums and various forms of exhibition, exposition, theatre and circuses, with a fourth taking up issues around travel and travel writing (Behdad, 1994; Kabbani, 1986; Melman, 1992; Poignant, 1997). There have been many excellent studies of the ways in which 'blackness' is deployed in art and narrative (Marcus, 1997; Stoler, 1995), of how 'whiteness' is created (Frankenberg, 1993, 1997; Hale, 1998; Lipsitz, 1998; Roediger, 1994). And finally, Said's discourse on orientalism has provided the ground from which have sprung a number of studies of 'occidentalism', an approach which has been rapidly taken up within anthropology and cultural studies (Carrier, 1995; Chen, 1995; Mathy, 1993; Young, 1990).

'Occidentalism' is a notion based upon, in James Carrier's (1995) formulation, the dialectical relationship between orient and occident which some readings of Said allow to emerge. It is an approach which seeks to deconstruct the homogenizing effects that 'orientalism' has upon anthropological understandings of 'the West' and its various forms are exemplified in a collection of papers, *Occidentalism. Images of the West* (1995) which Carrier edited. With one significant exception, the essays in this volume rest upon precisely the dialectical relationship which Bhabha (1994) identified as problematic in Said's rendering of Foucault's notion of discourse. In *Orientalism*, Bhabha says, Said's concept of discourse is 'undermined by what could be called the polarities of intentionality' (Bhabha, 1994: 72). In his view, Foucault's concept of power/knowledge 'places subjects in a relation of power and recognition that is not part of a symmetrical or dialectical relation – self/other, master/slave – which can then be subverted by being inverted'.

In utilizing 'occidentalism' as a mode of analysis, Carrier extends Said's reading of Foucault and, in doing so, shifts attention away from the specificities of 'orientalism' as discourse of power/knowledge which is geographically located and which is concerned essentially with reproducing a specific hierarchy. On the basis of the common processes of hierarchy by which differences are polarized, essentialized, homogenized and generalized, 'occidentalism' broadens the orient to a point where it can be found anywhere: in subordinated classes, remote villages, marginalized urban or rural populations. In doing so, it not only dislocates discourse from its normalizing power effects but it removes it from its location. These moves, in turn,

lead to the muffling of the political processes involved and power becomes almost impossible to trace. It is not surprising to find that in many of the fine essays brought together by Carrier under the rubric of 'occidentalism', the analyses could proceed just as effectively had the concept not been employed. The striking exception, referred to earlier, is Michael Herzfeld's (1992) analysis of the ways in which European notions of the orient and Hellenism inflect Greek political thought and action. In this context, occident takes on some of the meaning which both Said and Foucault might have attributed to it.

THE DREAM OF THE ORIENT

It will be clear by now, I trust, that anthropologists have read Said in very different ways. In addition to clear anthropological responses, Said's definition and placing of a Western knowledge of its 'orient' within the discursive enunciations of colonialism has been influential in history, cultural studies, literature and post-colonial studies and this commonality of interests has led to a broadening of anthropology's field and to a degree of interdisciplinarity. Rana Kabbani's elegant study of travel writing in *Europe's Myths of Orient* (1986) used a sensitive account of V.S. Naipaul's hostility to Islam to show it growing upon the wounds of colonialism itself. Said's work is fundamental to the essays collected in *Gender and Imperialism* (Midgley, 1998), to broader critiques of the discipline of Asian studies and to studies that seek to move away from it (Franco and Preisendanz, 1997). Mica Nava's (1998) recent work on popular orientalism in everyday life in metropolitan England, for example, attempts to reposition orientalism as a more productive trope, one providing a legitimate domain of fantasy which was not necessarily as xenophobic as other versions of 'othering' narratives. She argues for a commercial orientalism 'with a distinctive libidinal economy in which women were key players and cultural difference signalled not the abject and the excluded but the modern, the liberating and perhaps even – though this is more contentious – the progressive' (Nava, 1998: 182). Here indeed is a challenge to Said's 'discourse on the orient'.

Orientalism's ramifications are endless. Even where his proposals are contested, they produce interesting and challenging work. While a balanced assessment of Said's work remains to be carried out, the debates have been immensely productive. If those who engage with *Orientalism* cannot always accept Said's conclusions or even his premises, his critique has ensured not only that writing about 'other' cultures and 'other' lives can never be the comfortable and untroubled occupation it once was, but that writing about our 'selves' in terms that no longer require 'orientalism' and its favourite dreams is now just as difficult.

Like David Hwang's French diplomat, in his encounter with Islam Lévi-Strauss saw himself caught up in a mirrored world in which his sense of identity and his own world kept shifting. I quote again: 'I am only too well aware of the reasons for the uneasiness I felt in coming into contact with Islam: I rediscovered in Islam the world I myself had come from; Islam is the West of the East ... I cannot easily forgive Islam for showing me our own image ...' (Lévi-Strauss, [1955] 1976: 531). It is in this hall of oriental mirrors that he finds the beginning of the ending of his book, a book which ends with the disintegration of anthropology and the disintegration of his world. Hwang's fictional character, the diplomat, sees freedom and renounces it because his own identity rests upon an imaginary and hallucinatory 'other'. If he could renounce his dreams he would find both himself and his lover who waits beyond. As the discipline of 'difference' which manufactures those cultural 'others', anthropology faces *Orientalism*'s prison and choices in a particularly decisive way. And in anthropology's encounter with Islam, it faces them head on. *Orientalism* offers a challenge that strikes at the heart of the mind. Can anthropology lose itself and find at least a kind of freedom from the dream?

NOTES

1 Cited in Garber (1992), *New York Times*, 11 May 1986.

2 Marjorie Garber's (1992) astute and detailed analysis of Hwang's play and of cross-dressing and its politics makes many more important points about the role of transgression and transvestism.

3 In a perceptive discussion of 'the West' in anthropology, Henrietta Moore (1994: 158 n.1) notes that an uncritical notion of it as a unified entity remains fundamental to discussions of colonialism and post-colonialism in both cultural studies and sociology.

4 Bryan Turner's *Marx and the End of Orientalism* was published in the same year as *Orientalism* but there is a long tradition of critique from within British and French oriental studies which also interrogated the discipline. These critiques grew out of the disciplines themselves rather than from philosophical debates, as did earlier anthropological approaches to the political questions raised by the subjects of anthropological enquiry. Talal Asad had raised issues regarding anthropology and colonialism in 1973.

5 See J. Marcus (1990) for further comment on this tendency. James Clifford's detailed and thoughtful essay, 'Orientalism', brings in Said's politics towards the end but does not disclose his own. In this way he preserves his dominating authorial position.

6 In this passage Torgovnik refers to James Clifford's work and to Christopher Miller's book, *Black Darkness* (1989).

7 For studies of gender in the Middle East which do not take Said and orientalism as a focus, see Goçek and Balaghi (1994).

8 'My [Ahmed's] understanding of anthropology is based on the assumption that the anthropologist is the spectator par excellence, the public eye, the social analyst, the objective commentator of a particular group. At best the anthropologist transcends culture and race to represent the group. Above all, anthropology ideally is embedded in ... a 'strong humanitarian tradition'. Anthropology is a figleaf which still provides some dignity to humanity ... [anthropology] compares and contrasts societies and by describing how ordinary people live elsewhere it creates understanding and sympathy for them. Second, it does so broadly in the context of a wider humanitarian tradition. Finally, it counters the simplistic media images which, painting with a broad brush, often ridicule other cultures as odd, as comical or inferior' (Ahmed, 1991: 1).

REFERENCES

Ahmed, A.S. (1991) 'Anthropology "comes out"?', *Anthropology Today*, 7 (3): 1–2.

Asad, Talal (ed.) (1973) *Anthropology and the Colonial Encounter*. New York: Ithaca Press.

de Beauvoir, Simone (1953) *The Second Sex*. New York: Knopf.

Beck, Lois and Keddie, Nikki (eds) (1978) *Women in the Muslim World*. Cambridge, MA: Harvard University Press.

Behdad, Ali (1994) *Belated Travellers. Orientalism in the Age of Colonial Dissolution*. Durham, NC: Duke University Press.

Bhabba, Homi (1994) 'The other question: stereotype, discrimination and the discourse of colonialism', in *The Location of Culture*. London and New York: Routledge.

Carrier, James G. (ed.) (1995) *Occidentalism. Images of the West*. Oxford: The Clarendon Press.

Chen, Xiao-mei (1995) *Occidentalism. A Theory of Counter-discourse in Post-Mao China*. New York: Oxford University Press.

Clifford, James (1988) 'On *Orientalism*', in *The Predicament of Culture: Twentieth Century Ethnography, Literature, and Art*. Cambridge MA: Harvard University Press.

Clifford, James and Marcus, George E. (1986) *Writing Culture. The Poetics and Politics of Ethnography*. Berkeley and Los Angeles, CA: University of California Press.

Crapanzano, Vincent (1980) *Tuhami. Portrait of a Moroccan*. Chicago: University of Chicago Press.

Edwards, Elizabeth (1992) *Anthropology and Photography, 1860–1920*. New Haven, CT and London: Yale University Press and the Royal Anthropological Institute.

Franco, Eli and Preisendanz, Karin (eds) (1997) *Beyond Orientalism. The Work of Wilhelm Halbfass and Its Impact on Indian and Cross-cultural Studies*. Amsterdam: Rodopi.

Frankenberg, Ruth (1993) *White Women, Race Matters. The Social Construction of Whiteness*. Minneapolis, MN: University of Minnesota Press.

Frankenberg, Ruth (ed.) (1997) *Displacing Whiteness. Essays in Social and Cultural Criticism*. Durham, NC: Duke University Press.

Garber, Marjorie (1992) 'The Occidental Tourist: *M. Butterfly* and the scandal of transvestism', in Andrew Parker, Mary Russo, Doris Sommer and Patricia Yaeger (eds), *Nationalisms and Sexualities*. New York: Routledge.

Geertz, Clifford (1988a) 'The world in a text. How to read *tristes tropiques*', in *Works and Lives. The Anthropologist as Author*. Stanford, CA: Stanford University Press.

Geertz, Clifford (1988b) *Works and Lives. The Anthropologist as Author*. Stanford, CA: Stanford University Press.

Gilsenan, Michael (1996) *Lords of the Lebanese Marches. Violence and Narrative in an Arab Society*. Berkeley and Los Angeles, CA: University of California Press.

Goçek, Fatma Müge and Balaghi, Shiva (eds) (1994) *Reconstructing Gender in the Middle East. Tradition, Identity, Power*. New York: Columbia University Press.

Hale, Grace E. (1998) *Making Whiteness. The Culture of Segregation in the South, 1890–1940*. New York: Pantheon Books.

Hall, Catherine (1992) *White, Male and Middle Class. Explorations in Feminism and History*. Cambridge: Polity Press.

Herzfeld, Michael (1992) *The Social Production of Indifference. Exploring the Symbolic Roots of Western Bureaucracy*. New York: Berg.

Kabbani, Rana (1986) *Europe's Myths of Orient*. Bloomington, IN: Indiana University Press.

Lacoste, Yves ([1966] 1984) *Ibn Khaldun*. Paris: Librairie François Maspero/London: Verso.

Lévi-Strauss, Claude ([1955] 1976) *Tristes Tropiques*. Paris: Librairie Plon/London: Penguin.

Lipsitz, George (1998) *The Possessive Investment in Whiteness. How White People Profit from Identity Politics*. Philadelphia: Temple University Press.

Manderson, Lenore and Margaret Jolly (eds) (1997) *Sites of Desire, Economies of Pleasure. Sexualities in Asia and the Pacific*. Chicago and London: University of Chicago Press.

Marcus, George E. and Fischer, Michael M.J. (1986) *Anthropology as Cultural Critique*. Chicago: University of Chicago Press

Marcus, J. (1997) '"... like an Aborigine" – empathy, Elizabeth Durack, and the colonial imagination', *Olive Pink Society Bulletin*, 9 (1&2): 44–52.

Marcus, J. (1990) 'Anthropology, culture and postmodernity', *Social Analysis*, 27 (April): 3–16.

Marcus, J. (1992) *A World of Difference. Islam and Gender Hierarchy in Turkey*. Sydney: Allen and Unwin.

Mathy, Jean-Philippe (1993) *Extreme-Orient. French Intellectuals and America*. Chicago: University of Chicago Press.

Melman, Billie (1992) *Women's Orients. English Women and the Middle East, 1718–1918. Sexuality, Religion, and Work*. Ann Arbor: University of Michigan Press.

Mernissi, Fatma (1975) *Beyond the Veil*. New York: John Wiley & Sons.

Midgley, Clare (1998) *Gender and Imperialism*. Manchester: Manchester University Press.

Miller, Christopher (1989) *Black Darkness*. Chicago: University of Chicago Press.

Minh-ha, T. (1989) *Women, Native, Other*. Bloomington, IN: Indiana University Press.

Moore, Henrietta (1994) *A Passion for Difference*. Cambridge: Polity Press.

Nava, Mica (1998) 'The cosmopolitanism of commerce and the allure of difference. Selfridges, the Russian ballet and the tango, 1911–1914', *International Journal of Cultural Studies*, 1 (2): 163–96.

Poignant, Roslyn (1997) 'Looking for Tambo', *Olive Pink Society Bulletin*, 9 (1&2): 27–37.

Reed-Danahy, Deborah (1995) 'The Kabyle and the French: occidentalism in Bourdieu's theory of practice', in James Carrier (ed.), *Occidentalism. Images of the West*. Oxford: The Clarendon Press.

Reiter, Rayna (ed.) (1975) *Toward an Anthropology of Women*. New York: Monthly Review Press.

Rodinson, Maxime (1974) *Islam and Capitalism*. New York: Pantheon.

Roediger, David R. (1994) *Towards the Abolition of Whiteness. Essays on Race, Politics and Working Class History*. London and New York: Verso.

Rosaldo, Michelle and Lamphere, Louise (eds) (1974) *Women, Culture and Society*. Stanford, CA: Stanford University Press.

Said, E.W. (1978) *Orientalism*. London: Routledge and Kegan Paul.

Said, E.W. (1981) *Covering Islam*. London: Routledge and Kegan Paul.

Said, E.W. (1985) 'Orientalism reconsidered', *Race and Class*, 27 (2): 1–15.

Said, E.W. (1993) *Culture and Imperialism*. London: Chatto and Windus.

Spivak, G.C. (1990) *The Post-Colonial Critic*. London: Routledge.

Stoler, Ann Laura (1995) *Race and the Education of Desire. Foucault's 'History of Sexuality' and the Colonial Order of Things*. Durham, NC and London: Duke University Press.

Torgovnik, Marianna (1990) *Gone Primitive: Savage Intellects, Modern Lives*. Chicago and London: University of London Press.

Turner, Bryan S. (1978) *Marx and the End of Orientalism*. London: George Allen and Unwin.

Yegenoglu, Meyda (1998) *Colonial Fantasies: Towards a Feminist Reading of Orientalism*. Cambridge and New York: Cambridge University Press.

Young, Robert (1990) *White Mythologies. Writing History and the West*. London and New York: Routledge.

8

Ethnomethodology and Ethnography

MELVIN POLLNER AND ROBERT M. EMERSON

The overlap of genealogies, concerns and prefixes might lead one to expect a cordial relationship between ethnomethodology (EM) and ethnography (EG). Both perspectives are informed by the interpretive tradition, concerned with the lifeworld, respect the point of view of the social actor (hence 'ethno-'), and typically eschew quantitative and theoretical approaches. From a distance – the heights of, say, macro- or historical sociology – the family resemblances must seem striking. Despite the similarities, however, the relationship has not been congenial. Most ethnographers have ignored EM and its potential relevance for EG, while ethnomethodologists have often rebuffed invitations to the equivalent of family reunions with kindred perspectives (Maynard, 1998; Zimmerman and Wieder, 1970). Garfinkel (1991; see also Garfinkel and Wieder, 1992) reiterated the width of the schism by referring to EM as a radically 'incommensurable' respecification of sociology's topics and methods.

None the less, over the 30 years during which EM and EG have grown older together, once clearer boundaries have become blurred. Some ethnographers have appropriated EM concepts and concerns (cf. Dingwall, 1981; Emerson, 1987; Emerson et al., 1995) and both have been influenced by (and contributed to) intellectual currents such as postmodernism. EM's recent emphasis on deep immersion in the profession or activity under consideration – roughly equivalent to 'going native' – and references to 'ethnomethodologically informed ethnography' (e.g., Randall et al., 1995), make differences between some strains of EM and EG difficult to discern even by close-up observers. Finally, recent efforts to integrate EG and EM (Gubrium and Holstein, 1997; Silverman, 1993) suggest that the once pronounced differences may be dissolving into an integrated methodological sensibility.

We begin by providing an overview of EM's core concepts and taking note of divergences within contemporary EM. We are particularly concerned with the potential relevance of these EM concepts to EG, recognizing, of course, that, as this volume attests, EG itself is a diverse methodology with sometimes discordant characterizations of key concerns. We suggest that, often in the face of its own theoretical claims and stance, EM offers resources that buttress and deepen EG. For example, EM's insistence on the import of background knowledge for the very intelligibility of talk and action adds weight to the significance of EG's signature method – embodied presence in the social world. But EM also challenges key aspects of EG theory and practice. As we shall suggest in the second part of the chapter, EM faults EG for being both too involved in and too removed from the social worlds it studies, and for ignoring the problematics of its own efforts to represent such worlds. Finally, we conclude by suggesting that self-deconstructing aspects of EM provide good reasons for EG *not* to embrace EM initiatives too enthusiastically. Rather, EM insights can be used selectively to heighten sensitivity to fundamental methodological issues and to augment appreciation of the practices of both the subjects of ethnography and ethnographers themselves.

ETHNOMETHODOLOGY

Ethnomethodology originated in the context of the Parsonian orthodoxy of mid-century American sociology (Heritage, 1984). Despite its aspiration to be 'the' theory of social action, Parsons' (e.g., 1951) massive effort neglected or distorted significant aspects of the organization of social life. The emphasis on shared, internalized norms as an explanation of patterned social behavior, for example, disregarded the interpretive judgements necessarily involved in the application of a norm or rule (Cicourel, 1974a; Garfinkel, 1967); the emphasis on theoretical 'top-down' solutions to the problem of social order precluded examination of actual 'bottom-up' or lived ordering; the invocation of the ideals of scientific enquiry as a model of every-day rationality pre-empted consideration of how members indigenously organize and assess the 'rationality' of their own activities in everyday life (Schutz, 1962, 1964).

If concern with the social order as defined by Parsons privileged *sociological* methods, definitions of order, explanations and assessments, EM focused attention on *participants*' methods, definitions of order, explanations and assessments. Reduced to a phrase, EM directed attention to what has variously been referred to as the 'indigenous', 'endogenous' or 'lived order' (Goode, 1994; Heritage, 1984; Maynard and Clayman, 1991), that is, the orderliness of social life as experienced, constructed and used from within the concrete and particular contexts and activities of which the society is composed:

> The words 'lived' and 'order' refer to aspects of what actually occurs and is experienced in everyday social action. The word 'lived' alerts the observer to the essentially situated and historical character of everyday action (to paraphrase Garfinkel: that it is composed of just these people, at just this time, at just this place, doing just this – the 'justs' of everyday structures of everyday actions that are social in origin, such as taking turns in conversation, queuing up, getting directions, driving on the freeway, offering a description of what you are doing, and so on). The term 'lived order', then, calls our attention to both the contingent and socially structured ways societal members construct/enact/do/inhabit their everyday world. (Goode, 1994: 127)

Adverse to consolidation as a systematic theoretical position (Garfinkel, 1967; Heritage, 1984), ethno-methodology initially developed as a melange of exhibits and arguments. In general, EM injunctions and initiatives focused concern on the skills, prac-tices and assumptions constituting social settings, their deployment in particular temporally unfolding courses of activity, and the experiences for which they provide. EM has evolved over the 30 years since publication of Garfinkel's *Studies in Ethno-methodology* (1967), however, and is now marked by diverse theoretical, methodological and substan-tive concerns (Maynard and Clayman, 1991). Space limitations preclude complete coverage of the current diversity of EM; we have therefore opted to focus more selectively on EM work which has strong parallels with and direct relevance to the concerns of EG. In so doing we will make frequent use of classic EM works, generally confining ourselves to single

examples of issues and phenomena where multiple examples abound.

Despite increased diversity in focus and method, EM studies are guided by an overlapping set of ideas and directives. Many central ideas are in place early in EM's history and are subsequently elabo-rated, emphasized and combined in ways which produce the distinctive accents of earlier and later studies. Rather than reiterate major exegeses and syntheses of EM (e.g., Button, 1991; Gubrium and Holstein, 1997; Heritage, 1984; Lynch, 1993; Maynard and Clayman, 1991), and in the spirit of EM's antipathy to systematization, we overview a number of the key directives comprising the EM sensibility.

Constructive Analysis

The dissatisfaction with Parsonian theory was amplified into a comprehensive rejection of any a priori or external version of the achievement of the lived order. In one way or another, the commitment to conventional sociological explanation and description, EM argues, either diverts attention from the lived order, formulates it as epiphe-mena, and/or imposes concepts and mechanisms variously irrelevant or unintelligible to participants. At best, conventional sociological analyses 'con-struct' a highly abstract version of the processes through which the fabric of social life is created, experienced and sustained by participants. Such constructed versions of order are responsive to the criteria and concerns of the professional sociologi-cal community but (one might say 'and therefore') inherently incapable of providing insight into or even of recognizing the problematic of the lived order. Thus, advice to those aspiring to understand social life from an EM perspective would include a recommendation to divest oneself of all sociologi-cal concepts (but see Hilbert, 1992).

Constructive analysis is embodied in the various methods of the social sciences. In one way or another, social scientific techniques for securing and analysing data transform and reduce features of the lifeworld (Cicourel, 1964; Goode, 1994). Surveys, interviews, content analysis, experiments, and even conventional EG impose a priori or extrinsic definitions of pattern and order. The repre-sentations contrived through these techniques have a tenuous relation to the actual concerns and doings of practitioners and participants. Thus, for example, the use of accounts elicited through interviews may not only gloss or omit details but by virtue of their retrospective character impart a determinacy and inexorability that the recounted events did not possess as they were lived, experienced and struc-tured the 'first time through' (Garfinkel et al., 1981). Other methods pose yet greater and possibly irremediable limitations in recovering or recognizing the lived order. Thus, a second piece of advice to the aspiring EM might include the recommendation to abandon conventional sociological methodology.

Endogenous Order

The critique of constructive analysis emerges in tandem with an appreciation of the endogenous or lived order. At the risk of simplification, the lived order consists of how participants in the diverse, temporally developing, concrete circumstances comprising 'the society' concertedly organize, recognize, use and achieve whatever they regard or define as sensible, rational, intelligible or orderly. EM proposes in effect that the society consists of the ceaseless, ever-unfolding transactions through which members engage one another and the objects, topics and concerns that they find relevant. These interactions are accomplished as interactants deploy the resources and competencies they possess as members of the society, not as sociologists with special insight. The orderliness of social life ceases to be a problem raised and resolved by social theorists but a practically achieved phenomenon 'incarnate' in the interactions and activities of social actors in actual particular circumstances. Accordingly, the analyst of the lived or endogenous order is directed to detailed empirical examination of the 'detailed and observable practices which make up the incarnate production of ordinary social facts' (Lynch et al., 1983).

Accountable Features

To highlight the endogenous order, ethnomethodologists speak of 'accountable' features. The term is evocative of several concerns. First, an accountable feature refers to the features of a setting as and in the ways they are oriented to (that is, taken account of) and sustained in interaction, practice and experience (Garfinkel, 1967). Bereft of any theoretically driven criteria of significance or focus, EM's attention is directed to whatever participants take into account. Secondly, 'accountability' evokes appreciation that members do not casually take certain matters into account but assess and evaluate the adequacy of one another's recognition, assessment and use of those matters. As Garfinkel's (1967) early breaching experiments illustrated, for example, failure to participate in the web of practices undergirding even the most banal of interactions occasions confusion, concern and attributions of incompetence. Indeed, the aspect of accountability marks EM's distinctive domain: EM's focus is not on what members, each on their own, *might* take into account, but rather features and practices which are sanctionably, consequentially or warrantably invoked (cf. Heritage, 1984). Finally (and

classically), accountability – in the sense of capable of being represented within an account – connotes that members construct the identifiability or intelligibility of their activities. Any setting is understood to be a process whose very recognizability and formulability is the outcome of practices of interpretation and enactment.[1] As Garfinkel proposes:

> In exactly the way that a setting is organized, it *consists* of methods whereby its members are provided with accounts of the setting as countable, storyable, proverbial, comparable, picturable, representable – i.e., accountable events. (1967: 34; emphasis in original)

Ethnomethodological Indifference

EM's abstention from evaluative or ironic analysis of the activities it addresses – so-called 'ethnomethodological indifference' (Garfinkel and Sacks, 1970) – is reflected in the very term 'ethnomethodology'. The choice of the rubric was inspired by developments in the cultural anthropology of several decades ago. Various 'ethno-studies' such as ethno-medicine, ethno-botany and ethno-zoology, sought to understand the principles, practices and bodies of knowledge pertaining to their respective domains in non-Western societies. In the traditional anthropological manner, ethno-studies refrained from invidious comparison with Western understanding of appropriate scientific knowledge. Capitalizing on these connotations, 'ethnomethodology' was coined by Garfinkel (1974) to identify the knowledge and practices – the 'methods' – deployed by ordinary actors in their everyday lives. Although they did not necessarily comport well with the academic and scientific models of rational action (and participants might be oblivious to their existence), the knowledge and methods that members used were nevertheless the infrastructure of social life. From the outset, then, ethnomethodology as the study of ethnomethods was to maintain a posture of indifference to the ultimate value or validity of members' methods.

In general, EM indifference bids the researcher to refrain from assessing correctness, appropriateness or adequacy in articulating the practices and organization of the endogenous order. Whatever faults (or virtues) they may display when assessed by extrinsic criteria, these practices and their products constitute the social reality of everyday activities – in the home, office, clinic and scientific laboratory (Garfinkel et al., 1981). Thus, ethnomethodological indifference precludes characterizations of members as deficient, pathological or irrational (or superior, normal or rational). Of course, such characterizations are of interest as phenomena when they occur in the setting under consideration: critique and fault-finding are ubiquitous features of social life and thus comprise activities whose organization, use and consequences are to be explicated.

Resource and Topic

The taken-for-granted practices that comprise the lived order are frequently of such subtlety that they surreptitiously infiltrate professional social science. Consequently, processes that might otherwise be topics of enquiry – bodies of knowledge and artful practices – are unwittingly employed as 'resources' for analysis (Zimmerman and Pollner, 1970). The fusion and sometimes confusion of sociological and 'common sense' concepts and practices has profound implications for the study of social life. To the extent that practices such as 'counting', 'describing', 'theorizing' and even questing after 'truth' originate in the lifeworld, the unexplicated appropriation of these activities conflates sociology with its subject matter. Without explication of these primordial practices, analysis risks usurpation by the discursive practices and categories of the very order of affairs it seeks to analyse. From this point of view, the methodological problem is not one of 'going native' but of already being deeply and naively native.

Making the Familiar Strange

Although members are remarkably adept in recognizing, knowing and 'doing' the lived order, their practices are resistant to analytic recovery.[2] While they contribute to the constitution of meaning and intelligibility, these practices rarely comprise thematic concerns for participants. In fact, Garfinkel (1967: 7–8) suggests that participants are specifically and sanctionably 'uninterested' in the practices through which local order is achieved – and such uninterestedness is itself a feature of competence. Because these assumptions and practices are difficult to discern by participants and analysts alike, Garfinkel's (1967) initial efforts sought to make them 'visible' by destabilizing or disrupting ordinary activities in the (in)famous series of breaching experiments. Relatedly, EM takes advantage of 'perspicuous' persons or settings in which the ordinarily effaced infrastructure is (or can be made to be) transparent or thematic. To explore the taken-for-granted work of the construction of gender identity, for example, Garfinkel (1967) conducted extensive interviews with 'Agnes' who was born a biological male but presented and conducted herself as a woman. In other efforts to explore the role of the body in the lived order, Garfinkel (described in Robillard, 1999) developed procedures which temporarily disrupted ordinary bodily feedback, for example, wearing inverted lenses while conducting commonplace tasks. One of Garfinkel's former students describes the effects of another such procedure:

> Garfinkel also had us experience speaking by means of a machine that delayed hearing your own voice as you spoke. We saw that intelligible speaking is based on the almost instantaneous capacity to hear yourself. If the delay became too great, the ability to pronounce even familiar words quickly degenerated into something that produced only mush-mouth mumbles. (Robillard, 1999: 156)

Reflexivity

One sense of reflexivity emerges from Garfinkel's more or less explicit use of the term. Reflexivity refers to the simultaneously embedded and constitutive character of actions, talk and understanding. The intelligibility of an utterance, for example, appeals to and depends upon the ongoing sequence, retrospectively contributes to the sense of the sequence and extends the sequence into the future. Somewhat more complexly, social actors have a sense of the field of action, explicitly reason about the field of action, and act in the light of such understandings and reasonings in ways that variously affect (reproduce or change) the field of action. Reflexivity, then, refers to how what actors 'know about' or 'make of' and 'do in' a setting is itself constitutive of the setting and informed by it. As Garfinkel has characterized this process: 'such practices consist of an endless, ongoing contingent accomplishment ... carried on under the auspices of, and made to happen as events in, the same ordinary affairs that in organizing they describe' (1967: 1).

A second sense of reflexivity emerges from the appreciation that the 'ethno' in ethnomethodology refers to *every* category of member and activity, not only 'lay members' but professionals of every sort, and, by implication, ethnomethodologists themselves (Garfinkel, 1967). EM representation of reality, no less than that of the lay member, may be approached as an achievement:

> No inquiries can be excluded no matter where or when they occur, no matter how vast or trivial their scope, organization, cost, duration, consequences, whatever their successes, whatever their repute, their practitioners, their claims, their philosophies or philosophers. Procedures and results of water witching, divination, mathematics, sociology – whether done by lay persons or professionals – are addressed according to the policy that every feature of sense, of fact, of method, for every particular case of inquiry without exception, is the managed accomplishment of organized settings of practical actions, and that particular determinations in members' practices of consistency, planfulness, relevance, or reproducibility of their practices and results – from witchcraft to topology – are acquired and assured only through particular, located organizations of artful practices. (Garfinkel, 1967: 32)

The reflexive turn recognizes that ethnomethodological concepts and empirical studies are themselves examinable as embedded in taken-for-granted practices and presuppositions.[3] In actually taking the reflexive turn, the EM representation of a setting's practices and assumptions may itself be attended to as the product of practices and assumptions through which 'data' are collected, interpreted and textually rendered (Cicourel, 1981) into a determinate EM version of social reality (cf. Pollner and Goode, 1990).

Illustrative EM Phenomena

Given EM's concern with the lived or endogenous order, it is difficult, perhaps contradictory, to specify EM topics of concern in advance of actual enquiry. In EM's concern with 'everyday' interaction and institutional settings, however, analysts were sensitive to a number of (arguably) generic processes and practices.

Background understandings The importance of background knowledge in the intelligibility of everyday life is emphasized by any number of the intellectual tributaries drawn upon by EM. Schutz (1962, 1964), of course, highlighted the taken-for-granted meanings and assumptions which make interaction possible. In his description of the plight of the cultural stranger (1964), for example, he underscores the role of *general* cultural background meanings in providing orientation and understanding: while vocabulary and rules of syntax can be translated, background understandings which suffuse interaction defy articulation. Wittgenstein (1953) highlighted the role of *local* understandings in a 'primitive language game' in which one worker says 'slab!' to his colleague. Within this context, says Wittgenstein, the word is not merely naming an object, but functions as an order or request to hand over a slab. The locally competent understanding of 'slab!' as a request makes reference to and requires understanding of a complex of projects and relations comprising 'a form of life'. Thus, EM studies are especially sensitive to how intelligible or 'naturally accountable' action invokes and presupposes an unarticulated – and perhaps not totally articulable – background of knowledge and understanding.[4]

Interpretive practices Vivid examples of the role of background knowledge in the intelligibility of discourse and action are provided by actual EM studies. In an explication of conversational exchanges, for example, Garfinkel illustrated how the meaning of an utterance depended on placement in a developing and inferred context: 'their sense cannot be decided by an auditor unless he knows or assumes something about the biography and purposes of the speaker, the circumstances of the utterance, the previous course of conversation, or the particular relationship of actual or potential interaction that exists between user and auditor'

(Garfinkel, 1967: 40). Moreover, the irremediable 'indexicality' of expressions means that background understandings cannot be articulated without appeal to yet other unspoken understandings *ad infinitum*. Thus, while members may formulate their knowledge to a point, the very grasp of those formulations may require knowledge that is itself borne of experience within the order it describes (cf. Cicourel, 1974b).

Given the inherent indeterminacy of meaning, members are actively engaged in making sense of discourse – and indeed social life in general – through a process which Garfinkel (1967) termed the 'documentary method of interpretation'. Through the documentary method, manifest particulars are treated as referring to or 'documenting' a putatively underlying pattern, topic or theme, which in turn is used to elaborate the sense of the particulars. The actual ways in which parties to a range of settings engage in the documentary method to establish and sustain the meaning or 'sense' of one or another feature of a setting has emerged as a central process in a variety of everyday and professional settings.

Practical sociological reasoning In early efforts, EM took issue with Durkheim's (1951) critique of coroner's reasoning in determining the cause of suicide. Coroners, argued Durkheim, typically conducted a superficial investigation resulting in failure to identify the 'real' cause of suicide which Durkheim's subsequent analysis was intended to supersede. Rather than regard the coroner's reasoning as inadequate, the emerging EM attitude held that the reasoning of the coroner comprises a focal concern of any enquiry seeking to understand how a society constructs, sustains and applies the category 'suicide' (Atkinson, 1978; Garfinkel, 1967). The attitude is extended to members' reasoning about whatever features comprise their circumstances – persons, bodies, technology, organizations, nature and society. Once again, from the point of view of EM, members are not 'judgemental dopes' (Garfinkel, 1967) whose actions are mechanically determined by social conditions. Rather, they are actively engaged in appraising and reasoning about those circumstances, the products of which reflexively redound to the setting.[5]

Accounts and formulations Sacks' (1963) parable of a stranger encountering a machine composed of a 'doing part' and a 'narrating part' signaled EM's regard for representation. Sacks noted the limitations of using the narrating part as a description of the machine: the narrating part was another doing of the machine and thus itself an activity to be explicated rather than appropriated as an analytic resource. For EM, representation is an integral feature of the production of the endogenous order: a group's (self-) descriptions, conceptualizations and analyses are themselves socially organized practices. A host of everyday activities and specialized settings use or produce formal and informal categorizations, conceptualizations and formulations – that is, specific statements in which actors describe, summarize or explain 'in so many words' the 'gist' of what they are saying or doing (Garfinkel and Sacks, 1970). Accordingly, the construction and use of analyses and accounts – written and oral – is a naturally occurring (and increasingly important) social phenomenon addressed by EM. The work of physicists, physicians and phenomenologists – as they collect data and develop representations – comprise lived orders to which EM enquiry is addressed. Needless to say, social scientists are also involved in the production of accounts. Thus, the very constructive analyses EM faults in terms of their capacity to recognize or recover lived order comprise candidate topics of EM enquiry.

Embodiment   Recent work in EM has explored embodied competencies. On the one hand, several studies examine the ubiquitous but self-effacing role of the body in everyday activities. Goode's (1994) explorations of the lifeworlds of children rendered deaf, dumb and blind by rubella highlights the role of the body in the constitution of an intersubjective world. Robillard's (1999) account of the disruptions of the ordinary activities consequent to his progressive paralysis through Lou Gehrig's disease (or motor neurone disease) highlights the 'bodily achievements' involved in the most mundane tasks. Other studies, notably Sudnow's *Ways of the Hand* (1978), explore the acquisition of the embodied competencies involved in the performance of complicated worldly activities. Pursuing Garfinkel's recommendation to describe the is-ness or 'quiddity' of worldly action, Sudnow painstakingly and poetically describes his efforts to become competent in first 'going for the sounds' and then 'going for the jazz'. In his concluding commentary he notes:

> I had come to learn, overhearing and overseeing this jazz as my instructable hands' ways – in a terrain nexus of hands and keyboard whose respective surfaces had become known as the respective surfaces of my tongue and teeth and palate are known to each other – that this jazz music *is* ways of moving from place to place as singings with my fingers. To *define* jazz (as to define any phenomenon of human action) is to *describe* the body's ways. (1978: 146; emphasis in original)

The Unique Adequacy Requirement

From early on in its development one current within EM has emphasized active participation and the acquisition of indigenous skills and knowledge as means of capturing the lived order (cf. Bellman,

1975; Jules-Rosette, 1975). Such practices have taken on even more prominence as EM has refocused from studying the diffuse competencies and practices implicated in 'everyday' interaction to examining technical or otherwise esoteric settings. Instead of 'making the familiar strange' by developing 'amnesia for common sense' (Garfinkel, 1967), then, the ethnomethodologist is exhorted to acquire familiarity with opaque background knowledge and practices. For EM views these specialized settings as self-organizing ensembles of local practices whose ways and workings are only accessible through a competent practitioner's in-depth experience and familiarity. Thus, identification of the distinctive features of shamanism or mathematics requires the capacity for competent performance and actual participation in the form of life under consideration. As Garfinkel and Wieder (1992: 182) describe this 'unique adequacy requirement':

> ... for the analyst to recognize, or identify, or follow the development of, or describe phenomena of order in local production of coherent detail the analyst must be vulgarly competent in the local production and reflexively natural accountability of the phenomenon of order he is 'studying'.

'In plain ethnographic terms,' explains Lynch, 'Garfinkel seemed to be insisting on a strong participant observation requirement, through which his students would gain adequate mastery of other disciplines as a precondition for making ethnomethodological descriptions' (1993: 274). As EM focuses more intensely on specialized settings, the earlier methodological goal of making the familiar strange is replaced by efforts to make the strange familiar. For this recent development in EM, the fusion of local and analytic knowledge and competencies is not a 'problem', but a goal.

THE IMPLICATIONS OF EM FOR EG

Many ideas and initiatives of EM are resonant with those voiced in EG and the broader interpretive tradition. Both EM and EG insist that involvement in the form of life of a particular group or setting is indispensable for understanding local meaning and action. The critique of constructive analysis and EM's posture of indifference are recognizable as a variant of EG's injunction against a priori, ethnocentric or 'corrective' biases (Matza, 1969). Garfinkel's critique of the 'judgemental dope' is redolent of Blumer's (1969) version of symbolic interactionism. Indeed, it can be argued that field research and participant observation – frequently supplemented by or even focused primarily upon naturally occurring talk – have provided EM's primary method.

Yet significant differences between EG and EM remain. Because EM does not speak in a single voice (Maynard and Clayman, 1991), however, specifying these differences requires specifying a version of EM. An emphasis or permutation of one or another central initiative yields distinctive forms of EM enquiry such as cognitive sociology (Cicourel, 1974b), the reflexive program (McHugh et al., 1974) and conversation analysis.[6] Even the EM tradition most closely associated with Garfinkel and his students has differentiated. One aspect of the change is substantive: earlier EM was concerned with a diverse array of 'everyday' and institutional settings, while the recent studies focus on scientific activity. As Lynch's (1993) distinction between the earlier 'proto-' and more recent 'post-analytic' ethnomethodology suggests, however, the change in focus also involves a change in the nature and point of EM enquiry.

If EM is generally concerned with the lived order, then earlier EM is preoccupied with *ordering*, that is, the *practices* through which the lived order is organized. Generally, to gain purchase on taken-for-granted practices, the researcher strives to break the unwitting *communion* with his subjects and to achieve a measure of analytic *distance*. Hence, the various methodological caveats of EM indifference and topic-resource confusion warn of the dangers of becoming (naively) involved in or identifying with members' categories and concerns. The pursuit of practice is conducted with awareness that the pursuit has taken-for-granted practices of its own which are intertwined with (Garfinkel et al., 1981) and shape the very objects of enquiry. Thus, the enquiry is haunted by the possibility of a reflexive move in which the enquiry itself becomes the object of attention.

Recent EM, on the other hand, is concerned with '*living*' the lived order. Partly because the sophisticated sites of recent studies are accessible only by and to those with the competence to participate in them, the analyst must immerse him/herself ever more deeply in the actual practice or endeavor. Moreover, because any exogenous analysis or reflection is a diversion from the quiddity or 'just this' of the here and now, the EM seeks to eliminate any connection or concern external to the lived order. Even such bedrock EM concepts as 'detail', 'methods' and 'order' are used only as provisional place markers, to be forfeited or re-specified by whatever is accountable within the world under consideration (Garfinkel, 1991). Contrary to the caveats accompanying the pursuit of practice warning against communion, the pursuit of *presence* cautions against distance or disjuncture between the researcher and practitioner.[7] Indeed, rather than an aloof posture of EM indifference, the ethnomethodologist is invited to engage practitioners in a 'hybrid' discipline. At the end of the day, the ethnomethodologist is an auxiliary to the particular profession or work site under consideration.[8]

Criticisms of EG take varying form with these different versions of EM. The differing priority given to practice or to presence highlights distinctly different – even contradictory – ways in which EG misses or mistakes central phenomena. In the following pages we will examine three types of criticisms: first, EM holds that EG is typically so 'close' to the settings it studies that it may be unable to identify taken-for-granted practices and features of lived ordering. Secondly, EM also argues that the stance and practices of EG are too 'distant' from the social worlds it studies, again compromising its ability to recover the lived order. Finally, EM finds fault with EG's inattention to and unwillingness to examine its own essential assumptions and procedures. Just as the eye does not see itself seeing, EG effaces the very presence and practice through which it provides representations of the social world.

Too Close: Issues of Communion and Collusion

For anthropologists approaching a foreign culture, the dangers of 'going native' are familiar and evident: the prejudices of the home culture caution against appropriation of, say, oracular consultation as a technique of anthropological enquiry, or of local explanations of the efficacy of such consultation as anthropological analysis. For those describing the lived order of more familiar worlds, however, the problems are more subtle and insidious. EG is enmeshed in the very lived order and ordering activities it ought to study, and as a consequence its findings and analyses risk 'usurpation' by the lived order.

EG's vulnerability to co-optation by the social worlds it studies gives rise to two interrelated problems. First, in common with most sociology, EG fails to distance itself from conventional, culturally entrenched notions of a variety of 'natural facts' and hence remains oblivious to the social and interactional work that goes into their ongoing achievement. By virtue of membership in the larger common culture, the researcher may fail to attend to the problematic character of subjects' assumptions and practices, in this way *presupposing* and treating as factual and immutable what might otherwise be understood as contingent, artful interactional productions. Second, EG's unrecognized closeness to subjects' worlds may lead the researcher to treat members' concerns, distinctions and explanations as analytic resources. Ethnographers may engage indigenous concerns *critically* in order to produce a putatively more accurate or comprehensive account. Or they may *appropriate* and use these practices, offering them up as ethnographic characterizations and analyses, thereby using as a resource what EM maintains should be a topic. In either case,

EG risks 'missing' essential practices because of unwitting cultural communion between researcher and subject. Formulated as advice to EG, the response to these problems includes the following recommendations.

1 *Treat 'natural facts' as 'accomplishments'*. Garfinkel's work has sought to problematize what members take for granted as unalterably 'factual', that is, what they unthinkingly, naturally, unreflectively see/experience as part of the normal order of things. For example, Garfinkel et al. (1988: 146) explain that the term 'members' refers to what is 'efficaciously and witnessably known in common *without saying* and therein unworthy o[f] remark, specifically unnotice-able as a practical and local achievement' (emphasis added). At other points, he characterizes his concern with what is available to members immediately 'in the look of the thing'. What is 'evident' to members in this sense often eludes the attention of ethnographers in that they too accept the 'look of things' at face value. EM would then suggest that EG might well attend to the ways in which this order of 'natural fact' is interactionally produced and sustained.

EM treatment of 'natural facts' as social 'doings' involved recasting what most sociology viewed as 'ascribed' characteristics, as practical, interactional achievements. Garfinkel's (1967) analysis of Agnes as a case study of the practical, interactional achievement of *gender* provided the original and most influential instance of such an effort. Developing a position now well established, Garfinkel urged viewing gender not as a fixed attribute, but as an ongoing interactional accomplishment of a variety of situationally specific practices for passing as gendered as female (or male).

Moerman (1965) approached ethnicity in this fashion in looking at the actual occasions of identification as 'Lue' among a tribal people in Southeast Asia.[9] Moerman argued that it is impossible to identify the Lue on the basis of such standard anthropological tools as 'dialect divisions and trait distributions' (1965: 1218); there are greater language differences between some groups who identify themselves as Lue, for example, than between groups considered of different ethnicity but who 'speak as we do' (p. 1217). Moerman thus concluded that '[s]omeone is a Lue by virtue of believing and calling himself Lue and of acting in ways that validate his Lueness' (1965: 1222). Common ethnicity and ethnic identity, then, cannot be assumed; rather, in this particular case, the key issues are 'how and why the Lue can come across to their neighbors, themselves, and their ethnographer as "a group the members of which claim unity on the grounds of the their conception of a specific common culture"' (Moerman, 1974: 57, citing Nadel, 1942: 17). Furthermore, specific cultural traits (at least those the Lue themselves identify) should not be understood as objective qualities

determining ethnicity but as resources available to the Lue 'to *demonstrate* their ethnicity' (1974: 62; emphasis in original).

2 *Problematize practical sociological reasoning*. EM places great emphasis on the primacy of indigenous sense-making and interpretive practices, indeed insisting that EG's core project – to describe the ways, workings, and understandings of a social world – is derivative from and parallel to indigenous practices. Consider 'description', one of EG's signature activities. EM maintains that 'describing' is initially and foremost a folk activity; indigenous descriptions are in and part of the social world, ways of 'doing things with words' in that world. In their everyday lives, members routinely elaborate comprehensive formulations or explanations of local events, provide complex narrative accounts to themselves, other members and outsiders regarding the ways and workings, methods and meanings of the local setting (on laboratory scientists' descriptions to outsiders, see Lynch, 1985). A specific description, for example, may characterize members' circumstances in particular ways, thereby identifying specific meanings and hence excluding other meaning possibilities. In and through describing, then, members produce the order and orderliness of their daily lives and activities.[10] EG, however, fails to recognize the in-the-world character of these 'first order', indigenous descriptions, treating them instead as reports about 'real' events standing outside the social order described. To use such a situationally–produced characterization to represent a social world in a more or less authoritative, transcendent fashion, without reference to the specific local circumstances and purposes of its production, risks fundamental distortion.[11]

Bittner's (1964) analysis of the understanding of 'informal' structure in early qualitative studies of organizations provides an insightful examination of these issues. Bittner suggested that the standard sociological distinction between formal and informal organization begins by invoking an organization's explicit formal self-definition (for example, an organizational flow chart). Patterns and actions conforming to the chart are then treated as instances of the formal organization, allowing other patterns and actions to be designated 'departures' and consigned to the domain of 'informal' structures. As a result 'the sociologist finds himself in the position of having borrowed a concept from those he seeks to study in order to describe what he observes about them' (1964: 240). Although such borrowing is unavoidable up to a point, it becomes a significant problem when 'such concepts are expected to do the analytical work of theoretical concepts' (p. 241). Instead of appropriating the concept, recommends Bittner, the analyst ought to consider how members invoke and use definitions of formal and informal organization as a practice for achieving the local sense of the unity, meaningfulness and typicality of organizational actions.

Wieder (1974) extended EM treatment of these issues by examining EG's unselfconscious appropriation of members' practical sociological reasoning to describe and analyse the organization of prisons by reference to the 'convict code'. The classic sociological literature on prisons (e.g., Sykes, 1958) used the prisoners' own descriptions of the 'convict code' as a resource for explaining how prison life was organized; for example, to suggest that rehabilitative efforts were bound to fail because they ran counter to the requirements of the code. Wieder redirected attention to actual, in-situ references to the 'code' by residents of a half-way house for former drug addicts. Wieder showed how invoking the code or its specific tenets represented ways of taking action in the social organization of the house, an organization made relevant to this particular occasion by these very statements. For example, residents commonly responded to staff (or fieldworker) questions about personal matters by asserting 'You know I won't snitch.' This response, invoking the primary maxim of the convict code ('don't snitch'), 'multiformulated the immediate environment, its surrounding social structures, and the connections between this interaction and the surrounding social structures' (p. 168). The resident thus not only asserted that his refusal was not personal whim but a matter of sanctioned conformity to the local resident culture; but also indicated that he understood this particular 'personal question' as a request to 'snitch', that in such matters he stood with residents, against staff, etc. These situated, order-creating uses of the code are lost in their entirety when turned from members' accounts into sociological explanation.

Wieder's analysis of the convict code links directly with another central EM concern – criticism of EG's reliance on rules, definitions and meanings to provide causal explanations of order as defined by the analyst (Zimmerman and Wieder, 1970).[12] EM insists that order and orderliness (or, for that matter, disorder) are indigenously produced and appreciated features of social life. In their everyday and professional affairs, members of society recognize and explicitly attend to the coherence, connectedness, typicality, planful character of their circumstances. Accordingly, EM is concerned with how members of society go about the task of seeing, describing and explaining order in the world in which they live (Zimmerman and Wieder, 1970: 289). One way in which members establish the orderliness (or disorderliness) of what does or should occur is by invoking norms and rules. Many EG analyses, however, appropriate these member-invoked uses of norms or rules and convert them to inclusive causal explanations. The EM approach, in contrast, displaces or at least unsettles norms and rules as analytic resources, framing their use as topics in their own right.

In sum, one implication of EM's critique of the unrecognized conflation of resource and topic in EG's appropriation of members' sense-making procedures is the need to address explicitly the relationship between these procedures and the accounts that the ethnographer comes to offer. But a second implication is that EG should attend to indigenous sense-making – to members' descriptions, classifications and concepts – as *indigenous ethnography*. As Gubrium and Holstein (1997: 46) have suggested, subjects are ethnographers in their own right whose narratives reflect, interpret and constitute their social reality. From this point of view, descriptions are neither a resource for sociological investigation nor a dismissable competitor but a form of indigenous representation (Kirshenblatt-Gimblett, 1989) whose contexts, construction and consequences invite EG consideration.

Too Far: Issues of Disjuncture and Distance

Reluctant to participate completely or to acquire the requisite training for competent performance, the ethnographer is further denied access to the detailed richness of actual on-going activity. Needless to say, the commitment to sociology and the role of detached observer are not readily abandoned: they define the professional recognizability of EG. Owing to EG's commitment to sociology and perhaps to its very nature as EG, EG is disjoined from access to the lived order. Responsive to sociological concerns, EG's focus is deflected to secondary aspects of the local order while 'missing' a group's focal or defining activity; thus, numerous ethnographies of professions, but (until recently) little ethnographic consideration of actually making music (Sudnow, 1978) or solving mathematical proofs (Livingston, 1986). The radical solution (that is, becoming a practitioner) to what EM would suggest is EG's inherent superficiality, then, is more than most ethnographers would accept – indeed, more than most ethnomethodologists accept (Lynch, 1993). Nevertheless, the EM critique can be scavenged for pointers to what EG might be missing: specifically, EM suggests that by prioritizing non-involved observation over skilled performance within the field of action, by relying on redescription into exogenous concepts and categories rather than specifying endogenous focal concerns, and by not fully appreciating the detailed and temporally unfolding particulars of the lived order, the ethnographer is denied access to the 'quiddity' of social action. Stated as exhortations, the gist of EM's advice is: Do! Focus! Detail!

Not observation, but skilled participation The EM critique of detached observation appeared in early form in Bittner's (1973) commentary on the peculiar distortions evident in many ethnographic accounts. Specifically, as an unattached observer who can move more or less freely in and around the local scene, the ethnographer experiences choice and decision, not constraint and necessity. An observational stance and distanced experiences lead to representations that subtly transform members' worlds and experience in at least two distinct ways. First, EG overly subjectivizes and psychologizes the relation of participants to their social world: ethnographers frequently formulate what are objective matters for participants as matters depending on 'interpretation', 'beliefs' or 'concepts'. Secondly, EG frames as perceived, achieved or constructed what participants experience as simply there. In Bittner's words:

> the more he relies on his sensitivity as an observer who has seen firsthand how variously things can be perceived, the less likely he is to perceive those traits of depth, stability, and necessity that people recognize as actually inherent in the circumstances of their existence. Moreover, since he finds the perceived features of social reality to be perceived as they are because of certain psychological dispositions people acquire as members of their cultures, he renders them in ways that far from being realistic are actually heavily intellectualized constructions that partake more of the character of theoretical formulation than of realistic description. (1973: 123)

Subsequent EM critiques highlight the subjectivizing consequences of adopting an explicitly observational stance in various ethnographic studies of scientific practice. The work of Latour and Woolgar (1986), for example, had suggested that scientists might be profitably analogized to tribes and their products given no more or less analytic credence. Accordingly, the ethnographer of the scientific community approaches the laboratory as a site in which participants are engaged in the 'construction' of knowledge. The implication is that the accounts offered by the sciences are less than the 'objective' representation practitioners take them to be and more akin to narrative fabrications. For EM, such characterizations again reflect EG's distant view and its irreverence of the experienced 'depth, stability and necessity' of the lifeworld (Bittner, 1973: 121; Sharrock and Anderson, 1991).

For EM, adequate description requires not mere observation but embodied presence as a competent participant in the field of action. In the words of an earlier proposal to the same effect, the researcher must 'become the phenomenon' (Mehan and Wood, 1975). As noted earlier, Garfinkel has elaborated this insistence in the unique adequacy requirement, holding that the researcher who is not an active, adept and accredited participant will miss and distort central aspects and qualities of the lived order. Sudnow documents the depth of understanding that only skilled performance can provide – in effect filling in the meaning and relevance of advice that strikes the novice as empty or opaque:

> But for the most part I now follow one piece of advice – heard a long time before from jazz musicians, perhaps their most oft-voiced maxim for newcomers, literally overheard through my years of pursuing these notes on the records, regarded from my standpoint of novice and ethnographer as nothing but the vaguest of vague talk, accessible finally as the very detailed talk it was only when a grasp of the details to which it pointed were themselves successfully at hand – now my central instruction: SING WHILE YOU ARE PLAYING. (1978: 149)

The extent of involvement required for adequate understanding is illustrated in Garfinkel et al.'s (1988: 11) critique of Lynch's failure to become 'competent with the science he was studying': The researcher 'was not taken seriously' by laboratory researchers (p. 12); 'described the technical specifics of discovering axon sprouting though he did not know that work and could not recognize it for himself'; and was not required to and could not teach practices to practitioners as the latter did among and to one another.[13]

EM efforts to approximate more closely the actual life circumstances of the member may provide a more attractive model to EG than complete mastery of members' technical skills. Consider Goode's (1994) efforts to understand the worlds of the families and of the children who were born deaf and dumb because of rubella. While EG naturalism would recommend trying to grasp these worlds 'on their own terms', it is all too easy to assume that the child's world is limited, defective and incomplete. Goode framed the issue with regard to the child – Christina – as follows:

> I wanted a dialogue to begin between us but in her 'own terms'. The problem was how to recognize what her 'own terms' were. And there was this ever growing awareness that I was in a very real sense the greatest obstacle to being interior to Chris's world. [Consequently] ... a regular part of my work with Chris was thus work on and about myself. I sought by a series of exercises to 'clear myself out of the way'. (1994: 24)

In order to do so, to overcome his 'seeing, hearing, speaking self', Goode employed a number of unorthodox methodological practices; for example, simulating deaf–blindness by using ear stops and blindfolds. While recognizing the gulf between his efforts and Christina's congenital condition, Goode experienced something of the world of the deaf–blind: '[r]elying primarily on the kinesthetic sense and sense of smell makes the experiential world relatively "thin", immediate, unpredictable, and therefore dangerous' (1994: 25). He then came to recognize the pervasive and subtle power of his 'seeing, hearing, speaking self': the reflexively sustaining nature of his own 'perceptual bubble'.

Not exogenous concepts, but endogenous focal activities   EM offers a second, related criticism of EG, namely, that EG imports and imposes alien categories through perspectives virtually built into its very project. In addition to the detachment of mere observation, the exogenous pull of sociology variously deflects EG attention from and distorts representations of the lived social or professional order. EM articulates several variants of this critique.

First, EM insists that all sociological concepts and concerns are necessarily exogenous to and hence distortive of the lived order. Garfinkel et al. (1988) in fact uses the term 'analytic ethnography' to refer to EG accounts that rely on sociological concerns and categories to provide descriptions. Indeed, more extreme statements treat even EM concepts such as 'order', 'practice' etc., as having this alien, imposed character, and hence are to be used only in the most provisional fashion.

Secondly, EM contends that EG's reliance on exogenous sociological concerns leads it, even more specifically, to ignore or misapprehend the activities that stand at the core of and define a wide variety of social, professional and scientific enterprises. This criticism, directed broadly at sociological analyses as the problem of the 'missing what', is prefigured in Garfinkel's reflections on juror deliberations (1974), where he distinguished EM concerns from what might be learned from applying Bales' scheme for coding small-group interaction:

> The notion was that if we used Bales' procedures we could find a lot to say from these recorded conversations. From the transcriptions we could learn a great deal about how, in their conversations, they satisfied certain characteristics of small groups. The question that we had was, 'What makes them jurors?' (1974: 15)

That is, while a Balesian coding might reveal aspects of the jury as a small group, it yields little about the actual reasoning and deliberations through which participants conduct and construct themselves as jurors. Similarly, the typical orientation in sociological studies of work and occupations reduces observed activities to the familiar categories of the discipline: they are 'about' the occupation, rather than the actual 'what' or quiddity of the occupations themselves.[14] In his study of jazz musicians, Becker (1963) described a variety of concerns of professional musicians, especially their efforts to distance themselves from 'square' audiences; the work of playing music together never emerged as a topic. The activity at the heart of being a musician – actually making music – comprises the 'missing what'. Most relevantly for EM's current empirical concerns are omissions of the core activities of mathematics and the natural sciences.

Conventional concerns in the sociology of science have long addressed topics such as the distinctive normative order of science and the social factors shaping science policy and aspects of practice but neglected the very activities – proving, measuring, counting and so on – that comprise the actual doing of science.

In seeking to avoid sociological concepts in descriptions of the lifeworld of others, then, EM urges abandoning sociologists as an audience, instead addressing its descriptions to members or practitioners. From an EM point of view, descriptions must not only be produced by adept practitioners, but also should be delivered in the local vernacular in ways that are attentive to practitioners' central focal concerns.[15]

The value of lived detail   In addition to emphasizing the depth of descriptive detail needed to understand how the lived order is constructed and sustained, EM has also been especially concerned with the unique nature of experienced detail over and in the course of temporally unfolding and hence open or uncertain courses of action. Specifically, EM maintains that capturing endogenously relevant 'details' depends on providing 'real time' descriptions of events and actions. Real-time descriptions characterize events using only what is known at successive points as the event unfolds; the analyst must avoid using any 'end-point object' (Garfinkel et al., 1981: 137) as a resource for retrospectively analysing/characterizing prior stages of action. As a general principle, EM maintains that end-points or ultimate 'appearances are problematic as events-to-start-with' (Garfinkel et al., 1981: 136).

These matters are central to Garfinkel et al.'s analysis of the discovery of an optical pulsar, where descriptions of the discovered pulsar as a 'finished object' (that is, as represented in a scientific publication) distort or obscure the prior, contingent processes of making the 'discovery' in the first place. Reliance on the end-point of the finished pulsar dissolves its 'local historicity', that is, the temporally ordered details of 'discovering' an object that was not 'there' at an earlier point. Rather, analysis must address how, over the course of a number of successive 'runs' during one evening's work, physicists reconstituted the focus of their enquiries 'from an evidently-vague IT which was an object-of-sorts with neither demonstrable sense nor reference, to a "relatively finished object"', the discovered pulsar (1981: 135). For the collection of observations invoked to represent the discovered pulsar in subsequent publications 'was only obtainable, case-after-case, as an historicized series. The series was done as a lived orderliness, in real time. ... The crux of the matter is the historicity of their Runs' (p. 135). In these terms, then, EM would not only warn EG against description from an established end-point, but also urge attention to the sequenced, step-by-step unfolding of action ('case-after-case').[16]

EG as Practice

Garfinkel (1967) asserts that every form of enquiry – everyday or scientific – relies upon the deployment of taken-for-granted assumptions, knowledge and practices for organizing itself and its findings. Relatedly, EM has been attracted to activities pertaining to enquiry which have an epistemological cast – what Lynch (1993) refers to as 'epistopics': facticity, objectivity, description, truth. These core concerns with methods of enquiry and their practical accomplishment clearly might be applied to EG as a distinctive set of practices for producing and warranting findings: as a lived order and ordering informed from the outset by the goal of producing professionally sanctionable accounts of particular groups or settings, EG could be examined as a distinctive form of enquiry. In this way every aspect of the EG process – entry into the field, observation and embodied engagement of subjects, textual inscription from jottings to finished text, and remedial self-concern – would be regarded as moments of a lived order suffused by an infra-layer of practice.

Although EM has not produced a sustained examination of EG as a phenomenon and is dubious of EG's capacity to do so itself, it does offer analytic treatments of a number of core EG practices that provide possible starting points. These range from the problematics of accomplishing observation and of making sense of 'what's happening' in the field to the inscription of written texts.

Doing 'observer' Virtually any aspect of fieldwork recommends itself as a phenomenon, but several are especially noteworthy in light of the EM critique of EG's preference for limited observation. Indeed, analysis might start with the recognition that remaining an 'observer' in the midst of enticing events which variously engulf or seduce the researcher into deeper levels of participation is itself an achievement. Accordingly, Pollner and Emerson (1988) examined how an ethnographer, despite often feeling as if he or she is naturally and unproblematically 'just an observer,' must achieve and sustain the role of 'observer' in the face of various pulls and seductions to participate more fully in unfolding events. Ethnographers may, for example, anticipate and attempt to preclude overtures for consequential involvement, evade such overtures through vague or ambiguous responses, and even periodically 're-mind' themselves of their research goals and priorities in the face of inclusive tendencies (Pollner and Emerson, 1988: 242–51). Failure to do so may dissolve the very distinction between 'observer' and 'observed',

thereby threatening the very conditions underlying EG research itself (p. 252).

Making sense in the field Wieder's (1974: 183–214) treatment of his own interpretive use of the 'convict code' in a half-way house for ex-drug addicts provides one of the few EM-informed examinations of EG sensemaking (but see also Stoddart, 1974). Wieder found that residents regularly blocked his enquiries into underlife events at the house. While he initially interpreted such resident actions as mere resistance – distrust of him personally and as a researcher – he ultimately came to understand these refusals, and the accounts accompanying them, as specific instances of a wider code regularly invoked in interactions between residents and staff. Wieder reflexively suggests that the code provided him with 'a self-elaborating schema' with which to interpret and integrate a wide variety of events within the house:

> Equipped with what I understood to be a preliminary and partial version of the residents' definition of the situation ... I saw that other pronouncements of residents were untitled extensions of this same line of talk. I used whatever 'pieces' of the code I had collected at that point as a scheme for interpreting further talk as extensions of what I had heard 'up to now' ... [For example at a Monday night group] a resident has suggested that a baseball team be formed. He was then asked by the group leader (the program director) to organize the team himself. He answered, 'You know I can't organize a baseball team.' The program director nodded, and the matter was settled. Using my ethnography of the code as a scheme of interpretation, I heard him say, 'You know that the code forbids me to participate in your program in that way, and you know that I'm not going to violate the code. So why ask me?' (1974: 184–5)

Constructing and using texts EM has long been concerned with the construction, interpretation and use of texts by both members and by ethnographers themselves (Cicourel, 1968; Lynch and Woolgar, 1988; McHoul, 1982; Smith, 1988). One core theme in studies of written ethnographies has been textual practices through which transient experience is transformed into enduring observation and authoritative account (cf. Atkinson, 1990). One key practice, for example, involves the suppression of the presence and person of the observer as an active, relevant force in recounted events or incidents. Stoddart (1986: 115) pointed specifically to the common use of textual strategies in ethnographic methods accounts which 'display the features of a domain as they exist independently of the techniques employed to assemble them'. Ethnographers do so by presenting 'findings' as discovered as opposed to created by '(1) neutralizing or (2) invisibilizing their techniques of inquiry, and by (3) providing redundant demonstrations that what is reported was there independently of viewpoint' (p. 115).[17]

Ethnographers also establish the authority of their accounts by identifying some *general type* to which specific incidents are then linked as illustrations or examples. In this way, for example, the ethnographer not only identifies some tribal entity (for example, 'the Nuer') as the unit being described, but also arranges to have him- or herself speak on behalf of this category (Moerman, 1965). Similarly, sociological fieldwork accounts often refer to some category of general other – 'the police', 'students', etc. – characteristics of which are held to be represented by specific incidents. Through these and other textual choices and practices the ethnographer organizes the coherence of the phenomenon (Sharrock, 1974).

Finally, EM calls attention to differences and disjunctures between the texts produced by EG and the projects and the practical concerns of participants. Analysing several projects in which he provided extensive written descriptions of their activities to those studied, Bloor (1988: 169) found that 'members' purposes at hand ... produce distinctive member readings of and reactions to the sociologist's account'. Along these same lines, Emerson and Pollner (1988, 1992) examine the dynamics of participants' responses to EG representations when members of psychiatric emergency teams (PET teams) read preliminary reports of an extensive ethnographic enquiry. It was striking that one respondent characterized these ethnographic accounts as providing 'an outside view' of his own work circumstances, even though the ethnographers' intent was to describe PET decision-making 'from the inside'. Furthermore, this respondent emphasized the obvious consequences of these accounts for the local organizational evaluation of PET activities, even though the ethnographers presented their texts as analytic work lacking any practical import (Emerson and Pollner, 1992: 84–92). It then became clear that having those depicted in an ethnographic account become readers of/audiences for that account breaks down the standard separation between ethnography and participants, perhaps creating a moment of dialogue between them. Such dialogue 'is not merely a medium for resolving substantive differences – although it is that – but an occasion for revealing the suppositions, structures of relevances, and practices of two forms of life: that of participants and researchers. The very effort to resolve differences begins to reveal and elaborate the forms of life in relation to one another' (Emerson and Pollner, 1992: 94).

CONCLUSION

EM appears to offer double-binding advice to EG. EM cautions that EG does not go far or deep enough: the vital and vivid presence at the center of the lifeworld eludes EG because of EG's practical and discursive distance. EG, by virtue of its commitment to sociology, can never recover the lived order. But EM also cautions that EG is too close to the lifeworld: vital practices at the heart of the lifeworld elude EG because it naively partakes of the same practices and modes of discourse. And in turning its gaze to the doing of ethnography *per se*, EM's seemingly contradictory injunctions converge with special force. On the one hand, an ethnographer is extraordinarily well positioned for access to the practices comprising EG. Although an ethnographer may fail to satisfy the unique adequacy requirement with regard to the social worlds he or she studies, he or she necessarily satisfies it with regard to doing EG: the ethnographer is an ethnographer with competence and experience in 'doing' EG. Yet, as Garfinkel has argued, professional competence often includes a 'disinterestedness' in the contingent practices making up the day's work; professionals exhibit a finely honed indifference to the quiddity of their work exactly as part of that quiddity. Thus, though ethnographers are perfectly positioned to know the practices of EG, they are the least able and inclined to speak about them.

Many of these criticisms and insights, however, are known to EG. EG, for example, has long emphasized embodied presence in the world as a key to research. Park, after all, exhorted students to 'go get the seat of your pants dirty in real research' (reported by Becker in McKinney, 1966: 71), while Goffman (1989) honored deep immersion that would ultimately have the fieldworker acquire the rhythms and personal aesthetics of those studied. Furthermore, some EG researchers have sought to penetrate the world of their subjects in a literally embodied fashion. Estroff (1981), for example, took psychotropic medication to have the experience of former mental patients; Wacquant spent three years training as a boxer in order to experience and convey 'the passion, the love, the suffering, the sensual roots of [boxers'] experience of boxing' (1995: 491). Others advocate various kinds of more purely 'insider' or participatory styles (see Adler et al., 1986) which demand substantial investments of time and energy to learn the necessary skills to become a practicing, competent member. Similarly, at least from the publication of Whyte's famous methodological appendix, 'On the Evolution of *Street Corner Society*' (1955), EG has nourished and elaborated methodological self-consciousness. This tendency has become the hallmark of EG since the 1960s (Emerson, 1988: 9–13). And while EG has shown more inclination to pursue reflection rather than reflexivity (Pollner, 1991), a number of EG works have taken up deeply reflexive stances (e.g., Atkinson, 1990; Berger, 1981; Thorne, 1993). Thus, to some extent, EM augments and encourages themes and developments within EG.

What is perhaps most distinctive about EM is that it recommends extreme resolutions to persisting EG dilemmas. The consummate realization of each of the two differently accented versions of EM entertains a 'risk' (Gubrium and Holstein, 1997: 105–9) of analytic dissolution. Extreme immersion on the one hand and hyper-reflexivity on the other obliterate the very distinction between researcher and member, observer and observed, enquiry and object. The unmodulated pursuit of presence, for example, precludes any re-presentation which transforms the lived order into concepts and categories accountable within the sociological community. Drawn ever closer to presence, EM *disappears* through *implosion* by absorption into its field of study and abandoning any sociological commitment in favor of instructing *practitioners* about their lived order. Indeed, as noted earlier, Garfinkel et al. (1988) hold that EM studies of work and science are properly understood as 'hybrid disciplines' insinuated in and instructive to the particular disciplines and settings with which they are concerned. In its final expression, the EM of mathematics becomes mathematics (cf. Lynch, 1993: 274–6).[18]

If the pursuit of presence attenuates the relation of EM to sociology through immersive implosion, the pursuit of practice threatens the relation through a reflexive *explosion*. Taken to the extreme, the reflexive turn undermines representation by inviting the analyst to consider EM representation itself as the product of yet to be articulated practices (Woolgar, 1988). Centrifugally spun away from naive presence in order to grasp the practices of grasping, EM risks *disintegration* by ceaselessly reflexive preoccupation with the practices of the enquirer.

While these contradictory impulses (cf. Atkinson, 1988) might be eliminated, synthesized or modulated to create a consistent and 'safer' EM, they might alternatively be seen as a consummate expression of EM's animating concerns: an explication of the tensions and interpenetrations of immediate and unique features of social life on the one hand and the re-presention, re-flection or analysis of those features on the other. While the contradictory prongs of EM can be used as a platform for studies of presence or practice, appreciation of the simultaneous and contradictory movements within EM provide an 'edifying' (Rorty, 1979) commentary on the problematic (even impossible), yet nevertheless always (and sometimes effortlessly) accomplished sense of lived order.

EM's critique establishes asymptotically approachable limits – in terms of which EG might come to understand and gauge its own efforts to recover the 'point of view' or 'subjectivity' of its subjects. Indeed, the EM critique suggests that these cognitivizing terms are themselves borne of such a distance. Informed by this tension and these extremes, EG may learn about itself (and about the features of its phenomena) as and in the ways it falls short of completely recovering the lifeworld. A dialogue with EM then – as contentious and one-sided as it might be – nevertheless expands EG's appreciation of the depth, limits and complexity of its own practices and those of the persons and groups comprising its substantive focus.[19]

NOTES

1 EM 'brackets' (Garfinkel and Sacks, 1970; Gubrium and Holstein, 1997) a phenomenon notationally and conceptually to indicate that its ostensible character as an obvious or given feature of the lived order is to be understood as the on-going achievement of local practices.

2 Goode (1994) provides an insightful analysis and illustration of how methodic procedure – i.e., 'any systematic, rationally conceived set of data gathering activities that are reasoned to encode, record, capture, or reflect features of phenomena that are under investigation' (p. 130) – leaves out or distorts features of lived experience. More specifically, such procedures create 'forms of data whose relation to the lived order as produced and recognized by those involved is entirely problematic' (p. 135).

3 Lynch (1993) argues that Garfinkel uses 'reflexivity' exclusively in the first sense discussed above. Certainly Garfinkel does not explicitly invoke the term in this second sense, but its compatibility with every reference to and use of 'reflexivity' in his work would justify this extension by 'misreading'. See Pollner, 1991 for a fuller discussion of both meanings of reflexivity.

4 In general, EM has been concerned with how such tacit knowledge is invoked and deployed as a condition of competent membership rather than with articulating a substantive body of knowledge in any particular setting.

5 Although Garfinkel's (1967) critique of the judgemental dope resonates with a humanistic perspective, when EM addresses 'persons' and 'subjectivity' as courses of practical sociological reasoning the focus shifts from elaborating theoretical conceptions of personhood to studies of how versions of personhood, subjects or subjectivity are developed, used and sustained (cf. Coulter, 1974, 1989; Weinberg, 1997). In general, EM's focus is not the social actor but the organization of action (Peyrot, 1982).

6 Overviews of research in this area are provided by Atkinson and Heritage, 1984, Goodwin and Heritage, 1990, and Heritage, 1984: 233–92; key early statements include Sacks, 1992, Schegloff, 1968, and Sacks, Schegloff and Jefferson, 1974. Conversation analysis (CA) examines 'the methodical construction in and through talk of member-productive and analyzable social action and activity' (Maynard and Clayman, 1991: 396). It examines 'talk-in-interaction', and has distinctively addressed a wide variety of topics involved in the sequential organization of talk, most recently with special concern with talk in institutional settings (e.g., Drew and Heritage, 1992).

The relationship between EM and CA is close but contested: Maynard and Clayman characterize it as 'perhaps the most visible and influential form of EM research' (1991: 396), while Lynch contends that 'CA has lost its original relationship to ethnomethodology' (1993: 215) on becoming professionalized as a technical 'analytic discipline'. While CA shares some common concerns with EG, its focus on the organization and sequence of talk limits its concern with embodied presence; moreover, CA's concern with 'a context-free yet context-sensitive structure of turn-taking' (Silverman, 1993: 141) diverges from EG's approach to local context (see also Maynard and Clayman, 1991: 408). For discussion of these and other issues in the relationship of CA and EG, see Maynard (1998), Maynard and Clayman (1991), Moerman (1988) and Silverman (1993: 115–43).

7 The pursuit of presence shares certain features with the genre of naturalistic research which Gubrium and Holstein (1997) refer to as 'emotionalism'.

8 Perhaps the foremost expression of a 'hybrid discipline' occurs in recent EM-inspired studies of the meaning and use of technology in work settings (e.g., Button, 1993; Engestrom and Middleton, 1996; Suchman, 1987). Much of this research is explicitly concerned with combining EM sensitivities and modes of analysis with the design and planning of the organizational implementation of technology. Button and Dourish (1996: 7), for example, propose a relationship in which 'design adopts the analytic mentality of EM, and EM dons the practical mantle of design'.

9 It is probably not chance that this conceptualization of ethnicity as a 'doing' arose cross-culturally, i.e., in a context in which the researcher was not deeply enmeshed in the 'natural' or 'factual' character of local ethnic categories. For EG research on ethnic groups and ethnic identity, generally conducted in American society, have almost invariably taken for granted the existence and relevance of a given ethnic distinction. Most EG description and analysis assumes that there are 'blacks' and 'whites', that who falls into which category is generally obvious and unproblematic, and gives no attention to actual occasions of this categorization process (except in a few, presumably rare 'marginal' cases; e.g., a 'black passing for white').

10 EM further contends that EG descriptions and interpretations are in no fundamental way different from those members provide. Both professional and folk descriptions, for example, reflect the describer's purposes at hand; that the ethnographer's purposes are perhaps more 'theoretical' does not make his or her descriptions any less partial, selective, or perspectival than members' descriptions – only different. Similarly, both ethnographic and folk descriptions make frequent use of specific interpretive procedures such as the documentary method of interpretation to find and convey meaning and regularity.

11 EM research on school settings in particular (Cicourel and Kitsuse, 1967; Cicourel et al., 1974; Mehan, 1979; Mehan et al., 1986) has provided detailed analyses of how a wide variety of educational phenomena ordinarily viewed as matters of objective fact, ranging from 'correct' answers to teachers' questions during lessons to ability groupings, are products of educators' sense-making practices situated in highly local institutional circumstances.

12 In its classic form the convict code provides such a rule-following explanation: prisoners are socialized to the specific 'norms' of code and are subject to harsh sanctions from their peers for non-compliance; their behavior in the prison setting (and beyond) is thus depicted as products of their conformity to the provisions of the code. But EM maintains as a general principle that action cannot be explained in terms of rules or norms, since, following Hart's (1961) maxim, a rule cannot specify its application to particular circumstances, producing a fundamental indeterminacy.

13 Garfinkel et al. contrast Lynch's failure to become an adept, contributing member of his scientific worksite with Livingston's involvement in higher mathematics: 'Livingston spent seven years in graduate training as a mathematician and with this preparation conceived the work of proving mathematical structures and gathered analytically descriptive details of it' (1988: 11).

14 Similarly, although EM has not actually suggested this critique, this line of thinking would also fault studies of deviance which examine how forms of deviance were labeled and experienced for paying little attention to the in-situ commission of those acts. Katz (1988) develops this critique and pursues this line of enquiry.

15 In this vein, Garfinkel et al. (1988) fault Lynch not only for his lack of hands-on laboratory skills, but also for producing findings that 'are not results in neurobiology'.

16 The related emphasis Garfinkel et al. (1981) place on 'first time through' applies primarily to the discovering work of the hard sciences, suggesting that any sort of reconstruction of this process involves a replay which obscures the original sense of uncertainty and contingency. However, work processes that are more routine (e.g., criminal case settlement discussions) presumably are not so strictly subject to this 'first time through' requirement, or are subject to it in a different way; i.e., it is the 'first time through' with this particular case, these particular people, where these 'kinds of cases' or 'kinds of situations' in typified terms are deeply familiar.

17 Similarly, many classic anthropological accounts first invoke the field experiences of the ethnographer to warrant experiential claims to knowledge, then obscure the presence of this figure through such textual devices as the use of the third person narrative form. As Rabinow has described this practice (1986: 244): 'from Malinowski on, anthropological authority has rested on two textual legs. An experiential "I was there" element establishes the unique authority of the anthropologist; its suppression in the text establishes the anthropologist's scientific authority.'

18 Katz's (1999) analysis of the warrants for ethnography suggests formidable problems in establishing the contribution of hybird studies of professional practices. 'In effect, the ethnographer is told by the elite subject, "Here is what we do and why we do it," and then the ethnographer is asked, "What is there about us that we are

not already the experts in knowing?"' (p. 404). 'Once the researcher begins to make descriptive use of the culturally autonomous language of elite or charismatic [e.g., professional] practices,' Katz writes, 'sociological readers are likely to get glassyeyed and, for their part, expert practitioners may not grant that they have learned anything new' (p. 404).

19 Gubrium and Holstein (1997) have reinitiated invitations to such dialogue, seeking to extend EM concerns in synthesizing them with symbolic interactionist, ethnographic and postmodern interpretive sociologies. Early ethnomethodologists engaged in such dialogue, although at the cost of subsequent identification as 'proto-EM'. It is paradoxical that what was characterized as proto-ethnomethodology might well prove an expression of the more recent understanding of EM as a hybrid enterprise actively engaged with a host discipline and making contributions to it.

REFERENCES

Adler P.A., Adler P. and Rochford, E.B. (eds) (1986) 'The politics of participation in field research', *Urban Life*, 14: 4.

Atkinson, J.M. (1978) *Discovering Suicide: Studies in the Social Organization of Sudden Death*. London: Macmillan.

Atkinson, P. (1988) 'Ethnomethodology: a critical review', *Annual Review of Sociology*, 14: 441–65.

Atkinson, P. (1990) *The Ethnographic Imagination: Textual Constructions of Reality*. New York: Routledge.

Atkinson, J.M. and Heritage, J. (eds) (1984) *The Structures of Social Action: Studies in Conversation Analysis*. Cambridge: Cambridge University Press.

Becker, H.S. (1963) *Outsiders*. New York: The Free Press of Glencoe.

Bellman, B. (1975) *Village of Curers and Assassins: On the Production of Fala Kpelle Cosmological Categories*. The Hague: Mouton.

Berger, B.M. (1981) *The Survival of a Counterculture: Ideological Work and Everyday Life among Rural Communards*. Berkeley, CA: University of California Press.

Bittner, E. (1964) 'The concept of organization', *Social Research*, 3: 239–55.

Bittner, E. (1973) 'Objectivity and realism in sociology', in G. Psathas (ed.), *Phenomenological Sociology*. New York: Wiley. pp. 109–25.

Bloor, M.J. (1988) 'Notes on member validation', in R.M. Emerson (ed.), *Contemporary Field Research: A Collection of Readings*. Prospect Heights, IL: Waveland. pp. 156–72.

Blumer, H. (1969) *Symbolic Interactionism: Perspective and Method*. Englewood Cliffs, NJ: Prentice–Hall.

Button, G. (ed.) (1993) *Technoglogy in Working Order: Studies of Work, Interaction and Technology*. London: Routledge and Kegan Paul.

Button, G. (ed.) (1991) *Ethnomethodology and the Human Sciences*. Cambridge: Cambridge University Press.

Button, G. and Dourish, P. (1996) 'Technomethodology: paradoxes and possibilities'. Cambridge: Xerox Research Center Europe, Technical Report Series EPC-1996-101.

Cicourel, A.V. (1964) *Method and Measurement in Sociology*. New York: The Free Press.

Cicourel, A.V. (1968) *The Social Organization of Juvenile Justice*. New York: Wiley.

Cicourel, A.V. (1974a) 'Basic and normative rules in the negotiation of status and role', in D. Sudnow (ed.), *Studies in Social Interaction*. New York: The Free Press. pp. 229–58.

Cicourel, A.V. (1974b) *Cognitive Sociology: Language and Meaning in Social Interaction*. New York: The Free Press.

Cicourel, A.V. (1981) 'Notes on the integration of micro- and macro-levels of analysis', in K. Knorr Cetina and A.V. Cicourel (eds), *Analysis in Social Theory and Methodology: Toward an Integration of Micro- and Macro-Sociologies*. Boston, MA: Routledge and Kegan Paul. pp. 51–80.

Cicourel, A.V. and Kitsuse, J. (1967) *Educational Decision-Makers*. Indianapolis: Bobbs–Merrill.

Cicourel, A.V., Jennings, S.H.M., Jennings, K.H., Leiter, K.C.W., MacKay, R., Mehan, H. and Roth, D.R. (1974) *Language Use and School Performance*. New York: Academic Press.

Coulter, J. (1974) *The Social Construction of Mind*. London: Rowman and Littlefield.

Coulter, J. (1989) *Mind in Action*. Atlantic Highlands, NJ: Humanities Press.

Dingwall, R. (1981) 'The ethnomethodological movement', in G. Payne, R. Dingwall, J. Payne and M. Carter (eds), *Sociology and Social Research*. London: Routledge and Kegan Paul. pp. 124–38.

Drew, P. and Heritage, J. (eds) (1992) *Talk at Work*. Cambridge: Cambridge University Press.

Durkheim, E. (1951) *Suicide* (trans. J.A. Spaulding and G. Simpson). New York: The Free Press.

Emerson, R.M. (1987) 'Four ways to improve the craft of fieldwork', *Journal of Contemporary Ethnography*, 16: 69–89.

Emerson, R.M. (ed.) (1988) *Contemporary Field Research: A Collection of Readings*. Prospect Heights, IL: Waveland.

Emerson, R.M. and Pollner, M. (1988) 'On the uses of members' responses to researchers' accounts', *Human Organization*, 47: 189–98.

Emerson, R.M. and Pollner, M. (1992) 'Difference and dialogue: members' readings of ethnographic texts', in G. Miller and J.A. Holstein (eds), *Perspectives on Social Problems: A Research Annual*, vol. 3. Greenwich, CT: JAI Press. pp. 79–98.

Emerson, R.M., Fretz, R.I. and Shaw, L.L. (1995) *Writing Ethnographic Fieldnotes*. Chicago: University of Chicago Press.

Engestrom, Y. and Middleton, D. (eds) (1996) *Cognition and Communication at Work*. Cambridge: Cambridge University Press.

Estroff, S.E. (1981) *Making It Crazy: An Ethnography of Psychiatric Clients in an American Community.* Berkeley, CA: University of California Press.

Garfinkel, H. (1967) *Studies in Ethnomethodology.* Englewood Cliffs, NJ: Prentice–Hall.

Garfinkel, H. (1974) 'The origins of the term ethnomethodology', in R. Turner (ed.), *Ethnomethodology.* Harmondsworth: Penguin. pp. 15–18.

Garfinkel, H. (1988) 'Evidence for locally produced, naturally accountable phenomena of order, logic, reason, meaning, method, etc., in and as of the essential quiddity of immortal ordinary society (I of IV): an announcement of studies', *Sociological Theory,* 6: 103–9.

Garfinkel, H. (1991) 'Respecification: evidence for locally produced, naturally accountable phenomena of order, logic, reason, meaning, methods, etc. in and of the essential haecceity of immortal ordinary society (I) – an announcement of studies', in G. Button (ed), *Ethnomethodology and the Human Sciences.* Cambridge: Cambridge University Press. pp. 10–19.

Garfinkel, H. and Sacks, H. (1970) 'On formal structures of practical actions', in J.C. McKinney and E.A. Tiryakian (eds), *Theoretical Sociology: Perspectives and Developments.* New York: Appleton–Century–Croft. pp. 337–66.

Garfinkel, H. and Wieder, L. (1992) 'Two incommensurable, asymmetrically alternate technologies of social analysis', in G. Watson and R.M. Seiler (eds), *Text in Context: Studies in Ethnomethodology.* Newbury Park, CA: Sage. pp. 175–206.

Garfinkel, H., Lynch, M. and Livingston, E. (1981) 'The work of a discovering science construed with materials from the optically discovered pulsar', *Philosophy of the Social Sciences,* 11: 131–58.

Garfinkel, H., Livingston, E., Lynch, M., Robillard, A.B. and MacBeth, D. (1988) 'Respecifying the natural sciences as discovering sciences of practical action, I & II: doing so ethnographically by administering a schedule of contingencies in discussions with laboratory scientists and by hanging around their laboratories'. Unpublished manuscript, Department of Sociology, UCLA.

Goffman, E. (1989) 'On fieldwork', *Journal of Contemporary Ethnography,* 18: 123–32.

Goode, D. (1994) *A World without Words: The Social Construction of Children Born Deaf and Blind.* Philadelphia: Temple University Press.

Goodwin, C. and Heritage, J. (1990) 'Conversation analysis', *Annual Review of Anthropology,* 19: 283–307.

Gubrium, J.F. and Holstein, J.A. (1997) *The New Language of Qualitative Method.* New York: Oxford University Press.

Hart, H.L.A. (1961) *The Concept of Law.* Oxford: Oxford University Press.

Heritage, J. (1984) *Garfinkel and Ethnomethodology.* Cambridge: Polity Press.

Hilbert, R.A. (1992) *The Classical Roots of Ethnomethodology.* Chapel Hill, NC: University of North Carolina Press.

Jules-Rosette, B. (1975) *Vision and Realities: Aspects of Ritual and Conversion in an African Church.* Ithaca, NY: Cornell University Press.

Katz, J. (1988) *Seductions of Crime: Moral and Sensual Attractions in Doing Evil.* New York: Basic Books.

Katz, J. (1999) 'Ethnography's warrants', *Sociological Methods and Research,* 25: 391–423.

Kirshenblatt-Gimblett, B. (1989) 'Authoring lives', *Folklore Research,* 26: 123–49.

Latour, B. and Woolgar, S. (1986) *Laboratory Life: The Social Construction of Scientific Facts,* 2nd edn. Princeton, NJ: Princeton University Press.

Livingston, E. (1986) *The Ethnomethodological Foundations of Mathematics.* London: Routledge and Kegan Paul.

Lynch, M. (1985) *Art and Artifact in Laboratory Science: A Study of Shop Work and Shop Talk in a Research Laboratory.* London: Routledge and Kegan Paul.

Lynch, M. (1993) *Scientific Practice and Ordinary Action: Ethnomethodology and Social Studies of Science.* New York: Cambridge University Press.

Lynch, M. and Woolgar, S. (eds) (1988) *Representation in Scientific Practice.* Cambridge, MA: MIT Press.

Lynch, M., Livingston, E. and Garfinkel, H. (1983) 'Temporal order in laboratory work', in K. Knorr Cetina and M. Mulkay (eds), *Science Observed: Perspectives on the Social Study of Science.* London: Sage. pp. 205–38.

Matza, D. (1969) *Becoming Deviant.* Englewood Cliffs, NJ: Prentice–Hall.

Maynard, D.W. (1998) 'On qualitative inquiry and extramodernity', *Contemporary Sociology,* 27: 343–5.

Maynard, D.W. and Clayman, S.E. (1991) 'The diversity of ethnomethodology', *Annual Review of Sociology,* 17: 385–418.

McHoul, A. (1982) *Telling How Texts Talk: Essays on Reading and Ethnomethodology.* London: Routledge and Kegan Paul.

McHugh, P., Raffel, S., Foss, D.C. and Blum, A.F. (1974) *On the Beginning of Sociological Inquiry.* London: Routledge and Kegan Paul.

McKinney, J.C. (1966) *Constructive Typology and Social Theory.* New York: Appleton–Century–Croft.

Mehan, H. (1979) *Learning Lessons: Social Organization in the Classroom.* Cambridge, MA: Harvard University Press.

Mehan, H. and Wood, H. (1975) *The Reality of Ethnomethodology.* New York, NY: Wiley.

Mehan, H., Heertweck, A. and Meihls, J.L. (1986) *Handicapping the Handicapped: Decision Making in Students' Educational Careers.* Stanford, CA: Stanford University Press.

Moerman, M. (1965) 'Ethnic identification in a complex civilization: who are the Lue?', *American Anthropologist,* 65: 1215–30.

Moerman, M. (1974) 'Accomplishing ethnicity', in R. Turner (ed.), *Ethnomethodology.* Harmondsworth: Penguin. pp. 54–68.

Moerman, M. (1988) *Talking Culture: Ethnography and Conversation Analysis*. Philadelphia: University of Pennsylvania Press.

Nadel, S.F. (1942) *A Black Byzantium*. Oxford: Oxford University Press.

Parsons, T. (1951) *The Social System*. New York: The Free Press.

Peyrot, M. (1982) 'Understanding ethnomethodology: a remedy for some common misconceptions', *Human Studies*, 5: 261–83.

Pollner, M. (1991) 'Left of ethnomethodology: the rise and decline of radical reflexivity', *American Sociological Review*, 56: 370–80.

Pollner, M. and Emerson, R.M. (1988) 'The dynamics of inclusion and distance in fieldwork relations', in R.M. Emerson (ed), *Contemporary Field Research: A Collection of Readings*. Prospect Heights, IL: Waveland. pp. 235–52.

Pollner, M. and Goode, D. (1990) 'Ethnomethodology and person-centering practices', *Person Centered Review*, 5: 203–20.

Rabinow, P. (1986) 'Representations are social facts: modernity and post-modernity in anthropology', in J. Clifford and G.E. Marcus (eds), *Writing Culture: The Poetics and Politics of Ethnography*. Berkeley, CA: University of California Press. pp. 234–61.

Randall, D., Rouncefield, M. and Hughes, J.A. (1995) 'Chalk and cheese: BPR and ethnomethodologically-informed ethnography', in *CSCW, Proceedings of the Fourth European Conference on Computer Supported Cooperative Work*. Stockholm: Kluwer Academic Publishers. pp. 325–40.

Robillard, A.B. (1999) *Meaning of a Disability: The Lived Experience of Paralysis*. Philadelphia: Temple University Press.

Rorty, R. (1979) *Philosophy and the Mirror of Nature*. Princeton, NJ: Princeton University Press.

Sacks, H. (1963) 'Sociological description', *Berkeley Journal of Sociology*, 8: 1–16.

Sacks, H. (1992) *Lectures on Conversations*, vols 1 and 2. Cambridge, MA: Blackwell.

Sacks, H., Schegloff, E.A. and Jefferson, G. (1974) 'A simplest systematics for the organization of turn-taking for conversation', *Language*, 50: 696–735.

Schegloff, E.A. (1968) 'Sequencing in conversational openings', *American Anthropologist*, 70: 1075–95.

Schutz, A. (1962) *The Problem of Social Reality*. The Hague: Martinus Nijhoff.

Schutz, A. (1964) *Studies in Social Theory*. The Hague: Martinus Nijhoff.

Sharrock, W.W. (1974) 'On owning knowledge', in R. Turner (ed.), *Ethnomethodology*. Harmondsworth: Penguin. pp. 45–53.

Sharrock, W.W. and Anderson, B. (1991) 'Epistemology: professional skepticism', in G. Button (ed.), *Ethnomethodology and the Human Sciences*. Cambridge: Cambridge University Press. pp. 51–76.

Silverman, D. (1993) *Interpreting Qualitative Data: Methods for Analyzing Talk, Text and Interaction*. London: Sage.

Smith, D.E. (1988) *The Everyday World as Problematic*. Toronto: University of Toronto Press.

Stoddart, K. (1974) 'Pinched: notes on the ethnographer's location of argot', in R. Turner (ed.), *Ethnomethodology*. Harmondsworth: Penguin. pp. 173–9.

Stoddart, K. (1986) 'The presentation of everyday life: some textual strategies for "adequate ethnography"', *Urban Life*, 15: 103–21.

Suchman, L.A. (1987) *Plans and Situated Actions: The Problem of Human Machine Communication*. Cambridge: Cambridge University Press.

Sudnow, D.N. (1978) *Ways of the Hand*. Cambridge, MA: Harvard University Press.

Sykes, G. (1958) *The Society of Captives*. Princeton, NJ: Princeton University Press.

Thorne, B. (1993) *Gender Play: Girls and Boys in School*. New Brunswick, NJ: Rutgers University Press.

Wacquant, L. (1995) 'The pugilistic point of view: how boxers think and feel about their trade', *Theory and Society*, 24: 489–535.

Weinberg, D. (1997) 'The social construction of non-human agency: the case of mental disorder', *Social Problems*, 44: 217–34.

Whyte, W.F. (1955) *Street Corner Society*. Chicago: University of Chicago Press.

Wieder, D.L. (1974) *Language and Social Reality: The Case of Telling the Convict Code*. The Hague: Mouton.

Wittgenstein, L. (1953) *Philosophical Investigations*. New York: Macmillan.

Woolgar, S. (ed.) (1988) *Knowledge and Reflexivity: New Frontiers in the Sociology of Knowledge*. London: Sage.

Zimmerman, D.H. and Pollner, M. (1970) 'The everyday world as a phenomenon', in H. Pepinsky (ed.), *People and Information*. New York: Praeger. pp. 33–65.

Zimmerman, D.H. and Wieder, D.L. (1970) 'Ethnomethodology and the problem of order: comment on Denzin', in J.D. Douglas (ed.), *Understanding Everyday Life: Toward the Reconstruction of Sociological Knowledge*. Chicago: Aldine. pp. 285–98.

9

Phenomenology and Ethnography

ILJA MASO

In his essay on 'The Stranger', Alfred Schutz (1971) attempts to describe the typical situation of a stranger who endeavours to understand the culture of a group so as to know how to behave in the hope he will be accepted, or at least tolerated by its members. (The use of the male pronoun here and in the following discussion of Schutz reflects the usage of the original.) As an example of someone in such a situation Schutz chooses an immigrant. This is not surprising, for as a Jew he had to leave his homeland, Austria, in 1938 before it was occupied by Nazi Germany. In July 1939, having stayed for more than a year in Paris, he emigrated to the United States. His experiences of trying to adapt himself to American culture are partly reflected in 'The Stranger', which was originally published in 1944. In that essay Schutz deals not only with the experiences of a stranger in a strange land, but also with the experiences of those who by profession try to distance themselves from their own culture in order to describe it more or less objectively: that is, sociologists.

Initially, the stranger behaves like an 'unconcerned onlooker' who is able to place the culture of the new group competently in an interpretive framework provided by his own culture. He will, however, soon discover that in order to be able to participate in this group, this familiar framework does not suffice and that he is in need of a kind of knowledge that he does not yet possess:

> The discovery that things in his new surroundings look quite different from what he expected them to be at home is frequently the first shock to the stranger's confidence in the validity of his habitual 'thinking as usual'. Not only the picture which the stranger has brought along of the cultural pattern of the approached group but the whole hitherto unquestioned scheme of interpretation current within the home group becomes invalidated. It cannot be used as a scheme of orientation within the new social surroundings. For the members of the approached group *their* cultural pattern fulfils the functions of such a scheme. But the approaching stranger can neither use it simply as it is nor establish a general formula of transformation between both cultural patterns permitting him, so to speak, to convert all the co-ordinates within one scheme of orientation into those valid within the other. (Schutz, 1971: 99; emphasis in original)

According to Schutz there are two reasons why the stranger will not be able to overcome this problem. First, because in order to be able to orient oneself at all it is necessary to know where one stands. The stranger, however, cannot know this because he (still) does not have a position within the culture of the group. Secondly, because the unity that is represented by the scheme of orientation of the group – by their culture – cannot be known by the stranger. At the most he will be able to understand and apply parts of it, to the extent that they can be 'translated' into his own culture. In this way he can be quite sure that, for the time being, his interpretation will hardly ever coincide with the way the members of the group regard that aspect of their culture. Only after collecting a certain knowledge of the interpretive possibilities of the new culture can the stranger start to adopt this culture as the scheme of interpretation of his own expression. In Schutz's opinion, however, the stranger must still check everything he says or does to see if it has the desired effect. At the same time he has to be certain of everything members of the group say or do, and of the extent to which this behaviour is normal only to the person concerned or to the whole group. Although he will thus achieve an ever-greater understanding of the elements of the new culture and of the relationships between these elements, to him this culture will – for the time being – remain inconsistent, incoherent and unclear (Schutz, 1971: 103).

The stranger can only be seen as a true member of the group when he is able to assess normal social situations at a single glance and to react immediately to them in a proper way: that means when 'his acting shows all the marks of habituality, automatism, and half consciousness' (1971: 101) typical of anybody who has grown up in this kind of situation. However, both the fact that the new culture, as described above, has been (and may still be) a 'topic of investigation' to the stranger, and the bitter experience that the self-evident character of his original frame of interpretation has been questioned, provide – according to Schutz – for the more-or-less objective attitude that the stranger will have towards that new culture. This is something that a real member lacks. Whereas a real member in the role of a sociologist will also try to adopt an objective attitude, it will differ from that of the acculturated stranger. Contrary to the latter, the sociologist is – in Schutz's terms – disinterested in that he 'refrains from participating in the network of plans, means-and-ends relations, motives and chances, hopes and fears, which the actor within the social world uses for interpreting his experiences of it' (Schutz, 1971: 92). Instead of seeing the social world mainly as the domain of his actual and possible acts, he tries to 'observe, describe and classify the social world as clearly as possible in well-ordered terms in accordance with the scientific ideals of coherence, consistency, and analytical consequence' (p. 92).

Finally, Schutz points out that although he has sketched the stranger and the member of a group as opposites, everybody can in fact have some of the experiences of the stranger within his or her own culture. After all, when somebody is confronted with some unknown fact, she or he has to change their frame of interpretation, at least in such a way that the meaning of this unknown fact acquires a proper place within this frame.

Contours of an Ethnographic and Phenomenological Approach

With reference to Schutz's essay on the stranger, Hammersley and Atkinson (1995: 8) remark that 'ethnography exploits the capacity that any social actor possesses for learning new cultures, and the objectivity to which this process gives rise'. In this respect the use of that talent does not need to be restricted to new cultures outside one's own society but can also be used within it. After all, even within their own society researchers will hardly ever deal with people and groups that have exactly the same

culture as they themselves have. That is why, as Schutz himself pointed out, they could have more or less the same experiences as the stranger, though generally in a milder form. Insofar as sociological researchers find themselves on familiar territory, Hammersley and Atkinson recommend them to treat this area as 'anthropologically strange' because researchers will thus be able to make explicit the assumptions they take for granted as members of that culture. They can turn the familiar into an object available for study. In this way, Hammersley and Atkinson illustrate how Schutz's discussion of the stranger points to two kinds of strategies in ethnography, namely the 'anthropological destrangement' in which one tries to make the unknown known, and the 'anthropological estrangement' in which one tries to make the known unknown.

Contrary to what the preceding seems to suggest, however, Schutz was not so much concerned with the methodology of ethnography but with the development and application of a phenomenological sociology. To this end he pointed out that the study of social reality, that is 'the sum total of objects and occurrences within the social cultural world as experienced by the common-sense thinking of men living their daily lives among their fellow-men, connected with them in manifold relations of interaction' (Schutz, 1973c: 53), is to a large extent ignored. In his analysis of social reality he showed that, although in terms of commonsense thinking men have only a more or less personal, fragmentary, restricted, often inconsistent, and partly indistinct knowledge of the world, it is sufficient for coming to terms with this social reality. This is so, according to Schutz, because the social world is

from the outset an intersubjective world and because ... our knowledge of it is in various ways socialized. Moreover, the social world is experienced from the outset as a meaningful one ... We normally 'know' what the other [in his biographically determined situation] does, for what reason he does it, why he does it at this particular time and in these particular circumstances. (Schutz, 1973c: 55)

In this way we construct the others' typical motives, goals, attitudes and personalities – of which their actual conduct is just an instance or example – in a way that is sufficient for many practical purposes. The way a social scientist has to proceed, according to Schutz, is to form concepts of interrelated typical course-of-action patterns executed by interrelated typical actors, in various situations. The social scientist forms these objective, ideal-typical constructs by constructing the constructs – the typifications – formed in commonsense thinking. These 'second order' constructs must be verified to establish their validity (the postulate of consistency) and their compatibility with 'first-order' constructs of everyday life (the postulate of adequacy).

Through this kind of analysis, and because of the task of the social sciences as he saw it, Schutz has had an important influence on the development of phenomenological approaches in sociology. In this respect, his insights into the way first-order and second-order constructs are formed, and his postulate of adequacy were especially important. With this in mind it would appear worthwhile to examine the extent to which the ethnographic approaches pointed out by Hammersley and Atkinson in their reading of Schutz also have a phenomenological character. If they do, we shall have found two approaches to a phenomenological ethnography!

Each phenomenological approach chooses as its point of departure the phenomena insofar as, and the way in which, they present themselves to consciousness (Gadamer, 1976; Spiegelberg, 1971). This implies that phenomenologists will try their utmost to refrain from every certainty or uncertainty concerning the existence or origin of these phenomena, and from every other – more or less elaborate – preliminary idea about them. This strict 'bracketing' of all presuppositions and prejudices about phenomena makes it possible to experience them as they appear in their full richness to consciousness (Husserl, 1969; Spiegelberg, 1971). Nowadays this strict bracketing of all presuppositions and prejudices about phenomena must be considered a myth. Since Hanson we know that perception and interpretation are inseparable, which means that 'theories and interpretations are "there" in the observing, from the outset' (Hanson in Derksen, 1980: 273). To bracket them, if at all possible, would make perception, and therefore experience, impossible. This is why bracketing can at best refer to an attempt to refrain from those presuppositions and prejudices about phenomena that are sensed by phenomenologists as contaminating (from the outside) their pure experience of those phenomena.

What will be bracketed and what subsequently appears to consciousness will be dependent on who is bracketing. Not every phenomenologist will be aware of the same contaminating presuppositions and prejudices or will use the same theories and interpretations in his or her perception and experience. Even when these ideas and approaches originate from a more or less common culture and history, each phenomenologist will, at least because of his or her personal history – her or his biographically determined situation as Schutz put it – be different in this respect from every other phenomenologist. Because of the dominant culture and the inherent subjectivity of the bracketing procedure, some results of phenomenology can justly be criticized as representing a male, white, middle-class standpoint. That is why it is only right that some phenomenologists have chosen to refrain from bracketing ideas that represent the voice of those 'who have never been heard'.

On the basis of the bracketing procedure, or – as it has also been called – the phenomenological *epoche* (the Greek word for 'abstention'), Schutz's stranger can be seen as a willy-nilly phenomenologist. As long as he can remain an outsider to the culture of the new group he is able to fit what he perceives into his old frame of interpretation; he notices to his dismay that this does not suffice when he really has to understand it. In almost every situation he subsequently finds himself in, he will be forced to refrain from the way he habitually looked at and dealt with it. Only in this way will he in the long run be able to learn how to (re)act in a way that is appropriate within the new culture.

The sociologist described by Schutz who wants to study his own culture can at best be seen as a phenomenologist who has insufficiently bracketed his presuppositions and prejudices. For a phenomenological approach it is not enough to refrain as much as possible from the interests of everyday life in order to observe one's own culture successfully. (For this reason, critics of traditional ethnography hold that 'it is precisely because of this distancing of oneself as enquirer that interpretivists cannot engage in an explicitly critical evaluation of the social reality they seek to portray'; Schwandt, 1994: 131). With such an approach one must do one's utmost to refrain from the presuppositions and prejudices about that culture that are sensed by phenomenologists as contaminating, from the outside, their pure experience of it, and that is not what Schutz makes the stranger do. True, in a subsequent paper he states that the social scientist places that which he takes for granted in his daily life between brackets, but he also indicates that this does not imply that the scientific knowledge of that culture has to be placed in brackets too. In his opinion these may only be used if the researcher can supply good reasons for this approach (Schutz, 1973b: 36–9).

Although with 'The Stranger' Schutz does not explicitly intend to sketch a phenomenological approach to social research, the stranger and the sociologist can still both be seen as examples of the phenomenological approach that he recommends for sociology. In this respect it is remarkable that he indicates that, albeit for good reasons only, the phenomenological *epoche* may be executed in its totality. What those reasons are he fails to mention, although on the basis of his fable of the stranger we may assume that at least (scientific) unfamiliarity with phenomena or with a culture must be among them. However, the starting point of the phenomenological approach is to consider *every* phenomenon, including the known ones, as if they are presenting themselves for the very first time to consciousness. In this way we can (again) become aware of the fullness and richness of these phenomena. It is precisely this that represents the strength of the phenomenological approach, which is why there seems little reason to deviate from it. Although the ethnographic approaches Schutz describes – anthropological destrangement and estrangement – also seem to be inspired by the phenomenological *epoche*, this 'reduction' is not followed through radically enough for us to see them as more than a first start towards a phenomenological ethnography. So, in order to be able to formulate one that is fully fledged we must look for ethnographic approaches inspired by an *epoche* that represents such a radical process.

Two Illustrative Examples

Mrs Wera Kapkajew, born in Vilnius, interpreter at the court of law in Frankfurt, has been involved in the Auschwitz-case since 1959 and has translated more than eighty Polish and Russian witness accounts. 'I have put myself in their shoes ... their life has grown into a piece of my life ... in the evening and at night their destiny comes over me ... I have lived their life to such an extent that, in 1964, I have caught a typical concentration camp disease: phlegmon, a severe inflammation of the tissue with symptoms of poisoning and a high fever, exactly as the witnesses told me ...' (Jacobs and Stoop, 1965: 17–18)

When, a long time ago, I was struggling to understand phenomenology, this passage from a book about the Auschwitz trial in Frankfurt am Main (1963–5) seemed to be one of the two most important examples of the possibilities of a phenomenological approach. The other example concerned the assignment given a student by Harold Garfinkel: it involved spending some time in the home of her parents, viewing the activities of the latter while assuming she was a boarder in the household:

A short, stout man entered the house, kissed me on the cheek and asked, 'How was school?' I answered politely. He walked into the kitchen, kissed the younger of the two women, and said hello to the other. The younger woman asked me, 'What do you want for dinner, honey?' I answered 'Nothing'. She shrugged her shoulders and said no more. The older woman shuffled round the kitchen muttering. The man washed his hands, sat down at the table, and picked up the paper. He read until the two women had finished putting the food on the table. The three sat down. They exchanged idle chatter about the day's events. The older woman said something in a foreign language which made the others laugh. (Garfinkel, 1967: 45)

In her imagination the interpreter of Vilnius could place herself in the experiences of others in such a way that their experiences became her experience. Experiencing the experiences of others is called 'empathy' (Lauer, 1958: 152). This is the way in which, in a phenomenological approach, we are not only able to consider others as humans like ourselves (cf. Husserl, 1969: 420) but also to acquire an understanding of the experiences 'behind' their perceptible expressions. Because experiencing the experience of others is only possible by bracketing one's own contaminating presuppositions and prejudices about those expressions (except that we are now seeing them as expressions of experiences) empathy can be seen as a special case of the phenomenological *epoche*. However, this *epoche* of the interpreter, her empathy, was more radical than is usual within phenomenology. She not only bracketed her contaminating presuppositions and prejudices about the expressions of the inhabitants of the concentrations camp, but also the distinction – the distance – between the experiences of herself and those of the others. In this respect she seems to have overdone it, at least from a phenomenological standpoint. However, phenomenologists need not deem this negative for it can be turned into something positive if at a given moment they are able to look at those experiences in the unprejudiced and open manner that characterizes the true phenomenologist.

Something similar applies from the perspective of ethnography. The interpreter's anthropological estrangement has gone so far that for some time she refrained from the more or less objective attitude imperative for ethnographers which, according to Schutz, every acculturated stranger has towards his new culture. To ethnographers this need not be a problem as long as – at a given moment – they can recapture this more or less objective, unprejudiced attitude. With these notes the empathy of the interpreter from Vilnius can indeed be seen as a possible phenomenologically ethnographic approach: in which experiencing the fullness and richness of phenomena that are basically unknown to a researcher precedes their examination.

By taking the stance of a boarder, Garfinkel's student 'behaviourized' the activities of her parents (and another woman). That is, she tried to describe their activities without using her previous knowledge of who was who and of the daily household routine. Whereas in this respect she seems to apply the phenomenological *epoche*, she goes too far, phenomenologically speaking, by abstaining from the richness with which the phenomena concerned could have appeared to her consciousness: her possible experience of familiarity, warmth, affection, relatedness, being there and so on. Her description seems to be the result of the bracketing of this possible richness and in this respect falls short. There is also a problem if we try to see this as an example of an ethnographic approach. Although the student is able to render a description of the known by making it anthropologically strange, there is in the example no indication of an explication of the assumptions as advocated by Hammersley and Atkinson (1995). Still, we must not judge this example negatively. As it happens, the kind of observation of Garfinkel's student actually refers to ways of illuminating general assumptions in the everyday life of a culture, namely to the estrangement demonstrations that we know from ethnomethodology. Garfinkel, who devised these demonstrations with the purpose of illuminating everyday life assumptions, describes at least two types which we can also apply to the case of his student. The first is the observation of a well-known situation without adding anything to it that is not directly perceptible. In this way, for instance, persons, relationships and activities '[will be] described without respect for their history, for the place of a scene in a set of developing life circumstances, or for the scenes as texture of relevant events' (Garfinkel, 1967: 45) for the observer, or for his or her reasons, norms and values. In this way we can acquire an understanding of what we generally assume if we experience a sitation with our everyday attitude.

So students who carried out Garfinkel's assignment discovered to their amazement that in their parents' home:

> The business of one was treated as the business of the others. A person being criticized was unable to stand on dignity and was prevented by others from taking offence ... Displays of conduct and feeling occurred without apparent concern for the management of impressions. Table manners were bad, and family members showed each other little politeness. (Garfinkel, 1967: 45–6)

From these discoveries it is fairly easy to deduce some of the assumptions underlying the behaviour of family members.

The second type is to start with normal situations and to consider in what way this normality can be questioned so that the participants to the situation will feel uneasy and go out of their way to restore the normality of the situation. The insight into how to question the normality of a situation and the reactions of its 'victims' give us an indication of the assumptions we use in this kind of situation to allow them to appear normal. The reactions of parents who were not so much confronted with their children viewing their behaviour while assuming they were boarders, but with them acting out this assumption, is a fine example of this kind of estrangement demonstration:

> Family members were stupefied. They vigorously sought to make the strange actions intelligible and to restore the situation to normal appearances ... Explanations were sought in previous, understandable motives of the student: the student was 'working too hard' in school; the student was 'ill'; there had been 'another fight' with a fiancée. (Garfinkel, 1967: 47–8)

Although the value of estrangement demonstrations to ethnography is unmistakable it is, at this moment, uncertain if this also applies to the phenomenological approach in ethnography. In the next section we shall see that this is indeed the case. We shall see that the richness of the experiences caused by types of anthropological destrangement – such as empathy – can be enhanced by anthropological estrangement. The consequence is that the purpose of ethnography – learning a culture, its customs, attitudes and behaviour of the members of a group towards each other and their environment – will be served better still, as will the assumptions (or in Schutz's terms, the frame of interpretation).

FROM EXPERIENCE TO IDEA

Explaining assumptions, which is also the aim of ethnography, simultaneously points to a second, common practice of a phenomenological approach – namely *ideation*. Ideation means that we try to go from the particular to the general: starting from what appears to consciousness (because of the phenomenological *epoche*) we try to acquire an understanding of the idea that determines its meaningfulness (Giorgi, 1978; Moustakas, 1994). Or, to use the terms we have used already, we try to discover through which frame of reference – which typification or first-order construct – the experience purified of contaminating presuppositions and prejudices acquires its meaning.

Imagine I am doing phenomenologically ethnographic research on 'being in love'. I start to study my own experiences of 'being in love'. In the phenomenological *epoche* I refrain from wondering if I was really in love or how my infatuation came to be. I am not bothered about all possible scientific and other explanations and circumstances as to why, how and when I or other people fall in love, and I refrain from what I myself think being in love is. In other words, I bracket my knowledge *about* 'being in love' but not my knowledge *of* being in love as manifested in my recognition of the phenomenon 'being in love' (Giorgi, 1978: 76). In this way I am able to keep an open, unprejudiced mind to what appears to my consciousness. When, in the *epoche*, I study my own experiences, I have to be alert to the fact that language not only enables but also obscures the awareness of experience. This means that every time I put experience into words I have to look behind those words for possible experiences they could veil. If, for instance, I remember how attractive the object of my infatuation appeared to me, I must try to experience that feeling again and in this way establish what made the other so attractive – for instance the eyes. Having put that into words I must try to find out if some aspects of my experience of the eyes have been glossed over by these words – for instance, a feeling of recognition.

In the ideation I first have to realize that I am able to see a particular scene as 'being in love' on the basis of my own, now described, experience, of the observations of the behaviour of others, of what I have learned or fantasized about it one way or another (Husserl, 1969: 57) and of the idea of 'being in love' I have thus formed (Giorgi, 1978: 76). Next I compare (aspects of) these recollections with one another, to work out the basis on which all these different cases can be considered examples of 'being in love'. In this way I acquire an understanding of 'being in love' that I did not possess before. It is, as expressed by Merleau-Ponty (1970: 61) 'a question of replacing habitual concepts to which we pay no careful attention, by concepts which are consciously clarified'. In this way I could, for instance, discover one aspect of my idea of what 'being in love' is, namely 'recognizing a part of yourself in the other'. By seeking to perceive more expressions of 'being in love', by experiencing, recollecting or imagining it, my understanding of my idea of 'being in love' will become increasingly more explicit. In this sense the phenomenological approach is educating (Van Manen, 1990: 7).

However, phenomenological ethnography is not so much interested in my idea as it is in understanding more generally how in my own and/or in a strange group or culture 'being in love' is perceived. That is why I must subsequently not only bracket all contaminating presuppositions and prejudices about 'being in love', but for the time being also my own more or less explicit idea of it. In this way I can acquire the necessary openness to address myself to others (and other sources of information) to explain to me, in one way or another, what they (or these sources) consider as 'being in love'. For persons this means that, through a kind of open interview, I will ask and help them to discover (and to formulate) their own idea of 'being in love' in a way that is comparable with my own. In this sense they will become co-researchers (cf. Van Manen, 1990).

Empathy and demonstrations of estrangement can play an important role here. The questioning and helping of others to discover their own idea of 'being in love' should, generally speaking, occur as openly as possible. However, during this process I could, deliberately or through ignorance, offer descriptions of 'being in love' that are based on what is only directly perceivable, or I could create (hypothetical) situations that violate their idea of 'being in love'. The consequence of both possibilities will usually be that they try to elucidate what 'being in love' 'really is', and that will help them and me in the process of discovery. In addition there is the fact that the more insight I acquire into their experiences – through questioning and helping them and by demonstrations of estrangement – the more I shall be able to imagine myself in these experiences. Not only can this lead to a questioning and helping that increasingly complies with the experiences of others because these activities will be more complementary and affirmative, but also I will increasingly be able to discover the ideas of others by studying my own empathetic self. It goes without saying that the results of such a study have to be meticulously verified.

The purpose of questioning others (and other sources of information) is not to gloss over via mutual comparison and generalization the smaller and bigger differences for the benefit of 'the great insight'. Discovered differences should in phenomenological ethnography lead to further analysis – and, if necessary, further empirical research – to determine whether they are merely individual differences or represent different ways of looking at similar phenomena within this specific culture. When dealing with the first possibility, I must at least report these individual differences. When dealing with the latter, I must describe this extensively: for instance, I have discovered that in the researched culture women adhere to a different idea of 'being in love' than do men. Hence *the* idea as we have found it in a certain culture can never be less than a description of different and similar ways in which members of that culture look at and experience certain phenomena.

Only after having thus acquired a more or less clear understanding of the complex idea about how 'being in love' is seen within a culture, I am able to compare this with my own. As far as my research within my own culture is concerned, possible differences can lead to a correction of my idea and/or to additions to the collective idea. As far as I have researched another culture I will be able, by comparison, to show something of the differences and similarities between my idea and what can be found in this culture (which at the most can lead to amending my own idea of what 'being in love' is). The description of such a complex, culturally shared idea (on the basis of and/or illustrated by examples) is what is primarily at stake with a phenomenological approach in ethnography. In this respect we should not suppose that the idea we have found will fully coincide with *the* undoubtedly more complex idea that may be held in a certain culture. As Van Manen says, 'To do ... phenomenology is to attempt to accomplish the impossible: to construct a full interpretive description of some aspect of the lifeworld, and yet to remain aware that life is always more complex than any explication of meaning can reveal' (Van Manen, 1990: 18). What can best be accomplished by our description is that it is considered as a possible way in which the idea of each and everyone in that culture might be expressed (1990: 41, 122).

The phenomenologically trained reader will have noticed that the discussion of ideation (also called *eidetic reduction*) and idea (also called *essence* or *eidos*) deviates somewhat from what is customary in phenomenology. For example, when a phenomenologist studies a cube he or she will generally proceed as follows. One starts from the cube as it shows itself to consciousness within the phenomenological *epoche*. Then one will imagine other cubes – a cube with another colour, another size, made from other material, one that shows itself from another perspective, is differently lit, has other surroundings, a different background and so on. In this way one can discover that, despite all those differences, all these cubes show certain characteristics – rectilinearity, limitation to six sides and so on. To the phenomenologist all these fixed characteristics together form the unchanging essence of a cube (Schutz, 1973a: 114).

It is quite possible that an educated phenomenologist might thus discover the essence of a cube (irrespective of function: cf. Wittgenstein, 1976: 54–5). He or she will be able to do so because a cube has a clear definition and is perceptible to everyone. But this does not apply to a phenomenon such as 'being in love'. If we want to study this in a traditionally phenomenological way, we must (or must have been, or must yet) fall in love, or empathize with this feeling, for the phenomenon to present itself to consciousness. However, how do we know that we are (or have been, or have properly empathized to be) in love? After all, a new experience of 'being in love' might make us realize that our former experience was not really so. Moreover, how could we assume that every individual, group or culture, in each period of history, will as a matter of course have experiences of 'being in love' with a meaning that for all concerned leads to and originates from the same idea? A phenomenologist who thinks that he or she knows what it is 'to be in love' and who thinks that he or she could thus sufficiently imagine different forms of 'being in love' to reach its only, unchanging essence, is taking for granted presuppositions and prejudices about oneself and the world. That is why it will be better to bracket those assumptions. Only by collecting as many different forms as possible of 'being in love' – of one's own and of others within a certain group or culture – can one achieve an understanding of the prevailing idea of 'being in love' in that culture or group. We may not assume here that a fixed idea of being in love exists, nor that we shall be able to find it. It would already be something if the idea we find consists of some *family resemblances* (Wittgenstein, 1976: 31–2).

THE REFERENTS OF A CULTURALLY SHARED IDEA

In ethnography we generally do not want to limit ourselves to the description of an idea existing within a certain culture. Although the comparison of the different ideas of a culture's members might have resulted in the fact that we could thus distinguish different groupings, we generally find this insufficient. Usually we want to position the found, complex idea within the cultural, shared frame of interpretation of which it is a part.

Departing from a phenomenological analysis of the horizon on which every experience takes place (Husserl, 1969: 238–9; Schutz, 1973a: 108–9) we have *on the level of ideas* different possibilities to situate them within their cultural context. First, we can start from one or more discovered aspects of an idea. Imagine that I have come to the conclusion that the aspect of 'being in love' that I first found on my own – 'recognizing a part of oneself in the other' – is also shared to some degree by members of the culture I have studied. Imagine also that I have found another more or less shared aspect, namely 'being possessed by the other'. On the basis of these I shall be able to ask myself to what they refer and what their position is within these references. So, as to 'recognizing a part of oneself in the other' I can examine what other kinds of developments of self-knowledge appear in the culture concerned, and what the position of this aspect of 'being in love' is in relation to these developments. I can do the same with 'the relationship to the other' and with regard to 'obsessive thoughts and behaviours'.

Second, we can start from the idea itself and examine what it refers to and what relationship it represents. This implies that we must at least ask ourselves what our research shows us. In mine, for instance, I was compelled to distinguish 'being in love' from 'being one-sidedly in love', from love, and from friendship. I also observed among other things that from the beginning of puberty age has no influence on the idea of 'being in love', and that the gender of those in love is not important. In this way research can be used to acquire some understanding of what 'being in love' refers to and how it is related to that. On the basis of these referents we can possibly use our imagination, guided by our knowledge of the studied culture, to examine what these referents in turn are referring to. For example, love could refer to marriage, having children, respect and so on; friendship could refer to a shared past and/or interests, and so forth.

Third, and starting again from the idea itself, we can examine what might have occurred before and after the experiences concerned. Basically, our research will have yielded some understanding of this. In the case of 'being in love', for instance, we might have been confronted with different ways in which members of the culture meet, become acquainted, and show more than a usual interest in each other; we might have discovered some bad things and some good things to which 'being in love' could lead. We can thus situate the discovered idea of 'being in love' within these phenomena. The idea of 'being in love' that we have found can function as a focus to acquire an understanding of one part of a culture – namely of a shared frame of interpretation that directly (or possibly indirectly) is connected with this idea of 'being in love'. It will be clear that from each of the phenomena found to be connected with 'being in love' we shall have only a preliminary description until we have subjected them to a phenomenological approach.

From Research Question to Reporting

A phenomenological approach requires researchers to be profoundly engaged in a certain group of similar phenomena in order to discover to which idea they refer. It is almost impossible to do this properly if these activities do not stem from a real question. That is, a question to which researchers do not know the answer but that is sufficiently important to them that they are prepared to do their utmost to find an answer that will satisfy them (cf. Denzin, 1971: 167; Gadamer, 1990: 369; Maso, 1995: 12–13). What kind of research question could, for example, lead to phenomenologically ethnographic research on 'being in love'? Imagine that on several occasions I thought I was in love with someone but that people in my environment, nearest and dearest included, made it incessantly clear to me that what I was experiencing was not 'being in love'! In such a case it would matter a great deal to me to find out, to empathize, what 'being in love' is supposed to be. In that sense, I would have a real question.

With this question begins the collection and inspection of the information about the phenomenon to be researched. To this end we shall – after we have studied our own, sometimes empathized, experiences – read the relevant scientific and non-scientific literature, possibly consult informants, and perhaps put ourselves in situations in which we can perceive the phenomenon to be researched. This seems strange. After all, whereas the phenomenological *epoche* is supposed to bracket all contaminating presuppositions and prejudices about the phenomenon to be researched, this collecting of information seems to yield only more presuppositions and prejudices. In a sense this is indeed the case, but the collection and inspection of information produces more than this. All this information leads to confrontations, not only between the different assumptions, opinions, judgements, research findings and descriptions that these sources of information yield, but also between the presuppositions and prejudices that we are or will become conscious of through this confrontation. The result is that it will be a lot easier to bracket a considerable portion of our presuppositions and prejudices without replacing them with the often contradictory assumptions that originate from other sources (Maso, 1995: 13).

Besides these advantageous results, the collection and inspection of all possible information about the phenomenon to be researched also leads to a more extensive, clearer and more accessible idea of that phenomenon. The process of ideation, and positioning the outcome within the cultural shared frame of interpretation of which it is a part, will thus become more easy. Finally, phenomenological ethnographic research lends itself to various forms of representation as current in ethnography: the 'traditional' ethnographic text, 'dialogical' forms

of representation, feminist texts and postmodern arrangements (Atkinson, 1995). Hence researchers are able to report their findings in a way that is appropriate to the phenomenon they have studied.

Phenomenology and Phenomenological Ethnography

Phenomenologically ethnographic research is based on phenomenological and hermeneutic approaches in philosophy. These approaches know many directions, opinions and deviations. This had already started with Edmund Husserl (1859–1938), the father of phenomenology. Initially he assumed that consciousness and phenomena could not be separated (*intentionality*) and so talked about the intentional consciousness and intentional phenomena. Later, however, he reached the conclusion that only the transcendental consciousness has an independent existence. Initially he also assumed that the intentional consciousness and people are two separate, independent entities. Later he stated that the human world is an intersubjective world – a community of persons who live together in a mainly pre-objective, pre-scientific universe. The task peculiar to phenomenology is the investigation of the lifeworld (*Lebenswelt*), the description of the infinitely rich universe of the so-called predicative experience (Mora, 1962: 45).

Max Scheler (1874–1928) saw primarily in phenomenology 'not a method in the sense of a set of mental operations [as Husserl did] but a peculiar attitude or way of viewing [*Einstellung*]. In this attitude we enter into an immediate intuitive relationship with the "things"' (Spiegelberg, 1971: 241). Martin Heidegger (1889–1976), who claimed at first to be very much inspired by Husserl, was not concerned with consciousness, but with the meaning of being. Instead of bracketing 'every certainty or uncertainty concerning the existence' of whatever, he started to examine *Dasein* – human existence – as the entrance to uncover the meaning of being. Jean-Paul Sartre (1905–80) introduced 'interpretations of the sense of phenomena that run far beyond the direct evidence but are even apt to interfere with the unbiased description of the directly accessible phenomena' (Spiegelberg, 1971: 510), as advocated by Husserl. Maurice Merleau-Ponty (1908–61) was greatly influenced by the work of Husserl. He did not, however, see intentionality or transcendental consciousness as the prime phenomenon, but being-present-in-the-world.

These and many other directions, opinions and deviations in and of phenomenology and hermeneutics in philosophy have repercussions for the phenomenological approaches and patterns in the human and social sciences. They have brought with them all their own difficulties and possibilities. Confined as I am to the limits of a chapter, these differences and nuances have hardly been represented. I have thus limited myself to the presentation of a phenomenological approach that is currently used, at least with regard to the phenomenological *epoche* and ideation, and I have tried to present this in a way that is also feasible for empirical research.

Phenomenological ethnography occupies a middle position concerning the difference between naturalism and constructionism (Gubrium and Holstein, 1997). Phenomenological ethnographic research tries, like the naturalists, 'to get close to its subjects in order to capitalize upon their familiarity with the topic of study' (Gubrium and Holstein, 1997: 42) but, unlike them, they do not assume that they will find in this manner an 'underlying, shared, cognitive order' (1997: 53). Both in the *epoche* and the ideation, phenomenological ethnographers assume that there are individual differences as well as different ways of looking between each other and within a group. They consider it as taken for granted that these differences lead to, as well as being the result of, different constructions of reality.

REFERENCES

Atkinson, P.A. (1995) 'Ethnography: style and substance', in I. Maso, P.A. Atkinson, S. Delamont and J.C. Verhoeven (eds), *Openness in Research: The Tension Between Self and Other*. Assen: Van Gorcum. pp. 51–63.

Denzin, N.K. (1971) 'The logic of naturalistic inquiry', *Social Forces*, 50: 166–82.

Derksen, A.A. (1980) *Rationaliteit en wetenschap*. Assen: Van Gorcum.

Gadamer, H-G. (1976) 'The phenomenological movement', in D.E. Linge (ed.), *Hans-Georg Gadamer: Philosophical Hermeneutics*. Berkeley, CA: University of California Press.

Gadamer, H-G. (1990) *Hermeneutik I. Wahrheit und Methode: Grundzüge einer philsophischen Hermeneutik. Gesammelte Werke, Band I*. Tübingen: J.C.B. Mohr.

Garfinkel, H. (1967) *Studies in Ethnomethodology*. Englewood Cliffs, NJ: Prentice–Hall.

Giorgi, A. (1978) *Fenomenologie en de grondslagen van de psychologie*. Meppel/Amsterdam: Boom.

Gubrium, J.F. and Holstein, J.A. (1997) *The New Language of Qualitative Method*. Oxford: Oxford University Press.

Hammersley, M. and Atkinson, P. (1995) *Ethnography: Principles in Practice*, 2nd edn. London: Tavistock.

Husserl, E. (1969) *Ideas: General Introduction to Pure Phenomenology*. London: George Allen and Unwin.

Jacobs, H. and Stoop, B. (1965) *Het Auschwitz-proces: Berichten van de levenden en de doden*. Amsterdam: De Arbeiderspers.

Lauer, Q. (1958) *Phenomenology: Its Genesis and Prospect*. New York: Harper Torchbooks.

Maso, I. (1995) 'Trifurcate openness', in I. Maso, P.A. Atkinson, S. Delamont and J.C. Verhoeven (eds), *Openness in Research: The Tension Between Self and Other*. Assen: Van Gorcum.

Merleau-Ponty, M. (1970) *Primacy of Perception*. Evanston, IL: Northwestern University Press.

Mora, J.F. (1962) *Inleiding tot de moderne filosofie*. Utrecht: Het Spectrum.

Moustakas, C. (1994) *Phenomenological Research Methods*. Thousand Oaks, CA: Sage.

Schutz, A. (1971) 'The stranger: an essay in social psychology', in A. Broderson (ed.), *Alfred Schutz: Collected Papers II: Studies in Social Theory*. The Hague: Martinus Nijhoff. pp. 92–105.

Schutz, A. (1973a) 'Some leading concepts of phenomenology', in M. Natanson (ed.), *Alfred Schutz: Collected Papers I: The Problem of Social Reality*. The Hague: Martinus Nijhoff. pp. 99–117.

Schutz, A. (1973b) 'Common-sense and scientific interpretation of human action', in M. Natanson (ed.), *Alfred Schutz: Collected Papers I: The Problem of Social Reality*. The Hague: Martinus Nijhoff. pp. 3–47.

Schutz, A. (1973c) 'Concept and theory formation in the social sciences', in M. Natanson (ed.), *Alfred Schutz: Collected Papers I: The Problem of Social Reality*. The Hague: Martinus Nijhoff. pp. 48–66.

Schwandt, T.A. (1994) 'Constructivist, interpretivist approaches to human inquiry', in N.K. Denzin and Y.S. Lincoln (eds), *Handbook of Qualitative Research*. Thousand Oaks, CA: Sage. pp. 118–37.

Spiegelberg, H. (1971) *The Phenomenological Movement: A Historical Introduction*, 2 vols. The Hague: Martinus Nijhoff.

Van Manen, M. (1990) *Researching Lived Experience: Human Science for an Action Sensitive Pedagogy*. London: State University of New York Press.

Wittgenstein, L. (1976) *Philosophical Investigations*, 3rd edn. New York: Macmillan.

10

Semiotics, Semantics and Ethnography

PETER K. MANNING

Semiotics has evolved from de Saussure's radical revision of historical linguistics to a largely pragmatic, referential and empirical field in which signs are analysed for meaning in social and cultural contexts. In many respects, it remains a marginal and interdisciplinary field in which sociologists, anthropologists, philosophers and sociolinguists work. Semiotically inspired publications are found in the journals of these fields as well as in the *American Journal of Semiotics and Semiotica*, and dictionaries and encyclopediae of semiotics exist (Noth, 1990). Broad overviews, such as Eco's (1979), have done much to make the ideas accessible. Semiotic method has had little direct influence on social sciences, and its practitioners, with some exceptions like Thomas Sebeok and Umberto Eco, have not enjoyed international acclaim. Its influence is indirect, shaping the field-refined technique of anthropologists, and providing a vehicle in cultural and literary studies for current fashionable critiques of the practice of literature and philosophy. 'Semiotics' is often used merely as a metaphor for the analysis of symbolic action-representations, and their ordering.

Semiotics' complexities arise in part from its dualistic heritage – the ideas of de Saussure and Peirce – while semantics, the study of meaning, has become largely a specialized concern of linguistics. Semiotics claims all symbol systems as its own. Ethnography, the practice of cultural description, is the means by which 'context', the basis of meaning for both semiotics and semantics, is established, and conversely, the most powerful means to reveal the key problematics in these fields.

This chapter, devoted to semiotics, semantics and ethnography, begins with an example, the meaning of wearing an American baseball cap analysed from a semiotic perspective, and then provides definitions of key terms. A brief outline of the history of semiotics precedes a section illustrating the interconnections of ethnographic work and semiotics.

CAPPING

All social science begins with observation of a natural event or scene – a crowd, a wedding, a classroom, a meeting, with its setting, props, costumes, actors and action. From this natural event, with primary reality, abstractions or secondary reality, and further abstractions, can be laminated. Considerable evidence, both empirical and logical, supports the idea that actors typify their perceptions of the complex stimuli they encounter; they do not process raw data, but mini-concepts, typifications, tentative generalizations, that render complexity manageable. The depth, subtlety, intensity, generality and differentiation in these schema vary, as cognitive anthropology best illustrates. The work of semiotics, and to a lesser degree, semantics, is directed to sorting out and organizing what might be called 'the coding of the world'.

Below, I present an analysis of the American 'baseball' cap, rendering it within various perspectives forming a family of semiotic approaches to social analysis. Bear in mind that semiotics is the science of signs, or the study of how signs convey meaning, that it is characteristically, although not exclusively, human, and that it enables human beings to represent, to pun, or misrepresent or lie as well as to represent.

A Natural Scene with Caps

Walking across campus I note recently an increasing number of caps. A cap is a small hat covering only the top of the head with an extended rounded bill, and, when worn by baseball and softball players, was called a 'baseball cap'. I notice that although the shape remains fairly constant, close-fitting and of smooth texture, the colours and cap material vary; some caps are multi-coloured, some bills contrast with the main headpiece by colour or texture, but all the bills are consistent with the head size. Such hats are worn with almost all campus clothing, including coat and tie. Some display a name or manufacturer's logo, and range widely – names of designers, clothing manufacturers, products, teams, universities, businesses, places, country clubs, and vulgar exclamations, amongst others. Students, professors, campus employees, visitors (adults walking with apparent students on campuses), and workers briefly working on campus – television staff, electrical and construction people – all wear caps. Perhaps 25–30 per cent plus, even in the winter months, wear these caps. Both males and females wear them, in about equal number (perhaps more males). The bill offers a statement – they are worn with the bill forward, reversed, sideways, or tipped at odd angles, usually on the side.

These caps are sign vehicles, useful wearing apparel that are socially constituted, and communicate as well as serve utilitarian purposes. We require a socially grounded perspective informing us how these caps, seen as signs, or something that expresses something and has a content that is meaningful to people in a context, communicate. They express some culturally defined, or arbitrary, values if linked to a content. Expression and content require an interpretant or perspective to complete the sign by linking them. If 'cap' is the expression, what does it point to – what content completes the sign? I draw on my commonsense knowledge: the campus setting and other cues to locate these caps in the context of the lifestyles associated with campus life.

Since caps are an item of clothing, they are part of a fashion ensemble. Caps contrast with other items in an ensemble or set of garments (shirt, trousers, shoes, and perhaps underwear or outer garments), and with other types of headwear (other caps, hats, scarves), uncovered heads, and with each other. These are binary contrasts, based on either presence or absence, and produce differences between each of the above contrasts. These differences communicate social status, role or function.

As I walk, I observe a series of caps, associated in space and time, as part of a whole, 'student life'. They may be an ironic comment on other caps and hats (or lack thereof) off the campus, or as a metaphor, or way of symbolizing work, non-work or a lifestyle, and categories of people on the campus. These observations are more abstract, almost a code – I'm placing objects in categories, using expression, the cap, to point toward social content. In so doing, I identify social distinctions, such as the differences between caps of campus-based workers, staff and students. Caps, as sign vehicles, or that which conveys the sign, symbolize different roles and functions. I can create this analysis drawing on my intersubjective knowledge of campus life.

I can now regroup caps into social categories, signs about signs, that distinguish a segment of social life. Social categories such as 'student', 'parent', 'campus visitor', 'janitor', or 'grounds worker' are names, or signs about signs. Naming orders assigns meaning, and expresses an attitude toward a social object. Caps as signs (content and expression linked via a code) have several values (denotations) – instrumental value(s) as an eye shade, protecting against sun and rain, holding hair out of the face and eyes, as well as covering and concealing the eyes, face, or hair of the wearer. (Their origin was as a shade against the sun in cricket and later baseball games.) Caps also have an expressive value, a role in a fashion system or the complement of clothing (Barthes, 1983). They connote or imply social meanings that cluster into domains.

Caps can be placed in cognitive domains, or assemblages that cohere, such as work and leisure, and work/non-work: leisure/non-leisure. This yields six contrasts:

1   not-work/leisure;
2   work/not-leisure;
3   not work/work;
4   not-leisure/leisure;
5   not-work/not-leisure;
6   work/leisure.

These oppositions are created by combining contrasts into a semiotic square devised by Greimas (Jackson, 1985) which reveals contradiction as well as opposition. A cap may also connote mythological or ideological meanings, insofar as it is associated with political organizations and power (Barthes, 1970, 1972).

Within the identified domains there are 'minimeanings', the denotations and connotations of the cap. The cap is a self-referential iconic sign. It indicates or points to itself and the wearer. Denotations of a cap can be organized paradigmatically or metaphorically. The cap observed is like a baseball cap and the associations noted work by simile – they are like other caps. The connotations of a baseball-type cap can be encoded as instances of costume, fashion or leisure, as a part of an 'ensemble', as an instance of a 'costume', or a uniform in sport or work, as part of a uniform. It can stand alone, or be a salient sign, if its associations with other items in a clothing system is weak. The signification of a cap remains, in the absence of direct cues originating from a clothing system, but an ensemble, an 'outfit', costume, or uniform, is a more powerful message since it is additive, and incorporates a coherent set of signs. Several codes when collected constitute a field (Bourdieu, 1977). A given cap can be multiply coded and stand within a field comprised of several associated codes. A field here is used to refer to very broad types of organization of capital and resources, for example, work and play (Bourdieu, 1991: 14).

Now, can we organize these connections at a slightly higher level of abstraction? Coding is a necessary part of an interpretation – providing 'rules which generate signs as concrete occurrences ...' (Eco, 1979: 49). It is a logical basis for drawing connections between the components of a sign, signs clustered, and social organization. A code enables one to see signs as instances of rules and interpretations, as well as to map one set of signs on another. Once the cap is encoded (and decoded), the question of subjective meanings, those of the observer or the wearer, can be folded into the analysis. The analytic and syntactical analysis above assumes meanings and contrasts. Empirical research based on questioning wearers about what the cap means to them, or to observers, seeks to determine what and how the signs mean, to whom, and the resultant social consequences.

The physical make-up of the sign vehicle communicates. Consider the function of the bill of the cap as an indicator of mood and attitude. Any bill position communicates semiotically, just as the cap itself conveys or connotes an attitude and a mood. Altering it while wearing it is a direct sign. It can be coded as a sign of leisure, advertising, personal biography and identity, or merely coded as mood communication: 'I enjoy the feelings associated with drinking or serving or buying this beer; wearing, smelling or buying this perfume.' The bill can be worn 'straight ahead,' over the face of the wearer, shading the eyes; on the side (left or right placement does not seem to be differentiated); or 'reversed,' with the bill directly opposite the face of the wearer. Caps can also be positioned with the bill down (rather than more level with the ears) and reversed to either the left or right side. What do these positions, or the syntax or arrangement of the elements, mean? The bill worn directly ahead, especially by adults, does not strongly indicate a particular mood, but contrasts with any other position. (I have noticed that Dads visiting their children on campus wear caps straight ahead; serious leisure and identification perhaps.) Bills are reversed for functional or instrumental reasons – when playing certain positions in games (catcher, for example), or riding a motor scooter. When worn by students sideways, turned left or right, or reversed, it connotes leisure, and an adversarial attitude or mood. I have observed this style displayed by skate boarders. Wearing the cap at a slant and reversed connotes exotic leisure activities such as skate boarding, surfing and volleyball. A cap worn backwards (or askew), suggests a

message: 'I wear it this way because I do, like, or watch very active, demanding, or difficult outdoor activities during which the wind might remove my head covering.' But clearly, bills combine to send multiple messages. Caps with signs on the rear – smaller versions of the logo on the front crown – suggest announcing an identity, role or group relationship, and an attitude. Activity and attitude are connoted by the bill. Fully reversed and at an angle to the rear, the cap connotes 'a fool', or a very playful mood. Bill position conveys gender-specific meanings. Females associate a cap with an ensemble or a style and wear the cap almost always with the bill straight-ahead. The small hole at the rear above the strap can accommodate a 'pony tail' for men or women.

Caps facilitate play, misleading messages and lies (where known observed facts contradict the appearance). The cap is an all-purpose sign vehicle, sending abundant, complex or polysemic messages, and its meaning is context-dependent. As a context-dependent sign, it contributes to the blurring of class, race and gender differences in campus dress, conveys imagery and illustrates the commodification of clothing. Consider some anomalies.

1   Males can wear 'female caps' and vice versa. If a male wears a cap with 'Pi Beta Phi' (a sorority), or a seven-year-old wears a specific University cap, ambiguous messages are conveyed. The male may have received the cap as a 'favor' while attending a sorority dance; the child could be related to a student, staff or faculty. Although the cap signals social relationships, the actual connection, without other evidence, is unclear.

2   Caps elicit and display generalized imagery not closely tied to specific social relationships, social structure and signs about signs, or social organization. They communicate an attitude toward, and display desires or fantasies. For example, a 'Budweiser' cap communicates brand loyalty and advertises the beer, but may just be a cap. It may simply be worn as a convenience and have no specific expressive purpose.

3   Caps' team logos announce ambiguous identities. A cap may announce vicarious identification with a team, for example 'Detroit Tigers', 'Los Angeles Dodgers', or 'Detroit Pistons'; as such, the cap's emblem implicitly reads 'I support the Tigers' (Do you?). This announcement is directed to a specific generalized other, sports fans, but also offers a symbolic bond of support – manifest through claiming to be a fan and identifying with other fans (of the same team, of basketball, or of sports). It says: 'Hello! Have we anything in common?'

4   A cap without uniform points to something out of sight, or two things at once, leisure and work.

A cap can pun, or play on two known qualities at once: 'My wife ran away with my best friend, and I sure do miss him.' Since it is assumed that marriage is a closer bond than same-sex friendship, the pun is that the person wearing the cap misses him more than her. An ambiguous reference: 'Just do it' plays on the ambiguity of 'it'. 'It' is a context-dependent shifter for which the cap alone supplies no obvious referent.

5   A cap conveys ambiguous status claims and blurs lines of authority. Stalls along the Mall in Washington, DC sell caps with FBI on the front crown. Students wearing caps with 'FBI', 'Michigan State Police', or 'USS Tigercat', may not be members of these organizations. Since police are increasingly wearing caps (and jackets) with 'FBI', 'DEA', or 'East Lansing Police' on the crown, widespread wearing of caps with the same colour, shape and logo, and made with the same materials, diminishes the unique character of the cap to convey authority.

6   A cap with a place name or locality can mislead. Previously, a cap displaying the logo of a local team, it was assumed, was worn by a native of that area. I saw a student in the supermarket wearing an MSU baseball cap and a wool, leather-sleeved, American style 'letterman's jacket' with 'Oxford University' on the upper left quadrant. Given frequent travel, the mass merchandising of souvenir shirts, caps and sweat shirts, it is impossible to know if a person is a native, has traveled there, merely likes the place, is displaying a wish, or announcing an identity.

7   Caps blur time and place. They can signify nostalgia for an unknown time or exotic place. The past, present and future can be conflated. Some caps display the emblems of long-defunct teams: Brooklyn (now the Los Angeles) Dodgers, New York (now San Francisco) Giants or teams in the old Negro League – the past in the present. People who have never been to Minnesota, seen a timberwolf, or know anything about basketball, can wear a 'Minnesota Timberwolves' cap with pride.

DEFINITIONS

As the cap example shows, neither the sign, a meaningful representation of some kind, nor semiotics, the science of signs, have consensual definitions (Noth, 1990, Fig. Si. 3: 90). Thomas Sebeok's comment (1991: 20) suggests the ethnographic value of semiotics:

> ... some [definitions of semiotics] thrive, but all are misleading. For semiotics is not about something, unless you want to say it is about semiosis, and that does not

help much. Semiotics is something, something by means of which we can conjure reality from illusion by the use of signs ...

Although contemporary ethnographers may eschew the rather romantic notion that they 'conjure reality', in many respects, ethnography seeks to explicate 'the native's point of view' (Geertz, 1973) by connecting the existential grounds of experience (what people think, feel and remember) with its symbolic manifolds, or forms of representation. Jakobson, a noted sociolinguist, writes 'Language is the only system which is comprised of elements which are signifiers, yet at the same time signify nothing' (1981: 66). Music is close, but musical scores refer to a harmonic code and can be reproduced and repeated relatively easily to produce the same sound. What is signified by signs is mental. This proposition enables ethnographic work to parse out the elements of any communication event, whether it be a sidewalk conversation, a funeral, a wedding or a poem. Because people, whether preliterate or postmodern, live and interpret the one life they have in terms of the language(s) and other symbols they learn, they negotiate a fit between language, thought and action, and the constraints of social structure.

Semiotics, as used here, is not a theory or perspective, but a method, or general approach to social life, that begins with observation, identifying and pinning down connections between intersubjectivity or shared meanings, and patterned social relations. Since signs convey meaning in many ways, and are encoded variously, communicate by many vehicles (that which conveys the sign, be it person, animal, place or thing), work through many channels (modes of communication, electronic or physical), and are non-linguistic (signs, postures, gestures) as well as linguistic (words, discourse, texts), the scope of semiotics is vast (Sebeok, 1991).

Langer's (1942: 35–9; 54–67) distinction between (a) representative signs (names, symbols, pictures), which are 'motivated' and 'arbitrary' conveying culturally derived meanings, and (b) indicators (symptoms, signals, natural signs) standing 'closer' to their source is useful. In practice, semiotics can be very tightly articulated analysis or a very loose metaphor for deconstructing symbolic action. It can take a highly formal guise, with tight internal connections among signs, mathematical equations, codes, or kinship trees, or a rather vague descriptive assemblage mentioned in passing and used merely as a gloss for the study of symbolic structures.

Ethnography, the close study of representations, or in Langer's terms, 'representative signs', artifacts, and beliefs characteristic of a social group, provides the context within which signs, symbolic forms and content, are joined with meaning. Ethnography is a rendition of a culture as lived by particular people in particular places doing particular things at particular times (Van Maanen, 1995: 23). Systematic ethnography is attuned to the work of signs, referentially, communicatively and functionally, in a system. It is essential for a full semiotic study, and a requisite for the study of semiosis, or change(s) in meaning.

Sign work, when revealed and understood, points to the invisible. Consider the Roman Catholic Christian Mass: it contains signs with denotations – the cross, the costume of the priest, the wine and bread – (relatively narrow and circumscribed meanings) – and connotations – the suffering of Christ, the authority of the Church, the body and blood of Christ (more broadly extended meanings). Semiosis occurs – the signs change meaning during the course of the ritual: wine becomes the blood of Christ. All of the signs on the costume of the priest are connected to Christian myths and beliefs. These (visible sign) denotations and connotations symbolize the invisible, what is out of sight, transcendent multivalent concepts such as sanctity, sacrifice, immortality, salvation, forgiveness and grace. The power of the ritual lies not only in its content, but in its form of redundant sequences that refer only to itself.

If we consider denotations and connotations as sign functions and transcendent meanings as culturally lodged explanations, or signs about signs, identifying and explicating the key and lasting connections between these levels of meaning are the ethnographers' tasks. MacCannell and MacCannell (1982) suggest the felicitous term, 'ethnosemiotics', as the study of signs about signs. This concept points the way toward the integration of ethnography and semiotics because without the context of sign work they become merely marks.[1]

SEMIOTICS: A BRIEF REVIEW

Semiotic analysis remains an awkward blend of ideas drawn from Ferdinand de Saussure, a Swiss linguist, and two American philosophers, Charles S. Peirce and Charles Morris (Peirce's advocate and editor of the lectures of G.H. Mead, the founder of symbolic interactionism). Let us call Saussure's version 'semiotics' and the Peirce–Morris version 'pragmatics', even though this is somewhat misleading. Semiotics refers to Saussure's closed-system, ahistorical structural approach to signs, while pragmatics is associated with Peirce and Morris, who sought to identify signs in-use or sign-functions.

Because most modern ethnographic work is based on the pragmatic approach of Peirce and Morris, and the social psychologies of John Dewey and George Herbert Mead, we need only briefly review Saussure's ideas. The sign is a function of signifier and signified joined as a mental construct. Meaning comes from contrast, difference and ordering of signs. This is a 'closed' system in which sound and image are assumed to be one. This excludes external influences on language change, contrasts performance (*parole*) with structure (*la langue*), is ahistorical and obviates the role of interpretation and the hearer–speaker interaction.

The limitations of the Saussurian approach were also its strength. Saussure sought to replace the historical study of languages and their development (philology, grammar, syntax and semantics) with the study of language structure and function that was generic across all Indo-European languages. Notions of contrast, difference, levels of meaning, context and the functions of signs are abstract and stated at such a level that comparative semiotics was possible.

An expanded and alternative view of semiotics emerged in the early nineteenth century in New England. Charles Peirce (8 vols, 1931–58), a philosopher, mathematician and logician, clarified the relationship between perception, sign and interpretant in semiotic theory. While eschewing the closed system of Saussure, and introducing the notion of the interpretant as a source of meaning, Peirce redefined the sign, not as conjunction of signifier and signified within an assumed system of meanings, but as something that means something to an interpretant (a perspective, not a person). The interpretant completes the sign, connects its elements in the mind of someone. The signifying system and the pragmatics of communication are identical for Peirce, not separate entities as in Saussure. Peirce emphasizes an internal dialogue, and implies the self concept without developing it. He differentiates the perspective of the interpretant, 'a mediating representation', through the concepts of firstness, secondness and thirdness that roughly correspond to degree of abstract reference (Noth, 1990: 44–5; Peirce, vol. 2: 275). Peirce continued to modify his nomenclature throughout his lifetime and produce confusing listings. The concepts of self and perspective loom large in ethnographic work influenced by Peircian or pragmatic semiotics because Peirce felt that the meaning of a sign, indeed its creation, arose when representations were grounded in belief, values and attitudes. These in turn arose from semiosis, the creating and using of signs. A word conjures up a conception and the conception guides action, and when this action is shored up by belief, it sustains the conception.

Although not known as a semiotician, the philosopher G.H. Mead introduced a now widely used symbolic framework. His work was edited and expanded by Charles Morris, a University of Chicago trained philosopher who later taught Thomas Sebeok. Mead asked how does a sign (a symbol in his terms) become significant? He imagined a little scenario in which people gestured, indicated objects which in turn were suffused with meaning and action potential, and thus created a dialogue between the I, present action, the me, reflections on action, and the (significant and generalized) other. An interaction is shaped by all three. The triadic self is the source of perspective and reflection on past, present and future, and in effect is the source of shared, emergent meanings that guide interaction. The self includes the inner dialogue between the I (action) and the me (reflection) as well as the you or the other. These terms indicate the present (I), the past (me) and the future (the other) (Wiley, 1991: 14). Mead includes the biological and the emotional in his scheme, and sees the interpretation of symbols and signs by the self as the agency for socialization, progress and scientific endeavour itself. When a sign spurs action, or calls out a response, and a response results, it becomes meaningful. In the course of interactions and indications, joining selves and the response of others, semiosis results. Morris (1938) urged a tight distinction between signs and symbols, reserving the latter for arbitrarily motivated and interpreted representations. The sign was more narrowly connected, such as smoke to fire, or a footprint to its owner. (Some writers distinguish 'sign' from 'symbol' following Morris, while others consider 'sign' the generic and 'symbol' a sort of sign.) Mead's influence at the University of Chicago was extensive as well as deep, and influenced at least two generations of sociologists (Blumer and Hughes, and later, Goffman, Strauss and Becker), anthropologists (Redfield and Geertz), psychologists and philosophers (John Dewey).[2]

These pragmatists, Peirce, Mead and Morris, connected sign functions indicated by the (behavioral) consequences of responses to signs. They directed attention to the communicative and referential functions of signs, and explored the social role of the interpretant (that which makes the sign complete). Semiotics, until this time, could not account for the code–coder–message relationship – how actors, taking the role of the other and sustaining some kind of intersubjective reality, were able to communicate. Since interactions take place over time, biography and history are important features of the long-lagged interactions that shape societies; Saussure does not take into account the pause between signifier and the meaning attached to the signified, long-term changes in cultural context. In traditional semiotics, issues of power and authority seem by-passed or assumed. The selective use of signs to persuade, whether interpersonally or on mass audiences, is part of all market-oriented societies.

The triadic notion of Peirce, Morris and Mead extends Saussure's elegant two-sided and influential scheme to include the interpretant and the behavioural consequences of response to the sign. American semiotics (Morris, 1938) has three branches – syntax, the formal properties and grammar of sign systems; pragmatics, the relationships of signs and interpreters, and semantics, the relationship of signs to the objects to which they are applicable (meaning). Symbolic interactionists (following Mead) and leading American semioticians (such as Halton, MacCannell and MacCannell, and Sebeok) blend the ideas of pragmatists (C.S. Peirce, G.H. Mead, Charles Morris), insights of Roman Jakobson (1981, 1987) and the Italian novelist, philosopher and critic, Umberto Eco (1979).

Pragmatists introduced the idea of change through interaction. Semiosis, a process-oriented concept that integrates stages of the act with types of signs (Morris, 1938: 4), entails indication, response and completion. The degree of culturally determined, or 'arbitrary meaning' that signs convey, differs. 'Good manners', for example, can be indexical, an indicator of what a person at a dinner party has done, or can resonate widely into different class, cultural or ethnic tastes, but is always subject to discovery over time.

Most ethnographic work explores the communicative and referential functions of representative signs, but must consider indexical signs or indicators because they raise the culturally problematic matter of what is 'natural'. Witchcraft in southeastern Mexico is revealing. The cry of a wolf or dog at night indicates the presence of a witch in an animal's guise. Shades of meaning are also generally accepted. It is useful to identify three levels of sign meaning: denotative (narrow connection), connotative (broader implication) and ideological. The connotative and mythical level of interpretation results from unexamined non-empirical or belief-based connections drawn between denotative and connotative meanings (Barthes, 1972: 115ff.). Signs are conveyed by many vehicles (both material and symbolic), and the vehicle can at times 'rub off' on the sign – think of the mixture of feelings and thoughts aroused by seeing a mink-lined toilet bowl.

Recall, however, that semiotics identifies structural features and is a form for analysis that assumes an idealized communicative dyad. Questions of orientation, for example, are much more vexing when doing an analysis of a national monument, television, revolutionary rhetoric, organizational structure, or societal change. The flow or management of conversation requires the vocabulary of pragmatics. In some way, ethnographic work is perched between situational analysis and a structural or macro-cultural analysis of the constraints on speaking–hearing and communication.

Pragmatics (Levinson, 1983), a lively subfield within semiotics, has been a fruitful expansion of semiotics. Pragmatics considers the role of implicit deference in address and interactions, of deixis, anaphoria and conversation management, all of which indicate matters outside the speech act that influence meaning and social relationships (Levinson, 1983). It also entails the brilliant work glossed with the term 'conversational analysis' or

CA (Psathas, 1995). In CA, a general ethnographic account is eschewed, arguing that studies of 'natural language' reveal universal patterns – turn-taking, joking, interruption, topic selection, and opening and closing in English. An exception is the work of Heath (1986), who embeds his close analysis of doctor–patient interactions using CA (and other techniques) in carefully honed ethnographic materials.

Semantics' general theories of speech behaviour, usually including a semantic aspect, such as implicature theory, speech act theory, and presupposition-based theories (Levinson, 1983), as well as computer-based modeling of the mind, have failed to gain general acceptance. They are often biogenetic in origin, a notion that until recently has been rejected by social scientists other than psychologists. John Searle (1995), among others, contends this is not an obstacle to a sociocultural conception of communication. The loss of academic popularity of these theories is perhaps attributable in part to the recognition of the role of context (Harris, 1983), and the impact of Chomsky's work on theories of language learning and use. Chomsky truncated theoretically the assumed connection between grammar, syntax and semantics, showing that a 'deep structure' of understanding precedes and shapes meanings, and arguing conversely that language can produce grammatically correct but stupid phrases. Finally, such general theories were roundly assailed by philosophers such as Wittgenstein, Heidegger and Husserl, each of whom demolished assumptions and arguments that claimed that the structure of language captured the structure of the world, or mirrored it (Rorty, 1979). The fallacy of representation, in their words, was misleading, and thus interest in the world-creating functions of language superseded interest in the extent to which it represented, mirrored, or accurately reproduced the structure of the world. This principle did not obviate notions like causation because it was assumed that the material world 'acted' under different principles than the social world. When a tree falls due to physical forces, high winds, the processes differ from the human act of 'falling asleep'. The latter involves observation and interpretation, the former only changes in wind velocity.

The most systematic approaches to semantics relevant to ethnographic work emerged in the 1960s, developed by anthropologists influenced by biological taxonomies, cognitive psychology and mathematics. Romney, Metzger and D'Andrade extended ideas of fieldworkers toiling in the South Pacific, such as Goodenough, Frake and Conklin (Tyler, 1981). They elicited by detailed, forced comparisons classificatory terms from informants and then arrayed them to show how they organized key domains in a culture, such as colour, kinship and ethnobotanical categories. Later work systematized native notions of mental illness, weddings, firewood, lesions and law, and mapped taxonomies yielding Western, linear, hierarchical, exclusive, Aristotelian classifications. Such typologies and algorithms arranged using principles of hierarchy, contrast, opposition and differentiation, they argued, represented culturally sanctioned 'native' logics-in-use. Like artificial intelligence projects, they sought to model the connections between 'the mind' (more often the brain) and 'culture', or an aspect of culture. The limits of such cognitive schemes, the question of the head term, or what domain is being studied, and the ambiguity of use, drove the cognitive anthropologists to increasing formalization (Tyler, 1981). For example, if one takes a 'head term' for a domain from Western medicine, and asks peasants in the State of Chiapas, Mexico, initially about the existence of a series of symptoms – depression, lack of appetite, loss of sleep, low affect – these may be discovered (found in a sample), and found to form factors or domains. This mapping is culturally defined. Is the term 'depression' or 'schizophrenia', a cluster of symptoms that constitutes disease categories in the Euro-American world, thus extant in south-eastern Mexico? Anthropologists disagree (Fabrega, 1997).

An important variation on semiotics and sociolinguistics, the work of Basil Bernstein (1972, 1973; Atkinson, 1985), bridges the concerns of pragmatists and structuralists. Building on Durkheim's notion of language as both a structure of constraint and representation, Bernstein infers from discourse of school children codes – the elaborated or differentiated code and the restricted or more concrete code – that underlie their speech. He shows that the implicit character of the elaborated code, associated with some children (there is a class effect) grants them a broader perspective, a more differentiated sense of social relations, and a relativism that assists abstract learning. Combining Halliday's (1979) notion of language as a 'social semiotic', with Durkheim, Bernstein outlines a theory of learning, socialization and stratification. Most importantly, Bernstein demonstrates that the implicit links of coder (the hearer–speaker dyad), code (the paradigm within which speech is heard) and the encoded (the speech), render different experiences, social realities and life chances. The phenomenology of the actor, including the self, is explicitly taken into account in Bernstein's work. Bernstein fruitfully synthesized French thought and incorporated ideas such as classification (the degree of internal differentiation of a scheme) and code (the rules governing relationships between the items) with symbolic interactionism.

In the past fifteen years, a number of semiotically influenced works have appeared, ranging from highly abstracted theorizing in psychoanalysis (Kristeva, 1989; Silverman, 1983; Turkle, 1984), geography (Harvey, 1989; Soja, 1989), and science

(Hayles, 1994). Translations of writings of Michel Foucault, who marketed his own ambivalent version of structuralism, and of Pierre Bourdieu, who converted the doctrine into a materialist version of constraint, absent selves or actors as a locus of agency, became an American cottage industry. More convoluted versions of cultural semiotics spun out by Baudrillard (1993) have appeared.

In these works 'structure' is metaphoric and used by analogy to characterize massive moments of thought, historical trends and cultural change. A modified semiotics presently occupies a key role in social theorizing as the evolutionary paradigm once did in sociology. In these theories, the notion of 'self' is 'decentred' or absent, as in Saussure. The power of the code functions to 'translate' and apply the structure of signs (Dosse, 1997a, 1997b). In these approaches, the model of language, based loosely on semiotics, is used to depict social relations.

Ethnographic Work and Semiotics

Ethnography is essential to any semiotic analysis by a scientist because the problematic, context-based and arbitrary meaning of a representation must be pinned down and communicated to others in the scientific community through lectures, articles and books. Even if materials from, say an Amazonian pre-literate people are presented in a film, the visual presentation is accompanied by a 'voice over' narration; the images are embedded in talk and vice versa. This process is based on written and spoken language. Semiotics is a tool that must be expressed linguistically. While semiotics considers a multitude of sign systems, its findings are communicated primarily through written language.

In other words, semiotics is a fundamentally reflexive practice – written language(s) display the very problems analysed. Ethnographers use language as a tool to elicit data, often in the indigenous language, write up their findings to describe sociolinguistic behaviour, and communicate about symbols and signs as both cause and effect of behaviour. While semiotics is the science of signs, language is not only a model for studying other symbol systems, it is the primary channel by which analyses are communicated.

Consider how the French semiologist Roland Barthes defines semiotics. He avers that it is a branch of semiology, or the science of meaning, 'the world of signifieds is none other than that of language' (1970: 10). A sign links a signifier and signified in a given system, but full explication of the function of signifieds and associated signifiers requires not only an analysis of syntax and pragmatics, but of the context of use. Semiotics, Barthes argues, reveals the form in which signification is communicated, but it does not exhaust the subtle

questions of 'substance'. Here, he means what is being analysed – whether it be wrestling, wine, a film, or photographs. Barthes writes (1970: 40), 'the substance is that whole set of aspects of linguistic phenomena which cannot be described without resorting to extra linguistic premises ... for instance, the ideological, emotional, or simply notional aspects of the signified, its "positive meaning"'. Barthes here rejects a narrowly defined semiotics, a formalism that cannot capture the emotive and substantive aspects of communication, nor indeed, the non-verbal. He is also questioning a narrow behaviouristic conception of the sign. So, when we watch a wrestling match (World Wrestling Federation on American television) it is a spectacle (a struggle of good versus evil, not solely between two wrestlers), an unruly (literally, since the rules of wrestling are constantly violated, like hockey, with the complicity of the referees), vulgar, excessive, violent clash. The emotional epiphanies and nadirs are the essential feature of the scene, and words (symbols) fail to fully capture what we see. Since culture is fundamentally about the governing of emotions, this is a powerful window on modern societies.

Language is double-articulated because it refers to itself as well as to the social and material world. In a sentence, 'It is raining,' or 'I'm here,' 'It' and 'here' (both called 'shifters') refer to both the material world and require a context (what is brought to the speech event) to be understood. 'I' refers to the speaker, and here to some social place.

Barthes believes that the ambiguities and richness of language can be captured by his version of semiotics, or semiology. Semiotics remains a means to analyse language. In this sense, it is a meta-language, a language that refers to another language and to itself. Language, both its formal and substantive aspects, is embedded in and shapes social relations, while social relations shape language use (Hymes, 1964). Social relations, norms, roles, values and rules, as well as the tacit knowledge that underlies society, pin down the signified, or as Barthes explains, 'the relay of language extracts their signifiers ... and names their signifieds ...' (1970: 11). Think of how 'openings' and 'closings' work in an interaction at a bar asking for a drink, or in a British shop while buying a newspaper. Both involve a very complex and nuanced series of 'pleases', 'thank yous', and often 'small talk' – the weather, sport or current events dominate. Both the instrumental, buying and selling something, and the expressive, showing feelings and mutuality of emotions, animate the exchange. My analysis in the last sentence labels the signs and their meaning using written English, but much of what occurs is tacit, based on a kind of 'practical consciousness' (Giddens, 1984), more than signs.

Sociologists espouse their own heritage in ethnography and connect it especially with the 'Chicago school' (Becker, 1998). Works drawing on Mead and the broad symbolic interactionist tradition are varied and raise the question: How do semiotics and symbolic interactionism differ? Clearly, American semiotics, as practiced, is quite close to symbolic interactionism, and they both emerged at the University of Chicago. They both focus on the role of symbolization or signification in social life; emphasize the role of language in shaping social realities, and emphasize pragmatism as a philosophic tradition.

Consider, however, these three differences (Denzin, 1987). Peircian social semiotics draws a clear distinction between 'the interpretant' as perspective and the 'self'. There is no self in Pierce [to the reader: consider that sentence semiotically]. The self is the fundamental concept of symbolic interaction, regardless of the level of analysis employed. Semiotic analysis can proceed with an analysis of any symbol system (bearing in mind Barthes' points about language), in the absence of 'self' or a concept of meaning except one analytically derived as a function of difference. Semiotic analyses of flags, tourism or the function of pauses in conversation require no self, or the dance of gestures from which meanings arise. Semiotics posits a structural shape to meaning in advance, a part of its rationalist heritage, and relies on the model of language to direct its attention in advance to structures, signification and practices. As Lemert (1981) demonstrates, a structural metaphor serves well a variety of structuralisms, including Saussurian, Marxist and cultural Marxist approaches, and even embraces the quite metaphorical ramblings of Baudrillard. No such 'structuralist' assumptions lurk in symbolic interactionism, and some versions of it are quite elegantly sparse (Rock, 1977).

Analyses partaking of the semiotic tradition via Mead, such as dramaturgy or dramatism (Kenneth Burke, Erving Goffman, Hugh Dalziel Duncan), symbolic interactionism (Mead, Bulmer, and students), narrative (Czarniawska, 1998; Manning and Cullum-Swan, 1992) and discourse analysis (Reissman, 1993; Wagner-Pacifici, 1986, 1991), consider symbols and other representations, and the sign-referent function, but are inclined to slight analysis of social structure as lived experience.

Perhaps the most engaging social semiotician is Umberto Eco, a pragmatist and polymath philosopher who uses a semiotic perspective to illuminate his travels and observations on modern European and North American culture (1986), medieval murder (1983), and cinematic and textual practices (1984). Eco's semiotics and deep knowledge of medieval philosophy, especially the Augustinians, illuminates his lively texts. Other writers, seizing on the utility of the metaphor of a 'frame' (roughly analogous to the two-sided sign of Saussure) focus on system-level – explorations of meaning production and dissemination (Bateson, 1973; Lincoln, 1991). Wagner-Pacifici and Schwartz imaginatively

combine history and discourse analysis (1991). By extension, I would include the theorizing of Anthony Wilden, influenced by Lacan, Freud and Saussure, and Ulrich Beck, Niklas Luhmann and Orin Klapp.

Ethnographic works influenced by semiotics range from loose to rather tight in respect of systematic use of the semiotic heuristic. 'Tight' and 'loose' indicate the extent to which the framework and assumptions of semiotics, as traced from Saussure to Morris, are applied to social life using empirical materials. Recall the above definition of ethnography – the study of the meaning of what a particular people do in a particular time and place – and distinguish it from writing about this, or the process of textual representation (Atkinson, 1992).

Loose Semiotics

Many of the works influenced by symbolic interactionism are 'loosely semiotic' insofar as they explore the role of signs, symbols and discourse in shaping action choices (whether in texts or in natural activity). They adopt the central idea that communication is the foundation of social order, but the semiotic vocabulary, and heuristics, other than metaphor and myth, are suppressed or absent. Many well-known works that appeal to symbolization and even cite semiotics are better located in the 'symbolic interactionist tradition'. Works of Geertz, Gusfield, Richard Merelman, Murray Edelman and Lauren Edelman, eschew the sometimes belaboured vocabulary of semiotics. They combine fruitfully the ideas of Burke, Mead and Goffman, rather than a refined semiotic framework.

The artificial intelligence (AI) group at MIT and elsewhere sought to step back from describing culturally embedded logics to model actions that could be mistaken for those of a human. Here, the intersection of semiotics and ethnography is revealed in the attempt to simulate cognitive behaviour. The mission of AI parallels that of social and cultural anthropology. It seeks to experimentally recreate or simulate 'how people think', and how cultural assumptions, practices and actions are seen as culturally meaningful and 'human' (Neroponte, 1991).

The social context of the artificial intelligence experiments is well documented in Sherry Turkle's two virtuoso performances, *Life on the Screen* (1995) and *The Second Self* (1984), in which she details key transformations in the MIT AI program. She illustrates changes in conceptions of sign systems, language, culture and the brain–mind connection. Both representative and natural signs are cultural, social and/or biological in origin. The AI movement, like semiotics, aims to capture the meaning of 'a mental life outside our bodies' (Turkle, 1995: 22). She traces this quest using three principles which are consistent with the ideas traced here. She argues that, first we have (or should?) become accustomed to 'opaque' technology, for example icons that do not reveal what is functioning underneath (p. 23). Secondly, we take things at 'interface value' and seldom worry about whether 'representations' or 'real' is a meaningful distinction (p. 23) because 'if it works, it has all the reality it needs ...' (p. 24).

These two principles support the growth of a 'culture of simulation' that enables us to use our relationships to technology to reflect on the human-thinking-being as well as asking 'What do things think?' (pp. 24–5). Thirdly, the computer (PC) is personal, an 'intimate machine', a means to relate to others, change our selves, and ways of thinking (and feeling). She orchestrates an overview of developments in computing and AI that have changed our conception of the computer as well as of ourselves. Most importantly, self and body links have been reconceptualized via computer work – as emergent, 'bottom-up' parallel and multiple (several extant selves are working at once in the various windows of 'Windows 95'). This formulation, in many respects, challenges the Aristotelian logic of previous conceptions of the mind, and makes clear that the self can be several places at once, is not a single thing, nor does it remain continuous or bounded.

Consider some parallels in AI with the assumptions of semiotics, or the semiotic conceit. The objects (signs) are meaningful only in context and in relationship to a system (program, software) and other signs. The 'code', both literally (as a software program) and figuratively (that which links instances or signs to understanding), is invisible-there is no compulsion to look further for 'reality', or peek 'underneath' a sign or icon ('Netscape Navigator') to determine in detail how it 'works'. Language, like the machinations of computers, works. One can play with signs without fear of altering 'reality' because reality is, at least in part, a function of perspective, or the interpretant of the objects seen and manipulated. The connections made between expression and content are even magical since the mechanics and details of punching up a website are concealed by a single mouse click. Signs may be words in a chat room, icons on a screen such as 'my computer', images embedded in frames, texts, other images, or an HTML system. Some famous computer software programs, bots like 'Julia,' 'Depression 2' and 'Eliza,' actually 'present themselves as people' (Turkle, 1995: 88). This is simulation of person-like actions and feelings, and creates the tacit conception of a real ghost in the machine. The challenge of semiotics is present – merely simulating or repeating actions does not mean the actions are understood. Understanding requires a theory of sign function in which signs are connected to basic social concepts such as self, role, identity and significant others. In this

sense, semiotics, like statistics, is a tool that requires interpretation, and does not produce interpretations.

While Turkle argues that a multiplicity of selves is available as a result of computing, this multiplicity could be more felicitously stated as many 'identities' – who or what a person is in social terms – rather than as 'selves'. 'Self' here means the overall sense of process or continuity that people fashion. The extent and character of this organization of experience varies, over time, across cultures (Geertz, 1973), among groups and individuals.

The self arises again at this point. Turkle's work suggests that the integrative sense of self espoused by Mead, Blumer and symbolic interactionists may be a dated nineteenth-century notion. Roles, identities and 'selves' are not mutually exclusive, but may be emergent and parallel. This is a central question raised by semiotics, and leads to consideration of the issues of mind–body integrity, generational continuity, and epistemology (Heim, 1995). Alan Wolfe (1991, 1993), following Mead, argues that computer modeling of the mind tells us little about how the mind processes 'external reality', even if robots follow rules and procedures, because humans create and interpret rules, constitute meaning through interactions, and use both interpretive and natural signs (using Langer's vocabulary). Shifts in focus from modeling the mind using programs that could reproduce human problem-solving to creating 'agents' who act intelligently in parallel fashion to produce a network or society (Wolfe, 1991: 1087), are indicative of the search for 'a form of simulation of human intelligence or social relations, because it intends to create software and hardware that act as though they knew the rules' (Wolfe, 1991: 1084).

In short, AI experiments combine a form of semiotics, programming and mathematics, with applied ethnography to simulate cognitively based human choice. The 'social' and the 'mental', and even the 'substance' of interaction modeled by semiotics as a social meta-language, in AI becomes 'intelligence' inferred from human-like behaviour. In this sense, it parallels the aims of sociology and anthropology studying the self in cultural context.

Furthermore, this work suggests a needed direction in studies. Consider the self of the computer user. For some computer users, a heightened, self-reflexive focus results from intense, repeated, screen–self interactions (Heim, 1995; Turkle, 1984, 1995). The screen contains or reflects a micro-conflation of the inner dialogue and the dialogue between self and other, and the computer is often named and personalized ('My Computer' and 'My Briefcase' are condescending icons found on my 'Windows 95' screen). A screen, such as the television screen, also clearly has anxiety-producing, narcissistic and onamistic cues and images, some produced by e-mails, some by pictures and interactions on the internet, whether obviously 'pornographic' or not, some by the combination of voice, text and imagery, especially when combined by a fertile and flexible imagination. Like all pictures, it can be a source of the erotic and fantasies whether alone or with others.

A screen displays once-mediated communication, but content is also important. The self, which in Meadian thought (1934) is a holistic, integrative idea, is subject to re-shaping by processes of mediated communication via a screen and the viewing situation. The content of the screen also shapes identity. It should also be possible to speculate about the processes of semiosis of identities, given the interaction of screen, situation and content. Screens display objects that become internalized as a part of the self dialogue, and screens and their technologies become personalized and anthropomorphized. Screens reflect the thinking process and thus shape selves (Turkle, 1995). Thus, semiotic analysis of screens and identity, as well as of semiosis suggests that traditional interactionism and pragmatism, which focus on the representations or symbols as a kind of sign, and the interpersonal processes of self–other dialogue, should be expanded to include mediated communication, especially that mediated by screens (which in the digital world now means the capacity to transform messages into many forms when received), and explore the semiosis of self or selves.

More Scrupulous Examples

Research influenced by semiotics in a tighter fashion, not merely as a metaphor for symbolic analysis generally, include works of Dorst (1989), McGregor (1994) and Marling. Marling, drawing on semiotics in the American studies tradition, makes fascinating the world of 1950s television (1997), the Iwo Jima monument (with Weltenhall, 1991), and Elvis Presley's Graceland (1996). In the less tight, but still systematic category, I consider the works of Mary Douglas, Julian Pitt-Rivers (1970), and Dean MacCannell. A useful example is Douglas' extraordinary and charming explication of the structure of an English Sunday dinner (1975). In general, these works announce a symbolization, 'the sombrero', 'Elvis Presley's hair', or a monument, and explore the complex and changing connotations of it historically and culturally. In this sense, it shares interests and some methodological tendencies with cultural studies.

Police in the United States and the UK are moving to adopt crime mapping, a way of visually displaying data on crime and disorder on city maps. Icons are developed for each matter of interest – stolen cars, burglaries, traffic stops, gang locations – and placed on a map using a software program. Each of these can be laminated or layered, one on the other, to produce a complex picture of an area (neighbourhood, precinct, city block). The icons are linked to informatlon on the given offense; clicking on them produces a small window on the screen with date, time, offense and offender. This information can be organized using an object relations software that links co-offenders (those who have committed crimes together in the past), or a graphics package that will produce tables by time, date, offense, precinct, or city-wide.

Now think of this semiotically. Each icon is an expression that can be linked to a content to create a sign, a burglary at 101 Smith St with related data. These signs can be collected to create a metonymic series, all the burglaries on a given street, or at a given time period, or month. Or the signs can be collected, defined as a synecdochical string (one part contributes to forming a whole) defined by time periods. The icons can be seen as a metaphor for a 'problem' cluster of crimes or disorder.

Place these observations in a police culture, namely the investigative or detective culture, in a middle-sized city (Westville) I studied. Burglary detectives, for example, are assigned cases by their supervisors and expected to 'work' and 'clear' them ('cleared' is an organizational label and can vary from a case being transferred to another jurisdiction to an actual arrest). Each case is to be worked with a partner and without any necessary reference to other cases, prior or future, other offenses of the same type, a given offender, or the spatial or temporal distribution of such cases. Cases need not be linked to other investigations or investigators in the juvenile bureau, vice and drugs, robbery or homicide. Information sources are not linked – evidence from property, incident reports from dispatch, records from traffic stops and criminal records are kept in different databases that cannot be collated or merged. Social services information, emergency room information and city government files cannot be accessed. Police act semiotically in a sequential, metonymic fashion, taking and working cases one after the other, as if they were isolated symptoms of non-rational processes – sin, evil, greed, lust, moves and changes – yet recognizing that all crime is patterned. In a sense, the police act within a particular local culture with practices and tacit assumptions that sustain one reading of a very complex set of signs of crime. To display alternative reading would show how the signs can be clustered into problem groups for crime analysis, and to move the definition of 'crime' and events away from patrol officers' impressions and detectives' parochial, case-oriented perspective.

Tight Links and Usage of Semiotics

Works in the ethnographic tradition that advance semiotic analysis using 'tight' semiotics, are few – Barley (1983a, 1983b), Daniel (1984), Gottdiener (1995) (see also any issue of the journal

Semiotica, edited by Thomas Sebeok, and Manning, 1987). Through eliciting, diagramming and mapping on classification to everyday practices and routines, these authors successfully link ethnographic and semiotic strands. The cap example above uses semiotic figures and examples to show what caps as signs mean. It is an example of relatively tight use of the semiotic method.

SEMIOTICS AND FIELDWORK

Semiotics can guide and direct analysis based on fieldwork (Manning, 1987, 1988, 1990). Consider several examples. Manning used fieldwork to show that ecology, technology and subculture in the police communications system (PCS) affected communication semiotically. The textual information (message) created by the operators was shaped and altered systematically through technology (the contact or channel), the operators' and dispatchers' message-work (connotative, phatic and meta-lingual) and the meanings attributed to the message received by officers on the ground. Selectively sent forward, put in new contexts (with new referents), the signs (or words) used by citizens to describe a 'life-situation' or quasi-emergency, were transformed into a 'job' by officers (Manning, 1988).

Consider also an analogy which has animated anthropology for the past fifteen years. The focus of attention, a 'natural activity' such as a wedding, a healing ceremony, or head-hunting, is recorded (written, filmed, tape-recorded) and now must be analysed and 'written up'. The data, like the messages, are subjected to formative processes. These parallel social scientists' work as they convert talk into 'data', 'texts', and then to 'narratives' and publications (Atkinson, 1990, 1992). In each case, a social domain is mapped carefully using signs, their links and coherence, presented diagrammatically and embedded in social practices that make visible the implications of the systematics outlined. The mapping enables the ethnographer to imaginatively explore variations on the paradigms and metaphors discovered (the move to higher abstractions from the data) as well as to locate the meaningful consequences of such signwork in behavioural choices, actions and accounts for them. The pragmatics of signs are articulated, not left as allegorical glosses on human action. These works show that semiotics and semantics require systematic ethnography to produce clear connections between signs, social action and meaning.

Ethnographies enable exploration of semiosis, the central concern of pragmatically oriented semiotics, changes in meaning over time, space or group relations. A call to the police is an expression, or part of a sign, completed when the operator accepts it as an incident; an incident becomes the expression for an assignment when the dispatcher sends it out to a police unit to investigate; an assignment to an officer indicates an expression, a job, and a job, when the officer makes a call to the house of the caller, is work. Now note that each expression is linked to another content to make a sign, but the social connections involve different social roles (caller, operator, dispatcher, officer), and the signs are affected by the sequence in which they unfold. When the officer comes to the door to respond to a call (the citizen's first gesture, or expression), the two social worlds of caller/citizen and police meet and interact around the sign-based process, yet the sign created has quite different connotations for each member of the described social system. Officially, the call may be labeled 'domestic dispute', but the semiosis that results in the officer at the door has emotional and social meanings that differ. Conversely, the ability of each of the parties to imagine the experience and thoughts of the others enables a negotiated order to emerge.

Pinning down the interpretant in the field is a powerful way into perception, belief and practice. Signs are produced by interpretants, or social vehicles. The work of the interpretant, forging the links between signifier and signified, is phenomenological, and cannot be by-passed if signwork is to be located in a cultural context. Pragmatics should be linked to reflection, or reflexivity, thoughts about thoughts. Signs about signs produce differentiation which is fundamental in the study of social organization. A recent cartoon in the *New Yorker* (1 November 1999: 58) shows two people in an office (books in the background, a window with blinds), one with a goatee and rimless glasses seated taking notes in a suit and tie and another lying on a couch in shirt and slacks to the left and slightly behind the seated person. The person on the couch is scowling, the other is looking thoughtfully through his glasses and taking notes. Both wear baseball caps, one with the New York Yankees logo and the other with the New York Mets logo on the crown. What do the caps signify in this context? Granted, we draw on common-sense American knowledge since we have not done fieldwork. If the interpretant is the culture and repertoire of psychotherapy, this depicts two role-players, a 'Dr' or 'analyst' and a 'patient', one listening the other talking, bound together in a therapeutic quest, the patient perhaps to transfer his troubling feelings and thoughts to the analyst as a way of diffusing them, and working them through by placing trust in the analyst. If the interpretant is the male culture of competition and sports, represented by major league baseball, then the two are joined as baseball fans, fans of two New York teams, and as males, yet divided symbolically by loyalty to different local teams, each in a different league, yet potential opponents if they win their leagues. November is the end of the baseball season. The Yankees won their league, the Mets did not, and the Yankees subsequently won the World Series, the championship of American baseball. The scowl is a sign that represents the unhappiness of the analysand with his therapist-fan-opponent, and has an elliptical relationship to the content of the therapy session! Combining or juxtaposing these two interpretants produces humour. The cartoon is an ironic icon; it captures contradictory and irresolvable cultural themes.

Recall always that the central connection between person and society is the self, including the I and the me. Saussure saw signifier and signified as the components of the sign, and meaning as systemic, structural and ahistorical. He outlined a structural analysis of meaning, but excluded a self or locus of interpretation, as well as the 'referential object' (Noth, 1990: 59). Peirce's often changing work includes a triadic version of the sign. Combining these three implies a self, but Peirce 'never explained what part of the self was the sign, what part interpretant and what part object' (Wiley, 1991: 29). To some degree, the self is a dialogic cluster, or an internal dialogue, but this idea is underdeveloped in Peirce.

An ethnographic project would seem to require a central organizing concept, the self, or perspective by which sign and signifier are 'connected', and their meanings established in interaction-sourced reflections. Anthropologist Paul Stoller (1989) has laboured to interweave the body and sentient features of human relations such as smell, into their works. Cognitive thought and deciding, rational thought only fleetingly organizes human relations. The poetics and aesthetics of representation may be vividly present in texts, plastic arts, or speech, but each is a patterning feature of a representation (Jakobson, 1987). Conceptions of the body, and the body–self relationship, seem increasingly mediated by information technology (Barley, 1990; Zuboff, 1988). As signs are mediated, transmitted electronically and interpreted at a distance, the gap or difference between expression and content is more ambiguous. Embodied co-presence is a powerful arena for judging trust.

Conclusions

Semiotics, outlined originally by Saussure, was modified by Peirce and Morris, and by Mead and Dewey, shaped by Jakobson and Sebeok, and widely popularized by Eco. Barthes' assertion that semiology subsumes semiotics, the science of signs, remains a valid point, as are his ruminations on the powerful emotive 'substance' carried by language. The connections between semiotics and semantics are most revealed in pragmatics, where non-verbal aspects of language are used to sharpen assertions about language function. The study of deixis in particular has directed brilliant anthropological

work (Levinson, 1983). Social semiotics is shaping the study of cognitions, both in the field and in the laboratory. Work on artificial intelligence (AI), in particular, has highlighted the questions of the semiotics of the self, or selves, as have studies of information technology in organizational context. Ethnographic work illustrates the influence of semiotics in many respects.

In the past ten years, new tensions have arisen in both sociology and anthropology concerning the connections between 'fieldwork' 'data analysis' and 'writing up'. In many respects, this is dismissed by some scholars (see Denzin and Lincoln, 1992), who see unity in the writing itself. The poetics, aesthetics and style of the written work is the reality of interest, not the 'data' or 'empirical basis', if any other than reflections on personal experience. Most social scientists compromise, urging some fit between the subjective, psychic reality as experienced and the shared social reality in part captured by symbols and linguistically conveyed representations. This interface continues to animate and enliven debates about semiotics and ethnography.

Notes

1 Disagreement remains about the value and utility of a social semiotics, even when linked to ethnographic methods and history, and the pertinence of the linguistic analogy for social analysis (see Culler, 1975; Eco, 1979; Guiraud, 1973; Hawkes, 1977; Lemert, 1979, 1981). A most interesting overview of structuralism in France is Dosse's history (1997a, 1997b). These critiques are perhaps less salient for you, the readers of this chapter, than tracing the mutual interactions of semiotics and semantics with ethnography, and the value thereof.

2 The sociologist Erving Goffman, while not a semiotician, was a structuralist (i.e. he understood the prior character of constraint, externality, and expectations that patterned interpersonal deference) who shared assumptions with semiotics, and occasionally cited their works (Goffman, 1974: 529, n. 26).

References

Atkinson, Paul (1985) *Language, Structure and Reproduction.* London: Methuen.

Atkinson, Paul (1990) *The Ethnographic Imagination.* London: Routledge and Kegan Paul.

Atkinson, Paul (1992) *Understanding Ethnographic Texts.* Thousand Oaks, CA: Sage.

Barley, S. (1983a) 'Codes of the dead', *Journal of Contemporary Ethnography (Urban Life)*, 10: 459–71.

Barley, S. (1983b) 'Semiotics, and the study of organizational and occupational cultures', *Administrative Science Quarterly*, 28: 393–413.

Barley, S. (1990) 'Technology as an occasion for structuring', *Administrative Science Quarterly*, 31: 78–108.

Barthes, R. (1970) *Elements of Semiology*. New York: Hill and Wang.

Barthes, R. (1972) *Mythologies*. New York: Hill and Wang.

Barthes, R. (1983) *The Fashion System*. New York: Hill and Wang.

Bateson, G. (1973) *Steps Toward an Ecology of Mind*. New York: Ballantine Books.

Baudrillard, J. (1993) *Selected Writings* (ed. Mark Poster). Stanford, CA: Stanford University Press.

Becker, H.S. (1998) 'The Chicago School, so called', *Qualitative Sociology*, 22 (1): 3–12.

Bernstein, B. (1972) *Class, Codes and Conduct*. vol. I. London: Routledge and Kegan Paul.

Bernstein, B. (1973) *Class, Codes and Conduct*. vol. II. London: Routledge and Kegan Paul.

Bourdieu, P. (1977) *Outline of a Theory of Practice*. Cambridge: Cambridge University Press.

Bourdieu, P. (1991) *Language and Symbolic Power*. Cambridge, MA: Harvard University Press.

Culler, J. (1975) *Structuralist Poetics*. Ithaca, NY: Cornell University Press.

Czarniawska, B. (1998) *A Narrative Approach to Organization Studies*. Thousand Oaks, CA: Sage.

Daniel, E. Valentine (1984) *Fluid Signs*. Berkeley, CA: University of California Press.

Denzin, N. (1987) 'On semiotics and symbolic interactionism', *Symbolic Interaction*, 10: 1–19.

Denzin, N. and Lincoln, Y. (eds) (1992) *Handbook of Qualitative Research*. Thousand Oaks, CA: Sage.

Dorst, J. (1989) *The Written Suburb*. Philadelphia: University of Pennsylvania Press.

Dosse, F. (1997a) *A History of Structuralism. The Rising Sign, 1945–67*. vol. I. Minneapolis, MN: University of Minnesota Press.

Dosse, F. (1997b) *A History of Structuralism. The Sign Sets, 1967–Present*. vol. II. Minneapolis, MN: University of Minnesota Press.

Douglas, Mary (1975) *Implicit Meanings*. London: Routledge and Kegan Paul.

Eco, Umberto (1979) *The Theory of Semiotics*. Bloomington, IN: University of Indiana Press.

Eco, Umberto (1983) *The Name of the Rose*. New York: Harcourt Brace, Jovanovich.

Eco, Umberto (1984) *The Limits of Interpretation*. London and New York: Macmillan.

Eco, Umberto (1986) *Travels in Hyperreality*. New York: Harcourt Brace, Jovanovich.

Fabrega, H. (1997) *Evolution of Sickness and Healing*. Berkeley, CA: University of California Press.

Geertz, C. (1973) *The Interpretation of Cultures*. New York: Basic Books.

Giddens, A. (1984) *The Constitution of Society*. Berkeley, CA: University of California Press.

Goffman, Erving (1974) *Frame Analysis*. Cambridge, MA: Harvard University Press.

Gottdiener, M. (1995) *Postmodern Semiotics*. Oxford: Blackwell.

Guirard, P. (1973) *Semiology*. London: Routledge and Kegan Paul.

Halliday, M.A.K. (1979) *Language as Social Semiotic*. London: Edward Arnold.

Harris, Roy (1983) *Language, Saussure and Wittgenstein*. London: Routledge and Kegan Paul.

Harvey, D. (1989) *The Condition of Postmodernity*. Oxford: Blackwell.

Hawkes, T. (1977) *Structuralism and Semiotics*. Berkeley, CA: University of California Press.

Hayles, N.K. (1994) *The Cosmic Web*. Ithaca, NY: Cornell University Press.

Heath, C. (1986) *Body Movement and Speech in Medical Interaction*. Cambridge: Cambridge University Press.

Heim, P. (1995) *The Metaphysics of Virtual Reality*. New York: Oxford University Press.

Hymes, Dell (1964) *Sociolinguistics*. Philadelphia: University of Pennsylvania Press.

Jackson, B. (1985) *Semiotics and Legal Theory*. London: Routledge and Kegan Paul.

Jakobson, Roman (1981) *Six Lectures on Language and Meaning*. Cambridge: MIT Press.

Jakobson, Roman (1987) *Language in Literature*. Cambridge, MA: Harvard University Press.

Kristeva, Julia (1989) *The Black Sun*. New York: Columbia University Press.

Langer, Susan (1942) *Philosophy in a New Key*. New York: Signet.

Lemert, C. (1979) 'Language, structure, and measurement', *American Journal of Sociology*, 84: 929–57.

Lemert, C. (ed.) (1981) *French Sociology*. New York: Columbia University Press.

Levinson, S. (1983) *Pragmatics*. Cambridge: Cambridge University Press.

Lincoln, B. (1991) *Discourse and the Construction of Society*. New York: Oxford University Press.

MacCannell, D. and MacCannell, J.F. (1982) *The Time of the Sign*. Bloomington, IN: Indiana University Press.

McGregor, G. (1994) *EcCentric Visions*. Waterloo, Canada: Wilfred Laurier University Press.

Manning, Peter K. (1987) *Semiotics and Fieldwork*. Thousand Oaks, CA: Sage.

Manning, Peter K. (1988) *Symbolic Communication*. Cambridge, MA: MIT.

Manning, Peter K. (1990) *Organizational Communication*. Hawthorne, NY: Aldine.

Manning, Peter K. and Cullam-Swan, Betsy (1992) 'Semiotic and narrative analysis', in N. Denzin and Y. Lincoln (eds), *Handbook of Qualitative Research*. Thousand Oaks, CA: Sage.

Marling, K. (1996) *Graceland: Going Home With Elvis*. Cambridge, MA: Harvard University Press.

Marling, K. (1997) *As Seen on TV: The Visual Culture of Everyday Life in the 'Fifties'*. Cambridge, MA: Harvard University Press.

Marling, K. and Wetenhall, John (1991) *Iwo Jima: Mandate, Memories and the American Hero*. Cambridge, MA: Harvard University Press.

Mead, G.H. (1934) *Mind, Self and Society*. Chicago: University of Chicago Press.

Morris, C. (1938) *Foundations of a Theory of Signs.* Chicago: University of Chicago Press.

Neroponte, N. (1991) *Being Digital.* New York: Viking.

Noth, W. (1990) *The Encyclopedia of Semiotics.* Bloomington, IN: Indiana University Press.

Peirce, Charles (1931–1958) *Collected Works,* 8 vols. Cambridge, MA: Harvard University Press.

Pitt-Rivers, Julian (1970) 'The context of the model', *European Journal of Sociology.*

Psathas, George (1995) *Conversational Analysis.* Thousand Oaks, CA: Sage.

Rock, Paul (1977) *Symbolic Interactionism.* London: Macmillan.

Rorty, R. (1979) *Philosophy and the Mirror of Nature.* Princeton, NJ: Princeton University Press.

Reissman, Catherine (1993) *Narrative Analysis.* Thousand Oaks, CA: Sage.

de Saussure, F. ([1915] 1966) *Course in General Linguistics* (eds C. Bally and A. Secehaye, trans. W. Baskin). New York: McGraw–Hill.

Schwartz, Barry and Wagner-Pacifici, R. (1991) 'The Vietnam veterans memorial: commemorating a difficult past', *American Journal of Sociology*, 97: 376–420.

Searle, John (1995) *The Construction of Social Reality.* New York: The Free Press.

Sebeok, T. (1991) *Semiotics in America.* Bloomington, IN: Indiana University Press.

Silverman, Kaja (1983) *The Subject of Semiotics.* New York: Oxford University Press.

Soja, E. (1989) *Postmodern Geographies.* London: Verso.

Stoller, Paul (1989) *The Taste of Ethnographic Things.* Philadelphia: University of Pennsylvania Press.

Turkle, S. (1984) *The Second Self.* New York: Simon and Schuster.

Turkle, S. (1995) *Life on the Screen.* New York: Simon and Schuster.

Tyler, S. (ed.) (1981) *Cognitive Anthropology.* New York: McGraw–Hill.

Van Maanen, J. (ed.) (1995) *Representation in Ethnography.* Thousand Oaks, CA: Sage.

Wagner-Pacifici, R. (1986) *The Moro Morality Play.* Chicago: University of Chicago Press.

Wagner-Pacifici, R. (1991) *Discourse and Destruction.* Chicago: University of Chicago Press.

Wiley, Norbert (1991) *The Semiotic Self.* Chicago: University of Chicago Press.

Wolfe, Alan (1991) 'Mind, self, and society and the computer', *American Journal of Sociology*, 96: 1073–96.

Wolfe, Alan (1993) *The Human Difference.* Berkeley, CA: University of California Press.

Zuboff, Shoshana (1988) *In the Age of the Smart Machine.* New York: Basic Books.

11

Grounded Theory in Ethnography

KATHY CHARMAZ AND RICHARD G. MITCHELL

Grounded theory methods consist of flexible strategies for collecting and analysing data that can help ethnographers to conduct efficient fieldwork and create astute analyses. No more, no less. Take a fresh look at these methods and partake of them. Remember Barney G. Glaser and Anselm L. Strauss' (1967) original call for a systematic, yet flexible, approach to analysing qualitative data. Ethnographers can adopt and adapt grounded theory to increase the analytic incisiveness of their studies. Our approach to grounded theory builds upon a symbolic interactionist theoretical perspective and constructivist methods that assume the existence of multiple realities, the mutual creation of knowledge by researchers and research participants, and aims to provide interpretive understanding of the studied world (Altheide and Johnson, 1994; Charmaz, 1995b, 2000; Guba and Lincoln, 1994; Prus, 1987, 1996; Schwandt, 1994).[1] A constructivist approach to grounded theory complements the symbolic interactionist perspective because both emphasize studying how action and meaning are constructed.

All variants of grounded theory include the following strategies:

1 simultaneous data-collection and analysis;
2 pursuit of emergent themes through early data analysis;
3 discovery of basic social processes within the data;
4 inductive construction of abstract categories that explain and synthesize these processes;
5 integration of categories into a theoretical framework that specifies causes, conditions and consequences of the process(es).

Grounded theory methods move the research and the researcher toward theory development. In contrast, ethnography relies on developing a full description of a society or group of people and, thus, provides the details of their everyday life. As a method, ethnography refers to ways of studying, knowing and reporting about the world (see Atkinson, 1990). The term also connotes a frame of mind – an intent to be open to everything unknown; a suspension of disbelief.

Both grounded theory and ethnography have common roots in Chicago School sociology with its pragmatist philosophical foundations. Anselm Strauss brought Chicago School pragmatist, symbolic interactionist and field research traditions to grounded theory while Barney G. Glaser's emphasis on rigorous methods and empiricism derived from his training in survey research with Paul Lazarsfeld at Columbia University. Glaser and Strauss (1967) developed grounded theory methods to codify explicit procedures for qualitative data analysis and, simultaneously, to construct useful middle-range theories from the data.[2]

Glaser and Strauss' (1965, 1968) early works relied on extensive field research. Since then, grounded theory and ethnographic methods have developed somewhat differently; however, these approaches can complement each other. Using grounded theory methods can streamline fieldwork and move ethnographic research toward theoretical interpretation. Attending to ethnographic methods can prevent grounded theory studies from dissolving into quick and dirty qualitative research.

Earlier versions of grounded theory offer openended guidelines (Charmaz, 1983, 1990, 1995b; Glaser, 1978; Stern, [1980] 1994b; Strauss, 1987). Recent interpretations of grounded theory have taken a mechanistic turn (Creswell, 1998; Strauss and Corbin, 1990, 1998). Guidelines have become prescriptive procedures – and there are more of them. Realist critics question whether grounded theory methods actually provide a more rigorous means of processing information into ideas than other qualitative approaches (Lofland and Lofland, 1984; Sanders, 1995). Postmodernist critics question the positivistic methodological underpinnings and scientist writing style in many grounded theory works (Denzin, 1994). Grounded theory began with gentle guidelines, but now risks being reduced to rigid rules imposed on researchers and on research practices.

Methods are only a means, not an end. Our subjects' worlds and our renderings of them take precedence over methods and measures. A keen eye, receptive mind, discerning ear and steady hand bring us close to the studied phenomena and are more important than developing methodological tools.[3] Insightful industriousness takes an ethnographer further than mechanistic methods. Tools may neither bring us closer to realities we visit nor assist us to portray them in their fullness. Technical procedures do not ensure truth. Mere industry alone does not spawn insightful or important works.

Developing an array of methodological tools can be a false quest; they may make our work more scientist but not more significant. Grounded theory should not become *the* rules of *qualitative* method, *à la* Durkheim ([1895] 1982).

Subsequently, our methodological strategies differ from Strauss and Corbin's *Basics of Qualitative Research* (1990/1998) and, to a lesser extent, from Glaser's *Theoretical Sensitivity* (1978) and *Basics of Grounded Theory Analysis: Emergence vs. Forcing* (1992). Our epistemological stance also differs. Strauss, Corbin, and Glaser assume positivistic notions of science including objectivist enquiry despite their recent sharp differences (Charmaz, 2000). Our view comes closer here to Strauss' *Qualitative Analysis for Social Scientists* (1987) and Strauss and Corbin (1994), in that these works are less deterministic and more open-ended than *Basics* and are more imbued with pragmatism and constructivism than Glaser's (1992) refutation of the book. Strauss and Corbin (1990/1998) profess traditional positivistic concerns about reliability, validity and verification. In practice, these concerns may amount to a search for reproducible form and, thus, subvert discovering the depth and fulness of the studied reality. We are concerned with correspondence between reports we craft and human experience. We aim to construct a full account, to tell a meaningful story – not to reduce our craft to the canons of 'normal' science (Kuhn, 1970).

Because ethnography means full description of a specific world rather than just a segment of it, it is more than fieldwork or qualitative research. Participant observation, for example, may focus on an aspect of the scene, rather than an entire setting, and may not entail the extent or depth of involvement of an ethnography. Much work that claims to be ethnography consists of one type or another of focused participant observation. Much work that claims to be grounded theory is not; instead, it is description (see also, Stern, 1994a). Granted, ethnography and grounded theory have different emphases. Tensions between the two approaches are discernible. Irreconcilable? No. But there are points when decisions need to be made and directions taken. Our analysis aims to make such points explicit and to show how ethnography and grounded theory can complement and further each other.

Grounded theory techniques can sharpen the analytic edge and theoretical sophistication of ethnographic research. The benefits of combining ethnographic and grounded theory approaches go both ways. With ethnography, we can move grounded theory away from technology and turn it toward art. Grounded theory studies can be reclaimed as humanistic stories rather than stand as scientist reports. Ethnography encourages writers to locate themselves in their narratives and, therefore, lessens the distanced writing and objectified presentation of data typical of most grounded theory reportage (Charmaz and Mitchell, 1996). Ethnographic study can connect theory with *realities*, not just with research. Thus, it may prompt grounded theorists to go deeper into their studied phenomena to understand experience as their subjects live it, not simply talk about it.

GROUNDED THEORY SOLUTIONS TO PROBLEMS IN ETHNOGRAPHIC RESEARCH

A potential problem with ethnographic studies is seeing data everywhere and nowhere, gathering everything and nothing. The studied world seems so interesting (and probably is) that an ethnographer tries to master knowing it all. Mountains of unconnected data grow (see also Coffey and Atkinson, 1996) but they don't say much. What follows? Low-level description and, if a bit more sophisticated, lists of unintegrated categories. Ethnographers who leave data undigested seldom produce fresh insights and, sometimes, may not even complete their projects, despite years of toil.

Enter grounded theory. Its strategies can aid ethnographers in gaining a more complete picture of the *whole* setting than the former approach common in earlier ethnographic work. Ethnographers can make connections between events by using grounded theory to study processes. A grounded theory emphasis on comparative method leads ethnographers to (1) compare data with data from the *beginning* of the research, not after all the data are in; (2) compare data with emerging categories; and (3) demonstrate relations between concepts and categories. Grounded theory strategies can increase ethnographers' involvement in their *research enquiry*, despite however involved they might be in participating in their research setting. In this sense, grounded theory dispels the positivist notion of passive observers who merely absorb their surrounding scenes. Grounded theorists select the scenes they observe and direct their gaze within them. If used with care and thoroughness, grounded theory methods provide systematic procedures for probing beneath the surface and digging into the scene. These methods help in maintaining control over the research process because they assist the ethnographer in focusing, structuring and organizing it.

Glaser and Strauss' (1967; Glaser, 1978; Strauss, 1987) defining characteristics of grounded theory include:

1 simultaneous involvement in data collection and analysis;
2 analytic codes and categories developed from data, not from preconceived logically deduced hypotheses;
3 theory development during each step of data collection and analysis;
4 memo-making, an intermediate bridge between coding data and writing first drafts;
5 theoretical sampling aimed toward theory construction not for population representativeness;
6 a literature review conducted after developing an independent analysis.

These characteristics move ethnographic research toward theoretical development by raising description to abstract categories and theoretical explanation. (see also Bigus et al., 1992; Charmaz, 1983, 1990, 1995b; Glaser, 1992, 1994; Glaser and Strauss, 1967; Stern, [1980] 1994b; Strauss, 1987; Strauss and Corbin, 1990/1998, 1994). Ethnography suffered in the past from a rigid and artificial separation of data collection and analysis. Grounded theory methods preserve an open-ended approach to studying the empirical world yet add rigor to ethnographic research by building systematic checks into both data collection and analysis. The logic of grounded theory entails going back to data and forward into analysis then returning to the field to gather further data and refine the emerging theoretical framework. This logic aids in overcoming several ethnographic problems:

1 'going native';
2 lengthy unfocused forays into the field setting;
3 superficial, random data collection;
4 reliance on disciplinary stock categories.

Thin, unfocused data may tempt ethnographers to fall back on lifting stock concepts from their disciplinary shelves. Grounded theory prompts taking a fresh look and creating novel categories and concepts. That is the strength and the core of the method. Moving back and forth between data and analysis also helps to lessen feelings of being overwhelmed and, with them, tendencies to procrastinate.[4] Both are common results of collecting data without direction.

We are not passive receptacles into which data are poured (Charmaz, 1990, 1998; cf. Glaser, 1978; Glaser and Strauss, 1967). Neither observer nor observed come to a scene untouched by the world. Researchers and subjects hold worldviews, possess stocks of knowledge, and pursue purposes that influence their respective views and actions in the presence of the other. Nevertheless, researchers alone are obligated to be reflexive about what they see and how they see it.

CONDUCTING GROUNDED THEORY RESEARCH

What do grounded theorists do? The following list outlines basic steps in grounded theory research in approximate sequence. In practice, the process is less linear, more multi-dimensional, and considerably less clear-cut. Ethnographers can collect initial data on varied problems in the setting, focus on one direction, and, later, return to others. We discuss several major steps as they affect doing ethnography; more detailed descriptions of grounded theory are in Charmaz (1990, 1995b), Chenitz and Swanson (1986), Glaser (1978, 1992), Strauss (1987), and Strauss and Corbin (1990/1998, 1994).

- Collect data on what happens in the research setting.
- Code data line-by-line to show action and process.
- Compare data with data in memos.
- Raise significant codes to categories.
- Compare data with category in memos.
- Check and fill out categories through theoretical sampling.
- Compare category to category.
- Integrate categories into a theoretical framework.
- Write the first draft.
- Identify gaps and refine concepts.
- Conduct a comprehensive literature review.
- Rework the entire piece.

It all Starts with Data

Creditable qualitative research of any kind requires a solid empirical foundation. Current trends toward limited data and 'instant' theorizing[5] have long been associated with grounded theory and now permeate other methods, including ethnography. A competent ethnographic study demands time and commitment. Grounded theory can help trim excess work but the core tasks still need to be done. Gathering rich ethnographic data means starting by answering basic questions about the studied phenomena:

- What is the setting of action? When and how does action take place?
- What is going on? What is the overall activity being studied, the relatively long-term behavior about which participants organize themselves? What specific acts comprise this activity?
- What is the distribution of participants over space and time in these locales?
- How are actors organized? What organizations effect, oversee, regulate or promote this activity?
- How are members stratified? Who is ostensibly in charge? Does being in charge vary by activity? How is membership achieved and maintained?
- What do actors pay attention to? What is important, preoccupying, critical?
- What do they pointedly ignore that other persons might pay attention to?
- What symbols do actors invoke to understand their worlds, the participants and processes within them, and the objects and events they encounter? What names do they attach to objects, events, persons, roles, settings, equipment?
- What practices, skills, stratagems, methods of operation do actors employ?
- Which theories, motives, excuses, justifications or other explanations do actors use in accounting for their participation? How do they explain to each other, not to outside investigators, what they do and why they do it?
- What goals do actors seek? When, from their perspective, is an act well or poorly done? How do they judge action – by what standards, developed and applied by whom?
- What rewards do various actors gain from their participation? (Mitchell, 1991)

From these questions, an ethnographer learns about context and content, meaning and action, structures and actors. Grounded theory can aid ethnographers in getting into these areas; it should not be used as reason to side-step them. Our basic rule: find data, answer the foundational questions, then develop theory. This approach also remedies weaknesses in grounded theory studies, especially those that rely on single accounts given to field interviewers. What people say may differ from what they do. How they explain their actions to each other may not resemble their statements to an interviewer. Moreover, participants' most important explanations may consist of tacit understandings. If so, then participants seldom articulate them out loud, even among themselves, let alone to non-members.

Understanding derives most directly from the immediacy of participation in social actors'

inter-subjective experience (Prus, 1996). In practical terms, this means the researcher needs to share experiences, but not necessarily viewpoints, with those being studied. Bergson states, 'Philosophers agree in making a deep distinction between two ways of knowing a thing. The first implies going all around it, the second entering into it' (Bergson, [1903] 1961: 1). The ethnographer's job is to explore the second way. Grounded theory studies often move around an object; these methods generate a map of the object from the outside, but may not enter it. These studies look at phenomena from a variety of locations (see, for example, Glaser and Strauss, 1965, 1968). Ethnographers can go deep into experience to make an interpretive rendering (Duneier, 1992; Fine, 1986, 1996; Geertz, 1973; Whyte, 1993).

Throughout this chapter, we draw upon excerpts from Richard G. Mitchell's ethnographic study of survivalists in North America (Mitchell, forthcoming). What are survivalists?

1 Survivalists have been dubbed many things in the popular press; citizens' militias, tax and anti-government protesters, racial separatists and others. *Survivalist* is used to refer to the whole for practical and theoretical reasons; because participants themselves often do, and because one sort of survival, the creative transcendence of calamitous cultural change, lies at the root of these seemingly diverse events.

2 Survivalism accompanies the changes in modern times but not in the ways commonly understood from text-based analyses and other indirect theorizing. It is not diminished possessions, prestige or sense of autonomy that motivates. Survivalists do not, metaphorically, covet a larger share of the cultural pie. They want something more and different. They want a job at the bakery, writing the recipes, mixing the ingredients and watching the oven. It is the work of *culture-crafting* not the artifacts of culture to which survivalists are attracted. Survivalists desire a direct hand in economic production, exchange and valuation, not ownership or consumption. They seek to reinterpret the wisdom of science, not obedience to its laws. They want to reformulate the social contract, not the privileges of citizenship. But in modern, monolithic rationally ordered industrial society, formalized in bureaucratic routine, and driven by the ebb and flow of global capital, finding hands-on, creative, consequent work at the heart of these basic institutions is not easy.

3 Omnipresent modern culture comes ready-made; finished, sized, sorted, packaged and priced, on the shelf. The creative work of visionary individuals is over. Little is left to do but acquire and arrange possessions and perspectives at leisure,

passive leisure, inconsequential leisure. All around, a predictable plethora of general goods, standard knowledge, regularized relationships, and reasoned order. Only a few find the way out. The way of doubt.

4 To find places of consequence, survivalists fashion discourses of pending need, speculative circumstances of crisis and concern, wherein major social institutions face imminent serious erosion or total dissolution, *and* in which survivalists themselves play central roles in reprioritized revisioning, recovery and renewal. National boundaries, ethnic identities, political and economic structures, knowledge systems and other elements of culture weaken and need refurbishment, or deteriorate and require rebuilding. Breakdowns, crises, chaos, even doomsdays have latent allure. Survival discourse tailors widespread rancor and disorder to fit schemes for maximizing personal competence, actualization and relevance. Troubles draw near, but with them come opportunities to celebrate humanity's full *élan vital*, to achieve a sense of belonging, not to the comfortable mass at the center of stability but among the novel few on the cutting edge of change. Survivalism is a celebration of these changes in imaginative narrative and rehearsal.

The preceding argument was written after years of piecing together action and meaning in diverse scenes. On what kinds of ethnographic accounts is the argument based? In the following account, Mitchell (forthcoming) shows how mundane ethnographic description can frame a story. Ethnographers do count – participants, objects and events – as they gather information about the worlds they study, but from a grounded theory perspective, such counts must 'earn their way' (Glaser, 1978) into the analysis. In the story below, Mitchell uses counting as a rhetorical tactic to draw attention to disparities between subjects' grandiose claims and meager deeds. He crafts images with numbers and strips stereotypes of their conventional meanings. Mitchell enriches mundane data by locating them in context. In turn, these counts shape readers' images of aryanism and advance Mitchell's description of aryan worlds. We begin to sense meanings – of aryan warriors, of aryan 'nations', and of the ethnographic story-teller.

Countdown

It is to be an Aryan World Congress, a late-July three day Idaho gathering of Aryan elite from the millions of Anglo-Saxon, Germanic, Nordic, Basque, Lombardic, Celtic, and Slavic peoples around the globe.

Calls go out to all the Aryan Nations, all thirteen tribes, Manasseh, Ephraim, Ruben, Simeon, Judah, Dan, Napthali ... And to the thousands actively sympathetic here in North America.

At least seven hundred are coming, organizers claim two weeks before.

Three hundred will be here, Aryan Nations' founder, Richard Butler, tells the press on Thursday.

One hundred and thirty are found in the late Saturday head count. (But not all count. Twenty-two women and ten children need protection. And the twenty skinheads don't care.)

Fifty-seven go to church to hear Pastor Butler preach.

Fifty-two stay through the sermon.

Forty-nine stay awake.

Then comes the alarm, broadcast over the camp loudspeakers. Attention! Attention! Uniformed Officers report to the guard house! Trouble at the entrance way! Aryan pride at stake!

Thirteen Aryan Warriors answer the call, scuttle to the gate, take up positions behind the cattle fence.

Twelve wear long pants.

Eleven have both shoes on.

Seven have regulation uniforms.

In the excerpt above, Mitchell uses counts to show that something quite different is happening than given in first impressions and standard media accounts. Grand titles obscure petty accomplishments. Mitchell sets the stage for building his interpretive analysis of aryan worlds.

'What is happening here?' is the fundamental question for grounded theorists when entering a research setting. This question leads the researcher to focus on identifying basic social processes. Glaser and Strauss (1967; Glaser 1978, 1992) imply that what is happening is obvious; suitable data are there for the taking, and categories inhere in them. None of that may be true. Rather, processes, data and categories reflect the mutual production of experience, including interaction, by the observer and observed. Similarly, Glaser and Strauss (1967), Glaser (1978, 1992) and Strauss and Corbin (1990/ 1998, 1994) assume data have objective status. The world has obdurate qualities but data consist of researchers' and subjects' mutual constructions. Core categories arise from researchers' reconstructions of those constructions rather than inhering in the data. Categories may not be readily apparent. They may lack internal consistency, appear ambiguous, or reflect multiple realities within the setting.

Finding out what is happening in a setting is problematic. We may encounter puzzles, party lines and paradoxes. Glaser (1992) is correct when he says that initial fieldwork changes an earlier research proposal. Bergson ([1903] 1961) insisted that we cannot know a scene until we are in it. Glaser (1992) says research participants will tell us what the problems are. Perhaps. They might tell us what they see as problems, what they think we should know, or what they think we want to hear. But they may not tell us what is most important. They might take some things for granted or gloss over untoward topics. Nor are their perceptions ours. Tapping implicit actions and meanings takes effort. The best ethnography is difficult, arduous and tenuous work.

Coding the Data

Coding begins the analysis. Because it raises analytic questions about the data, coding is the first step in developing theoretical categories. Through coding, researchers start to define what their data are all about. If wrong, subsequent data collection and coding provides checks. This initial stage of coding encourages researchers to take their data apart and to look at them anew with an analytic eye. Grounded theory codes arise *from* analysing data, rather than from applying concepts from earlier works *to* data. When coding, researchers take an active stance toward their data. Thus, grounded theory ethnographers interact with their data, not just their subjects. They must ask questions of these data. Simultaneously, they begin to create the correspondence between experience and social scientific portrayals of them. For example, ethnographers can use *in vivo* codes directly from members' discourse.

Grounded theory researchers begin with open or initial coding and then try to code everything they see *in* the data. In contrast to Miles and Huberman's (1994) advice to plan a set of codes beforehand, grounded theorists adhere to the basic premise of developing the codes directly from data through an emergent process. Never force data into pre-existing codes (Glaser, 1978, 1992). Shorthand, active codes specify, classify, sort, summarize and synthesize data. Keeping codes active and as specific as possible gives a researcher grist for the analytic mill.

Coding provides the shorthand synthesis for making comparisons between:

1 different people, objects, scenes, or events (for example, members' situations, actions, accounts, or experiences);
2 data from the same people, scenes, objects, or type of event (for example, individuals with themselves at different points in time);
3 incident with incident (Charmaz, 1983, 1995b; Glaser, 1978, 1992).

Then, through early memo-making, the researcher can elaborate the relationships within these comparisons and begin to address their meanings.

During one of Mitchell's early forays into the field, he had a lengthy conversation with Tim, a part-time tree planter by vocation, a survivalist by inspiration. Tim cautions Mitchell about things.

I think a lot of things that are coming up demand a lot of security. Don't trust everybody that comes along just 'cause they say they're into LFI [a survivalist organization called Live Free, Inc.] and all ... The only man down there that I trust, other than you, is Henry and his

family and that's it. He found me after I'd been active about a year and he's the one that put a group together.

How might we code Tim's statement using grounded theory? 'Socialization,' a perfectly good concept, makes a poor grounded theory code here and elsewhere. Though useful for drawing initial sketches, this concept paints scenes with too wide a brush. It is also preconceived. 'Socializing Potential Members?' A little better, but flat and dull. What is happening? What seems to be portrayed in these statements? 'Coaching?' 'Imparting Warnings?' 'Revealing Self?' 'Taking Caution?' 'Talking Caution?' 'Limiting Trust?' 'Drawing Boundaries?' 'Roping a Prospect?' 'Shattering Myths?' None of these codes? Might Tim's statements mean something else? Mitchell found that Tim's story juxtaposed organizational troubles within the survivalist movement against Tim's identities and actions. Tim's story unfolds:

Tim confessed that organizing survivalism had proven cheerless and elusive. After years of work he remained a phenomenon unto himself. Aurora Borealis (a survivalist field project) showed him as he often was, a lone voice in the dark:

I'm still an active integral movement ... but I failed you know, I mean to actually put a group together here ... I've got hundreds of man-hours in helping LFI get on its feet. I'll never give up. But do you realize that of all that time – other than you and Henry and a couple of other people – do you realize that after three years you're the only ones. I mean really. There's no group in Republic [town] ... there never really was ...

Tim the survivalist was a character apart from Tim the part-time tree planter. Tree-planter-Tim was well known and clearly defined by his neighbors of twenty years as an affable, quirky, unskilled woods-worker of little import in a rural timber town. Survivalist-Tim took less substantial form in the weak social bonds of irregular correspondence, the author's imagined readership, and the vicarious adventures of his fictive and historic heroes. Survivalist-Tim, the center of practical action and effects, was a fragile fabrication at constant risk of dissolution by others' disregard and his own personal disappointments. But Survivalist-Tim had resources. At his disposal lay an array of symbols and arguments that made his position less tenuous and more attractive than the non-survivalist might recognize. Like other survivalists, Tim could read, imagine and tell, and publish stories, which included a provocative place for himself, and he could invite others into the story-telling. He could master a few skills with a few implements and, like the Dutch boy by the leaky dike, accomplish much with one digit, perseverance and good timing. Warrior survivalism was not all Tim did, but a part of his life that added animation and an alternative to humdrum times.

Mitchell uses a general code titled 'Organizing Survivalism'. Specific codes include 'Survivalist

Story-telling', its connections with 'Tree-planter-Tim' and 'Survivalist-Tim'. Note how the codes recede into the background as Mitchell frames the story. Mitchell's excerpt reveals the ethnographer's advantage in coding: the individual cases and separate incidents shape descriptive and theoretical understanding of the larger process and, simultaneously, an emerging grasp of the larger process provides context for interpreting specifics. Details of Tim's life illuminate what happens in organizing survivalism and, in turn, Mitchell's growing awareness of the world of survivalism gives him a frame for constructing conceptual meanings of Tim's life. An ethnographer's immediate access to the empirical world complements the grounded theorist's methods of comparing data to data.

Three points merit underscoring:

1 data do not stand alone;
2 apparent disclosures may not reflect a subject's crucial concerns;
3 an emerging analysis takes varied forms – depending on what the researcher takes as creditable data.

We could make a case for each code taken separately or together. When Mitchell talked further with Tim, he found that Tim's cares lay elsewhere than in the 'security' issues he first espoused. Not only are literal fieldnote excerpts acontextual, but entire interviews may take researchers away from subjects' primal foci. Interpretations of data are not unidimensional. If researchers agree on what is 'in' data, their agreement flows from shared presuppositions about the world, the context and the specific scene. Furthermore, what researchers bring to the data places a silent frame on what they see and hear.

Line-by-line coding (Glaser, 1978) poses an area of potential tension with ethnography. Any set of data already has some level of interpretation written into its collection. Line-by-line coding works well with interviews and structured conversations but not with all observations and anecdotes. Line-by-line coding stays close to the data. If data consist of observed mundane behavior with little contextual framing, line-by-line coding may not be helpful. Mitchell's tape-recorded reflections about observed mundane actions in the field proved invaluable in making sense of them and in filling in gaps between them. Coding whole anecdotes, scenarios and sketches may work better for ethnographic observations than line-by-line coding.

Grounded theorists use line-by-line coding to stay close to the data, although many of them treat data as self-evident and non-problematic – simply there. They are not. Line-by-line coding imposes conceptual limits when conducted acontextually. Potential multiple meanings of data remain unrecognized.[6] An organization's written documents are often taken as reflecting some kind of inherent truth about it. Consider how Mitchell might have portrayed survivalists had he taken their documents as reproductive of reality, followed with line-by-line coding, then built categories on the resulting acontextual constructions.

At Ranger meetings, nearly everyone brought something informative to share; handouts, advertisements, news clippings, finds on bargain supplies, letters from other groups or personal correspondence. At one meeting 28 pieces of material comprised of 161 photocopied pages were shared by the nine persons in attendance. Kermit brought literature from the American Pistol and Rifle Association; 'Communism vs. Gun Ownership,' 'When Will it Happen?' i.e. the Russian ultimatum, 'Will the Government Confiscate Your Guns?', 'The Right of the People,' and four more. The Todds handed out, 'Water!' a guide to building solar stills at retreats, and the 'Personal Survival Equipment Checklist.' John had copies of a flyer he received from a friend in Spokane describing the 'Countelpro Sting ...' soon to be based by the FBI [Federal Bureau of Investigation] against survivalists. Dale also brought ammunition reloading hints, though he did no reloading himself. Ric brought a must-have book list. And so it went.

At our first few meetings, we sociologists were fascinated by all of this material, the lurid magazines, the conspiratorial flyers, the odd advisories and warnings. We asked for copies, borrowed others, and at home poured over our bounty. Here was text, the written word, the 'facts' of survivalism, quotable material, sensational, stationary, ready for sociological analysis. We missed the point.

As months passed, then years, we understood this process better. Every survivalist is an intelligence officer to a degree, not an arbiter of final fact but a librarian, an archivist, an organizer of data and themes, from which others may choose and make sense in their own ways. The ritual of passing along interesting tidbits of information brings the group together in a mutual tolerance of diverse views. Sharing of data is good survivalist citizenship, not a way of asserting one truth over another. Much passing along, pamphleteering, and redistributing is done as a courtesy, relatively independent of content.

The object of survivalism is never the discovery of new authorities to replace old ones, the supplanting of one superordinate metanarrative with another. It may appear so from the outside, when only one voice is heard, or de-animated texts made sense of out of context. But always, survivalism is a way of creative renarration of the self, and often one's companions, into tales of aesthetic, consequent action. The actions of gathering and disseminating, of passing along, photocopying, mailing, handing out, are essential manifestations of survivalist identity. Survivalists have information to share, and the generosity and will to share it. But they don't have the truth, the facts, the final words. What the handouts and copies say is not what they mean. Content is not important. Sharing is.

Selective coding is more focused and more conceptual than line-by-line coding (Charmaz, 1983, 1995; Glaser, 1978). These codes account for the most data and categorize them more precisely than other codes.[7] Selective coding integrates earlier codes that it subsumes. Hence, selective coding provides a more abstract and comprehensive conceptual handle on the data than open, or initial coding. These focused codes not only serve to synthesize large amounts of data, but also to organize earlier codes into a coherent framework.

From a grounded theory perspective, coding involves developing comparisons. Selective coding prompts the researcher to make comparisons between emerging categories. A substantial amount of data is necessary to engage in effective selective coding. In the example above, Mitchell avoids an inherent hazard in grounded theory – gathering too little data. Comparing what participants did with their written materials with the content of survivalist events as well as survivalists. He also made comparisons between multiple incidents, experiences, actions and individuals. Had he not, Mitchell might have used the written ideological statements for his selective coding without realizing what this ideology meant to participants and how they behaved toward it.

Memo-making

Memo-making is the crucial step between coding and a first draft of a paper. Memos bring analytic focus to data collection and to the researcher's ideas. Amorphous ideas and ambiguous questions gain clarity. An ethnographer can play with ideas, try them out and check their usefulness by going back and forth between written pages and studied realities. Memos are preliminary, partial and correctable. Constructing them is much like free-writing or pre-writing (Charmaz, 1995b; Elbow, 1981; see also Becker, 1986). Memo-making involves researchers in an on-going process of analysing and writing and therefore reduces writer's block and increases fluidity and depth. These memos may stand as private conversations with self in which researchers record ideas and information and state confirmed facts and conjectures.

Memo-writing elaborates material subsumed by a code. A careful definition of a code begins to get beneath the surface. The grounded theorist identifies its fundamental properties, looks for its underlying assumptions, and shows how, when and why it develops and changes. Codes grow beyond mere means for sorting data and become processes to explore. Treating codes analytically transforms them into theoretical categories. Comparisons can be written right into memos such as between individual and individual or between incident and

incident. Making explicit comparisons helps ethnographers discern patterns and establish variations from which they can outline theoretical relationships.

Using comparative methods brings data into the narrative from the start. Analysis proceeds from the ground up. Data are raised through increasingly abstract levels of conceptual analysis. These data should not become invisible or distant as a researcher's memos become more analytic. Rather the researcher brings the selected data forward in each successive memo. Building a memo on raw data anchors ideas and, ultimately, balances evidence with the theoretical argument. This approach increases the usefulness of the final product because the researcher establishes and measures its analytic boundaries. Weaving the raw data in from the start also allows for easy retrieval to obtain more information, if needed. Researchers need to provide enough verbatim data to make their abstract analyses strong, compelling and persuasive.

A grounded theory emphasis on keeping codes active and specific from the start accrues advantages. Ethnographers see and connect actions and contexts early in their research. In later memos, active codes enable ethnographers to show how categories are connected in a larger, overall process.

Grounded theorists look for patterns. So do ethnographers but how they treat and portray those patterns may differ. Grounded theorists explicitly analyse a pattern to develop middle-range theory; ethnographers strive to describe how action is played out in the social world and within the lives of its members. The analytic features of the pattern remain more implicit; they are subjugated to fuller ethnographic accounts or stories. Thus, ethnographers build substantially more description and more discussion into their memos than do grounded theorists. Lengthy tales about subjects' lives abound in ethnographic narratives. Grounded theorists also use respondents' stories, but likely as only short excerpts within analytic memos.

The excerpt below is one of Mitchell's memos presented in narrative form. The analytic edge of grounded theory can frame and shape a story. Mitchell defines his category, 'Aryan Idle Time', through illustration. The category is a topic here; the scenes on which Mitchell constructs it are processes. The topic is specific and evocative. Note that Mitchell does not say 'leisure time' or 'free time.' It's 'idle time' – *aryan* idle time. As Atkinson (1990) points out, titles can cue readers that they are about to enter an esoteric world. Mitchell's title suggests such entry by implying that aryan idle time has special qualities. He describes the slow pace and fragmented talk of aryan idle time, observes what the category leaves out, and notes what participants do not do. Mitchell builds his category with sorted and synthesized observations. He reproduces tempo and social space as well as a bit of aryan talk in his rendering of this category. The pace slows further through how he places description on the page. By bringing the description right into the category, Mitchell not only keeps the category grounded but also builds the reader's interest.

Aryan Idle Time

Aryan idle time is not easily filled. Butler's participants have few ideas of their own, few thought-out programs to promote or personal insights to share, few favored topics to animate dialogue, consolidate interest, focus attention. There is no talk of secret technology or hidden health aids, no plans for democratic reform or dietary discipline.

Transcribed and trimmed, edited and organized onto the page, Aryan interlude talk may look cohesive, to the point. It was not. Talk was listless, unfocused. It came in snippets and grunts, 'Yep's and 'You bet's, in brief, disconnected anecdotes, that ran down to stillness in a minute or two. Putty talk. It matches the surroundings and fills the cracks between silences, but provides no unifying strength. My tapes are full of it, lapses, coughs, ahems, bench shifting, scratching and remarks meant to meet civil obligations, not move or inform.

One starts, tries a topic, tells a story. Another adds a word or two. A third nods. Story ends. Wait. Wait for something to happen. Wait for someone to begin again.
Listen.

Forty-five minutes of tape sounds like this ...

'You know those Shakers, own all that rich farm land in Pennsylvania? Not very many of them left. They are all octogenarians, 80, 90 years old, all gonna die pretty soon. They've been leaving that property to each other for generations and generations. Now they've only got one member that is gonna live much longer. He's 43, just converted to the Shaker religion.'

'He's a Jew?'

'Yep. He's not dumb.'

'He'll get all that land.'

'You know, Jews are smart. You have to admit it.'

'Not so smart as sneaky.'

'Sneaky, yeah, sneaky.'

Pause. Scratch.

'Growing up we had Jews in our neighborhood. I don't mean it was a Jewish neighborhood, but we had some Jews there. We used to torment 'em, We'd make 'em line up against the wall, wear yellow swastikas, yellow stars, we stuck on 'em.'

'Yeah. We used to do that, too, where I lived. We had a tough gang. We used to beat up on 'em all the time. Beat 'em up, and beat 'em up, and they never fight back.'

'Jews and niggers, they never fight back.'

Pause. Stare at the ground.

Theoretical Sampling

Theoretical sampling means going back to the field to gather specific data to fill gaps within categories,

to elaborate the analysis of these categories, and to discover variation within and between them. This sampling is aimed to develop a theoretical analysis or to fill out ethnographers' accounts or stories, *not* to approximate any statistical representation of the population parameters. By this stage in the analytic process, the researcher has already defined relevant issues and allowed significant data to emerge.[8]

Researchers become more selective than earlier about what, when, where, why and from whom data are obtained. A researcher's focus may change from individuals or events to certain experiences or issues to develop needed theoretical categories.

Theoretical sampling helps the researcher to 'saturate' categories. According to grounded theory policy statements, saturation means the researcher's categories are filled with data. No significant new information or ideas emerge with additional data. Variation has been established and accounted for. In practice, grounded theorists use the notion of saturated categories loosely – and sometimes glibly. The point of saturation remains unclear. Janice M. Morse (1995) suggests that researchers invoke two criteria: (1) investigator proclamation or (2) the adequacy and comprehensiveness of the results. This term, 'saturation', serves to justify a small number of cases – at least that's how a number of grounded theorists seem to have used it. Constructed categories may be 'saturated', but are they the most telling categories? Might not a longer, fuller view of studied realities lead in different directions and net other categories? Early saturation leads to narrow, superficial categories and premature closure. Strong ethnographic work requires saturation of a wide range of categories, located in their cultural, historical or organizational contexts.

Whether theoretical sampling advances ethnographic study depends on researchers' working and writing styles. This step can help those who lean toward explicit techniques and analytic development of their material. For those who treat enquiry and writing as emergent art, theoretical sampling may seem too mechanical. An ethnographic story-teller may not use theoretical sampling as grounded theorists outline. A naturalistic study, a particular research problem, and a narrative turn in *thinking* as well as in writing can reduce the usefulness or necessity of theoretical sampling. Mitchell went back into fields – not 'the' field – to obtain more data because his research required multiple sites and scenes. Neither static institutional structures, nor stable social worlds beckoned his return. Even tracing specific individuals proved elusive. Survivalism remained a slippery phenomenon. Mitchell's discovery of meanings took more than sampling checks could yield, though many observations eventually shaped, then later, confirmed his ideas. Worlds of survivalism felt amorphous, mysterious, its meanings too nuanced and subtle to emerge with merely technical grounded theory prodding. An ethnographer needs to grasp the whole phenomenon and that may not always occur incrementally. Mitchell found that different social actors held a constellation of meanings about survivalism. These meanings grew apparent through writing the monograph, but long before then Mitchell pursued a narrative style. It shaped how he thought about his work, the questions he asked, and how he developed his ideas.

Integrating the Analysis

Grounded theorists develop their categories in relation to each other, as well as through elaborating their unique properties. Hence, a researcher may construct a nascent theoretical framework while building categories. Conditional statements and propositions show the theoretical relationship between categories and integrate them into a theory. Glaser (1978) contends that studying a basic social process leads to a logically integrated theoretical analysis. His perspective assumes that researchers readily find single unifying themes in their research. That may not be so – there may be many.[9] Organizing ethnographic materials around a basic process builds action into the analysis and, thus, gives it movement and direction, establishes causality and leads to delineating consequences. Convenient, neat, seemingly complete, but also potentially arbitrary and Procrustean. The world may not be as simple as the sense we make of it. More commonly, integrating categories results from trial and error, from locating and mapping while keeping empirical locations in mind. Diagramming how categories fit within a conceptual map can help enormously. Whatever integrative frames researchers construct, *how* they present them becomes a problem in writing for audiences.

Once researchers have developed and integrated their analyses around their fresh take on the empirical reality, it is time to complete their literature review. However, the grounded theory principle to delay the literature review is only partly useful. Glaser and Strauss (1967) contend that delaying it reduces researchers' potential reliance on extant theory and interpretations from a parent discipline. Those are concerns – particularly for novices who might be entranced by earlier works. Some researchers cannot extricate themselves from logico-deductive theory. Yet only in fields with borrowed or undeveloped theory do researchers remain unaffected by earlier ideas and information.[10] Not even grounded theorists need to advocate that researchers wear theoretical blinders. Instead, grounded theorists can use extant theories to sensitize them to certain issues and processes in their data (Blumer, 1969; van den Hoonard, 1997).

Theory can breathe through ethnographic and grounded theory research and animate it (Charmaz,

1998). And we can give old theories new life through comparing our fresh analyses with them.

Writing Ethnography, Writing Grounded Theory

Analysis proceeds into the writing. It does not stop when an ethnographer has framed a story or when a grounded theorist has integrated categories.[11] Nor does its relative effectiveness. Laurel Richardson (1994) is right when she says that many published ethnographies are boring – unpublished ones may be worse. How writers present their material reflects their approach and their view of the audience. How an audience responds may belie the writer's presuppositions. Yet writing should fit the author's purpose, material and audience.

Writing ethnography often poses different problems from writing grounded theory. Many ethnographers offer telling descriptive accounts or stories (Duneier, 1992; Liebow, 1967; Loseke, 1992). Some develop analytic renderings (Fine, 1986, 1996; Kondo, 1990; Lofland, 1993; Morrill, 1995; Snow and Anderson, 1993). Few construct grounded theories. Their products range from objectified reports to impressionist tales of the field (Van Maanen, 1988). An ethnographic story can preserve experiential form and process as well as content.

When writing ethnographic stories, researchers imbed their categories in the narrative. They may use these categories as a means of organizing their description. Such categories tend to be more general and fewer than those in grounded theory analyses. The more the ethnography takes story form, the more imbedded the categories – even if the story contains theoretical import. Here, the author's perspective and use of key phrases directs the story. In 'Countdown', Mitchell turns mundane enumeration into a story. He builds the counts to move the story forward to the culminating event. The term, 'countdown', transcends clever description and becomes a category itself as Mitchell shows how the event wanes as the numbers dwindle:

> At least seven hundred are coming ... Three hundred will be here ... One hundred and thirty are found in the late Saturday head count. (But not all count. Twenty-two women and ten children need protection. And the twenty skinheads don't care.)
> Fifty-seven go to church ...
> Fifty-two stay through the sermon.
> Forty-nine stay awake ...
> Thirteen Aryan Warriors ...
> Twelve wear long pants.
> Eleven have both shoes on.
> Seven have regulation uniforms.

In this way, the meanings of 'simple sums' expand and reveal hidden images of the survivalists' world. This short ethnographic tale reveals players and paradoxes – survivalism is not what we had supposed.

In grounded theory writing, researchers' analytic treatment of theoretical categories takes precedence over narrative. This emphasis strengthens theory-building, or at least the appearance of it, but readability suffers. When grounded theorists construct explicit concepts and make their fit within the work apparent, readers can assess it. They can take the parts apart. They can apply either Glaser's (1978) or Strauss and Corbin's (1990/1998) criteria for evaluation of a given piece but such criteria pale with a powerful ethnographic story. Criteria for evaluating ethnographic stories include correspondence with the studied reality, illumination of it and generic understanding. Is the written word congruent with experience? Does the story illuminate the studied world? Does the reader gain new and deeper understanding of human experience more generally?

The purposes of ethnographic writing vary, depending on research objectives, reporting style and potential audiences. Ethnographers can use description to tell stories, form scenes, describe players and demonstrate actions. Grounded theory works typically reverse this emphasis. Conceptual analysis takes center-stage; stories and scenes and, therefore, individuals play minor parts on the illustrative sidelines. Grounded theorists include snippets of stories and fragments of experience rather than entire narratives. Thus, grounded theory works may sacrifice subtlety and nuance for clarity and explicitness. Explicit conditions, fine distinctions, discrete boundaries and crisp comparisons move grounded theory works toward establishing causality and prediction. Despite these differences, both ethnographer and grounded theorist insist on grappling with studied life and anchoring their theoretical and policy arguments firmly in their analyses of it.

Neither ethnographic nor grounded theory works always fit standard modes of professional writing. Grounded theory recipe writing comes closer because it divides studies into familiar categorized sections. In addition, grounded theorists may provide a more or less theoretical 'list' of propositions. Yet little that purports to be grounded theory *is* theory. It is grounded description instead.

The following excerpts juxtapose Kathy Charmaz's (1995a) grounded theory analysis of adapting to an impaired body with Mitchell's ethnographic story-telling delineated in preceding excerpts. We chose the category below, 'surrendering to the sick body', because the grounded theory treatment within it is quite explicit. Charmaz first defines surrendering by explicating its properties and the assumptions on which it rests. Then she provides data from Arnold Beisser's (1988) autobiographical account that simultaneously shows how he experienced surrendering and provides evidence for her theoretical category.

Surrendering to the sick body

Surrendering means to stop pushing bodily limits, to stop fighting the episode or the entire illness. The quest for control over illness ceases and the flow with the bodily experience increases. Surrender means awareness of one's ill body and a willingness and relief to flow with it (cf. Denzin, 1987a, 1987b). A person ceases to struggle against illness and against a failing body at least at this specific time. Through surrendering, the person anchors bodily feelings in self. No longer does he or she ignore, gloss over, or deny these feelings and view the ill body as apart from self.

Conditions for surrender to occur include (1) relinquishing the quest for control over one's body, (2) giving up notions of victory over illness, (3) affirming, however implicitly, that one's self is tied to the sick body. Ill people may surrender and flow with the experience in the present but hope for improvement in the future. Yet they are unlikely to entertain false hopes. At this point, the person views illness as integral to subjective experience and as integrated with self (see also LeMaistre, 1985; Monks and Frankenberg, n.d.).

Surrendering differs from being overtaken by illness, resigning oneself to it, or giving up (cf. Charmaz, 1991; Radley and Green, 1987). Being overtaken occurs without choice; surrendering is an active, intentional process. However silently and tacitly, ill people agree to surrender. When surrender is complete, the person experiences a new unity between body and self ... Becoming resigned means yielding to illness, acquiescing to its force, or to the devalued identities attributed to it. Such resignation means accepting defeat after struggling against illness. When people give up, they lose hope and crumble inward. Passivity, depression, and debility follow. They are overtaken by illness. Under these conditions, people with chronic illnesses can become much more disabled than their physical conditions warrant ... In contrast, surrender means permitting oneself to let go rather than being overtaken by illness and despair.

Resisting surrender means holding on and, with advanced illness, refusing to die. Fear may propel critically ill people. When they struggle against illness and try to impose order upon it and their lives, they are unlikely to surrender during the midst of crisis. But later, learning to live with residual disability can teach them about surrender. As Arnold Beisser (1988) acknowledges, he learned about surrender through facing defeat. Like many other men, Beisser had earlier believed, then later hoped, that his sustained effort would force change to occur and victory to prevail. Yet no amount of effort changed the fact of his disability. Beisser (1988: 169–70) reflects:

> Defeated on all fronts, I had to learn how to surrender and accept what I had become, what I did not want to be.
>
> Learning to surrender and accept what I had not chosen gave me knowledge of a new kind of change and a new kind of experience which I had not anticipated. It was a paradoxical change.

When I stopped struggling, working to change, and found means of accepting what I had already become, I discovered that that changed me. Rather than feeling disabled and inadequate as I anticipated that I would, I felt whole again. I experienced a sense of well-being and a fullness I had not known before. I felt at one not only with myself but with the universe.

(Charmaz, 1995a: 672–3)

Note that Charmaz starts by defining and describing the category. She builds comparisons into her definition as well as throughout the analysis as she distinguishes surrendering from other stances toward illness. She tells what surrendering is and what it is not. She outlines conditions under which the category is visible. She looks at thought and feeling in addition to describing choice and action. By building upon an explicit personal account of surrendering, the properties and process of surrendering come alive. In these ways, Charmaz moves from description into analysis of a theoretical category.

CONCLUSION

Our discussion above takes us full circle back to method and forward into art. We end by renewing our invitation to ethnographers and by challenging grounded theorists. Methods should bring us closer to our studied phenomena and spark our ideas. Grounded theory offers ethnographers useful guidelines for conducting research. We invite ethnographers to apply and adapt these guidelines to increase control over and clarity within their work. Rather than constraining ethnographers, we see possibilities for revision and renewal of grounded theory methods to advance ethnographic work. Ethnographers can modify these methods, as grounded theorists themselves modify their theories, to work within the worlds they study. But as several of Mitchell's excerpts show, ethnographers may not be able to endorse these methods wholesale. They need to be adapted for specific objectives of a study and for the style of the researcher.

Grounded theory provides powerful guidelines – they can aid us in our progress and can enhance our conceptual grasp of empirical phenomena. But we must use them well. Access to powerful guidelines does not compensate for using them poorly. Reductionist, limited, acontextual grounded theory research neither advances theory nor contributes to substantive knowledge. We cannot sidestep the work that makes our studies shine. Adopting ethnographic sensibilities can further grounded theory research.

We challenge grounded theorists to adopt perspectives ethnographers have long shared – an appreciation and knowledge of context, a sensitivity to unstated and unrecognized meanings, and an awareness of layers of meaning in language. If grounded theory becomes more of a mechanical operation and less of a reflexive enterprise, its potential strength will diminish. Grounded theory strategies and guidelines can be reclaimed and used to achieve the kind of depth and breadth represented in the best ethnographies.

Simultaneously, grounded theorists can move away from a quest for elegant method and move toward writing with grace and style. We can develop greater appreciation of aesthetic standards in our work and pursue them with diligence. We need to make our written products symbolic of the worlds we visit, rather than distilled abstractions of actions. We must try to make our written works resonate with meanings palpable within the research settings.

As we narrate our stories and construct our analyses, we also struggle with language. How do we frame our writing and shape our research accounts? How should we? Must we adopt a single frame for presenting our written products, whatever form that frame takes? No. We must be self-conscious and reflexive in our choices and in direction. We can create a frame that fits our material and suits our audience. When we are reflexive, we sense the distance between our words and worlds. As our awareness of that distance grows, we realize that struggling with language reflects our struggles with complexities of the field. The obdurate qualities of the world do not diminish with our departure from the field. Yet we can see these qualities, and keep seeing them anew. We may struggle with them. And we should search for words that recognize the obdurate qualities of empirical worlds while revealing the evanescence of experience within them.

Acknowledgements

Thanks for reading an earlier version of this chapter are due to Charles Gallagher, Lyn Lofland, Sarah Phoenix, two anonymous reviewers and Sonoma State University Faculty Writing Program members Wanda Boda, Maureen Buckley, Noel Byrne, Scott Miller, Elisa Valasquez and Elaine Wellin.

NOTES

1 Earlier major grounded theory statements took a more objectivist position (see Glaser and Strauss, 1967; Glaser, 1978; Strauss and Corbin, 1990/1998).

2 Glaser (1978, 1992) has always argued that grounded theory methods may also be used with quantitative methods. Strauss (1987) focused on qualitative research.

3 For a critique of current debates on grounded theory, see Kathy Charmaz, 'Grounded theory: objectivist and constructivist methods' (2000).

4 Coffey and Atkinson (1996) address problems of being overwhelmed and procrastinating directly.

5 Grounded theory studies have long been accused of building analyses on skimpy data (Lofland and Lofland, 1984). Creswell (1998) views grounded theory as primarily based upon a limited number of interviews (20–30), but does not challenge using a small sample. Depending on the purpose and the quality of data and analysis, a limited sample might be sufficient. But it is unlikely for a dissertation or major study.

Now the tendency to shortcut data collection permeates all kinds of methods, including ethnography. We agree with Schneider (1997) that the rush to theorizing reflects political and career decisions beyond specific research problems to the detriment of both theory and research.

6 Alasuutari (1996) makes a similar point when he argues that coding is not theoretically 'innocent' (p. 373). The act of coding presupposes a perspective. Further, line-by-line coding does not give a sense of the whole story, which is important for narrative analysis as well as ethnography.

7 Researchers who follow Strauss and Corbin's (1990/1998) approach to grounded theory may engage in axial coding before selective coding. Axial coding is intended to develop the sub-categories of a category by looking at their properties and dimensions. Thus, a researcher must have categories to work with before using this technique. From other perspectives, including Glaser's (1992), axial coding makes grounded theory unduly complex and forces the data into categories.

8 Otherwise, early theoretical sampling may bring premature closure to the analysis. Strauss (1995), in contrast, moves to theoretical sampling early. He contends that following this step early sharpens the subsequent analysis. However, the line between early theoretical sampling and forcing data into preconceived categories is not clear, as Glaser (1992) might note.

9 For some years, I tried to define a basic social process that chronically ill people experienced – one that subsumed all other processes. I couldn't find one and looking was another source of delay. A search for a unitary basic process preconceives the frame of analysis and forces the data into boxes – quite a paradox within a paradigm in which progenitors argue vehemently against forcing the data.

10 If researchers are active scholars, the notion of delaying the literature review is rather silly and disingenuous. They are apt to be steeped in specific literatures for a variety of purposes beyond a specific research project.

11 Unfortunately, some researchers from both schools do stop there. That weakens their work and results in rejected manuscripts. Stopping at this point leads to sketchy ethnographic stories and grounded theory works reading like mechanical lists.

REFERENCES

Alasuutari, Pertti (1996) 'Theorizing in qualitative research: a cultural studies perspective', *Qualitative Inquiry*, 2: 371–84.

Altheide, David L. and Johnson, John M. (1994) 'Criteria for assessing validity in qualitative research', in Norman K. Denzin and Yvonna S. Lincoln (eds), *Handbook of Qualitative Research*. Thousand Oaks, CA: Sage. pp. 485–99.

Atkinson, Paul (1990) *The Ethnographic Imagination: Textual Constructions of Reality*. London: Routledge.

Becker, Howard S. (1986) *Writing for Social Scientists*. Chicago: University of Chicago Press.

Beisser, Arnold R. (1988) *Flying without Wings: Personal Reflections on Being Disabled*. New York: Doubleday.

Bergson, Henri ([1903] 1961) *An Introduction to Metaphysics* (trans. Mabelle L. Andison). New York: Philosophical Library.

Bigus, Odis E., Hadden, Stuart C. and Glaser, Barney G. (1994) 'The study of basic social processes', in Barney G. Glaser (ed.), *More Grounded Theory Methodology: A Reader*. Mill Valley, CA: Sociology Press. pp. 38–64.

Blumer, Herbert (1969) *Symbolic Interactionism*. Englewood Cliffs, NJ: Prentice–Hall.

Charmaz, Kathy (1983) 'The grounded theory method: an explication and interpretation', in Robert M. Emerson (ed.), *Contemporary Field Research*. Boston, MA: Little, Brown. pp. 109–26.

Charmaz, Kathy (1990) 'Discovering chronic illness: using grounded theory', *Social Science and Medicine*, 30: 1161–72.

Charmaz, Kathy (1991) *Good Days, Bad Days: The Self in Chronic Illness and Time*. New Brunswick, NJ: Rutgers University Press.

Charmaz, Kathy (1995a) 'Body, identity, and self: adapting to impairment', *The Sociological Quarterly*, 36: 657–80.

Charmaz, Kathy (1995b) 'Grounded theory', in J.A. Smith, R. Harré and L. Van Langenhove (eds), *Rethinking Methods in Psychology*. London: Sage. pp. 27–49.

Charmaz, Kathy (1998) 'Research standards and stories: conflict and challenge', Plenary Presentation, Qualitative Research Conference. University of Toronto, Toronto, Ontario, 15 May.

Charmaz, Kathy (2000) 'Grounded theory: objectivist and constructivist methods', in Norman K. Denzin and Yvonna S. Lincoln (eds), *Handbook of Qualitative Research*, 2nd edn. Thousand Oaks, CA: Sage. pp. 509–35.

Charmaz, Kathy and Mitchell, Richard G. (1996) 'The myth of silent authorship: self, substance, and style in ethnographic writing', *Symbolic Interaction*, 19: 285–302.

Chenitz, W. Carol and Swanson, Janice M. (eds) (1986) *From Practice to Grounded Theory: Qualitative Research in Nursing*. Reading, MA: Addison–Wesley.

Coffey, Amanda and Atkinson, Paul (1996) *Making Sense of Qualitative Data: Complementary Research Strategies*. Thousand Oaks, CA: Sage.

Creswell, John W. (1998) *Qualitative Inquiry and Research Design: Choosing Among Five Traditions*. Thousand Oaks, CA: Sage.

Denzin, Norman K. (1987a) *The Alcoholic Self*. Newbury Park, CA: Sage.

Denzin, Norman K. (1987b) *The Recovering Alcoholic*. Newbury Park, CA: Sage.

Denzin, Norman K. (1994) 'The art and politics of interpretation', in Norman K. Denzin and Yvonna S. Lincoln (eds), *Handbook of Qualitative Research*. Thousand Oaks, CA: Sage. pp. 500–15.

Duneier, Mitchell (1992) *Slim's Table: Race, Respectability, and Masculinity*. Chicago: University of Chicago Press.

Durkheim, Emile ([1895] 1982) *The Rules of Sociological Method*. New York: Macmillan.

Elbow, Peter (1981) *Writing with Power*. New York: Oxford University Press.

Fine, Gary Alan (1986) *With the Boys: Little League Baseball and Preadolescent Culture*. Chicago: University of Chicago Press.

Fine, Gary Alan (1996) *Kitchens: The Culture of Restaurant Work*. Berkeley, CA: University of California Press.

Geertz, Clifford (1973) *The Interpretation of Cultures*. New York: Basic Books.

Glaser, Barney G. (1978) *Theoretical Sensitivity*. Mill Valley, CA: The Sociology Press.

Glaser, Barney G. (1992) *Basics of Grounded Theory Analysis: Emergence vs. Forcing*. Mill Valley, CA: The Sociology Press.

Glaser, Barney G. (1994) *More Grounded Theory Methodology: A Reader*. Mill Valley, CA: The Sociology Press.

Glaser, Barney G. and Strauss, Anselm L. (1965) *Awareness of Dying*. Chicago: Aldine.

Glaser, Barney G. and Strauss, Anselm L. (1967) *The Discovery of Grounded Theory*. Chicago: Aldine.

Glaser, Barney G. and Strauss, Anselm L. (1968) *Time for Dying*. Chicago: Aldine.

Guba, Egon G. and Lincoln, Yvonna S. (1994) 'Competing paradigms in qualitative research', in Norman K. Denzin and Yvonna S. Lincoln (eds), *Handbook of Qualitative Research*. Thousand Oaks, CA: Sage. pp. 105–18.

Kondo, Dorinne K. (1990) *Crafting Selves: Power, Gender and Discourses of Identity in a Japanese Workplace*. Chicago: University of Chicago Press.

Kuhn, T.S. (1970) *The Structure of Scientific Revolutions*. Chicago: University of Chicago Press.

LeMaistre, Joanne (1985) *Beyond Rage: The Emotional Impact of Chronic Illness*. Oak Park, IL: Alpine Guild.

Liebow, Elliott (1967) *Talley's Corner*. Boston, MA: Little, Brown.

Lofland, John (1993) *Polite Protestors: The American Peace Movement of the 1980s*. Syracuse, NY: Syracuse University Press.

Lofland, John and Lofland, Lyn H. (1984) *Analyzing Social Settings*, 2nd edn. Belmont, CA: Wadsworth.

Lofland, John and Lofland, Lyn H. (1994) *Analyzing Social Settings*, 3rd edn. Belmont, CA: Wadsworth.

Loseke, Donileen, R. (1992) *The Battered Woman and Shelters: The Social Construction of Wife Abuse*. Albany, NY: State University of New York Press.

Miles, Matthew B. and Huberman, A. Michael (1994) *Qualitative Data Analysis: A Sourcebook of New Methods*. Thousand Oaks, CA: Sage.

Mitchell, Richard G. (1991) 'Field notes', Unpublished ms., Oregon State University, Corvallis, OR.

Mitchell, Richard G. (forthcoming) *Dancing to Armageddon: Survivalism, Chaos, and Culturecraft in Modern Times*. Chicago: University of Chicago Press.

Monks, Judith and Frankenberg, Ronald (n.d.) 'The presentation of self, body and time in the life stories and illness narratives of people with multiple sclerosis'. Unpublished MS, Brunel University, London.

Morrill, Calvin (1995) *The Executive Way: Conflict Management in Corporations*. Chicago: University of Chicago Press.

Morse, Janice M. (1995) 'The significance of saturation', *Qualitative Health Research*, 5: 147–9.

Prus, Robert C. (1987) 'Generic social processes: maximizing conceptual development in ethnographic research', *Journal of Contemporary Ethnography*, 16: 250–93.

Prus, Robert C. (1996) *Symbolic Interaction and Ethnographic Research: Intersubjectivity and the Study of Human Lived Experience*. Albany, NY: State University of New York Press.

Radley, Alan and Green, Ruth (1987) 'Illness as adjustment: a methodology and conceptual framework', *Sociology of Health and Illness*, 9: 179–206.

Richardson, Laurel (1994) 'Writing: a method of inquiry', in Norman K. Denzin and Yvonna S. Lincoln (eds), *Handbook of Qualitative Research*. Thousand Oaks, CA: Sage. pp. 516–29.

Sanders, Clinton R. (1995) 'Stranger than fiction: insights and pitfalls in post-modern ethnography', in Norman K. Denzin (ed.), *Studies in Symbolic Interaction*, 17: 89–104.

Schneider, Mark A. (1997) 'Social dimensions of epistemological disputes: the case of literary theory', *Sociological Perspectives*, 40: 243–64.

Schwandt, Thomas A. (1994) 'Constructivist, interpretivist approaches to human inquiry', in Norman K. Denzin and Yvonna S. Lincoln (eds), *Handbook of Qualitative Research*. Thousand Oaks, CA: Sage. pp. 118–37.

Snow, David A. and Anderson, Leon (1993) *Down on Their Luck: A Study of Homeless People*. Berkeley, CA: University of California Press.

Stern, Phyllis N. (1994a) 'Eroding grounded theory', in Janice M. Morse (ed.), *Critical Issues in Qualitative Research Method*. Thousand Oaks, CA: Sage. pp. 210–13.

Stern, Phyllis N. ([1980] 1994b) 'The grounded theory method: its uses and processes', in B.G. Glaser (ed.), *More Grounded Theory: A Reader*. Mill Valley, CA: Sociology Press. pp. 116–26.

Strauss, Anselm L. (1987) *Qualitative Analysis for Social Scientists*. New York: Cambridge University Press.

Strauss, Anselm (1995) 'Notes on the nature and development of general theories', *Qualitative Inquiry*, 1: 7–18.

Strauss, Anselm and Corbin, Juliet A. (1990/1998) *Basics of Qualitative Research: Grounded Theory Procedures and Techniques* (2nd edn 1998). Newbury Park, CA: Sage.

Strauss, Anselm and Corbin, Juliet A. (1994) 'Grounded theory methodology: an overview', in Norman K. Denzin and Yvonna S. Lincoln (eds), *Handbook of Qualitative Research*. Thousand Oaks, CA: Sage. pp. 273–85.

Whyte, William F. (1993) *Street Corner Society*, 4th edn. Chicago: University of Chicago Press.

Van den Hoonard, Will C. (1997) *Working with Sensitizing Concepts*. Thousand Oaks, CA: Sage.

Van Maanen, John (1988) *Tales of the Field*. Chicago: University of Chicago Press.

PART TWO

Introduction to Part Two

Ethnography is a useful method: it is a method (or group of methods) that has survived and flourished for over a century because it is an appropriate way of collecting data on (and in) a plethora of settings. From the psychiatric ward to the hippie commune, from the stockyard to the newsroom, from three-year-olds to nonagenarians, from Tokyo to Tierra del Fuego, from the post-doctoral mathematician to the severely mentally retarded, ethnography is a method that works. Precisely because ethnography is robust and flexible there are many applications which could have been subjects for inclusion in this book. We have chosen the specific empirical examples for this volume because they are areas in which the method has been developed and refined while the investigators were producing their accounts of particular settings and generating grounded theory. The chapters in this section focus on health and illness (Bloor), education (Gordon et al.), crime and deviance (Hobbs), paid employment (Smith), science (Hess), childhood (James), material culture (Tilley), cultural studies (Van Loon), communication (Keating) and visual communication (Ball and Smith).

Some of these areas have been central to ethnographic endeavour for over a century. The earliest anthropologists focused on work in 'savage' societies, such as farming, fishing and weaving. The earliest sociologists who used ethnography focused on how Americans earned their living. Other topics, such as science, are relatively recent foci for the ethnographic gaze. We have included a spread from classic topics to modern ones.

In some respects the authors commissioned to write about empirical areas and ethnographic applications had the hardest task. They had to decide on what priorities to set and what exclusions to make from very large literatures. Coverage is a problem which has at least five dimensions: depth versus breadth of coverage: national versus international spread: disciplinary versus interdisciplinary focus: studies important in the past versus important now; and the extent to which contemporary sensitivities around gender and race should be 'back projected'. On all these dimensions our authors differed from our referees, and sometimes both differed from us, the editorial team.

Depth versus breadth is a problem for all the authors in this section. Even if it were possible for an author to mention all the important empirical studies the result would be both superficial and tedious to read. It would also become out of date very quickly. The reader would not find the chapter useful in a decade's time. We asked the authors to analyse the literature, and focus on the interesting studies. Referees often queried the choices made by authors: we asked the authors to clarify and make explicit their reasoning but not to change it. We wanted analytic accounts of the area, not exhaustive catalogues.

National versus international spread is a second dimension. Few authors in Britain, the United States or Australia are familiar with research from continental Europe. Scholars outwith the United States are not necessarily up to date with American research, while Americans are rarely well read in the non-American literature. Some of our authors have been more successful than others in covering the world; some referees were more distressed by ethnocentrism than others. We have not managed to reconcile these opposing views: some of our chapters are more cosmopolitan than others. For example, Smith's chapter on work is predominantly about the American literature, while Gordon et al. deal with education on three continents and in ten countries.

Anthropology and sociology are separate disciplines. Some of our authors have written only from the perspective of either sociology or anthropology. Others, such as Hess on science, have made a point of covering studies from both disciplines. In contrast, Hobbs (on crime and deviance) has stayed inside his own discipline of sociology. Few of our referees were anxious about this, and we have given our authors freedom to make their own choice on this dimension.

As disciplines develop, and both sociology and anthropology are at least 150 years old, the landmark studies change. Once fashionable projects are forgotten, while others are re-discovered. In the history of anthropology, Zora Neale Hurston is an example of a scholar whose ideas are being 're-discovered' after a long period in obscurity. In sociology, domestic work was an important topic in the early years of the Chicago School, and was then ignored for sixty years before re-emerging as a subject for investigation. Writing in 2000, our authors had to decide whether to focus on studies that are seen as path-breaking, pioneering, or seminal today, or on those that were lauded in their own era when deciding on their structures; they had to choose to write either thematic or chronological accounts, and where to lay their emphases. Once again, we encouraged our authors to make their own choices, and to defend them. Hobbs has chosen a largely chronological framework, while Keating's is more analytic. Whichever pattern the author has chosen, the reader will be able to share the insights of a leading researcher.

Perhaps most contentiously, there is an issue around gender and race. Contemporary scholarship privileges differences of gender and race, whereas earlier authors were often blind to them. The scholarships of women and people of colour, and the empirical research on these groups, has frequently been lost to the official histories of the discipline. Deegan (1987) shows this for the work done by and on women in Chicago before 1945; McRobbie and Garber (1976) for British research on 'youth'. We did not ask our authors to focus on race and gender, but we did ask our referees to apply 'adequate coverage' of these topics as a judgement criterion. Some of the male authors wrote drafts that ignored women altogether, both as scholarly authors and as the focus of empirical studies. Some of the male referees did not even notice that this omission had occurred. As an editorial team, however, we have requested the authors to address issues of gender and ethnicity, if only to remark on their absence from the majority of the studies they have chosen.

We have chosen analyses of four classic areas – health, education, deviance and work – to open Part Two. Many of the most famous ethnographers of the past fifty years have chosen to investigate these four topics, and they are, as these essays show, vibrant today. In contrast, Hess and James deal with areas that have become popular more recently – science and childhood. All these chapters share a focus on research done in specific settings such as hospitals, schools, prisons, factories, laboratories and homes. Then the focus changes. The last four chapters in this section of the book focus on aspects of culture. Keating on oral communication, Van Loon on cultural studies, Tilley on material culture and Ball and Smith on visual communication, are covering empirical topics of a contemporary kind. These are the topics around which ethnographic methods will be developed in the next twenty years. The classic empirical areas will still be studied, but the scholarly gaze will also be focused on these developing areas.

REFERENCES

Deegan, M.J. (1987) *Jane Addams and the Men of the Chicago School, 1890–1918.* New Brunswick, NJ: Transaction Books.

McRobbie, A. and Garber, J. (1976) 'Girls and subcultures', in S. Hall and T. Jefferson (eds), *Resistance through Rituals.* London: Hutchinson.

12

The Ethnography of Health and Medicine

MICHAEL BLOOR

Like other contributions to this volume, this chapter views ethnography as a broad field. Studies that involve an immersing participation in the lives of others are deemed ethnographic for the purposes of this chapter, even if the main form of data collection was not observation. If we take, for example, Williams' (1990) careful study of the health beliefs of the elderly citizens of the Scottish city of Aberdeen, he went well beyond the collection of conventional, one-time interviews. Over many months, he interviewed seventy respondents drawn from two social circles (snowballing from a retirement club in a middle-class district and from a pensioners' association on a working-class estate), with many of his respondents interviewed more than once; he participated in older people's social events, called socially on more than half of his respondents (and indeed saw some key informants on several occasions) and even developed his Scottish Fiddle technique through repeated home instruction from one willing respondent. Given the barriers of convention against any extended observation of respectable Scottish households, no researcher could have done more to develop an ethnographic account of the health beliefs of this group of people that would also be consonant with their notions of douce reticence and household privacy.

It is not the case that observational studies of health and illness behaviour are wholly lacking in developed societies, but those studies that have been conducted have often been observations of everyday health and illness within non-medical institutions, for example, observational studies of illness behaviour in the school (Prout, 1986), in the workplace (Bellaby, 1990) and in a common lodging house (Bloor, 1985). Neither street ethnographies nor community studies have normally had health as a generic focus, although some specific aspect of health and illness – such as drug use (Preble and Casey, 1969), or burial customs (Vallee, 1955), or drinking patterns (Wight, 1993) – may sometimes be a central topic of analysis. Estroff's (1981) study of deinstitutionalized chronically ill mental patients, which ranged over treatment settings, community settings and patients' homes, perhaps comes closest to the goal of a community ethnography with health as a generic topical focus. Most ethnographic studies have, of course, taken place in treatment settings, with a focus on medical decision-making, or training, or patient behaviour, or interprofessional relationships. An overview of ethnographies of health and illness in developing societies is outside the scope of this handbook, despite their inspirational impact on many ethnographies in developed societies.

A thematic treatment of medical ethnographies has been preferred as a principle of organization to classification by topic, although it is recognized that the corpus of medical ethnography contains a number of studies (Goffman's (1961) *Asylums*, Becker and his colleagues' (1961) *Boys in White*) with a fame and influence far beyond the boundaries of medical sociology, and icons are resistant to any classification. Four themes have been identified: first, the theme of symbolic interactions in medical institutions; secondly, that of the socially constructed character of professional medical categories; thirdly, that of the experience of illness and the sociology of the body; and fourthly, that of the contemporary challenges facing medical ethnography – the challenges of postmodern fragmentation, of policy relevance, and of the revolt of the subject. This division has the disadvantage that the topics of professional socialization, regulation and interprofessional practice are only viewed from the perspective of institutional interactions or medical decision-making. A synoptic approach has been aimed for; comprehensive[1] coverage is beyond the scope of this Handbook and beyond the reach of this author.

SYMBOLIC INTERACTIONS IN MEDICAL INSTITUTIONS

Early 1960s ethnographies in medical settings were concerned largely with the topics of professional socialization (such as *Boys in White*), or the experience of patienthood (such as *Asylums*), or the doctor–patient relationship (for example, Roth's classic 1963 study of bargaining over the treatment timetable in a TB sanatorium). Although many of the early medical ethnographers were Chicago-trained, their principles of methodological conduct owed relatively little to the prewar urban ethnographies of the Chicago School (see Atkinson and Hammersley, 1994), but they did share a theoretical background in Chicagoan symbolic interactionism. It is arguable that the interactionists' *theoretical* concern with emergent meanings and everyday work as a practical accomplishment was a more potent influence on the conduct of 1960s ethnographies than 1920s and 1930s ethnographic *methods*: symbolic interactionist theory became a template for symbolic interactionist methods. Symbolic interactionism likewise influenced the topical foci of those early medical ethnographies. Thus, social organizations were conceived, not as structures, but as sites of interactions between individuals and groups, ordered by fluid and provisional negotiations between those individuals and groups – the hospital as a negotiated order (Strauss et al., 1963; see Dingwall and Strong, 1985 for an overview of this approach). Likewise, medical work was seen largely as a matter of medical conduct – the professional worker in interaction with peers and laity (although Strauss and colleagues attempted a more task-centred formulation of medical work in later years – Strauss et al., 1985). And the experience of illness was seen as mediated through social action, shaped by the sufferers' dealings with treatment agencies and fellow-patients, as in Goffman's depiction of the moral career of the mental patient (Goffman, 1961).

Choosing one study as an exemplar of the strengths of this type of medical ethnography is naturally invidious, but Strong's (1979) study of pediatric outpatient consultations was written late enough to incorporate a mature understanding of earlier symbolic interactionist work in medical institutions. Drawing on observations of over a thousand clinic consultations in three hospitals in the UK and the United States, Strong used Goffman's frame analysis (Goffman, 1975) to understand how these complex clinic interactions were smoothly accomplished. Most clinic consultations unfolded within a 'bureaucratic role format' where doctor and parent adopted complementary roles to produce collaboratively a ceremonial clinic order: clinicians acted with courtly gentility to idealize mothers and find appropriate excuses for their seeming misdemeanours and shortcomings, while parents idealized the competence of the clinicians, ignoring previous lapses and blunders; yet each party to the consultation would seek to manipulate the frame to their own advantage, albeit with more medical than parental success.

Strong's analysis of interactions between physicians and parents was paralleled by other studies reporting on medical encounters across the divides of ethnicity, class, age and gender, with studies of gender in medical consultations being particularly well represented (see West, 1993). Similarly, ethnographers described the conduct of many different occupational groups found in medical settings from clinical psychologists (Rushing, 1964) to hospital kitchen workers (Paterson, 1981), with studies of nursing, psychiatric nursing, midwifery and health visiting being particularly well represented: early ethnographic studies of the training of nurses and allied professionals (Dingwall, 1977; Olesen and Whittaker, 1968) contributed largely to the sociology of work and occupations as well as to the sociology of health and illness.

Despite the work of Strong and others in showing the limitations of patient influence, the interactionists' topical focus on social interaction in medical settings was thought by some to be distortive, for example, in a lack of attention to constraint and coercion in organizational relationships (Maines, 1977). And, less obviously, the selective attention to particular study settings inadvertently influenced general understandings of medical practice and illness behaviour. So, for example, it was an accidental or incidental circumstance that much early sociological documentation of doctor–patient interaction related to long-stay hospital patients, well-schooled by fellow patients and highly committed to influencing the course of their treatment either overtly (as where Roth's (1963) TB patients might threaten to discharge themselves if their treatment timetable was not accelerated) or covertly (as where Braginsky et al.'s (1969) long-stay schizophrenic patients were able indirectly to influence psychiatric assessments of their fitness for transfer to an open ward or their unfitness for discharge). As a consequence, some early medical sociology texts probably overemphasized the extent to which many routine medical consultations assumed a negotiated character: in the great majority of primary care consultations (such as in British General Practice) it is unlikely to be a relevant pursuit for patients to exercise overt or covert influence on their consultation outcome, unless their expectations of the routine character of the consultation prove unfounded (Bloor and Horobin, 1975).

In recent years the equation in early ethnographies of medical work with medical conduct has been a focus of particular criticism (Atkinson, 1995; Berg, 1992): it is suggested that the focus on social action has left unexamined the central, cognitive aspects of medical work; this issue is discussed in more detail in the next section. Another recent and more thoroughgoing criticism relates to the epistemological position of ethnographic work. Mere direct observation has always been recognized as no guarantee of understanding. An extended example of spiralling misinterpretation by an observer is to be found in the autobiography of the nineteenth-century anarchist revolutionary Prince Peter Kropotkin, who chanced to come across the damning account by a government agent of his own (Kropotkin's) journey from Paris to London: the most sinister interpretation is put upon Kropotkin's chance befriending of a monoglot Greek Orthodox priest unable to make himself understood in the Calais station buffet; Kropotkin's kind offer to the priest that he travel with Kropotkin's party compounded the agent's misplaced suspicions, since the party conversed throughout the journey in Russian – a language seemingly chosen for security in a crowded carriage; finally, the agent records that, on their arrival in London, the party delayed their departure from the station until all their fellow-travellers had left in the hope that their destination would be unobserved – Kropotkin comments that they were expecting to be met at the station, but when no one arrived to meet them they eventually made their own way to their lodgings (Kropotkin, 1899: 288–91). To guard against such misunderstandings, ethnographers have stressed that ethnographic practice entails not just prolonged and careful observation, but also Weberian empathy with research subjects – 'close-in contact with far-out lives' (Geertz, 1988: 6). The epistemological basis for ethnography is hermeneutics, with its concern for immersive understanding; the methodological basis for ethnography is an obsessive concern with the relationship between observer and observed. But it has been suggested that this quest for immersive understanding is a form of essentialism, an attempt to apprehend an authentic reality behind the veil of forms and appearances. This ethnographic quest for authenticity is equated by critics with the Romantic movement in nineteenth-century art, literature and music and is seen as a quest for the unattainable (Silverman, 1989). Medical ethnographies, in this reading, cannot tell eager medical professionals what their reticent patients 'really' feel, think and aspire to: there is no final, authentic reality awaiting ethnographic revelation. This is a topic to be revisited in the final section of this chapter.

Although late-modern ethnography is under challenge, some of the early medical ethnographies have been highly influential in social science, clinical practice and public policy: vivid sociological reports of the everyday life of long-stay psychiatric patients combined in a strange alliance with radical psychiatrists like R.D. Laing and with proponents of new pharmacological treatments to undermine the intellectual credibility of residential psychiatric care at a time when funders were simultaneously seeking to find ways of cutting the costs of residential services provision – and the outcome in the UK was the mishmash of community psychiatric care (Sedgwick, 1982). On the whole, however, these early medical ethnographies probably had a stronger impact on professional practice than on public policy. Ethnographers, like researchers using other qualitative methods, sought to represent the viewpoints of their research subjects and the centre of their practice was what Lincoln and Denzin, in their own contribution to their celebrated *Handbook of Qualitative Research* identified as a 'humanistic commitment' (Lincoln and Denzin, 1994: 575). This humanistic commitment to authentic representation made the end-products of ethnographic research less readily assimilated by health services managers and policy-makers, who sought to weigh the comparative efficiency and effectiveness of different services. As a consequence, professional practitioners might value ethnography and use its insights to modify their everyday practices (see Bloor, 1997), but policy-makers have preferred quantitative data which offered (seemingly) more clear-cut criteria for executive action.

This policy marginalization of ethnography has been unfortunate, but it has also been unjust, since ethnographic data may serve to qualify policy judgements based on quantitative research. Take for example the question of whether hospice care should be routinely available for dying patients, or whether dying patients may be adequately accommodated on general hospital wards. A Californian randomized controlled trial (RCT) was conducted of hospice care and care of the dying on general hospital wards, with dying patients being randomly allocated to hospice or ward (Kane et al., 1984). The results were unequivocal: on measure after measure (cost, pain relief, reported symptoms, survival time, therapeutic procedures undertaken, activities of daily living) the hospice performed no better (and sometimes worse) than the hospital ward. Only on one measure, patient satisfaction, did the hospice clearly out-perform the ward: even carers were little more likely to be satisfied with the hospice care than with the care their spouse or relative received on the ward. The authors of the study were therefore cautious about the spread of expensive hospice facilities, where they seemed to convey so little extra benefit. However, a Canadian ethnographic study comparing hospice and hospital terminal care, where the researcher disguised himself as a terminally ill patient (Buckingham et al., 1976), was able to highlight a number of features of the hospice and hospital regimes which were sources of patient satisfaction with the hospice and dissatisfaction with the hospital. For example, in the hospice, staff would talk at length to patients on a one-to-one basis, sitting on the patient's bed; in the ward, clinicians would typically speak to their patients only on their ward rounds, standing by the bedside and surrounded by other staff, and while nurses were prepared to interact individually with patients, the demands of high technology care else-where on the ward would make their bedside visits to dying patients brief and superficial. By seeking to report the experience of patienthood, Buckingham and colleagues were able to elucidate features of the greater quality of care experienced in the hospice which were inadequately conveyed by a simple summary measure of 'patient satisfaction' in the later RCT: the Canadian ethnography leads us to doubt the policy conclusions of the RCT, despite its 'gold standard' RCT methodology.[2]

THE SOCIAL CONSTRUCTION OF MEDICINE

With hindsight, the above early medical ethno-graphies were restricted in scope in that they did not address at all the topic of medical work, only the topic of medical conduct. From the social construc-tionist perspective, neither professional medical diagnoses nor lay diagnoses have a privileged epistemological status: they are arrived at by essen-tially similar routine processes of enquiry and inter-pretation, shaped by the purposes at hand and social interests of the enquiring subject. This approach to clinical science is Kuhnian, rather than Popperian (Kuhn, 1970). Medical diagnoses and prognoses are invested with professional authority and usually have a demonstrable pragmatic utility in the treat-ment of disease, but they are constituted by a process of social construction, amenable to socio-logical description and analysis. From the stand-point of Kuhnian sociology of science, it is not only the mistakes of medicine which are explicable through social science, but also the triumphs of pre-vailing clinical science (Latour, 1988).

A social science which takes for granted the truth status of medical judgements is likely to adopt the methods of social epidemiology, but a social con-structionist approach which problematizes medical judgements is likely to accord high status and prior-ity to the ethnographic observation of everyday medical practice and medical decision-making. Nevertheless, ethnographers were not the first to set out a broadly social constructionist approach to medical work: the first such writings are probably those of the philosopher of science and eminent pathologist, Lester King (1954), writing out of the same philosophical position, Jamesian pragmatism, as the sociologists of the Chicago School. Nor were ethnographers the popularizers of social construc-tionism in medical sociology: the laurels here

should probably go to Eliot Freidson's *Profession of Medicine* (Freidson, 1970). But there were a number of ethnographic studies of medical work in the 1960s and 1970s which emphasized the consti-tutive character of routine medical work practices.

One such early medical ethnography was Sudnow's *Passing On* (Sudnow, 1967), based on more than a year's fieldwork at two contrasting hospitals – 'County', a large charity hospital on the West Coast, and 'Cohen', a private general hospital in the Midwest. Sudnow described the operational procedures – major and minor, sober and absurd – surrounding hospital deaths. For example, the Catholic chaplain at County, while on his rounds of the wards, would consult an index file to discover which Catholic patients on the ward had been newly 'posted' on the 'critical patients list' (posted patients were identifiable by the red plastic border placed on their index cards). The chaplain would duly admini-ster extreme unction to each newly posted patient and then would return to the index file to stamp the index card of the patient with a rubber stamp:

Last Rites Administered

Date_____ Clergyman_____

Sudnow dryly but correctly remarked that 'his stamp serves to prevent him from performing the rites twice on the same patient' (Sudnow, 1967: 73). The ethno-grapher's objective here was to produce a *procedural* definition of dying, a description of the social proce-dures which constituted death for hospital personnel. Sudnow borrowed the term 'social death' from the chair of his dissertation committee at Berkeley, Erving Goffman, to depict how an institutionally organized death differs from 'clinical death' or 'bio-logical death'. Social death may have preceded clinical death, as where two resident physicians at County discussed together the forthcoming autopsy at the bed of the dying patient, or where a nurse routinely attempted to close the eyelids of dying patients *prior* to death, for the convenience of the orderlies or aides who would later come to wrap the corpse (Sudnow, 1967: 74). Social death was an organizational category which oriented the work of clinicians, nurses, morgue attendants, chaplains and others and which was associated with a number of routine procedures, which in turn structured the experience of dying: the sub-title of *Passing On* is *The Social Organization of Dying* – formal and infor-mal hospital procedures do not influence the process of dying, they *constitute* dying in the hospital.

This interest in everyday organizational practices certainly represented a broadening of focus from earlier work. Nevertheless, early social construc-tionist studies still left the topic of clinical medical work largely unaddressed (Atkinson, 1995). Just as Sudnow focused on 'social death' rather than 'clinical death', so Sudnow's ethnographer-contemporaries have tended to leave aside the processes of clinical examination, interpretation and disposal, an omission the more surprising when it is considered that philosophers of science have continued to make everyday medical thinking a topic of philosophical investigation (King, 1982). Berg (1992) was able to point to earlier isolated examples of ethnographies of clinical medical work (for example, Bloor, 1976) but argued that it was developments in the sociology of scientific knowledge in the 1980s that provided the intellectual basis for subsequent ethnographies of medical work. Berg drew on ethnographic studies of laboratories investigating scientific knowledge in the making (Fujimura, 1987; Knorr Cetina, 1981; Latour and Woolgar, 1986) to describe how physicians in everyday clinical practice constructed medical disposals, using data collected by two years' participant observation as a house officer (an extraordinary achievement, given all the various pressures to which junior doctors are subject). Just as laboratory scientists arrive at scientific knowledge through practical reasoning and collegial negotiations rather than through universal rules, so also Berg's physicians arrived at medical disposal decisions through following time-tested 'routines', or recipes for action, which supplied a framework that delineated what was proper action and what was not – following routines makes the disposal decision 'obvious'. Medical work, from this perspective, is not a careful, exhaustive and processual collection of a range of evidence (history, clinical signs, test results), followed by a weighing of competing explanations to arrive at a diagnosis, followed by further investigations to explore different possible disposals. Indeed, no practical distinction between diagnosis and treatment is possible, as routines lead physicians to an image of the patient's disorder which automatically indicates the appropriate disposal.

Berg's physicians were practising in group settings and collegial interactions were a fundamental aspect of many medical routines: as the old joke has it, hospitals are places where the clinical professions go to talk about patients. An increasingly important strand of social constructionist analyses of medical practice has been the analysis of medical talk: not analyses of professional interactions with patients (as in symbolic interactionist studies of medical conduct), but analyses of inter-professional and intra-professional interactions which establish consensual images of patients' difficulties and appropriate treatment responses. These collegial interactions are the focus of Atkinson's (1995) ethnography of an American hospital haematology service,[3] appropriately entitled *Medical Talk and Medical Work*. Drawing on audio-recordings of weekly lunchtime review conferences and particularly of daily 'rounds' – not the walking tours of the wards found in UK hospitals, but office gatherings of little groups of haematologists of varying degrees of seniority – Atkinson shows how junior physicians

and medical students had to deploy rhetorical skills to pass as clinically competent in the judgement of their seniors and their peers: they had to present the cumulative work of clinical investigation, laboratory tests and radiographic imaging in the form of convincing accounts of the patient's condition, justifying past actions and current plans. But there is more going on during these 'rounds' than the production of convincing accounts. In a memorable passage, Atkinson also analyses a long transcript extract of a conversation between a senior 'Attending' physician and a student sharing a single microscope with multiple eye-pieces: the senior guides the seeing of the junior as they both observe a blood smear; the extract displays 'the oral transmission of the craft skill of recognition' (Atkinson, 1995: 78), but it also shows how both parties come to share the same view of the object they are observing, how intersubjective understanding is practically accomplished. This conversation at the microscope is an exemplar of how the product of these collegial meetings is a shared, sometimes negotiated, sometimes jointly constituted, case-picture. Medical talk produces the object of medical work.

A leading American ethnographer of medical talk has been Jay Gubrium, beginning with his 1975 analysis of care planning conferences for nursing home residents (Gubrium, 1975, 1980). In his co-authored analysis of professional descriptions of care in a physical rehabilitation unit (Gubrium and Buckholdt, 1982), Gubrium and his collaborator showed how patients' rehabilitation was framed quite differently for different audiences. In working with patients, hospital staff described clinical activity in educational terms: patients were told that staff could not cure, they could only teach patients how to minimize their handicaps – successful rehab was as much about patient motivation as about clinical intervention. In contrast, communications with medical insurers reinterpreted patient progress as a product of successful medical management rather than of patient motivation. And in communications with patients' families, staff would ascribe successes to clinical intervention and lack of progress to poor patient motivation or inadequate learning. The meaning of rehabilitation thus depends crucially on the framings of communicative activity; consensual images of patients may be elaborated within a local organizational culture (as in Atkinson's rounds), but they are then diversely and selectively recast for different outside audiences in the promotion of service policy (Gubrium, 1989).

THE LIVED EXPERIENCE OF ILLNESS
AND THE SOCIOLOGY OF THE BODY

As Charmaz and Olesen (1997) have pointed out, early ethnographic studies of chronic illness (such as Davis' (1963) study of child polio victims and their families) developed an alternative to the structuralist views of illness found in the work of Parsons (1953) and his successors. Those first studies on chronic illness were soon joined by many others: by studies of pain and suffering (for example, Basanger, 1989); by a wealth of feminist analyses of women's experiences of illness, of patienthood and of gendered strategic relationships between doctors and patients (see, for example, Fisher, 1986, and Todd, 1989); and by a smaller number of studies of the health and illness experiences of ethnic minorities (for example, Ong, 1995). It would be naive to claim that these studies gave voice to the silenced, as if ethnographers were mere transparent vessels or mouthpieces, but they certainly undermined the dominance of physician discourses on health and illness and offered a social science alternative to psychological interpretations of patients' behaviours. In emphasizing, for example, the social meanings that drug injectors attached to the sharing of needles and syringes as emblematic of intimacy and trust (as in Howard and Borges' (1970) now-celebrated, pre-AIDS ethnography of drug use in Haight-Ashbury), ethnographers drew attention to the *situated rationality* of illness behaviour and risk behaviour, in contrast to discourses that portrayed such behaviour as irrational, ignorant or pathological. Moreover, as Charmaz and Olesen (1997) have also pointed out, these ethnographic studies of the lived experience of illness pre-figured a new sociology of the body.

The object of all professional clinical work from obstetrics to pathology, from childbirth to postmortem, is the patient's body. Indeed, the paradigm shift that marks the foundation of modern medicine is the movement towards the objectification of the patient's body under the 'clinical gaze', first found in the Paris *cliniques* at the end of the eighteenth century (Foucault, 1973). Foucault's followers have argued that a sociology of the body should be at the centre of sociological theorizing, since the body is the focus of the rationalizing disciplines of modernity and late modernity. The previously discussed ethnographies of professional medical work are therefore understandable as ethnographies of how the body is 'read' authoritatively and collectively, through history-taking, examination, lab testing, X-ray reading and other procedures (see, for example, Atkinson, 1995: 60–89). However, very few recent ethnographies have taken 'bodywork' as their central focus. Indeed, one of the surprising features of the recent literature on the sociology of the body is how the tide of complaint about the claimed 'disembodied' nature of sociology rises from a literature that is itself overwhelmingly theoretical and/or textual. Two significant exceptions are Lawler's very accessible ethnography of Australian nurses' body care work (Lawler, 1991) and Monaghan's recent ethnography of South Wales bodybuilders (Monaghan, 1999): Lawler deals with the intimate work which nurses undertake on the privatized body – not least their responses to the sexuality of male patients – and shows how body care work is a practical accomplishment which is simultaneously invisible, neither a topic for social discourse nor nursing knowledge; and Monaghan shows how experienced bodybuilders become ethnophysiologists, lay experts in the training, nutritional and pharmacological regimens required for the project of shaping their bodies to the standards of the bodybuilding subculture (giving a new, literal twist to the phrase 'the social construction of the body').

CONTEMPORARY CHALLENGES TO MEDICAL ETHNOGRAPHY

Three challenges are of particular note – the epistemological challenge of postmodernism, the challenge of policy relevance and the challenge posed by the revolt of the subject. None of these difficulties is unique to ethnographic work in health and medicine, but they have been posed in this field with particular acuteness.

In respect of the last of these challenges, the revolt of the subject, this has been acutely felt in studies of health and illness: persons with disabilities, for example, have questioned whether researchers without disabilities have the capacity to conduct disability research (cf. Oliver, 1996). However, ethnographers have generally been better placed than health and illness researchers using other methods to respond to the concerns of research subjects, pre-sensitized by the ethnographer's perennial concern over fieldwork relationships. The very term 'research subjects' has an old-fashioned ring to it, as many ethnographers now signal the involvement of those research subjects in all stages of the research process by a preference for the term 'research participants'. While the utility of early group meetings with research subjects has long been recognized for securing research access, project steering groups with research subject representation are now a commonplace exercising oversight of a project from beginning to end, and many ethnographers make special provision for the early feedback of results to their research subjects (sometimes with disastrous results – cf. Emerson and Pollner's (1988) account of the feedback process in their ethnography of the work of psychiatric emergency teams). This incorporation of research subjects in the research process is often given institutional legitimization by funding agencies and medical research ethics committees. Epstein (1996) has provided an empirical account of the incorporation of AIDS activists into the research process.

As noted earlier, the main epistemological underpinning of ethnography has been found in hermeneutic philosophy. Ethnographic *verstehen* is the product of an engagement with a culture, of the immersion of the ethnographer in a 'form of life', and guarantees of the observer's understanding are to be found partly in analytic techniques to avoid selective attentiveness and partly in a reflexive concern with the relationship between researcher and research subjects. This pursuit of immersive understanding should not to be conflated with the quest for an essentialist authenticity. From a phenomenological standpoint, the intersubjectivity of observer and observed is a social accomplishment of the 'natural attitude', a provisional and unexamined assumption which makes social interaction possible; it is not a merging of minds. And the trust between ethnographer and collectivity member is similarly a social accomplishment, subject to disruption and re-examination; it is not an indissoluble bond.

However, the ethnographer's understanding of the problematics of fieldwork has only been proof against one kind of epistemological challenge. The postmodern epistemological challenge concerns not the relationship between observer and observed, but the relationship between the ethnographer–author and the ethnographic text. Foucault (1979), Geertz (1988) and Latour (1987), all from rather different premises, have argued that scientific writings convince as texts partly because of the impact of the author's 'signature' – idiosyncratic devices of vocabulary, rhetoric and the organization of an argument. This challenge to the verisimilitude of ethnography is particularly acute in the fields of health and medicine, because medical ethnographers so frequently work cheek-by-jowl with clinical scientists operating in the positivist scientific tradition. Evidence-based medicine has, for the most part, moved towards a cautious acceptance of qualitative research, where that qualitative research adheres to rigorous, explicit standards of data collection and analysis. But scientific medicine boggles at the suggestion that the verisimilitude of ethnography rests, not on scientific procedures alone, but crucially on authorly discursive practices.

If there is any remedy for this postmodern challenge it lies not in quietly ignoring the discursive character of ethnographic writing, nor yet in abandoning ethnography for the study of texts, but in an embracing awareness of the literary discursive character of ethnographic writings, a reflexive awareness of the relationship with the page as well as with the research subject (Atkinson, 1992). There is, of course, nothing very new in such a remedy: after all, Scott Fitzgerald began *The Beautiful and the Damned* (first published in 1922) with a short (and very late-modern) disquisition on irony and the need for his main character to live with his ironic knowledge and be 'a man who was aware that there could be no honor and yet had honor, who knew the sophistry of courage and yet was brave' (Fitzgerald, 1966: 9). Ethnographic authorship

must retain a commitment to veracious description and systematic method alongside a reflexive awareness of the ethnopoetics of scholarship. What is perhaps surprising is that so much autobiographical information is so often suppressed in ethnographic writing, when the very scientific methods used lean so heavily on personal experience: what Geertz calls 'author-evacuated texts' (Geertz, 1988: 9) seem to be a wilful aberration that could be abandoned with relief.

The challenge of policy relevance cannot be entirely disentangled from the toils of epistemology, since policy-makers are unlikely to be impressed by findings they believe to be scientifically suspect. But the already-noted preference of policy-makers for quantitative studies over ethnography probably has more to do with the generalizability of ethnographic findings than issues of epistemology. There can be few areas of public policy formulation that are more influenced by scientific evidence than the area of health and medicine, and this receptiveness is likely to increase over time rather than diminish as 'evidence-based medicine' is promoted as a means of the rational deployment of scarce resources for maximum benefit to public health. But ethnography seems unlikely ever to play a large independent part in this evidence base while the representativeness of ethnographic work (invariably conducted in just one or two sites) remains problematic.

This impression is confirmed by policy studies. Thus, beginning with Becker's 'Becoming a Marihuana User' (Becker, 1953), there have been many valuable ethnographies of drug use; ethnography has proved its worth as a method able uniquely to access the subcultures of drug use and, for example, to document the social contexts in which HIV-related risk behaviour occurs. In addition, public policy on drug use has undergone a profound change since the early 1980s in many European countries and in Australasia and Canada: 'harm reduction' policies, such as syringe exchanges and methadone maintenance schemes, have been adopted as policy alternatives to zero tolerance 'war on drugs' policies. But Berridge's analysis of changes in British drugs policies in response to the HIV/AIDS epidemic (Berridge, 1996, 1998) shows only a marginal role for ethnographic research in the shaping of policies. While Berridge points out that the UK government's main advisory body on drugs policy, the Advisory Council on Drugs Misuse, accepted in 1982 the longstanding sociological view of the 'normality' of drug use, the crucial research evidence on harm minimization was provided by a controlled trial of oral methadone prescribing (Berridge and Thom, 1996), and the introduction of pilot syringe exchange schemes in 1987 was accompanied by newly commissioned quantitative evaluative research. In America, methadone treatments are widely available, but syringe exchanges remain illegal in most states and the use of federal funds for syringe exchanges is prohibited; ethnographic research has been funded as part of the National Institute on Drug Abuse's AIDS intervention programmes and ethnographers' findings have contributed to the design and re-design of local demonstration outreach programmes to drug users, but ethnography's part has remained a comparatively small one in the mixed economy of US research on social aspects of AIDS (Wiebel, 1996).

As stated earlier, practitioners have often been a more responsive audience for ethnographic findings than policy-makers. Practitioners working in the fields of health and illness have the professional autonomy to modify their everyday work practices in response to research findings and ethnographies of everyday professional practice may have such rich descriptions of everyday practice that practitioner audiences are able imaginatively to juxtapose their own everyday practices with the research description. Some ethnographic work on therapeutic communities has contributed to practice changes in this way (Bloor, 1997; Bloor et al., 1988). These processes of practitioner influence follow closely traditional processes of policy influence – 'the Enlightenment model' (Hammersley, 1995) – but other kinds of relationships are also possible between ethnography and practitioner practice. Thus, Shaw (1996) has argued that qualitative methods can provide a paradigm or exemplar for practitioners seeking to reflect upon and modify their work practices. More radically, street ethnographers have sometimes opted for a dual role of both researcher and service provider, both street ethnographer and outreach worker (cf. Broadhead and Fox, 1990, on ethnography and drugs outreach; McKeganey and Barnard, 1996, on ethnography and prostitution outreach). And street ethnographers have also increased the policy relevance of their research by opting for a dual research role. Thus, McKeganey and Barnard's (1996) street prostitution ethnography, not only functioned in addition as an outreach project providing free condoms and syringes, it also functioned additionally as an epidemiological study: anonymous saliva samples were collected from research subjects for HIV prevalence estimation; and the size of the street prostitution population was estimated using a variant of mark–recapture techniques, whereby the size of the hidden (uncontacted) population is estimated by plotting the changing ratio of new to repeat fieldwork contacts over the fieldwork period (McKeganey et al., 1992, 1993).

CONCLUSION

Despite a number of classic studies, medical ethnographies as a group exhibit no distinctive theoretical or methodological features. Indeed, early studies

borrowed much from the sociology of work and occupations and from the sociology of deviance, while many later studies have been indebted to feminist studies and to the sociology of scientific knowledge. However, the field of health and medicine is one which is particularly rich in ethnographic studies. This may be due in part to funding opportunities and due in part, no doubt, to the patronage of a medical profession which has been sufficiently secure in prestige and authority to seek evidence of good and bad professional performance and unmet medical need. But the enormous volume of medical research ensures that medical ethnographies will remain highly marginal to clinical practice while constituting a significant fraction of all ethnographic research. Marginality of course has its advantages as well as its disadvantages.

Recent studies of topics such as risk behaviour and the conduct of scientific work have ensured that medical ethnographies have contributed prominently to contemporary sociological theory, although the scarcity of ethnographic studies of body work is surprising. Medical ethnography contains many examples of imaginative responses to the challenge of policy relevance. Concerns about the implications of viewing ethnographic writing as a set of discursive practices have perhaps been slower to surface, but a developing reflexive awareness of the tools of the narrative craft should ensure the continuing theoretical relevance of medical ethnographic research.

For reasons that should now be obvious, I feel it is appropriate to end this overview with a bit of autobiography. In the summer of 1969 I was about to start a newly constituted postgraduate course in medical sociology at the Medical Research Council's Medical Sociology Unit, then located in Aberdeen, Scotland. But I had still to graduate from Cambridge, because the authorities wisely declined to process would-be graduates until they had paid their college bills. So I spent that summer working double shifts as a bus conductor, paying off my debts. Having next-to-no advance knowledge of medical sociology, I dutifully bought the recommended text, Mechanic's (1968) *Medical Sociology*, as preparatory reading. I am inclined now to lay the blame on the noisome atmosphere of the Derby Corporation Omnibus Department canteen, a place as conducive to study as a First World War trench during a gas attack, where even *Kidnapped* or *Lucky Jim* would seem less than compelling. But, whatever the reason, those reports of studies of 'the inclination to adopt the sick role', and the rest, failed to charm. I wondered if I was making a big mistake and, if I had possessed any career prospects outside the Omnibus Department, I might never have travelled north to Aberdeen in the autumn.

Needless to say, gentle reader, on my arrival at the Medical Sociology Unit and the Aberdeen Sociology Department all my doubts were dispelled. I found a group of staff enthused by a flood of new

American symbolic interactionist and ethnomethodo-logical studies and texts. Goffman's *Asylums* had just been reprinted by Penguin and after that I quickly consumed the unit library's copies of other 1960s hospital ethnographies – *Boys in White, Psychiatric Ideologies and Institutions, Passing On, Timetables*. Eliot Freidson was editor of the *Journal of Health and Social Behavior* and publishing street ethnographies like Davis and Munoz's (1968) 'Heads and freaks: patterns of meaning of drug use among hippies'; Freidson's *Profession of Medicine*, his overview of a social constructionist approach to health and medicine, was published during my post-graduate year.

My path was set. And if I trace an element of continuity in medical ethnographies over the past thirty years, this is hardly surprising, since I am tracing what I fondly suppose to be my own intel-lectual development.

NOTES

1 For a lengthy overview which is as near-comprehensive as any reader has a right to expect, see Charmaz and Olesen (1997).

2 I am grateful to Clive Seale for pointing out how Buckingham's ethnography and the Californian RCT could be felicitously juxtaposed.

3 Atkinson also conducted a limited amount of parallel observation of UK haematologists.

REFERENCES

Atkinson, P. (1992) *Understanding Ethnographic Texts*. London and Newbury Park, CA: Sage.

Atkinson, P. (1995) *Medical Talk and Medical Work*. London and Thousand Oaks, CA: Sage.

Atkinson, P. and Hammersley, M. (1994) 'Ethnography and participant observation', in N. Denzin and Y. Lincoln (eds), *Handbook of Qualitative Research*. London and Thousand Oaks, CA: Sage. pp. 248–61.

Basanger, I. (1989) 'Pain: its experience and treatment', *Social Science and Medicine*, 29: 425–34.

Becker, H.C. (1953) 'Becoming a marihuana user', *American Journal of Sociology*, 59: 235–42.

Becker, H.C., Greer, B., Hughes, E.C. and Strauss, A.L. (1961) *Boys in White: Student Culture in Medical School*. Chicago: University of Chicago Press.

Bellaby, P. (1990) 'To risk or not to risk? Uses and limi-tations of Mary Douglas on risk acceptability for under-standing health and safety at work and road accidents', *Sociological Review*, 38: 465–83.

Berg, M. (1992) 'The construction of medical disposals. Medical sociology and medical problem solving in clini-cal practice', *Sociology of Health and Illness*, 14: 151–80.

Berridge, Virginia (1996) *AIDS in the UK: The Making of Policy, 1981–1984*. Oxford: Oxford University Press.

Berridge, V. (1998) 'AIDS and British drug policy', in M. Bloor and F. Wood (eds), *Addictions and Problem Drug Use: Issues in Behaviour, Policy and Practice*. Research Highlights in Social Work No. 33. London: Jessica Kingsley. pp. 85–106.

Berridge, V. and Thom, B. (1996) 'Research and policy: what determines the relationship?' *Policy Studies*, 17: 23–34.

Bloor, M. (1976) 'Bishop Berkeley and the adeno-tonsillectomy enigma: an exploration of variation in the social construction of medical disposals', *Sociology*, 10: 43–61. (Reprinted in M. Bloor (1997) *Selected Writings in Medical Sociological Research*. Aldershot: Ashgate.)

Bloor, M. (1978) 'On the routinised nature of work in people-processing agencies: the case of adenotonsil-lectomy assessments in ENT out-patient clinics', in A. Davis (ed.), *Relationships between Doctors and Patients*. Farnborough: Gower. pp. 29–47.

Bloor, M. (1985) 'Observations of abortive illness behav-iour', *Urban Life*, 14: 300–16. (Reprinted in M. Bloor (1997) *Selected Writings in Medical Sociological Research*. Aldershot: Ashgate.)

Bloor, M. (1997) 'Addressing social problems through qualitative research', in David Silverman (ed.), *Quali-tative Research: Theory, Method and Practice*. Thousand Oaks, CA: Sage. pp. 221–38.

Bloor, M. and Horobin, G. (1975) 'Conflict and conflict resolution in doctor–patient relationships', in C. Cox and A. Mead (eds), *A Sociology of Medical Practice*. London: Collier–Macmillan. pp. 271–84.

Bloor, M., McKeganey, N. and Fonkert, D. (1988) *One Foot in Eden: A Sociological Study of the Range of Therapeutic Community Practice*. London: Routledge.

Braginsky, B.M., Braginsky, D.D. and Ring, K. (1969) *Methods of Madness: The Mental Hospital as a Last Resort*. New York: Holt, Rinehart and Winston.

Broadhead, R. and Fox, K. (1990) 'Takin' it to the streets: AIDS outreach as ethnography', *Journal of Contem-porary Ethnography*, 19: 322–48.

Buckingham, R., Lack, S., Mount, B., MacLean, L. and Collins, J. (1976) 'Living with the dying: use of the technique of participant observation', *Canadian Medical Journal*, 115: 1211–15.

Charmaz, K. and Olesen, V. (1997) 'Ethnographic research in medical sociology', *Sociological Methods and Research*, 25: 452–94.

Davis, F. (1963) *Passage Through Crisis: Polio Victims and their Families*. Indianapolis: Bobbs–Merrill.

Davis, F. and Munoz, L. (1968) 'Heads and freaks: patterns and meanings of drug use among hippies', *Journal of Health and Social Behavior*, 9: 156–65.

Dingwall, R. (1977) *The Social Organisation of Health Visitor Training*. London: Croom Helm.

Dingwall, R. and Strong, P. (1985) 'The interactional study of organizations: a critique and a reformulation', *Urban Life*, 14: 205–31. (Republished in G. Miller and R. Dingwall (eds) (1997) *Context and Method in Qualitative Research*. London and Thousand Oaks, CA: Sage.)

Emerson, R. and Pollner, M. (1988) 'On the uses of members' responses to researchers' accounts', *Human Organization*, 47: 189–98.

Epstein, S. (1996) *Impure Science: AIDS, Activism and the Politics of Knowledge*. Berkeley, CA: University of California Press.

Estroff, S. (1981) *Making It Crazy: An Ethnography of Psychiatric Clients in an American Community*. Berkeley, CA: University of California Press.

Fisher, S. (1986) *In the Patient's Best Interest: Women and the Politics of Medical Decisions*. New Brunswick, NJ: Rutgers University Press.

Fitzgerald, F.S. ([1922] 1966) *The Beautiful and the Damned*. Harmondsworth: Penguin.

Foucault, M. (1973) *The Birth of the Clinic*. London: Tavistock.

Foucault, M. (1979) 'What is an author?', in J.V. Harari (ed.), *Textual Strategies*. Ithaca, NY: Cornell University Press.

Freidson, E. (1970) *Profession of Medicine*. New York: Dodds Mead. (Republished 1988 by University of Chicago Press.)

Fujimura, J. (1987) 'Constructing do-able problems in cancer research: articulating alignment', *Social Studies of Science*, 17: 257–93.

Geertz, C. (1988) *Work and Lives: The Anthropologist as Author*. Cambridge: Polity Press.

Goffman, E. (1961) *Asylums: Essays on the Social Situation of Mental Patients and Other Inmates*. New York: Doubleday.

Goffman, E. (1975) *Frame Analysis*. Harmondsworth: Penguin.

Gubrium, J. (1975) *Living and Dying at Murray Manor*. New York: St Martins Press.

Gubrium, J. (1980) 'Doing care plans in patient conferences', *Social Science and Medicine*, 14A: 659–67.

Gubrium, J. (1989) 'Local cultures and service policy', in D. Silverman (ed.), *The Politics of Field Research: Sociology Beyond Enlightenment*. London and Newbury Park, CA: Sage. pp. 94–112.

Gubrium, J. and Buckholdt, D. (1982) *Describing Care: Image and Practice in Rehabilitation*. Boston, MA: Oelgeschlager, Gunn and Hain.

Hammersley, M. (1995) *The Politics of Social Research*. London: Sage.

Howard, J. and Borges, P. (1970) 'Needle-sharing in the Haight: some social and psychological functions', *Journal of Health and Social Behavior*, 11: 220–30.

Kane, R.L., Wales, J., Bernstein, L., Leibowitz, A. and Kaplan, S. (1984) 'A randomised controlled trial of hospice care', *Lancet*, i: 890–4.

King, L. (1954) 'What is disease?', *Philosophy of Science*, 21: 193–203.

King, L. (1982) *Medical Thinking: A Historical Preface*. Princeton, NJ: Princeton University Press.

Knorr Cetina, K. (1981) *The Manufacture of Knowledge*. Oxford: Pergamon Press.

Kropotkin, Prince Peter (1899) *Memoirs of a Revolutionist*, vol. II. London: Smith, Elder & Co.

Kuhn, T. (1970) *The Structure of Scientific Revolutions*. Chicago: University of Chicago Press.

Latour, B. (1987) *Science in Action: How to Follow Scientists and Engineers through Society*. Milton Keynes: Open University Press.

Latour, B. (1988) *The Pasteurization of France*. Cambridge, MA: Harvard University Press.

Latour, B. and Woolgar, S. (1986) *Laboratory Life: The Construction of Scientific Facts*. Princeton, NJ: Princeton University Press.

Lawler, J. (1991) *Behind the Screens: Nursing, Somology and the Problem of the Body*. Edinburgh: Churchill Livingstone.

Lincoln, Y. and Denzin, N. (1994) 'The fifth moment', in N. Denzin and Y. Lincoln (eds), *Handbook of Qualitative Research*. Thousand Oaks, CA: Sage.

McKeganey, N. and Barnard, M. (1992) *AIDS, Drugs and Sexual Risk: Lives in the Balance*. Milton Keynes: Open University Press.

McKeganey, N. and Barnard, M. (1996) *Working on the Streets: Female Prostitutes and their Clients*. Milton Keynes: Open University Press.

McKeganey, N., Barnard, M. and Bloor, M. (1993) 'Estimating prostitute numbers: epidemiology out of ethnography', in Mary Boulton (ed.), *Methodological Advances in Behavioural Research on AIDS*. Brighton: Falmer Press.

McKeganey, N., Barnard, M., Leyland, A., Coote, I. and Follet, E. (1992) 'Female streetworking prostitution and HIV infection in Glasgow', *British Medical Journal*, 305: 801–4.

Maines, D. (1977) 'Social organization and social structure in symbolic interactionist thought', *Annual Review of Sociology*, 3: 235–59.

Mechanic, D. (1968) *Medical Sociology*. New York: The Free Press.

Monaghan, L. (1999) 'Creating "The Perfect Body": A Variable Project', *Body and Society*, 5: 267–90.

Olesen, V. and Whittaker, E. (1968) *The Silent Dialogue: The Social Psychology of Professional Socialization*. San Francisco: Jossey–Bass.

Oliver, M. (1996) *Understanding Disability: From Theory to Practice*. London: Macmillan.

Ong, A. (1995) 'Making the biopolitical subject: Cambodian immigrants, refugee medicine and cultural citizenship in California', *Social Science and Medicine*, 40: 1243–57.

Parsons, T. (1953) *The Social System*. New York: The Free Press.

Paterson, E. (1981) 'Food-work: maids in a hospital kitchen', in P. Atkinson and C. Heath (eds), *Medical Work: Realities and Routines*. Farnborough: Gower.

Preble, E. and Casey, J. (1969) 'Taking care of business: the heroin user's life on the street', *International Journal of the Addictions*, 4: 1–24.

Prout, A. (1986) '"Wet children" and "little actresses": a primary school's hidden curriculum of the sick role', *Sociology of Health and Illness*, 8: 111–36.

Roth, J. (1963) *Timetables*. New York: Bobbs–Merrill.

Rushing, W. (1964) *The Psychiatric Professions: Power, Conflict and Adaption in a Psychiatric Hospital Staff.* Chapel Hill, NC: University of North Carolina Press.

Sedgwick, P. (1982) *Psycho Politics*. London: Pluto Press.

Shaw, I. (1996) *Evaluating in Practice*. Aldershot: Ashgate.

Silverman, D. (1989) 'The impossible dreams of reformism and romanticism', in J. Gubrium and D. Silverman (eds), *The Politics of Field Research: Sociology beyond Enlightenment*. London and Newbury Park, CA: Sage. pp. 30–48.

Strauss, A.L., Fagerhaugh, S., Suczek, B. and Wiener, C. (1985) *Social Organisation of Medical Work*. Chicago: University of Chicago Press.

Strauss, A.L., Schatzman, L., Bucher, R., Ehrlich, D. and Sabshin, M. (1963) 'The hospital and its negotiated order', in Eliot Freidson (ed.), *The Hospital in Modern Society*. New York: The Free Press.

Strong, P. (1979) *The Ceremonial Order of the Clinic: Parents, Doctors and Medical Bureaucracies*. London: Routledge.

Sudnow, D. (1967) *Passing On: The Social Organization of Dying*. Englewood Cliffs, NL: Prentice–Hall.

Todd, A.D. (1989) *Intimate Adversaries: Cultural Conflict between Doctors and Women Patients*. Philadelphia: University of Pennsylvania Press.

Vallee, F. (1955) 'Burial and mourning customs in a Hebridean community', *Journal of the Royal Anthropological Institute*, 85: 119–31.

West, C. (1993) 'Reconceptualizing gender in physician–patient relationships', *Social Science and Medicine*, 36: 57–66.

Wiebel, W. (1996) 'Ethnographic contributions to AIDS intervention strategies', in T. Rhodes and R. Hartnoll (eds), *AIDS, Drugs and Prevention: Perspectives on Individual and Community Action*. London: Routledge.

Wight, D. (1993) *Workers not Wasters: Masculine Respectability, Consumption and Employment in Central Scotland*. Edinburgh: Edinburgh University Press.

Williams, R. (1990) *A Protestant Legacy: Attitudes to Death and Illness among Older Aberdonians*. Oxford: The Clarendon Press.

13

Ethnographic Research in Educational Settings

TUULA GORDON, JANET HOLLAND
AND ELINA LAHELMA

I sat in classes for days wondering what there was to 'observe'. Teachers taught, reprimanded, rewarded, while pupils sat at desks, squirming, whispering, reading, writing, staring into space, as they had in my own grade-school experience, in my practice teaching in a teacher-training program, and in the two years of public school teaching I had done before World War II. What should I write down in my empty note book?

(Spindler and Spindler, 1982: 24)

When American anthropologist Spindler started fieldwork in 1950 in West Coast elementary schools, he could not see the strangeness in the situation, because it was a mirror of his own cultural strangeness (Spindler and Spindler, 1982). For anthropologists, making the strange familiar is the usual task. But school is familiar for all of us and in opposition to the task of anthropological research in culturally remote settings, the task of a school ethnographer is to make the familiar strange (Delamont and Atkinson, 1995; Spindler and Spindler, 1982).

Definitions of ethnography vary. We regard ethnography in education as 'research on and in educational institutions based on participant observation and/or permanent recordings of everyday life in naturally occurring settings' (Delamont and Atkinson, 1995: 15). Ethnographic study requires 'direct observation, it requires being immersed in the field situation' (Spindler, 1982: 154) with the researcher as a major instrument of research. A range of data is collected – mostly qualitative, but also quantitative.

In educational ethnographic research, researchers are further implicated in their field, since they have usually themselves experienced schooling as a participant; issues of authenticity and authority are particularly poignant in ethnographic research (cf. Coffey, 1996).

Educational ethnography has its roots in cultural anthropology, and this tradition has been and still is strong in the research conducted in the United States, while the British tradition is in sociology of education. Delamont and Atkinson conducted a comparative review of research from the two traditions (Atkinson and Delamont, 1980; see also Delamont and Atkinson, 1995). They suggested that American anthropologists focused particularly on ethnic differences in classrooms, where teachers are agents of cultural imposition, whilst British sociologists were more interested in social class and structures that constrain both teachers and pupils. Smith (USA), in her introduction to Martyn Hammersley's (UK) book *Classroom Ethnography* (1990) 'was struck by the fact that Martyn and I both had been doing classroom ethnography for a couple of decades, but that we have been living in two different cultures if not worlds' (1990: 1).

In the United States, ethnographic methods became popular in educational research in the late 1970s, but Wolcott (1982) argued that this positive interest came from evaluators rather than educators. As an example he described the reception of his ethnographic research by head teachers (Wolcott, 1973). In the 1970s classroom research blossomed in Britain. Ethnographic work has also been conducted in Canada and Australia. An example of the growing interest in ethnographic research in other European countries in the 1990s is a European network *Ethnography in Education* and a Nordic network *Classroom Studies and Ethnography*. Research conducted in the Nordic and Central European countries is often hidden from the Anglophone mainstream through the language gap. Unfortunately, here we have also to limit our review to texts that are written in English.

Ethnographic research in educational settings has an intensive history of more than three decades in a number of countries, and, broadly defined, educational settings exist in a whole range of locations. Atkinson (1984) argued that much of the ethnographic research on educational settings has been concerned with students aged 7–16 in mainstream classes in state schools. This is still the case, although studies with other foci do exist. Ethnographic research with very young children has been sparse, and the lives of children have often been interpreted from adult perspectives, although for example Corsaro's (1981) research entered into the child's world and demonstrated the fragility of the social organization of peer interaction in the pre-school playground. Interesting work among very young school children took place in the 1990s from different methodological perspectives (Connolly, 1998; Davies, 1993; Thorne, 1993).

Ethnographers have studied adult education (Hammons-Bryner, 1995; Larsson, 1993; McFadden, 1996), teacher education (Beach, 1996; Hatton, 1997), postgraduate studies in universities (Delamont et al., 1997; Holland and Eisenhart, 1990), situational learning of university graduates during their first year of work in an organization (Coffey, 1996) and special schools, for example for teenage mothers (Holm, 1995). Atkinson (1984) conducted research on the bedside teaching of medical students, and compared this with teaching in school (Delamont and Atkinson, 1995). Schools have also been compared and contrasted for example with factory work (Foley, 1990).

Rather than using a thematic or discipline-based approach to structure our review, we have chosen a more analytical starting point. We have chosen what we see as the broad theoretical, conceptual and methodological approaches that have shaped the field. They fall under the headings: social interaction research, cultural studies, critical ethnography, feminism, studies that focus on difference and diversity, postmodern and poststructural ethnography and materialist approaches. The review draws predominantly on the UK literature, but includes material from North America, Australia and Europe. Where a work is seen as particularly important or influential it is described in some detail, but with such a wide field to cover, only brief reference can be made to most of the material. We have tried to read extensively but are aware that the choice of text is ours and there are lots of interesting and important studies that we have not included in this review.

SOCIAL INTERACTION

Much of the ethnographic educational research taking place in recent decades has its theoretical basis in social interaction studies influenced by ethnomethodology, phenomenology and symbolic interactionism. The main focus from this perspective is a concern for the creation and change of symbolic orders through social interaction (e.g. Silverman, 1993), and for understanding how people actually get through the day, the week and the year (Delamont and Atkinson, 1995). Woods (1996) defines the interactionist perspective in an educational context, highlighting a common feature of all teaching and learning situations as 'construction of meanings and perspectives, the adaptation to circumstances, the management of interests in the ebb and flow of countless interactions containing many ambiguities and conflicts, the strategies devised to promote those interests, and the negotiation with others' interests' (Woods, 1996: 7).

Although Jackson may not be classified as an interactionist or ethnographic researcher, his classic book *Life in Classrooms* (1968) has been widely used as an inspiration among interactionists. He argued that school is taken for granted: 'we simply note that our Johnny is on his way to school' (1968: 3), and tried to address some of the complexities of the life in classrooms. The book was a notable landmark in that it helped to legitimate and popularize the hidden curriculum as an area of study. In his book *The Divided School*, Woods' (1979) interest was in interpersonal relations and processes, within a social context linked to the wider social framework. His initial concern was with the broad questions: 'What do people do in school and what do they do to each other?' (1979: 8). He examined teacher strategies in guiding pupils into making 'right' choices, and concluded that school serves the interests of the stratified society, regardless of teachers' intentions.

The negative impact of streaming and different treatment of working-class boys was highlighted by the studies of Lacey (1970) and Hargreaves (1967), conducting their studies in boys schools. Lambart (1976) is exceptional in undertaking research on girls (in a grammar school) at this point. In *Beachside Comprehensive*, Ball (1981) took up the issue of class and asked what social mechanisms operating in schools can explain the disappointing performance of working-class pupils. Ball combined interactionist and structural perspectives to explore the social construction of pupils' identities and school careers in the process of educational innovation. His aim was to understand the school as a social system through the participants' own interpretations whilst analytically placing these in a wider social context, and so moving beyond those interpretations. In 1990 Hammersley reviewed the research by Hargreaves (1967), Lacey (1970) and

Ball (1981), suggesting that their work could be seen as a cumulative research programme, since they focus on interrelated theoretical ideas, although applying them in different settings. He considers this unique in sociology of education and calls the theory that lies at the heart of the work of Hargreaves, Lacey and Ball 'differentiation–polarization theory'. 'This theory claims that if pupils are differentiated according to an academic-behavioural standard, for example by being streamed or banded, their attitudes to that standard will become polarized. In particular, those given the lowest rankings will reject it and the values it embodies' (Hammersley, 1990: 104–5).

With a starting point in the classic texts, some common themes and important concepts have emerged in classroom research from an interactional perspective in recent decades. In this tradition, power in classrooms and other educational settings can be described as a process of negotiation (Delamont, 1976; Larsson, 1993). In classroom settings, the creation and the negotiation of the order-that-is-to-be (Davies, 1983) often takes place during the initial encounters of teachers and new students, and as a result, this period has been the focus of several ethnographic studies (e.g. Ball, 1984; Benyon, 1985; Davies, 1983; Delamont and Galton, 1986; Harris and Ruddock, 1993; Garpelin and Lindblad, 1994; Lahelma and Gordon, 1997; Larsson, 1993; Measor and Woods, 1984). Ball (1984) argued that it is not easy for a researcher to be able to observe or participate in these initial encounters, since teachers, not unreasonably, are reluctant to be observed at this stage. But the presence of the researcher is particularly useful, since in these initial encounters the investigator is in the same knowledge state as the participants, and rules, norms and procedures are more likely to be made explicit (Delamont and Galton, 1986). As Benyon (1985: 2) has argued, in initial encounters 'teachers cannot hide behind routines, they must establish them'.

The ORACLE-project (e.g. Delamont and Galton, 1986; Galton et al., 1980) was a series of interrelated studies on teaching and learning in primary classrooms and on transfer to secondary school. *Inside Secondary Classrooms* by Delamont and Galton (1986) discussed areas of ethnography that were relatively neglected at that time; for example, by focusing on issues such as 'danger', 'time', 'movement and immobility' they challenged the familiarity of the classroom. Delamont also published material from the ORACLE project in the book *Sex Roles and the School* (1980; second edition, 1990), which was a ground-breaking feminist text on the impact of gender in schooling.

In an early investigation of students' informal life in schools, Furlong (1976) studied girls in secondary school. He criticized the social psychological model of the study of school, in which the process of pupil interaction in the classroom is assumed to take place within the context of peer or friendship groups. He argued for an alternative understanding of classroom interaction, where the pupils are seen to be continually adjusting their behaviour to each other, and norms of behaviour are not consistent. His definition of interaction was where individuals come to a common definition of the situation, draw on similar commonsense knowledge, and make common assessments of appropriate action. In criticizing classroom interaction studies, Llewellyn (1980: 50) uses Furlong's research as an example; 'he neglects to incorporate into his analysis the crucial factor that the "pupils" he studied were girls and West Indian'.

Social interactionism has also examined processes of control in schools (cf. Denscombe, 1985). Wax and Wax (1971), for example, characterized schools as battlefields. In his essay on the organization of pupil participation based on research on an inner-city secondary modern school, Hammersley (1990) drew attention to the structure of interaction in the school in which the teacher demands and is accorded the right routinely to command, interpret and judge answers; this symbolizes and reinforces the teacher–pupil relationship as a superordinate–subordinate one. Students' resistance to, negotiation and challenge of this relationship, 'sussing out the teachers' (Benyon, 1985) is emphasized and even romanticized in several studies which we will discuss in the cultural studies section.

A long-term focus in ethnographic research has been on teachers and teaching. In the United States in the 1970s there was a concern to identify a good teacher (Leacock, 1971) stressing the use of ethnography for evaluation (Wolcott, 1982). In Britain, Woods conducted research with a focus on teachers in several projects. He emphasized the collaboration between researchers and teachers, because 'if educational improvement is to be made through research, it has to be done by teachers' (Woods, 1996: 10–11).

The effect of educational policies on teachers' work – for example the 1992 Education Act in England and the ideas of new technicist professionalism, as well as rationalization and standardization of teaching in the United States – has been investigated in several ethnographic studies (Ball and Bowe, 1992; Gillborn, 1994; Hargreaves, 1994; Mac an Ghaill, 1992; McNeill, 1986; Troman, 1996). The micro-politics of the school is highlighted when the importance of school responses to macro reforms is analysed (Ball, 1987; Gillborn, 1994). Troman (1996), for example, argued that he did not find a totally compliant workforce or the creation of a new form of technicist professionals in his study of a primary school, but professionals who both comply with some of the educational reforms which have restructured their work, and resist others; there is a 'strategy of resistance within accommodation' (1996: 485). But this kind of strategy is self-evidently not always possible. Gillborn's (1994) study highlighted the *multiple* factors involved in the implementation of the new policies in a single school.

The Richness of Interactionist and Ethnomethodological Perspectives

Approaches in classroom research that derive from linguistics and ethnomethodology are often linked to social interaction studies. Following Garfinkel (1967), 'ethnomethodology attempts to understand "folk" (ethno) methods (methodology) for organizing the world. It locates these methods in the skills ("artful practices") through which people come to develop an understanding of each other and of social situations' (Silverman, 1993: 60). Education researchers describe work influenced by ethnomethodology in different ways; for example, Mehan (1978) refers to 'constitutive ethnography' and Erickson and Mohatt (1982) write of a 'micro ethnographic' approach. Micro ethnography is concerned with the local and situated ecology obtaining among participants in face-to-face interactional engagements, constituting societal and historical experience (Garcez, 1997: 187). Common to these approaches is a resolute attention to detail, and the use of quantitative as well as qualitative data. Hammersley (1990: 93) argued that in classroom ethnography the concern of such approaches is in 'specifying the cultural resources used by teachers and pupils in constructing their interactions with one another'.

The interpretative school in the United States was influenced by ethnomethodology, sociolinguistics and symbolic interactionism. It concentrated on the internal life of schools and home–school relations, and close analysis of videotapes of classrooms was frequently employed (Mehan, 1992). The study of basic rules and competences has tended to focus on the ability of pupils to recognize what teachers want, and the teachers' reciprocal ability to recognize the competences that these pupils already have (Hargreaves and Woods, 1984; Mehan, 1978). Studies have also been concerned with language in the classroom (Heath, 1982; Warren, 1982), and bilingual and bi-cultural children. Ethnography of communication has revealed important aspects of communication in children's worlds in the school and at home (Farah, 1997). Often these projects extend beyond the school to the 'community'. In Britain, ethnomethodologists have been concerned with how teachers maintain classroom order or how they define knowledge (Hargreaves and Woods, 1984). Focus has often been on the content of school curriculum, both manifest and latent (Mehan, 1992).

Delamont and Atkinson (1995), for example, suggest that the British sociologists' sensitivity to the negotiation of everyday life within schools and classrooms has tended to obscure relationships between schooling, local culture and local social structure. Hammersley (1990), again, has criticized ethnographic research that is inspired by symbolic interactionism for its failure to produce cumulative theoretical knowledge.

The social (symbol) interactionist paradigm in ethnographic studies has been rich in the United States and in Britain, and has increased understanding of everyday processes in schools, and other educational contexts. Hargreaves and Woods (1984: 4) suggested that 'the Chicago interactionist and ethnomethodological traditions with their respective emphases on control as against order, strategies as against rules, provide two of the most powerful influences on contemporary ethnographic work, often combined'.

The political implication and contribution of social interactionist studies has been to interpret and give voice to those who lack power (Wax, 1971), describing the negative consequences of control in classroom and school, from a liberal humanist position. The impact of gender, social class and 'race'/ethnicity have been neglected in many (although not all) of these studies; we will discuss these dimensions of difference below.

Cultural Studies

Cultural studies' approaches to educational ethnography began from a position of frustration with the social interactionist approach. An example is provided by Sharp's (1981) review of Ball's *Beachside Comprehensive*, in which she criticized sociology of education in Britain, suggesting that 'because of its failure to develop any rigorous theoretical conception of the nature of the society which state schooling serves ... [it] is always running behind real events' (1981: 281). Sociology of education, Sharp argued, was too concerned with policies to grasp 'the "whole" with its richness of texture and underlying structural logic'. Sharp continued that Ball was 'preoccupied by constraints and inhibitions' and so the processes he describes seem inevitable, as he does not provide evidence of contradictory processes in class reproduction and the potential to politicize these; this 'can only lead to disillusionment, resignation and cynicism' (1981: 283). Sharp and Green (1975) took the critique of sociology of education further, arguing that it was suffering from a paradigmatic crisis. Sharp's main arguments are in particular with social interaction research, and her critique was shared by many researchers, and echoed work in cultural studies as well as in critical ethnography. Conservative educational politics gave an edge to the frustration with research which did not deal with 'big questions' of 'class domination', and which was characterized by positivism and empiricism (Sharp and Green, 1975).

A profound effect on educational research in general, and ethnographic research in education in particular, has been exercised by the mode of cultural studies undertaken in the Centre for Contemporary Cultural Studies in the University of Birmingham, led by Stuart Hall. This group concentrated on reproduction and resistance in youth. In *Learning to Labour* (1977), Willis studied a group of non-academic working-class boys at school and into the early months of work. He argued that although their countercultures provided the 'lads' with critical insights into the working of relations of domination in a capitalist society, at the same time they were preparing themselves to take their allotted places as manual labourers. Willis had argued that it is important to listen to the 'partial penetrations' of the lads despite their limitations, and the sexism and racism which was part of their youth culture. Willis (along with other male academic researchers) has been criticized for celebrating 'resistant' boys, and there were calls for a much more subtle model of pupil adaptations than those which portray them as simply pro- or anti-school.

Willis' approach to ethnography is ambivalent. He suggests that an ethnographic account 'can allow a degree of the activity, creativity and human agency' (1977: 3), but he is critical of a tendency towards naturalism in such accounts, and argues that the method is 'patronizing'. Willis concludes that, for all its faults, an ethnographic account can render human agency and experiences visible. Similar ambivalent views on ethnography are found in the book *Resistance through Rituals: Youth Subcultures in Post-war Britain*, edited by Hall and Jefferson (1997). Ethnographic research is interpreted as writing naturalistic accounts; this is evident in such titles as 'Naturalistic Research into Subcultures and Deviance' (Roberts, 1977) and 'Ethnography through the Looking-glass' (Pearson and Twohig, 1977). Corrigan (1979), like Willis, studied working-class boys who were disaffected and critical at school, and examined the control practices they encountered, and their response to these practices. The structure of the school was antipathetic to these boys; the leisure activities of the boys were as antipathetic to the school. The boys inhabited a separate world of working-class youth, where 'doing nothing' is an activity in itself. In these studies, expressions of culture, including style (cf. Hebdige, 1979) were explored, and important avenues in cultural studies were opened. Subcultural studies have influenced educational research, though youth studies and school research are largely conducted by different researchers.

Willis' study has been criticized for romanticizing resistance (cf. Walker, 1986), neglecting the new middle class (Watson, 1993) and for an uncritical acceptance of the 'lads' sexism and racism. Stanley (1989) argues that ethnographers have been interested in disaffected 'youth' whose 'replies are much the same' whether in Britain, the United States or Australia (1989: 173). McRobbie and Garber (1977) noted that for subcultural studies 'youth' meant boys. Girls were rendered invisible or described through

the eyes of boys in accounts that emphasized boys' countercultural activities. Feminist subcultural researchers wanted to redress the balance arguing that girls were oppressed by patriarchy as well as by capitalism. Early studies seem to almost mirror the work done by male researchers – discussing how working-class girls were steered towards romantic love, marriage and motherhood and the ways in which working-class girls might use sexuality in schools as a form of resistance. The girls were 'fascinated with marriage, partly because of the status it would confer on them and partly because it was the only possible means through which their sexuality could be expressed legitimately' (McRobbie, 1978: 105–6); the type of sexist talk and practices cited by Willis controlled the activities of girls. These studies suggested that working-class girls face limitations as a result of their class position, and through their own responses they are locked within femininity and domesticity, whilst working-class boys are locked into working-class jobs.

Christine Griffin was influenced by Willis (1977) in her study on *Typical Girls?* (1985), and aimed to follow a group of young working-class women from school into the job market. She found it difficult to conceptualize and analyse her material within what she called the 'gang of lads' framework employed in studies of male youth by male academics. 'Young women are particularly likely to be lumped together into a "faceless bunch" of "typical girls", rendered silent and invisible behind a haze of stereotypes and assumptions' (Griffin, 1985: 6). She drew attention to the absence of 'typical girls', highlighting the complex interaction between the simultaneous points of transitions in labour, marriage and sexual marketplaces which girls had to negotiate.

Davies (1984), from an interactionist perspective, attempts to retrieve girls as active and resistant, rather than passive and overdetermined, using the concepts of power and script. In her study of the young women in Gladstone High, she found that those who were working class or with lower academic achievement, employed sexuality, as had been found in studies by Anyon (1983) and McRobbie (1978); they used feminine wiles, invoked the female-as-sex-object ideology as a 'powerful source of resistance'. McLaren (1986) also discussed rituals of resistance in the culture of working-class schoolgirls in Canada. Blackman (1995) identifies a different stance of 'critical conformity' amongst a group of 'boffin girls', middle-class, pro-school pupils who had an instrumental approach towards the school. For these boffin girls 'The school and the family combine in the promotion of middle-class individualism with competitive relations and explicit rules for achievement, but in the peer group these relations also become relations of support, collaboration and affirmation' (1995: 148).

It is now easy to read the early cultural studies work as limited and naive in its romanticizing of resistant activities, but this work did address the problems raised by Sharp. The focus on culture brought new dimensions into ethnographic studies in education, connecting micro-level processes to macro-level structures, and mounting a critique of the type of determinism exemplified, for example, by Bowles and Gintis (1976). Bowles and Gintis argued for a correspondence principle between education and work through which social relationships in education replicate the hierarchical division of labour in production.

British cultural studies has also influenced North American educational research. Anthropologists have highlighted cultural processes in studies that examined schools and communities; for example, Foley (1990) analyses the school and the community in a city in Texas, drawing on and developing Willis' work, and Holland and Eisenhart (1990) draw on this work in their ethnography of women in college. Interest in resistance has continued, but there have also been attempts to problematize the concept as one-dimensional, and studies have focused on high achieving school students. Undertones of scorn for 'conformism' are less likely to be found in more recent texts.

The cultural dimension has been important in recent ethnographic research in educational studies, though the work is more multifaceted, and less connected to the resistance/conformity binary. Interest has extended to middle-class students; for example, Aggleton (1987) examined the transmission of middle-class cultural capital between generations. Skeggs (1997) studied working-class females in caring courses and argues that class as a concept and working-class women as a group have been ignored by feminist and cultural theory. McDermott and Varenne (1995) question the label of disability, and argue that disabilities are cultural constructions of institutional significance rather than properties of persons. Heterosexuality, homophobia and masculinities have been the object of the ethnographic gaze in schools (Epstein, 1997; Kehily and Nayak, 1996, 1997; Mac an Ghaill, 1994; Nayak and Kehily, 1996; Parker, 1996; Skelton, 1997). Kehily and Nayak (1996) have studied ways in which working-class girls and boys in schools bring informal relations into the classroom to alter the pedagogic relation. Nayak (1999) suggests that postmodernist theories have been critical of the assumption that youth cults form homogeneous groupings and interactions of British youth culture are hybrid. These later studies have moved on from a focus on resistance to broader challenges to cultural hegemonies.

CRITICAL ETHNOGRAPHY

Critical ethnography draws on cultural studies, neo-Marxist and feminist theories and research on critical pedagogy. The aim is to theorize social structural constraints and human agency, as well as the interrelationship between structure and agency in order to consider paths towards empowerment of the researched. 'The overriding goal of critical ethnography is to free individuals from sources of domination and repression' (Anderson, 1989: 249). Corson (1998) suggested that, in critical ethnography, study of a single school is combined with critical insights into how wider structures are mediated and produce change. Critical ethnography is thus simultaneously hermeneutic and emancipatory (May, 1997).

Critical ethnographers are sceptical of micro-ethnographic approaches. Sharp and Green (1975), for example, aimed to situate teachers' views and practices 'within the context of social and physical resources and constraints which they may or may not perceive, but which structure their situation and set limits to their freedom of action through the opportunities and facilities made available to them and the constraints and limitations imposed on them' (1975: 30). As a result, the work of teachers can have many unintended consequences, as Sharp and Green in their analysis of child-centred classroom practices demonstrate. These authors argued that the control practices of teachers restrict the opportunities of some school students, who develop alienated identities and the 'social stratification of knowledge and ignorance which characterizes the wider society thus impinges on the child in his [*sic*] earliest encounters with formal institutional mechanisms' (1975: 221). Jordan and Yeomans (1995) wanted to take critical ethnography 'a step further', suggesting that it needs to challenge its own institutional relations and practices inherited from ethnography as generally practised. They argued that practices need to be related to notions of 'really useful knowledge' (Johnson, 1979), action research and postmodernism.

Knowledge was a central concern of the 'new sociology of education' on which critical ethnographers draw, particularly as discussed by a number of authors in *Knowledge and Control* (1971), edited by Michael F.D. Young. The question raised is what 'counts as knowledge' in curricular content. Nell Keddie (1973), for example, described how in a liberal humanities department, a new study course relied on assumptions that were more available to students in higher than in lower streams.

In *Schooling as a Ritual Performance*, McLaren (1986) integrated post-structuralist and post-colonial theory with critical ethnography. He analysed the school as a cultural site in which a struggle for symbolic capital takes place in the form of ritual dramas, and argued that resistance by students to the school's attempts to marginalize their street culture is the primary cultural narrative that defines school life: 'Critical theorists begin with the premise *that men and women are essentially unfree and inhabit a world rife with contradictions and asymmetries of power and privilege'* (McLaren, 1998: 171; emphasis in original). Kincheloe and McLaren (1994) argue that critical ethnography is still in its infancy as a research approach and lacks that obviousness of meaning that would secure its disciplinary status; it therefore continues to redefine itself through alliances with recent theoretical currents. In critical ethnography the boundaries between ethnographic and other critical research are blurred, and work done in the context of critical pedagogy can be drawn upon. Taylor (1993), in a contribution to this fusion, took exception to impositional critical pedagogy which ignores the experiences of students, and the meanings these experiences have for them (see Lather, 1997). She argued that there are pressures on young people to incorporate socially acceptable definitions of masculinity and femininity into their own identity. Critical pedagogy must start from where the students are at, and so build on the romances and teenage soap operas which have meaning for them.

Social interactionism has been characterized by liberal humanist perspectives; critical ethnographers take a more radical political stance and make explicit their aim to change the world.

FEMINISM

Feminist ethnographers seek to observe processes in the construction of gender hierarchy and gendered power relations at the level of the micro politics of the educational institution, and take many of the perspectives outlined and illustrated in other sections of this review. In educational ethnography, as in other fields, the task for feminists has been to insert the previously invisible woman, or move her to the centre of the observation and analysis, as when early feminist critics of cultural studies challenged the invisibility of girls in studies of youth cultures (McRobbie and Garber, 1977). Llewellyn argued that 'we don't actually know what girls do either at school or outside it' (1980: 42).

An early and influential collection of feminist research edited by Deem (1980) includes several feminist ethnographic studies. Clarricoates (1980; see also Butters, 1978) studied four primary schools in England and suggested that the ways in which the gender code is transmitted and patriarchal relationships reproduced varied from one establishment to another. She emphasized that the process of constructing definitions of femininity and masculinity is complex, drawing on the sexual division of labour and class culture which exists in the community around the given school, as well as on the beliefs and ideologies held by parents, children and teachers. Although 'femininity' varied according to the area in which the school was situated,

Clarricoates argued that girls remain subordinated in all versions. Llewellyn (1980) reported an intensive participant observation study of (230) girls at two urban single-sex schools. She argued that 'there are always distinct "female" and "male" experiences of any situation, as well as shared levels of meaning through being working-class or successful within the classroom' and continues: 'Crucially, girls' and women's experiences are structured in response to male definitions, and not simply "filled in" because it raises crucial questions as to how the previous work has been understood' (1980: 45). She shows how different groups of girls operate with different stereotypes of femininity and a variety of notions of gender-appropriate behaviour, and how gender is relevant to their experiences both inside and outside the school. Fuller's (1980) research on a group of black girls of West Indian parentage in London schools showed how gender and ethnicity overlap. She was one of the first to draw attention to the way existing research on ethnicity told us little about the experience of black girls in schools. She suggested that black girls' behaviour within the classroom was 'intimately connected with their positive identity as black and female' (1980: 61) and that they took an instrumental approach to the accreditation which the school can provide.

Wolpe (1988) conducted an ethnographic study in a London co-educational comprehensive school in the 1970s. Her focus was on gender formation of girls and boys within the context of schooling. She shows how the gender formation of boys and girls is mediated in the school by disciplinary control, sexuality and the curriculum (see Riddell, 1992 for a study of the way subject choice is used by schools to bring about traditional gender divisions in the curriculum). Wolpe's research was conducted in the era when girls' low school achievement had aroused the interest of feminist researchers. She challenged arguments about the function of patriarchal control of girls, and demonstrated that girls themselves are active in the construction of gender difference.

In the early feminist ethnographic research, discrimination against girls and girls' underachievement, especially in mathematics and science, were often the starting points. In the 1980s and 1990s, feminist interpretations which emphasized differences among girls and among boys have displaced the former dualist thinking. Black feminist researchers, gay and lesbian studies and research on disabled women, for example, have challenged the monolithic picture of girls and boys in education (e.g. Epstein, 1996; Grant, 1992; Mirza, 1992). High achievement of some girls has also been highlighted; for example Mirza (1992) explored a group of Afro Caribbean high achieving girls with strong and high career aspirations – but for female occupations.

Within research on informal relations in school, theories of girls' and boys' separate worlds have been challenged in Thorne's ethnographic research on young children's friendships in two working-class elementary schools in California (Thorne, 1992, 1993). She argued that gender separation in schools is a variable and complicated process, and far from total and criticized research that emphasizes the 'different cultures' of girls and boys, and suggests that they are always 'apart' with no theoretical attention paid to 'the moments of "with" and comfortable sharing' (Thorne, 1993: 90). She found such moments in her data along with moments of 'apart' (cf. Goffman, 1977). Thorne questions how girls and boys separate into gender-defined and relatively boundaried collectivities and asks in what contexts and through what processes they interact in less gender-divided ways (Thorne, 1992). This enabled her to see more nuances in children's play. Other studies have delineated the influence of the peer group culture on the construction of gendered and sexual identity for young women in school (Kehily, 1999) and college (Holland and Eisenhart, 1990).

Acker (1995) studied female teachers. She described two aspects of teachers' work: caring for the children and caring for each other, and discussed these against the cultural script for caring which is traditionally associated with women. In their research on feminist college teachers, Maher and Thompson-Tetreault (1993) found that these teachers struggled with issues of mastery, voice, authority and positionality with their students, and concluded that these themes can also be lenses for a new ethnographic approach: 'Like feminist teachers with their students, we have had to construct knowledge with our informants as well' (1993: 31).

Feminist researchers have taken up the methodological and ethical issues raised by ethnographic research (e.g. Lather, 1997; Stacey, 1988). Stacey discusses ethical questions involved in an intervention in systems of relationships and notes that the researcher is far freer to leave than the researched. Ethnographic research depends on human relationships, including engagement and attachment, and thus 'places research subjects at grave risk of manipulation and betrayal by the ethnographer' (1988: 23). Stacey asks whether there can in fact be a feminist ethnography and answers that there 'can and should be feminist research that is rigorously self-aware and therefore humble about the partiality of its ethnographic vision and its capacity to represent self and other' (1988: 26).

DIVERSITY AND DIFFERENCE

The feminist researchers discussed above were concerned to explore and expose both the position of women and processes of the production and construction of gender relations in education (and other institutional and structural locations). In social theory

and research they were recovering the invisible woman. As we have seen earlier, they inserted gender into approaches that employed a class analysis, and difference was associated with differences between women and men (Anyon, 1981, 1983; Clarricoates, 1980; Griffin, 1985; McRobbie, 1978, 1982). Many of these researchers initially worked within a reproduction framework, including Connell et al. (1982), although they were critical of its limitations in the face of practice in schools. But for Connell and his collaborators, once in the field, gender difference moved into a more central position, as did the need for theorizing an active relationship between social structures and individual practices in personal lives. Their study mapped the lives of 100 young people in independent schools and state comprehensives in two cities in Australia, with parents in particular fractions of the working and middle class. The researchers analysed the effects and interaction of gender and class codes in school and family, but they stressed that their aim was 'to reach through the categories ... to the relations and processes behind them' (1982: 212). They introduced the useful explanatory concept of 'gender regime'.

An early extensive and intensive ethnography on educational inequality in the United States, Ogbu (1974), with a conceptual framework drawing on Durkheim and Merton, studied school failure among subordinate minorities in Burgherside. In this classic and influential study, Ogbu argued that there had been a group adaptation amongst the subordinate minorities (blacks and Mexican Americans) to continuing educational failure and this was maintained by three factors: first, a loss of desire to perform or compete effectively in school due to inequality in educational rewards; secondly, the way that teachers interacted with Burghersiders treating them as *not* equal participants, based on a folk definition of them as culturally or mentally inferior; thirdly, the way the school defined educational problems in psychological and clinical terms, and based their actions on the ideas and policies of the dominant group.

In Fordham's (1996) fascinating study of black identity formation and school achievement in the United States, in which a narrative, post-structuralist approach is employed, she argued that the high-achieving black students feared 'acting white' and being named as the Other in their own community, and that they engaged in resistance through conformity. She suggested that their community has a deep-rooted cultural system which favours egalitarianism and group cohesion which is in opposition to the individualistic, competitive demands of academic success. Unlike Ogbu (1974), she was particularly interested in success rather than failure, although she did study low-achieving students whose practices at school were characterized by avoidance. Fordham suggested that the most conflict-laden of the students studied were high-achieving males. For them, issues associated with gender took precedence over race issues. High-achieving females tended to act as though social limitations did not exist. Many of the students sought 'to be consumed by the Other, not only because it is officially sanctioned in school, but because it is a way of minimizing their affiliation with the disparaged Black Self' (1996: 336).

Hemmings (1998) discusses African American student achievers, and their attempts to transform their multiple selves as black, gendered and classed, moving between multiple worlds of their families, schooling and peers. Their strategies were self-negation, self-fragmentation and self-synthesis. Cordeiro's (1993) study of Hispanic achievers focuses on key life events such as positive reinforcement in early school years, on home cultures where parental strictness was associated with the choice of high-achieving peer groups. They had Hispanic identities, but valued individualism, and did not experience the burden of 'acting white'.

As we see here, the categories of difference with which researchers and social theorists worked were increasingly challenged and expanded from class and gender to 'race' and ethnicity, disability and sexuality. Major challenges came from the social movements associated with feminism, anti-racism, gay rights and disability, through which a developing politics of identity emerged. For example, a black feminist critique of white feminism was important in drawing attention to the differences between women, rather than between women and men (Aziz, 1992; Brah, 1992).

Identity politics was the mobilization of particular oppressed groups around a shared identity on the basis of which hierarchical power structures could be challenged and rights sought. With the growing influence of postmodern and post-structuralist arguments, these identities themselves, having served a political purpose for a period, appeared too static, and the focus moved to diversity within and fluidity between identities. As Stuart Hall puts it for 'race': 'What is at issue here is the recognition of the extraordinary diversity of subjective positions, social experiences and cultural identities which compose the category "black"' (Hall, 1992: 254). This has led to a new politics of cultural difference critical of the notion of shared identity, regarding identity as 'constituted through a range of subjectivities that cannot be contained within a singular category' (Haywood and Mac an Ghaill, 1998: 127).

Mac an Ghaill (Haywood and Mac an Ghaill, 1998) described his own ethnographic investigation of gender in school as caught in the tension between these two positions (Mac an Ghaill, 1994). He used ideal types to characterize different groups of male students, which suggested 'a fixity of male student styles' but this was in contrast to 'the accompanying use of the new politics of cultural difference to argue that heterosexual masculinities could not be understood as unitary wholes or be seen as static or unchangeable since they are always in the process of production and reproduction' (Haywood and Mac an Ghaill, 1998: 128). Mac an Ghaill was able to deal with these contradictions by refocusing his book (1994) on gay male students in the secondary school in which his study was located, who gave a critical account of heterosexuality from their position as outsiders. He concludes that '[t]hey offer evidence that supports feminist analysis that sex/gender regimes are a fundamental organizing principle within schools, which underpins the individual and collective construction of student and teacher identities' (1994: 168).

In a year-long ethnographic study of a multiethnic, inner-city primary school, Connolly (1995a, 1995b, 1998) examined the ways in which racialized and gendered cultural identities are formed amongst 5- and 6-year old boys. He stressed the active role that infant children themselves play in negotiating and forming social relationships, and discussed the way the friendship group he follows (the 'Bad Boys') make sense of and actively construct their own identities as black, boys and children, calling on discourses of childhood, masculinity, racism and sexuality. Their competent displays of masculinity caused feelings of insecurity and threat amongst the white boys, and Connolly argues that the Bad Boys draw on black cultural forms and a 'hard' streetwise image in response to the racism that they experience in school.

Following on from early ethnographies examining the experience of young black people in the UK (Fuller, 1980; Furlong, 1984), from the mid-1980s a number of ethnographic studies were undertaken on this issue in secondary schools (Foster, 1990; Gillborn, 1990; Mac an Ghaill, 1988; Mirza, 1992; Wright, 1986), and in primary schools (Connolly, 1998; Troyna and Hatcher, 1992; Wright, 1992a, 1992b, 1998). Almost all of these studies indicated that black and white pupils experience schooling differently. They suggest that even well-intentioned white teachers who are committed to equality of opportunity as an ideal may nevertheless act in ways that unwittingly reproduce racial stereotypes, generate conflict (especially with African Caribbean young men) and perpetuate existing inequalities (Gillborn, 1995). Foster (1990), in contrast to this body of work, concluded from his study of a multiethnic school in the north of England that 'ethnic minority students enjoyed equal opportunities with their white peers' (1990: 174). Foster and colleagues went on to criticize the work of other ethnographic researchers in this area as methodologically unsound, arguing that their conclusions were therefore unconvincing (examples of this critique are Foster, 1992, and Hammersley and Gomm, 1993). Gillborn (1995) provides a deconstruction of Foster's critique of his own work. The argument in this debate turns around the construction and validation of social science knowledge.

Work on 'difference' then has moved from a focus on 'difference between' to 'difference within' social categories and identities related to class, gender, 'race'/ethnicity, dis/ability (impairment) and sexuality (discussed here and in other sections of this chapter). It has been undertaken from various perspectives, from early reproduction theory and social interactionist work on class and gender, through to approaches drawing heavily on the post-structural and textual turn in social theory and ethnography. The move from identity politics to the new politics of cultural difference in educational ethnography as in other areas of social research, has led to problems in relation to the desire for political action and empowerment of the researched which has underpinned many approaches to research in the past.

Postmodern and Post-structuralist Ethnographies

Postmodern and post-structuralist ethnographies are characterized by a turn to the textual (Clifford and Marcus, 1986) and away from 'the ideal of objective ethnographic accounts' (Foley, 1990: xix). Foley (1990) discusses these shifts in ethnographic work; experimental narratives problematize authoritative texts as realist, and call for more dialogic accounts which write the researchers into the text. Foley finds these developments puzzling, particularly as some of the postmodern texts remain inaccessible, and seem more concerned with epistemology and ethnographic writing than what is written about. Nevertheless, he notes that he has been influenced by these debates and has developed a more dialogic style of writing, and concedes that ethnographic research will undoubtedly change in the coming years.

Despite influential discussions on the ethnographic genre, the impact of postmodernism and post-structuralism has not been great in the field of educational research. Taking these on is perhaps more problematic in education than in other fields; we have referred to the (changing) political and emancipatory goals of educational researchers; it is difficult to remain dispassionate when studying schools. Researchers emphasize their commitment to social change, to the improvement of education, to equality and social justice; for them postmodern critiques of humanism, and the fluidity of postmodern and post-structuralist accounts, do not lend themselves to political concerns.

Many educational researchers who engage with postmodernism and post-structuralism combine this approach with the critical ethnographic genre, and emphasize their engagement. Fordham (1996) discussed the gaze of the ethnographer, split personhood and multiple subjectivities and placed her own positionality/ies in the foreground of the discussion.

But this did not prevent her engagement. She suggested that her 'involvement is not laminated by textual claims of scientific objectivism or lack of engagement. I *was* engaged, and in far more than classroom observation. Indeed, I was involved in the school and community' (1996: 340). Hemmings' (1998) emphasis on 'new cultural pluralism' suggests postmodern influences, evident in the focus and the vocabulary she uses, but otherwise her approach shares common ground with social interactionism.

But Foley's concern for concentration on the writing rather than what is written about does have some resonance. Postmodern and post-structuralist ethnographers concentrate a great deal on how research is conceived and written about; many texts concentrate on issues about ethnography rather than issues about education. Chaudhry (1997) suggests that post-structuralist and post-colonialist theories stress that identity is fluid and the self is multiple and contingent on power relations. As there is no authentic self except in a contextual performance and representation, postmodernists are compelled to problematize their own identities, and Chaudhry asks 'Why do I go out to seek other Pakistani Muslim women and investigate their marginality, hybridity, resistance, and empowerment, when I keep going back to the history of my own consciousness?' (1997: 450). Chaudhry's discussion is useful in acknowledging the stake which researchers have in their research. Reflecting on doing postgenre is popular, and the development of post-research may be overtaken by criticism of the textual turn before more empirical work develops.

Wexler (1992) disengaged with both objective realist and subjective imaginative accounts. Although clearly influenced by the postmodern turn in an interest in polyvocality, he criticized 'the seriously coded premise of playfulness contained by field workers' reflections on their methods – we have already reached the point at which such reflections displace the work itself to a protective cultural regime' (1992: 159). Though his account is described as a historical artefact, he emphasized the importance of empirical work and suggested that there has been enough deconstruction of the ethnographic approach, arguing that what is needed now is 'to write ethnography from the vantage point of the future' (1992: 160). His is a social psychological study of 'becoming somebody' in school.

Raissiguier (1995) poses a seemingly simple question about how working-class female students of Algerian descent construct themselves in a French vocational school, but debates emerging from postmodernism and feminism make the question a great deal more complex. How does one, Raissiguier asks, 'frame a non-essentialist analysis of the construction of subjectivity that allows for agency while still recognizing the existence of material and discursive boundaries within which the agent is constituted?' (1995: 79). It is difficult to give up the notion of subjectivity when studying people who have previously been denied access to it. Raissiguier analyses identity formation and ways in which the girls (de)construct themselves, discovering neither 'pure resistance' nor 'pure accommodation'. The marginal positioning of the girls puts them 'at crossroads of several contradictory discourses' (1995: 91); for this reason, they put more value on non-economic outcomes of their education than do girls of French descent (Raissiguier, 1993).

Davies (1983) was interested in how discourses position young girls and boys, and how they position themselves. She explored micro-processes in classrooms and playgrounds, but her analysis focused on how gender, social class and race differences were constructed, and the approach is therefore broader than those of micro-ethnographers. Davies also emphasized her own positioning as a researcher and an interpreter. Her insights on young children's agency in the negotiation of the social order in the classroom are important, and the subject of feminist debates on post-structuralism (cf. Davies, 1983; Jones, 1993).

Rhedding-Jones (1996) has conducted research among a small group of schoolgirls. Narratives written by the girls formed an important part of her data; she approached these narratives not as reflections of experience but as discursive productions. Discussing her study from a post-structural perspective, Rhedding-Jones argues:

> The girls whose subjectivity I was concerned with were different from me. But the 'me' who used to be a schoolgirl, the 'me' who used to be a primary school teacher, and the 'me' who used to be a mother of two young girls and two young boys was constantly engaged in what happened with the research project. Further, my own desire to tell the truth was complicated by the post-structural knowledge that there is not one truth but many; and that claims to truth are claims to power. (1996: 26)

This example illustrates the way in which postmodern and post-structuralist approaches question the authority of the author, whilst they reach for multi-layered accounts with many voices.

MATERIALISM

The post-structuralist and textual turn in ethnography (Clifford and Marcus, 1986), as in other disciplines and methods, brings with it the fear of loss of an understanding of the material conditions of existence (McRobbie, 1997; Morley, 1997). Morley (1997) argued that the post-structural moment, particularly in cultural studies – itself moving towards the ethnographic method – may have tipped the balance too far into the textual, and quoted in support Probyn's (1993) comment on ethnography: 'just as practitioners in other disciplines seem to be drawn

to ethnography because of its promise to delve into the concrete (in the hope of finding real people living "real" lives), ethnography is becoming increasingly textual' (Probyn, 1993: 61). Morley and Probyn are taking up an argument with the influential work of Clifford and Marcus (1986) which set the groundwork for a predominantly textual approach in postmodern ethnography, and their desire was to know what is the relationship between the textual and the real. Morley wanted to avoid the disabling of empirical research by what he saw as a muddled relativism that eschews the notion of truth.

Roman notes that feminists have tried to develop research approaches that go beyond both objectivism and subjectivism; neither neutrality nor relativity are sufficient guises for the researcher. She calls for the consideration of 'underlying structures, material conditions, and conflicting historically specific power relations and inequalities' (Roman, 1993: 282). Like McRobbie (1996, 1997), she calls for ethnographic accounts that do not dematerialize the social and the cultural. Thus feminist approaches can no longer assume themselves to be inherently egalitarian, nor other approaches to be essentially reifying or masculinist. Materialist analyses have also been mapped out in Roman and Eyre (1997), though the analyses are not ethnographic. Roman's ethnographic study on girls in punk cultures combines materialism and feminism. Her work included participant observation in schools, but its main focus was in leisure settings.

Hey (1997) has studied girls and their interrelationships in two secondary schools in London. She criticized subcultural theories which have not addressed gender, and argued that 'it is only through theorizing struggles between girls as embodying/ embodied forms of cultural and material power that we can connect the networks of supposedly private forms of subjectivity and identity to the making of cultural hegemony' (1997: 131). Kenway and Willis (1998) draw on post-structuralism and materialist approaches to study feminist initiatives in schools in Australia. Though their data have been gathered using a range of methods, the broader methodological approach is little discussed, but does not appear to draw particularly on the ethnographic tradition. Gordon, Holland and Lahelma (2000) combine post-structuralism, feminist, cultural and material approaches in their comparative, cross-cultural study of secondary schools in London and Helsinki. The material approach is particularly evident in their analysis of the 'physical school', focusing on spatiality and embodiment.

CONCLUSIONS

Although researchers have sought materialist theories in order to address problems of the textual turn, as well as difficulties attached to social interactionism, materialism, of course, is not new. Critical ethnographers with a Marxist orientation have drawn on historical materialism, and analysts of cultures have suggested that cultures express material experiences and relations, though cultural forms are not determined by these, but actively produced. The structure of this chapter does not then reflect a solid evolution from one broad perspective to another. Instead we have looked for an interpretive approach as a way to understand such a fast-changing field. Social (and symbolic) interactionism is a tradition that is alive and well, as plenty of recent studies testify. Although the highly influential studies of subcultures can now seem dated, they are still frequently addressed, and not only in an overview such as this. Moreover, cultural studies, like symbolic interactionism, is constantly developing and critical ethnographic work also continues.

Research in the field of education is often connected to particular ways of wanting to improve schools/education/societies; critical approaches are interested in making connections between research and practice, and want to combine theory with radical pedagogy. The post-structural turn has taken place rather late in educational research, and postmodern research is still rather sparse, as are the latest materialist approaches. Feminist educational research is ongoing, though it is currently more likely to be influenced by attention to difference. Intersecting analyses focusing on lives of children, young people and adults in educational settings still need to be developed beyond foci of single perspectives. This is a great challenge for educational research, and one that the ethnographic approach in particular, with its focus on complex and multi-layered practices and the meanings attached to such process and practices, is in a strong position to meet.

REFERENCES

Acker, Sandra (1995) 'Carry on Caring: The Work of Women Teachers', *British Journal of Sociology of Education*, 16 (1): 21–36.

Aggleton, Peter (1987) *Rebels without a Cause? Middle Class Youth and the Transition from School to Work*. London: Falmer Press.

Anderson, Gary L. (1989) 'Critical ethnography in education: origins, current status, and new directions', *Review of Educational Research*, 59 (3): 249–70.

Anyon, Jean (1981) 'Elementary schooling and distinctions of social class', *Interchange*, 12: 118–32.

Anyon, Jean (1983) 'Intersections of gender and class: accommodation and resistance by working-class and affluent females to contradictory sex-role ideologies', in Stephen Walker and Len Barton (eds), *Gender, Class and Education*. Lewes: Falmer Press. pp. 19–37.

Atkinson, Paul (1984) 'Wards and deeds: taking knowledge and control seriously', in Robert G. Burgess (ed.), *The Research Process in Educational Settings: Ten Case Studies*. Lewes: Falmer Press. pp. 163–85.

Atkinson, Paul and Delamont, Sara (1980) 'The two traditions in educational ethnography: sociology and anthropology compared', *British Journal of Sociology of Education*, 1: 139–52.

Aziz, Razia (1992) 'Feminism and the challenge of racism: deviance or difference?', in Helen Crowley and Susan Himmelweit (eds), *Knowing Women: Feminism and Knowledge*. Cambridge: Polity Press. pp. 291–305.

Ball, Stephen (1981) *Beachside Comprehensive*. Cambridge: Cambridge University Press.

Ball, Stephen (1984) 'Initial encounters in the classroom and the process of establishment', in Martyn Hammersley and Peter Woods (eds), *Life in School: The Sociology of Pupil Culture*. Milton Keynes: Open University Press. pp. 108–20.

Ball, Stephen J. (1987) *The Micro-Politics of the School. Towards a Theory of School Organization*. London: Routledge.

Ball, Stephen J. and Bowe, Richard (1992) 'Subject departments and the "implementation" of National Curriculum Policy: an overview of the issues', *Journal of Curriculum Studies*, 24 (2): 97–115.

Beach, Dennis (1996) 'Social material structuration and educational change', *Nordisk Pedagogik*, 16 (4): 203–12.

Benyon, John (1985) *Initial Encounters in the Comprehensive School*. London: Falmer Press.

Benyon, John (1989) '"A school for men": an ethnographic case study of routine violence in schooling', in Stephen Walker and Len Barton (eds), *Politics and the Processes of Schooling*. Milton Keynes: Open University Press. pp. 191–218.

Blackman, Shane J. (1995) *Youth: Positions and Oppositions*. Aldershot: Avebury.

Bowles, Samuel and Gintis, Herbert (1976) *Schooling in Capitalist America*. London: Routledge and Kegan Paul.

Brah, Avtar (1992) 'Difference, diversity and differentiation', in James Donald and Ali Rattansi (eds), *'Race', Culture and Difference*. London: Sage, with Open University. pp. 126–45.

Butters, Steve (1978) 'The logic-of-enquiry of participant observation', in Stuart Hall and Tony Jefferson (eds), *Resistance through Rituals: Youth Subcultures in Postwar Britain*. London: Hutchinson (first published 1975).

Chaudhry, Lubna Nazir (1997) 'Researching "my people", researching myself: fragments of a reflexive tale', *Qualitative Studies in Education*, 10 (4): 441–53.

Clarricoates, Katherine (1980) 'The importance of being Ernest ... Emma ... Tom ... Jane. The perception and categorization of gender conformity and gender deviation in primary schools', in Rosemary Deem (ed.), *Schooling for Women's Work*. London: Routledge and Kegan Paul. pp. 26–41.

Clifford, Janet and Marcus, George E. (eds) (1986) *Writing Culture: The Poetics and Politics of Ethnography*. Berkeley, CA: University of California Press.

Coffey, Amanda (1996) 'The power of accounts: authority and authorship in ethnography', *Qualitative Studies in Education*, 9 (1): 61–74.

Connell, R.W., Ashenden, D.J., Kessler, S. and Downsett, G.W. (1982) *Making the Difference*. Sydney: Allen and Unwin.

Connolly, Paul (1995a) 'Racism, masculine peer-group relations and the schooling of African/Caribbean infant boys', *British Journal of Sociology of Education*, 16 (1): 75–92.

Connolly, Paul (1995b) 'Boys will be boys? Racism, sexuality and the construction of masculine identities amongst infant boys', in Janet Holland and Maud Blair (with Sue Sheldon) (eds), *Debates and Issues in Feminist Research and Pedagogy*. Clevedon: Multi-lingual Matters with Open University. pp. 160–95.

Connolly, Paul (1998) *Racism, Gender Identities and Young Children*. London: Routledge.

Cordeiro, Paula A. (1993) 'How a minority of the minority succeed: a case study of twenty hispanic achievers', *Qualitative Studies in Education*, 6 (4): 277–90.

Corrigan, Paul (1979) *Schooling the Smash Street Kids*. London: Macmillan.

Corsaro, William A. (1981) 'Entering the child's world – research strategies for field entry and data collection in a preschool setting', in Judith L. Green and Cynthia Wallat (eds), *Ethnography and Language in Educational Settings*. Norwood, NJ: Ablex. pp. 117–46.

Corson, David (1998) *Changing Education for Diversity*. Buckingham: Open University Press.

Davies, Bronwyn (1983) 'The role pupils play in the social construction of classroom order', *British Journal of Sociology of Education*, 4 (1): 55–69.

Davies, Bronwyn (1993) *Shards of Glass: Children Reading and Writing Beyond Gendered Identities*. Cresskill: Hampton Press.

Davies, Lynn (1984) *Pupil Power: Deviance and Gender in School*. Lewes: Falmer Press.

Deem, Rosemary (ed.) (1980) *Schooling for Women's Work*. London: Routledge and Kegan Paul.

Delamont, Sara (1976) 'Beyond Flanders fields', in Michael Stubbs and Sara Delamont (eds), *Explorations in Classroom Observation*. Chichester: Wiley.

Delamont, Sara ([1980] 1990) *Sex Roles and the School*. London: Routledge.

Delamont, Sara and Atkinson, Paul (1995) *Fighting Familiarity: Essays on Education and Ethnography*, Cresskill, NJ: Hampton Press.

Delamont, Sara and Galton, Maurice (1986) *Inside the Secondary Classroom*. London: Routledge and Kegan Paul.

Delamont, Sara, Parry, Odette and Atkinson, Paul (1997) 'Critical mass and pedagogic continuity: studies in academic habitus', *British Journal of Sociology of Education*, 18 (4): 533–45.

Denscombe, Martyn (1985) *Classroom Control: A Sociological Perspective*. London: George Allen and Unwin.

Epstein, Debbie (1996) 'Keeping them in their place: hetero/sexist harassment, gender and the enforcement of heterosexuality', in Janet Holland and Lisa Adkins (eds), *Sex, Sensibility and the Gendered Body*. London: Macmillan. pp. 202–21.

Epstein, Debbie (1997) 'Boyz' own stories: masculinities and sexualities in schools', *Gender and Education*, 9 (1): 105–15.

Erickson, Frederick and Mohatt, Gerald (1982) 'Cultural organisation of participation structures in two class-rooms of Indian students', in George D. Spindler (ed.), *Doing Ethnography of Schooling*. New York: Rinehart and Winston. pp. 132–71.

Farah, Iffat (1997) 'Ethnography of communication', in Nancy H. Hornberger and David Corson (eds), *Research Methods in Language and Education*. Dordrecht: Kluwer. pp. 125–34.

Foley, Douglas E. (1990) *Learning Capitalist Culture*. Philadelphia: University of Pennsylvania Press.

Fordham, Signithia (1996) *Blacked Out: Dilemmas of Race, Identity, and Success in Capital High*. Chicago: University of Chicago Press.

Foster, Peter (1990) *Policy and Practice in Multicultural and Anti-racist Education*. London: Routldege.

Foster, Peter (1992) 'Equal treatment and cultural difference in multi-ethnic schools; a critique of the teacher ethnocentrism theory', *International Studies in Sociology of Education*, 2 (1): 89–103.

Fuller, Mary (1980) 'Black girls in a London comprehensive school', in Rosemary Deem (ed.), *Schooling for Women's Work*. London: Routledge and Kegan Paul. pp. 52–65.

Furlong, Viv (1976) 'Interaction sets in the classroom: towards a study of pupil knowledge', in Michael Stubbs and Sara Delamont (eds), *Explorations in Classroom Observation*. Chichester: Wiley. pp. 23–44.

Furlong, Viv (1984) 'Black resistance in the liberal comprehensive', in Sara Delamont (ed.), *Readings on Interaction in the Classroom*. London: Methuen. pp. 212–36.

Galton, Maurice, Simon, Brian and Croll, P. (1980) *Inside the Primary Classroom*. London: Routledge and Kegan Paul.

Garcez, Pedro M. (1997) 'Microethnography', in Nancy H. Hornberger and David Corson (eds), *Research Methods in Language and Education*. Dordrecht: Kluwer. pp. 187–96.

Garfinkel, E. (1967) *Studies in Ethnomethodology*. Englewood Cliffs, NJ: Prentice–Hall.

Garpelin, Anders and Lindblad, Sverker (1994) 'On students' life projects and micropolitical strategies. A progress report from explorations of Swedish comprehensive schools'. Paper presented at the AERA meeting in New Orleans, April 1994.

Gillborn, David (1990) *'Race', Ethnicity and Education: Teaching and Learning in Multi-ethnic Schools*. London: Unwin–Hyman/Routledge.

Gillborn, David (1994) 'The micro-politics of macro reform', *British Journal of Sociology of Education*, 15 (2): 147.

Gillborn, David (1995) *Racism and Antiracism in Real Schools*. Buckingham: Open University Press.

Goffman, Erving (1977) 'The arrangement between the sexes', *Theory and Society*, 4: 301–36.

Gordon, Tuula, Holland, Janet and Lahelma, Elina (2000) *Making Spaces: Citizenship and Difference in Schools*. London: Macmillan and New York: St Martin's Press.

Grant, Linda (1992) 'Race and the schooling of young girls', in Julia Wrigley (ed.), *Education and Gender Equality*. London and Washington, DC: Falmer Press. pp. 91–113.

Griffin, Christine (1985) *Typical Girls? Young Women from School to the Job Market*. London: Routledge and Kegan Paul.

Hall, Stuart (1992) 'New ethnicities', in James Donald and Ali Rattansi (eds), *'Race', Culture and Difference*. London: Sage. pp. 252–9.

Hall, Stuart and Jefferson, Tony (eds) (1997) *Resistance Through Rituals: Youth Subcultures in Post-war Britain*. London: Hutchinson.

Hammersley, Martyn (1990) *Classroom Ethnography: Empirical and Methodological Essays*. Milton Keynes: Open University Press.

Hammersley, Martyn (ed.) (1993) *Social Research. Philosophy, Politics and Practice*. London: Sage.

Hammersley, Martyn and Gomm, Roger (1993) 'A response to Gillborn and Drew on "race", class and school effects', *New Community*, 19 (2): 348–53.

Hammons-Bryner, Sue (1995) '"Crystal stair": rural women's collegiate enrollment and persistence', *Qualitative Studies of Education*, 8 (2): 121–36.

Hargreaves, Andy (1967) *Social Relations in Secondary School*. London: Routledge and Kegan Paul.

Hargreaves, Andy (1994) *Changing Teachers, Changing Times: Teachers' Work and Culture in the Postmodern Age*. London: Cassell.

Hargreaves, Andy and Woods, Peter (eds) (1984) *Classrooms and Staffrooms. The Sociology of Teachers and Teaching*. Milton Keynes and Bristol: Open University Press.

Harris, Susan and Ruddock, Jean (1993) 'Establishing the seriousness of learning in the early years of secondary schooling', *British Journal of Educational Psychology*, 63: 322–36.

Hatton, Elizabeth (1997) 'Teacher educators and the production of bricoleurs: an ethnographic study', *Qualitative Studies in Education*, 10 (2): 237–57.

Haywood, Chris and Mac an Ghaill, Máirtín (1998) 'The making of men: theorizing methodology in "uncertain" times', in Geoffrey, Walford (ed.), *Doing Research about Education*. London: Falmer Press.

Heath, Shirley Brice (1982) 'Questioning at home and at school: a comparative study', in George Spindler (ed.), *Doing Ethnography of Schooling*. New York: Rinehart and Winston. pp. 102–31.

Hebdige, Dick (1979) *Subculture: The Meaning of Style*, London: Methuen.

Hemmings, Annette (1998) 'The self-transformations of African American achievers', *Youth and Society*, 29 (3): 330–58.

Hey, Valerie (1997) *The Company She Keeps: An Ethnography of Girls' Friendship*. Milton Keynes: Open University Press.

Holland, Dorothy C. and Eisenhart, Margaret A. (1990) *Educated in Romance: Women, Achievement, and College Culture*. Chicago: University of Chicago Press.

Holm, Gunilla (1995) 'Handled but not heard: the managed lives of teenage mothers in school', *Qualitative Studies in Education*, 8 (3): 253–64.

Jackson, Philip W. (1968) *Life in Classrooms*. New York: Holt, Rinehart and Winston.

Johnson, Richard (1979) 'Really useful knowledge, 1790–1848', in J. Clarke, C. Critcher and Richard Johnson (eds), *Working Class Culture: Studies in History and Theory*. New York: St Martin's Press. pp. 75–102.

Jones, Alison (1993) 'Becoming a "girl": post-structuralist suggestions for educational research', *Gender and Education*, 5 (2): 157–66.

Jordan, Steven and Yeomans, David (1995) 'Critical ethnography: problems in contemporary theory and practice', *British Journal of Sociology of Education*, 16 (3): 89–108.

Keddie, Nell (ed.) (1973) *Tinker, Tailor ... the Myth of Cultural Deprivation*. Harmondsworth: Penguin.

Kehily, Mary Jane (1999) 'Learning Sex and Doing Gender: Pupil Sexual Cultures in the Secondary School'. Unpublished PhD thesis, Institute of Education, University of London.

Kehily, Mary and Nayak, Anoop (1996) '"The Christmas kiss": sexuality, story-telling and schooling', *Curriculum Studies*, 4 (2): 211–27.

Kehily, Mary Jane and Nayak, Anoop (1997) '"Lads and laughter": humour and the production of heterosexual hierarchies', *Gender and Education*, 9 (1): 69–87.

Kenway, Jane and Willis, Sue with Blackmore, Jill and Rennie, Leonie (1998) *Answering Back*. London: Routledge.

Kincheloe, Joe L. and McLaren, Peter L. (1994) 'Rethinking critical theory and qualitative research', in Norman K. Denzin and Yvonna S. Lincoln (eds), *Handbook of Qualitative Research*. London: Sage. pp. 138–57.

Lacey, Colin (1970) *Hightown Grammar*. Manchester: Manchester University Press.

Lahelma, Elina and Gordon, Tuula (1997) 'First day in secondary school: learning to be a "professional pupil"', *Educational Research and Evaluation*, 3 (2): 119–39.

Lambart, Audrey (1976) 'The sisterhood', in Martyn Hammersley and Peter Woods (eds), *The Process of Schooling*. London: Routledge and Kegan Paul. pp. 152–9.

Larsson, Staffan (1993) 'Initial encounters in formal adult education', *Qualitative Studies in Education*, 6 (1): 49–65.

Lather, Patti (1997) 'Drawing the line at angst: working the ruins of feminist ethnography', *Qualitative Studies in Education*, 10 (3): 285–304.

Leacock, Eleanor B. (1971) 'Theoretical and methodological problems in the study of schools', in Murray L. Wax, Stanley Diamond and Fred D. Gearing (eds), *Anthropological Perspectives on Education*. New York: Basic Books. pp. 169–79.

Llewellyn, Mandy (1980) 'Studying girls at school: the implications of confusion', in Rosemary Deem (ed.), *Schooling for Women's Work*. London: Routledge and Kegan Paul. pp. 42–51.

Mac an Ghaill, Máirtín (1988) *Young, Gifted and Black: Student–Teacher Ratios in the Schooling of Black Youth*. Milton Keynes: Open University Press.

Mac an Ghaill, Máirtín (1992) 'Teachers work: curriculum restructuring, culture, power and comprehensive school', *British Journal of Sociology of Education*, 13 (2): 177–99.

Mac an Ghaill, Máirtín (1994) *The Making of Men*. Buckingham: Open University Press.

Maher, Frances A. and Thompson-Tetreault, Mary Kay (1993) 'Doing feminist ethnography: lessons from feminist classrooms', *Qualitative Studies in Education*, 8 (1): 19–32.

May, Stephen A. (1997) 'Critical ethnography', in Nancy H. Hornberger and David Corson (eds), *Research Methods in Language and Education*. Dordrecht: Kluwer. pp. 197–206.

McDermott, Ray and Varenne, Herve (1995) 'Culture as disability', *Anthropology and Education Quarterly*, 3 (26): 324–8.

McFadden, Mark G. (1996) '"Second change" education: accessing opportunity or recycling disadvantage?', *International Journal of Sociology of Education*, 6 (1): 87–110.

McLaren, Peter (1986) *Schooling as a Ritual Performance: Towards a Political Economy of Educational Symbols and Gestures*. London: Routledge and Kegan Paul.

McLaren, Peter (1998) *Life in Schools: An Introduction to Critical Pedagogy in the Foundations of Education*, 3rd edn. London: Longman.

McNeill, Linda (1986) *Contradictions of Control: School Structure and School Knowledge*. New York: Routledge and Kegan Paul.

McRobbie, Angela (1978) 'Working class girls and the culture of femininity', in Women's Studies Group, CCCS (eds), *Women Take Issue: Aspects of Women's Subordination*. London: Hutchinson. pp. 96–108.

McRobbie, Angela (1982) 'Settling accounts with subcultures: a feminist critique', *Screen Education*, 34.

McRobbie, Angela (1996) 'Looking back at the new times and its critics', in Chen Kuan-Hsing and David Morley (eds), *Stuart Hall: Critical Dialogues in Cultural Studies*. London: Routledge. pp. 238–61.

McRobbie, Angela (1997) 'The Es and the anti-Es: new questions for feminism and cultural studies', in Marjorie Ferguson and Peter Golding (eds), *Cultural Studies in Question*. London: Sage.

McRobbie, Angela and Garber, Jenny (1977) 'Girls and subcultures', in Stuart Hall and Tony Jefferson (eds), *Resistance through Rituals: Youth Subcultures in Post-war Britain*. London: Hutchinson (first published 1975). pp. 209–22.

Measor, Linda and Woods, Peter (1984) *Changing Schools*. Milton Keynes: Open University Press.

Mehan, Hugh (1978) 'Structuring school structure', *Harvard Educational Review*, 48 (1): 32–64.

Mehan, Hugh (1992) 'Understanding inequality in schools: the contribution of interpretive studies', *Sociolology of Education*, 65 (January): 1–20.

Mirza, Heidi Safia (1992) *Young, Female and Black: Do Schools Make a Difference*. London: Routledge.

Morley, David (1997) 'Theoretical orthodoxies: textualism, constructivism and the new ethnography in cultural studies', in Marjorie Ferguson and Peter Golding (eds), *Cultural Studies in Question*. London: Sage. pp. 121–37.

Nayak, Anoop (1999) '"Ivory lives": race, ethnicity and practice of whiteness amongst young people'. PhD Thesis, Department of Geography, University of Newcastle upon Tyne.

Nayak, Anoop and Kehily, Mary Jane (1996) 'Playing it straight: masculinities, homophobias and schooling', *Journal of Gender Studies*, 5 (2): 211–20.

Ogbu, John L. (1974) *The Next Generation: An Ethnography of Education in an Urban Neighborhood*. New York: Academic Press.

Parker, Andrew (1996) 'The construction of masculinity within boys' physical education', *Gender and Education*, 8 (2): 141–57.

Pearson, Geoffrey and Twohig, John (1977) 'Ethnography through the looking-glass', in Stuart Hall and Tony Jefferson (eds), *Resistance through Rituals: Youth Subcultures in Post-war Britain* (first published 1975). London: Hutchinson. pp. 119–25.

Probyn, Elizabeth (1993) *Sexing the Self: Gendered Positions in Cultural Studies*. London: Routledge.

Raissiguier, Catherine (1993) 'Negotiating work, identity and desire: the adolescent dilemmas of working-class girls of French and Algerian descent in a vocational high school', in Cameron McCarthy and Warren Crichlow (eds), *Race, Identity and Representation in Education*. London: Routledge.

Raissiguier, Catherine (1995) 'The construction of marginal identities: working-class girls of Algerian descent in a French school', in Marianne H. Marchand and Jane L. Parpart (eds), *Feminism/Postmodernism/ Development*. London: Routledge. pp. 79–93.

Rhedding-Jones, Jeanette (1996) 'Researching early schooling: poststructural practices and academic writing in an ethnography', *British Journal of Sociology of Education,* 17 (1): 21–37.

Riddell, Sheila I. (1992) *Gender and the Politics of the Curriculum*. London: Routledge.

Roberts, Brian (1977) 'Naturalistic research into subcultures and deviance', in Stuart Hall and Tony Jefferson (eds), *Resistance Through Rituals: Youth Subcultures in Post-war Britain* (first published 1975). London: Hutchinson. pp. 243–52.

Roman, Leslie G. (1993) 'Double exposure: the politics of feminist materialist ethnography', *Educational Theory*, 43 (3): 279–308.

Roman, Leslie G. and Eyre, Linda (eds) (1997) *Dangerous Territories. Struggles for Difference and Equality in Education*. New York: Routledge.

Sharp, Rachel (1981) 'Review of *Beachside Comprehensive*', *British Journal of Sociology of Education*, 2 (3): 278–84.

Sharp, Rachel and Green, Anthony, with Lewis, Jacquine (1975) *Education and Social Control: A Study in Progressive Primary Education*. London: Routledge and Kegan Paul.

Silverman, David (1993) *Interpreting Qualitative Data. Methods for Analysing Talk, Text and Interaction*, London: Sage.

Skeggs, Beverley (1997) *Formations of Class and Gender*. London: Sage.

Skelton, Christine (1997) 'Primary boys and hegemonic masculinities', *British Journal of Sociology of Education*, 18 (3): 349–69.

Smith, Louis M. (1990) 'Critical introduction: whither classroom ethnography?', in Martyn Hammersley (ed.), *Classroom Ethnography: Empirical and Methodological Essays*. Milton Keynes: Open University Press. pp. 1–12.

Spindler, George (ed.) (1982) *Doing the Ethnography of Schooling: Educational Anthropology in Action*. New York: Holt, Rinehart and Winston.

Spindler, George and Spindler, Louise (1982) 'Roger Harkes and Schönhausen: from the familiar to the strange and back', in George Spindler (ed.), *Doing the Ethnography of Schooling. Educational Anthropology in Action*. New York: Holt, Rinehart and Winston. pp. 20–47.

Stacey, Judith (1988) 'Can there be a feminist ethnography?', *Women's Studies International Forum*, 11 (1): 21–7.

Stanley, Julia (1989) *Marks on the Memory: Experiencing School*. Milton Keynes: Open University Press.

Taylor, Sandra (1993) 'Transforming the texts: towards a feminist classroom practice', in Leslie K. Christian-Smith (ed.), *Texts of Desire: Essays on Fiction, Femininity and Schooling*. London: Falmer Press. pp. 126–44.

Thorne, Barrie (1992) 'Girls and boys together ... but mostly apart: gender arrangements in elementary schools', in Julia Wrigley (ed.), *Education and Gender Equality*. London: Falmer Press. pp. 115–30.

Thorne, Barrie (1993) *Gender Play: Girls and Boys in Schools*. Buckingham: Open University Press.

Troman, Geoff (1996) 'The rise of the new professionals? The restructuring of primary teachers' work and professionalism', *British Journal of Sociology of Education*, 17 (4): 473–87.

Troyna, Barry and Hatcher, Richard (1992) *Racism in Children's Lives: A Study of Mainly White Primary Schools*. London: Routledge.

Walker, J.C. (1986) 'Romanticising resistance, romanticising culture: problems in Willis' theory of cultural production', *British Journal of Sociology of Education*, 17 (1): 59–80.

Warren, Richard L. (1982) 'Schooling, bi-culturalism, and ethnic identity: a case study', in George Spindler (ed.), *Doing Ethnography of Schooling*. New York: Rinehart and Winston. pp. 382–409.

Watson, Ian (1993) 'Education, class and culture: the Birmingham ethnographic tradition and the problem of the new middle class', *British Journal of Sociology of Education*, 14 (2): 179–97.

Wax, Murray L. (1971) 'Comparative research upon the schools and education: an anthropological outline', in Murray L. Wax, Stanley Diamond and Fred Gearing (eds), *Anthropological Perspectives on Education*. New York: Basic Books. pp. 293–9.

Wax, Murray and Wax, Rosalie (1971) 'Great tradition, little tradition, and formal education', in Murray L. Wax, Stanley Diamond and Fred Gearing (eds), *Anthropological Perspectives on Education*. New York: Basic Books. pp. 3–27.

Wexler, Philip, with the assistance of Warren Crichlow, June Kern and Rebecca Martusewicz (1992) *Becoming Somebody: Toward a Social Psychology of School*. London: Falmer Press.

Willis, Paul (1977) *Learning to Labour: How Working Class Kids Get Working Class Jobs*. Farnborough: Saxon House.

Wolcott, Harry F. (1973) *The Man in the Principal's Office*. New York: Holt, Rinehart and Winston.

Wolcott, Harry F. (1982) 'Mirrors, mods, and monitors: educator adaptations of the ethnographic innovation', in George Spindler (ed.), *Doing the Ethnography of Schooling. Educational Anthropology in Action*. New York: Holt, Rinehart and Winston. pp. 68–95.

Wolpe, Ann Marie (1988) *Within School Walls. The Role of Discipline, Sexuality and the Curriculum*. London and New York: Routledge.

Woods, Peter (1979) *The Divided School*. London: Routledge and Kegan Paul.

Woods, Peter (1996) *Researching the Art of Teaching: Ethnography for Educational Use*. London and New York: Routledge.

Wright, Cecile (1986) 'School processes – an ethnographic study', in J. Eggleston, D. Dunn and M. Anjali (eds), *Education for Some: The Educational and Vocational Experiences of 15-18-Year Old Members of Minority Ethnic Groups*. Stoke-on-Trent: Trentham.

Wright, Cecile (1992a) 'Early education: multiracial primary school classrooms', in D. Gill, B. Mayor and M. Blair (eds), *Racism and Education: Structures and Strategies*. London: Sage. pp. 5–41.

Wright, Cecile (1992b) *Race Ratios in the Primary School*. London: David Fulton. pp. 191–23.

Wright, Cecile (1998) '"Caught in the crossfire": reflections of a black female ethnographer', in Paul Connolly and Barry Troyna (eds), *Researching Racism in Education: Politics, Theory and Practice*. Buckingham: Open University Press. pp. 67–78.

Young, Michael F.D. (ed.) (1971) *Knowledge and Control*. London: Collier–Macmillan.

14

Ethnography and the Study of Deviance

DICK HOBBS

Ethnographies of deviant behaviour are amongst the most popular within the sociological genre, identifying studies that require a commitment to 'personal observation, interaction, and experience [as] the only way to acquire accurate knowledge about deviant behavior' (Adler, 1985: 11). Inevitably in such a review there will be omissions, particularly of studies that constitute a cocktail of methodologies, although every attempt has been made to cover as wide a spectrum as possible and not merely to round up the usual suspects. The chapter will cross and re-cross anthropology, sociology and criminology in an effort to highlight research that encounters deviance in its natural setting. Consequently, ethnographies of deviant action in the context of policing, courts and prisons are excluded. The central principle that drives the chapter, and underpins the better studies, is that deviants, '[like] any group of persons ... develop a life of their own that becomes meaningful, reasonable, and normal once you get close to it and ... a good way to learn about any of these worlds is to submit oneself in the company of the members to the daily round of petty contingencies to which they are subject' (Goffman, 1968: lx–x).

Broadly, the chapter is organized chronologically, as it is felt that such a structure best illustrates the emergent theoretical and methodological themes. As a starting point, mid-nineteenth-century London, both the centre of the world's most powerful military and trading empires and a byword for urban squalor and social decay, is a suitably ambiguous site to commence. Complex social phenomena within a modern urban social setting featured in the work of a number of nineteenth-century commentators, for instance, the journalism and fiction of Dickens, or Engels' analysis of the political economy. However, the work of Henry Mayhew marks the first attempt both to document social phenomena via personal engagement, and analyse it utilizing a methodology that is identifiable to contemporary social scientists.

Mayhew wrote eighty-two 10,000-word articles for the *Morning Chronicle*,[1] describing the material conditions and lived experiences of the poor, and by the craven standards of contemporary criminology boldly locates deviant behaviour within these conditions. Whether he wrote of prostitution amongst needlewomen,[2] begging and homelessness,[3] theft,[4] pickpockets,[5] or drunkenness,[6] deviance is richly and sympathetically described. Situated within the political economy of the era, deviant behaviour is seen by Mayhew as an inevitable response to irregular work: 'It is a moral impossibility that the class of labourers who are only occasionally employed should be either generally industrious and temperate – both industry and temperance being habits produced by constancy of employment and uniformity of income' (Vol. 1: 83, 30/10/1849).

Mayhew also wrote at some length about coster-mongers, itinerant street traders who were distinguished by their language, by their attitude to employment, their disruptive pastimes such as dog fighting and gambling, their dismissal of religion and formal marriage, and their violence and physical opposition to authority.[7] More than any other aspect of his work, the unearthing of the coster-mongers should be seen as a forerunner of the appreciative work on deviant subcultural life that emerged a century later. (See also Mayhew and Binney, [1862] 1968 on professional crime.)

THE CHICAGO TRADITION

The influence of the University of Chicago's sociology department is an inescapable theme from this point onwards (see Chapters 1 and 2). Echoing the work of Mayhew, and reflecting the concerns of journalistic contemporaries such as Jacob Riis and Lincoln Steffens. Robert Park inspired some of the most exhilarating and methodologically unsophisticated ethnographies of deviance. The Chicagoan combination of ecology, formalism and journalism is at the heart of the ethnographic tradition. Prompted by Park's exhortations to his students to '... go get the seat of your pants dirty in real research' (Becker, cited in McKinney, 1966: 71), the Chicago School's early studies of the urban poor often indicated deviance as a feature of the diversity of distinct communities, which due to their occupant's socioeconomic niche as immigrants, was an essential part of communal identities in the process of assimilation. Consequently, 'The life of the slum is lived almost entirely without the conventional world' (Zorbaugh, 1929: 152), and the conventional world was hostile. The sense of difference, separateness and normality within a milieu of rapid change set the scene for the classic ethnographies of deviant life that were to follow. Few could be described as pure ethnographies, and they tended to employ a range of methodologies, but it is the ethnographic content and the ensuing insights for which they are so rightly celebrated, being based on close observation and interviews carried out in their natural setting.

Nels Anderson ceased being an itinerant worker when he commenced his academic career, and with the benefit of an absence of methodological training wrote *The Hobo* ([1923] 1975).[8] Anderson details the social world of the hobo, using sixty life histories, interviews and descriptions and 'what he knows', to highlight five types of homeless men, and depict a complex cultural universe integral to both the reality and myth of the United States. An itinerant mobile workforce in effect built the country and was as essential to the nation's economy as were the inhabitants of the rookeries to mid-nineteenth century London.

The inclusion of Thrasher's study of Chicago youth gangs ([1927] 1963) in this chapter may appear contentious, for the methodology is a bizarre and often unspecified mixture of 'census and court records, personal observation, and personal documents collected from gang boys and from persons who had observed gangs in many contexts' (Short, 1963: xviii). The observational data situates gang activity within interstitial areas of the city, identifying an astonishing 1,313 gangs operating within the city's poverty belt, consisting of 25,000 members. Virtually every possible youthful lower class street collaboration, 'from loose knit groups of drug users and institutionalized sports clubs to violent groups of street pirates' (Hobbs, 1997: 803), feature in the study. The interview segments now read quite stiff and formal, and the twenty-one life histories written by gang members even more so. Yet an ethnographic richness does pervade, particularly in the location of gangs within delinquency areas, which are typified by social disorganization amongst immigrant communities, and in the multiple conflicts that are organized around working-class territorial imperatives. The notion of deviant groups being interstitial, filling the voids left by various forms of urban disorganization, has been enormously influential, and will be returned to later.

Cressey's *Taxi-Dance Hall* (1932) was also concerned with a social world, that of a commercial dance hall where women are employed as dance partners. Cressey concentrated upon the meaning of the hall for the working women and the patrons, their special language, and the values, upon which their social world was structured. Having failed initially to gain the cooperation of the hall proprietors, Cressey sent a team into the halls to act as participant observers. The structural arrangements upon which working-class single male leisure is examined, as the unsentimental social world of the Taxi-Dance Hall is recreated for the reader, exposing 'the distinct vocabulary and ways of acting, the interpretations of activities, the code, the organization and structure, and the dominant schemes of life ...' (Cressey, 1932: 53).[9]

Whyte's *Street Corner Society* is also a study of social order and organization, and successfully refutes social disorganization as a prime factor in producing deviance, for as Whyte explains, 'Cornerville's problem is not lack of organization but failure of its own social organization to mesh with the structure of the society around it' (Whyte, [1943] 1955: 273). Whyte produced 'a documented hierarchy of personal relations based on a system of reciprocal obligations' ([1943] 1955: 272), via an ethnography based on his relationship with 'Doc', his sponsor or gatekeeper to the world of 'Cornerville'. Whyte describes structural arrangements based on cooperative action rooted in the political and social economic foundations of a community configured upon mutual obligations, within which a range of deviant activity featured as normal. Whyte succeeds in setting a tone that is genuinely appreciative and is afforded a political dimension. Whyte achieves this by richly describing everyday activities in fine detail that succeed in convincing the reader that the narrator has produced an authentic account.[10]

In a study of equal importance to that of Whyte, Suttles (1968) worked as an assistant at a boys club in order to gain access to a slum neighbourhood under threat of demolition. He lived on Chicago's West Side for three years, and via his participation in the community, reinforced much of Whyte's thesis regarding the existence of gangs as informal organizations whose primary function is to protect the 'defended neighbourhood' from intruders. This is achieved by stressing the evolution of street corner cultures featuring community-specific, essentially functional attributes that are intrinsic to the local community. The street gang consists of youths who are 'hardly the unruly and unreachable youths that we are led to expect ... The street corner groups not only make their members known to the remainder of the neighborhood, but create a network of personal acquaintances that augment those already in existence' (Suttles, 1968: 172–3). The perception of deviance being crucial to the local social order is pivotal to the ethnographic work of Whyte and Suttles, and the informality that is apparent in both studies emphasizes a local order within which agglomerations of youth thrive more in harmony than in conflict with their locale. Both Whyte and Suttles stress deviant action that is less structured, but more functional than the early studies of delinquent youth, yet succeed in retaining the spirit and dynamism that was first expressed in the work of Thrasher.

Liebow's *Tally's Corner* is based upon 18 month's participant observation in a black neighbourhood in Washington. As a white Jewish male, Liebow studied the day-to-day lives of two dozen men, focusing upon 'the streetcorner man as breadwinner, father, husband, lover and friend' (Liebow, 1967: 12). Deviance in the form of gambling, drinking and a healthy cynicism towards some aspects of straight culture is presented as an integral part of local community life, much of which thrives on the street. The methodological appendix, written in a narrative reminiscent of Whyte, tells the personal story of Liebow's project and deals rather unconvincingly with the issue of race, for instance his presence as the only white male at a dance of a thousand people is mentioned virtually in passing. However, his discussion of the relationship that developed with Tally is rather more instructive, and should be considered along with other famous researcher, gatekeeper/key informant associations.

Underdog Sociology

The massive influence of Chicago continued into the postwar period, and ethnographies of deviance featured prominently amongst the work of scholars of the 'second Chicago School' (Fine, 1995). In Becker's covert study of dance musicians (1951), the author worked as a musician and uncovered a learnt environment, a social world that is partially deviant. This paved the way for Becker's seminal study of marijuana use (1953), an activity that is presented in terms of a three-stage learning process: learning the technique, learning to perceive the effects, and learning to enjoy the effects. Becker's 1963 collection (Becker, 1963) created a flagship for both a method and a theory, for as the sociology of deviance emerged, so interactionism gained

ground, competing with conventional criminology which Becker described as, 'a practical pursuit, devoted to helping society deal with those it found troublesome' (Becker, 1964: 1).

Goffman (1968) located the troublesome by working as assistant to the athletic director of a large federal mental hospital in Washington. Through his informal interactions with patients, he focused upon the means by which the treatment of deviant behaviour creates conformity amongst individuals via the professionalization of informal control mechanisms and the creation of a moral order. Goffman's subjects were not therefore mentally ill, but sufferers of hospitalization, a process that required an adjustment to a new stage in their moral career. Goffman's study is, of course, a study of institutions rather than deviance, but his work has been hugely influential on ethnographic-based studies in related areas, for instance in the sociology of policing,[11] and criminal courts.[12] Becker and Goffman succeeded in laying down a body of work that has assumed almost iconic status amongst successive generations of scholars. The interactionist/labelling school marked a total break from legalism and focused the reader's attention upon social control institutions. Consequently 'deviance is not a quality of the act the person commits but rather a consequence of the application by others of rules and sanctions to an offender' (Becker, 1963: 9). As Sumner explains, 'The individual always made a choice and reigned sovereign over social forces' (Sumner, 1994: 242).

This sociology of the underdog, of 'nuts, sluts and preverts' (Liazos, 1972), which was to be crudely savaged on political grounds from the left by Gouldner (1975) and the right by Turk (1969), peaked in Polsky's celebration of low life ([1967] 1971). This study, ostensibly of poolroom hustling, is actually five freestanding essays on subjects such as 'beat' culture and pornography. The central essay on 'The Hustler' (pp. 43–114) provides the only ethnographic material. Based upon the author's poolroom experiences, he describes the workings of a profession rooted in the sub-cultural world of urban deviance. However, Polsky is best known for a coruscating chapter on the morality and pragmatics of ethnographic work with deviants (pp. 115–47), a chapter that has been used as a rough guide by a great number of ethnographers (for instance, Adler, [1985] 1993; Hobbs, 1988), in which he slaughters traditional criminological endeavour and waves the flag for ethnography.

Radical Ambiguity

During the 1960s a dissatisfaction with both conventional criminology and with the limitations of interactionism created the environment for what seemed at the time to many commentators to be a serious intellectual and political movement (Cohen, 1971: ch. 1). What emerged was a loose knit confederacy of 'Anarchists, CND, Young Communists and International Socialists' (Cohen, 1974: 27), a 'dynamic hotchpotch of interactionists, anarchists, phenomenologists, and Marxists' (Sumner, 1994: 262), where deviancy was viewed as part of the struggle waged by the lower orders against the forces of repression. The formation of the National Deviancy Conference in 1968 spawned a number of symposia, several edited collections and one of the most influential criminology texts of the postwar era (Taylor et al., 1973) The 'New Criminologists' considered that 'For us, as for Marx ... deviance is normal – in the sense that men are now ... asserting their human diversity' (Taylor et al., 1973: 282). This rhetoric promoted ethnographic work as an alternative to the instrumental positivism typified by 'mainstream criminology' (Cohen, 1974: 1–40), and initially the underdog ethnographies of the interactionists were embraced (Cohen, 1971: 9–24), the notion of a sceptical approach to the study of crime and deviance ideally complimented the sense of irony that is central to many ethnographic projects (Matza, 1969; Atkinson, 1990: 170–4). Yet despite the apparent championing of ethnography, at the first fourteen symposia, consisting of seventy papers, less than ten featured ethnographic work of any type.

However, with the tantalizing prospect of a 'fully social' (Taylor et al., 1973: 268–82) theory of deviance apparently imminent, some scholars did eschew the internal wrangling that blighted the New Criminology project (Taylor et al., 1975: 203–44) to discuss as integral to their ethnographic work, the structural arrangements that construct the social parameters within which deviant worlds are created. Archard (1979), in his ethnography of skid row alcoholics in London, succeeds in blending the political drive of the New Deviancy theorists with the theoretical rigour of symbolic interactionism. Archard attended soup runs, magistrates courts, common lodging houses, parks and other venues frequented by alcoholics. He also interviewed professionals working with alcoholics and with alcoholics themselves, but most importantly, he entered several skid row drinking schools, and describes the routine of drinking, begging and buying drink that constituted the world of the skid row alcoholic. During his 15 months in the field he 'went native' on several occasions, as the drink took its toll and note-taking ceased. Archard focuses upon skid row alcoholism in terms of efforts to contain and control it, yet given the heroic nature of the fieldwork, the study lacks a deep description of the drinkers' social world, relying upon segments of interviews to reinforce theoretical points.

Corrigan's study of working-class youth in the North East of England (1979) is based upon ethnographic work that locates the routine nature of deviance in the context of schooling. There is, contrary to Archard's fulsome fieldwork chapter, hardly any account of his fieldwork practice, and Corrigan explains youth deviance in terms of the imposition of mass education, and the everyday relationship between youths and agents of control: 'the major aspect of rules for these boys is the power of the enforcer rather than the existence of the rules in abstract' (1979: 140).

It is an interesting phenomenon of this era that the unpalatable realities of such distinctly unheroic deviancy as burglary, or crimes against women, tended to be avoided. Indeed before many of the same cast reassembled under the banner of 'Left Realism' (Lea and Young, 1984; Kinsey, Lea and Young, 1986), the ideologically imposed limits of ethnography were found in any form of working-class deviance not interpreted as constituting resistance to the oppressive heel of capitalism. However, this era also produced one of the most enduring ethnographies of deviance in Paul Willis' *Learning to Labour* (1977). In his ethnographic work with male teenagers, Willis shows how deviance functions as a way of formalizing, via the school, conflictual relations with middle-class culture, and prepares working-class youth for their inherited position on the labour market. Links between the culture of the school and the culture of work are skilfully established by Willis, indicating the futile nature of 'lads' deviance at school, and the irony of its consequences. Willis also avoids the celebratory analysis that is prevalent in some studies of this era, and highlights the contradictory nature of state-run institutions and the authority that they claim. The methodology that Willis used to explore the 'subordinate culture' of 'the lads' (as opposed to the culture of the 'ear'oles', who subscribed to the school's ethos of hard work and academic success), involved Willis sitting in on classes 'as a pupil', accompanying the fifteen boys in his sample during their leisure hours, and carrying out observations and interviews at work, and his analysis of the way in which symbolic resistance reinforces class relations remains as compelling as his description of mass production and mass employment are dated.

WOMEN, ETHNOGRAPHY AND DEVIANCE

Robert Park addressed his famous exhortation for his students to get the seats of their pants dirty to 'Gentlemen', and although some of the most influential work mentioned in this chapter has been carried out by women, particularly in the respective fields of gangs and drugs (see the work of Patricia Adler, Anne Campbell, Joan Moore and Louise Dunlap), ethnographies of deviance, both authorship and subject, are dominated by men. Whether or not this is disproportionate to the male/female ratio found amongst, for instance, demographers is hard to tell, but there is undoubtedly a paucity of ethnographic studies of female deviance (cf. Downes and Rock, 1998), and as a consequence the female offender remains 'elusive' (Hudson, 1990). Mayhew located the female deviant as a fallen woman whose agency (like that of working-class men) was restricted to coping with economic oppression (see above). Although female deviants were often dismissed by an earlier generation of male scholars (cf. Cohen, 1955),[13] since Carol Smart's thought-provoking work in the late 1970s, debates concerning male bias in criminology have been a feature of the discipline, and it is beyond the rubric of this chapter to provide a review of feminist critiques of male criminology, indeed this has been carried out at length elsewhere (Gelsthorpe, 1997; Gelsthorpe and Morris, 1988; Heidensohn, 1996; Smart, 1976), and criticisms of male ethnographies feature as essential parts of these critiques (McRobbie, 1980; Millman, 1975; see also Hedderman and Hough, 1994).

Male ethnographers, particularly those concerned with gangs and subcultures, have tended to situate their female subjects as bit part players in various (usually violent) adolescent psycho dramas (Robins and Cohen, 1978; Patrick, 1973),[14] and amongst contemporary criminologists, both male and female, there is a tendency to view women principally as victims.[15] However, Carlen (1983, 1985, 1988),[16] in her studies of convicted, mainly property offenders, and Mcleod (1982) and Miller (1986), in their studies of prostitution, afford the same degree of agency to women that has traditionally been afforded to male deviants, rewarding them with 'a better standard of living, an outlet for energies and talents, and a network of non judgemental friends' (Carlen, 1988: 106–10).[17] In her ethnography of prostitution in Spain, Hart (1998) emphasizes the ambiguity that is integral to the often taken-for-granted power relationship between female deviants and men, represented here by prostitute and client. This anthropological study also represents one of the most consistently reflexive ethnographic enterprises, with Hart explicitly locating herself amongst the data throughout the book, as she hung around a barrio bar with the women and their clients.

The emergence of deviant female identities that complement normative notions of being female (Fountain, 1993; Dunlap et al., 1994; Hobbs, 1995: ch. 1) is particularly evident in Miller's ethnography of prostitution (1986), indicating that prostitute women conduct relatively orderly careers, careers that are enabled by older women in the extended family taking responsibility for the children. In turn, prostitute women will return to the domestic realm to take their turn at looking after their grandchildren when it is their daughters turn to pick up the trade. Likewise, Taylor's drug addicts were coping with

their habits while simultaneously dealing with pregnancy and child rearing (Taylor, 1993).

Anne Campbell's (1984) depiction of girl members of violent delinquent gangs situates female gang members within the structural constraints of class and ethnicity as well as gender. Spending six months with each of three girl gangs in New York, Campbell focused in particular upon one gang member in each gang, and highlighted the reproduction of normative gender roles within gangs establishing violence as a particularly ambivalent feature, which both contradicts and enforces normative images of femininity. Campbell simultaneously questions a number of female stereotypes, whilst identifying the control exerted over the girls by male gang members and the seduction of the stable marriage and beautiful home, while indicating that violence in defence of turf was a distinct characteristic of both male and female gang membership. Campbell succeeds in teasing out parallels between deviant life in the gang and the non-gang world, and stresses that for young women the attractions of gang membership should be understood in the context of the isolation, poverty and welfare dependency that constitutes their inevitable futures.

DEVIANT YOUTH

British Youth

The three ethnographies of deviance that emanated from doctoral theses written at the London School of Economics during the mid-1960s to early 1970s have been hugely influential upon subsequent generations of sociologists and criminologists. All three authors were involved in the National Deviancy Symposium, but their lineage can be traced back to the Chicagoan ecological study of Morris (1957). Downes' study (1966), which featured amongst more orthodox methods of studying delinquent youth, 'informal observation', involving 6 months' fieldwork in youth clubs, pubs and a late night 'caff',[18] located socialization in school as the prime reason for working-class youth accepting low level work. Most importantly, however, Downes denied the existence of the youth gangs so vividly described by American researchers, rather he discovered the existence of 'street corner groups', loose knit friendship groups linked to territoriality via which youths acknowledge the futility of work, and dissociate themselves from middle-class-oriented aims and practices by engaging in deviant action.

Young's study of illicit drug use (1971), although based on his own experiences in London during the late 1960s, is more concerned with deviancy amplification than deviant action. Young attacked the preconceptions of control agents and questioned the authority and validity of dominant moralities, pointing out their role in construction of deviant stereotypes. There is no discussion of methodology in this highly influential book, and although steeped in interactionism, there is no evidence of systematic observation or participation, rather a set of propositions regarding the role of the police in the deviancy amplification process (1971: 169–97).

Stanley Cohen's study of the 'moral panic' that emanated from the public holiday battles between Mods and Rockers at British seaside towns in the 1960s is also based upon a mixture of methodologies, including documentary analysis and interviews, and questionnaires (1973: 205–10). Cohen worked as a volunteer on a project designed to provide shelter for youths attending the holiday festivities, and used this as a base for interviews and observations. He also conducted observational work during public holidays at two sites over a two-year period, and rather coyly refers to 'one Bank Holiday ... [when] the method came closer to what sociologists un-humorously refer to as "participant observation" in that I wore what could roughly be called Mod clothes and enjoyed the days with various groups on the beaches and the nights in the clubs' (1973: 210).[19] The resultant study brought to public attention the concept of moral panic, a concept that in Cohen's study is represented by the perceived threat to societal values of 'A condition, episode, person or group of persons ...' (1973: 9). The mass media are the principal agents of the dramatization of what contemporaneously seems mundane youth deviancy, and Cohen's distinctly Durkheimian take on the functionality of deviance, his utility of symbolic interactionism within an acknowledgement of the structural arrangements of class society, and his sensitive rendition of subcultural meaning and membership, results in one of the most satisfying ethnographically orientated studies of the era.

Somewhat removed from the concerns of the New Criminologists, were the group of researchers that emanated from Liverpool University, and in particular the work of John Mays, a Liverpool youth worker. Utilizing a range of methods including ethnography, Mays work is closer than most British researchers to the Chicago tradition of neighbourhood ethnographies. Mays (1954) located delinquency as a social tradition of neighbourhoods characterized by 'a long history of poverty, casual employment and bad housing' (1954: 147). Howard Parker, also engaged as a community worker, in his Liverpool study (1974), found that 'The Boys' were born into a structured, clearly defined delinquent territory, and that both the adolescents and adults shared the basic structural constraints and social inequalities of the 'Roundhouse Estate'. Consequently, deviance constituted an accommodation to their structural situation, rather than a rejection of, or resistance to, dominant values.

Gill (1977: 94), also a Liverpool community worker, found that the corner boys of 'Casey's Corner' inherited a neighbourhood delinquent tradition that Gill linked to a specific housing policy (1977: 117). For the Luke Street kids unemployment was a norm that had to be accepted (p. 110), and if work was found, it would be monotonous, badly paid and uncongenial. The result was a subcultural tradition featuring a range of deviant behaviour from 'hanging about', to petty theft and riot.

Football hooliganism is a highly visible form of deviance with its roots in working-class youth culture, and its relative accessibility has yielded a number of valuable studies featuring observational work (Giulianotti, 1991; Robins, 1984). However, Armstrong's (1998) ten-year study constitutes the richest ethnographic account. With at times more detail than all but the most committed reader will need to know about 'away days to Hull', Armstrong details the context and practice of committed football fandom, situating football hooliganism within a milieu of industrial masculinity and the gentrification of working-class leisure. Armstrong is also one of the few contemporary ethnographers unafraid to oppose the authoritarian tendencies of administrative criminologists, and has produced via some rich descriptions of provincial territorial violence on the streets and in the pubs of Sheffield, a truly appreciative account of deviant action.

The only researcher to claim the existence of American-style gangs in Britain is Patrick (1973), who, like Liebow, May, Parker, Gill and others, used his occupation to gain access to deviant youth. Yet unlike these writers, Patrick's fieldwork was conducted covertly. He worked as a teacher in a Scottish approved school, and became aware via the inmates of teenage gang activity in Glasgow. One of the inmates, Tim, acted as a gatekeeper to the world of 'The Young Team', and for four months Patrick became a weekend peripheral member of a violent teenage gang. Patrick gives an account of territorial-based fighting gangs that conform to Thrasher's structured gang, in terms of leadership and designated roles, within a loose collectivity that is orientated towards spontaneous violence. Patrick claims that the gangs emerge from long-established working-class neighbourhoods that suffer levels of deprivation unmatched elsewhere in Britain (1973: 118), resulting in an enduring gang subculture hinging on dissociation from middle-class norms.[20]

AMERICAN GANGS

Youth deviance continued to prove a most fruitful field for ethnographic study, and gang studies in the USA provide a consistent ethnographic strand linking the first Chicago school to the millennium. Although for many years Thrasher's study has been massively influential, the notion of gangs being the product of disorganized newly arrived poor immigrant communities, relies on a notion of deviant behaviour being interstitial existing between the disorganized culture of the new arrivals, and the stable environments of the respectable working class. Youths were expected to abandon gang life when blue-collar employment beckoned. However, contemporary ethnographers regard this model as being out of date. Moore (1978) stresses the way in which, excluded from the mainstream of economic life, informal Chicano culture forms gangs which were territorially based, segregated by age, and were violent and drug-orientated. This study underlines the way in which Mexican Americans are isolated from mainstream socioeconomic life and it is this isolation that formulates the context of gang formation. Using Chicano ex-convicts as research associates, the study revealed the life-long role of the territorially based, age-graded, violent, drug-dealing gang. Its interaction with the criminal justice system was also a major feature, as the high rate of Mexican American incarceration created prison gangs that provided continuities with gang life on the street, assuring ethnic solidarity and cohesion. Moore's later work (1991) highlighted the decline of Chicano neighbourhoods, and further emphasized the role of the political economy in making the gang, in the absence of legitimate institutions, an alternative neighbourhood government.

Of the current generation of gang researchers, there is no more passionate advocate of ethnography than Hagedorn (1988). Hagedorn's study evolved from his role as a community activist, and he worked closely with an ex-gang leader, in order to interview forty-seven gang members in researchers' homes or offices. The ethnographic sensibility of this study informed the shape of the enquiry, and enabled the interviews to take place. Hagedorn traces the emergence of gangs in Milwaukee during the 1980s, locating the economic conditions of black and Hispanic communities as the trigger for contemporary gang membership. More specifically, Hagedorn points to the relatively high levels of employment that existed when Thrasher was carrying out his seminal study, and the fact that in contemporary society there is 'no industrial ladder to step on' (1988: 42), reducing the chance that gang youth will 'mature out' of gang banging. As a consequence, a permanent underclass now exists that includes gangs as integral parts of minority communities (see Glick, 1990).

Vigil (1988) also gained access to gangs via his role as a local activist who shared many core biographical features with gang members. His Los Angeles study features life histories, qualitative interviews, the use of key informants and participant observation as the basis of the research strategy, in a book that locates the 'multiple marginality' of contemporary youths as structuring the basis of gang membership (Vigil, 1988).

Taylor's (1990) study also indicates how far gangs are now removed from Thrasher's original model. Taylor went back to his old neighbourhood in Detroit with a team gleaned from his own security and investigation company to observe and interview members of corporate gangs (representing the future), and scavenger gangs (representing the past), and succeeded in redefining the youth problem in terms of the entrepreneurial imperialism of the drugs trade (Taylor, 1990). Padilla's entrepreneurial 'Diamonds', a Puerto Rican street gang, echo many of these themes (1992). Although the author's ethnography is restricted by his desire to avoid violence and drug dealing, therefore concentrating on peripheral social relationships and off-duty gang activity, he succeeded in persuading Chicago gang members to 'help Felix write our story' (1992: 20). The story indicates that contemporary gangs based upon entrepreneurship are similar to the street gangs of the early twentieth century, who utilized rudimentary organizational structures based upon race, class and territory to evolve into America's principal organized crime groups (Lacey, 1991: ch. 3; Ianni, 1972).

Decker and Van Winkle (1996) utilized three years of ethnographic work in St Louis to inform the interviews carried out with gang members and their families. The richness of this departure into the family life of deviants is a most welcome humanizing innovation within the genre of gang studies, and the results of this study go a long way to establishing the normality of group deviance amongst disadvantaged urban youth. The study also indicates that the process of becoming a gang member marks an alignment with a loose confederation within whose informality is to be found protection from violence, and a confirmation of the weakening of gang members' ties with formal institutions and a confirmation of deviant identity.

Sanchez-Jankowski (1990), in his ten-year study of gangs in Los Angeles, New York and Boston, gained access to gangs via local community institutions. He claims to have participated fully in gang activity, yet avoided illegality, which, given that so much gang action revolves around crime and deviance, is somewhat hard to comprehend. None the less, he suffered physical attack both as part of initiation rituals, and as a result of being (falsely) accused of being an informant. Sanchez-Jankowski skilfully portrays the deviant as a rational actor selecting gang membership as a means of achieving collective benefits, benefits that are superior to those that can be acquired by the individual. In turn, the gang is viewed as an organization generating goals that supersede those of the rational actors that constitute its members, and as an organization that generates an ambivalent response from its host community by acquiring insulation from economic, ethnic and class marginality, constructing identities around a form of 'local patriotism' (Sanchez-Jankowski, 1990: 99).

Sullivan's comparative ethnography of three inner city neighbourhoods in New York (1989) constitutes a robust response to the conventional questionnaire- or survey-based approach that limits the scope of many studies of youth deviance. The focus of this study is the relationship between crime and unemployment and the role of acquisitive crime as a surrogate for legitimate employment. Unusually for an ethnography of deviance, Sullivan places a great deal of stress upon the policy implications of his findings, highlighting the needs of communities rather than punitive action against individuals.

DEVIANCE IN THE ADULT WORLD

Access to deviant youth can be gained via local schools, community initiatives etc. However, non-incarcerated deviant adults are not usually subjected to the same levels of surveillance as deviant youths, and so constitute hidden populations, who by utilizing both various forms of cultural capital and violence are able to protect their privacy. For instance, Hunter Thompson was severely beaten after spending a period with the Oakland chapter of the Hells Angels (1966). Thompson's book has been influential upon ethnographers. There is some excellent socio/historical scene-setting, a concise rendition of a moral panic, and a glimpse of early gonzo in his celebration of motorbike riding. However, Wolf's (1991) is an underrated ethnography that should now be regarded as the standard work. His exploration of his own deviant past enabling his total immersion in biker culture (the author acquired the club name of 'Coyote'), produced a genuinely appreciative study of a classic deviant subculture.

Humphreys' enlightening and controversial study (1970) of anonymous sexual encounters in the men's toilet of a Chicago public park is a landmark study. For the purposes of the research, Humphreys became a 'watch queen', a highly specialized role as a look-out for police or homophobic attack. In this role he was able to observe, and later describe in graphic detail, the sexual comportment of the participants, the roles that they adopted and, most controversially, how the sexuality of their home lives contradicted their tearoom activities.[21] In one of the more sociologically sound accounts of fieldwork (1970: 16–44), Humphreys describes how his field role evolved, the systematic nature of his observations, issues of sampling and analysis, and is refreshingly candid regarding ethics (pp. 161–73). He also describes, and to this reader justifies, his use of car registrations in order to trace the names and addresses of tearoom clientele (pp. 37–40). Further subterfuge followed when Humphreys, working on a social health survey, approached his tearoom sample regarding a range of demographic and personal issues, and was able to surreptitiously interrogate their straight sexual identities (pp. 41–4).[22] His findings expose the irony and ambiguity that is integral to deviant behaviour, indicating the thin façade of normality behind which deviant action thrives as part of discrete social worlds that provide, 'self-esteem, relief from torment, and important training on how to avoid conflict with the law' (Humphreys, 1970: 166).

Klockars' 'professional fence' (1975), in common with so many of the ethnographies mentioned in this chapter, began life as a doctoral thesis. The focus of Klockars' study is Vincent, who is a dealer in stolen goods. Klockars frames Vincent's practice within a historical context, before proceeding to spend time at work and leisure with him, learning the business of fencing and the drives and motivations of the proprietor of 'Vincent's Place'. Klockars closely observed Vincent in his domestic and commercial domains, where, 'Everybody's looking for a bargain ... 9 out of 10 people got larceny. Maybe even 99 out of 100 ... If the price is right and a man can use the merchandise, he's gonna buy. No question about it' (1975: 62). The result is an extremely candid account of deviant enterprise at the point where criminal and non-criminal commerce converge, where upper and underworld meet to trade and seek out bargains. Klockars' book also has the benefit of a very personal methods chapter, featuring in particular some of the problems of access faced by ethnographers (pp. 197–226), and there is a real sense of ethnographic work in itself being a fraught enterprise, beset by the petty and personal details of everyday life.[23]

Heyl's study of a career in prostitution (1979) also started out as a PhD thesis, and constitutes an ideal companion study to that of Klockars. Heyl charts the career of 'Anne', who after ten years as a prostitute works her way up to become the madam of her own 'service business'. Anne's life history is complimented by interviews with colleagues and family, and what emerges is a highly detailed account both of the construction and eventual deconstruction of a deviant identity, and the maintenance of a deviant enterprise. Heavily influenced by the work of Becker, Heyl's analysis is more sophisticated than that of Klockars, particularly in the negotiation of conflict with prostitutes, pimps and the police, but lacks Klockars' ability to frame deviance within historical and economic constraints, a common problem with studies explicitly wedded to interactionism. However, the detail provided in Heyl's study is outstanding, albeit derived principally from accounts as opposed to observation. Of particular note are the sequential stages of career development, and the complexity of managing an enterprise that shares many of the problems with legitimate business (for instance, frozen pipes in winter, unsuitable premises, disputes with business partners, uncooperative workforce), while possessing few of the advantages.

In ethnographic studies method and biography often merge in a reflexive soup of experiential reflection, and it is not uncommon for ethnographers to utilize their own biographies in order to gain and maintain access to deviant groups. Patricia Adler used her familiarity with southern California's drug culture to study upper level drug dealers and smugglers, in a remarkable project that focuses upon successful drug entrepreneurs. Adler illustrates, within a constantly evolving commercial framework, the overlapping business and social affiliations of a group who are 'secretive, deceitful, mistrustful, and paranoid' (Adler, 1985: 110). The six years of fieldwork with sixty-five dealers and smugglers, and their assorted wives, friends and family, unearthed careers dedicated to deviant work and hedonistic behaviour. Life was lived 'as a party' (Shover and Honaker, 1991), and Adler identifies a craving for pleasure, and legitimate societies' repression of pleasure-seeking through the routinization of everyday life, as providing the context for individuals to engage with upper level dealing and smuggling.[24]

A contrary use of the researcher's biography, that of the naive outsider, is to be found in Fielding's (1981) ethnography of an extreme right political group. Like most post-Gouldner ethnographies of deviance, great care is taken in piecing together the various sociohistorical aspects of the relevant phenomena, and in Fielding's study it is the evolution of British right-wing ideology that provides the context for the moral careers of 'National Front' members.

DEVIANT WORK, DEVIANCE AS NORMAL

Petty theft and 'fiddling' has provided suitably ambiguous areas of study for ethnographers of deviance. These studies highlight the artificial distinction between honest and dishonest, legal and illegal, and in different ways focus upon the way in which legitimate society accommodates low-level deviance as it becomes integral to the normative order. Henry's (1978) study of stolen goods trading networks was derived from a doctoral thesis. He used periods spent working in a number of jobs to generate interviews with twenty individuals operating within different networks. He also exploited relationships with friends, neighbours, colleagues and a number of probation referrals. Henry's concern was the linking of relationships that were formed around the trade in stolen goods, and is curiously negligent of the influence of class in both the formation and maintenance of these networks. The segments of interview data skilfully establish

the moral ambiguity that is at the core of this 'normal crime', as participants operate as skilled consumers in a market that relies as much upon reciprocity as the desire to reap a profit. However, his sober conclusion, reiterating his claim on the special nature of these networks, includes advocating community-based criminal justice, distributing sanctions based upon shaming the offender, and is a dampening feature that invites the wrath of Polsky.

Jason Ditton's study of fiddling in an English bread factory (1977) is one of the more sociologically satisfying ethnographies of deviance. Overtly influenced by Donald Roy and Erving Goffman, Ditton worked in a bakery, first during his student vacations, and then as a covert observer posing as a plant operative. His vacation work had ensured that he experienced no problems of acceptance at the bakery, although he did have some initial problems covertly taking notes. Indeed Ditton's comments on the merits and demerits of taking surreptitious notes on waxed toilet paper are a lesson to us all (1977: 5). His study became somewhat less covert and he embarked upon an ill-fated questionnaire before concentrating on an ethnography of fiddling in the bakery's dispatch department and then as a salesman. Ditton's skilful description of the process of acceptance and trust that he experienced is hugely insightful. Refusing to duck problems of ethics, he proclaims that, 'participant observation is inevitably unethical by virtue of being interactionally deceitful. It does not become ethical merely because this deceit is openly practiced. It only becomes inefficient' (1977: 10). He supplemented the 4,560 hours of observation with thirty-four taped interviews, and presents fiddling as a subculture of business 'somewhere between the inhuman accounts so often found in criminological literature, and the subhuman ones given by journalists' (p. 11).

The part-time criminals in Ditton's study are following a moral career, in which they learn and apply sometimes quite intricate techniques of theft, distribution and control while avoiding the adoption of a deviant identity by maintaining the activities' essential part-time nature. The bread salesmen's fiddling was carried out within an informal series of interlocking networks of knowledge and competence, the economic consequences of which are fully integrated into the commercial structure of the bakery by its management.

Hobbs' ethnography of East London has much in common with these studies of the hidden economy. The emphasis is upon the means by which the socioeconomic conditions inherited by the denizens of East London created a cultural response that, like that of East End detectives, is distinctly entrepreneurial.[25] This entrepreneurial culture is also, according to Hobbs, common to detectives who share with East Enders an essentially informal deviant identity. Hobbs emphasizes his own biography as an important factor in gaining access and dealing with ethical issues, claiming that the ethics of his informants and not those of academic life are those that he adhered to in this largely covert study. Deviant behaviour, presented here in descriptions of commercial burglary, theft from work, and dealing in stolen goods, is presented as a culturally sanctioned action that sits side by side with the hidden economy, self-employment and non-criminal buying and selling. Deviance is therefore normal; an 'Everyman Performance' integral to the existence of certain working-class communities, proffering opportunities for the utilization of culturally condoned action that emphasizes sharp practice and monetary gain.[26]

AT THE HEAVY END

This commercial imperative is also a feature of studies of more serious levels of deviance, for instance professional and organized crime, areas that have been colonized, relatively unambiguously by criminologists and journalists utilizing data generated by criminal justice agencies. Bourgois' (1995) ethnography of crack, culture and community in Spanish Harlem brings together many aspects of the classic Chicago community studies, coupled with late modern sensibilities that touch gender, race, crime and mutating commercial forces. His three years spent living in El Barrio with his family enabled Bourgois, a white male, albeit an 'honorary nigga' (1995: 41) to detail the careers of Puerto Rican crack dealers, and in particular the interactions in and around the local crack house. The normalization of serious deviation is presented in the context of economic as opposed to moral depravity, where individualism and pecuniary advantage reign over communal priorities. This study, along with the work of Williams, Padilla and Taylor, is someway removed from specialized academic concerns, and takes contemporary gangs and the communities that spawned them into what is sometimes presented as a more rarefied deviant zone, that of organized crime.

Professional and organized criminals, what Block calls the 'serious crime community' (1991), constitute a hidden population *par excellence.* Consequently, this community is ideal subject matter for ethnographers, particularly those with a penchant for covert investigation or those with, as indicated by many of the above studies of gangs, biographies that afford them special access. Even for these individuals research in this field is inevitably dangerous. Ken Pryce, who wrote an outstanding ethnography of the reproduction of urban Caribbean hustling culture in Bristol (1979), was murdered when he extended his interests into Jamaican organized crime.

Chambliss possessed no particularly biographical advantages when he walked into a Seattle bar 'with two days' growth of beard, a pair of khaki pants and an old shirt' (1978: 14), and commenced his study of organized crime and corruption. Nor as far as any reader can tell did Potter in his highly detailed study of organized crime in 'Moorisburg'[27] (1994; see also Rawlinson, 1996). However, Ianni used his Italian heritage to good effect by gaining access to the 'Lupollo' crime family. This study of the social system that constitutes organized crime is based on overt fieldwork, constituting access to family gatherings, private dinners and interviews with informants. Ianni concentrated not on the criminal activities of the family, but upon the 'codes and rules by which members of the Lupollo family organize their universe and behavior' (1972: 188). His subsequent refutation of many of the law enforcement generated myths concerning organized crime, based on his three years of fieldwork, constitutes a valuable and highly practical ethnographic enquiry.

The appreciative stance generated by ethnographic work has been particularly effective in studies of drug use, which in direct contrast to alternative methodologies, tend to stress elements of autonomy, and intelligence being applied to developing strategies designed to cope with the rigours of the political economy of urban street life. In Finestone's (1964) study of black male drug users, he highlights the value placed upon their 'kicks' and 'hustle', a world of imagination and innovation that is at odds with the liberal correctional consensus that was emerging as criminology. Preble and Casey's (1969) ethnography of heroin users, like Finestone's study, has been hugely influential. Observational work was supplemented by 200 life history interviews, and revealed a vibrant lifestyle that had the quest for heroin at the core of an existence that would otherwise be dominated by the monotonous constraints of grinding poverty. In this study, 'The quest for heroin is the quest for a meaningful life' (Preble and Casey, 1969: 3; see Sutter, 1966; Taylor, 1993).

Agar, working from an institutional base, utilized simulated situations to generate data for his ethnography of heroin addicts (Agar, 1973: ch. 3: 133–56). These simulations allowed Agar to develop themes based upon categories generated by his informants, and concentrate upon a cognitive approach to junkie culture. Although undoubtedly strengthened by the wealth of semantic analysis he derived from the simulations, the study is somewhat weakened by the lack of context that creates the parameters of the addicts' universe.

The ethnographic work generated by the National Development and Research Institute, and its associates is amongst the best contemporary work on deviance available. Principally concerned with drug use and its attendant trades, the Institute's output is sufficiently voluminous to merit savage editing in such a brief review as this, but the following studies warrant special mention. Dunlap et al.'s (1994) study of a female crack dealer normalizes a modern urban demon, and establishes the role of women in the drug trade as having close parallels with their role in the legitimate economy (see also Bourgois and Dunlap, 1992; Dunlap et al., 1990). Terry Williams' two studies of the crack trade (1989, 1992) show how apprenticeships into adult deviant groups are no longer necessary, as youths groups can evolve quite quickly into substantial illegal concerns in their own right (Williams, 1989: 14–61), reinforcing many of the points made by contemporary gang researchers concerning the entrepreneurial shift that gang culture has taken. Similarly, Mieczkowski's study of the crack trade in Detroit (1990), stresses the small size and relative isolation of the entrepreneurial units that typify the distribution of the drug.

One of the most successful and consistent academics to study persistent adult criminals is Neal Shover. Shover has published valuable studies of persistent thieves since the early 1970s, and although the criminal justice context of his data gathering excludes a detailed consideration of his work in this chapter, his ability to maintain long-term relationships with inmates on their release, and his use of 'free world' interviews to supplement his prison data betray a certain ethnographic sensibility that makes his work of inestimable value to any scholar with an interest in criminal careers (Shover, 1973, 1985, 1996; Shover and Honaker, 1991).[28]

However, using variations on ethnographic technique, some writers have ventured into 'free world' research with this category of deviant. Hobbs' (1995) study structured around case studies of British professional criminals based on fieldwork and interviews, is an ethnography emphasizing changes wrought upon the profession of crime over several decades. The study emphasizes the shift towards an entrepreneurial criminal culture that mirrors shifts in the legitimate worlds of industry, commerce and work.

Wright and Decker's work is as methodologically innovative as Hobbs is traditional (1994, 1997). Wright and Decker studied the 'cognitive script(s)' (1994: 204), of residential burglars (1994; see also Cromwell et al., 1991), and armed robbers (Wright and Decker, 1997), by employing an ex-offender with excellent contacts amongst the street and criminal fraternities of St Louis as an intermediary between the academic and criminal worlds. This intermediary 'established contacts and trust in the criminal subculture and [vouched] for the legitimacy of the research' (Wright and Decker, 1994: 18). The resulting 'snowball' referral effect (Wright et al., 1992), led to interviews being conducted with 105 and 86 offenders respectively, and although their informants were paid, the authors clearly state that the prime motivation for involvement was 'the opportunity to be in a book, albeit

anonymously, as a powerful acknowledgment of their competence' (1994: 26). The researchers then visited, with offenders, the location of recent burglaries and armed robberies to discuss the precise details of the act, in order to develop some notion of typicality. This latter methodology constitutes a remarkable use of ethnographic interviewing technique, lending the study an ethnographic sensibility that would have been lacking in more orthodox studies that rely upon some form of criminal justice or corrections referral.

CONCLUSIONS

This brief review of ethnographies of deviance suggests that most studies begin life as doctoral theses, indicating that the ethnographer's craft is practised for the most part by younger academics just launching a career. A large number of studies, particularly those focusing on the deviance of youth, tend to utilize social service agencies within the host community to facilitate access. The other common strategy in the negotiation of access is the researcher's individual biography; from Nels Anderson onwards, researchers have used ethnography as a tool to explore their own pasts. Aspects of class, gender and ethnicity, occupational or demographic knowledge, or indeed the researcher's own vices, all provide tools with which to negotiate access to deviant details hidden from the gaze of civilians.

For some researchers interviews feature as the prominent source of data, and ethnographic work involves nurturing relationships with deviant groups and their host communities, developing sufficient trust to enable interviews to take place. In studies such as these the fieldwork enables the researcher or research team to learn the language of the host community, and most pertinently, what questions to ask. This strategy was particularly prevalent where the researcher was excluded from membership of a deviant group, or where the researcher had reached the ethical or pragmatic boundaries of their involvement. Covert ethnographies do not have this problem, for deviance can be reported first hand rather than relying upon accounts of action from informants, but the practicalities of covert research on deviance, both ethically and practically, are immense.

The length of time researchers spent in the field also varies enormously. For some it was a weekend/part-time commitment, fitted in whenever the rigours of job or family permitted. At the other end of the scale ethnographers lived in the field for years, sharing the material world of the deviant. The extent to which ethnographers experienced the deviant's world therefore varies tremendously; a handful of weekends hardly constitutes the kind of situated intensity envisaged for instance by

Goffman (1989). However, deviant fraternities are not crofting communities in the Shetlands, and ethnographic work with deviants, who by definition constitute a hidden population, where secrecy is often the norm, can be difficult. As a consequence the reader must take what he can get, and a convincing account of a rarefied social field is often as good as it gets. For some researchers access to the community that housed deviant activity was sufficient; others sought out deviant actors, while for others access to deviant action provided the focus.

From the sociology of the Chicago School, through the interactionist studies of the 1950s and 1960s, and Marxist-inspired critics, to those contemporary scholars who in practice have enhanced rather than competed with their Chicagoan inheritance, there is an overwhelming bias towards ethnographies of deviant young men. Given the stress afforded by commentators of both the left and the right to the redundancy of men in the post-industrial age, and the subsequent danger that they pose to the normative social order, it is difficult to see an end to this long-term trend.

Each ethnographer brings different possibilities, tactics, responsibilities and tolerances to the field, and ethnographies of deviance proffer opportunities for social scientists to explore worlds that may be ordinary, or exotic, mundane or dangerous. The analysis of these worlds will then lend themselves to a range of descriptive, critical and theoretically adventurous styles. Ethnography is an adaptable tool, which, like deviants themselves, will continue to evolve. But as criminology and criminal justice studies have come to dominate the academic study of transgression, the modern criminologist's bookshelf has become overloaded with policy orientated criminal justice repair kits sitting spine to spine with a few token theoretical tomes.

The ethnographer of deviance will be well aware of the wisdom of Polsky's warning over thirty years ago: 'Until the criminologist learns to suspend his personal distaste for the values and lifestyles of the untamed savages, until he goes out into the field to the cannibals and head-hunters and observes them without trying to civilize them or turn them over to colonial officials ... he will only be a jail house or court house sociologist ...' (Polsky, [1967] 1971: 145). Legalism and its myriad processes along with the terminal timidity of bourgeois academics dictate agendas, and ethnographies of deviance are increasingly rare, which makes the inheritance richer, and the challenge to delay the funeral, or at least extend the wake, all the more enticing.

NOTES

1 Mayhew's *Morning Chronicle* work is available in many forms, but this chapter refers to the six-volume edition published in 1980. This edition has the advantage of a subject index, and an illuminating introduction by Peter Razzell. It also features material unavailable elsewhere, and is presented in the original sequence. Selections of the more picaresque of Mayhew's writings are also to be found in *Mayhew's London* (edited by P. Quennell, Bracken Books, London, 1984), which features selections from the three-volume version of *London Labour and the London Poor* first published in 1851, and *Mayhew's Underworld* (edited by P. Quennell, Bracken Books, London, 1983), which features selections from the fourth volume, published in 1862. In addition, *Mayhew's Characters* (edited by P. Quennell, Spring Books, London, 1951) features selections from all four volumes.

2 Mayhew, 1980: vol. 1, 13/11/1849; 23/11/1849.

3 Vol. 2, 15/1/1850; vol. 3, 18/1/1850; 22/1/1850; 25/1/1850; 29/1/1850; 31/1/1850.

4 Vol. 3, 31/1/1850; vol. 4, 25/10/1850; 29/3/1850; 25/4/1850.

5 Vol. 3, 29/1/1850.

6 Vol. 2, 11/12/1849; 21/12/1849; 25/12/1849; 28/12/1849; 1/1/1850; 4/1/1850 and 8/1/1850; 8/1/1850; vol. 4, 11/3/1850; vol. 5, 27/6/1850; 25/7/1850.

7 Vol. 1, 27/11/1849; vol. 11, 30/11/1849.

8 The 1961 Phoenix edition contains an invaluable introduction by Anderson, in which he reflects upon his early life, his family and his years as an itinerant worker travelling America. For students, it also contains in full the only methodological instruction Anderson was to receive from Robert Park: 'Write down only what you see, hear and know, like a newspaper reporter' (1961: xii). See also Anderson's reflective article in *Urban Life* (1983).

9 Two life histories also emerged during this classic period, Shaw's *The Jack Roller* (1930), a study of a delinquent career, and Sutherland's *The Professional Thief* (1937). (For a discussion of life histories, see Plummer, [1983] 2001.) Case studies were part of the methodological armory of the Chicago School, and deserve some mention here for their part in the continuation of Chicago's disputed methodological heritage (Platt, 1994). These two 'jointly told tales' (Van Maanen, 1988: 137) take deviant careers and succeed in creating contexts for activities that might otherwise be regarded in terms of individual pathologies. For although they feature some elements of observation, they lack the kind of participatory action that might be expected of a conventional ethnography (see Chambliss, 1972 for another excellent example). The deviant's lifeworld is afforded some structure and as a consequence the predominant Chicagoan notion of crime emerging from social disorganization is clearly contradicted (see Matza, 1969 for a discussion).

10 The highly personal methodological appendix that first appeared in the 1955 edition can be recommended as an introduction to fieldwork. Although Whyte's account of the crass naivety of some of his early efforts (p. 289) are frankly difficult to believe, they do serve to highlight the hard-won competence that is represented by the finished article (see Atkinson, 1990: 107–8).

11 Manning, 1977.

12 Carlen, 1976.

13 Thrasher, who located only six gangs of his massive sample as female, claimed that a combination of an inherent lack of aggression and the intense supervision of young women led to a lack of female gang involvement. An interesting, and most underrated refutation of such reactionary views on female deviance is provided by Sheila Welsh (1981), who via her ethnographic work stresses the centrality of the search for excitement amongst both male and female adolescents in their encounters with the police.

14 Paul Cressey's *Taxi-Dance Hall* (1932), however, remains an eloquent and sensitive portrayal, written by a man, of prostitute women and their clients.

15 An interesting and largely ignored ethnography of domestic violence in London and the normality of domestic violence (Hood-Williams and Bush, 1995).

16 Pat Carlen's work fully deserves to be mentioned here despite the prison environment of much of her interview-based studies. The consistent linking of gender to class, and the unsentimental empathy that she has shown to her informants, makes her work stand out in a field that is consistently marked by a lack of engagement with deviants.

17 However, Kathleen Daly indicates that of the five major routes into crime for women, only three have parallels with the careers of male offenders (1994).

18 Downes also gives an interesting insight into the problems of interviewing working-class informants (1966: 195–8).

19 Despite British sociology's obsession with spectacular youth sub-cultures during the 1960s and 1970s, and their relative accessibility compared with most deviant groups, we do not have any ethnography of, for instance 'Teddy Boys', 'Mods' or 'Punks'. However, speculative accounts abound (Hall and Jefferson, 1976).

20 Studies of 1990s British youth have tended to stress hedonism, and a number of these studies have utilized ethnographic techniques (Rietveld, 1993; see also McKay, 1996). However, given the relative lack of ethnographic detail available at the time of writing, the best overview of this era is that of Collin (1997). See also Shapiro, 1998.

21 Reiss, 1961 employed observational work amongst an array of techniques, and found those young men who 'hustle' adult gay men are engaged not in homosexual behaviour but are merely extending their delinquent activity.

22 For a damning critique of Humphrey's use of deception, see Warwick, 1973.

23 Another excellent study of the fence at work is that of Cromwell, Olson and Avery (1993), which was conducted partly from the backroom of the fence's place of business.

24 The 1993 edition of Adler's book features two invaluable new chapters. Chapter 10 deals with the relevant literature and policy innovations regarding drug enforcement. However, Adler continues her ethnographic quest in Chapter 9, in which she traces thirteen of her original sample in order to extend our knowledge of deviant careers, and improve our understanding of the various processes that impact upon the reintegration of former deviants into legitimate society.

25 A significant part of this study relates to the deviance of police officers, and although space does not permit a detailed discussion of ethnographic studies of police deviance, several outstanding studies do deserve attention being brought to them as they situate deviance within an ambiguous enacted environment that is dominated by the occupational culture of the lower ranks. These studies refer both to criminal activity and to the informal practices that emerge as a result of attempting to carry out police work within the constraints of both legal edicts and organizational rules. Consequently they function as healthy alternatives to the contemporary diet of criminological and sociolegal accounts of police work that stress policy over practice, whilst simultaneously valorizing deviant elements within the agency of the oppressed. Among the most important ethnographic studies of police work that contain significant references to police deviance are Fielding, 1988; Holdaway, 1983; Manning, 1977, 1980; Manning and Redlinger, 1977; Muir, 1977; Norris, 1989; Punch, 1985; Van Maanen, 1973, 1974.

26 Damer, in his study of Glasgow (1974, 1989), also goes to some pains to explain how socioeconomic conditions, and specifically local housing policy, create 'dreadful enclosures', deviant neighbourhoods that are stigmatized and develop a distinct deviant identity. At a time in most de-industrialized economies when working-class families and communities are coming under unprecedented pressure from government agencies, a revival of interest in Damer's work is long overdue.

27 Potter's superb study, although in common with so many ethnographically orientated studies is lacking in what doctoral supervisors continue to call a 'methods chapter', contains a most elegant critical review of the American academic literature on organized crime.

28 Dorn et al. (1992) deserve a mention for the way in which they have used ethnographic interviews to interview police, drug dealers and users in their multi-method, highly authoritative study of drug markets and enforcement in Britain.

REFERENCES

Adler, P. ([1985] 1993) *Wheeling and Dealing: An Ethnography of an Upper Level Drug Dealing and Smuggling Community*, 2nd edn. New York: Columbia University Press.

Agar, M. (1973) *Ripping and Running*. New York: Seminar.

Anderson, N. ([1923] 1975) *The Hobo: The Sociology of the Homeless Man* (Phoenix edn). Chicago: University of Chicago Press.

Anderson, N. (1983) 'A stranger at the gate: reflections of the Chicago School of Sociology', *Urban Life*, 11: 396–406.

Archard, P. (1979) *Vagrancy, Alcoholism and Social Control*. London: Macmillan.

Armstrong, G. (1998) *Football Hooligans: Knowing the Score*. Oxford: Berg.

Atkinson, P. (1990) *The Ethnographic Imagination.* Routledge: London.

Becker, H. (1951) 'The professional dance musician and his audience', *American Journal of Sociology*, 57: 136–44.

Becker, H. (1953) 'Becoming a marijuana user', *American Journal of Sociology*, 59: 235–42.

Becker, H. (1963) *Outsiders: Studies in the Sociology of Deviance.* New York: The Free Press.

Becker, H. (ed.) (1964) *The Other Side.* New York: Macmillan.

Block, A. (1991) *The Business of Crime.* Boulder, CO: Westview Press.

Bourgois, P. (1995) *In Search of Respect.* Cambridge: Cambridge University Press.

Bourgois, P. and Dunlap, L. (1992) 'Exorcising sex-for-crack prostitution: an ethnographic perspective from Harlem', in M. Ratnet (ed.), *Crack Pipe as Pimp: An Eight City Ethnographic Study of the Sex for Crack Phenomenon.* Lexington, MA: Lexington Books. pp. 97–132.

Campbell, A. (1984) *The Girls in the Gang.* New York: Blackwell.

Carlen, P. (1976) *Magistrates Justice.* Oxford: Martin Robertson.

Carlen, P. (1983) *Women's Imprisonment.* London: Routledge and Kegan Paul.

Carlen, P. (ed.) (1985) *Criminal Women.* Cambridge: Polity Press.

Carlen, P. (1988) *Women, Crime and Poverty.* Milton Keynes: Open University Press.

Chambliss, W.J. (1972) *Box Man.* New York: Harper and Row.

Chambliss, W.J. (1978) *On the Take.* Bloomington, IN: Indiana University Press.

Cohen, A.K. (1955) *Delinquent Boys. The Culture of the Gang.* New York: The Free Press.

Cohen, S. (1971) 'Introduction', in S. Cohen (ed.), *Images of Deviance.* Harmondsworth: Penguin.

Cohen, S. (1973) *Folk Devils and Moral Panics.* London: Paladin.

Cohen, S. (1974) 'Criminology and the sociology of deviance in Britain', in P. Rock and M. McIntosh (eds), *Deviance and Social Control.* Tavistock: London. pp. 1–40.

Collin, M. (1997) *Altered State.* London: Serpents Tale.

Corrigan, P. (1979) *Schooling the Smash Street Kids.* London: Macmillan.

Cressey, P. (1932) *The Taxi-Dance Hall.* Chicago: University of Chicago Press.

Cromwell, P., Olson, J. and Avery, D. (1991) *Breaking and Entering: An Ethnographic Analysis of Burglary.* Newbury Park, CA: Sage.

Cromwell, P., Olson, J. and Avery, D. (1993) 'Who buys stolen property? A new look at criminal receiving', *Journal of Crime and Justice,* 56 (1): 75–95.

Daly, K. (1994) *Gender Crime and Punishment.* New Haven, CT: Yale University Press.

Damer, S. (1974) 'Wine alley: the sociology of a dreadful enclosure', *Sociological Review,* 22: 221–48.

Damer, S. (1989) *From Moorpark to Wine Alley: The Sociology of a Dreadful Enclosure.* Edinburgh: Edinburgh University Press.

Decker, S. and Van Winkle, B. (1996) *Life in the Gang.* Cambridge: Cambridge University Press.

Ditton, J. (1977) *Part Time Crime.* London: Macmillan.

Dorn, N., Murji, K. and South, N. (1992) *Traffickers.* London: Routledge.

Downes, D. (1966) *The Delinquent Solution: A Study in Subcultural Theory.* London: Routledge and Kegan Paul.

Downes, D. and Rock, P. (1998) *Understanding Deviance.* Oxford: The Clarendon Press.

Dunlap, E., Johnson, B. and Manwar, A. (1994) 'A successful female crack dealer: case study of a deviant career', *Deviant Behaviour,* 15: 1–25.

Dunlap, E., Johnson, B., Sanabria, H., Holliday, E., Lipsey, B., Barnett, M., Hopkins, W., Sobel, I., Randolph, D. and Chin, K. (1990) 'Studying crack users and their criminal careers', *Contemporary Drug Problems,* Spring, pp. 121–4.

Fielding, N. (1981) *The National Front.* London: Routledge and Kegan Paul.

Fielding, N. (1988) *Joining Forces.* London: Routledge.

Fine, G. (ed.) (1995) *The Second Chicago School.* Chicago: University of Chicago Press.

Finestone, H. (1964) 'Cats, kicks and color', in H. Becker, (ed.), *The Other Side.* New York: The Free Press.

Fountain, J. (1993) 'Dealing with data', in D. Hobbs and T. May (eds), *Interpreting the Field.* Oxford: Oxford University Press. pp. 145–73.

Gelsthorpe, L. (1990) 'Feminist methodologies in criminology: a new approach or old wine in new bottles?' in L. Gelsthorpe and A. Morris, *Feminist Perspectives in Criminology.* Milton Keynes: Open University Press.

Gelsthorpe, L. (1997) 'Feminism and criminology', in M. Maguire, R. Morgan and R. Reiner, *The Oxford Handbook of Criminology.* Oxford: Oxford University Press. pp. 511–34.

Gelsthorpe, L. and Morris, A. (1988) 'Feminism and criminology in Britain', *British Journal of Criminology*, 28 (2): 93–110.

Gelsthorpe, L. and Morris, A. (1990) *Feminist Perspectives in Criminology.* Milton Keynes: Open University Press.

Gill, O. (1977) *Luke Street: Housing Policy, Conflict and the Creation of the Delinquent Area.* London: Macmillan.

Giulianotti, R. (1991) 'Scotland's Tartan Army in Italy: the case for the carnivalesque', *Sociological Review*, 39: 503–30.

Glick, R. (1990) 'Survival income and status: drug dealing in the Chicago Puerto Rican community', in R. Glick and J. Moore (eds), *Drugs in Hispanic Communities.* New Brunswick, NJ: Rutgers University Press. pp. 77–101.

Goffman, E. (1968) *Asylums.* Harmondsworth: Penguin.

Goffman, E. (1989) 'On fieldwork', *Journal of Contemporary Ethnography*, 18: 123–32.

Gouldner, A. (1975) *For Sociology.* Harmondsworth: Pelican.

Hagedorn, J. (1988) *People and Folks: Gangs, Crime and the Underclass in a Rustbelt City.* Chicago: Lake View.

Hall, S. and Jefferson, T. (eds) (1976) *Resistance through Rituals.* London: Hutchinson.

Hart, A. (1998) *Buying and Selling Power.* Boulder, CO: Westview Press.

Hedderman, C. and Hough, M. (1994) 'Does the criminal justice system treat men and women differently?'. Research Findings No. 10. London: Home Office.

Heidensohn, F. (1996) *Women and Crime*, 2nd edn. Basingstoke: Macmillan Press.

Henry, S. (1978) *The Hidden Economy.* Oxford: Martin Robertson.

Heyl, B.S. (1979) *The Madam as Entrepreneur.* New Brunswick, NJ: Transaction Books.

Hobbs, D. (1988) *Doing the Business: Entrepreneurship, the Working Class and Detectives in the East End of London.* Oxford: Oxford University Press.

Hobbs, D. (1995) *Bad Business: Professional Criminals in Modern Britain.* Oxford: Oxford University Press.

Hobbs, D. (1997) 'Criminal collaborations' in M. Maguire, R. Morgan and R. Reiner (eds), *The Oxford Handbook of Criminology.* Oxford: Oxford University Press. pp. 801–40.

Holdaway, S. (1983) *Inside the British Police.* Oxford: Blackwell.

Hood-Williams, J. and Bush, T. (1995) 'Domestic violence on a London housing estate', in C. Byron (ed.), *Home Office Research Bulletin*, No. 37.

Hudson, A. (1990) 'Elusive subjects: researching young women in trouble', in L. Gelsthorpe and A. Morris (eds), *Feminist Perspectives in Criminology.* Milton Keynes: Open University Press. pp. 115–23.

Humphreys, L. (1970) *Tea-Room Trade: Impersonal Sex in Public Places.* Chicago, IL: Aldine.

Ianni, F. (1972) *A Family Business: Kinship and Social Control in Organized Crime.* New York: Russell Sage Foundation.

Kinsey, R., Lea, J. and Young, J. (1986) *Losing the Fight Against Crime.* Oxford: Blackwell.

Klockars, C. (1975) *The Professional Fence.* London: Tavistock.

Lacey, R. (1991) *Little Man.* New York: Little, Brown.

Lea, J. and Young, J. (1984) *What is to be Done about Law and Order?* London: Pluto.

Liazos, A. (1972) 'The poverty of the sociology of deviance: nuts sluts and perverts', *Social Problems*, 20: 103–20.

Liebow, E. (1967) *Tally's Corner.* Boston, MA: Little, Brown.

Manning, P. (1977) *Police Work: The Social Organisation of Policing.* Cambridge, MA: MIT Press.

Manning, P. (1980) *The Narcs Game.* Cambridge, MA: MIT Press.

Manning, P. and Redlinger, J. (1977) 'Invitational edges of corruption', in P. Rock (ed.), *Drugs and Politics.* New Brunswick, NJ: Transaction Books.

Matza, D. (1969) *Becoming Deviant.* Englewood Cliffs, NJ: Prentice–Hall.

Mayhew, H. ([1861] 1980) *The* Morning Chronicle *Survey of Labour and the Poor.* London: Caliban Books, vols 1–6.

Mayhew, H. and Binney, J. ([1862] 1968) *The Criminal Prisons of London and Scenes of Prison Life.* London: Frank Cass.

Mays, J. (1954) *Growing Up in the City: A Study of Juvenile Delinquency in an Urban Neighbourhood.* Liverpool: Liverpool University Press.

McKay, G. (1996) *Senseless Acts of Beauty: Cultures of Resistance since the Sixties.* London: Verso.

McKinney, J. (1966) *Constructive Typology and Social Theory.* New York: Appleton–Century–Croft.

Mcleod, E. (1982) *Women Working.* London: Croom Helm.

McRobbie, A. (1980) 'Settling accounts with subcultures: a feminist critique', *Screen Education*, 39: 37–49.

Mieczkowski, T. (1990) 'Crack distribution in Detroit', *Contemporary Drug Problems*, 17 (1): 19–30.

Miller, E. (1986) *Street Women.* Philadelphia: Temple.

Millman, M. (1975) 'She did it all for love: a feminist view of the sociology of deviance', in M. Millman and R. Moss Kanter (eds), *Another Voice.* New York: Anchor Books.

Moore, J. (1978) *Homeboys: Gangs, Drugs, and Prison in the Barrios of Los Angeles.* Philadelphia: Temple University Press.

Moore, J. (1991) *Going Down to the Barrio: Homeboys and Homegirls, in Change.* Philadelphia: Temple University Press.

Morris, T. (1957) *The Criminal Area.* London: RKP.

Muir, W.K. (1977) *Police Streetcorner Politicians.* Chicago: Chicago University Press.

Norris, C. (1989) 'Avoiding trouble', in M. Weatheritt (ed.), *Police Research: Some Future Prospects.* Aldershot: Avebury.

Padilla, F. (1992) *The Gang as an American Enterprise.* New Brunswick, NJ: Rutgers University Press.

Parker, H. (1974) *View from the Boys: A Sociology of Down Town Adolescents.* Newton Abbott: David and Charles.

Patrick, J. (1973) *A Glasgow Gang Observed.* London: Eyre Methuen.

Platt, J. (1994) 'The Chicago School and firsthand data', *History of the Human Sciences*, 7 (1): 57–80.

Plummer, K. (1983) *Documents of Life.* London: Unwin. (2nd edn., Sage, 2000.)

Polsky, N. ([1967] 1971) *Hustlers, Beats and Others.* Harmondsworth: Pelican.

Potter, G. (1994) *Criminal Organisations.* Prospect Hills, IL: Waveland Press.

Preble, E. and Casey, J. (1969) 'Taking care of business: the heroin user's life on the streets', *International Journal of the Addictions*, 4 (1): 1–24.

Pryce, K. (1979) *Endless Pressure: A Study of West Indian Lifestyles in Britain.* Harmondsworth: Penguin.

Punch, M. (1985) *Conduct Unbecoming: The Social Construction of Police Deviance and Control.* London: Tavistock.

Rawlinson, P. (1996) 'Russian organised crime: a brief history', *Transnational Organised Crime*, 2 (2/3): 28–52.

Reiss, (1961) 'The social integration of queers and peers', *Social Problems*, 9: 102–20.

Rietveld, H. (1993) 'Living the dream', in S. Redhead (ed.), *Rave Off: Politics and Deviance in Contemporary Youth Culture*. Aldershot: Avebury. pp. 41–78.

Robins, D. (1984) *We Hate Humans*. Harmondsworth: Penguin.

Robins, D. and Cohen, P. (1978) *Knuckle Sandwich: Growing Up in the Working-Class City*. Harmondsworth: Penguin.

Sanchez-Jankowski, M. (1990) *Islands in the Street: Gangs in American Urban Society*. Berkeley, CA: University of California Press.

Shapiro, H. (1998) 'Dances with drugs', in N. South (ed.), *Drugs: Cultures, Controls and Everyday Life*. London: Sage.

Shaw, C.R. (1930) *The Jack Roller*. Chicago: University of Chicago Press.

Short, J. (1963) 'Introduction' to 1963 abridged version of F. Thrasher, *The Gang* (1927). Chicago: University of Chicago Press. pp. xv–liii.

Shover, N. (1973) 'The social organisation of burglary', *Social Problems*, 20: 499–514.

Shover, N. (1985) *Aging Criminals*. Beverly Hills, CA: Sage.

Shover, N. (1996) *Great Pretenders*. Boulder, CO: Westview Press.

Shover, N. and Honaker, D. (1991) 'The socially bounded decision making of persistent property offenders', *The Howard Journal*, 31 (November): 276–93.

Smart, C. (1976) *Women, Crime and Criminology*. London: Routledge and Kegan Paul.

Sullivan, M. (1989) *Getting Paid*. Ithaca, NY: Cornell University Press.

Sumner, C. (1994) *The Sociology of Deviance: An Obituary*. Buckingham: Open University Press.

Sutherland, E. (1937) *The Professional Thief*. Chicago: University of Chicago Press.

Sutter, A. (1966) 'The world of the righteous dope fiend', *Issues in Criminology*, 2 (2): 177–222.

Suttles, G. (1968) *The Social Order of the Slum*. Chicago: University of Chicago Press.

Taylor, A. (1993) *Women Drug Users: An Ethnography of a Female Injecting Community*. Oxford: The Clarendon Press.

Taylor, C. (1990) *Dangerous Society*. East Lansing: Michigan State University Press.

Taylor, I., Walton, P. and Young, J. (1973) *The New Criminology*. London: Routledge and Kegan Paul.

Taylor, I., Walton, P. and Young, J. (eds) (1975) *Critical Criminology*. London: Routledge and Kegan Paul.

Thompson, H. (1966) *Hells Angels*. Harmondsworth: Penguin.

Thrasher, F. ([1927] 1963) *The Gang*. Chicago: University of Chicago Press.

Turk, A.T. (1969) *Criminality and the Legal Order*. Chicago: Rand McNally.

Van Maanen, J. (1973) 'Observations on the making of a policeman', *Human Organisation*, 32 (4): 407–18.

Van Maanen, J. (1974) 'Working the street', in H. Jacob (ed.), *The Potential for Reform of Criminal Justice*. Beverly Hills, CA: Sage.

Van Maanen, J. (1988) *Tales of the Field*. Chicago: University of Chicago Press.

Vigil, J. (1988) *Barrio Gangs: Street Life and Identity in Southern California*. Austin, TX: University of Texas Press.

Warwick, D.P. (1973) *Tearoom Trade: Means and Ends in Social Research*. The Hastings Centre Studies, 1, pp. 27–38.

Welsh, S. (1981) 'The manufacture of excitement in police–juvenile encounters', *British Journal of Criminology*, 21 (3): 257–67.

Whyte, W. ([1943] 1955) *Street Corner Society: The Social Organisation of a Chicago Slum*. Chicago: University of Chicago Press.

Williams, T. (1989) *The Cocaine Kids*. Reading, MA: Addison–Wesley.

Williams, T. (1992) *Crack House*. Reading, MA: Addison–Wesley.

Willis, P. (1977) *Learning to Labour: How Working Class Kids Get Working Class Jobs*. London: Saxon House.

Wolf, D. (1991) *The Rebels: A Brotherhood of Outlaw Bikers*. Toronto: University of Toronto Press.

Wright, R. and Decker, S. (1994) *Burglars on the Job: Streetlife and Residential Break-ins*. Boston, MA: Northeastern University Press.

Wright, R. and Decker, S. (1997) *Armed Robbers in Action: Stick-Ups and Street Culture*. Boston, MA: Northeastern University Press.

Wright, R., Decker, S., Redfern, A. and Smith, S. (1992) 'A snowball's chance in hell: doing fieldwork with active residential burglars', *Journal of Research in Crime and Delinquency*, 29 (2): 148–61.

Young, J. (1971) *The Drugtakers*. London: Paladin.

Zorbaugh, H. (1929) *The Gold Coast and the Slum*. Chicago: University of Chicago Press.

15

Ethnographies of Work
and the Work of Ethnographers

VICKI SMITH

The purpose of this chapter is to map out studies that provide rich and contextualized understandings of work, workplaces and occupations through observation, participation and/or immersion – research commonly accepted as constitutive of an ethnographic approach. In order to identify and evaluate what ethnographic field researchers have actually done, and the kinds of claims that ethnographic research can generate, I explore studies that deploy a variety of temporal criteria and methodological strategies, and take a variety of analytic foci, including labor processes, organizations, occupations, industries and combinations of all four.[1]

The list of themes and topics found in social science, ethnographic studies of work is lengthy. Hodson (1998) and Morrill and Fine (1997), for example, have identified a large number of salient themes in this literature, including autonomy, citizenship, informal relations, meaning, environments, ethics and change. In this chapter I focus on three thematic areas, deliberately selecting them to illuminate the advantages of using an ethnographic approach: how routine jobs are complex; how complex jobs are routine; and how power, control and inequality are sustained. I emphasize throughout how researchers use their own experiences as a source of understanding and insight in workplace studies.

I then discuss the unresolved dilemmas of time and access, in order to identify the very arduous journey fieldworkers have undertaken to generate these findings. I do this not only to convey a sense of the quite substantial collective investments that have been made to build this important field of research, but also to provide a frank appraisal of the time spent, the anxieties raised and rejections incurred in conducting ethnographies of work. Such

an appraisal may deter even the most determined researchers from using an ethnographic approach to study work, but that is not my intention. Rather, such an appraisal should enable ethnographers of work to take stock of the unique barriers to entry to the field, as well as the more universal problem of demands on their time. These barriers are worrisome for all ethnographers; here, I wish to demonstrate the particular ramifications of these barriers for researchers who study work and workplaces.

AN OVERVIEW

As is true of ethnographic researchers more generally, social scientists who use ethnographic approaches to study work – whether relying principally on participant observation as a mode of enquiry (Burawoy et al., 1991) or privileging particular styles of textual representation over others (Van Maanen, 1988) – cannot be accused of being armchair academics who examine the world at arm's length. On the contrary, they are an impressively polyvalent and engaged lot, having labored in a spectrum of work sites that encompasses factories, offices, hospitals, restaurants and homes. By becoming paid workers, many have capitalized on an avenue into the research field – getting a job, learning by laboring – not readily available to researchers in other domains.

Fully immersed for often considerable amounts of time, sociologists and anthropologists have been employed as domestic workers in private households (Rollins, 1985), paralegals (Pierce, 1995), food servers and cocktail waitresses (Paules, 1991; Spradley and Mann, 1975), lettuce (Thomas, 1985) and strawberry (Wells, 1996) pickers, phone sex operators (Flowers, 1998), nightclub hostesses (Allison, 1994) and locomotive repairers (Gamst, 1980). They have toiled as machine operators (Burawoy, 1979), mechanics (Juravich, 1985), furnace stokers (Burawoy and Lukás, 1992), longshoremen (Finlay, 1988), changed the clothes and diapers and moisturized the bodies of the elderly (Diamond, 1992), and trimmed fat and meat off hog bellies (Fink, 1998). They have worked on a variety of assembly lines: auto (Chinoy, [1955] 1992; Graham, 1995), electronics (Lee, 1998), lingerie (Roberts, 1994), auto parts and garments (Salzinger, 1997) and confectionery (Kondo, 1990).

Short of full immersion and regular employment, ethnographic scholars, often quite creatively, have studied work worlds through a prism of organizational spaces, routines and events. They have observed police detectives tending to dead bodies (Jackall, 1997), and doctors performing surgeries (Bosk, 1979) and abortions (Simonds, 1996). They have assisted genetics counselors, consulting with parents who are grieving over seriously ill children or shell shocked at the news that their future offspring might be genetically damaged (Bosk, 1992). They volunteer as reserve police officers (Martin, 1980), attend Tupperware and Amway parties (Biggart, 1989), sit through countless training sessions (Chetkovich, 1997; Leidner, 1993; Pierce, 1995; Smith, 1990; including training in sexual massage, Chapkis, 1997), vocational classes (Diamond, 1992; Fine, 1996) and corporate and workplace meetings (Kanter, [1977] 1993; Kleinman, 1996; Kunda, 1992). They hang out in union halls (Finlay, 1988), bars and workers' homes (Burawoy and Lukás, 1992; Wells, 1996). In short, they have 'gained the point of view, the reality-as-experienced' (Harper, [1987] 1992: 204) of industrial and postindustrial; intellectual-, manual-, service- and sex-based; blue-, pink- and white-collar; semi-professional, professional and working-class workers.

Field researchers who study work conduct their research and write about it in a variety of ways. A close reading of studies of work reveals that while some conform to a model of ethnography based on sustained immersion and participant observation, many others draw on data that can be called ethnographic – observational, interview, experiential – but have derived that data from fieldwork that is intermittent, partial and disrupted. In some, ethnography is simply equated with qualitative research,[2] which may satisfy methodological but not representational criteria (see Clifford and Marcus, 1986; Van Maanen, 1988 for discussions of the claim for ethnography as a process of representing culture in written texts).

I neither attempt to resolve the issue, a perennial one for ethnographers across the board, of what might constitute a 'true' or 'best' ethnography, or to untangle whether ethnographic studies meet what

Van Maanen (1988: xi) worries are the 'overrated' criteria of reliability, validity and generalizability, issues that have been amply addressed elsewhere (e.g., Friedman and McDaniel, 1998; Hammersley, 1992; Hodson, 1998; Morrill and Fine, 1997). Rather, I map out a broad spectrum of studies that exemplify what ethnographic approaches can tell us about worlds of work. For this reason I avoid exclusively using a strict and narrow label of 'ethnographies of work', a label that suggests that there is a singular type of ethnography. In order to reflect the field itself I deliberately use multiple labels for the studies I consider, calling them, for example, 'ethnographic approaches to work' as well as 'ethnographies of work', and calling practitioners 'ethnographic field researchers', or simply 'field workers' as well as 'ethnographers'.

HIGHLIGHTING HOW ROUTINE JOBS ARE COMPLEX

No single approach to the study of work has been more effective than the ethnographic in uncovering the tacit skills, the decision rules, the complexities, the discretion and the control in jobs that have been labeled routine, unskilled and deskilled, marginal and even trivial. Researchers working to this end have debunked hegemonic conceptions of the unskilled job, challenging the idea that the 'truly' skilled job is an industrial or professional one, or that it is a job held only by a male worker.[3] They have shown how assumptions about what constitutes an unskilled or routine job have been socially and historically constructed, and that how managers describe such jobs may have little relation to the skills the job in fact entails.

Researchers have used the ethnographic method to dissect how workers do their jobs: the conceptual tools and the strategies workers use to accomplish their work when faced with mechanical failures, bottlenecks, speedups, defective materials, or the need to take shortcuts to finish their work in a timely way; how they reconcile the contradictory demands between efficiency and quality; and the individual- and group-level processes by which workers maintain dignity and control over and against supervisors and customers. Observing workers and their interactions with co-workers, managers and clients over extended periods of time; talking endlessly with workers about how they make decisions about what they do; and actually working in order to experience the organizational arrangements of and social relations in work that shape lived experience and construct workers' interests, are just some of the ways that ethnographers have advanced social science knowledge about work.

One approach to this issue has been inspired by the work of Marx, by way of the critical analyses of Harry Braverman (1974) and Ken Kusterer (1978).

In his now-classic argument about deskilling, Braverman suggested that under conditions of monopoly capitalism, employers and managers wrest planning and control from workers, depoliticize, marginalize and otherwise exploit them, in order to profit from their labor. Kusterer (1978) soon thereafter pointed out that such overly-deterministic assertions about deskilling ignored the degree to which nearly all types of jobs, even those that appear to be mindless and highly routinized, require some degree of worker consent, initiative and insight gained through time and experience (a point about the importance of tacit skill corroborated by Manwaring and Wood, 1984). Often as participant observers, subsequent researchers tackled these claims, investigating whether or not capitalists continually deskilled and degraded workers, robbing them of opportunities for involvement, for decision-making and for personal meaning (see Smith, 1994 for a review of their findings).

Juravich's (1985) study of 'National', which focused on industrial jobs often regarded as repetitive, meaningless and devoid of planning and initiative, is an exemplar of the investigation of tacit skill. Juravich worked as a mechanic in a small plant manufacturing wire and explored the unique types of craft knowledge possessed by, mostly female, wire assemblers. His struggles to get the job done with shoddy equipment and deficient material enabled him to understand the complexity of thought and action workers needed to do the job. Their insider knowledge, he argued, enabled assemblers to minimize the chaos springing from management's decisions about how to organize the line, enabled them to make improvements in the production process, and indeed to complete their workloads everyday. Juravich's findings, uncovered in the course of his own participation, corrected social science assumptions that managers exercise unilateral control, that managerial planning is wholly rational, and that monopoly capitalism inevitably strips all decision-making from factory workers.

The excavation of insider, craft and tacit skill, particularly as a basis of worker control and autonomy, has been conducted in a range of occupations and work sites. Waiting tables in a restaurant for 18 months gave Paules (1991) first-hand knowledge of the informal strategies waitresses used to serve their customers quickly (serving their bosses' interests) and at the same time manipulate managerial policies to maximize their own interests – doing what they could to earn a generous tip.

Finlay (1988), contra Braverman, argued that despite massive automation of longshoremen's work, workers continued to exercise skills not necessarily visible to the casual observer. Working as a longshoreman, he explored the initiative and concentration required of cab operators, winch men and tractor drivers after the introduction of container technology for loading and unloading ships. Finlay demonstrated that even if employers hoped to cut costs and minimize workers' input with the adoption of containers, this transformation, instead, only changed the skills required. Building on Zuboff's (1988) theory of 'intellective skill', Finlay argued that in the newly automated era of longshore work, skill had become less physical but more intellectual, and no less critical to getting the job done. His conclusions match those of Vallas, who noted in his study of how new technologies changed the labor processes of telephone workers, that 'management has been unable to reduce or eliminate the need for conceptual skills in workers' jobs ... the company has merely shifted the locus of expertise' (1993: 137).

The study of the unacknowledged, the hidden, the insider knowledge, the unwritten but pervasive rules governing jobs also has influenced many ethnographies that focus on 'understudied occupations', occupations often considered unskilled and sometimes considered to be marginal or trivial. Some studies, such as Gamst's (1980) monograph about 'hogheads' (men who service rail locomotives), thickly describe the inner workings of a job but are narrow in theoretical scope and generalizability. Others use the daily experiences and interactions within understudied occupations to shed light on a larger population of occupations, or link them to broader economic, political, or social issues, exemplifying the extended case method which 'looks for specific macro determination in the micro world' (Burawoy, 1991: 279).

Diamond (1992), for example, studied nursing home workers to critically analyse how the health care industry has commodified care for the elderly in order to turn a profit. Working as a nursing assistant in three separate homes for three to four months at a time, he burrowed into this female-dominated, 'unskilled' occupation, and the deceptively simple job description for workers in it, calling them to 'assist as needed'. Assisting as needed, he discovered, required him to learn to engage in a host of simultaneous, shifting, physically arduous and emotionally draining activities: to think, listen, see, feed, touch, change, clean and talk to people who were angry, demoralized, frail, ill and depressed (1992: 156). Managers in nursing homes depended on nursing assistants' understanding and mastery of these unarticulated skills to process the maximum number of elderly bodies in the most efficient and rapid way possible.

Flowers (1998) worked as a phone sex operator – another understudied occupation that, in her view, is too easily dismissed as trivial or deviant – and compellingly made the case that it was exemplary of many service jobs in the American economy. Phone sex operators had to engage in extensive emotional labor and acquire a tacit craft knowledge. She struggled up a long learning curve, mastering knowledge of how to keep clients on the line but simultaneously discouraging them from becoming too obsessed with her personally. Doing so satisfied supervisors' criteria for productivity and enabled her and other operators to keep their jobs.

Barley (1986) observed radiologists and technicians to theorize about how technological change affected organizational structure; Fine (1996) went behind the scenes to tap the complex negotiated order of restaurant kitchen workers in order to illuminate theories of organizations; Chapkis (1997) went even further behind the scenes, nearly underground, to study prostitutes and other workers who gave sexual massage, shedding surprising light on the emotional labor of sex workers; Orr (1996) worked in front of the scenes but in an occupation commonly overlooked in accounts of skilled jobs – photocopy machine technician – in order to shed light on the unique triangle of worker/manager/ customer relations in modern service jobs (as did Flowers (1998) for phone sex operators, Hochschild (1983) for flight attendants and bill collectors, and Leidner (1993) for fast food and insurance sales workers).

In earlier work (Smith, 1996), I analysed the tacit skills of another understudied group, those workers who actually operate the photocopy machines that were maintained by Orr's technicians, to illuminate the impact of broader corporate restructuring processes on low-level service workers. In-depth and up-close studies of the labor and skills of family planning workers (Joffe, 1986), abortion clinic workers (Simonds, 1996), and mechanics (Harper, [1987] 1992) have similarly analysed rarely studied occupations to draw attention to larger political, technological and economic currents in American society.

HOW COMPLEX JOBS ARE ROUTINE

Conversely, ethnographic researchers have taken the work of professionals and semi-professionals and rendered them ordinary, accessible and routinized. Here, too, the vantage point of ethnographic researchers – the direct experiences, the sustained observations, or the immersion – has allowed a degree of penetration into the inner workings of an occupation or a work setting that is not easily attained by other approaches. Sustained involvement and observation have been especially productive because the defining features of professional work – unpredictability, variety, the formal absence of routinization of tasks and activities – necessitate that researchers be available to observe the unexpected (Bosk, 1979: 14), to opportunistically focus on events and interactions as they arise (Buchanan et al., 1988; Kunda, 1992: 236).

One population of studies – studies of medical practitioners, including surgeons, nurses, genetic counselors, and physicians – illustrates the unique contribution that ethnography has made to this

enquiry. Two substantive concerns tie these works together. First, many follow Everett Hughes' (1958) call to examine how the crises of some, such as patients and their families, constitute the routines of others. Researchers have sought to understand how workers – in the case of medical workers, those who deal with illness, death, ethical dilemmas, individual and family catastrophe, day in and day out – accommodate to and live with their jobs, how they depersonalize the deeply traumatic personal circumstances of others. A second concern has been to translate and demystify professional work, to give what seem to be chaotic, challenging, uncertain work settings a sense of order, of familiarity and repetition.

Bosk, for example, sought to understand the 'shared and socially patterned ways that surgeons treat deaths and complications' (1979: 31), serving as a participant observer for 18 months in two hospitals. He was a gofer, he scrubbed and assisted on operations as needed, observed meetings where cases were evaluated, and served variously as a 'sounding board', a 'referee', and a 'historian', a source of organizational memory for the groups of surgeons he studied. This intense engagement and the high trust he earned in the process enabled him to observe patterns in the ways surgeons routinely distanced themselves from their own and their colleagues' professional errors.

Chambliss (1996) uncovered how nurses detached themselves from and even objectified the dead, turning death into an 'organizational act' rather than experiencing it as a human tragedy. (Sudnow (1967) had drawn similar conclusions about the strategies of doctors and nurses who worked in wards for the terminally ill.) The doctors that Fox (1959) observed for more than 10 months in a research hospital experienced a moral conflict between their professional imperative to heal patients and their organizational mandate to dispense experimental drugs and conduct experimental tests. They coped with this dilemma by joking, wagering on patients' diseases, test outcomes and probabilities for surviving, and 'counter transferring' to their patients by showering special treatment on them. These routinely enacted mechanisms enabled them to stabilize their everyday practices and reconcile their two very different orientations to the practice of medicine.

EXPOSING AND EXPLAINING POWER, CONFLICT AND INEQUALITY

Ethnographic research also has had a premier influence on our understanding of social-relational dynamics and lived experiences related to class control and inequality. Fieldworkers have observed relations between workers, between workers and their managers, and between managers. They have participated in everyday shopfloor and office relations that reveal the drudgeries and satisfactions of job tasks, as well as unsanctioned, informal activities (following classic studies of informal work groups done by Blau, [1955] 1963; Dalton, 1959; Roy, 1954). They have been squarely positioned to detect how power is exercised, control asserted and maintained, conflict and resistance expressed, and social inequalities manipulated and recreated.

Laboring side-by-side workers in their natural settings has enabled fieldworkers to experience the same emotional reactions, bodily pains and injuries, personal humiliations, compromises, ambivalences about mobility and resentment about blocked opportunities. Fieldworkers' shared experience itself thus has been an important and unique source of insight and data. Fink (1998) worked in a meatpacking plant for five months, tapping into the degradation to which assembly workers in a 'new breed' of meatpacking plants were subjected. She discovered, nearly having a physical breakdown in the process, how management's unrelenting and coercive control, the brutalities, the speed and the arduousness in the job of butchering hogs, created a near-inescapable cycle for the working-class labor force, trapping them in a life of economic and spiritual impoverishment. As a front-line worker Fink directly observed the ways in which management at this 'new breed' plant, which was rural and non-unionized, mapped its coercive practices onto the regional stratification system, exploiting primarily non-white, newly immigrated and women workers.

Other researchers have observed and experienced the costs to workers' dignity, authenticity and sense of self, when they are required to labor and perform, not so much physically, but interpersonally and emotionally, in jobs that require significant levels of interactions with customers (Leidner, 1993). Making home visits with insurance salesmen and attending their training seminars enabled Leidner to explain how the potential dehumanization that salesmen might feel – from having to make repeatedly hard-hitting, patently manipulative sales pitches to clients who frequently deflected their goal of making a sale – was offset by their hope that eventually they would profit handsomely from these questionable interactions and that they would move up into management positions. Graham (1995) found that, when she worked on the line in an auto plant where a participative work model had been introduced, she was pressured to develop both new physical, productive skills and new interpersonal skills. Her direct experience provided a core insight about the confusing and destabilized nature of control and domination inherent in a model that many call progressive: she and her co-workers felt, at various points, embarrassed, resentful, critical, but at the same time immobilized, 'chained psychologically to the line' (1995: 113).

Immersion, participation, observation have also yielded our most enduring typologies for understanding class control. Engagement on shop and office floors over extended periods of time gives researchers a sense of the depth of particular strategies for control, as well as the distinctiveness of patterns across diverse work sites. Theories of coercive and hegemonic control emerged from Burawoy's (1979) study of blue-collar machine operators; autocratic control from Juravich's (1985) study of blue-collar assemblers; paternalistic and craft control from Vallas' (1993) study of operators, clerical workers and craft workers in A T&T; and bureaucratic control from Jackall's studies of bank branch clerical workers (1978) and corporate middle managers (1988), and Kanter's ([1977] 1993) study of managers and secretaries in a huge bureaucratic firm: all studies based, if not on sustained participant observation (Burawoy, Juravich, Kanter), on extensive observation and interviews (Vallas, Jackall).

Notions of cultural control have increasingly gained currency from fieldwork conducted in, to name a few: 'High Technologies Corporation' (Kunda, 1992), 'American Security Bank' (Smith, 1990), 'Ethicon-Albuquerque', a Johnson & Johnson subsidiary (Grenier, 1988), and a Subaru–Isuzu plant in Indiana (Graham, 1995). Looking at everyday work practices and interviewing workers about their subjective impressions of new cultural norms, in-depth field researchers have been particularly successful in uncovering the disjuncture between rhetoric and experience, as 'progressive' cultural frameworks, introduced by managers to improve organizational performance, fail to map onto existing cultures and elicit unanticipated forms of resistance from corporate employees.

The counterpart to understanding systems of control has been the identification of modes of conflict and resistance. Because conflict and resistance are dynamic social processes, apprehension of which requires ongoing observation of action and interaction, and interpretation of meaning, ethnographers can claim a near-monopoly on this issue. Fieldworkers have been well positioned to observe, wait out, listen for and experience the dissonances between formal systems of control and the reactions of workers to them. Virtually every study mentioned above has looked at workers' individual- and group-level resistances to management's efforts to control their bodies and their minds. Ethnographers have uncovered how workers refuse to do what supervisors and managers tell them to do, do their jobs differently from the methods dictated by management, withhold information from supervisors and engineers about the most efficient method of working, sabotage production processes, play games on the job, and collaborate with fellow workers to finish their work.

Morrill's (1995) innovative ethnography of executive action in private corporations examined conflict, not as an expression of class conflict *per se*, but as a reflection of the ways different organizations structure hierarchy and authority at their highest levels. Over the course of two years of fieldwork in three different firms he observed and interviewed high-ranking managers, extensively studied grievance patterns, and attended a variety of executive meetings. Only prolonged exposure to diverse organizational contexts could have generated this compelling comparative account of patterns of conflict enactment and management. Prolonged observation and participation in the field similarly made possible Kleinman's (1996) vivid understanding of gender- and occupational-based conflict in an organization of holistic health workers.

Finally, ethnographic studies have effectively pinpointed how gender and race are central categories upon which the workplace is organized. Arguing that it is insufficient to study work and the labor process through the lens of class hierarchy alone, researchers have found that gender and race constitute parallel systems of control, often inextricably bound up in class power and authority relations. Kondo's (1990) brilliant examination of gender, family and economic organization in Japan demonstrated how gendered conceptions of identity formed an enduring foundation for the sexual division of labor and for unequal modes of participation in paid work. Biggart (1989) explored the work/family linkage in the direct sales industry in the United States; Roberson (1998) also studied the work/family linkage as a participant observer in a Japanese metals firm, as did Roberts (1994), who spent 12 months working on a female-dominated lingerie packing assembly line in Japan. Allison (1994) 'hostessed' for four months in a nightclub in Tokyo, examining how women's sexual and work identities intersected with and were exploited by large corporations' efforts to colonize their male workers' lives.

Ethnographers also have uncovered how work sites recreate gender and race stratification over time, thus explaining how the workplace acts as a major institution in the persistence of inequality. Exploring Acker's (1990) claim that work organization jobs, compensation schemes and interactional expectations are structured differently for women and men, many have traced the depth to which work organizations are gendered, explicitly and subtly. Hossfeld (1990), Hsiung (1996), Lee (1998), Pierce (1995), Salzinger (1997) and Thomas (1985) found that gendered and racialized discourses were constructed, manipulated and incorporated into the way jobs were defined, compensation determined, members valued and workers controlled. Salzinger (1997), for example, conducting extensive observations in three plants in Mexico and working on the line in two, documented how shopfloor managers appropriated gendered assumptions and stereotypes quite flexibly to control female assembly workers,

advancing our understanding of how pervasive yet how malleable social categories such as gender are, and how readily available they are as a source of control and social organization.

Researchers have tapped into the ways that male police officers discourage and even jeopardize the lives of female officers in routine practice and in crisis (Martin, 1980); how women firefighters precariously navigate through a deeply masculinized work culture – built on intense gender unity between men of different racial groups counterposed against a woman of any color (Chetkovich, 1997); and how, in workplace meetings and interactions, the expression of emotions is privileged when done by men but devalued when done by women (Kleinman, 1996). In so doing, they have facilitated our understanding of why jobs, occupations and positions of formal authority that appear to be opening up to women continue to discourage and block them from participating on terms comparable to men. Participant observation, interviews and sustained observation enable researchers to go beyond numbers that indicate women's occupational mobility and success, to see continued inequalities within aggregate categories. Precisely for this reason, Reskin and Roos (1990) used a set of ethnographic case studies to document the 'integration–resegregation' process: how formerly male-dominated occupations – officially opening up and showing greater statistical representation of women – continued to resegregate women workers into the lowest, less prestigious levels of each occupation.

In short, ethnographers of work, like ethnographers writ large, have problematized what we often take for granted. By highlighting the complex in the routine and the routine in the complex, and by examining the reproduction of power and inequality, they have made enduring and unique contributions to the social science understanding of the dynamic nature of workplaces. These insights would not otherwise be available from study methods that cannot go deeply into organizations and occupations, study process, experience relationships and events firsthand, listen for voices, hesitations and silences, unpack and interpret meaning, and account for the effects of historical context.

THE DUAL CONSTRAINTS ON ETHNOGRAPHIC RESEARCHERS WHO STUDY WORK: ACCESS AND TIME

In key respects the substantial size and the integrity (Hodson, 1998) of the population of ethnographic workplace studies is surprising given a set of inextricably connected obstacles researchers have faced getting into work sites and spending significant periods of time in them. I complete the mapping of this field of studies by highlighting researchers' struggles to enter workplaces, focusing especially on the ways in which organizational gatekeepers – those who have the authority to permit field researchers to enter work organizations and carry out their research (Morrill et al., 1999; Schwartzman, 1993: 48–51) – have thrown obstacles in the way of completing research. Invariably, all ethnographers must contend with the twin problems of access and time. Here, I identify ways in which these problems can shape and limit the research activities of scholars who study work and workplaces in particular.

Methods appendices and fieldwork reflections are replete with examples of the appreciable amount of time it can take simply to get permission to enter a particular work site or set of work sites. It took Thomas (1994) fully one year, approaching fifteen different firms before he finally received approval to conduct a case study with significant organizational, ethnographic depth. As he noted, firms were all too happy to let him interview a handful of key management personnel, or to give him the official tour they reserved for business-school faculty (1994: 262), but balked when he requested 'broad and relatively unrestricted access to people and documentation in order to do a thorough study of the decision processes surrounding technological change' (1994: 34). Jackall's request to conduct research in large bureaucratic organizations was rejected by thirty-six corporations over the course of 10 months (1988: 13); only personal ties, including a chance meeting over a game of tennis between one of his academic colleagues and a well-placed executive, ultimately paved his way for the fieldwork for *Moral Mazes*. From the time he began planning his research, it took Morrill 18 months to gain access to the first firm he was allowed to enter, even though he was assisted in his search by a close relative who was 'a longtime management consultant and a respected member of the local business community' (1995: 233).

I have written elsewhere (Smith, 1997a) about my frustrating and anxiety-provoking experiences trying to obtain permission to study temporary workers *in situ* in a well-known high-technology firm. My difficulties were two-pronged: first, I spent many discouraging months seeking approval from a number of firms to go in and conduct research. I was on the verge of being granted permission to work on the shopfloor as a temp worker in one computer manufacturing plant when the site manager who had authorized my access left the company to take a better position in a rival firm. Despite his assurance that the person assuming his position would be delighted to have me conduct this research (music to my naive ears), his successor, to the discouragement and surprise of no one but myself, never returned my phone calls.[4]

Once having made a connection with an individual in the type of site I was seeking, who both had

the power to let me in and was enthusiastic about my research interests, it took five more nerve-wracking months before all the details of my access had been hammered out. Her delayed delivery of pertinent phone numbers that I could call to begin my work was sandwiched in between her staggeringly busy schedule as a personnel director, her need to clear my proposal with one of the corporate lawyers, and her desire to brief some of my prospective interviewees about my project. It was at this time that I began seriously to ponder research projects that would leave me less vulnerable to the inescapable realities of the corporate work world, realities that seemed to thwart my goals at every turn.

Some writers convey the sense that obtaining access was seamless and effortless, that the researcher simply decided what site or sites she or he wished to study, asked for permission, and received it with nary a rejection (e.g., Fine, 1996: 240–5). But the preponderance of evidence suggests that organizational gatekeepers tend to deny and delay researchers because they are concerned – not unreasonably from their point of view – about the uses to which the research data will be put. They may worry, for example, that research reports will be used to expose company practices to the public, or be used in lawsuits against the firm. They cite the need for confidentiality, both for individuals and for firms. They worry about their liability for company practices that might be revealed in the course of the research. Such issues might be potentially explosive, such as when researchers uncover evidence about sex or race discrimination, about violations of labor law, or about the use of informal policies which run counter to official company regulations (Friedman and McDaniel, 1998). In the course of my research on workplace flexibility I have been required to sign non-disclosure forms, addressing company managers' desires to protect details of products and specific technology innovations, and to avoid having these details revealed in articles or books, an agreement that Thomas (1994) also made with managers in the companies he studied.

Obviously, gatekeepers' resistances to researchers present a story or set of data about the organization itself. As Burawoy (Burawoy and Lukás, 1992: 4) noted about his travails getting into Hungarian firms, 'As so often happens in fieldwork, the genealogy of research – entry, normalization, and exit – reveals as much about the society as the research itself. Resistance to novel and potentially threatening research, such as that we undertook, exposes deeply held values and interests of the actors – both the ties that bind and the conflicts that divide.' Yet such insight and potential can be of little reassurance to the field researcher whose time clock is ticking, whether because a leave from teaching is coming to an end, a summer break is almost over, a grant is about to expire, or repeated failure has battered self-esteem and sense of mastery.

Some might argue that the obvious, even desirable solution is to enter companies covertly, unencumbered by any obligation to people or persons with power. In fact, the number of researchers who conduct their studies anonymously and covertly is small. That most researchers obtain permission and do their research overtly reflects a constellation of factors. First, in the United States the American Sociological Association's Code of Ethics identifies a very limited number of conditions under which sociologists can conduct covert research and as a general guideline advocates obtaining informed consent from research participants (American Sociological Association, 1997: Section 12; on covert research see Section 12.05). Then, researchers understandably worry they cannot get where they want to go inside the work organization, and thus will not be able to develop a picture with meaningful depth, unless they are authorized. Working covertly, for example as a paid employee, can restrict researchers' access to a narrow range of interactions, events and relationships.[5] Lack of depth can compromise one of the main advantages of ethnographic research, which is to grasp faithfully the meanings that individuals hold, the factors shaping those meanings, a full rather than partial perspective on work organizations, and the dynamic nature of work life.

It is, nevertheless, a fine line to walk. Although researchers may accomplish their goals with official authorization they also run the risk that they are being allowed contacts with and glimpses of people, situations and events carefully selected by company managers. Struggling with and overcoming this tension is a significant source of labor – strategizing, negotiating – for all field researchers. Ethnographers of work, though, often strive to descend well into organizations in their studies. They worry that they may have only partial views into one area or one workgroup, and so strive to supplement or cross-check their participant observation or observational data with other types of data. Ethnographic fieldworkers extensively draw on depth interview and focus group data with a variety of participants from the setting they are studying. They have done surveys (Kanter, [1977] 1993), analysed company documents, such as personnel files, production records, newsletters, memos and annual reports, some quantifying the data taken from such sources (Burawoy, 1979; Kanter, [1977] 1993; Morrill, 1995; Thomas, 1985; Vallas, 1993).

Many companies have on-site libraries open to their employees and to the public, filled with publications for general audiences about the business world in general and more specialized publications – reports and documents – internal to the firm itself. However, this archival source, I have found, is vulnerable, hence unreliable. When I conducted a qualitative case study of the Bank of America in the mid-1980s, for example, I initially used their corporate library extensively, but arrived one day to discover that the library had been closed to the public without advance warning. The official explanation was that this was necessitated by reduced resources for serving the public, but since the bank was in a period of major financial crisis, its history, its practices and its mistakes scrutinized daily in the local, national and international press, it seemed plausible to me that corporate-level managers had become wary of making their internal documents conveniently available to the public. This reversal of company policy, and its implications for my study goals, underscores Buchanan, Boddy and McCalman's (1988) observation that opportunism is an asset when doing field research. Fieldworkers never know what organizational door will close in their faces, what meeting will be convened to which researchers are spontaneously invited, or what change in organizational fortunes may lead investigators down new avenues of enquiry. For these reasons, many ethnographic scholars self-consciously approach the field using multiple research tactics to develop broadly sketched, multi-layered portrayals of work.

Once in the field, ethnographers have structured their research time in a number of different ways. Some work or are involved full-time in a research setting for long periods of time, while others do fieldwork part-time and continuously, or part-time discontinuously. A great many of the studies considered for this chapter are based on fieldwork carried out for longer than six months, and a not-insignificant minority were carried out for several years. Months and years can pass in between the completion of one case study and the beginning of another.

Fieldwork appendices and texts reveal that the diversity of approaches is not due to insensitivity to ethnographic standards, to flaws in research designs, or to methodological sloppiness. Instead, very often they reflect the real constraints governing the conditions under which researchers can and cannot conduct qualitative field research. Here, difficulties with gaining access merge with constraints on the time that social scientists can spend doing uninterrupted fieldwork. In addition to aspects of work organizations themselves that limit when social scientists can get into them, the pace at which they can collect their data, and how long they can spend there, researchers face professional, community and familial obligations that restrict one's ability to commit to sustained fieldwork, particularly to fully immersed participant observation. Researchers rarely articulate the stories of how personal life – the births of children, the deaths of friends and family, physical illness and emotional upheavals (both of self and others), breakups of family and friendships, changes in job fortunes – shape the conduct of research and the writing of books and articles. We glean these stories from reading between the lines, usually in authors' acknowledgments.

It is the rare researcher who has maintained a consistent, steady track record, continually immersing themselves in the ethnographic fieldwork enterprise for long periods of time over a matter of many years, but it is instructive to look at those who do. Burawoy, to use one example, visited Hungary two and three times a year over the course of seven years, at times spending entire semesters off from teaching (Burawoy and Lukás, 1992: xiv) for his co-authored research monograph on Hungary's transition from socialism. He has continued this pattern of immersion in the field in more recent research in the Soviet Union (personal communication). This model of work is impressive but obviously difficult to sustain.

Zussman (1992) diagnosed this problem and its implications in his own methods appendix. His frank, lucid reflections, expressing his weariness after several years of fieldwork in two hospitals, are worth quoting at length.

> Although the claim would be difficult to document, it is my impression that (with a good number of notable exceptions) an unusually high proportion of social scientists who have produced superb first books based on fieldwork have then either failed to produce second books, taken a very long time to do so, or turned to different methods. I suspect that most of us, myself very much included, simply find fieldwork too exhausting, too time consuming (especially if undertaken in conjunction with a full-time teaching position) and too inefficient to justify the effort. (1992: 231)

The time-consuming nature of using an ethnographic approach to work is reflected in one direct indicator: the length of time between the beginning of fieldwork and the publication of the fifty-three research monographs considered for this chapter. The average length between the start of fieldwork and publication of the fifty books for which information was provided was 8.14 years.[6] (To be sure, this length of time is extended by the nine anthropologists in the sample; their average was 10.7 years. Taking out the anthropologists, the average is still impressive at 7.6 years.) This figure would be more striking (dismally so) if I were able to calculate the amount of time from the design or inception of the project to publication, since a significant amount would have to be added for the period of time during which field researchers were trying to get into workplaces to do their research.

Clearly, the time conceptualizing, planning, researching, coding and analysing, and writing, is a considerable amount to wait to see the fruition of one's work. A more indirect indicator is an observation about the origins of the books and articles I have reviewed here. Of the 57 authors whose work resulted in a book *or* article considered in this chapter, 32 (56%) indicated that the study originated in

their dissertation research, thus done during a stage in one's academic career where individuals have greater flexibility and latitude to stay in the field (compared to the time when one is on a tenure track and must contend with, not only research and publishing pressures, but teaching, advising, administrative and committee work).[7]

Ethnographic field research in general is notorious for its time- and labor-intensiveness. Ethnographic researchers, whether immersed in communities, in social movement organizations, in the military, or in laboratories, all must struggle with the time and access dilemma. Why in particular does the time-consuming nature of ethnographies of work – the research and the production of texts – matter? As Bosk (1992) pointed out, studying work and work processes can have a time-delimited aspect to it. Writing about his research on genetics counselors, he noted that with the passage of the ten years between doing his fieldwork and publishing the book, new technologies, testing procedures and scientific knowledge itself had changed enough that he worried whether his conclusions would still hold. Much field research in work organizations is historically specific, trying to document how particular forces and trends in the larger political economy shape and reshape work structures and relationships. Studying current trends – organizational (restructuring or flattening), technological (the effects of computer technology), demographic (the entrance of white women and men and women of color into the labor force and diverse work settings), or labor market (the explosion of temporary work) – is problematic for scholars whose data may not be as relevant or whose conclusions will be dated if published a considerable time after collected. Work ethnographers thus have an extra dimension of complexity in their deliberations about how long to stay in the field, how long to take to analyse findings and write them up (usually in books), and about the limitations of their analysis.

Finally, it should be noted that too often researchers only hint at these difficulties rather than acknowledge them explicitly. There is a wide range of representational styles, including accounts that deeply implicate the self of the researcher in the story of work (e.g., Diamond, 1992; Kondo, 1990; Swerdlow, 1998), those that do not place the researcher at center stage yet tell the story from deep within organizations and labor processes (e.g., Burawoy, 1979; Juravich, 1985), and those whose authors were less involved observers but use their observational data with rich and vivid effect (e.g., Hossfeld, 1990). Representations of methods, the confessions of fieldworkers, similarly vary from the straightforward ('I did this, then I did that') to the critically self-reflexive; from standard methods appendices that serve a kind of scientific legitimating function, in which researchers justify each methodological tactic and account for all time spent (e.g., Morrill, 1995), to cases in which reflections in and on the field are fully and fluidly part of the text itself (e.g., Bosk, 1992).

But as Van Maanen (1988) has pointed out, the great majority of ethnographic studies are written in a realist voice, a style of writing about fieldwork that implies unquestionable authority, objectivity, detachment and confidence about the research and the writing of the text. Although few writers are assuming or objectifying enough that they discuss their field roles in the third person, as was more characteristic of earlier generations of qualitative case studies,[8] objectivist, realist voices pervade the majority of ethnographic studies of work. These voices convey to the reader a sense that the researcher's observations were clear-cut, that they are imparting a truth about a knowable entity, the organization and social relationships of work. Importantly, realist accounts rarely acknowledge the uncertainties, the flaws, the confusions, and the ambivalences that authors feel about the process of their work.

CONCLUSION

Ethnographic studies have been invaluable for the contemporary understanding of work. Researchers have mined the situations and perspectives of workers through their own lived experience as participant observers, both as workers and as witnesses (Bosk, 1992: 12). By engaging in the same social processes, confronting the same organizational, technological, and administrative structures, and being implicated in the same relations of power and control, ethnographic field researchers have acquired a type of data that is simply unattainable using other modes of enquiry. They reveal to us things that we cannot know by conducting a survey, by interviewing individuals out of context, by doing archival research, or by performing experiments in carefully controlled settings. In particular, fieldworkers using ethnographic approaches convey vivid, dynamic and processual portrayals of lived experience.

I have outlined three key areas which ethnographers have pioneered. But I have also suggested that there is reason to be concerned about how effectively this enterprise can be maintained. Between the restrictions placed by those guarding the gateways to businesses and work organizations, on the one hand, and the pressing demands of professional and familial obligations, on the other, researchers' ability to conduct sustained observation and participation seems to me to be in jeopardy. This is especially troubling when thinking about doing research that gets at how work, occupations, labor processes and work organizations are changing, and how those changes affect different groups of workers who ordinarily stand to benefit from the insights of ethnographic research.

One of the major goals of social science research on work, I would argue, should be not merely to describe, but to explain, to determine how modern work organizations change opportunity structures, serve as vehicles of inequality, and transform the nature of power and control. Trends in work arrangements in postindustrial workplaces are reconfiguring production arrangements and employment relations in fundamental ways (Smith, 1997b). If field researchers – with a keen eye toward understanding both structure and agency, the ways in which action is situated, objective constraints and subjective experiences – cannot fully explore these trends, we will have a partial view, a view that will keep us from pinpointing causal forces, identifying ameliorating policies and theorizing alternatives. We may miss out on how inequalities are maintained, or, conversely, how workplace participants embrace, in surprising ways, new forms of work, participation, or employment.

In other words, if we are confined to talking to workers at the end of the workday, or to managers and personnel directors who tell selective stories about the causes and consequences of particular work arrangements, we lose the ethnographic edge and thus lose knowing what is transpiring at work. Not all fieldworkers must get jobs in the organizations they study, but my reading of the field strongly suggests they should have the 'broad and relatively unrestricted access to people' that Thomas (1994) held out for in his multi-case study of technology systems. These dilemmas, discussed intermittently and often relegated to margins and the back pages of scholarly texts, remain unresolved but central to this field.

Acknowledgements

My warmest thanks go to Anna Muraco for compiling the reference section for this chapter. For invaluable critical comments on the chapter I thank Charles Bosk, Randy Hodson, Carole Joffe, Robin Leidner, Ming-cheng Lo and two anonymous reviewers. Thanks also to Lyn Lofland for ushering this through to completion.

NOTES

1 Because of spatial constraints I don't consider ethnographic monographs that shed considerable light on work but focus primarily on other institutions and social processes such as family (Ong, 1987; Stacey, 1990; Wolf, 1992; Zavella, 1987), community (Halle, 1984), social movements (Blum, 1991; Fantasia, 1988), secondary schools and labor markets (MacLeod, 1987; Powers, forthcoming; Weis, 1990; Willis, 1977), and professional

schools (Becker et al., 1961; Granfield, 1992), to name just a very few. It is worth noting that there is a substantial literature on work and occupations that is ethnographically evocative, which uses primarily interviews, surveys and documentary analysis to generate thick descriptions of work: some examples include research on domestic workers (Constable, 1997; Dill, 1994; Glenn, 1986); blue-collar women (Eisenberg, 1998); longshoremen (DiFazio, 1985); men in female-dominated occupations (Williams, 1995) and women in male-dominated institutions (Zimmer, 1986); and industrial workers (Dudley, 1994; Milkman, 1997). Vaughn's (1996) innovative historical organizational ethnography, a study of engineers and managers at NASA, is similarly evocative. See Schwartzman (1993) for a *history* of workplace studies with an ethnographic orientation or component.

2 Although some explicitly disavow such an equation; e.g., Manning (1977) emphatically noted that his qualitative fieldwork study of police officers was not in and of itself an ethnography.

3 For this reason, the studies discussed in this section have a strong affinity with comparable worth studies. The latter deconstruct the ways in which definitions of what is more and less skilled have been infused heavily with implicit biases within work organizations that value men's job tasks and qualifications more highly than women's (Blum, 1991).

4 Another organizational variable, one that lengthens the time spent trying to get into work organizations, is the notorious difficulty of making person-to-person contact with organizational gatekeepers – middle managers and personnel staff – in order to broach the topic of doing research in their firm, and seeking their permission for the project. In large companies, it is an axiom that these individuals do not *ever* answer their own telephones unless you have a prearranged phone appointment. Even then, secretaries usually answer the phones and transfer the call to the correct person. Researchers don't often write about the wait involved as they play a long game of phone tag, leaving multiple messages on voice mail, speaking to secretaries, as well as the wait involved for the time and day, usually weeks away, that the individual can fit you into their frantic schedules for a phone appointment. All this is only the prelude to making an in-person appointment to talk about research possibilities, usually scheduled a few weeks down the road. I have learned never to rely on a person to return my call, and instead, pursue him or her as aggressively as possible. I find that keeping a phone log is quite useful, which I use to track when I have called people and to remind myself of when to call them next.

5 Human subjects review committees also discourage fieldworkers when they prohibit covert research because it might put subjects at risk or violate their privacy.

6 Authors usually indicate the year, and often the month of the year, in which they began their fieldwork: in the text, in a methods appendix, acknowledgements, footnotes or in tables summarizing data collected by the author. In some cases dates of fieldwork are not included but can be approximated from the timing of key events that are mentioned in the data analysis (for example, Bosk (1979)

noted that he brought newspapers to the surgeons he studied during the Watergate affair, dating his research at approximately the early 1970s), or from the timing of earlier publications on the research. Technology facilitated my search for information about this since I was able to e-mail some people directly to ask them when they did their fieldwork and whether or not their research started as a dissertation.

7 Additional, anecdotal evidence supports my point. Four authors included in the population of studies I reviewed for this chapter have multiple research monographs (Bosk, 1979, 1992; Burawoy, 1979; Burawoy and Lukás, 1992; Jackall, 1978, 1988, 1997; and Thomas, 1985, 1994). One of these authors published their second book 9 years after the first (Thomas), one, 10 years after the first (Jackall), and two, 13 years after the first (Bosk, Burawoy), all fairly substantial amounts of time. Needless to say, all four published other things in the intervening years (articles and edited collections), but the studies listed above are the monographs reporting the results of their major ethnographic research projects.

8 See Blau's ([1955] 1963) comments, for example, about how people reacted to his observer role in two government agencies: 'In both agencies *the observer* was introduced to the staff as a sociologist by a senior official ... Many believed *he* was a member of a government commission ... and not a social scientist, as *he* claimed' (p. 3; emphasis added). It is profound to compare his distanced voice to the involved voice of someone like Diamond (1992), whose description of his anxiety and care in helping a nearly-100-year-old woman slip on her sweater, delicately 'coaxing her eggshell-brittle, pencil-thin arms into sleeves' (p. 140), as well as many other instances of caring for the frail and the sick when he worked as a nursing assistant, so vividly conveys the lived experience of the participant observer.

REFERENCES

Acker, Joan (1990) 'Hierarchies, bodies, and jobs: a theory of gendered organizations', *Gender and Society*, 4 (2): 139–58.

Allison, Anne (1994) *Nightwork: Sexuality, Pleasure, and Corporate Masculinity in a Tokyo Hostess Club*. Chicago: University of Chicago Press.

American Sociological Association (1997) *Code of Ethics*. Toronto, Canada.

Barley, Stephen (1986) 'Technology as an occasion for structuring: evidence from observations of CT scanners and the social order of radiology departments', *Administrative Science Quarterly*, 31 (1): 78–108.

Becker, Howard, Geer, B., Hughes, E.C. and Strauss, A. (1961) *Boys in White: Student Culture in Medical School*. Chicago: University of Chicago Press.

Biggart, Nicole Woolsey (1989) *Charismatic Capitalism: Direct Selling Organizations in America*. Chicago: University of Chicago Press.

Blau, Peter M. ([1955] 1963) *The Dynamics of Bureaucracy: A Study of Interpersonal Relations in Two*

Government Agencies. Chicago: University of Chicago Press.

Blum, Linda (1991) *Between Feminism and Labor: The Significance of the Comparable Worth Movement.* Berkeley, CA: University of California Press.

Bosk, Charles L. (1979) *Forgive and Remember: Managing Medical Failure.* Chicago: University of Chicago Press.

Bosk, Charles L. (1992) *All God's Mistakes: Genetic Counseling in a Pediatric Hospital.* Chicago: University of Chicago Press.

Braverman, Harry (1974) *Labor and Monopoly Capital.* New York: Monthly Review Press.

Buchanan, D., Boddy, D. and McCalman, J. (1988) 'Getting in, getting on, getting out, and getting back', in Alan Bryman (ed.), *Doing Research in Organizations.* London: Routledge. pp. 53–67.

Burawoy, Michael (1979) *Manufacturing Consent: Changes in the Labor Process Under Monopoly Capitalism.* Chicago: University of Chicago Press.

Burawoy, Michael (1991) 'Teaching participant observation', in Michael Burawoy, A. Burton, A. Ferguson et al. (eds), *Ethnography Unbound: Power and Resistance in the Modern Metropolis.* Berkeley, CA: University of California Press. pp. 291–300.

Burawoy, Michael and Lukás, Janos (1992) *The Radiant Past: Ideology and Reality in Hungary's Road to Capitalism.* Chicago: University of Chicago Press.

Burawoy, Michael, Burton, A., Ferguson, A., Fox, K., Gamson, J., Gartrell, N., Hurst, L., Kurzman, C., Salzinger, L., Schiffman, J. and Ui, S. (eds) (1991) *Ethnography Unbound: Power and Resistance in the Modern Metropolis.* Berkeley, CA: University of California Press.

Chambliss, Daniel (1996) *Beyond Caring: Hospitals, Nurses, and the Social Organization of Ethics.* Chicago: University of Chicago Press.

Chapkis, Wendy (1997) *Live Sex Acts: Women Performing Erotic Labor.* New York: Routledge.

Chetkovich, Carol (1997) *Real Heat: Gender and Race in the Urban Fire Service.* New Brunswick, NJ: Rutgers University Press.

Chinoy, Ely (1955/1992) *Automobile Workers and the American Dream*, 2nd edn, with introduction by Ruth Milkman. Urbana, IL: University of Illinois Press.

Clifford, James and Marcus, George E. (1986) *Writing Culture: The Poetics and Politics of Ethnography.* Berkeley, CA: University of California Press.

Constable, Nicole (1997) *Maid to Order in Hong Kong: Stories of Filipina Workers.* Ithaca, NY: Cornell University Press.

Dalton, Melville (1959) *Men Who Manage: Fusion of Feelings and Theory in Administration.* New York: John Wiley & Sons.

Diamond, Timothy (1992) *Making Gray Gold: Narratives of Nursing Home Care.* Chicago: University of Chicago Press.

DiFazio, William (1985) *Longshoreman: Community and Resistance on the Brooklyn Waterfront.* New York: Bergin and Garvey.

Dill, Bonnie Thornton (1994) *Across the Boundaries of Race and Class: An Exploration of Work and Family Among Black Female Domestic Servants.* New York: Garland Publishing.

Dudley, Kathryn Marie (1994) *The End of the Line: Lost Jobs, New Lives in Postindustrial America.* Chicago: University of Chicago Press.

Eisenberg, Susan (1998) *We'll Call You if We Need You: Experiences of Women Working Construction.* Ithaca, NY: ILR/Cornell University Press.

Fantasia, Rick (1988) *Cultures of Solidarity: Consciousness, Action, and Contemporary American Workers.* Berkeley, CA: University of California Press.

Fine, Gary Alan (1996) *Kitchens: The Culture of Restaurant Work.* Berkeley, CA: University of California Press.

Fink, Deborah (1998) *Cutting into the Meatpacking Line: Workers and Change in the Rural Midwest.* Chapel Hill, NC: University of North Carolina Press.

Finlay, William (1988) *Work on the Waterfront: Worker Power and Technological Change in a West Coast Port.* Philadelphia: Temple University Press.

Flowers, Amy (1998) *The Fantasy Factory: An Insider's View of the Phone Sex Industry.* Philadelphia: University of Pennsylvania Press.

Fox, Renee (1959) *Experiment Perilous: Physicians and Patients Facing the Unknown.* Glencoe, IL: The Free Press.

Friedman, Raymond and McDaniel, Darren (1998) 'In the eye of the beholder: ethnography in the study of work,' in K. Whitfield and G. Strauss (eds), *Researching the World of Work: Strategies and Methods in Studying Industrial Relations.* Ithaca, NY: ILR/Cornell University Press. pp. 113–26.

Gamst, Frederick (1980) *The Hoghead: An Industrial Ethnology of the Locomotive Engineer.* New York: Holt, Rinehart and Winston.

Glenn, Evelyn Nakano (1986) *Issei, Nisei, War Bride: Three Generations of Japanese-American Women in Domestic Service.* Philadelphia: Temple University Press.

Graham, Laurie (1995) *On Line at Subaru–Isuzu: The Japanese Model and the American Worker.* Ithaca, NY: ILR/Cornell University Press.

Granfield, Robert (1992) *Making Elite Lawyers.* New York: Routledge.

Grenier, Guillermo (1988) *Inhuman Relations: Quality Circles and Anti-Unionism in American Industry.* Philadelphia: Temple University Press.

Halle, David (1984) *America's Working Man: Work, Home, and Politics among Blue Collar Property Owners.* Chicago: University of Chicago Press.

Hammersley, Martyn (1992) *What's Wrong With Ethnography?* London: Routledge.

Harper, Douglas (1987/1992) *Working Knowledge: Skill and Community in a Small Shop.* Berkeley, CA: University of California Press.

Hochschild, Arlie (1983) *The Managed Heart: Commercialization of Human Feeling.* Berkeley, CA: University of California Press.

Hodson, Randy (1998) 'Organizational ethnographies: an underutilized resource in the sociology of work', *Social Forces*, 76 (4): 1173–208.

Hossfeld, Karen (1990) '"Their logic against them": contradictions in sex, race, and class in the silicon valley', in Kathryn Ward (ed.), *Women Workers and Global Restructuring*. Ithaca, NY: ILR/Cornell University Press. pp. 149–78.

Hsiung, Ping-Chun (1996) *Living Rooms as Factories: Class, Gender, and the Satellite Factory Industry System in Taiwan*. Philadelphia: Temple University Press.

Hughes, Everett C. (1958) *Men and Their Work*. Glencoe, IL: The Free Press.

Jackall, Robert (1978) *Workers in a Labyrinth: Jobs and Survival in an Bank Bureaucracy*. Montclair, NJ and New York: Landmark Studies.

Jackall, Robert (1988) *Moral Mazes: The World of Corporate Managers*. New York: Oxford University Press.

Jackall, Robert (1997) *Wild Cowboys: Urban Marauders and the Forces of Order*. Cambridge, MA: Harvard University Press.

Joffe, Carole (1986) *The Regulation of Sexuality: Experiences of Family Planning Workers*. Philadelphia: Temple University Press.

Juravich, Tom (1985) *Chaos on the Shop Floor: A Worker's View of Quality, Productivity, and Management*. Philadelphia: Temple University Press.

Kanter, Rosabeth Moss (1977/1993) *Men and Women of the Corporation*. New York: Basic Books.

Kleinman, Sherryl (1996) *Opposing Ambitions: Gender and Identity in an Alternative Organization*. Chicago: University of Chicago Press.

Kondo, Dorinne (1990) *Crafting Selves: Power, Gender, and Discourse of Identity in a Japanese Workplace*. Chicago: University of Chicago Press.

Kunda, Gideon (1992) *Engineering Culture: Control and Commitment in a High-Technology Firm*. Philadelphia: Temple University Press.

Kusterer, Ken (1978) *Know-How on the Job: The Important Working Knowledge of 'Unskilled' Workers*. Boulder, CO: Westview Press.

Lee, Ching Kwan (1998) *Gender and the South China Miracle: Two Worlds of Factory Women*. Berkeley, CA: University of California Press.

Leidner, Robin (1993) *Fast Food, Fast Talk: Service Work and the Routinization of Everyday Life*. Berkeley, CA: University of California Press.

MacLeod, Jay (1987) *Ain't No Makin' It: Aspirations and Attainment in a Low-Income Neighborhood*. Boulder, CO: Westview Press.

Manning, Peter (1977) *Police Work: The Social Organization of Policing*. Boston, MA: MIT Press.

Manwaring, Tony and Wood, Stephen (1984) 'The ghost in the machine: tacit skills in the labor process', *Socialist Review*, 74: 55–94.

Martin, Susan (1980) *Breaking and Entering: Policewomen on Patrol*. Berkeley, CA: University of California Press.

Milkman, Ruth (1997) *Farewell to the Factory: Auto Workers in the Late Twentieth Century*. Berkeley, CA: University of California Press.

Morrill, Calvin (1995) *The Executive Way: Conflict Management in Corporations*. Chicago: University of Chicago Press.

Morrill, Calvin and Fine, Gary Alan (1997) 'Ethnographic contributions to organizational sociology', *Sociological Methods and Research*, 25 (4): 424–51.

Morrill, C., Buller, D., Buller, M.K. and Larkey, L. (1999) 'Toward an organizational perspective on identifying and managing formal gatekeepers', *Qualitative Sociology*, 22 (1): 51–72.

Ong, Aihwa (1987) *Spirits of Resistance and Capitalist Discipline: Factory Women in Malaysia*. Albany, NY: State University of New York Press.

Orr, Julian (1996) *Talking About Machines: An Ethnography of a Modern Job*. Ithaca, NY: ILR/Cornell University Press.

Paules, Greta Foff (1991) *Dishing it Out: Power and Resistance Among Waitresses in a New Jersey Restaurant*. Philadelphia: Temple University Press.

Pierce, Jennifer (1995) *Gender Trials: Emotional Lives in Contemporary Law Firms*. Berkeley, CA: University of California Press.

Powers, Brian (forthcoming) *Making Marginality: How High Schools Create Inequality in the City*. New Haven, CT: Yale University Press.

Reskin, Barbara F. and Roos, Patricia A. (1990) *Job Queues, Gender Queues: Explaining Women's Inroads Into Male Occupations*. Philadelphia: Temple University Press.

Roberson, James (1998) *Japanese Working Class Lives: An Ethnographic Study of Factory Workers*. London: Routledge.

Roberts, Glenda (1994) *Staying on the Line: Blue-Collar Women in Contemporary Japan*. Honolulu, HI: University of Hawai'i Press.

Rollins, Judith (1985) *Between Women: Domestics and their Employers*. Philadelphia: Temple University Press.

Roy, Donald (1954) 'Efficiency and the "fix": informal intergroup relations in a piecework machine shop', *American Journal of Sociology*, 54: 255–66.

Salzinger, Leslie (1997) 'From high heels to swathed bodies: gendered meanings under production in Mexico's export processing industry', *Feminist Studies*, 23 (3): 549–74.

Schwartzman, Helen B. (1993) *Ethnography in Organizations*. Newbury Park, CA: Sage. (Volume 27 in *Qualitative Research Methods series*.)

Simonds, Wendy (1996) *Abortion at Work: Ideology and Practice in a Feminist Clinic*. New Brunswick, NJ: Rutgers University Press.

Smith, Vicki (1990) *Managing in the Corporate Interest: Control and Resistance in an American Bank*. Berkeley, CA: University of California Press.

Smith, Vicki (1994) 'Braverman's legacy: the labour process tradition at 20', *Work and Occupations*, 21 (4): 403–21.

Smith, Vicki (1996) 'Employee involvement, involved employees: participative work arrangements in a white-collar service occupation', *Social Problems*, 43 (2): 166–79.

Smith, Vicki (1997a) 'Ethnography bound: taking stock of organizational case studies', *Qualitative Sociology*, 20 (3): 425–35.

Smith, Vicki (1997b) 'New forms of work organization', *Annual Review of Sociology*, 23: 315–39.

Spradley, J.P. and Mann, B. (1975) *The Cocktail Waitress: Women's Work in a Men's Place*. New York: Wiley.

Stacey, Judith (1990) *Brave New Families: Studies of Domestic Upheavals in Late Twentieth Century America*. New York: Basic Books.

Sudnow, David (1967) *Passing On: The Social Organization of Dying*. Englewood Cliffs, NJ: Prentice–Hall.

Swerdlow, Marian (1998) *Underground Woman: My Four Years as a New York City Subway Conductor*. Philadelphia: Temple University Press.

Thomas, Robert (1985) *Citizenship, Gender, and Work: Social Organization of Industrial Agriculture*. Berkeley, CA: University of California Press.

Thomas, Robert (1994) *What Machines Can't Do: Politics and Technology in the Industrial Enterprise*. Berkeley, CA: University of California Press.

Vallas, Steven (1993) *Power in the Workplace: The Politics of Production at AT&T*. Albany, NY: State University of New York Press.

Van Maanen, John (1988) *Tales of the Field: On Writing Ethnography*. Chicago: University of Chicago Press.

Vaughn, Diane (1996) *The Challenger Launch Decision: Risky Technology, Culture, and Deviance at NASA*. Chicago: University of Chicago Press.

Weis, Lois (1990) *Working Class Without Work: High School Students in a De-industrializing Economy*. New York: Routledge.

Wells, Miriam J. (1996) *Strawberry Fields: Politics, Class, and Work in California Agriculture*. Ithaca, NY: Cornell University Press.

Williams, Christine (1995) *Still a Man's World: Men Who Do Women's Work*. Berkeley, CA: University of California Press.

Willis, Paul (1977) *Learning to Labor: How Working Class Kids Get Working Class Jobs*. New York: Columbia University Press.

Wolf, Diane (1992) *Factory Daughters: Household Dynamics and Rural Industrialization in Java*. Berkeley, CA: University of California Press.

Zavella, Patricia (1987) *Women's Work and Chicano Families: Cannery Workers of the Santa Clara Valley*. Ithaca, NY: Cornell University Press.

Zimmer, Lynn (1986) *Women Guarding Men*. Chicago: University of Chicago Press.

Zuboff, Shoshana (1988) *In the Age of the Smart Machine: The Future of Work and Power*. New York: Basic Books.

Zussman, Robert (1992) *Medical Ethics and the Medical Profession*. Chicago: University of Chicago Press.

16

Ethnography and the Development of Science and Technology Studies

DAVID HESS

Because the term 'ethnography' has widely variant meanings across the disciplines, it should not be surprising that, within an interdisciplinary field such as Science and Technology Studies (STS), the practices of fieldwork and the conventions of ethnographic writing also vary dramatically. This chapter will explore some of the differences between two 'generations' or networks of ethnographic researchers in the STS field, then discuss some possible standards for a good ethnography in the field. The heuristic of two generations provides a useful, albeit simplified, point of entry into the literature, its methods and its theoretical frameworks.

METHODOLOGICAL ISSUES
IN THE FIRST GENERATION

During the early 1980s, social scientists (primarily sociologists) published several fieldwork-based studies that are sometimes referred to as the anthropology of science. The first generation of STS ethnographers included both Europeans and non-Europeans (mostly Americans), but during the early 1980s the British dominated the field.[1] Overall, the first generation occurred within a current of STS known as the sociology of scientific knowledge (SSK), which contrasted with the largely American sociology of science (or scientific institutions) associated with Robert Merton (1973) and colleagues. For SSK the central research concept was the social construction of knowledge, that is, the problem of how decisions about the credibility of knowledge claims and methods involve a mix of social and technical factors. The first generation of STS ethnographies

tended to be defined in contrast with a naive view of scientific work as a purely rational process of representing a nature that revealed itself in transparent observations. The term 'rational' in this context suggests that universalistic, technical decision criteria such as concerns with evidence and consistency are the dominant shaping factors in the outcomes of controversies and other decisions regarding theories, methods and knowledge claims in science. Instead, the SSK researchers emphasized the way in which concerns with evidence and consistency were interwoven with situationally contingent events, local decision-making processes, negotiation among a core set of actors in a controversy, the interpretive flexibility of evidence, additions and deletions of rhetorical markers (modalities) to knowledge claims, and other social or non-technical factors that shape the outcome of what comes to be constituted as accepted knowledge and methods in a field.

Notwithstanding the common ground of SSK ethnographies, there were substantial differences. For example, although this group of studies is known sometimes as 'laboratory studies', some of the ethnographies went beyond observations of laboratory science. Theoretical judgements about the nature of knowledge had implications for the choice of fieldwork site and method. For example, Collins' (1983a) emphasis on the role of community negotiation led to fieldwork in broader research communities rather than laboratories (e.g., Collins and Pinch, 1982) and to an interpretive method that he termed 'participant comprehension' in contrast with the more positivistic term 'participant observation' (Collins, 1983b). Collins and Pinch (1982: 20) were concerned with the problem of achieving competence in the sciences of the field site; like anthropologists in a foreign culture, they viewed a core ethnographic problem to be achieving understanding across the different disciplinary cultures of the social sciences and the field site science. In contrast, Latour and Woolgar ([1979] 1986) were more concerned with the rhetorical markers of the persuasion process that converted observations into widely accepted facts, and consequently their fieldwork focused on the laboratory and writing processes. They also were more concerned with the problem of going native, that is, accepting scientists' accounts of their work at face value. As a result, they emphasized the value of playing stranger to the experimental culture of the laboratory.[2]

Another major difference involved the changing conceptualization of the construction rubric. Over time the tradition of empirical studies of science took an increasing 'turn to technology' (Woolgar, 1991), and concern with the co-shaping of knowledge (or technology) and society displaced microsociological accounts. New terms such as 'co-construction' or simply 'construction' tended to displace the older term 'social construction'. Research methods also tended to be based more on documentary sources and interviews than on fieldwork; however, fieldwork-based research in this tradition continued to take place into the 1990s.[3] Actor–network theory is an influential example of the increasing concern with technology and with the co-construction problem (Callon, 1986, 1995). Of significance for ethnographic method is the theoretical question of how non-human entities achieve a delegated agency within sociotechnical networks. A trivial but simple example is the role of a traffic light in a busy intersection, which constitutes a sociotechnical network of pedestrians, drivers, police, traffic laws, vehicles, roads, crosswalks, etc. The light has a delegated agency that shapes human action in the system. A theoretical position on the agency of things will influence fieldwork choices about how to define a fieldwork site. Likewise, a well-chosen fieldwork site (such as the nocturnal traffic culture of urban Brazil) might lead to interesting theorizing of the cultural contingency of agency in sociotechnical systems.

In a few cases, researchers associated with the SSK ethnographies made excessive claims that suggested they believed that the consensus knowledge of a scientific field at any point in its history was solely the product of social factors. In other words, they suggested a plasticity to the interpretation of observations and production of evidence that left little room for the material world to intervene as a constraining force in scientific research or a decisive factor in the resolution of controversies. The excessive epistemological relativism of the radical versions of constructivism led to strong reactions from some philosophers and eventually from scientists of science wars fame. The latter tended to want to return to a pre-constructivist era in which histories and ethnographies of science excluded consideration of the social shaping of content. It is probably fair to say that neither extreme is feasible to many in the STS community today. For example, the outcome of controversies is frequently shaped by battles of evidence; thus, there is no doubt that a technical, universalistic decision criterion is influential and that the world has a kind of agency in decision-making of this sort. However, the ability to produce good evidence is shaped by research traditions that govern its interpretation, access to resources that govern its production, control over what counts as good methods, and the ability to mobilize rhetoric and colleagues to win arguments over the interpretation of data. Yet, even when taking such strong social factors into account, it is also the case that outgroups are sometimes able to defeat the orthodoxies of a scientific field based on higher quality evidence or more logical argumentation, even when the orthodox methods are used to judge such evidence and argumentation. Thus, a moderate view of constructivism suggests a both–and framework for interpreting the outcome of controversies and other scientific decision processes.

THE NEUTRALITY QUESTION IN STS

Some of the first generation of STS ethnographies were informed by the basic methodological principles known as the 'strong program'. The program involved four basic principles: causality, impartiality, symmetry and reflexivity (Bloor, [1976] 1991: 7). Causality meant that social studies of science would explain beliefs or states of knowledge. The impartiality principle held that social scientific accounts of science would be impartial with respect to the truth or falsity, rationality or irrationality, or success or failure of knowledge. The symmetry principle held that the same types of causes would explain both true and false beliefs; in other words, one would not explain 'true' science by referring it to nature and 'false' science by referring it to society. Reflexivity held that the same explanations of science would also apply to the social studies of science. Although the principles were formulated for SSK, presumably they could be extended to the study of technology.

Not all ethnographies of science were influenced by the strong program, nor were all of the principles equally influential. Latour and Woolgar made explicit and favorable reference to the strong program (1986: 105), particularly its principles of impartiality (p. 149) and symmetry (p. 23). Likewise, Collins and Pinch (1982: 17) adopted a position of impartiality regarding true and false beliefs in their study of a parapsychology controversy, and subsequently Collins articulated his own research program with the strong program's symmetry principle (1983a: 86; see also 1996). Woolgar (1988) later developed the reflexivity tenet in relationship to ethnography. In contrast, for Lynch the overall orientation was ethnomethodological, and mention of the strong program was more as a point of comparison (1985: 200; 1992). Likewise, Chubin and Restivo (1983) developed an opposing 'weak' program that in some ways antedates the developments of the second generation of ethnography.

Although the question of influence is complicated, the strong program does provide a point of reference for the first generation, and the principles of impartiality and symmetry serve as a valuable point of comparison between the first and second generations of ethnography in STS. As methodological principles, impartiality and symmetry proved to be, up to a point, valuable heuristics to guide empirical research projects, particularly those focused on the origins and outcomes of scientific controversies. In brief, the principles prevented a presentist type of explanation. For example, position A of a controversy won because it was based on the truth as we understand it today, whereas position B lost because it was biased by social factors. Although one might draw on today's knowledge and conclude that advocates of position A may have indeed developed a more accurate map of the world, one cannot assume that the evidence for A was better at the time of the controversy, that arguments for the evidence for A were more persuasive, that evidence itself was the only factor that led to the closure of the controversy, or that today's knowledge may not be reversed at some later point in time. In practice, the principles of impartiality and symmetry led to more nuanced explanations of empirical material in which social and technical explanations were interwoven. In the context of ethnography, the principles invited – although did not always lead to – a perspective that began with the views of the scientists of the field site, rather than with categories imposed by the observing ethnographer. As starting points, the principles therefore had value in helping researchers to avoid some methodological pitfalls.

Notwithstanding the value and general influence of the impartiality and symmetry principles as methodological heuristics, the principles were at the heart of ongoing debates and criticisms. Some criticisms were largely internal to SSK and were the result of continuing attempts to extend the symmetry principle, such as to the analysis of humans and things mentioned above regarding actor–network theory (see Bijker, 1993, and the epistemological chicken debate in Pickering, 1992). However, the more profound criticisms came from outside SSK. For example, SSK researchers argued that they had opened the black box of the content of science, but critics charged that upon opening the black box, they had found it politically empty (Winner, 1993) or that the strong program principles represented the academic depoliticization of STS' roots in activist struggles (Martin, 1993). One reading of the symmetry and impartiality principles is that they underplay or

even fail to make distinctions between the truth and falsity of scientific claims or the success and failure of technological designs. If one accepts the reading, then there are no grounds for making a decision about what course of action one ought to take, as in a policy recommendation. The broader topic of the politics of impartiality and symmetry received substantial attention during the 1990s (for example, from Ashmore and Richards, 1996; Radder, 1998). In some ways the second generation of ethnography begins with the recognition that the task of ethnography cannot be limited to the objectivizing framework of pure description/explanation and to the politics of scientific and value neutrality.

METHODOLOGICAL ISSUES
IN THE SECOND GENERATION

The second generation or network of ethnographic studies in STS has a different social address: there are more anthropologists, feminists and cultural studies researchers in this network, and it has a more American flavor.[4] Second generation ethnographies have tended to be more oriented toward social problems (environmental, class, race, sex, sexuality, and colonial) in addition to theoretical problems in the sociology and philosophy of knowledge. Consequently, the second generation tends to have a wider field site than the laboratory or core set of a controversy. Second generation examinations of knowledge and technology also tend to go outside the citadel of expert knowledge to the viewpoints of lay groups, activists, social movements, the media and popular culture; to examine the contours of orthodoxy and heterodoxy in a discipline's development, including the political, institutional and economic forces that govern the selection of research fields and programs; and to examine variations in expert knowledge and technology across cultures. Consequently, the research tends to be 'multi-sited' (Marcus, 1998; Rapp, 1999a), and ethnographic projects tend to require more time in the field. In fact, some of the projects span more than a decade of field research.

The concepts of culture and power (and the related family of concepts that includes gender, race, class, sexuality and nationality) are generally more central to theoretical frameworks of the second generation than the concept of the construction of knowledge and technology. Although the claim that scientific knowledge is in some sense socially constructed is widely accepted, the claim no longer seems to require proof. Indeed, when one takes into account the broad comparative perspective that includes studies of an immense literature on non-Western knowledges and material cultures, it is clear that each society produces a knowledge about the world that encodes its cultural traditions even as it maps real structures and processes in the material and social worlds. 'Western science' is no different – for example, in the resonances of key concepts such as natural law, atomism and evolution with similar concepts in the political and social systems (for example, legislative law, individualism and progressivism). It is probably more accurate to say that in the second generation the construction problem shifts from the SSK focus on how social and technical factors are interwoven in knowledge and technology production (social construction) or how sociotechnical networks and societies are mutually constituted (co-construction) to how cultural meanings or legitimating power relations are embedded in science and technology (cultural and political construction) and how different actors interpret science and technology (reconstruction).

Researchers in the second wave have tended to avoid the science wars problems that emerged in SSK partly because they often view the knowledge–culture relationship as both–and rather than either–or (Toumey, 1998). In other words, the cultural and political shaping of knowledge does not prevent it from also providing reasonably accurate maps of the world. For example, a hunter–gatherer people may have a complex mythological system that organizes categories of plant classification, but at the same time categories of plant classification follow empirical observations about structural and functional differences among species. The structures of both nature and culture co-determine knowledge; in other words, moderate or realistic constructivism is a starting, rather than ending, point of a research tradition. The view is not necessarily in conflict with the strong program; Bloor recognizes that 'there will be other types of causes apart from social ones which will cooperate in bringing about belief' (1991: 7). However, the applications of the strong program emphasized social variables in their explanations.

A second point of comparison and contrast with SSK in general and the strong program in particular is the relationship between the principle of cultural relativism and the strong program principles of impartiality and symmetry. Just as the strong program principles suggest an analysis that begins with the frameworks of the participants of a field site or controversy – what Bloor (1991: 176) calls 'methodological symmetry' – so the methodological principle of cultural relativism holds that ethnographic research should begin with the point(s) of view on one's informants. However, ethnographers in the anthropological/feminist/cultural studies traditions are careful to distinguish the moment of cultural interpretation in the research process from the complete analysis. Analysis may begin with local interpretations and meanings, but it does not end there. In the process, the second wave of ethnographers tends to distinguish cultural

relativism as a methodological heuristic from epistemological or moral relativism. Failure to engage in the 'stepping in' and 'stepping out' process constitutes 'going native', which is usually rejected as a departure from a completed analysis (Forsythe, 2001; Powdermaker, 1966). Like Collins and Pinch, the first concern is to understand how the world works from the point of view of one's informants, thus to achieve competence in the culture. The distancing or strangeness that Latour and Woolgar wanted occurs with the stepping back process of social scientific analysis of one's observations. In a way, a contrast in the first generation of ethnography comes together as two phases of a research project in the second generation.

The analytical half of second-wave STS ethnography implies asymmetry, and the most frequently given example is belief in supernatural phenomena. Social scientists and historians generally do not believe in supernatural phenomena, and they do not take supernatural forces into account in their explanations of, for example, witchcraft or sorcery as social phenomena. Likewise, Bloor recognizes a higher level asymmetry in the Afterword to the second edition of *Knowledge and Social Imagery* (1991: 176). He argues that a sociological explanation of witchcraft – that is, as opposed to a supernatural explanation – 'will logically imply that the witchcraft beliefs (taken at their face value) are false' (1991: 176). The logical asymmetry implicit in a sociological explanation of witchcraft is distinguished from the methodological symmetry of asking why members of a culture would choose the false belief – witchcraft is based on supernatural powers – over the true belief that witchcraft is not (p. 177). Bloor recognizes the problem of higher-level asymmetry that arises from methodological symmetry, but his exploration of the implications of higher-level asymmetry is limited.

Consider the complexities of the play of symmetry and asymmetry that occur in a social scientific explanation of the genesis and outcome of a scientific controversy. The explanation is inherently asymmetrical because it presumes that the social scientist's account can be, even if it is not always in fact, superior to the more limited explanations provided by most scientist-participants in the controversy. Participants generally have access to less complete technical and social information about the controversy than do post-hoc analysts, and they also do not have access to the accumulated science studies research on controversies. In this sense, scientists' accounts of controversies are like the traditional accounts of anthropologists' informants; they need to be analysed in light of an accumulated, cosmopolitan base of research as well as all sources of knowledge local to the controversy. However, there is a difference in the asymmetries of a social scientific explanation of, for example, why one shaman defeats another and why one side of a scientific or technical controversy prevails. An emic explanation of the outcome of a shamanic conflict would hold that one shaman defeated another because the first had stronger supernatural power or access to stronger spirits. The emic explanation would not enter into the social scientist's account except to the extent that belief in the emic explanation had an effect on the outcome. By extension, one might argue that a social scientist's account of the outcome of a scientific controversy would not rely on emic explanations such as stronger evidence or logic except to the extent that belief in stronger evidence and logic had an effect on the outcome. Yet, this application of symmetry precludes the social scientist from making the claim that whereas one side of the controversy believed it had better evidence and logic, in fact it only had access to greater resources, better rhetoric, or more political clout. Whereas few if any social scientists would want to make a similar distinction for shamanism (for example, one side had stronger supernatural power versus stronger social clout), for the analysis of scientific controversies in a policy-making context such an ability should not be surrendered.

The higher-level asymmetry that I am defending goes together with a higher-level partiality. At the second, higher-level of analysis, when one reassesses all the evidence and argumentation, and puts it together with all the social factors, it is possible to arrive at the conclusion that the minority or lost position was in fact 'better'. Rejected technologies such as the gas refrigerator (Cowen, 1985) or rejected theories such as the infectious etiology of cancer (Hess, 1997a) may have been wrongly rejected, at least partially or in some circumstances, and there are defensible grounds for making that evaluation. One can ground the verdict on the very standards that were used to dismiss the lost choices, such as cost and efficiency for a technological choice or evidence and consistency for a research program choice. Such a strategy is the most convincing, but one can also move up a level of analysis to argue that the methods or standards of evaluation in place at the time were biased in favor of the status quo, and an alternative set of criteria that inverts the established orthodoxy would better serve a general public interest. The necessity of beginning an analysis with a principle of cultural relativism, which I have shown to have some parallels with the impartiality and symmetry principles, is therefore linked to the equal and opposite necessity of concluding the analysis with a framework that is partial and asymmetrical, and likewise that is grounded in an epistemological and moral anti-relativism. The back-and-forth movement is essential if the social scientific analysis of science is to escape the incoherences revealed by critiques of the strong program and to move on to contribute to policy debates of public importance.

What Constitutes a Good Ethnography of Science and Technology?

The ethnography of science and technology shares several features with other contemporary ethnographic projects, but it also has some relatively unique features. First, as has occurred with much contemporary anthropological ethnography (Marcus, 1998), the traditional anthropological fieldwork narrative of the lone ethnographer who goes off to a remote village is clearly not appropriate. Fieldwork sites in the ethnography of science and technology are rarely remote, rarely disconnected from the world system, and frequently part of one's own society. Second, the ethnography of science and technology shares with contemporary ethnographic projects a new relationship with informants. As Michael Fischer (1998) has pointed out, in the traditional fieldwork model the ethnographer is the naive child or student who learns the culture from informants or teachers. In contrast, in ethnographies of emerging worlds the rapidly changing character of the field site(s) and sciences/technologies means that ethnographers and informants are groping together to understand what is going on. Third, there is usually an existing social science or historical literature on the science or technology in question, and ethnographers are challenged to produce something new against a backdrop of a pre-existing interdisciplinary social science literature. As occurs in, for example, medical anthropology, this epistemo-political situation will tend to drive the ethnography of science and technology toward a social science, as opposed to a humanities, orientation.

In the STS context there are some additional twists that are less common in other contemporary ethnographic projects. As Forsythe (2001) noted, ethnographers are likely to be collaborating with informants who will read very carefully what they write. While the situation is shared with some other contemporary ethnographic projects, in the science and technology context there are some cases in which ethnographers are also employed by their informants. Likewise, there is a much greater frequency in which informants or their colleagues serve as reviewers of the work of ethnographers. The situation creates the possibility that informants can directly restrict what the ethnographer can or cannot say. For example, Forsythe became involved in a legal battle over who owned her fieldnotes.

A second difference, at least of emphasis, between the ethnography of science and technology and some of the other contemporary ethnographic projects is that a social or cultural analysis is frequently taken as threatening in and of itself. Because the frameworks of the scientists tend to equate the 'social' or 'cultural' with the non-scientific or unscientific (that is, they assume an asymmetrical framework as a starting point), any attempts to show how their work is social and cultural will tend to be interpreted as a discrediting maneuver. In the context of heightened competition for funding and public support, such interpretations can lead to counterattacks on the ethnographer. Consequently, any sociocultural analysis of science will therefore tend to produce discomfort that could trigger the science wars.

How, then, does one assess the quality of an ethnography of science and technology? In the STS context, the term 'fieldwork' comes to include many points of exposure and triangulation: attending conferences (for the second wave of STS ethnographies, probably a preferred field site to laboratories), working in laboratories and schools, attending virtual chat rooms and real-world colloquia, interviewing a wide range of persons associated with the community, reading a vast technical literature, working in archives, developing long-term relationships with informants (who may, over time, become friends or even co-researchers), interviewing outsiders and laypeople about their perceptions of the expert community and its products, becoming a part of activist and social movement organizations, and providing services and help to the community (such as writing or lecturing on social, historical, or policy aspects of the community). Over time – generally at least two years of sustained contact but frequently five or ten years – a deep knowledge of the field community develops, so that the ethnographer achieves a rigorous standard of fieldwork quality. In George Marcus' phrase, the standard means 'being able to inform someone of your own community (scholarly and otherwise) what is going on in the frame of your project and fieldsite to the full extent of his or her curiosity' (1998: 18).

From the perspective of this standard of 'good ethnography', the ethnographer develops near native competence in the technical aspects of the science and technology involved. The standard of near native competence does not mean that one necessarily could pass, for example, a general doctoral exam that covers a wide variety of sub-fields in, for example, biology. Rather, the technical competence of the fieldworker tends to be within a narrow band – limited to specific sub-fields – where one's control of the literature is equivalent to that of the experts and, in some cases, superior to it. (The latter circumstance occurs most frequently when one delves into the archives that are often unread by contemporary researchers, who may have a bias against reading literature that is more than five years old and therefore may not know how current controversies repeat old ones.) More generally, the standard of near-native competence means that good ethnographers are able to understand the content and language of the field – its terminology, theories, findings, methods, and controversies – and they are able to analyse the content competently with respect to the social relations, power structures, cultural meanings and history of the field.

This is a high standard that often requires years of research.

In addition to a standard of competence, there are other criteria that should be included in a standard of a 'good ethnography' of science and technology. In the direction of the humanities, good ethnographies frequently interrogate or complexify the taken-for-granted, such as commonsense categories employed by social scientists, policy-makers, activists and scientists. Good ethnographies usually involve an element of surprise or subversion; the fieldworker finds phenomena, meanings, terms, practices, social relations, institutions, capital flows, culture–power connections, and so on that might not have been expected. Here, the ethnographic voice is one of thick description (Geertz, 1973), as in the work of historical interpretation or textual exegesis, although not necessarily restricted to the textualist limitations of Geertzian interpretive anthropology.

I also submit that good ethnographies are positioned explicitly with respect to a social science research tradition, either theoretical or empirical, and they move the tradition forward by providing new concepts and categories, new empirical findings, new explanations or explanatory models, or reasons for questioning unquestioned theoretical assumptions. The second, social science-direction is more evident in the classical ethnographic debates over, for example, kinship, but also in the more recent ethnographies that are situated in interdisciplinary social science research traditions such as social studies of medicine, science, and technology. There is a tension between the tendency to immerse oneself in the complexities of ethnographic detail and the tendency to produce an explicit contribution to a research tradition of theoretical models and empirical findings, but I would maintain that good ethnography can and should do both. In short, good ethnographies reveal competence, interpret complexity, interrogate the taken-for-granted, and make an explicit empirical or theoretical contribution to a literature.

MAKING GOOD ETHNOGRAPHY BETTER

Some ethnographers would argue that the standard described above is good enough. Can a mere contribution to the STS literature justify the tremendous investment of an intelligent, educated citizen, not to mention taxpayer dollars that might have supported the research project? An additional criterion for a good ethnography is that ethnographers develop ways of intervening in their field sites as citizen-researchers and of making their competence applicable to policy problems. The concept of policy does not have to be restricted to government science and technology policy; following Beck (1997), the policy application may be more at the 'subpolitical' level of how scientific and technical communities might change practices to achieve goals such as increased participation from underrepresented groups.

As a social scientist who understands the relevant science and technology at a level close to or equivalent to the experts *and* who understands the social/cultural/political aspects of the field in ways that often surpass the grasp of the experts in the field, the ethnographer has not only the unique opportunity, but also the civic obligation, to become part of the conversation about the relationship between the research field and the broader public that ultimately supports it. One therefore tends to find STS anthropologists speaking openly of 'intervention' and activism (Downey and Dumit, 1997). Against this position some have criticized all talk of intervention or activism as sacrificing explanatory or interpretive rigor on the altar of politics. However, the issue should be seen as both–and rather than either–or. One can maintain a high standard of descriptive analysis while at the same time providing the grounds for making prescriptive recommendations for ongoing policy problems. Furthermore, grappling with policy and prescriptive issues often tends to clarify descriptive work.

In this way, a good second generation STS ethnography can be described as post-constructivist. Rather than focusing on how knowledge and technology are socially constructed, the analysis examines ways in which they might be *better* constructed, with the criteria of 'better' defined explicitly and their contestability openly acknowledged as both epistemological and political. For example, what alternatives are there to the current configuration of the production of content in a specific field of science and technology? Usually, research fields are polarized by controversies over roads not taken, over research programs that have become dominant while others have fallen into backwater status. The polarization of fields along lines of orthodoxies and heterodoxies is particularly true in the applied fields such as medicine, public health, agriculture, management, policy, education and engineering. Often the connections are not obvious until one follows out the linkages between basic research and its applications.

Another approach is to ask similar questions about existing social institutions in science. For example, why are there so few women and underrepresented ethnic groups in most research fields in science, and what are the experiences of those who stay and leave? How do national research communities in a scientific field form a hierarchy, how do they relate to each other, and what is the experience of scientists in post-colonial societies? The institutional focus of the topic may appear to be old-fashioned to the SSK ethnographers, but here is another way in which a post-constructivist STS

differs from its constructivist predecessor. The institutional or 'Mertonian' side of science studies should not be rejected as a backwater or outdated paradigm. Indeed, it should be reconjugated with ethnographic research to reveal insights from the perspective of policy and intervention. For example, we now know that when underrepresented groups enter scientific fields, they tend to see biases of both theory and method that were not evident before, and they tend to lead innovations in the content of the field (Haraway, 1989). We also know that, in the United States at least, the educational process for technical fields such as engineering (Downey, 1998) involves socialization into a habitus that is most comfortable for white males and less so for women and members of underrepresented ethnic groups. Scientific fields such as artificial intelligence (Forsythe, 2001) and physics (Traweek, 1988) are not only dominated by men but also constructed around practices, slang and methods that embody masculine values. Ethnographically based research of this sort suggests that policy discussions need to involve more than the pipeline problem; in other words, the gender and ethnic problems in the social composition of scientific and technical professions will not be solved by getting more underrepresented groups into the pipeline. Rather, good ethnography points the way to ideas for redesigning the pipe itself.

INTERVENTION: SOME COMPARISONS

Within the second generation of STS ethnography there is a tendency to move toward a prescriptive discourse that engages various types and levels of policy questions. Although the concept of intervention is no more universally accepted in the second generation than symmetry and impartiality were in the first, intervention may have a comparable role as a point of reference. For example, the concept of intervention provides the framework for the introductory essay for the volume *Cyborgs and Citadels* (Downey and Dumit, 1997), which provides a prominent sampling of the second generation of ethnography in STS.

The scope and meaning of intervention as a central concept remains controversial. Eglash (1999b) suggests that the concept can be stretched too thinly, for example by arguing that a critique of theory – that is, a 'theoretical intervention' either within STS or within the science of the field site – might water down the concept of intervention to the point of inaction. Likewise, in a multi-sited ethnography of the Bhopal disaster and global environmentalism, Fortun (2001) queries the concept of intervention through her analysis of environmental advocacy. She suggests that the idealized ways of conceptualizing advocacy are inadequate because they underestimate the amount of uncertainty that advocates must confront. In environmental disputes such as Bhopal, advocates move in a world of dubious facts and ambiguous political alliances. Because a similar situation also characterizes most of science at the research front, as well as in many applied fields, her arguments can be generalized. As in the case of other ethnographers of this generation, Fortun played an active role in her field site; she provided her activist informants/partners with skills and labor in a mode that might be characterized as partnership action or participant action. However, as a writer–analyst she is skeptical of the prescriptive discourse that characterizes some of the other intervention projects in the second wave of ethnography. As she writes, 'Heroic images of scholars as activists without double-bind madden as much as they lure' (2001, Postscript: 2).

Gary Downey and colleagues provide a model of intervention that involves positioning the ethnographer within a research community. Downey and Lucena describe 'hiring in' as involving 'a willingness on the part of social researchers to allow their work to be assessed and evaluated in the theoretical terms current in the field of analysis and intervention' (1997: 119). They regard 'hiring in' as a subcategory of various types of 'partner theorizing', or short-term cooperative work relationships between ethnographers and, in this case, scientists or engineers (Downey and Rogers, 1995). Working in the belly of the beast creates opportunities to influence technical research and institutions directly, for example by challenging engineers to revise their curriculum to make it more friendly to a more diverse student body. However, at the same time Downey and Lucena recognize that the role creates 'complementary risks of cooptation and social engineering' (1997: 120).

Although Downey and Lucena suggest that 'hiring in' does not necessarily involve becoming the employee of scientists, the development did occur with Forsythe (2001). Her research demonstrates some of the dilemmas that can occur when 'hiring in' involves putting the ethnographer in the position of an employee of her scientist informants. Forsythe's early papers showed how the technicist assumptions of artificial intelligence (AI) engineers led to the design of systems that could have been more successful if the engineers had had a more ethnographically grounded understanding of what knowledge is and how it can be elicited. Although a member of the SSK network attacked her critiques as ethnocentric and asymmetrical (Fleck, 1993), Forsythe was writing as a member of the AI lab who was engaged in ongoing dialogue with the 'boys' in the lab, who valued her alternative perspective. The relationship was one of mutual criticism – often focused on gender issues – combined with mutual respect. As time went on, her work and that of other ethnographer colleagues became influential in the AI community, and eventually AI researchers adopted ethnographic methods in the design of expert systems. The development is most interesting from the perspective of a theory of ethnography as intervention and the unintended consequences that all historical action carries in its wake. Forsythe and colleagues won the battle and lost the war: ethnography became accepted in the AI field, but ethnography was redefined by the AI researchers. Furthermore, funding for her work dried up while ethnography by the 'natives' remained well-funded. The dual development led Forsythe to another level of criticism, in which she argued that the AI scientists' understanding of ethnography was colored by the same technicist assumptions that she originally documented for the AI culture, and therefore would produce similar failures.

Partner theorizing and hiring in belong to the same family of interventions that Heath (1997) characterizes as 'modest interventions'. As part of her fieldwork on a genetic disorder known as Marfan syndrome, Heath organized roundtable discussions at a conference that brought together researchers, clinicians and advocates in an open-ended discussion (1997: 79; see also Martin, 1996). The encounter between her scientist-informant and frustrated patients created some tensions, and Heath found her scientist-informant somewhat annoyed by the threat to autonomy that the ethnographer's intervention had created. At the same time, the scientist-informant also saw her research in new light, that is, as embedded in a more complex social context that, when taken into account, could lead to shifts in research priorities.

A less modest approach to intervention (perhaps some would call it 'immodest intervention') is developed in my own research project on alternative medicine, which brings ethnographic research to bear on a well-recognized policy failure: the war on cancer (Hess, 1997a, 1999; Wooddell and Hess, 1998). The project develops the issue of intervention around the concept of 'evaluation': how one should evaluate lost or suppressed therapies and research traditions, current clinical and research practices, and ongoing failures in regulatory and research policy. Situated alongside a social movement of clinicians, patients and researchers who are advocating changes in cancer research and treatment, I might also be described as a partner theorist or advocate. As in other communities, the alternative cancer therapy community itself is quite diverse and even internally split on crucial issues, so there is no easy way to advocate policy changes from 'the' community's perspective. The focus on evaluation provides a model of how differences both within the alternative medicine community and between it and conventional medicine might be resolved in a more universalistic way that serves a broader public interest than current policies allow. Through ethnographic interviews, I crystallize the community's knowledge into a framework for opening up the evaluation question to a complex set of epistemological/policy proposals that better serves the broad public interests of patients and their clinicians. In addition to presenting such work in academic fora, I have tried to bring the ideas into the general public sphere of debate through trade books, radio interviews, networking with patients and activists, presentations at alternative medicine conferences, and literature supplied to a congressional committee that was holding hearings on the failure to research alternative medicine.

A general issue that emerges from the comparisons made here is the willingness to engage in prescriptive discourse – such as calls for policy reform – within the ethnographic text, as opposed to banishing such writing and action to a separate sphere of action as a citizen. Debates over the scope and meaning of intervention seem likely to characterize the second wave of ethnography in a way similar to debates over constructivism in the first wave. Whereas debates over constructivism often took the form of the value of realism versus relativism, debates over intervention seem to be developing on the parallel issues of the relative emphasis on a policy focus versus language-symbolism focus in styles of intervention, or the relative place of prescriptive discourse within versus outside the ethnographic text.

Conclusion

Whereas the first generation of STS ethnographies focused on opening the black box of the social content of science and technology, second generation ethnography of science and technology has tended to open the brown, yellow, purple, red, pink and other multicolored boxes of the culture and politics of science and technology. Just as feminism taught that the personal is the political, so this approach to STS teaches that the technical is the cultural and the political. To develop an analysis that is both culturally profound and politically relevant, one must have a point of comparison and some sense of an alternative, and perhaps no method is better suited to developing alternatives – or even to having the ability to perceive them in the first place – than is wide-ranging, multi-sited fieldwork. It is perhaps the sense of alternatives that underlies both the scope of ethnographic enquiry in the second generation (outside the laboratory or even the expert community of science and technology producers) and the concern with intervention. The alternative perspective might be found in the viewpoint of a Japanese physicist, a Mexican oncologist, a woman engineering student, or a religious, working-class amniocentesis patient. The power of an ethnography rooted in alternative perspectives is the ability to

perceive science and technology differently, and consequently to imagine the design of new research programs, technologies and policies.

Furthermore, the ability to articulate alternatives puts the ethnographer in a unique position of being able to become a voice of leadership in policy discussions of public interest. To restrict the ethnographer's voice to one of social scientific explanation or humanistic interpretation represents a failure of nerve when confronted with the prospect of intervention. Rather, ethnographers need to meet the opportunity and obligation to provide much-needed leadership as articulators of public interest, even as they face their own double-binds and senses of uncertainty. Such leadership is increasingly important in a world characterized by the globalization of capital and the privatization of public spheres.

Acknowledgements

My thanks to Ron Eglash, Ernst Schraube, the Rice University Anthropology Department and two anonymous reviewers for comments on an earlier version of the chapter.

Notes

1 Prominent studies include Collins and Pinch (1982), Knorr Cetina (1981), Latour and Woolgar ([1979] 1986), Lynch (1985), and Zenzen and Restivo (1982). Those studies and others are reviewed in Knorr Cetina (1983, 1995) and listed in Lynch (1985: xiii–xiv); see Shapin (1995) and Hess (1997c) for points of entry into the SSK literature in general.

2 See Collins (1994a, 1994b) for a further discussion of his view of the stranger concept in the context of ethnography and social scientific research. The ethnomethodologist Lynch (1985: 2) also drew attention to the problem of achieving competence in a field of science.

3 Examples of the empirical case studies in the technology vein are the volumes edited by Bijker, Hughes and Pinch (1987) and Bijker and Law (1992). Two very different examples of continued fieldwork-based or observational research in the SSK tradition are Knorr Cetina (1998) and Wynne (1996), which, like Traweek (1988) and the work of some of the American sociologists (e.g., Casper and Clarke, 1998; Fujimura, 1996; Star, 1989, 1995; also Bowker and Star, 1999), are examples of projects that cross the two-generation heuristic. Likewise, see Kleinman (1998) for a laboratory study that includes an analysis of macrostructural issues.

4 See reviews by Downey and Dumit (1997); Franklin (1995); Franklin, Lury and Stacey (1991); Hakken (1993); Harding (1998); Hess (1995, 1997b, 1997c); Traweek (1993); and Watson-Verran and Turnbull (1995). Examples of recent ethnographic projects (including some mixings of ethnography and history) that comprise this second network of researchers include Allen (1999);

Blomberg (1997); Casper (1998); Clarke (1998); Davis-Floyd and Dumit (1998); De Laet (1998); Downey (1998); Dubinskas (1988); Dumit (1997, 2000); Eglash (1999a); Fischer (1999); Fortun (2001); Forsythe (2001); Franklin (1997); Franklin, Lury and Stacey (1991: Part Three); Gamradt (1997); Gusterson (1996); Hakken and Andrews (1993); Haraway (1989, 1997); Heath (1997); Heath and Rabinow (1993); Helmreich (1998); Hess (1997a, 1999); Hogle (1999); Horn (1994); Koenig (1988); Layne (2001); Martin (1987, 1994); Morgan and Michaels (1999); Nader (1996); Nardi (1993); Nardi and Reilly (1996); Nyce and Bader (1993); Orr (1997); Perin (1998); Pfaffenberger (1992); Rabinow (1996); Rapp (1999b); Stone (1996); Suchman (2000a, 2000b); Taussig (in press); Timmermans (1999); Toumey (1994); Traweek (1988, 1992); and Zabusky (1994).

REFERENCES

Allen, Barbara (1999) 'Making sustainable communities'. PhD dissertation, STS Department, Rensselaer Polytechnic Institute.

Ashmore, Malcolm and Richards, Evelleen (eds) (1996) 'Special issue on "the politics of SSK"', *Social Studies of Science*, 26 (2): 219–468.

Beck, Ulrich (1997) *The Reinvention of Politics*. Cambridge: Polity Press.

Bijker, Wiebe (1993) 'Do not despair: there is life after constructivism', *Science, Technology, and Human Values*, 18 (1): 113–38.

Bijker, Wiebe and Law, John (eds) (1992) *Shaping Technology/Building Society*. Cambridge, MA: MIT Press.

Bijker, Wiebe, Hughes, Thomas and Pinch Trevor (eds) (1987) *The Social Construction of Technological Systems*. Cambridge, MA: MIT Press.

Blomberg, Jeannette (1997) 'Constructing technological objects: reconfiguring the sociotechnical divide'. Paper presented at the annual meeting of the American Anthropological Association, Washington, DC.

Bloor, David ([1976] 1991) *Knowledge and Social Imagery*, 2nd edn. Chicago: University of Chicago Press.

Bowker, Geoffrey and Star, Susan Leigh (1999) *Sorting Things Out: Classification and Its Consequences*. Cambridge, MA: MIT Press.

Callon, Michel (1986) 'Some elements of a sociology of translation', in John Law (ed.), *Power, Action, and Belief*. London: Routledge. pp. 196–233. (Sociological Review Monograph 32.)

Callon, Michel (1995) 'Four models of the dynamics of science', in Sheila Jasanoff, Gerald E. Markle, James C. Peterson and Trevor Pinch (eds), *Handbook of Science and Technology Studies*. Thousand Oaks, CA: Sage. pp. 29–63.

Casper, Monica (1998) *The Making of the Unborn Patient*. New Brunswick, NJ: Rutgers University Press.

Casper, Monica and Clarke, Adele (1998) 'Making the pap smear into the "right tool" for the job', *Social Studies of Science*, 28 (2): 255–91.

Chubin, Daryl and Restivo, Sal (1983) 'The "mooting" of science studies', in Karin Knorr Cetina and Michael Mulkay (eds), *Science Observed*. London: Sage. pp. 53–84.

Clarke, Adele (1998) *Disciplining Reproduction*. Berkeley, CA: University of California Press.

Collins, Harry (1983a) 'An empirical relativist pro-gramme in the sociology of scientific knowledge', in Karin Knorr Cetina and Michael Mulkay (eds), *Science Observed*. Beverly Hills, CA: Sage. pp. 85–114.

Collins, Harry (1983b) 'The meaning of lies', in G. Nigel Gilbert and Peter Abell (eds), *Accounts and Action*. Aldershot: Gower House. pp. 69–76.

Collins, Harry (1994a) 'Dissecting surgery', *Social Studies of Science*, 24: 311–3.

Collins, Harry (1994b) 'Scene from afar', *Social Studies of Science*, 24: 369–89.

Collins, Harry (1996) 'In praise of futile gestures', *Social Studies of Science*, 16: 229–44.

Collins, Harry and Pinch, Trevor (1982) *Frames of Meaning*. London: Routledge.

Cowen, Ruth Schwartz (1985) 'How the refrigerator got its hum', in Donald MacKenzie and Judy Wajcman (eds), *The Social Shaping of Technology*. Philadelphia: Open University Press. pp. 202–18.

Davis-Floyd, Robbie and Dumit, Joe (eds) (1998) *Cyborg Babies*. New York: Routledge.

De Laet, Marianne (1998) 'Intricacies of technology trans-fer', *Knowledge and Society*, 11: 213–33.

Downey, Gary (1998) *The Machine in Me*. New York: Routledge.

Downey, Gary and Dumit, Joe (eds) (1997) *Cyborgs and Citadels*. Santa Fe, NM: School of American Research.

Downey, Gary and Lucena, Juan (1997) 'Engineering selves', in Gary Downey and Joe Dumit (eds), *Cyborgs and Citadels*. Santa Fe, NM: School of American Research. pp. 117–41.

Downey, Gary and Rogers, Juan (1995) 'On the politics of theorizing in a postmodern academy', *American Anthropologist*, 97 (2): 269–81.

Dubinskas, Frank (1988) 'Janus organizations', in Frank Dubinskas (ed.), *Making Time*. Philadelphia: Temple University Press. pp. 170–232.

Dumit, Joe (1997) 'A digital image of the category of the person', in Gary Downey and Joe Dumit (eds), *Cyborgs and Citadels*. Santa Fe, NM: School of American Research Press. pp. 83–102.

Dumit, Joe (2000) 'When explanations rest: 'good enough' brain science and the new sociomedical disorders', in Margaret Lock, Allan Young and Alberto Cambrosio (eds), *Living and Working with the New Medical Technologies: Intersections of Inquiry*. Cambridge: Cambridge University Press.

Eglash, Ron (1999a) *African Fractals*. New Brunswick, NJ: Rutgers University Press.

Eglash, Ron (1999b) 'Review of *Cyborgs and Citadels*', *Ethnos*, 64 (1): 134–6.

Fischer, Michael (1998) 'Seminar on STS'. Delivered at Rensselaer Polytechnic Institute, November.

Fischer, Michael (1999) 'Worlding cyberspace'. Unpublished ms.

Fleck, James (1993) 'Knowing engineers? A response to Forsythe', *Social Studies of Science*, 23: 445–77.

Forsythe, Diana (2001) *Toward an Anthropology of Artificial Intelligence*. Stanford, CA: Stanford University Press.

Fortun, Kim (2001) Advocacy after Bhopal. *Environmentalism, Disaster, New World Orders*. Chicago: University of Chicago Press.

Franklin, Sarah (1995) 'Science as culture, cultures of science', *Annual Review of Anthropology*, 24: 163–84.

Franklin, Sarah (1997) *Embodied Progress*. New York: Routledge.

Franklin, Sarah, Lury, Celia and Stacey, Jackie (1991) *Off-Centre: Feminism and Cultural Studies*. New York: HarperCollins.

Fujimura, Joan (1996) *Crafting Science*. Cambridge, MA: Harvard University Press.

Gamradt, Jan (1997) 'Innovation, risk, and the anthropology of learning in a professional community'. Paper presented at the annual meeting of the American Anthropological Association, Washington, DC.

Geertz, Clifford (1973) *The Interpretation of Cultures*. New York: Basic Books.

Gusterson, Hugh (1996) *Nuclear Rites*. Berkeley, CA: University of California Press.

Hakken, David (1993) 'Computing and social change: new technology and workplace transformation, 1980–1990', *Annual Review of Anthropology*, 22: 107–12.

Hakken, David and Andrews, Barbara (1993) *Computing Myths, Class Realities*. Boulder, CO: Westview Press.

Haraway, Donna (1989) *Primate Visions*. New York: Routledge.

Haraway, Donna (1997) *Modest Witness@Second Millenium*. New York: Routledge.

Harding, Sandra (1998) *Is Science Multicultural?* Bloomington, IN: Indiana University Press.

Heath, Deborah (1997) 'Bodies, antibodies, and modest interventions', in Gary Downey and Joe Dumit (eds), *Cyborgs and Citadels*. Santa Fe, NM: School of American Research. pp. 67–82.

Heath, Deborah and Rabinow, Paul (1993) 'Biopolitics: the anthropology of the new genetics and immunology', Special issue of *Culture, Medicine, and Psychiatry*, 17 (1).

Helmreich, Stefan (1998) *Silicon Second Nature*. Berkeley, CA: University of California Press.

Hess, David (1995) *Science and Technology in a Multicultural World*. New York: Columbia University Press.

Hess, David (1997a) *Can Bacteria Cause Cancer?* New York: New York University Press.

Hess, David (1997b) 'If you're thinking of living in STS', in Gary Downey and Joe Dumit (eds), *Cyborgs and Citadels*. Santa Fe, NM: School of American Research. pp. 143–64.

Hess, David (1997c) *Science Studies*. New York: New York University Press.

Hess, David (1999) *Evaluating Alternative Cancer Therapies*. New Brunswick, NJ: Rutgers University Press.

Hogle, Linda (1999) *Recovering the Nation's Body*. New Brunswick, NJ: Rutgers University Press.

Horn, David (1994) *Social Bodies: Science, Reproduction, and Italian Modernity*. Princeton, NJ: Princeton University Press.

Kleinman, Daniel (1998) 'Untangling context: understanding a university laboratory in the commercial world', *Science, Technology, and Human Values*, 23 (3): 285–314.

Knorr Cetina, Karin (1981) *The Manufacture of Knowledge*. New York: Pergamon.

Knorr Cetina, Karin (1983) 'The ethnographic study of scientific work', in Karin Knorr Cetina and Michael Mulkay (eds), *Science Observed*. Beverly Hills, CA: Sage. pp. 115–40.

Knorr Cetina, Karin (1995) 'Laboratory studies', in Sheila Jasanoff, Gerald E. Markle, James C. Peterson and Trevor Pinch (eds), *Handbook of Science and Technology Studies*. Thousand Oaks, CA: Sage. pp. 140–66.

Knorr Cetina, Karin (1998) *Epistemic Cultures*. Cambridge, MA: Harvard University Press.

Koenig, Barbara (1988) 'The technological imperative in medical practice', in M. Lock and D.R. Gordon (eds), *Biomedicine Examined*. Dordrecht: Kluwer. pp. 465–96.

Latour, Bruno and Woolgar, Steve ([1979] 1986) *Laboratory Life: The Social Construction of Scientific Facts*, 2nd edn. Princeton, NJ: Princeton University Press.

Layne, Linda (2001) *Motherhood Lost*. New York: Routledge.

Lynch, Michael (1985) *Art and Artifact in the Laboratory*. London: Routledge.

Lynch, Michael (1992) 'Extending Wittgenstein', in Andrew Pickering (ed.), *Science as Practice and Culture*. Chicago: University of Chicago Press. pp. 215–65.

Marcus, George (1998) *Ethnography Through Thick and Thin*. Princeton, NJ: Princeton University Press.

Martin, Brian (1993) 'The critique of science becomes academic', *Science, Technology, and Human Values*, 18 (2): 247–59.

Martin, Brian (1996) 'Sticking a needle into science', *Social Studies of Science*, 26: 245–76.

Martin, Emily (1987) *The Woman in the Body*. Boston, MA: Beacon Press.

Martin, Emily (1994) *Flexible Bodies*. Boston, MA: Beacon Press.

Merton, Robert (1973) *The Sociology of Science*. Chicago: University of Chicago Press.

Morgan, Lynn and Michaels, Meredith (1999) *Fetal Subjects, Feminist Positions*. Philadelphia: University of Pennsylvania Press.

Nader, Laura (1996) *Naked Science*. New York: Routledge.

Nardi, Bonnie (1993) *A Small Matter of Programming*. Cambridge, MA: MIT Press.

Nardi, B. and Reilly, B. (1996) 'Interactive ethnography', *Innovation*, 15: 22–5.

Nyce, J. and Bader, G. (1993) 'Fri att valja? Hierarki, individualism och hypermedia vid tva amerikanska gymnasier [Hierarchy, individualism and hypermedia in two American high schools]', in L. Ingelstam and L. Sturesson (eds), *Brus over Landet. Om Informationsoverflodet, kunskapen och Manniskan.* Stockholm: Carlsson. pp. 247–59.

Orr, Julian (1997) *Between Craft and Science.* Ithaca, NY: IRL Press.

Perin, Constance (1998) 'Operating as experimenting', *Science, Technology, and Human Values*, 23 (1): 98–128.

Pfaffenberger, Bryan (1992) 'Technological dramas', *Science, Technology, and Human Values*, 17: 282–312.

Pickering, Andrew (ed.) (1992) *Science as Practice and Culture.* Chicago: University of Chicago Press.

Powdermaker, Hortense (1966) *Stranger and Friend.* New York: W.W. Norton.

Rabinow, Paul (1996) *Making PCR.* Chicago: University of Chicago Press.

Radder, Hans (1998) 'The politics of STS', *Social Studies of Science*, 28 (2): 325–31.

Rapp, Rayna (1999a) 'On new reproductive technology, multiple sites', in Adele Clarke and Virginia Olesen (eds), *Revisioning Women, Health, and Healing.* New York: Routledge. pp. 119–135.

Rapp, Rayna (1999b) *Testing Women, Testing the Fetus.* New York: Routledge.

Shapin, Steve (1995) 'Here and everywhere: sociology of scientific knowledge', *Annual Review of Sociology*, 21: 289–321.

Star, Susan Leigh (1989) *Regions of the Mind.* Stanford, CA: Stanford University Press.

Star, Susan Leigh (ed.) (1995) *Ecologies of Knowledge.* Albany, NY: State University of New York Press.

Stone, Sandy (1996) *The War of Desire and Technology at the Close of the Mechanical Age.* Cambridge, MA: MIT Press.

Suchman, Lucy (2000a) 'Embodied practices of engineering work', in C. Goodwin and N. Ueno (eds), special issue of *Mind, Culture, and Activity.* San Diego, CA: University of California Press.

Suchman, Lucy (2000b) 'Organizing alignment: a case of bridge-building', in S. Gherardi (ed.), special issue of *Organization.* London: Sage.

Taussig, Karen-Sue (in press) *Just Be Ordinary.* Berkeley, CA: University of California Press.

Timmermans, Stephen (1999) *Sudden Death and the Myth of CPR.* Philadelphia: Temple University Press.

Toumey, Christopher (1994) *God's Own Scientists.* New Brunswick, NJ: Rutgers University Press.

Toumey, Christopher (1998) 'The scholarship and the personality of the orphan anthropologist'. Paper presented at the annual meeting of the American Anthropological Association, Philadelphia.

Traweek, Sharon (1988) *Beamtimes and Lifetimes.* Cambridge, MA: Harvard University Press.

Traweek, Sharon (1992) 'Border crossings', in Andrew Pickering (ed.), *Science as Practice and Culture.* Chicago: University of Chicago Press. pp. 429–65.

Traweek, Sharon (1993) 'An introduction to cultural and social studies of sciences and technologies', *Culture, Medicine, and Psychiatry*, 17: 3–25.

Watson-Verran, H. and Turnbull, D. (1995) 'Science and other indigenous knowledge systems', in Sheila Jasanoff, Gerald E. Markle, James C. Peterson and Trevor Pinch (eds), *Handbook of Science and Technology Studies.* Thousand Oaks, CA: Sage. pp. 115–39.

Winner, Langdon (1993) 'Upon opening the black box and finding it empty', *Science, Technology, and Human Values*, 18 (3): 362–78.

Wooddell, Margaret and Hess, David (1998) *Women Confront Cancer.* New York: New York University Press.

Woolgar, Steve (ed.) (1988) *Knowledge and Reflexivity.* Beverly Hills, CA: Sage.

Woolgar, Steve (1991) 'The turn to technology in social studies of science', *Science, Technology, and Human Values*, 16 (1): 20–50.

Wynne, Brian (1996) 'Misunderstood misunderstandings', in Alan Irwin and Brian Wynne (eds), *Misunderstanding Science?* Cambridge: Cambridge University Press. pp. 19–46.

Zabusky, Stacia (1994) *Enduring Diversity.* Princeton, NJ: Princeton University Press.

Zenzen, Michael and Restivo, Sal (1982) 'The mysterious morphology of immiscible liquids', *Social Science Information*, 21: 447–73.

17

Ethnography in the Study of Children and Childhood

ALLISON JAMES

In its literal translation, the term 'ethnography' means writing about people and it is the argument of this chapter that it is the use of ethnography as a research methodology which has enabled children to be recognized as people who can be studied in their own right within the social sciences. In this sense ethnographic methods have permitted children to become seen as research participants and, increasingly therefore, it is ethnography which is fast becoming a new orthodoxy in childhood research (see Qvortrup, 2000). In thus detailing this progressive journey, one which has witnessed the shift from children as objects to their being subjects in the research process, this chapter has two aims: first to detail the history and present scope of ethnographic research with children; secondly, to explore along the way the potential which ethnography has unleashed for our contemporary understanding of children's lives and thus for the study of childhood itself, both inside and outside the academy. In this sense, then, while ethnography may not in the past have been deemed a central methodology in applied or policy oriented social research, the research considered in this chapter demonstrates the appropriateness of its application (Wallman, 1997).[1]

Indeed, it may not be too far fetched to claim that the *social* study of childhood – and here I include some of the research contemporarily being carried out by sociologists, anthropologists, educationalists, psychologists, historians, NGOs (non-governmental organizations) and those working in applied social research – has only been made possible through the use of ethnographic approaches, for what ethnography permits is a view of children as competent interpreters of the social world. This involves a shift from seeing children as simply the raw and uninitiated recruits of the social world to seeing them as making a contribution to it, a changed perspective which has steered researchers towards doing work 'with' rather than 'on' children (Alderson, 1995). This reflects the developments occurring with respect to children's rights outside the academy – such as the UN Convention 1989 and, in England and Wales, the Children Act 1989 – which, in turn, represent broader perspectival shifts with regard to the social status and position of children: first, a recognition that, although children are members of an age category nominally called 'the child' to which particular expectations and values are ascribed, they participate and share in a cultural space termed 'childhood' which varies extensively across time and in social space; second, that through their participation as members of this particular generational space, through occupying a particular position in the life course, children themselves can be said to help constitute that space in culturally and historically distinctive forms.[2,3] And it is has been through the use of ethnography that the everyday articulation of some of these latter processes has been able to be described and, later, theoretically accounted for (James et al., 1998).

What then is meant by 'ethnography'? Although it is not my intention here to show directly what the study of children has done for ethnography – albeit along the way some observations might be made in passing – a working definition is necessary at the outset for, as Hammersley and Atkinson (1995: 1–3) note, the term has been variously and vicariously employed. This chapter takes as its starting point, therefore, the anthropologist Clifford Geertz's (1973) definition of doing 'ethnography' as being an interpretive act of 'thick description'. He writes that 'what we call our data are really our own constructions of other people's constructions of what they and their compatriots are up to' (1973: 9). What ethnographers do, he suggests, is to try to analyse or make sense of the 'structures of signification' which inform people's actions (1973: 9–10). This interpretive understanding evolves but slowly; through immersion in the lives of those we seek to understand, over a lengthy period of time, across a range of social contexts, and involving a variety of different kinds and levels of engagement between the researcher and his/her informants. In this way the 'doing' of ethnography might encompass a range of different qualitative research techniques within its orbit; from unstructured interviews through to casual conversations, from the simple observation of the comings and goings of people in their everyday lives to full participation alongside them in different kinds of work (Hammersley, 1990; Hammersley and Atkinson, 1995).[4] What remains central throughout, however, is the commitment to an interpretive approach for, although by no means the only method for studying children and childhood, ethnography expressly facilitates the desire to engage with children's own views and enables their views and ideas to be rendered accessible to adults as well as to other children.

The following sections outline the progress made towards this position. This is followed by a discussion of some of the methodological and ethical considerations which arise when conducting ethnographic research with children. In doing so the chapter charts, then, the shift from a predominantly adult-focused concern with child socialization and acculturation to a more child-centred view which sees children as social actors, a movement which has been largely facilitated through the widespread and increasing popularity of ethnography as a method for researching children's lives.

EARLY ETHNOGRAPHIES OF THE SOCIALIZATION PROCESS

It is within social anthropology that some of the earliest examples of ethnographic work with children are to be found and although these studies are marked extensively by what Boas has termed the 'cult of childhood', through which children are seen as the 'paradigm of the Ideal man', these very early accounts already bear witness to the potential ethnography has for the study of childhood (1966: 9).

For example, despite being steeped in evolutionist and racist assumptions about the proximity of 'the noble savage' to the natural world, Kidd's (1906) study of Kafir children, based on participant observation fieldwork, offers a detailed and descriptive account of children's play and social lives comparable with many contemporary accounts in its close observation of what children do. However, although

the use of ethnographic methods produced some fascinating insights into children's lives in the developing world in the first part of the twentieth century,[5] like the studies that were to follow, these early ethnographers' accounts of childhood were part of a larger project in which the study of children *per se* was simply a means to a greater end. In this instance their studies were shaped by the overarching concern of that era with social evolution and cultural development. The ethnographers were not concerned to articulate children's own perspectives. Rather they hoped to prove that the historic roots of Western civilization were to be found in so-called 'primitive' societies and, for them, 'savage childhood' – Kidd's book goes by this title – thus clearly held out the promise of a natural laboratory for such an endeavour; here, if anywhere, were surely to be found the earliest roots of modern society? Thus, for example, in his critique of Kidd's study, Raum notes that

> Kidd is obviously far too anxious to show in the mental development of the Kafir child the emergence of those logical confusions between the self and its environment which formed part of the then prevailing theory of animism. (Raum, 1940: 27)

This use of childhood and the study of children as the location for the study of broader social values, and that of ethnography as a method for observing their inculcation in children through daily life, later became a hallmark of what has become known as the culture and personality school of American anthropology which flourished during the 1930s and 1940s. Most famously this is represented by the work of Margaret Mead and Ruth Benedict. However, interest in culture and personality has continued within social anthropology, albeit less prominently, with the publication in the 1960s of, for example, Whiting's (1963) study of childrearing in six cultures and, more recently, Le Vine et al.'s (1994) account of child care cross-culturally. What unites all the researchers within this tradition is their use of ethnographic methods, particularly participant observation, to observe in everyday life how it is that children learn to take on or are taught the core social values of their particular society.

Thus, for example, in her 1930 account of childhood in New Guinea Mead's intention is stated clearly in the opening paragraph. Using Manus society as 'one kind of laboratory', she wishes to explore the 'way in which each human infant is transformed into the finished adult' and to see 'how much or how little and in what ways it is dependent upon early training, upon the personality of its parents, its teachers, its playmates, the age into which it is born' ([1930] 1968: 9).

And it is the ethnographic method of participant observation which she hails as the key to achieving such an understanding:

> The religious beliefs, sex habits methods of discipline, social aims, of those who constitute the child's family,

can all be arrived at by an analysis of culture itself. ([1930] 1968: 211)

In Mead's view it is the ethnological training of the anthropologist – a familiarity with the native language, knowledge of kinship systems and so on – which facilitates this understanding. The ethnographer as a participant observer in another society,

is willing to forsake the amenities of civilised life and subject himself [*sic*] for months at a time to the inconveniences and unpleasantness of life among a people whose manners, methods of sanitation and ways of thought are completely alien to him. He is willing to learn their language, to immerse himself in their manners, get their culture sufficiently by heart to feel their repugnances and sympathise with their triumphs. ([1930] 1968: 213)

Thus, in her account of growing up in New Guinea, it is this daily immersion in the everyday lives of the children and adolescents which enables Mead to provide rich and detailed documentation of family relations, early education, children's work and social lives, to recount young people's attitudes towards sex and the relationship between children and adults in Manus society. It is this method which also allows her to argue for the cultural shaping of personality. She notes, for example, that Manus parents have a very different attitude from their American counterparts towards helping children adapt to the dangers of the external environment, a difference in child-rearing practices which, she argues, shapes later, adult personalities. She illustrates this through a detailed description of an often observed and everyday childhood occurrence:

a [Manus] child who, after having learned to walk, slips and bumps his head, is not gathered up in kind, compassionate arms while mother kisses his tears away, thus establishing a fatal connection between physical disaster and extra cuddling. Instead the little stumbler is berated for his clumsiness, and, if he has been very stupid, slapped soundly into the bargain. ... The next time the child slips, he will not glance anxiously for an audience for his agony as so many of our children do; he will nervously hope that no one has noticed his *faux pas*. This attitude, severe and unsympathetic as it appears on the surface, makes children develop perfect motor coordination. ([1930] 1968: 30)

The later study by Le Vine et al. of Gusii society in the 1970s similarly draws on in-depth, observational fieldwork to explore the processes through which Gusii children are taught to become adult members of Gusii society. The fieldwork methods which were adopted were described thus:

each child would be studied with naturalistic observations at home and in a setting amenable to video recording ... The interpersonal environment of the child and the nature of caregiving and interactions between the baby and others, were to be in the foreground of the research. (1994: 277)

This was to be achieved by detailed, minute by minute observations, carried out at particular points in the day, observations which could then be interpreted by placing them within the framework of a more generalized understanding of Gusii society achieved through the long-term familiarity which participant observation fieldwork provides. Like Mead, this method enabled Le Vine et al. to offer comment on Gusii cultural understanding of how it is that children learn to become members of Gusii society. Thus, for example, in direct contrast to the values ascribed to in Manus society, as depicted by Mead, the Gusii conceive of exploration by young children as a dangerous, rather than a normal aspect of child development, and take steps to discourage it:

Satisfaction with the developmental accomplishment of walking is qualified by the concern that the child might stumble into the cooking fire or otherwise become injured. Thus at 12 to 15 months of age the sample infants were still being held or carried in 42% of daytime observations, though most had been able to walk since 9 months. (1994: 253)

And in contrast to American mothers,

praise is explicitly rejected by Gusii mothers as a verbal device that encourages conceit and would make even a good child rude and disobedient. (1994: 254)

However, in such ethnographic studies children's own views on the process of socialization are given but little prominence when contrasted with the emphasis given to the child's perspective in more recent work (see below).[6] The interpretations offered derive largely from the ethnographic observation of adult–child interactions and adults', rather than children's, accounts of what cultural learning involves. In part, as noted earlier, this is because their focus is on the larger question of *what* adults teach children about culture through their child-rearing practices, rather than *how* those lessons are learned by children. But, in demonstrating the quality and value of the data to be derived from empirical and closely observed ethnographic accounts of child-rearing practices, the culture and personality studies did, none the less, pave the way for the 'new paradigm' for childhood studies in the 1970s for, within this, ethnography too has become championed as a method (James and Prout, 1997).

Through their use of ethnography, the culture and personality studies offered, therefore, an early platform from which to begin to mount a serious challenge to universalistic accounts of childhood and children's development. In this way they represented a stark contrast to the purely theoretical accounts of socialization being offered from within sociology which, up until the 1960s, remained wedded to a unitary developmental perspective on childhood (James and Prout, 1997; James et al., 1998). Drawing extensively on Piagetian psychology, within this tradition socialization was regarded as a more or less one-way process – as what adults do to children – and as a process in which children themselves had little part to play. It was accounted for theoretically in terms of a thesis about cultural reproduction which endeavoured to explain how children learn or, more correctly, how they are taught their social roles in society (see for example, Elkin and Handel, 1972). Devoid of any empirical account of real children's life experiences, comparable with those offered by the culture and personality writers, these studies simply and uncritically imported what Rafky has termed 'a vague, somewhat muddled ... excess of "psychologising" into the sociological arena' (1973: 44). They took little account of the cultural specificities of the socialization process which make the experience of childhood for children far from a shared and universal experience and it was, I suggest, the absence of any empirical ethnographic work with children that enabled such a perspective to be sustained – and for so long.

ETHNOGRAPHY AND THE SOCIAL STUDY OF CHILDHOOD

Ethnography, then, has been critical to the development of a perspective on childhood which, in acknowledging its culturally constructed character, enables a view of children as social actors who take an active part in shaping the form that their own childhoods take. And perhaps nowhere is the value of this approach more demonstrable than within contemporary developmental psychology where, despite a long history of positivistic laboratory-based research and a commitment to childhood universals, ethnography is now appreciated for the insight which it can yield into the social aspects of children's development in particular cultural contexts. Dunn (1988), Dunn and Kendrick (1982) and Woodhead (1996, 1997) among others, now routinely employ ethnographic methods to further their social psychological work on child development and have been able to offer a radical critique of the homogeneous models of childhood which, hitherto, have dominated the psychological account. Dunn (1988), for example, combined observational and interview methods to produce an ethnographic account of young children's involvement in family life and their interaction with parents and siblings. She provides a ground-breaking account of their emotional and interpersonal relations. Similarly, through utilizing the more naturalistic method of interviews combined with detailed and close observation of children in their everyday lives at home and school in parts of the developing world, rather than conducting traditional psychological experiments with children in the laboratory, Woodhead offers evidence of the failure of traditional developmental psychology to acknowledge the cultural

diversity of children's childhoods. His ethnographic-based approach recognizes that 'children do not grow up in a vacuum, nor do child care programmes function in isolation. Both are embedded in a dynamic social context of relationships, systems and cultural values' (1996: 10). Woodhead's work extends, therefore, the pioneering work of the culture and personality school to argue for the initiation of culturally sensitive child development programmes in developing contexts which are, what he terms, *paced* – that is, appropriate to the context of early development in any particular location.

Schieffelin's (1990) work on the language socialization of Kaluli children in Papua New Guinea is significant in this respect for she shows that what is regarded by Kaluli adults as necessary for children's language development is rather different from the view held by developmental sociolinguistics. Thus, during her lengthy period of fieldwork, when she was making her recordings and transcriptions of child–adult interactions or those that take place between children she would be told that certain exchanges were 'to no purpose' (1990: 30–2). However, in Schieffelin's view, they 'turned out to be rich in terms of displaying children's discourse and metalinguistics skills' (1990: 32). And it was through hearing such exchanges on a daily basis that she is able to argue that,

> in addition to an ethnographic view that considers what Kaluli say must occur for their children to talk and act like Kaluli, there is a complementary view from developmental sociolinguistics and psycholinguistics that suggests important developmental processes that should be examined in comparative perspective. (1990: 32)

The importance of this concern to identify what are regarded as culturally appropriate forms of child-rearing within a particular local context, and the importance of ethnography to this enterprise, is graphically demonstrated by the work of Briggs (1986). Her account of childhood among the Inuit reveals the very different views the Inuit hold concerning children's needs and interests.[7] Briggs' long engagement as a participant observer in Inuit society exposed her to a very particular and, for her, unusual form of adult–child interaction. Inuit adults play games with children which deliberately provoke, tease and frighten them. Such games, which might well be regarded as abusive within Western contexts, are, Briggs argues, one of the ways in which the Inuit encourage their children to develop an acute sensitivity to and awareness of the dangers of the external social and physical environment in which they are growing up.

One game described by Briggs was played with a small 3-year-old boy, Saila. Taking place within the immediate family but also involving a wider circle of neighbours and friends, the little boy becomes the butt of teasing, a teasing focused upon the potential loss of his penis:

Jona picked up a seal fetus, which was being used as a toy by his daughters. It was lying on the floor with a string around its neck. He brought the fetus towards [Saila's] penis and said: 'It's going to bite your penis'. Saila watched him with a stiff 'frightened' face. Other adults of both sexes and various ages came in to visit and entered the game, to a total of eight or nine. All of them poked their fingers into Saila's fly and pretended to pull his pants down. They pretended the fetus would bite and eat the penis. And they brought in Susi's puppy and pretended it too would bite and eat the penis. Susi and her four-year-old sister were told to do these things, too, and they did. (1986: 12–13)

Out of its cultural context this extract would seem to describe an episode of tormenting and sexual play between adults and children. In Briggs' opinion it is not; it is, in fact, just one of a series of legitimate educational games which adults play with their children. These games, which may teasingly threaten that a child's mother might die or tempt a child to risk his or her own life, Briggs argues, are the ways in which Inuit children are taught to be observant and cautious of the world around them. They are lessons for the future when, as adults, they must survive the precariousness of Inuit life.

Through ethnography, therefore, the possibility has at last been opened up of seeing children's life experiences as being contextualized by both the cultures and societies in which they live, as well as the biology which shapes their mental and physical development. Furthermore, what ethnography has achieved is a view of children themselves as active participants in, rather than simply subject to, the vagaries of these processes. Through their social interactions and engagement with their peers and adult care-takers ethnographic accounts have shown how children contribute to the shape and form which their own childhood takes. The next section indicates the range of such studies.

SOCIAL CHILDREN: 'DOING' ETHNOGRAPHIC RESEARCH WITH CHILDREN

Pioneered during the 1970s by Hardman (1973) in her study of children's games and social relations in a school playground in Oxford, England, as noted above, ethnographic approaches are central to the new paradigm for the study of childhood (James and Prout, 1997). Ethnography, it is suggested, allows children to be seen as competent informants about and interpreters of their own lives and of the lives of others and is an approach to childhood research which can employ children's own accounts centrally within the analysis. Thus it is that contemporary social scientific accounts of children's social worlds are able to shed new light on many different aspects of children's lives through the presentation of those lives from the children's own perspectives. With

ethnography now the central methodology, research with children has extended beyond its traditional location in the school into other settings such as the hospital (Alderson, 1993; Bluebond-Langner, 1978), the club (James, 1986), the home (McNamee, 1998) and the community (Baker, 1998). It has also moved beyond the study of socialization and schooling to explore other aspects of children's lives: for example, how children learn to take on particular kinds of childhood identities among their peers (James, 1993); children's acquisition of health knowledge (Mayall,1996); children's understanding and experience of sickness (Christensen, 1999; Prout, 1987); the taking on of gendered and ethnic identities during childhood (Connolly, 1998); and the experience of work (Nieuwenhuys, 1994; Reynolds, 1996; Solberg, 1994) and that of play (Thorne, 1993).

Although much of this contemporary ethnographic work with children is largely concerned to explore children's everyday social lives – their games, their friendships and interactions with their peers, their participation in work, their health beliefs and attitude – an overarching interest in socialization remains central to many of these and other studies (see, for example, Schieffelin, 1990; Stafford, 1995). However, through the use of ethnography, its point of contemporary departure is radically changed. First, it assumes that an understanding of *how* children learn, not simply *what* they learn, is central to the comprehension of processes of cultural learning. A second, and closely linked assumption is that it is not sufficient simply to observe adults' behaviour towards children; it is important also to see children as social actors in their own right, to observe and understand what it is that children do with one another as well as with their adult care-takers and, most importantly, to canvass children's own views and opinions directly.

Such a perspective is explored by Corsaro (1997) in his account of socialization as a process of 'interpretive reproduction'. Drawing on extensive ethnographic fieldwork with children in both Italy and America Corsaro argues that children's cultural learning takes place, not as the linear progression advocated by traditional developmental psychology but, rather, as a collective process of reproduction:

children do not simply imitate or internalize the world around them. They strive to interpret or make sense of their culture and to participate in it. In attempting to make sense of the adult world, children come to *collectively produce* their own peer worlds and cultures. (1997: 24; emphasis in the original)

And it is through the detailed observation and recording of little children's everyday interactions and conversations with each other and with him that Corsaro is able to substantiate this claim. For example, in one of his early ethnographic studies of nursery school children, Corsaro (1985) described in detail a sequence of behaviours which he observed and which, for him, illustrates part of the process whereby children collectively learn and reproduce the social rules and expectations of a given society. Two children, Richard and Barbara, have been building things and sitting near one another, although they have not spoken and do not appear to be playing together. However, when another child – Nancy – approaches, Richard says to Barbara 'We're friends right?' and they begin to coordinate their play activities to the exclusion of Nancy. Corsaro's later analysis of this sequence of behaviours places children's perspectives centrally as he endeavours to interpret their actions and words from the child's points of view:

> Resistance of access attempts seems uncooperative or selfish to adults, including parents and most teachers ... But it is not that the children are refusing to cooperate or are resisting the idea of sharing. In fact, as we see in this example, the defenders of the interactive space are often intensively involved in creating a sense of sharing during the *actual course of playing together* and often mark this discovery with references to affiliation ('We're friends, alright?'). In simple terms, the children *want to keep sharing what they are already sharing* and see others as a threat to the community they have established. (1997: 124)

James (1993) has a comparable example in her ethnographic study of nursery school children where a 4-year-old girl, playing on her own, attempts to draw a boy by-stander into her play:

> You're out of my house' she says to no one in particular as she brings plates and cups to a table. 'I haven't no peas in my house.' (To a boy standing watching): 'Will you look after my food? ... You're daddy right? Come on, hurry. You can have milk shake and I've got some peas. I know where they are ... lost them ... in the pink jug. Where's the milk jug because I need it?. No. We don't need it there. I gave it to dad and he was losing it. I'm going home.' (To the boy again:) 'You come to my house, dad, there's your hat.' (She gives him a straw hat). 'Go away.' (She pushes away another boy who attempts to join in). On another day, hanging around outside the Wendy House in the reception class and refused access by the girls for the third time, five-year old Saul reluctantly announced: 'I'll go off to work again.' (1993: 187)

Such examples of young children's early attempts at collective and shared social action clearly demonstrate that they have already learnt some of the rules of social engagement which are a prerequisite for membership in the social world. They are, however, very conventional and fleeting instances of social action and, as such, are not readily amenable to the processes of testing, questioning or recall upon which other kinds of research methodologies rely. In both instances, therefore, it can be argued that it was precisely the everyday and

ethnographic familiarity of the researcher with the context, and of the children with the researcher, which permitted these very commonplace occurrences, first, to be remarked and noted down in the flow and buzz of social action and, second, to be later interpreted as having a particular significance and meaning. As Geertz has observed:

> It is with the kind of material produced by long-term, mainly (though not exclusively) qualitative, highly participative, and almost obsessively fine-comb field study in confined contexts that the mega-concepts with which contemporary social science is afflicted ... can be given the sort of sensible actuality that makes it possible to think not only realistically and concretely *about* them, but, what is more important, creatively and imaginatively *with* them. (1973: 23)

The above examples amply illustrate the potential ethnography has for accessing what has often been regarded as the separate and secret world of childhood (Opie and Opie, [1959] 1977). However, in the proliferation of studies of childhood which has occurred during the past twenty years, there are some differences emerging concerning ways of carrying out ethnographic research with children (James et al., 1998). Notwithstanding that the appearance of these distinctions seems to affirm Hammersley's (1990) observation that it is increasingly difficult to assess what actually counts as 'ethnography', central to the social study of childhood remains the commitment to understanding the everyday social worlds of children as children do, and to seeing children as informed and engaged social actors. These twin perspectives provide a common and uniting thread between the various accounts and approaches which can now be found.

Many ethnographic studies of children's lives continue to employ traditional participant observation as a mainstay research technique for it is this which many regard as having the greatest potential to engage children actively with the research. However, there is variation as to exactly where emphasis is placed during the research process. In the school setting, for example, teacher–pupil interactions are often the focus for research, the intention being to explore the formal and informal educational processes at work during the school day (see King, 1978, 1984; Pollard, 1985; Walkerdine, 1985). Within this group of studies what constitutes participant observation varies extensively. Slukin (1981), for example, in researching children's play and games as an aspect of growing up in the playground, combined times for strict observation with those for conversation with the children about their play. King (1984), by contrast, adopted what he calls a non-participant observation approach. Finding it problematic that the nursery children regarded him as a teacher-surrogate, King's strategy was to be as unobtrusive as possible. By on occasion using the 'unoccupied Wendy House as a convenient hide', he eventually achieved a situation where the children ignored his presence amongst them (1984: 123).

Others, however, have adopted a more fluid and conventional participatory approach, akin to that of an anthropologist working in another culture. Of some more recent fieldwork, for example, Pollard and Filer write:

> I was certainly viewed as being somewhat 'strange'. Here was an adult who was often at school, but who did not behave like a teacher, a parent, dinner supervisor or classroom assistant. He wandered around the classroom and the playground, watching activities, chatting with children and occasionally asking questions and recording their replies in his notebook. When asked what he was doing he would explain that he was, 'writing a story about what children think about school'. The children, with no other experience, accepted their pet researcher and joked about him. 'Was I a spy?' 'Was I Superman?' ... As in my previous research with pupils, I found that children loved to be listened to and have their views taken seriously. This, of course, was simple for me because, unlike their teachers and parents, I had no responsibility for the children and no position to protect. Whilst I was never required to 'tell them off', I could indulge the children simply by being interested in them. (1996: 294)

Barrie Thorne in her study of gender and childhood fleshes out in more detail what such an approach actually involves for the ethnographer in her account of doing participant observation in an American school:

> I set out to learn about gender in the context of kids' interactions with one another. I began to accompany fourth- and fifth-graders in their daily round of activities by stationing myself in the back of Miss Bailey's classroom, sitting on the scaled-down chairs and standing and walking around the edges, trying to grasp different vantage points. I was clearly not a full participant; I didn't have a regular desk and I watched and took notes, rather than doing classroom work. As the kids lined up, I watched and then walked alongside, often talking with them, as they moved between classroom, lunchroom, music room and library. At noontime I sat and ate with the fourth- and fifth-graders at their two crowded cafeteria tables, and I left with them when they headed for noontime recess on the playground. (1993: 13)

Using participant observation as an ethnographic research technique for studying children's lives, others have ventured outside the school setting. Indeed, Bluebond-Langner's (1978) study of children with leukemia is remarkable for its early insights, not only into the worlds of dying children, but for its recognition of the value ethnography has for working with children in the twin settings of the hospital and home. Bluebond-Langner spent nine months on the children's ward of a hospital in mid-west America and, during this time, not only carried out interviews with children but was able to

participate in their lives as patients and also to visit them at home. During their long period of hospitalization she played with them, listened to their stories, comforted them and observed their interactions with their parents, with medical staff and with one another: 'Like a volunteer, and like most anthropologists in the field, I willingly did whatever they [the hospital staff] told me. I played with the children, helped with the meals, accompanied the children to various parts of the hospital, and assisted in procedures' (1978: 251).

Similarly, in her research into children's working lives in South India, Nieuwenhuys (1994) employed the traditional holistic ethnographic techniques of participant observation. For Nieuwenhuys this involved living for over a year in a small community in South India where she got to know the families and their children very well across a variety of different settings simply through living alongside them. However, it was the switch to systematic observation of children's work, a method which then slowly evolved into more participatory methods, which proved 'a crucial moment in the research' (1994: 33). And it was crucial in that it enabled her to begin to engage with the children as people in their own right whose opinions were to be valued:

> I found nevertheless support from the children whom I met while they were at work. They did not think it awkward that I should show some interest in what they did. The thought that I was interviewing them to write down what they said excited them. Some became spontaneously my informants, reporting to me all the news that used to go from mouth to mouth. A few even sought in me their patroness, asking me for small loans with which to start a business or for loans to buy the necessities for going to school. (1994: 5–6)

Reynolds (1989), in her study of children as healers, also confirms how it was participant observation techniques – 'playing, talking, walking, eating and working with the children both in their homes and outside' – for over a year, which allowed her to contextualize her understanding of 7-year-old black South Africans' view of the world (1989: 8; see also Reynolds, 1996).

In depicting the broad range of qualitative research on childhood currently being carried out, James, Jenks and Prout (1998) suggest that ethnographic research with children is beginning to embrace, as part of its method, different kinds of research techniques. These are designed to both engage children's interests and to exploit their particular talents and abilities. For example, what James et al. (1998) term 'task-centred activities' are research techniques adapted from those commonly used in development work for participatory rural appraisals. These techniques involve children in using media other than 'talk' – for example, drawing maps or pictures, filling in charts, grouping objects together – to reveal in visual and concrete form their thoughts and ideas about a particular research question. They are now being used in qualitative research with children either as stand alone techniques in group work, in combination with qualitative interviewing, or as additional research tools during participant observation work with children (Christensen and James, 2000). O'Kane (2000), for example, describes how in a study of children's decision-making in relation to foster care placements in Britain such participative techniques permitted children to articulate their concern to be consulted about their present and future care.[8] As her work shows, their value and particular pertinence for childhood ethnography lies in their ability to provide researchers with a highly focused body of data around a discrete topic but, additionally and perhaps most importantly, they encourage children themselves to be reflexive about the outcomes of the data production process in which they are involved.

As part of her participant observation study of children's attitudes towards difference and disability, James (1993), for example, shows how the use of group story-telling led children to reflect on some of their own prejudices. The children were given the outline of a story about a child who had no friends and they then had to decide why this was the case and what he or she would have to do to make friends. In their stories, the 6–9-year-old children collectively agreed that it was children who looked different – ugly, dirty, fat children – and those who behaved anti-socially – those who stole, who fought, who swore – who would be children without friends. To gain friends a child would have to change their behaviour, a move which, the children decided, would be reflected in the child's changed, physical appearance. On two occasions this parallel change in the physical body was challenged by one member of the group. The first time was when a boy insisted that the girl in the story could not stop being ugly just because she was now good, a proposition which, once it had been articulated, led the other children to stop and reconsider. As James notes, 'eventually, and somewhat charily, they concluded that although she was still ugly, the girl's friends "don't care any more because she is good"' (1993: 132). On the second occasion a girl was described in the story as being friendless because she was in a wheelchair and could not run about. When trying to work out what then would happen if this girl were to try to make friends the group reached an impasse. James describes the discussion that ensued among the children:

> how could this situation be ameliorated? How could the girl's body be made to be the kind of body a girl with friends would have? They chose a magical resolution, a fairy-tale ending: the heroine fell out of her wheelchair and suddenly found that she could walk again. (1993: 132)

In the move towards greater reflexivity in the research process and, in particular, with regard to ethnographic practice, the use of such task-centred activities are a significant development in childhood research. Not only do they draw children in as research participants, thereby furthering the research dialogue, they also encourage childhood researchers to be reflexive: about the data that is produced by children and about what, as ethnographers, they will reproduce as a written and authoritative text about childhood (Clifford and Marcus, 1986; Marcus and Fischer, 1986).

REFLECTIONS ON CHILDHOOD ETHNOGRAPHY

While ethnographic work with children may permit adults to see the world as a 7-year-old does, and thus is to be applauded, this new vision does carry with it an additional burden of responsibility. The first of these centres on the power relations between adult researcher and child informant. As noted by Pollard and Filer above, the researcher is, for example, often not regarded as a 'normal' kind of adult by the children and children may not therefore see the researcher as occupying an adult position of power (see Mayall, 2000). Recalling various pieces of fieldwork in schools, Corsaro, for example, depicts the way in which the simple difference of size between child and researcher has to be negotiated and a new status taken on in the ethnographic encounter:

> In my ethnographic research in preschools in the United States and Italy my goal is always to discover the children's perspectives, to see what it is like to be a child in the school. To do this I have to overcome the children's tendency to see me as a typical adult. A big problem is physical size; I am much bigger than the children. In my early work I found that a 'reactive' method of field entry into children's worlds works best. In simple terms I enter free play areas, sit down, and wait for the kids to react to me ... After a while the children begin to ask me questions, draw me into their activities and gradually define me as an atypical adult. Size is still a factor, however, and the children come to see me as a big kid, often referring to me as 'Big Bill' ... To the Italian children, as soon as I spoke in my fractured Italian I was peculiar, funny, and fascinating. I was not just an atypical adult but also an incompetent one – not just a big kid but sort of a big, dumb kid. (1997: 29)

But the researcher is not a child. She/he can always revert to their adult role, by choice or by circumstance. This is why the question of the researcher's role has become one of the central issues in research with children. Fundamentally, it engages with the vexed question of the power differentials that exist between the child and the adult researcher and various solutions to this dilemma have been proffered.

Mandell (1991), for instance, describes her status *vis-à-vis* her child subjects during her research as that of being 'least adult' and details how she accomplished this. Rejecting the research role of detached observer, Mandell opted for complete involvement, refusing the position of an authoritative adult in the children's world. She climbed into the sand pit and joined the children on the swings, arguing that through such participatory activities she was able to distance her adult self from the children. Others have questioned the validity and utility of such a stance. Fine and Sandstrom (1988), for example, argue that it is never possible for adults to 'pass unnoticed' in the company of children: age, size and authority always intervene, something which in fact Mandell also rather reluctantly notes. But asking in what circumstances these differences assume significance and importance, and when they are irrelevant, may tell us much about children's position in the social world. As Fine has observed: 'there is methodological value in maintaining the differences between sociologists and children – a feature of interaction that permits the researcher to behave in certain "non kid" ways – such as asking ignorant questions' (1988: 17). If, as Geertz (1983) argues, anthropologists do not have to turn native in order to argue from the natives' point of view, then it is clear also that childhood researchers need not pretend to be children. Indeed, as Mayall (2000) argues, the inevitable differences between children and ourselves have to be accepted. Only when it is openly acknowledged that, however friendly we are, adult researchers can only ever have a semi-participatory role in children's lives, can the power differentials which separate children from adults begin to be effectively addressed. In this sense ethnography is powerfully placed to initiate this process.

A second issue which arises in relation to childhood ethnography concerns the siting of the research itself. From the examples given throughout the chapter, it is clear, for instance, that the school is increasingly being used as an ethnographic setting for purposes other than the study of the education process *per se*: for research into children's social relations with their peers and/or adults, the acquisition of cultural knowledge, gender socialization etc. And, this really comes as no surprise: the structural features of the school system help constitute an ideal and ready-made cultural setting for the ethnographic study of childhood. However, this being so, it is all the more important that researchers continue to remain reflexive about the impact this setting has both for the process and the product of the ethnographic method. James et al. underline the importance of such a reflexive awareness:

how often are reflections offered on the ways in which the school as a research site works to naturalise the model of the socially developing child within our studies? As an age-based institution which is hierarchically

organized into age classes and shot through with particular power relations, might it not shape the form and style of the research process? To what extent, for example, are we led to design our research with the age stratification of the school in mind and what implications might this have for our research? Would findings about sexuality, gender, ethnicity, friendship, bullying, play and work, for example, look different if they had been gathered outside the context of the school or other child-specific, age-based institutions such as youthclubs or day-care centres. (1998: 176)

A third and related issue concerns the question of access and informed consent for, it must be noted, that although perhaps providing easy ethnographic access to children the school does not automatically therefore guarantee children's research consent. The importance of this can be underlined by examples of research that engages children in the researcher's project in settings where access has proved more difficult. In these projects children are engaged as informants in semi-structured ethnographic interviews or as participants in focus groups or other kinds of group work and although such techniques represent a more formal and perhaps a more restrictive ethnographic methodology, what they do is to encourage researchers to be attentive to the issues of children's own consent.

Alderson's (1993) study of children's consent to surgery, for example, draws extensively on child interviews, setting these in the context of other qualitative ethnographic data gathered during weeks of observation carried out in the hospital by the research team. Children were directly asked if they wished to participate in the research and those who did gave their consent. The virtue of using semi-structured interviews with children, conducted in a quiet space either with children alone or in friendship groups, is that they can facilitate a more focused and private discussion than would be possible in the hustle and bustle of the everyday public life of the classroom or school yard and thereby help ensure children's informed participation. The interview may also prove especially useful for collecting data of a personal and sensitive kind such as children's experiences of divorce (Neale and Smart, 1998) or of being in foster care (O'Kane, 2000), where the necessity of establishing some parameters for informed consent would seem particularly critical.

In this respect the home is an important research site in childhood research precisely because it does not easily lend itself to the more fluid ethnographic techniques of participant observation, especially in Western urban contexts where the 'black box' of the family remains a largely privatized social space. Strangers (and researchers) enter by adult invitation only. Those interested to research children's lives at home are faced, then, with not only the more generalized difficulty of gaining access to such a protected sphere but also the fact that children do not usually occupy positions of power within the domestic arena. Children can rarely act as the gatekeepers to family life. Those wishing to carry out research with children in their homes may, therefore, have to resort to using the more formal technique of the semi-structured interview.

Often, however, this is only possible with prior parental approval for the project and, even when this is obtained, children may be made marginal to the research process precisely because they occupy positions of relative powerlessness within the family. James (1993: 40–1), for example, describes how in the course of interviewing children and parents at home, it was the parents – often the mother – who took charge of the interview. She most often directed its course and signalled to her children when their participation was required. However, although children in such instances may often be powerless either to assent to or to refuse researchers' access to their lives at home, what the unstructured interview *can* achieve for children is the possibility for they themselves, rather than the researcher, to control and direct the ebb and flow of the conversation. Here, for example, a mother and daughter are discussing with the researcher what happened when Paula, the daughter, received specialist help for dyslexia:

Mother: You recognize the letter and the sound it makes, and you slowly build it up. Now also they've got to learn the alphabet frontwards, backwards, from the middle, you name it.

Paula: [*challengingly*] I didn't do that.

Although as James acknowledges in this particular instance the daughter ultimately failed in her challenge to assert the authority of her own account, the interview had provided her with at least the possibility of doing so. Similarly, Neale and Smart (1998: 20–7) describe how, when interviewing children about their experiences of divorce, not only did the children often decide where they should be interviewed and limit their parents' involvement, but they also used the occasion of the interview as a vehicle to talk through problems and issues which were of concern to them. Alderson's work, too, confirms the empowering role which the semi-structured interview can offer children whose position as minors may mean that their opinions and views are either not asked for or risk being reinterpreted if they conflict with those held by their adult care-takers. Sensitive to the ethical issues which her research about consent might raise for the children, and also aware that the interview did not constitute a therapeutic encounter, Alderson none the less shows its value both for the research and for the children themselves in offering a full and rounded picture of the child's perspective:

semi-structured interviews offer people time to have second thoughts. This raises complications for analysis. The initial quick response could be the best guide to young people's conscious hopes about surgery. Their later thoughts might refer to less conscious hopes, or prompt new motives as they spoke. Simply by asking questions we started new ideas. (1993: 85)

Within settings where participant observation research is possible and access is not an obstacle, the relative powerlessness of children may be less visible and obvious. It becomes, therefore, an even more important issue for ethnographers to address: whether in schools, youth clubs or clinics, children may be vulnerable to the expectations from authoritative adults that they will participate in the research. They may not be able to opt out. Alternatively, as Nieuwenhuys (1994) relates, adults may not wish children to be involved and may place obstacles in their path. In the account of her fieldwork in India, Nieuwenhuys, for example, describes the difficulties she and her research assistant had in eliciting children as informants in a cultural milieu where children are regarded as having low social status:

we had noticed that children felt uncomfortable speaking freely in front of me. Adults never failed to require from children to behave with respect and modesty towards me, forcing them to do so if need be. They felt that going into detail about a child's normal routine, was much too mundane a subject to talk about with a foreigner and ran contrary to general notions of etiquette. They would therefore make derisory comments or even scold children who attempted to answer my questions seriously. As it was impossible for me to speak to the children without their parents' interference, it finally was Mohanakumari, herself born and brought up in Pommkara, who took it upon herself to carry on the interviews in our home. I would afterwards discuss with her the interviews she had recorded and translated. (1994: 34)

In such instances, then, the semi-structured interview provides a ballast for children against demands set by the adult world and permits children to engage more freely with the research, to actively give their permission at any time and to choose to withdraw from participating in the project (Alderson, 1995).

CONCLUSION

Ethnography in all its guises has, therefore, proved critical to the social study of childhood. Its key strength as a method lies in the ways in which, through close attention to the everyday and familiar through which the social world is both created and sustained, it has enabled the voices of those who would otherwise be silent to be heard. The 'mutedness' of children's voices, noted in the 1970s by Hardman, has been largely ended through the development of a paradigm for childhood research in which children themselves are regarded as key social actors, whose own views and perspectives are to be taken into account. Increasingly, they may also be working jointly with researchers in the production of data about their own lives and the lives of those significant others with whom they engage (see Christensen and James, 2000). Through such examples of what Clifford and Marcus (1986) have called 'dialogical textual production', childhood ethnographies can be said, therefore, to be at the forefront of the experimental and poetic moment in ethnography's own history. It is in this sense, then, that ethnography has enabled the social study of childhood finally to come of age.

NOTES

1 In this respect it is significant that the majority of studies funded under the ESRC children 5–16 Research programme, which has an explicit policy agenda, employ qualitative research methods which might loosely be grouped together as 'ethnographic'.

2 It was in the work of Phillipe Aries (1962), a French historian, that the socially constructed character of childhood was first described through his assertion that in medieval society childhood did not exist. Though this claim has since been tempered by other historians, the main thrust of his argument remains: that although children have always existed the social institution of childhood through which the age status category of 'the child' gains its form has varied across time and in space. For a discussion of these issues see James et al., 1998.

3 Acknowledgement of the cultural relativity of childhood is problematic, however, for those concerned to implement such policies (see Boyden, 1997).

4 Taking this definition I would not, therefore, regard historical work on the social worlds of children as 'ethnographic work', although historians such as Hendrick have made a very significant contribution to the social study of childhood (see Hendrick, 1994, 1997) and, indeed, helped recover children's own perspectives from history (see Hendrick, 2000).

5 Raum (1940) provides a comprehensive overview of this body of work.

6 Mead's own work is exceptional in this respect for its early inclusion, albeit somewhat limited, of children's own views and verbal interactions with their peers and their parents (see also *Coming of Age in Samoa*, [1928] 1963).

7 See Woodhead, 1997 for a discussion of children's needs and interests, in which he argues against the possibility of a universal account.

8 For example, the diamond-ranking exercise asked children to evaluate which decisions about care were the most important for them; the pots and beans activity enabled children to evaluate how much say individuals involved in their care had over decisions taken about their lives.

REFERENCES

Alderson, P. (1993) *Children's Consent to Surgery.* Buckingham: Open University Press.

Alderson, P. (1995) *Listening to Children. Children, Ethics and Social Research.* London: Barnardo's.

Aries, P. (1962) *Centuries of Childhood.* London: Cape.

Baker, R. (1998) 'Runaway street children in Nepal: social competence away from home', in I. Hutchby and J. Moran-Ellis (eds), *Children and Social Competence.* London: Falmer. pp. 46–64.

Bluebond-Langner, M. (1978) *The Private Worlds of Dying Children.* Princeton, NJ: Princeton University Press.

Boas, G. (1966) *The Cult of Childhood.* London: Warburg Institute.

Boyden, J. (1997) 'Childhood and the policy makers: a comparative perspective on the globalization of childhood', in A. James and A. Prout (eds), *Constructing and Reconstructing Childhood.* London: Falmer. pp. 190–230.

Briggs, J. (1986) 'Expecting the unexpected: Canadian inuit training for an experimental lifestyle'. Paper delivered to the Fourth International Conference on Hunting and Gathering Societies, London School of Economics.

Christensen, P. (1999) 'The cultural performance of sickness amongst Danish schoolchildren'. PhD thesis, Hull University.

Christensen, P. and James, A. (2000) 'Childhood: diversities, conformities and methodological insights', in P. Christensen and A. James (eds), *Research with Children.* London: Falmer.

Clifford, J. and Marcus, G.E. (1986) *Writing Culture: The Poetics and Politics of Ethnography.* California: University of California Press.

Connolly, P. (1998) *Racism, Gender Identities and Young Children.* London: Routledge.

Corsaro, W.A. (1985) *Friendship and Peer Culture in the Early Years.* Norwood, NJ: Ablex.

Corsaro, W.A. (1997) *The Sociology of Childhood.* Thousand Oaks, CA: Pine Forge Press.

Dunn, J. (1988) *The Beginnings of Social Understanding.* Cambridge, MA: Harvard University Press.

Dunn, J. and Kendrick, C. (1982) *Siblings: Love, Envy and Understanding.* Cambridge, MA: Harvard University Press.

Elkin, F. and Handel, G. (1972) *The Child and Society: The Process of Socialization.* New York: Random House.

Fine, G.A. and Sandstrom, K.L. (1988) *Knowing Children. Participant Observation with Minors* (Qualitative Methods Series). Newbury Park, CA: Sage.

Geertz, C. (1973) *The Interpretation of Culture.* London: Hutchinson.

Geertz, C. (1983) *Local Knowledge: Further Essays in Interpretive Anthropology.* New York: Basic Books.

Hammersley, M. (1990) *Reading Ethnographic Research.* London: Longman.

Hammersley, M. and Atkinson, P. (1995) *Ethnography: Principles in Practice*, 2nd edn. London: Tavistock.

Hardman, C. (1973) 'Can there be an anthropology of children?', *Journal of the Anthropology Society of Oxford*, 4 (1): 85–99.

Hendrick, H. (1994) *Child Welfare. England, 1872–1989.* London: Falmer.

Hendrick, H. (1997) *Children, Childhood and English Society, 1880–1990.* Cambridge: Cambridge University Press.

Hendrick, H. (2000) 'The child as social actor in historical sources: problems of identification and interpretation', in P. Christensen and A. James, *Research with Children.* London: Falmer. pp. 36–62.

James, A. (1986) 'Learning to belong: the boundaries of adolescence', in A.P. Cohen (ed.), *Symbolising Boundaries.* Manchester: Manchester University Press. pp. 155–71.

James, A. (1993) *Childhood Identities: Self and Social Relationships in the Experience of the Child.* Edinburgh: Edinburgh University Press.

James, A. and Prout, A. (1997) *Constructing and Reconstructing Childhood,* 2nd edn. Basingstoke: Falmer Press.

James, A., Jenks, C. and Prout, A. (1998) *Theorising Childhood.* Cambridge: Polity Press.

Kidd, D. (1906) *Savage Childhood.* London: Adam and Charles Black.

King, R.A. (1978) *All Things Bright and Beautiful.* Chichester: Wiley.

King, R.A. (1984) 'The man in the Wendy House: researching infants' schools', in R.G. Burgess (ed.), *The Research Process in Educational Settings: Ten Case Studies.* Lewes: Falmer Press. pp. 117–39.

Le Vine, R.A., Dixon, S., Le Vine, S., Rickman, A., Leiderman, P.H., Keefer, C.H. and Brazelton, T.B. (1994) *Child Care and Culture: Lessons from Africa.* Cambridge: Cambridge University Press.

Mandell, N. (1991) 'The least-adult role in studying children', in F. Waksler (ed.), *Studying the Social Worlds of Children.* London: Falmer Press. pp. 38–60.

Marcus, G.E. and Fischer, M.M.J. (1986) *Anthropology as Cultural Critique.* Chicago: University of Chicago Press.

Mayall, B. (1996) *Children, Health and the Social Order.* Buckingham: Open University Press.

Mayall, B. (2000) 'Conversations with children: working with generational issues', in P. Christensen and A. James (eds), *Research with Children.* London: Falmer. pp. 120–36.

McNamee, S. (1998) 'Youth, gender and video games: power and control in the home', in G. Valentine and T. Skelton (eds), *Geographies of Youth Culture.* London: Routledge.

Mead, M. ([1928] 1963) *Coming of Age in Samoa.* Middlesex: Penguin.

Mead, M. ([1930] 1968) *Growing Up in New Guinea.* Middlesex: Penguin.

Neale, B. and Smart, C. (1998) *Agents or Dependents?: Struggling to Listen to Children in Family Law and Family Research.* Working Paper 3. University of Leeds: Centre for Research on Family, Kinship and Childhood.

Nieuwenhuys, O. (1994) *Children's Life Worlds: Gender, Welfare and Labour in the Developing World.* London: Routledge.

O'Kane, C. (2000) 'The development of participatory techniques: facilitating children's views about decisions which affect them', in P. Christensen and A. James (eds), *Research With Children.* London: Falmer Press. pp. 136–60.

Opie, I. and Opie, P. ([1959] 1977) *The Lore and Language of Schoolchildren.* Oxford: Oxford University Press.

Pollard, A. (1985) *The Social World of the Primary School.* London: Holt, Rinehart and Winston.

Pollard, A. and Filer, A. (1996) *The Social World of Children's Learning.* London: Cassell.

Prout, A. (1987) 'An analytical ethnography of sickness absence in an English primary school'. Unpublished PhD thesis, Keele University.

Qvortrup, J. (2000) 'Macroanalysis of childhood', in P. Christensen and A. James (eds), *Research with Children.* London: Falmer. pp. 77–98.

Rafky, D.M. (1973) 'Phenomenology and socialization', in H.P. Dreitzel (ed.), *Childhood and Socialization.* London: Macmillan.

Raum, O.F. (1940) *Chaga Childhood.* Oxford: Oxford University Press.

Reynolds, P. (1989) *Children in Cross-roads: Cognition and Society in South Africa.* Claremont: David Phillip.

Reynolds, P. (1996) *Traditional Healers and Childhood in Zimbabwe.* Ohio: Ohio University Press.

Schieffelin, B.B. (1990) *The Give and Take of Everyday Life: Language Socialization of Kaluli Children.* Cambridge: Cambridge University Press.

Slukin, A. (1981) *Growing Up in the Playground.* London: Routledge and Kegan Paul.

Solberg, A. (1994) '*Negotiating Childhood: Empirical Investigations and Textual Representations of Children's Work and Everyday Lives*', Stockholm: Nordic Institute for Studies in Urban and Regional Planning.

Stafford, C. (1995) *The Roads of Chinese Childhood.* Cambridge: Cambridge University Press.

Thorne, B. (1993) *Gender Play: Girls and Boys in School.* New Brunswick, NJ: Rutgers University Press.

Walkerdine, V. (1985) 'Child development and gender: the making of teachers and learners in the classroom', *Early Childhood Education: History, Policy and Practice.* Bulmershe Research Publication 4.

Wallman, S. (1997) 'Appropriate anthropology and the risky inspiration of "capability" Brown: representations of what, by whom and to what end?', in A. James, J. Hockey and A. Dawson (eds), *After Writing Culture.* London: Routledge. pp. 244–64.

Whiting, B.B. (ed.) (1963) *Six Cultures: Studies of Child Rearing.* London: Wiley.

Woodhead, M. (1996) 'In search of the rainbow: pathways to quality in large-scale programmes for young disadvantaged children', *Early Childhood Development: Practice and Reflections,* 10. The Hague: Bernard van Leer Foundation.

Woodhead, M. (1997) 'Psychology and the cultural construction of children's needs', in A. James and A. Prout (eds), *Constructing and Reconstructing Childhood,* 2nd edn. Basingstoke: Falmer Press.

18

Ethnography and Material Culture

CHRISTOPHER TILLEY

The definition of material culture adopted here is catholic: any humanly produced artefact from a crisp packet to a landscape in the past or in the present. The category is ambiguous insofar as a boundary demarcation between culture and nature cannot be clearly defined. Such things as domestic animals and cultivated plants and landscapes are simultaneously artefacts of humanity and yet the form of their production clearly differs from that involved in making an axe. The human body is as much public artefact on which an identity is marked as a personal thing. Material culture is a reflexive category insofar as its analysis includes itself. Thus museum collections are designed to display and educate us about material forms but are simultaneously pieces of contemporary material culture themselves. Material culture is a relational and critical category leading us to reflect on object–subject relations in a manner that has a direct bearing on our understanding of the nature of the human condition and social Being in the world.

OBJECTS AND LANGUAGE

Lévi-Strauss' appropriation of Saussurian linguistic theory to study non-verbal aspects of human culture provides an essential foundation for modern material culture studies. While the overwhelming focus of his work remained the explication of social relations, the grand master of structuralism was aware, from the very beginning, of the potentialities of a language of things (Lévi-Strauss, 1968, 1973, 1988; see Tilley, 1990a). The abiding legacy of his version of structuralism for material culture studies is the general idea that things communicate meaning like a language. Artefacts can be considered as

signs bearing meaning, signifying beyond themselves. From this perspective material culture becomes a text to be 'read' and a semiotic discourse to be 'decoded'. Advocacy of this position has generated a large number of innovative material culture studies over the past twenty years with various attempts being made to locate a silent grammar of the artefact and investigate its social significance (see, for example, Faris, 1972; Gottdiener, 1995; Hanson, 1983; Hodder, 1982; Humphrey, 1971; Korn, 1978; Layton, 1991; Munn, 1973; Riggins, 1994; Vastokas, 1978; Washburn, 1983). In contrast to Lévi-Strauss' own work, these studies have all tended to be contextually and historically specific: local and temporally specific, rather than universal grammars of things.

Formal analyses of artefacts have been undertaken in order to isolate an underlying grammar, or set of rules, capable of accounting for their forms. Attention has focused on obviously stylistic attributes such as surface designs. The concern has been with understanding formal properties of designs, such as forms of symmetry, and the generative constituents of patterns. So a particular combination of zigzags, ovals, lines and circles may be held to generate a 'poisonous snake' in Nuba (Sudan) body art (Faris, 1972: 103). Faris shows how, by combining a small repertoire of shapes, a wide variety of different designs can be generated. Similarly, Korn isolates a series of rules which ovals obey in Abelam (Papua New Guinea) art, such as: 'ovals can be attached upwards to smaller ovals and circles, but not if they have a rim of white dots' (Korn, 1978: 172). Some structural analyses have been conducted without reference to a wider social meaning. Being able to identify a grammar of things, equivalent to a grammar of language, has been deemed a sufficient end in itself. In most cases, however, the aim has been to socially contextualize the results of design grammars in order to graft meaning onto them. Munn, for example (1973), demonstrates the wide meaning ranges of even the simplest Walbiri (Australian Aborigine) designs and relates her analysis of design structure in a general way to a consideration of gender relations, mythological beliefs and ideas about landscape. Hanson (1983) attempts to demonstrate homologous relations (one-to-one correspondences) between Maori (New Zealand) art styles and properties of social systems, associating a preoccupation with disrupted symmetry in art forms with social forms of competitive reciprocity. Gell (1998) comments that Hanson's approach fails to be convincing because of its lack of cultural specificity. Disruptive symmetry is encountered cross-culturally and cannot be claimed to be a distinctive feature of Maori design structure. It therefore seems unlikely to be a manifestation of specific cultural features of Maori social organization.

Many studies of material culture have gone beyond a rather narrow consideration of artefact design structures and expanded to consider a much wider range of relationships and their associations with power and hierarchies. Kaeppler (1978) attempts to demonstrate a series of similar conceptual structures in Tongan music, dance and forms of bark cloth production and design regarding these as material transformations of each other, products of the same conceptual structure. She comments that 'these underlying features may be some of the unconscious, or at least unstated, principles by which individuals help to order their lives' (Kaeppler, 1978: 273). Adams (1973) similarly attempts to adduce sets of structural principles linking different aspects of Sumbanese (Indonesia) society. For example, designs on textiles are organized in terms of a dyadic–triadic set and the same principle is manifest in village organization, marriage systems, patterns of gift exchange and seating patterns taken in formal negotiations. In another paper, Adams (1975) demonstrates links between Sumbanese methods of the processing of raw materials, art and ritual.

The overwhelming emphasis in structuralist approaches to material culture has been the identification of systematic and recurrent rules of transformation linking different material and social practices, structural principles that systematically link different domains which are claimed to be the basic building blocks or essential constituents of the material and social worlds that people inhabit. The idea that there is a language of things has proved to be a fruitful one. The main drawback with the approach is an often excessive formalism, in which all the emphasis is on system and code, a position in which the actual practices of social agents tends to be ignored. The material grammars found are invariably claimed passively to reflect wider social grammars rather than acting to create them.

BEYOND LANGUAGE: THE MATERIALITY OF THINGS

Melanesian anthropologists have noted over and over again an extreme reluctance on the part of their informants to talk about the artefacts they invest so much time and energy in making and decorating. Forge (1970, 1979) has made a highly influential argument on the basis of this observation. He suggests that the significance of Abelam art is simply not amenable to linguistic translation in terms of individual design elements themselves signifying particular things or concepts beyond the artistic system itself. The meanings of the designs reside *within* the designs themselves rather than referring to anything external such as the art being a visual representation of myth. Art forms a powerful medium for socialization precisely because of its autonomy from spoken discourse. The material medium creates and defines what it means to be a member of society in just the same way as speaking a language, but through a material medium. It is a distinct system of knowledge in its own right.

While some of the most exciting and innovatory studies of material culture during the past thirty years have exploited analogies between language and things in terms of both being communication systems, we know that things are not texts or words and that to attempt to communicate even the simplest sentence such as 'it is raining' with things would be a completely redundant exercise. Things communicate in a different way, such that if I could say it, why would I dance it, or paint it, or sculpt it? etc. Things often 'say' and communicate precisely that which cannot be communicated in words. A silent discourse of the object may permit the cultural unsaid to be said, or marked out. So, for example, in societies characterized by extreme sexual antagonism, as in Melanesia, a discourse of material forms exemplified by artefacts such as the net bag (MacKenzie, 1991) or canoes (Tilley, 1999) may speak about the complementarity of male and female roles in the reproduction of social life in a way that is otherwise denied, negated or obfuscated in contexts of social action and speaking.

Language works through sequences of sounds that unfold their meaning in a linear way. Objects, by contrast, are what Langer (1953) refers to as 'presentational' forms. There is no starting point to 'reading' a pot or an axe: the whole artefact is present to us simultaneously. We might look at it from top to bottom, side to side, start glancing at the middle etc. Objects relate to far wider perceptual functions than words, they have multidimensional qualities relating to sight, sound, smell, taste and touch enabling remarkably subtle distinctions to be made: 'try to describe in words the difference in smell between two kinds of fish, or the shape of two different kinds of shirts' (Miller, 1994a: 407). The distinctions between things, contributing to their meaning, can be created in an enormous variety of ways. Sheer size and lack of portability may be important, for example, monuments and shrines one must visit, located in a particular place. Or the significant feature might be smallness and portability – the ability to carry things around and display them. Things may acquire value by having a high degree of public visibility or by being kept secret. An absence of something may be as crucial as its presence. It may be 'invisibly foregrounded' (Battaglia, 1994). Things may be valued because they are local and available to all, or foreign and 'exotic' goods. Weight or lightness may be desirable qualities or colours, dullness or brilliance, textures, roughness or smoothness. These are all ways of employing and creating distinctions and difference in the world of objects and are virtually inexhaustible.

Such distinctions are rarely unidimensional, but relate to a thickly textured phenomenological experience of the thing with which we may engage with the full range of our senses: a synaesthetic interaction and knowledge. Things perform work in the world in a way that words cannot. Their relative permanence compared with the fleeting spoken word is important in this respect. They usually have a practical use-value as well as a sign value. The two are intertwined and cannot be meaningfully separated out in terms of 'functional' and 'stylistic' parameters. Material forms such as pots can equally perform the function of containing things while taking a wide variety of different forms (Miller, 1985). Styles may have functions and functions have styles (Boast, 1997). Material forms are practically, or performatively, as well as discursively produced, maintained and given significance.

OBJECTIFICATION PROCESSES

The usual way we tend to think about things in contemporary Western society is to set up a categorical opposition between things as objects and persons as subjects. Things are dead, inert matter that only acquire their significance, or become personalized, through the actions of social agents. This perspective actively blocks an understanding of the significance of things. One of the most influential theoretical perspectives informing contemporary material culture studies has been an emphasis on objectification: that through making things people make themselves in the process (Bourdieu, 1977, 1984; Miller, 1987, 1997; Munn, 1977, 1986; Strathern, 1988). There is a dialectic at work. This

perspective overcomes an object/subject dualism in which the former becomes regarded as passive and the latter as active. In functionalist and structuralist approaches it has been assumed that material forms simply reflect or symbolize various kinds of social relations and practices. These come first and the artefacts merely serve to signify already established social distinctions of whatever kind.

A perspective emphasizing objectification processes emphasizes instead that material forms play a fundamental part in the creation and establishment of forms of sociality. In other words, they are generative of thought and action. Thus the meanings that people give to things through their production exchange and consumption are part and parcel of the same process by means of which they give meaning to their lives. Our cultural identity is simultaneously embodied in our persons and objectified in our things. Things may be attributed agency, not in the sense that they have minds and intentions, but because they produce *effects* on persons. As Gell (1992a, 1998) points out, an elaborately decorated Trobriand canoe prowboard, in the context of the exchange of *kula* valuables, is not just a form of code, a non-verbal mode of signification communicating meaning, but part of its purpose is to trap, beguile, enchant so as to impress others to yield up their valuables. For Gell art is not so much a matter of symbolizing and communicating as *doing* things in the world, creating social effects and realizing outcomes.

STRUCTURATION: KNOWLEDGE AND AGENCY

Adopting a broadly structuration perspective (Giddens, 1984), Morphy's (1991) study of Yolungu (Australian Aboriginal) art emphasizes the multiplicity of meanings of the graphic designs as both a system of communication and a system of knowledge from an action frame of reference. Meaning is created out of situated, contextualized social action which is in continuous dialectical relationship with generative rule-based structures forming both a medium for and an outcome of action. What Yolungu art means is produced through its use in relation to individual and group practices and institutional structures. Its very production may involve the changing of its structure. The art is structured internally through the manner in which it encodes meaning. The artistic system is in a continuous process of structuration through its articulation with the sociocultural system. Key factors here are the system of restricted knowledge dividing seniors from juniors and men from women in Yolungu society and the system of clan organization. Yolungu art both orders knowledge by the way it is encoded and, as an institutional practice, orders the way that knowledge is acquired. The meanings in the art and the manner in which it articulates with the sociocultural system are reproduced or changed through individual actions. Paintings give power to persons and make them strong. They encode spiritually powerful ancestral designs owned by clans and store information about ancestral events in the mythological 'Dreamtime'.

The meaning of paintings in ceremonies is highly complex. Here Morphy (1991: ch. 7) identifies (i) iconographic meanings denoted by elements in the paintings (for example, a line may represent a sand ridge); (ii) reflectional meanings (such as what the use of white paint means as a component of ancestral law); (iii) thematic meanings (for example, selection of a painting for a specific purpose in the context of a particular ceremony); (iv) particularistic meaning (the association of a painting with a specific event with its own individual significance, such as the burial of a relative); (v) sociological meaning (for example, the association of the form of a painting with a clan and its land). Denotative and connotative meanings are both created and released in the context of ceremonies. On the one hand, paintings have meanings independent of the specific ceremony because of the iconographic and sociological meanings encoded in them. On the other hand, connotative meanings are related to the use of paintings in previous ceremonies and the associations that build up around them. Meanings are also created through the association of the paintings with individuals, and the ceremonial and societal events and themes with which they are integrated. This creates multiple layers of meaning and the knowledge of these meanings can be restricted and controlled in order to legitimate power and authority. As a person moves through life their initial status as an outsider who does not possess this knowledge and cannot produce or reproduce it moves to various degrees to that of an insider who knows, and can be creative.

POST-STRUCTURALISM: POLYSEMY AND RECEPTION THEORY

Post-structuralist positions in the analysis of material culture have stressed in a similar manner to structuration and objectification perspectives, the polysemic and often contradictory meanings of things. They have also emphasized the multiple ways in which they may be 'read', interpreted and understood. Preston-Blier (1995) has discussed West African Vodun (sculptural) art from the multiple perspectives of the artist who makes the underlying figure, the producer who empowers it with various surface additions before or during its use, the users and audiences who interact with it and 'cultural spokespersons' (diviners, priests, family heads etc.) who guard information on these objects. Each

sculpture is, as a result, thick with signification. No single interpretation can suffice. The artist is but one individual in a ramifying network of meanings, inexhaustibly altering according to social and material context. Each individual, in effect, creates and constructs his or her own artwork, including the analyst but within distinctive 'communities' of viewers the sculptures may also be said to have certain shared meanings (1995: 57). Artists, producers, users and audiences all act on the sculptures, which in turn act on them so as to transpose their features and transfer their properties. Depicting human bodies wrapped and clothed in a kaleidoscopic variety of materials, the sculptures perform protective and therapeutic functions in relation to human agency and play a critical role in forming and forging personal identities and destinies. The most salient features of these sculptures, according to Preston-Blier, are the powerful human emotions they evoke, their potency is a manifestation of their psychological power to disorientate, disturb and grip the human imagination: force, fear, fury, schock, disorder and deception play critical roles in their reception and use.

METAPHOR AND MATERIAL CULTURE

What are the cognitive processes at work in the connection between persons and things? The structuralist answer is a digital logic of binary oppositions taking the raw materials of experience and processing them in exactly the same way. The functionalist approach leads us to believe that things mirror, represent and act so as to maintain pre-established ideas manifested in particular sets of social relations. Structuration and objectification approaches usefully stress a generative dialectic between things and persons in which neither is granted primacy. Avoiding a mind/body dualism a recursive relationship between thought (in various ways regarded as providing principles, 'rules' and particular sets of dispositions for action) and agency is argued to be mediated through practical (embodied) activity in the world. Bourdieu (1977, 1984), in particular, stresses the contingent, improvised and provisional character of these processes and their manifestation in routinized social action: knowing how to go on in the world without this entering into public discourse which is what Giddens (1984) refers to as 'practical consciousness'.

Where this literature is weak is in its generality: the relative lack of attention to specifying exactly what goes on in an embodied mind in relation to activity in the world. This is the missing link. I have recently argued that a concept of metaphor, if suitably conceptualized, provides a new way to link together thought, action and material forms (Tilley, 1999). Only aspects of some of the arguments can be briefly summarized here.

Some cognitive psychologists have forcefully argued that metaphors are not an embellishment or elaboration of an originary and primary literal language (the traditional theory of metaphor going back to Aristotle) but constitute its very essence as a mode of communication. 'Dead' metaphors are so ubiquitous and embedded in our thought that we rarely realize that we are even using them when we speak (for example, expressions such as the leg of a table, the face of a clock, I *see*, that is, I understand, what you mean). To be human is to think through metaphors and express these thoughts through linguistic utterances (Gibbs, 1994; Lakoff, 1987; Lakoff and Johnson, 1980). The essence of metaphor is to work from the known to the unknown, to make connections between things so as to understand them. A metaphorical logic is thus an analogic logic. Metaphors serve to map one domain in terms of another. This is precisely what we do in all interpretative work in the social sciences. Core theories of the social are all heavily metaphorical. So, in functionalism society is likened to being a machine, or an organism; in structuralism, society is like a language; in ethnomethodological approaches, we write of persons as performing roles, settings and stages for social actions etc. The metaphors used in language are all culturally relative and historically determined. Japanese metaphors will not necessarily have any meaning in English and vice versa.

The counterpoint to linguistic metaphor is 'solid metaphor' – the metaphorical qualities of things which are equally ubiquitous, hence the widespread occurrence of animism (a belief that stones, trees, artefacts etc. have souls, embody ancestral or spirit powers etc.) and personification (a belief that objects can variously take the form of subjects) as ascribed qualities of things present in all known societies. Material metaphors differ from linguistic metaphors in their relative density of metaphorical compression (because material forms are synaesthetic, making them inherently ambiguous and polysemic in nature). Nevertheless, within a particular cultural context many of the metaphorical links will be motivated, or relatively non-arbitrary, for example, linking redness with blood, white with milk or semen or employing types of metonymic (part-whole) connections, for example, referring to a body by depicting a body part. Metaphoric extensions of the notion of containers and containment can serve to link such diverse forms as pots, houses, bodies, skulls. Notions of wrapping can link gift giving, clothing, food, houses (Hendry, 1993). A path metaphor may be a way of linking things and persons in terms of sequence, method, technique or strategy thus technological processes follow their paths as do people. There may be varying degrees of coherence, or contradiction, between metaphors operating in different material domains (body metaphors, house metaphors, animal metaphors, artefact metaphors etc.).

OBJECTS AND SPACE

Consider the arrangement of chairs in a room. Their spatial arrangement in a circle, or in rows, has a direct bearing on the types of social interactions that will take place in terms of relative degrees of formality/informality and the types of social interactions deemed desirable and possible. Once a building is erected it physically channels movement, creating a frame for experience that may both enable or constrain forms of social interaction. The arrangement of furniture and artefacts in a room, houses in a village, settlements in a landscape, all have profound effects on people and their social relationships.

Both generated and generative, material forms distributed in social space-times are both the medium and outcome of human actions in the world. An excellent exposition of this general thesis is Munn's ethnography of canoe building and exchange on Gawa island (Papua New Guinea) (Munn, 1977, 1983, 1986). These are shown to be successive spatio-temporal transformations of social identities. The manufacture and exchange of the canoes involves converting a heavy, rooted, immobile object (the tree) into a material form that is light and mobile and moves from the island context to the outside world. On Gawa the canoe enters exchange pathways in which it moves from wife-giving to wife-receiving matrilines mediated by yam transactions. It is then converted into a wider sphere of influence by means of its exchange for *kula* shell valuables. Armbands and necklaces are circulated in opposite directions around a ring of islands exchanged principally between men. The various named parts of the shells are heavily anthropomorphized; labelled after body parts, they are said to have a voice and a gender, follow prescribed exchange pathways, and have a rank order of importance. The most famous have individual names and individual histories according to who has possessed them. Kula exchange partners can only acquire their fame and identity through holding and subsequently passing on the shells. Men further transact these shells and in so doing convert them into personal fame and the ability to move distant minds, that is, receive shells from others. Men's names are remembered even by persons they have never met in the exchange ring through their connections with the shells that they have held. In this manner the circulating shells become detached mobile elements of personal identities.

A great deal of recent attention has been devoted in ethnographic studies of material culture to issues of space and place and landscape and the manner in which they encode, produce and reproduce, alter and transform patterns of sociability (e.g. Basso and Feld, 1996; Bender, 1993; Hirsch and O'Hanlon, 1995; Lovell, 1998; Tilley, 1994).

The house, of course, is a primary locus for the production and reproduction of social relations. What makes a house a home is that it is far more than a physical structure providing shelter. To enter a house is to enter a body, a mind, a sensibility, a specific mode of dwelling and being in the world (Chevalier, 1998; Csikszentmihalyi and Halton, 1981; Halle, 1996). Houses are material forms with very special characteristics: complex artefacts consisting of standardized parts that are arranged and organized into a totality. They are collective in that people collect together and organize themselves through them. Hence many social groups are referred to as 'houses' (Carsten and Hugh Jones, 1995). Houses actively produce, and serve to reproduce, distinctive forms of action and agency. Bourdieu's influential study of the Kabyle house (1977) shows how it is organized according to a set of oppositions such as cooked:raw, fire:water, high:low, light:shade day:night, east:west, male: female. Going beyond an ordinary structuralist analysis, Bourdieu shows how the symbolic divisions of the house are constantly invoked through the practical actions and social strategies of social actors rather than being an inherent feature of the internal space: a dialectic between agency, structure and meaning. A large number of other studies have emphasized the almost limitless biographic, metaphoric, social and symbolic qualities of domestic spaces. For example, houses and house parts are frequently anthropomorphized as bodies. They may provide cosmological models of the world in minature, reflect and structure hierarchy, gender and a host of other social divisions and practices (see e.g. Guidoni, 1975; Humphrey, 1974; Kent, 1990; Neich, 1996; Pandya, 1998; Preston-Blier, 1987; Waterson, 1991).

ARTEFACTS, TIME AND MEMORY

Variable times are both inside and outside artefacts forming fundamental elements of their meanings and relationships to people. In a long-standing ethnographic tradition I am referring here to social time rather than time conceived as an empty linear universal reference and measurement dimension. We are all born into a preconstituted artefactual world. The child sees and touches, manipulates and experiences the world through all the senses before being able to speak. Language acquisition and the development of social skills are relatively late in the development of the self. The first and primordial world of the child is a sensory-motor interaction with things in which even the breast may have more objective than subjective qualities.

The social meaning and value of things are contextually and historically relative. Age and durability may be the significant factor. Things, like antique furniture, acquire a patina of age (McCracken, 1988) which works best in the 'correct' spatial context (a stately home rather than an ordinary home). Or it may be novelty and ephemerality that is significant, as in many consumer goods where the aesthetics of their sign value usually predominates over their practical use-value. The sheer length of time and complexity in making a thing may add to its value or the speed and simplicity of its manufacture. Things may be important in and for themselves, their uniqueness and the inability to replace them but more usually because they may be converted into other things and social relationships in time. For example, transformative principles may be stressed: exchange valuables can attract other valuables. Even the production of food may be largely geared to exchange. To consume prized yams may be wasteful because such things can be converted into establishing social relationships: a full belly is, in effect, a lost relationship (Munn, 1986).

Durable artefacts such as stone monuments or an antique chest, in which time is literally inscribed as age, preserve collective and personal memories forming parts of the biographies of individuals and societies but sheer physical presence is not necessary for memory work. In collections throughout the world there are over 5,000 complex and intricate wooden Malangan carvings from New Ireland (Papua New Guinea) (Küchler, 1987, 1992). They are still produced and play a fundamental role in social and ritual life but the paradox is that there is hardly a single one to be seen on the island. Despite the intricacy of the carvings, Küchler has demonstrated a remarkable constancy in form of particular types produced more than a century apart. These carvings are used in death rituals and were traditionally thrown away into the forest to rot after display for a few hours during which the soul of the deceased is thought to leave the corpse and enter the carving. The smell of the rotting carving was a sign of its symbolic death in which the imagery was set free and converted into a memorized image. After colonization the alternative to allowing the sculpture to rot was simply to sell it. The significant point here is that the sacrifice of the carvings creates time not as a history visible on the surface of a durable thing but as *memory* which, as imagery, is subject to reproduction in future carvings. These ephemeral carvings confound time, and thus are central to the production of memory in culture and society, not through their permanence but through their *renewal* in which the new carving is reminiscent of another seen in the past. The example of object sacrifice and its relationship to memory serves to undermine the distinction we commonly hold between material things and mental representations. While *malangan* are material objects, their physical existence is brief.

BIOGRAPHIES OF THINGS

When Hoskins was interested in recording personal life histories in Sumba, Indonesia, she found that the only way in which it was possible to elicit this information was to get people to talk about things. Personal identities were wrapped around and embedded in objects such as a betel bag, a drum, a spindle. Talking about things was a way of constructing, materializing and objectifying the self, for things contain and preserve memories, embody personal experiences. Without the things identity construction was well-nigh impossible. The betel bag contained ancestral words, the spindle was a lost husband, the drum evoked female receptivity to a male voice. The social impact of the death of a young woman could only be recounted through using the metaphor of a shattered green bottle (Hoskins, 1998). This challenges a view of life histories and identities being somehow self-evident and complete in themselves. While words so often fail us as communication and representational devices, our possessions and the homes in which we live, silently speak volumes. A narrative of the self is constructed through a metaphoric language of things.

Things, like persons, may be said to have biographies and go through various phases in their life cycles from the moment of their production to their consumption and destruction or re-use (Kopytoff, 1986). Tracing the biographies of things, their social lives, has proved to be a most fruitful way of analysing material culture. Such a perspective emphasizes the manner in which the meanings of things change through time, as they are circulated and exchanged and pass through different social contexts. Consider a hut: it might start out as a family dwelling, then become a house for a widow, be converted into a kitchen and finally a goat house before termites eat it and it collapses. A new shirt may at first be reserved for special occasions, then become everyday wear, then used for painting or gardening and finally become a series of cleaning cloths. From this processual perspective we can appreciate that things can have radically different meanings according to the stages that they have reached in their life cycles. So those things labelled commodities are not one type of thing rather than another but only one phase in the life cycle of certain types of things.

What sorts of things can have what kinds of biographies becomes critical to trace. We can posit a relationship of relative homology between the biographies of persons and things. The multiple and uncertain social identities characteristic of 'postmodern' industrial societies become paralleled by a much greater degree of potential variability and ambiguity in the meaning and significance of things to different people. In small-scale societies, by contrast, the ranges of meanings of things and the kinds of distinct biographies they may have are relatively stable. For example, certain items may only circulate in restricted spheres of exchange and follow relatively prescribed social pathways. This is much more a matter for social contestation and choice in Western industrial societies than in small-scale societies not dominated by a market economy.

TECHNOLOGIES

The ways in which artefacts are made, the types of raw materials used, their sources, the manner in which they become combined and transformed through technological processes, the time and effort required, and consideration of the social relations of production have been a long-standing concern in ethnographic studies of material culture. The traditional functionalist approach has been to investigate these parameters in terms of environmental constraints, the maximization of efficiency and the effects technologies have on culture and society. More recent approaches have suggested that technology and techniques may be far better understood as cultural choices or social productions intimately linked to systems of knowledge and value (e.g. Gosselain, 1992; Hauser-Schäublin, 1996; Hosler, 1996; Latour, 1993a, 1993b; Lemonnier, 1986, 1989, 1993; Rowlands and Warnier, 1993; Sigaut, 1994; Sillar, 1996). This moves us away from viewing technologies as mechanical actions applied to objects and requires us to think instead about the way actions on the material world are embedded in a broader symbolic, social and political system. Technical traditions have to be understood as part of a broader logic of cultural choice and local representations of techniques, which is why the same kinds of objects are often made in totally different ways in different societies. Uses of raw materials, tools and techniques are not only socially informed but draw on historical traditions:

> it happens, for example, that, because they are conceptualized and 'classified' by a given society as 'wild' (or 'feminine', or 'impure', or 'foreign', or 'poor', or whatever), a raw material (a species of wood, a kind of ground, a particular metal) or a tool ... [is] included in some techniques and not in others. Another society reverses the choices ... Conversely, because it is used in a given technique, an element is mentally associated with or rejected for some other use for which it was perfectly suited from a purely material point of view. In turn, the technical function of an element affects its place in various classifications. (Lemonnier, 1993: 3)

Studies of technologies in small-scale societies reveal that technical knowledges are inseparable from ideas of spiritual or ancestral involvement in the production process. Techniques and tools are common metaphors for talking about society and social relations. Weaving provides a common analogue for talking about social relations, readily evoking ideas about connectedness or tying. Participants in life cycle celebrations and in death rituals often emphasize the gift of cloth as a continuous thread binding kin groups, the ancestors and the living (Weiner and Schneider, 1989), ideas about vegetation growth and rootedness bind people to the land, making a basket becomes analagous to making a person (Guss, 1989).

A theoretical emphasis on choice, rather than constraint, leads us to understand that the production, acceptance or rejection of new technologies is 'art' rather than objectified calculating 'science'. New ethnographic studies of technological systems force us to abandon the old tired distinction between a realm of 'efficient' rational material practices and a realm of arbitrary cultural meaning grafted onto them. An old technicist evolutionism would claim that the modern world differs from the primitive one by virtue of the sweeping away of 'magic', 'mysticism' and 'irrational' thought to arrive at a 'purity' of truth, efficiency and profitability. But as Latour points out, when we actually ethnographically observe the ways in which technologies get produced and scientific practices are conducted and their results accepted our own world stops being modern because it looks no different from the others (Latour, 1993b).

EXCHANGE: GIFTS AND COMMODITIES

An opposition has been set up in some of the anthropological literature between gift exchange and commodity exchange, 'us' and 'them', clan-based versus class-based societies. Deriving from the work of Mauss ([1925] 1990), this position has been most fully elaborated by Gregory (1982), who draws the following distinctions:

alienable	inalienable
independence	dependence
quantity (price)	quality (rank)
objects	subjects
commodities	gifts

The argument is that in clan-based societies things cannot be separated from the persons who make them. They have an inalienable quality compared with alienated objects not intimately connected with their producers characteristic of capitalist production. The relationship between persons in gift exchange is primary. By contrast, transactors engaged in commodity exchange have an impersonal independent relationship, strangers in which price is the mark of value of a thing. In gift exchange the fundamental principle at work is the dominance of the giver over the receiver and the social production of indebtedness. The gift must be returned after a variable degree of delay. The exchange relationship of a commodity is a relationship between things of price which creates a system of equivalence with money acting as a universal medium for equating relationships between all things. While commodities have their prices, gifts have their rank. Commodity exchange is a relationship between objects, gift exchange is a relationship between persons. In many societies to give away a woman is to make the ultimate gift cementing social relationships and alliances. From a commonsense Western perspective this is to treat the woman as if she were merely another exchange object, that is, it is to reify her, to treat the person as if she were a thing. But if we deny the relevance of the basic presupposition underlying this position – a subject/object dualism – then an entirely different conclusion will be reached.

The entire theory of 'primitive' exchange developed from Mauss emphasizes in various ways that the meanings and qualities ascribed to things are in basic ways homologous to those given to persons. Things are like subjects and subjects are like objects. Gifts are inalienable because they have within themselves attributes which cannot be detached from the giver who is part of them. Thus to give away a woman is not to devalue her *as* a thing but to treat persons and things in just the same way. Social agency is both invested in things and emanates from things. Strathern's particular argument is that in a commodity economy both persons and things take the form of things whereas in a gift economy persons and things take the form of persons (Strathern, 1988: 176–82). The mechanisms at work are reification in the first case, in which objects appear as things and persons (for example, in selling their labour) are treated like things, and personification in the second in which objects appear as persons and are treated like subjects.

This contrast between class and clan societies, commodities and gifts, has both been exaggerated and overdrawn (Appadurai, 1986; Carrier, 1995; Miller, 1987; Thomas, 1991). There is a need to move away from an ahistorical essentialism depicting reciprocity rather than trade as a diacritical marker of the 'savage'. Distinctions between societies in which the commodity form or gifts dominate in the circulation and exchange of things is simply a matter of degree, or emphasis. These should be regarded as only being *analytical* distinctions. In traditional Melanesian societies all manner of things could be bought and sold as commodities from dances to magical spells to details of ritual performances to styles of house and artefact design (Gell, 1992a; Harrison, 1993). In modern Western societies it is not difficult to distinguish a social sphere of gift-giving located in the relationships between households, family, friends and neighbours and a much more anonymous world of 'economic' activities, of work, buying things in shops and trading in markets characterized by commodity relations. A crucial distinction does hold between the way things are produced and consumed in 'clan-' and 'class-' based societies. In clan-based societies most possessions are made locally and, even if they are not produced by their owners, the owners will usually influence their form, the materials used and know the producer. This contrasts with the alienation of the modern Western consumer from the anonymous production process in which the choices become what to purchase, where and when.

ALIENABLE AND INALIENABLE WEALTH

Weiner (1985, 1992, 1994) argues that rather than considering exchange systems in terms of rules for equivalent returns, the classical Maussian perspective, it is the desire to keep, the dread of loss, which underlies acts of reciprocity. She explains exchange through examining non-exchange: why some things are not given away and remain out of circulation: inalienable wealth. These objects are granted powers and cosmological authenticity through their links to ancestral forces or the gods. Such qualities imbue objects such as Australian Aboriginal tjurunga boards and Maori feather cloaks, the British crown jewels or things such as the Elgin marbles, whose ownership is under dispute. Such things are symbolically 'dense' (Weiner, 1994: 394), filled with cultural meanings and values, and this density accrues through association with its owners, ancestral histories, sacred connotations etc. In the West we would generically refer to such things as the 'family silver', items that even in the direst of economic circumstances should not be sold while less dense things may be circulated with impunity. Keeping a highly prized object against all the demands for its exchange is a way of emphasizing the owner's difference and singularity. In his classic essay Mauss, citing the example of Maori gift exchange, referred to the *hau* of the gift – according to him, a mystical and spiritual quality within the gift that compels its return and gives it a quality of inalienability. Weiner's novel explanation for the *hau* in gifting is that it is simply a means of reconciling the social imperative to give while keeping: one can give something away but still retain its essence or soul. Exchange, rather than creating equivalence, establishes difference. The control of exchange objects through keeping while giving allows the emergence of rank and political hierarchies.

CONSUMPTION

Studies of consumption in contemporary Western societies have formed a major focus for material culture studies during the past fifteen years and this has replaced a more traditional Marxist emphasis on processes of production and distribution in the constitution of culture and society (e.g. Appadurai, 1986; Carrier, 1995; Clarke, 1998; Douglas and Isherwood, 1979; Miller, 1987, 1994b, 1995, 1997). From the nineteenth-century Paris arcades to the contemporary shopping malls of the United States, the development of various practices and sites for consumption has been claimed to be the new key to unlock an understanding of our modernity and the way in which we come to know ourselves. If alienation is an intrinsic condition of our relationship to goods in Western society, it has been recognized that people convert these alienated things into meaningful possessions through endowing them with subjective meaning in relation to ethnicity, gender, social roles and statuses (Bourdieu, 1984; de Certeau, 1986). The enormous array of distinctions in consumption preferences both reflect and serve to reproduce key social distinctions. Theorizing consumption as a social process rather than as an isolated moment of economic exchange has led to new ways of understanding the significance of commodities and theorizing the construction of social identities. The recognition that it is increasingly through the social practices of the consumption and the use of commodities that persons define themselves, create and re-create their identities, means that we require in our analyses a detailed focus on the dialectics of subject–object relationships and the various cultural milieu through which objects are given social meaning from the clothes that people wear, to the manner in which they decorate and furnish their homes, the way they create their gardens, the food that they cook etc. In this manner objects move from being impersonal public commodities to personalized tokens in a domestic 'gift' economy. Recent research on consumption has stressed that the meanings and associations things have for people are always performatively produced, embodied, worked through contextually in relation to specific persons, groups, social networks, places and times.

From such a perspective shopping has been fundamentally reconceptualized as a network of activities of which the actual moment of purchase is only a small element in the production and reproduction of a much wider social and moral order (Miller et al., 1998: 14). Shopping becomes not a simple matter of individualized 'economic' calculation in relation to commodity signs but much more to do with the manner in which a person's experience of the qualities of objects (from the visual to the tactile) becomes mediated by themes such as love and sacrifice (Miller, 1998b; Miller et al., 1998), that is, shopping and shopping malls are part of a process by which goods communicate, and are communicated as, social relationships: symbolic and expressive acts.

THE GLOBAL AND THE LOCAL

We have seen that the identities of persons and things are mutually entangled, one cannot be understood without considering the other. On a much broader scale, the history of colonial encounters is a history of object entanglement in which the meanings of things become shifted, appropriated, blurred and transformed according to social context. Thomas succinctly makes the point: 'to say that black bottles were given [to natives in trade] does not tell us what was received' (Thomas, 1991: 108). What things get reconceptualized and how depends on specific social and historical circumstances, specifically the manner in which they can be adapted, or conflict with, existing systems of categorization.

Transnational flows of material goods, services, populations, money, information and the explosive growth of the tourist industry have led to claims about cultural homogenization and the erosion of local tradition. Products such as Coca-Cola and McDonald's hamburgers have been used as meta symbols of capitalist dominance on a global scale, with local cultures seemingly unable to resist their allure. Detailed ethnographic studies of material culture have shown this perspective to be somewhat simplistic. The effects of globalization have, in fact, turned out to be cultural differentiation, 'revivals' and inventions of ethnicity. It has been shown that localized places and global processes intersect in an increasingly creolized and hybridized world of peoples and experiences in which a search for cultural 'authenticity' seems particularly fruitless. The cultural realities are of bricolage in which things take on local meanings and are adapted to local circumstances (Appadurai, 1990, 1997; Clifford, 1997; Lash and Friedman, 1992; Miller, 1995; Palumbo-Liu and Gumbrecht, 1997). Miller (1998c), for example, shows the manner in which Coca-Cola becomes ethnically contextualized within a general system of drinks within Trinidad, becoming a black sweet drink with strong Black African associations, contrasting with red sweet drinks connoting Indianness. Coca-Cola as brand and in its generic form as a black sweet drink becomes an image which develops through local contradictions in popular culture and this has crucial effects on its marketing and consumption. In such a perspective, focusing on the materiality of things, we encounter capitalism in a rather different manner than is normally the case: as a highly contextualized mode of production rather than a formalized economic logic, always the same irrespective of locality.

Global processes organize diversity rather than produce homogeneity. The recent emergence of objectified national cultures in places like Belize in the Carribean (Wilk, 1995) or Vanuatu in the south Pacific (Jolly, 1992; Tilley, 1997) are clear examples of the production of difference on a global scale. Everywhere in the 'third' and 'fourth' worlds local peoples are putting their material culture on display for a tourist market. This has led to a great deal of analysis of ethnic and tourist arts (e.g. Graburn, 1976; Jules-Rosette, 1984; Marcus and Myers, 1995; Steiner, 1994). Early analyses stressed the manner in which tourist or 'airport' art radically changed traditional forms through such means as choosing or altering forms so as to be more likely to appeal to a Western audience, through simplification of design and through miniaturization. The emphasis was on the corrosive demise of traditional culture, an acceptance of consumerism and the values of the West. Material things are thus used by Westerners as signs of an irretrievable loss of a 'primitive' identity. The equation is far too simple. In an increasingly globalized world the significances of things are in a constant process of contextualization and recontextualization as they move across borders and between peoples. Historically this is nothing new, as Thomas has made clear in his studies of colonialism in the Pacific (Thomas, 1991, 1994, 1997). It is just that the tempo and speed of these processes has heated up. Shields were a traditional item of warfare in Whagi (Papua New Guinea) culture which fell out of use after pacification following 'first contact' with the white Australian authorities in the 1930s. O'Hanlon's study of contemporary Whagi shield designs (1995) shows how their form and substance has become revitalized since the 1980s, with the use of advertising slogans and exogenous designs to express distinctively local issues. Moral virtue can now be expressed by representing 'good guys' like Superman; ancestral support can be summoned up by written inscriptions.

Globalization has resulted in issues of multiculturalism, modernity and postmodernity, tradition and primitivism coming to the fore. In the context of this the ownership, ascribed meanings and uses of artefacts and art in and outside museums and galleries has increasingly become the subject of intense contestation through the critical impact of studies emphasizing a relativized sense of cultural worth and value which recent ethnographic considerations of material culture have done so much to promote (Clifford, 1988, 1997; Karp and Lavine, 1991; MacClancey, 1997; O'Hanlon, 1993). In an era of decolonization and revivals of ethnicity, local communities are demanding that their artefacts be returned, which become central signifying mediums in conflicts over values, rights and interests. The outcome of this has been the recognition of the politics of heritage and forms of representation more generally. Who are the meanings for? And why? From what perspective? Whose interests do they represent? It is now recognized that art can also be used as a political weapon, something used by indigenous peoples to boost perceptions of their own identities and to attack the manner in which others represent them. Given the contemporary traffic in art from the ethnographic Other to the West, studies of art forms have tracked the processes at work from the indigenous communities to the use and reception of these works in the institutionalized settings of Western art worlds. Attention has focused on how the meanings of things radically alter once 'primitive' culture gets put in 'civilized places' (Price, 1989) in which ritualized disinterested aesthetic contemplation of the object for its own sake as 'art' replaces its original highly specific uses, as artefact, in traditional ceremonial settings. The effects of an external market in the local context on production, form, content and meaning have also been extensively studied.

Indigenous reactions to Western consumer goods range along a continuum. In some cases, such as in the Cameroon, the acquisition and use of Western clothing, furniture etc. represents a tangible and immediate way to convey success and status (Rowlands, 1995). By contrast, amongst the Sa traditionalists of South Pentecost in Vanuatu imported food weakens the body because its production is not grounded in tradition (Jolly, 1991). Among the Yeukana of southern Venezuela foreign objects such as plastic buckets are regarded as insipid with none of the symbolic power of locally produced artefacts (Guss, 1989).

The repatriation of objects to their place or people of origin may help to revitalize a local sense of identity. It may also serve to re-kindle inter-ethnic rivalries (Saunders, 1997).

A focus on material culture in relation to issues of the global and the local has not only served to transcend and thoroughly blur these two categories, it has also fostered increasingly self-reflexive studies in which the person doing the representation (the anthropologist) becomes as much a focus of attention as the people being represented. Increasingly from such a perspective attention shifts away from the traditional anthropological question of what does this thing mean to a rather different one: what intellectual and symbolic resource does it represent, and to whom?

CONCLUSION

Ethnographic studies of material culture have undergone a profound transformation during the past twenty years and may now be claimed to be one of the most dynamic and innovatory areas of anthropological research. This is reflected in an impressive volume of research activity, the publication of a new international journal, the *Journal of Material Culture*, and a flood of books, edited collections and papers devoted to this theme. The study of things may now be claimed to be at the forefront of the discipline. The study of material forms represents

another way of telling about social relations, one that moves us away from a narrow and traditional social anthropological focus on those relations themselves and directs us instead towards the wider sets of material practices in which these relations are embedded.

The great paradox, or aporia, of all material culture studies is that to write about things is to transform, domesticate and strip away the fundamental non-verbal qualities of the things we are investigating through this very process (Tilley, 1991). Although a sub-discipline of visual anthropology exists, going beyond a traditional concern with the anthropology of art (Banks and Morphy, 1997; Collier and Collier, 1986; Devereaux and Hillman, 1995; Edwards, 1992; Pinney, 1998), and two journals are currently devoted to this field, the primary purpose of the visual illustrations still remains as a foil for, and means to authenticate the words (Wright, 1998: 20). We cannot adequately capture or express the powers of things in texts. All we may conceivably hope to do is to evoke. This is why experimentation with other ways of telling, in particular with exploiting media that can more adequately convey the synaesthetic qualities of things, in particular the use of imagery and film, must become of increasing importance to the study of material forms in the future.

REFERENCES AND FURTHER READING

Adams, J. (1973) 'Structural aspects of a village art', *American Anthropologist*, 75 (1): 265–79.
Adams, J. (1975) 'Style in southeast Asian materials processing: some implications for ritual and art' in H. Letchman and R. Merill (eds), *Material Culture. Style, Organization and the Dynamics of Technology*. New York: West Publishing.
Andersen, C. and Dussart, F. (1988) 'Dreaming in acrylic: western desert art', in P. Sutton (ed.), *Dreamings: The Art of Aboriginal Australia*. New York: Asia Galleries.
Appadurai, A. (ed.) (1986) *The Social Lives of Things*. Cambridge: Cambridge University Press.
Appadurai, A. (1990) 'Disjuncture and difference in the global cultural economy', *Public Culture*, 2: 1–24.
Appadurai, A. (1997) 'Consumption, duration and history', in D. Palumbo-Liu and H. Gumbrecht (eds), *Streams of Cultural Capital*. Stanford, CA: Stanford University Press.
Banks, M. (1997) 'Representing the bodies of the Jains', in M. Banks and H. Morphy (eds), *Rethinking Visual Anthropology*. New Haven, CT: Yale University Press.
Banks, M. and Morphy, H. (eds) (1997) *Rethinking Visual Anthropology*. New Haven, CT: Yale University Press.
Barlow, K. and Lipset, D. (1997) 'Dialogics of material culture: male and female in Murik outrigger Canoes', *American Ethnologist*, 24: 4–36.

Basso, K. and Feld, S. (eds) (1996) *Senses of Place*. Albuquerque, NM: University of New Mexico Press.

Battaglia, D. (1990) *On the Bones of the Serpent*. Chicago: University of Chicago Press.

Battaglia, D. (1994) 'Retaining reality: some practical problems with objects as property', *Man*, 29: 631–44.

Bender, B. (ed.) (1993) *Landscape: Politics and Perspectives*. Oxford: Berg.

Boast, R. (1997) 'A small company of actors: a critique of style', *Journal of Material Culture*, 2 (2): 173–98.

Bourdieu, P. (1977) *Outline of a Theory of Practice*. Cambridge: Cambridge University Press.

Bourdieu, P. (1984) *Distinction*. London: Routledge.

Carrier, J. (1995) *Gifts and Commodities*. London: Routledge.

Carsten, J. and Hugh-Jones, S. (1995) *About the House*. Cambridge: Cambridge University Press.

Cerny, C. and Seriff, S. (eds) (1996) *Recycled, Re-Seen: Folk Art from the Global Scrap Heap*. New York: Harry N. Abrams.

de Certeau, M. (1986) *The Practice of Everyday life*. Berkeley, CA: University of California Press.

Chevalier, S. (1998) 'From woollen carpet to grass carpet: bridging house and garden in an English suburb', in D. Miller (ed.), *Material Cultures*. London: UCL Press.

Clarke, A. (1998) 'Window shopping at home: classifieds, catalogues and new consumer skills', in D. Miller (ed.), *Material Cultures*. London: Routledge.

Classen, C. (1993) *Worlds of Sense: Exploring the Senses in History and Across Cultures*. London: Routledge.

Clifford, J. (1988) *The Predicament of Culture*. Cambridge, MA: Harvard University Press.

Clifford, J. (1997) *Routes: Travel and Translation in the Late Twentieth Century*. Cambridge, MA: Harvard University Press.

Collier, J. and Collier, M. (1986) *Visual Anthropology: Photography as a Research Method*. Albuquerque, NM: University of New Mexico Press.

Coote, J. and Shelton, J. (eds) (1992) *Anthropology, Art and Aesthetics*. Oxford: The Clarendon Press.

Csikszentmihalyi, M. and Halton, E. (1981) *The Meanings of Things*. Cambridge: Cambridge University Press.

Devereaux, L. and Hillman, R. (eds) (1995) *Fields of Vision: Essays in Film Studies, Visual Anthropology and Photography*. Berkeley, CA: University of California Press.

Douglas, M. and Isherwood, B. (1979) *The World of Goods*. London: Penguin.

Edwards, E. (ed.) (1992) *Anthropology and Photography*. New Haven, CT: Yale University Press.

Faris, J. (1972) *Nuba Personal Art*. London: Duckworth.

Forge, A. (1970) 'Learning to see in New Guinea', in P. Mayer (ed.), *Socialisation: The View from Social Anthropology*. London: Tavistock.

Forge, A. (1979) 'The problem of meaning in art', in S. Mead (ed.), *Exploring the Visual Art of Oceania*. Honolulu: University of Hawaii Press.

Foucault, M. (1977) *Discipline and Punish*. New York: Vintage.

Gell, A. (1992a) 'The technology of enchantment and the enchantment of technology', in J. Coote and A. Sheldon (eds), *Anthropology, Art and Aesthetics*. Oxford: The Clarendon Press.

Gell, A. (1992b) 'Inter-tribal commodity barter and reproductive gift exchange in old Melanesia', in C. Humphrey and S. Hugh-Jones (eds), *Barter, Exchange and Value*. Cambridge: Cambridge University Press.

Gell, A. (1995) 'The language of the forest: landscape and phonological iconism in Umeda', in E. Hirsch and M. O'Hanlon (eds), *The Anthropology of Landscape*. Oxford: The Clarendon Press.

Gell, A. (1996) 'Vogel's net: traps as artworks and artworks as traps', *Journal of Material Culture* 1 (1): 15–38.

Gell, A. (1998) *Art and Agency*. Oxford: The Clarendon Press.

Gibbs, R. (1994) *The Poetics of Mind*. Cambridge: Cambridge University Press.

Gibson, J. (1986) *The Ecological Approach to Visual Perception*. Mahwah, NJ: Lawrence Erlbaum Associates.

Giddens, A. (1984) *The Constitution of Society*. Cambridge: Polity Press.

Gosselain, O. (1992) 'Technology and style: potters and pottery among the Bafia of Cameroon', *Man*, 27 (3): 559–86.

Gottdiener, M. (1995) *Postmodern Semiotics*. Oxford: Blackwell.

Graburn, N. (ed.) (1976) *Ethnic and Tourist Arts*. Berkeley, CA: University of California Press.

Gregory, C. (1982) *Gifts and Commodities*. London: Academic Press.

Guidoni, E. (1975) *Primitive Architecture*. London: Faber and Faber.

Guss, D. (1989) *To Weave and Sing: Art, Symbol and Narrative in the South American Rainforest*. Berkeley, CA: University of California Press.

Halle, D. (1996) *Inside Culture*. Chicago: Chicago University Press.

Hanson, F. (1983) 'When the map is the territory: art in Maori culture', in D. Washburn (ed.), *Structure and Cognition in Art*. Cambridge: Cambridge University Press.

Harrison, S. (1993) 'The commerce of cultures in Melanesia', *Man*, 28: 139–58.

Hauser-Schäublin, B. (1996) 'The thrill of the line, the string, and the frond, or why the Abelam are a non-cloth culture', *Oceania*, 67 (2): 81–106.

Hendry, J. (1993) *Wrapping Culture. Politeness, Presentation, and Power in Japan and Other Societies*. Oxford: The Clarendon Press.

Hirsch, E. and O'Hanlon, M. (eds) (1995) *The Anthropology of Landscape*. Oxford: The Clarendon Press.

Hodder, I. (1982) *Symbols in Action*, Cambridge: Cambridge University Press.

Hoskins, J. (1998) *Biographical Objects*. London: Routledge.

Hosler, D. (1996) 'Technical choices, social categories and meaning among the Andean potters of Las Animas', *Journal of Material Culture*, 1 (1): 63–92.

Howell, S. (1989) 'Of persons and things: exchange and valuables among the Lio of eastern Indonesia', *Man*, 24: 419–38.

Howes, D. (ed.) (1991) *The Varieties of Sensory Experience: A Sourcebook in the Anthropology of the Senses*. Toronto: Toronto University Press.

Humphrey, C. (1971) 'Some ideas of Saussure applied to Buryat magical drawings', in E. Ardener (ed.), *Social Anthropology and Language*. ASA Proceedings. London: Tavistock.

Humphrey, C. (1974) 'Inside a Mongolian tent', *New Society* (October): 21–8.

Jay, M. (1993) *Downcast Eyes. The Denigration of Vision in Twentieth Century French Thought*. Berkeley, CA: University of California Press.

Jolly, M. (1991) 'Gifts, commodities and corporeality: food and gender in South Pentecost, Vanuatu', *Canberra Anthropology*, 14: 45–66.

Jolly, M. (1992) 'Custom and the way of the land: past and present in Vanuatu and Fiji', *Oceania*, 62 (4): 330–54.

Jules-Rosette, B. (1984) *The Messages of Tourist Art*. London: Plenum Press.

Kaeppler, A. (1978) 'Melody, drone and decoration: underlying structures and surface manifestations in Tongan art and society', in M. Greenhalgh and V. Megaw (eds), *Art in Society*. London: Duckworth.

Karp, I. and Levine, S. (eds) (1991) *Exhibiting Cultures: The Poetics and Politics of Museum Display*. Washington, DC: Smithsonian Institution Press.

Kent, S. (ed.) (1990) *Domestic Architecture and the Use of Space*. Cambridge: Cambridge University Press.

Knauft, B. (1989) 'Bodily images in Melanesia: cultural substances and natural metaphors', in M. Feher, R. Nadaff and N. Tazi (eds), *Fragments for a History of the Body, Part Three*. New York: Zone Books.

Kopytoff, I. (1986) 'The cultural biography of things: commoditization as a process', in A. Appadurai (ed.), *The Social Lives of Things*. Cambridge: Cambridge University Press.

Korn, S. (1978) 'The formal analysis of visual systems as exemplified by a study of Abelam (Papua New Guinea) paintings', in M. Greenhalgh and V. Megaw (eds), *Art in Society*. Duckworth: London.

Küchler, S. (1987) 'Malangan: art and memory in a Melanesian society', *Man*, 22 (2): 238–55.

Küchler, S. (1992) 'Making skins: Malangan and the idiom of kinship in northern New Ireland', in J. Coote and A. Sheldon (eds), *Anthropology, Art and Aesthetics*. Oxford: The Clarendon Press.

Lakoff, G. (1987) *Women, Fire and Dangerous Things: What Categories Reveal about the Mind*. Chicago: Chicago University Press.

Lakoff, G. and Johnson, M. (1980) *Metaphors We Live By*. Chicago: Chicago University Press.

Langer, S. (1953) *Feeling and Form, A Theory of Art*. London: Routledge and Kegan Paul.

Lash, S. and Friedman, J. (eds) (1992) *Modernity and Identity*. Oxford: Blackwell.

Latour, B. (1993a) *We Have Never Been Modern*. Cambridge, MA: Harvard University Press.

Latour, B. (1993b) 'Ethnography of a "high-tech" case', in P. Lemonnier (ed.), *Technological Choices*. London: Routledge.

Layton, R. (1991) *The Anthropology of Art*. Cambridge: Cambridge University Press.

Lemmonier, P. (1986) 'The study of material culture today: toward an anthropology of technical systems', *Journal of Anthropological Archaeology*, 5: 147–86.

Lemmonier, P. (1989) 'Bark capes, arrowheads and Concorde: on social representations of technology', in I. Hodder (ed.), *The Meanings of Things*. London: Unwin Hyman.

Lemmonier, P. (ed.) (1993) *Technological Choices*. London: Routledge.

Lévi-Strauss, C. (1968) *Structural Anthropology*. London: Penguin.

Lévi-Strauss, C. (1973) *Tristes Tropiques*. London: Jonathan Cape.

Lévi-Strauss, C. (1988) *The Way of the Masks*. Seattle, WA: University of Washington Press.

Lovell, N. (ed.) (1998) *Locality and Belonging*. London: Routledge.

MacClancey, J. (ed.) (1997) *Contesting Art*. Oxford: Berg.

MacKenzie, M. (1991) *Androgynous Objects: String Bags and Gender in Central New Guinea*. Melbourne: Harwood Academic Press.

Malinowski, B. (1922) *Argonauts of the Western Pacific*. London: Routledge and Kegan Paul.

Marcus, G. and Myers, F. (eds) (1995) *The Traffic in Culture*. Berkeley, CA: University of California Press.

Mauss, M. ([1925] 1990) *The Gift*. London: Routledge.

McCracken, G. (1988) *Culture and Consumption*. Bloomington, IN: Indiana University Press.

Miller, D. (1985) *Artefacts as Categories*. Cambridge: Cambridge University Press.

Miller, D. (1987) *Material Culture and Mass Consumption*. Oxford: Blackwell.

Miller, D. (1988) 'Appropriating the state on the council estate', *Man*, 23: 353–73.

Miller, D. (1994a) 'Artefacts and the meanings of things', in T. Ingold (ed.), *Companion Encyclopedia of Anthropology*. London: Routledge.

Miller, D. (1994b) *Modernity: An Ethnographic Approach*. Oxford: Berg.

Miller, D. (ed.) (1995) *Acknowledging Consumption*. London: Routledge.

Miller, D. (1997) *Capitalism: An Ethnographic Approach*. Oxford: Berg.

Miller, D. (ed.) (1998a) *Material Cultures*. London: UCL Press.

Miller, D. (1998b) 'Coca-cola: a black sweet drink from Trinidad', in D. Miller (ed.), *Material Cultures*. London: UCL Press.

Miller, D. (1998c) *A Theory of Shopping*. Cambridge: Polity Press.

Miller, D., Jackson, P., Thrift, N., Holbrook, B. and Rowlands, M. (1998) *Shopping, Place and Identity*. London: Routledge.

Moore, H. (1986) *Space, Text and Gender*. Cambridge: Cambridge University Press.

Moore, H. (1994) *A Passion for Difference*. Cambridge: Polity Press.

Morphy, H. (1991) *Ancestral Connections*. Chicago: University of Chicago Press.

Morphy, H. (1992a) 'Aesthetics in a cross cultural perspective: some reflectives on native American basketry', *Journal of the Anthropological Society of Oxford*, 23 (1): 1–16.

Morphy, H. (1992b) 'From dull to brilliant: the aesthetics of spiritual power amongst the Yolungu', in J. Coote and A. Sheldon (eds), *Anthropology, Art and Aesthetics*. Oxford: The Clarendon Press.

Morphy, H. (1994) 'The anthropology of art', in T. Ingold (ed.), *Companion Encyclopedia of Anthropology*. London: Routledge.

Munn, N. (1973) *Walbiri Iconography*. Chicago: Chicago University Press.

Munn, N. (1977) 'The spatiotemporal transformation of Gawa canoes', *Journal de la Société des Océanistes*, 33: 39–53.

Munn, N. (1983) 'Gawan kula: spatiotemporal control and the symbolism of influence', in J. Leach and E. Leach (eds), *The Kula*. Cambridge: Cambridge University Press.

Munn, N. (1986) *The Fame of Gawa*. Cambridge: Cambridge University Press.

Neich, R. (1996) *Painted Histories*. Auckland: Auckland University Press.

Nunley, J. (1996) 'The beat goes on', in C. Cerny and S. Sheriff (eds), *Recycled, Re. Seen: Art from the Global Scrap Heap*, New York: Harry N. Abrams.

O'Hanlon, M. (1993) *Paradise: Portraying the New Guinea Highlands*. London: British Museum.

O'Hanlon, M. (1995) 'Modernity and the "graphicalization" of meaning: New Guinea Highland shield design in historical perspective', *Journal of the Royal Anthropological Institute*, 1: 469–93.

Ong, W. (1967) *The Presence of the Word*. New Haven, CT: Yale University Press.

Palumbo-Liu, D. and Gumbrecht, H. (eds) (1997) *Streams of Cultural Capital*. Stanford, CA: Stanford University Press.

Pandya, V. (1998) 'Hot scorpions, sweet peacocks. Kachchhe art, architecture and action', *Journal of Material Culture*, 3 (1): 51–76.

Pinney, C. (1998) *Camera Indica*. London: Reaktion Books.

Preston-Blier, S. (1987) *The Anatomy of Architecture*. Chicago: Chicago University Press.

Preston-Blier, S. (1995) *African Vodun*. Chicago: Chicago University Press.

Price, S. (1989) *Primitive Art in Civilized Places*. Chicago: Chicago University Press.

Radcliffe-Brown, A. (1922) *The Andaman Islanders*. Cambridge: Cambridge University Press.

Renne, E. (1996) 'Virginity cloths and vaginal coverings in Ekiti, Nigeria', in H. Hendrickson (ed.), *Clothing and Difference*. Durham, NC: Duke University Press.

Riggins, H. (ed.) (1994) *The Socialness of Things*. Berlin: Mouton de Gruyter.

Rowlands, M. (1993) 'The role of memory in the transmission of culture', *World Archaeology*, 25 (2): 141–51.

Rowlands, M. (1995) 'The material culture of success', in J. Friedman (ed.), *Consumption and Identity*. Melbourne: Harwood Academic Press.

Rowlands, M. and Warnier, J-P. (1993) 'The magical production of iron in the Cameroon grassfields', in T. Shaw, P. Sinclair, B. Audah and A. Okpoko (eds), *The Archaeology of Africa*. London: Routledge.

Saunders, B. (1997) 'Contested ethnie in two Kwakwaka'wakw museums', in J. MacClancey (ed.), *Contesting Art*. Oxford: Berg.

Sigaut, F. (1994) 'Technology', in T. Ingold (ed.), *Companion Encyclopedia of Anthropology*. London: Routledge.

Sillar, B. (1996) 'The dead and the drying: techniques for transforming people and things in the Andes', *Journal of Material Culture*, 1 (3): 259–90.

Steiner, C. (1994) *African Art in Transit*. Cambridge: Cambridge University Press.

Stoller, P. (1989) *The Taste of Ethnographic Things*. Philadelphia: University of Pennyslvania Press.

Strathern, M. (1988) *The Gender of the Gift*. Berkeley, CA: University of California Press.

Thomas, N. (1991) *Entangled Objects*. Cambridge, MA: Harvard University Press.

Thomas, N. (1994) *Colonialism's Culture*. Princeton, NJ: Princeton University Press.

Thomas, N. (1997) *In Oceania*. Durham, NC: Duke University Press.

Tilley, C. (ed.) (1990a) *Reading Material Culture: Structuralism, Hermeneutics and Post-Structuralism*. Oxford: Blackwell.

Tilley, C. (1990b) 'Claude Lévi-Strauss: structuralism and beyond', in C. Tilley (ed.), *Reading Material Culture*. Oxford: Blackwell.

Tilley, C. (1991) *Material Culture and Text: The Art of Ambiguity*. London: Routledge.

Tilley, C. (1994) *A Phenomenology of Landscape*. Oxford: Berg.

Tilley, C. (1997) 'Performing culture in the global village', *Critique of Anthropology*, 17 (1): 67–90.

Tilley, C. (1999) *Metaphor and Material Culture*. Oxford: Blackwell.

Vastokas, J. (1978) 'Cognitive aspects of Northwest Coast art', in M. Greenhalgh and V. Megaw (eds), *Art in Society*. London: Duckworth.

Washburn, D. (ed.) (1983) *Structure and Cognition in Art*. Cambridge: Cambridge University Press.

Waterson, R. (1991) *The Living House*. Oxford: Oxford University Press.

Weiner, A. (1976) *Women of Value, Men of Renown*. Austin, TX: University of Texas Press.

Weiner, A. (1985) 'Inalienable wealth', *American Ethnologist*, 12: 210–27.

Weiner, A. (1992) *Inalienable Possessions*. Berkeley, CA: University of California Press.

Weiner, A. (1994) 'Cultural difference and the density of objects', *American Ethnologist*, 21: 391–403.

Weiner, A. and Schneider, J. (eds) (1989) *Cloth and Human Experience*. Washington, DC: Smithsonian Press.

Wilk, R. (1995) 'Learning to be local in Belize: global systems of common differences', in D. Miller (ed.), *Worlds Apart: Modernity Through the Prism of the Local*. London: Routledge.

Williams, D. (1975) 'The brides of Christ', in S. Ardener (ed.), *Perceiving Women*. London: Dent.

Wright, C. (1998) 'The third subject: perspectives on visual anthropology', *Anthropology Today*, 14 (4): 16–21.

19

Ethnography: A Critical Turn in Cultural Studies

JOOST VAN LOON

Cultural studies designates a wide-ranging and expanding domain of research questions concerning processes and structures of sense-making and, more specifically, the way in which 'sense' becomes 'lived' in practices of everyday life. It is, to paraphrase Geertz, 'an ensemble of stories we tell ourselves about ourselves' (Inglis, 1993: xi). It is not a discipline, but merely a catch-phrase for an ensemble of perspectives, analyses, research frameworks, approaches and debates that can be situated anywhere between and across the social sciences and humanities (Denzin, 1999). It is distinctive in its eclectic appropriation of various theoretical infrastructures (basic assumptions), research questions and methodologies (McGuigan, 1997) as well as in its persistent refutation of any attempt to 'integrate' theory, methodology and empirical research into a single paradigm (Johnson, 1986/1987). Hence, the incorporation of, for example, an ethnographic tradition in cultural studies has always been a *partial* event, one that has always been mediated by various resonances of other research traditions. If there are any limitations to cultural studies then they are more likely to be found in terms of geographical location as most of what is labelled as such has taken place in the context of British, Australian and North American societies. Although its international profile is increasing, it is still safe to say that the primary location of cultural studies is still very much the English-speaking parts of the Western world.[1]

None the less, it is possible to identify a set of historical trajectories through which 'cultural studies' has evolved in the UK, North America and Australia, and within which ethnography has emerged as a particularly effective and popular approach to researching cultural processes (G. Turner, 1990).

The starting point of this chapter is therefore a very abbreviated and necessarily schematic overview of historical trajectories of approaches in/to cultural studies. The discussion touches upon the distinction between culturalism and structuralism made by Stuart Hall in the early 1980s, but also incorporates more recent interventions which have engendered major implications for the way in which 'ethnography' has become a more established tradition in cultural studies. The discussion continues with a more specific focus on the way in which ethnography has contributed to cultural studies. In turn, ethnography has also been influenced by the eclectic mixture of theories and perspectives developed by cultural studies. In particular, we shall see how the 'linguistic turn' (Alasuutari, 1995: 24) in cultural studies has produced a sensitivity to culture as an ensemble of sense-making practices that demand a dialogic and reflexive engagement, rather than expert interpretation (Davies, 1995). The main impact of cultural studies on ethnography has been that the latter has become not only a subject but also an instrument of a continuous process of critical engagement with our own being-in-the-world, beyond the taking for granted of that which already exists.

HISTORICAL TRAJECTORIES

Although most histories of cultural studies (Alasuutari, 1995; Davies, 1995; Hall, 1980; Inglis, 1993; Storey, 1993) locate its emergence in the 1950s with the works of Raymond Williams and Richard Hoggart, they all insist that the roots of 'studies of culture' are longer and extend into the nineteenth century when various comments were written about the state of society under industrial modernization. What allows us to speak of 'cultural studies' as a specific domain, however, has been a significant break in the relationship *between* cultural research and cultural criticism. Whereas during the century before 1950 cultural criticism, that is the valorization of particular 'opinions' in moral and philosophical terms, was the main directing force behind specific studies of cultural products (for example, to determine the canon of English literature), cultural studies emerged as an inversion of that relationship. 'The issue was not *What Books?* but under what conditions did reading or making books, watching or making films *matter?*' (Davies, 1995: 6).

This particular *English* trajectory of cultural studies was from the outset framed within a series of encounters with 'Marxism'. They were aimed to extend Marxist analyses of culture beyond the rather reductionist agendas of the Communist Party which saw culture as nothing but an epiphenomenon of the capitalist mode of production. Instead, they developed a notion of culture as lived, and historically formed, and hence to be analysed and studied on its own terms. In particular, the studies focused on interpreting the historical traces of English working-class culture in the forms of expression and forms of content of the literary tradition. This is what Stuart Hall (1980) referred to as *culturalism*, which is one of the two central paradigms he identifies within cultural studies, the other being *structuralism*.

According to Hall, culturalism refers to a particular research tradition which was mainly concerned with the construction of a historiography of English 'working-class culture' – and more specifically the way in which it evolved in a more, rather than less, antagonistic relationship with the official national British/English 'Culture'. Crucially, this historiography was based on the assumption of a continuity between particular cultural manifestations and their underlying socioeconomic 'logic'. This continuity could be revealed only through a historical analysis of cultural changes, which were usually of a very *longue durée*. Moreover, this historical continuity of cultural change took place on the mundane and banal level of 'everyday life' and 'common sense'. More specifically in the work of Raymond Williams, it was *experience* that mediated between 'being' and 'consciousness', between that which exists and that which makes sense. Essential for research associated with the culturalist tradition, therefore, is the emphasis on 'meanings' that were actively attributed to particular cultural phenomena by the members of a particular society or group on the basis of their own life experiences. Through these attributions, members were able to exercise *agency* and thus to construct their own sense of being-in-the-world. Hence there exists a deeply rooted connection between culturalism and the ethnographic tradition. Both emphasized the

centrality of culture as 'everyday life' and their 'meaningfulness' according to the members themselves. Moreover, the strong historical focus of 'culturalism' echoes the necessary emphasis in ethnography on tracing particular instances of sense-making in lived experience within a more holistic and commonsense oriented understanding of the development of *local knowledge* (Geertz, 1995; Inglis, 1993: 168). For example, in his famous work on a group of working-class school leavers ('the lads'), Paul Willis (1977) argued that ethnography is an effective tool of cultural research against theoretical reductionism (Turner, 1990: 175). For Willis, it was the agency of these lads that provided both the experiences and the strategies for coping with the class divisions in British society. The reproduction of these divisions was not something that just happened, but because people actively engaged in it. This illustrates the way in which ethnography was invoked by cultural studies as a way in which (abstract) 'theory' could be properly placed in relation to the 'real world'; and hence reinforced the imagined split between sense as abstraction and as actuality, with ethnography privileging the latter.

Structuralism, in contrast, has a very different trajectory, whose origins are almost entirely outside of the English tradition. The roots of structuralism are usually traced back to the work of the Swiss linguist Ferdinand de Saussure, and the Belgian anthropologist Claude Lévi-Strauss. Structuralism was a dominant paradigm in French philosophy, literary criticism and the social sciences and reigned supreme until the late 1960s, when its strong associations with the French Communist Party became highly problematic in the wake of the repression of the Prague Spring and the Party's inability to support the workers and students protests in France in 1968. As with culturalism, the development of a structuralist trajectory within the English tradition of cultural studies was predominantly framed through a Marxist paradigm. One must bear in mind, however, that structuralism originates from a rather different set of basic assumptions and questions about the nature of social order. Moreover, its incorporation into what was until then a very English intellectual tradition has never been smooth and often accompanied by a wide range of misunderstandings and misreadings.

The most prominent incorporation of structuralism into cultural studies has been around debates in Marxism, in particular concerning issues of ideology and determination. Here the influence of the French philosopher Louis Althusser (1971) has been particularly noteworthy. He developed a notion of ideology which no longer referred to 'false consciousness', but to 'the imaginary relationship of human beings to their real conditions of existence' (1971: 162). Ideology thus became conceptually linked to what psychoanalysts call 'the unconscious'. This link forced any critique of ideology, which became, in effect, the essence of structuralist cultural studies, to deal with that which escapes our awareness – as that which constitutes our very subjectivity and to a large degree irrespective of our own understanding of it. The influence of Althusser on cultural studies has been phenomenal. It engendered a tradition of research and theory that was no longer content with interpreting reality as an empirical-historical presence. Instead, it enabled theory and research to engage with different levels of abstraction and critique, beyond accepting 'that which exists' as either a historical or an empirical 'factuality'.

Whereas the label culturalism refers to a historiographical tradition of research, which is based on an assumed continuity between essence and appearance, structuralism emerges from a categorical rejection of such a principal unity (which can be uncovered through a careful historiography). That is to say, there remains a radical rupture between 'structures' and 'manifestations' as a consequence of which structures always remain (partly) concealed from the meaningfulness attributed to manifestations by members of society. In contrast to the culturalist trajectory in which experience provides *the* linchpin that connects being and sense, indeed between theory and practice, for structuralists experience was itself not primary to the structures of being, it belonged to the world of manifestations and appearances. Experience was itself *an effect of* structure.

Given this radical departure from the centrality of 'experience', it is obvious that within a structuralist framework ethnography could never engender the necessary theoretical insights to make sense of that which governs the everyday experiences of members of a society. An analysis of the structures which enabled particular sense to be made, indeed particular meanings to be constructed, required 'abstraction'. Whereas ethnography was still widely used (particularly in anthropology), it was only to provide illustrations to already existing abstractions of the logic of manifestation of expressions and experiences. That is to say, whatever meanings are being attributed by members to processes of their everyday life, structuralist analysis would only take into account the degree to which they are able to express the structural logic that informs them.

Towards the end of his essay in which he discusses culturalism and structuralism as the two main paradigms in cultural studies, Stuart Hall (1980) assesses the strengths and weaknesses of both trajectories and suggests a third way that combines the focus on structures of domination (abstracted logic) with a more historically embedded logic of everyday life experiences of members of society. This would enable cultural studies to both take into account the situatedness of subjectivity as well as the moments of active intervention and agency through which people enforce change more deliberately and intentionally. Hall suggests that an effective merging of the two traditions can already be found in the work of Marx, but more specifically in the work of the Italian Marxist Antonio Gramsci who has been and still is a major source of inspiration to many proponents of cultural studies, including Hall himself. However, in the 1980s, cultural studies would take a much more dramatic turn than Hall's attempted synthesis. The exposure of cultural studies to, for example, post-structuralism, postmodernism, feminism and 'post-colonialism' led to an immense fragmentation of theory and research and a multiplication of trajectories of engagement. It is impossible to engage thoroughly with any of these interventions. Instead, I will focus on one particular problematic that has crucial implications for the relationship between cultural studies and ethnography. This is the problematic of *language*.

THE LINGUISTIC TURN

In the previous section, the structuralist trajectory was discussed in some detail to stress how it imposed a particular problem for ethnographic research, basically relegating it to the provision of 'illustrations' of abstract theory. When Derrida ([1967] 1978) wrote his now famous axiom that 'there is nothing beyond the text', the general mood in continental philosophy and Anglo-Saxon social theory was still heavily inscribed by a legacy of structuralism in the former and Marxism in the latter. Derrida's relationship with the then-dominant force in French philosophy, Louis Althusser, was rather uncomfortable, and as a consequence, many of his writings were simply ignored by proponents of cultural studies (Easthope, 1988). The idea that culture could be studied as a text, however, was not entirely alien to cultural studies. The Lacanian aphorism that 'the unconscious is structured like a language' (Lacan, [1973] 1977), and Claude Lévi-Strauss and Emile Benveniste's structural analyses of the universal grammar of culture and meaning, were very much part of the canon of, for example, those associated with the film journal *Screen*, who were certainly at the heart of cultural theory in the UK during the 1970s (Davies, 1995; Heath, 1975).

Indeed, alongside Althusserean 'structuralist' Marxism, cultural studies became increasingly influenced by Roland Barthes' semiology. Barthes' famous work *Mythologies* ([1957] 1993) can be seen as one of the classic texts in cultural studies and a key example of the linguistic turn. The analysis of such banal cultural phenomena as advertisements and children's toys and cultural practices such as wrestling and stripping as 'texts', proved to be a model for a lot of cultural studies of, for example, youth sub-cultures, adolescent magazines, popular music, newspapers and television. What these studies had in common was the objective of revealing the way in which 'meaning' was structured and formed by those cultural practices. It was argued that such structures of meaning were derived from a wider 'logic' that was part and parcel of the social, economic and political order in which they took place (for example, in the analyses of how cultural practices and phenomena were influenced by dominant ideologies). This logic was structured by particular 'codes' through which messages operated (Hall et al., [1980] 1992). These codes could be analysed through semiology – the study (science) of signs. At one and the same time therefore, codes were seen as structuring devices and as analytical tools, allowing the cultural researcher direct access to 'meaning', without having to go through people's individual consciousness or reasoning.

Initially, this thesis of mythology could be seen as a further extension of the general structuralist premise that everything, including grammar itself, was grounded in and therefore governed by 'universal structures' that exceed each individual experience of it. However, already in *Mythologies*, but more clearly in his later writings, Barthes' own position shifted. Whereas in the concrete analyses of myths he did not question where these came from, in his concluding chapter, he suggested that they were the result of a historical process of *production*. This immediately puts question marks behind the assertion of universal myths, including the Universal Myth itself. Barthes realized that this structuralist tendency to abstract to the most general and (allegedly) universal category, was itself governed by mythology, that is, it is itself a moment in the 'fixation' of history into a natural essence. This prompted him to suggest, in *The Pleasure of the Text* (1980), that it was not the author that grounds the meaning of texts, but the reader. Having broken the silent equivalence between 'author' and 'structure', texts were subsequently 'set free' for any type of analysis, and thus for any type of violation of authorial intention. This was referred to as 'the death of the author'. In other words, language could no longer be appropriated as if it were a transparent medium for expressing universal categories. Language itself became infected by its own appropriation and reproduction.

This constitutes the essence of post-structuralism. Like structuralism, it does not maintain that subjectivity constitutes the grounds for experience, but unlike structuralism, it does not suggest that therefore 'universal structures' express the entire history of meaning and sense. Instead, it offers a perspective in which every structure, every grammar, is always in a process of being undone, that is, every structure is merely in a process of construction, but this process is never completed because ultimately, it works against

itself. This is what Derrida ([1967] 1974) termed 'deconstruction'.

Deconstruction had a fundamental impact on cultural research in general. This impact was both methodological and theoretical. By conceptualizing cultural practices and phenomena in terms of 'discourse', cultural researchers could systematize their analyses as forms of 'textual analyses'. In semiology, the separation of signifiers and signifieds, together with the concepts of 'codes' and 'myth', established a set of tools which enabled an analysis of 'culture-as-text' as if it was an objective structure existing independently of any subjective interpretation of it. However, with the notion of discourse, it became more and more obvious that although the authors might still be irrelevant, subjectivities are not. What matters was the way in which discourses engender and construct particular subjectivities, which in turn acted through, and thereby upon, particular discourses (Morley, [1980] 1992). The turn to discourse created a strategic space for the development of research methods that were neither objectivist nor subjectivist.

Similarly, the turn to discourse allowed for a theoretical move away from the structure–agency dilemma that had created a stalemate in cultural studies between structuralists and culturalists. As discourse was neither a product of consciousness nor the unconscious, cultural theory could embrace both the intentionality of action, as well as the relatively invisible multiplicity of forces that constitute the power relations which both structure and enable actions and intentions. Foucault's (1980) notion of power as productive, relational, infinitesimal and all-pervasive generated a 'third space' for understanding the social and symbolic organization of our being-in-the-world. Discourse points towards practices rather than structures of social and symbolic organization that are at once 'orderly' (as sense is orderly) and 'fragile' (as sense is temporary).

The undermining of structuralism in the 1970s had similar detrimental consequences for the allegiance between cultural studies and Marxism. Indeed, those associated with ethnographic work in cultural studies, such as Phil Cohen ([1980] 1992) and Paul Willis (1977) had already stressed that culture was never a simple epiphenomenon of a dominant ideology, but instead a site of resistance. The emphasis on cultures of resistance was realized by particular 'readings' of cultural practices and phenomena. For example, in his analysis of 'punk culture', Dick Hebdige (1979) argued that the appropriation of 'waste' by 'punks' was a sign of their refusal of capitalism and its mindless consumerism. By turning waste into fashion, that is, by aestheticizing what is refused by the dominant capitalist consumer culture, punks asserted a counter-identification, a cultural logic that refused the dominant ideology. Such analyses perfectly fitted the tradition of British cultural studies as it was initiated by Williams and Hoggart, by merging a thoroughly historical approach with what could be called a romanticized version of popular working-class culture.

However, what these ethnographic-Marxist perspectives lacked was the provision of an explanation of what motivates this resistance. This work could only remain 'Marxist' if this motivation was somehow related to a sense of class-struggle. Indeed, whereas they would by no means endorse the Althusserean notion of a 'Universal Subject' as the first effect of ideology (in general), Cohen, Willis and Hebdige all implicitly worked with a notion of working-class agency as the expression of a *universalized* subject. Yet it became obvious that many experiences of youths could not be easily subsumed under notions of class and class struggle. This prompted an engagement with other notions of 'resistance' structured by antagonisms that were relatively autonomous from those of capitalism, for example those of race and gender. Rather than a relative autonomy from capitalism (which would still endorse the notion of class as somehow more universal than other forms of subjectification), gender and race constituted a far more radical autonomy of identification and resistance.

THE RADICAL AUTONOMY OF DIFFERENCE

Until the 1980s, ethnography in cultural studies was predominantly concerned with ways in which lived experiences were marked by and were articulations of wider economic, political and social structures and/or histories. However, whereas these concerns were predominantly phrased within a framework of analysis that was deeply inspired by Marxism, it became rather apparent that the latter's predominant concern with forces and relations of production, and more specifically class struggle, made it more difficult for cultural research of this kind to provide a similarly clear understanding of, for example, gender relations or racism. Here we must note the impact of feminism and – at a somewhat later stage – work associated with the rather peculiar label of 'post-colonialism'.

Although the impact of feminism on cultural studies dates from well before the 1980s, the steep increase in books and articles directly engaged in feminist cultural studies marks one of the most remarkable developments in cultural studies as a whole. The writings of, for example, Dorothy Hobson, Angela McRobbie and Judith Williamson quickly became a central part of cultural research. More importantly perhaps, the influence of feminism extended beyond the particular domain of women's studies and entered all aspects of popular culture. Furthermore, the proliferation of debates within

feminism has resulted in a rapid fragmentation of political agendas, issues and perspectives, to a degree that it has become common place to speak of feminisms in the plural (Gray, 1997).

Whereas post-structuralist interventions in cultural studies intensified the notion of 'language', 'meaning' and 'subjectivity' as constructions in a way that was not entirely incompatible with the ethnographic tradition, feminism's interventions in cultural studies engendered a more thorough concern for ethnography by focusing on the importance of 'lived experience' (Gray, 1997; Smith, [1974] 1996). 'The personal is political' – one of the famous slogans of 1970s feminism – could also be seen as the perfect definition of a cultural studies approach to 'lived experience'. At the same time, lived experience has always been a central concern in ethnographic research. However, under the guise of (quasi-)scientific objectivism of traditional anthropology, ethnographic work also had a legacy of neglecting the deeply political aspects of personal experience. This was a major concern for those working within cultural studies, who always maintained a strong adherence to 'critical' research that entailed a direct recognition of the involvement of the researcher in relations of domination, confrontation and conflict (Turner, 1990).

The feminist intervention in cultural studies could thus be seen as, on the one hand, engendering a generic interest in 'lived experiences', and on the other hand, a politicization of researching these experiences (Gray, 1997; Stacey, 1998). In both cases, the starting point was that of women's lived experiences. A key issue in these analyses was the notion of 'pleasure' – as it became obvious that a critique of popular culture in relation to women's lived experience could not but positively address the active involvement of women in the consumption of, for example, romance novels, soaps, beauty magazines and Hollywood melodrama (Coward, 1984; Radway, 1987; Stacey, 1995; also see Storey, 1993). As a result, the 'politics' of feminist cultural studies had to engage with the ambivalence of desire, as at once an expression of women's agency and a discursively constructed node of (patriarchal) power-relations. For example, it was no longer possible to simply read women's magazines as instruments of patriarchal domination, as the main consumers of these magazines were women who actually enjoyed them. Yet at the same time, as part of a critical and political movement, feminist cultural studies could not blindly celebrate such forms of popular culture as if they had no implications for the perpetuation of patriarchal domination in women's lives.

Although the impossibility of unifying a critical voice with an adequate appreciation of experiences of pleasure and desire in women's lives could easily be seen as producing a stalemate in feminist research, it actually engendered a proliferation of feminisms, whose influence stretched far beyond the domains of women's studies and cultural studies. Indeed, many feminists have positively embraced this ambivalence to critically engage with aspects of 'women's lives' and beyond. A crucial issue in this engagement became the notion of 'difference'. What enabled feminist critique to extend beyond women's studies was the fact that until the 1980s, cultural studies had been predominantly concerned with notions of class, in particular working-class culture. Tied in a Marxist framework of analysing class (the universalized subject) as a fundamental constituent of capitalist social formations, such a focus placed a strong emphasis on fleshing out the relationship between socioeconomic social structures and cultural formations.

However, it became increasingly difficult to maintain that gender differences, and the relations of domination they entailed, were merely derived from a capitalist mode of production (Barret, 1980). Hall's (1980) invocation of a Gramscian notion of 'hegemony', which enabled an extension of understanding political power towards other social relationships than those of class, could be seen as a first step to differentiate the notion of 'power' beyond those of class domination. However, whereas the charge that mainstream cultural studies had done little in terms of the analysis of gender, and thus had to take on board a gender-differentiated notion of power, was not without consequences. It invited a further proliferation of understanding power. Not only were classes internally differentiated, the two genders were equally forged with differentiations, most notably those of class, race, ethnicity and sexual orientation. 'The woman' which was held as 'the' (universalized) subject of feminism, was itself an homogenized construct that masked fundamental divisions which were as important as those between women and men. Women of colour, lesbians and women within working-class movements all forcefully argued that what was traditionally seen as 'feminism' was in fact nothing more than a very culturally specific set of concerns derived from the lives of middle-class, white, heterosexual women. Indeed, the emergence of the notion of 'difference' could be seen as the hallmark of cultural studies at the turn of the 1990s. The most prolific advocacy of differentialism has arguably been delivered by what has been labelled 'post-colonialism'.

Although issues over race, ethnicity and nationhood are evidently crucial to any understanding of culture in modern society, it is remarkable that they have not been very central to cultural studies, and only began to appear on the horizon in the late 1980s. Despite widely acclaimed and influential critical studies of racism and Western ethnocentrism by, for example, Franz Fanon (1986) and Edward Said (1978), understanding race, ethnicity and nationhood has been predominantly left to anthropologists and to a lesser degree sociologists and

historians. However, cultural studies became rapidly overwhelmed with a turning towards an understanding of race, ethnicity and nationhood that would radically upset the then still rather manageable categories of identity and subjectivity such as class and gender. This also had a huge impact on the way in which 'race' and 'ethnicity' were conceptualized. The traditions of culturalism and (post-) structuralism which framed most work labelled as cultural studies well into the 1980s, brought a new sensitivity to the importance of understanding both historical and literacy traditions as vital dimensions of the way in which identities were being (de)constructed and reconstructed. The critical edge of such approaches shifted away from the sociological preoccupation with status and wealth and the psychological preoccupation with identity in terms of 'dispositions' (for example 'authoritarian personality' as a key factor in understanding racism), towards the *longue durée* of particular constructions of race and ethnicity as resonances of, for example, colonialism and slavery systems (e.g. Davies, 1995; Goldberg, 1993; Spivak, 1988; Young, 1990).

Such writings cannot be understood without appreciating the deep influence of post-structuralism on understanding the relationships between subjectivity and identity as profoundly (con)textual and historiographical. This influence was already very present in Edward Said's famous thesis on orientalism (1978). Essential here is the argument that no identity is ever simply 'present' or 'given'; all identities are temporal and symbolic constructions that engage in determining boundaries and establish relationships (between selves and others). These boundaries may be discursively presented as 'fixed'; however the complexity of everyday life processes of *identification* inevitably reveals their deeply permeable and unstable character.

Homi Bhabha's (1994) work has often been cited as one of the leading theoretical attempts to rethink notions of subjectivity and identity under 'postcolonialism'. His work is deeply influenced by an English literary tradition, as well as by the 'poststructuralist' writings of Jacques Derrida and Julia Kristeva. His most famous writings concern the predicament of national identity in the experience of ethnic displacement. His starting point is the estrangement that engenders identification in a post-colonial experience. The becoming-signified, which is identification, is a form of ethnography that mobilizes various other writings: literary, biographical, autobiographical. A truly intertextual event, identification always bears the mark of difference, of that which cannot be subsumed into the unity of the self. One always finds oneself somewhere else – one is always displaced – one is never One. This is the experience of migration, of exile, of diaspora. Bhabha's force lies in stressing that such experiences are at the heart of understanding identification and nationhood.

The impact of such an unsettled notion of 'identity' as an intertextual-intersubjective construction on ethnography within cultural research has been enormous. It radically undermines the authority of identification which the traditional ethnographer had to impose in order to delineate 'his' or 'her' subjects. For example, the collection of essays edited by of Clifford and Marcus (1986) clearly shows how the ethnographic authority maintained by mainstream anthropology has been radically undermined not only by the notion of 'data' but also of 'interpretation' as anything but a temporal injunction of writing by the ethnographer him/herself (Rosaldo, 1986). In the wake of this recognition, it became commonplace to describe ethnography as a 'journey' (Chambers, 1994; Tyler, 1986: 140); as 'translation' (Asad, 1986; Bhabha, 1994; Clifford, 1992) or – when the two are combined – as border crossings (Chambers, 1994; Haraway, 1990). All these metaphors indicate the transience of ethnographic writing as itself an intersubjective and spatially and temporally contingent enterprise. As a result, the notion of invoking an ethnographic 'authority' is nothing but an attempt to transform such contingent observations into fixed and static accounts, that is, to transfer the permeable into the permanent.

Indeed, the radical autonomy of difference that became the hallmark of cultural studies in the 1980s, enabled a revival of interest in ethnography – but one stripped of its traditional authority. If grand theoretical claims have been undermined by a decline of faith in universal categories central to modern thought, a turn towards more modest, empirical work seems a logical outcome. Moreover, with a decline of trust in existing (party-) political formations and established ideologies ('isms'), the charge that ethnographic work often leads to political quietism also lost the self-evident association with automatic dismissal. Indeed, the political and epistemological critique of postmodernism problematizes that which in traditional ethnography, even in the work of Clifford Geertz, has been taken rather unproblematically – the notion of representation.

THE PROBLEM OF REPRESENTATION

The crucial problem with the movement against the universalized subject of class, in favour of a radical autonomy of difference, is that it becomes a process without end. Any difference has the potential to become a site of struggle and a moment of subjectification. This notion difference as 'diversity' thus ultimately results in the dissolution of difference. If all differences are equal then all differences are the same. Indeed, difference as diversity is still grounded in a sense of 'identity'. That is, in order for a difference to be actualized, all one requires is

the identification of an element that has been subsumed under another category (for example, the way in which women of colour have been subsumed under the category of 'women' in many feminist discourses, or under 'race' in many anti-racist discourses). Indeed, such a notion of difference is derived from the identification of a particular 'essence' that subsequently grounds its identity.

The infinite differentiation of identities into a collage of diversity in which all differences are ultimately the same, is highly unsatisfactory for any of the aforementioned political engagements over class, gender and race (because of its inherent fragmentation). Moreover, it poses significant problems for ethnography as well. This becomes particularly clear when focusing on the notion of 'participation' in the classical ethnographic technique of 'participant observation'. Much of the writings about the ethics and politics of ethnography have dealt with the relationship between the ethnographer and his or her research subjects (Davies, 1995: 94–5; Turner, 1990: 178). Questions about, for example, the authorship of ethnography and whether ethnographers can or even should aspire to understand their research subjects (empathy), mark the more fundamental question of difference.

The language of ethnography is the language of 'representation'. Representation refers to, at one and the same time, a social and a symbolic relationship. In the social sense, representation is generally associated with 'speaking for', as in political representation. Here the relationship between a delegate and his or her constituency is one in which the delegate takes the place of a larger collective. In the symbolic sense, representation also refers to 'standing in for' or 'taking the place of'. Most generally, this representation refers to the relationship between signs and referents as signs stand in for referents in symbolic practices. Crucial to any notion of representation is that of *presence*. Indeed, the essence of representation is the process of 'returning to presence'. The post-structuralist critique that prompted the linguistic turn was in fact a realization that all grounding, all structures, were contaminated by the tools (discourses) of their own 'construction'. The doubling of the problematics of speaking for (the universalizing subject) and standing-in (the Universal Subject), must always be taken together to understand that difference is always more than diversity. That is to say, what has been forgotten is the linguistic turn itself – namely the irreducibility of the sign to the referent; there always remains a difference that is not derived from an identity.

This other difference is Derrida's ([1972] 1982) 'concept' of *differance*: an amalgamation of the verbs to differ and to defer. Differance points to the impossibility of bringing phenomena into full presence; their presencing is always an event in which something escapes; a difference that is deferred, like the signified is always deferred because one signifier always slides into another (Sarup, 1989: 48–9). This is the tragedy of the structuralist quest for original grammar, the pure *langue* (like the unconscious) can never be revealed, for its existence depends on its absence. Derrida's post-structuralism is in effect a philosophy of contamination (as it refers to the impossibility of 'pure' meaning). This contamination is what we call history; and it is that which always escapes us. History is a trajectory of deviation, of structures that fail to accomplish a full closure of their arbitrariness (de Certeau, 1984). History is thus an ensemble of traces of transgressions; traces of violence (Derrida, [1967] 1978). These traces are what Derrida also refers to as 'writing' – the practice of inscription. Writing is a practice through which signifiers come into a form of being that is not 'presence' (as in speech). Writing is always meaning-deferred, a difference that escapes us.

It is with the notion of writing, or discursive practice, that we can see how cultural theory has effectively appropriated ethnography. Ethnography essentially refers to the writing (*graphe*) of others (*ethne*). This is evident in the anthropological fascination with (primitive) otherness as a point of difference from which we may begin to understand the fundamental unity (origin) of human being. Indeed, Derrida's philosophy of differance is nothing but a turn to ethnography – the writing of difference. Derrida's desire is not to uncover the true unity beneath the difference. His notion of difference (differance) is not the opposite of identity. It is not restrained by that mythological figure of representation: the reflection. It is not contained by Plato's cave; it neither refers to the Ideas, nor the Real Objects which cast their shadows on the wall (Derrida refers to this as 'the metaphysics of presence – Van Loon, 1996). Indeed, the difference emerges from those shadows; those strange absent–presents that corrupt the minds of the prisoners of the cave, yet make up their entire being-in-the-world (also see Deleuze, [1968] 1994).

Writing always presupposes differance. Inscription 'takes' place and it 'takes' time; the 'origin' of writing is therefore always deferred. At the same time, writing always presupposes an otherness that is suspended, preserved, deferred. Writing's otherness is that of becoming. Every writing engenders a trace; it can never bring itself into full presence. This becomes more clear if we simply take the example of a 'classic' ethnographic situation of the observer, observing the unfolding of an event. The bearing-witness of the event can only become part of ethnography if it is being written, inscribed into a text. The writing engenders a difference between the unfolding and its inscription. In ethnography, the event is always doubled – its taking place as unfolding is 're-enacted' in a taking place as inscription. The ethnographic event is always

deferred from our immediate presence; its presence is merely a trace inscribed by the writing of the event (Clifford, 1988).

Returning to ethnography the doubling of representation in social and symbolic terms constitutes two key questions: first, 'does the ethnographer adequately represent his/her subjects in writing?' and secondly, 'does his/her writing adequately represent that which is really happening?' In both cases, the central focus is on correspondence. However, such an ideal of correspondence suffers from a metaphysics of presence as it assumes that difference, be it that of research subjects or of the enfolding event, can be subordinated to the presence of writing. That is, to assume that adequate representation is merely a matter of correspondence is to forget that the ethnographer can never become his or her research subject, and that the unfolding event is never the same as its written inscription.

The point to make here is simply that ethnography cannot be anything else than a writing of difference; even if it claims to generate an adequate correspondence between ethnographer and research subjects, and between the reality of the event and its written representation. The fallacy of this claim of adequate correspondence, however, does pose some serious problems for those engaged in researching cultures of resistance; as there is often an assumed necessity of 'engagement'. If the ethnographer can never truly speak in the voice of his/her research subjects, then, it is often assumed, he is an impostor and a voyeur who merely appropriates his or her research subjects for his or her own career benefits. To argue that the claim to empathy is an impossible vanity is often seen as a direct assault on the political engagement of ethnography. Consequently, it has been easier to dismiss the post-structuralist critique and continue to engage with a politics of representation based on the ideal of correspondence, than to try to rework what ethnography might be otherwise.

The relationship between French and continental philosophy and Anglo-Saxon sociohistorical empiricism has never been a completely smooth one. One major cause for this is the reluctance of the latter to engage in philosophical debates. These are often regarded as irrelevant in the face of either 'the real world', or 'the real political issues' of the day. This real, however, could be easily replaced with the term 'urgent'. The call to arms against philosophy is often embroiled in a mobilization of a sense of urgency – an urgency to act, to declare, to represent, to render an account. This politics of speed runs counter to the temporization that is necessary to engage in philosophy and the cultivation of a sensibility guided by a desire to think rather than to act.

However, a politics of speed cannot be a major force in ethnography – speed runs counter to the ethos of ethnographic work which is to describe practices as they happen; in terms that are understood by or at least reflect the sensibilities of those engaged in those practices. Speed destroys a good ethnography. In haste, one overlooks the detail that is necessary for the cultivation of sensibility; speed inhibits the development of the necessary trust to establish genuine relationships between the participants in the ethnographic practice; speed de-activates what Paul Atkinson (1990) describes as the ethnographic imagination. Speed and urgency are the enemies of ethnography. Ethnography requires differance – a deferral of judgement – a differing of perspectives – and a patience to be surprised (Gray, 1997).

The Future of Ethnography in Cultural Research

In a recent article in the *European Journal of Cultural Studies*, Norman Denzin (1999) describes the uneasy relationship between cultural studies and mainstream sociology in North American academia. The main charges raised against cultural studies are that it has been done before and that it lacks academic rigour in the sense of having a clear methodology which is often equated with a 'realist ethnography'. This 'realist ethnography' is central to the long-standing ethnographic tradition in American sociology as, for example, embodied by the Chicago School, symbolic interactionism and – to some degree – ethnomethodology. The essence of this approach is that it imposes an ideal of correspondence between the unfolding of an event and its writing as a rendering of an account of the event. This does not mean that the advocates of realist ethnography believe that such a correspondence is actually possible, but merely that it is the ideal.

Against this perspective, Denzin argues that the quest for an ideal correspondence, even if under the acknowledgement of its impossibility, is not only futile, but also limiting more creative and theoretically informed encounters with the ways in which people actually make sense of the world in which they live. He argues that cultural studies has a lot to offer on these counts. It enables the researcher to remain attuned to the 'politics of everyday life'. The quest for facticity always engenders a depoliticization of the issues at stake because the situatedness of factual knowledge must, out of necessity, be forgotten. This relates particularly well to the previous sections which sketched some implications of the theoretical interventions in cultural studies by poststructuralism. The inherent hostility to positivism is given a more constructive and creative turning in the affirmation of difference, of reflexivity (Gray, 1997) and thus – we might add – of accountability. If ethnography is the writing of difference, and thereby takes place as a problematization of the representational, then the situatedness of the

ethnographer becomes affirmed as, rather than a limitation to, the formation of 'understanding' (Atkinson, 1990; also see Haraway, 1988). This 'understanding' is nothing but an active acknowledgement of and participation in the construction of 'sense' in everyday life settings. Lived experience is simply irreducible to the sociological categories that we may invoke to impose on them a 'structure of sense' that lies beyond the experience itself. Denzin argues that such an affirmative approach to difference always entails a reminder of the mediated character of lived experiences. These experiences are never 'present at hand', but always being enpresented. Citing Hall, Denzin argues that 'humans live in a second hand world of meanings and have no direct access to reality' (1999: 123).

However, apart from a strong defence of cultural studies against the charges offered by mainstream (cultural) sociology, Denzin also sketches some of the developments that are emerging from cultural studies towards the turn of the millennium. He argues that we are witnessing a turn towards a more performance-based cultural studies. This claim is linked to an argument he made in *The Cinematic Society* (1995). In the cinematic society everything is transformed into visual categories, that is, everything is being visualized as if being filmed. Moreover, the way in which we construct our sense of being in the world is equally structured cinematically, for example through particular narratives, often derived from or in conjunction with those of (Hollywood) films. Indeed, this has led to a commodification of souls in visual culture. As the cinematic links quite well to, for example, discipline and surveillance (including self-monitoring), but equally well to consumer culture, character-based identifications and narrative sequencing, we can furthermore see how 'sense' is not simply the produce of individuals as free-agents, but structured socially, culturally, economically, politically and technologically. This echoes Walter Benjamin (1973) who, in 'The Work of Art in an Age of Mechanical Reproduction', already argued that cinematic technology has irreversibly transformed our aesthetic experiences (including those of space and time) and thereby also the way in which we engage ourselves politically. A further extension of this could be found in the way in which telematics are currently transforming our sense of being-in-the-world, as well as the conditions under which we can engage ourselves 'politically'.

Like Benjamin, Denzin does not regress into nostalgic contemplation of a world that is no longer retrievable but senses that such transformations in our being-in-the-world engender new opportunities to engage with this world, and provide a better 'understanding' of the sense we make. He suggests that in order to understand people's sense of their own everyday experiences, we need to turn our attention to (a) the performative aspects of sense-making and (b) the auto/biographical aspects of our own involvement as 'ethnographers'. The emphasis on the performative resonates quite well with the work of Judith Butler (1993), whose theory of subjectivity offers a radical alternative to the psychoanalytic insistence on original myths such as the Oedipus complex. Moreover, Denzin argues that the performative affirms the constructedness of all sense, including that produced by the ethnographer's account.

> In the moment of performance, these [performance] texts have the possibility of overcoming the biases of an ocular, visual epistemology. They undo the voyeuristic, gazing eye of the ethnographer, bringing audiences and performers into an jointly felt and shared field of experience. These works unsettle the writer's place in the text, freeing the text and the writer to become interactional productions. (Denzin, 1999: 130)

This immediately relates to the emphasis on the auto/biographical.[2] The use of biographical and autobiographical research has, of course, a long-standing tradition in literature studies. Moreover, biography has already enjoyed a strong revival within the social sciences and humanities (e.g. Stanley, 1992). What is central here is a turn to the biographical as a writing of life stories – the revelation of the unfolding of selves through literary means. More specifically, the active affirmation of the writing process becomes visible in the 'auto' that becomes inseparable from the biographical. Through autobiography we can investigate the complex historiographies of the construction of self-hood as an intersection with our own reflections, thoughts and experiences (Steedman, 1997). Again it is obvious that the situatedness of knowledge is not seen as a limitation, but as a very productive point of departure. More importantly perhaps, Steedman shows that what is at stake in autobiography is not some romanticized turn towards the privilege of the inner perspective, but the way they index 'the historical relationship between stories – the circulation of particular narratives – and societies' (1997: 107). She refers to the way in which writing autobiographies is already a 'taught and learned' skill, particularly through education and particularly English teaching.

One of the best examples of how such autobiographical work may operate within a cultural studies approach, is a recent book by Jackie Stacey entitled *Teratologies*. It gives a fascinating account of the production of multiple embodied subjectivities in discourses of disease and (alternative) medicine. Theoretical accounts, based on, for example, a feminist critique of medicalization, theories of the body, self-discipline as well as a range of theories currently in vogue in and around alternative medicine, are intersected with deeply personal and intimate autobiographical reflections on her own experiences with cancer, its diagnosis, treatment and its aftermath.

Although at first sight, autobiography may seem the opposite of ethnography, as it refers to writing the self, rather than writing the other, it becomes obvious when reading Stacey's careful blending of her own experiences with more general cultural theoretical writing, that autobiography is very much a writing of difference. The difference here is that which Kristeva (1988) refers to as 'the strangers to ourselves' – the strangeness within. The diseased body can be read as an example of estrangement – a becoming other of the self. This estrangement, however, is simultaneously a self-disclosure. Through her painful experiences with cancer, and especially cancer treatment, Stacey is confronted with the alien-ness of her own body which is engendered in the alien-ness of discourses of medicalization as well as the 'holistic' metaphysics of 'alternative medicine'. Although she completely recovered, the 'end' is never a perfect reunion, an erasure of the difference embodied by the stranger within. The difference cannot be resolved; only rewritten.

Through Stacey's magnificent book, we can see how every autobiography is always an ethnography. This is not just an inversion of Clifford and Marcus' (1986) claim that every ethnography is also an autobiography. Self and other are not on equal territory here. Surely, every account of the other, of difference, must succumb to the homogenizing force of language, if it is to become meaningful; but this does not mean that the self-same is the starting point. It does not mean that we are locked to ourselves, chained to the walls of Plato's cave. We are always already incorporated into something larger than ourselves. The self is an accomplishment of the temporary differing-deferral (differance) of the otherness-within. The body is never simply there, it is made, practised and processed. This processing, the becoming-body, embodiment, is the work of ethnography. Autobiography is therefore a specific type of ethnography; an ethnography that is turned towards the becoming-self; an ethnography that is primarily concerned with the reflexive sensibility that informs all sense-making practices of being in the world.

Acknowledgements

I would like to thank Neal Curtis, the anonymous referees and the editors for their comments, suggestions and encouragement.

NOTES

1 See, for example, Alasuutari (1999: 91–108) and Horak (1999: 109–15) for the way in which cultural studies has been introduced in Finland and Germany/Austria respectively.

2 I use autobiography, testimony and life story as similar; see Gray, 1997: 100–3 for a clarification of their distinctions.

References

Alasuutari, P. (1995) *Researching Culture. Qualitative Method and Cultural Studies*. London: Sage.

Alasuutari, P. (1999) 'Cultural studies as a construct', *European Journal of Cultural Studies*, 2 (1): 91–108.

Althusser, L. (1971) *Lenin and Philosophy and Other Essays*. London: NLB.

Asad, T. (1986) 'The concept of cultural translation in British social anthropology', in J. Clifford and G. Marcus (eds), *Writing Culture: The Poetics and Politics of Ethnography*. Berkeley, CA: University of California Press. pp. 141–64.

Atkinson, P.A. (1990) *The Ethnographic Imagination: Textual Construction of Reality*. London: Routledge.

Barret, M. (1980) *Women's Oppression Today. The Marxist Feminist Encounter*. London: Verso.

Barthes, R. ([1957] 1993) *Mythologies*. London: Vintage.

Barthes, R. (1980) *The Pleasure of the Text*. Oxford: Blackwell.

Benjamin, W. (1973) 'The work of art in an age of mechanical reproduction', in *Illuminations*. (trans. H. Zohn). London: Fontana. pp. 219–53.

Bhabha, H. (1994) *The Location of Culture*. London: Routledge.

Butler, J. (1993) *Bodies that Matter. On the Discursive Limits of 'Sex'*. London: Routledge.

de Certeau, M. (1984) *The Practice of Everyday Life*. Berkeley, CA: University of California Press.

Chambers, I. (1994) *Migrancy, Culture, Identity*. London: Routledge.

Clifford, J. (1988) *The Predicament of Culture. Twentieth-Century Ethnography, Literature and Art*. Cambridge, MA: Harvard University Press.

Clifford, J. (1992) 'Traveling cultures', in L. Grossberg, C. Nelson and P. Treichler (eds), *Cultural Studies*. London: Routledge. pp. 96–112.

Clifford, J. and Marcus, G. (eds) (1986) *Writing Culture: The Poetics and Politics of Ethnography*. Berkeley, CA: University of California Press.

Cohen, P. ([1980] 1992) 'Subcultural conflict and working-class community', in S. Hall, S. Hobson, A. Lowe and P. Willis (eds), *Culture, Media, Language*. London: Routledge. pp. 78–87.

Coward, R. (1984) *Female Desire. Women's Sexuality Today*. London: Paladin.

Davies, I. (1995) *Cultural Studies and Beyond. Fragments of Empire*. London: Routledge.

Deleuze, G. ([1968] 1994) *Difference and Repetition*. London: Athlone.

Denzin, N.K. (1995) *The Cinematic Society*. London: Sage.

Denzin, N.K. (1999) 'From American sociology to cultural studies', *European Journal of Cultural Studies*, 2 (1): 117–36.

Derrida, J. ([1967] 1974) *Of Grammatology* (trans. G. Chakravorty Spivak). Baltimore, MD: Johns Hopkins University Press.

Derrida, J. ([1967] 1978) *Writing and Difference*. Chicago: University of Chicago Press.

Derrida, J. ([1972] 1982) *Margins of Philosophy* (trans. A. Bass). Hemel Hamsptead: Harvester Wheatsheaf.

Easthope, A. (1988) *British Post-Structuralism since 1968*. London: Routledge.

Fanon, F. (1986) *Black Skin White Masks*. London: Pluto Press.

Foucault, M. (1980) *Power/Knowledge. Selected Interviews and Other Writings 1972–1977*. New York: Pantheon.

Geertz, C. (1995) *After the Fact. Two Countries, Four Decades, One Anthropologist*. Cambridge, MA: Harvard University Press.

Goldberg, D.T. (1993) *Racist Culture. Philosophy and the Politics of Meaning*. Oxford: Blackwell.

Gray, A. (1997) 'Learning from experience: cultural studies and feminism', in J. McGuigan (ed.), *Cultural Methodologies*. London: Sage. pp. 87–105.

Hall, S. (1980) 'Cultural studies: two paradigms', *Media Culture and Society*, 2: 57–72.

Hall, S. ([1980] 1992) 'Encoding/decoding', in S. Hall, S. Hobson, A. Lowe and P. Willis (eds), *Culture, Media, Language*. London: Routledge. pp. 128–38.

Hall, S., Hobson, S., Lowe, A. and Willis, P. (eds) ([1980] 1992) *Culture, Media, Language*. London: Routledge.

Haraway, D. (1988) 'Situated knowledges: the science question in feminism and the privilege of partial perspective', *Feminist Studies*, 14 (3): 575–99.

Haraway, D. (1990) 'A manifesto for cyborgs: science, technology and socialist feminism in the 1980s', in L.J. Nicholson (ed.), *Feminism/Postmodernism*. New York: Routledge/Chapman and Hall. pp. 190–233.

Heath, S. (1975) 'Film and system: terms of analysis: Part 1', *Screen*, 16 (1): 7–77.

Hebdige, D. (1979) *Subculture: The Meaning of Style*. London: Methuen.

Horak, R. (1999) 'Cultural studies in Germany (and Austria): and why there is no such thing', *European Journal of Cultural Studies*, 2 (1): 109–15.

Inglis, F. (1993) *Cultural Studies*. Oxford: Blackwell.

Johnson, R. (1986/1987) 'What is cultural studies anyway?', *Social Text*, Winter: 38–80.

Kristeva, J. (1988) *Étrangers à nous-même*. Paris: Fayard.

Lacan, J. ([1973] 1977) *The Four Fundamental Concepts of Psychoanalysis*. Harmondsworth: Penguin.

McGuigan, J. (ed.) (1997) *Cultural Methodologies*. London: Sage.

Morley, D. ([1980] 1992) 'Texts, readers, subjects', in S. Hall, S. Hobson, A. Lowe and P. Willis (eds), *Culture, Media, Language*. London: Routledge. pp. 163–73.

Radway, J. (1987) *Reading the Romance. Women, Patriarchy, and Popular Literature*. London: Verso.

Rosaldo, R. (1986) 'From the door of his tent: the field-worker and the inquisitor', in J. Clifford and G. Marcus (eds), *Writing Culture: The Poetics and Politics of Ethnography*. Berkeley, CA: University of California Press. pp. 77–97.

Said, E. (1978) *Orientalism. Western Conceptions of the Orient*. London: Routledge and Kegan Paul.

Sarup, M. (1989) *An Introductory Guide to Post-structuralism and Postmodernism*. Athens, GA: University of Georgia Press.

Smith, D. ([1974] 1996) 'Women's perspective as a radical critique of sociology', in E. Fox Keller and H.E. Longin (eds), *Feminism and Science*. Oxford: Oxford University Press. pp. 17–27.

Spivak, G. (1988) *In Other Worlds. Essays in Cultural Politics*. London: Routledge.

Stacey, J. (1995) *Stargazing. Hollywood Cinema and Female Spectatorship*. London: Routledge.

Stacey, J. (1998) *Teratologies. A Cultural Study of Cancer*. London: Routledge.

Stanley, L. (1992) *The Auto/Biographical I*. Manchester: Manchester University Press.

Steedman, C. (1997) 'Writing the self: the end of the scholarship girl', in J. McGuigan (ed.), *Cultural Methodologies*. London: Sage. pp. 106–25.

Storey, J. (1993) *An Introductory Guide to Cultural Theory and Popular Culture*. Hemel Hempstead: Harvester Wheatsheaf.

Turner, G. (1990) *British Cultural Studies: An Introduction*. London: Routledge.

Tyler, S. (1986) 'Post-modern ethnography: from document of the occult to occult document', in J. Clifford and G. Marcus (eds), *Writing Culture: The Poetics and Politics of Ethnography*. Berkeley, CA: University of California Press. pp. 122–40.

Van Loon, J. (1996) 'A cultural exploration of time: some implications of temporality and mediation', *Time and Society*, 5 (1) 61–84.

Willis, P. (1977) *Learning to Labour. How Working Class Kids Get Working Class Jobs*. London: Saxon House.

Young, R. (1990) *White Mythologies. Writing History and the West*. London: Routledge.

20

The Ethnography of Communication

ELIZABETH KEATING

In the 1960s Dell Hymes, John Gumperz and their students launched an innovative program for researching language called the ethnography of speaking, later broadened to the ethnography of communication (see Gumperz and Hymes, 1964). The project was initiated and named with the publication of a 1962 paper by Hymes called 'The Ethnography of Speaking', in which Hymes proposed combining ethnography, the description and analysis of culture, with linguistics, the description and analysis of language. His idea was that such a synthesis would elucidate important relationships between language and culture. The program was innovative for a number of reasons. For the first time a non-linguistic unit, the speech event, was used as the basis for the analysis and interpretation of language. Actual language use was to be the focus of research and particular importance was paid to matters of context of use. Culturally defined categories or native taxonomies of ways of speaking were acknowledged as important tools in the analysis of talk, and the approach was cross-disciplinary.

Hymes' and Gumperz's conception of an ethnography of speaking was in part a response to Chomskian linguistics, which had shifted linguistics radically from its anthropologically oriented antecedents.[1] In the 1960s linguists began to organize departments of linguistics in American universities, a development linked both to the view that syntax should be at the core of any study of language as well as a demand for the autonomy of linguistics from its previous academic environments – humanistic literary traditions and behaviorist psychology (Ochs et al., 1996: 2). The study of language in the new linguistics departments was conceived as independent of culture, pragmatics or issues of context. The focus was on 'an ideal speaker–listener, in a completely homogeneous speech-community' (Chomsky, 1965). Hymes encouraged linguists to expand on Chomsky's introspective methodology and 'move outward into the exploration of speech behavior and use' (1962: 193), but linguistics departments and anthropology departments continued on separate paths. Within anthropology, linguistics lost its former authority (Boas had shaped American anthropology as a study of culture through language, and linguistics had provided influential structuralist paradigms) and became the least represented among the four American sub-fields (physical, cultural, archaeology and linguistics).[2] Hymes sought to re-synthesize the two fields.

Hymes' ethnography of speaking framework promoted the description of the 'many different ways of speaking which exist in the community' (Sherzer and Darnell, 1972). The term 'speaking' in ethnography of speaking was used to differentiate his project from the static notion of 'language' as it had been conceived by structural linguistics. Later broadened to the ethnography of communication, this approach included a reinvisioning of the nature of meaning from an emphasis on the truth value[3] of utterances, a focus of linguists, to a conception of meaning dependent on shared beliefs and values of a community and dependent on social and cultural context. The study of language to Hymes was the 'use of the linguistic code(s) in the conduct of social life' (Duranti, 1988: 212). Chomsky had also moved towards the study of meaning (which had not been a focus of Bloomfield, his influential predecessor), but from an entirely different vantage point.[4]

The ethnography of communication was thus a new form of language research, but had important roots in a number of traditions, both European and American. It was highly influenced by the anthropological tradition of ethnography and cross-cultural comparison, for example, Malinowski's notion of context as fundamental in understanding speech. Firth's situational approach to language and call for linguistically centered social analysis (1957) is also relevant here. Emerging at the same time as the ideas of Gumperz and Hymes (to study communication ethnographically) were a number of other influential frameworks for studying the nature of meaning and culture, for example Turner's ideas about communitas and ritual and Geertz's ideas about ethnographic practice, also other work in symbolic and cognitive anthropology. Hymes' program of comparative language ethnography aimed to claim a place in anthropology and to redress a lack – the fact that there were no books devoted to the cross-cultural study of speaking 'to put beside those on comparative religion, comparative politics and the like' (Hymes, 1972b: 50). The ethnography of speaking was influenced by what Hymes called anthropology's 'traditional scientific role' (Hymes, 1972b) – the testing of universality and empirical adequacy, actually 'a blend of scientific and humanistic approaches' (Saville-Troike, 1982: 177). Hymes' call for cross-cultural comparative work on communicative practices was also influenced by traditional anthropological concerns with the evolution of society: 'mankind cannot be understood apart form the evolution and maintenance of its ethnographic diversity' (Hymes, 1972b: 41).

In addition to anthropology, the ethnography of speaking was influenced by linguistics, not only as a response to Chomsky but because of an interest in language forms as well as a strong precedence for links between anthropological and linguistic enquiry in the American tradition. Boas had made linguistics essential to anthropological investigation, a necessary part of understanding human cognitive strategies as well as social life (Boas, 1911). His student Sapir closely investigated the principle that grammatical categories both reflect and construct local ways of thinking about and acting in the world. Labov's (1972c) work demonstrated innovative ways to study differences in language use. Gumperz and Hymes and their students continued these trajectories but also introduced the ethnography of speaking as a new form of linguistic enquiry: turning from an investigation of language as a referential[5] code, to an investigation into social meaning, diversity of practices, and actual language use in context. Emphasis was on exchanges of talk between speakers rather than the elicitation of grammatical structures by interviewing native speakers, or the structural analysis of myth. Hymes was as interested as linguists in identifying universal patterns, but he characterized his approach as essentially different from the leading linguistic thought of the time: 'Chomsky's type of explanatory adequacy leads away from speech, and from

languages, to relationships possibly universal to all languages, and possibly inherent in human nature. The complementary type of explanatory adequacy leads from what is common to all human beings and all languages toward what particular communities and persons have made of their means of speech' (Hymes, 1974: 203). This characterization of moving from the general to the particular accurately characterizes the majority of the work done in the ethnography of communication approach.

The ethnography of communication has roots not only in the practice of linguistics in America, but in Europe as well. Drawing on ideas developed by the Prague school of linguistics, particularly some of Jakobson's formalizations of enquiry (Jakobson, 1960), ethnographers of communication focus on relationships between form and content as consequential to meaning, for example, how poetic patterns can create semantic relations (see, for example, Fox, 1974; Sherzer, 1983; Sherzer and Urban, 1986; Tedlock, 1972, 1983).

Other important influences on the development of the ethnography of speaking include sociolinguistic methods of inferring patterns of variation on the basis of controlled sampling (see, for example, Labov, 1972b, 1972c; Sankoff, 1974), and Austin's ideas about speech as action (Austin, 1962). Developments in folklore studies have influenced and been influenced by the ethnography of speaking, especially in theorizing cultural practices as emergent performances (see Paredes and Bauman, 1972).[6] Concurrent developments in sociology complemented Hymes' focus on the description of language in real situations. Goffman (1961, 1963, 1971) had begun to study the organization of conduct, including talk,[7] in face-to-face interaction with methods that were both anthropological and influenced by social psychology. Garfinkel introduced the concept of ethnomethodology (Garfinkel, 1967), the study of the 'mundane' knowledge and reasoning procedures used by ordinary members of society, which then made possible the field of conversation analysis, the study of structures of talk (see, for example, Sacks et al., 1974; Schegloff, 1968). These concurrent developments in sociology were represented in the 1964 special issue of the *American Anthropologist* in which the Ethnography of Communication was introduced to a wide anthropological audience, and the influential 1972 volume by Gumperz and Hymes, *Directions in Sociolinguistics: The Ethnography of Communication*. The inclusion of these papers indicates the strong affinity between these various approaches (Bauman and Sherzer, 1975: 101).

Hymes' and Gumperz's basic aim then was to merge ethnographic and linguistic approaches as fully as possible and to describe language in its social settings (Hanks, 1996: 188). Hymes felt that traditional descriptions of language had been limited to only a portion of the complexity of human communicative practice. His goal, however, was to inspire anthropologists to theorize about the interaction of language with social life, to define 'some universal dimensions of speaking' and propose 'explanation within social theory of certain constellations of them' (Hymes, 1972b: 49). Language was defined broadly to include all forms of speech, writing, song, speech-derived whistling, drumming, horn calling, gesturing, etc. A general theory of the interaction of language and social life would encompass the multiple relations between linguistic means and social meaning (Hymes, 1972b: 39). Adequate theory-building could only be accomplished by drawing on extant theoretical contributions from 'all the fields that deal with speech', including such fields as rhetoric and literary criticism (1972b: 51). In addition, descriptive analyses from a variety of communities utilizing a mode jointly ethnographic and linguistic were needed before such a general theory of the interaction of language and social life could be developed. The understanding of ways of speaking necessitated a complete inventory of a community's speech practices. The first steps toward an ethnography of speaking were classificatory: 'we need taxonomies of speaking and descriptions adequate to support and test them' (Hymes, 1972b: 43).[8] The call for descriptive studies in the new research paradigm was answered by a number of scholars and led to a profusion of new and stimulating research to be discussed further below.

New methodologies to study the social uses of speech were devised when it was recognized that those developed to study the referential uses of speech would not be appropriate. Neither linguists nor anthropologists had generated adequate units of description for speech use and an outline of a new methodology was formulated in an important paper by Sherzer and Darnell (1972). Hymes advocated the use of Jakobson's framework of paradigmatic and syntagmatic relations (Jakobson and Halle, 1956), as well as Jakobson's notion of the speech event as primary tools necessary to do an ethnography of speaking in various societies.

COMMUNICATIVE COMPETENCE

An ethnography of speaking is centrally concerned with 'communicative competence' (Hymes, 1972c), what speakers need to know to communicate appropriately in a particular speech community, and how this competence is acquired. Competence includes rules pertaining to language structure and language use as well as cultural knowledge – for example, which participants may or may not speak in certain settings, which contexts are appropriate for speech and which for silence, what types of talk are appropriate to persons of different statuses and roles,

norms for requesting and giving information (of particular concern to ethnographers), for making other requests, offers, declinations, commands, the use of non-verbal behaviors in various contexts, practices for alternating between speakers, for constructing authority, etc. This focus on the skills members of a community display when communicating with each other entails a broader notion of competence than linguists advocated. Hymes included communicative as well as grammatical competence in conditions of appropriate speech use, embracing aspects of communication such as gestures and eye-gaze, whereas Chomsky cautioned that to incorporate aspects such as beliefs and attitudes into a study of language would mean that 'language is chaos that is not worth studying' (Chomsky, 1977: 153).

> We have ... to account for the fact that a normal child acquires knowledge of sentences, not only as grammatical, but also as appropriate. He or she acquires competence as to when to speak, when not, and as to what to talk about with whom, when, where, in what manner. In short, a child becomes able to accomplish a repertoire of speech acts, to take part in speech events, and to evaluate their accomplishment by others. This competence, moreover, is integral with attitudes, values, and motivations concerning language, its features and uses, and integral with competence for, and attitudes toward, the interrelation of language, with the other codes of communicative conduct. (Hymes, 1972c: 277–8)

The study of communicative competence includes describing and analysing contexts and situations where it is appropriate to sound incompetent in a language. Examples of this are in Burundi, where people are expected to speak in a hesitating and inept manner to those of higher rank, but to speak fluently to peers or those of lower rank (Albert, 1972). In Wolof, conversely, certain incorrectness in speech is expected of the high nobles (Irvine, 1974). Describing what is 'appropriate' communication in certain contexts in particular societies can contribute legitimacy to power relations which are expressed through such organization of linguistic forms and the ethnographer must be aware of his or her role in this process (Fairclough, 1989: 8). More recent work by those looking at situated language addresses not only local ideas of appropriate language use but how these ideas can be used as means to legitimate or delegitimate language practices of certain members of society.

UNITS OF ANALYSIS

One of the most important contributions of the ethnography of speaking approach involved the introduction of new units of analysis. Gumperz and Hymes (1964) extended the boundaries of linguistic enquiry to units such as speech event, speech situation and speech community, and looked at the relation of these units to other components of speech use (Sherzer and Darnell, 1972: 550) as well as aspects of culture.

> People who enact different cultures do to some extent experience distinct communicative systems, not merely the same natural communicative condition with different customs affixed. Cultural values and benefits are in part constitutive of linguistic relativity. (Hymes, 1966: 116)

The ethnography of speaking as conceptualized by Hymes utilizes Pike's paradigm[9] of etic and emic analysis (Pike, 1954) as a way of talking about the general and particular goals of an ethnography of communication. An emic account is the ultimate goal, that is, the identification of categories which are meaningful to members of the community. The etic perspective, categories meaningful to the analyst, is considered useful for initial data gathering as well as for cross-cultural comparison. The two perspectives, etic and emic, are seen as interrelated. A sensitivity to native speaker categories is held to be congruent with the categories organized in Hymes' research model, which he introduced with the mnemonically ordered term 'SPEAKING', where each letter represents a component of the paradigm (to be discussed below).

Isolating taxonomic categories and the dimensions and features underlying them is an essential part of the methodology. Hymes thought categories would be found to be universal and 'hence elementary to descriptive and comparative frames of reference' (1972b: 49). He gave examples of ways taxonomies could be used in cross-cultural comparison, for example speech settings could be compared (Blom and Gumperz, 1972), or languages could be compared in terms of features like quantity of talk considered ideal. Ways of speaking could be characterized and contrasted using terms like voluble or reserved. An example is J. Fischer's (1972) study of two related Micronesian languages, Pohnpeian (formerly Ponapean) and Chuukese (formerly Trukese). Fischer posits a relationship between linguistic form and social structure, characterizing Pohnpeians as valuing conciseness and emotional restraint and Chuukese in contrast valuing loquacity and a greater show of emotion. He argues that this dichotomy extends to speech styles, leading to less 'forceful' consonant clusters in Pohnpeian, as opposed to Chuukese. Hymes justified dichotomies as necessary for the establishment of elementary categories. However, some of the difficulties of cross-culturally relevant classification, comparison and generalization can be seen in the Pohnpeian example. For instance, discourses about the nature of emotion in Micronesia have been shown to be saliently different from Western ideas about emotion (Lutz, 1988), and Pohnpeians do not always

value conciseness in the transmission of information, but often engage in strategies of concealment (Keating, 1998; Peterson, 1993). The taxonomic enterprise within the ethnography of communication has clear roots in linguistics as well as aspects of anthropology, but together with the notion of cross-cultural comparison and generalization has recently been the subject of extensive criticism within anthropology (see, for example, Marcus and Fischer, 1986). Indeed, the ways of speaking about and constructing 'difference' between groups of people and between investigator and investigated have altered dramatically. The relationship between the researcher's norms and the norms of the system they are analysing is now considered a subject worthy of study by anthropologists (see, for example, Ochs and Schieffelin, 1984) and can add a new level of understanding of the relationships between discourses and culture.

SPEECH COMMUNITIES

Hymes used the term speech community as an important beginning unit of analysis in an ethnography of communication, and considered this a social rather than a linguistic entity. Few other terms in linguistic anthropology or sociolinguistics have undergone such a sustained critique, pointing both to the complexity of characterizing everyday speech practice and to the pitfalls of generalizations about 'shared' communicative competence. Most criticisms of the term 'speech community' stem not from the initial formulation of the idea, but rather from the realization of the idea in ethnographic and sociolinguistic work. Even though the definition of speech community Hymes assumes is one based on the premise that all speech communities are linguistically and socially diverse, the actual realization of the notion in ethnographies of speaking has more often than not amplified what is shared and neglected what is not[10] (a notable exception is some gender and language studies). Descriptions have focused, for example, on the common aspects of a speech community through the notions of communicative repertoire, speech event, speech act, shared language attitudes etc. The speech community is analytically more imagined than real, more unified than diverse (see Pratt, 1987; Romaine, 1982; Walters, 1996a for an extended discussion of the criticisms of the notion of speech community).

Without necessarily addressing some of the problems within the taxonomy of the ethnography of speaking itself, Hymes is clear that a speech community is not homogeneous. Not only is no community limited to a single way of speaking, but sharing the same language does not necessarily mean sharing the same understandings of its use and meanings in various contexts (Hymes, 1972a, 1972b). As

Ervin-Tripp shows in her work on sociolinguistic rules (1972: 223), having a language in common does not necessarily entail a common set of sociolinguistic rules (see, for example, Mitchell-Kernan, 1972; Morgan, 1996, 1998, for examples in African American English). In spite of the tendency to reify the idea of conformity, the notion of the speech community, constructed through frequency of social interaction and communication patterns (Bauman and Sherzer, 1975: 113), is felt by many to be indispensable as a starting point for analysis (see for example, Romaine, 1982).

COMMUNICATIVE REPERTOIRE

Each speech community is recognized to have a repertoire (Gumperz, 1964) of language codes and ways of speaking, including 'all varieties, dialects, or styles used in a particular socially defined population, and the constraints which govern the choice among them' (Gumperz, 1977). An ethnography of communication is concerned with the totality of this linguistic repertoire or patterned ways of speaking, and an explication of relationships between speech systems and other aspects of culture. Identifying and recording this repertoire through observation of communicative behaviors and consultation with members of the community is an important part of an ethnography of speaking, as well as documenting contexts and appropriateness of use. Strategies of communication are recognized to index certain social features such as status, setting and relationships between members. Non-verbal behavior, for example, is an important communicative resource for indicating status as well as affect and stance. It is recognized that individuals' command of the communicative repertoire varies.

Some of the most interesting work on the analysis of repertoire has been on code-switching and style-shifting, for example, Gumperz's work (e.g. 1982; see also Auer, 1998). Code-switching refers to speakers' shifts in languages or language varieties within a single speech event. Style-shifting refers to shifts in features associated with social attributes such as age, gender, class and contextual aspects such as formality or informality. Code-switching has been shown to co-occur with changes in topic, participants, a redefinition of the situation, and can be used to mark features of identity between participants (Blom and Gumperz, 1972).

Studying the communicative repertoire involves looking through a framework of three other units of analysis suggested by Hymes (1972b): speech situation, speech event and speech act. Originally Hymes formulated a difference between 'events' that would be impossible to conduct without speech (for example, a telephone conversation or a lecture) and 'situations' where speech plays a minor role, and where speech does not define the event (for example, fishing or making clothes, hunts, meals). Speech events are governed by rules and norms for the use of speech, but speech situations are not governed by one set of rules. This dichotomy between event and situation has not proved to be a useful one, and speech event has emerged as a more general term (Bauman and Sherzer, 1975: 109) for characterizing the point of interest for ethnographers of speaking. Work in conversation analysis (e.g. Sacks et al., 1974) has shown that so-called ordinary conversation is in fact highly structured (event-like) and aspects of conversation are highly ritualized (for example, greetings and leave-takings), making the original distinction less justifiable. Most of the work in the ethnography of speaking framework has focused on formal or ritual speech (speech events according to Hymes' definition).

SPEECH EVENTS OR COMMUNICATIVE EVENTS

The focus on speech event has emerged as one of the most important contributions of ethnographers of speaking in the analysis of speech habits of communities. It is to the analysis of verbal interaction 'what the sentence is to grammar' (Gumperz, 1972: 16–17). An expansion of the analytical unit to the speech event actually goes beyond the sentence and is a shift from an emphasis on text or an individual speaker to an emphasis on interaction, and this is a significant departure from traditional analyses of language.

The analysis of speech events largely focuses on sequences that are conceived of as distinct from 'everyday' talk. Speech events are categorized as the type of sequences members of societies recognize as routines, are usually named, and are shaped by special rules of language and non-verbal behaviors. Examples are ceremonial events, such as those surrounding marriages or births, and the telling of jokes. Switching languages or language varieties or styles sometimes distinguishes between types of speech events. For example, as part of the constitution of a marriage ceremony certain words are spoken by certain participants. This is in addition to other components which construct the ceremony, such as spatial relationships among participants. What is of interest to ethnographers of speaking is how speakers use various linguistic resources and how others make sense of or interpret these choices.

Speech events are recognized to be embedded within other speech events and can be discontinuous, for example if someone is interrupted during a meeting by a telephone call. An important part of any ethnography of speaking is discovering not only the range of speech events, but attitudes toward different speech events; prior to the 1970s there existed almost no systematic information on attitudes toward speech (Gumperz and Hymes, 1972: 36). The Ashanti of Nigeria consider infants' vocalizations to be a special language, interpretable only by men with certain guardian spirits. Thus according to local language ideology adult language is each person's second language (Hymes, 1972b: 39). Speakers of Malagasy do not believe speech should necessarily meet the informational needs of the listener (Keenan, 1974). Similarly, Pohnpeian speakers execute a disclaimer before or after telling historical narratives; the formulaic phrase attests that they have purposely 'twisted' the narrative, and it is up to each listener to set it straight (Keating, 1998).

Local taxonomies of speech events are important, though not all types of talk are named. For the Yakan of the Philippines, for example, native categories include *mitin* 'discussion', *qisun* 'conference', *mawpakkat* 'negotiation' and *hukum* 'litigation' (Frake, 1969). Melpa speakers in New Guinea categorize types of oratory as *el-ik* 'arrow talk' or 'war talk', *ik ek* 'veiled speech' or 'talk which is bent over and folded', and *ik kwun* 'talk which is straight' (Strathern, 1975), the Kuna of Panama recognize three basic patterns in speech events *namakke* (chanting), *sunmakke* (speaking) and *kormakke* (shouting) (Sherzer, 1974).

SPEECH ACT OR COMMUNICATIVE ACT

Speech events are composed of speech acts, which mediate between grammar and the rest of a speech event or situation. Communicative acts are embedded in larger units such as genres and discourse structures. The notion of speech act, the theory that words perform actions in the world, was borrowed from Austin (1962), but expanded. An ethnography of communication entails a broader notion of context than Speech Act Theory, and a broader range of acts than speech, including gesture and paralinguistic communication. A communicative act in the ethnography of communication tradition is usually taken to have one interactional function, for example, a request or a command (but see Schegloff, 1984 on the many 'jobs' questions can do interactionally).

Research in the ethnography of speaking framework has resulted in important discussions of the relationship between the notion of speech act as first proposed by Austin and culturally diverse theories of communication and interpretation. Local notions of self, strategies of interpretation, speakers' ability to control interpretation, the relevance of 'sincerity', intentionality and the organization of responsibility for interpretation all have implications for the nature of speech acts cross-culturally (Duranti, 1988: 222; see also Hill and Irvine, 1993). (For an application of Austin's theory of speech

acts in an ethnography of speaking see Duranti, 1997: 227–44; Foster, 1974; Rosaldo, 1973.)

COMPONENTS OF SPEECH: THE SPEAKING MODEL

In order to organize the collection of data about speech events and speech acts in numerous societies with an eye towards cross-cultural comparison, Hymes formulated a preliminary list of features or components of these events to be described. The list was intended to be a 'useful guide' (Hymes, 1964) towards identifying components of speech considered to be universal. Eight particular components of events were chosen based on Hymes' study of ethnographic material. The model is also based on Jakobson's (1960) paradigm of six factors or components in any speech event: addresser, addressee, message, contact, context and code, each of which corresponds to a different function of language: emotive, conative, poetic, phatic, referential and metalingual.[11] Hymes' model includes the following dimensions, which he formulated as the 'mnemonically convenient' (Hymes, 1972b: 59) title 'SPEAKING', where each letter in the word 'speaking' represents one or more important components of an ethnography of speaking. The features of the list can be grouped generally into a concern with describing setting (time and place, physical circumstances) and scene (psychological setting), purposes (functions and goals), speech styles and genres, and participants (including speaker, addressor, hearer, addressee), as well as the interrelationships among them. The SPEAKING model is an etic scheme but meant to be made relevant to individual societies and eventually result in an emic description that prioritizes what is relevant to the local participants. The goal of this descriptive tool is to force attention to structure and reveal similarities and differences between events and between ways of organizing speaking. From the investigative categories represented in the model, Hymes proposed ethnographers would develop a universal set of features that could easily be compared in order to learn about differences such as important relationships between rules of speaking and setting, participants and topic, and begin to define the relationships between language and sociocultural contexts.

The components of the SPEAKING model – **s**etting, **p**articipants, **e**nds, **a**ct sequences, **k**ey, **i**nstrumentalities, **n**orms and **g**enres – are discussed in turn.

Setting Aspects of setting to be described in an ethnography of communication include temporal and spatial aspects of speech – time of day, season, location, spatial features – and includes the social valuing of these aspects of setting. An ethnographer asks: how do individuals organize themselves temporally and spatially in an event? Frake's discussion of the Yakan house in the Philippines is emblematic of some of the culture-specific complexities of spatial and temporal arrangements. He shows that a house, even a one-roomed Yakan house, is not just a space, but a structured sequence of settings where social events are differentiated not only by the position in which they occur but also by the positions the actors move through and the manner in which they have made those moves (1975: 37). In some cultures it is common to find different settings for many kinds of speech events – rooms for classes, structures for religious observances, buildings for litigation, entertainment, etc.

Participants The composition of the social group participating in different speech events is part of an ethnography of speaking. Aspects to be described include, for example, age, ethnicity, gender, relationships of persons to each other. Hymes expands the traditional speaker–hearer dyad to four categories of participants: speaker, addressor, hearer and addressee.

Ends An ethnography of communication includes descriptions of the purposes of the speech event, such as outcomes and goals. As Hymes states: 'communication itself must be differentiated from interaction as a whole in terms of purposiveness' (1972b: 62). Ends are differentiated from personal motivations of social actors in a speech event, which can be quite varied. What Hymes has in mind are the 'conventionally expected or ascribed' outcomes, important because rules for participants and settings can vary according to these aspects (see also Levinson, 1979 on goals and social activities).

Act sequences According to Hymes (1972b) this term refers to the way message form and content interdependently contribute to meaning, or '*how* something is said is part of *what* is said' (1972b: 59, emphasis in original). Act sequences can include silence, co-participants' collaborative or supportive talk, laughter, gesture, as well as restrictions on co-occurrence of speech elements (Ervin-Tripp, 1969: 72). Irvine (1974) and Salmond (1974) discuss how act sequences are related and negotiated among participants. Saville-Troike (1982) and Duranti (1985) interpret act sequences to refer to sequential aspects of communicative events, and as separate from form and content.

Key This refers to the tone, manner or spirit in which a speech act is performed, or the emotional tone of the speech event, indicated by choice of language or language variety, gesture or paralinguistic cues such as intonation, laughter, crying. Acts which are similar in terms of setting, participants and message form can differ in terms of key, for example mock vs. serious (Hymes, 1972b: 62). Key signals can be simple or complex; complex types tend to occur at the boundaries of events (Duranti, 1985: 216).

Instrumentalities This term also relates to message form, but on a larger scale than act sequences. It refers to form in terms of language varieties, codes, or registers. Instrumentalities includes 'channels' (Hymes, 1972b: 62), media of transmission, such as oral, written, or gestural. Two important goals of recording instrumentalities, according to Hymes, are descriptions of their interdependence and the 'relative hierarchy among them' (1972b: 63).

Norms This aspect is divided into norms of interaction and norms of interpretation and concerns shared understandings. Examples of community norms are whether it is appropriate to interrupt or not, the allocation of speaking turns, etc. The full description of norms necessitates an analysis of social structure and social relationships (Hymes, 1972b: 64). The question of 'norms' has proven to be problematic in sociolinguistic studies (particularly studies of 'gendered' language behavior), where one group is posited as the norm and others are evaluated against this framework.

Genres Genre refers to categories such as poem, tale, riddle, letter, as well as attitudes about these genres. Although genres often coincide with speech events, Hymes conceives them as analytically independent.

Hymes felt a great deal of empirical work was needed to clarify interrelations between these eight components. Attention to the emergent and unique properties of individual speech events is also important (Bauman and Sherzer, 1975: 111). Sherzer (1983), in what has been called the first full-scale ethnography of speaking (Urban, 1991), describes the complex set of sociolinguistic resources of the Kuna of Panama, including not only grammar, but styles, terms of reference and address, lexical relationships, the musical patterns and shapes of chanted speech, and the gestures accompanying speech. He discusses the unique set of speech acts and events associated with three forms of ritual: politics, curing and magic, and puberty rites. Everyday forms of talk are also described, for example, greetings, conversation, gossip. Ways of speaking are related to larger issues such as the nature of verbal art and performance in non-literate societies, the search for universal features of language use, the role of speech among American Indians, the relationships between ritual and everyday forms of speech as well as relationships between speech and other socio-cultural patterns found in a society.

FIELD RESEARCH

Tasks for ethnographers of speaking include working with an increasingly complex notion of what a speech community is, identifying recurrent communicative events and their components, including everyday events across a range of speakers, as well as relationships between such events and other aspects of the society, describing attitudes and ideas about language use, the acquisition of competence in communicative events, and linking the use of language with the constitution of society. Fieldwork involves observing and participating in speech events and other activities, asking questions, interviewing, as well as more recently video and audio recording speech events.[12] Videotaping and audiotaping are important strategies in describing contexts of use of varieties of communicative behaviors, since speakers often have a limited awareness (Silverstein, 1981) of their language habits. At the same time, consulting with native speakers about the recorded speech data can clarify important points about what features of context are salient for understanding the repertoire (see Goodwin, 1993 for an excellent guide to videotaping interaction).

A precise and focused guide on exactly how to proceed in the ethnographic study of speech use is provided in Sherzer and Darnell (1972). The guide lists questions to be asked by ethnographers interested in speech behavior and is designed with Hymes' idea in mind – to document the range of cross-cultural variability in the use of speech. The research questions were originally formulated on the basis of a study of seventy-five societies designed to serve both as a rough guideline and stimulus for fieldwork. Five areas are delineated: analysis of the social uses of speech, attitudes toward the use of speech, acquisition of speaking competence, the use of speech in education and social control, and typological generalizations. In the case of the acquisition of speaking competence, questions deal with issues such as native theories of language acquisition, interpretation of infant utterances and transmission of communicative skills. A field manual by Slobin (1967) also proposes relevant research questions for the study of language use.

Saville Troike (1982: 117) considers the following data part of a complete ethnography of communication: (a) background information on the speech community, including history, topographical and population features, patterns of movement, employment, religious practices, educational practices; (b) material artifacts, including written means of communication, radios, drums, etc; (c) information about social organization, including formal and informal organizations, association patterns, power relations, etc; (d) legal information, that is, practices of social control, particularly about language use; (e) common knowledge or unstated presuppositions about the interpretation of language and language habits; (f) beliefs about language use, including attitudes towards speech the types of entities considered appropriate speech participants; and (g) data on the linguistic code, including paralinguistic and non-verbal features. Hymes (1970) recommends a pretest before attempting a large-scale data collection, including an exploration of who can be interviewed, how people within a community exchange information, and what forms of questions are appropriate.

Data collection methods such as participant observation, interviewing, videotaping and audiotaping are not without shortcomings. Briggs (1986) has focused on some problems with the speech event of interviewing which is not considered an appropriate way to communicate information in many cultures. (See also Duranti, 1997 for a discussion of videotaping as one of the technologies for capturing aspects of communicative encounters that are often ignored or misinterpreted.)

ETHNOGRAPHIES OF SPEAKING

It is impossible to describe here all the important and ground-breaking work done in the ethnography of communication, so I will mention some representative studies and direct the reader to collections by Gumperz and Hymes (1964, 1972), Bauman and Sherzer (1974, 1975), Baugh and Sherzer (1984), Giglioli (1972), Blount (1974), as well as work described in Saville-Troike (1982). Philipsen and Carbaugh (1986) have compiled a bibliography of over 200 studies conducted within the paradigm. Many descriptions and analyses of individual communicative events in diverse communities have appeared.

Some of the most important early work using the ethnography of communication framework looked at classroom interactions between teachers and students. The approach was used productively to address educators' concern with the failure of minority children to achieve in school settings (Cazden et al., 1972; Green and Wallat, 1981; Gumperz, 1981). Ethnographic investigations were conducted of various groups of school children in interactions with teachers who had been trained in the EuroAmerican tradition of schooling, with its attendant culture-specific patterns for organizing knowledge and measuring learning. Classrooms were studied in order to understand how children with different culturally acquired language patterns for expert–novice interactions could be disadvantaged or misinterpreted within the dominant white, middle-class framework. Ethnographers examined classrooms of African American children (Heath, 1983; Kochman, 1972; Labov, 1972c; Michaels, 1981), Native American children (e.g. Cazden and John, 1972; Philips, 1983), Hawaiian children (Au, 1980; Boggs, 1972), rural Appalachian white children (Heath, 1983) and working-class British children (Bernstein, 1964). Some studies combined the ethnography of speaking methods with those developed by conversation analysts (e.g. Gumperz and Herasimchuck, 1973). In an important study Heath (1982) analyses correlations between the organization of language events at home and children's performance in 'literacy events' at school. More recently Street (1995) builds on this work but broadens the notion of literacy as a situated social practice and discusses the multiple character of literacy practices (see also Besnier, 1988; Schieffelin and Gilmore, 1986).

Scholars working in the ethnography of speaking framework have focused on the description of linguistic resources, the analysis of particular speech events and the role of speech in specific areas of social and cultural life (Sherzer, 1983: 12). There have been a number of key concerns: systems and functions of communication, the nature and definition of speech community, aspects of communicative competence, relationships of language to world-view and social relations, language attitudes, and linguistic and social universals. The following list is by no means comprehensive, but shows the range of studies and topics. Work in this tradition includes, for example, Basso's investigation of patterns of language and attitudes towards language use among the Western Apache, encompassing the importance of silence in situations where social relations are uncertain (K. Basso, 1970: 227, 1988) as well as Philips' (1983) description of speech patterns and attitudes at the Warm Springs Indian Reservation in Oregon. In other work, Gossen comprehensively describes a rich array of Chamula ways of speaking and identifies a central metaphor used to organize concepts of speech (1972, 1974), Stross discusses some 416 terms for speaking in Tzeltal (1974), Reisman (1974) describes speech routines in Antigua. Jackson critically engages the notion of speech community with a description of language and identity among the Vaupes in Columbia (1974). Friedrich describes important implications of historical Russian pronoun shifts used to index social meanings (1972, 1979), Kirshenblatt-Gimblett links narrative and social relations in specific contexts (1975), Blom and Gumperz (1972) look at the interrelationship of cultural values and language rules in Norway, Albert among the Burundi (1972), and Hill and Hill (1978) investigate the use of honorifics in Nuahtl. Bauman discusses historic language practices and attitudes among Quakers (1974), and shows how verbal art should be studied as emergent within a specific

context, as a form of practice, rather than as a continually recounted text (1977, 1986). Fox (1974) describes and analyses the role of oral poetry based on couplets in Roti in Indonesia; Bricker (1974) similarly discusses couplet poetry among the Maya, Tedlock (1972, 1983) analyses verbal art among the Zuni. Haviland (1977) looks at gossip in Zincantan, Gal (1978) at language change and its relationship to gender in Austria, the Scollons (1979) at linguistic convergence at Fort Chipewyan, Alberta. Walters (1996a, 1996b) shows that shared and contested variables of language are important in Tunisia.

Ochs and Schieffelin (1984), Ferguson (1964) and Blount (1972) investigate the development of children's communicative competence (see also Goodwin and Goodwin, 1987); Boggs (1978) and M. Goodwin (1990) also analyse children's language use. Mitchell-Kernan (1972) discusses ways of speaking among the African-American community, as do Labov (1972a), Kochman (1972), Abrahams (1970, 1983) and Ward (1971). These studies show how sociolinguistic rules for interpretation differ from other English-speaking communities. Research on language use in legal, medical and educational settings includes work by Erickson and Schultz (1982) and Philips (1982).

The speech event unit has proved to be a useful tool and resulted in many important studies of political events (e.g. Brenneis and Myers, 1984; Duranti, 1984, 1994; Foster, 1974; Kuipers, 1984; Sherzer, 1974), child-rearing practices (e.g. Schieffelin and Ochs, 1986; Schieffelin, 1990), literacy activities (e.g. Anderson and Stokes, 1984; Cook-Gumperz, 1986; Heath, 1982, 1983; Philips, 1974, 1983; Schieffelin and Gilmore, 1986; Scollon and Scollon, 1981; Street, 1993, 1995), counseling (e.g. Erickson and Schultz, 1982; Watson-Gegeo and White, 1990), and narrative (e.g. Darnell, 1974; Finnegan, 1967; Schuman, 1986).

Ethnographers of speaking have played a central role in studies of pidginization and creolization (Bauman and Sherzer, 1975; see, for example, Hymes, 1971). By looking at patterns of social uses of language, these studies provide ways of understanding linguistic borrowing and language change. The approach has also led to a number of important debates (Hanks, 1996: 188), for example, raising important questions about Native American discourse (Woodbury, 1985). Work in the ethnography of communication tradition has led to the development of a sophisticated framework for describing verbal performance (see Bauman, 1977, 1986, 1993; Bauman and Briggs, 1990; Briggs, 1988; Hanks, 1984; Hymes, 1975; Sherzer, 1983). Within this framework, certain aspects of language that are typically neglected in linguistic study become central, for example the cues that mark a shift into performance (as differentiated from 'everyday' speech), and the role of the audience. Analytical attention is redirected from verbal art as an object to verbal art as performance.

A main tenet of ethnographers of communication is of course that language practices are not only culturally specific, but are a central locus for the creation and transmission of culture. In 1987 Sherzer introduced the idea of a 'discourse centered' approach to culture, with the idea of making language even more central and investigating the notion of culture from socially circulating discourse, especially 'verbally artistic and playful discourse' (Sherzer, 1987: 295), a view utilized and further developed by Urban in his study of South American discourse patterns (1991).

CRITICISMS OF THE MODEL AND CURRENT DIRECTIONS

Despite its appeal to a variety of researchers around the world, the ethnography of communication has been criticized for a lack of theoretical unity, for its functionalist leanings, and for its underestimation of the difficulties of totally describing all the ways of speaking of any language (Hanks, 1996: 188). While Hymes envisioned cross-cultural comparison, most of the studies that use his methodology concentrate, not on building a theory of relationships between speech and context in societies in general, but on describing speech practices that are meaningful to a specific society (Duranti, 1988: 219). There are some exceptions in studies that have explicated some general areal patterns from local studies (e.g. Abrahams, 1983; Roberts and Forman, 1972; Sherzer and Urban, 1986), Brown and Levinson's (1978) cross-cultural study on politeness, Irvine's (1979) discussion of four universal aspects of formality, and Ochs and Schieffelin's work on language acquisition (1984, 1995). Of course, difficulties and questions inherent in cross-cultural comparison have become a recent focus across sub-disciplines in anthropology. While Hymes broadened the notion from 'speaking' to 'communication' in his articles, in most work the emphasis remained on speaking (Joel Sherzer, personal communication).

One of the original goals of the ethnography of speaking was to avoid reducing language to a series of fundamental precepts, to generalize but also to retain in descriptions the complexity of language and interpretation. This has proved to be an extremely challenging and difficult task. The approach has been criticized for transforming speech into 'another exotic object to be described by the ethnographer's metadiscursive procedures' (Maranhao, 1993). When Hymes spoke of generalizations, he seemed to be looking for common categories of speech events that were shared among cultures. The focus on speech events, however, has

been critiqued as likely to ignore those interactions which are not recognized as units of some sort by members of the speech community (Duranti, 1988: 220). The distinction between speech situation and speech event was found to be difficult to operationalize. The emphasis on formal genres such as ritualized speech (Bloch, 1976), and the very dichotomy of speech into formal and informal has also been critiqued (Irvine, 1979).

While early studies in the ethnography of speaking tended to treat the speech event as an object rather than as something achieved by people in interactions over time (Ochs et al., 1996: 7), the notion of speech event has been recognized as an important way to approach the analysis of language. Duranti notes that using 'speech event' as a theoretical notion 'referring to a perspective of analysis rather than to an inherent property of events' (1985: 201) is a constructive way to look at interaction from the perspective of the speech used in it, and a useful way to make sense out of discourse patterns. At the same time, Gumperz and others have stressed the importance of looking at the larger sociopolitical contexts within which culturally situated communication takes place in an effort to understand communicative practice.

The ethnography of communication has been criticized for its lack of attention to integration with other branches of linguistics and anthropology (Leach, 1976) as well as other disciplines, a criticism perhaps based on Hymes' visionary goal to utilize insights from various academic fields in understanding the social aspects of language meaning, certainly an ambitious project. Recent studies by scholars who incorporate the ethnography of speaking among other approaches show a far greater integration of some of the fields cited as important to Hymes: anthropology, linguistics, sociology, folklore and psychology (for example Bauman and Briggs, 1990; Capps and Ochs, 1995; Duranti and Goodwin, 1992; Feld, 1982; Gumperz and Levinson, 1996; Hanks, 1990; Ochs, 1996; Ochs and Schieffelin, 1995; Sherzer and Urban, 1986).

It has been widely recognized that the ethnography of communication framework has had a great influence in the practice of linguistic anthropology. The approach is recognized for its potential to offer solutions for practical problems (Bauman and Sherzer, 1975), for its attention to the important relationship between language and culture, and for its emphasis on documenting and analysing actual speech in use. Work in the ethnography of communication framework has led to an increasing sophistication in both the recording of communicative events and the analysis of language in use. Recent studies of relationships between language and social life have focused on ethnopoetics (for example E. Basso, 1985; Bright, 1982; Graham, 1995; Kuipers, 1990; Tedlock, 1983), analysis of talk-in-interaction (e.g. Alvarez-Caccamo, 1996; Duranti, 1994; Goodwin, 1990; Hanks, 1990; Jacquemet, 1996; Keating, 1998; Moerman, 1988), and links with psychology (e.g. Capps and Ochs, 1995; Ferrara, 1994), analysis of discourse (e.g. Sherzer, 1987; Urban, 1991), cognition (e.g. Brown and Levinson, 1993; Danziger, 1996), gesture (e.g. Farnell, 1995; Goodwin, 1994; Kendon, 1990) and combinations of these approaches (e.g. Besnier, 1995; Brown, 1993; Cicourel, 1992; Haviland, 1991; Hill and Irvine, 1993; Kulick, 1992; Philips, 1992; Street, 1995; Valentine, 1995; Walters, 1996b; Wilce, 1998). Currently linguistic anthropologists use a number of strategies for fieldwork and analysis, but many acknowledge the influence of the ethnography of communication approach in focusing their work and in orienting fieldwork and analysis towards actual language in use. The ethnography of communication tradition continues to be conducted in varied and diverse ways, and to serve as an inspiration for continued contributions to the formation of new ideas and directions of research.

CONCLUSIONS

Ethnographers of speaking focus on understanding the large range of resources speakers have for the production and interpretation of language. Part of the goal of those working in this tradition has been to address the lack of information on ways of speaking in different speech communities, as well as to design procedures for the collection of data. The comparative approach to fieldwork was advocated as the best way to isolate different groups' 'theories of speaking' (Gumperz and Hymes, 1972: 36). The approach entailed a major shift in the choice of units of analysis in language research (Duranti, 1992: 25), framing research in terms of social units rather than linguistic units. This ethnographically grounded research paradigm has influenced a wide range of research into relationships between language and culture, including identity, social stratification, ethnicity, ideology, multilingualism, acquisition of language and culture, power relationships, aesthetics, conflict, literacy, representation, cognition and gender. The ideas formulated by Hymes and Gumperz and developed as the ethnography of communication continue to be highly influential.

Acknowledgements

I would like to express my appreciation to Sandro Duranti, Madeline Maxwell, Joel Sherzer, Keith Walters and two anonymous reviewers for their generous comments on earlier versions of this chapter. Any remaining errors or omissions are, of course, my own responsibility.

NOTES

1 Bloomfieldians had called linguistics an 'anthropological science' (Trager, 1968).

2 Part of the reason grammar lost its centrality among cultural anthropologists was a move away from a temporal structural analyses toward a focus on temporally and spatially situated practices (Ochs et al., 1996: 6).

3 Linguists use the idea of truth values to suggest that meaning can be defined in terms of the conditions in the 'real world' under which a person can use a sentence to make a true statement. This approach to meaning is different from other approaches such as Speech Act Theory, which defines meaning in terms of the use of sentences in communication.

4 Chomsky was interested in formulating a theory of mental structure or mind.

5 The term 'reference' is used in linguistics for the entity (object, state of affairs, etc.) in the external world to which a linguistic expression refers, for example, the referent of the word feasthouse is the physical object 'feasthouse'.

6 Although the field of pragmatics also studies language usage and choices speakers make, the ethnography of communication approach is different from pragmatic analysis in its stronger concern for the sociocultural context of language use, the relationship between language and local systems of knowledge and social order, and a lesser commitment to the relevance of logical notation in understanding the strategic use of speech in social interaction (Duranti, 1988: 213).

7 For an interesting discussion of Goffman's hesitancy to use linguistics see Ochs et al., 1996: 14.

8 Garfinkel has pointed out that classifying itself is a social act, meaningful within particular local contexts.

9 Pike distinguishes between emic and etic (from the terms phonemic and phonetic). His dichotomy has had a wide influence in American cultural anthropology.

10 Bloomfield remarks that ignoring differences within speech communities should only be done 'provisionally' (1933: 45) in order to employ a 'method of abstraction, a method essential to scientific investigation', but the results obtained from such abstraction have to be corrected 'before they can be used in most kinds of further work' (1933: 45).

11 See Lyons, 1977 for an account of Jakobson's introduction of these ideas into linguistics.

12 Initially many ethnographies of speaking were based on texts and notes written down in the field by ethnographers.

REFERENCES

Abrahams, Roger (1970) *Positively Black*. Englewood Cliffs, NJ: Prentice–Hall.

Abrahams, Roger (1983) *The Man-of-words in the West Indies: Performance and the Emergence of Creole Culture*. Baltimore, MD: Johns Hopkins University Press.

Albert, Ethel (1972) 'Culture patterning of speech behavior in Burundi', in John Gumperz and Dell Hymes (eds), *Directions in Sociolinguistics: The Ethnography of Communication*. New York: Blackwell. pp. 72–105.

Alvarez-Caccamo, Celso (1996) 'Building alliances in political discourse: language institutional authority and resistance', in Helga Kotthoff (ed.), *Folia Linguistica*, XXX (3/4), Special Issue on Interactional Sociolinguistics.

Anderson, A.B. and Stokes, S.J. (1984) 'Social and institutional influences on the development and practice of literacy', in H. Goelman, A. Oberg and F. Smith (eds), *Awakening to Literacy*. London: Heinemann. pp. 24–37.

Au, Kathryn Hu-pei (1980) 'Participation structures in a reading lesson with Hawaiian children: analysis of a culturally appropriate instructional event', *Anthropology and Education Quarterly*, XI (2): 91–115.

Auer, Peter (ed.) (1998) *Code-Switching in Conversation: Language, Interaction, and Identity*. London: Routledge.

Austin, John (1962) *How to Do Things With Words*. Oxford: Oxford University Press.

Basso, Ellen (1985) *A Musical View of the Universe: Kalapalo Myth and Ritual Performances*. Philadelphia: University of Pennsylvania Press.

Basso, Keith (1970) 'To give up on words: silence in the western Apache culture', *Southwest Journal of Anthropology*, 26: 213–30.

Basso, Keith (1988) 'Speaking with names: language and landscape among the western Apache', *Cultural Anthropology*, 3 (2): 99–130.

Baugh, John and Sherzer, Joel (1984) *Language in Use: Readings in Sociolinguistics*. Englewood Cliffs, NJ: Prentice–Hall.

Bauman, Richard (1974) 'Speaking in the light: the role of the Quaker minister', in R. Bauman and J. Sherzer (eds), *Explorations in the Ethnography of Speaking*. Cambridge: Cambridge University Press.

Bauman, Richard (1977) *Verbal Art as Performance*. Rowley, MA: Newbury House.

Bauman, Richard (1986) *Story, Performance, and Event*. Cambridge: Cambridge University Press.

Bauman, Richard (1993) 'Disclaimers of performance', in Jane Hill and Judith Irvine (eds), *Responsibility and Evidence in Oral Discourse*. Cambridge: Cambridge University Press.

Bauman, Richard and Briggs, Charles (1990) 'Poetics and performance as critical perspectives on language and social life', *Annual Review of Anthropology*, 19: 59–88.

Bauman, R. and Sherzer, J. (eds) (1974) *Explorations in the Ethnography of Speaking*. Cambridge: Cambridge University Press.

Bauman, R. and Sherzer, J. (eds) (1975) 'The ethnography of speaking', *Annual Review of Anthropology*, 4: 95–119.

Bernstein, Basil (1964) 'Elaborated and restricted codes: their social origins and some consequences', in J. Gumperz and Dell Hymes (eds), *The Ethnography of Communication*. Special issue of *American Anthropologist*, 66 (6), Part II: 55–69.

Besnier, Niko (1988) 'The linguistic relationship of spoken and written Nukulaelae registers', *Language*, 64 (4): 707–36.

Besnier, Niko (1995) *Literacy, Emotion, and Authority: Reading and Writing on a Polynesian Atoll*. Cambridge: Cambridge University Press.

Bloch, Maurice (1976) 'Review of R. Bauman and J. Sherzer (eds), *Explorations in the Ethnography of Speaking*', *Language in Society*, 5: 229–34.

Blom, Jan-Petter and Gumperz, John (1972) 'Social meaning in linguistic structures: code switching in Norway', in John Gumperz and Dell Hymes (eds), *Directions in Sociolinguistics: The Ethnography of Communication*. New York: Blackwell. pp. 407–34.

Bloomfield, Leonard (1933) *Language*. New York: Holt.

Blount, Ben (1972) 'Aspects of socialization among the Luo of Kenya', *Language in Society*, 1: 235–48.

Blount, Ben (ed.) (1974) *Language, Culture, and Society: A Book of Readings*. Cambridge, MA: Winthrop Publishers.

Boas, Franz (1911) 'Introduction', in F. Boas (ed.), *Handbook of American Indian Languages*. Washington, DC: Smithsonian Institution, Bureau of American Ethnology.

Boggs, Stephen (1972) 'The meaning of questions and narratives to Hawaiian children', in Courtney Cazden, Vera John and Dell Hymes (eds), *Functions of Language in the Classroom*. Prospect Hills, IL: Waveland Press. pp. 299–327.

Boggs, Stephen (1978) 'The development of verbal disputing in part-Hawaiian children', *Language in Society*, 7: 325–44.

Brenneis, D. and Myers, F. (eds) (1984) *Dangerous Words: Language and Politics in the Pacific*. New York: New York University Press.

Bricker, Victoria (1974) 'The ethnographic context of some traditional Mayan speech genres', in R. Bauman and J. Sherzer (eds), *Explorations in the Ethnography of Speaking*. Cambridge: Cambridge University Press. pp. 366–88.

Briggs, Charles (1986) *Learning How to Ask: A Sociolinguistic Appraisal of the Role of the Interview in Social Science Research*. Cambridge: Cambridge University Press.

Briggs, Charles (1988) *Competence in Performance: The Creativity of Tradition in Mexicano Verbal Art*. Philadelphia: University of Pennsylvania Press.

Bright, William (1982) *Poetic Structure in Oral Narrative in Spoken and Written Language: Exploring Orality and Literacy*. Norwood, NJ: Ablex.

Brown, Penelope (1993) 'Gender, politeness, and confrontation in Tenejapa', in D. Tannen (ed.), *Gender and Conversational Interaction*. New York: Oxford University Press. pp. 144–62.

Brown, Penelope and Levinson, Stephen (1978) *Politeness*. Cambridge: Cambridge University Press.

Brown, Penelope and Levinson, Stephen (1993) '"Uphill" and "downhill" in Tzeltal', *Journal of Linguistic Anthropology*, 3 (1): 46–74.

Capps, Lisa and Ochs, Elinor (1995) *Constructing Panic: The Discourse of Agoraphobia*. Berkeley, CA: University of California Press.

Cazden, Courtney and John, Vera (1972) 'Learning in American Indian children', in M. Wax, M.S. Diamond and F. Gearing (eds), *Anthropological Perspectives on Education*. New York: Basic Books. pp. 252–72.

Cazden, Courtney, John, Vera and Hymes, Dell (1972) *Functions of Language in the Classroom*. Prospect Hills, IL: Waveland Press.

Chomsky, Noam (1965) *Aspects of the Theory of Syntax*. Cambridge, MA: MIT Press.

Chomsky, Noam (1977) *Language and Responsibility. Based on Conversation with Mitsou Ronat* (trans. J. Viertel). New York: Pantheon.

Cicourel, Aaron (1992) 'The interpenetration of communicative contexts: examples from medical encounters', in Alessandro Duranti and Charles Goodwin (eds), *Rethinking Context: Language as an Interactive Process*. Cambridge: Cambridge University Press. pp. 291–310.

Cook-Gumperz, Jenny (1986) *The Social Construction of Literacy*. London: Cambridge University Press.

Danziger, E. (1996) 'Parts and their counter-parts: social and spatial relationships in Mopan Maya', *Journal of the Royal Anthropological Institute (N.S.)*, incorporating *MAN*, 2 (1): 67–82.

Darnell, Regna (1974) 'Correlates of Cree narrative performance', in R. Bauman and J. Sherzer (eds), *Explorations in the Ethnography of Speaking*. Cambridge: Cambridge University Press. pp. 315–36.

Duranti, Alessandro (1984) 'Lauga and Talanoaga: two speech genres in a Samoan political event', in Donald L. Brenneis and Fred R. Meyers (eds), *Dangerous Words: Language and Politics in the Pacific*. New York: New York University Press. pp. 217–42.

Duranti, Alessandro (1985) 'Sociocultural dimensions of discourse', in T.A. van Dijk (ed.), *Handbook of Discourse Analysis I*. New York: Academic Press. pp. 193–210.

Duranti, Alessandro (1988) 'Ethnography of speaking: toward a linguistics of the praxis', in Frederick J. Newmeyer (ed.), *Linguistics: The Cambridge Survey*. Cambridge: Cambridge University Press. pp. 210–28.

Duranti, Alessandro (1992) 'Language in context and language as context: the Samoan respect vocabulary', in A. Duranti and C. Goodwin (eds), *Rethinking Context*. Cambridge: Cambridge University Press. pp. 77–99.

Duranti, Alessandro (1994) *From Grammar to Politics*. Berkeley, CA: University of California Press.

Duranti, Alessandro (1997) *Linguistic Anthropology*. Cambridge: Cambridge University Press.

Duranti, Alessandro and Goodwin, Charles (eds) (1992) *Rethinking Context: Language as an Interactive Process*. Cambridge: Cambridge University Press.

Erickson, R. and Schultz, J. (1982) *The Counselor as Gatekeeper: Social Interactions in Interviews*. New York: Academic.

Ervin-Tripp, Susan M. (1969) 'Sociolinguistics', in Leonard Berkowitz (ed.), *Advances in Experimental Social Psychology*. New York: Academic Press. pp. 91–165.

Ervin-Tripp, Susan M. (1972) 'On sociolinguistic rules: alternation and co-occurrence', in John Gumperz and Dell Hymes (eds), *Directions in Sociolinguistics: The Ethnography of Communication*. New York: Blackwell. pp. 213–50.

Fairclough, Norman (1989) *Language and Power*. London: Longman.

Farnell, Brenda (1995) *Do You See What I Mean? Plains Indian Sign Talk and the Embodiment of Action*. Austin, TX: University of Texas Press.

Feld, Stephen (1982) *Sound and Sentiment: Birds, Weeping, Poetics, and Song in Kaluli Expression*. Philadelphia: University of Pennsylvania Press.

Ferguson, Charles A. (1964) 'Baby talk in six languages', in John Gumperz and Dell Hymes (eds), *The Ethnography of Communication*. Special Issue of *American Anthropologist*, 66 (6), Part II: 103–14.

Ferrara, Kathleen (1994) *Therapeutic Ways with Words*. New York: Oxford University Press.

Finnegan, Ruth (1967) *Limba Stories and Story-Telling*. Oxford: The Clarendon Press.

Firth, J.R. (1957) *Selected Papers of J.R. Firth, 1952–1959*. London: Oxford University Press.

Fischer, John (1972) 'The stylistic significance of consonantal sandhi in Trukese and Ponapean', in John Gumperz and Dell Hymes (eds), *Directions in Sociolinguistics: The Ethnography of Communication*. New York: Blackwell. pp. 498–511.

Foster, M.K. (1974) 'When words become deeds: an analysis of three Iroquois longhouse speech events', in R. Bauman and J. Sherzer (eds), *Explorations in the Ethnography of Speaking*. Cambridge: Cambridge University Press.

Fox, James (1974) '"Our ancestors spoke in pairs": Rotinese views of language', in R. Bauman and J. Sherzer (eds), *Explorations in the Ethnography of Speaking*. Cambridge: Cambridge University Press. pp. 65–85.

Frake, Charles (1969) 'Struck by speech: the Yakan concept of litigation', in Laura Nader (ed.), *Law in Culture and Society*. Chicago: Aldine. pp. 106–29.

Frake, Charles (1975) 'How to enter a Yakan house', in M. Sanches and B. Blount (eds), *Sociocultural Dimensions of Language Use*. New York: Academic Press. pp. 25–40.

Friedrich, Paul (1972) 'Social context and semantic feature: the Russian pronominal usage', in John Gumperz and Dell Hymes (eds), *Directions in Sociolinguistics: The Ethnography of Communication*. New York: Blackwell. pp. 270–300.

Friedrich, Paul (1979) 'The linguistic sign and its relative non-arbitrariness', in *Language, Context and the Imagination: Essays* (selected and introduced by A. Dil). Stanford, CA: Stanford University Press. pp. 1–62.

Gal, Susan (1978) 'Peasant men can't get wives: language change and sex roles in a bilingual community', *Language in Society*, 7: 1–16.

Garfinkel, Harold (1967) *Studies in Ethnomethodology*. Englewood Cliffs, NJ: Prentice–Hall.

Giglioli, P.P. (ed.) (1972) *Language and Social Context*. Harmondsworth: Penguin.

Goffman, Erving (1961) *Encounters: Two Studies in the Sociology of Interaction*. Indianapolis: Bobbs–Merrill.

Goffman, Erving (1963) *Behavior in Public Places: Notes on the Social Organization of Gathering*. New York: The Free Press.

Goffman, Erving (1971) *Relations in Public: Microstudies of the Public Order*. New York: Harper and Row.

Goodwin, Charles (1993) 'Recording human interaction in natural settings', *Pragmatics*, 3 (2): 181–209.

Goodwin, Charles (1994) 'Professional vision', *American Anthropologist*, 96 (3): 606–33.

Goodwin, Marjorie (1990) *He-Said-She-Said: Talk as Social Organization Among Black Children*. Bloomington, IN: Indiana University Press.

Goodwin, Marjorie and Goodwin, Charles (1987) 'Children's arguing', in Susan U. Philips, Susan Steele and Christine Tanz (eds), *Language, Gender and Sex in Comparative Perspective*. Cambridge: Cambridge University Press. pp. 200–48.

Gossen, Gary (1972) 'Chamula genres of verbal behavior', in A. Paredes and R. Bauman (eds), *Toward New Perspectives in Folklore*. Austin, TX: University of Texas Press. pp. 145–67.

Gossen, Gary (1974) 'To speak with a heated heart: Chamula canons of style and good performance', in R. Bauman and J. Sherzer (eds), *Explorations in the Ethnography of Speaking*. Cambridge: Cambridge University Press. pp. 389–416.

Graham, Laura (1995) *Performing Dreams: Discourses of Immortality among the Xavante of Central Brazil*. Austin, TX: University of Texas Press.

Green, Judith and Wallat, Cynthia (1981) 'Mapping instructional conversations: a sociolinguistic ethnography', in Judith Green and Cynthia Wallat (eds), *Ethnography and Language in Educational Settings*. Norwood, NJ: Ablex. pp. 161–208.

Gumperz, John (1964) 'Linguistic and social interaction in two communities', in John J. Gumperz and Dell Hymes (eds), *The Ethnography of Communication*. Special issue of *American Anthropologist*, 66 (6), Part II: 137–54.

Gumperz, John (1972) 'Introduction', in J.J. Gumperz and D. Hymes (eds), *Directions in Sociolinguistics: The Ethnography of Communication*. New York: Blackwell. pp. 1–15.

Gumperz, John (1977) 'Sociocultural knowledge in conversational inference', in Muriel Saville-Troike (ed.), *Linguistics and Anthropology*. Washington, DC: Georgetown University Press. pp. 191–212.

Gumperz, John (1981) 'Conversational inference and classroom learning', in Judith Green and Cynthia Wallat (eds), *Ethnography and Language in Educational Settings*. Norwood, NJ: Ablex. pp. 3–23.

Gumperz, John (1982) *Discourse Strategies*. Cambridge: Cambridge University Press.

Gumperz, John and Herasimchuck, E. (1973) 'Conversational analysis of social meaning', in R. Shuy (ed.), *Sociolinguistics: Current Trends and Prospects*. (Georgetown University Monographs in Language and Linguistics.) Washington, DC: Georgetown University Press.

Gumperz, J. and Hymes, D. (1964) *The Ethnography of Communication*. Special issue of *American Anthropologist*, 66 (6): Part II.

Gumperz, John and Hymes, Dell (eds) (1972) *Directions in Sociolinguistics: The Ethnography of Communication*. New York: Blackwell.

Gumperz, John and Levinson, Stephen (eds) (1996) *Rethinking Linguistic Relativity*. Cambridge: Cambridge University Press.

Hanks, William (1984) 'Sanctification, structure, and experience in a Yucatec ritual event', *Journal of American Folklore*, 97: 131–66.

Hanks, William F. (1990) *Referential Practice*. Chicago: University of Chicago Press.

Hanks, William (1996) *Language and Communicative Practices*. Boulder, CO: Westview Press.

Haviland, John (1977) *Gossip, Reputation, and Knowledge in Zinacantan*. Chicago: University of Chicago Press.

Haviland, John (1991) '"That was the last time I seen them, and no more": voices through time in Australian aboriginal autobiography', *American Ethnologist*, 18 (2): 331–61.

Heath, Shirley Brice (1982) 'What no bedtime story means: narrative skills at home and at school', *Language in Society*, 11: 49–76.

Heath, Shirley Brice (1983) *Ways with Words: Language, Life, and Work in Communities and Classrooms*. London: Cambridge University Press.

Hill, Jane and Hill, Kenneth (1978) 'Honorific usage in Modern Nahuatl', *Language*, 54 (1): 123–55.

Hill, Jane and Irvine, Judith (eds) (1993) *Responsibility and Evidence in Oral Discourse*. Cambridge: Cambridge University Press.

Hymes, Dell (1962) 'The ethnography of speaking', in T. Gladwin and W. Sturtevant (eds), *Anthropology and Human Behavior*. Washington, DC: Anthropological Society of Washington. pp. 15–53.

Hymes, Dell (1964) 'Introduction: toward ethnographies of communication', in J.J. Gumperz and D. Hymes (eds), *The Ethnography of Communication*. Special issue of *American Anthropologist*, 66 (6), Part II.

Hymes, Dell (1966) 'Two types of linguistic relativity', in William Bright (ed.), *Sociolinguistics*. The Hague: Mouton. pp. 114–67.

Hymes, Dell (1970) 'Linguistic aspects of comparative political research', in R. Holt and J. Turner (eds), *The Methodology of Comparative Research*. New York: The Free Press. pp. 295–341.

Hymes, Dell (1971) *Pidginization and Creolization of Languages*. London: Cambridge University Press.

Hymes, Dell (1972a) 'Toward ethnographies of communication', in P.P. Giglioli (ed.), *Language and Social Context*. Harmondsworth: Penguin. pp. 21–44.

Hymes, Dell (1972b) 'Models of the interaction of language and social life', in John Gumperz and Dell Hymes (eds), *Directions in Sociolinguistics: The Ethnography of Communication*. New York: Blackwell. pp. 35–71.

Hymes, Dell (1972c) 'On communicative competence', in J.B. Pride and J. Holmes (eds), *Sociolinguistics*. Harmondsworth: Penguin. pp. 269–85.

Hymes, Dell (1974) *Foundations in Sociolinguistics: An Ethnographic Approach*. Philadelphia: University of Pennsylvania Press.

Hymes, Dell (1975) 'Breakthrough into performance', in D. Ben-Amos and K. Goldstein (eds), *Folklore: Performance and Communication*. The Hague: Mouton. pp. 11–74.

Irvine, Judith (1974) 'Strategies of status manipulation in the Wolof greeting', in Richard Bauman and Joel Sherzer (eds), *Explorations in the Ethnography of Speaking*. Cambridge: Cambridge University Press. pp. 167–91.

Irvine, Judith (1979) 'Formality and informality in communicative events', *American Anthropologist*, 81: 773–90.

Jackson, Jean (1974) 'Language identity of the Colombian Vaupes Indians', in R. Bauman and J. Sherzer (eds), *Explorations in the Ethnography of Speaking*. Cambridge: Cambridge University Press. pp. 50–64.

Jacquemet, Marco (1996) *Credibility in Court: Communicative Practices in the Camorra Trials*. Cambridge: Cambridge University Press.

Jakobson, R. (1960) 'Closing statement: linguistics and poetics', in T.A. Sebeok (ed.), *Style in Language*. Cambridge, MA: MIT Press. pp. 398–429.

Jakobson, R. and Halle, M. (1956) *Fundamentals of Language*. The Hague: Mouton.

Keating, Elizabeth (1998) *Power Sharing: Language, Rank, Gender and Social Space in Pohnpei, Micronesia*. New York: Oxford University Press.

Keenan, Elinor Ochs (1974) 'Norm-makers, norm-breakers: uses of speech by men and women in a Malagasy community', in R. Bauman and J. Sherzer (eds), *Explorations in the Ethnography of Speaking*. Cambridge: Cambridge University Press. pp. 125–43.

Kendon, Adam (1990) *Conducting Interaction: Patterns of Behavior in Focused Encounters*. Cambridge: Cambridge University Press.

Kirshenblatt-Gimblett, Barbara (1975) 'A parable in context', in D. Ben-Amos and K. Goldstein (eds), *Folklore: Performance and Communication*. The Haugue: Mouton. pp. 105–30.

Kochman, Thomas (ed.) (1972) *Rappin' and Stylin' Out: Communication in Urban Black America*. Urbana, IL: University of Illinois Press.

Kuipers, Joel (1984) 'Place, names, and authority in Weyewa ritual speech', *Language in Society*, 13: 455–66.

Kuipers, Joel (1990) *Power in Performance: The Creation of Textual Authority in Weyewa Ritual Speech*. Philadelphia: University of Pennsylvania Press.

Kulick, Don (1992) *Language Shift and Cultural Reproduction: Socialization, Self, and Syncretism in a Papua New Guinean Village*. Cambridge: Cambridge University Press.

Labov, William (1972a) 'Rules for ritual insults', in D. Sudnow (ed.), *Studies in Social Interaction*. Englewood Cliffs, NJ: Prentice–Hall. pp. 120–69.

Labov, William (1972b) 'The study of language in its social context', in P.P. Giglioli (ed.), *Language and Social Context*. Harmondsworth: Penguin. pp. 283–308.

Labov, William (1972c) *Sociolinguistic Patterns*. Oxford: Blackwell.

Leach, E. (1976) 'Social geography and linguistic performance', *Semiotica*, 16: 87–97.

Levinson, Stephen (1979) 'Activity types and language', *Linguistics*, 17: 365–99.

Lutz, Catherine (1988) *Unnatural Emotions*. Chicago: University of Chicago Press.

Lyons, John (1977) *Semantics*, vols. 1 and 2. Cambridge: Cambridge University Press.

Maranhao, Tullio (1993) 'Fieldwork conversations', in Jane Hill and Judith Irvine (eds), *Responsibility and Evidence in Oral Discourse*. Cambridge: Cambridge University Press. pp. 181–200.

Marcus, George and Fischer, Michael (1986) *Anthropology as Cultural Critique*. Chicago: University of Chicago Press.

Michaels, Sarah (1981) 'Sharing time: children's narrative styles and differential access to literacy', *Language in Society*, 10 (3): 423–42.

Mitchell-Kernan, Claudia (1972) 'Signifyng and markng: two Afro-American speech acts', in John Gumperz and Dell Hymes (eds), *Directions in Sociolinguistics: The Ethnography of Communication*. New York: Blackwell. pp. 161–79.

Moerman, Michael (1988) *Talking Culture: Ethnography and Conversation Analysis*. Philadelphia: University of Pennsylvania Press.

Morgan, Marcyliena (1996) 'Conversational signifying: grammar and indirectness among African American women', in E. Ochs, E. Schegloff and S. Thompson (eds), *Interaction and Grammar*. Cambridge: Cambridge University Press. pp. 405–34.

Morgan, Marcyliena (1998) 'More than a mood or attitude: discourse and verbal genres in African-American culture', in S. Mufwene, J. Rickford, G. Bailey and J. Baugh (eds), *African American English: Structure, History and Use*. New York: Routledge.

Ochs, Elinor (1996) 'Linguistic resources for socializing humanity', in J. Gumperz and S. Levinson (eds), *Rethinking Linguistic Relativity*. Cambridge: Cambridge University Press. pp. 407–37.

Ochs, Elinor and Scheiffelin, Bambi (1984) 'Language acquisition and socialization: three developmental stories', in R. Schweder and R. Levine (eds), *Culture Theory: Essays on Mind, Self, and Emotion*. Cambridge: Cambridge University Press.

Ochs, Elinor and Schieffelin, Bambi (1995) 'The impact of language socialization on grammatical development', in P. Fletcher and B. MacWhinney (eds), *The Handbook of Child Language*. Oxford: Blackwell. pp. 73–94.

Ochs, Elinor, Schegloff, Emanuel and Thompson, Sandra (1996) *Interaction and Grammar*. Cambridge: Cambridge University Press.

Paredes, A. and Bauman, R. (eds) (1972) *Toward New Perspectives in Folklore*. Austin, TX: University of Texas Press.

Peterson, Glenn (1993) 'Kanengamah and the politics of concealment', *American Anthropologist*, 95: 334–52.

Philips, Susan (1974) 'Warm Springs "Indian Time": how the regulation of participation affects the progress of events', in R. Bauman and J. Sherzer (eds), *Explorations in the Ethnography of Speaking*. Cambridge: Cambridge University Press. pp. 92–109.

Philips, Susan (1982) 'The language socialization of layers: acquiring the "cant"', in George Spindler (ed.), *Doing the Ethnography of Schooling*. New York: Holt, Rinehart and Winston. pp. 176–209.

Philips, Susan (1983) *The Invisible Culture: Communication in Classroom and Community on the Warm Spring Indian Reservation*. New York: Longman.

Philips, Susan (1992) 'The routinization of repair in courtroom discourse', in A. Duranti and C. Goodwin (eds), *Rethinking Context: Language as an Interactive Process*. Cambridge: Cambridge University Press. pp. 311–22.

Philipsen, Gerry and Carbaugh, Donal (1986) 'A bibliography of fieldwork in the ethnography of communication', *Language in Society*, 15: 387–98.

Pike, Kenneth (1954) *Language in Relation to a Unified Theory of the Structure of Human Behavior*. Glendale, CA: Summer Institute of Linguistics.

Pratt, Mary Louise (1987) 'Linguistic utopias', in Nigel Fabb, Derek Attridge, Alan Durant and Colin MacCabe (eds), *The Lingusitics of Writing: Arguments Between Language and Literature*. Manchester: Manchester University Press. pp. 48–66.

Reisman, Karl (1974) 'Contrapuntal conversations in an Antiguan village', in R. Bauman and J. Sherzer (eds), *Explorations in the Ethnography of Speaking*. New York: Cambridge University Press. pp. 110–24.

Roberts, J. and Forman, M. (1972) 'Riddles: expressive models of interrogation', in John Gumperz and Dell Hymes (eds), *Directions in Sociolinguistics: The Ethnography of Communication*. New York: Blackwell. pp. 180–209.

Romaine, Suzanne (ed.) (1982) *Sociolinguistic Variation in Speech Communities*. London: Edward Arnold.

Rosaldo, Michelle (1973) 'I have nothing to hide: the language of Ilongot oratory', *Language in Society*, 2: 193–223.

Sacks, Harvey, Schegloff, Emanuel and Jefferson, Gail (1974) 'A simplest systematics for the organization of turn-taking for conversation', *Language*, 50: 696–735.

Salmond, Anne (1974) 'Rituals of encounter among the Maori: sociolinguistic study of a scene', in R. Bauman and J. Sherzer (eds), *Explorations in the Ethnography of Speaking*. Cambridge: Cambridge University Press. pp. 192–212.

Sankoff, Gillian (1974) 'A quantitative paradigm for the study of communicative competence', in R. Bauman and J. Sherzer (eds), *Explorations in the Ethnography of Speaking*. Cambridge: Cambridge University Press. pp. 18–49.

Saville-Troike, Muriel (1982) *The Ethnography of Communication: An Introduction*. Oxford: Blackwell.

Schegloff, Emanuel (1968) 'Sequencing in conversational openings', *American Anthropologist*, 70: 1075–95.

Schegloff, Emanuel (1984) 'On some questions and ambiguities in conversation', in J.M. Atkinson and J. Heritage (eds), *Structures of Social Action: Studies in Conversation Analysis*. Cambridge: Cambridge University Press. pp. 28–52.

Schieffelin, Bambi (1990) *The Give and Take of Everyday Life*. Cambridge: Cambridge University Press.

Schieffelin, Bambi and Gilmore, Perry (eds) (1986) *The Acquisition of Literacy: Ethnographic Perspectives*. Norwood, NJ: Ablex.

Schieffelin, Bambi and Ochs, Elinor (1986) *Language Socialization Across Cultures*. Cambridge: Cambridge University Press.

Schuman, A. (1986) *Storytelling Rights: The Uses of Oral and Written Texts by Urban Adolescents*. Cambridge: Cambridge University Press.

Scollon, Ronald and Scollon, Suzanne (1979) *Linguistic Convergence: An Ethnography of Speaking at Fort Chipewyan*. Alberta, NY: Academic Press.

Scollon, R. and Scollon, S.K. (1981) *Narrative, Literacy, and Face in Interethnic Communication*. Norwood, IL: Ablex.

Sherzer, Joel (1974) 'Namakke, Sunmakke, Kormakke: three types of Cuna speech events', in R. Bauman and J. Sherzer (eds), *Explorations in the Ethnography of Speaking*. Cambridge: Cambridge University Press. pp. 263–82.

Sherzer, Joel (1983) *Kuna Ways of Speaking: An Ethnographic Perspective*. Austin, TX: University of Texas Press.

Sherzer, Joel (1987) 'A discourse-centered approach to language and culture', *American Anthropologist*, 89 (2): 295–309.

Sherzer, Joel and Darnell, Regna (1972) 'Outline guide for the ethnographic study of speech use', in J. Gumperz and D. Hymes (eds), *Directions in Sociolinguistics: The Ethnography of Communication*. New York: Blackwell. pp. 548–54.

Sherzer, Joel and Urban, Greg (eds) (1986) *Native South American Discourse*. Berlin: Mouton de Gruyter.

Silverstein, Michael (1981) 'The limits of awareness', *Working Papers in Sociolinguistics*. No. 84. Austin, TX: Southwestern Educational Library.

Slobin, Dan (1967) *A Field Manual for Cross-cultural Study of the Acquisition of Communicative Competence*. Berkeley, CA: University of California (ASUC Bookstore).

Strathern, Andrew (1975) 'Veiled speech in Mount Hagen', in Maurice Bloch (ed.), *Political Language and Oratory in Traditional Society*. New York: Academic Press. pp. 185–203.

Street, Brian (1993) *Cross-Cultural Approaches to Literacy*. Cambridge: Cambridge University Press.

Street, Brian (1995) *Social Literacies: Critical Approaches to Literacy in Development, Ethnography, and Education*. London: Longman.

Stross, Brian (1974) 'Speaking of speaking: Tenejapa Tzeltal metalinguistics', in R. Bauman and J. Sherzer (eds), *Explorations in the Ethnography of Speaking*. Cambridge: Cambridge University Press. pp. 213–39.

Tedlock, Dennis (1972) 'On the translation of style in oral narrative', in A. Paredes and R. Bauman (eds), *Toward New Perspectives in Folklore*. Austin, TX: University of Texas Press. pp. 114–33.

Tedlock, Dennis (1983) *The Spoken Word and the Work of Interpretation*. Philadelphia: University of Pennsylvania Press.

Trager, George (1968) 'Review of Hockett', *Studies in Linguistics*, 20: 77–84.

Urban, Greg (1991) *A Discourse-Centered Approach to Culture*. Austin, TX: University of Texas Press.

Valentine, Lisa (1995) *Making it their Own: Seven Ojibwe Communicative Practices*. Toronto: University of Toronto Press.

Walters, Keith (1996a) 'Gender, quantitative sociolinguistics, and the linguistics of contact', in Mary Bucholtz, A.C. Liang, Laurel Sutton and Caitlin Hines (eds), *Cultural Performances: Proceedings of the Third Berkeley Women and Language Conference*. Berkeley, CA: Berkeley Women and Language Group. pp. 757–76.

Walters, Keith (1996b) 'Language, gender and the political economy of language', *Language in Society*, 26: 515–56.

Ward, Martha (1971) *Them Children*. New York: Holt, Rinehart and Winston.

Watson-Gegeo, Karen and White, Geoffrey (eds) (1990) *Disentangling: Conflict Discourse in Pacific Societies*. Stanford, CA: Stanford University Press.

Wilce, James (1998) *Eloquence in Trouble: The Poetics and Politics of Complaint in Rural Bangladesh*. New York: Oxford University Press.

Woodbury, Anthony C. (1985) 'The functions of rhetorical structure: a study of central Alaskan Yupik Eskimo discourse', *Language in Society*, 14: 153–90.

21

Technologies of Realism? Ethnographic Uses of Photography and Film

MIKE BALL AND GREG SMITH

INTRODUCTION: IMAGES IN THE AGE OF THEIR
TECHNICAL REPRODUCTION

This chapter considers methodological and theoretical contexts for the employment of still photographs and moving film in ethnographic reports. It sketches these uses in light of the historical development of fieldwork, ethnography and participant observation in order to show how they reflect theoretical and epistemological concerns. On to our historical consideration of these methods we chart developments in photographic, film and video representational technologies. From within this framework we ask, what role do pictorial and filmic materials play in the predominantly written inscriptions of ethnographic reports?

The chapter consequently draws upon studies in visual sociology and visual anthropology[1] to explore the scope and potential of photography and film in ethnography. Our examination differs from earlier surveys (e.g. Ball and Smith, 1992; Chaplin, 1994; Grady, 1996; Harper, 1994; Henney, 1986)[2] in that it frames ethnographic usage of visual methods in terms of broad shifts in visual technology and associated viewing competences. In particular we want to articulate the significance of the linkage between photography, the realism debates it engenders and modernity. We further wish to suggest some of the potential and problems associated with ethnographic applications of the emergent representational forms characteristic of what are variously and contentiously described as late modern (Giddens, 1990) or postmodern societies (see Table 21.1).

Our cultural and historical approach is designed to throw into relief changing conceptions of visual methods. The application by ethnographers of visual methods occupies the interface between what technological developments make possible and current conceptions of ethnography. As each of these alters, applications of visual methods will change. Currently this is exemplified by developments within the new information and communication technologies (ICTs), especially digitalization and the multimedia opportunities afforded by the increasing availability of computer technology and the rapid growth of the Internet. The broad shifts in the character of visual culture resulting from technological developments can be summarized ideal-typically as in Table 21.1. This conceptualization extends themes from Benjamin's ([1936] 1973) essay on the fate of the work of art when technical methods permit its easy reproduction.

Benjamin ([1936] 1973) asked how art was changed when it can be readily reproduced by mechanical – or, better, 'technical' (Snyder, 1989) – methods. Film and photography (and other recording technologies) allow large quantities of copies to be made of an art work. Yet, for Benjamin, the notable feature of the art work in premodern societies was its *aura* arising from its unique existence and its embeddedness in tradition.

In premodern societies, paintings and other art objects possessed a secure meaning, which arose from their clear anchorage in the ceremonial practices of particular social groups. The 'presence' generated by the art object, the sense of reverence it elicited, stemmed from its location in tradition. The art work was an original 'text' in the sense that it existed in a specific place and could only be seen and appreciated *in situ*. According to Benjamin's argument, art objects were encapsulated in a 'pod' of awe.

Table 21.1 *Types of society, modes of pictorial representation and their associated reading positions*

Traditional society	Autographic (handmade) images	Worshippers
Modernity	Photographic and cinematographic images	Viewers
Late modernity/ postmodernity	Electronic images	Interactive users

The power of a work of art derived from its singularity and its location in tradition that lent it aura.

Efficient and accurate methods of reproduction, Benjamin argues, dislocate art from tradition. Once art is subject to non-traditional interpretation the way is paved to its politicization. Benjamin also draws attention to an art object's 'exhibition value', which he traces to the development of photography and film. Benjamin further suggests that methods of technical reproduction introduce new, more precise standards of depiction that significantly alter perceptual schemes.

Benjamin's theory of aura and reproduction can be adapted to understand some very general features of modes of pictorial representation and the position of the perceiver. This is summarized in Table 21.1. The visual representational technologies (photography, film) associated with modernity change our relation to the seen world. Generalizing, with the emergence of modern society there is a shift in the position of the perceiver of visual imagery from worshipper to viewer. The easy availability of photographic images in modern societies annuls the sense of aura historically attached to visual representations in premodern societies. The conjecture we wish to explore in the latter part of this chapter is that image perceivers' position is changing again with the increasing accessibility of electronic images characteristic of late modern or postmodern societies. This shift has implications for ethnographic practice using pictorial materials since sociology and anthropology are decidedly creatures of modernity (Clifford, 1988; Nisbet, 1967). Born around the same time and place, sociology, anthropology and photography (Becker, 1975; Pinney, 1992) share similar preoccupations with realism.

As Benjamin's discussion of aura implies, photography and film are each nineteenth-century technical innovations that have made a major impact on the development and apprehension of the visual cultures of modernity and late modernity. In the following sections we consider how photography and film have promoted a concern with the realistic representation of the world – a claim that needs to be approached cautiously.

REALISM AND THE DOCUMENTARY
TRADITION

We begin with a brief review of significant technical developments in the history of photography and film before moving to a consideration of the documentary tradition, the photographic and filmic genre that stands closest to the realist concerns of ethnography. Interestingly, there are broad parallels in the development of the documentary tradition and ethnographic method. The following section traces the reprising of realist themes in the early history of ethnographic photography and film.

Cameras existed long before photographs did. The *camera obscura* was in widespread use as a drawing aid by the sixteenth century, although the principle on which it was based (light entering a small room or box through an aperture or lens throws an inverted image against the back wall) was known to the ancients. Photography is a modernist technology whose history is a complex and contested story. In one version Fox Talbot invented modern photography around 1839. For most of the nineteenth century photography remained in the hands of a group of technical specialists. The first Kodak camera appeared in 1888 but it was only the marketing in 1899 of the Brownie box camera that put photography into the hands of large sections of European and North American societies. In 1895 the brothers Louis and Auguste Lumière invented the cinematograph, a portable movie camera. Other landmarks include the marketing in 1923 of the Leica, the first SLR 35mm camera; the invention of the Polaroid camera in 1947; the instamatic camera, which simplified the loading and taking of pictures, first appeared in 1963. Video cameras and recorders became widespread in the early 1980s and their price and weight has continued to fall since then; affordable digital cameras are a mid-1990s phenomenon. These inventions have facilitated the easy production of images. They have democratized image-making, stimulating a large vernacular practice – a middle-brow art (Bourdieu et al., 1990) – alongside the professional specialisms.

The documentary tradition of photography and film emerged in the late nineteenth century in Europe and America as a socially conscious endeavour to depict graphically the actualities of the world. Documentary has a rich and varied history. In the early decades of the twentieth century Lewis Hines' photographs of industrial working conditions influenced US reform movements and legislation. *Let Us Now Praise Famous Men* (1941) by James Agee and Walker Evans dramatically conveyed the personal costs of drought and the Depression on small farmers in 1930s America. In Europe, the pictures of Parisian street scenes and café life made by Henri Cartier-Bresson and Brassai reached wide audiences (Westerbeck and Meyerowitz, 1994). At a time when television was still in its infancy, documentarists found a mass outlet for their work through the new and influential occupation of photo-journalism. That documentary found such a ready audience in the 1930s, in both Europe and America, has to be understood as part of wider social currents that showed a new sensitivity towards the description of the experiences of the ordinary person.

One of the first motion pictures ever produced showed workers leaving the Lumières' factory. The Lumières used their new invention to cast fresh light on aspects of daily life both at home and abroad; a primary function of cinematography was a documentary impulse to capture life *sur le vif* ('on the fly'). Indeed, they coined the term *documentaires* to describe their short travel films. Although Hollywood quickly exploited film for entertainment purposes, its capacity to document ways of life was not neglected. One milestone was Robert Flaherty's account of Eskimo life in *Nanook of the North* (1922). The ideological potential of documentary was rapidly recognized and exploited – in the Soviet Union, by *Kinopravda* (film truth) cinematographers, and in Nazi Germany, where Leni Riefenstahl's epic documentary of the 1934 Nazi Party national rally, *Triumph of the Will*, added new dimensions to the propaganda function of film.

It is customary to distinguish documentary from fictional work. Documentary is about reporting, not inventing, whatever is in the world. According to Michael Renov (1986; cited in Winston, 1995: 6), 'every documentary issues a "truth claim" of a sort, positing a relationship to history which exceeds the analogical status of its fictional counterpart'. The realist impulse is paramount: documentary photographs and film aim to exhibit the facts of a situation. Documentary,

> defies comment; it imposes its meaning. It confronts, us, the audience, with empirical evidence of such nature as to render dispute impossible and interpretation super-fluous. All emphasis is on the evidence; the facts them-selves speak ... since just the fact matters, it can be transmitted in any plausible medium ... The heart of documentary is not form or style or medium, but always content. (Stott, 1973: 14)

But documentary is also designed to encourage viewers to come to a particular conclusion about how the world is and the way it works, much as occurs in ethnographic texts. Documentary starts off by avowing merely descriptive concerns, 'telling it like it is'. As one distinguished exponent, Dorothea Lange, put it, 'documentary photography records the social scene of our time. It mirrors the present and documents for the future' (quoted in Ohrn, 1980: 37). Routinely, however, these realist concerns of documentary are linked to persuasive ones, enjoining the viewer to take a particular attitude to what is

depicted. For example, John Grierson, the Scottish film-maker who is widely regarded as a pivotal figure in the development of British and North American documentary film in the 1930s and 1940s, considered cinema as a modernist pulpit. His approach was to exploit the observational potential of film in order to construct a picture of reality that would realize cinema's destiny as a social commentator and source of inspiration for social change (see Barnouw, 1974).

Documentary thus capitalizes upon photography's immense descriptive potential. Photographs provide a precise record of material reality, what is indubitably there in the world. This is the doctrine of photographic causality. Photography has been described as 'a benchmark of "pictorial fact"' (Snyder and Allen, [1975] 1982: 66) arising from the automatism of the process through which photographs are produced (by the machine-generated exposure of light to chemically treated paper). Photography seems to remove human agency from this process and yield a representation possessing an authenticity and objectivity that autographic forms (for example, easel painting) can never obtain. In John Berger's (1989: 96) summary, 'Photographs do not translate from appearances. They quote them.' The camera is, in the famous slogan, 'a mirror with a memory'. These are all powerful claims on behalf of photographic realism. But they do not support the more exaggerated affirmation that artifice is foreign to photography, nor do they support a hard and fast contrast between documentary (or scientific) and art photography. Art photography emerges around the recognition that photographs are not simply documents but are also aesthetic objects. As Susan Sontag (1978: 85) put it: 'nobody ever discovered ugliness through photographs. But many, through photographs, have discovered beauty.' Some of the issues at stake can be summarized in Table 21.2.

What Table 21.2 sets out are not two distinct types of photographic practice but rather two dimensions for appraising photographic images. Indeed, the most credible view to take is that documentary is defined by its use; documentary pictures are those which are used in documentary ways (Snyder, 1984). This also allows aesthetic considerations a place in documentary photography: a powerful image is often the most effective way of driving home the facts of some situations. The persuasiveness of documentary is achieved through the artful fusion of descriptive and aesthetic concerns: production decisions about pose, light, composition, lenses, types of film and focus, as well as editing judgements such as cropping and the like, are guided by the photographer's sense of what will make an effective image.

The realism of documentary is thus a professional ideology. In its most simple form it rests on two questionable assumptions: that the camera takes pictures and never lies, and that the camera

Table 21.2   *Conceptions of photographic practice*

Art photography	*versus*	Documentary photography
The photographer as seer		The photographer as witness
Photography as expression		Photography as reportage
Theories of imagination and conceptual truth		Theories of empirical truth
Affectivity		Information value
Symbolism		Realism

Source: Adapted from Sekula, 1975

faithfully records the world as it appears (Ruby, 1976). Against the first assumption it must be remembered that people, not cameras, take pictures and those pictures are always taken from some point of view that has an arbitrary component. Here 'arbitrary' does not mean happenchance; it means it could have been otherwise – another, different picture could easily have been made. Henri Cartier-Bresson famously spoke of waiting for the 'decisive moment' to create his arresting pictures of fugitive moments of Parisian life. The second assumption also cannot be accepted without qualification. Photographs do not unambiguously and transparently record reality. The sense we make of any photograph depends upon a variety of factors. Viewer-centred factors include our cultural and personal knowledge, and that elusive quality we call visual literacy. Text-centred factors include the location of the picture's publication and its title or caption or commentating text. Thus what the viewer actually sees in a photograph is profoundly shaped by language, its accompanying description (Price, 1994).

Ethnographic applications of both photography and film employ a broadly documentary approach. At present there is a notable asymmetry between anthropology and sociology. Visual anthropologists have overwhelmingly concentrated on the production and use of moving images (ethnographic films) while visual sociologists have been more at home with stills (photo-essays). Furthermore, sociologists have made nothing like the quantity of ethnographic film and photography produced by anthropologists. No doubt there are a number of reasons for the asymmetry, including the differing historical trajectories of the two parent disciplines and the differing place they accord ethnographic fieldwork. Anthropology has taken observation and description very much more seriously than sociology, which has tended towards the analytical and explanatory. It has been easier to justify the anthropological use of the camera because the discipline's traditional topic-matter is 'exotic' and because it is a discipline that is committed to exploring cultural difference. Sociology for much of its history has not only lacked these legitimations, it has been faced with the presence of non-sociological visual documentarists in the societies it studies. So why is there no body of sociological films corresponding to the

rich tradition built up over the course of a century in anthropology? In one respect this may be considered a production issue. Anthropological film can be seen as a technique originating in the Western academy that in its early years aimed to record facts about native life. Sociologists, however, stand in a different relation to their 'people'. The societies sociologists study offer specialist qualifications and careers in documentary film production. The would-be sociological film-maker has to compete with a technically proficient indigenous tradition. Anthropology may have its Jean Rouch but sociology has yet to find even its Henri Cartier-Bresson.

ORIGINS OF THE USE OF VISUAL METHODS IN ANTHROPOLOGICAL AND SOCIOLOGICAL ETHNOGRAPHY

The Torres Straits expedition of 1898, led by A.C. Haddon, was the first to use cinematography to record sociocultural arrangements. Modelled on natural history expeditions, Haddon's team sought to base its enquiries on direct contact with the islanders (Urry, 1972: 50). Equipped with a 35mm Newman and Guardia camera (Long and Laughren, 1993), they produced what is probably the first recognizably 'ethnographic' film, in contrast to film that could be put to ethnographic or ethnological purposes (such as Regnault's film made in 1895 of a Berber woman making a pot; Barnouw, 1974: 29). Only four and a half minutes of the fragile Torres Straits film still remain, depicting fire-making and ceremonial dances. These were scenes that were staged for the camera (Banks, 1998), a practice which was to become commonplace in subsequent ethnographic film.

The natural sciences furnished the broad intellectual temper of the team. As an integral part of their research they conducted a range of physiological and psychological tests, including Rivers' investigations into colour vision and perception, and Myers' studies of the sense of smell. The interest of Rivers, Myers and others in aspects of the physical capabilities and characteristics of people in what were then referred to as 'savage societies' had its roots firmly in physical anthropology. Indeed, as soon as still photography was developed and the technology commercially available, physical anthropology started to employ it to advance its analytical concerns. In the late nineteenth century, influenced by pre-Darwinian evolutionist theories, physical anthropology and anthropometry made extensive use of photography to reveal the putative differences between the Mongol, Negro and Caucasian 'racial' groups. Guided by Huxley and Lamprey's attempts to systematize and record the physiological measurement of body mass and skeletal size in a manner that would enable reliable comparative morphometric data to be collected, anthropometric photography became established (Boas, 1974; Spencer, 1992).

Rivers, Haddon et al. recognized how important it was for professional anthropologists to collect their own data in the field,[3] in contrast to the earlier practice of relying on the secondhand data collected incidentally by traders, missionaries, travellers, administrators and the like (Kuper, 1977). Radcliffe-Brown underscored the new departure that an ethnographically grounded anthropology marked, observing that 'Haddon urged the need of "intensive" studies of particular societies by systematic field studies of competent observers' (Kuper, 1977: 54). Since 1874 the British Association for the Advancement of Science's handbook, *Notes and Queries on Anthropology*, had been used to assist and guide laypersons in the types and categories of information relevant to professional anthropologists. As Urry (1972: 51) observed, *Notes and Queries* evolved to the stage where it was 'not so much a guide for travellers as a manual of advice for more highly trained observers; a handbook for a new era of anthropological research to be based on more exact methods'. Indeed, by the time Malinowski went into the field equipped with a copy, *Notes and Queries* was in its fourth edition. Furthermore, Malinowski's fieldwork exemplar effectively relegated it to the second division of ethnographic method.

In significant part, the movement towards professional fieldwork practice occurred for the purpose of documenting forms of life that were rapidly changing or vanishing. This has been called 'salvage ethnography' (Clifford, 1987). Approximately contemporaneous to the Torres Straits expedition was the American Jesup North Pacific expedition, organized under Boas' direction while he was assistant curator in the department of anthropology at the American Museum of Natural History (Boas, 1974). The expedition resulted in more than seventeen published volumes, a copious collection of artifacts for the museum, photographs and later – film[4] of the peoples of the Northwest Coast of America. In common with the Rivers and Haddon expedition, the visual record included illustrative reconstructions (Jacknis, 1984, 1992). Fifteen years after the Jesup expedition, Boas followed Curtis in photographing and filming

reconstructions of native behaviour and ceremonial, including a potlatch ceremony and dance, even himself posing in native attire (Curtis, 1915; Jacknis, 1992). Visually recorded reconstructions thus became an acceptable – indeed invaluable – addition to fieldwork reports.

Following the Torres Straits expedition, both Rivers and Haddon canvassed tirelessly for the widespread adoption within the emerging discipline of anthropology of what they referred to as 'fieldwork'.[5] This concept was 'a term apparently derived from the discourse of field naturalists, which Haddon seems to have introduced into that of British anthropology' (Stocking, 1983: 80). For Rivers and Haddon fieldwork was a team enterprise, whereas post-Malinowskian fieldwork tended to be conducted by a solo researcher (or occasionally a man and woman partnership). Direct observation and enquiry into native beliefs and practices lay at its core. What fieldwork stands for – the close observation of a group's beliefs and practices that can be obtained only by prolonged immersion in its way of life – is now the staple of various styles of qualitative research.

Fieldwork is an essential constituent of the professional training of British social and American cultural anthropologists. At the centre of anthropology is comparative ethnographic study. To descriptively map human cultures became an implicit ultimate goal of anthropological ethnography, a residue of anthropology's association with the highly ambitious Victorian ethnological enterprise, which sought to fashion an all-inclusive historical explanation of humankind. Radcliffe-Brown and others made a great effort to distinguish the anthropological enterprise from a broader ethnology.[6] Claiming positivistic science as a licence for the ethnographic enterprise, Radcliffe-Brown emphasized key methodological and theoretical issues. Ethnography, involving a substantial spell of fieldwork, became established as the distinctive activity of anthropologists. But this project was to be carried forward by Malinowski, not Radcliffe-Brown.

In part through his success as a self-publicist, Malinowski's ethnography has come to be treated as a watershed in professional anthropological fieldwork techniques. His Trobriand research (beginning with Malinowski, 1922) set the mould for anthropology as an empirical discipline. The modern idea of ethnographic research did not originate with Malinowski: it was his followers who disseminated this fieldwork validating myth (Stocking, 1983: 109). By the second half of the twentieth century, Malinowski had become so firmly established euhemeristically as the influential ancestor who pioneered fieldwork techniques that those who pointed him in that direction were often overlooked. Even if we accept Leach's quip that 'there was plenty of good ethnography long before Malinowski went to the Trobriands' (Leach, 1957: 120), it has become difficult to afford these earlier researches the same significance. What distinguished Malinowski's ethnography was the time he devoted to it, and its quality: between one and two years in the field alongside the obligation to acquire competence in the native vernacular.

In common with Radcliffe-Brown, Malinowski actively sought to establish the scientific credentials of an ethnographically based anthropology. Malinowski's approach proposed a practical merger of functional theory and fieldwork methods. This observational and ethnographic enterprise would produce 'objective' and 'naturalistic' social scientific descriptions that represented the 'native's point of view'.

Malinowski presented himself to his readers as 'striving after the objective, scientific view of things' (Malinowski, 1922: 6) and saw photography 'purely as a visual aid to his science' (Young, 1998: 13). Yet Malinowski's published ethnographies deploy considerable textual persuasion to convince the reader of their authoritative and realistic character (Geertz, 1988). His photographs helped to emphasize that his ethnography addressed the brute 'facts' of Trobriand life with a minimum of subjective construction and artifice. Young (1998: 5) observes that 'no other anthropologist of Malinowski's generation made photographs work so hard in the service of ethnographic narrative'. There is a high ratio of photographs to text. Malinowski's camera work results in a characteristic style. He eschewed close-ups and panoramas, preferring horizontally framed middle distance shots in which the camera matches the height of the subject. The photographs invariably include contextual cultural features and the same scene was often 'snapped' in quick succession from varying viewpoints (Young, 1998: 16–17).

As his posthumously published personal diaries make plain (Malinowski, 1967), the photographic construction of a visual record was a central element of his fieldwork practice. He frequently sought refuge in the technicalities of photographic practice to escape the vicissitudes and ennui of being in the field. One example:

> 1.25.18. Friday. Gusaweta. I cannot write the diary. Dissipation, I take up novel reading. Developing films and thinking aloud about a number of things. Radical longing only for E.R.M. – Intellectual and emotional turmoil abates. Exhaustion, headache. (Malinowski, 1967: 195–6)

Even a cursory review of Malinowski's published ethnographic reports on aspects of Trobriand life reveal that he made copious use of photography. For example, in *Argonauts* he employs some seventy-five photographs to display aspects of the culture. Malinowski also makes effective use of photographs to establish his ethnographic presence: several photographs show Malinowski and his equipment on Trobriand alongside Trobrianders.

At the core of Malinowski's use of photographs is the recourse he makes to their documentary character, an attribution that also aids the establishment of his ethnographic authority. While Malinowski's text describes Trobriand culture, his photographs have the power to authenticate the text. They appeal to what Sekula (1975) calls 'the myth of photographic truth', the apparent semantic autonomy of the photographic image. In the context of ethnographic monographs, photographs of fieldwork are generally treated as unmediated, mechanical transcriptions of the transparent facts.

Malinowski's ethnographic texts on Trobriand culture serve as a classical benchmark for what became the conventional ethnographic use of photography in fieldwork. Malinowski's published ethnographies used photographs as evidence of the following: photographs of persons, items of material culture with and without persons, symbolic items, unusual events such as rituals and ceremonies, commonplace activities, and culture as the embodiment of abstract theories (Ball, 1998b). A broadly similar range of categories was employed by those who followed Malinowski.

As Table 21.1 indicates, drawings, paintings and sketches are widely regarded as less realistic than photographs. Pinney draws attention to how 'pre-photographic representations always depend on the trustworthiness of the author/artist' (Pinney, 1997: 18). If ethnography had developed as a systematic research method prior to photography, then an earlier 'Malinowski' would have depended solely on such autographic images.[7] Yet drawings and paintings have persisted in anthropological ethnographies. While forms of representation may be tied to types of society – photography and sociology are both documentary creatures of modernity – in actual ethnographic reports the photographic and the autographic have overlapped and mutually reinforced each other.

Historically, photography and film have occupied a much smaller place within sociological ethnography. When the sociological literature is examined for an equivalent fieldwork classic to place against Malinowski's *Argonauts*, then the disciplinary wisdom offers *Street Corner Society* (Whyte, 1943) as the best fit. Like Malinowski, Whyte also placed great store by the empirical, factual and naturalistic potential of fieldwork. Yet camera-generated data played no part in his investigation. This was true of the work of other notable sociological ethnographers. For example, Erving Goffman told his Shetland informants that he was working out of the Social Anthropology department at the University of Edinburgh and his Leica camera appears to have drawn their attention (Winkin, 1999), but visual data did not figure in the reports of his three major fieldwork-based studies (for Shetland see Goffman, 1953; for St Elizabeths, Goffman, 1961; for Las Vegas, Goffman, 1967).

Thus, photographs are far less common within sociological ethnographies. Indeed, if we search for a sociological classic which makes extensive use of photography, then the choices are few, but the Chicago School offers *The Hobo* (Anderson, 1923) as an example. *The Hobo* was a product of what Denzin (1995: 8) has termed interactionism's canonical phase. It includes some fourteen photographs. Perhaps more is at stake than the sheer 'familiarity' of those researched rendering photography redundant when carrying out fieldwork 'at home'. It also concerns the sociological researcher's conscious attempt to render both the research subjects and their location anonymous (Gold, 1989), an endeavour only rarely found in anthropological research.

Anderson's use of photographs followed a brief but significant episode in American sociology between 1896 and 1916, when the *American Journal of Sociology* published social problems-oriented articles that included photographs (Stasz, 1979). But with the exception of Thrasher's *The Gang* (Thrasher, 1927), few other Chicago works employed photographs. Thrasher's and Anderson's pictures now resemble documentary photographs: fascinating photographic studies that visually convey aspects of the ambience of the time. Viewed from a new century, their photographic subjects look every bit as exotic as Malinowski's Trobrianders. The neglect of visual data by sociological participant observers is founded in a preoccupation with the verbal elicitation of native points of view combined with a concern to protect subjects' anonymity.[8] We now address a more fundamental epistemological issue, the marginalization of visual images in ethnographic texts.

A VISUAL FOUNDATION FOR ETHNOGRAPHY?

For ethnography, photographs alone do not inform; rather it is the analysis that the ethnographer is able to accomplish with these records of persons, places and activities (Schwartz, 1989). Ethnographies that include photographs inevitably and necessarily also employ written description. Mary Price's (1994: 5) proposal that for the interpretation of still photographs 'it is the act of describing that enables the act of seeing' is persuasive. This is evident in such exemplary studies as Bateson and Mead (1942) and Goffman (1979).

Balinese Character (Bateson and Mead, 1942) is an example of a post-Malinowskian problem-centred ethnography with a pointedly visual emphasis. Bateson and Mead were seeking to use visual methods to describe and analyse the 'ethos' of the Balinese, the cultural organization of their instincts and emotions. If Malinowski can be said to have established the conventional ethnographic use of photography as an illustrative adjunct to anthropological ethnographic work, then Bateson and Mead opened up the potential of photography and film as both data repositories and analytical tools. Equipped with a theory relating ethos to personality development, Bateson and Mead amassed some 25,000 photographs and 22,000 feet of film. They worked as a team, Bateson filming and photographing while Mead took notes and interviewed. In the report of the research, *Balinese Character*, 759 photographs are thematically organized into a 100 'plates' with an accompanying text on the facing page. Bateson and Mead's work is innovatory because it requires the reader to scrutinize still photographs alongside the written text to make sense of the analysis. In this way Bateson and Mead's book reveals elusive and intangible aspects of culture that hitherto the artist had better captured than the social scientist (Bateson and Mead, 1942: xi–xii). Their achievement was to show how still photographs, together with a descriptively precise and theoretically informed commentating text, can serve to illuminate and further ethnographic understanding. Bateson and Mead's skilful interweaving of text and photograph has led to its deserved valuation as an exemplar of visual analysis (Harper, 1989; Jacknis, 1988). Arguably, its long-run impact seems to have been more consequential for visual sociology than visual anthropology (Harper, 1994). Yet it has been an exemplar that has spawned few offspring.[9]

Gender Advertisements (Goffman, 1979), another exemplar of visual analysis, echoes elements of Bateson and Mead's method. Around 500 images are organized into a collection of categories and sub-categories, underpinned by a sophisticated theoretical framework. In encountering Goffman's text we are set puzzles to solve that involve looking as well as reading. Informed by Goffman's laconic commentary, the reader has to scan and sort to find the precise sense of the points that Goffman makes (Smith, 1996). While images cannot 'talk' for themselves but demand to be spoken for, Goffman's analysis draws more than most on the reader's active engagement with the text. What distinguishes Goffman's book from other analytic visual ethnographies, such as Whyte's (1980) notable use of timelapse photography to study sociability on urban streets, is the artful manner in which the success of the analysis depends upon the co-opting of the reader's visual literacy.

To characterize data as unable to 'talk' for itself is to employ a conversational trope. In the English language, for example, visualist tropes and metaphors are commonplace descriptive resources (Fernandez, 1986). Coulter and Parsons (1991) enumerate the diverse range of English verbs to describe forms of visual orientation. Language can be powerfully visualist in its representational function, so much so that linguistic modes can often substitute for visual modes of representation. The logocentric bias this lends ethnography 'is the price that must be paid for making language do the work of the eyes' (Tyler, 1986: 137).

The communicative and interpretive dimensions of linguistic and visual representations are indexical (Garfinkel, 1967) and polysemic in character. This is not immediately obvious because photographs apparently yield 'fugitive testimony' to a fleeting moment; they seem 'to constitute a message without a code' (Barthes, 1977: 43). According to Barthes, rather than 'pure denotation', photographic images are 'floating chains of signifieds' that are anchored by linguistic messages.[10] Sometimes, however, photographs can include information not mentioned by the ethnographer. They may contain an 'excess of meaning' that the ethnographer cannot control. Stored visual images are signs or communicative forms that depend upon other sign systems for their meaning. Hence the camera's value as an ethnographic tool is similar to the audio tape recorder: it provides an accurate trace of events that still leaves an enormous scope for analytic interpretation.

REALISM AND REPRESENTATION IN VISUAL ETHNOGRAPHY

Two decades after Becker's (1979: 7) observation that 'visual social science isn't something brand new ... but it might as well be', priorities have not changed substantially, although the visual dimension is beginning to occupy an established corner in ethnographic work. Visual ethnography is emerging as a distinct but diverse specialism. Like other domains of ethnographic work its realist assumptions have been assailed by a variety of critiques often lumped together as 'postmodern'. However, there has been no simple substitution of one for the other. Indeed, in many respects visual ethnographers have been quite resistant to the blandishments of postmodern theory, perhaps because their unusual mode of working has already sensitized them to the partial, artefactual, reflexive character of their enterprise (recall Bateson and Mead's (1942: xii) sensitivity to 'the steps by which workers in a new science solve piecemeal their problems of description and analysis' in acknowledging the experimental character of their investigation). A review of current ethnographic uses of film and photography shows that a variety of stances toward the vaunted 'crisis of representation' coexist.

The realist assumptions of the documentary tradition continue to inspire ethnographic uses of photography. Documentary's influence is evident, for example, in the ethnographically informed photo essays of Jon Rieger (1996) and Dona Schwartz (1997). Using photographs of rural and small-town American settings, Rieger (1996) considers the method of rephotographing the same site or persons or activities and processes in order to study social change. Rieger suggests that while photographs can graphically exemplify change, it is often necessary to additionally use non-visual methods since some issues of evidence and inference can only be settled by drawing upon documentary or interview materials. Schwartz's study of the social organization of an American sporting spectacle, the 1992 Super Bowl, adopts the visual diary method (see also Prosser and Schwartz, 1998) and is presented from the point of view of an observer who enjoyed privileged access but who was not swept along by the domain assumptions of commercial photographers covering the event. Like commercial photography's coverage, Schwartz's pictures vividly convey the excitement and excess of the event. But unlike commercial photography, her pictures and purposefully interleaved text also address aspects of the political protests, hype, exploitation and backstage organization of this media-saturated phenomenon.

The analysis of indigenous uses of visual imagery was advanced by Sol Worth. Trained as a media professional, Worth modified the tradition that was established by Bateson and Mead, from a general visual anthropology to studies in visual communication (Worth, 1980). Worth encouraged the analysis of 'found' visual data (advertising, popular art forms etc.) rather than the researcher-generated kind. The emphasis on the analysis of indigenous imagery has stimulated ethnographic studies of the 'codes' informing professional photographic practices (Rosenblum, 1978; Schwartz, 1992). A different example of film serving as data is Worth and Adair's (1972) 'experiments' in indigenous image production with the Navajo. Working from a visual variant of the Sapir–Whorf hypothesis, Worth and Adair equipped cinematically untrained Navajo with 16mm cameras. The films they produced enabled Worth and Adair to empirically investigate 'Navajo' ways of seeing that were manifest in what they filmed, how they used the equipment and the meaning they assigned to their images. Other notable studies of indigenous image production include Chalfen's (1987, 1998) ethnographies of home photography and movie-making. Developing the anthropology of visual communication approach pioneered by Worth, Chalfen submits that family photography can be characterized as a 'home mode' of communication, that is, images produced in the home for consumption in the home. Chalfen proposes a general descriptive framework consisting of 'communication events' (planning, shooting, editing, and exhibition events) that can be characterized in terms of five 'components' (participants, settings, topics, message form and code). Chalfen's framework provides a basis for ethnographic descriptions of the home mode of visual communication that encourages comparative analysis.

At roughly the same time, Collier (1967) (see also Collier and Collier, 1986) advocated photography as a method of data collection, recommending its power to record material culture and to depict the physiognomy of social interaction (see Whyte, 1980 for a celebrated example). Collier also recommended its use within ethnographic interviews as a device to prompt and stimulate discussion ('photo elicitation'). In a noted study, Harper (1987) employed the technique to examine the work of an upstate New York mechanic, often spending two to four hours at a time eliciting the meanings of the photographs.

Indigenous imagery is also the topic of a branch of social studies of science that focuses on scientific uses of pictorial materials. Drawing on his own extensive research, Lynch outlines significant developments in natural scientific uses of visual materials (Lynch, 1998; Lynch and Woolgar, 1990). The study of scientific visual representations can be framed by studies of scientific work as text, discourse and practice. Hence there is an emphasis on the practical work involved in rendering 'scientific' matters accountable and seeable through visual devices.

This approach to 'scientific' ways of seeing overlaps with ethnomethodological studies of action in natural settings. In ethnomethodology visual and audio recordings that are rough by professional standards can serve as data for analysis (Bellman and Jules-Rosette, 1977; Garfinkel et al., 1981; Heath, 1986, 1997; Lebaron and Streeck, 1997). For example, Hindmarsh and Heath (1998) have analysed aspects of the visual and audio channels from a video recording of a brief strip of practical decision-making in a work organization, the Restoration Control Room of a telecommunications company. The analysis explores the unfolding of courses of action in time and space, and shows how the precise sense and relevance of computer displays and documents is constituted through participants' actions. Videotaped data permits close analysis of the local intelligibility of objects in an environment in which the visual intertwines with the spoken (Hindmarsh and Heath, 1998).

Visual ethnographers in anthropology, as already noted, tend to be concerned more with moving film and video while those affiliated to sociology generally concentrate on still photographic imagery. As Banks observes, 'until recently, visual anthropology was understood by many anthropologists to have a near-exclusive concern with the production and use of ethnographic film' (Banks, 1998: 9). Banks proposes a much broader notion of visual anthropology, a 'rethinking' that might include, for instance, the study of art, material culture, media studies and the like (Banks and Morphy, 1997). Nevertheless, the contrasting stills/movies orientations of visual sociology and visual anthropology continue to be reflected in the content of the current major specialist journals: *Visual Sociology, Visual Anthropology* and *Visual Anthropology Review.*

The last quarter of the twentieth century saw the establishment and institutionalization of the sub-discipline of visual anthropology.[11] There is now a market for ethnographic films. Many of these films seek to 're-present' in another medium themes drawn from conventional written ethnographic reports, using film to retell aspects of the ethnography (Crawford and Turton, 1992). While many ethnographic films are based upon a written report 'film brings people and cultures alive on the screen, capturing the sensation of living presence, in a way that neither words nor even still photos can' (Barbash and Taylor, 1997).

Ethnographic films can be considered a 'subset of documentary films more generally' (Loizos, 1993: 5). It is very difficult to establish hard and fast distinctions between ethnographic and documentary film. At the end of the twentieth century, Loizos' legitimation of ethnographic film is similar to Malinowski's much earlier claims for the ethnographic method: it fundamentally strives to fashion a 'realist', 'factual' account of social arrangements. But for Loizos the technology of photography can no longer be regarded as offering a simple guarantee. While the documentary style claims to furnish a more or less faithful record, as Loizos points out, 'there are dozens of filmic ways of creating a documentary "feel"' (Loizos, 1993: 5). *Cinema vérité* and *Direct Cinema* present some of the more arresting examples of this experimentation (Barnouw, 1974; Corner, 1996; Nichols, 1991; Renov, 1993; Stoller, 1992; Winston, 1995).

From the arrival of moving film, ethnographic film practice has been influenced by technical changes. These have included the replacement of highly flammable early film by more stable versions, the addition of a sound channel (first a separate task but, with the advent of 'synch-sound shooting' from around 1960, it became possible to shoot films solo) and the introduction of colour film and fast film that can be shot in low light conditions (Heider, 1976). Noting that 16mm film is relatively expensive, Henley (1989) anticipated salvation through 'the on-going video revolution'. The video 'revolution' has been so extensive, that it is not uncommon for film and video production to be treated as though they were the same (Rabiger, 1987 is representative of this approach). These changes have made the technical aspects of film-making simpler and easier: ordinary people can record the events once only accessible to trained film-makers. This offers new opportunities for collaboration and participation by the subjects of the film.

Academic disciplines are primarily 'disciplines of words' (Mead, 1995: 4), which has implications for the place and legitimacy of ethnographic film. The standard ethnographic product is a textual report and the ethnographic film is fundamentally a second order construct. Ethnographic films are thus based upon the framework of a written ethnographic report, extracted themes from it serving as a basis of the film's storyline. Loizos (1993) and Chiozzi (1989) make this point, although they also maintain that film can be used for constructive purposes different in character from text. A common asymmetry in the assessment of ethnographic film is for the anthropologist to concentrate upon the accuracy of the anthropological content and to treat the filmic and aesthetic components as secondary. As Henley assures us, in a consideration of the relationship of film to text, 'Film-making is simply an alternative means of representing certain aspects of social reality, which in certain contexts may be more effective than writing a text but which in others, is certainly less effective' (Henley, 1998: 55).

Ethnographic films have often resulted from collaboration between an anthropologist and a film-maker. David Turton, who had a highly successful working relationship with the film-maker Leslie Woodhead, is a good example of such collaboration. They made a collection of films for the *Disappearing World* series that explored cultural aspects of the East African Mursi and Kwegu peoples (Singer and Woodhead, 1988; Turton, 1992; Woodhead, 1987). While such collaborations have served a generation of anthropologists and film-makers, they are fraught with potential tensions and difficulties (see Barbash and Taylor, 1997: 74–84). For Henley (1989) and others the ideal is for the anthropologist to simultaneously also serve as the film-maker. Dan Marks' 1992 film *My Crasy Life* (shown in the BBC *Fine Cut* series), which deals with gang warfare, is a case in point. Video technology, which simplifies some of the technical aspects of film-making, assists the realization of this ideal. In Britain a number of television series devoted to making and showing anthropological films have received much critical acclaim, including Granada's *Disappearing World* and the BBC's *Worlds Apart* and *Under the Sun*. The licensing of British terrestrial television stations demanded a compulsory educational element (a practice that started with the BBC). This demand has ensured a budget for the production of informed, high quality programmes. In other parts of the world public service broadcasting and the emergence of specialist television channels seems to ensure a niche market for ethnographic film.

Technical aspects of film-making are a prominent part of the literature on ethnographic film (Devereaux and Hillman, 1995; Hockings, 1995; Hockings and Omori, 1988; Loizos, 1993; Rollwagen, 1988). There is frequently a close correspondence between the topic-matters of written ethnographic reports and those of ethnographic films. Indeed, many of the classical written ethnographies have had ethnographic films made about

photogenic themes within them. For instance, several of the films about Trobriand (each of them made after Malinowski's death) are haunted at every turn by his ethnography. Notable among them is Powell's film *The Trobriand Islanders* (1951), which was made after a period of fieldwork and which illustrates aspects of mythology, garden magic and Kula exchange. More recently, Weiner brought a women's perspective to bear on Trobriand culture, and a *Disappearing World* film was based around her research (*The Trobrianders of Papua New Guinea*, 1990; Weiner, 1988). There have also been films based around other classic ethnographies, such as Evans-Pritchard's studies of the Nuer and Azande (Heider, 1976; Singer and Woodhead, 1988).

Two relatively distinct sets of questions can be identified in debates around realism and representation in visual ethnography. The more conventional critique of documentary complains that what has been captured is a rehearsed construction rather than naturally occurring actuality. Prior to a photograph or moving film being taken, a scene has been 'set up'. A classic example cited in the literature is Andrew Gardner and colleagues' photographs of the aftermath of the Battle of Gettysburg in the American Civil War. Here it seems that the same corpse was dressed up in the uniforms of first one side and then the other, positioned appropriately, and photographed (Fulton, 1988). This pro-filmic event must be regarded differently from other decisions made immediately prior to the instant of picture-taking, such as the selection of the angle of the shot, the lighting, lens, film type and so forth. Artifice can also be constructed *after* the photograph or moving film has made its record. The alteration that is possible at this stage depends on the technology, ranging from tampering with negatives in early photography and film, to digitally modifying an image to produce something that is akin to a collage (Chaplin, 1998). A classic example of tampering with an image after it has been recorded is the Russian revolution photograph of Lenin engaging in public oratory with, in the original, comrade Trotsky close by – a position from which he was removed in the versions of the photograph endorsed by Stalin (see Wyndham and King, 1972: 151). While it is widely known that photographs can be faked in these ways, this knowledge does little to shake our belief in the photograph as evidence.

The critique associated with postmodern theory (though having diverse sources and containing some ideas that would not have been foreign to Max Weber) suggests that cultural description of any kind is a good deal more complex and political than envisaged by conventional accounts of fieldwork practice and ethnographic film-making. Attempts to establish a definitive set of criteria of ethnographic adequacy of film, such as Heider's (1976) fourteen variables, are regarded as a set of scientistic 'dicta' that are rarely if ever realized fully in practice (Weinberger, 1994). Why should long takes and 'whole bodies' be preferred as universally yielding full representations of social activities? Others, such as the MacDougalls, have challenged the single authorial voice of conventional ethnographic film and its politics and ethics of representation by incorporating dialogic formats into the films they have produced. When organized thus ethnographic film 'can be read as a compound work, representing a crossing of cultural perspectives' (MacDougall, 1994: 55) that does not re-tell extant anthropological knowledge but rather provokes the discovery of new knowledge through its making. In this conception, the professional anthropologist's knowledge is simply another narrative with no privileged status.

These critiques draw attention to important features of the production and consumption of ethnographic film: the film-maker's purpose or 'intention', the making of the product or 'event', through to the way it is received, the audience 'reaction' (Banks, 1992). These categories allow the scope of the debates about realism to be expanded. In particular they give attention to the role of the audience in the reception of the text.

A difficulty with earlier debates about photographic realism and the evidentiary status of the photograph and film is their tendency to focus on the process and circumstances of image production while omitting to give commensurate attention to viewers' and audiences' interpretations of the image. Brian Winston (1998: 66) proposes 'moving the legitimacy of the realist image from *representation* – the screen or the print – where nothing can be guaranteed to *reception* – by the audience or the viewer where nothing need be guaranteed'. In this view photography ceases to be a reflection of the world's properties. Photography's authenticity or truthfulness comes to be assessed in relation to our commonsense understanding of the world and the other kinds of evidence available to us about what is depicted.

This conception of image interpretation does not give sovereign interpretive authority to the viewer, as some versions of postmodernism seem to aver. Rather, it places great store by the overworked but none the less essential notion of context. Once an image has been recorded and placed in the public domain, it is then open to all manner of interpretation, for as Becker has argued, 'Photographs get meaning, like all cultural objects, from their context' (Becker, [1995] 1998: 88). Withholding information about context is a device often used by art photographers to lend an air of mystery to their work. Providing contextual detail – the stuff of all good ethnography – is what is needed to make images intelligible.

CONCLUSION: THE WORK OF ETHNOGRAPHY IN THE AGE OF DIGITAL REPRODUCTION

We conclude with a discussion of recent and ongoing technical developments and sketch some of their possibilities for visual analysis in ethnography. New digital technologies herald the end of photography's dependence upon chemical and mechanical processes and thus seem to decisively undermine the 'pencil of nature' (Fox Talbot)/ 'stencil off the real' (Sontag) realist claims traditionally associated with photographic representation. In certain respects, the 'digital revolution' looks set to extend the realms of the hyperreal at realism's expense. Digitalization is a process through which a picture is divided in a grid into small elements ('pixels'). Each pixel is assigned a number from a code of colours or brightness. By changing the values of the pixels or removing them, a photograph can be readily and seamlessly slightly modified or drastically transformed. As the popular press nowadays often shows us, persons who could not possibly have met can be depicted in a seamless photograph. Movies now contain shots constructed as simulations from angles that no human cameraperson would be capable of filming, affording perspectives that once could only be imagined. The production of mass-mediated images is coming to be more a matter of computing proficiency than camera, darkroom or editing skills. Digitalization techniques seem to permit an unprecedented enhancement and manipulation of pictorial representations.

These changes strike at the heart of the notion of photographic causality and the easy conceptions of realism it supports, severing the necessary tie between photographs and their referents. Digitalization finally puts an end to documentary's 'innocent arrogance of objective fact' by 'removing its claim on the real' (Winston, 1995: 259). When placed alongside such cognate developments as multimedia applications, the growth of the Internet, the emergence of large electronic data banks and virtual reality technologies, these changes lead some to suggest that the 'post-photographic' age has arrived.

Some consider the changes thus signalled to be as momentous as those postulated by Benjamin's ([1936] 1973) classic essay. Digitalization can promote the emergence of new forms of pictorial representation, for example the pop video that exemplifies such key postmodern themes as collage, heterogeneity, pastiche and fragmentation. While there is a basis for claiming that digitalization might provide new grounds for perception, claims about the death of photography need to be treated more circumspectly. Such claims rest on an oversimple technological determinism and overlook the dependence of the new technologies on older skills, knowledges and ways of seeing. Continuities always co-exist with technologically driven ruptures. Moreover, the 'postmodern' world is increasingly hybrid or intertextual in character, where all kinds of borrowing and pastiche are permissible (Lister, 1997). The more portentous claims about a post-photographic era are probably premature. Claims about photographic realism have always been properly understood in qualified terms: 'seeing is believing' is an adage that has long been ironically framed. Digitalization now renders claims about, for example, documentary realism, transparently ideological – it 'destroys the photographic image as evidence of anything except the process of digitisation [*sic*]' (Winston, 1995: 259). One may gloomily prognosticate that digitalization may be regarded as just another symptom of what Baudrillard has termed 'the triumph of signifying culture'.

Such developments might seem to run the risk of pushing ethnographers' productions even further in the direction of – in a pejorative construal that buys into simple conceptions of realism – 'fictions'. New technologies may readily offer the opportunity for misrepresentation but they may just as easily enhance the possibilities for 'adequate' representation. As always, the key issues lie to either side of the technology and concern how the new technologies are used for ethnographic purposes. We incline to the more optimistic view that new technologies can offer ethnographers tools to sharpen their visual perception. We end this chapter with a brief survey of studies suggestive of such ethnographic potential.

Digitalization's implications help to shift attention away from the putatively distinctive characteristics of the photographic representation towards the reception and interpretation of these images. In an intriguing reconsideration of the 1942 classic *Balinese Character*, Dianne Hagaman (1995) has argued that digitalization and related computer-based multimedia technologies would have considerably aided Bateson and Mead's research process and product. Computers could efficiently handle many of their data management and analysis problems. For example, photographs could be scanned into computer files that would also permit their ready storage, retrieval and comparison. Images could be readily exchanged with colleagues at the analysis stage. Devices like hypertext links could aid Bateson and Mead's presentation by more effectively cross-referencing their images. Film sequences could also be integrated into the presentation of stills. Hagaman's mental experiment suggests ways in which the computer can facilitate the combination and recombination of pictorial and written textual representations, and thus encourage shifts in thinking and the emergence of new visual literacies (see also Chaplin, 1998 for comments on how information technologies can assist constructionist approaches).

The new technology also offers tools for the more precise collection and analysis of dynamic visual media such as television news. Priest (1998) shows the usefulness of one software program for capturing and viewing video clips, comparing and categorizing the clips, creating stills and transcribing the soundtrack. For presentational purposes the hypertext link, which can provide a direct link from a point in the author's written text to one image or collection of images, has much to recommend it over paper-based alternatives of search-and-look (see Jewitt's (1997) study of images of men for one example and Thoutenhoofd's (1998) examination of the culturally distinct visuality of deaf communities for another). Here electronic journals have led the way. There are other multi-media possibilities. It is already possible to insert videoclips into the published report (e.g. McGettigan, 1998) and even to include transcripts of the soundtrack in the text adjacent to the videoclip (e.g. Lomax and Casey, 1998). It does seem that there are real benefits for presenting ethnographic work in a far more vivid fashion than ever before (Slack, 1998). New forms of reader and viewer engagement with the ethnographic text are emerging. On the other hand, there is evidently a risk of technological determination parallel to the worries about intellectual convergence and stultification that may follow the widespread adoption of qualitative packages (Coffey et al., 1996; Lee and Fielding, 1996).

Our discussion of contemporary ethnographic uses of photography and film are diagrammatically summarized in Figure 21.1.

We trust that this chapter has signposted some of the opportunities for ethnographers that photography and film potentially offer. Visual methods have been utilized in ethnography almost since the inception of anthropology and sociology. With certain notable exceptions, that use has been primarily illustrative rather than analytical – to amend Ruby's remark, visual methods have only rarely been considered a way of *doing* ethnography. The chapter has traced the uses of visual methods and reviewed directions taken by the work of ethnographers interested in the medium. The greater use of visual methods is not a panacea for all of ethnography's ills nor is it the touchstone to startling ethnographic discoveries. These methods may, nevertheless, go some way towards countering ethnography's logocentric bias, allowing eyes to do the work so often assumed by language in ethnographic accounts. Lastly, it needs to be remembered that when doing fieldwork, ethnographers engage all of their senses, of which vision is but one (the observational metaphor). This chapter, then, might be read as a review of and plea for (to coin a phrase) CSEW – Camera-Supported Ethnographic Work.[12]

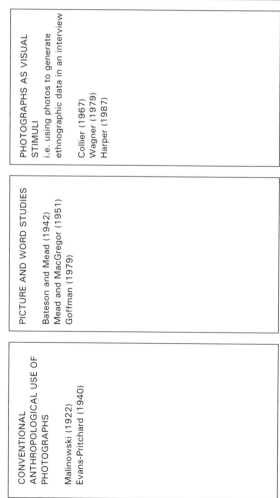

Figure 21.1 *Summary of contemporary ethnographic uses of photography and film*

NOTES

1 We do not wish to get caught up in debates about the meaning, defining orientations and limits of visual sociology and visual anthropology. While most work in these sub-areas has concentrated on the use of photography and film, other kinds of visual record are not precluded (cf. Grady, 1996). As *images* appear to be at the centre of both sub-areas, there is much to recommend Prosser's (1996, 1998) 'image-based qualitative methodology' if an ethnographic generic is sought.

2 Chaplin's book and Harper's chapter address implications of the cultural turn for visual sociology. Henney gives a historical account and annotated bibliography of the development of visual sociology up to the mid-1980s. Ball and Smith review ethnographic methods for the analysis of visuality. Grady provides a judicious analysis of the scope of visual sociology.

3 The Torres Straits expedition resulted in some five published volumes of detailed information, the collection of over 2,000 cultural artifacts, film and photographs (Haddon, 1901).

4 Jay Ruby (1980) suggests that Boas' use of still photography in the field dates from 1894 while his use of motion picture cameras came much later (around 1930). Nevertheless, the significance of Boas cannot be underestimated:

> it is not an overstatement to suggest that Franz Boas should be regarded as a father figure in visual anthropology. He is at least partially responsible for making picture-taking a normative part of the anthropologist's field experience – a characteristic which has distinguished us from other students of the human condition. (Ruby, 1980: 6)

5 The early fieldwork of Rivers and Haddon et al. was not exclusively qualitative in orientation. It included various forms of quantification, survey work and the experimental method.

6 As he wrote in 1931, when the separation from ethnology was still not healed, and the Durkheimian influence on his thinking was powerful:

> The progress of our studies required that they be separated, and this separation has been taking place during the last four decades. Out of social anthropology there has grown a study which I am going to speak of as comparative sociology. (Radcliffe-Brown, 1958: 55)

7 Indeed, it was common for general anthropological work prior to Malinowski to contain an abundance of images such as drawings and sketches. For example, E.B. Tylor's classic text of 1881, *Anthropology*, includes some seventy-eight illustrative figures, mainly sketches of people and items of material culture. Later work, such as that of Malinowski's student Evans-Pritchard, also contains sketches of persons and items of material culture, alongside a substantial corpus of photographs (Evans-Pritchard, 1940).

8 Anonymizing the people studied also featured in the anthropology of Europe from its modern beginning in the 1950s. Misgivings about the practice have emerged more recently and over the past decade or so the practice has fallen into disuse.

9 Indirectly this bears testimony to the immense amount of fieldwork and deskwork that went into the study: as Harper (1994: 404) observes, 'There have been no visual ethnographies that equal *Balinese Character* in depth or comprehensiveness.' Anthropologists have increasingly preferred the medium of film while systematic sociological interest in visual analysis is thinner and more recent (dating from the late 1960s). Mead went on to produce a similar study concentrating on childhood development (Mead and MacGregor, 1951), but otherwise there have been few attempts to follow the opening. Goffman's (1979) *Gender Advertisements* is probably the closest that academic sociology has come to rivalling *Balinese Character*. Bateson and Mead set the exemplar; an opportunity still exists to develop a tradition of work.

10 Semiology has spawned a number of investigations of visual imagery, particularly when refracted through the concerns of cultural studies (see Burnett, 1995; Evans and Hall, 1999; Kress and van Leeuwen, 1996 for significant reviews and recent developments).

11 Perhaps best known is the Granada Centre for Visual Anthropology at the University of Manchester in the UK and the Center for Visual Anthropology at the University of Southern California in the United States.

12 In coining this usage, we borrow from the established field of Computer-Supported Co-operative Work (CSCW) that investigates ways of working with computing technologies. Just as in CSCW there is a clear resistance to simple forms of technological determinism that downgrade the practicalities of the diverse ways that computers can be used, so too CSEW might profit from retaining a recognition of the centrality of context for the interpretation of camera-generated images. As Benjamin recognized in 1936, the camera has an enormous potential as a tool of perception. The photographer:

> increases insight into the necessities that govern our existence, by using close-ups from the environment, by emphasizing hidden details ... by investigating banal milieus while directing his lens in an inspired manner, he manages ... to ensure for us a massive and undreamed of latitude. We seem to be hopelessly encircled by our pubs, our city streets, our offices and furnished rooms, our railway stations and factories. Then came the film and blew-up our prison world with the dynamite of tenths of a second, so that we now casually undertake adventurous journeys among its widely scattered ruins. It thus becomes obvious that a different nature speaks to the camera from the one that speaks to the eye. (Benjamin, 'Work of art ...', as translated from the German by Joel Snyder; quoted Snyder, 1989: 171)

REFERENCES

Agee, J. and Evans, W. (1941) *Let Us Now Praise Famous Men*. Boston, MA: Houghton Mifflin.

Anderson, N. (1923) *The Hobo*. Chicago: University of Chicago Press.

Ball, M. (1998a) 'Remarks on visual competence as an integral part of ethnographic fieldwork practice: the visual availability of culture', in J. Prosser (ed.), *Image-Based Research: A Sourcebook for Qualitative Researchers*. London: Falmer Press. pp. 131–47.

Ball, M. (1998b) 'The visual availability of culture', *Communication and Cognition*, 31 (2/3): 179–96.

Ball, M. and Smith, G. (1992) *Analyzing Visual Data*. Newbury Park, CA: Sage.

Banks, M. (1992) 'Which films are the ethnographic films?' in P. Crawford and D. Turton (eds), *Film as Ethnography*. Manchester: Manchester University Press in association with the Granada Centre for Visual Anthropology.

Banks, M. (1998) 'Visual anthropology: image, object and interpretation', in J. Prosser (ed.), *Image-Based Research: A Sourcebook for Qualitative Researchers*. London: Falmer Press. pp. 9–23.

Banks, M. and Morphy, H. (eds) (1997) *Rethinking Visual Anthropology*. New Haven, CT: Yale University Press.

Barbash, I. and Taylor, L. (1997) *Cross-Cultural Film-making: A Handbook for Making Documentary and Ethnographic Films and Videos*. Berkeley, CA: University of California Press.

Barnouw, E. (1974) *Documentary: A History of Non-Fiction Film*. New York: Oxford University Press.

Barthes, R. (1977) *Image–Music–Text*. London: Fontana.

Bateson, G. and Mead, M. (1942) *Balinese Character* (Special Publications vol. 2). New York: New York Academy of Sciences.

Becker, H.S. (1975) 'Photography and sociology', *Afterimage*, 2: 22–32; reprinted in *Doing Things Together: Selected Papers*. Evanston, IL: Northwestern University Press (1986).

Becker, H.S. (1978) 'Do photographs tell the truth?', *Afterimage*, 5: 9–13; reprinted in *Doing Things Together: Selected Papers*. Evanston: IL: Northwestern University Press (1986).

Becker, H.S. (1979) 'Preface', in J. Wagner (ed.), *Images of Information*. Beverly Hills, CA: Sage.

Becker, H.S. ([1995] 1998) 'Visual sociology, documentary photography and photojournalism: it's (almost) all a matter of context', in J. Prosser (ed.), *Image-Based Research: A Sourcebook for Qualitative Researchers*. London: Falmer Press. pp. 84–96.

Bellman, B. and Jules-Rosette, B. (1977) *A Paradigm for Looking: Cross-Cultural Research with Video Media*. Norwood, NJ: Ablex.

Benjamin, W. ([1936] 1973) 'The work of art in the age of mechanical reproduction' in *Illuminations*. London: Fontana.

Berger, J. (1989) 'Appearances', in J. Berger and J. Mohr, *Another Way of Telling*. Cambridge: Granta. pp. 81–129.

Boas, F. (1974) 'Remarks on the theory of anthropometry' in G.W. Stocking, Jr (ed.), *A Franz Boas Reader.* Chicago: University of Chicago Press.

Bourdieu, P., Boltanski, L., Castel, R. and Chamboredon, J-C. (1990) *Photography: A Middle-Brow Art*. Cambridge: Polity Press.

Burnett, R. (1995) *Cultures of Vision: Images, Media and the Imaginary*. Bloomington, IN: Indiana University Press.

Chalfen, R. (1987) *Snapshot Versions of Life*. Bowling Green State University: Popular Press.

Chalfen, R. (1992) 'Picturing culture through indigenous imagery: a telling story', in P.I. Crawford and D. Turton (eds), *Film as Ethnography*. Manchester: Manchester University Press.

Chalfen, R. (1998) Interpreting family photography as pictorial communication', in J. Prosser (ed.), *Image-Based Research: A Sourcebook for Qualitative Researchers*. London: Falmer Press.

Chaplin, E. (1994) *Sociology and Visual Representation*. London: Routledge.

Chaplin, E. (1998) 'Would you trust a photograph? Common knowledge and social theory in the age of the digital image', *Communication and Cognition*, 31 (2/3): 197–212.

Chiozzi, P. (ed.) (1989) *Teaching Visual Anthropology*. Florence: Published under the Auspices of the European Association for Visual Studies of Man.

Clifford, J. (1987) 'Of other peoples: beyond the "Salvage Paradigm"', in H. Foster (ed.), *Discussions in Contemporary Culture*. Seattle, WA: Bay Press. pp. 121–30.

Clifford, J. (1988) *The Predicament of Culture*. Cambridge, MA: Harvard University Press.

Clifford, J. and Marcus, G.T. (eds) (1986) *Writing Culture*. Berkley, CA: University of California Press.

Coffey, A., Holbrook, B. and Atkinson, P. (1996) 'Qualitative data analysis: technologies and representations', *Sociological Research Online*, 1 (1). http://www.socresonline.org.uk/socresonline/1/1/4.html

Collier, J. (1967) *Visual Anthropology*. New York: Holt, Rinehart and Winston.

Collier, J. and Collier, H. (1986) *Visual Anthropology*. Albuquerque, NM: University of New Mexico Press.

Corner, J. (1996) *The Art of Record*. Manchester: Manchester University Press.

Coulter, J. and Parsons, E.D. (1991) 'The praxiology of perception: visual orientations and practical action', *Inquiry*, 33: 251–72.

Crawford, P. and Turton, D. (eds) (1992) *Film as Ethnography*. Manchester: Manchester University Press in association with the Granada Centre for Visual Anthropology.

Curtis, E.S. (1915) 'The Kwakiutl', in *The North American Indian*, volume 10 (cited in Jacknis 1992).

Denzin, N. (1995) *The Cinematic Society*. Newbury Park, CA: Sage.

Deveraux, L. and Hillman, R. (eds) (1995) *Fields of Vision: Essays in Film Studies, Visual Anthropology and Photography*. Berkeley, CA: University of California Press.

Evans, J. and Hall, S. (eds) (1999) *Visual Culture: The Reader*. London: Sage.

Evans-Pritchard, E.P. (1940) *The Nuer*. Oxford: The Clarendon Press.

Fernandez, J.W. (1986) *Persuasions and Performances: The Play of Tropes in Culture*. Chicago: University of Chicago Press.

Fulton, M. (1988) *Eyes of Time: Photojournalism in America*. New York: New York Graphical Society.

Garfinkel, H. (1967) *Studies in Ethnomethodology*. Englewood Cliffs, NJ: Prentice–Hall.

Garfinkel, H., Lynch, M. and Livingston, E. (1981) 'The work of a discovering science constructed with materials from the optically discovered pulsar', *Philosophy of the Social Sciences*, 11: 131–58.

Geertz, C. (1988) *Works and Lives*. Stanford, CA: Stanford University Press.

Giddens, A. (1990) *The Consequences of Modernity*. Cambridge: Polity Press.

Goffman, E. (1953) 'Communication conduct in an island community'. PhD dissertation, Department of Sociology, University of Chicago, December.

Goffman, E. (1961) *Asylums: Essays on the Social Situation of Mental Patients and Other Inmates*. New York: Doubleday.

Goffman, E. (1967) 'Where the action is', in *Interaction Ritual: Essays on Face-to-Face Behavior*. New York: Doubleday.

Goffman, E. (1979) *Gender Advertisements*. Basingstoke: Macmillan.

Gold, S.J. (1989) 'Ethical issues in visual field work', in G. Blank, J.L. McCartney and E. Brent (eds), *New Techology in Sociology: Practical Applications in Research and Work*. New Brunswick, NJ: Transaction Books. pp. 99–109.

Grady, J. (1996) 'The scope of visual sociology', *Visual Sociology*, 11 (2): 10–24.

Haddon, A.C. (1901) *Headhunters: Black, White and Brown*. London: Methuen.

Hagaman, D.D. (1995) 'Connecting cultures: Balinese character and the computer', in S.L. Star (ed.), *Cultures of Computing*. Oxford: Blackwell/The Sociological Review. pp. 85–102.

Harper, D. (1982) *Good Company*. Chicago: University of Chicago Press.

Harper, D. (1987) *Working Knowledge: Skill and Community in a Small Shop*. Chicago: University of Chicago Press.

Harper, D. (1989) 'Visual sociology: expanding sociological vision' in G. Blank, J.L. McCartney and E. Brent (eds), *New Technology in Sociology: Practical Applications in Research and Work*. New Brunswick, NJ: Transaction Books. pp. 81–97.

Harper, D. (1994) 'On the authority of the image: visual methods at the crossroads' in N. Denzin and Y. Lincoln (eds), *Handbook of Qualitative Research*. Thousand Oaks, CA: Sage.

Heath, C.C. (1986) *Body Movement and Speech in Medical Interaction*. Cambridge: Cambridge University Press.

Heath, C.C. (1997) 'The analysis of activities in face to face interaction using video', in D. Silverman (ed.), *Qualitative Research*. London: Sage.

Heider, K.G. (1976) *Ethnographic Film*. Austin, TX: University of Texas Press.

Henley, P. (1989) 'Signs of life: teaching visual anthropology in Britain', in P. Chiozzi (ed.), *Teaching Visual Anthropology*. Florence: Published under the Auspices of the European Association for Visual Studies of Man.

Henley, P. (1998) 'Film-making and ethnographic research', in J. Prosser (ed.), *Image-Based Research: A Sourcebook for Qualitative Researchers*. London: Falmer Press. pp. 42–59.

Henney (1986) 'Theory and Practice of Visual Sociology' *Current Sociology* 34 (3).

Hindmarsh, J. and Heath, C. (1998) 'Video and the analysis of objects in action', *Communication and Cognition*, 31 (2/3): 111–30.

Hockings, P. (1995) *Principles of Visual Anthropology*, 2nd edn. The Hague: Mouton.

Hockings, P. and Omori, Y. (eds) (1988) *Cinematographic Theory and New Dimensions in Ethnographic Film*. Osaka: Senri Ethnological Studies, No. 24.

Jacknis, I. (1984) 'Franz Boas and photography', *Studies in Visual Communication*, 10 (1): 2–60.

Jacknis, I. (1989) 'Margaret Mead and Gregory Bateson in Bali: their use of photography and film', *Cultural Anthropology*, 3 (2): 160–77.

Jacknis, I. (1992) 'George Hunt, Kwakiutl photographer', in E. Edwards (ed.), *Anthropology and Photography, 1860–1920*. New Haven and London: Yale University Press in association with The Royal Anthropological Institute, London. pp. 143–51.

Jewitt, C. (1997) 'Images of men: male sexuality in sexual health leaflets', *Sociological Research Online*, 2 (2). http://www.socresonline.org.uk/socresonline/2/2/6.html

Kress, G. and van Leeuwen, T. (1996) *Reading Images: The Grammar of Visual Design*. London: Routledge.

Kuper, A. (1977) *Anthropology and Anthropologists: The British School, 1920–1970*. Harmondsworth: Penguin.

Latour, B. (1986) 'Visualization and cognition: thinking with eyes and hands' *Knowledge and Society*, 6, pp. 1–40

Leach, E.R. (1957) 'The epistemological background to Malinowski's empiricism', in R. Frith (ed.), *Man and Culture*. London: Routledge and Kegan Paul.

Lebaron, C.D. and Streeck, J. (1997) 'Built space and the interactional framing of experience during a murder interrogation', *Human Studies*, 20 (1): 1–25.

Lee, R.M. and Fielding, N. (1996) 'Qualitative data analysis: representations of a technology: a comment on Coffey, Holbrook and Atkinson', *Sociological Research Online*, 1 (4). http://www.socresonline.org.uk/socresonline/1/4/lf.html

Lister, M. (1997) 'Photography in the age of electronic imaging' in L. Wells (ed.), *Photography: A Critical Introduction*. London: Routledge.

Loizos, P. (1993) *Innovation in Ethnographic Film*. Manchester: Manchester University Press.

Lomax, H. and Casey, N. (1998) 'Recording social life: reflexivity and video methodology', *Sociological Research Online*, 3 (2). http://www.socresonline.org.uk/socresonline/3/2/1.html

Long, C. and Laughren, P. (1993) 'Australia's first films: facts and fables. Part Six: Surprising survivals from Colonial Queensland', *Cinema Papers*, 96: 32–7, 59–61.

Lynch, M. (1998) 'The production of scientific images: vision and revision in the history, philosophy, and sociology of science', *Communication and Cognition*, 31 (2/3): 213–28.

Lynch, M. and Woolgar, S. (ed.) (1990) *Representation in Scientific Practice*. Cambridge: MIT Press.

MacDougall, D. (1994) 'Whose story is it?', in L. Taylor (ed.), *Visualizing Theory: Selected Essays from V.A.R., 1990–1994*. New York: Routledge.

Malinowski, B. (1922) *Argonauts of the Western Pacific.* London: Routledge and Kegan Paul.

Malinowski, B. (1967) *A Diary in the Strict Sense of the Term*. London: Routledge and Kegan Paul.

McGettigan, T. (1998) 'Reflections in an unblinking eye: negotiating identity in the production of a documentary', *Sociological Research Online*, 3 (1). http://www.socresonline.org.uk/socresonline/3/1/7.html

Mead, M. (1995) 'Visual anthropology in a discipline of words', in P. Hocking (ed.), *Principles of Visual Anthropology*. The Hague: Mouton.

Mead, M. and MacGregor, F.C. (1951) *Growth and Culture: A Photographic Study of Balinese Childhood.* New York: G.P. Putnam's Sons.

Nichols, B. (1991) *Representing Reality*. Bloomington, IN: Indiana University Press.

Nisbet, R.A. (1967) *The Sociological Tradition.* London: Heinemann.

Ohrn, K.B. (1980) *Dorothea Lange and the Documentary Tradition*. Baton Rouge, LA: Louisiana State University Press.

Pinney, C. (1992) 'The parallel histories of anthropology and photography', in E. Edwards (ed.), *Anthropology and Photography, 1860–1920*. New Haven, CT and London: Yale University Press in association with The Royal Anthropological Institute, London. pp. 74–95.

Pinney, C. (1997) *Camera Indica*. London: Reaktion Books.

Price, M. (1994) *The Photograph: A Strange Confined Space*. Stanford, CA: Stanford University Press.

Priest, R. (1998) 'TV news: using computer technology to enhance the study of dynamic visual media', *Visual Sociology*, 13 (1): 61–70.

Prosser, J. (1996) 'What constitutes an image-based qualitative methodology?', *Visual Sociology*, 11 (2): 25–34.

Prosser, J. (ed.) (1998) *Image-Based Research: A Sourcebook for Qualitative Researchers*. London: Falmer Press.

Prosser, J. and Schwartz, D. (1998) 'Photographs within the sociological research process', in J. Prosser (ed.), *Image-Based Research: A Sourcebook for Qualitative Researchers*. London: Falmer Press.

Rabiger, M. (1987) *Directing the Documentary*. Boston, MA: Focal Press.

Radcliffe-Brown, A.R. (1922) *The Andaman Islanders*. Cambridge: Cambridge University Press.

Radcliffe-Brown, A.R. (1958) *Method in Social Anthropology: Selected Essays by A.R. Radcliffe Brown* (ed. M.N. Srinivas). Chicago: University of Chicago Press.

Renov, M. (ed.) (1986) 'Re-thinking documentary: towards a taxonomy of mediation', *Wide Angle*, 8 (3/4): 71–7.

Renov, M. (ed.) (1993) *Theorizing Documentary.* London: Routledge.

Rieger, J. (1996) 'Photographing social change', *Visual Sociology*, 11 (1): 5–49.

Rollwagen, J. (1988) *Anthropological Film-making.* London: Harwood Academic Press.

Rosenblum, B. (1978) 'Style associal process' *American Sociological Review*, 43 (3): 422–38.

Ruby, J. (1976) 'In a pic's eye: interpretive strategies for deriving meaning and significance from photographs', *Afterimage*, 3 (1): 5–7.

Ruby, J. (1980) 'Franz Boas and the early camera study of behavior', *Kinesics Report*, 3 (1): 6–11.

Sharrock, W.W. and Anderson, D. (1979) 'Directional hospital signs as sociological data' *Information Design Journal*, 1 (2): 81–94.

Schwartz, D. (1989) 'Visual ethnography: using photography in qualitative research', *Qualitative Sociology*, 12 (2): 119–55.

Schwartz, D. (1992) 'To tell the truth: codes of objectivity in photojournalism' *Communication*, 13: 95–108.

Schwartz, D. (1997) *Contesting the Superbowl*. London: Routledge.

Sekula, A. (1975) 'On the invention of photographic meaning', *Artforum*, 13: 36–45.

Simmel, G. (1921) 'Sociology of the senses: visual interaction', in R.E. Park and E.W. Burgess (eds), *Introduction to the Science of Sociology*. Chicago: University of Chicago Press. pp. 356–61.

Singer, A. and Woodhead, L. (1988) *Disappearing World.* London: Boxtree.

Slack, R.S. (1998) 'On the potentialities and problems of a WWW based naturalistic sociology', *Sociological Research Online*, 3 (2). http://www.socresonline.org.uk/socresonline/3/2/3.html

Smith, G. (1996) '*Gender Advertisements* revisited: a visual sociology classic?', *Electronic Journal of Sociology*, 2 (1). http://www.sociology.org/vol002.001/Smith.Article.1996.html

Smith, G. (1998) 'Tie-signing *The Conversation*: information and expression in an anonymous world', *Communication and Cognition*, 31 (2/3): 131–44.

Snyder, J. (1984) 'Documentary without ontology', *Studies in Visual Communication*, 10 (1): 78–95.

Snyder, J. (1989) 'Benjamin on reproducibility and aura: a reading of "The Work of Art in the Age of its Technical Reproducibility"', in Gary Smith (ed.), *Benjamin: Philosophy, History, Aesthetics*. Chicago: University of Chicago Press. pp. 158–74.

Snyder, J. and Allen, N.H. ([1975] 1982) 'Photography, vision, and representation', in T. Barrow and S. Armitage (eds), *Reading Into Photography*. Albuquerque, NM: University of New Mexico Press. pp. 61–91.

Sontag, S. (1978) *On Photography*. Harmondsworth: Penguin.

Spencer, F. (1992) 'Some notes on the attempt to apply photography to anthropometry during the second half of the nineteenth century' in Elizabeth Edwards (ed.), *Anthropology and Photography, 1860–1920*. New Haven, CT and London: Yale University Press in association with The Royal Anthropological Institute, London.

Stasz, C. (1979) 'The early history of visual sociology', in J. Wagner (ed.), *Images of Information*. Beverly Hills, CA: Sage. pp. 119–36.

Stocking, Jr, G. (ed.) (1983) *Observers Observed*. Madison, WI: University of Wisconsin Press.

Stoller, P. (1992) *The Cinematic Griot: The Ethnography of Jean Rouch*. Chicago: University of Chicago Press.

Stott, W. (1973) *Documentary Expression and Thirties America*. New York: Oxford University Press.

Sudnow, D. (1972) 'Temporal parameters of interpersonal observation in D. Sudnow (ed.) *Studies in Social Interaction*. New York: Free Press.

Thoutenhoofd, E. (1998) 'Method in a photographic enquiry of being deaf', *Sociological Research Online*, 3 (2). http://www.socresonline.org.uk/socresonline/3/2/2.html

Thrasher, F. (1927) *The Gang*. Chicago: University of Chicago Press.

Turton, D. (1992) 'Anthropology on television. What next?', in P.I. Crawford and D. Turton (eds), *Film as Thenography*. Manchester: Manchester University Press.

Tyler, S.A. (1986) 'Post-modern ethnography: from document of the occult to occult document', in *Writing Culture: The Poetics and Politics of Representation* (ed. J. Clifford and G.F. Marcus). Berkeley, CA: University of California Press. pp. 122–40.

Tylor, E.B. (1881) *Anthropology*. London: Macmillan.

Urry, J. (1972) '*Notes and Queries on Anthropology* and the development of field methods in British anthropology 1870–1920', *Proceedings of the Royal Anthropological Institute for 1972*, pp. 45–57.

Wagner, J. (1979) *Images of Information: Still Photography in the Social Sciences*. Beverly Hills, CA: Sage.

Weinberger, E. (1994) 'The camera people', in L. Taylor (ed.), *Visualizing Theory: Selected Essays from V.A.R., 1990–1994*. New York: Routledge.

Weiner, A.B. (1988) *The Trobrianders of Papua New Guinea*. New York: Harcourt Brace Jovanovich.

Westerbeck, C. and Meyerowitz, J. (1994) *Bystander: A History of Street Photography*. London: Thames and Hudson.

Whyte, W.F. (1943) *Street Corner Society*. Chicago: University of Chicago Press.

Whyte, W.H. (1980) *The Social Life of Small Urban Spaces*. Washington, DC: The Conservation Press.

Winkin, Y. (1999) 'Erving Goffman: What is a life? The uneasy making of an intellectual biography', in G. Smith (ed.), *Goffman and Social Organization*. London: Routledge.

Winston, B. (1995) *Claiming the Real: The Griersonian Documentary and Its Legitimations*. London: British Film Institute.

Winston, B. (1998) '"The camera never lies": the partiality of photographic evidence', in J. Prosser (ed.), *Image-Based Research: A Sourcebook for Qualitative Researchers*. London: Falmer Press. pp. 60–8.

Woodhead, L. (1987) *A Box Full of Spirits*. London: Heinemann.

Worth, S. and Adair, J. (1972) *Through Navajo Eyes*. Bloomington, IN: Indiana University Press.

Worth, S. (1980) 'Margaret Mead and the shift from "visual anthropology" to the "anthropology of visual communication"', *Studies in Visual Communication*, 6 (1): 15–22.

Wyndham, F. and King, D. (1972) *Trotsky: A Documentary*. Harmondsworth: Allen Lane/Penguin.

Young, M.W. (1998) *Malinowski's Kiriwina: Fieldwork Photography, 1915–18*. Chicago: University of Chicago Press.

PART THREE

Introduction to Part Three

The third section of this handbook brings together contributions that contemplate ethnographic presents and futures. The chapters here share common ground by focusing on some of the contemporary preoccupations and conceptualizations of ethnographic enquiry. The range of topics and themes covered is testimony to the calls to diversity which now (and indeed have always) captured the field.

The section has three overarching strands which run through and between chapters. First, a number of the chapters are concerned with the practice of ethnography. Ethnographic labour encapsulates craft skills of data collection, analysis and writing. As more scholars, from a widening range of disciplines, have turned to qualitative research, there has been an increasing need to illuminate and document the methods and strategies of ethnography. The recognition that ethnography is skilful work, and that those skills can be articulated and transferred has transformed the ethnographic landscape. While this handbook should not be seen as a recipe book of 'how to do' ethnography, many of the chapters in this section provide detailed and reflective accounts of the variety of approaches available to the discerning ethnographer. These include strategies for collecting data – participant observation, interviewing, life history; analytic techniques – narrative, computer assisted, biographical; and representational options – writing, scripting, dramatization, hypermedia, poetry, biography. The process of ethnography is also considered as ethical, political (and powerful) work.

The second linking strand of this section might well be termed ethnographic futures, or issues of reflexivity and representation. Several of the contributions provide commentary and contemplation on the present positioning and possible futures of

ethnography. A recurring theme is the (re)location of ethnographic work alongside theoretical and epistemological fluidity. Hence chapters address relationships betwixt and between ethnography and postmodernism, post-structualism, (post-) feminism and (post-) critical theory. In particular ethnographic praxis and representation are re-imagined.

Thirdly, many of the chapters in this section reaffirm the interweaving of ethnographic work with (auto)biography. The labour of ethnography is emotional and potentially intimate. Identity work and the (re)construction of the self is part and parcel of the ethnographic endeavour. More generally the concern of ethnography with 'lives' is foreshadowed. Hence a number of authors address the complexities and nuances of these relationships between ethnography, biography and selfhood, and reflect upon their consequences – both for the present positioning and future directions of ethnographic enquiry and representation.

The section has an internal order, although, as we have indicated, there are connections between and across the contributions. Wellin and Fine open the section with a chapter that seeks to locate ethnography as a distinct form of work and labour process. Ironically, although there have been many ethnographic studies *of* work and occupations, the work of ethnography has been almost completely neglected. Reflections on the ethnographic process have been confessional in tone, rather than applying sociological perspectives on work and organizations to the personal and institutional practices of ethnographic research. Murphy and Dingwall follow on from this with a comprehensive essay on the ethics and politics of ethnography. They ground their discussion in ethical theory, and consider the rights, responsibilities and risks of field work. Their discussion on autonomy and self-determination is particularly helpful in rethinking the issues of power which lie within the research process.

Emerson, Fretz and Shaw (on participant observation and fieldnotes) and Heyl (on ethnographic interview) demonstrate the craft nature of ethnography. Emerson and his colleagues pay careful consideration to the production, reading and usage of fieldnotes. As well as dealing with strategies and styles for writing, they also pick up on the emotional and biographical qualities that fieldnotes imbue. Heyl's chapter takes a walk through the histories and changing conceptualizations of this research strategy. As well as providing an exemplary review of shifting literatures, Heyl also contemplates the ways in which ethnographic interviewing has itself shifted in response to changing times. She reflects on the consequences for interview practice of postmodernism, feminism and increased calls to reflexivity.

The chapters by Cortazzi and Plummer both address the theme of narrative within ethnographic research. Plummer considers the call of life histories, distinguishing between different forms of life story and their applicability to social research. He looks at the ways in which life histories are scripted and draws attention to current movements towards autobiographical ethnography. Plummer also addresses the analytic purchase which life histories offer. This is a topic which Cortazzi elaborates on in his chapter on the role of narrative analysis in ethnographic enquiry. As well as providing a systematic rationale and schema for narrative analysis, Cortazzi also considers the representational and biographical work of narrative research. This is a perspective which is elaborated upon by Reed-Danahay in a comprehensive and insightful piece on autobiography and intimacy. Reed-Danahay considers ethnography as a form of 'life-writing'

and the issues of power and representation that are raised by such an approach. Power is also central to the chapter on feminist ethnography. By articulating the feminist spaces in the ethnographic landscape, Skeggs addresses issues of power, politics and epistemology. This chapter draws on historical and contemporary perspectives, and considers the theoretical intersections on which feminist ethnography is positioned. Skeggs makes an important contribution to both feminist and ethnographic debates on methodology, ethics and research praxis.

The final four chapters in this section address, in different ways, ethnographic representation and futures. Spencer provides a cogent exegesis of the debates surrounding ethnographic writing after postmodernism, and offers his own critique and interpretation. Mienczakowski considers one particular direction that such debate has led – focusing on alternative and experimental representational forms. Here he draws on his own work in ethnodrama and performance texts, to illuminate the limitations and possibilities of such innovative approaches. Fielding is also concerned with innovation and potential in his chapter on the use of computer applications in qualitative research. As well as providing a systematic synthesis of current packages and their general features, Fielding looks towards possible technological futures for ethnography.

This section, and indeed the handbook, ends with a thought-provoking piece from Patti Lather, in which she situates ethnography in postmodern, post-structural and post-foundational times. Lather states that her hope is to create a text that will 'work against itself in disavowing prescription, tidy tales and successor regimes'. The resultant text succeeds in this claim, while providing much to ponder over as to where ethnography has been and where it is going. A good place to start and to end.

22

Ethnography as Work: Career Socialization, Settings and Problems

CHRISTOPHER WELLIN AND GARY ALAN FINE

Whatever else it may be, ethnography is work. This reality and its implications for the doing of and institutional support for ethnography[1] has largely been neglected. None the less, in addition to being a form of cultural critique (Clifford and Marcus, 1986), a set of literary or rhetorical traditions (Atkinson, 1990; Hunter, 1990), a research tool for policy-makers (Akins and Beschner, 1979) and a set of techniques for gathering and analysing data (Agar, 1980; Becker, 1970; Emerson, 1981, 1983; Spradley, 1980; Strauss, 1987), ethnography is, we repeat, ultimately a kind of work. However, only rarely is ethnography *central* to the job descriptions of practitioners, whatever their disciplinary or institutional affiliations. Therein lies the rub. Almost never does one answer an advertisement for 'Ethnographer'. There are, to be sure, exceptions to this rule, such as in the growing world of evaluation and applied research (Loseke, 1989; Patton, 1990; Steele and Iutcovich, 1997) or for those under contract to governments, private foundations or industrial employers (Baba, 1998; Fetterman, 1989; Riley, 1967).

Some ethnographers embrace the more direct connection to social practice and grounded theorizing afforded in various kinds of 'action' research (Cancian, 1993; Lyon, 1997; Whyte, 1984, 1995). But, the occupational dilemmas in this choice are encapsulated by the very term – non-academic research – which has traditionally been used to denote activity not primarily oriented to publishing and developing theory. Here we detect a fateful career contingency in fieldwork, a tension that Wright (1967) found to be strong among graduate students: a reformist versus a scientific orientation. Our discussion of role problems suggests that this tension reflects the institutional and political pressures to which researchers are subject as conditions of employment. These tensions are especially salient among ethnographers who, like the theater's Blanche DuBois, must depend on the kindness of strangers. Being dependent on informants' consent fosters empathy, as well as ambiguous obligations of reciprocity.

For most in academic jobs, however, concerns about the practical impact of their research – Robert Lynd's still troubling question, *Knowledge For What?* (1939) – are less pressing than the problems of conducting and publishing research based on fieldwork, and gaining respect from disciplinary peers. Hence the perennial sub-text of much writing about ethnography is, in Clinard's (1970) phrase, the 'quest for respectability'. In our insistent digging into the underside of social ideals and institutions, and our alliances with those at society's margins, we may be discredited by association (Stinchcombe, 1984). Ironically, though central to the public image of social research (Gans, 1997) and to its appeal for the undergraduates who help subsidize academic sociology, fieldwork may be derided as the academic equivalent of 'dirty work' (Hughes, 1984: 338–47).[2]

Our agenda is: (1) to identify an approach, concepts and empirical problems relevant to understanding ethnography as work; (2) to show how an ethnography-as-work perspective helps one to connect separate streams of writing about practitioners and their careers; and (3) to help delineate an agenda for future research.

We need to clarify our scope at the outset: first, while our focus is on fieldworkers, we readily concede that many problems we discuss arise in different forms in the careers of other kinds of researchers, including quantitative ones (see, for example, Szenberg, 1998, on craft in economics);

secondly, our discussion reflects the normative and institutional conditions for doing research in the United States, and may not apply elsewhere, given different systems of training and promotion. Problems we discuss below, such as incorporating community groups and agendas into research, are probably smaller in nations where tenure is rare and scholars receive more sponsorship from outside the academy. We hope that this chapter prompts those working in different styles, and in other places, to contrast their experiences.

ETHNOGRAPHY AS WORK: A NEGLECTED PERSPECTIVE

By taking this perspective we subject our practices to the same scrutiny that fieldworkers have applied to other occupations. In Barley's (1989: 41–65) review of the 'Chicago School' of work, revolving around Everett Hughes, he argues that its essential (if often implicit) contribution was to reveal the recursive interconnections between careers, identities and institutions through which society itself is sustained and transformed. An occupational analysis of ethnography sheds light on the history of the method (Vidich and Lyman, 1994; Wax, 1970: 21–41) and on dilemmas that practitioners are likely to face in the future. Fieldwork cannot be understood by an exclusive focus on its internal logics, which, as Burawoy (1998: 12) shows, have often been invoked to provide justification in a ritualized dispute between reflexive and positivist 'models of science'. This dichotomy, useful for generating methodological discourse and occupational networks, obscures the institutional constraints felt in common by diverse researchers, regardless of method.

As in other occupations, ethnographers' ideals and practices coincide and diverge over time, depending on the business at hand and the interests (and power) of observers. Ideals are desirable, even essential, for occupational communities. But understanding work as a 'going concern' (Hughes, 1984: 52–64) requires that one pay equal attention to the *drama* of work: its informal organization (for example, the constraints on and conflict over resources); cooperative ties linking practitioners, sponsors, clients and 'regulators'; frustrations and thrills that animate encounters among these participants; and the forces that produce patterns in the diversity of individual careers. Also, occupational groups are neither static nor unified, but forever *in process*, through changes in internal specialization and external alliances (Bucher and Strauss, 1961).

Sadly, journals that publish ethnography pay scant attention to recurring problems of work; ethnographic monographs include methodological appendices, but these tend either to be defensive (regarding problems in research design), topical (elaborating generic fieldwork problems), or personally confessional (Van Maanen, 1988). Not even in the autobiographical writings of prominent researchers (such as Berger, 1990; Hammond, 1964; Reinharz, 1984; Riley, 1988) do we learn much about mundane pressures, pettiness or collegial sustenance in employing institutions (but see Shaffir et al., 1979).[3] Like other workers, we are often blind to organizational dynamics shaping our careers (Rosenbaum, 1989). Consulting the index of Denzin and Lincoln's (1994) *Handbook of Qualitative Research* reveals virtually no reference to the categories 'work', 'funding', 'occupation', or 'career', nor do the articles indexed (but see chapters by Greene, Morse, and Punch). Promising exceptions to this neglect in American social science can be found in feminist narratives of academic life, centered on the women's movement (Laslett and Thorne, 1997; Orlans and Wallace, 1994), but here, too, attention to the practice of research is peripheral. The richest cache of data on managing fieldwork and other demands is, as Rabinow writes, still to be found in 'corridor talk'. But, 'the micropractices of the academy might well do with some scrutiny ... When corridor talk becomes discourse, we learn a good deal' (1986: 253).

The 'Chicago School', Work and Method

The roots of fieldwork in sociology can be traced to the Chicago School and, in turn, to its connections with social problems and social reform (Bulmer, 1984; Fine, 1995; Turner and Turner, 1990). In the resurgence of ethnography among sociologists in the 1950s and 1960s, scholars developed methodological rationales for fieldwork in social research. This was partly a response to Merton's (1968: 39–72) ecumenical call to develop theories of the middle-range, as well as to the growing number in government agencies and foundations willing to fund social research but unsure about its validity. In papers such as Becker's (1970) 'Problems of inference and proof in participant observation', Bensman and Vidich's 'Social theory in field research' (1960) and Gold's (1958) 'Roles in sociological field observations' sociologists analysed fieldwork and its relation to theorizing in ways that anthropologists, as carriers of an oral tradition, had generally not done (for example, Freilich, 1970; Golde, 1970). This literature enhanced both the practice and prestige of field research.

For sociologists of work, however – especially those in the tradition exemplified by Hughes and his students during the 'Second Chicago School' (Fine, 1995; Solomon, 1968) – no attempt to understand an occupation, nor the careers of its members, could get very far by uncritically accepting lofty ideals, or ignoring the 'dirty work' of making a living. Superiors and clients must be kept at bay; autonomy and honor are seldom won for good. If Hughes and his colleagues seemed subversive, asking the same questions of the 'proud' professions as of those in more 'humble' lines, it was not an exercise in irony or contrarism. Rather, the core insight of the Hughesian approach is that occupational ideals, routines, achievements and indignities are shaped by institutional arrangements, disparities of power and the legacies of local and societal cultures. To a puzzling degree the work of ethnographers has escaped this venerable kind of scrutiny. Perhaps the problem is that the tasks and issues 'internal' to ethnography – gaining access, forging roles and relationships, constructing and recording data, ethics, analysis, writing – have been treated with such care separately that authors seldom have integrated them with other features of work and careers. Writings about ethnography have tended to remove and abstract particular work problems (for example, gaining access, ethics, data collection, writing/ rhetoric), and to subject them to philosophical or methodological scrutiny. Yet, these topics have seldom been integrated or discussed in the context of 'external' career constraints or contingencies. This lack of *occupational* self-reflection among ethnographers is striking, however, after a decade defined by the most thoroughgoing and reflexive critiques of this research genre.

From Work *in* Methods, to the Work *of* Methods

One, parallel line of analysis has explored the social relations and constraints *in* (as opposed to *of*) field methods. The thrust of these writings has been methodological – that is, rejecting or responding to criticisms about ethnography *as science*. So, Katz (1983: 147) describes fieldwork and data analysis as a social system, in which researchers, informants, and (later) readers jointly define and interpret findings. He notes that 'In its present state, the methodological literature assumes that reactivity in participant observation is a contaminating problem. But if we examine how research procedures shape the meaning of the study to members, we may conclude that field research without a formal design makes interaction between researcher and member into a substantive data resource'. Wellin and Shulman (1995) argue that placing field data in theoretical 'frames' involves negotiation between researchers and those – including mentors and reviewers – with the authority to judge. In these encounters the validity of field data, central to realist claims, is bracketed; fieldnotes and interview transcripts become vehicles for demonstrating ethnographic competence, creative induction, or knowledge of substantive domains. Others analyse conversational practices, emergent meanings and coding decisions of survey researchers (Hak and Bernts, 1996; Holstein and Staples, 1992; Maynard and Schaeffer,

1997). These authors elaborate Garkfinkel's argument that:

> The investigator frequently must elect among alternative courses of interpretation and enquiry to the end of deciding matters of fact, hypothesis, conjecture, fancy, and the rest, despite the fact that in the calculable sense of the term 'know', he does not and even cannot 'know' what he is doing prior to or while he is doing it. Fieldworkers, most particularly those doing ethnographic and linguistic studies in settings where they cannot presuppose a knowledge of social structures, are perhaps best acquainted with such situations. (1967: 77–78)

These and similar studies implicitly provide evidence about recurring work problems facing ethnographers. But revealing the fluidity of meaning within research encounters is different from documenting the obdurate institutional contexts in which such fluidity is either glossed over or resolved in routine ways. This paradox is common in occupational sociology: for instance, we recognize the discursive construction of medical diagnoses (for example, Waitzkin, 1991), but do not ignore the question of how institutional authority and procedures order work lives in hospitals.

SALIENT CONCEPTS IN THE SOCIOLOGY OF WORK AND OCCUPATIONS

Three concepts and processes basic to the sociology of work and occupations are helpful in analysing ethnographers' work: occupational socialization and culture, tensions of bureaucratic (and disciplinary) organization, and careers.

Socialization and the Legacy of 'Classical' Anthropologists

For ethnographers, idealized work images and identities are inherited partly from cultural anthropologists, whose rigorous process of penetrating others' cultural and language groups is extended metaphorically to fieldwork in one's 'own backyard'. Paradoxically, for anthropologists doing fieldwork has been at once more central to occupational socialization and identity, and less subject to critical reflection, than among sociologists (Freilich, 1970). We do not refer here to the broad, political and literary critiques of ethnography and its linkages to colonial power, in which anthropologists have been in the vanguard (Clifford and Marcus, 1986). Cultural anthropologists treat initiation into fieldwork with the deep affect and autobiographical nuance befitting its status as an occupational rite of passage. However, because the rite is culturally sanctioned as a solitary, transformative ordeal in an anthropological career, reflections by neophytes have produced little in the way of collective, institutional definitions of work problems, let alone solutions to the problems of how to sustain fieldwork throughout a career.

The guiding metaphors by which anthropologists define and transmit problems in ethnography often reinforce individualistic, quasi-mystical imagery: one is made to 'sink or swim', in an encounter that commonly demands total and prolonged immersion in a 'foreign' culture and language. The author of an influential textbook chapter on ethnography as method and product acknowledges that the neophyte:

> has little advance preparation for the methodological and technical problems which will confront him in his field research. This is partly because of the subtlety of the ethnographic research process ... and partly because, until very recently, it was widely assumed that the process need not, and perhaps could not, be taught, that it was an ability or knack which came naturally or not at all. (Berreman, 1968: 340)

Similarly, in a memoir Laura Nader reports having received a grant to support nine months of fieldwork in Mexico. Though she lacked even a 'textbook' knowledge of fieldwork, she writes that her advisor, Clyde Kluckhohn 'told me that he thought I had been in the library too long ... I accepted the grant ... I packed several good ethnographies, a copy of *Notes and Queries* (written for nonanthropologists), and a pack of medicines, and off I went' (Nader, 1970: 98).

Coffey and Atkinson survey the dense domain of meanings associated with 'fieldwork' in anthropology, based on interviews with a graduate student and faculty member. They find it connotes both ordeal and reward in the process of training; fieldwork is central to 'semantic relationships' that organize (for both parties) the student's emerging identity along dimensions of place, inclusion, product, emotions and time (1996: 92–107). These meanings anchor researcher identities both projectively – as aspirants await validation through the crucible of fieldwork – and retrospectively – as one narrates theoretical insights in terms of biographical detail and personae. As Geertz (1988: 79) concludes, 'To be a convincing "I-Witness" one must first, it seems, become a convincing "I".'

The possessive identification, common among earlier cohorts of anthropological fieldworkers with *their* tribe or community, is analogous to the therapeutic relationship in psychoanalysis; this helps explain the almost mystical aura around cultural translation and personal transformation of the neophyte from a student of culture to an anthropologist. There was, in this tradition, little emphasis on prescriptive training or protocols since, after all, 'How can one program the unpredictable?' (Freilich, 1970: 15).[4]

This theme in the culture of anthropological fieldwork endures. In a revealing essay entitled

'I am a fieldnote', Jean Jackson explores the feelings and careers of seventy cultural anthropologists she interviewed, most of whom reported never having before publicly discussed this central activity in their work lives. In their accounts, fieldnotes themselves, for all their personal idiosyncrasy and context-dependence, embody the practice of ethnography. On the one hand, they signal the acceptance of the collective ritual of initiation into fieldwork, a membership defined by a rejection of uniformity:

> A general pattern for most interviewees is to couch their answers in terms of how much their fieldwork – and hence fieldnote-taking – differs from the stereotype. In part, this signals a defensiveness about one's fieldwork not living up to an imagined standard ... A substantial number of interviewees expressed pride in the uniqueness of their field sites, in their own iconoclasm, and in being autodidacts at fieldnote-taking. (Jackson, 1990: 19)

Anthropologists accept, even celebrate, the resistance of their practices to routinization. In turn, they reinforce the image of ethnography as an elusive combination of theoretical orientation, spontaneous insight and bodily presence. This individualistic image of ethnographic practice makes a virtue of the necessity of going it alone, and continues to define the ways in which new practitioners assess their performance and are seen by teachers. Because these evaluations are 'characterological', many ethnographers perceive their methodological stance as more salient than their discipline or topics of interest. As, Kleinman, Stenross and McMahon (1994: 4) argue, those using non-ethnographic approaches see them as 'techniques rather than [as] identities ... Field workers are more likely to identify with their method, and the perspective that underlies it, than with substantive areas. This occurs because each new study might bring us into a different substantive area.'

Sociologists have inherited the anthropological ethos that ethnography is a creative, ineffable accomplishment, borne, by necessity, of long, solitary removal from one's familiar haunts – especially given that teamwork in field studies is uncommon, despite such well-known exceptions as *Boys in White* (Becker et al., 1961) and valuable discussions like those by Olesen et al. (1994), Mitteness and Barker (1994), and Shaffir et al. (1980). The ordeal of fieldwork is seen not as a pedagogical or institutional shortcoming, but as inevitable. As a result, a connection exists between the silence in the literature regarding ethnographic careers, and the prescribed images by which aspirants embrace the role of the ethnographer. To acknowledge social and institutional constraints in ethnographers' work lives is to reveal the benign, humdrum, perhaps arbitrary nature and consequences of such constraints for ethnography itself.

Training, Identity Formation and Early Career Problems

As Pavalko notes, occupational socialization can be understood with reference either to aspirants' patterned subjective appraisals of work, or to salient features and demands of their social context. But, as he reminds us, 'Clearly, not all occupations have elaborate, formal training and socialization processes, and in many occupations socialization occurs on the job' (1988: 117). For ethnographers, socialization is embedded in a process of academic apprenticeship which, though intimate and subject to negotiation, is also regulated by evaluations and dependence on mentors. Thus, for ethnographic researchers, the learning of the craft is: (1) idiosyncratic across aspirants; (2) dependent on immersion in 'the field' at a distance from schools and mentors; and (3) equated symbolically with competence and occupational membership. These conditions, in turn, reinforce the solitary ethos of the work, the strong subjective identification with ethnography, even among many whose daily work lives all but preclude ongoing involvement in the method (Kleinman et al., 1994); and the absence of accurate 'anticipatory socialization' or of collective strategies that might help students cope with uncertainty in ways similar to those Becker and colleagues (1961) found true of medical students.

These conditions of uncertainty regarding performance, evaluation and temporal markers of progress compound the emotional paralysis or 'hang-ups' that Stinchcombe (1986) discusses as characteristic generally of graduate training. The tendency to become identified with method is also a product of the delay in graduate training before one can tackle a concrete project. Uncertainty about one's substantive direction is managed partly by the acquisition of research skills, which, in turn, is often a basis for matching students with mentors. The minority status of fieldwork students in most disciplines and departments reinforces the need to justify and identify with the method.

The degree of disciplinary consensus regarding goals and evaluative standards influences the strength and timing of methodological commitment, as it does the reception work receives. Where scholars are chronically divided over research approaches – as in sociology, education, psychology – choices about method are tantamount to career choices (Schatzman and Strauss, 1974: 3). Furthermore, role conflicts embedded in training or employing institutions are overlaid by those inherent in field relations (Adler and Adler, 1987; Wax, 1957). Negotiating field roles involves both practical and psychological demands. For instance, we must reconcile our schedules to those of our informants; and we must choose field settings in which we are 'allowed' if not comfortable, given our age, ethnic

and gender statuses.[5] To these demands is usually added that of learning the specialized knowledge or language required to be a competent member and observer of the social world.[6] And, as Wax argues, we must teach our informants to assume roles that will allow us to learn (1957).

Moving from graduate training these logistical and emotional demands produce a 'hangover' effect following the completion of ethnographic dissertations, coinciding with the pressure, certainly in academic jobs, to begin a new project. Also, any new project will be measured against the dissertation by peers plotting one's research trajectory, despite junior professors' inability to invest the time and single-minded devotion to research demanded of graduate students. There are long-term costs of failing to manage these pressures – not to mention those of family life – in the transition from student to professional. Although books are often favored by ethnographers, they take longer to complete and are subject to more variable criteria of evaluation than are articles (Clemens et al., 1995). Thus, in the early career, one finds an especially large part of ethnographers' occupational identity and hopes riding on a single product.

WORK SETTINGS AND DILEMMAS OF OCCUPATIONAL IDENTITY

Few scholars work primarily as ethnographers. The majority of ethnographic researchers are hired for positions in which teaching, advising, publishing, consulting, or service are the practical activities that must be performed. This reality, now taken for granted, is anomalous given the roots of sociological fieldwork in social reform and the emphasis in anthropology on ethnography as immersion. Shaffir and colleagues introduced their collection of essays on fieldwork processes and problems by claiming *marginality* to be an 'especially well-suited adjective that describes the social experiences of fieldwork' (1980: 18). They view fieldworkers as marginal in several ways: in our desire to know the situated and subjective realities of people, we stand outside of their communities, suspected of being spies or inept. In turn, we are marginal to the social sciences and closer to the humanities. In rejecting positivism, we are marginal to standards that have regulated much academic research and evaluation. Excepting anthropologists, ethnographers are often marginal to their own disciplines.

Ironically, the ethnographer-as-marginal theme coexists with a counter-theme, based on the protected and quasi-elite status we enjoy by virtue of class, educational and institutional affiliations. Joined to postmodern enquiries into the method's colonial roots, this critique cast ethnographic practice and writing into a period of deep, even crippling, introspection through the early 1990s (e.g., Gans, 1999). The postmodern movement has none the less given rise to a vigorous and cohesive community of scholars, whose writings and exegeses of earlier texts sustained ethnography as an intellectual genre, based in academe. Here we note Nader's (1998) injunction to distinguish ethnography as practice (that is, the sustained, first-hand study of cultural meanings and processes) from scholarship that is *ethnographic* (also see Wolcott, 1990). An anthropologist, she is among those who regard the growing popularity of the genre as, ironically, concurrent with a dilution of ethnography's standards and aspirations. For Gans, the introspective, postmodern genre of ethnographic writing, unlike sustained fieldwork, is

> a nearly perfect adaptation to today's academic economy. [It] can be done by one person, working at home, and in bits and pieces between teaching one's classes – or even in class ... Moreover, the ethnographic product can be turned into articles ... In this respect, ethnography is similar to today's computerized quantitative research, which, at the acceptable level of quality required by its peer reviewers, can also produce the number of refereed articles needed for tenure. (1999: 7)

In *Living the Ethnographic Life*, Rose (1990: 10) too is concerned that 'our corporate way of life constrains our pursuit of ethnographic knowledge'. While this might be dismissed as romantic naivete, kindred researchers do give up their protected status as organizational employees. Diamond (1995), for example, took leave from a tenured faculty position – and his health insurance benefits – partly to experience the vulnerability that millions of Americans face in securing medical coverage in the hodgepodge of care provision. This commitment to bodily immersion in the field harkens back to such classical realist studies as Nels Anderson's *The Hobo* (1923), the 'research' for which began as the author rode the rails between work in mines and lumber camps, years before he wrote of 'Hobohemia' as a student at the University of Chicago. Goffman (1989: 125–6), reflecting on the essence of fieldwork, offered that:

> It's [a way] of getting data, it seems to me, by subjecting yourself, your own body and your own personality, and your own social situation, to the set of contingencies that play upon a set of individuals ... You are in a position to note their gestural, visual, bodily response to what's going on around them, and you're empathetic enough – because you've been taking the same crap they're taking. To me, that's the core of observation. If you don't get yourself in that situation, I don't think you can do a piece of serious work.

These scholars occupy a place on a continuum whose other pole is planted firmly in the worker's institutional setting and roles, including those who rely on 'one-shot' interviews, 'hit and run' fieldwork, or narrative analysis of extant texts. However, we are more than any of our field roles; these images obscure fieldworkers as workers who, like other workers, must negotiate and justify multiple tasks, roles and relationships. Depending on the task and audience, workers invoke multiple rhetorics, each reflecting and seeking to sustain occupational identities (Fine, 1996).

Work Problems and Role Conflict

Writings on *membership roles* in field research (e.g., Adler and Adler, 1987; Gold, 1958) have placed more emphasis on how they shape the collection and interpretation of data than how they may conflict with or disrupt other roles in researchers' daily lives. Studies of occupational socialization examine the development of and conflict between work roles (Pavalko, 1988: 84–120). Some studies reflect a 'structural' conception of roles, following Merton and Ralph Linton; others, an interactionist one, following Mead, Blumer, Becker, and others (Colomy and Brown, 1995; Hewitt, 1984). In structural terms, Merton (1957, 1968) argued that we do not occupy single roles, but are members of *role sets* with their competing expectations. In theory, conflicting pressures in role sets are attenuated by differences in the importance attached to various roles. But, fieldworkers' most immediate and visible *institutional* roles – teacher, departmental citizen, advisor – may be less central to identity than one's subjective commitment to that of ethnographer. Much interactionist attention to role conflict centers on the *dynamics of inclusion and distance* in field relations (Emerson, 1983: 235–52). These tensions, of intimacy, trust and translation, can only be managed, never resolved. This can result in a *dual-consciousness* regarding our work lives. A parallel is that which Dorothy Smith and others long proclaimed was true for women scholars, torn between their lived experience and the abstract concepts dominant in sociology (see DeVault, 1999: 46–55).

The character of and investment in academic roles varies based on method, which can be seen across the settings in which ethnographers work. One's institutional affiliation can, depending on one's field milieux, be irrelevant or even harmful to the maintenance of field relations (as when 'low status' informants are alienated or threatened by researchers' associations with the government or with elites). One class of career problems among fieldworkers are, then, rooted in the combination of their reformist orientation, topical concerns (institutional power, social inequalities) and reciprocal obligations with both sponsors and informants. Fieldworkers often reflect the grievances and hopes of those whose worlds they enter. This is why realist claims – which some postmodern critics reject as quaint or trivialize as a literary trope – are better seen as social facts, imposed on us by all sides in our work. Both oppressed people, who see one as an instrument for articulating their critique, and more privileged informants, seeking absolution for institutional failure, see the fieldworker as a tangible embodiment of the more abstract promise implicit in ethnography: that empathic understandings can matter in exposing and shaping realities.

Further, as fieldworkers we assume complex burdens in our institutional roles. As mentors, we supervise beginning fieldworkers in a system of apprenticeship. To guide students in field projects responsibly requires much time and talk; issues of access, field roles, data sources and 'making sense' of material is far less amenable than most research genres to prescriptive advice (Schatzman, 1991). Often, students are drawn to topics in which they feel a personal stake, thereby adding to mentors' pedagogical role, a therapeutic one.

ETHNOGRAPHY AS WORK, BUREAUCRATIZATION AND DISCIPLINES

Even when the products of ethnography, such as publications, reports, or policy recommendations, fit readily into the system of occupational duties and rewards, few institutional allowances are made for the demands of this labor-intensive method of enquiry. But, on the other horn of this dilemma, compromising standards of methodological rigor to those sponsors accept may offend one's scholarly integrity and bring the scorn of fellow ethnographers. However central to one's identity and research program ethnography is, accomplishing it is peripheral to the bureaucratic timetables and record-keeping that govern work in employing institutions.

In a historical essay, 'Professionalization of sociology', Janowitz (1972: 105) argues that, 'To speak of sociology as a profession is to focus on a relatively neglected aspect of the organization of the discipline, namely, its clients and the dilemmas of client relations ... But strictly speaking, the clients of the sociologist, as researcher, are relatively ambiguous.' Janowitz (1972: 106) concludes that sociology is best seen as, 'a staff-type profession based on the fusion of research and teaching roles most effectively institutionalized in a university structure.' Adler and Adler (1995) confirm this pattern among fieldworkers. They tallied characteristics of authors who had submitted work to the *Journal of Contemporary Ethnography* (over 800 manuscripts) between 1986 and 1994, and reported that roughly 90 per cent were academically based. We have, then, the anomalous situation of a craft-like activity that has no direct constituency, and is almost entirely dependent upon an institutional infrastructure.

The overall benefits of this arrangement for the establishment of academic disciplines have been costly for field researchers. Thus situated, social researchers have been subject to bureaucratization (Mills, 1959; Sjoberg and Vaughan, 1993), both in the allocation and management of research support and in their evaluation for tenure and promotion. This trend has had distinctly different effects on scholars, depending upon their styles of research: theorists or those who rely on archival data are better suited to careers inside academic institutions, provided that library resources are readily available. The bureaucratic context is favorable too for those who analyse large-scale survey research, in line with what Sjoberg and Vaughan (1993: 5) term 'the natural science model':

> Grantsmanship in sociology is closely-interwoven with commitment to the natural science model ... By relying on established data sets, the researcher can anticipate, in general terms, the results of the findings. These are defined by the nature of the questions included in the survey. This situation greatly reduces the risk of failure, and the funding agency generally can be assured that numerous publications will result from the project.

Efforts to control costs in higher education – pervasive in the United States – may promote the natural science model, independent of the status of various research styles (but see Lidz and Ricci, 1990 for advice). One sign is the increasingly common requirement that academic job-seekers demonstrate 'a track-record of securing external funding'; these data sets and funds are, in turn, important in the training of graduate students in many research universities, and cannot but shape their own research ideals and practices.

Disciplinary Contexts and Career Problems

Many bureaucratic controls in academic life are mediated by departments and their affiliated disciplines. Field researchers are especially vulnerable to a set of career problems arising from work being subject to *disciplinary* evaluation and politics. As in academic life generally, the 'politics' are both institutional (selecting personnel and allocating resources) and ideological (shaping knowledge production). Whether separately or in tandem, these have myriad effects on ethnographers. Rather than having our work appraised and our status assigned primarily by those within the 'guild' – the *sine qua non* both of traditional craft control and of professional dominance (Freidson, 1970) – ethnographers must translate their work into terms that are acceptable to disciplinary peers who may have little direct experience with the craft of ethnography. Moreover, promotion and tenure decisions are based on criteria that are even further removed from research or teaching practice, that rest on indices of reputation among disciplinary peers (citations, publications in prestigious journals, grants), that committee members and deans outside the field can accept.[7] Stinchcombe (1990: 338) argues that universities 'rent reputations, ... by paying [faculty] to do research whose value to the university will come mainly when they are senior scholars who are known to be first-rate by a wide community of scholars outside the university'.

This administrative fact makes a virtue of disciplinary consensus, which (at least in sociology and anthropology) is weak. Under these conditions, evaluators and grant-review committees can either fetishize those methods that have gained the highest status, or, they can rely for their judgements on more transient and morally charged criteria, such as 'interestingness' (Stinchcombe, 1994). Whereas emphasizing method works to the disadvantage of fieldworkers (as Plattner et al., 1987 found of NSF funding in anthropology), the latter may be a benefit, as long as the work is not defined as trivial or 'popular'. In a world with increasingly polycentric disciplines (Becker, 1986: 209–20), where innovative thinking spawns 'hybrid' fields (Dogan and Pahre, 1989), we ethnographers have carved out spaces with our own institutions, such as scholarly societies and publishing outlets. But, in the United States, the most esteemed journals featuring field studies, the *Journal of Contemporary Ethnography* and *Qualitative Sociology*, solicit and feature work from a wide range of disciplines, thus confusing the reception authors may enjoy among departmental peers.[8] And these spaces are themselves under pressure by researchers favouring different goals and criteria of evaluation.

Careers of fieldworkers in academic jobs and the fortunes of the method more generally are also tied, then, to factors that interact with and transcend disciplinary affiliations. Three factors we see as important are:

1   *Institutional contexts*: employing institutions differ in their definition and ranking of work products in promotion decisions; Clemens and her colleagues (1995) found that in large state and research universities, journal articles are 'the coin of the realm', whereas liberal arts colleges are more accepting of books, even or perhaps especially those which find a broad scholarly and lay audience. The same contradiction between the public and academic reception given ethnography and other qualitative work is apparent in Gans' (1997) review of 'best-sellers in sociology', whose virtues and readership often overlap with those of journalism (Ragin, 1994: 17–24).

2   *The timeliness of research topics* and their linkage with social problems agendas advanced by government agencies and foundations. The connection between field research and social problems agendas is especially apparent when one considers that a great many of the 'classic' post-war American studies – of poverty, family, ethnicity, and cities – were sponsored by such federal agencies as the National Institutes of Mental Health (NIMH), as part of their commitment to an expanded model of the etiology and treatment of mental illness (Duhl and Leopold, 1968; Felix, 1961). More recent federal policy to wage a 'drug war' and, it is assumed, stem street crime, has led the National Institutes of Drug Abuse (NIDA) consistently and generously to sponsor field research. Whatever its impact on the policies in question, and granting the moral and political hazards this dependence may pose for researchers, knowledge of fieldwork and of society have been enhanced by this support (e.g., Agar, 1973; Akins and Beschner, 1979; Weppner, 1977). Many in the postwar cohorts are nostalgic for the days when funding for field research was more plentiful, because it afforded them time away and relief from the academic career pressures discussed above.[9]

3   *Movements within social theory* create change and dynamism in careers. Ethnographers have both instigated and benefitted from movements that bridge and transcend disciplinary discourse. For instance, narrative analysis has infused enquiry in history, psychology, linguistics, even clinical medicine, which, in turn, has stimulated interest in pinning down linkages between narrative and context via ethnography (Riessman, 1993). The same synergy can be seen between ethnography and the dramatic growth of research on gender, and constructionist studies of social problems and of science.

APPLIED, EVALUATION AND INDUSTRIAL ETHNOGRAPHY

We would be remiss if we did not say that much of the growth in ethnography – both in numbers and in its influence on practice – is in non-academic settings. The traditional denigration of 'applied', versus 'basic', research, as well as the insularity of academic life, are to blame for the collective ignorance of the promise and problems in such settings (but see Baba, 1998; Fetterman, 1989; Lyon, 1997; Patton, 1990). Lyon examines and refutes conventional concerns that have impeded the growth of applied ethnography, concluding that: 'Given the increasing acceptance, and frequent advocacy, of practice- and policy-related ethnography, it is remarkable that it is not more widespread' (1997: 23).[10] Indeed, Mobley and Spitler (1998: 24) report that 'a majority of those with sociological training at both the undergraduate and graduate level choose to work in applied settings upon graduation'. According to a 1984 'Career Guide for Anthropologists', 'a majority of practicing anthropologists report that they are employed in areas of administration, management, and service, rather than in research' (Chambers, 1984: 338). In the United States then, applied ethnographers are both more numerous and more informative for understanding the changing role and market for the method than is generally reflected in the literature.

Given their academic training, it is understandable that many of the problems facing ethnographers in non-academic settings have to do, first, with role and identity problems (Fetterman, 1983; Mobley and Spitler, 1998; Riley, 1967) and, secondly, with the demands of justifying the method to those whose expectations are vague or irrelevant to the logics of field research. Many practitioners 'straddle the fence' between academic and applied research, finding problems distinctive to their location. Those in non-academic settings tend to have an easier time forging collaborative relations with co-workers and in seeing how their work can inform practice. Yet, as Brownstein (1990) explains from his position as an analyst in a government agency, if they are to survive, qualitative researchers must demonstrate the utility of their approach for addressing pre-existing organizational questions; and they face a greater need to 'sell' both the efficacy of the methods and themselves as practitioners, than is true in academic jobs. Fetterman (1983) elaborates on problems ethnographers, working under contract as evaluators, are likely to face. In addition to a shortened time-frame (which may involve the need to report findings on-site), contract workers often must mediate between contending organizational factions. If under government contract, they are seen as agents of government, which, in turn, is liable for the actions of researchers. As a result, ethnographers must negotiate 'up-front' and explicitly the terms, boundaries and results of research (including whether and in what form findings may be disseminated). As with those linked to government and its construction of social problems, applied researchers may be judged among informants as 'guilty by association' with institutional authorities and goals.

In contrast, those conducting applied or evaluation research from an academic base, face logistical and status problems in translating this work into the reward structure of tenure and promotion. For example, contract researchers may accept agreements regarding confidentiality, such that limits on the use of data or potential revelation of the case undercuts scholarly publication. In addition, the short time-frame of contract research may yield a level of ethnographic depth or understanding that is too superficial to inform theoretical articles. Finally, research reporting on the fate of a particular policy intervention in ways unflattering either to the sponsors of the research or to powerful stakeholders, may expose the investigator to public, even legal, challenges that, in turn, could threaten relations with academic and private employers. Finally, when the goal of qualitative evaluation is to assess the effectiveness or efficiency of programs – that is, an 'engineering', as opposed to an 'enlightenment' model of research (Weiss, 1977) – fieldworkers inherit the positivist burden of demonstrating validity, in response to concerns that, 'This is an interesting portrayal of the program, but where are the hard facts?' And, 'With all these different views of the program, how do I know which one is true?' (Greene et al., 1988: 353; Morse, 1994). Solutions to these troubles, on which fieldworkers depend for their continuing acceptance in this career niche, can involve external audits, in which outside researchers inspect both data and findings for threats for bias or sloppiness. Such practices collide with the researcher-as-instrument ethos and may ultimately produce a convergence between ethnographic methods and those of private detectives who uncover 'dirty data' in their investigation of lies and deception (Shulman, 1994), with as yet unexamined occupational and ethical implications.

Lyson and Squires (1984) acknowledge that applied and contract research offers an alternative 'career niche' during times when competition for secure academic jobs is high (Hartung, 1993). But they detect a danger that such research will appropriate the methods and prestige of social science without either enriching theoretical understanding or altering relations of power. None of these problems is insurmountable (Weiss, 1977), nor are they sufficient to dissuade those (Bogdan and Taylor, 1990; Loseke, 1989; Lyon, 1997; Mobley, 1997; Whyte, 1995) who see qualitative evaluation work as uniquely well positioned to reveal the moral and organizational dimensions of social problems, in more direct ways than are possible when we translate the problems into abstract theory.

Ethnography in and for Industrial Settings

There is also a long-standing tradition of ethnography in industrial work organizations (Baba, 1998; Burawoy, 1979b; Sachs, 1999; Schwartzman, 1993). Occupational problems in this tradition have turned on the relationship of fieldwork and managerial control. Between roughly 1930 and 1960, and including the 'Hawthorne Studies' of informal work organization, ethnographers were consulted by and worked with the highest levels of industrial management. This period was followed by the critical, Neo-Marxian line of enquiry that Braverman (1974) established with *Labor and Monopoly Capital*. In this period (circa 1960–1980) attention to applied questions was rejected in favor of documenting forms of managerial exploitation and the presence (or lack thereof) of worker resistance (Baba, 1998; Burawoy, 1979a, 1979b).

Since the early 1980s we see a new intellectual paradigm and a new occupational niche for ethnographic research in industry. This research has been animated by questions central to established theoretical schools. For example, Orr's (1996) study of oral culture among Xerox copier technicians, applies the concerns of ethnomethodology to work in which formal (and textual) authority is largely irrelevant. Barley and Orr's (1997) edited book on the new technical labor force, relies heavily on workplace ethnography to re-think labor divisions, politics and theory in relation to this fast-growing sector of workers.

These researchers can as likely be found in ethnographic 'shops', like those at Xerox (Suchman and Orr, 1999), NYNEX (Sachs, 1999), Sun Micro-Systems or 'E-Lab', than in academic departments. Whatever their scholarly concerns, these practitioners must also justify their work in terms of direct benefit to product design or process innovations, for employers with whom they often do not share even the tenuous connection that university-based fieldworkers have with disciplinary or departmental colleagues. New forms and uses of data strain against academic standards and rules guiding ethnography. The *Financial Times* (5 December 1997) reports that:

> Observational research ranges from the distant to the intimate. For some projects, studying footage of people browsing in a shopping mall or negotiating their way through an airport can be appropriate. For others, researchers spend time with subjects as they use the product at home or work ... One factor driving the growth of observational research is technology. Advances in photography and video recording make it easier to obtain and analyse the observations – increasing the research's value.

Finally, industrial ethnographers have increased pressure to master such technical skills as are used in the workplaces they study, and are vulnerable, once producing detailed accounts of local work practices, to the managerial goals that such knowledge may inform (Sachs, 1999; Suchman and Orr, 1999). On the positive side, industrial ethnographers tend to have significantly more time and continuity in fieldwork projects (often spanning years) than even the most privileged academics. They also enjoy great autonomy, since few in their immediate milieux are apt to question or even care about the details of how data are collected or interpreted, so long as the work, in the aggregate, informs product or process innovation (Suchman and Orr, 1999). In this sense, ethnographers in industrial settings 'make out' by finding spaces for spontaneity and independence, much as those in the machine shop Burawoy studied (1979a); and like workers in the arts, they may trade a measure of organizational status for greater continuity

and autonomy in the practice of their craft, seen holistically (Wellin, 1993).

Career Lines and Cumulation of Knowledge

Many authors of important ethnographic books, having made widely acknowledged contributions to theory, move on to new settings and topics. In doing so they violate the expectation, embedded in processes of promotion and tenure, that scholarly enquiry and individual careers be marked by continuity and cumulativeness. As Kleinmann et al. (1994) show, ethnograhers' focal concerns tend to be defined broadly, in terms of social process, or identity formation, or organizational change, rather than by discrete substantive areas. Still, given our orientation to work careers, it bears mention that such catholic scholarship is likely to be better accepted (and rewarded) from senior scholars than from junior ones, who need to establish credibility in substantive niches. Although we write of ethnographic careers, it is sobering to recognize that relatively few ethnographers sustain this research activity after completing a dissertation.

This is surely not to denigrate the quality or impact of work by younger scholars. Consider as an illustration the genre of workplace ethnography in the United States: Chinoy's *Automobile Workers and the American Dream* (1955), Gouldner's *Patterns of Industrial Bureaucracy* (1954), Blauner's *Alienation and Freedom* (1964), Bosk's *Forgive and Remember* (1979), Burawoy's *Manufacturing Consent* (1979a), Halle's *America's Working Man* (1984), Smith's *Managing in the Corporate Interest* (1990), Kunda's *Engineering Culture* (1992), Leidner's *Fast Food, Fast Talk* (1993), Morrill's *The Executive Way* (1995) and Nippert-Eng's *Home and Work* (1996) – each an important if not a classic study – were revisions of doctoral dissertations, published by top university presses. Each has contributed to theory, been a valuable book for teaching, and provides a model for ethnography.

A significant implication of the tendency for ethnography to be conducted and published by graduate students and junior faculty, however, is that the pool of practioners is especially beset by those pressures that rest most heavily on people early in their careers (that is, new or large classes, demands for publication and for university service). Even junior scholars who manage to revise their dissertations for publication – itself becoming harder, given the fiscal pressures in academic publishing – may require heroic efforts to conduct a second ethnographic project. Finally, despite encouraging recent changes, those writing articles based on ethnography have traditionally strained against the stylistic and methodological preferences of the editors of the prestigious journals.

Clearly the conditions of graduate study can provide a combination of compulsion and support – material and intellectual – that is both conducive for sustained ethnographic research and difficult to re-create afterward. The fact that ethnography is labor-intensive, while not being capital-intensive (in contrast to survey research) makes it compatible with graduate training. While there are, of course, ethnographers who continue to practice the method later in their careers, they are exceptional.[11] A worthwhile project would be a collection of statements of how, or under what personal and occupational circumstances, they have managed this feat.

In occupational terms, this realization has several important implications. First, it is notable that so many exemplars of any craft should, at the same time, be relative neophytes; rather few of the writings by which ethnography has its impact on social theory and policy are products of cumulative experience by seasoned scholars. This minimizes comparative research across related settings, and longitudinal research or retrospective interpretation of earlier fieldwork, which is more common among anthropologists (e.g., Nader, 1990; Wolf, 1992).[12]

Conversely, the scope and richness of ethnography that reflects more extensive, cumulative experience suggests the method's even greater potential contribution, were more researchers to continue doing fieldwork (see Wiseman, 1987). Both Burawoy and Lukács' (1992) research on industrial work organization through the transition from state socialism to capitalism in Eastern Europe, and Nader's (1990), on how a range of local institutions and cultural practices mediate global expansions of power, are inspiring examples of how seasoned scholarship and ethnography can inform one another. Adams reports a fascinating account of her years-long odyssey, studying followers of the American rock band The Grateful Dead (1998). Along with her increasing involvement and visibility in this 'community', (to the consternation of some colleagues and public watchdogs), she discovered that her ideas, access to 'data', modes of teaching and effect on the wider public expanded and informed one another.

CONCLUSIONS

As in most case studies of work groups, ours betrays both a conceit and a moral stance. The conceit is to impose typicality on career stages and responses which are (as we make clear) complexly varied. The stance is avidly sympathetic; and, while essential for seeing problems from workers' viewpoints, it is all the more natural because we share those problems. In addition to the inherent interest in revealing work problems (which here will be most keen for those who are non-ethnographers),

we hope to have shown the collective impact of these pressures for practitioners and for the stock of knowledge that is available to inform social theory and practice. There is a distinctive value to research that immerses one bodily and morally in others' social worlds. But this work activity places considerable demands, not only on practitioners, but on the institutions and personal networks in which the researchers are lodged.

Though ethnography is not an occupation in the strict sense, we regard problems facing practitioners as *occupational*; our warrant for the term is justified, first, by workers' subjective identification with the method, which (identity) is a basis for career choices and patterns; secondly, we have seen that such workers are sought out and hired by a range of employers who somehow rely on the distinctive practices and knowledge fieldworkers provide.

Like other work communities, ethnography is defined by ideals, as well as by drudgery; by the sacred and the mundane; even by self-serving myths or lies (Fine, 1993) that aim to preserve reputation and the tenuous mandate ethnographers enjoy *vis-à-vis* sponsors, employers, students and consumers. Institutional work problems that ethnographers share are important – for individuals and for the larger 'guild' – however obscured they are at times by abstract debates over epistemology and representation. Still, in their backstage moments, ethnographers are commonly preoccupied by just such workaday problems. Examples abound: typically out-numbered – if not isolated – in their departments, ethnographers struggle with the burden of practicing and teaching a labor-intensive research 'craft' in bureaucratic institutions, among colleagues whose understanding and support may be limited. A similar tension arises with granting agencies or human subjects committees, whose demands for certainty about research methods, timetables and outcomes may collide with the ethnographer's injunction to maintain an inductive and flexible posture regarding data and theory.

Counter-balancing these pressures on ethnography as work are others that help sustain the enterprise. If practitioners are few and have marginal status in their departments, their occupational networks are relatively strong and resourceful. At the university level, ethnographers are joining, across disciplinary boundaries, colleagues from psychology, communication, education, nursing, social work and performance studies. Combined with the recognition in policy circles (notably those concerned with AIDS, drug abuse, homelessness, and educational reform) that ethnographic knowledge is critical to major public concerns, the future of ethnography appears hopeful.

For ethnographers, occupational and organizational membership bring with them distinctive challenges. First, field research places ethnographers in practical and moral worlds outside the academy, where demands and obligations can be as compelling as those within it. Secondly, fieldwork tasks, such as discussing tentative ideas with informants or colleagues, and 'open coding' with data (Strauss, 1987) are so idiosyncratic – between workers and across projects for the same worker – as to strain conventional definitions of what the word 'work' means. Aside from inhibitions regarding 'not knowing what's going on' in a project, one often avoids sharing such tasks with peers due to ethical concerns about confidentiality or pragmatic ones about preserving access to research sites. But share we must, since managing fieldwork problems and developing theoretical narratives are, no less than fieldwork itself, social processes. Thirdly, the 'packaging' of ethnographic knowledge to fit into pre-established theoretical categories and sub-fields is more complicated than in survey research, where questions are more explicit and circumscribed at the outset.

Ultimately we claim that ethnographers as social scientists need to recognize that they are workers, and that the concepts and theories that they have applied successfully to other domains of labor apply within the scholarly workforce. As we began, so do we end, whatever else it may be, ethnography is a form of work, interpretable as such.

Clearly, we have merely charted, rather than mined, the territory involved. We hope to have sharpened interest in further reflections on and empirical investigation of problems herein. Among them: *To what extent, and how, do career and role conflicts shape the topics ethnographers study?* One would expect important gender differences here – given the unequal division of domestic labor – though we found little public discussion of this problem. *How do different national, historical and disciplinary contexts provide distinctively different problems (or opportunities) from those we discuss?* And, finally, with Adams (1998), we ask, *How can we foster career conditions and rewards which recognize the process, as well as the products, of field research?*

Notes

1 We use the terms 'ethnography' and 'fieldwork' interchangeably. Both convey sustained first-hand involvement in research settings, which we distinguish from research based solely on interviewing or the analysis of audio or video tapes.

2 Similar status problems, arising in work groups that mediate between abstract theory or discourse and local practices, have been noted by Barley and Orr (1997) and Orr (1996) with respect to technicians in the labor force.

3 An important exception is Orlans and Wallace's (1994) collection of essays on Berkeley Women Sociologists. There, the goal of revealing gender barriers,

faced by an important cohort of scholars, overcame the tendency publicly to narrate one's career in cosmopolitan terms. Perhaps it was only after these authors became generally celebrated, however, that they determined such candor was possible without reinforcing stereotypes about women's marginal status in academic institutions.

4 Fieldwork culture in anthropology has not been static. Prior to the postmodern critique, there were efforts to codify practice, as in Campbell and Levine's (1970) 'Field Manual' aimed at facilitating replication of prior studies in elaborate schemes of cross-cultural comparison. Smith and Crano (1977: 364) conducted factor analyses, based on ethnographic data from over 800 societies, 'for the dual purposes of sorting out spurious results attributed to particular methods of analysis and also of developing an empirical model of the dimensional structure of culture'. Such a model of ethnography as a basis for a formal, cumulative body of knowledge, is unusual (Noblit and Hare, 1988).

5 Of these, age has been notably absent in writings about fieldwork (but see limited treatment, e.g., in Delamont, 1984 and Honigman, 1970). In addition to increasing career demands over time for individual fieldworkers, are constraints rooted in the age-grading of social life in Western societies, in which it is 'deviant' for older people to take part in many groups and activities of interest to researchers. This is especially true given that the social problems many field studies address (e.g., drug use, informal economy, occupational socialization, schooling) predominantly involve young people. Of course, younger investigators may have poorer access to some elite settings.

6 The acquisition of local competence in the doing of fieldwork is rarely discussed. In academically oriented fieldwork, the threshold is minimal – to know enough to 'pass' with informants, and to confirm or refine theory during fieldwork. For ethnographers in program evaluation or under contract in industry, the standards of competence, needed to collaborate in large, diverse teams of practitioners, are higher.

7 These career problems are exacerbated for sociologists by what Dean (1989) has shown is a shortage of available publication space, relative to other disciplines.

8 This same dilemma has been evident for writers on women's studies, who have often found their publications in specialty journals discounted in the eyes of disciplinary colleagues.

9 This point was confirmed through discussions between the first author and several members of that cohort, including Howard S. Becker, Herbert Gans, Lillian B. Rubin and Leonard Schatzman. We appreciate their help.

10 For valuable insights into the problems of informing policy with such work, see Rist, 1994.

11 In trying to confirm and amplify this trend, we had helpful correspondence from two experienced and respected sociology editors. Douglas Mitchell of the University of Chicago Press, and Naomi Schneider of the University of California Press. They estimate that between one-third and one-half of their ethnographic books are revisions of doctoral dissertations.

12 In a self-fulfillng prophecy, this tendency is taken as confirmation by those (including funders) charging that ethnographic research is overly descriptive, ahistorical and micro-oriented. In turn, fewer resources and allowances are made available to support fieldwork, *vis-à-vis* other, supposedly more scientific approaches.

REFERENCES

Adams, Rebecca G. (1998) 'Inciting sociological thought by studying the deadhead community: engaging publics in dialogue', *Social Forces*, 77 (1): 1–25.

Adler, Patricia A. and Adler, Peter (1987) *Membership Roles in Field Research*. Newbury Park, CA: Sage.

Adler, Patricia A. and Adler, Peter (1995) 'The demography of ethnography', *Journal of Contemporary Ethnography*, 24: 3–29.

Agar, Michael H. (1973) *Ripping and Running*. New York: Seminar Press.

Agar, Michael H. (1980) *The Professional Stranger*. San Diego, CA: Academic Press.

Akins, Carl and Beschner, George (eds) (1979) *Ethnography: A Research Tool for Policymakers in the Drug and Alcohol Fields*. Rockville, MD: US Department of Health and Human Services.

Anderson, Nels (1923) *The Hobo*. Chicago: University of Chicago Press.

Atkinson, Paul (1990) *The Ethnographic Imagination*. London: Routledge.

Baba, Marietta (1998) 'The anthropology of work in the Fortune 1000: a critical retrospective', *Anthropology of Work Review*, Summer: 17–28.

Barley, Stephen R. (1989) 'Careers, identities, and institutions: the legacy of the Chicago School of Sociology', in Michael B. Arthur et al. (eds), *Handbook of Career Theory*. New York: Cambridge University Press. pp. 41–65.

Barley, Stephen R. and Orr, Julian (eds) (1997) *Between Craft and Science: Technical Work in U.S. Settings*. Ithaca, NY: Cornell/ILR Press.

Becker, Howard S. (1970) *Sociological Work*. New Brunswick, NJ: Transaction Press.

Becker, Howard S. (1986) 'What's happening to sociology?', in *Doing Things Together*. Evanston, IL: Northwestern University Press. pp. 209–20.

Becker, Howard S., Geer, Blanche, Hughes, Everett C. and Strauss, Anselm L. (1961) *Boys In White*. Chicago: University of Chicago Press.

Bensman, Joseph, and Vidich, Arthur J. (1960) 'Social theory in field research', *American Journal of Sociology*, 65 (6): 577–84.

Berger, Bennett (ed.) (1990) *Authors of Their Own Lives*. Berkeley, CA: University of California Press.

Berreman, Gerald D. (1968) 'Ethnography: method and product', in James Clifton (ed.), *Introduction to Cultural Anthropology*. New York: Houghton Mifflin.

Blauner, Robert (1964) *Alienation and Freedom*. Chicago: University of Chicago Press.

Bogdan, Robert and Taylor, Steven J. (1990) 'Looking at the bright side: a positive approach to qualitative policy and evaluation research', *Qualitative Sociology*, 13 (2): 183–92.

Bosk, Charles (1979) *Forgive and Remember*. Chicago: University of Chicago Press.

Braverman, Harry (1974) *Labor and Monopoly Capital*. New York: Monthly Review Press.

Brownstein, Henry H. (1990) 'Surviving as a qualitative sociologist: recollections from the diary of a state worker', *Qualitative Sociology*, 13 (2): 149–67.

Bucher, Rue and Strauss, Anselm L. (1961) 'Professions in process', *American Journal of Sociology*, 66: 352–34.

Bulmer, Martin (1984) *The Chicago School of Sociology: Institutionalization, Diversity, and the Rise of Sociological Research*. Chicago: University of Chicago Press.

Burawoy, Michael (1979a) *Manufacturing Consent*. Chicago: University of Chicago Press.

Burawoy, Michael (1979b) 'The anthropology of industrial work', *Annual Review of Anthropology*, 8: 231–66.

Burawoy, Michael (1998) 'Critical sociology: a dialogue between two sciences', *Contemporary Sociology*, 27 (January): 12–20.

Burawoy, Michael, and Lukács, Janos (1992) The *Radiant Past*. Chicago: University of Chicago Press.

Campbell, Donald T. and Levine, Robert A. (1970) 'Field-manual anthropology', in Raoul Narroll and Ronald Cohen (eds), *A Handbook of Method in Cultural Anthropology*. Garden City, NY: The Natural History Press. pp. 366–87.

Cancian, Francesca (1993) 'Conflicts between activist research and academic success: participatory research and alternative strategies', *The American Sociologist*, Spring: 92–106.

Chambers, Erve (1984) 'Career guides for anthropologists', *American Anthropologist*, 86 (June): 337–40.

Chinoy, Ely (1955) *Automobile Workers and the American Dream*. Boston, MA: Beacon Press.

Clemens, Elizabeth S., Powell, Walter W., Mallwaine, Kris and Okamoto, Dina (1995) 'Careers in print: books, journals, and scholarly reputations', *American Journal of Sociology*, 101 (2): 433–94.

Clifford, James, and Marcus, George E. (1986) *Writing Culture: The Poetics and Politics of Ethnography*. Berkeley, CA: University of California Press.

Clinard, Marshall B. (1970) 'The sociologist's quest for respectability', in William J. Filstead (ed.), *Qualitative Methodology: Firsthand Involvement with the Social World*. Chicago: Markham. pp. 63–74.

Coffey, Amanda and Atkinson, Paul (1996) *Making Sense of Qualitative Data*. Thousand Oaks, CA: Sage.

Colomy, Paul and Brown, J. David (1995) 'Elaboration, revision, polemic, and progress in the second Chicago School', in Gary Alan Fine (ed.), *A Second Chicago School?* Chicago: University of Chicago Press. pp. 17–81.

Dean, Dwight G. (1989) 'Structural constraints and the publications dilemma: a review and some proposals', *The American Sociologist*, Summer: 181–7.

Delamont, Sara (1984) 'The old girl network', in Robert G. Burgess (ed.), *The Research Process in Educational Settings*.

Denzin, Norman K. and Lincoln, Yvonna S. (eds) (1994) *Handbook of Qualitative Research*. Newbury Park, CA: Sage.

DeVault, Marjorie L. (1999) 'Institutional ethnography: a strategy for feminist inquiry', in *Liberating Method: Feminism and Social Research*. Philadelphia: Temple University Press. pp. 46–54.

Diamond, Timothy (1995) 'Breaking the dichotomy between theory and research: the method of institutional ethnography'. Paper read at the Annual Meeting of the American Sociological Association, Washington, DC.

Dogan, Mattei and Pahre, Robert (1989) 'Hybrid fields in the social sciences', *International Social Science Journal*, 121 (August): 457–70.

Duhl, Leonard J. and Leopold, Robert L. (1968) *Mental Health and Political Process*. New York: Basic Books.

Emerson, Robert M. (1981) 'Observational field work', *Annual Review of Sociology*, 7: 351–78.

Emerson, Robert M. (ed.) (1983) *Contemporary Field Research*. Prospect Heights, IL: Waveland Press.

Felix, Robert H. (1961) 'A comprehensive community mental health program', in *Mental Health and Social Welfare*. New York: Columbia University Press. pp. 3–21.

Fetterman, David M. (1983) 'Guilty knowledge, dirty hands, and other ethical dilemmas: the hazards of contract research', *Human Organization*, 42 (3): 214–24.

Fetterman, David M. (1989) *Ethnography Step by Step*. Newbury Park, CA: Sage.

Fine, Gary Alan (1993) 'Ten lies of ethnography', *Journal of Contemporary Ethnography*, 22 (3): 267–94.

Fine, Gary Alan (ed.) (1995) *A Second Chicago School?* Chicago: University of Chicago Press.

Fine, Gary Alan (1996) 'Justifying work': occupational rhetorics as resources in restaurant kitchens', *Administrative Science Quarterly*, 41: 90–115.

Freidson, Eliot (1970) *Professional Dominance*. Chicago: Aldine.

Freilich, Morris (ed.) (1970) *Marginal Natives: Anthropologists at Work*. New York: Harper and Row.

Gans, Herbert J. (1997) 'Best-sellers by sociologists: an exploratory study', *Contemporary Sociology*, 26 (2): 131–5.

Gans, Herbert J. (1999) 'Participant observation in the era of ethnography', *Journal of Contemporary Ethnography*, 28 (5): 540–8.

Garfinkel, Harold (1967) *Studies in Ethnomethodology*. Engelwood Cliffs, NJ: Prentice–Hall.

Geertz, Clifford (1988) *Works and Lives: The Anthropologist as Author*. Stanford, CA: Stanford University Press.

Goffman, Erving (1989) 'On fieldwork', *Journal of Contemporary Ethnography*, 18 (Summer): 123–32.

Gold, Ray L. (1958) 'Roles in sociological field observations', *Social Forces*, 36: 217–23.

Golde, Peggy (1970) *Women in the Field*. Chicago: Aldine.

Gouldner, Alvin W. (1954) *Patterns of Industrial Bureaucracy*. New York: Free Press.

Greene Jennifer C., Doughty, Joan, Marquart, Jules M., Ray, Marilyn L. and Roberts, Lynn (1988) 'Qualitative evaluation audits in practice', *Evaluation Review*, 12 (4): 352–75.

Hak, Tony and Bernts, Tom (1996) 'Coder training: theoretical training or practical socialization?', *Qualitative Sociology*, 19 (2): 235–58.

Halle, David (1984) *America's Working Man*. Chicago: University of Chicago Press.

Hammond, Phillip E. (ed.) (1964) *Sociologists at Work*. New York: Basic Books.

Hartung, Beth (1993) 'Academic labor markets and the sociology temporary', in Ted Vaughan, Gideon Sjoberg and Larry T. Reynolds (eds), *A Critique of Contemporary American Sociology*. Dix Hills, NY: General Hall. pp. 269–88.

Hewitt, John P. (1984) *Self and Society: A Symbolic Interactionist Social Psychology*, 3rd edn. Newton, MA: Allyn and Bacon.

Holstein, James A. and Staples, William G. (1992) 'Producing evaluative knowledge: the interactional bases of social science findings', *Sociological Inquiry*, 62 (1): 11–35.

Honigman, John J. (1970) 'Field work in two northern Canadian communities', in Morris Freilich (ed.), *Marginal Natives: Anthropologists at Work*. New York: Harper and Row.

Hughes, Everett C. (1984) *The Sociological Eye*. New Brunswick, NJ: Transaction Books.

Hunter, Albert (1990) *The Rhetoric of Social Research*. New Brunswick, NJ: Rutgers University Press.

Jackson, Jean (1990) ' "I am a fieldnote": fieldnotes as a symbol of professional identity', in Roger Sanjek (ed.), *Fieldnotes*. Ithaca, NY: Cornell University Press. pp. 3–33.

Janowitz, Morris (1972) 'Professionalization in sociology', in *Varieties of Political Expression in Sociology*. Chicago: University of Chicago Press. pp. 105–35.

Katz, Jack (1983) 'A theory of qualitative methodology: the social system of analytic fieldwork', in Robert M. Emerson (ed.), *Contemporary Field Research*. Prospect Heights, IL: Waveland Press. pp. 127–48.

Kleinman, Sherryl, Stenross, Barbara and McMahon, Martha (1994) 'Privileging fieldwork over interviews: consequences for identity and practice', *Symbolic Interaction*, 17 (1): 37–50.

Kunda, Gideon (1992) *Engineering Culture*. Philadelphia: Temple University Press.

Laslett, Barbara and Thorne, Barrie (eds) (1997) *Feminist Sociology: Life Histories of a Movement*. New Brunswick, NJ: Rutgers University Press.

Leidner, Robin (1993) *Fast Food, Fast Talk*. Berkeley, CA: University of California Press.

Lidz, Charles W. and Ricci, Edmund (1990) 'Funding large-scale qualitative sociology', *Qualitative Sociology*, 13 (2): 113–26.

Loseke, Donileen R. (1989) 'Evaluation research and the practice of social services: a case for qualitative methodology', *Journal of Contemporary Ethnography*, 18 (2): 202–23.

Lynd, Robert S. (1939) *Knowledge for What? The Place of Social Science in American Culture*. New York: Grove Press.

Lyon, Eleanor (1997) 'Applying ethnography', *Journal of Contemporary Ethnography*, 26 (1): 3–27.

Lyson, Thomas A. and Squires, Gregory D. (1984) 'The promise and perils of applied sociology: a survey of nonacademic employers', *Sociological Inquiry*, 54 (1): 1–15.

Maynard, Douglas W. and Schaeffer, Nora Cate (1997) 'Toward a sociology of social scientific knowledge: survey research, ethnomethodology, and conversation analysis'. Paper read at the Annual Meetings of the ASA, Toronto, Canada.

Merton, Robert K. (1957) 'The role-set: problems in sociological theory', *British Journal of Sociology*, VIII (June): 106–20.

Merton, Robert K. (1968) *Social Theory and Social Structure*. New York: The Free Press.

Mills, C. Wright (1959) 'The bureaucratic ethos', in *The Sociological Imagination*. New York: Oxford University Press. pp. 100–18.

Mitteness, Linda S. and Barker, Judith (1994) 'Managing large projects', in Jaber F. Gubrium and Andrea Sankar (eds), *Qualitative Methods in Aging Research*. Thousand Oaks, CA: Sage. pp. 82–104.

Mobley, Catherine (1997) 'Toward a new definition of accountability', *Journal of Contemporary Ethnography*, 26 (1): 75–97.

Mobley, Catherine and Spitler, Hugh (1998) 'To be or not to be? Some comments on the professional identity of applied sociologists in non-academic settings', *Journal of Applied Sociology*, 15 (1): 24–43.

Morrill, Calvin (1995) *The Executive Way: Conflict Management in Organizations*. Chicago: University of Chicago Press.

Morse, Janice M. (1994) 'Designing funded qualitative research', in Norman K. Denzin and Yvonna S. Lincoln (eds), *Handbook of Qualitative Research*. Newbury Park, CA: Sage. pp. 220–35.

Nader, Laura (1970) 'From anguish to exultation', in Peggy Golde (ed.), *Women in the Field*. Chicago: Aldine. pp. 96–116.

Nader, Laura (1990) 'Controlling processes: tracing the dynamic components of power', *Current Anthropology*, 38 (5): 711–32.

Nader, Laura (1998) Personal communication with Wellin.

Nippert-Eng, Cristena E. (1996) *Home and Work*. Chicago: University of Chicago Press.

Noblit, George W. and Hare, R. Dwight (1988) *Meta-Ethnography: Synthesizing Qualitative Studies*. Newbury Park, CA: Sage.

Olesen, Virginia, Droes, Nellie, Hatton, Diane, Chico, Nan and Schatzman, Leonard (1994) 'Analyzing together: recollections of a team approach', in Alan Bryman and Robert G. Burgess (eds), *Analyzing Qualitative Data*. London: Routledge. pp. 111–28.

Orlans, Kathryn P. Meadow and Wallace, Ruth A. (eds) (1994) *Gender and the Academic Experience: Berkeley Women Sociologists*. Lincoln, NB: University of Nebraska Press.

Orr, Julian E. (1996) *Talking About Machines*. Ithaca, NY: Cornell/ILR Press.

Patton, Michael Quinn (1990) *Qualitative Evaluation and Research Methods*, 2nd edn. Newbury Park, CA: Sage Publications.

Pavalko, Ronald M. (1988) *Sociology of Occupations and Professions*, 2nd edn. Itasca, IL: F.E. Peacock.

Plattner, Stuart, Hamilton, Linda and Madden, Marilyn (1987) 'The funding of research in socio-cultural anthropology at the national science foundation', *American Anthropologist*, 89 (4): 853–66.

Rabinow, Paul (1986) 'Representations are social facts', in James Clifford and George E. Marcus (eds), *Writing Culture*. Berkeley, CA: University of California Press. pp. 234–61.

Ragin, Charles C. (1994) *Constructing Social Research*. Thousand Oaks, CA: Pine Forge Press.

Reinharz, Shulamit (1984) *On Becoming a Social Scientist*. New Brunswick, NJ: Transaction Books.

Riessman, Catherine Kohler (1993) *Narrative Analysis*. Newbury Park, CA: Sage.

Riley, John W., Jr (1967) 'The sociologist in the non-academic setting', in Paul Lazersfeld (eds), *The Uses of Sociology*. New York: Basic Books. pp. 789–805.

Riley, Matilda White (ed.) (1988) *Sociological Lives*. Newbury Park, CA: Sage.

Rist, Ray (1994) 'Influencing the policy process with qualitative research', in Norman K. Denzin and Yvonna S. Lincoln (eds), *Handbook of Qualitative Research*. Thousand Oaks, CA: Sage. pp. 545–58.

Rose, Dan (1990) *Living the Ethnographic Life*. Newbury Park, CA: Sage.

Rosenbaum, James E. (1989) 'Organization career systems and employee misperceptions', in Michael B. Arthur, Douglas T. Hall and Barbara S. Lawrence (eds), *Handbook of Career Theory*. New York: Cambridge University Press. pp. 329–53.

Sachs, Patricia (1999) Personal Interview with Wellin.

Schatzman, Leonard (1991) 'Dimensional analysis: notes on an alternative approach to the grounding of theory in qualitative research', in David Maines (ed.), *Social Organization and Social Process*. New York: Aldine de Gruyter. pp. 303–14.

Schatzman, Leonard and Strauss, Anselm L. (1974) *Field Research: Strategies of a Natural Sociology*. Englewood Cliffs, NJ: Prentice–Hall.

Schwartzman, Helen B. (1993) *Ethnography in Organizations*. Newbury Park, CA: Sage.

Shaffir, William B., Marshall, Victor and Haas, Jack (1979) 'Competing commitments: unanticipated problems of field research', *Qualitative Sociology*, 1 (1): 56–71.

Shaffir, William B., Marshall, Victor and Haas, Jack (1980) *Fieldwork Experience*. New York: St Martins Press.

Shulman, David (1994) 'Dirty data and investigative methods', *Journal of Contemporary Ethnography*, 23 (2): 214–53.

Sjoberg, Gideon and Vaughan, Ted (1993) 'The bureaucratization of sociology: its impact on theory and research', in Ted Vaughan, Gideon Sjoberg and Larry T. Reynolds (eds), *A Critique of Contemporary American Sociology*. Dix Hills, NY: General Hall. pp. 54–113.

Smith, Frank J. and Crano, William D. (1977) 'Cultural dimensions reconsidered: global and regional analyses of the ethnographic atlas', *American Anthropologist*, 79 (2): 364–87.

Smith, Vickie (1990) *Managing in the Corporate Interest: Control and Resistance in an American Bank*. Berkeley, CA: University of California Press.

Solomon, David N. (1968) 'Sociological perspectives on occupations', in Howard S. Becker, Blanche Geer, David Riesman and Robert S. Weiss (eds), *Institutions and the Person*. Chicago: Aldine. pp. 3–13.

Spradley, James P. (1980) *Participant Observation*. New York: Holt, Rinehart and Winston.

Steele, Stephen F. and Iutcovich, Joyce M. (1997) *Directions in Applied Sociology*. Arnold, MD: Society for Applied Sociology.

Stinchcombe, Arthur L. (1984) 'The origins of sociology as a discipline', *Acta Sociologica*, 27 (1): 51–61.

Stinchcombe, Arthur L. (1986) 'On getting "Hung-Up" and other neuroses', in *Stratification and Organization*. New York: Cambridge University Press.

Stinchcombe, Arthur L. (1990) *Information and Organizations*. Berkeley, CA: University of California Press.

Stinchcombe, Arthur L. (1994) 'Disintegrated disciplines and the future of sociology', *Sociological Forum*, 9 (2): 279–91.

Strauss, Anselm L. (1987) *Qualitative Analysis for Social Scientists*. New York: Cambridge University Press.

Suchman, Lucy, and Orr, Julian (1999) Personal Interview with Wellin. Xerox, Palo Alto Research Center.

Szenberg, Michael (ed.) (1998) *Passion and Craft: Economists at Work*. Ann Arbor, MI: University of Michigan Press.

Turner, Stephen P. and Turner, Jonathan H. (1990) *The Impossible Science: An Institutional Analysis of American Sociology*. Newbury Park, CA: Sage.

Van Maanen, John (1988) *Tales of the Field*. Chicago: University of Chicago Press.

Vidich, Arthur J. and Lyman, Stanford M. (1994) 'Qualitative methods: their history in sociology and anthropology', in Norman K. Denzin and Yvonna S. Lincoln (eds), *Handbook of Qualitative Research*. Thousand Oaks, CA: Sage. pp. 23–59.

Waitzkin, Howard B. *The Politics of Medical Encounters: How Patients and Doctors Deal with Social Problems*. New Haven, CT: Yale University Press.

Wax, Rosalie, H. (1957) 'Twelve years later: an analysis of field experience', *American Journal of Sociology*, 63: 133–42.

Wax, Rosalie H. (1970) *Doing Fieldwork: Warnings and Advice*. Chicago: University of Chicago Press.

Weiss, Carol H. (ed.) (1977) *Using Social Research in Public Policy-Making*. Lexington, MA: Lexington.

Wellin, Christopher (1993) 'Careers in art worlds: dilemmas of mobility in theater work', in Muriel G. Cantor and Cheryl L. Zollars (eds), *Current Research on Occupations and Professions: Creators of Culture*, vol. 8. Greenwich, CT: JAI Press. pp. 247–76.

Wellin, Christopher and Shulman, David (1995) 'Theorizing in field research as negotiation'. Paper read at the Annual Meetings of the ASA, Washington, DC.

Weppner, Robert S. (ed.) (1977) *Street Ethnography: Selected Studies of Crime and Drug Use in Natural Settings*. Beverly Hills, CA: Sage.

Whyte, William Foote (1984) *Learning from the Field*. Beverly Hills, CA: Sage.

Whyte, William Foote (1995) 'Encounters with participatory action research', *Qualitative Sociology*, 18 (3): 289–300.

Wiseman, Jacqueline P. (1987) 'The development of generic concepts in qualitative research through cumulative application', *Qualitative Sociology*, 10 (4): 318–38.

Wolcott, Harry F. (1990) 'Making a study "more ethnographic"', *Journal of Contemporary Ethnography*, 19 (1): 44–72.

Wolf, Margery (1992) *A Thrice-Told Tale*. Stanford, CA: Stanford University Press.

Wright, Charles R. (1967) 'Changes in the occupational commitments of graduate sociology students', *Sociological Inquiry*, 37: 55–62.

23

The Ethics of Ethnography

ELIZABETH MURPHY AND ROBERT DINGWALL

The ethics and the politics of ethnography are not clearly separable. Questions about the right way to treat each other as human beings, within a research relationship, are not wholly distinct from questions about the values which should prevail in a society, and the responsibility of social scientists to make, or refrain from, judgements about these. For ethnographers, ethical issues are also inextricably related to views about the ontological and epistemological foundations of their work. Our assumptions about the nature of reality, the possible knowledge of that reality, the status of truth claims and so on, all have significant implications for our judgements about the ethnographer's responsibilities. The lack of consensus about methodology, which marks contemporary debates in and about ethnography, is reflected in discussions about its ethics. This chapter explores the challenges that confront ethnographers as they design and carry out studies, and as they analyse, interpret and publish findings. It opens with an outline of different theoretical approaches to research ethics and the ways in which these are conventionally translated into guiding principles. We then consider the application of these principles to research practice, relating the discussion of ethics to wider political and methodological concerns.

ETHICAL THEORY

How can we form judgements about what will count as ethical practice in ethnography? *Consequentialist* approaches focus on the outcomes of research. Have participants been harmed in some way, or, if they have been harmed, has this been outweighed by the research's benefits? They can be contrasted with *deontological* approaches, which focus on the inherent *rights* of research participants, such as the right to privacy, the right to respect, or the right to self-determination. In Kantian terms, researchers have a duty to avoid treating participants as a means to an end, rather than as an end in themselves (Kelman, 1982; Macklin, 1982). Ethical research does not just leave participants unscathed but also avoids infringing their rights. Have these been acknowledged, protected or violated (Beauchamp et al., 1982)? Consequentialist and deontological ethics are not necessarily in competition. Like all researchers, ethnographers have a responsibility not only to protect research participants from harm, but also to have regard to their rights.

These dual concerns with outcomes and rights are often translated by ethicists into sets of principles to guide research practice. The following list, from Beauchamp et al. (1982: 18–19), is typical:

Non-maleficence: that researchers should avoid harming participants.
Beneficence: that research on human subjects should produce some positive and identifiable benefit rather than simply be carried out for its own sake.
Autonomy or *self-determination:* that the values and decisions of research participants should be respected.
Justice: that people who are equal in relevant respects should be treated equally.

The first two principles are essentially consequentialist while the latter are primarily deontological.

At this level of abstraction, there is a wide measure of agreement among researchers, irrespective of whether they are using qualitative or quantitative methods. This ethical consensus, however, reflects the assumptions of welfare liberalism as understood in the United States in the post-war period: about the rights to be afforded to individuals over collectivities, about the virtue of autonomy and about the nature of justice (Benatar, 1997). The consensus does not, for example, acknowledge that a collective interest could sometimes override individual rights. Most research ethicists live in Western societies at a historical moment when autonomy and self-determination are strongly valued. This esteem is not universal. The conventional approach is also troubled by the problem of 'false consciousness': what if the exercise of autonomy and self-determination by research subjects is at odds with the researcher's perception of their interest? Finally, the principle of justice struggles with the difficulty of defining what constitute 'relevant respects'.

Most controversy about the ethics of ethnography has, however, arisen at the level of practice, rather than principle. Professional ethical codes have been developed in an attempt to give effect to the abstract propositions of ethical theory. There has been wide criticism of the mechanical application to ethnographic research of codes and regulatory systems, including human subjects review, devised for biomedical and/or quantitative research (Barnes, 1979; Cassell, 1978, 1979, 1982; Dingwall, 1980; Finch, 1986; House, 1990; Kelman, 1982; Merriam, 1988; Punch, 1994; Thorne, 1980; Walker, 1980; Wax, 1980). This process raises two problems. First, ethical codes that are not method-sensitive may constrain research unnecessarily and inappropriately. Secondly, and just as importantly, the ritualistic observation of these codes may not give real protection to research participants but actually increase the risk of harm by blunting ethnographers' sensitivities to the method-specific issues which do arise. This is not to suggest that different ethical standards should be applied to different kinds of research so much as to recognize that common principles may need to be operationalized in different ways. We now consider each of the ethical principles outlined above and the contingencies that affect their application to ethnography.

Principles in Practice

Non-maleficence and Beneficence

These two principles are commonly combined to argue that research is ethical if its benefits outweigh its potential for harm. In biomedical research this has led to subject risk–benefit analyses. Researchers should only proceed where they can show that the anticipated benefits of a study outweigh its potential risks. The difficulties of applying such calculations to ethnography arise from the different nature and positioning of risk. Any harm caused to the subjects of biomedical experiments is likely to arise directly from the researcher's intervention in administering a drug or a new surgical treatment. The potential benefits are likely to be equally obvious. The argument against extending such analyses to ethnographic research is not, as some suggest, that its potential for harm is negligible. Admittedly, the risks associated with an ethnographic study are not normally of the same order as those which arise in trialling a new drug or surgical technique (Brewster Smith, 1979; Cassell, 1978; Diener and Crandall, 1978; Pattullo, 1982). Nevertheless, ethnography is not risk-free and its potential for harm cannot be lightly dismissed (Bakan, 1996).

Ethnographers can harm the individuals or groups they study. Research participants may experience anxiety, stress, guilt and damage to self-esteem during data collection. In observational fieldwork, participants may form close relationships with the observer and experience loss when the study is completed and the observer withdraws (Cassell, 1978, 1979; Patai, 1991; Stacey, 1991). Interview informants may feel embarrassed – about the opinions they hold or because they do not hold opinions on matters about which the interviewer expects them to have opinions (Kelman, 1982). Voysey (1975) described how some participants in her study of the parents of disabled children became distressed during interviews. In ethnography, however, harm is more likely to be indirect than direct, and open to interpretation. For example, a study of the division of household labour might include informal interviews, which lead some women to focus on their unequal domestic workloads. They may become dissatisfied and challenge current arrangements. This outcome could be regarded either as beneficial (increased self-awareness leading to positive change) or harmful (the disruption of previously happy and stable family arrangements), depending upon one's ideological position. As Patai (1991) has observed, any defence of research as 'consciousness-raising' risks the charge of arrogance. We cannot assume that increased self-knowledge is necessarily a benefit for all research participants in all circumstances (Brewster Smith, 1979). Similarly, claims about the cathartic effects of research interactions (see, for example, Bar-On, 1996; Miller, 1996) must be treated with caution. The harms or benefits derive from the participant's unpredictable response to the interactions rather than from the researcher's intentions. To recall W.I. Thomas's great aphorism, it is not the reality of the interview but the perception of it that leads to the consequences, whether negative or positive. That reaction is not directly controlled by the researcher and may not even be a stable one. Positive or negative feelings immediately after an interview may reverse later.

Perhaps the most significant difference between biomedical experiments and ethnography lies in the temporal positioning of risk. In biomedical research, the risk of harm is concentrated during the experimental manipulation. The greatest risk in ethnography, however, arises at the time of publication (Cassell, 1978, 1979; Wax and Cassell, 1979). Here, the indeterminacy of risk becomes most obvious (Patai, 1991). Researchers have relatively limited control over the use of their findings in the public domain (Schneider, personal communication, cited in Brettell, 1993; Richardson, 1996). As Burgess (1985) has commented, ethnographic studies typically increase knowledge of the adaptive behaviours that actors use to accommodate to structural and institutional pressures. By uncovering such behaviours, ethnographers offer tools for those with power to control or manipulate those without. Nicolaus' attack on the American Sociological Association at its 1968 meeting in Boston, during the heyday of the New Left and the movement against the war in Vietnam, is a classic formulation of this charge:

> Sociology is not now and never has been any objective seeking out of objective truth or reality. Historically, the profession is an outgrowth of 19th century European traditionalism and conservatism, wedded to 20th century American corporation liberalism ... Sociologists stand guard in the garrison and report to its masters on the movements of the occupied populace. *The more adventurous sociologists don the disguise of the people and go out to mix with the peasants in the 'field'*, returning with books and articles that break the protective secrecy in which a subjugated population wraps itself, and make it more accessible to manipulation and control. (Nicolaus, 1969; emphasis added)

The experience of being written about may be a matter for concern in its own right: 'I worry intensely about how people will feel about what I write about them. I worry about the experience of being "writ down", fixed in print, formulated, summed up, encapsulated in language, reduced in some way to what the words contain. Language can never contain a whole person, so every act of writing a person's life is inevitably a violation' (Josselson, 1996b: 62). Research participants may be wounded not only by what is contained in a report, but also by what has been left out: this may seem to treat as trivial or unimportant something which has great significance for them. Ethnographers who think of themselves as sensitive, respectful and caring people, may be surprised and chagrined to discover how their published accounts offend and distress those about whom they have written (Ellis, 1995). There is ample evidence that publications from ethnographic fieldwork can, and do, cause hurt and offence to those studied (Ellis, 1995; Messenger, 1989; Scheper-Hughes, 1982; Vidich and Bensman, 1958, 1964).

Ethnographic reports may be sensationalized by mass media in ways that cause distress or embarrassment to participants, even where anonymity is preserved (Gmelch, 1992; Greenberg, 1993;

Rosaldo, 1989). However careful researchers may be in their own writing, they cannot guarantee it will not be used to produce offensive characterizations of participants or settings. Social science researchers are currently under considerable pressure from sponsors to disseminate their findings beyond the academic community, increasing the likelihood that research will be taken up in ways over which the authors have minimal control or influence.

The widening dissemination of social science research increases the significance of the general obligations to protect participants' anonymity and to keep data confidential (cf. Beauchamp et al., 1982; Bulmer, 1982; Punch, 1994). However, these raise difficulties specific to ethnographic research (Finch, 1986). In quantitative research, anonymity and confidentiality can be treated as technical matters and managed through rigorous procedures for data anonymization and storage. Since most ethnographies are carried out in a single setting, or a very small number of settings, it is much more difficult to ensure that data are totally unattributable: fieldnotes and interview transcripts inevitably record sufficient detail to make participants identifiable.

Ethnographers can do much to protect settings and participants by removing identifying information at the earliest possible opportunity, routinely using pseudonyms, and altering non-relevant details (Burgess, 1985; Tunnell, 1998). However, they are rarely able to give *absolute* guarantees that the identities of people and places will remain hidden. Where fieldwork is overt, many people come to know that it is taking place and will be able to identify the source of data after publication. As Morgan (1972) discovered, a refusal to disclose the site of observations may not be enough to prevent journalists uncovering it (see also Lieblich, 1996). Even where anonymity is preserved beyond the setting, members are likely to recognize themselves and one another (Ellis, 1995). Burgess (1985), for example, described the impact on staff at Bishop MacGregor School when he presented some findings to them. While his report used pseudonyms, this was not completely effective in disguising individuals. His research had focused on one department within the school. Since this only involved four members of staff, it was not difficult for the head teacher and others to make educated guesses about who was involved in various reported incidents.

However successful ethnographers may be in protecting the anonymity of those they study, participants and informants will remain identifiable to themselves. This raises the possibility that publication will cause private (or community) shame, even where it does not lead to public humiliation (Ellis, 1995; Hopkins, 1993). If the purpose of ethnographic research is more than the mere reproduction of participant perspectives, it is possible that the researcher's analysis will disrupt the assumptions that participants make about their world (Borland, 1991; Messenger, 1989; Scheper-Hughes, 1982). The publication of ethnographic accounts may expose individuals to other versions of reality held by those close to them, breaking down protective silences. As Lieblich reflected, 'The most painful reaction [to the publication of her work] was that of family members who became aware, through the pages of the book, of memories, opinions, and feelings that belonged to their family life and relationships that had never been discussed among them before' (1996: 182).

Accepting that positivism is the currently dominant epistemology, participants are likely to expect an ethnographic report to define reality in some objective sense, whatever the author's position (Josselson, 1996a). Ethnography, however, treats all versions of the social world as just some of a set of possible formulations (Dingwall, 1980: 873). Given the conditions of intimacy that arise in prolonged periods of fieldwork, this sociological stance may be experienced as betrayal or rejection by participants who expect researchers to affirm or endorse their version. In the nature of sociological analysis, people's views of themselves and their social worlds are likely to be deflated (Becker, 1964: 265–6). It is not always straightforward for ethnographers to decide what will and will not cause offence (Davis, 1993). The translation of individual accounts into examples of larger social phenomena, with the attendant loss of uniqueness, may be disconcerting (Chase, 1996). Responses to this problem have included suggestions that reports should be co-produced in dialogue between researcher and researched (Horwitz, 1993; McBeth, 1993), or that participants should be offered a 'right to reply' (Blackman, 1992; Lawless, 1992). Indeed, research participants may exercise such a right quite independently, through, for example, the letters pages of the local press.

Autonomy/Self-determination

Deontological discussions have conventionally focused on autonomy. Research participants are said to have certain rights, notably to privacy, respect or self-determination, that may be infringed. As MacIntyre (1982) observed, people can be wronged, even when they are not harmed. Historically, much of the debate about these rights has centred on the ethics of covert research. Discussions of privacy have been fuelled by the occasionally hostile response to ethnographic reports from the communities studied and from native (or nativist) anthropologists (Brettell, 1993; Davis, 1993; Ellis, 1995). The rights of research subjects in ethnographic work will not be respected simply because consent forms have been signed: indeed, as in much biomedical research,

these forms may offer more protection to the researcher than to the subject in the event of litigation. Moreover, as Price (1996) noted, signed consent forms may actually jeopardize the confidentiality of participants by making them identifiable. There are genuine difficulties about the means of respecting rights to autonomy and self-determination. The answers depend more on the moral sense of the researcher and their ability to make reasoned decisions in the field than upon regulative codes of practice or review procedures.

Critics of covert research (such as Bulmer, 1980; Dingwall, 1980; Erikson, 1967; Warwick, 1982) hold that such studies violate participants' right to autonomy. Defenders of covert observational studies (for example, Bolton, 1995; Holdaway, 1982; Homan, 1980; Humphreys, 1970) tend to justify their position in consequentialist terms, arguing that the research benefits outweighed any compromise of participants' rights. Indeed, Bolton (1995), who actively participated in sexual relations while studying the gay scene in Brussels, without always disclosing his research interests to his partners, suggested that informed consent was only relevant where there was a possibility of harm to those being studied.

Recent work has recognized that the distinction between covert and overt research is less straightforward than sometimes imagined. In complex and mobile settings, it may simply be impractical to seek consent from everyone involved. Unlike experimental researchers, ethnographers typically have limited control over who enters their field of observation. All research lies on a continuum between overtness and covertness. If ethnographers, whether radical constructivists or not, accept that there is no single true version of a setting, the same must be true for the accounts of their proposed research that they present in negotiating access. They cannot combine a commitment to multiple perspectives in data collection and analysis with a naive assertion that the simple, unmediated truth about the research has been communicated to the participants. The versions they offer are both necessarily and appropriately designed for their audiences. Otherwise they might well be true but incomprehensible. This is a particular concern in sociological (and anthropological) research where it may be difficult fully to explain the objectives 'without sending informants and cohabitants to graduate school' (Brewster Smith, 1979: 14). Signed consent forms do not guarantee participants' understanding, although, as Wong (1998) suggests, they may be a useful, albeit uncomfortable, reminder to both parties of the nature of their relationship.

The ethical concerns raised by the opacity of sociological and anthropological interests to non-social scientists (Glazier, 1993) are further complicated by the emergent nature of research design and analysis in ethnography (Josselson, 1996a). At the point of negotiating access, researchers typically do not have all the information that fully informed consent might require. At the outset of the study cited earlier, Voysey saw the outcome as a description of the problems facing families with a disabled child in order to improve health and social care services. This goal seems both comprehensible and likely to be attractive to the parents approached to participate. However, her focus was transformed in the course of the research. She came to recognize that her interviews were irreducibly social encounters and must be analysed as 'situationally appropriate accounts' where participants sought to present themselves as 'good parents'. The initial consent was clearly not fully informed. This was, though, unavoidable, both because her approach changed as the study progressed and because the sociological issues addressed in her final analysis were unlikely to have been fully accessible to the parents. This also suggests some caution about the current enthusiasm for depositing qualitative data in archives accessible to other researchers. The problem is not just that the data may be used to harm participants but that the original investigator may have a duty to respect the autonomy of participants and the information about the purpose of the study on which their consent was based.

Conventionally, discussions about openness in research have focused on what participants are told about the objectives and nature of the fieldwork and analysis. More recently, a number of researchers, particularly feminist and post-colonial anthropologists, have raised concerns about deception in relation to self-disclosure. Diane Wolf (1996a) described her unease at having lied to her Indonesian informants about her religious affiliation, marital status and finances, at the same time as seeking frankness from them on the same issues. Blackwood (1995) hid her lesbian orientation from the people in her fieldwork village, maintaining a fiction about a fiancé at home. She described her discomfort at this, which 'at worst established my superiority over the people in the village because it implied they should not, or did not need to, know such things about "their" anthropologist' (p. 57). In both cases, the researchers' reluctance to disclose arose from concerns that their identities would make them unacceptable to potential participants and compromise their fieldwork. Edelman (1996) has discussed some of the discomfort associated with his reluctance to reveal his Jewish identity in some field settings. This led to a false presentation of self, colluding with the tacit assumption that he was a Christian and with those who held negative images of Jews.

The concern with self-disclosure is related to wider issues about the power relations between researcher and researched. Once again these have particularly exercised feminist and post-colonial researchers. At the extreme, they have argued that the research relationship is irreducibly oppressive and exploitative and that truly ethical research is impossible (Patai, 1991). Particular concerns include the way in which research objectifies participants and then controls and exploits them during fieldwork and in subsequent publications (D. Wolf, 1996b). Such arguments are often associated with suspicion of expertise, which is seen as elitist (Eisner, 1997). Researchers who claim special competence to devise and design research and to analyse and interpret data may be regarded as authoritarian. Their claims to 'know' are inappropriate in a post-colonial world (Brettell, 1993). In the light of this critique, feminists have experimented with more collaborative approaches, where participants have been invited to join in defining research questions and designs, using models of action research or participative enquiry (D. Wolf, 1996b). These experiments have raised a number of practical problems, not least the unwillingness of some participants to engage in such collaborative approaches (Chase, 1996; Swadener and Marsh, 1998). Moreover, collaborations do not necessarily lead to agreement and the researcher cannot escape the residual responsibility for deciding how to 'respond to, negotiate or present disagreement, and, in so doing, she continues to exercise control over the research process' (Chase, 1996: 51).

Both Hammersley (1992a) and Eisner (1997) have questioned the underlying assumption that researcher control is necessarily wrong or an offence against participants' autonomy. Hammersley argued that researchers' claim to expertise is not made *ex cathedra*. In Eisner's terms, this expertise is 'attained' rather than 'ascribed' and is subject to critical evaluation. From an explicitly feminist position, Marjorie Wolf (1996) has observed that power differentials between researchers and researched do not necessarily lead to exploitation. Exploitation only occurs when ethnographers use their superior power to achieve their objectives at real cost to those they are studying. Research should be judged in terms of its effects, particularly on the collectivity, rather than in relation to issues of power and control. Here she is balancing a deontological concern with participants' rights against a consequentialist focus on effects.

Some feminist researchers (Finch, 1984; Oakley, 1981, for example) have attempted to redress the power imbalances between researcher and researched by replacing the hierarchical stance of the 'neutral researcher', characteristic of conventional approaches, with more intimate, 'authentic' and 'sisterly' relations with those studied (Patai, 1991; Reinharz, 1983). Others (for example, Stacey, 1991) have responded with caution, pointing out that the development of closer, more empathic relationships between researcher and researched may mask 'a deeper, more dangerous form of exploitation' (Stacey, 1991: 113) and create more subtle opportunities for manipulation. Research participants may be *more* likely to disclose private information to those they consider friends than to those adopting a more traditional fieldwork stance (D. Wolf, 1996b). As Diane Wolf (1996b) and Reinharz (1992) have suggested, attempts at down-playing inequalities and developing reciprocal relationships with participants may be disingenuous, not least because researchers have the privilege of eventually leaving the field. Any attenuation of the power imbalance between researcher and researched is likely to be temporary (D. Wolf, 1996b). Reinharz (1992: 265) observed, 'Purported solidarity is often a fraud perpetuated by feminists with good intentions.' Moreover, participants may not want a reciprocal relationship or aspire to friendship (Ribbens, 1989): as Altork's informant, Goldie, so frankly remarked, 'I wanted you to use it [interview material] for something. That meant more to me than our friendship idea, because I have lots of friends. I do!' (Altork, 1998: 20).

It is also important to recognize that the distribution of power is often less clear-cut in ethnographic than in other kinds of research (Sheehan, 1993). In experimental studies, once consent has been granted, power lies almost exclusively with the researcher, manipulating passive subjects who have surrendered their right to self-determination for the duration of the intervention. This asymmetrical relationship is attenuated in ethnographic research. The different 'positionalities' (D. Wolf, 1996b) of researcher and researched, in terms of race, class, nationality, gender, education etc., may render participants vulnerable to exploitation (Patai, 1991). However, participants still have substantial capacity for exerting power over ethnographers (Hammersley, 1992a; Wong, 1998). A number of researchers have described how powerful actors obstructed access to communities and prevented them from taking full control of their research design (see Abbott, 1983; Abu-Lughod, 1986; Brown, 1991, cited in D. Wolf, 1996b). Wong (1998) observed that the women he studied actively controlled the direction and temper of his ethnographic encounters with them. Participants may use the research for their own ends: Bilu (1996) described how the participants in his research into the life of a legendary rabbi-healer were able to use his involvement as a way of legitimating the mythologization and popularization of the rabbi-healer as a saint.

A preoccupation with not objectifying participants has called into question some principles that were previously treated as axiomatic by ethnographers. Until recently, an embargo on sexual relations between researcher and researched largely went unchallenged (in principle, if not in practice). Indeed some, including Lincoln (1998), still see sex in the field as an 'oxymoron'. However, a number of, mainly gay, lesbian and post-colonialist, researchers (Blackwood, 1995; Bolton, 1995; Dubisch, 1995; Kulick, 1995) have begun to argue

that refusing to consider a sexual relationship with participants reflects the objectification of them as 'Alien or Other' (Blackwood, 1995: 71). The consequence, Bolton argued, may be to increase rather than decrease 'ethnocentrism, racism, homophobia, religious intolerance, and sexism' (Bolton, 1995: 140). By contrast, he suggested, 'sex is arguably the ultimate dissolution of boundaries between individuals'. If this is the case, then sexual relations with participants seem to raise, in even starker form, the problems, discussed above, which emerge when researchers seek to develop close reciprocal friendships with the researched. Whether the participant is harmed or not, the opportunities for exploitation and manipulation are greatly increased.

Concerns about participants' rights have also been raised in relation to the research product (Sheehan, 1993; D. Wolf, 1996b). Arguably, the career and financial benefits that researchers derive from their work are expropriated from research participants (Dubisch, 1995). Some (for example, Razavi, 1993; Scheper-Hughes, 1992) have attempted to counter-balance such potential exploitation by acts of reciprocity during the fieldwork or by sharing royalties from publications with participants (Glazier, 1993; Shostak, 1989). Others have tried, in various ways, to 'return the research to participants'. However, as Patai (1991) observed, participants are not always particularly interested in follow-up and researchers must be wary of further burdening them with expectations of intense involvement, arising more from their own needs for affirmation than from any need or desire among the participants themselves. The argument that the product should be 'returned' to participants as a means of empowering them and undermining their hierarchical relationship with the researcher, is particularly problematic when the participants represent perspectives or political positions which are abhorrent to the researcher. As Blee (1993) observed, in the context of her study of former members of the Ku Klux Klan, even where the researcher does not actively seek to strengthen the political agendas of such groups, the mere acts of eliciting, recording and publishing such accounts may have this effect.

Alongside rights to autonomy and self-determination, some researchers have argued that research participants should be accorded the right to self-definition (Stanley and Wise, 1983). This concern is related to the so-called 'crisis of representation' (Clifford and Marcus, 1986). If, as Clifford (1986) argued, ethnography is 'always caught in the invention, not the representation of cultures' (p. 2), then questions are raised about the authority of ethnographers to 'invent' a version of participants' realities which they may not acknowledge. If ethnographic texts are indeed based on 'systematic and contestable exclusions' (Clifford, 1988: 7), issues arise about the 'representational politics' (Neumann, 1996) of the ethnographer's authority. Who has the right to interpret another's reality, to define what should or should not be excluded and what meanings should or should not be attributed, and by what right do they do so?

Some postmodernists have called for a democratization of representation and rejected the writer's right to interpret any experience other than his or her own. Attempts to interpret the experience of others have been seen as a new form of colonization (Fine, 1994; Price, 1996). The concern about usurping participants' rights to self-definition has been associated with a growing enthusiasm for auto-ethnography (see, for example, Kolker, 1996; Ronai, 1996; Tillman-Healy, 1996). Neumann (1996) suggested that auto-ethnography may offer an opportunity to 'confront dominant forms of representation and power in an attempt to reclaim ... representational spaces that marginalize individuals and others' (1996: 189). Auto-ethnography is a 'discourse from the margins and identifies the material, political and transformative dimensions of representational politics' (1996: 191). However, auto-ethnography does not escape ethical problems. Authors present accounts of events, interactions and relationships in which they are intimately involved: Ronai (1996), for example, described her experience as the child of a 'mentally retarded' mother. At one level, auto-ethnography appears to resolve some of the ethical problems generated by studying other people's lives. If one's research subject is oneself then the issues around autonomy and informed consent may be solved at a stroke. However, the author is never represented in a social vacuum. Auto-ethnography typically presents the actions and interactions of others from the author's perspective. What is the basis of the auto-ethnographer's authority to represent those others in this way? Should the consent of other players in the auto-drama not be obtained before publication? Are those judged to be the villains of a narrative to be denied privacy and autonomy but not the heroes/heroines? Does the auto-ethnographer not have a duty of beneficence and non-maleficence to those about whom (s)he writes?

Concern that researchers are usurping research participants' right to self-definition is related to the particular weight granted to the authorial voice in our culture (Josselson, 1996a). Critics of conventional ethnographic accounts argue that the rhetorical construction of ethnographic texts elevates the researcher's definition of the situation to a status that makes it impossible, or at least very difficult, for the participants to sustain alternative definitions of their situation. Some argue that the *only* legitimate role for researchers is to *reproduce* participants' perspectives: to go beyond this usurps the right of people to define their own reality. This position is linked to preoccupations about 'voice' and has given rise to calls for multivocality, polyphony and 'messy texts' in research reports

(Fox, 1996; Ginsberg, 1993). The ethnographer's interpretations may represent a powerful, uninvited intrusion into participants' lives which robs them of some element of their freedom to make sense of their own experience (Josselson, 1996b). The ethical issues of interpretative authority are particularly marked where the analyst treats a participant's account as an exercise in narrative persuasion, rather than as the literal description originally intended (Ochberg, 1996).

The debate on interpretative authority again brings together a complex of representational, epistemological and ethical issues that it is important to disentangle. At the level of presentation, there can be little disagreement that ethnographers are, at least potentially, able to exploit their authorial position by imposing interpretations on their data. Nor is there any doubt that, in doing so, they may disempower and abuse research participants. The capacity for doing so is particularly great where authors are rendered invisible in the text so that the authority of their interpretations is assumed and ascribed rather than attained. It is therefore incumbent upon researchers to make themselves visible in the texts they write (Chase, 1996) and to present the evidence upon which their interpretations are based. By making the process of data analysis 'public and reproducible' (Dingwall, 1992) and separating out the data from the researcher's interpretation, authors open the possibility that their interpretations may be challenged.

However, for some ethnographers the ethical issues surrounding interpretative authority are more complex. The issue is not the *validity* of the interpretations, but the question of control over the interpretative process (Chase, 1996). Some, particularly feminist, researchers have argued that only by sharing control of interpretation, can we break down the hierarchical relationship between researcher and researched and avoid exploiting participants. Chase (1996), on the other hand, has suggested that we need to acknowledge our interests and the extent to which they may differ from those of participants. The analyst's concern to construct second-order accounts that generalize individual experiences inevitably involves reshaping the originals. Moreover, we must acknowledge that participants may not be in a position fully to grasp all the relevant aspects of context. Borland (1991) described the particular problems which this raises for feminist researchers: 'We hold an explicitly political vision of the structural conditions that lead to particular social behaviours, a vision that our field collaborators, many of whom do not consider themselves feminists, may not recognize as valid' (1991: 64). Experience cannot be treated as the sole source of authority (Hammersley, 1992a). We do not necessarily understand a phenomenon just because we have experienced it. Oppressed groups may experience oppression but have little understanding of it (M. Wolf, 1996). It is for researchers to take responsibility for the interpretative processes they engage in. Perhaps, as Chase (1996) suggests, the ethical problem raised by our interpretations is less that we usurp participants' rights to self-definition than that, in negotiating access, we fail to alert participants to the ways in which we will re-frame their versions.

There are problems in naively asserting that the researcher's sole responsibility is to 'let the people speak'. As Hammersley observed, reliance on participants' definitions ignores the fact that these are, at least in part, products of the context: as context and audience change so will narratives. Even more fundamentally, this position raises the problem of how participants' interpretations of the situation are to be accessed. In practice, this depends heavily on participant accounts, verbal or written, involving what Atkinson and Silverman described as 'neo-Romantic celebrations of the speaking subject' (1977: 305). As Borland (1991) observed, reflecting upon the conflicts of interpretation arising from her analysis of a narrative elicited from her grandmother, such accounts are always governed by the narrator's 'assumption of responsibility to an audience for a display of communicative competence' (Bauman, 1977: 11).

At times, these concerns about the usurpation of interpretative authority involve an elision of epistemological, political and ethical issues. Where ethnographers endorse the radical solipsism of some versions of postmodernism, which make truth-claims a matter of choice, then it is indeed difficult to see how the ethnographer could make any claim to authoritative interpretation. His or her interpretation can only be placed alongside those of any other participant (or indeed non-participant) and, since multiple, contradictory realities can exist, there is no basis for choosing between them. It is at this point that some ethnographers appeal to consequentialist ethics, claiming that the justification for usurping the interpretative authority of those one researches lies in the power of the research to produce valued social outcomes (Fine, 1994). This, though, simply raises the problem of how to value social outcomes (Price, 1996).

Not all ethnographers endorse radical relativism. Many seek to combine a commitment to social constructionism with the pursuit of truth as a regulative ideal. Such 'subtle realism' (Hammersley, 1992b) leads to an alternative perspective on the issues around interpretative authority. Subtle realists accept the possibility of multiple, *non-contradictory* versions of reality which, although different from one another, may nevertheless all be true. However, they reject the possibility of multiple, *contradictory* versions of reality which are nevertheless true. This opens up the possibility that participants' versions of events may be 'reality tested' through empirical

work. The researcher is not obliged to treat any particular version as authoritative simply because it is offered by a participant. The ethical imperative shifts to a concern with fair dealing, discussed in the next section.

Justice

The issue of fair dealing is an expression of the final ethical principle, that research participants should be treated equally. For some the argument that all research is inevitably shaped by values has led to the question, 'Whose side are we on?' (Becker, 1967). Researchers have been warned against a deferential posture, privileging the perspective of the elite or powerful in the research setting and paying scant attention to the less powerful (Guba and Lincoln, 1989; Marshall, 1985; Sandelowski, 1986; Silverman, 1985). Set against this is the concern that preoccupation with the so-called under-dog has led to a neglect of the powerful and privileged (Dingwall, 1980, 1992; Silverman, 1993). As a result, elites are sometimes presented as 'cardboard cutouts who are either misguided or wilfully putting their own interests first' (Voysey, 1975: 61). Similarly, Blee has reported some of the challenges she encountered in studying former members of reactionary race-hate groups (Blee, 1993). Traditionally, the emphasis had been upon 'caution, distance, and objectivity in interviews with members of elites and egalitarianism, reciprocity, and authenticity in interviews with people outside elites.' (1993: 597). Studying former members of the Ku Klux Klan highlighted the 'epistemological dichotomy' and 'romantic assumptions about the subjects of history from the bottom up' that are implicit in such recommendations. The principle of justice demands that the ethnographer should aspire to even-handed treatment of all participants or informants. This does not mean the suspension of all personal moral judgements. Indeed, acknowledging such responses may be vital to the ethnographer's reflexive engagement with data. However, it does demand that the researcher remains committed to developing an analysis which displays an equally sophisticated understanding of the behaviour of both villains and heroes – or heroines (Dingwall, 1992).

This is, in some respects, a return to Weber's argument, that the vocation of science requires 'the intellectual integrity to see that it is one thing to state facts, to determine mathematical or logical relations or the internal structure of cultural values, while it is another thing to answer questions as to the *value* of culture and its individual contents and the question of how one should act in the cultural community and in political associations ... the prophet and the demagogue do not belong on the academic platform' (Gerth and Mills, 1970: 146).

Of course, others may see the adoption of such a position as a political challenge. Much of what is sometimes known as 'standpoint ethnography' rests upon the argument that science is an inherently political activity. Mies (1991: 65), for example, asserts the need 'to question contemplative science, which veils power and exploitation ... [and to create] an alternative scientific paradigm which supports emancipatory movements and does not limit them as dominant science does'. Mies happens to be writing from a feminist perspective but her arguments have many echoes in other writers associated with queer, black or post-colonial studies. 'Truth' does not depend on 'the application of certain methodological principles and rules, but on its potential to orient the processes of praxis towards progressive emancipation and humanization' (Mies, 1983: 124). As Hammersley (1992a) has pointed out, however, the problem is to determine what actually constitutes 'emancipation and humanization' and for whom. It may be as much an expression of a sectional interest as the dominant ideology to which it is counterposed and it is unclear what right the researcher has, other than self-appointment, to speak for the oppressed interest. The Weberian approach acknowledges the difficulty of separating questions of fact and value. However, it has the virtue of setting a goal for investigators to strive towards and of creating a disciplinary regime that regulates the possibilities of interpretation rather than leaving these wholly to the fancy or interest of the researcher. As Oakley (1998) notes, the cause of women may in practice be advanced much more by systematically disinterested work than by an obvious fitting of data to a prior position. Having said that, one is still left with the problem of 'partial truths' (Clifford, 1986: 18) in that what may appear to be 'systematically disinterested' is constantly changing and reflects both the historical and political context in which it is defined. In Clifford's words, 'a great many portrayals of "cultural" truths now appear to reflect male domains of experience'. The corollary of this is that the partiality of current versions of reality will in time also be seen as partial. As Denzin (1997) has argued, theory, writing and ethnography are inseparable. What is required is a reflexive form of writing that exposes theory to ethnography and ethnography to theory. Truth and facts may be irreducibly socially constructed but this need not undermine the self-conscious pursuit of the separation of fact and value as a regulative goal.

CONCLUSION

Like all research that involves human participants, ethnography raises significant ethical concerns. All researchers share the same minimal responsibility to protect participants from harm even where such participants may, themselves, be cavalier about the risks they are taking. Similarly, the justification for research lies at least partly in the belief that it will 'make a difference', although the benefits may well accrue to the collectivity rather than to the particular individuals who take part in the research. However, these concerns with beneficence and non-maleficence do not exhaust the ethical imperatives encountered by ethnographers, who must also be concerned with the extent to which their research practice affects the rights and interests of participants. These obligations are complex and will not be fulfilled through simple adherence to a prescriptive list of requirements. Indeed, given the diversity and flexibility of ethnography, and the indeterminacy of potential harm, a prescriptive approach may be positively unhelpful. It can fail to protect participants and, perhaps even more importantly, may deflect researchers from the reflective pursuit of ethical practice.

REFERENCES

Abbott, S. (1983) '"In the end you will carry me in your car": sexual politics in the field', *Women's Studies*, 10: 161–78.

Abu-Lughod, L. (1986) *Veiled Sentiments: Honor and Poetry in a Bedouin Society*. Berkeley, CA: University of California Press.

Altork, K. (1998) 'You never know when you might want to be a redhead in Belize', in K. de Marrais (ed.), *Inside Stories: Qualitative Research Reflections*. Mahwah, NJ: Lawrence Erlbaum. pp. 111–25.

Atkinson, P. and Silverman, D. (1997) 'Kundera's *Immortality*: the interview society and the invention of the self', *Qualitative Inquiry*, 3: 304–25.

Bakan, D. (1996) 'Some reflections about narrative research and hurt and harm', in R. Josselson (ed.), *Ethics and Process in the Narrative Study of Lives*. Thousand Oaks, CA: Sage. pp. 3–8.

Barnes, J. (1979) *Who Should Know What? Social Science, Privacy and Ethics*. Harmondsworth: Penguin.

Bar-On, D. (1996) 'Ethical issues in biographical interviews and analysis', in R. Josselson (ed.), *Ethics and Process in the Narrative Study of Lives*. Thousand Oaks, CA: Sage. pp. 9–21.

Bauman, R. (1977) *Verbal Art as Performance*. Prospect Heights, IL: Waveland.

Beauchamp, T., Faden, R., Wallace, R.J. Jr and Walters, L. (1982) 'Introduction', in T. Beauchamp, R. Faden and R. Wallace (eds), *Ethical Issues in Social Science Research*. Baltimore, MD: Johns Hopkins University Press. pp. 3–39.

Becker, H.S. (1964) 'Problems in the publication of field studies', in A.J. Vidich, J. Bensman and M.R. Stein (eds), *Reflections on Community Studies*. New York:

Wiley. (Reproduced in G.J. McCall and J.L. Simmons) (eds), *Issues in Participant Observation: A Text and Reader*. Reading, MA: Addison Wesley. pp. 9–21.

Becker, H.S. (1967) 'Whose side are we on?', *Social Problems*, 14: 239–48.

Benatar, S. (1997) 'Just healthcare beyond individualism: challenges for North American bioethics', *Cambridge Quarterly of Healthcare Ethics*, 6: 397–415.

Bilu, Y. (1996) 'Ethnography and hagiography: the dialectics of life, story and afterlife', in R. Josselson (ed.), *Ethics and Process in the Narrative Study of Lives*. Thousand Oaks, CA: Sage. pp. 151–71.

Blackman, M. (1992) *During my Time: Florence Edenshaw Davidson, a Haida Woman*, rev. edn. Seattle, WA: University of Washington Press.

Blackwood, E. (1995) 'Falling in love with an-Other lesbian', in D. Kulick and M. Willson (eds), *Taboo: Sex, Identity and Erotic Subjectivity in Anthropological Fieldwork*. London: Routledge. pp. 51–75.

Blee, K.M. (1993) 'Evidence, empathy and ethics: lessons from oral histories of the Klan', *Journal of American History*, September: 596–606.

Bolton, R. (1995) 'Tricks, friends and lovers: erotic encounters in the field', in D. Kulick and M. Willson (eds), *Taboo: Sex, Identity and Erotic Subjectivity in Anthropological Fieldwork*. London: Routledge. pp. 140–67.

Borland, K. (1991) '"That's not what I said": interpretive conflict in oral narrative research', in S. Gluck and D. Patai (eds), *Women's Words: The Feminist Practice of Oral History*. New York and London: Routledge. pp. 63–76.

Brettell, C. (1993) 'Introduction: fieldwork, text, and audience', in C. Brettell (ed.), *When They Read What We Write: The Politics of Ethnography*. Westport, CT: Bergin and Garvey. pp. 1–24.

Brewster Smith, M. (1979) 'Some perspectives on ethical/political issues in social science research', in M. Wax and J. Cassell (eds), *Federal Regulations: Ethical Issues and Social Research*. Boulder, CO: Westview Press. pp. 11–22.

Brown, K. (1991) *Mama Lola: A Voudou Priestess in Brooklyn*. Berkeley and Los Angeles, CA: University of California Press.

Bulmer, M. (1980) 'Comment on the ethics of covert methods', *British Journal of Sociology*, 31: 59–65.

Bulmer, M. (1982) *Social Research Ethics*. London: Macmillan.

Burgess, R. (1985) 'The whole truth? Some ethical problems of research in a comprehensive school', in R.G. Burgess (ed.), *Strategies of Educational Research: Qualitative Methods*. Lewes: Falmer Press. pp. 141–62.

Cassell, J. (1978) 'Risk and benefit to subjects of fieldwork', *American Sociologist*, 13: 134–43.

Cassell, J. (1979) 'Regulating fieldwork: of subjects, subjection and intersubjectivity', in M. Wax and J. Cassell (eds), *Federal Regulations: Ethical Issues and Social Research*. Boulder, CO: Westview Press. pp. 129–44.

Cassell, J. (1982) 'Does risk–benefit analysis apply to moral evaluation of social research?', in T. Beauchamp,

R. Faden, R. Wallace and L. Walters (eds), *Ethical Issues in Social Science Research*. Baltimore, MD: Johns Hopkins University Press. pp. 144–62.

Chase, S. (1996) 'Personal vulnerability and interpretive authority in narrative research', in R. Josselson (ed.), *Ethics and Process in the Narrative Study of Lives*. Thousand Oaks, CA: Sage. pp. 45–59.

Clifford, J. (1986) 'Introduction: partial truths', in J. Clifford and George E. Marcus (eds), *Writing Culture: The Poetics and Politics of Ethnography*. Berkeley, CA: University of California Press. pp. 1–26.

Clifford, J. (1988) *The Predicament of Culture*. Cambridge, MA: Harvard University Press.

Clifford, J. and Marcus, G. (1986) *Writing Culture*. Berkeley, CA: University of California Press.

Davis, D. (1993) 'Unintended consequences: the myth of "the return" in anthropological fieldwork', in C. Brettell (ed.), *When They Read What We Write: The Politics of Ethnography*. Westport, CT: Bergin and Garvey. pp. 27–35.

Denzin, N.K. (1997) *Interpretive Ethnography: Ethnographic Practices for the 21st Century*. Thousand Oaks, CA: Sage.

Diener, E. and Crandall, R. (1978) *Ethics in Social and Behavioural Research*. Chicago: University of Chicago Press.

Dingwall, R. (1980) 'Ethics and ethnography', *Sociological Review*, 28: 871–91.

Dingwall, R. (1992) 'Don't mind him – he's from Barcelona: qualitative methods in health studies', in J. Daly, I. McDonald and E. Willis (eds), *Researching Health Care*. London: Tavistock/Routledge. pp. 161–75.

Dubisch, J. (1995) 'Lovers in the field: sex, dominance and the female anthropologist', in D. Kulick and M. Willson (eds), *Taboo: Sex, Identity and Erotic Subjectivity in Anthropological Fieldwork*. London: Routledge. pp. 29–50.

Edelman, M. (1996) 'Devil, not-quite-white, rootless cosmopolitan *Tsuris* in Latin America, the Bronx, and the USSR', in C. Ellis and A.P. Bochner (eds), *Composing Ethnography: Alternative Forms of Qualitative Writing*. Walnut Creek, CA: AltaMira Press. pp. 267–300.

Eisner, E. (1997) 'The new frontier in qualitative research methodology', *Qualitative Inquiry*, 3: 259–73.

Ellis, C. (1995) 'Emotional and ethical quagmires in returning to the field', *Journal of Contemporary Ethnography*, 24: 68–98.

Erikson, K. (1967) 'A comment on disguised observation in sociology', *Social Problems*, 14: 366–73.

Finch, J. (1984) '"It's great to have someone to talk to": the ethics and politics of interviewing women', in C. Bell and H. Roberts (eds), *Social Researching: Policies, Problems and Practice*. London: Routledge and Kegan Paul. pp. 70–85.

Finch, J. (1986) *Research and Policy: The Uses of Qualitative Methods in Social and Educational Research*. Lewes: Falmer Press.

Fine, M. (1994) 'Working the hyphens: reinventing self and other in qualitative research', in N.K. Denzin and

Y.S. Lincoln (eds), *Handbook of Qualitative Research*. Thousand Oaks, CA: Sage. pp. 70–82.

Fox, K.V. (1996) 'Silent voices: a subversive reading of child sexual abuse', in C. Ellis and A.P. Bochner (eds), *Composing Ethnography: Alternative Forms of Qualitative Writing*. Walnut Creek, CA: AltaMira Press. pp. 330–56.

Gerth, H.H. and Mills, C.W. (1970) *From Max Weber*. London: Routledge and Kegan Paul.

Ginsberg, F. (1993) 'The case of mistaken identity', in C. Brettell (ed.), *When They Read What We Write: The Politics of Ethnography*. Westport, CT: Bergin and Garvey. pp. 163–76.

Glazier, S. (1993) 'Responding to the anthropologist: when the spiritual baptists of Trinidad read what I write about them', in C. Brettell (ed.), *When They Read What We Write: The Politics of Ethnography*. Westport, CT: Bergin and Garvey. pp. 37–48.

Gmelch, S. (1992) 'From beginning to end: an irish life history', *Journal of Narrative and Life History*, 2: 29–38.

Greenberg, O. (1993) 'When they read what the papers say we wrote', in C. Brettell (ed.), *When They Read What We Write: The Politics of Ethnography*. Westport, CT: Bergin and Garvey. pp. 107–18.

Guba, E.G. and Lincoln, Y.S. (1989) *Fourth Generation Evaluation*. Newbury Park, CA: Sage.

Hammersley, M. (1992a) 'On feminist methodology', *Sociology*, 26: 187–206.

Hammersley, M. (1992b) 'Ethnography and realism', in M. Hammersley (ed.), *What's Wrong With Ethnography?* London: Routledge. pp. 43–56.

Holdaway, S. (1982) '"An inside job": a case study of covert research on the police', in M. Bulmer (ed.), *Social Research Ethics: An Examination of the Merits of Covert Participant Observation*. London: Macmillan. pp. 59–79.

Homan, R. (1980) 'The ethics of covert methods', *British Journal of Sociology*, 31: 46–59.

Hopkins, M. (1993) 'Is anonymity possible? Writing about refugees in the United States', in C. Brettell (ed.), *When They Read What We Write: The Politics of Ethnography*. Westport, CT: Bergin and Garvey. pp. 121–9.

Horwitz, R. (1993) 'Just stories of ethnographic authority', in C. Brettell (ed.), *When They Read What We Write: The Politics of Ethnography*. Westport, CT: Bergin and Garvey. pp. 131–43.

House, E. (1990) 'An ethics of qualitative field studies', in E. Guba (ed.), *The Paradigm Dialog*. Newbury Park, CA: Sage. pp. 158–201.

Humphreys, L. (1970) *Tearoom Trade*. Chicago: Aldine.

Josselson, R. (1996a) 'Introduction', in R. Josselson (ed.), *Ethics and Process in the Narrative Study of Lives*. Thousand Oaks, CA: Sage. pp. xi–xviii.

Josselson, R. (1996b) 'On writing other people's lives: self-analytic reflections of a narrative researcher', in R. Josselson (ed.), *Ethics and Process in the Narrative Study of Lives*. Thousand Oaks, CA: Sage. pp. 60–71.

Kelman, H. (1982) 'Ethical issues in different social science methods', in T. Beauchamp, R. Faden, R. Wallace and L. Walters (eds), *Ethical Issues in Social Science Research*. Baltimore, MD: Johns Hopkins University Press.

Kolker, A. (1996) 'Thrown overboard: the human costs of health care rationing', in C. Ellis and A.P. Bochner (eds), *Composing Ethnography: Alternative Forms of Qualitative Writing*. Walnut Creek, CA: AltaMira Press. pp. 132–59.

Kulick, D. (1995) 'Introduction', in D. Kulick and M. Willson (eds), *Taboo: Sex, Identity and Erotic Subjectivity in Anthropological Fieldwork*. London: Routledge. pp. 1–28.

Lawless, E. (1992) '"I was afraid someone like you ... an outsider ... would misunderstand": negotiating interpretive differences between ethnographers and subjects', *Journal of American Folklore*, 105: 302–14.

Lieblich, A. (1996) 'Some unforeseen outcomes of narrative research', in R. Josselson (ed.), *Ethics and Process in the Narrative Study of Lives*. Thousand Oaks, CA: Sage. pp. 172–84.

Lincoln, Y.S. (1998) 'The ethics of teaching in qualitative research', *Qualitative Inquiry*, 4: 315–27.

McBeth, S. (1993) 'Myths of objectivity and the collaborative process in life history research', in C. Brettell (ed.), *When They Read What We Write: The Politics of Ethnography*. Westport, CT: Bergin and Garvey. pp. 146–62.

MacIntyre, A. (1982) 'Risk, harm and benefits assessments as instruments of moral evaluation', in T. Beauchamp, R. Faden, R. Wallace and L. Walters (eds), *Ethical Issues in Social Science Research*. Baltimore, MD: Johns Hopkins University Press. pp. 175–89.

Macklin, R. (1982) 'The problem of adequate disclosure in social science research', in T. Beauchamp, R. Faden, R. Wallace and L. Walters (eds), *Ethical Issues in Social Science Research*. Baltimore, MD: Johns Hopkins University Press. pp. 193–214.

Marshall, C. (1985) 'Appropriate criteria of the trustworthiness and goodness for qualitative research on educational organizations', *Quality and Quantity*, 19: 353–73.

Merriam, S. (1988) *Case Study Research in Education: A Qualitative Approach*. San Francisco, CA: Jossey Bass.

Messenger, J. (1989) *Inis Beag Revisited: The Anthropologist as Participant Observer*. Salem, WI: Sheffield Publishing.

Mies, M. (1983) 'Towards a feminist methodology for feminist research', in G. Bowles and R. Duelli Klein (eds), *Theories of Women's Studies*. Boston, MA: Routledge and Kegan Paul. pp. 117–39.

Mies, M. (1991) 'Women's research or feminist research? The debate surrounding feminist science and methodology', in M.M. Fonow and J.A. Book (eds), *Beyond Methodology: Feminist Scholarship as Lived Research*. Bloomington, IN: Indiana University Press. pp. 60–84.

Miller, M.E. (1996) 'Ethics and understanding through interrelationship: I and thou in dialogue', in R. Josselson (ed.), *Ethics and Process in the Narrative Study of Lives*. Thousand Oaks, CA: Sage.

Morgan, D.H.J. (1972) 'The British Association scandal: the effect of publicity on a sociological investigation', *Sociological Review*, 20 (2): 185–206.

Neumann, M. (1996) 'Collecting ourselves at the end of the century', in C. Ellis and A.P. Bochner (eds), *Composing Ethnography: Alternative Forms of Qualitative Writing*, Walnut Creek, CA: AltaMira Press. pp. 172–98.

Nicolaus, M. (1969) Remarks at ASA Convention, Boston, 1968. *Catalyst* (Spring): 103–6.

Oakley, A. (1981) 'Interviewing women: a contradiction in terms', in H. Roberts (ed.), *Doing Feminist Research*. London: Routledge and Kegan Paul. pp. 30–61.

Oakley, A. (1998) 'Gender, methodology and people's ways of knowing: some problems with feminism and the paradigm debate in social science', *Sociology*, 32 (4): 707–31.

Ochberg, R.L. (1996) 'Interpreting life stories', in R. Josselson (ed.), *Ethics and Process in the Narrative Study of Lives*. Thousand Oaks, CA: Sage. pp. 97–113.

Patai, D. (1991) 'US academics and Third World women: is ethical research possible?', in S. Gluck and D. Patai (eds), *Women's Words: The Feminist Practice of Oral History*. New York: Routledge. pp. 137–53.

Pattullo, E. (1982) 'Modesty is the best policy: the federal role in social research', in T. Beauchamp, R. Faden, R. Wallace and L. Walters (eds), *Ethical Issues in Social Science Research*. Baltimore, MD: Johns Hopkins University Press. pp. 373–90.

Price, J. (1996) 'Snakes in the swamp: ethical issues in qualitative research', in R. Josselson (ed.), *Ethics and Process in the Narrative Study of Lives*. Thousand Oaks, CA: Sage. pp. 207–15.

Punch, M. (1994) 'Politics and ethics in qualitative research', in N. Denzin and Y. Lincoln (eds), *Handbook of Qualitative Research*. Thousand Oaks, CA: Sage. pp. 83–97.

Razavi, S. (1993) 'Fieldwork in a familiar setting: the role of politics at the national, community and household levels', in S. Devereux and J. Hoddinott (eds), *Fieldwork in Developing Countries*. Boulder, CO: Lynne Rienner. pp. 152–63.

Reinharz, S. (1983) 'Experiential analysis: a contribution to feminist research', in G. Bowles and R. Duelli Klein (eds), *Theories of Women's Studies*. London: Routledge. pp. 162–91.

Reinharz, S. (1992) *Feminist Methods in Social Research*. New York: Oxford University Press.

Ribbens, J. (1989) 'Interviewing – an "Unnatural Situation"?', *Women's Studies International Forum*, 12: 579–92.

Richardson, L. (1996) 'Ethnographic trouble', *Qualitative Inquiry*, 2: 227–9.

Ronai, C.R. (1996) 'My mother is mentally retarded', in C. Ellis and A.P. Bochner (eds), *Composing Ethnography: Alternative Forms of Qualitative Writing*. Walnut Creek, CA: AltaMira Press. pp. 109–31.

Rosaldo, R. (1989) *Culture and Truth: The Remaking of Social Analysis*. Boston, MA: Beacon Press.

Sandelowski, M. (1986) 'The problem of rigor in qualitative research', *Ans-Advances in Nursing Science*, 8: 27–37.

Scheper-Hughes, N. (1982) *Saints, Scholars and Schizophrenics: Mental Illness in Rural Ireland*. Berkeley, CA: University of California Press.

Scheper-Hughes, N. (1992) *Death Without Weeping: The Violence of Everyday Life in Brazil*. Berkeley, CA: University of California Press.

Sheehan, E. (1993) 'The student of culture and the ethnography of Irish intellectuals', in C. Brettell (ed.), *When They Read What We Write: The Politics of Ethnography*. Westport, CT: Bergin and Garvey. pp. 75–89.

Shostak, M. (1989) '"What the wind won't take away": the genesis of Nisa – the life and words of a !Kung woman', in Personal Narratives Group (ed.), *Interpreting Women's Lives: Feminist Theory and Personal Narratives*. Bloomington, IN: Indiana University Press. pp. 228–40.

Silverman, D. (1985) *Qualitative Methodology and Sociology*. Aldershot: Gower.

Silverman, D. (1993) *Interpreting Qualitative Data: Methods for Analysing Talk, Text and Interaction*. London: Sage.

Stacey, J. (1991) 'Can there be a feminist ethnography?', in S.B. Gluck and D. Patai (eds), *Women's Words: The Feminist Practice of Oral History*. New York: Routledge, Chapman and Hall. pp. 111–19.

Stanley, L. and Wise, S. (1983) *Breaking Out: Feminist Consciousness and Feminist Research*. London: Routledge and Kegan Paul.

Swadener, B. and Marsh, M. (1998) 'Reflections on collaborative and not-so-collaborative research in early childhood settings', in K. de Marrais (ed.), *Inside Stories: Qualitative Research Reflections*. Mahwah, NJ: Lawrence Erlbaum Associates. pp. 161–72.

Thorne, B. (1980) '"You still takin' notes?" Fieldwork and problems of informed consent', *Social Problems*, 27: 284–97.

Tillman-Healy, L. (1996) 'A secret life in a culture of thinness: reflections on body, food and bulimia', in C. Ellis and A.P. Bochner (eds), *Composing Ethnography: Alternative Forms of Qualitative Writing*. Walnut Creek, CA: AltaMira Press. pp. 16–108.

Tunnell, K. (1998) 'Interviewing the incarcerated: personal notes on ethical and methodological issues', in K. de Marrais (ed.), *Inside Stories: Qualitative Research Reflections*. Mahwah, NJ: Lawrence Erlbaum, Associates. pp. 127–37.

Vidich, A. and Bensman, J. (1958) 'Freedom and responsibility in research: comments', *Human Organization*, 17: 1–7.

Vidich, A. and Bensman, J. (1964) 'The Springdale Case: academic bureaucrats and sensitive townspeople', in A. Vidich, J. Bensman and M. Stein (eds), *Reflections on Community Studies*. New York: John Wiley and Sons. pp. 313–49.

Voysey, M. (1975) *A Constant Burden: The Reconstitution of Family Life*. London: Routledge and Kegan Paul.

Walker, R. (1980) 'The conduct of educational case studies: ethics, theory and procedures', in W. Dockerell and D. Hamilton (eds), *Rethinking Educational Research*. London: Hodder and Stoughton.

Warwick, D. (1982) 'Tearoom trade: means and ends in social research', in M. Bulmer (ed.), *Social Research Ethics*. London: Macmillan. pp. 38–58.

Wax, M. (1980) 'Paradoxes of consent to the practice of fieldwork', *Social Problems*, 27: 272–83.

Wax, M. and Cassell, J. (1979) 'Fieldwork, ethics and politics: the wider context', in M. Wax and J. Cassell (eds), *Federal Regulations: Ethical Issues and Social Research*. Boulder, CO: Westview Press. pp. 85–102.

Wolf, D. (1996a) 'Preface', in D. Wolf (ed.), *Feminist Dilemmas in Fieldwork*. Oxford: Westview Press. pp. ix–xii.

Wolf, D. (1996b) 'Situating feminist dilemmas in fieldwork', in D. Wolf (ed.), *Feminist Dilemmas in Fieldwork*. Oxford: Westview Press. pp. 1–55.

Wolf, M. (1996) 'Afterword: musing from an old gray wolf', in D. Wolf (ed.), *Feminist Dilemmas in Fieldwork*. Oxford: Westview Press. pp. 215–21.

Wong, L. (1998) 'The ethics of rapport: institutional safeguards, resistance and betrayal', *Qualitative Inquiry*, 4: 178–99.

24

Participant Observation and Fieldnotes

ROBERT M. EMERSON, RACHEL I. FRETZ AND LINDA L. SHAW

Participant observation – establishing a place in some natural setting on a relatively long-term basis in order to investigate, experience and represent the social life and social processes that occur in that setting – comprises one core activity in ethnographic fieldwork. Until recently, ethnographers restricted their interest in participant observation to such issues as the vagaries of establishing such a place, the need for empathetic immersion in the daily life and meaning systems of those studied, and the ethical and political issues arising with these efforts. But participant observation involves not only gaining access to and immersing oneself in new social worlds, but also producing *written accounts and descriptions* that bring versions of these worlds to others. Geertz's early insistence on the centrality of *inscription* in ethnography, calling attention to the fact that 'the ethnographer "inscribes" social discourse, he writes it down' (1973: 19), sparked growing recognition that the ethnographer is the scribe as well as the explorer and quasi-insider of both exotic and familiar social worlds.

By the 1980s, ethnographers increasingly recognized the centrality of these more mundane and unromantic writing activities for participant observation techniques and began to give close attention to ethnographic writing. Some of these efforts have focused on clarifying the presuppositions evident in polished (published) ethnographic accounts and monographs, proposing concepts ranging from 'inscription' (Geertz, 1973) and 'transcription' (Clifford, 1990) to 'textualization' (Clifford, 1986; Marcus, 1986) and 'translation' (Crapanzano, 1986) to depict the general character of ethnographic representation. A second strand of theorizing has sought to identify specific textual and rhetorical properties of ethnographic accounts. Richardson (1990a, 1990b) points to the centrality of 'narrating' in ethnographic writing: the ethnographer both elicits and records lay narratives as a primary form of field 'data', and then rewrites and reconstructs these narratives into polished ethnographic texts. Others address issues of how authority and authenticity are established in ethnographic texts (Atkinson, 1990; Clifford, 1983), the pervasive use of core literary devices such as synedoche and metaphor in ethnographic writing (Atkinson, 1990; Richardson, 1990b), and variations in voice in ethnographic accounts (Atkinson, 1990; Richardson, 1990b).

Only in the past decade or so have ethnographers moved beyond analysing the rhetorical strategies of finished ethnographies (and of some of the embedded fieldnote accounts they contain) to consider another, more mundane form of ethnographic inscription – the writing processes whereby a participating observer transforms portions of her lived experience into written fieldnotes. Ethnographers have begun to give attention to the character of fieldnotes as written texts, to variations in style and approach to writing fieldnotes, and to how to effectively train fieldwork novices to write more sensitive, useful and stimulating fieldnotes.[1] The recent 'discovery' of fieldnotes is ironic, for it can be argued that writing fieldnotes, rather than writing finished ethnographies, provides the primal, even foundational moments of ethnographic representation: for most ethnographic monographs rely upon, incorporate and may even be built from these initial fieldnotes.

This movement has been advanced by several key works. Van Maanen's *Tales of the Field* (1988) explores the differences between extended fieldnote accounts written in 'realist', 'confessional', and 'impressionist' styles. Sanjek's edited volume *Fieldnotes: The Making of Anthropology* (1990a) provides a collection of symposium papers examining 'what anthropologists do with fieldnotes, how they live with them, and how attitudes toward the construction and use of fieldnotes may change through individual professional careers' (1990b: xii). In *The Ethnographic Imagination* (1990), Atkinson provides close analyses of various rhetorical and textual devices common to ethnographies, giving special attention to several extended fieldnote extracts (pp. 57–63). The latest edition of the Loflands' *Analyzing Social Settings* (1995) includes a lengthy chapter on 'Logging Data', which examines both observing and writing fieldnotes as well as conducting and writing up interviews. And finally, in *Writing Ethnographic Fieldnotes* (1995), Emerson, Fretz and Shaw offer an extended treatment of the processes of writing fieldnotes from first contacts in the field to producing final ethnographies.

In the following pages we review these and other recent treatments of the actual processes of writing fieldnotes as a core activity in ethnography and participant observation. We do not consider analyses of fieldnotes included in finished ethnographies; the latter are not only polished and highly selected, but they also are tied into specific themes or arguments used to construct and organize the ethnography as a whole. Rather we are concerned with fieldnotes as 'original texts' (Mulkay, 1985: 237–8), with 'raw' fieldnotes written (for the most part) more or less contemporaneously with the events depicted.

The following section first identifies some distinctive features of fieldnotes, then considers variations among ethnographers in their understandings and uses of fieldnotes. The subsequent section examines fieldnotes as a distinctive form of ethnographic writing, first considering the intrusion of writing concerns into the core ways an ethnographer participates in and orients to events in the field, then reviewing the actual processes of writing sustained, evocative and reexaminable accounts of what one has seen, heard and experienced while so observing/participating. The final section addresses some issues that arise in incorporating, using and transforming fieldnotes into finished ethnographic texts.

The Meanings and Uses of Fieldnotes in Ethnography

Ethnography is created through what Atkinson (1992: 5) characterizes as 'a double process of textual production and reproduction'. Although culminating in an integrated, coherent ethnographic account, this process begins with the day-by-day writing up of fieldnotes 'observations and reflections concerning "the field"' (1992: 5). Indeed, at their core, fieldnotes are writings produced in or in close proximity to 'the field'. Proximity means that fieldnotes are written more or less *contemporaneously* with the events, experiences and interactions they describe and recount. As one ethnographer comments: 'Anthropologists are those who write things down at the end of the day' (Jackson, 1990: 15).[2]

Fieldnotes are a form of *representation*, that is, a way of reducing just-observed events, persons and places to written accounts. And in reducing the welter and confusion of the social world to written words, fieldnotes (re)constitute that world in preserved forms that can be reviewed, studied and thought about time and time again. As Geertz (1973: 19) has emphasized, in writing down social discourse, the ethnographer 'turns it from a passing event, which exists only in its own moment of occurrence, into an account, which exists in its inscription and can be reconsulted'.

As representations, fieldnote texts are inevitably *selective*. The ethnographer writes about certain things that seem 'significant', ignoring and hence 'leaving out' other matters that do not seem significant. In this sense, fieldnotes never provide a 'complete' record (Atkinson, 1992: 17). But fieldnotes are also selective in what they do include, since they inevitably *present or frame* the events and objects written about in particular ways, hence 'missing' other ways that events might have been presented or framed.

Furthermore, fieldnotes are intended to provide *descriptive* accounts of people, scenes and dialogue, as well as personal experiences and reactions, that is, accounts that minimize explicit theorizing and interpretation. Description, however, it not a simple matter of recording 'facts', of producing written accounts that 'mirror' reality (Atkinson, 1992: 17; Emerson et al., 1995: 8–10). Rather descriptive writing embodies and reflects particular purposes and commitments, and it also involves active processes of interpretation and sense-making.

Finally, fieldnotes accumulate set-by-set over time into a larger *corpus*. That is, fieldnotes are produced incrementally on a day-by-day basis, without any sustained logic or underlying principle and on the assumption that not every observation will ultimately be useful for a larger/finished project. As a result, a fieldnote corpus need have little or no overall coherence or consistency; it typically contains bits and pieces of incidents, beginnings and ends of narratives, accounts of chance meetings and rare occurrences, and details of a wide range of unconnected matters. Ethnographers, moreover, treat their corpus of fieldnotes as a loose collection of possibly usable materials, much of which will never be incorporated into a finished text.

Within these general features of fieldnotes, however, researchers express considerable divergences over the specific forms of writing that they term 'fieldnotes', over when and how fieldnotes should be written, over how they understand 'the field', and about the place and value of fieldnotes in ethnographic analyses.

In the first place, ethnographers often have different forms of written records in mind when they refer to 'fieldnotes'. Sanjek (1990c) found that ethnographers talked about fieldnotes in many different ways, including 'headnotes', 'scratch notes', 'fieldnotes proper', 'fieldnote records', 'texts', 'journals and diaries', and 'letters, reports, papers'.

Behind the disagreements over what constitutes fieldnotes lie different takes on the distinctiveness of writing about others and writing about (and for) oneself. Some field researchers consider fieldnotes to be writings that record *both* what they learn and observe about the activities of others *and* their own actions, questions and reflections. But others insist on a sharp distinction between records of what others said and did – the 'data' of fieldwork – and writings incorporating their own thoughts and reactions. Some of these ethnographers view only the former as fieldnotes and consider the latter as personal 'journals' or 'diaries'; others hold a diametrically opposed view and '*contrast* fieldnotes with data, speaking of fieldnotes as a record of one's reactions, a cryptic list of items to concentrate on, a preliminary stab at analysis, and so on' (Jackson, 1990: 7).

Despite near consensus on writing fieldnotes in or close to the field, ethnographers take different approaches to the actual timing and organization of writing fieldnotes. Many compose fieldnotes only as 'a running log written at the end of each day' (Jackson, 1990: 6). But others contrast such 'fieldnotes proper' with 'fieldnote records' that involve 'information organized in sets separate from the sequential fieldwork notes' (Sanjek, 1990c: 101). Furthermore, some field researchers try to write elaborate notes as soon after witnessing relevant events as possible, typically sitting down to type complete, detailed observations after every foray into the field. Others initially produce less detailed records, filling notebooks with handwritten entries to be elaborated and 'finished' upon leaving the field. And still others postpone the bulk of writing until they have left the field and begun to grapple with writing a coherent ethnographic account.

It is important to recognize that these differences in terminology and practice reflect not only personal styles and preferences but also arise from different assumptions ethnographers hold about the nature of ethnography and participant observation. If, for example, one sees the core of ethnography as writing observations that would be more or less available to any trained observer, one can reasonably separate the 'findings' from the processes of making them and 'data' from 'personal reactions'.

Similarly, differing priorities about how closely fieldnotes should be written to the observed event reflect notions of the degree of detail required for different ethnographic projects – for example, capturing broad patterns as opposed to tracking day-to-day routines and processes.

But differences in terminologies and writing practices regarding fieldnotes are also directly tied to ethnographers' varied understandings of 'the field' and 'fieldwork'. Indeed, a number of ethnographers emphasize the 'the field' not as 'a pre-given natural entity' but 'something we construct, both through the practical transactions and activities of data collection and through the literary activities of writing fieldnotes, analytic memoranda, and the like' (Atkinson, 1992: 5). Specifically:

> the field is produced (not discovered) through the social transactions engaged in by the ethnographer. The boundaries of the field are not 'given'. They are the outcome of what the ethnographer may encompass in his or her gaze; what he or she may negotiate with hosts and informants; and what the ethnographer omits and overlooks as much as what the ethnographer *writes*. (1992: 9)

Similarly, Clifford (1997: 186) conceives of 'fieldwork' as 'an embodied spatial practice' calling for both 'displacement' (that is, 'physically going out' from 'home' to some other 'different' place or setting)[3] and also 'focused, disciplined attention'. The latter involves a series of discipline-specific methodological and theoretical commitments along with related practices – learning a local language, conducting observations and interviews, and conceptualizing events in terms of deep or implicit structures (1997: 201).

In recognizing 'the field' as a construction, one can appreciate the ways in which the implicit assumptions and routine practices that produce it, in turn, shape and constrain the writing of fieldnotes. Gubrium and Holstein, for example, contrast the different conceptions of the field implicitly assumed in different approaches to qualitative methods: classic ethnographic naturalism views the field as a geographical place, whereas ethnomethodology's 'field' lies 'wherever reality-constituting interaction takes place' (1997: 52); those concerned with examining the emotions focus on inner lived experience in ways that blur any distinction between 'the field and its representational venue' (1997: 71), while postmodern conceptions of 'hyperreality' displace any equation of 'the field' with fixed, spatial location (1997: 77–9). These different core assumptions about 'the field' not only shape general methods of enquiry, but they also provide specific taken-for-granted ways of orienting to ongoing social life; different moments and happenings, for example, become framed as occasions for making and recording observations.

Furthermore, ethnographers' assumptions about and practices in 'the field' reflect and incorporate specific *theoretical* interests and commitments. These discipline-based interests and commitments shape what are considered important and relevant matters to take note of and what is interesting or significant content to write up in fieldnotes; for example, in classic British structural anthropology, kinship matters (but not contemporary political factions and issues) comprised appropriate topics. In all of these ways, 'the field' is constructed by subjecting particular ongoing settings, events and discourse to the 'ethnographer's gaze' (Atkinson, 1992); and different gazes constitute different events and happenings as observable/writable-about matters for fieldnotes.

Ethnographers also vary in their approaches to fieldnotes because of different understandings of the ultimate *value* of fieldnotes. At one extreme, some ethnographers place fieldnotes at the core of the ethnographic project. They view the essence of field research as a process of accumulating a corpus of detailed fieldnotes which provides the foundation and inspiration for subsequent writings and analyses. Thus they emphasize writing detailed fieldnotes close to their field observations, mining these notes systematically through qualitative coding techniques, and producing 'grounded' analyses tied closely and specifically to the original fieldnote corpus (Emerson et al., 1995; Glaser and Strauss, 1967). Rich, detailed fieldnotes thus provide means for developing and working through new theoretical connections and analytic understandings; theoretical insight and compelling ethnographic monographs depend upon the close, careful analysis and comparison of the full fieldnote record.

At the other extreme, ethnographers regard fieldnotes as a relatively marginal or preliminary activity. Some emphasize the pure 'doing' of ethnography, suggesting that putting too much effort into writing fieldnotes interferes with the fieldwork. One anthropologist told Jackson (1990: 23): '*This* is what I would call fieldwork. It is not taking notes in the field but is the interaction between the researcher and the so-called research subjects.' Similarly, some ethnographers maintain that detailed personal fieldnotes provide little more than crutches to help the field researcher deal with the stresses and anxieties of living in another world while trying to understand it from the outside. And still others point out that fieldnotes simply cannot capture the depth and subtlety of the ethnographer's intellectual and personal encounter with others' ways of living:

> Fieldwork, at its core, is a long social process of coming to terms with a culture. It is a process that begins before one enters the field and continues long after one leaves it. The working out of understandings may be symbolized by fieldnotes, but the intellectual activities that support such understandings are unlikely to be found in the daily records. The great dependency commonly claimed to exist

between fieldnotes and fieldworkers is not and cannot be so very great at all. (Van Maanen, 1988: 117–18)

Indeed, in this view fieldnotes may even stymie in-depth understanding, getting in the way of deep experience, intuitive understandings and coming to grasp the 'big picture'. As one anthropologist quoted by Jackson noted (1990: 13): '[Without notes there is] more chance to schematize, to order conceptually ... [and to be] free of niggling exceptions, grayish half-truths you find in your own data.' From this perspective deeper understandings can get lost beneath 'too many facts' or 'too much detail'.

Again, these seemingly minute, pragmatic differences with regard to the writing and value of fieldnotes reflect recurrent tensions, dilemmas and choices endemic to all ethnography. For on the one hand, ethnographic fieldwork requires both close observation and immersion; both types of activities can be recorded and preserved. This record of observations and experiences can be examined and mined for insights and connections, even after fieldwork has been completed. But on the other hand, spending long periods of time participating in other ways of life can generate deep, intuitive insight and perception without day-to-day note-taking. Thus one anthropologist reported gaining 'insight into Australian Aboriginal symbolism about the ground while on the ground' (Jackson, 1990: 25): 'You notice in any kind of prolonged conversation, people are squatting, or lie on the ground. I came to be quite intrigued by that, partly because I'd have to, too ... endless dust.' Here analysis proceeds more or less independently of specific fieldnotes. In practice most ethnographers take something from both these approaches: for some purposes they seek to create and work with a strong fieldnote record; for others they draw upon deeper intuition and understandings to find issues and make connections.

FIELDNOTES AS A FORM OF ETHNOGRAPHIC WRITING

The close-to-the-field transformations of experiences and observations provided by fieldnotes represent a distinctive form of ethnographic writing. Fieldnotes are not written in accord with some tightly pre-specified plan or for some specifically envisioned, ultimate use. Rather, composed day-by-day, open-endedly, with changing and new directions, fieldnotes are an expression of the ethnographer's deepening local knowledge, emerging sensitivities and evolving substantive concerns and theoretical insights. Fieldnotes are therefore unruly or 'messy' (Marcus, 1994), changing form and style without attention to consistency or coherence; they have the 'loose', shifting quality of working, preliminary and transitory, rather than final, or fixed, texts.

The unruly content and style of fieldnotes is directly related to the ethnographer's actual and envisioned audiences. For the most part, fieldnotes are not written as finished, comprehensible-in-themselves, 'readerly' (Atkinson, 1992: 8) texts, intended for outside audiences; rather, the ethnographer ordinarily writes fieldnotes immediately for herself as a future reader. As a result most fieldnote accounts are literally *incomprehensible* to others.[4] Indeed, one ethnographer defines a fieldnote as 'something that can't be readily comprehended by another person' (Jackson, 1990: 20). Thus, specific fieldnote entries often have an opaque, idiosyncratic, reader-unfriendly quality.

The transformation of observed and experienced realities into fieldnote texts is simultaneously facilitated, shaped and constrained by writing conventions. As Atkinson argues: 'The ethnographer encounters a problematic and complex social world that is not closed or bounded. By contrast, he or she represents that world within the confines of a given textual form. The limits of what can be understood about the world are set by the boundaries of what can be written and what can be read' (1992: 8). In the following pages we examine key issues that mark the process of writing fieldnotes.

Pre- and Initial Writing

Writing fieldnotes begins in the field, as the ethnographer participates in local scenes and activities in order to experience them directly and immediately and to accumulate a series of observations to be written up into fieldnotes. Although most of what will ultimately be turned into full fieldnotes remains in the head of the ethnographer, many field researchers actively write brief, preliminary reminders while still in the field about key features of incidents or encounters they regard as significant. This process entails moving from mental notes to jotted notes to full fieldnotes, in the terms used by Lofland and Lofland (1995: 89–97) and Emerson et al. (1995: 17–65), and from scratch notes to fieldnotes proper to fieldnote records, in Sanjek's (1990b: 95–103) terms. Mental and/or jotted notes facilitate writing detailed, elaborate fieldnotes as close to the field experience as possible in order to preserve the immediacy of feelings and impressions and to maximize the ethnographer's ability to recall happenings in detail.

Mental notes In attending to ongoing scenes, events and interactions, field researchers take mental note of certain details and impressions. For the most part, these impressions remain as 'headnotes' only. Lofland and Lofland describe the process as follows:

> The first step in the process of writing fieldnotes is to orient your consciousness to the task of remembering items [such as who and how many were there, the physical character of the place, who said what to whom,

who moved about in what way] ... This act of directing your mind to remember things at a later point may be called making *mental notes*. You are preparing yourself to be able later to put down on paper what you are now seeing. (1995: 90)

Emerson et al. (1995: 17–19) suggest that when an ethnographer enters the field with the intent to remember and write details about events, he adopts a 'participating-in-order-to-write' approach. Here the fieldworker seeks to 'get into place' to observe interesting, significant events in order to produce a detailed written record. At an extreme, the fieldworker might self-consciously look for events that should be written down for research purposes; he might position himself in these unfolding events to be able to observe and write; and he might explicitly orient to events in terms of 'what is important to remember so that I can write it down later'.

At other moments, by deliberately suspending concern with producing written records of these events, field researchers participate in ongoing events in an 'experiential style' to maximize immersion in local activities and the experiences of others' lives. In practice, most field researchers employ both experiential and participating-to-write approaches, now participating without thought about writing up what is happening, now focusing closely on events in order to write about them.

Jotted notes The very first writing for many ethnographers occurs when they jot down key words and phrases while literally in or very close to the field. Indeed, many field researchers act as blatant scribes, moving around, note pad in hand, visibly recording bits of talk and action as they occur. Jottings translate to-be-remembered-observations into writing as quickly rendered scribbles about actions and dialogue. Fieldworkers use these words, written at the moment or soon afterwards, to jog the memory later in the day in order to recall and reconstruct in close detail significant scenes and events.

Field researchers record jottings in different ways. While some fieldworkers learn a formal transcribing system such as shorthand or speedwriting, many simply develop their own private systems of symbols and abbreviations. These procedures not only facilitate getting words on a page more quickly, but they also make jotted notes incomprehensible to onlookers who ask to see them and thus protect the confidentiality of these writings.

In some field situations, ethnographers openly jot notes. By adopting this practice from the very first contacts with those studied, the ethnographer can establish a 'note-taker' role and thus increase the likelihood that writing at the scene will be accepted (or at least tolerated). Indeed, people often develop expectations about what events and topics the fieldworker should record and question why the fieldworker is or is not taking note of particular events. They may even feel slighted if she fails to make jottings on what they are doing or see as important, even when these matters appear sensitive or controversial.

Yet even when most of those studied tacitly or explicitly accept open writing in their presence, some may become upset when the researcher pulls out his pad and begins to write down their words and actions. Fieldworkers try to become sensitive to, and avoid jotting down, those matters which participants regard as secret, embarrassing, overly revealing, or potentially harmful. And, many ethnographers try to avoid challenges and to facilitate open, extensive note-taking by positioning themselves on the margins of interaction (cf. Pollner and Emerson, 1988). Given the delicacy of these situations, fieldworkers constantly rely upon interactional skills and tact to manage open jottings and their implications. Thus, some ethnographers calibrate jottings to the unfolding context of the interaction. However, even making jottings 'off-phase', as recommended by Goffman (1989: 130) as a means of minimizing reactive effects (that is, 'don't write your notes on the act you're observing because then people will know what it is you're recording'), may offend others when the focus of the jotting appears to be the *current* activity or topic.

In other field situations, ethnographers rigorously avoid any and all writing in the presence of those studied. Making open jottings not only reminds those studied that the fieldworker, despite constant proximity and frequent expressions of empathy, has radically different (perhaps unknown) commitments and priorities (Thorne, 1980); making such jottings could also distract and deflect the fieldworker's attention from what is happening in the immediate scene.

One way to avoid such open violations of trust, and possibly awkward or tense encounters, is to try to conceal the act of making jottings while in the field. Indeed, even ethnographers who usually write open jottings may at other times make jottings privately, when out of presence of those studied. Leaving a scene, incident, or conversation that has just occurred, the ethnographer withdraws to a private place to jot down key words and highlights. Here fieldworkers often exploit the ways members of the setting themselves use to take 'time out' or 'get away'. Fieldworkers have reported retreating to private places such as bathrooms, deserted lunchrooms, stairwells and supply closets to record such covert jottings.

Other field researchers avoid all writing in the field setting but immediately upon leaving the field, pull out a notebook to jot down reminders of the key incidents, words, or reactions they wish to include in full fieldnotes. This procedure allows the fieldworker to signal items that she does not want to forget without being seen as intrusive.

Ethnographers often experience deep ambivalence about whether, when, where and how to write jottings. On the one hand, the ethnographer may wish to preserve the immediacy of the moment by jotting down words as they are spoken and details of scenes as they are enacted; on the other hand, he may feel that openly writing jottings will ruin the moment and plant seeds of distrust. For it is a defining moment in field relations when an ethnographer takes out a pad and begins to write down what people say and do in his very presence: participants tend to see those who act in this way as proclaiming strong outside commitments and to react to such writing as efforts to turn intimate and cherished experiences into objects of scientific enquiry. As a result, ethnographers' approaches to making jottings vary widely both across and within projects and both shape and are shaped by their understanding of the setting and by their relationships within it.

Writing Fieldnotes: Diverse Styles and Strategies

Sitting down to write full fieldnotes involves a turning away from the field toward the worlds of research and writing. Through such writing, the ethnographer turns remembered and jotted scenes into text, taming and reducing complex, lived experience to more concise, stylized, re-examinable written accounts. However, descriptive fieldnotes can be written in a variety of different styles.

Van Maanen (1988) has identified three major writing or representational styles used to organize and depict fieldwork accounts, both in whole ethnographies and in extended fieldnote segments. Rhetorical conventions, he points out, undergird and produce even the most 'studied neutrality' of *realist tales*, which are accounts marked by 'the almost complete absence of the author from most segments of the finished text' (1988: 46–7). The resulting effect of reporting 'objectively' a world-out-there derives from several sources: by describing concrete details of daily life and routines as well as what typical people commonly say, do and think; by depicting events and meanings as though 'from the native's point of view'; and by presenting the whole account as a 'no-nonsense' report devoid of self-reflection and doubt, in what Van Maanen terms 'interpretive omnipotence' (p. 51). *Confessional tales*, in contrast, move the person and experiences of the researcher to stage center. Though these tales generally describe the research process itself in detail, relying upon the ethnographer's authority and point of view, the writing clearly separates the personal and methodological confessions from the social and cultural life depicted in the ethnography proper. Finally, *impressionist tales* are organized around 'striking stories' intended 'not to tell readers what to think of an experience but to show them the experience from beginning to end and thus draw them immediately into the story to work out its problems and puzzles as they unfold' (p. 103). This style of ethnographic representation employs the conventions of textual identity, fragmented knowledge, characterization and dramatic control (pp. 103–6). Van Maanen suggests that finished ethnographic writings routinely mix and combine these different styles.

But, in contrast to such published texts, initial fieldnotes are marked by particularly unruly mixes and combinations of these and other styles. Indeed, in considering stylistic features of working fieldnotes, one finds a wide, often quite idiosyncratic, range of writing conventions and rhetorical effects. Nevertheless, one can notice and characterize some commonly used strategies in fieldnote-writing.

Fieldnotes as 'writer's prose' In actually sitting down and writing fieldnotes, the ethnographer often experiences an outpouring of memories, thoughts and words. Knowing that memories fade as time passes, most fieldworkers write fieldnotes in a rush, using whatever phrasing and organization seem most accessible, convenient and do-able at the time. Thus, fieldnotes have a distinctive writing style marked by flowing, even hurried, outbursts of words, often dashed down on the page in uncensored, yet focused ways. Lofland and Lofland capture this style in the following advice:

> You need not attempt to employ totally correct grammar, punctuate with propriety, hit the right keys, say only publicly polite things, be guarded about your feelings, or use any of the other niceties most people affect for strangers. The object in fieldnotes, rather, is to get information down as correctly as you can and be as honest with yourself as possible. (1995: 95–6)

Fieldnotes can be written in this loose fashion because they are 'behind the scenes' documents (Lofland and Lofland, 1995: 96), not intended – at least initially – for any audience other than the researcher herself as the future reader. Some analysts recognize such initial, dashed-off compositions as '*writer's prose*', which though intended only for their own eyes, contains the kernel vision and ideas for subsequent, more polished work (Lanham, 1983). The wording, sentence structure and organization of this style might be incomprehensible to a reader other than the author. However, at the same time, in dashing off these initial fieldnotes, the ethnographer might also envision possible future audiences and, at that moment, be inspired to write more detailed and comprehensive descriptions (Emerson et al., 1995: 44–5). Though not yet revised into '*reader's prose*' or edited for others (Lanham, 1983), such fieldnotes move beyond the hazards of idiosyncratic styles – which could be unintelligible in the future, even to the author – because the writer has imagined what others might want to know.

In this initial writing, the field researcher grapples with a series of practical writing and analytic issues about what to write and how to write. Ethnographers choose, whether from habit or through deliberation, what kinds of writings to produce by deciding whose voices and actions to depict, what sort of diction to use and point of view to take, and how to organize the chaos of life on a linear page.

Most ethnographers write highly descriptive fieldnotes, recording slices of observed social life in detailed texts.[5] As Lofland and Lofland emphasize: 'For the most part, fieldnotes are a running description of events, people, things heard and overheard, conversations among people, conversations with people' (1995: 93). Although fieldnote descriptions are not mere reports of 'the facts', but rather implicitly theorized accounts, ethnographers generally seek to avoid explicit analysis and interpretation as much as possible. Indeed, they compose fieldnotes in what is a predominantly 'naturalistic' or 'realist' frame of mind, in the sense that they intend to record in almost classic journalistic fashion 'the Who, What, When, Where, and How of human activity' in a fieldnote that 'tells who said or did what, under stated circumstances' (Schatzman and Strauss, 1973: 100). Descriptive fieldnotes, however, often move beyond the news-worthy facts of a bare-boned report. In addition to reporting events, descriptive fieldnotes also can include detailed accounts of the fieldworker's initial impressions, key events and incidents observed in the setting along with the observer's personal reactions, what people in the setting treat as especially important, and any unusual happenings that depart from the routine and ordinary (Emerson et al., 1995: 26–30).

Until recently most ethnographers treated such descriptive writing as a more or less transparent process, primarily a matter of putting on paper what had been seen and heard. Writing detailed description, many implied, requires only a sharp eye, a good memory and conscientious effort. But contemporary ethnographers recognize that even seemingly straight-forward, descriptive writing is fundamentally a process of representation and construction. Fieldnotes, like all descriptions, 'are selective, purposed, angled, voiced, because they are authored' (Emerson et al., 1995: 106). Through the writer's stylistic preferences – diction, point of view, and organization – that day's fieldnotes present a *version* of a world that functions more as a filter than a mirror reflecting the 'reality' of events. Certainly, the writer creates a world-on-the-page, not only through her analytic commitments and participation in the field, but also through the moment-by-moment writing choices which in sum create a particular rhetorical effect.

Inscriptions and transcriptions Analysts notice that fieldnotes tend to focus on description of action or on talk, perhaps because attention to dialogue can be all-consuming. Atkinson distinguishes between two forms of descriptive fieldnotes: *inscriptions*, written accounts that represent events and activities in some portion of the social world; and *transcriptions*, some 'representation of informants' or other social actors' own words' (1992: 16, 22). Similarly, Emerson et al. distinguish between '*description* as a means of picturing through concrete sensory details the basic scenes, settings, objects, people, and actions the fieldworker observed', and fieldnote representations of *dialogue*, 'conversations that occur in their presence or that members report having had with others' (1995: 67, 74). Furthermore, Emerson et al. point out that these types of fieldnotes are not mutually exclusive: descriptions often encompass talk, by quoting snippets of verbatim dialogue or by inserting members' terms and expressions; and, whether transcribed from tapes or jotted down verbatim, most dialogues may and often do include depiction of related actions (1995: 68, 74).

Recalling and ordering During the process of writing fieldnotes, ethnographers recall their experiences in different ways and, thus, order their memories to highlight certain features. One strategy traces noteworthy events in the chronological sequence in which one observed and experienced them. Another strategy details some 'high point' or incident and then considers, in some topical fashion, other significant events, incidents, or exchanges. Or, the ethnographer can focus more systematically on incidents related to specific topics of interest. Wanting to turn memories quickly into words on the page, ethnographers often combine or alternate between strategies in a stream of consciousness flow.

In recalling and ordering their jottings and memories, ethnographers also choose whether to write from some known 'end-point' of more or less complete knowledge, or whether to represent events unfolding 'in real time' from a perspective of incomplete or partial knowledge (Emerson et al., 1995: 60–3). In describing many happenings and situations, field researchers make full use of what they ultimately came to know and understand about the outcomes and meanings. Paralleling the conventions Van Maanen describes in both realist and confessional ethnographies, this approach incorporates 'facts' or understandings subsequently established in order to characterize what was going on at earlier stages. Drawing primarily on those understandings gained by some 'end point' realization, the ethnographer describes what happened at earlier moments even though she may not have initially understood, or only partially or even incorrectly comprehended, what was taking place. However, in real-time descriptions, the writer aims to characterize events by relying only on what he knows, at

discrete moments, as the event unfolds. Thus, the writer avoids using information that ultimately comes out, but that he does not know in the scene he is depicting. As though a player in an improvisational drama, he describes events as he saw and now re-envisions them emerging.

Representing action and dialogue In addition to ways of ordering memories, ethnographers also rely on other commonly-known writing conventions for depicting scenes and representing dialogues. Emerson et al. (1995: 85–99) discuss a number of these rhetorical strategies, frequently employed in writing inscriptions or descriptions. In a *sketch*, the fieldworker describes a scene primarily through detailed imagery. Struck by a vivid impression, the writer looks out on the scene and depicts the sensory details as though a still-life portrait or a snapshot. As in a photograph, the scene portrays arrested action, and thus sequencing does not dominate the description.

In contrast, an *episode* recounts action and moves through time. The writer tells an incident as one continuous action or interaction and thus constructs a more or less unified entry. Though some episodes might build to a climax, others simply recount one character's routine, everyday actions. Episodes are easily strung together to recreate an event on the pages. In describing a particular event, for example, ethnographers often connect a series of episodes that center on the same characters or similar activities. The ethnographer might also perceive the episodes as linked because actions progress, develop over time and seem to lead to immediate outcomes.

When making such connections between episodes, the ethnographer writes a *fieldnote tale*. In narrating such tales, researchers not only link episodes, but also might recount developing actions and depict fully realized characters. In so doing, however, they do not ordinarily create a unified narrative, but rather try to recount action as it unfolded, to tell the event as they saw it happen. As a consequence, fieldnote tales tend to be episodic, a string of action chunks put down on the page, one after another. Thus, both in structure and content, fieldnote tales generally differ from constructed, dramatic narratives. The highly crafted narratives of published writers not only describe actions chronologically, but they also 'make something happen' by building suspense into the unfolding action and by creating motivated characters whose consequential actions lead to instructive, often dramatic outcomes. But most of everyday life does not happen like dramatic stories in which one action neatly causes the next and results in clear-cut consequences. Instead, much of life unfolds rather aimlessly. Describing life in a narrative form, by fitting events into cause-and-effect conventions, might overdetermine the links between actions as well as the movement toward an outcome or climactic resolution.

Representing *dialogue* also requires the use of writing conventions. Writing fieldnotes that incorporate dialogue is not a simple task of remembering talk or literally replaying every word. People talk in spurts and fragments. They accentuate or even complete a phrase with a gesture, facial expression, or posture. They send complex messages through incongruent, seemingly contradictory or ironic verbal and non-verbal expressions, such as in sarcasm or polite put-downs. To transpose naturally occurring speech to a page, therefore, requires extreme reductions, which necessarily employ writing conventions, including orthography, punctuation and type-setting (Atkinson, 1992: 23). Furthermore, ethnographers must decide how to represent non-verbal expression – tone of voice, pauses, volume, pace – in order to convey the speaker's meanings as well (cf. Fine, 1984). But in relying upon these and other conventions, the ethnographer faces a number of difficult choices, notably, those involving a balance between 'accessibility' and 'authenticity'. As Atkinson argues, 'the more *comprehensible* and readable the reported speech, the less "authentic" it must be. The less the ethnographer intervenes, the more delicately he or she transcribes, the *less* readable becomes the reported speech' (1992: 23).

Stance Regardless of the conventions used to depict social life and to transcribe talk, the writer more deeply filters observed events through a particular *stance*, that is, an underlying orientation towards the people he studies and their ways of living. Stance not only shapes how the ethnographer observes and participates in the field, thus shaping the content of fieldnotes; but stance also prefigures how the ethnographer orients to his 'writing subject' in composing fieldnotes (Emerson et al., 1995: 42–6). Stance is reflected in such matters as how the ethnographer identifies with (or distances himself from) those studied: for example, in writing about them sympathetically (or not); in selecting certain kinds of local activities, which draw his attention, to write about in more detailed descriptions; and in prioritizing and framing certain topics and thus writing more fully about those events he sees as relevant. Shaped by disciplinary training, theoretical interests, and moral and political commitments, an ethnographer's stance may be evident in the content, comprehensiveness and shadings of descriptions. Certainly, the tone of descriptions, as expressed through word choice, definitely reflects the writer's stance.

Point of view The ethnographer's orientation towards the world studied may also influence her point of view – whether or not to write as the omniscient scholar, or to report in third person the observed actions and overheard voices of members,

or to stick to a first-person perspective (Abrams, 1988: 144–8; Emerson et al., 1995: 53–60).[6] Each point of view offers a different angle from which to report the scene, and because of its constraints, inclines the writer to balance personal insights and the voices of others in certain ways.

A first-person perspective 'limits the point of view to what the narrator knows, experiences, infers, or can find out by talking with other characters' (Abrams, 1988: 146). In writing fieldnotes in the first person, the researcher presents only the details she saw, experienced and now remembers from her own perspective and in her own voice. First-person writing is particularly effective when the ethnographer is also a member of the group she is studying. Seeing incidents through her eyes allows the reader an insider's view of actions as filtered through her concerns as an ethnographer. In addition, the first-person point of view encourages the writer to present the natural unfolding of experience as seen from her participant's viewpoint.[7]

In contrast, when writing in the *third person*, the ethnographer can convey the words and actions of others very effectively. In addition, if he entirely excludes his presence from the fieldnotes, or if he refers to himself in the third person, then the ethnographer-as-author can achieve a tone of detachment, distance and 'objectivity'. Inevitably, this perspective focuses the writer's attention on others, on describing their actions and documenting their voices, more so than on his own.

When writing in the third person, the ethnographer can easily slip into an *omniscient point of view*, assuming 'privileged access to the characters' thoughts and feelings and motives, as well as to their overt speech and action' (Abrams, 1988: 145). Because this point of view positions the writer as a detached observer above or outside events, she can depict characters and actions with near-divine insight into prior causes and ultimate outcomes. For this reason, the omniscient point of view holds particular dangers for fieldnotes, in that it tends to

> merge the ethnographer's participatory experience with reports from others; conceal the complex processes of uncovering the varied understandings of what an event is about; reduce and blend multiple perspectives into accounts delivered in a single, all-knowing voice; and ignore the highly contingent interpretations required to reconcile and/or prioritize competing versions of the event. (Emerson et al., 1995: 59)[8]

Writing about Personal Feelings and Emotions

Until fairly recently, anthropological ethnographers tended to separate writings describing others' actions and talk from their writings about their own emotions, reactions and anxieties, relegating the latter to personal journals or diaries (Sanjek, 1990c). At least from the 1960s, most sociological ethnographers have advocated including accounts of personal feelings and emotional reactions in core fieldnotes accounts, sometimes only peripherally in descriptions of one's methodological doings (Schatzman and Strauss, 1973: 101), sometimes as an exclusive or core component of the ethnographic project (Emerson et al., 1995; Johnson, 1975; Kleinman and Copp, 1993; Lofland and Lofland, 1995).

Lofland and Lofland identify three purposes for entering personal and emotional reactions into one's fieldnotes. First, as Goffman (1989) emphasized, the fieldworker's emotional responses to events in the field may mirror those that naturally occur in the setting. For example, in feeling 'that some person in the setting is getting unjustly treated by a turn of events, and getting privately angry over it, you may also discover later that many other people felt the same way' (Lofland and Lofland, 1995: 94–5). Second, even if not shared by others, emotional reactions may provide important analytic leads. And finally, recording one's emotions over time enables the ethnographer to read through fieldnotes to identify biases and prejudices as well as the changing attitudes toward people and events.

Writing about the personal and the emotional has emerged as the central concern of recent practitioners of experiential or emotional ethnography (for example, Ellis, 1991, 1995; Ellis and Bochner, 1992). Arguing that most social science accounts neglect the subjective aspects of lived experience, these ethnographers explore the deeply intimate aspects of human relations and, thus, seek to integrate private and social experience through the use of personal *introspection* and 'auto-ethnography' as research methods. Rather than providing dispassionate descriptions of events and outcomes, experiential ethnographers advocate writing fieldnotes about the fieldworker's own 'lived emotional experience' of unfolding events and interactions (Ellis, 1991: 25). Fieldnotes then facilitate turning the ethnographer's 'private processing ... of memory, detail, feeling, recognition, physiological response, language, cognition, and tone of voice' into written texts (Ellis, 1991: 25).

For example, in her 'experimental ethnography' *Final Negotiations* (1995), Ellis tells the story of attachment, chronic illness and loss in her nine-year relationship with her partner who died of emphysema. Concentrating on the details of conversations and interactions, she wrote extensive notes on the day-to-day events entailed in grief and grief work, filling specific scenes, episodes and sketches with dialogue in order to show rather than tell about emotions such as anger or grief. In these ways, Ellis shares much in common with those ethnographers who write fieldnotes in order to convey social life from the points of view of people in the settings they study (Emerson et al., 1995: ch. 5). But unlike those who seek to provide a window into the experiences of others, Ellis' attempts to convey the immediacy and intensity of emotions by saturating her fieldnotes (and finished ethnographies) with intimate discussions of her own and others' emotional experiences. Placing herself at the centre as both the narrator and the main character, she attempts to communicate feelings and thoughts directly to the reader.

While some ethnographers have misgivings about such 'author saturated' texts (Geertz, 1988: 97), fieldnotes that directly recount these kinds of experiences offer major advantages for developing and refining methodological and theoretical insights. Such emotionally evocative fieldnotes may, for example, facilitate reconstruction of features of a setting or scene at some later point in time. Most importantly, by focusing attention on emotions as an aspect of social life worthy of attention in their own right, evocative fieldnotes may provide particularly rich accounts of the processual nature and full complexities of experience which cannot be conveyed through descriptions of behaviors obtained by direct observation or interview questions alone (Ellis, 1991: 33–4).[9]

Analytic Writing in Fieldnotes

Although the primary purpose of writing fieldnotes is to describe situations and events, as well as people's understandings of and subjective reactions to these matters, fieldnotes also provide a critical, first opportunity to write down and hence to develop initial interpretations and analyses. In writing the day's events, an ethnographer tends to assimilate and to understand her observations and experiences, seeing previously unappreciated meanings in particular happenings, making new linkages with or contrasts to previously observed and written-about experiences. To capture these ruminations, reflections, and insights, and to make them available for further thought and analysis, field researchers engage in various kinds of analytical writing during or close to the initial production of fieldnotes.

Schatzman and Strauss (1973: 100–1), for example, urge ethnographers to regularly write theoretical notes, to be labeled 'TN', in contrast to observational notes (ON) and methodological notes (MN). They suggest that such theoretical notes

> represent self-conscious, controlled attempts to derive meaning from any one of several observational notes. The observer as recorder thinks about what he has experienced, and makes whatever private declaration of meaning he feels will bear conceptual fruit. He interprets, infers, hypothesizes, conjectures; he develops new concepts, links these to older ones, or relates any observation to any other in this presently private effort to create social science. (1973: 101)

Similarly, Lofland and Lofland note that in writing fieldnotes, 'analytic ideas and inferences will begin to occur to you', and they emphasize that it is critical to 'put all of them into the fieldnotes', no matter how obvious or how far-fetched they seem (1995: 94). All analyses, they propose, should be clearly marked as separate from descriptive fieldnotes by simply putting them in brackets.

Finally, Emerson et al. (1995: 105) emphasize the importance of 'in-process analytic writing', contrasting such initial insights while actively writing fieldnotes to the more systematic, analytic procedures of coding and memoing in the final stages of fieldwork. This initial writing enables the field researcher to carry forward analysis contemporaneously with the collection of field data; the more explicitly the fieldworker identifies analytic themes, the better able he is to 'check out' different alternatives, making and recording observations that confirm, modify, or reject inprocess interpretations. Emerson et al. discuss three such devices – asides, commentaries and in-process memos (1995: 100–5).

Asides are brief, reflective bits of analytic writing that succinctly clarify, explain, interpret, or raise questions about some specific happening or process described in a fieldnote. Asides may also be used to offer personal reflections or interpretive remarks on a matter just considered. Ethnographers frequently use asides, for example, to convey their explicit 'feel' for or emotional reactions to events; putting these remarks in asides keeps them from intruding into the descriptive account.

A *commentary* is a more elaborate reflection on some specific event or issue that is generally placed in a separate paragraph and set off with parentheses. Commentaries require a shift of attention from events in the field to imagined audiences, who might be interested in something the fieldworker has observed and written-up. Again, in contrast to descriptive fieldnotes, commentaries may explore problems of access or emotional reactions to events in the field, suggest ongoing probes into likely connections with other events, or offer tentative interpretations. Commentaries are also used to record the ethnographer's own doings, experiences, and reactions during fieldwork, both in observing-participating and in writing up. Finally, commentaries can raise issues of what terms and events mean to members, can make initial connections between some current observation and prior fieldnotes, and can suggest points or places for further observation.

Finally, *in-process memos* are products of more sustained analytic writing and, thus, require a more extended time-out from actively composing fieldnotes. Often ethnographers write memos after completing the day's fieldnotes. In-process memos are used both to address practical, methodological questions and to explore emerging theoretical possibilities. Such memos not only provide initial theoretical materials, but they also help to focus and to guide future observations and analyses.

FIELDNOTES AND FINISHED
ETHNOGRAPHIC TEXTS

Fieldnotes in finished texts are inevitably transformations of initial fieldnotes in the original corpus that the ethnographer produced in the field. While the extent of transformation may vary, fieldnotes in completed ethnographies are drastically reordered and often substantially rewritten as the ethnographer selects and molds them with some analytic or representational purpose. Although consideration of developing and writing published ethnographic texts is beyond the scope of this review, we examine three issues in the use of fieldnotes: differences in the value accorded initial fieldnotes in producing final ethnographies; the processes of revising fieldnotes for inclusion in a published text; and different strategies for working fieldnote excerpts into the finished ethnography.

The Value and Uses
of the Fieldnote Corpus

Ethnographers differentially use and value initial fieldnotes in creating polished ethnographic accounts. Some ethnographies provide texts that make minimal use of fieldnotes. Some postmodern ethnographies, in particular, self-consciously displace fieldnotes from the centre of the text and its organization. Dorst's (1989) 'post ethnography' of the small Pennsylvania community of Chadds Ford, for example, is an organized 'collection/collage' of local 'auto-ethnographies and souvenirs' – 'postcards, texts from brochures, the words of Chadds Ford natives, ... excerpts from travel literature, fiction and popular history, photographs, reproductions' (1989: 5). Dorst does include a number of his own 'verbal representations of objects, scenes and events', as in accounts of the scene of and some participants in an annual craft fair (Chapter 4); but in so doing, he instructs the reader to treat any such account as 'just another textual fragment of the same order as the other souvenirs' (1989: 5).

Most ethnographers, however, draw heavily upon a corpus of original fieldnotes and incorporate large selections of these fieldnotes into their polished texts. Those advocating procedures for grounded theory fall at an extreme in this regard; such ethnographers treat the original fieldnote record – although expanded and elaborated by subsequent analytic coding and memoing – as the primary, if not exclusive, focus for generating ethnographic analyses. Many other styles of ethnography also rely upon a fieldnote corpus as a central resource in producing published texts. Indeed, many ethnographies experimenting with alternative styles of representation build directly upon the base provided by original fieldnotes to compose final texts. Thus Ellis draws directly upon her extensive introspective fieldnotes to construct her auto-ethnographic writings. Similarly, almost all efforts at dialogic representation (such as Dwyer, 1982) incorporate notes or transcriptions of talk. Moeran describes his 'fictionalized' *Okubo Diary* (1985) as a gradually rewritten 'fieldwork journal' constructed around successive revisions of these original fieldnotes (Moeran, 1990: 345–8).

However, some ethnographers highlight the limitations of fieldnotes for developing analyses and composing finished texts. Van Maanen (1988: 118), in particular, argues that the fieldnote corpus does not provide a set of fixed materials for analytic enquiry, as initial fieldnotes are constantly re-examined and reinterpreted in light of new concerns and understandings. Furthermore, in some instances, fieldnotes provide only surface summaries that almost inevitably fail to capture the intuitive, holistic understandings that are critical for ethnographic insight and analysis. By way of illustration, Van Maanen contrasts a fieldnote as originally written and the subsequent extended account of a police chase (1988: 109–15) used to exemplify the impressionist tale:

> nowhere in my fieldnotes does this story appear in a form even remotely comparable to the shape, tone, concern for detail, background information, or personal posturing that I've given it here. My fieldnotes, hastily composed the morning after the incident, contain a terse, two-page descriptive statement typed in fractured syntax and devoid of much other than what I took then to be the incidental highlights of the episode. (1988: 117)

Thus, selected fieldnote segments may be suggestive but they often must fundamentally be recast and rewritten in order to provide more than embryonic insight.

Editing and Revising Fieldnotes

When incorporating fieldnotes into finished texts, ethnographers routinely edit them for wider audiences to eliminate material extraneous or irrelevant to the argument and to provide anonymity to the people, institutions and communities studied (Emerson et al., 1995: 186–94). But ethnographers also edit to make fieldnotes comprehensible to readers, and in so doing, face a series of choices between preserving 'the vividness and complexity of the original fieldnotes' and producing clear, readable accounts (Emerson et al., 1995: 192; see also Atkinson, 1992). Hence, excerpts about specific events and local scenes often need to be rewritten to include pertinent information about context and background and to clarify allusions to people, places or procedures external to the fieldnote. In addition, earlier representations of natural speech may have to be edited to balance the reader's need for clarity against a commitment to providing detailed renderings of peoples' local speech (Atkinson, 1992: 26–9).

But such editing decisions reflect the ethnographer's underlying sense of the nature and sanctity of fieldnotes as originally written. Some ethnographers wish to preserve as much as possible of the flavor and actual content of original fieldnotes in any published account, thus tending to minimize editorial and other changes. These ethnographers incorporate (selected) fieldnotes without extensive editing, assuming that earlier writing composed at the time of the event better captures immediacy and local meanings than does later writings. Such ethnographers might implicitly treat the original fieldnote rendering of an event as a fixed 'datum' to be used to formulate and 'test' theoretical propositions; thus, basic alterations in fieldnote excerpts take on the connotation of 'changing the data to fit the theory.'

Ethnographers who develop alternative forms of textual representation (cf. Atkinson, 1992: 37–50; Richardson, 1994) question these practices and assumptions. Whereas some seemingly reject almost any fieldnote representation, others make heavy use of fieldnotes to construct their finished texts yet refuse to treat 'original' fieldnotes as sacrosanct writings. The latter frequently use fieldnotes to compose a 'secondary, analytic text' (Mulkay, 1985: 237–8); but they refashion these fieldnotes and other accounts of '"real" utterances and exchanges' 'into new arrangements and ... mould them into a range of different formats' (Atkinson, 1992: 46). Ellis, for example, advocates using original fieldnotes as resources to create texts that lead readers 'through a journey in which they develop an "experiential sense" of the events ... and come away with a sense of "what it must have felt like" to live through what happened' (Ellis and Bochner, 1992: 80). Thus, in *Final Negotiations*, Ellis substantially reworks fieldnotes – constructing unwitnessed conversations, condensing several experiences into a single episode – in order to intensify the emotional impact of the final text.[10] Similarly, Moeran (1990) relies heavily upon his original fieldnote journals in writing his *Okubu Diary* but uses its 'literary' format to authorize not only significant changes in chronological sequences and the creation of composite characters, but also the depiction of his experiences as occurring during 'one continuous period of fieldwork'. His fieldnotes thus provide a flexible set of materials for writing in which, for example, 'what had been said by one ... person in the course of a "real" conversation could ... be expressed by a different, or at least composite, character' (1990: 348).

Working Fieldnote Excerpts into Finished Texts

Ethnographers incorporate fieldnotes into finished texts in a variety of ways. One strategy interpolates units of fieldnotes and interpretive commentary. Seemingly more characteristic of sociological than anthropological ethnographies (cf. Atkinson, 1992: 20), this *excerpt strategy* (Emerson et al., 1995: 179–80) visually marks off fieldnote extracts from the allied commentary and interpretation, usually by indenting and/or italicizing. This procedure not only highlights the discursive contrast between descriptive fieldnotes and analytic writing, but also frames the former as accounts composed in the past, close to events in the field. In this sense, excerpting shapes fieldnote bits as 'evidence', as 'originally recorded' voices and events, standing in contrast to subsequent interpretation. Using this strategy, the ethnographer employs fieldnotes as 'exemplars' of a claimed pattern, producing a text which achieves its 'persuasive force' from the resulting 'interplay of concrete exemplification and discursive commentary' (Atkinson, 1990: 103).[11]

A different textual strategy weaves together fieldnote and interpretation. This *integrative strategy* (Emerson et al., 1995: 179) produces a smooth, thematically focused text with minimal spatial markings to indicate where the fieldnote ends and interpretation begins. In the text, fieldnotes and ideas merge into flowing prose, written in a single authorial voice. Having reworked original fieldnote accounts, the ethnographer recounts some happening as an illustration of an analytic claim or interpretation. Rather than textually offsetting fieldnotes recorded in the past from present interpretations, the author simply indicates these shifts through transitional phrases such as 'for example', 'in a telling episode', or 'in one instance'.

Integrative strategies allow more flexible, 'literary' versions of fieldnotes in ethnographic representation. An integrative style facilitates consistently writing in the first person and hence encourages more reflective narrative accounts (e.g. Thorne, 1993). It is also particularly suited for presenting extended fieldnote episodes, with complicated background circumstances, as one continuing story, and for bringing together observations and occurrences, scattered in different places in the fieldnote record, to create a coherent story or account. For these reasons, some ethnographers interested in alternative modes of representation have adopted and pushed to extreme the use of integrative strategies (cf. Ellis and Bochner, 1996).

Multiple Voices in Final Texts

Ethnographers confront further issues in reporting speech and representing voices in final ethnographies. While the possibilities in this regard are directly constrained by the content and style of previously written fieldnotes, the problematics of 'giving voice' to those studied lie deeper in the very assumptions about representation. An analyst cannot provide meaningful access to others' worlds simply by 'retelling their stories'. As Atkinson points out: 'Informants cannot "speak" for themselves. In order to give an impression of it we have to select, edit and *represent* their spoken narratives' (1992: 23). At every turn, the ethnographer recreates voices, whether or not she quotes from fieldnotes, tapes, or film, or if she reconstructs her memory of voices. For, as Riessman notes: 'Informants' stories do not mirror a world "out there". They are constructed, creatively authored, rhetorical, replete with assumptions, and interpretive' (1993: 4–5).

The excerpt strategy provides a particularly effective device for highlighting dialogues between the voices of the ethnographer–author and the social actors in the setting. Though recorded by the ethnographer, the voices of local people can be heard in the excerpt. In the analytic text, the author then can engage those member voices in various ways, for example, by augmenting them, by supplementing them with additional information, or by highlighting the implicit contradictions in what they said.[12]

In addition to textual dialogues between the ethnographer–analyst and social actors, the ethnographer–author also can stage a conversation among the multiple voices of social actors, who express different views on a topic. Whereas Atkinson discusses the voice of social actors as one generic voice, Emerson et al. (1995) encourage ethnographers to document and write about the multiple voices of local people and their divergent views arising from their various positions and roles. Richardson (1990b) discusses various ways the writer can persuasively quote the voices so carefully documented. For example, the author may cluster a set of single-line quotes with each expressing a contrasting viewpoint, in order to emphasize the diverse responses people have to a similar situation. Or, the writer might choose to embed quoted voices in the text, or even within the author's sentence. Longer quotations are critical to showing how a situation evolves and how the person constructs a story about the event (1990b: 40–4).

In addition, the excerpt strategy allows the ethnographer to speak in two different voices – as fieldworker describing the experience depicted in the excerpt ('here is what I heard and observed') and as author now explaining those events to readers ('here is the sense that I *now* make of it') (Atkinson, 1990). For example, by presenting herself as a participant in an event and witnessing insider actions, the ethnographer can convince by showing how she learned about a process. Or, when juxtaposing the superficial understanding of the novice fieldworker to the views of the informed ethnographer-as-analyst, the writer can persuade by demonstrating that there is something more complex going on than what an outsider sees.

Finally, even those ethnographers who use an integrative strategy may rely on member voices for rhetorical effects, to persuade and convince the readers. For, whether or not ethnographers present fieldnote excerpts, those authors who insert voices from the field construct a tone of authenticity in their texts. In effect, the writer says to the reader, 'I was there and here is what I heard someone say'. By presenting vivid characters who speak in their own idioms, the ethnographer creates an engaging text which invites the reader not only to think about the argument, but also vicariously to experience the moment. Such rhetorical strategies persuade.

Conclusion

Recent years have witnessed growing recognition of writing fieldnotes as one of the central methods of participant-observation-based ethnography. Fieldnotes include a variety of writings produced in or near the field which provide written accounts of an evolving array of experiences and observed events. While fieldnotes inevitably provide selective and partial reductions of these lived and observed realities, they fix those realities in examinable forms, that is, in written texts that can be read, considered, selected and rewritten in order to produce polished ethnographic analyses and monographs. But in contrast to these finished texts, original fieldnotes are unruly, in-process writings: produced in initial versions solely or primarily for the ethnographer, reflecting shifting concerns, contradictory claims and varied writing styles, accumulating day-by-day without close pre-planning and overall structure.

The process of writing fieldnotes often begins in advance of any actual writing, as the fieldworker orients to 'the field' as a site for observing/writing, such that the 'ethnographer's gaze' takes in particular qualities and happenings as noteworthy. But the key moment comes when the ethnographer withdraws from the immediate field to begin to record observed events in private. As close-to-the-scene recordings of people, places, talk and events, fieldnotes are self-consciously descriptive in character; that is, they generally provide accounts of 'what happened' that minimize explicit analysis and extensive interpretation. In writing fieldnotes ethnographers face constant choices not only in what to look at and take note of, but also in how to write down these matters. As texts fieldnotes are through and through products of a number of writing conventions, varying not only in content but in style, voice, focus and point of view.

Ethnographers orient to, write and use fieldnotes in constructing finished ethnographies in different ways. Some ethnographers treat original fieldnotes as a primary, sacrosanct 'data set', seeking to ground subsequent analyses tightly in these materials, and to preserve as much as possible their original qualities, styles and meanings. Others place less reliance on their fieldnote corpus, feeling it provides only pale reflections of the richness of actual encounters and observations, at best serving as jumping-off points for subsequent analyses.

While interest in fieldnotes in ethnography is growing, it is important to note a recurrent tension in the nature of this interest. Some ethnographers take a 'readerly' interest (Atkinson, 1992), attending to fieldnotes as a 'completed act', as part of 'the finished product of the writing of ethnography' (Moeran, 1990: 339). This approach contrasts with 'writerly' interests directed toward 'what takes place during the act of writing', and focusing on processes of writing (Moeran, 1990: 339). Moeran (1990: 340–1) suggests that those in the first camp, represented by Clifford and Marcus' 1986 collection, approach ethnographies from the point of view of the *literary critic*, the latter from the point of view of working *author*. He cites deMan (1983: 43) on this difference as follows: 'The work changes entirely with the point of view from which it is being examined, depending on whether one considers it as a finished form (*forma formata*) or, with the artist, as a form in the process of coming into being (*forma formans*)'. These different approaches generate very different concerns and sensitivities with regard to fieldnotes: the writing ethnographer has to make writing choices in real time; the analyst looking over what has been so produced has a completed product, definite end points and arguments, that is, choices already made, to focus on and examine.

Notes

1 The long-standing neglect of processes of writing fieldnotes is particularly evident in 'how to do it' manuals of field work, which have long provided extensive guidelines on how to manage access and relations in the field while offering only occasional, ad hoc commentary on how to write about what has been observed. Schatzman and Strauss (1973), and more recently, Lofland and Lofland (1995), stand as notable exceptions to this tendency. None the less, recent treatments of field research methods which give sustained attention to issues of writing (e.g., Fetterman, 1989; Richardson, 1990b; Wolcott, 1990) concentrate on writing finished ethnographic analyses rather than original, close-to-the field fieldnotes.

2 Writing fieldnotes as close to withdrawal from the field as possible not only preserves the 'idiosyncratic, contingent character [of observed activities] in the face of the homogenizing tendencies of retrospective recall', but it also helps to capture the subtle experiences of processes of learning and resocialization at the core of participant observation (Emerson et al., 1995: 13–14).

3 Anthropological fieldwork has long emphasized this 'going out' and the related radical separation between 'the field' and 'home,' conceiving of the former as a far-away, exotic and pastoral place unaffected by contemporary development and technology (Gupta and Ferguson, 1997). 'The field' is the site of 'fieldwork' (part of which involves writing fieldnotes as data); 'home' is 'where analysis is conducted and the ethnography is written up'. While this field/home separation appears in some classic sociological ethnographies (e.g. Whyte, 1955), much sociological fieldwork involves 'subway ethnography' in which the field/home split is relatively ephemeral and hence less pervasive.

4 This obscurity is not only a consequence of abbreviations and lack of socially identifying information; more fundamentally, in writing up some current episode, the ethnographer omits matters of background, context and significance that have already been described and recounted in prior notes or that she/he anticipates can easily be recalled or reconstructed at a later point.

5 Postmodern ethnography provides a major exception, at least in principle, to this descriptive emphasis of fieldnotes, as well as challenging the very project of writing fieldnotes in the first place. As Rosenau (1992: 92) emphasizes, 'most postmodernists are anti-representational'; 'skeptical' postmodernists see representation as deeply 'dangerous and basically "bad"', while 'affirmative' postmodernists view it as 'fraudulent, perverse, artificial, mechanical, deceptive, incomplete, misleading, insufficient, wholly inadequate for the postmodern age' (1992: 94–5; see also Gubrium and Holstein, 1997: ch. 5). Much postmodern ethnography eschews fieldnotes entirely, taking at its 'field' existing texts – 'indigenous ethnographic texts' (Dorst, 1989: 206), already published ethnographies, or 'the corpus of texts written about doing ethnographic research' (Gubrium and Holstein, 1997: 84). On the other hand, some ethnographers deeply influenced by postmodern ideas continue to view writing fieldnotes as a central research activity (Ellis, 1995; Richardson, 1994), but with strong emphasis on fieldnote writing 'as an opportunity to expand ... habits of thought, and attentiveness to your senses' (Richardson, 1994: 525).

6 Although an ethnographer's ideological or theoretical orientation might incline toward writing in one point of view her stance does not rigidly determine this outcome. In a strict sense, differing points of view are simply technical strategies for presenting the angle through which the action will be seen. As such, each point of view offers differing writing opportunities and limitations.

7 In a strict adherence to first person, ethnographers quote only those voices of others they actually heard or can quote as reported speech. The voices of others, and their diverse views, thus not only are filtered through the eyes and ears of the ethnographer-as-participant, but their representation also is circumscribed by the writing perspective taken. Though advantaging the ethnographer-as-insider voice, this point of view can mute the voices of others, if used exclusively.

8 In contrast to fieldnotes, some final publications effectively take an omniscient point of view, in order to give equal voice to a variety of persons and positions (cf. Richardson, 1990b). Thus, Van Maanen (1988: 45–72) notes that realist tales depend heavily upon omniscient qualities – the absence of the author from the text, minutely detailed descriptions and overviews, 'interpretive omnipotence'; and Brown (1977) sees the omniscient point of view as fundamental to many classic ethnographies, as when the ethnographer chooses which members' voices to present and shifts from one person's view to another's.

9 Evocative first-person fieldnotes also assure that the ethnographer does not write himself out of the text, thus enhancing, at least initially, 'authorial responsibility' (Rosenau, 1992: 27).

10 To do so she relied upon a process of 'emotional recall' to relive situations in order to remember in detail the experiences in which she had previously felt particular emotions (Ellis, 1995: 310).

11 Emerson et al. (1995) suggest that the excerpt strategy allows for maximum presentation of unexplicated details and qualities of events observed in the field: containing more than the ethnographer chooses to discuss and analyse, such excerpts give depth and texture to ethnographic texts, contributing to readers' tacit understanding of the scenes or events being described and analysed. Thus excerpts contribute to the 'weblike character' of well-crafted ethnographies which may allow readers to use data offered in support of one idea to confirm or disconfirm other ideas (Katz, 1988: 142).

12 Atkinson (1990: 93–4) suggests that the juxtaposition of social actor's and ethnographer's voices does more than duplicate and reinforce. In his discussion of Cressey's (1971) ethnography of taxi-dancers, he writes:

> [T]he two voices combine to produce a collaborative, almost antiphonal account. The two voices are not equivalent, but contribute to the ethnographic text's complexity. It is easy to see that the quotation from 'Case No. 12' does not provide anything like conclusive evidence for the sociologist's assertions ... Again, we should not really expect there to be a direct correspondence between the two levels of text: their functions are complementary rather than identical. The full force of the passage is derived from the switching of perspective between the two voices. (Atkinson, 1990: 93–4)

Clearly, these dialoguing voices can render a more complex understanding of the situation than either could do alone.

REFERENCES

Abrams, M.H. (1988) *A Glossary of Literary Terms*, 5th edn. New York: Holt, Rinehart and Winston.

Atkinson, P. (1990) *The Ethnographic Imagination: Textual Constructions of Reality*. New York: Routledge.

Atkinson, P. (1992) *Understanding Ethnographic Texts*. Newbury Park, CA: Sage.

Brown, R.H. (1977) *A Poetic for Sociology: Toward a Logic of Discovery in the Human Sciences*. Cambridge: Cambridge University Press.

Clifford, J. (1983) 'On ethnographic authority', *Representations*, 1: 118–46.

Clifford, J. (1986) 'On ethnographic allegory', in J. Clifford and G.E. Marcus (eds), *Writing Culture: The Poetics and Politics of Ethnography*. Berkeley, CA: University of California Press. pp. 98–121.

Clifford, J. (1990) 'Notes on (field)notes', in R. Sanjek (ed.), *Fieldnotes: The Making of Anthropology*. Ithaca, NY: Cornell University Press. pp. 47–70.

Clifford, J. (1997) 'Spatial practices: fieldwork, travel, and the disciplining of anthropology', in A. Gupta and J. Ferguson (eds), *Anthropological Locations: Boundaries and Grounds for a Field Science*. Berkeley, CA: University of California Press. pp. 185–222.

Clifford, J. and Marcus, G.E. (eds) (1986) *Writing Culture: The Poetics and Politics of Ethnography*. Berkeley, CA: University of California Press.

Crapanzano, V. (1986) 'Hermes' dilemma: the masking of subversion in ethnographic description', in J. Clifford and G.E. Marcus (eds), *Writing Culture: The Poetics and Politics of Ethnography*. Berkeley, CA: University of California Press. pp. 51–76.

Cressey, P.G. (1971) 'The taxi-dance hall as a social world', in J.F. Short Jr (ed.), *The Social Fabric of the Metropolis: Contributions of the Chicago School of Urban Sociology*. Chicago: University of Chicago Press. pp. 193–209.

Dorst, J.D. (1989) *The Written Suburb: An American Site, An Ethnographic Dilemma*. Philadelphia: University of Pennsylvania Press.

Dwyer, K. (1982) *Moroccan Dialogues: Anthropology in Question*. Baltimore, MD: Johns Hopkins University Press.

Ellis, C. (1991) 'Sociological introspection and emotional experience', *Symbolic Interaction*, 14: 23–50.

Ellis, C. (1995) *Final Negotiations: A Story of Love, Loss, and Chronic Illness*. Philadelphia: Temple University Press.

Ellis, C. and Bochner, A.P. (1992) 'Telling and performing personal stories: the constraints of choice in abortion', in C. Ellis and M.G. Flaherty (eds), *Investigating Subjectivity: Research on Lived Experience*. Newbury Park, CA: Sage. pp. 79–101.

Ellis, C. and Bochner, A.P. (eds) (1996) *Composing Ethnography: Alternative Forms of Qualitative Writing*. Walnut Creek, CA: AltaMira Press.

Emerson, R.M., Fretz, R.I. and Shaw, L.L. (1995) *Writing Ethnographic Fieldnotes*. Chicago: University of Chicago Press.

Fetterman, D.M. (1989) *Ethnography: Step by Step*. Newbury Park, CA: Sage.

Fine, E.C. (1984) *The Folklore Text: From Performance to Print*. Bloomington, IN: University of Indiana Press.

Geertz, C. (1973) 'Thick description: toward an interpretive theory of culture', in *The Interpretation of Culture*. New York: Basic Books. pp. 3–30.

Geertz, C. (1988) *Works and Lives: The Anthropologist as Author*. Stanford, CA: Stanford University Press.

Glaser, B.G. and Strauss, A.L. (1967) *The Discovery of Grounded Theory: Strategies for Qualitative Research*. Chicago: Aldine.

Goffman, E. (1989) 'On fieldwork', *Journal of Contemporary Ethnography*, 18: 123–32.

Gubrium, J.F. and Holstein, J.A. (1997) *The New Language of Qualitative Method*. New York: Oxford University Press.

Gupta, A. and Ferguson, J. (eds) (1997) *Anthropological Locations: Boundaries and Grounds for a Field Science*. Berkeley, CA: University of California Press.

Jackson, J.E. (1990) '"I am a fieldnote": fieldnotes as a symbol of professional identity', in R. Sanjek (ed.), *Fieldnotes: The Making of Anthropology*. Ithaca, NY: Cornell University Press. pp. 3–33.

Johnson, J.M. (1975) *Doing Field Research*. New York: The Free Press.

Katz, J. (1988) 'A theory of qualitative methodology: the system of analytic fieldwork', in R.M. Emerson (ed.), *Contemporary Field Research: A Collection of Readings*. Prospect Heights, IL: Waveland Press. pp. 127–48.

Kleinman, S. and Copp, M.A. (1993) *Emotions and Fieldwork*. Newbury Park, CA. Sage.

Lanham, R.A. (1983) *Analyzing Prose*. New York: Scribner.

Lofland, J. and Lofland, L.H. (1995) *Analyzing Social Settings: A Guide to Qualitative Observation and Analysis*, 3rd edn. Belmont, CA: Wadsworth.

deMan, P. (1983) *Blindness and Insight: Essays in the Rhetoric of Contemporary Criticism*, 2nd edn. London: Methuen.

Marcus, G.E. (1986) 'Afterword: ethnographic writing and anthropological careers', in J. Clifford and G.E. Marcus (eds), *Writing Culture: The Poetics and Politics of Ethnography*. Berkeley, CA: University of California Press. pp. 262–6.

Marcus, G.E. (1994) 'What comes (just) after "post"? The case of ethnography', in N.K. Denzin and Y.S. Lincoln (eds), *Handbook of Qualitative Research*. Thousand Oaks, CA: Sage. pp. 563–74.

Moeran, B. (1985) *Okubo Diary: Portrait of a Japanese Valley*. Stanford, CA: Stanford University Press.

Moeran, B. (1990) 'Beating about the brush: an example of ethnographic writing from Japan', in R. Fardon (ed.), *Localizing Strategies: Regional Traditions of Ethnographic Writing*. Edinburgh: Scottish Academic Press. pp. 339–57.

Mulkay, M. (1985) *The Word and the World: Explorations in the Form of Sociological Analysis*. London: George Allen and Unwin.

Pollner, M. and Emerson, R.M. (1988) 'The dynamics of inclusion and distance in fieldwork relations', in R.M. Emerson (ed.), *Contemporary Field Research: A Collection of Readings*. Prospect Heights, IL: Waveland. pp. 235–52.

Richardson, L. (1990a) 'Narrative and sociology', *Journal of Contemporary Ethnography*, 19: 116–35.

Richardson, L. (1990b) *Writing Strategies: Reaching Diverse Audiences*. Newbury Park, CA: Sage.

Richardson, L. (1994) 'Writing: a method of inquiry', in N.K. Denzin and Y.S. Lincoln (eds), *Handbook of Qualitative Research*. Thousand Oaks, CA: Sage. pp. 516–29.

Riessman, C. (1993) *Narrative Analysis*. Thousand Oaks, CA: Sage.

Rosenau, P.M. (1992) *Post-Modernism and the Social Sciences: Insights, Inroads and Intrusions*. Princeton, NJ: Princeton University Press.

Sanjek, R. (ed.) (1990a) *Fieldnotes: The Making of Anthropology*. Ithaca, NY: Cornell University Press.

Sanjek, R. (1990b) 'Preface', in R. Sanjek (ed.), *Fieldnotes: The Making of Anthropology*. Ithaca, NY: Cornell University Press. pp. xi–xviii.

Sanjek, R. (1990c) 'A vocabulary for fieldnotes', in R. Sanjek (ed.), *Fieldnotes: The Making of Anthropology*. Ithaca, NY: Cornell University Press. pp. 92–121.

Schatzman, L. and Strauss, A. (1973) *Field Research: Strategies for a Natural Sociology*. Englewood Cliffs, NJ: Prentice–Hall.

Thorne, B. (1980). '"You still takin' notes?" Fieldwork and problems of informed consent', *Social Problems*, 27: 284–97.

Thorne, B. (1993) *Gender Play: Girls and Boys in School*. New Brunswick, NJ: Rutgers University Press.

Van Maanen, J. (1988) *Tales of the Field: On Writing Ethnography*. Chicago: University of Chicago Press.

Whyte, W.F. (1955) *Street Corner Society*. Chicago: University of Chicago Press.

Wolcott, H.F. (1990) *Writing Up Qualitative Research*. Newbury Park, CA: Sage.

25

Ethnographic Interviewing

BARBARA SHERMAN HEYL

Researchers in an ever-increasing number of disciplinary and applied fields have been turning to ethnographic interviewing to help gather rich, detailed data directly from participants in the social worlds under study. Indeed, the substantial number of chapters in this volume devoted to different substantive and disciplinary-related areas attests to the wide variation in research contexts within which ethnographic interviewing takes place today. For example, beyond anthropology and sociology, the fields of medicine, education, psychology, communication, history, science studies and art have seen a dramatic increase in projects utilizing qualitative methods of various kinds, including ethnographic interviewing.

Ethnographic interviewing is one qualitative research technique that owes a major debt to cultural anthropology, where interviews have traditionally been conducted on-site during lengthy field studies. However, researchers from a variety of disciplines conduct on-site, participant observational studies, although typically shorter than those carried out by anthropologists. In addition, researchers regularly devise non-participant research projects that center on a set of unstructured, in-depth interviews with key informants from a particular social milieu or with people from a variety of settings and backgrounds who have had certain kinds of experiences. The question arises whether these are all examples of ethnographic interviewing. Given that there is a great deal of overlapping terminology in the areas of qualitative research and ethnography (Atkinson and Hammersley, 1994; Reinharz, 1992: 18, fn. 3, 4; 46, fn. 5; Silverman, 1993: 23–9), the definition of ethnographic interviewing here will include those projects in which researchers have established respectful, on-going relationships with their interviewees, including enough rapport for

there to be a genuine exchange of views and enough time and openness in the interviews for the interviewees to explore purposefully with the researcher the meanings they place on events in their worlds.

Thus, both the time factor – duration and frequency of contact – and the quality of the emerging relationship help distinguish ethnographic interviewing from other types of interview projects by empowering interviewees to shape, according to their world-views, the questions being asked and possibly even the focus of the research study.[1] Also central to traditional ethnographic research is the focus on cultural meanings (Wolcott, 1982). As Spradley notes in *The Ethnographic Interview*, 'The essential core of ethnography is this concern with the meaning of actions and events to the people we seek to understand' (1979: 5), and the researcher's job in the ethnographic interview, then, is to communicate genuinely, in both subtle and direct ways that 'I want to know what you know *in the way that you know it.* ... Will you become my teacher and help me understand?' (p. 34; emphasis added).[2] Life history interviewing fits comfortably within the ethnographic tradition, since it is usually conducted over time, within relationships characterized by high levels of rapport, and with particular focus on the meanings the interviewees place on their life experiences and circumstances, expressed in their own language (Becker, 1970; Spradley, 1979: 24). These key definitional characteristics allow ethnographic interviewing to be distinguished from survey interviewing, including interviews with open-ended questions, because there is no time to develop respectful, on-going relationships.

In the 1990s interest in ethnographic interviewing has grown, partly in response to the limitations of the quantitative research methodologies that, in the last half of the twentieth century, dominated such fields as sociology, criminology, education and medicine. Researchers in increasing numbers have turned to ethnographic interviewing out of a growing recognition of the complexity of human experience, a desire to hear from people directly how they interpret their experiences, as well as an interest, at times, in having the results of their research efforts be relevant and useful to those studied. The 'up close and personal' characteristics of ethnographic interviewing make it appealing on all these grounds. Yet, ethnographic enquiry today, as the chapters in this volume clearly indicate, is contested terrain. Debates since the 1980s about epistemology in the social sciences and humanities in general, and feminist and post-positivist concerns about ethnography in particular, have raised a number of important questions that are clearly relevant to ethnographic interviewing. In particular, the debates have highlighted issues concerning the relationship between the researchers and their 'subjects', as well as considerations about what can be known in the interview process.

This chapter will describe the most recent literature on ethnographic interviewing, emphasizing how we can do ethnographic interviewing in a way that incorporates what we have learned about the impact of the interviewer/interviewee relationship on the co-construction of knowledge. Many researchers today find themselves doing ethnographic interviewing in a middle place in their disciplines, surrounded by debates about what can be known (for example, can scientific methods access the real world?) and challenged by issues raised by poststructuralist, feminist and multicultural scholars (Eisner and Peshkin, 1990; Kvale, 1996). The debates bring to the fore incongruous positions and differing emphases about what is most important to consider in interviewing. And yet, as we will see in this chapter, among the many voices there is still agreement on these goals: when we carry out ethnographic interviewing, we should

1 listen well and respectfully, developing an ethical engagement with the participants at all stages of the project;
2 acquire a self awareness of our role in the co-construction of meaning during the interview process;
3 be cognizant of ways in which both the ongoing relationship and the broader social context affect the participants, the interview process, and the project outcomes; and
4 recognize that dialogue is discovery and only partial knowledge will ever be attained.

Even those voicing serious concerns about ethical and epistemological issues in contemporary interviewing do not reject the method altogether (Denzin, 1997: 265–87; Ellis, 1995: 94; Scheurich, 1995: 249). There is a broad-based commitment

to continue to try to *do it* – and do it ethically, bringing no harm, and indeed, doing it, as Laurel Richardson (1992: 108) has said, 'so that the people who teach me about their lives are honored and empowered, even if they and I see their worlds differently'.

CHANGING CONCEPTIONS OF
ETHNOGRAPHIC INTERVIEWING

The theory and practice of ethnography have been scrutinized in the international debate during the 1980s over qualitative methods and methodology, alongside the broader debates over epistemology and the crisis of authority and representation in most humanities and social sciences (Alasuutari, 1995; Atkinson and Coffey, 1995; Clifford and Marcus, 1986; Clough, 1998; Denzin, 1997; Denzin and Lincoln, 1994b; McLaren, 1992; Stacey, 1988). The literature focusing specifically on the implications of these debates for ethnographic interviewing is considerably smaller than that devoted to the issues of writing up and representing the results of those research efforts (see Chapter 32). Still, in the past few years several major works have focused specifically on doing interviewing with an awareness of the postmodern and feminist critiques in anthropology and sociology (Briggs, 1986; Kvale, 1996; Maso and Wester, 1996; Michrina and Richards, 1996; Mishler, 1986; Reinharz, 1992; Rubin and Rubin, 1995). These researchers stress that interviewing involves a complex form of social interaction with interviewees, and that interview data are co-produced in these interactions. Furthermore, they recognize that *what* the interviewees in each study choose to share with the researchers reflects conditions in their relationship and the interview situation. Central to this process is how interviewees reconstruct events or aspects of social experience, as well as how interviewers make their own sense of what has been said.

Recognition of the co-construction of the interview, and its reconstruction in the interpretation phase, shifts the basic assumptions that for many years defined the interview process. These assumptions are embodied in Kvale's (1996: 3–5) two alternative metaphors of the research interviewer: one as a miner, and another as a traveler. In the miner metaphor (which contains traditional research assumptions about how to gather objective data), the interviewer goes to the vicinity of the 'buried treasure' of new information in a specific social world, seeks out good sources ('She was a walking, talking gold mine'), and carefully gathers up the data – facts waiting to be culled out and discovered by the interviewer's efforts. The miner metaphor can also be extended to the taking of the accumulated treasure home, as Kvale describes:

The precious facts and meanings are purified by transcribing them from the oral to the written mode. The knowledge nuggets remain constant through the transformations of appearances on the conveyor belt from the oral stage to the written storage. By analysis, the objective facts and the essential meanings are drawn out by various techniques and molded into their definitive form. Finally, the value of the end product, in degree of purity, is determined by correlating it with an objective, external, real world or to a realm of subjective, inner, authentic experiences. (1996: 3–4)

The ideal is to distill interviews into 24-carat gold.

In contrast, the traveler metaphor sees the interviewer as on a journey from which he or she will return with stories to tell, having engaged in conversations with those encountered along the way. Kvale (1996: 4) notes that the original Latin meaning of *conversation* is 'wandering together with'. The route may be planned ahead of time, but will lead to unexpected twists and turns as interviewer-travelers follow their particular interests and adjust their paths according to what those met along the way choose to share. As is true with any traveler today, what one receives in new knowledge and experiences is influenced by just how one manages to connect to the people one meets along the way and how long one stays to talk, learn and build a relationship with them. Both the traveler and those met are changed by those relationships involving meaningful dialogue (DeVault, 1990; Heyl, 1997; Narayan, 1993; Roman, 1993; Warren, 1988: 47).

As researchers approach the interviewing process, they bring with them a 'vocabulary of method' that shapes how they proceed (Gubrium and Holstein, 1997). This vocabulary has roots in the researcher's own discipline and in the sub-disciplines that make up research approaches – predilections and prescriptions for conducting research in specific ways. Some of these approaches facilitate 'mining' and some encourage 'traveling'. Gubrium and Holstein's (1997: 5) premise is that the social science researchers use language that 'organizes the empirical contours of what is under investigation'. Such organization includes whether they will 'mine' or 'travel'.[3]

LITERATURE ON STAGES IN THE INTERVIEW PROJECT

Developing Challenges to a Positivistic Framework

Tracing the literature on ethnographic interviewing in sociology reveals the historical roots of current ideas in a series of developments that increasingly challenged the position of interviewer as an autonomous 'miner'. The Chicago School of the 1920s and 1930s is generally seen as the birthplace

of ethnographic interviewing in sociology. Robert Park's experience as a journalist and his familiarity with anthropological methods played a role in his demand that his graduate students go out into the city and 'get the seat of your pants dirty in real research' (Bulmer, 1984: 97). Park, who had been especially affected by the teachings of William James, writes in an autobiographical essay about a particular lecture by James titled 'On a Certain Blindness in Human Beings':

The 'blindness' of which James spoke is the blindness each of us is likely to have for the meaning of other people's lives. At any rate, what sociologists most need to know is what goes on behind the faces of men, what it is that makes life for each of us either dull or thrilling. For 'if you lose the joy you lose all'. But the thing that gives zest to life or makes life dull is, however, as James says, 'a personal secret', which has, in every single case, to be discovered. Otherwise we do not know the world in which we actually live. (Park, 1950: viii; cited in Bulmer, 1984: 93)

The Chicago School sociologists in the 1920s developed informal interviewing and observation techniques that were very different from the large-scale, standardized surveys being conducted by political scientists of the time (Bulmer, 1984: 102, 104). They emphasized the need to 'speak the same language' as those one wanted to understand, and Nels Anderson, Paul Cressey and Frederic Thrasher had each at some points taken on covert researcher roles in the settings they were studying. They and Ernest Burgess, especially, developed the life history method as a way of getting 'objective data' on interviewees' own interpretation of their circumstances and key events. Bulmer (1984: 108) sees the lasting effects of the field research methods of the Chicago School in the use of documentary sources of all kinds, in the establishment of participant observation as a standard sociological research method, and in an openness to using diverse research methods. Although the Chicago School sociologists were comfortable using a mix of quantitative and qualitative approaches, Hammersley (1989: 89–112) notes that after the arrival of William F. Ogburn in the late 1920s, the department began a shift toward quantitative methods and a positivist paradigm, as did most sociology departments in the nation.

Although the Chicago School tradition has sustained criticism from scholars representing a wide variety of perspectives,[4] it has had a significant impact on generations of sociologists and other scholars interested in carrying out field research projects. Indeed, Joseph Gusfield (1995: xi) notes that his cohort at the University of Chicago in the 1950s, which included Howard Becker and Erving Goffman, shared some 'tacit perspectives' about doing sociology, and that, 'While diversely stated and applied, these perspectives had much in common with that first Chicago School and the tradition it formed.' The work of this cohort has been so influential in sociology as to warrant consideration as a 'Second Chicago School' (Fine, 1995).

Thus, ethnographic interviewing has long been utilized in sociology as a way of shedding light on the personal experiences, interpersonal dynamics and cultural meanings of participants in their social worlds. Researchers today have a rich literature available to help them consider how to proceed with their interview projects using this approach. Beginning in the 1970s, a set of texts appeared which has formed a body of 'classic' sociological literature on field methods and in-depth interviewing; it has offered guidance on the multitude of decisions to be made at every stage of the project (Bogdan and Taylor, 1975; Denzin, 1978; Johnson, 1975; Lofland, 1971; Schatzman and Strauss, 1973; Spradley, 1979). Central to these classic works in methodology is a symbolic interactionist stance, which, by virtue of its focus on interviewing as emergent interaction, contrasts sharply with a positivistic approach to interviewing (Silverman, 1993: 94).

The postmodern and feminist challenges to traditional fieldwork techniques opened up room for considering *how* to approach doing ethnographic research while keeping these new challenges in mind. By the 1980s and early 1990s, books on field methods emphasized the constructivist nature of fieldwork (Bailey, 1996; Glesne and Peshkin, 1992; Hammersley and Atkinson, 1983; Maso and Webster, 1996; Roberts, 1981; Weiss, 1993; Wolcott, 1995). And most recently, books that focus directly on interviewing address ways to conceptualize and carry out new styles of ethnographic interview projects following the linguistic, postmodern turn (Holstein and Gubrium, 1995; Kvale, 1996; Michrina and Richards, 1996; Mishler, 1986; Rubin and Rubin, 1995; Silverman, 1993).

The literature on the methodology of ethnographic interviewing published over the past three decades shows a consistent pattern of challenging a positivistic framework. The 'classic' sociological[5] works on field methods of the 1970s described stages in a field study, such as how to gain entrée to a setting, explain the research project to gatekeepers and key informants, gain trust and rapport, decide on space and time sampling, interview key informants in an open-ended or semi-structured style, develop fieldnotes, analyse the fieldnotes and interview transcriptions, exit the field and write up the results of the analyses. Although there was often a linear presentation of steps in these descriptions, the researcher was typically encouraged to consider analytical issues throughout the data-gathering process; especially for Strauss, early analysis of fieldnotes was central to locating other sources for additional interviews and observations which could

strengthen the developing conceptual framework (Schatzman and Strauss, 1973: 108; Strauss and Corbin, 1990).

The authors of these 1970s sociological works on fieldwork were already grounded in and aware of sociology's own 'crisis of objectivity'. Alvin Gouldner's (1970) *The Coming Crisis of Western Sociology* had critiqued a social science that premised (after the natural sciences) 'that man might be known, used, and controlled like any other thing: it "thingafied" man' (1970: 492). Gouldner posited instead a reflexive social science in which 'both the inquiring subject and the studied object are seen not only as mutually interrelated but also mutually constituted' (1970: 493). Reflecting the spirit of the times, the classic sociological texts on fieldwork written in the 1970s posed the critical question: could social scientific methods, no matter how carefully done, generate objective data? For example, John Johnson in his introduction to *Doing Field Research* (1975: 1–12) discusses in detail a whole series of contemporary ideas undermining the fundamental concept of social science objectivity. These challenges include:

1 the 'tacit political meanings' embedded in social science knowledge;
2 the documented conclusions from social psychology that 'what an individual perceives or regards as fact is highly variable' and is contingent on the social context; and
3 that language not only is the medium of reporting but influences 'what it is one observes' (Johnson, 1975: 10–12).

Finally, recognizing that both gathering data and conducting analyses are dependent on the researchers and influenced by their characteristics and personal values, Johnson notes that researchers are urged to make their personal values 'explicit' in their work. But Johnson (1975: 23) goes further, positing as equally important the impact of the researchers' 'commitment to theories and methodologies', including their membership in their discipline and community of like-minded scholars. These issues and insights in the 1970s presaged key points in the major debates of the next two decades on research on the social sciences and humanities.

In the meantime, anthropology was anticipating its own 'coming crisis', epitomized by Edward Said's *Orientalism* (1979), a broad attack on writing genres developed in the West for depicting non-Western societies, and calls to 'reinvent' anthropology (Hymes, 1969), since the knowledge produced and disseminated through ethnographic monographs was linked to colonial systems of oppression. George Marcus and Michael Fischer (1986) trace the wave of critiques, and responses to them, in cultural anthropology. Challenges to classic fieldwork approaches focused especially on the issue of a 'scientific' basis for social research and added a whole set of new questions, such as those catalogued by Clifford Geertz:

> Questions about discreteness ... questions about continuity and change, objectivity and proof, determinism and relativism, uniqueness and generalization, description and explanation, consensus and conflict, otherness and commensurability, and the sheer possibility of anyone, insider or outsider, grasping so vast a thing as an entire way of life and finding the words to describe it. (Geertz, 1995: 42–3)

Ruth Behar (1996: 162) notes that the discipline has weathered a range of daunting crises: 'complicity with conquest, with colonialism, with functionalism, with realist forms of representation, with racism, with male domination'. Behar feels that in weathering such storms, the discipline has become more inclusive and knows itself better, but she worries about the current pressures to reconnect anthropology to 'science'. Behar (1996: 162–4) traces this latter pressure to those who claim that all the disparate voices in modern anthropology – postmodern, multicultural, feminist – leave the discipline fragmented and vulnerable in today's academy. However, I feel that even if fragmented,[6] cultural anthropologists' debates and reflections on their discipline have helped the rest of us consider the issues at stake in doing ethnographic research. And with each new well-written ethnography, we can appreciate what the struggles and reflections mean in action (for example, Brown, 1991; Jackson, 1989; Latour, 1996; Leonardo, 1991, 1998; Myerhoff, 1994; Smith and Watson, 1992; Williams, 1988).

Conducting Ethnographic Interview Projects after 'The Turn'

The effects of the rise of the different voices Behar mentions – those voices representing postmodern, feminist and multicultural positions in the 1980s and early 1990s – gradually became known as 'the turn'. Denzin and Lincoln (1994b) trace the stages of its historical development. This section focuses on those writings since 'the turn' that present ethnographic interviewing as method while taking these challenges into account, providing concrete suggestions to researchers on ways to conduct interview projects in this era. Steinar Kvale's *InterViews* (1996) centers on the idea that interviews are first and foremost interaction, a conversation between the researcher and the interviewee. The knowledge that is produced out of this conversation is a product of that interaction, the exchange and production of 'views'. His book is designed to be helpful to researchers in a variety of disciplines, and he presents an in-depth analysis of the stages of an interview project, addressing ethical issues that can arise at each stage. Kvale sets out seven stages of an interview investigation:

1 thematizing;
2 designing;
3 interviewing;
4 transcribing;
5 analysing;
6 verifying;
7 reporting.

The 'thematizing' stage involves the researcher in thinking through the goals and primary questions of the study in ways that can help guide the many subsequent decisions that must be made (Kvale, 1996: 94–8). It involves actively planning for the interview project by identifying and obtaining (from literature searches and even preliminary fieldwork), a 'preknowledge' of the subject matter of interest, clarifying the purpose of the project, and acquiring skills in different types of interviewing and analysis approaches and deciding which to apply.

In *The Active Interview*, Holstein and Gubrium (1995) also take as their major premise that the researcher and the interviewee are active creators in all phases of the interview process. Indeed, Holstein and Gubrium assert that a careful transcription from an audio or video tape of the interview will allow the researcher to observe and document how meaning got produced during the conversation. To introduce their approach, Holstein and Gubrium (1995: 14) resurrect the remarkably prescient position taken by Ithiel de Sola Pool in 1957:

> The social milieu in which communication takes place [during interviews] modifies not only what a person dares to say but even what he thinks he chooses to say. And these variations in expressions cannot be viewed as mere deviations from some underlying 'true' opinion, for there is no neutral, non-social, uninfluenced situation to provide that baseline. (Pool, 1957: 192)

Pool (1957: 193) goes on to assert that the interview situation 'activates' opinion, such that 'every interview [besides being an information-gathering occasion] is an interpersonal drama with a developing plot'. Holstein and Gubrium pursue the implication of having both an active interviewer and an active respondent constructing meaning, or creating a plot, throughout the interview process. For example, respondents can turn to different stocks of knowledge in answering a single question. Holstein and Gubrium (1995: 33–4) cite tell-tale phrases respondents use that signal shifts in roles and frames of reference: 'speaking as a mother now', 'thinking like a woman', 'wearing my professional hat', 'now that you ask', and 'if I were in her shoes'. If respondents shift around and give what may appear to be contradictory answers, it could be unnerving to a conventional interviewer. But the 'active interviewer' is interested in tracing how the interviewee develops a response, so that the shifts, with their attendant markers – including hesitations and expressions indicating a struggle to formulate a coherent answer – are keys to different identities and meanings constructed from these different positions. Which responses are valid? Holstein and Gubrium (1995: 34) posit 'alternative validities' based on recognition of the different roles and the 'narrative resources' they provide for the respondent.

Even though this approach is built on flexibility throughout the interview process, the pursuit of both subjective information about specific aspects of individuals' lives as well as data on how meaning gets made, calls for certain research strategies. Holstein and Gubrium (1995: 77) emphasize the importance of acquiring background knowledge relevant to the research topic, as well as knowledge of the 'material, cultural, and interpretive circumstances to which respondents might orient'. Decisions about sampling should include consideration of whose voices will get heard, as well as recognition that respondents selected because of specific positions or roles may complicate the sampling plan later when they spontaneously 'switch voices' and speak from different positions (1995: 25–7, 74–5). The 'active interview' data can be analysed not only for *what* was said (substantive information) and *how* it was said (construction of meaning), but also for showing the ways the *what* and *how* are interrelated and 'what circumstances condition the meaning-making process' (Holstein and Gubrium, 1995: 79).[7] As exemplified here, current literature on conducting ethnographic interviewing moves beyond an interest in the interview interaction, and addresses specific techniques for systematic interpretation of the text that is produced out of that interaction (Silverman, 1993).

FEMINISTS ON INTERVIEWING

Collaborative Relationships: Language and Listening

Feminist researchers are pursuing their studies in a wide range of substantive areas, utilizing varied methodological approaches (Fonow and Cook, 1991; Gluck and Patai, 1991; Harding, 1987; Nielsen, 1990; Olesen, 1994; Reinharz, 1992; Warren, 1988). However, feminists have found ethnography and ethnographic interviewing particularly attractive because they allow for gathering data experientially, in context, and in relationships characterized by empathy and egalitarianism (Stacey, 1988: 21). Indeed, Shulamit Reinharz (1992: 18) opens her review of feminist interview research with Hilary Graham's conclusion that 'The use of semi-structured interviews has become the principal means by which feminists have sought to achieve the active involvement of their respondents in the construction of data about their lives.' Feminist researchers appreciate ethnographic interviewing for

the chance to hear people's ideas, memories and interpretations in their own words, to hear differences among people and the meanings they construct, and to forge connection over time to the interviewees.

Today's feminist scholars view ethnographic interviewing as a 'conversation', and as such, many of them focus on the talk going on in interviews and how it is shaped by both parties. Marianne Paget (1983) has characterized this conversation as involving both the researcher and the interviewee in a 'search' process whereby they locate a collaborative basis for developing the question–response sequences and the co-construction of meaning. Thus, in those cases of feminist research that involve women interviewing women, the participants can utilize a tradition of engaging in 'woman talk' (DeVault, 1990: 101) to facilitate this search for partnership in the interview.

Though there are wide variations in interviewing style among feminist researchers (Reinharz, 1992), a theme runs through the literature of the need for careful listening to the actual talk of the interview. Marjorie DeVault (1990) proposes specific recommendations for interviewing women, noting that language is so influenced by male categories that when women talk, the right words are not easily available that fit their experience. For example, the categories of 'work' and 'leisure' fail to describe well the host of household and family-related tasks in which many women are involved for hours of their day. DeVault urges the researcher to avoid importing too many categories from outside women's experience, including those from social science, in order to be open to respondents' ways of describing their lifeworlds. If the available vocabulary does not quite fit, the interviewee has to translate, to work at describing her experiences. When researchers listen carefully to the actual talk, they can hear these moments of translation, which can sensitize the analysis to these aspects of women's lives where language is found wanting.

Emotions During Interviewing

Judith Stacey (1988) has raised a concern about feminist interviewing that is related to the possibility of building an equal relationship with the interviewees. Though drawn to ethnographic methods as a feminist, she found some of her experiences troubling and wondered if the close relationships in the field can mask other forms of exploitation because of the inherent inequality connected to the researcher's freedom to exit that social world. Stacey's view was influenced by her experience in the field: one informant confided in her secrets involving others in the community, leaving Stacey feeling 'inauthentic' in her dealings with those others. This 'up close and personal' style of interviewing can indeed produce discomfort and ethical dilemmas. When one moves away from the separations imposed by the 'scientific' approach (stay distant and thereby 'neutral'), then all the messiness of everyday life can intrude. In this approach, emotions become an important part of fieldwork (Kleinman and Copp, 1993; Krieger, 1991), and especially intense field relationships or interview topics can leave the researcher, as well as the informants, feeling vulnerable (Ellingson, 1998; Ellis et al., 1997; Krieger, 1983). In describing the emotions raised for Barbara Katz Rothman (1986), whose research involved interviewing women who had undergone an amniocentesis followed by an abortion, Carol Warren notes:

> Emotions are evoked in the fieldworker while listening to the respondent's accounts of their own lives. Fieldwork, like any interaction of everyday life, evokes the whole range of feelings associated with everyday life. But transference or identification – in fieldwork as in everyday life – is evoked mainly through talking with others, in conversation, or (as with Katz Rothman's research) interviews. (1988: 47)

Ethnographic interviewers are increasing their efforts to understand such dynamics. Interviewees can feel affirmed and empowered from being genuinely listened to (Opie, 1992), and they can choose how 'deep' to go in answering questions (Heyl, 1997). Michelle Fine urges researchers to develop an awareness of the interpersonal politics of the interview encounter – how the 'self' and 'other' of both parties to the dialogue are created and defined through the talk. For researchers to become more aware of this complex process, Fine suggests interviewers try ways of 'working the hyphen' in this self–other connection:

> Working the hyphen means creating occasions for researchers and informants to discuss what is, and is not, 'happening between', within the negotiated relations of whose story is being told, why, to whom, with what interpretation, and whose story is being shadowed, why, for whom, and with what consequences. (1994: 72)

LEVELS OF EMPOWERMENT
IN INTERVIEWING

Several themes in the recent literature on ethnographic interviewing focus on goals that are consonant with those of feminist researchers. Of particular interest in this literature are the concepts of empowerment and reflexivity. The next two sections address the issues involved in empowering respondents and developing reflexivity as interviewers.

Eliot Mishler (1986) presents a strong rationale for interviewers to empower respondents – a rationale he developed out of his critique of traditional interview techniques. His critique shows that

far from being a 'neutral' research procedure, structured interviewing decontextualizes the respondents by separating the individuals and their responses from the context of their daily lives. The structured interview protocol interferes with the respondents' ability to develop detailed, coherent narratives and to trace with the interviewer how they have made sense of events and experiences. To obtain such responses, the interviewer needs to share power over the interview process with the interviewee (Mishler, 1986: 122–32). Mishler identifies three types of relationships between the interviewers and interviewees: informants and reporters, research collaborators, and learners/actors and advocates. Each successive set increases the empowering component in the interview relationship.

Informants and Reporters

When an interviewer acts as a reporter, his or her goal is to report on 'members' understandings', but this approach is far from the miner metaphor discussed earlier. At this first level of empowerment, the researcher's awareness of how the interview itself shapes the outcome shifts the research toward the 'traveler' metaphor. The reporter empowers the respondent (now elevated to an 'informant') by listening carefully and respectfully, allowing the informants to 'name' the world in their own terms, rather than reacting to terminology or categories introduced by the researcher. Another empowering shift from traditional practice can occur at this level by reporting the informants' real names in the text, if that is what they would like, having considered potential future repercussions for them or for others who could be identified by association with the named informants (Mishler, 1986: 123–5; see Myerhoff, 1994: 36 on the desire of the elderly Jews in her study to have their real names used in the book so that there would be some permanent documentation of their life stories).

Other researchers have pointed out that the admonition to listen carefully and respectfully applies not only to what the researcher does during the interview but also to the 'listening' that is done later when the researcher reviews and analyses tapes and transcripts. DeVault (1990), Holstein and Gubrium (1995), Opie (1992) and Poland and Pederson (1998) urge making close transcription of taped interviews, and then, through careful reviewing of transcripts (and re-playing of the tapes), listening for respondents' hesitations, contradictions, topics about which little is said, and shifts in verbal positioning (taking different points of view), all of which help to highlight the complexities in what the respondents are saying. This 'listening' after the interview also helps heighten the researcher's awareness of the way the interview text was co-produced. By focusing on the immediate context of the interview, including just how the interviewer asked a question or responded to the informant's last utterance, the interviewer can better understand why the informant answered in a particular way. In what can be viewed as a linguistic approach to interview analysis, these researchers are urging more explicit study and appreciation of the ways in which actual talk in the interview proceeds.[8]

Paying attention to when talk does *not* proceed can also be part of respectful listening. Poland and Pederson (1998: 295, 300) note that traditionally ethnographic interviewers are taught to 'keep informants talking' (Spradley, 1979: 80); however, silences may be indicators of complex reactions to the questions and self-censorship. Researchers need to respect respondents' right to remain silent and to appreciate that, for some respondents, the research interview may not be an appropriate place to 'tell all'. Poland and Pederson (1998: 307) also urge researchers to attend to a broader context than that of the interview itself; they refer to the 'many silences of (mis)understanding embedded in qualitative research that is not grounded in an appreciating of the "objective" material/cultural conditions in which social and personal meanings are shaped and reproduced ... '. They reference Bourdieu's (1996: 22–3) call for qualitative researchers to have not just 'a well intentioned state of mind' but extensive knowledge of the social conditions within which people live. These recommendations for interviewers to be cognizant of both interaction and context of the interview – for interpreting talk, silences, and even underlying social and cultural structures – acknowledge that researchers have considerable control over the 'reporting' and the outcome, while still striving to empower the respondents through respectful listening.

Research Collaborators

Mishler's (1986) second level of empowering shifts the interviewer/interviewee relationship to one of research collaborators. This shift can be managed in a number of ways. Mishler notes, for example, that Laslett and Rapoport (1975: 974) urge researchers to tell respondents how the data will be used. In collaborative research the interviewee is included in discussions up front about what information is being sought and what approaches to the topics might be most fruitful to the endeavor for both participants. Similarly, Smaling (1996) feels that the shift to research collaborators is dependent on developing trust and the basis for genuine dialogue. With the shift to collaboration, the interviewer acknowledges that the interviewee influences the content and order of questions and topics covered. The interviewee participates in interpreting and re-interpreting questions and responses, clarifying what their responses meant, and even re-framing

the research questions (Lather, 1986; Smaling, 1996). The collaboration can result in rich narrative data, since the interviewer has multiple opportunities to expand at length on topics and angles of relevance to him or her.

At the same time, however, researchers can sometimes find themselves wondering how the expanded responses all relate to the research project. Indeed Mazeland and ten Have (1996: 108–13) have concluded that there are always 'essential tensions' in the research interview, due to three separate orientations at work throughout the interview; interviewees are attending first to their lifeworld, secondly to the interview situation itself, and thirdly to the research question. Using conversation analysis to examine transcripts of (semi-) open interviews, Mazeland and ten Have found that interviewers and interviewees engage in negotiations over the relative precedence of the lifeworld orientation versus the research orientation:

> Interviewers in open interviews seem to take an ambivalent stance in these negotiations, on the one hand calling for a free and natural telling, while on the other often displaying a preference for a summarized answer, that can be easily processed in terms of the research project. (1996: 88)

Mazeland and ten Have found that interviewees in fact lobbied for ways to present their story; they actively engaged the interviewers in the 'essential tension' over the question: 'Is this about *me*, or about your *research*?' If pursuing consciously collaborative interviewing, interviewers can be aware of these essential tensions and promote negotiations that are respectful of interviewees' desire to control the telling of their stories.

Another dimension of collaboration in interviewing is including the participants in the interpretation process. This may begin with follow-up questions or interviews wherein the researcher presents his or her initial interpretations and asks for clarification. This approach may extend to sharing with the interviewee copies of interview transcripts or drafts of research papers and reports. Interestingly, this aspect of collaboration builds on the long-standing procedure known as 'member validation' (Bloor, 1988; Emerson, 1981; Emerson and Pollner, 1988; Hammersley and Atkinson, 1983: 195–8; Heyl, 1979: 1–9, 181–9; Schatzman and Strauss, 1973; Schmitt, 1990). In checking for misinterpretations that could stem from different communication norms, Charles Briggs (1986: 101) has consulted his interviewees but found that it was also helpful to talk with others in the community about his data and interpretations because 'interviewees themselves are less likely to point out the ways in which the researcher has violated the norms of the speech situation or misconstrued the meaning of an utterance than are persons who did not participate in the initial interview'. Certainly, the researcher would involve the initial interviewees in any decision to share their interview transcripts with others and consider carefully any ethical and social ramifications of such sharing.

Moshe Shokeid (1997) details his experience in 'member validation' and collaboration while studying a gay synagogue in New York City. He had asked one member of the synagogue (no longer actively involved) to read his manuscripts and help check his interpretations. This led to numerous debates and detailed, intense negotiations up to the final moments before publication. He notes that the collaboration took on a life of its own and was more than he had bargained for at some points, but in the end it was something he was glad to have accomplished. Shokeid felt that the discussions about his interpretations with this key project participant, as well as other synagogue members, and later with a feminist editor at his publishing house, improved the final book manuscript. His experience did, however, raise questions about the researcher's authority to determine the final product (Nussbaum, 1998; see also Chapter 32 in this volume). Researchers who use the collaborative model will be called upon to give up some control and to respect those whom they have involved in their research projects.

Learner/Actors and Advocates

Eliot Mishler (1986: 129) proposes a third level of empowerment that shifts the relationship between the interviewee and interviewer still further to that of 'learners/actors and advocates'. At this level, the researcher as advocate promotes the interests of those connected to their projects (Erikson, 1976; Mies, 1983). This shift allows the interviewees numerous opportunities to benefit directly from their involvement in the research through learning more about their circumstances, including possible alternatives to their situation, and then acting on this new awareness. 'Participatory action research', as well as emancipatory research in feminist and critical ethnography are several forms of research where the researcher's efforts are focused on empowering individuals involved in their projects (Carspecken, 1996; Kincheloe and McLaren, 1994; Lather, 1991; Reason, 1994; Roman, 1993; Thomas, 1993; Whyte et al., 1989).

REFLEXIVITY IN ETHNOGRAPHIC INTERVIEWING

We turn now to the on-going debate in the recent literature on ethnography about what it means to practice 'reflexivity' as a researcher in order to understand and allow for the interconnections and mutual influence between the researcher and those being 'researched'. In earlier sections of this chapter we encountered recommendations for researchers to develop sophisticated levels of awareness as part of the interview process. Two such examples are Michelle Fine's (1994) call for interviewers to 'work the hyphen' (develop awareness of the complex interplay of 'self' and 'other' during interviews) and Bourdieu's (1996) call for researchers to use knowledge of the material context of the respondents to understand their stories, and help empower them to transform their circumstances. Today's discussion of reflexivity finds an interesting echo in Alvin Gouldner's 1970 urgings for a new 'praxis' of sociology – a genuine change in how we carry out research and how we view ourselves. This shift to a 'reflexive sociology' has a radical component because sociologists would be consciously seeking to transform themselves and the world outside themselves. In terms that anticipate Woolgar's (1988a: 21–2) definition of 'radical constitutive reflexivity', Gouldner proclaims,

> We would increasingly recognize the depth of our kinship with those whom we study. They would no longer be viewable as alien others or as mere objects for our superior technique and insight; they could, instead be seen as brother sociologists, each attempting with his varying degree of skill, energy, and talent to understand social reality. (Gouldner, 1970: 490)

Current discussion of reflexivity since the 'interpretative turn' in the social sciences covers a variety of topics. For example, as a research strategy in fieldwork and interviewing endeavors, reflexive practice is proposed as a way to bridge differences between researcher and respondents (Wasserfall, 1997), to help researchers to avoid unexamined assumptions (Karp and Kendall, 1982), to promote the reconstruction of theories (Burawoy, 1998), and to create a protected space within which the respondents can tell their life stories as well as increase the interviewers' understanding of those stories (Bourdieu, 1996). More broadly, the debates about reflexivity have centered primarily on issues of representation, authority and voice (Hertz, 1997; Woolgar, 1988b). Thus, these varied goals emphasize that reflexivity applies not only to the phases of active interaction during interviewing, but also to the phases of interpretation, writing and publication.

Rahel Wasserfall (1997) describes a 'weak' and a 'strong' reading of reflexivity in the literature. The 'weak' reading focuses on the researcher's 'continued self-awareness about the ongoing relationship between a researcher and informants' (1997: 151). In this view, the researcher makes a steady effort to be cognizant of her own influences on the construction of knowledge by continuously 'checking on the accomplishment of understanding' (p. 151). This reading is similar to the form of reflexivity Woolgar (1988a: 22) calls 'benign introspection'. Those taking this approach have urged investigators to be sensitive to the ways in which their personal characteristics and biographies affect the interaction and production of knowledge during the research project (Reinharz, 1983; Shostak, 1981). The 'strong' reading assumes researchers can proceed in ways that will go beyond recognition of difference and influence in order to deconstruct their own authority (in favor of more egalitarian relationships between researcher and informants) and actively try to bridge class or power differentials. Wasserfall is skeptical that researchers can enact the 'strong' reading when the differences between the researcher and respondents involve strongly held, opposing value commitments. However, she feels that when differences are not great, both the weak and strong approaches to reflexivity can help minimize exploitation of informants and allow the researcher to 'take responsibilities for the influences her study has on her informant's life' (1997: 162).

Karp and Kendall (1982: 250) emphasize what reflexivity requires of the ethnographic researcher – the challenge of 'turning the anthropological lens back upon the self'. The process of widening the research lens to include the researcher and her place in the research not only enlarges 'the fieldworker's conceptual field, but reorganizes it. It poses challenges to the fieldworker's most fundamental beliefs about truth and objectivity' (1982: 250).[9] Karp and Kendall (1982: 260–2) note that one frequently only becomes truly reflexive following a moment of 'shock' – when either the interviewer or interviewee respond in ways unexpected by the other – because only at that moment are assumptions on either side uncovered.

Similarly, Michael Burawoy (1998: 18) finds that moments of 'shock' between what the researcher expects, based on previous work, and what he or she suddenly encounters during observing or interviewing, are important in forcing revisions in their on-going theorizing. Indeed, for Burawoy, theorizing is at the heart of the 'reflexive model of science', which he proposes can co-exist with the positivist model of science. Both models of science may be useful, each with its own strengths and weaknesses, and the choice between them may depend primarily on how we choose to orient to the world: 'to stand aside or to intervene, to seek detachment or to enter into dialogue' (1998: 30). Burawoy's four principles of reflexive science include recognition that we

1   intervene in the lives of those we study;
2   analyse social interaction;
3   identify those local processes that are in mutual determination with external social forces; and
4   reconstruct theories based on what we have learned in dialogue with those involved in our research projects.

Burawoy proposes a reflexive interview method that follows these principles: the interaction during a reflexive interview is interventionist, dialogic, designed to uncover processes in situationally specific circumstances, as well as in broader social contexts, and results in a reconstruction of a theory that fits what has emerged from the dialogue. The resulting theory is also part of dialogue with ideas in the researcher's profession. The published theories (or oral versions of them) will return to the lives of ordinary citizens, including the original study participants, who may adopt them, refute them, or extend them in unexpected ways, and send them, via the next visit by a researcher, back into 'science'. Burawoy (1998: 16, fn. 11) notes that 'Anthony Giddens (1992) has made much of this interchange between academic and lay theory, arguing that sociology appears not to advance because its discoveries become conventional wisdom'. Burawoy's (1998) reflexivity during interviewing and in his 'extended case method' feed into the reflexivity of social theorizing.

Pierre Bourdieu (1996: 18) advocates a 'reflex reflexivity', which is 'based on a sociological "feel" or "eye", [that] enables one to perceive and monitor on the spot, as the interview is actually being carried out, the effects of the social structure within which it is taking place'. The structure of the interview relationship is asymmetric in two ways: first, the investigator starts the game and sets the rules, and secondly, the interviewer likely enters the game with more social capital, including more linguistic capital, than the respondent. Bourdieu combats this asymmetry through 'active and methodical listening'. Active listening consists of 'total attention', which he notes is difficult for interviewers to maintain since we have so much practice in everyday life of categorizing people's stories and turning inattentive. Methodical listening is based on the researcher's 'knowledge of the objective conditions common to the entire relevant social category' for each respondent (1996: 19). Such listening requires an interviewer to have 'extensive knowledge of her subject, acquired sometimes in the course of a whole life of research or of earlier interviews with the same respondent or with informants' (1996: 23). Important here as well is the process that promotes collaboration with the respondents, such that they can 'own' the questioning process themselves. In his latest research Bourdieu (1996: 20) encouraged members of his interview team to select their respondents from among people personally known to them, noting that 'Social proximity and familiarity in effect provide two of the social conditions of "non-violent" communication'. However, he notes that such a strategy can limit research possibilities if only people in like-positions can interview one another. Bourdieu concludes – similarly to Anselm Strauss (1969: 156–9) three decades earlier – that it is more difficult, but still possible, to conduct reflexive interviews with respondents different from oneself:

The sociologist may be able to impart to those interviewees who are furthest removed from her socially a feeling that they may legitimately be themselves, if she knows how to show them, both by her tone and, most especially, the content of her questions, that, without pretending to cancel the social distance which separates her from them ... she is capable of *mentally putting herself in their place*. (Bourdieu, 1996: 22; emphasis in original)

Clearly, the concept of reflexivity during the research process is a multifaceted one, and it is being called on today to do yeoman's duty. But the goals are worthy ones. Our success will be partial, yet our efforts can contribute to identifying processes and power relations at work (both inside the interview situation and outside in the lifeworlds of those with whom we talk), hearing stories respondents feel empowered to tell, and forging connections to one another across different life circumstances. These relational outcomes of ethnographic interviewing resemble Denzin's (1997: 271–87) goals for future ethnographers. Although Denzin (1997: 265–84) is skeptical of the power of reflexivity to transform traditional ethnographic practice, he underscores the primacy of collaborative and empowering relationships when he urges researchers to adopt a 'care-based ethical system' (Ryan, 1995: 148) and follow feminist, communitarian values in their research. Unlike the 'scientist-subject' model, the care-based ethical model asks the researcher 'to step into the shoes of the persons being studied' (Denzin, 1997: 272–3). This issue of whether we can put ourselves in another's place, as Bourdieu also proposes, is addressed eloquently by Elliot Liebow (1993) in his study of homeless women:

This perspective – indeed, participant observation itself – raises the age-old problem of whether anyone can understand another or put oneself in another's place. Many thoughtful people believe that a sane person cannot know what it is to be crazy, that a white man cannot understand a black man, a Jew cannot see through the eyes of a Christian, a man through the eyes of a woman, and so forth in both directions. In an important sense, of course, and to a degree, this is certainly true; in another sense, and to a degree, it is surely false, because the logical extension of such a view is that no one can know another, that only John Jones can know John Jones, in which case, social life would be impossible.

I do not mean that a man with a home and family can see and feel the world as homeless women see and feel it. I do mean, however that it is reasonable and useful to try to do so. Trying to put oneself in the place of the other lies at the heart of the social contract and of social life itself. (1993: xiv–xv)

CONCLUSION

This chapter focuses on a set of interrelated themes in the recent literature on ethnographic interviewing. It highlights the ways in which the interview situation itself constitutes a site of meaning construction that emerges out of the immediate interaction, but also out of the on-going relationship, between interviewer and interviewee. Indeed, the concern with the relationship emphasizes one of the defining characteristics of ethnographic interviewing over other types of interviewing – the significant time invested in developing, through repeated contacts and multiple interviews over time, a genuine relationship involving mutual respect among the participants and mutual interest in the project out of which meaning evolves. Although this definition reflects my personal bias (and other researchers from a variety of disciplines may bring their favorite practices and theoretical predilections to ethnographic interviewing), the literature cited in this chapter emphasizes the need for awareness of ways in which the relationship between the interviewer and interviewee affects how the research topics and questions are approached, negotiated, and responded to – indeed, how the co-construction of meaning takes place. This literature review identifies increasing interest in linguistic analysis of interview talk, feminist and empowering methods of research, and development of reflexivity as a goal. Though not uncontested, these approaches provide some encouraging notes and resources to those researchers from a variety of disciplines interested in conducting ethnographic interview research 'after the turn'.

NOTES

1 From this position, interviewing projects based on one-shot interviews would also not constitute ethnographic interviewing.

2 Certainly this stance, with the researcher as novice and the interviewee as teacher, contrasts sharply with other kinds of interviews, such as depositions and interrogatory interviews, during which interviewers maintain both their positions of greater authority and their continued control over the interview process. Interestingly, interviews done as part of mental health counseling could meet some of the characteristics of ethnographic interviewing, with relationships of long duration, built on trust and mutual respect, and in-depth discussions of the meanings and interpretations of the client's life experiences, however, with therapeutic, rather than research, goals as central to the process (Kvale, 1996: 74–9).

3 While critically analysing four approaches to qualitative research, Gubrium and Holstein (1997: 11–4) probe how the approaches differ and how the 'method talk' of each approach guides, limits and constrains the outcomes of the research. Interestingly, the authors also identify common threads that run through such diverse research languages as naturalism, ethnomethodology, emotionalism and postmodernism; these include having a 'working

skepticism', a commitment to close scrutiny, a search for the 'qualities' of social life, a focus on process, an appreciation for subjectivity, and a tolerance for complexity.

4 See Denzin (1992: 46–70) for a detailed discussion of the critiques and responses to them.

5 Though in cultural anthropology, fieldwork studies remain central to work in the discipline, anthropologists have been less likely to write 'methods' texts for their novice fieldworkers (Narayan, 1993; Michrina and Richards, 1996). In her autobiography of her earlier years, Margaret Mead (1972: 140) noted, 'I really did not know very much about fieldwork. ... There was, in fact, no *how* in our education. What we learned was *what* to look for.'

6 For one related arena of debate, see Jacoby (1995) for an in-depth analysis of the conflicting viewpoints among post-colonial scholars.

7 Gubrium and Holstein further developed their active interviewing project in *The New Language of Qualitative Method* (1997). Since their approach bridges epistemological positions associated with different sub-disciplines in sociology, it is open to critique from several stances; see *Contemporary Sociology*'s (1998) symposium of reviews by Douglas Maynard (from a conversation analytic/ ethnomethodological approach), Nancy Naples (from a feminist perspective) and Robert Prus (from an interactionist perspective).

8 Briggs (1983, 1986) notes that the norms governing what and how one communicates in the informant's social world may well differ from the expectations the researcher brings to the interview, and he offers a range of strategies for identifying and analysing problems that interviewers' questions can cause for the informant.

9 There are critics of such efforts to be reflexive. Clough (1998: xxiv) argues that reflexivity in the form of being self-reflective is doomed: 'The idea of self-reflection in the self-conscious scientist has been exhausted in the growing awareness of the violence of making the other nothing but a reflective apparatus for the scientist' (1998: xxiv).

REFERENCES

Alasuutari, Pertti (1995) *Researching Culture: Qualitative Method and Cultural Studies*. Thousand Oaks, CA: Sage.

Atkinson, Paul and Coffey, Amanda (1995) 'Realism and its discontents: on the crisis of cultural representation in ethnographic texts', in Barbara Adam and Stuart Allan (eds), *Theorizing Culture: An Interdisciplinary Critique after Postmodernism*. New York: New York University Press. pp. 41–57.

Atkinson, Paul and Hammersley, Martyn (1994) 'Ethnography and participant observation', in Norman K. Denzin and Yvonna S. Lincoln (eds), *Handbook of Qualitative Research*. Thousand Oaks, CA: Sage Publications. pp. 248–61.

Bailey, Carol A. (1996) *A Guide to Field Research*. Thousand Oaks, CA: Pine Forge Press.

Becker, Howard S. (1970) 'The relevance of life histories', in Norman K. Denzin (ed.), *Sociological Methods: A Sourcebook*. Chicago: Aldine. pp. 419–28.

Behar, Ruth (1996) *The Vulnerable Observer: Anthropology that Breaks Your Heart*. Boston, MA: Beacon Press.

Bloor, Michael J. (1988) 'Notes on member validation', in R. Emerson (ed.), *Contemporary Field Research*. Prospect Heights, IL: Waveland. pp. 156–72.

Bogdan, Robert and Taylor, Steven (1975) *Introduction to Qualitative Research Methods*. New York: John Wiley.

Bourdieu, Pierre (1996) 'Understanding', *Theory, Culture and Society*, 13 (2): 17–37.

Briggs, Charles L. (1983) 'Questions for the ethnographer: a critical examination of the role of the interview in fieldwork', *Semiotica*, 46 (2/4): 233–61.

Briggs, Charles L. (1986) *Learning How to Ask: A Sociolinguistic Appraisal of the Role of the Interview in Social Science Research*. Cambridge: Cambridge University Press.

Brown, Karen McCarthy (1991) *Mama Lola: A Vodou Priestess in Brooklyn*. Berkeley, CA: University of California Press.

Bulmer, Martin (1984) *The Chicago School of Sociology: Institutionalization, Diversity, and the Rise of Sociological Research*. Chicago: University of Chicago Press.

Burawoy, Michael (1998) 'The extended case method', *Sociological Theory*, 16 (1): 4–33.

Carspecken, Phil Francis (1996) *Critical Ethnography in Educational Research: A Theoretical and Practical Guide*. New York: Routledge.

Clifford, James and Marcus, George E. (eds) (1986) *Writing Culture: The Poetics and Politics of Ethnography*. Berkeley, CA: University of California Press.

Clough, Patricia Ticineto (1998) *The End(s) of Ethnography: From Realism to Social Criticism*. New York: Peter Lang Publishers.

Denzin, Norman K. (1978) *The Research Act: A Theoretical Introduction to Sociological Methods*, 2nd edn. New York: McGraw–Hill.

Denzin, Norman K. (1992) *Symbolic Interactionism and Cultural Studies: The Politics of Interpretation*. Cambridge, MA: Blackwell.

Denzin, Norman K. (1997) *Interpretive Ethnography: Ethnographic Practices for the 21st Century*. Thousand Oaks, CA: Sage.

Denzin, Norman K. and Lincoln, Yvonna S. (eds) (1994a) *Handbook of Qualitative Research*, 2nd edn. Thousand Oaks, CA: Sage.

Denzin, Norman K. and Lincoln, Yvonna S. (1994b) 'Introduction: entering the field of qualitative research', in N.K. Denzin and Y.S. Lincoln (eds), *Handbook of Qualitative Research*. Thousand Oaks, CA: Sage. pp. 1–17.

DeVault, Marjorie L. (1990) 'Talking and listening from women's standpoint: feminist strategies for interviewing and analysis', *Social Problems*, 37 (1): 96–116.

Eisner, Elliot W. and Peshkin, Alan (eds) (1990) *Qualitative Inquiry in Education: The Continuing Debate*. New York: Teachers College Press.

Ellingson, Laura L. (1998) '"Then you know how I feel": empathy, identification, and reflexivity in fieldwork', *Qualitative Inquiry*, 4 (4): 492–514.

Ellis, Carolyn (1995) 'Emotional and ethical quagmires in returning to the field', *Journal of Contemporary Ethnography*, 24 (1): 68–98.

Ellis, Carolyn, Kiesinger, Christine E. and Tillmann-Healy, Lisa M. (1997) 'Interactive interviewing: talking about emotional experience', in Rosanna Hertz (ed.), *Reflexivity and Voice*. Thousand Oaks, CA: Sage. pp. 119–49.

Emerson, Robert M. (1981) 'Observational field work', *Annual Review of Sociology*, 7: 351–78.

Emerson, Robert M. and Pollner, Melvin (1988) 'On the uses of members' responses to researchers' accounts', *Human Organization*, 47 (3): 189–98.

Erikson, Kai T. (1976) *Everything in Its Path: Destruction of Community in the Buffalo Creek Flood*. New York: Simon and Schuster.

Fine, Gary Alan (ed.) (1995) *A Second Chicago School?: The Development of a Postwar American Sociology*. Chicago: University of Chicago Press.

Fine, Michelle (1994) 'Working the hyphens: reinventing self and other in qualitative research', in N.K. Denzin and Y.S. Lincoln (eds), *Handbook of Qualitative Research*. pp. 70–82.

Fonow, Mary Margaret and Cook, Judith A. (eds) (1991) *Beyond Methodology: Feminist Scholarship as Lived Research*. Bloomington, IN: Indiana University Press.

Geertz, Clifford (1995) *After the Fact*. Cambridge, MA: Harvard University Press.

Giddens, Anthony (1992) *The Consequences of Modernity*. Stanford, CA: Stanford University Press.

Glesne, Corrine and Peshkin, Alan (1992) *Becoming Qualitative Researchers: An Introduction*. White Plains, NY: Longman.

Gluck, Sherna Berger and Patai, Daphne (1991) *Women's Words: The Feminist Practice of Oral History*. New York: Routledge.

Gouldner, Alvin W. (1970) *The Coming Crisis of Western Sociology*. New York: Basic Books.

Gubrium, Jaber and Holstein, James A. (1997) *The New Language of Qualitative Method*. New York: Oxford University Press.

Gusfield, Joseph (1995) 'The Second Chicago School?', in Gary Alan Fine (ed.), *A Second Chicago School?: The Development of a Postwar American Sociology*. Chicago: University of Chicago Press. pp. ix–xvi.

Hammersley, Martyn (1989) *The Dilemma of Qualitative Method: Herbert Blumer and the Chicago Tradition*. London: Routledge.

Hammersley, Martyn and Atkinson, Paul (1983) *Ethnography: Principles in Practice*. New York: Tavistock. (2nd edn 1995.)

Harding, Sandra (ed.) (1987) *Feminism and Methodology: Social Science Issues*. Bloomington, IN: Indiana University Press.

Hertz, Rosanna (ed.) (1997) *Reflexivity and Voice*. Thousand Oaks, CA: Sage.

Heyl, Barbara Sherman (1979) *The Madam as Entrepreneur*. New Brunswick, NJ: Transaction Books.

Heyl, Barbara Sherman (1997) 'Talking across the differences in collaborative fieldwork: unanticipated consequences', *The Sociological Quarterly*, 38 (1): 1–18.

Holstein, James A. and Gubrium, Jaber F. (1995) *The Active Interview*. Thousand Oaks, CA: Sage.

Hymes, Dell (ed.) (1969) *Reinventing Anthropology*. New York: Pantheon Books.

Jackson, Michael (1989) *Paths Toward a Clearing: Radical Empiricism and Ethnographic Inquiry*. Bloomington, IN: Indiana University Press.

Jacoby, Russell (1995) 'Marginal returns: the trouble with post-colonial theory', *Lingua Franca*, 5 (6): 30–7.

Johnson, John M. (1975) *Doing Field Research*. New York: The Free Press.

Karp, Ivan and Kendall, Martha B. (1982) 'Reflexivity in field work', in Paul F. Secord (ed.), *Explaining Social Behavior: Consciousness, Human Action, and Social Structure*. Beverly Hills, CA: Sage. pp. 249–73.

Kincheloe, Joe and McLaren, Peter (1994) 'Rethinking critical theory and qualitative research', in Norman K. Denzin and Yvonna S. Lincoln (eds), *Handbook of Qualitative Research*. Thousand Oaks, CA: Sage. pp. 138–57.

Kleinman, Sherryl and Copp, Martha A. (1993) *Emotions and Fieldwork*. Newbury Park, CA: Sage.

Krieger, Susan (1983) *The Mirror Dance: Identity in a Women's Community*. Philadelphia: Temple University Press.

Krieger, Susan (1991) *Social Science and the Self: Personal Essays on an Art Form*. New Brunswick, NJ: Rutgers University Press.

Kvale, Steinar (1996) *InterViews: An Introduction to Qualitative Research Interviewing*. Thousand Oaks, CA: Sage.

Laslett, Barbara and Rapoport, Rhona (1975) 'Collaborative interviewing and interactive research', *Journal of Marriage and the Family*, 37 (4): 968–77.

Lather, Patti A. (1986) 'Feminist research perspectives on empowering research methodologies', *Women's Studies International Forum*, 11 (6): 569–82.

Lather, Patti A. (1991) *Getting Smart: Feminist Research and Pedagogy With/In the Postmodern*. New York: Routledge.

Latour, Bruno (1996) 'Not the question', *Anthropology Newsletter*, 37 (Mar.): 1, 5.

Leonardo, Micaela di (1991) *Gender at the Crossroads of Knowledge: Feminist Anthropology*. Berkeley, CA: University of California Press.

Leonardo, Micaela di (1998) *Exotics at Home: Anthropology, Others, and American Modernity*. Chicago: University of Chicago Press.

Liebow, Elliot (1993) *Tell Them Who I Am: The Lives of Homeless Women*. New York: The Free Press.

Lofland, John (1971) *Analyzing Social Settings: A Guide to Qualitative Observation and Analysis*. Belmont, CA: Wadsworth.

Marcus, George and Fischer, Michael M.J. (1986) *Anthropology as Cultural Critique: An Experimental Moment in the Human Sciences*. Chicago: University of Chicago Press.

Maso, Ilja and Wester, Fred (eds) (1996) *The Deliberate Dialogue*. Brussels: VUB University Press.

Maynard, Douglas W. (1998) 'On qualitative inquiry and extramodernity', *Contemporary Sociology*, 27 (4): 343–5.

Mazeland, Harrie and ten Have, Paul (1996) 'Essential tensions in (semi-) open research interviews', in Ilja Maso and Fred Wester (eds), *The Deliberate Dialogue*. Brussels: VUB University Press. pp. 87–113.

McLaren, Peter (1992) 'Collisions with otherness: "traveling" theory, post-colonial criticism, and the politics of ethnographic practice – the mission of the wounded ethnographer', *Qualitative Studies in Education*, 5 (1): 77–92.

Mead, Margaret (1972) *Blackberry Winter: My Earlier Years*. New York: Morrow Press.

Michrina, Barry P. and Richards, Cherylanne (1996) *Person to Person: Fieldwork, Dialogue, and the Hermeneutic Method*. Albany, NY: State University of New York Press.

Mies, Maria (1983) 'Towards a methodology for feminist research', in Gloria Bowles and Renate D. Klein (eds), *Theories of Women's Studies*. London: Routledge and Kegan Paul.

Mishler, Eliot G. (1986) *Research Interviewing: Context and Narrative*. Cambridge, MA: Harvard University Press.

Myerhoff, Barbara (1994) *Number Our Days: Culture and Community among Elderly Jews in an American Ghetto*. New York: Meridan.

Naples, Nancy A. (1998) 'Traversing the new frontier of qualitative methodology', *Contemporary Sociology*, 27 (4): 345–7.

Narayan, Kirin (1993) 'How native is a "native" anthropologist?', *American Anthropologist*, 95: 671–86.

Nielsen, Joyce McCarl (ed.) (1990) *Feminist Research Methods: Exemplary Readings in the Social Sciences*. Boulder, CO: Westview Press.

Nussbaum, Emily (1998) 'Return of the natives: what happens when an anthropologist's manuscript is edited by his subjects?', *Lingua Franca*, 1998: 53–6.

Olesen, Virginia (1994) 'Feminisms and models of qualitative research', in Norman K. Denzin and Yvonna S. Lincoln (eds), *Handbook of Qualitative Research*. Thousand Oaks, CA: Sage Publications. pp. 158–74.

Opie, Anne (1992) 'Qualitative research, appropriation of the "other" and empowerment', *Feminist Review*, 40: 52–69.

Paget, Marianne A. (1983) 'Experience and knowledge', *Human Studies*, 6: 67–90.

Park, Robert E. (1950) 'An autobiographical note', in *Race and Culture*. Glencoe, IL: The Free Press. pp. v–ix.

Poland, Blake and Pederson, Ann (1998) 'Reading between the lines: interpreting silences in qualitative research', *Qualitative Inquiry*, 4 (2): 293–312.

Pool, Ithiel de Sola (1957) 'A critique of the twentieth anniversary issue', *Public Opinion Quarterly*, 21: 190–8.

Prus, Robert (1998) 'The new language of qualitative method: enabling device or dialectics of obscurity?', *Contemporary Sociology*, 27 (4): 347–9.

Reason, Peter (1994) 'Three approaches to participatory inquiry', in Norman K. Denzin and Yvonna S. Lincoln (eds), *Handbook of Qualitative Research*. Thousand Oaks, CA: Sage. pp. 324–39.

Reinharz, Shulamit (1983) 'Experiential research: a contribution to feminist research', in G. Bowles and R. Klein (eds), *Theories of Women's Studies*. London: Routledge and Kegan Paul. pp. 162–90.

Reinharz, Shulamit (1992) *Feminist Methods in Social Research*. New York: Oxford University Press.

Richardson, Laurel (1992) 'Trash on the corner: ethics and technology', *Journal of Contemporary Ethnography*, 21: 103–19.

Roberts, Helen (ed.) (1981) *Doing Feminist Research*. London: Routledge and Kegan Paul.

Roman, Leslie (1993) 'Double exposure: the politics of feminist materialist ethnography', *Educational Theory*, 43 (3): 279–308.

Rothman, Barbara Katz (1986) 'Reflections: on hard work', *Qualitative Sociology*, 9: 48–53.

Rubin, Herbert J. and Rubin, Irene S. (1995) *Qualitative Interviewing: The Art of Hearing Data*. Thousand Oaks, CA: Sage.

Ryan, K.E. (1995) 'Evaluation ethics and issues of social justice: contributions from female moral thinking', in Norman K. Denzin (ed.), *Studies in Symbolic Interaction: A Research Annual*, vol. 19. Greenwich, CT: JAI Press. pp. 143–51.

Said, Edward (1979) *Orientalism*. New York: Random House.

Schatzman, Leonard and Strauss, Anselm (1973) *Field Research*. Englewood Cliffs, NJ: Prentice–Hall.

Scheurich, James Joseph (1995) 'A postmodernist critique of research interviewing', *Qualitative Studies in Education*, 8 (3): 239–52.

Schmitt, Raymond L. (1990) 'Postscript: an adaptable strategy for optimizing the effectiveness of insider evaluations of an ethnography', in Norman K. Denzin (ed.), *Studies in Symbolic Interaction*, vol. 11. Greenwich, CT: JAI Press. pp. 241–53.

Shokeid, Moshe (1997) 'Negotiating multiple viewpoints: the cook, the native, the publisher, and the ethnographic text', *Current Anthropology*, 38 (4): 631–45.

Shostak, M. (1981) *Nisa: The Life and Words of a !Kung Woman*. Cambridge, MA: Harvard University Press.

Silverman, David (1993) *Interpreting Qualitative Data: Methods for Analysing Talk, Text and Interaction*. London: Sage.

Smaling, Adri (1996) 'Qualitative interviewing: contextualization and empowerment', in Ilja Maso and Fred Wester (eds), *The Deliberate Dialogue*. Brussels: VUB University Press. pp. 15–28.

Smith, Sidonie and Watson, Julia (eds) (1992) *De/Colonizing the Subject: The Politics of Gender in Women's Autobiography*. Minneapolis: University of Minnesota Press.

Spradley, James P. (1979) *The Ethnographic Interview.* Orlando, FL: Harcourt Brace Jovanovich.

Stacey, Judith (1988) 'Can there be a feminist ethnography?', *Women's Studies International Forum*, 11 (1): 21–7.

Strauss, Anselm L. (1969) *Mirrors and Masks: The Search for Identity.* San Francisco, CA: The Sociology Press.

Strauss, Anselm and Corbin, Juliet (1990) *Basics of Qualitative Research: Grounded Theory Procedure and Techniques.* Newbury Park, CA: Sage.

Thomas, Jim (1993) *Doing Critical Ethnography.* Newbury Park, CA: Sage.

Warren, Carol A.B. (1988) *Gender Issues in Field Research.* Newbury Park, CA: Sage.

Wasserfall, Rahel R. (1997) 'Reflexivity, feminism, and difference', in Rosanna Hertz (ed.), *Reflexivity and Voice.* Thousand Oaks, CA: Sage.

Weiss, Robert (1993) *Learning from Strangers: The Art and Method of Qualitative Interview Studies.* New York: The Free Press.

Whyte, W., Greenwood, D. and Lazes, P. (1989) 'Participatory action research', *American Behavioral Scientist*, 32: 513–51.

Williams, Brett (1988) *Upscaling Downtown: Stalled Gentrification in Washington, DC.* Ithaca, NY: Cornell University Press.

Wolcott, Harry F. (1982) 'Differing styles of on-site research, or, "If it isn't ethnography, what is it?"', *Review Journal of Philosophy and Social Sciences*, 7 (1, 2): 154–69.

Wolcott, Harry F. (1995) *The Art of Fieldwork.* Walnut Creek, CA: AltaMira Press.

Woolgar, Steve (1988a) 'Reflexivity is the ethnographer of the text', in Steve Woolgar (ed.), *Knowledge and Reflexivity: New Frontiers in the Sociology of Knowledge.* London: Sage.

Woolgar, Steve (ed.) (1988b) *Knowledge and Reflexivity: New Frontiers in the Sociology of Knowledge.* London: Sage.

26

Narrative Analysis in Ethnography

MARTIN CORTAZZI

There is increasing recognition of the importance and usefulness of narrative analysis as an element of doing ethnography. This is hardly surprising. Narrative is now seen as one of the fundamental ways in which humans organize their understanding of the world. Most social science and human disciplines have recently turned to narrative analysis for the human involvement in reporting and evaluating experience (Cortazzi, 1993; Polkinghorne, 1988; Riessman, 1993; Toolan, 1988). Narrating is, after all, a major means of making sense of past experience and sharing it with others. Most narratives are told about things which, at one level or another, matter to the teller and audience. Therefore, a careful analysis of the topics, content, style, context and telling of narratives told by individuals or groups under ethnographic study should, in principle, give researchers access to tellers' understandings of the meanings of key events in their lives, communities or cultural contexts. This is to analyse narrative as text or product, but narrative can also be analysed as a social process or performance in action. Narrating can be considered an interactive process of jointly constructing and interpreting experience with others, therefore narrative analysis is potentially a means of examining participant roles in constructing accounts and in negotiating perspectives and meanings (Edwards, 1997). Both these orientations to narrative – as text and as process – can inform reflexive analyses of various stages of doing ethnography.

The term 'narrative' covers a variety of understandings and a range of types of talk and text. At its most abstract, the term is used to refer to structures of knowledge and storied ways of knowing. Oral narrative genres include recounts describing past events, reports which may be more explanatory, anecdotes and stories of personal experiences,

news and media stories, folktales and urban or traditional myths and legends, occupational stories reflecting professional beliefs and practices, oral histories told by different tellers about the same events. Generally, these narratives are highly structured, reportable ways of talking about the past with an understood chronology. Written genres include transcriptions or summaries of oral narratives, and respondent diaries, logs, journals, quoted incidents in case studies and other research accounts. Narratives will form a key element in life stories, biographies, and historical accounts, though these also draw on other forms of documentation. While these are predominantly verbal and factual accounts there is a role for the narrative analysis of film, dance, song, poetry, fiction or fantasy in ethnography where they are influential on social practices. Commonly, narrative is mixed and blended into other genres. This is seen when narrative frames or forms significant parts of the write-ups of ethnographic research itself.

Narrative analysis can be used for systematic interpretations of others' interpretations of events. This can be an especially powerful research tool if the narratives are accounts of epiphanic moments, crises, or significant incidents in people's lives, relationships or careers. Every narrative is a version or view of what happened. Most narratives do not simply report events but rather give a teller's perspective on their meaning, relevance and importance. This perspective can often be seen in structural analysis by dividing the parts of a narrative into at least three major structural categories: an event structure, which reports happenings; a description structure, which gives background information on time, place, people and context necessary to understand the narrative; and an evaluation structure, which shows the point of telling the narrative by presenting the speaker's perspective or judgement on the events, marking off the most important part. This is elaborated in several models of narrative analysis (Labov, 1972; Linde, 1993; Polanyi, 1989) (see below). By collecting and analysing a number of narratives from one or more informants it should be possible to distil the tellers' perspectives on the events recounted or on particular themes or processes. Narrative analysis gives a researcher access to the textual interpretative world of the teller, which presumably in some way mediates or manages reality. Narrative analysis is therefore a useful research tool to complement the use of other ethnographic research strategies.

However, simply analysing narrative structures or contents is not sufficient in ethnographic research. Account needs to be taken of the functions of particular narratives, the cultural conventions and the contexts within which they occur; together with the speaker's motive and intention, these construct the meaning for the teller. Since narratives are interactive, occasioned tellings, it is also crucial to consider performance aspects and how narratives do social work among participants in speech events. This may mean that narratives given in interviews differ from those that emerge in ordinary conversation or in ceremonial events. Such functional, contextual, performative aspects of narrative have implications for a rationale of narrative analysis. Before outlining a rationale, a narrative example is given which will be discussed at several points below.

AN EXAMPLE OF A NARRATIVE

This example comes from a study of racism and corporate discourse (Van Dijk, 1993: 152–3). A manager (M) of a supermarket chain in Holland recounted to an interviewer (I) how his board had agreed to allow Muslim women cashiers to wear scarves at work. He had previously denied that there was any discrimination among the company personnel.

> *M:* I know one of our stores, where someone like that was offered by the employment agency, like, 'we have someone who could work for you, it is a fundamentalist Muslim who wears one of those scarves'. And then the store manager he got his personnel together, his own personnel in the canteen, and they had a discussion about that, shall we do it or won't we. Personnel said, yes, what are we fussing about, it is so difficult to get people, and we can't bypass someone like that. That would be very stupid. And he said, 'Let her come'. And she also worked at the cash register, and … the customers stayed away. They did not queue up at her cash, but at the others.
>
> *I:* Even after a while, when they got used to it?
>
> *M:* Yes, and then, well, then they said … and there was rather a big perceptible difference it was, a marked

difference, for the other customers. Then the manager, who panicked, again got his employees together, and again had discussions about, come and have a look at what's happening. And again the employees said, we should not be put off, we go on with this, and then those women should stay away, we don't care, and then they persisted and after some time she got other, so there were other customers, I don't know, or the same customers, who went to her, and it was quite a bright girl, it was really a very good girl.

The manager concludes this story of his organization's affirmative action and discrimination by customers by explaining that the employee was extraordinarily friendly with the customers yet some customers threw the money on the floor instead of handing it to the cashier. Also she was still being taken to work by her father ('that was really quite a different culture'). He continues with a second episode about the store manager's effort to promote the cashier.

> *M:* He wanted that she would go to work as a supervisor, because she was simply a very good girl. But then he really had to, because in that case she would have to be transferred to another store, but that man went to great lengths, also in these meetings with his personnel, with his supervisors to get this settled, that she would be transferred. Yes, and then she nearly had to be sanctified, and he got away with that, but what happens, as usual, she is taking a vacation in Turkey, stays away for 4 weeks, and she doesn't come back.
>
> *I:* That is not exactly inspiring.
>
> *M:* Yes, but you have to place yourself in the position of that manager, how he feels. Damn it! Then you think, then he thinks, he thinks, this is once, but never more. Why did I go through all this trouble? … That shows how it is a very difficult matter, and that it is also very difficult to have people accept using different values and norms, that it is a very slow process, you have to do that very carefully, but at the same time not evade it.

A RATIONALE FOR NARRATIVE ANALYSIS

Four major reasons for doing narrative analysis as part of ethnography can be suggested: concern with the meaning of experience, voice, human qualities on personal or professional dimensions, and research as a story.

The first reason is that narratives share *the meaning of experience*. That is, in recounting events in narratives, tellers also directly or indirectly give their own interpretations and explanations of those events. They also evaluate, in their own terms, the principal people and others featuring in narratives, the meaning of events and wider relevant contexts. In the example above, the company is portrayed as an equal opportunities employer which employs members of ethnic minority groups despite the actions of some racist customers. This is not simply stated but is demonstrated and dramatized through narrative. The store manager is presented positively as someone who faces predicaments of outside discrimination against his staff and goes to great lengths to get good people from minorities promoted, yet finds that it is difficult to accept personnel from other cultures. The cashier's co-workers support the policy even when the manager panics. An extended analysis of the story should probably relate it to other narratives, discourses and schemata of racism (Van Dijk, 1987).

The importance of this interpretative aspect is underlined by a variety of representative definitions and epithets used to describe narratives in a range of research contexts. Thus Polkinghorne (1988: 11), in a careful examination of the nature of narrative in history, literature and the cognitive and social sciences, defines narrative as 'the primary scheme by means of which human existence is rendered meaningful'. Bruner (1990: 35), in the context of his work in autobiography, psychology and education, defines narrative as the 'organizing principle' by which 'people organize their experience in, knowledge about, and transactions with the social world'. Bruner (1986) has also made the influential distinction between *paradigmatic* and *narrative* cognition; the former involves categorizing and classifying the world, while the latter involves interpreting, showing the significance, and creating explanations for experience. In media studies, Branigan (1992: 3) has defined narrative as 'a perceptual activity that organizes data into a special pattern which represents and explains experience', while Chafe (1990: 79) in linguistics has argued that narratives are 'overt manifestations of the mind in action: as windows to both the content of the mind and its ongoing operations'. From these perspectives, narrative research offers the possibility of allowing a fairly immediate investigation into the organization of social and cognitive interpretations, whether the focus is on the process of interpretation or on the events interpreted. If, as White (1981) claims, narratives translate knowing into telling (so that to tell is to come to know), then to carry out research through narrative analysis is to look at the telling to get back to the ways of knowing and ways of experiencing. This emphasis on experience is justified by the event-centred nature of narrative and its personal involvement, which is held to be understandable by others. Thus Zeller (1995: 75), discussing case reports, cites many researchers who explore narrative 'as a mode of communication more resonant with human experience than traditional social science rhetoric and, thus, inherently more understandable'. Goodson (1995: 89), focusing on teacher education, similarly stresses how narrative research genres 'have the potential for

advancing educational research in representing the lived experience of schooling'.

This concern with the representation of experience is related to a second reason for carrying out narrative analysis, which is the representation of *voice*, that is, the sharing of the experience of particular groups, so that others may know life as they know it. In the supermarket story, we hear the corporate voice of the personnel manager and, implicitly, the voice of the store manager who probably recounted the events to personnel. This concept of voice has overtones of a felt need for certain groups to be heard, so that narrative research may adopt an interventionist stance of advocacy from, say, a feminist or ethnic minority perspective. In the example, the voice of the cashier is notably absent, as are the views of other employees or those of the customers; however, further narrative data with interpretations from these key participants might be juxtaposed with the example in hand. In professional or occupational contexts paying attention to voice gives importance to sharing the meaning of experience of less-heard groups with other colleagues, or with decision-makers and the public at large. In educational research, for example, there is a strong movement to develop approaches to educational biography (Erben, 1998; Goodson, 1992; Goodson and Walker, 1991), teachers' stories (Jalongo and Isenberg, 1995; McLaughlin and Tierney, 1993; Nelson, 1993; Thomas, 1995; Trimmer, 1997), teacher's careers (Huberman, 1993), and what might be called educational narratology (McEwan and Egan, 1995; Witherell and Noddings, 1991) to allow the voices of teachers and, less often, of learners to be heard. This movement partly aims to explore participants' personal and professional identities and factors which, in narrative, are seen to be formative. At the same time, the act of narrating, for example, when pre-service teachers tell of early experiences, is also itself formative since it is part of the social construction processes of professional identity and self-understanding (Rosenwald and Ochberg, 1992). Narrative and its analysis is therefore a feature of professional development. The concern with voice and biography is related to how key events are significant not only for the teller but for other groups and in relation to social and research issues.

The publicizing aspect of voice is related to a third reason for conducting narrative research, which is to give higher public profiles to *human qualities*, often to reveal crucial, but probably generally unappreciated, personal and professional qualities involved in many occupations and professions. Essentially, narrative analysis can be used to portray the insider's view of what a particular job is 'really' like. In the supermarket example, the manager's panic, persistence and frustration are shown, as are the supposed difficulties of putting policies into practice. Yet the story also gives some (unintended) insight into a lack of understanding of religious customs (the cashier is 'a fundamentalist' who 'wears one of those scarves') and incomprehension (at the employee's failure to reappear). Attempts at human portrayal through narrative include Fletcher's (1991) study of American police, Cortazzi's (1991) study of British primary-school teachers, and Myerhoff's (1978) work with elderly Jewish Americans. This ethnographic concern emerges partly in the details of event description but mostly in the evaluations of stories, which may stress such humane values as love, dedication, patience, enthusiasm, sacrifice, struggle through hard work, and humour. An appreciation of such qualities emerges in narrative analysis perhaps more than in other ethnographic methods. It is often evident in the tone of a narrative or is conveyed non-verbally in gesture and facial expression, but also in prosodic and paralinguistic features of communication, such as intonation, pitch and voice quality.

This effort to feature the human interest through narrative research also relates to a fourth reason, which is to see ethnographic research itself *as a story*. This means that readers of ethnographic reports and those who write up such research need to be aware, at a metanarrative level, of how ethnography is often constructed as a narrative account of a quest, discovery and interpretation – the journey from outsider to insider – using story conventions to persuade readers effectively (Atkinson, 1990; Golden-Biddle and Locke, 1997; Polkinghorne, 1995). This calls for reflexivity in a kind of narrative self-research to recognize this narrative plotting and any autobiographical elements in narrative research which are not apparently autobiographical (Okely and Callaway, 1992; Swindells, 1995). Ethnographers make stories; they construct meanings as co-authors in the relaying and interpreting of informants' accounts (Mishler, 1995), but there are problematic elements and ethical dilemmas in how the story is told and how the author and participants are represented and credited (Van Maanen, 1988, 1995).

SOME FUNCTIONS OF NARRATIVES

Narratives are one of the most frequently occurring and ubiquitous forms of discourse but they have a variety of functions. Particular functions shape the structure of any set of narratives and arguably the structures cannot be understood by an analyst without considering what exactly the narratives are doing: socially, psychologically, culturally and so on. Stories of personal experiences, for example, crop up repeatedly in informal conversation, in doctor–patient talk, in the proceedings of law courts, in therapeutic and counselling discourse, in media reporting and in research interviews. These narratives do not only have the function of conveying news or information. Some will have the problem-solving functions of enabling the audience – a medical practitioner or counsellor, for example – to diagnose a problem or clarify a situation for a patient or client. In some social contexts, like focus group meetings, stories may help a group to define an issue or a collective stance towards it. In other contexts, the narratives of salespersons or witnesses are told as evidence or testimony as part of, or substitute for, argument; such narratives are designed to persuade but courtroom narratives are orchestrated by others and the teller may not be fully aware of the underlying intent of the person who elicits the story.

In the supermarket narrative, the teller is reporting events in order to present a positive image of his company. The narrative is given as evidence in an argument to show social responsibility and openness to change, to elicit positive evaluations about company recruitment and promotion practices; any problems with this are imputed to outsiders (racist customers or people of a different culture). The account is designed to give credibility.

In other contexts, telling stories of personal experience is a way of looking at the past and evaluating it. The narratives told in support groups such as Alcoholics Anonymous may not be news to the audience but they confirm the audience's own stories. The narratives help not only the teller but also the hearers to understand their own experience and, perhaps, to overcome it. Occupational stories are not only told in professional and training contexts as exemplars for novices but also to entertain, to express rapport and solidarity, to ratify group membership, to convey collective values and a sense of history and progress. This social transmission of experience through narrative therefore has an institutional role in the continuity and reproduction of organizations, communities and cultures. What matters is the function in relation to both teller and the audience. The same story given to different audiences can have different purposes. Thus, in medical contexts, Hunter (1991) sees stories as repositories of medical knowledge but also advocates narratives told to doctors to provoke ethical reflection in practitioners and as means to help doctors confront pain and suffering. Kleinman's (1988) and Garro's (1992) ethnographic accounts enable health care practitioners to enter the patient's cultural world to understand how chronic illness disrupts life. Here stories function in professional training. Erickson (Rosen, 1991) as a therapist retold patient's tales to other patients so that they would see their own situation in a new way – stories were the treatment. Other ethnographic studies (Good, 1995; Mattingly, 1998; Mattingly and Garro, 1994) show how chronically ill patients and doctors or therapists co-construct clinical narratives in the mid-stream of therapy to create desire, instil hope and plan the next steps; these 'therapeutic emplotments' reframe perceptions and experiences of illness with the function of projecting future action. Some narratives, such as parables, mystic tales and proverbial stories, can exercise social and moral control by provoking analogical reflective thinking. An ethnographer hearing stories, or rehearing them in recordings, needs to reflect carefully on their functions before coming to narrative conclusions.

Narrative also has an individual or collective role in the formation and maintenance of identity. Through life stories individuals and groups make sense of themselves; they tell what they are or what they wish to be, as they tell so they become, they *are* their stories. The supermarket story is the kind of institutional tale which might become embedded in management circles as an exemplar of attempting to put policy into practice, a part of institutional identity. Or it may bolster the professional self of the teller – as person or as personnel – as might be seen in the slippage into his own and others' relayed attributions and personal interpretations ('fundamentalist', 'a very good girl', 'those women', 'as usual ... she doesn't come back', 'Damn it! Then you think ... this is once, but never more').

All this means that narrative analysis can be a method to develop an understanding of the meanings people themselves give to themselves, to their lives and to their contexts. Because narratives occur frequently and naturally, they should, in principle, be easy to gather, whether they are elicited in research interviews or conversations, told incidentally to a researcher or others as part of some other activity, overheard in participant observation or read in other discourses. However, as the range of functions of narratives outlined above indicates, it is important for researchers to be aware of the likely functions of the particular narratives under investigation since these functions relate to the teller's motivation and affect the structure, content and style of the story. A narrative told in a research interview may not be the same at all as a narrative told by the same person, and reporting roughly the same events, told in a conversation among peers. Stories and accounts are shaped by the teller's perception of the audience and of ongoing interaction, but this is not necessarily a single perception. Most narratives are multifunctional.

The Elements of Narrative Context

On the face of it, narrative analysis could consist of a content analysis of whatever stories are to hand. Since narratives can be about any topic, the strategy of collecting stories and accounts on a topic which is of research interest may be useful. An outline of the elements of the common context of narratives, however, indicates that a simple content analysis will miss many of the contextual complications which make narrative analysis more difficult yet perhaps more rewarding as a research tool in ethnography. Context is not only an issue for the analyst but also for narrators. It is therefore vital to consider the elements of narrative context.

A full narrative will, by definition, involve an *event* or series of events (what happened or what is presumed to have happened in the past), *experiences* (the images, reactions, feelings and meanings ascribed to recounted events) and the *narrative* (the linguistic – or perhaps visual or musical – form of the telling of the events). A narrative gives coherence to experiences by plotting them in time and place, and often interpreting them in terms of causality, teleology or rationalization. The elements of narrative analysis therefore not only involve stories, variously defined, and their content as units of analysis, but other elements too, which take account of an ethnographic regard for a holistic concern with context and integral aspects of cultural interpretation. Besides the actual story – *the told* – other elements include the *teller*, and the *audience*, and their respective *relationships* to each other and to the told.

How the teller sees this context and how this affects a narrative trajectory is further mediated by preceding non-narrative talk. This talk can be quite crucial (and this is an argument for not being too hasty to isolate narratives in transcripts), given the current sociolinguistic understanding that context is socially constructed and sustained interactionally (Duranti and Goodwin, 1992). Essentially, this means that participants and their talk are part of the context, and that while talk relies partly on context it also contributes to it, shaping both later talk and context. Hence, talk is the context and medium for narrative but any narrative is itself formative for the subsequent context and talk, including later narratives.

The *researcher* might be a person other than the immediate audience at the time of telling, or, if it is the same person then it is the same person later in time, and quite probably, with other, more analytic, concerns than the audience hearing a story. Similarly, the teller may be a separate person from a *principal* figure in the story, either because the story is about others or because the teller as principal is the same person later in time, quite possibly with different concerns as teller now to the person in the story then. These relationships indicate that a further element of *the telling* may also be more complex than it may initially appear to be, for three reasons. First, because the story is generally about a past event but rarely simply replays the chronology of the past as it occurred. Rather, in the interests of being newsworthy or tellable, events are selected, compressed, shaped, recreated and reconstructed for the occasion of the telling. This presentation is, of course, affected by processes of memory, too, which are themselves shaped by perceptions then and later retrospective interpretations and current concerns of the teller (Neisser, 1982). This effectively doubles the interpretive aspect of a narrative from the teller's point of view: it concerns both interpretations made at the time of the events and those made later in or through the telling. This latter kind of interpretation means that narratives in interviews are a dialogue between past and present; the present telling is also a dialogue between teller and audience (Briggs, 1986). A second reason for the complexity of the telling is that many narratives are also affected by performance factors, such as the dramatizing of the telling for entertainment or audience interest, to make a good story, or by features connected with the teller's presentation of self to project an image, including the image of being a good narrator (Bauman, 1986). A third complexity is that there are cultural variations in both narrative structures or forms and in ways of telling, including performance. Cross-culturally, unacknowledged variations can lead to quite different perceptions of a narrative, to distortions to the received story, or even to whether an intended narrative is recognized as being such (Brumble, 1990; Sarris, 1993; Scollon and Scollon, 1981).

Context as a key element in narrative is at once an aspect relating to each of the other elements (the context of: the told, the teller, the principal, the audience, the researcher, the telling) and to the combination of all of them and their relation to wider social, institutional, historical and other broader contexts. A focus of interest in much narrative analysis, such as life histories, is precisely to explore relationships between events and the individuals prominent in them and such wider contexts.

In addition to the elements outlined above, the research process is also part of the context of narrative analysis (Riessman, 1993). As a minimum, this involves key stages of perception, transformation and interpretation of narrative events. The teller perceives (sees, hears of, takes part in) a stream of events, probably involving complex interactions, some of which are selectively remembered or reconstructed for some reason, before they are interpreted and fashioned into a narrative format which is told to some audience for some purpose. The telling is mediated by this audience (see below). A researcher, who may not have been present in, or who knows little of, the original events, listens to a recording of the story and transcribes it (or overhears it, takes field notes and reconstructs it later). After this transformation (or even interpretation, given the loss of non-verbal and performance information) the analyst selects, categorizes, analyses, interprets the data with much re-reading and, therefore, re-interpreting. In conjunction with other narratives or other data sources, an overall meaning or interpretation is constructed. With due critical reflection, and in the light of whatever research purpose and theoretical frameworks are in hand, including models of narrative, the results are then written up and shaped for some further audience, perhaps in a narrative format. This is a linear account but it is more likely recursive in a sequence of interviews perhaps divided into life cycle stages (Atkinson, 1998). It may be mediated by other academic processes such as ongoing reading, talking or teaching. It might be further mediated by checking interpretations with the informants, often some time after the original telling, by showing a written version of what was said in interaction. This apparently simple confirmation challenges the informant to recall both the experience and the told, both the interaction and the telling, besides overcoming any reluctance to relinquish what may be heartfelt experience to anonymous outside readers.

Narrative research in ethnography is clearly complex. It is multi-layered in interpretation. There is no simple transmission from teller to researcher. There are difficulties in maintaining text integrity and teller's intentions. There are further complex relations concerning readers of the analysis (Denzin, 1997) who may presume that the interpretation, like the transcript, is somehow fixed in a permanent interaction-less present tense. A major problem for the analyst is how much context is needed to understand a story (depending on purpose). A saving grace here is the fortunate fact that it is a key characteristic of narratives that tellers generally provide a sufficient minimum context (in the sense of background information concerning the events) within the narrative itself to enable it to be understood (depending on the teller's perception of audience knowledge and topical relevance). A parallel problem is how much context the researcher should provide for the reader and how to be sure that instances of narrative are representative. There are clearly many potential gaps in contextual knowledge between experience – narrative – analysis – reading.

NARRATIVES IN INTERVIEWS AND CONVERSATIONS

Some narratives may be found in the literature or non-narrative research documents. Others might be noted as overheard or told in general conversation. While many narratives can certainly be gathered in this way there is no guarantee that any topics or themes relating to a research focus will arise. For this reason many ethnographic researchers rely on interviews as a context in which to gather stories.

To get a sense of the narrative workings of interviews it is worth reflecting on how interviews are communicative events in which asymmetric roles and speaking rights are normally assigned to participants (Mishler, 1986). It cannot be assumed, especially across cultures, that all participants have the same understanding of this. Thus interviewers ask questions and what interviewees say is construed as answers. A narrative, as an answer, ensures an uninterrupted turn once started, although some interviewers cut off narratives or discard them from data sets in the belief that they are merely anecdotal. This is evidently a mistake from several points of view, given the rationale outlined earlier. As answers, narratives are crucially shaped by questions; a different question might lead to a quite different narrative or to none at all. Some interviewees use narratives to avoid other kinds of answers or to satisfy the interviewer, even if the narrative is quite untrue (Sarris, 1993: 254).

As part of a communicative event, a narrative is likely to reflect the history of the developing interview discourse. This includes the interviewer's feedback to previous responses ('OK. Good. Uh-huh.') through which the respondent progressively interprets not only how a previous answer was evaluated but what sort of answers the interviewer expects. That interviewees seek such evaluation is indicated by such metacomments as 'Is this what you want?' or 'Have I answered your question?' This can, of course, work in favour of eliciting narratives but it should be recognized how the narrative is, in fact, jointly constructed in interviews (or other kinds of talk). Narratives are not simply answers. They are not pre-packaged inside the person of the respondent, waiting to be expressed in response to the eliciting stimulus of a question. They are interactive co-productions (Lieblich et al., 1998; Mishler, 1997).

This point can be elaborated with reference to the Conversational Analysis model of narrative analysis. This model, based on the work of the sociologist Sacks, is particularly useful to see how stories are woven into the texture of talk (Cortazzi, 1993; Nofsinger, 1991; Psathas, 1995). A conversational narrative is often framed in 'adjacency pairs'. These are pairs of utterances, produced successively by different speakers, which form an identifiable sequence (question–answer; complaint–apology). Given the first, the second is expected; when the second arises, it is interpreted as completing the first. Such pairs can build up larger sequences. A narrative is often preceded by such a pair: a 'proposal' to tell a story ('Did you hear about the time when ... ') and an 'acceptance' to hear it ('No, do go on.') Silence also signifies acceptance. The narrative itself is often paired with a following 'receipt', some utterance (or a nod, a smile or commiserating groan) which shows that, and how, the story was understood. Silence here probably signals non-acceptance. A second story from another speaker is itself a receipt of a first, and so the chain may continue, with each story bettering the previous one in some way.

This model illustrates some of the mechanisms of joint story construction. It further shows how a skilful interviewer who is aware of such systems can indirectly elicit narratives but may also be involved in shaping them. An interviewer can obtain interviewee narratives by telling a story first. The model helps analysts to understand how stories are co-constructed or co-narrated, not only in interviews but in group settings, such as committee meetings or family mealtimes (Ochs et al., 1996; Tannen, 1984).

This also raises some wider issues. It problematizes the common understanding of an interview as a question and answer sequence with a carefully controlled interviewer role (Briggs, 1986; Mishler, 1986). In fact, from the narrative perspective, if the interview is controlled narratives tend to be less natural or conversational and hence less authentic. It provokes the question of who, in fact, tells a story, especially in groups. If the story belongs to the group then this tends to validate the meanings and evaluations in the story. However, this in turn raises fundamental questions of ownership, authorship and voice, and what the role of the researcher might be. Accounting for conversational narratives is not easy. It is noticeable how some of these issues also apply to written narratives, such as teachers' stories written as part of professional courses, once the interactive context of their genesis is examined.

A further issue is that of performance. Many narratives are performed or dramatized with voice, expression, gestures and particular grammatical features. This is seen in the supermarket story, for example in the teller's exclamation ('Damn it') and the switch to the narrative present tense ('he thinks') rather than the simple past (he thought) in the attribution of the moral of the story to the manager ('never more. Why did I go through all this trouble?'). Such performance features often give a rhetorical underlining to the point of the story. Wolfson (1982) argued that whereas conversational narratives are performed those told in interviews are not. This would be an important distinction since performance may imply that norms of evaluative interpretation are shared between teller and audience and that therefore a conversational narrative is a fuller form in which to share the meanings of experience, while interview narratives tend to become reports or summaries. However, this depends on the nature of the interview. Hymes (1981) found that direct questions or imperatives to Native Americans ('Tell me all the stories you know about .... ') elicited summaries only but that more culturally appropriate means led informants to tell fully performed stories. Cortazzi (1991) found that some questions in interviews ('What was the best time ... ?'; 'What is the funniest thing that has happened?') elicited performed narratives, partly because the interviewer, like the tellers, was a teacher. While performance may be a criterion for a full narrative, the real issue is to examine the nature of the performance, to see how it may be mutually signalled and developed, and to appreciate the extent to which narrative meaning is in the performance (Bauman, 1986; Briggs, 1986). As Denzin (1997) argues, the performance text is the most powerful way for ethnography to recover yet interrogate the meanings of lived experience. This means that the cultural meanings of the original performance of a narrative cannot entirely be captured by most analyses. The analysis of such texts and its reporting in conventional formats arguably needs to include a re-telling or, better, a re-performing. This is a telling point, for culture is performance; it is a verb as much as a noun.

MODELS OF NARRATIVE ANALYSIS

One of the best-known models for analysing oral narrative is the sociolinguistically oriented model of Labov (1972). This examines narrative structures in relation to social functions but does not consider the conversational context as Conversational Analysis does (Cortazzi, 1993; Linde, 1993; Toolan, 1988). Labov's model has also been used for analysing written narrative.

Labov suggests a six-part structure: an *abstract* to summarize the point or state a general proposition which the narrative will exemplify; an *orientation* to give details of time, place, persons and situation; a *complication* to give the main event sequence and show a crisis, problem or turning point; an *evaluation* to highlight the point, marking out from the rest; a *resolution* to show the result or solution to the complication; and a *coda* to finish the story. These elements can occur in various sequences and combinations. The evaluation can occur anywhere and it can overlap with other parts, since it is a rhetorical underlining of the narrative's meaning (and hence a major focus of analysis). It is realized by a wide variety of syntactic and prosodic devices which make it stand out from the rest of the narrative (Labov, 1972; Linde, 1993; Peterson and McCabe, 1983; Polanyi, 1989).

The supermarket story could be analysed as having the following narrative structure (after Van Dijk, 1993: 153–4):

Abstract: This is an example of discrimination.
Orientation: Hiring personnel in one of the supermarkets.
Complication 1: One applicant is a Muslim fundamentalist who wears a scarf.
Resolution 1: Personnel agreed to hire her; management allowed her to wear the scarf.
Complication 2: Some customers avoided her; one threw money on the floor.
Resolution 2: Personnel decided to keep her and ignored the discriminatory acts.

Evaluation 1: She was a very good and friendly employee.
Orientation 2: The manager did his best to get her promoted.
Complication 3: She went to Turkey and did not come back.
Evaluation 2: The manager was very frustrated.
Evaluation 3: It is very difficult to have personnel from a different culture.

As this example might show, some analyses may need a contextual expansion and further interpretation, which depends on some familiarity with the situation (Labov and Fanshel, 1977). Such expansion fits an ethnographic stance and quest for teller's meanings. Polanyi (1989) has extended Labov's model in a cultural direction by giving close attention to information foregrounded in the telling by evaluation and using lengthy expansions to show culturally salient values and beliefs by asking what is interesting and worthy of narration. Linde (1993) extends the model to life stories by seeing how evaluation partly expresses the sense of self and defines relationships and group membership.

Other culturally orientated models include Longacre's (1976) and Grimes' (1975, 1978), which have been used to show enormous cultural diversity of narrative structures around the world (Brewer, 1985). Longacre's model includes six parts: an *aperture*, which is an optional formulaic opening; the *stage*, which gives information about time, place and participants; a series of *episodes*, each of which may have sub-sections of an inciting moment which gets something going, a developing conflict which intensifies the situation, and a climax or resolution; a *denouement*, a crucial final event after the episodes; a *conclusion*, which gives optional narrator's comments or interpretations; and a *finish*, which is a formulaic closing. Marked attention is given by tellers to *peaks*, or main points, through paraphrase, repetition, grammatical shifts, dialogue and dramatization.

The choice of model for narrative analysis can make a difference. Hymes (1996: 168ff.), in a powerful account of narrative, takes up a story analysed by Labov (1972: 367). Where Labov had not found evaluation, Hymes uses narrative divisions into lines, verses, stanzas and scenes to seek an overall design of the story (see also Gee, 1996 for a version of this increasingly popular model). This ethnopoetic approach draws on anthropological studies. Hymes uses it to show that evaluation is, in fact, present in recurrent parallels and culminating segments. This shows that narrative analysis is not simply a matter of segmenting a story into narrative categories. It should also take into account rhythms and repetitions, and the overall patterning of the story. As argued earlier, it should also consider several levels of context.

Further ranges of models of narrative analysis are discussed, classified and exemplified by Bamberg (1997), Cortazzi (1993), Lieblich et al. (1998), Mishler (1995), Peterson and McCabe (1983), Riessman (1993), Toolan (1988). The choice of model should ultimately be determined by research purpose and the type of narratives in hand. The models mentioned here (of Sacks, Labov, Polanyi, Linde, Longacre, Grimes, Hymes and Gee) all have slightly different origins and emphases, but all are suitable for ethnographic enquiry.

A FURTHER EXAMPLE

The following example takes Carrithers' (1992: 92–116) ethnographic account of a story told among the Jain religious community in Maharashtra, India, but with an interpretation from Cortazzi and Jin (1999). Carrithers had asked a number of businessmen about the teachings of the Jain religion. In one such research interview in the office of a dealer in agricultural supplies, 'Mr P' was philosophizing at some length about key concepts when he was called out on a business matter. A shabby older man, 'Mr S', who had been sitting silently in a corner, then took up the discourse:

> This is a story my grandfather told me. This is very important. Write this down [pointing to the author's notebook]. There was a great man, a hero, a 'mahapurus', who lived right near here, and one time that man went out to the bulls. While [cleaning the dung out of the stalls] one of them stood on his hand. What did he do? He did nothing! He waited and waited, and finally the bull's owner came and saw what was happening! The owner struck the bull to make it move, and the great man told him to stop, that the bull did not understand! **That** is 'dharma' [true religion]. **That** is genuine 'jainadharma' [Jainism]! (Carrithers, 1992: 96)

Later Carrithers read this story in the printed biography of Siddhasaga, a local saint who lived about a hundred years ago. The evaluation in the narrative is easy to locate in the last two sentences, in which the word 'that' is twice heavily stressed, though it may be more problematic to say what this means exactly. Carrithers found that Europeans and Indians unsympathetic to the Jain religion thought the hero was insane or stupid to let an Indian bull (nearly two metres high at the shoulder) stand on his hand without protest. Their evaluation of the narrative is negative. But this evaluation is not that of those inside the culture. The narrative followed Mr P's explanation of 'ahimsa', the Jain teaching of harmlessness and non-violence. This central religious value includes vegetarianism, being truthful, having kindly speech and helping all beings. Hence, for the teller, the story portrays exemplary self-control and non-violence. In one sense, this

meaning of the story was given in advance by the preceding talk about ahimsa; without such cultural knowledge the story cannot be understood as intended. The researcher–informant relationship (with Mr P) had been negotiated as serious and was akin to a student–teacher relation. This was picked up by the overhearing Mr S. The setting of 'learning about religious truths' is a vital context which rules out negative evaluation as the insiders' meaning of the story. For teller and hearer the context of relationship and circumstance are part of the meaning.

The story performs other evaluative work. Since it followed a lengthy philosophical exposition, Carrithers thought (then and later) that the telling is informative in ways that logical argument is not. After the vehement words, 'That is genuine Jainism', it is as if the teller had added, 'and not what Mr P has been telling you'. The telling of deeds is thus implied criticism of the non-narrative exposition, but it is still a move in the overall argument.

To Carrithers, the ethnographer, this story within the lived experience of the teller's family gave him a different orientation to the flow of relationships and interactions in local villages. He began to understand 'how the local Jain world often reverberates with stories of great or minor deeds' (1992: 108); how it is through the responses to such stories that Jains themselves come to understand their cultural and religious heritage. Socialization takes place through hearers' evaluations of narratives. Telling such stories is a key part of the process of self-realization of individual and collective identity. Carrithers' report of this event in the ethnographic study is itself in a narrative format: through his narrative he understands, presents, and evaluates his research. His meta-evaluation of this story is: 'It is an ethnographic gem, the sort of illustration of the way of life that ethnographers happen across with pleasure and use in their books with immense satisfaction' (1992: 92).

While Carrithers did check the oral narrative with available printed texts, he does not say if he checked his understanding with local Jains. However, Dr Ramesh Mehta of the Jain Centre in Leicester, UK (personal communication, 1998) confirms that such stories are taught to children as part of moral and religious education to socialize them into Jain ways of thinking. Many such stories are embodied in statues and symbols in Jain temples, such as the one at Leicester. Mehta confirmed the foregoing evaluation as being essentially correct and added that the story embodies four levels of non-violence: in action (the saint doesn't push the bull away); in mind (he doesn't think badly about the bull); and in relation to others (he doesn't encourage the owner to push the bull away or for him to think badly of it); and in relation to his 'karma' (he endures the pain in silence to break the cycle of the effects of past actions in previous reincarnations). An understanding of these levels depends on the meaning of the key words in the story ('dharma' or religion and 'jainadharma' or Jainism) and the concept of 'ahimsa', which was woven into the pre-narrative text. This implies an interplay between linguistic and cultural meanings (of key terms) and sociocultural aspects of the context. The story embodies key cultural knowledge. To the ethnographer, the storytelling and his narrative analysis was an epiphanic moment in coming to understand participants' interpretations of this key cultural knowledge.

REFERENCES

Atkinson, P. (1990) *The Ethnographic Imagination: Textual Constructions of Reality*. London: Routledge.

Atkinson, R. (1998) *The Life Story Interview*. Thousand Oaks, CA: Sage.

Bamberg, M. (1997) *Narrative Development: Six Approaches*. Mahwah, NJ: Lawrence Erlbaum Associates.

Bauman, R. (1986) *Story, Performance and Event*. Cambridge: Cambridge University Press.

Branigan, E. (1992) *Narrative Comprehension and Film*. London: Routledge.

Brewer, W.F. (1985) 'The story schema: universal and culture specific properties', in D.A. Olsen, N. Torrance and A. Hildyard (eds), *Literacy, Language and Learning*. Cambridge: Cambridge University Press. pp. 167–94.

Briggs, C.L. (1986) *Learning How to Ask: A Sociolinguistic Appraisal of the Role of the Interview in Social Science Research*. Cambridge: Cambridge University Press.

Brumble, H.D. (1990) *American Indian Autobiography*. Berkeley, CA: University of California Press.

Bruner, J. (1986) *Actual Minds, Possible Worlds*. Cambridge, MA: Harvard University Press.

Bruner, J. (1990) *Acts of Meaning*. Cambridge, MA: Harvard University Press.

Carrithers, M. (1992) *Why Humans have Cultures: Explaining Anthropology and Social Diversity*. Oxford: Oxford University Press.

Chafe, W. (1990) 'Some things that narrative tell us about the mind', in B.K. Britton and A.D. Pellegrini (eds), *Narrative Thought and Narrative Language*. Hillsdale, NJ: Lawrence Erlbaum. pp. 79–98.

Cortazzi, M. (1991) *Primary Teaching, How It Is – A Narrative Account*. London: David Fulton.

Cortazzi, M. (1993) *Narrative Analysis*. London: Falmer Press.

Cortazzi, M. and Jin, L. (1999) 'Evaluating evaluation in narrative', in S. Hunston and G. Thompson (eds), *Evaluation in Text*. Oxford: Oxford University Press. pp. 102–20.

Denzin, N. (1997) *Interpretive Ethnography: Ethnographic Practices for the 21st Century*. Thousand Oaks, CA: Sage.

Duranti, A. and Goodwin, C. (1992) *Rethinking Context: Language as an Interactive Phenomenon*. Cambridge: Cambridge University Press.

Edwards, D. (1997) *Discourse and Cognition*. London: Sage.

Erben, M. (ed.) (1998) *Biography and Education: A Reader*. London: Falmer Press.

Fletcher, C. (1991) *What Cops Know*. London: Macdonald.

Garro, L.C. (1992) 'Chronic illness and the construction of narratives', in M.D. Good, P.E. Brodwin, B.J. Good and A. Kleinman (eds), *Pain as Human Experience: An Anthropological Perspective*. Berkeley, CA: University of California Press. pp. 100–37.

Gee, J.P. (1996) *Social Linguistics and Literacies: Ideology in Discourses*, 2nd edn. London: Taylor and Francis.

Golden-Biddle, K. and Locke, K.D. (1997) *Composing Qualitative Research*. Thousand Oaks, CA: Sage.

Good, M.D. (1995) *American Medicine: The Quest for Competence*. Berkeley, CA: University of California Press.

Goodson, I.F. (ed.) (1992) *Studying Teachers' Lives*. London: Routledge.

Goodson, I.F. (1995) 'The story so far: personal knowledge and the political', in J.A. Hatch and R. Wisniewski (eds), *Life History and Narrative*. London: Falmer Press. pp. 89–98.

Goodson, I.F. and Walker, R. (1991) *Biography, Identity and Schooling*. London: Falmer Press.

Grimes, J.E. (1975) *The Thread of Discourse*. The Hague: Mouton.

Grimes, J.E. (ed.) (1978) *Papers on Discourse*. Dallas, TX: Institute of Linguistics.

Huberman, M. (1993) *The Lives of Teachers*. London: Cassell.

Hunter, K.M. (1991) *Doctors' Stories: The Narrative Structure of Medical Knowledge*. Princeton, NJ: Princeton University Press.

Hymes, D. (1981) *In Vain I Tried to Tell You: Essays in Native American Ethnopoetics*. Philadelphia, PA: University of Pennsylvania Press.

Hymes, D. (1996) *Ethnography, Linguistics, Narrative Inequality: Towards an Understanding of Voice*. London: Taylor and Francis.

Jalongo, M.R. and Isenberg, J.P. (1995) *Teachers' Stories: From Personal Narrative to Professional Insight*. San Francisco: Jossey–Bass Publishers.

Kleinman, A. (1988) *The Illness Narratives: Suffering, Healing, and the Human Condition*. New York: Basic Books.

Labov, W. (1972) 'The transformation of experience in narrative syntax', in W. Labov, *Language in the Inner City*. Philadelphia, PA: University of Pennsylvania Press. pp. 352–96.

Labov, W. and Fanshel, D. (1977) *Therapeutic Discourse: Psychotherapy as Conversation*. New York: Academic Press.

Lieblich, A., Tuval-Mashiach, R. and Zilber, T. (1998) *Narrative Research: Reading, Analysis and Interpretation*. Thousand Oaks: Sage.

Linde, C. (1993) *Life Stories: The Creation of Coherence*. New York: Oxford University Press.

Longacre, R. (1976) *An Anatomy of Speech Notions.* Lisse: Peter de Ridder.

Mattingly, C. (1998) *Healing Dramas and Clinical Plots: The Narrative Structure of Experience.* Cambridge: Cambridge University Press.

Mattingly, C. and Garro, L.C. (eds) (1994) 'Narrative representations of illness and healing', Special issue of *Social Science and Medicine*, 38.

McEwan, H. and Egan, K. (eds) (1995) *Narrative in Teaching, Learning and Research.* New York: Teachers College Press.

McLaughlin, D. and Tierney, W.C. (eds) (1993) *Naming Silenced Lives: Personal Narratives and Processes of Educational Change.* London: Routledge.

Mishler, E.G. (1986) *Research Interviewing: Context and Narrative.* London: Harvard University Press.

Mishler, E.G. (1995) 'Models of narrative analysis: a typology', *Journal of Narrative and Life History*, 5 (2): 87–123.

Mishler, E.G. (1997) 'The interactional construction of narratives in medical and life history interviews', in B.L. Gunnarson, P. Linnell and B. Nordberg (eds), *The Construction of Professional Discourse.* London: Longman. pp. 223–44.

Myerhoff, B. (1978) *Number Our Days.* New York: Simon and Schuster.

Neisser, U. (1982) *Memory Observed: Remembering in Natural Contexts.* San Francisco: Freeman.

Nelson, M.H. (1993) *Teacher Stories: Teaching Archetypes Revealed by Analysis.* Ann Arbor, MI: Prakken Publications.

Nofsinger, R.E. (1991) *Everyday Conversation.* Newbury Park, CA: Sage.

Ochs, E., Smith, R.C. and Taylor, C.E. (1996) 'Detective stories at dinnertime: problem solving through co-narration', in C.L. Briggs (ed), *Disorderly Discourse, Narrative, Conflict, and Inequality.* New York: Oxford University Press. pp. 95–113.

Okely, J. and Callaway, H. (eds) (1992) *Anthropology and Autobiography.* London: Routledge.

Peterson, C. and McCabe, A. (1983) *Developmental Psycholinguistics: Three Ways of Looking at a Child's Narrative.* New York: Plenum Press.

Polanyi, L. (1989) *Telling the American Story: A Structural and Cultural Analysis of Conversational Storytelling.* Cambridge, MA: The MIT Press.

Polkinghorne, D.E. (1988) *Narrative Knowing and the Human Sciences.* Albany, NY: State University of New York Press.

Polkinghorne, D.E. (1995) 'Narrative configuration in qualitative analysis', in J.A. Hatch and R. Wisniewski

(eds), *Life History and Narrative.* London: Falmer Press. pp. 5–24.

Psathas, G. (1995) *Conversation Analysis: The Study of Talk-in-Interaction.* Thousand Oaks, CA: Sage.

Riessman, C.K. (1993) *Narrative Analysis.* Newbury Park, CA: Sage.

Rosen, S. (1991) *My Voice Will Go With You: The Teaching Tales of Milton H. Erickson, M.D.* New York: W.W. Norton.

Rosenwald, G.C. and Ochberg, R.L. (eds) (1992) *Storied Lives: The Cultural Politics of Self-understanding.* New Haven, CT: Yale University Press.

Sarris, G. (1993) 'Keeping slug woman alive: the challenge of reading in a reservation classroom', in J. Boyarin (ed.) *The Ethnography of Reading.* Berkeley, CA: University of California Press. pp. 238–69.

Scollon, R. and Scollon, S. (1981) *Narrative, Literacy and Face in Interethnic Communication.* Norwood, NJ: Ablex.

Swindells, J. (1995) *The Uses of Autobiography.* London: Taylor and Francis.

Tannen, D. (1984) *Conversational Style: Analyzing Talk Among Friends.* Norwood, NJ: Ablex.

Thomas, D. (ed.) (1995) *Teachers' Stories.* Buckingham: Open University Press.

Toolan, M.J. (1988) *Narrative: A Critical Linguistic Introduction.* London: Routledge.

Trimmer, J.F. (ed.) (1997) *Narration as Knowledge: Tales of the Teaching Life.* Portsmouth, NH: Boynton Cook.

Van Dijk, T.A. (1987) *Communicating Racism: Ethnic Prejudice in Thought and Talk.* London: Sage.

Van Dijk, T.A. (1993) *Elite Discourse and Racism.* Newbury Park, CA: Sage.

Van Maanen, J. (1988) *Tales of the Field: On Writing Ethnography.* Chicago: University of Chicago Press.

Van Maanen, J. (ed.) (1995) *Representation in Ethnography.* Thousand Oaks, CA: Sage.

White, H. (1981) 'The value of narrativity', in W.J.T. Mitchell (ed.), *On Narrative.* London: University of Chicago Press. pp. 1–25.

Witherell, C. and Noddings, N. (eds) (1991) *Stories Lives Tell: Narrative and Dialogue in Education.* New York: Teachers College Press.

Wolfson, N. (1982) *The Conversational Historic Present in American English Narrative.* Dordrecht: Foris.

Zeller, N. (1995) 'Narrative strategies for case reports', in J.A. Hatch and R. Wisniewski (eds), *Life History and Narrative.* London: Falmer Press. pp. 75–88.

## 27

The Call of Life Stories in Ethnographic Research

KEN PLUMMER

I have often thought that there has rarely passed a life of which a judicious and faithful narrative would not be useful ...

(Samuel Johnson, *c*.1760)

We are safe in saying that personal life records, as complete as possible, constitute the *perfect* type of sociological material.

(W.I. Thomas and Florian Znaniecki, 1918)

We want our lives to have meaning, or weight, or substance, or to grow toward some fullness ... if necessary we want the future to 'redeem' the past, to make it part of a life story, which has sense or purpose, to make it up in a meaningful unity ... because we cannot but orient ourselves to the good ... we must inescapably understand our lives in narrative form, as a quest ...

(Charles Taylor, 1989)

Virtue is a social construction. People make morality when they construct narratives of virtuous people.

(George Noblit and Van Dempsey, 1996)

Writing a personal narrative is perhaps worth a try because the prize is very great: that of some degree of transcendence of differences, of reaffirmation of common humanity ...

(Pat Caplan, 1997)

To tell the story of a life may be one of the cores of culture, those fine webs of meaning that help organize our ways of life. These stories – or personal narratives – connect the inner world to the outer world, speak to the subjective and the objective, and establish the boundaries of identities (of who one is and who one is not). Life stories cross the embodied and emotional 'brute being' with the rational and irrational 'knowing self'. They make links across life phases and cohort generations revealing historical shifts in a culture. They help establish collective memories and imagined communities; and they tell of the concerns of their time and place. They bridge cultural history with personal biography. And they become moral constructions, tales of virtue and non-virtue, which may act to guide us in our ethical lives. Indeed, the stories we construct of our lives may well become the 'stories we live by'. What matters to people keeps getting told in their stories of their life. Listening carefully to these stories may well be one of the cornerstones of ethnographic enquiry. To describe and analyse the ways of life which is a culture must mean describing and analysing the stories of its lived lives (cf. Anderson, 1983; McAdams, 1993; Noblitt and Dempsey, 1996).

All this has long been recognized, though the ways in which these stories have been told has changed dramatically. Throughout most of human history, telling the stories of lives has largely been an oral tradition – passed down across generations, suitably modified and reconstructed, feeding into the great myths we may later come to live by (Vansina, 1985). The tales of religious figures – of Christ and Buddha, of Mohammed and of ancestors long worshipped – all these lives feed into the cultural bricolage. With the earliest depiction of lives etched into Stone Age drawings on walls, their depictions become more elaborate some 3000 years BC with the elite hieroglyphics of Pharaohs preserving records of their lives and riches in the great tombs, temples and pyramids: as with the famous Tutankhamun. Here indeed are stories that enable the historian, the archaeologist and the writer routes into understanding the cultures of the past – limited and partial as they may be. Yet it is with the arrival of print, and the slow emergence of a culture of individualism putting great store on the individual life, that the written tale of a self and its others becomes more common. Some argue it is the *Confessions* of St Augustine around 400 AD admitting sins in order to be saved, which set the major pattern of coherence for the next fourteen centuries (Marcus, 1994; Olney, 1998). By the turn of the nineteenth century, social science was clearly coming to recognize the value of such an approach (Allport, 1942; Bennett, 1981; Plummer, 1983). Now, at the beginning of a new millennium, life stories are everywhere: a curious preoccupation with life narratives has become 'a defining feature of Western societies, linking phenomena as disparate as the documentary evidence occasionally collected to enliven quantitative research and the sensational outbursts filling in the intervals between TV commercials on the reality-show catwalk' (Simeoni and Diani, 1995: 1).

Life stories today come though many sources – biographies, autobiographies, letters, journals, short interviews, photos, video diaries, home web pages and the like. They exist in many forms: long and short, past and present, specific and general, fuzzy and focused, surface and deep, ordinary and extraordinary stories. And they are denoted by a plethora of terms: self stories, life stories, life histories, auto/biographies, personal documents, life documents, life narratives, oral histories, 'documents of life'. They have spawned major new academic groupings, archives and journals like *Life Histories, Oral History, Auto/Biography*; annual book series like *The Narrative Study of Lives* (see, for example, Josselson, 1996) and the *Year Book of Life Histories*; and many more popular outlets from the monthly magazine *Biography* (which has its slogan: 'Every life has a story'), television's *This is Your Life* and radio's *In the Psychiatrist's Chair* with Anthony Clare. It is, then, a field of enquiry that is voluminous and variegated.

Further, the interest in life stories stretches across both continents and countries, as well as across disciplines. From small communities across the world where there are 'memory groups', 'oral history societies' and 'camcorder clubs' keen to record local lives through to diverse 'International Congresses' on life history – the desire to record and analyse the stories of lives has almost the fervour of a global social

movement. (For discussions of some of the cultural variations in all this, see Bertaux, 1981: 6; Chalasinski, 1981; Chanfrault-Duchet, 1995 and for some overviews of the international scene, see Dunaway and Baum, 1996: Part 5). In what follows, I can only select a few themes in all this work to consider. My concerns will be fourfold: form, perspective, truth and ethics.

FORM AND VARIETY

There have been many attempts to distinguish different forms of life story, and there are indeed many varieties. In this chapter, I wish to highlight three overarching, though connected, types: the everyday naturalistic, the researched and the reflexive-recursive (for wider classifications, see Atkinson, 1998; Denzin, 1989; Stanley, 1992).

The first concerns life stories that are naturally occurring in culture. These are the stories that people tell as part of their everyday life space. I call these *naturalistic life stories*. They are simply there in cultures and have not been shaped at all by the social scientist. Yet they can be collected to become the objects of study for social scientists – in effect constituting a species of non-obtrusive gathering. They are documents that await a cultural analysis. Not artificially assembled, they just happen *in situ*. Much ethnographic work depends upon immersion and hanging around in settings where people then proceed to tell others their life stories. Naturalistic life stories believe in telling it as it is, 'the claiming authentic representation, of a natural fidelity to the world, of listening to voices speak, and hence of removing prior assumptions whilst faithfully representing the voice' (Gubrium and Holstein, 1997: ch. 2). Such stories can be heard in naturalistic settings – when the elderly reminisce, teenagers chat on the phone, criminals confess, job applicants are interviewed; and they may also be heard increasingly as media voices: on talk radio, in the letters pages, on chat shows. They are omnipresent in that most popular form of publishing: the biography and autobiography. Thus, for example, Diane Bjorklund has gathered some 200 North American autobiographies written over a span of 200 years and analysed their content, themes and links to the historical and cultural moment; whilst Wendy Simonds has studied the self-help confessional tales that abound in North American culture. (Bjorklund, 1999; Simonds, 1992). In a culture such as ours, flooded with biographical musings, here indeed is a rich mine for the ethnographer.

A second genre concerns life stories that are specifically gathered by researchers with a wider and usually social science goal in mind. I call these *researched life stories*. These do not naturalistically occur in everyday life: rather, they have to be seduced, coaxed and interrogated out of subjects, often in special settings using special implements (tape recorders, videos, psychiatric couches). Oral history, sociological life history, psychological case studies – all these can bring life stories into being that would not otherwise have happened in everyday life. The role of the researcher is crucial to this activity: they shape and assemble them, and indeed without them there would be no life story. Many of the classics of life story – *The Polish Peasant in Europe and America, The Jack Roller, Children of Sanchez, Letters to Jenny, Children of Crisis* or *Jane Fry* – are of this type (cf. Plummer, 2000). A more recent study of this form is the controversial story of Rigoberta Menchú, a 23-year-old Quiché Indian woman who speaks of her experience as a member of one of the largest of twenty-two ethnic groups in Guatemala; speaking for all the Indians of the American continent, she talks of her relationship with nature and of her community's discriminations, oppression, defeat and genocide. The story was gathered by Elizabeth Burgos-Dubray, in Spanish, over a period of a week in her Paris flat in 1982. It started with a schematic outline – the usual chronology from childhood onwards – but was soon deflected into much more political issues, and indeed a centrepiece of the book becomes the torturing, death and funeral of members of Menchú's family at the hands of government agents. The discussions were recorded, transcribed and edited into 500 pages of transcript. All Burgos' questions were deleted as the record was turned into thirty-four chapters (and 250 pages of book) – starting with 'The family' and 'Birth ceremonies', and moving through such topics as 'Life in the community', 'Attack on the village by the army', 'The torture and death of her little brother, burnt alive in front of members of his family and the community', 'In hiding in the capital', 'Hunted by the army'. To capture the flavour, here are two brief extracts:

> I worked from when I was very small, but I didn't earn anything. I was really helping my mother because she had to carry a baby, my little brother, on her back as she picked coffee. It made me very sad to see my mother's face covered in sweat as she tried to finish her workload, and I wanted to help her. But my work wasn't paid, it just contributed to my mother's work. I either picked coffee with her or looked after my little brother, so she could work faster. My brother was two at the time ... (Menchú, 1984: 33)

Much of the story is given over to detailed cultural description of daily life in the village – of work, religious ritual, family and children. Curiously, at one point she speaks of the importance of not disclosing the village secrets – 'Indians have been very careful not disclose any details of their communities, and the community does not allow them to talk about Indian things. I too must abide by this' (p. 9; cf. p. 188). This is either hard to

reconcile with the vivid descriptions she supplies, or it suggests that what she has told in the story is heavily screened by this taboo. Another quote:

> It was in 1979, I remember that my younger brother died, the first person in my family to be tortured. He was sixteen years old, ... It's an unbelievable story. We managed to find out how he died, what tortures were inflicted on him from start to finish. They took my brother away, bleeding from different places. When they'd done with him, he didn't look like a person any more. His whole face was disfigured from beating, from striking against stones, the tree-trunks; my brother was completely destroyed. His clothes were torn from his falling down. After that they let the women go. When he got to the camp, he was scarcely on his feet, he couldn't walk any more. And his face, he couldn't see any more, they'd even forced stones into his eyes, into my brother's eyes. Once he arrive in the camp, they inflicted terrible tortures on him to make him tell where the guerrilla fighters were and where his family was ... [a long description of torture follows] (Menchú, 1984: 174)

The tale of Rigoberta Menchú has rapidly become a classic: noted for the account of the way the Guatemalan army killed her two brothers and parents. A better seller than most 'life stories', it has made her a hero of the international human rights movement, led to her being awarded a Nobel Peace Prize in 1992; and has brought a storm of controversy. For the relationship between Elizabeth Burgos-Dubray and Rigoberta Menchú has been questioned; the veracity of her story has been challenged; and the potential use of such stories for political ends has been put under scrutiny. I shall return to all this later (cf. Stoll, 1999).

On the border, between the naturalistic life story and the researched life story, is the ethnographic auto/biography: many ethnographies may be seen as partly composed of the stories people tell of their lives. In the classic *Street Corner Society*, not only does the presence of 'Doc', the key informant, loom large – so too do the stories of Chick Morelli, Tony Cataldo, the Nortons and the Shelby Street Boys. Tally figures prominently in the classic *Tally's Corner* (Liebow, 1967), whilst 'Slim' is at the heart of *Slim's Table* (Duneier, 1992). Slim, for example, is 'a black mechanic in a back alley garage in the ghetto', a regular patron of the 'Valois' "See Your Food" cafeteria' in Chicago. He is contrasted in part with Bart: white, ten years older, a filing clerk, who died alone in his small studio. Likewise, David Goode's recent, neglected study *A World without Words* takes two children as its core – Christina and Bianca, who were born deaf, 'dumb', blind and mentally disabled as a result of pre-natal German measles during the Rubella epidemic of the 1960s. The study gets close to their experiences – and though they are the centre of the stories, they are linked to an array of significant others reacting to them: professionals, parents, other children. Here the focus is the ethnographic study of lives, whilst broad theoretical links are made to communication and ethnomethodology (Goode, 1994).

A third main kind of life story are the *reflexive and recursive life stories*, life stories that bring with them a much greater awareness of their own construction and writing, and flag the drift towards postmodern and feminist social enquiry (Dickens and Fontana, 1994; Stanley, 1992). Whilst the first two genres bring with them a sense that they are telling the story of a life, these latter kinds of stories are much more reflective and self-conscious: they see story-telling as a fabrication, as an act of speech, as a mode of writing; and whatever else they may say, they do not simply tell the tale of a life.

In some of both the naturalistic and research life stories located above, we can see the beginnings of 'messy texts' (Marcus, 1994: 567): making the writer a part of the writing. This is part of what has been variously called 'the crisis of representation', 'the postmodern turn' and the 'experimental moment' (Marcus and Fisher, 1986). The 'autoethnograph' and the 'new biography' for instance both bring the author firmly into the text with a heightened self-consciousness of the textual production; whilst by the time we reach the fictional autobiographical ethnography, the distinction of forms is completely 'blurred'. Here is an emerging sociological form where the life story becomes a composite, where real research and real lives is written in fictional form. Thus, for example, Michael Angrosino (1998) spent years – as volunteer and observer – in a home for retarded adults in Florida, but he writes his tale in a fictional form covering the same ground but making it more accessible and readable. He tells the stories of a dozen inhabitants of Opportunity House.

Most recently this kind of work has blossomed into research where the social scientist, and his or her life, moves into the heart of the ethnography. A host of new words have been invented for this enterprise: 'sociological introspection', 'narratives of the self' (Ellis, 1991), 'mystories' (Ulmer, 1990), 'autoethnography' (Neumann, 1998; Okely and Callaway, 1992; Pratt, 1991) and ethnographic biography. Here the social scientist is writing about his or her life whilst including within it the sense of other concerns coming from a social science understanding. Sometimes these are book length – as in the late Irving Zola's *Missing Pieces*. Here he describes 'an unusual experiment in living' (1982: 5) as his own life in a wheelchair is recounted side by side with his visits to Het Dorp in the Netherlands (he calls it a social-autobiography (p. 6). Whilst documenting the trials and tribulations of daily living with severe disabilities he relates 'little things that fill a day'. Sometimes, these are short pieces that ring out a different style and sensitivity for doing sociology. Thus, Carol Rambo Ronai tells her story of what it is like to be both a striptease dancer

(Ronai, 1992) as well as the daughter of a 'mentally retarded' mother – teeming with her personal resentments at pretending to be a 'normal family' and of her mother 'not taking care of me' (Ronai, 1996). In the work of Susan Krieger (1996) and Laurel Richardson (1998), there is a very clear tendency towards getting personal in their writing: using the self as a source for social science.

In this genre, Carolyn Ellis' *Final Negotiations* (1995) has caused some controversy because of the way she treads such a difficult line between the emotionality of its author, its personal writing style, and its links to social science. Her book reads like a hybrid between a novel, a fiction, an autobiography and a research tract. Officially she calls it 'experimental ethnography', and it is based on 'daily field notes'. It is subtitled – 'A story of Love, Loss and Chronic Illness' – which does not immediately suggest a sociological treatise! And what it provides is a 350 page first-person account of the sociologist author's experience of her relationship with a teacher (the sociologist Gene Weinstein based at the University of New York at Stony Brook) – as they first negotiate their attachment 'through a maze of jealousy, attraction, love and arguments' (1995: 10) with her in the more subordinate role, and then how they renegotiate their relationship as they come to terms with the impending death of Gene. Within this study, the story is presented in the present tense – 'which invites the reader to share in the immediacy' – whilst sociological commentaries and personal reflections are woven into the past tense. This is an intriguing study, almost certainly unacceptable to the more formal scientific academic community because it highlights both speaking of personal experience alongside narrative prose as a way of knowing. But the study takes us into the sociology of love, relationships, emotions, and death.

Whilst only a relatively small amount of social science is taking this personal, narrative path, there are nevertheless signs here of a shift. The 'autoethnography' brings the author firmly into the text with a heightened self-consciousness of the textual production. Once this happens it may be only a small step away to the 'fictional autobiographical ethnography', where the distinction of forms becomes completely 'blurred'. Indeed, what is 'fiction' and what is 'faction' is hard to distinguish. When social science starts to write fiction, and fiction writers start to write biographies, distinctions around life stories become very tenuous.

Increasingly found is the dissolution of the straightforward realist text and an intense problematizing of the whole field (Clough, 1992). In the wake of the drift (for some) towards postmodern methods (Dickens and Fontana, 1994) – what Denzin has suggested is the fifth and sixth waves of ethnography (Denzin, 1997) – and the search for a 'new language of qualitative methods' (Gubrium and Holstein, 1997), we find that many of the traditional working assumptions of life history and autobiographical research have been seriously challenged. As elsewhere, the drift towards a Derridean deconstructive turn with its emphasis on writing texts has almost obliterated the idea of a human life being told. The slogan of many of these critics might well be: 'out of the streets, into the armchairs' (Best, 1995: 128). What has come speedily into the place of conventional life history has been a cacophony of 'multiple voices', 'polyvocal texts', 'experiential texts', 'performance texts' and 'narratives of the self'. There is almost an extreme preoccupation with novelty and self-analysis. What seems to have gone missing is the straightforward sense of a person's life as they tell it.

PERSPECTIVES AND APPROACHES

The postmodern turn makes a number of analytic distinctions necessary. What perspectives may be taken towards a life? Most straightforwardly, life stories may be seen as *resources*. Here we study lives because they will help us understand something – a life, a life cycle, a culture. We read the classic text-length stories of Stanley, the Jack Roller (or mugger) (Shaw, 1966), or Wladek, the Polish peasant (Thomas and Znaniecki, 1958), because we wish to understand delinquency and migration; and this is what they tell us about. This is an approach which eschews the postmodern turn, seeks out a realist tale, and sees the life story as providing a beam of light on something important that needs understanding.

By contrast, we can approach the life story as a *topic*. Here we are less concerned with what the story tells us than with understanding the processes through which the life is composed, constructed, created. It looks at the ways in which men and women compose meanings in their lives, interpreting the mechanisms by which they do this. Here life stories become 'a constructed understanding of the constructed native's constructed point of view' (Crapanzano, 1986: 74; cf. Bateson, 1989). When life stories are viewed this way, they are usefully seen as *joint actions*. Life stories are joint actions assembled through social contexts into texts by authors and readers. Drawing from the work of George Herbert Mead, Herbert Blumer and Howard Becker, the social world may be approached as being constituted through joint actions, where people are doing things together (cf. Plummer, 1990). Life stories in this view become collective enterprises: we compose, construct, write the stories of our lives with the aid of others. Indeed, a life story depends on others – there must be a teller, but there must also be people who will hear and listen. Such a model of life stories may be depicted quite simply, as in Figure 27.1.

Tellers compose their life stories through a flood of joint actions and significant others. One task of the life researcher here may be to sense the social sources of constructing lives: from what bricolages and fragments does a person come to assemble their stories? There are, for instance, *significant others* like parents, loved ones, teachers and friends who are the important people in a life who tell you the story of your life – of what you were like as a child, of how you were at school, of what happened on that first date. The stories they tell you feed back into the stories of your life. These others often tell you 'the kind of person you are' and remind you of what you did in the past. Then there are the *personal props*: from diaries and photo albums, to collections of clothes, books and records, 'props' are deposited in a trail behind a life as it is lived. They can be regathered to enable a telling of a life. And a scanning of these helps to 'restory the life'; to bring alive times, places and people long since forgotten. Closely weaved into all this must be the social acts of remembering (cf. Plummer, 1995: 40).

Finally, the life story may come to be seen as a *narrative text*. The narrative of a life is clearly not *the* life; and it conforms much less to the contours of the life as lived than it does to the conventions and practices of narrative writing. Even unselfconscious tales that are simply 'told' are likely to be immersed in the narrative conventions of a culture, for 'narrative is the fundamental scheme for linking individual human actions and events into interrelated aspects of an understandable composite' (Polkinghorne, 1988: 13). Indeed, if it is not drawing from those narrative conventions, most readers will find it hard – even impossible – to understand as a life. Thus life story research must be closely linked to narrative analysis, which takes the very story itself as the topic of investigation (Edwards, 1997; Hillis Miller, 1990). Life story analysis must be part of the so-called 'narrative turn', and there are many approaches to this: hermeneutic, discourse, dramatist, formalist, structuralist, dialogic, psychoanalytic, semiotic.

Thus, and very briefly, within a narrative perspective, a life story must usually have a *plot*: a dynamic tension which moves the story on, adds momentum, and provides some coherence. In general, we speak of the plot 'thickening' to indicate events that grab the reader's interest. And in life stories these become important too. As Kenyon and Randall pithily say: 'no trouble, no tale; no ill, no thrill; no agony, no adventure' (Kenyon and Randall, 1997: 67). Indeed, very frequently a life story is organized around a major tension or crisis – what Denzin (1989) calls an epiphany. Dan McAdams highlights several other features. *Nuclear episodes* that can be identified, which detail 'specific autobiographical events which have been reinterpreted over time to assume a privileged status in the story'; *thematic lines*, which indicate 'recurrent

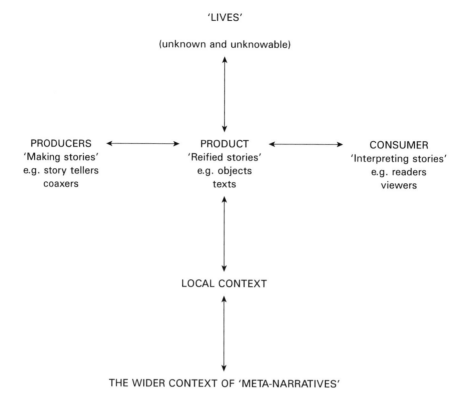

Figure 27.1 *Elements of the social action story process*

content clusters in stories' such as 'power' and 'intimacy'; and *characters* – where the life story has recognizable 'stereotypes' or 'storytypes' (McAdams, 1985: 62, 63). Usually, too, plots take on a sequence – a beginning, middle and end (though in some experimental modernist and all postmodern plots, linear time is dissolved or seriously weakened). All the classic life stories have linear time that organizes their plots. Many plots and characters become clustered into recognizable types or *genres*, such as the tragic, the comic, the romantic or the satirical (White, 1973). Life stories usually have a *point of view*: are written or told from 'an angle', be it author, narrator, protagonist, or reader. Finally, they can also be seen as 'conversational units', as linguistic units governed by language rules (Linde, 1993). (For a fuller discussion on all this, see Edwards, 1997: ch. 7; Lieblich et al., 1998; McAdams, 1985, 1993; Plummer, 2000: ch. 9; Riesmann, 1993).

TRUTHS AND MEMORIES

If ever anyone did hold the view that biographies told a simple 'realist truth' about the life – that the story told simply accessed reality – few can or do

these days. The problem of the link between lives, narratives of those lives, the production of stories of lives and fiction/truth is squarely on the agenda. Most life story researchers no longer believe a simple, linear or essential, real truth about a life can be gleaned through a life story; or indeed that a researcher can have any clear, superior access to knowledge about a life. As a leading contemporary proponent of the method, Jerome Bruner, puts it thus:

> there is no such thing as a 'uniquely' true, correct or even faithful autobiography; ... 'an autobiography is not and cannot be a way of simply signifying or referring to a 'life as lived'. I take the view that there is no such thing as a 'life as lived' to be referred to. On this view, a life is created or constructed by the act of autobiography. It is a way of construing experience – and of reconstruing and reconstruing it until our breath and our pen fails us. Construal and reconstrual are interpretative. (Bruner, 1993: 39; 38)

But if we accept, as I think we must, that all lives are composed – that the stories of our lives are indeed constructed, fabricated, invented, made up – this does not mean that all the stories we hear are equally valid or invalid, truthful or deceptive. To say that lives are invented is not to force us into a situation where we can no longer say that some stories are 'better' than others. Indeed, I believe it is just the opposite: to recognize that lives are constructed means that we then need to search out ways for evaluating just what it is that is being constructed, and how their constructions may lead to different kinds of 'truths'. The leading Italian oral historian, Allessandro Portelli, for example, recognizes that life stories are not and cannot be objective: they are always 'artificial, variable and partial'. But at the same time he believes that this does not weaken them. We may even know that some statements are factually wrong: and yet such 'wrong' statements may still be psychologically 'true': 'this truth may be equally as important as factually reliable accounts' (Portelli, 1998: 72, 68). We need, then, various criteria for appraising the different connections between life stories and 'truth'. (Other discussions of this may be found in Denzin, 1989: 23–5; Plummer, 1995: ch. 11; Riessman, 1993: 64–70).

There are many ways in which life stories may be evaluated. One approach is to think of a continuum of objectivity and subjectivity. At one end, there is the search for an objective life – as far as possible, given what has been said above. Classically, the task here has been to make 'reality checks' on the life story: to look at its internal consistency, its correspondence with external events, the sincerity with which it has been told. Most classic studies adopt this more objectivist or 'realist' approach: Clifford Shaw, for example, remarks that the numerous contacts he had with the delinquent boy, Stanley, as well as a close matching with official records etc., means that the sincerity of Stanley 'cannot be questioned' (Shaw, 1966: fn. 47). This may be seen as a historical truth – getting closer and closer to the reality of the life.

Further along this continuum comes narrative truth. Here what matters is the way in which the story enables the reader to enter the subjective world of the teller – to see the world from their point of view, even if this world does not 'match reality'. And at the extreme of this continuum comes narrative and fictional biography – when the story told is seen to be made up entirely. Fiction, by definition, does not make any claims to reality – but it does make claims to provide imagination, insight, art, creativity. Here, the ground is difficult. For instance, in a famous life story – that of Don Juan, the Yacqui sorcerer – his tale is told by a social scientist, Carlos Castaneda, and much debated, only later to be discovered as a hoax. Now the hoax matters ethically, but does it matter in terms of the story? Could a clearly invented story be of use within social science? I think the answer is yes. And, indeed, recently some social researchers see more and more of a role for the fictional narrative in social science (Banks and Banks, 1998).

All this leads to a further way of evaluating the life stories. Here the concern is no longer with the inner veridicality of the life story, but rather with outer pragmatics. In short, life stories can be evaluated in terms of their uses, functions and the role they play in personal and cultural life. Judged this way, stories need to have rhetorical power enhanced by aesthetic delight. The dry old tale told banally by a boring social scientist who hedges the tale in with the dust of theory and jargon will never meet such higher criteria! Writing skills, the craft of telling, art, imagination – all these now come into their own; and help us distinguish the valuable social science 'life story' from the less valuable one. Thus, for instance, James Bennet's articulate study of the life stories of delinquents suggests that for such stories to be successful they have to be written so as to attract an audience (something most social science usually cannot manage!), to help the reader see the phenomenon, and finally – most importantly – to persuade the reader to hold certain views (like the views that 'juvenile delinquents are not alien beings', and the 'good person becomes bad by interacting in a crimogenic environment' (Bennett, 1981: 258–9). Life stories are now seen as rhetoric, and can be evaluated through their power to persuade (cf. Atkinson, 1991).

Life stories may also be seen as ways of 'reading cultures'. This value may lie in the ways in which they come to reflect the culture but also display how the culture talks about itself, how it allows certain kinds of life stories to be told – and by implication, not others. And often, as we shall see, this takes us into moral worlds. The life story is in and of the culture.

The Problem of Memory

Closely connected to 'truth' is the issue of memory. Indeed, since all life story work is selective work, 'memories' are often seen as a major path to this selection and life stories become 'memory books' (cf. Terkel, 1970). Life story work involves recollecting, re-membering, re-discovering, along with the active processes of memorializing and constructing history. As Frisch vividly puts it:

> What happens to experience on the way to becoming memory? What happens to experiences on the way to becoming history? As an era of intense collective experience recedes into the past, what is the relationship of memory to historical generalisation. (Frisch, 1998: 33)

Oral history in particular may be seen as a 'powerful tool for discovering, exploring and evaluating the nature of the historical memory – how people make sense of their past, how they connect individual experience and its social context, how the past becomes part of the present, and how people use it to interpret their lives and the world around them' (Frisch, 1990: 188).

Analytically, 'memory' may work on at least four levels. First, there is what most people would readily recognize as *psychological or individual memory*, where the focus is upon what a person can recall, how well they can recall it (which often varies by time of day, mental tiredness and the like) along with various failures to recall – the most extreme versions being pathologies like Alzheimer's disease. In most respects, this is the best-trod path, with a long literature of critiques and debates. And in this view, life histories are concerned with dredging up the memories from the past. Yet this view has recently been under siege from some psychologists: as Jerome Bruner has remarked:

> I believe that the ways of telling stories and the ways of conceptualising that go with them become so habitual that they finally become recipes for structuring experience itself, for laying down routes into memory, for not only guiding the life narrative up to the present but directing it into the future. (Bruner, 1987: 31)

Secondly, there is *narrative memory*, where the focus is on the narratives that people tell about their past, and where highly selective stories dredged from the past somehow seem to have taken on a life of their own. They are somewhat akin to what Gordon Allport once called 'autonomous motives', whereby he argued that whatever 'motives' may have initiated a conduct in the first place, they ultimately came to be ruled by laws unto themselves – by motives which, so to speak, take on their own life. Likewise, memories often become – as Bruner once said – 'our best stories', the stories we tell so often that we come to believe them as true. Clearly, this version of memory fits well with the current interest in story-telling and narratives.

Thirdly, there is *collective memory*, where the focus becomes 'the social frameworks of memory'. For Maurice Halbwachs (1877–1945) – the most distinguished proponent of this view – 'no memory is possible outside frameworks used by people living in society to determine and retrieve their recollections' (Halbwachs, 1992: 43). Thus, life stories can only be told once a societal framework becomes available for them to be told: stories of gay men and lesbians 'coming out' or North American blacks 'up from slavery' can only be told once a social framework which organizes them becomes accessible. Many stories and histories simply cannot be told when the social frameworks are not there. The local community, and a sense of belonging to a generation, may become keys to unlocking such 'frames'. Thus *generational memory* may highlight the ways in which memories can become identified with events that happened generations earlier, 'to encompass the memories which individuals have of their own families' history, as well as more general collective memories about the past' (Haraven, 1996: 242). It could be suggested that the late Alex Haley's book (and subsequent highly successful TV drama) *Roots: The Saga of an American Family*, which documented the search for black America's roots in Africa, helped lay down frameworks and

the craft of genealogy for others to locate or 'construct' their memories within. Some have also suggested that memories of important world events – political, economic etc. – are often structured through generations, with people referring back 'disproportionately to a time when the respondents were in their 'teens or early twenties' (Schuman and Scott, 1989). Life stories have been assembled around the Holocaust, AIDS, wars and other major events which help provide a shape and a meaning not only to the lives being told but also to a re-claimed historical past.

Closely allied to the above is *popular memory*, where the focus is a form of 'political practice' which helps 'give voice' to stories that have either never been told or which have been lost, returning such memories to their communities where they may be reworked for the present. Here are the memories of class, traditional communities, oppressed minorities, indigenous peoples, the colonized, the marginalized, the depressed and oppressed.

ETHICS AND THE MORAL 'LIFE'

I hope to have shown so far how important the life story is for ethnographic research whilst also suggesting some of its difficulties arising from its 'constructed' and 'textual' nature. In this concluding section I want to come to the heart of the matter; and suggest why I see this approach as so core. For me, *composing a life is always bound up with political and moral processes*.

First, life stories and the 'memories' they bring with them always have a latent political structure: people tell their stories – or do not tell their stories – in conditions that are not entirely of their own making within a circuit of power. Some people can elaborate long and detailed stories: others are silenced. Some are always being heard, others never. The understanding of the ways in which people come to tell their stories – and what they say and cannot say, and even how they say it – must be seen as an important part of the politics of the ethnographic project. There are of course the 'heard voices' – but what allows them to be heard? Then there are stories that have been told but have had their day – why do some stories stop being told? There are voices within waiting in the wings to tell their stories – what social conditions allow for new tellings? And then of course, there are the silenced stories: do we know what they may be, and will they ever be heard? But in any event, whoever's story may be being told, whose voice entraps it? Are there certain kinds of ways – dominant narratives – in which stories are told that limit other ways of telling that story? Judith Stacey, in a classic of feminist ethnography, gets it right when she challenges 'The research product is ultimately that of the researcher. With very rare exceptions it is the researcher who narrates, who "authors" the ethnography ... a written document structured primarily by *a researcher's purposes,* offering a *researcher's interpretations,* registered in a *researcher's voice'* (Stacey, 1988: 22; emphasis added).

The Ethics of Life Story Research

This takes us into the ethics of doing such research. The act of telling the story of a life to a researcher is riddled with ethical issues – of confidentiality, deception, honesty, consent, exploitation, betrayal (Plummer, 2000: ch. 12). The potential for harm in such research becomes enormous. Consider what is involved: that someone is coaxed to let you have their story; that you are presumptuous enough to want it and believe you should have it; that you can then publish it, or seek some other reward for it, and often under your own name; and that they may read their story at a distance, with whatever pain and angst that may generate for them. Indeed, there may be a whole 'afterlife of a life story' which hangs around lives for a long time – changing them, haunting them, even damaging them (Blackman, 1992; Lieblich, 1996: 181; Snodgrass, 1982). Often this whole process is masked by simply assuming that the researcher is a 'nice guy', a good human being just doing the best they can. Maybe. But in practice life story research always means you are playing with another person's life in a number of ways. There is always an asymmetrical relation between researcher and researched: as Peneff remarks, 'life stories appear not to call into question the privileges carried by the interviewer's social group' (Simeoni and Diani, 1995: 4–5). There is always the presumption that a researcher can bring others to voice better than they can themselves – a kind of arrogance long noted by seasoned researchers (see Coles, 1997; Malcolm, 1990). And there is always a potential risk of harm and damage through the intrusion into someone else's life. There is the *hurt and harm* that may befall the subjects through the researcher's meddling.

In the hands of a seasoned researcher, it is true, there has to be a hope that there is a deep awareness of the complicated ethical involvements which research brings to bear on a subject's life: telling their story could literally destroy them – bring them to a suicidal edge, to murderous thoughts, danger. More modestly, subjects may be severely traumatized. The telling of a story of a life is a deeply problematic and ethical process in which researchers are fully implicated. But in the hands of some novice researchers – and especially, say, a student rushing in to gather a life story for a dissertation – such awareness may be very thin and the damage that could be done enormous. A process imbued with deep ethical significance, it is an act drenched

in the possibility of power, abuse and exploitation. All life story collection involves ethical troubles and no life story-telling in social science is ethically neutral. What Janet Malcolm says of journalism is surely true of life story research:

> Every journalist who is not too stupid or too full of himself to notice what is going on knows that what he does is morally indefensible ... The catastrophe suffered by the subject is no simple matter of an unflattering likeness or a misrepresentation of his views; what pains him, what ranks and sometimes drives him to extremes of vengefulness, is the deception that has been practiced on him. On reading the article or book in question, he has to face the fact that the journalist – who seemed so friendly and sympathetic, so keen to understand him so fully, so remarkably attuned to his vision of things – never had the slightest intention of collaborating with him on his story but always intended to write a story of his own. The disparity between what seems to be the intention of an interview as it is taking place and what it actually turns out to have been in aid of always comes as a shock. (Malcolm, 1990: 3)

The trouble is that when we write about others – and especially if it purports to be their story and often told in their words – they feel it. If they read it, they may disagree with it after the words have been said; they may find it hovers over their life and has some impact upon them. Consider the case told by Amia Lieblich about one of her respondents who allowed her to print her story of life in a kibbutz but then read the story provided by her children ...

> An older woman, Genia, who also read the first draft was the person I respected more than any other member of the kibbutz. After the joint meeting with all the 'readers', Genia asked to see me in private. 'I am shocked' she said, 'I cried so much' ... she explained what caused her all this pain were the stories of her two daughters, which were included in the book. I realised that both of them said in so many words that Genia had been a 'bad mother'. During their childhood, she dedicated all her time to the affairs of the kibbutz whilst they felt neglected and rejected. Although remorseful tears were shed in our conversation, Genia did not ask me to change a word in her or her daughters' narratives because she accepted their authenticity ... (Lieblich, 1996)

The Moral Call of Stories

But issues of ethics and morality enter life story research in more ways than this. Indeed, I suggest they enter into the very act of telling a life, which may be one of the key routes into the moral world of a culture. That is: people try through their life stories to give some coherence, some point to their existence, even when this fails. In one sense such stories all become 'ethical tales', struggling to show the different choices that people have faced and how they dealt with them. In doing this, they start to provide pragmatic guides to the ways in which a culture organizes its ethical practices. And this is a concern that moves right across the life span – from the moral tales told by little children to the reminiscing of the elderly (e.g. Bornat, 1994; Gubrium, 1993); from the stories told in men's lives to those told in women's (e.g. Gilligan et al., 1992); and from the tales of the 'normal' to those of the 'different' (e.g. Bogdan, 1974). There is not a concern here with abstract systems of morality, but rather the lived experiences of lives.

And it is in these stories that people struggle to tell, that they reveal, as probably nowhere else, the moral worlds they construct; and these in turn help to provide markers and guidelines to that culture's moral life. Looking at the tales told around a school – always rich in stories both formal and less formal – can guide a person into the moral life of a school (Noblit and Dempsey, 1996; cf. Witherell and Noddings, 1991). Listening to feminist-inspired autobiographies can lead to a better understanding of moral textures and social change in the public sphere (Lara, 1998). And reading the tales of black autobiography – including the slave narratives – can help in the political and moral formation of a Black Public Sphere (1995). Life stories perform major moral work.

IN CONCLUSION

It has long seemed to me to be that at the heart of the liberal-humanist tradition (in which I would locate the life story approach, cf. Plummer, 2000) is the concern with a human life story. In understanding a life and in listening to the lives of others are laid bare the struggles around morality and ethics that help organize any culture. Telling the stories of a life not only enables pathways into a culture, but also pathways into prescriptions for living the ethical life, even in these postmodern times (cf. Baumann, 1993). I am certainly not saying here that such a path leads us to any clear foundational views of ethics; indeed, it is does not. But it does leads us to see lives as moral struggles, embedded in specific contexts, shaped by particular conventions of time and place. The moral tales of a life are always collectively embedded in various communities and traditions, they do not arise out of nowhere (Barber, 1992).

There is a call to the telling of our lives that goes much deeper than simply being, in the words of W.I. Thomas which opened this chapter, 'a perfect sociological method', or a good tool for the ethnographic imagination. As many writers have long known, the telling of stories – and especially life stories – goes to the heart of the moral life of a culture (Coles, 1989). We tell and 'construct'; we hear and 'remember'; and all the time we are assembling ethical worlds. In this chapter, I have selectively reviewed some of the forms, perspectives and 'truths' such life stories may assume in this task.

REFERENCES

Allport, Gordon (1942) *The Use of Personal Documents in Psychological Science*. New York: Social Science Research Council.

Anderson, Benedict (1983) *Imagined Communities*. London: Verso.

Angrosino, Michael V. (1998) *Opportunity House: Ethnographic Stories of Mental Retardation*. London: AltaMira Press.

Atkinson, Paul (1991) *The Ethnographic Imagination*. London: Routledge.

Atkinson, Robert (1998) *The Life Story Interview*. London: Sage.

Banks, Anna and Banks, Stephen P. (eds) (1998) *Fiction and Social Research: By Ice or Fire*. London: AltaMira Press.

Barber, Benjamin (1992) *An Aristocracy of Everyone: The Politics of Education and the Future of America*. New York: Oxford University Press.

Bateson, Mary Catherine (1989) *Composing a Life*. New York: Penguin/Plume.

Baumann, Z. (1993) *Postmodern Ethics*. Oxford: Blackwell.

Bennett, James (1981) *Oral History and Delinquency: The Rhetoric of Criminology*. Chicago: University of Chicago Press.

Bertaux, Daniel (ed.) (1981) *Biography and Society: The Life History Approach in the Social Sciences*. London: Sage.

Best, Joel (1995) 'Lost in the ozone again: the postmodern fad and interactionist foibles', *Studies in Symbolic Interaction*, 17: 125–30.

Bjorklund, Diane (1999) *Interpreting the Other: Two Hundred Years of American Autobiography*. Chicago: University of Chicago Press.

Black Public Sphere (eds) (1995) *The Black Public Sphere: A Public Culture Book*. Chicago: University of Chicago Press.

Blackman, Margaret (ed.) (1992) 'The afterlife of the life history', *Journal of Narrative and Life History*, 2 (1): 1–9.

Bogdan, R. (1974) *Being Different: The Autobiography of Jane Fry*. London: Wiley.

Bornat, Joanne (ed.) (1994) *Reminiscence Reviewed: Perspectives, Evaluations, Achievements*. Buckingham: Open University Press.

Bruner, Jerome (1987) 'Life as narrative', *Social Research*, 54 (1): 11–32.

Bruner, Jerome (1993) 'The autobiographical process', in Robert Folkenflik (ed.), *The Culture of Autobiography: Constructions of Self Representation*. Stanford, CA: Stanford University Press. pp. 38–56.

Caplan, Patricia (1997) *African Voices, African Lives*. London: Routledge.

Chalasinski, Josef (1981) 'The life records of the young generation of Polish peasants as a manifestation of contemporary culture', in Daniel Bertaux (ed.), *Biography and Society: The Life History Approach in the Social Sciences*. London: Sage. pp. 119–31.

Chanfrault-Duchet, Marie Francoise (1995) 'Biographical research in former West Germany', in Daniel Simeoni and Marco Diani (eds), *Biographical Research, Current Sociology*, 43 (2/3).

Clough, Patricia (1992) *The End(s) of Ethnography*. London: Sage.

Coles, R. (1989) *The Call of Stories: Teaching and the Moral Imagination*. Boston, MA: Houghton–Mifflin.

Coles, R. (1997) *Doing Documentary Work*. Oxford: Oxford University Press.

Crapanzano, V. (1986) 'Hermes' dilemma: the masking of subversion in ethnographic description' in J. Clifford and G.E. Marcus (eds), *Writing Culture: The Poetics and Politics of Ethnography*. Berkeley, CA: University of California Press.

Denzin, Norman K. (1989) *Interpretative Biography*. London: Sage.

Denzin, Norman K. (1997) *Interpretative Biography: Ethnographic Practices for the 21st Century*. London: Sage.

Denzin, Norman K. and Yvonna S. Lincoln (eds) (1994) *Handbook of Qualitative Research*. London: Sage.

Dickens, David R. and Fontana, Andrea (eds) (1994) *Postmodernism and Social Inquiry*. London: UCL Press.

Dunaway, D.K. and Baum, W.K. (1996) *Oral History: An Interdisciplinary Anthology*. Walnut Creek, CA: AltaMira Press.

Duneier, Mitchell (1992) *Slim's Table: Race, Respectability and Masculinity*. Chicago: University of Chicago Press.

Edwards, D. (1997) *Discourse and Cognition*. London: Sage.

Ellis, Carolyn (1991) 'Emotional sociology', in Norman K. Denzin (ed.), *Studies in Symbolic Interaction*. Greenwich, CT: JAI Press.

Ellis, Carolyn (1995) *Final Negotiations: A Story of Love, Loss and Chronic Illness*. Phildelphia: Temple University Press.

Ellis, Carolyn and Bochner, Arthur P. (eds) (1996) *Composing Ethnography: Alternative Forms of Qualitative Writing*. London: Sage.

Ellis, Carolyn and Flaherty, Michael G. (eds) (1992) *Investigating Subjectivity: Research on Lived Experience*. London: Sage.

Frisch, Michael (1990) *A Shared Authority: Essays on the Craft and Meanings of Oral and Public History*. Albany, NY: State University of New York Press.

Frisch, Michael (1998) 'Oral history and hard times: a review essay', in Robert Perks and Alaistair Thompson (eds), *The Oral History Reader*. London: Routledge.

Gilligan, Carole et al. (1988) *Mapping the Moral Domain*. Cambridge, MA: Harvard University Press.

Gilligan, Carole and Brown, Lyn Mikel (1992) *Meeting at the Crossroads: Womens Psychology and Girls' Development*. Cambridge, MA, and London: Harvard University Press.

Goode, David (1994) *A World without Words: The Social Construction of Children Born Deaf and Blind*. Philadelphia: Temple University Press.

Gubrium, Jaber (1993) *Speaking of Life*. New York: Aldine de Gruyter.

Gubrium, Jaber F. and Holstein, James H. (1997) *The New Language of Qualitative Method*. Oxford: Oxford University Press.

Halbwachs, Maurice (1992) *On Collective Memory* (ed. and trans. Lewis A. Coser). Chicago: University of Chicago Press.

Haraven, Tamara (1996) 'The search for generational memory', in David K. Dunaway and Willa K. Baum (eds), *Oral History: An Interdisciplinary Anthology*. London: AltaMira Press. pp. 241–56.

Hillis Miller, J. (1990) 'Narrative', in Frank Lentricchia and Thomas McLaughlin (eds), *Critical Terms for Literary Study*. Chicago: University of Chicago Press.

Josselson, Ruthellen (1996) *Ethics and Process in the Narrative Study of Lives*. London: Sage. (vol. 4 of The Narrative Study of Lives Series.)

Kenyon, Gary M. and Randall, William L. (1997) *Restorying Our Lives: Personal Growth Through Autobiographical Reflection*. London: Praeger.

Krieger, Susan (1996) *The Family Silver: Essays on Relationships Among Women*. Berkeley, CA: University of California Press.

Lara, Maria Pia (1998) *Moral Textures: Feminist Narratives in the Public Sphere*. Cambridge: Polity Press.

Lieblich, Amia (1996) 'Some unforeseen outcomes of conducting narrative research with people of one's own culture', in Ruthellen Josselson (ed.), *Ethics and Process in the Narrative Study of Lives*. London: Sage. pp. 172–84. (vol. 4 of The Narrative Study of Lives Series.)

Lieblich, Amia, Tuval-Mashiach, Rivka and Zilber, Tamar (1998) *Narrative Research*. London: Sage.

Liebow, Elliot (1967) *Tally's Corner*. Boston, MA: Little Brown.

Linde, Charlotte (1993) *Life Stories: The Creation of Coherence*. Oxford: Oxford University Press.

Malcolm, Janet (1990) *The Journalist and the Murderer*. New York: Vintage.

Marcus, Laura (1994) *Auto/Biographical Discourses: Theory. Criticism. Practice*. Manchester: Manchester University Press.

Marcus, G.E. (1994) 'What comes (just) after 'Post'? The case of ethnography', in Norman K. Denzin and Yvonna S. Lincoln (eds), *Handbook of Qualitative Research*. London: Sage.

Marcus, G.E. and Fischer, M. (1986) *Anthropology as Cultural Critique*. Chicago: University of Chicago Press.

McAdams, Dan (1985) *Power, Intimacy and the Life Story*. New York: Guilford Press.

McAdams, Dan (1993) *The Stories We Live By: Personal Myths and the Making of the Self*. New York: Guilford Press.

Menchú, Rigoberta (1984) *I, Rigoberta Menchú: An Indian Woman in Guatemala* (ed. Elizabeth Burgos-Debray). London: Verso.

Neumann, Mark (1998) 'Collecting ourselves at the end of the century', in Carolyn Ellis and Arthur P. Bochner (eds), *Composing Ethnography: Alternative Forms of Qualitative Writing*. London: Sage. pp. 172–98.

Noblitt, George W. and Dempsey, Van O. (1996) *The Social Construction of Virtue: The Moral Life of Schools*. Albany, NY: State University of New York Press.

Okely, Judith and Callaway, H. (eds) (1992) *Anthropology and Autobiography*. New York: Routledge.

Olney, James (1998) *Memory and Narrative: The Weave of Life Writing*. Chicago: University of Chicago Press.

Perks, Robert and Thompson, Alaistair (eds) (1998) *The Oral History Reader*. London: Routledge.

Plummer, Ken (1983) *Documents of Life: An Introduction to the Problems and Literature of a Humanistic Method*. London: Allen and Unwin. (2nd edn, Plummer, 2000.)

Plummer, Ken (1990) 'Herbert Blumer and the life history tradition', *Symbolic Interaction*, 11 (2): 125–44.

Plummer, Ken (1995) *Telling Sexual Stories*. London: Routledge.

Plummer, Ken (2000) *Documents of Life – 2. An Invitation to a Critical Humanism*. London: Sage. (2nd edn of Plummer, 1983.)

Polkinghorne, Donald E. (1988) *Narrative Knowing and the Human Sciences*. Albany, NY: State University of New York Press.

Portelli, Alessandro (1998) 'What makes oral history different?', in Robert Perks and Alaistair Thompson (eds), *The Oral History Reader*. London: Routledge. pp. 63–74.

Pratt, Mary Louise (1991) 'Arts of the contact zone', *Profession*, 91: 33–40.

Prieur, Annick (1998) *Mema's House: On Transvestites, Queens and Machos*. Chicago: University of Chicago Press.

Richardson, Laurel (1998) *Fields of Play: Constructing an Academic Life*. New Brunswick, NJ: Rutgers University Press.

Riessman, Catherine Kohler (1993) *Narrative Analysis*. London: Sage.

Ronai, Carol Rambo (1992) 'The reflexive self through narrative: a night in the life of an erotic dancer/researcher', Carolyn Ellis and Michael Flaherty (eds), *Investigating Subjectivity: Research on Lived Experience*. London: Sage. pp. 102–24.

Ronai, Carol Rambo (1996) 'My mother is mentally retarded', in Carolyn Ellis and Arthur P. Bochner (eds), *Composing Ethnography: Alternative Forms of Qualitative Writing*. London: Sage. pp. 109–31.

Schuman, H. and Scott, J. (1989) 'Generations and collective memory', *American Sociological Review*, 54 (June): 359–81.

Shaw, Clifford (1966) *The Jack Roller: A Delinquent Boy's Own Story*. Chicago: University of Chicago Press.

Simeoni, Daniel and Diani, Marco (eds) (1995) 'Biographical research', *Current Sociology*, 43 (2/3).

Simonds, Wendy (1992) *Women and Self-Help: Reading Between the Lines*. Brunswick, NJ: Rutgers University Press.

Snodgrass, Jon, and The Jack Roller (1982) *The Jack Roller at Seventy*. Lexington, MA: D.C. Heath.

Stacey, Judith (1988) 'Can there be a feminist ethnography?', *Women's Studies International Forum*, 11 (1): 21–7.

Stanley, Liz (1992) *The Auto/Biographical I: Theory and Practice of Feminist Auto/Biography*. Manchester: Manchester University Press.

Stoll, David (1999) *Rigoberta Menchú and the Story of All Poor Guatemalans*. Oxford: Westview Press.

Taylor, Charles (1989) *Sources of the Self*. Cambridge, MA: Harvard University Press.

Terkel, Studs (1970) *Hard Times: An Oral History of the Great Depression*. London: Allen Lane.

Terkel, Studs (1974) *Working*. Middlesex: Penguin.

Thomas, William I. and Znaniecki, Florian (1958) *The Polish Peasant in Europe and America*. New York: Dover Books (originally published 1918–21).

Ulmer, G. (1990) *Teletheory*. London: Routledge.

Vansina, J. (1985) *Oral Tradition as History*. Madison, WI: University of Wisconsin Press.

White, Hayden (1973) *Metahistory*. Baltimore, MD: Johns Hopkins University Press.

Whyte, William Foote (1943) *Street Corner Society: The Social Structure of an Italian Slum*. Chicago: University of Chicago Press.

Witherell, Carol and Noddings, Nel (eds) (1991) *Stories Lives Tell: Narrative and Dialogue in Education*. New York: Teachers College Press.

Zola, Irving (1982) *Missing Pieces: A Chronicle of Living with a Disability*. Philadelphia: Temple University Press.

28

Autobiography, Intimacy and Ethnography

DEBORAH REED-DANAHAY

Ethnographers have long displayed themselves and others as individuals through photographs, biography, life history and autobiography. While disclosure of intimate details of the lives of those typically under the ethnographic gaze (the informants) has long been an acceptable and expected aspect of ethnographic research and writing, self-disclosure among ethnographers themselves has been less acceptable and much less common. As Ruth Behar (1996: 26) has written, 'In anthropology, which historically exists to "give voice" to others, there is no greater taboo than self-revelation'. Writing about the private lives of both ethnographers and their informants has been subject to debates about the humanistic versus scientific validity of a focus on individuals. In recent decades, three prominent genres of writing have influenced thinking about the relationship between ethnography and the self of both the ethnographer and the 'native' informant:

1 native anthropology, in which people who were formerly the subjects of ethnography become authors of studies of their own groups either as professional anthropologists or indigenous ethnographers;
2 ethnic autobiography: personal narratives in which ethnic or cultural identity is foregrounded in the life story;
3 autobiographical ethnography, in which professional researchers incorporate their own personal narratives into their ethnographic texts.

Social theory that emphasizes social agency and practice influences this trend (Cohen, 1994; Giddens, 1991), as do approaches of social and cultural poetics (Fernandez and Herzfeld, 1998;

Lavie et al., 1993). A more general trend toward 'reflexivity' in ethnographic writing (Cole, 1992), influenced by both postmodernism and feminism, also informs the increasing emphasis on self-disclosure and self-display. Anthropologists and sociologists are becoming more explicit in their exploration of the links between their own autobiographies and their ethnographic practices (Ellis and Bochner, 1996; Okely and Callaway, 1992). At the same time, the 'natives' are increasingly telling their own stories and have become ethnographers of their own cultures (Jones, 1970; Ohnuki-Tierney, 1984). Researchers as well as their informants/collaborators have become aware of the politics of representation and of the power relations inherent in ethnographic accounts (Archetti, 1994; Behar and Gordon, 1995; Clifford, 1983; Fox, 1991; Harrison, 1997; Hymes, 1974; Marcus and Fischer, 1986; Moore, 1994; Okely and Callaway, 1992; Strathern, 1987). This growing trend in ethnographic writing that foregrounds self-narratives can be characterized with the term 'autoethnography' – referring to self-inscription on the part of the ethnographer, the 'native', or both (see Reed-Danahay, 1997b).

In this chapter I will review ethnographic practices that use life writing, and the various issues of power and representation that these raise. This literature review will depend most heavily on sources in English or English translation, but will also include French sources. This reflects my own linguistic limitations and I apologize in advance for my neglect of ethnographic productions in other languages. This chapter aims to be interdisciplinary in its coverage of ethnography, drawing from qualitative studies in sociology, education and communication studies, but depends most heavily on writings in cultural anthropology. I will first review approaches to life history, and then turn to the autobiographical practices of ethnographers themselves, before pointing to newer hybridizations in ethnographic writing.

LIFE HISTORY

The methods of life history have been central to ethnography, particularly in the United States, but nevertheless remain in an ambiguous relationship to participant observation fieldwork. Recent approaches to the study of lives have introduced concepts of life stories and personal narrative, as well as 'ethnographic biography' (Herzfeld, 1997b), to this tradition. While Watson and Watson-Franke (1985: 1) describe the marginal role of life history in social science methods, Peacock and Holland write that 'life histories have become standbys in American ethnography' (1993). The neglect of life history in their review article on ethnographic texts by Marcus and Cushman (1982), is perhaps most indicative of the position of this methodological approach in the wider discipline. Bertaux and Kohli (1984) remarked upon the retrenchment of autobiographical and biographical methods in anthropology, particularly during the 1970s, and attributed this to a trend toward 'scientism'. However, the same neglect by Marcus and Cushman, who can hardly be placed in the camp of 'scientism', shows the wider biases in ethnography that have worked against an emphasis on life stories.

Several essays and entire volumes discuss methods of life history and its relationship to ethnography. Recent writers such as Angrosino (1989), Atkinson (1992), Denzin (1989), Linde (1993), Peacock and Holland (1993), Rosenwald and Ochberg (1992), and Watson and Watson-Franke (1985) have identified various genres of writing and introduce typologies of terminologies in this field. An example of this would be the distinction drawn between life history – elicited by another person – and autobiography – self-initiated (Watson and Watson-Franke, 1985: 2). Watson and Watson-Franke further distinguish 'biography', which involves more rearranging of material than life history, so that it becomes a 'recorder's report of the subject's life' (1985: 3), and 'diary' – life recorded in an 'immediate perspective' (1985: 3). Angrosino (1989: 3) differentiates between genres of biography, autobiography, life history, life story and personal narrative.

Bruce Shaw (1980) suggests four elements in most definitions of anthropological approaches to life history: '(1) they emphasize the importance of the teller's sociocultural milieu; (2) they focus on the perspectives of one, unique individual; (3) they have a time depth, so that a personal history reveals also matters relevant to a region's or group's local history; (4) they relate the local history from the point of view of indigenous narrators' (1980: 229). This standard view, while still prevalent among many researchers, has shifted ground somewhat in more recent approaches that focus on interactions between ethnographer/interlocutor and autobiographer, and on issues of individual creativity and emotion. These will be discussed later in the chapter.

Brandes (1982) identifies 'ethnographic autobiography' as a form of first-person narrative, recorded and edited by a professional anthropologist (or someone in a related discipline). Texts of this sort are, he writes, usually non-Western narratives, and the anthropologist generally takes an interest in the psychosocial and developmental stages of an individual's life. In advocating the use of life histories, Brandes argues that 'autobiographies, more than any other research tool, demonstrate that complex and subtle considerations motivate individuals; people are not automatons, responding blindly to the vague factors and forces that are said to compel this or that type of action' (1982: 190). Anticipating current trends, Brandes notes that 'ethnographers themselves are becoming increasingly autobiographical in their presentation of data, showing that the study of society is rooted as much in the anthropologist's personality, and the purely fortuitous circumstances into which he or she is thrust' (1982: 190). In his essay, Brandes also discusses editing choices made, and other methodological issues in ethnographic autobiography. Blauner (1987), who includes a useful literature review of methods, also comments on methodological issues of editing first-person narratives – such as those of voice and selection.

National trends in uses of life history have been identified by various scholars. Angrosino defines the American (as opposed to European) approach to life history as one continually searching for the extraordinary individual who is representative of their culture (especially Native Americans). This person's life comes to express change and to illustrate factors of acculturation. In the European study of life history, according to Angrosino, there is a more collective approach to personal narratives in order to show 'society as a whole' (intact). Angrosino attributes these differences in approach to historical factors, such as the influence of nationalism on European approaches and to the influence of psychology on American approaches (1989: 15–16). In the collective approach, there is more emphasis on the life cycle, on aging and on socialization – features not unique to the individual.[1]

There are several key histories and reviews of life history in ethnography to which the reader may turn. The earliest, and now classic, statement on methods of life history is Dollard (1935). This was followed by the also classic interdisciplinary 1945 collection *The Use of Personal Documents in History, Anthropology, and Sociology*, by L. Gottschallk, C. Kluckhohn and R. Angell. Two decades later, Langness provided a short but dense 1965 text which contains a comprehensive review of the literature on anthropological uses of biography and methods of life history research up until the 1960s. Langness' bibliography shows that there was an impressive amount of work already produced by that time. Despite the volume of work, however, Langness criticizes its lack of focus or method (cf. Crapanzano, 1984). A later review of the life history approach was *Lives: An Anthropological Approach* (Langness and Franke, 1981). A more recent comprehensive bibliography of life history (Grimes, 1995) lists the major texts.

The earliest uses of life history by social scientists in the United States focused on Native Americans (Kroeber, 1908; Landes, [1938] 1997; Radin, 1926; Simmons, [1942] 1979) and immigrants from Europe (Thomas and Znaniecki, 1918–1920; Whyte, 1943). These studies used personal narratives, diaries, autobiography and the editorial methods of life history in order to present first-person accounts of individuals in the midst of culture change. An edited collection of fictionalized Native American personal narratives written by anthropologists who used composite portraits of their informants also appeared in this earlier period (Parsons, [1922] 1967). The concerns of those ethnographers who used life history methods in the early twentieth century were connected to debates about the relationship between creativity and cultural constraints, issues of getting the native point of view, and psychological foci on the modal personality (DuBois, 1944). Ruth Landes ([1938] 1997) collected life histories of Ojibwa women to show that generalizations about culture must be nuanced by individual life stories, in order to portray individual differences rather than to focus on lives that were representative of the culture. In later research among Native Americans in both North and Central America, life histories were used to identify and chronicle cultural change and deviance (Lewis, 1964; Sewid and Spradley, [1969] 1978; Spindler, 1962).

Such concerns can still be seen in more recent work. Several newer themes have, however, emerged. The therapeutic use of life history among the elderly and the mentally and physically ill has been advocated by Angrosino (1989), Crapanzano (1980), Church (1995), Frank (1995), Kaufman (1986) and Myerhoff (1978). Langness and Frank (1981: 107) suggest that life history can play a role in 'repair work' to repair identities among stigmatized populations, such as that of transsexuals. There has also been a growing emphasis on the study of women's life histories, as a way to compensate for previous research with a male bias that ignored the 'woman's point of view' (see Personal Narratives Group, 1989). Three early examples are Landes ([1938] 1997), Reichard (1934) and Underhill ([1936] 1985). Key recent texts include Marjorie Shostak's life history of a !Kung woman named

Nisa ([1981] 1983), Caroline Brettell's work among Portuguese migrant women (1982) and on her own mother's life (1999), Lila Abu-Lughod's work on Bedouin women's stories (1993), Ruth Behar's volume on a Mexican peasant woman (1993), and Sally McBeth's collaboration with Esther Burnett Horne on the life story of a Shoshone teacher (1998).

Current theoretical debates in life history research are about issues of cultural constructions of selfhood, of truth and representation (see Bertaux, 1981; Mintz, 1979), issues of the generalizing versus particularizing nature of this research (that is, is this person 'representative' and does this matter?), and questions of voice. At issue, according to Watson and Watson-Franke (1985), is not so much the truth or representativeness of the individual life story, but rather the degree to which this narrative is revealing of concepts of the 'ideal self' in a given cultural context. They propose a method through which the individual's comments on 'self-appraisal' are analysed (1985: 188–9), and in which such material can be used in a comparative cross-cultural framework.

James Peacock and Dorothy Holland (1993) draw attention to the ways in which changing concepts of the self in recent theoretical approaches influence life history research. Such approaches raise questions about the universality of the traditional Western view of the 'unified' self, and present a view of the self as fragmented and context-dependent. Given this changing concept of the self, Peacock and Holland prefer the term 'life story' to that of life history (since the latter connotes a more unified and coherent narrative). They identify two dominant approaches to life stories. The first is the 'life-focused' approach, which emphasizes the individual's life and is dependent upon 'truth' and historical fact (1993: 369). The second is the 'story-focused' approach, advocated by Linde (1993), which emphasizes narrative form, techniques and the subjective experience of the narrator. In order to reconcile these two approaches, Peacock and Holland propose a synthesis – which they call a processual approach. In this method, they write, 'the telling of life stories, whether to others or to self alone, is treated as an important, shaping event in social and psychological processes, yet the life stories themselves are considered to be developed in, and the outcomes of, the course of these and other life events' (1993: 371). This view of life stories helps to erase the older objective vs. subjective dichotomy that has marked life history research from the beginning.

In addition to the processual approach, two other alternatives to a supposedly objective, factual approach to autobiography can be identified: a hermeneutic or phenomenological approach (Little, 1980; Watson, 1976), and an interactionist approach (Angrosino, 1989). In the hermeneutic approach, which Little traces back to Paul Radin, the focus is on interpretation and meaning – in particular, the individual's own interpretation of his or her life experiences. The aim is not to get at cultural patterns, but, rather, to focus on the aesthetics of the life history and the emotions it portrays. In his volume *Documents of Interaction: Biography, Autobiography and Life History in Social Science Perspectives*, Angrosino (1989) argues that autobiographical materials should be treated as part of an interaction between 'a subject recounting his or her life experiences and an audience, either the researcher recording the story or the readers of the resulting text' (1989: 1). Drawing from Catani (1981), he suggests that life history is the product of 'encounter' (1981: 17), and cites Vincent Crapanzano's work as a useful method for this approach. In his book *Tuhami*, Crapanzano (1980) explicitly shows the researcher's role in shaping the text in his discussions of his encounters with Tuhami. Elsewhere, Crapanzano (1984) critiques life history approaches for their lack of analysis. He suggests that ethnographers pay more attention to indigenous notions of rhetoric and narrative technique (1984: 957).

There is in increasing emphasis on story, on the interaction between the research and narrator, and on issues of narrativity in life history research. The uses of personal narratives that may not include an entire autobiography have become key tools of cultural study. Thus, Ginsburg (1987) made use of 'procreation stories' to study abortion activists; Herzfeld (1985) examined 'thieving stories' to study concepts of masculinity and self-presentation among Cretan shepherds; Rosaldo (1989) has examined 'hunting stories' among the Ilongot; Kleinman (1988) and Frank (1995) have looked at 'illness narratives' in order to understand interactions between culture and illness; and Reed-Danahay (1997b) and Luttrell (1997) have turned to 'schooling stories' to examine cultural constructions of education and literacy. Lawuyi (1989) analyses Yoruba obituaries as a form of biographical expression with interest for life history research. Attention has also been drawn in recent studies to the ethnographic uses of diaries (Bunkers and Huff, 1996; West, 1992) and other forms of everyday autobiographical productions (Smith and Watson, 1996).

Beyond the Written

In the area of cultural studies, three recent works point to forms of self-inscription that come from popular culture, and in which the social agency of local populations is expressed. Anne Goldman (1996) shows that recipes, midwife narratives and work narratives among working-class ethnic American women constitute important sites for self-narration and self-display. In her work with the autobiographical genres of Mexicanas, Jewish and African-American women, Goldman sheds

important light on everyday, autoethnographic productions. Two other studies show nicely the ways in which personal narrative is not necessarily dependent upon oral or written expression. John Dorst (1989) analyses local festival displays, including arts and crafts, in semi-rural Chester County, PA, as a form of autoethnography. Social and cultural artifacts constitute a form of self-inscription and self-referentiality, he argues. Dorst's work calls attention to everyday practices of personal narrative that may elude the ethnographer looking for oral or written forms.

In another study, Hertha Wong (1989) has contributed to the understanding of Native American autobiography by showing that Native Americans used pictographs as personal records. Previous scholars overlooked the significance of pictographs as means of individual expression, she writes, because it was assumed that notions of individualism were exclusively Western (1989: 295). Plains Indian males, she argues, described heroic feats in pictures as well as in words. Pictographs constitute visual narratives of accomplishments and of processes of cultural conversion (forced acculturation). Wong shows that we need to rethink 'autobiographical activity' through her analysis of pictographs by artists White Bull and Zo-Tom in the late nineteenth century. Zo-Tom's 'cultural conversion narrative' embodied in pictographs depicts a classroom in Fort Marion at the Indian School. 'Instead of the long-haired, brilliantly attired and ornamented Kiowa warriors of his earlier drawings, he draws seven clean-cut Indian students in blue pants and snug black coats who sit, lining a long school bench, at a long desk. Mrs. Gibbs, the teacher, stands prim and pleasant, to the left' (Wong, 1989: 304).

Both Wong and Goldman critique anthropological methods of life history and offer their own work as correctives to its biases. Their attempts to uncover native voices depend upon two different types of critiques, however. Wong argues that anthropologists were biased in seeking the 'individual' in the Native American self-narrative that was, she suggests, more dependent upon the communal. In contrast, Goldman argues that anthropologists undertaking life histories sought the cultural representative at the expense of the individual, and she claims that her work restores the sense of individual social agency to the subjects of ethnographic research. These two contrasting critiques, coming from outside of the discipline, underscore continued debates within the discipline about the politics of representation, self-representation and self-disclosure. They also point to unresolved debates on cross-cultural studies of subjectivity. Is the 'individual' a strictly Western invention, or does it have cross-cultural validity? Can we construct life history and autobiography without recognizing issues of gender, class and culture? More recent collaborative approaches in life history research, to be discussed later in this chapter, attempt to address these concerns.

THE 'PERSONAL APPROACH' IN ETHNOGRAPHY

Although, as Judith Okely writes, 'the personal is often denigrated in anthropological monographs' (1996: 30), there has been sufficient use of this mode to warrant numerous overviews and discussions of the personal approach. The conventions of self-disclosure in ethnographic writing have been discussed at length by Angrosino (1989), Atkinson (1992), Denzin (1989), Friedman (1990), Okely and Callaway (1992), Reed-Danahay (1997b), Tedlock (1991) and Van Maanen (1988).

Ethnographers intensified efforts to chronicle their fieldwork experiences in ways that foregrounded the researcher as person during the mid-twentieth century. Although many overviews of ethnographic writing propose a chronological development from realist ethnographic writing that strove for objectivity to newer forms of autoethnographic writing, there have long been modes of ethnographic writing that incorporated the self of the ethnographer (Arana, 1988; Cole, 1992; Pratt, 1986; Stivers, 1993; Tedlock, 1995). In many cases, these represented parallel worlds to the ethnographic writing products that established a scholar's reputation through ethnographic theory and description. As Bruner (1993: 3) writes, 'Until the past few decades ... the majority decision was to sharply segment the ethnographic self from the personal self.' Similarly, ethnographers who used life history methods kept their own lives outside of the life history narratives they recorded (see Brandes, 1982). Mary Louise Pratt has also taken note of the parallel tropes of ethnographic writing. She writes 'Of these pairs of books, the formal ethnography is the one that counts as professional capital and as an authoritative representation; the personal narratives are often deemed self-indulgent, trivial, or heretical in other ways. But despite such "disciplining", they have kept appearing, kept being read and above all kept being taught within the borders of the discipline, for what one must assume are powerful reasons' (Pratt, 1986: 31). She argues that the persistence of personal narrative is due to the mediating role it plays between the contradictions of personal and scientific authority connected to ethnographic, participant observation research. During the late 1970s and 1980s the dichotomy between personal and scientific writing began to change, with experimental writing projects that blended the genres of ethnography, biography and autobiography. Works from this period will be discussed later in the chapter.

It is instructive to recall some key texts from the 1970s and 1980s in which debates about 'personal'

ethnography were played out, especially in the pages of *Current Anthropology*, which published several essays (Honigmann, 1976; Mandelbaum, 1973; Nash and Wintrob, 1972; Sangren, 1988; Strathern, 1987). These articles and the responses to them dealt with the tension between what is often phrased, falsely many argue, as the 'personal' and the 'objective'. Autobiographical and reflexive methods have long been viewed by many within the social science paradigms of positivism as unscientific, and at odds with objective, standardized forms of research. Other critiques point out the cultural biases in an emphasis on the individual. Nash and Wintrob identified an increasing trend to insert anthropologists 'into the field picture' (1972: 527), and pointed to the difficulties historically experienced by anthropologists who attempted to publish personal accounts of fieldwork. Their perspective was that since anthropology is a science, there is a need to see ways in which individual biases affect this science. Nash and Wintrob identified the current conditions that were undermining 'naive empiricism':

1 an increasing personal involvement of ethnographers with their subjects;
2 the 'democratization' of anthropology;
3 multiple field studies of the same culture;
4 assertions of independence by native peoples.

This latter trend, they suggested, was chipping away at the self-confidence of anthropologists, associated as they were with colonial powers on the decline.

In his 1976 essay, Honigmann defended the personal approach, pointing to Kroeber's earlier attempts to incorporate such methods, as well as Evans-Pritchard's interest in hermeneutics. This article relied, however, on the dichotomy between objective and subjective, a dubious dichotomy, as pointed out by Charles Keil in his response to Honigmann (1976: 253). Foreshadowing critiques of the 1980s and 1990s, Keil argued for the adoption of 'extended autobiographies before fieldwork and candid diaries during fieldwork' and the insistence that 'investigators work in multicultural collectivities with the people and for the people rather than on the people for us' (1976: 253). In a more recent discussion of the 'personal approach,' Steven Sangren (1988) cautioned that such approaches rely narrowly upon Western notions of individualism. Sangren broadened the definition of 'individualism', beyond its connections to commodity fetishism, to mean 'the privileging of the subject or "experience" in theoretical constructions of reality' (1988: 423). Sangren writes that 'in short, the privileging of "experience" or the actor's point of view reproduces a bourgeois, Western, individualistic ideology' (p. 423). He called for closer attention to the contexts in which anthropological careers as well as texts are produced and reproduced.

Since they appeared in 1980s, critiques of ethnographic realism put forth by Clifford (1983) and Marcus and Cushman (1982) have been highly influential in thinking about the history of self-disclosure in ethnography. British anthropologists writing in the classic phase of what has come to be called 'ethnographic realism' included discussions of fieldwork, but in forms that bracketed the essential business of the ethnography itself. Marcus and Cushman identify the key features of this approach, which 'seeks to represent the reality of a whole world or form of life' (1982: 29), as 'unintrusive presence of the ethnographer in the text', combined with the use of photos to demonstrate 'having been there'.[2] The ethnographer is thus visually portrayed as present in the work if not explicitly signified in the writing. The writing, they suggest, leaned toward a focus on 'native point of view'.

Clifford (1983) suggests, however, that the validity of ethnographic research was originally established through texts that incorporated explicit discussion of the fieldwork. He cites the examples of classic ethnographies written by Malinowski (*Argonauts*), Mead (*Coming of Age in Samoa*) and Firth's *We the Tikopia*. Evans-Pritchard wrote of fieldwork experiences in his introduction to *The Nuer* (1940). Malinowski described fieldwork in his introduction to *Argonauts of the Pacific* (1922), and also in his Appendix to *Coral Gardens and their Magic* (1935). Later, however, fieldwork accounts became less necessary, Clifford argues, as the authority of anthropology as a discipline became more established. Godfrey Lienhardt's brief statement at the beginning of *Divinity and Experience*, 'this book is based upon two years' work among the Dinka, spread over the period 1947–1950' (1961: 124), is an example. There is no other discussion of the work itself. The growing prestige of the 'fieldworker–theorist' (that is, Evans-Pritchard and *The Nuer*), led to the eventual bifurcation of the personal and ethnographic modes. Clifford writes that 'we are increasingly familiar with the separate fieldwork account (a sub-genre that still tends to be classified as subjective, "soft", or unscientific). But even within classic ethnographies, more or less stereotypic "fables of rapport" narrate the attainment of full participant-observer status' (Clifford, 1983: 132). Newer forms of writing about fieldwork that went beyond stereotypic accounts began to appear in the late 1970s, such as those by Dumont ([1922] 1978), Favret-Saada (1980), Rabinow (1977) and Shostak ([1981] 1983).

Fables of Rapport

Accounts of fieldwork have been referred to by Van Maanen (1988) as 'confessional tales' and by Clifford (1983) as 'fables of rapport'. Both critics agree that one of the most important aims of such accounts is to establish authority – to establish that the ethnographer was really there (see also Pratt, 1986). Moreover, Van Maanen suggests that they also work to establish intimacy with readers and to convince them of the human qualities of the fieldworker (1988: 75). Marcus and Cushman (1982: 26) contrast the methodological orientation of confessional fieldwork literature in the past to more recent ethnographies whose main aim is to 'demystify the process of anthropological fieldwork whose veil of published secrecy has been increasingly embarrassing to a "scientific" discipline'. Self-disclosure in ethnographic writing can serve either a confessional autobiographical approach, according to Marcus and Cushman (1982), or one more intellectual, concerned with the epistemology of knowledge. Tedlock (1991) identifies a trend of movement from the 'ethnographic memoir' to the 'narrative ethnography'. She writes that 'in contrast to memoirs, narrative ethnographies focus not on the ethnographer herself, but rather on the character and process of the ethnographic dialogue or encounter' (1991: 78). The narrative ethnography deals with the personal experiences of the ethnographer, but also incorporates cultural analysis. Bruner (1993: 6) expresses these concerns about confessional modes and memoir in his statement that 'the danger is putting the personal self so deeply back into the text that it completely dominates so that the work becomes narcissistic and egotistical.'

There are those, such as Carolyn Ellis and Susan Krieger, who would deny a dichotomy between the personal and the intellectual, between memoir and ethnography. Ellis (Ellis and Bochner, 1996) argues that personal, autobiographical modes of writing are vital for knowledge production in the social sciences. She proposes an 'evocative autoethnography' (1997), and an 'emotional sociology' (Ellis, 1991) that draws upon Denzin's emphasis on personal epiphanies to advocate the study of not only the emotional lives of those ethnographers studied but also the emotions of researchers as legitimate foci of study. In much of her work, Ellis makes use of 'introspective narrative' – revealing personal narratives written by researchers (see Ellis and Bochner, 1996) that may have less than obvious connections to conventional ethnographic concerns than have previous 'fables of rapport'. Krieger (1991: 48) similarly argues that 'inner experience' in social life should be more developed in social science writing. She writes 'it may not be best to organize an account around an intellectual idea when the subject is one's own experience. For me, it is desirable to structure a description in terms of the emotional content of an experience' (1991: 50–1) (see also Richardson, 1994).

Another proponent of personal narrative in ethnography, Judith Okely, writes in her essay on 'The Self and Scientism' that 'there is a need for more explicit recognition of fieldwork as personal experience instead of sacrificing it to a false notion of scientific objectivity' (1996: 27). She further suggests that 'since almost nothing about the people studied is dismissed as private, taboo or improper for investigation, the same should apply to the investigator' (p. 29). In her recent writing, Ruth Behar also illustrates the refusal to distinguish between emotional forms of knowledge and intellectual forms. In a book subtitled *Anthropology that Breaks Your Heart* (1996), Behar utilizes a highly intimate mode of writing in order to express personal concerns and professional issues that go much beyond those of fieldwork itself. She urges ethnographers to write 'vulnerably'. Behar cautions, however, that 'vulnerability does not mean that anything personal goes. The exposure of the self who is also a spectator has to take us somewhere we couldn't otherwise go. It has to be essential to the argument, not a decorative flourish, not exposure for its own sake' (1996: 14). Renato Rosaldo (1989) has also written a narrative of emotion which explicitly links his own experiences of grief over the death of his wife to his understanding of the Ilongot headhunters he studied during many years of fieldwork. He draws upon his own emotions to gain ethnographic insights on the emotional life and culture of the Ilongot.

It was in American anthropology, and among female anthropologists, that the use of personal narratives of fieldwork experiences became established as a separate genre from the ethnographic monograph (Arana, 1988; Tedlock, 1995). Observers of this trend have raised the possibilities of different subjectivities for males and females (Behar and Gordon, 1995; Cole, 1992). Reflections by Jean Jackson (1986), Judith Okely (1996) and Anne-Marie Fortier (1996) make use of personal narratives of fieldwork and the role of gender in order to critique theory and writing in ethnography. Barbara Tedlock (1995) suggests a gendered division of labor in textual productions by male and female ethnographers. She argues that the 'narrative mode', with less structure, and less authority in its prose, is more often adopted by females. This issue has also been addressed by Arana (1988) and Stivers (1993). In her article 'Works and Wives' Tedlock (1995) points out that husband and wife teams in ethnography (among them Victor and Edith Turner, Elizabeth and Robert Fernea) generally reflected a gendered approach to writing. Bruner (1993: 5) suggests that 'husbands would do the ethnography and wives would tell the story of the field experiences'.[3]

The earliest ethnographic memoirs were written by female anthropologists. One of the first deliberate attempts to describe the ethnographer's experience of fieldwork, foregrounding the 'self' of the researcher, was written in 1930 by Frederica DeLaguna, but was not published until 1977. A student of Boas, Benedict and Reichard, DeLaguna writes that she was frustrated that there were no accounts of fieldwork to which the beginning student could turn, and that this inspired her own autobiographical excursions. However, the lack of an intellectual climate in which such an account would be well received prohibited her from publishing this until many decades later. In this account of first fieldwork in Greenland during the summer of 1929, DeLaguna details her personal experiences with a combination of narrative, direct quotes from her fieldnotes and letters exchanged between herself and her family.

One of the first published accounts of fieldwork was Alice Lee Marriott's (1952) *Greener Fields: Experiences among the American Indians*. Another early account came in the form of a 1954 novel, *Return to Laughter*, written pseudonymously as Elinore Bowen by Laura Bohannan. This book chronicles an anthropologist's experiences during fieldwork in Africa, and is generally viewed as a thinly disguised autobiography, although Rosalie Wax has suggested that it 'may be a fictionalized pastiche composed of the tales of several persons and numerous trips' (1971: 37). Jean Briggs' *Never in Anger: Portrait of an Eskimo Family* (1970) is a similarly novelesque rendering, full of humorous self-disclosure, of a fieldwork experience among the Inuit. Two other volumes attempted to meld narratives of fieldwork with discussions of and training in fieldwork methodology. In her 1966 book *Stranger and Friend*, Hortense Powdermaker writes that the project 'attempts to present a case history of how an anthropologist lives, works, and learns; how he thinks, and feels, in the field. Other readers may also find it useful and interesting to go backstage with an anthropologist, and see what lies behind the finished performance' (1966: 15). Rosalie Wax (1971) used three of her own fieldwork experiences to discuss methods in her guide to fieldwork, and the bibliography usefully includes other accounts of fieldwork that had been written before 1970. A similar approach to incorporating personal experiences in ethnography for didactic purposes is taken by Peter McLaren (1989), who makes use of his early teaching journal as a way to teach about the approach of critical pedagogy.

Gerald D. Berreman's (1962) *Behind Many Masks: Ethnography and Impression Management in a Himalayan Village* also provided an account of fieldwork, but one that refused to present itself as a model for methods. Berreman's objective was to discuss the ways in which presentation of self by both the ethnographer and those they study comes into play, and the various forms of impression management, including secrecy and concealment, involved. This account of fieldwork in a highly stratified, caste-based Indian village underscores the complexities of fieldwork in such a setting.[4]

There are now scores of volumes written by ethnologists that explore their fieldwork experiences in candid accounts. These include both monographs and edited volumes of essays. A significant departure from the earlier 'realist' fieldwork accounts was taken by Jean-Paul Dumont, who attempts to blend the two genres of ethnographic monograph and personal narrative. He begins his book *The Headman and I* with the statement: 'This book is about the Panare Indians of Venezuelan Guiana and me, the investigating anthropologist' (1992: 3). Written in 1978, Dumont's book represents a significant turning point in the relationship between ethnography and autobiography. While Rabinow (1977) had, some feel, raised the fieldwork account to a new level of intellectual sophistication, Dumont's book was one of the first to gain acclaim as an *ethnography* that is also autobiographical. Elizabeth Fernea (1969, 1975) had earlier done much the same thing, but she received less attention. Also receiving less attention is an account of fieldwork written by Miriam Slater that aimed to be 'a cross between the personal and the objective' (1976: 1). She explicitly rejects, she writes, the tactic of writing two books (the monograph and the memoir), and hoped to intersect the two in her narrative ethnography.

The autobiographical fieldwork account persists as a separate genre from other forms of ethnographic writing. There is also a continued production of 'confessional tales' written by ethnographers, despite Tedlock's (1991) prediction that ethnographic narrative would supersede memoir. A recent book by Daniel Bradburd, *Being There, The Necessity of Fieldwork* (1998), makes use of anecdotes from fieldwork in Iran to convey, as the author writes, 'out-of-the-ordinary, unplanned elements of my field experience' (1998: xiii). Bradburd previously published another book that was 'more formal', and conformed to more conventional forms of ethnographic writing. He positions the newer personal approach as a response to what he labels the postmodern critique of fieldwork offered by James Clifford, Mary Louise Pratt and others. The defense of fieldwork as the hallmark of anthropology may also be seen in Geertz (1998: 69), who similarly criticizes what he terms the 'non-immersive, hit-and-run ethnography' of cultural studies writers such as Clifford. Geertz, however, does not advocate the 'fables of rapport' approach taken by Bradburd and others.

Autobiographical accounts of fieldwork have in recent years become too numerous to mention all of them here. Examples of books that propose to show the intimate experiences of the fieldworker 'in the field' include Anderson (1990), Barley (1986), Cesara (1982), Hayano (1990), Raybeck (1996), Turner (1987), Van den Berghe (1989), Wachtel (1994) and Ward (1989). The everyday process of fieldwork, especially the issues of domestic arrangements in an anthropological household in the field, are also illustrated by Elizabeth Fernea in her vivid accounts of fieldwork in the Middle East (1969, 1975).

Most published fieldwork stories are shorter than book-length, and collected in numerous edited volumes that have appeared since the 1960s. The relative absence of such volumes during the 1980s and abundance of them during the 1990s should be noted. Many of these edited collections are shaped around particular themes. The first, Casagrande's 1960 *In the Company of Man: Twenty Portraits of Anthropological Informants*, took up the issue of relationships between informants and fieldworkers, with an emphasis on the humanity of the informant. It has been followed by the more recent volume *Bridges to Humanity: Narratives on Anthropology and Friendship* (Grindal and Salamone, 1995), in which the emphasis has turned to the humanity of the anthropologist. Several more general anthologies of discussions of fieldwork have appeared, starting with the 1964 volume *Reflections on Community Studies* (Vidich et al., 1964), and then *Anthropologists in the Field* (Jongmans and Gutkind, 1967). These have been followed, in chronological order, by Frielich (1970), Spindler (1970), Kimball (1972), Beteille and Madan (1975), Shaffir and Stebbins (1991), DeVita (1992), Hobbs and May (1993), Jackson and Ives (1996), and Lareau and Shultz (1996). Here, one can see a shift in emphasis from techniques of scientific research, with autobiography used only anecdotally, to the proliferation of a more personal mode of writing about fieldwork experiences. In Jongmans and Gutkind (1967), for example, Edmund Leach writes of fieldwork from a strictly technical perspective. An exception in that volume is the essay by Köbben (1967), who mentions his experiences of emotional stress during fieldwork in Surinam. More recent volumes of the 1990s foreground the personal experiences of the ethnographers. A similar comparison could be drawn, in sociology, between Hammond (1964) and Ellis and Bochner (1996).

Several volumes of fieldwork narratives are organized around particular themes. For example, there are edited collections, beginning with Golde's 1970 *Women in the Field*, that deal with issues of gender and/or sexuality in the field. Golde's landmark volume drew attention to the particular issues facing female anthropologists, and opened discussions about feminist approaches to fieldwork. It has been followed by Whitehead and Conway (1986), Altorki and El-Solh ([1988] 1992) and Bell, Caplan and Karim (1993). Behar and Gordon (1995) echo early concerns in a recent volume devoted to gender and the writing of ethnography. Sexuality in the field, which will be discussed further below, has been addressed in the edited collections by Kulick and Wilson (1995), Lewin and Leap (1996) and Markowitz and Ashkenazi (1999).

Other themes that have prompted edited collections of fieldwork accounts include issues of children and family in the field (Butler and Turner, 1987; Cassell, 1987; Fernandez and Sutton, 1998;

Flinn et al., 1998), and the personal and professional aspects of long-term fieldwork (Fowler and Hardesty, 1994). There are also volumes devoted to fieldwork in a particular part of the world – DeVita (1990) on the Pacific; Srinivas et al. (1970) on India; and Altorki and El-Solh ([1988] 1992) on the Middle East. The volume *Distant Mirrors: America as a Foreign Culture* (DeVita and Armstrong, [1993] 1998) contains personal essays by non-US anthropologists who have conducted fieldwork there, inverting some of the usual ethnographic constructions of 'otherness.' The essays in Anthony Jackson's *Anthropology at Home* (1987) similarly deal with issues of place and fieldwork, this time when fieldwork is not 'away', but 'home.'

Another set of collections focus on autobiography, ethnography and narrative forms of writing; and on the intersections of literature and ethnography. The essays in the ground-breaking *Anthropology and Autobiography* (Okely and Callaway, 1992) are reflexive in their uses of biographical genres to discuss fieldwork experiences, bringing issues of theory, method and writing together. Other volumes that relate these issues include Myerhoff and Ruby (1982), Bruner (1984), Benson (1993), Lavie et al. (1993), Daniel and Peck (1996), Reed-Danahay (1997b), Tierney and Lincoln (1997) and Hertz (1997).

Ethnographers, Intimacy and Sexuality

In most autobiographical ethnography, there has been scant mention of the sexuality of the researcher. This taboo was famously broached when Malinowski's diaries (1967) were published, and his own struggles with sexual repression and expression were brought out of the closet. In his discussion of the publication of the diaries, George Stocking (1974) mentions that many people had informally told him that sexuality was an issue for them during fieldwork, despite the lack of public discourse on this subject. Paul Rabinow's (1977) candid description of accompanying his informants in pursuit of sexual encounters with local girls in Morocco was unusual at the time for its acknowledgment of sexual activity on the part of the anthropologist. Karl Poewe's (Cesara, 1982) fieldwork memoir was ground-breaking in its open discussion of gender and sexuality for a female anthropologist in the field (see also Weber, 1989). Several anthropologists, such as Shostak ([1981] 1983) and Herdt (1982), have written of the intimate sexual behaviors of their informants (with Shostak, in particular, alluding to her own youthful interest in the older Nissa's sexual experiences), but to write about one's own sexuality is much less common.

Two males have written in detail about their marriages to 'native' women, in books that reveal intimacies in cross-cultural encounters that raise various issues of the crossing of boundaries in anthropological fieldwork. These texts romanticize the male's erotic attractions to these women. A German scientist, who worked closely with anthropologists, detailed his own marriage to a much younger !Kung woman (Heinz and Lee, 1979) in a text that blends confessional autobiographical writing with ethnographic description. Of his wife, Heinz writes 'Here was fundamental woman in a sort of simple splendor, a basic creature whose femininity bared her emotions, sometimes fierce, mostly gentle, genuine and good. And I, so worldly and corrupt, so cultured by degrees and academia, had won her heart' (1979: 99). In her foreword to this book, Margaret Mead comments that it stands as a strong counterpoint to the image of the cold, distant researcher, and 'depends upon keeping the mother-in-law taboos oneself' (1979: xiii). Photos include the author, always captioned 'Dr Heinz' and always fully clothed, and his wife, usually with naked breasts exposed and always captioned simply 'Namkwa'. In a more recent text, anthropologist Kenneth Good (1991) has written an autobiographical account of his work among the Yanomama that chronicles his courtship of and subsequent marriage to a young native girl, whom he eventually tries to settle in suburban New Jersey. Pictures of his naked pubescent future wife are included in the text, as are intimate photos of the couple lounging in their hammock. As with Dr Heinz, Dr Good is always fully clothed. In both books, cross-cultural marriage is used as an entry to ethnographic observations and knowledge of the 'other'. A female counterpart to these male writers is Joana Varawa (1989), who has chronicled her experiences of marriage to a Fijian fisherman.

Several edited collections have appeared in recent years that directly explore issues of sexuality and fieldwork (Kulick and Wilson, 1995; Lewin and Leap, 1996; Markowitz and Ashkenazi, 1999). These collections are informed by the experimental ethnographic writing of the 1980s with their critiques of 'objectifying' accounts of both the anthropologist and his/her informants, and by the gender studies and feminist approaches in anthropology in the decades since the 1970s. In the first such volume to appear, Kulick and Wilson (1995) deal more explicitly with issues of sexuality than previous work, tying them to broader themes of reflexivity and subjectivity in ethnographic research (see also Probyn, 1993). Kulick and Wilson are so sensitive to previous prohibitions against disclosures of sexual intimacy in the field that Kulick makes the disclaimer in his introduction that 'this volume is not a catalogue of ethnopornography' (1995: 5). He points out that sex itself has always been a part of anthropology and that 'anthropology has always trafficked in the sexuality of the people we study' (1995: 2). Nevertheless, he continues, 'throughout all the decades of concern with the sex lives of others, anthropologists have remained very tightlipped about their own sexuality' (p. 3). Kulick cites Wengle's (1988) conclusion from his review of ethnographic reports that ethnographers have generally remained celibate during fieldwork. Silences about this topic are connected, Kulick suggests, to three features of ethnography: the absence of the ethnographer in text; disdain for personal narratives in the discipline; and general cultural taboos about discussing sex. With this volume, the editors and chapter authors hoped to open the conversation about the 'erotic subjectivity of the ethnographer' (Kulick and Wilson, 1995: 23).

One example from this volume is Jill Dubisch's chapter 'Lovers in the field'. In her acknowledgments, she thanks (with an ironic tone?) 'various friends and lovers in Greece' (1995: 48). As a scholar with long-term field experience in Greece, Dubisch has made numerous field trips, and has had various encounters with Greek males during different stages of her life and career. In her discussion of this, Dubisch is not explicit about the sex itself, but engages with issues of gender and sexuality, marriage, attachment, cultural and class differences in approaches to sexuality. Most interestingly, Dubisch shows that fieldwork raises issues of selfhood for the ethnographer and describes how she came to self-understanding through fieldwork in Greece. Through her encounters with many informants, friends, lovers and collaborators (not a mutually exclusive list, she lets us know), Dubisch came to see a blurring of the concept of the 'authentic unified self'. Each time she returns to Greece, she is different, and she explores different aspects of her selfhood during each fieldtrip. On the topic of sexuality, Dubisch writes 'Sexuality is one dimension of the self, and a dimension which may be particularly challenged in the field, whether by the felt necessity for abstinence, the sexual temptations offered to us, the fears of professional consequences of sexual indulgence, and/or the reactions of those we encounter to our perceived nature as sexual beings' (1995: 47). Nothing in our training as ethnographers, Dubisch concludes, prepares us for this.

The next volume to follow was Lewin and Leap's (1996) collection of essays on gay and lesbian anthropologists and sexuality in fieldwork. Some of the most candid discussions of sexuality and the field are to be found in the writings of gay and lesbian anthropologists, despite the heterosexual bias of most anthropological research on sexuality.[5] While there has been silence about sexuality in the field, the silences about gay and lesbian anthropologists have been even more pronounced. As Lewin and Leap write, 'Speaking openly is a step toward stripping homosexuality and lesbian and gay identity of their stigma' (1996: xi). For gay and lesbian anthropologists who do research on gay and lesbian issues, there are additional issues about this particular form of 'insider' research, or autoethnography (see especially Kennedy, 1996; Weston, 1996).

The most recent volume to appear on anthropology and sexuality (Markowitz and Ashkenazi, 1999) is informed by previous contributions in this field, and works to link theory to personal narratives of experiences of sexuality in the field. As the editors write, 'Sex and sexuality are not novel topics in anthropology, nor is a consideration of participant observation as method and epistemology. What is new is linking these two themes in the person of the anthropologist' (Ashkenazi and Markowitz, 1999: 5). A major contribution of this recent volume is its focus on the cultural construction of sexuality and the ways in which anthropologists' discussions of their personal and erotic relationships in the field can help in understandings of the ways in which both anthropologists and their 'field partners' ('informants') are 'positioned' in systems of power and meaning. One example of this is the essay by Michael Ashkenazi and Robert Rotenberg (1999) in which the authors compare their experiences of undertaking fieldwork in cultural settings (Japan and Vienna) that include public nudity during public bathing. While avoiding overly 'confessional' accounts of their personal encounters with nudity in various spheres, through their discussions of social discomfort, the authors convey the ways in which the erotic is socially constructed in different cultures. They also vividly address the effects of doing fieldwork in the nude on concepts of authority and intimacy. As they write, 'Observing, participating with, and interviewing nude people of both genders while nude oneself has unexpected consequences' (Ashkenazi and Rotenberg, 1999: 92). While anthropologists have often conducted fieldwork fully clothed in settings where the 'natives' were naked or partially naked (cf. Malinowski, 1967), this essay illustrates the more recent sensitivity among anthropologists to issues of power and representation in ethnography. Discussions of sexuality and fieldwork speak to issues of intimacy and their representation in ethnographic writing, to the ways in which both ethnographer and informant are constructed as individuals in ethnographic accounts, and to the ways in which sexuality is culturally constructed and informed by systems of power and authority.

Intellectual Memoirs

One biographical genre that is often overlooked in discussions of ethnography and autobiography is that of the intellectual autobiography and biography by the professional ethnographer. Zussman (1996) points out that anthropologists have produced much more such autobiographical writing than have sociologists, but works appear in both disciplines. Sociologist William Foote Whyte's (1994) *Participant-Observer: An Autobiography*, is a notable exception (see also Goetting and Fenstermaker, 1995; Riley, 1988; Williams, 1988). Since the theme of this chapter is ethnography, intellectual autobiographies written by social scientists who are not ethnographers fall outside of the scope; however, it is worth noting that there have been a number of such texts produced (i.e., Dews and Law, 1995).

Two of the most famous autobiographies in anthropology are *Blackberry Winter*, by Margaret Mead ([1972] 1995) and *Tristes Tropiques*, by Claude Lévi-Strauss ([1955] 1992). These two books focus on the intellectual and professional development of the scholar, and on their theoretical concerns. Fieldwork is mentioned, but not in the 'confessional mode' to the same degree as are 'fables of rapport' or narratives of fieldwork experiences *per se*. We learn less about the foibles and personal experiences, less explicitly about the inner life of the scholar, in such intellectual reports. There is more explicit discussion of theory in Mead and Lévi-Strauss' memoirs, although descriptions from the field also play a role in legitimizing the authority of each anthropologist through discussions of their 'having been there'.

Clifford Geertz's *After the Fact* (1995) is his own contribution to the genre of intellectual autobiography. In these essays, Geertz refrains from the confessional mode to detail his professional experiences and the development of much of his thinking. It is in many ways an anti- 'fable of rapport', illustrating Geertz's famous mistrust of the anthropologist's ability to adopt the 'native point of view'. Geertz writes 'field research in such times, in such places, is not a matter of working free from the cultural baggage you brought with you so as to enter, without shape and without attachment, into a foreign mode of life. It is a matter of living out your existence in two stories at once' (1995: 94). This volume, while written in the form of personal essays, is a discussion of the directions in which anthropology has developed during Geertz's career, and engages much more with anthropology and anthropologists than with the informants Geertz has encountered.

In a review of the literature on biographies and autobiographies of professional anthropologists, Zamora and Stegall (1980) look at issues of what influenced these scholars to become anthropologists. They call for more research and writing on what they term 'professional turning', particularly among Third World scholars. Since that article, several such essays have appeared in the journal *Ethnos* and in the *Annual Review of Anthropology*: see, for example, T.O. Beidelman (1998), Andre Beteille (1993), Paul Bohannan (1997), Ottar Brox (1996), Ernestine Friedl (1995), John Hostetler (1992), Ida Magli (1991), Robert Paine (1998)

and M.N. Srinivas (1997). Edward Hall (1992) has also written a memoir of his career as an anthropologist, while several essays in Fowler and Hardesty (1994) deal with issues of career and intellectual development (see also Goldfrank, 1978; Hurston, [1942] 1991; Miller, 1995).

Illness and Self-disclosure

Another genre of personal narrative that ethnographers have written is that of the 'illness narrative' (Kleinman, 1988). While there has been little written about illness during fieldwork, self-disclosure associated with issues of emotion, death and illness has developed into an identifiable genre of writing by ethnographers. Anthropologists Robert Murphy (1987) and Susan DiGiacomo (1987) have written about their own chronic illnesses and the medical profession with the keen insights of an ethnographer. Murphy, who conducted decades of research in South America, compares his spinal cord disease, which left him paralysed, to an 'extended anthropological field trip' (1987: ix). DiGiacomo (1987) who suffers from cancer, also writes of entering a new field site: 'the kingdom of the sick'. In sociology, Irving Zola (1982) and Arthur Frank (1991) have also written extensively of personal illness from the perspective of a social scientist. While all four of these authors applied previous ethnographic insights to their new experiences of illness, Kathryn Church (1995) moves in a different direction, making use of her own experiences of physical and mental breakdown during an ethnographic study of the professionalization of treatment for the mentally ill and psychiatric 'survivors'. She labels her approach that of 'critical autobiography' (Church, 1995: 3), following David Jackson (1990). This entails a form of ethnographic narrative whereby the aim, as she says, is 'to write myself into my own work as a major character' (1995: 3). In her book *Final Negotiations* (1995), Carolyn Ellis uses a personal approach to the ethnography of illness as she details her affair and subsequent marriage to another sociologist, who suffers from a fatal illness and eventually dies. The interest in illness narratives as written by the ethnographers parallels interest in the study of 'illness narratives' as a mode of research noted earlier in this chapter.

FUTURE DIRECTIONS

There has been an enduring interest in the personal, intimate lives of others among those who read and write ethnography. Collaboration between researchers and informants, and convergence between the personal narratives of each, are among the prominent trends that one can notice in recent work. As the 'natives' become increasingly literate, the need for 'life history' that speaks for the other will lessen, and the 'natives' will tell their own stories (perhaps with the aid of the ethnographer – as in the case of Horne and McBeth, 1998). The 'field' of ethnography is broadening, to include 'home', 'self', fiction and other textual productions, as well as visual culture. The construct of 'the field' as a site of ethnographic research (Gupta and Ferguson, 1997) is being questioned.

Recent attention to native forms of autobiography, biography and ethnography have led to hybrid forms and experimentations with established genres of life history and ethnography. The edited volumes by Driessen (1993) and Brettell (1993) both address the encounters, particularly through published ethnographic writing, between professional anthropologists and the subjects of their research. They also draw attention to the issues of power and representation raised in ethnographic writing. In Brettell's volume, Ginsburg (1993) discusses her work among abortion activists in order to highlight the politics of academic research and the ways in which colleagues react to certain forms of research. Elsewhere, Blackman (1992) reviews the ways in which Native American life histories have been received by Native American audiences.

The increasing production of ethnography by 'native anthropologists' working in their own cultural milieu has also led to discussions of selfhood, voice and authority in ethnographic writing. Kondo (1990) explores these issues through a blending of ethnography and personal narrative, in a study of Japan by a Japanese-American woman who stands in an ambiguous role *vis-à-vis* her Japanese informants – looking Japanese but not acting or talking like a 'real' Japanese person. Ethnic autobiography has inspired Trinh T. Minh-ha's book *Women, Native, Other* (1989) which deals with issues of self-presentation and displays of self (and other) through discussions of conventions of anthropological writing. Minh-ha uses photos, poems, fiction and personal narrative in her discussions of gender and 'nativism'. Her book represents an example of the blending of anthropological theory and personal narrative, in a genre form that rejects the claim that the two must be in opposition.

Michael Herzfeld (1997b) has produced an 'ethnographic biography' that uses genres of life history, biography and ethnography to discuss the life and work of Greek novelist and left-wing political figure Andreas Nenedakis. Herzfeld explores important cultural and historical themes in Greek culture through the eye of the anthropologist (himself) and the eye of the novelist (Nenedakis). More than this, however, the book shows that the long-time friendship between these two men and their wives (Cornelia Meyer Herzfeld and Eli-Maria Komninou) has been fruitful to the anthropologist's understandings of culture and history. No contradiction is posited between friendship, intellectual intimacy and anthropological objectivity; for Herzfeld, such a dichotomy is false. Other experimentations with autobiography, biography and ethnography include the work of Brettell (1999), Brown (1991), Kendall (1988) and Narayan (1989).

An interest in the practices of ethnography and self-disclosure among those who were traditionally the subject of the ethnographic gaze has produced several important models of collaborative research and understandings of the 'practical knowledge' (Bourdieu, 1980) of both researchers and their informants. There is a growing tendency to produce texts that are presented as autobiographical, first-person accounts by the subject him or herself, rather than mediated life histories. The growth of schooling and literacy has enhanced this trend. Examples of this form of autoethnography are Laye ([1954] 1994), Roughsey (1984), Saitoti (1986) and Horne and McBeth (1998). Ethnographers increasingly view informants as collaborators and autobiographers in their own right. One example is Janet Hoskins' (1985) discussion of Maru Kaku, an Indonesian man who assisted several anthropologists, and who created an autobiography that uses his own poetic traditions. Hoskins describes this as a lament about choices made. Although Kaku's own native oral tradition does not include self-presentation, this boundary-crosser innovated, combining conventional narrative genres in his own tradition with more Western individualistic genres of autobiography.[6] Susan Rodgers (1993) has written about an Indonesian Batak writer who, while not explicitly autobiographical in his writings, makes use of autoethnographies and autorepresentations of ethnicity and culture. This writer, suggests Rodgers, is writing his own culture through a form of self-presentation. Autoethnography of this sort is also described by Herzfeld (1997a, 1997b), Kideckel (1997), Reed-Danahay (1997a) and Warren (1997).

Among the topics for narrative ethnography and ethnographic memoir that have not yet been addressed as much as others cited in this chapter, are issues of danger in fieldwork and physical or mental illness in the field (see Howell, 1990; Lee, 1995). There has also been relatively little candid writing about ethnographer careers (mentorship, education and employment issues, family and work issues, career success and failure). Perhaps these will be the next 'taboos' broached in intimate ethnographic writing!

Acknowledgements

I would like to thank Tara Martinez for her help in locating sources for this chapter.

NOTES

1 See also Heinritz and Rammstedt, 1991 and Morin, 1980 on the use of life history methods in France; Markiewicz-Lagneau, 1976 on Poland; Rammstedt, 1995 on Italy; and Guillestad, 1996 on Norway. Bertaux and Kohli, 1984 review what they term more generally as 'the continental approach'. For contemporary British approaches to social science uses of autobiography, see Stanley, 1993.

2 See also Charity et al., 1995 and Edwards, 1992 on the use of photographs in ethnography.

3 For a more recent collaborative work by a husband and wife, see Stoller and Olkes, 1987. See also Turner, 1987.

4 See also Gilmore, 1991 for a discussion of issues of social class, politics, and fieldwork in Spain.

5 In addition to the essays in Lewin and Leap, see also Bolton, 1995; Herdt, 1997; Lunsing, 1999; Newton, 1993.

6 See also Turner (1983) on 'Muchona the Hornet: Interpreter of Religion'.

REFERENCES

Abu-Lughod, Lila (1993) *Writing Women's Worlds: Bedouin Stories*. Berkeley, CA: University of California Press.

Altorki, Oraya and El-Solh, Camillia Fawzi (eds) ([1988] 1992) *Arab Women in the Field: Studying Your Own Society*. Syracuse, NY: Syracuse University Press.

Anderson, Barbara G. (1990) *First Fieldwork: The Misadventures of an Anthropologist*. Prospect Heights, IL: Waveland.

Angrosino, Michael V. (1989) *Documents of Interaction: Biography, Autobiography and Life History in Social Science Perspectives*. Gainesville, FL: University of Florida Press.

Arana, R. Victoria (1988) 'Examining the acquisition of cross-cultural knowledge: women anthropologists as autobiographers', *A/B: Autobiographical Studies*, 4 (1): 28–36.

Archetti, Eduardo P. (ed.) (1994) *Exploring the Written: Anthropology and the Multiplicity of Writing*. Oslo: Scandinavian University Press.

Ashkenazi, Michael and Markowitz, Fran (1999) 'Introduction: sexuality and prevarication in the praxis of anthropology', in Fran Markowitz and Michael Ashkenazi (eds), *Sex, Sexuality and the Anthropologist*. Urbana, IL: University of Illinois Press. pp. 1–21.

Ashkenazi, Michael and Rotenberg, Robert (1999) 'Cleansing cultures: public bathing and the naked anthropologist in Japan and Austria', in Fran Markowitz and Michael Ashkenazi (eds), *Sex, Sexuality and the Anthropologist*. Urbana, IL: University of Illinois Press. pp. 92–114.

Atkinson, Paul (1992) *Understanding Ethnographic Texts*. London: Sage.

Barley, Nigel (1986) *Ceremony: An Anthropologists' Misadventures in the African Bush*. New York: Henry Holt.

Behar, Ruth (1993) *Translated Women: Crossing the Border with Esperanza's Story*. Boston, MA: Beacon Press.

Behar, Ruth (1996) *The Vulnerable Observer: Anthropology that Breaks Your Heart*. Boston, MA: Beacon Press.

Behar, Ruth and Gordon, Deborah A. (eds) (1995) *Women Writing Culture*. Berkeley, CA: University of California Press.

Beidelman, T.O. (1998) 'Making the time: becoming an anthropologist', *Ethnos*, 6 (2): 273.

Bell, D., Caplan, Pat and Karim, W.J. (eds) (1993) *Gendered Fields: Women, Men, and Ethnography*. London: Routledge.

Benson, Paul (ed.) (1993) *Anthropology and Literature*. Urbana, IL: University of Illinois Press.

Berreman, Gerald (1962) *Behind Many Masks. Ethnography and Impression Management in a Himalayan Village*. Monograph No. 4. Ithaca, NY: Society for Applied Anthropology.

Bertaux, Daniel (ed.) (1981) *Biography and Society: The Life Story Approach in the Social Sciences*. Beverly Hills, CA: Sage.

Bertaux, Daniel and Kohli, Martin (1984) 'The life story approach: a continental view', *Annual Review of Sociology*, 10: 215–37.

Beteille, Andre (1993) 'Sociology and anthropology: their relationship to one person's career', *Contributions to Indian Sociology*, 27 (2): 291–304.

Beteille, Andre and Madan, T.N. (eds) (1975) *Encounter and Experience: Personal Accounts of Fieldwork*. Honolulu, HI: University Press of Hawai'i.

Blackman, Margaret B. (1992) 'Introduction: the afterlife of the life history', *Journal of Narrative and Life History*, 2 (1): 1–9.

Blauner, Bob (1987) 'Problems of editing "first person" sociology', *Qualitative Sociology*, 10 (1): 46–64.

Bohannan, Paul (1997) 'It's been a good fieldtrip', *Ethnos*, 62 (1): 117–36.

Bolton, Ralph (1995) 'Tricks, friends, and lovers: erotic encounters in the field', in Don Kulick and Margaret Wilson (eds), *Taboo: Sex, Identity, and Erotic Subjectivity in Anthropological Fieldwork*. London: Routledge. pp. 140–67.

Bourdieu, Pierre (1980) *Le Sens Pratique*. Paris: Editions de Minuit.

Bowen, Elinore Smith [Laura Bohannan] (1954) *Return to Laughter*. New York: Harper.

Bradburd, Daniel (1998) *Being There: The Necessity of Fieldwork*. Washington, DC and London: Smithsonian Press.

Brandes, Stanley (1982) 'Ethnographic autobiographies in American anthropology', in E. Adamson Hoebel, Richard Currier and Susan Kaiser (eds), *Crisis in Anthropology: View from Spring Hill*, 1980. New York: Garland.

Brettell, Caroline (1982) *We Have Already Cried Many Tears: Portuguese Women and Migration*. Cambridge, MA: Schenkman.

Brettell, Caroline (ed.) (1993) *When They Read What We Write: The Politics of Ethnography*. Wesport, CT: Bergin and Garvey.

Brettell, Caroline (1999) *Writing Against the Wind: A Mother's Life History*. Wilmington, DE: Scholarly Resources.

Briggs, Jean (1970) *Never in Anger: Portrait of an Eskimo Family*. Cambridge, MA: Harvard University Press.

Brown, Karen McCarthy (1991) *Mama Lola: A Voudou Priestess in Brooklyn*. Berkeley, CA: University of California Press.

Brox, Ottar (1996) 'My life as an anthropologist', *Ethnos*, 61: 1–2.

Bruner, Edward M. (ed.) (1984) *Text, Play and Story: The Construction and Reconstruction of Self and Society*. Washington, DC: American Ethnological Society.

Bruner, Edward M. (1993) 'Introduction: the ethnographic self and the personal self', in Paul Benson (ed.), *Anthropology and Literature*. Urbana, IL: University of Illinois Press. pp. 1–26.

Bunkers, Suzanne L. and Huff, Cynthia A. (eds) (1996) *Inscribing the Daily: Critical Essays on Women's Diaries*. Amherst, MA: University of Massachussets Press.

Butler, Barbara and Turner, Diane Michalski (eds) (1987) *Children and Anthropological Research*. New York: Plenum Press.

Casagrande, Joseph (ed.) (1960) *In the Company of Man: Twenty Portraits of Anthropological Informants*. New York: Harper and Row.

Cassell, Joan (ed.) (1987) *Children in the Field: Anthropological Experiences*. Philadelphia: Temple University Press.

Catani, Maurizio (1981) 'Social-life history as ritualized oral exchange', in Daniel Bertaux (ed.), *Biography and Society*. Beverly Hills, CA: Sage. pp. 211–24.

Cesara, Manda [Karla Poewe] (1982) *Reflections of a Woman Anthropologist: No Hiding Place*. London: Academic Press.

Charity, Ruth et al. (eds) (The Photographers Gallery) (1995) *The Impossible Science of Being: Dialogues between Anthropology and Photography*. London: The Photographer's Gallery.

Church, Kathryn (1995) *Forbidden Narratives: Critical Autobiography as Social Science*. New York: Gordon and Breach.

Clifford, James (1983) 'On ethnographic authority', *Representations*, 2: 118–46.

Cohen, Anthony P. (1994) *Self Consciousness: An Alternative Anthropology of Identity*. Routledge: London.

Cole, Sally (1992) 'Anthropological lives: the reflexive tradition in a social science', in Marlene Kadar (ed.), *Essays on Life Writing: From Genre to Critical Practice*. Toronto: University of Toronto Press. pp. 113–27.

Crapanzano, Vincent (1980) *Tuhami: Portrait of a Moroccan*. Chicago: University of Chicago Press.

Crapanzano, Vincent (1984) 'Review of lives: an anthropological approach to biography', *American Anthropologist*, 86 (4): 953–60.

Daniel, E. Valentine and Peck, Jeffrey M. (1996) *Culture/Contexture: Explorations in Anthropology and Literary Studies*. Berkeley, CA: University of California Press.

DeLaguna, Frederica (1977) *Voyage to Greenland: A Personal Initiation into Anthropology*. New York: W.W. Norton.

Denzin, Norman K. (1989) *Interpretive Biography*. Newbury Park, CA: Sage.

DeVita, Philip R. (ed.) (1990) *The Humbled Anthropologist: Tales from the Pacific*. Belmont, CA: Wadsworth.

DeVita, Philip R. (ed.) (1992) *The Naked Anthropologist: Tales from Around the World*. Belmont, CA: Wadsworth.

DeVita, Philip R. and Armstrong, James D. (eds) ([1993] 1998) *Distant Mirrors: America as a Foreign Culture*. Belmont, CA: Wadsworth.

Dews, C.L. Barney and Law, Carolyn Leste (1995) *This Place So Far from Home: Voices of Academics from the Working Class*. Temple, PA: University of Pennsylvania Press.

DiGiacomo, Susan M. (1987) 'Biomedicine as a cultural system: an anthropologist in the kingdom of the sick', in Hans A. Baer (ed.), *Encounters with Biomedicine: Case Studies in Medical Anthropology*. New York: Gordon and Breach Science Publishers. pp. 315–46.

Dollard, John (1935) *Criteria for the Life History. With Analysis of Six Notable Documents*. New Haven, CT: Yale University Press.

Dorst, John D. (1989) *The Written Suburb: An American Site, an Ethnographic Dilemma*. Philadelphia: University of Pennsylvania Press.

Driessen, Henk (ed.) (1993) *The Politics of Ethnographic Reading and Writing: Confrontations of Western and Indigenous Views*. Saarbrucken and Ft Lauderdale, FL: Verlag Breitenbach.

Dubisch, Jill (1995) 'Lovers in the field: sex, dominance and the female anthropologist', in Don Kulick and Margaret Wilson (eds), *Taboo: Sex, Identity and Erotic Subjectivitiy in Anthropological Fieldwork*. London: Routledge. pp. 29–50.

DuBois, Cora (1944) *The People of Alor*. Minneapolis, MN: University of Minnesota Press.

Dumont, Jean-Paul ([1978] 1992) *The Headman and I: Ambiguity and Ambivalence in the Fieldworking Experience*. Prospect Heights, IL: Waveland.

Edwards, Elizabeth (ed.) (1992) *Anthropology and Photography, 1860–1920*. New Haven, CT: Yale University Press.

Ellis, Carolyn (1991) 'Emotional sociology', *Studies in Symbolic Interaction*, 12: 123–45.

Ellis, Carolyn (1995) *Final Negotiations*. Philadelphia: Temple University Press.

Ellis, Carolyn (1997) 'Evocative autoethnography', in William G. Tierney and Yvonna S. Lincoln (eds),

Representation and the Text: Re-Framing the Narrative Voice. Albany, NY: State University of New York Press. pp. 115–42.

Ellis, Carolyn and Bochner, Arthur P. (eds) (1996) *Composing Ethnography: Alternative Forms of Qualitative Writing.* Walnut Creek, CA: AltaMira.

Evans-Pritchard, E.E. (1940) *The Nuer. A Description of the Modes of Livelihood and Political Institutions of a Nilotic People.* Oxford: The Clarendon Press.

Favret-Saada, Jeanne (1980) *Deadly Words: Witchcraft in the Bocage* (trans. Catherine Cullen). Cambridge: Cambridge University Press.

Fernandez, James and Herzfeld, Michael (1998) 'In search of meaningful methods', in H. Russell Barnard (ed.), *Handbook of Methods in Cultural Anthropology.* Walnut Creek, CA: AltaMira. pp. 89–130.

Fernandez, Renate and Sutton, David (eds) (1998) 'Special issue – in the field and at home: families and anthropology,' *Anthropology and Humanism,* 23 (2).

Fernea, Elizabeth W. (1969) *Guests of the Sheik. An Ethnography of an Iraqi Village.* New York: Anchor Books.

Fernea, Elizabeth W. (1975) *A Street in Marrakech: A Personal View of Women in Morocco.* Garden City, NJ: Doubleday.

Fischer, Michael M.J. (1986) 'Ethnicity and the post-modern arts of memory', in James Clifford and George E. Marcus (eds), *Writing Culture: The Poetics and Politics of Ethnography.* Berkeley, CA: University of California Press. pp. 194–233.

Flinn, Juliana, Marshall, Leslie B. and Armstrong, Jocelyn (eds) (1998) *Fieldwork and Families: Constructing New Models for Ethnographic Research.* Honolulu, HI: University of Hawai'i Press.

Fortier, Anne-Marie (1996) 'Troubles in the field: the use of personal experiences as sources of knowledge', *Critique of Anthropology,* 16 (3): 303–23.

Fowler, Don D. and Hardesty, Donald L. (eds) (1994) *Others Knowing Others: Perspectives on Ethnographic Careers.* Washington, DC: Smithsonian Press.

Fox, Richard G. (ed.) (1991) *Recapturing Anthropology: Working in the Present.* Santa Fe, NM: School of American Research.

Frank, Arthur W. (1991) *At the Will of the Body: Reflections on Illness.* Boston, MA: Houghton–Mifflin.

Frank, Arthur W. (1995) *The Wounded Storyteller: Body, Illness and Ethics.* Chicago: University of Chicago Press.

Freilich, Morris (ed.) (1970) *Marginal Natives: Anthropologists at Work.* New York: Harper Row.

Friedl, Ernestine (1995) 'The life of an academic: a personal record of a teacher, administrator, and anthropologist', *Annual Review of Anthropology,* 24: 1–19.

Friedman, Norman L. (1990) 'Autobiographical sociology', *The American Sociologist,* 21 (1): 60–6.

Geertz, Clifford (1995) *After the Fact: Two Countries, Four Decades, and One Anthropologist.* Cambridge, MA: Harvard University Press.

Geertz, Clifford (1998) 'Deep hanging out: review of James Clifford, routes: travel and translation in the late 20th century and Pierre Clastres, chronicle of the Guyaki Indians', *The New York Review of Books,* 45 (16): 69.

Giddens, Anthony (1991) *Modernity and Self-Identity: Self and Society in the Late Modern Age.* Stanford, CA: Stanford University Press.

Gilmore, David D. (1991) 'Subjectivity and subjugation: fieldwork in the stratified community', *Human Organization,* 59 (3): 215–24.

Ginsburg, Faye (1987) 'Procreation stories: reproduction, nurturance, and procreation in the life narratives of abortion activitists', *American Ethnologist,* 14 (4): 623–36.

Ginsburg, Faye (1993) 'The case of mistaken identity: problems in representing women on the right', in Carolyn B. Brettell (ed.), *When They Read What We Write: The Politics of Ethnography.* Wesport, CT: Bergin and Garvey. pp. 163–76.

Goetting, Ann and Fenstermaker, Sarah (eds) (1995) *Individual Voices, Collective Visions: Fifty Years of Women in Sociology.* Philadelphia: Temple University Press.

Golde, Peggy (ed.) (1970) *Women in the Field: Anthropological Experiences.* Chicago: Aldine.

Goldfrank, Esther Schiff (1978) *Notes on an Undirected Life: As One Anthropologist Tells It.* Flushing, NY: Queens College Press.

Goldman, Anne E. (1996) *Take My Word: Auto-biographical Innovations of Ethnic American Working Women.* Berkeley, CA: University of California Press.

Good, Kenneth, with David Chanoff (1991) *Into the Heart: One Man's Pursuit of Love and Knowledge among the Yanomama.* New York: Simon and Schuster.

Gottschalk, Louis R., Kluckhohn, Clyde and Angell, Robert C. (1945) *The Use of Personal Documents in History, Anthropology and Sociology.* New York: Social Science Research Council.

Grimes, Ronald L. (ed.) (1995) *Life History Bibliography.* http://wings.buffalo.edu/anthropology/Documents/life_historybib.txt

Grindal, Bruce and Salamone, Frank (1995) *Bridges to Humanity: Narratives on Anthropology and Friendship.* Prospect Heights, IL: Waveland.

Guillestad, Marianne (1996) *Everyday Life Philosophers: Modernity, Morality, and Autobiography in Norway.* Oslo: Scandinavian University Press.

Gupta, Akhil and Ferguson, James (eds) (1997) *Anthropological Locations: Boundaries and Grounds of a Field Science.* Berkeley, CA: University of California Press.

Hall, Edward T. (1992) *An Anthropology of Everyday Life: An Autobiography.* New York: Doubleday.

Hammond, Philip E. (ed.) (1964) *Sociologists at Work: The Craft of Social Research.* New York: Basic Books.

Harrison, Faye V. (ed.) (1997) *Decolonizing Anthropology: Moving Further Toward an Ethnography of Liberation,* 2nd edn. Arlington, VA: Association of Black Anthropologists, American Anthropological Association.

Hayano, David M. (1990) *Road Through the Rain Forest: Living Anthropology in Highland Papua New Guinea.* Prospect Heights, IL: Waveland.

Heinritz, Charlotte and Rammstedt, Angela (1991) 'L' Approche biographique en France', *Cahiers Internationaux de Sociologie*, XCI: 331–70.

Heinz, Hans-Joachim and Lee, Marshall (1979) *Namkwa: Life Among the Bushmen* (foreword by Margaret Mead). Boston, MA: Houghton–Mifflin.

Herdt, Gilbert (1982) *Rituals of Manhood: Male Initiation in Papua New Guinea.* Berkeley, CA: University of California Press.

Herdt, Gilbert (1997) 'Preface', in *Same Sex, Different Cultures: Gays and Lesbians Across Cultures.* Boulder, CO: Westview Press.

Hertz, Rosanna (ed.) (1997) *Reflexivity and Voice.* Thousand Oaks, CA: Sage.

Herzfeld, Michael (1985) *The Poetics of Manhood: Contest and Identity in a Cretan Mountain Village.* Princeton, NJ: Princeton University Press.

Herzfeld, Michael (1997a) 'The taming of revolution: intense paradoxes of the self', in Deborah E. Reed-Danahay (ed.), *Auto/Ethnography: Rewriting the Self and the Social.* London: Berg. pp. 169–94.

Herzfeld, Michael (1997b) *Portrait of a Greek Imagination: An Ethnographic Biography of Andreas Nenedakis.* Chicago: University of Chicago Press.

Hobbs, Dick and May, Tim (1993) *Interpreting the Field: Accounts of Ethnography.* Oxford: The Clarendon Press.

Honigmann, John J. (1976) 'The personal approach in cultural anthropological research', *Current Anthropology*, 17 (2): 243–51.

Horne, Esther Burnett and McBeth, Sally (1998) *Essie's Story: The Life and Legacy of a Shoshone Teacher.* Lincoln, NB: University of Nebraska Press.

Hoskins, Janet Alison (1985) 'A life history from both sides: the changing poetics of personal experience', *Journal of Anthropological Research*, 41 (2): 147–69.

Hostetler, John A. (1992) 'An Amish beginning', *The American Scholar*, 61 (4): 552–62.

Howell, N. (1990) *Surviving Fieldwork: A Report of the Advisory Panel on Health and Safety in Fieldwork.* Washington, DC: American Anthropological Association.

Hurston, Zora Neale ([1942] 1991) *Dust Tracks on a Road: An Autobiography.* New York: Harper Collins.

Hymes, Dell (ed.) (1974) *Reinventing Anthropology.* New York: Vintage Books.

Hymes, Dell (ed.) (1987) *Reinventing Anthropology.* New York: Random House.

Jackson, Anthony (ed.) (1987) *Anthropology at Home.* ASA Monograph No. 25. London: Tavistock Publications.

Jackson, Bruce and Ives Edward D. (eds) (1996) *The World Observed: Reflections on the Fieldwork Process.* Urbana, IL: University of Illinois Press.

Jackson, David (1990) *Unmasking Masculinity: A Critical Autobiography.* London: Unwin Hyman.

Jackson, Jean (1986) 'On trying to be Amazon', in Tony L. Whitehead and Mary Ellen Conway (eds), *Self, Sex,*

and Gender in Cross-Cultural Fieldwork. Urbana, IL: University of Illinois Press. pp. 263–74.

Jones, Delmos J. (1970) 'Towards a native anthropology', *Human Organization*, 29 (4): 251–9.

Jongmans, D.G. and Gutkind, P.C.W. (eds) (1967) *Anthropologists in the Field.* Assen: Van Gorcum.

Kaufman, Sharon R. (1986) *The Ageless Self: Sources of Meaning in Later Life.* Madison, WI: University of Wisconsin Press.

Keil, Charles (1976) 'Comment on Honigmann "The personal approach in cultural anthropological research"', *Current Anthropology*, 17 (2): 253.

Kendall, Laurel (1988) *The Life and Hard Times of a Korean Shaman: Of Tales and the Telling of Tales.* Honolulu, HI: University of Hawai'i Press.

Kennedy, Elizabeth L. with Madeline Davis (1996) 'Constructing an ethnohistory of the Buffalo lesbian community: reflexivity, dialogue and politics,' in Ellen Lewin and William L. Leap (eds), *Out in the Field: Reflections on Lesbian and Gay Anthropologists.* Urbana, IL: University of Illinois Press. pp. 171–99.

Kideckel, David A. (1997) 'Autoethnography as political resistance: a case from socialist Romania', in Deborah E. Reed-Danahay (ed.), *Auto/Ethnography: Rewriting the Self and the Social.* London: Berg. pp. 47–70.

Kimball, Solon T. (1972) 'Learning a new culture', in S.T. Kimball and J.B. Watson (eds), *Crossing Cultural Boundaries: The Anthropological Experience.* San Francisco: Chandler. pp. 182–92.

Kleinman, Arthur (1988) *The Illness Narratives: Suffering, Healing and the Human Condition.* New York: Basic Books.

Kluckhohn, Clyde (1945) 'The personal document in anthropological science', in Louis Gottschalk, Clyde Kluckholn and Robert Angell (eds), *The Use of Personal Documents in History, Anthropology, and Sociology.* New York: Social Science Research Council. pp. 78–173.

Köbben, A.F.J. (1967) 'Participation and quantification: field work among the Djuka (Bush Negroes of Surinam)', in D.G. Jongmans and P.C.W. Gutkind (eds), *Anthropologists in the Field.* Assen: Van Gorcum. pp. 35–55.

Kondo, Dorinne K. (1990) *Crafting Selves: Power, Gender and Discourses of Identity in a Japanese Workplace.* Chicago: University of Chicago Press.

Krieger, Susan (1991) *Social Science and the Self: Personal Essays on an Art Form.* New Brunswick, NJ: Rutgers University Press.

Kroeber, Alfred L. (1908) 'Ethnology of the Gros Ventre: war experiences of individuals', *Anthropological Papers of the American Museum of Natural History*, 1 (4): 192–222.

Kulick, Don and Wilson, Margaret (eds) (1995) *Taboo: Sex, Identity and Erotic Subjectivitiy in Anthropological Fieldwork.* London: Routledge.

Landes, Ruth ([1938] 1997) *The Ojibwa Woman.* Lincoln, NB: University of Nebraska Press.

Langness, L.L. (1965) *The Life History in Anthropological Sciences.* New York: Holt, Rinehart and Winston.

Langness, L.L. and Frank, Geyla (1981) *Lives: An Anthropological Approach*. Novatol, CA: Chandler and Sharp.

Lareau, Annette and Shultz, Jeffrey (eds) (1996) *Journeys through Ethnography*. Boulder, CO: Westview Press.

Lavie, Smadar, Narayan, Kirin and Rosaldo, Renato (eds) (1993) *Creativity/Anthropology*. Ithaca, NY: Cornell University Press.

Lawuyi, Olatunde Bayo (1989) 'The story about life: biography in the Yoruba obituaries', *Diogenes*, 148: 92–111.

Laye, Camara ([1954] 1994) *The Dark Child: The Autobiography of an African Boy*. New York: Farrar, Strauss and Giroux.

Lee, Raymond M. (1995) *Dangerous Fieldwork*. Thousand Oaks, CA: Sage.

Leinhardt, Godfrey (1961) *Divinity and Experience: The Religion of the Dinka*. Oxford: Clarendon Press.

Lévi-Strauss, Claude ([1955] 1992) *Tristes Tropiques* (trans. John and Doreen Weightman). New York: Penguin Books.

Lewin, Ellen and Leap, William L. (eds) (1996) *Out in the Field: Reflections on Lesbian and Gay Anthropologists*. Urbana, IL: University of Illinois Press.

Lewis, Oscar (1964) *Pedro Martinez: A Mexican Peasant and His Family*. New York: Random House.

Linde, Charlotte (1993) *Life Stories: The Creation of Coherence*. Oxford: Oxford University Press.

Little, Kenneth (1980) 'Explanation and individual lives: a reconsideration of life writing in anthropology', *Dialectical Anthropology*, 5 (3): 215–26.

Lunsing, Wim (1999) 'Life on Mars: love and sex in fieldwork on sexuality and gender in urban Japan', in Fran Markowitz and Michael Ashkenazi (eds), *Sex, Sexuality, and the Anthropologist*. Urbana, IL: University of Illinois Press. pp. 175–97.

Luttrell, Wendy (1997) *Schoolsmart and Motherwise: Working-Class Women's Identity and Schooling*. New York and London: Routledge.

Magli, Ida (1991) 'A journey in search of the white man', *Revue International de Sociologie/International Review of Sociology*, 3: 7–44.

Malinowski, Bronislaw (1922) *Argonauts of the Western Pacific*. New York: E.P. Dutton.

Malinowski, Bronislaw (1935) *Coral Gardens and their Magic*. London: G. Allen and Unwin.

Malinowski, Bronislaw (1967) *A Diary in the Strict Sense of the Term*. New York: Harcourt, Brace Jovanovich.

Mandelbaum, David G. (1973) 'The study of life history: Gandhi', *Current Anthropology*, 14 (3): 177–206.

Marcus, George E. and Cushman, Dick (1982) 'Ethnographies as texts', *Annual Review of Anthropology*, 11: 25–69.

Marcus, George E. and Fischer, Michael J. (1986) *Anthropology as Cultural Critique: An Experimental Moment in the Human Sciences*. Chicago and London: University of Chicago Press.

Markiewicz-Lagneau, Janina (1976) 'Autobiography in Poland or the social usage of a sociological technique', *Revue Française de Sociologie*, 17 (4): 591–613.

Markowitz, Fran and Ashkenazi, Michael (eds) (1999) *Sex, Sexuality and the Anthropologist*. Urbana, IL: University of Illinois Press.

Marriott, Alice (1952) *Greener Fields: Experiences Among the American Indians*. Garden City, NJ: Doubleday.

McBeth, Sally (1993) 'Myths of objectivity and the collaborative process in life history research', in Caroline Brettell (ed.), *When They Read What We Write: The Politics of Ethnography*. Wesport, CT: Bergin and Garvey. pp. 144–62.

McLaren, Peter (1989) *Life in Schools: An Introduction to Critical Pedagogy in the Foundations of Education*. White Plains, NY: Longman.

Mead, Margaret ([1972] 1995) *Blackberry Winter: My Earlier Years*. New York: Kodansha International.

Miller, Elmer S. (1995) *Nurturing Doubt: From Mennonite Missionary to Anthropologist in the Argentinian Chaco*. Urbana, IL: University of Illinois Press.

Minh-ha, Trinh T. (1989) *Women, Native, Other: Writing Postcoloniality and Feminism*. Bloomington, IN: Indiana University Press.

Mintz, Sidney M. (1979) 'The anthropological interview and the life history', *Oral History Review*, 7: 18–26.

Moore, Henrietta (1994) *A Passion for Difference: Essays in Anthropology and Gender*. Bloomington, IN: Indiana University Press.

Morin, Francoise (1980) 'Pratiques anthropologiques et histoire de vie', *Cahiers Internationaux de Sociologie*, LXIX: 313–39.

Murphy, Robert F. (1987) *The Body Silent*. New York: Henry Holt.

Myerhoff, Barbara G. (1978) *Number Our Days*. New York: Simon and Schuster.

Myerhoff, Barbara and Jay, Ruby (eds) (1982) *A Crack in the Mirror: Reflexive Perspectives in Anthropology*. Philadelphia: University of Pennsylvania Press.

Narayan, Kirin (1989) *Storytellers, Saints, and Scoundrels*. Philadelphia: University of Pennsylvania Press.

Nash, Dennison and Wintrob, Ronald (1972) 'The emergence of self-consciousness in ethnography', *Current Anthropology*, 13 (5): 527–42.

Newton, Esther (1993) 'My best informant's dress: the erotic equation in fieldwork', *Cultural Anthropology*, 8: 3–23.

Ohnuki-Tierney, Emiko (1984) 'Critical commentary: "native" anthropologists', *American Ethnologist*, 11: 584–6.

Okely, Judith (1996) *Own or Other Culture*. London: Routledge.

Okely, Judith and Callaway, Helen (eds) (1992) *Anthropology and Autobiography*. London: Routledge.

Paine, Robert (1998) 'Anthropology by chance, by choice – a personal memoir', *Ethnos*, 63 (1): 133.

Parsons, Elsie Clews (ed.) ([1922] 1967) *American Indian Life*. Lincoln, NB: University of Nebraska Press.

Peacock, James L. and Holland, Dorothy C. (1993) 'The narrated self: life stories in process', *Ethos*, 21 (4): 367–83.

Personal Narratives Group (1989) *Interpreting Women's Lives: Feminist Theory and Personal Narratives.* Bloomington, IN: Indiana University Press.

Powdermaker, Hortense (1966) *Stranger and Friend: The Way of an Anthropologist.* New York: W.W. Norton.

Pratt, Mary Louise (1986) 'Fieldwork in common places', in James Clifford and George E. Marcus (eds), *Writing Culture: The Poetics and Politics of Ethnography.* Berkeley, CA: University of California Press. pp. 27–50.

Probyn, Elspeth (1993) *Sexing the Self: Gendered Positions in Cultural Studies.* New York: Routledge.

Rabinow, Paul (1977) *Reflections on Fieldwork in Morocco.* Berkeley, CA: University of California Press.

Radin, Paul (1926) *Crashing Thunder.* New York: D. Appleton.

Rammstedt, Angela (1995) 'Biographical research in Italy', *Current Sociology*, 43 (2–3): 179–207.

Raybeck, Douglas (1996) *Mad Dogs, Englishmen, and the Errant Anthropologist: Fieldwork in Malaysia.* Prospect Heights, IL: Waveland.

Reed-Danahay, Deborah E. (1997a) 'Leaving home: schooling stories and the ethnography of autoethnography in rural France', in Deborah E. Reed-Danahay (ed.), *Autoethnography: Rewriting the Self and the Social.* Oxford: Berg. pp. 123–44.

Reed-Danahay, Deborah E. (ed.) (1997b) *Autoethnography: Rewriting the Self and the Social.* Oxford: Berg.

Reichard, Gladys A. (1934) *Spider Woman: A Story of Navajo Weavers and Changers.* New York: Macmillan.

Richardson, Laurel (1994) 'Writing: a method of inquiry', in Norman K. Denzin and Yvonna S. Lincoln (eds), *Handbook of Qualitative Research.* Thousand Oaks, CA: Sage.

Riley, Matilda White (1988) *Sociological Lives.* Newbury Park, CA: Sage.

Rodgers, Susan (1993) 'A Batak antiquarian writes his culture: print literacy and social thought in an Indonesian society', in Paul Benson (ed.), *Anthropology and Literature.* Urbana, IL: University of Illinois Press. pp. 89–106.

Rosaldo, Renato (1989) *Culture and Truth: The Remaking of Social Analysis.* Boston, MA: Beacon Press.

Rosenwald, George C. and Ochberg, Richard L. (eds) (1992) *Storied Lives: The Cultural Politics of Self-Understanding.* New Haven, CT: Yale University Press.

Roughsey, Elsie (1984) *An Aboriginal Mother Tells of the Old and the New* (ed. Paul Memmott and Robyn Horsman). New York: Penguin Books.

Saitoti, Tepilit Ole (1986) *The Worlds of a Masai Warrior: An Autobiography.* Berkeley, CA: University of California Press.

Sangren, P. Steven (1988) 'Rhetoric and the authority of ethnography', *Current Anthropology*, 29 (3): 405–35.

Sewid, James P. and Spradley, James ([1969] 1978) *Guests Never Leave Hungry. The Autobiography of James Sewid, a Kwakiutl Indian.* Montreal: McGill–Queen's University Press.

Shaffir, William and Stebbins, Robert A. (eds) (1991) *Experiencing Fieldwork: An Inside View of Qualitative Research.* Newbury Park, CA: Sage.

Shaw, Bruce (1980) 'Life writing in anthropology: a methodological review', *Mankind*, 12 (3): 226–32.

Shostak, Marjorie ([1981] 1983) *Nisa: The Life and Words of a !Kung Woman.* New York: Vintage Books.

Simmons, Leo W. ([1942] 1979) *Sun Chief: The Autobiography of a Hopi Indian.* New Haven, CT: Yale University Press.

Slater, Miriam K. (1976) *African Odyssey: An Anthropological Adventure.* Garden City, NJ: Anchor Books.

Smith, Sidonie and Watson, Julia (eds) (1996) *Getting a Life: Everyday Uses of Autobiography.* Minneapolis, MI: University of Minnesota Press.

Spindler, George (ed.) (1970) *Being an Anthropologist: Fieldwork in Eleven Cultures.* New York: Holt, Rinehart and Winston.

Spindler, Louise (1962) *Menomoni Women and Cultural Change.* Menasha, WI: American Anthropological Association.

Srinivas, M. Narasimhacher, A.M. Shah and E.A. Ramaswamy (eds) (1979) *The Fieldworker and the Field: Problems and Challenges in Sociological Investigation.* Delhi: Oxford University Press.

Srinivas, M.N. (1997) 'Practicing social anthropology in India', *Annual Review of Anthropology*, 26: 1–24.

Stanley, Liz (1993) 'On auto/biography in sociology', *Sociology*, 27 (1): 41–52.

Stivers, Camilla (1993) 'Reflections on the role of personal narrative in social science', *Signs*, 18 (2): 408–25.

Stocking, George W., Jr (1974) 'Empathy and antipathy in the heart of darkness', in Regna Darnell (ed.), *Readings in the History of Anthropology.* New York: Harper and Row. pp. 281–7.

Stoller, Paul and Olkes, Cheryl (1987) *In the Sorcerer's Shadow: A Memoir of Apprenticeship among the Songhay of Niger.* Chicago: University of Chicago Press.

Strathern, Marilyn (1987) 'Out of context: the persuasive fictions of anthropology', *Current Anthropology*, 28 (3): 251–81.

Tedlock, Barbara (1991) 'From participant observation to the observation of participation: the emergence of narrative ethnography', *Journal of Anthropological Research*, 47 (1): 69–94.

Tedlock, Barbara (1995) 'Works and wives: on the sexual division of textual labor', in Ruth Behar and Deborah A. Gordon (eds), *Women Writing Culture.* Berkeley, CA: University of California Press. pp. 267–86.

Thomas, William I. and Znaniecki, Florian (1918–1920) *The Polish Peasant in Europe and America: Monograph of an Immigrant Group.* Chicago: University of Chicago Press.

Tierney, William G. and Lincoln, Yvonne S. (1997) *Representation and Text: Re-Framing the Narrative Voice.* Albany: State University of New York Press.

Turner, Edith (1987) *The Spirit and the Drum: A Memoir of Africa.* Tucson, AZ: The University of Arizona Press.

Turner, Victor (1983) *The Forest of Symbols: Aspects of Ndembu Ritual*. Ithaca, NY: Cornell University Press.

Underhill, Ruth ([1936] 1985) *Papago Woman*. Prospect Heights, IL: Waveland.

Van den Berghe, Pierre L. (1989) *Stranger in their Midst*. Niwot, CO: University Press of Colorado.

Van Maanen, John (1988) *Tales of the Field: On Writing Ethnography*. Chicago: The University of Chicago Press.

Varawa, Joana McIntyre (1989) *Changes in Latitude: An Uncommon Anthropology*. New York: Harper and Row.

Vidich, Arthur J., Bensman, J. and Stein, M.R. (eds) (1964) *Reflections on Community Studies*. New York: John Wiley and Sons.

Wachtel, Nathan (1994) *Gods and Vampires: Return to Chiapas* (trans. Carol Volk). Chicago: University of Chicago Press.

Ward, Martha C. (1989) *Nest in the Wind: Adventures in Anthropology on a Tropical Island*. Prospect Heights, IL: Waveland.

Warren, Kay B. (1997) 'Narrating cultural resurgence: genre and self-representation for Pan-Mayan writers', in Deborah E. Reed-Danahay (ed.), *Auto/Ethnography: Rewriting the Self and the Social*. Oxford: Berg. pp. 21–46.

Watson, Lawrence C. (1976) 'Understanding the life history as a subjective document: hermeneutical and phenomenological perspectives', *Ethnos*, 4 (1): 95–131.

Watson, Lawrence C. and Watson-Franke, Maria-Barbara (1985) *Interpreting Life Histories: An Anthropological Inquiry*. New Brunswick, NJ: Rutgers University Press.

Wax, Rosalie H. (1971) *Doing Fieldwork: Warnings and Advice*. Chicago: University of Chicago Press.

Weber, Florence (1989) *Le Travail A-côté: etude d'ethnographie ouvriére*. Paris: INRA.

Wengle, John L. (1988) *Ethnographers in the Field: The Psychology of Research*. Tuscaloosa, AL: University of Alabama Press.

West, Barbara A. (1992) 'Women's diaries as ethnographic resources', *Journal of Narrative and Life History*, 2 (4): 333–54.

Weston, Kath (1996) 'Requiem for a street fighter', in Ellen Lewin and William L. Leap (eds), *Out in the Field: Reflections on Lesbian and Gay Anthropologists*. Urbana, IL: University of Illinois Press. pp. 274–86.

Whitehead, Tony Larry and Conway, Mary Ellen (eds) (1986) *Self, Sex, and Gender in Cross-Cultural Fieldwork*. Urbana, IL: University of Illinois Press.

Whyte, William Foote (1943) *Street Corner Society*. Chicago: University of Chicago Press.

Whyte, William Foote (1994) *Participant-Observer: An Autobiography*. New York: ILR Press.

Williams, Norma (1988) 'A Mexican American woman encounters sociology: an autobiographical perspective', *The American Sociologist*, 19 (4): 340–6.

Wong, Hertha D. (1989) 'Pictographs as autobiography: plains Indians sketchbooks of the late nineteenth and early twentieth centuries', *American Literary History*, 1 (Summer): 295–316.

Wong, Hertha D. (1994) 'Plains Indian names and "the autobiographical act"', in Kathleen Ashley, Leigh Gilmore and Gerald Peters (eds), *Autobiography and Postmodernism*. Amherst, MA: University of Massachusetts Press. pp. 212–39.

Zamora, Mario D. and Stegall, Pamela (1980) 'Professional enculturation and turning in life history', *The Eastern Anthropologist*, 33 (3): 255–62.

Zola, Irving K. (1982) *Missing Pieces: A Chronicle of Living with a Disability*. Philadelphia: Temple University Press.

Zussman, Robert (1996) 'Autobiographical occasions', *Contemporary Sociology*, 25 (2): 143–8.

29

Feminist Ethnography

BEVERLEY SKEGGS

This chapter maps the topography of feminist ethnography. Both of the terms feminism and ethnography should be in plural as there is no one feminism nor one ethnography, and when combined we have a multitude of different routings, objects and enquiry that can be fitted into the space of feminist ethnography. But as with most spaces, the boundaries are permeable and so for the purposes of clarity the term feminist is used to signify the political stance that motivates and brings the practice of ethnography to life and to our attention.

The chapter is organized into five sections. The first examines the different historical routes and disciplinary engagements that have framed the formations of feminist ethnographies, leading into the second section which explores how the historical entry point impacts upon the type of feminist ethnography that is created. The third and fourth sections examine how epistemological questions, different theories and different ethical positions shape the feminist ethnography. The final section develops these debates through an analysis of representation. Feminist politics, of whatever variant, is always concerned with power: how it works, how to challenge it. The final section brings this to bear on the actual process of ethnography and asks who has the power to do, write, authorize and distribute research in the name of feminist ethnography.

Different intersections with other areas and disciplines leads to the continual transformation of ethnography and to the different use made of it by feminists. Ethnography's association with demography, phrenology and Aristotle's physiognomonein, has led to long-standing epistemological assumptions such as the belief that appearance is the sign of the soul; it is part of the scopic economy of Western knowledge in which the observable is semiotically rendered into meaning. What this should suggest is that it is the use, the politics of the researcher and the context in which interpretation takes place, that defines what sort of ethnography we have. So for Reinharz (1992) it is ethnography in the hands of feminists that renders it feminist. Culling aspects from different histories and traditions and for the purposes of clarity in this chapter I define ethnography as a theory of the research process – an idea about how we should do research. It usually combines certain features in specific ways: fieldwork that will be conducted over a *prolonged period of time*; utilizing different research techniques;[1] conducted *within the settings* of the participants, with an understanding of how the context informs the action; *involving the researcher in participation* and observation; involving an account of the development of relationships between the researcher and the researched and focusing on how experience and practice are part of wider processes.

This is why feminism and ethnography can suit each other. They both have experience, participants, definitions, meanings and sometimes subjectivity as a focus and they do not lose sight of context. Just like any feminist research, the ethnographer maps out the physical, cultural and economic possibilities for social action and meaning. For some feminists the desire is not just with the interaction between the structure and agency at the site of the social, but it is to enable participants to establish research agendas, to enable women participants to have some say in how they are studied. Ultimately, I would argue (and see the later discussion on feminist standpoint), feminist ethnography is about understanding process, and to do this, it has to occur across both time and space.

However, it is impossible to have one water-tight definition as ethnography is used to mean different things when it emerges in different disciplinary spaces.[2] Some researchers will define their work as ethnographic if it is based on a small number of interviews and some human contact; whereas others will stress the necessity of time and intensity of different forms of contact with great attention to context. I have drawn on examples only where feminists define themselves as ethnographers and therefore do not include the huge numbers of qualitative research studies that rely on just interviewing.

This self-defining is, however, not without difficulties. Compare the differences between Jackie Stacey's (1994) *Star Gazing*, which uses letters and questionnaires from female Hollywood cinema spectators and which defines itself as ethnographic because its focus is on the audience (as opposed to the text of the film), Kath Melia's (1987) *Learning and Working*, which is an analysis of the occupational socialization of nurses conducted through forty one-hour interviews and which defines itself as 'within the scope of ethnography', Amanda Coffey's (1999) account in *The Ethnographic Self* of her participation in accountancy culture, including doing book-keeping classes, and the initial accountant's training programme (including the homework) and participation in the extra-curricula social life, my ethnography *Formations of Class and Gender* (Skeggs, 1997) based on 3 years living and participating in the culture of a group of young working-class women, with periods of follow-up participation (over an 11-year period) which drew on a wide variety of sources for supplementary contextual and biographical information, and Faye Ginsburg's (1989) *Contested Lives* study of the abortion debate in a US town, based on initial context visits, 12 months living in the area conducting fieldwork (over a 2-year period) and follow-up visits, which does not even bother to label itself as ethnographic because it comes from the discipline of anthropology where it is expected that all fieldwork is ethnographic. The definition as ethnographic is based on not just the methods used, but the questions asked and how they are analysed. These are part of the strategic use of the term in relation to history and discipline as the next sections will show.

Historical Routes

Feminist ethnography has many different routes/ roots. It emerged from a variety of disciplines with different histories and trajectories. It was as much the product of debates between classical scholars and historians as it was between anthropologists, Marxists and feminists. Ethnography was used as one of the main technologies of the Enlightenment to generate classifications and knowledge about 'others'. Lynette Finch (1993) shows how it was deployed in Australia, relying heavily on an interpretation of women's bodies to generate formulations of what came to be known as the working class. Ethnography was central to investigations and classifications of morality, an investigation deemed achievable only through observation, interpretation and representation, as Harvey (1989) notes:

> The Enlightenment project, for example, took it as axiomatic that there was only one possible answer to any question. From this it followed that the world could be controlled and rationally ordered if we could only picture and represent it rightly. (1989: 27)

There is nothing about ethnography that makes it feminist. In fact its history should suggest otherwise as it has been a method deployed for highly dubious ends: a number of anthropologists used ethnography to spy for the US government[3] for instance; and it is well known as a legitimating source of the colonial endeavour (Clifford, 1983, 1986). Yet it has also been used to provide important information about women's lives. Another genealogy is through the travel literature of nineteenth-century radical feminists, epitomized by Frances Wright's (1821) *View of Society and Manners in America, in a Series of Letters from that Country to a Friend in England during 1818, 1819, 1820* and in Harriet Martineu's (1837) *Society in America* (see Reinharz, 1992). This tradition continues within 'local stories' and novels which use an ethnographic focus: Bell (1993) lists Zora Neale Hurston's (1937) *Their Eyes Were Watching God*, Kate Simon's (1982) *Bronx Primitive* and Maxine Hong Kingston's (1975) *The Woman Warrior* as examples of this ethnographic tradition.

Four main contemporary locations have used ethnography: anthropology, sociology, education and cultural studies. It is from these areas where different feminist debates have taken place, not always connecting with each other, but always connecting with contemporaneous debates in feminism more generally. These debates have dialectically forged feminist theory.

The first location for feminist ethnography is anthropology where ethnography is the central methodology. Here it has been strongly framed by colonialism (see Chapters 3, 4 and 7) and heterosexuality. The tradition of the heterosexual couple – him the distinguished anthropologist, her the interested and helpful wife, travelling to distant continents to spend years living in a 'culture' in order to understand it – has led to the production of some exceedingly reflexive accounts (for instance, Mary Smith's (1954) *Baba of Karo*, Elizabeth Warnock Fernea's (1969) *Guests of the Sheikh* and Margery Wolf's (1968) *The House of Lim*; see Bell, 1993b for a full account). It has also led Bell (1993b) to ask if the 'anthropologist's husband' would have produced such reflexive, gendered accounts. Attention to gender is significant in the

earliest women anthropologists such as Margaret
Mead, Ruth Benedict, Hortense Powdermaker and
Peggy Golde, as was reflection on their own impact,
effect and power in the discipline of anthropology.[4]
Critiques of anthropology by post-colonial theorists, feminists and postmodernists have led to what
has been defined as a recent 'crisis' in which the
authority of the anthropologist and the authorizing
power of fieldwork has come under attack (see n. 2,
pp. 437 below and journals such as *Critique of
Anthropology*). Abu-Lughod (1990) argues that what
feminist ethnography can contribute to anthropology is an unsettling of the boundaries that have
been central to its identity as a discipline based on
the colonial method of 'studying the other'.

Sociology is the second location where feminist
sociologists have used ethnography to put women's
lives on the main disciplinary agenda to challenge
the complacency of previous research, to highlight
its gendered assumptions and to generate new
theory more fitted to exploring the complexities of
gender, race and class (see Afshar and Maynard,
1994). Ethnography has been deployed to study work,
the take-up of services, occupational socialization
and identity formation and is usually interview-
based qualitative research (see below under Realist
ethnographies; see also Pilcher and Coffey, 1996).
In the third location, education, usually informed by
sociology, feminist educational ethnographies have
likewise challenged accepted theory, put feminist
issues onto an agenda and provided new knowledge
of both education and girls and women's lives more
generally (see Griffiths, 1995; Hay, 1997). They
have also explored the intersections between race,
class and gender (see Mac an Ghaill, 1988; Mirza,
1992).

The fourth location is in cultural studies, an area
that was forged out of debates within feminism
alongside race and class (see Brunsdon, 1996;
Franklin et al., 1991). Feminists in cultural studies
have generated a form of ethnography which pays
close attention not only to experience in context, but
also to the ways in which representations shape
the lived context. Ellen Seiter's (1995a) study *Sold
Separately* of the impact of media advertising, magazines and TV on parenting practices and the emotional production of guilt, or Sarah Franklin's
(1997) *Embodied Progress*[5] study of assisted conception which explores the production of medical
knowledge, the understanding of technology, the
reformulating of parenthood and kinship, alongside
the production of desperateness by those who experience infertility, are beautifully nuanced studies of
how we are positioned by and can take up limited
(often media-influenced) understandings and emotional responses to our situation. A tangential but
important shaping influence in cultural studies
ethnography has been the media-focused audience-
response research. This fuses the cultural studies influence with understandings of audience and focuses

on responses to particular texts (for example a TV
programme or film). Studies such as Marie Gillespie's
(1995) *Television, Ethnicity and Cultural Change*
have explored how the medium of television
enables the recreation of cultural traditions within
the 'South Asian' diaspora in London and Janice
Radway's (1987) *Reading the Romance* study of a
group of women reading Harlequin romances
showed how a sense of identity, space and place
was generated through reading. Andrea Press
(1998) examines how television and the conversations it generates sets limits on how abortion is discussed and politicized. Seiter (1999) maps the
development of 'new media audiences' showing
how the different traditions merge.[6]

However, because of the intersection within cultural studies of literary traditions with sociological
ones, confusion often occurs over the term ethnography and it is sometimes used to refer to *any* form
of empirical analysis, be it an interview or even
analysis of questionnaire responses (Skeggs, 1994,
1995). The confusion appears to date from literary
theorist Stanley Fish's (1980) study of interpretative communities of readers which is based on what
he calls 'ethnographic interviews'. This is a very
different understanding to that of anthropology and
sociology which demand a level of intensity and
temporal duration far beyond one interview.
However, it has produced some interesting in-depth
analyses of the problems faced by intensity-
interviewing (see Seiter, 1990, 1995b).

Feminist researchers are thus placed within these
different traditions, and naming work as ethnographic which is as much about historical placement
and disciplinary location as it is about the methods
employed. The unbalanced attention drawn here to
cultural studies is because of the internal claim for
authority between audience researchers and those
who focus solely on the text. Whereas in sociology
the term is often used interchangeably with qualitative research, in cultural studies (and film studies) it
is a strong sign of on which side of the political
fence the researcher sits. And just as there are multiple routes into ethnography, there are many different
feminist ways through it.

FEMINIST ACCESS ROUTES

Many of the arguments about research that have
been explored by feminists are not just limited to
feminists. As Pat Caplan (1988) argues, feminist
research is often dismissed as just another specialization, where in fact its arguments have wider
relevance to other forms and types of research.
Male postmodernists positioned themselves as new
and different by ignoring how feminists had
been labouring over issues of fragmentation and
multiple-subjectivity for some time (Morris, 1988).

Wolf (1990) and Strathern (1987a) show how many issues in contemporary ethnography debates (especially the post-structural and postmodern) have a very long history:

> Before reflexivity was a trendy term, feminists were examining 'process' in our dealings with one another – questioning the use of power and powerlessness ... examining closely the politics of seemingly apolitical situations, evaluating the responsibilities we bore toward one another, and so on. (Wolf, 1990: 132)

Bell (1993b) argues that it is reflexivity and attention to gender that distinguishes feminist ethnography from the traditional. Sandra Harding (1991) argues that feminists might now expect serious engagement with the work they have already done.[7] But, she notes that this is a rare occurrence. There is always a politics to citation and whereas feminists have had to know about non-feminist research, the reverse is rarely the case.

Debates in feminist theory impact upon how feminist ethnography is framed.[8] Feminist ethnography has two main citational frames: first, it converses with the general debates in feminist theory about politics, methodology, ethics and epistemology, and secondly, with debates that constitute ethnography outside of feminism. Following from the late 1970s feminist researchers have debated which methods produce the greatest explanatory power in order to understand women's lives (and more recently men's lives as well). Beginning as a theory of gender oppression when women began sharing experiences with each other (de Lauretis, 1990), feminism is now in auto-critique. Gender is no longer seen as the primary determinant of women's lives and the constitutions and disruptions of other categorizations such as race and class are seen to be as important as gender. The traditional object of feminism 'woman' has come under critique (Ahmed et al., 2000; Riley, 1987) and there has been a shift from ethnographies on women to ethnographies informed by feminist theory.

Feminist ethnographers take up their place in relation to these debates, depending upon their entry into academia and their disciplinary location. For instance, entering into feminist ethnography in the early 1980s as I did, forced an engagement with the topical radical feminist ideas of male-stream knowledge as well as an understanding of the traditional imperialist anthropological debates. I forged my particular type of ethnography from my location as a sociologist, inspired by the disciplinary shattering debates in cultural studies and my education in historical materialism. As I moved through different theoretical debates – Althusser, Gramsci, Foucault, Butler, Haraway, Bourdieu – my analysis changed. I was able to draw on different resources for understanding my empirical data. For others who entered at different times, from different spaces, the take-up of positions and movements through debates will be different (see Skeggs, 1995).

It is essential to state at this point that very few feminists have ever believed in a feminist methodology,[9] even in 1983 Dickens argued:

> Demands that feminists produce a unique methodology act to circumscribe the impact of feminism ... We feel it is time to abandon what amounts to a defensive strategy. It has to be recognized that feminist research is not a specific, narrow, methodology, but one that is informed at every stage by an acknowledged political commitment. (1983: 1)

Rather feminists have tactically crafted ethical and political stances out of feminism more generally and applied these to the research process. It is how these political/ethical proscriptions are applied that makes the research identifiably feminist. One of the earliest proscriptions was that any feminist research should be based on women for women to produce research which would alleviate the conditions of oppression: Helen Roberts (1981), Angela McRobbie (1982) and Liz Stanley and Sue Wise (1983) framed the early debates, with Chris Griffin (1980) providing a ground-breaking, but not easily available, stencilled paper from CCCS[10] on feminist ethnography. Many of the early feminist debates ran parallel with debates about other forms of oppression, namely working-class and race. The initial impetus behind the claims for feminist research was for visibility. These initial studies tried to break down traditional male-centred research agendas which made women invisible and normalized the male gender. Important contestations were made on many fronts and Dale Spender's (1981) *Men's Studies Modified* mapped out how and where these challenges were being made.

One of the initial arguments of these feminist researchers was that all knowledge, hence all research is carried out in the interests of particular people/groups. Taking up historical-sociological debates from Marx and Weber, feminists argued that no research is value-free or objective (Roberts, 1981; Stanley and Wise, 1983). This led to the critique of objectivity and rationality and a rather problematic assertion of the subjective as the ideal focus for feminist research. The feminist critique of positivism (phallocentrically derided as 'if it moves measure it') overstated the case for understanding the subjective, emotional and irrational, unwillingly reproducing the binary categories that should have been demolished. Another impetus was from the direct political organizing involved in rape crisis and domestic violence, whereby it was argued that feminist research should have a direct political impact, rather than a purely scholarly imperative.[11] These different debates provided the impetus for feminist researchers to concentrate on qualitative research, to focus on women's experience and to listen and explore the shared meanings between women with an aim to reformulate traditional research agendas. 'Giving voice' was a mantra that was frequently evoked and ethnography was perfectly poised to provide the mechanism for doing so.

Ethnography provided an excellent methodology for feminists, with its emphasis on experience and the words, voice and lives of the participants, enabling what bell hooks (1989) describes as a 'view from below'. Paul Willis (1977) articulates this as showing the cultural viewpoint of the oppressed, their 'hidden' knowledges and resistances. He shows how agency – the entrapping 'decisions' that men make – produces 'structure'. This is the project, he argues, of showing the capacities of the working class to generate, albeit ambiguous, complex and often ironic, collective and cultural forms of knowledge, are not reducible to the bourgeois forms. This he identifies as one of the bases for political change.[12] Willis' articulation fed into the feminist desires for a more participant-centred methodology. In the early 1980s government funding bodies were hesitant to capitalize on the feminist enthusiasm for research and so feminist researchers appropriated parts of more mainstream methodology debates and transformed them through engagement with feminist politics. In this act of translation it is important to note how possibilities for new ethnographic formations were generated.

Marcus (1986) defines Willis' approach scathingly as 'the ethnographer as midwife', in which the oppressed are given life and voice by the ethnographer. Willis' position raises three important points for understanding feminist ethnography. First, the link made between structure and agency gestures towards some feminists' concerns to link the political to the subjective. Secondly, just as feminist theory has shown that women are not just women (Riley, 1987), feminists are not just feminists, they too have interests and investments in matters other than gender, such as class and race. For Willis, ethnography provided the technology to excavate the meanings of the oppressed; for feminists it offered the same potential in which different categorizations could be interlinked; for some it was the potential of ethnography to explore these intersections that made it more useful than other methods. Thirdly, what is relevant to note is the repositioning of ethnography from colonial method to liberatory strategy. It is the deployment rather than the methodology itself that makes the difference. The points raised above will now be discussed in more detail.

THEORETICAL INTERSECTIONS

Feminist researchers in general and those who do ethnography are not a homogeneous group. Different questions to be asked, disciplinary locations, theoretical investments as well as different political aims all inform the shape that the ethnography will take. All feminist research is related to wider political positions. These political positions are generated from the different understandings of why and how women are oppressed and what solutions are possible. Liberal, revolutionary, Marxist, socialist, post-structural and postmodern positions taken by feminist ethnographers will inform what focus is chosen for the study, the questions asked and what type of epistemological underpinnings structure the analysis. So whilst all feminist research is premised on a theory of gender, the form it takes is widely divergent. As an example, my ethnographic research *Formations of Class and Gender: Becoming Respectable* (1997) initially drew on three strands: on Marxist analysis which had been fused with Gramsci's concerns about how hegemony was achieved in practice; understandings of sub-cultural formations through the sociological work of Becker, Matza and Miller. This in turn was fused with feminist work which combined history and psychoanalysis with another variant of Marxism that focused on the multiple locations of subjectivities (for example, Walkerdine, 1981). Ethnography was chosen as a method because I wanted to explore how working-class women 'consented' to their own subordination (a Gramscian paraphrase) and I thought I could only find out by understanding the processes by which subordination is achieved. Valerie Walkerdine (1981) and Christine Griffin (1985) were already doing interesting work which questioned the traditional understandings of class and explored how it was lived as a form of subjectivity. My interest in this area is itself related to my own feminist politics and intellectual autobiography. Different interests, say in parliamentary representation, would have been generated through a different biography, a different exposure to feminism, different concerns and a desire for a different outcome. I wanted to know about how the everyday contributes to the maintenance of power in molecular and temporal ways. Whilst I generally wanted oppression to cease and equality to exist I did not have a more pragmatic, less idealist aim in mind. The scope and scale of the idea also informs the use to which ethnography is put. Sarah Franklin (1997) writes in the personal dedication to her ethnography of assisted conception 'for all of us trying to conceive of a new world order'. She has since gone on to study 'life itself'. This is somewhat different to the more specific, more focused studies, which have a direct aim. Rosabeth Moss Kanter (1977), for instance, wanted to explore women in corporations in order to promote equal opportunities. Her frame suggests a different historical location, a different political perspective and subsequently a different aim; and probably something which is a great deal more achievable.

Other differences occur in relation to the position the feminist ethnographer holds on epistemology (a theory of knowledge) and ontology (a theory of being). These beliefs can traverse disciplines and history. For instance, *naturalist* ethnography is usually associated with anthropology and underpinned by the ontological assumption that you can only know about people through their 'natural' settings. Naturalist ethnographers believe that you can provide a truth about a people: traditional anthropologists such as Malinowski would be an obvious case. Remnants of naturalism inform contemporary feminist ethnography such as Judith Stacey (1988). Marcus (1992) distinguishes between *realist* and *modernist* ethnography. Realist ethnographers believe in coherence, community, historical determination and structure. Their difference from naturalist ethnographers is, he argues, in the emphasis on structure. They also believe that there is a reality 'out there' which can be discovered and identified. The feminist studies of work draw upon these realist traditions (such as Cavendish, 1982; Pollert, 1981; Purcell, 1988; Stafford, 1991 and Westwood, 1984). Alternatively, modernist ethnographers do not concentrate on communities but on the complex formation of identity across a range of sites in relation to wider global issues. The modernist problematic, as defined by Marcus (1992), is the question of who or what controls and defines the identity of individuals, social groups, nations and cultures. They emphasize the role of re-presenting when discussing reality (for example, Griffin, 1985; Visweswaran, 1994). There are also *social constructionist* ethnographers who believe in the power of representation to construct the lives of the people they are studying (Steier, 1991). These should not be confused with *postmodern* or *critical* ethnographers who do not believe that there is a reality that can be known beyond the discursive representation of it (for example, Franklin, 1997; Harvey, 1996; Walkerdine, 1986). Some feminists can incorporate parts of each type of ethnography, but what is essential when noting the differences are the assumptions that are made about what can be known and how truth is defined.

Just as questions of epistemology and ontology inform the type of ethnography to which feminists subscribe, these issues also inform how analysis proceeds and the relationship between theory and practice. Feminists use and generate theory in the same multitudinous ways as other researchers. Feminists often begin within the analytic-induction tradition outlined by Robinson (1952) in which a study begins with a sensitizing concept (Blumer, 1969) or pre-emptive suppositions (Schutz, 1972) and proceeds to use participants' understandings of their experiences to develop and contest such speculations. This can either be seen to modify theory – by using the twin pronged attack of feminist theory and participants' understandings (see Griffin,

1985); or to 'improve pre-existent theory', which Burawoy et al. (1991) define as a significant outcome of most ethnography. Or ethnography can be used as 'grounded theory' in which theories are used as examples of empirical experience (Glaser and Strauss, 1967). A great deal of feminist ethnography has used empirical research to counter the assertions of previously taken-for-granted analysis and to articulate that which was previously invisible (see the 'Bell debate' later). Ethnography can be seen as one way in which theoretical deliberation is conducted within a context (de Saussure, 1960). Explanatory power is one of the major ways in which feminists have used and created theory, that is, by searching for the most effective explanation for conceptualizing the process, matter, person, issue, event or context (or all of them together) that need explaining.

In order to understand the status and authority of knowledge generated through a feminist ethnography researchers often engage with and take a position on the debates in feminist epistemology. These range from feminist empiricism – the belief that all feminist knowledge derives from experience – include feminist standpoint theories, which can assume that truth and reality are present in women's experiences, and can be found through research and different variants of post-structuralism and postmodernism, which assume, following Foucault, that truth is codified error – truth is made true – and that experience can only be understood through discursive analysis of the production of power and knowledge. Hennessy (1993) argues that in most research there is a failure adequately to explain the movement between the discursive materiality of feminism and the empirical materiality of women's lives. As ethnography is always premised upon experience, so it is to this issue that we now turn.

Experience can mean anything. Experience, Lazreg (1994) shows, is rarely defined in a systematic way. It is usually taken as a given, a self-explanatory concept that each feminist specifies in her own way. This is used to refer to feelings, emotions, the personal, personality, subjectivity and such like. Or experience is represented as unmediated: spoken words are placed directly on a page with no account given of how and where they came from, the power relations involved, the publishing deals signed, the editing and selection processes. The earlier discussed idea of 'giving voice' deflects attention away from all the institutional power relations involved in actually producing a text. Or researchers take as self-evident the identities of those whose experience is being documented, that is, they are already assumed to be classed, raced, gendered in specific ways as they are allocated to categories. This always leads to the reproduction of these categories intact. When both of these processes are utilized (giving voice and allocated identity categories) to gain authority, Scott (1992) argues they simply reflect on the facts of historical location. But it is location that is ignored when priority is given to experience itself. It is to assume that ontology is the ground of epistemology, that what I am determines what and how I know. But how do I know who I am? In historicism the answer is easy: I am my differences, which have been given to me by history.[13] We are thus left with a constant defining descriptor and all that changes are the descriptions which are sometimes squeezed to fit. Often experience is set against thinking and theorizing, as if they are different from practical experience.

Feminist standpoint theories encompass different takes on experience: Dorothy Smith (1997) reiterates her original point that she first made in 1987, that 'experience is a method of speaking that is not pre appropriated by the discourse of the relations of ruling' (1997: 394). She argues that when women first started speaking to each other as women (as a category of political mobilization) they discovered dimensions of experience that had no prior discursive definition. The authority of experience, she argues, is foundational to the women's movement (1997: 394). It is 'tacit knowing' (that is, the knowledge of how to do the everyday things without thinking about what we do) that means we know as a matter of doing (1997: 395). Taking women's standpoint and beginning in experience gives access to a knowledge of what is tacit. Although Smith argues that she is not making a claim for the privileging of women's experience, her arguments centre on the empirical belief (and those associated with this position are often called empiricist feminists)[14] that knowledge springs from experience and that women's experience carries with it special knowledge and that this knowledge is necessary to challenge oppression.[15] From this perspective ethnography would be the means for excavating the processes from which tacit knowledge is produced.

Patricia Hill Collins (1990, 1997, 1998) has a different take on standpoint. For her a standpoint is always a group production and related to how groups are positioned in structures of inequality and difference. She specifically explores the standpoints of African American women. To ignore power relations, she argues, is to misread standpoint theory (1997: 376). She maintains that standpoints emerge from and express the world-views of specific communities of practitioners. She shows how, in *Fighting Words* (1998), the privileged appropriate the standpoints of others to increase their knowledge whilst abandoning the politics associated with marginalized others' positions. In 1990 she argued that it is the standpoints of the marginalized group which generate epistemic privilege:[16] only those who have the appropriate experience of oppression are able to speak about it. This reduces knowledge to a formula of being = knowing, a formula which had dogged philosophers since Kant. It also grants

an authority and hierarchy to certain groups and silences others (Bar-On, 1993), leading to confrontations over identities in which differences are collapsed into a 'listen to me' 'hear my difference' power play (Probyn, 1990). This has led to a form of identity politics based on the idea of 'authentic subjective experience' which restricts politics to the personal.[17] She clarifies this position in 1998 when she insists that it is the political understanding arising from experiences of power that enable standpoints to offer a superior vantage point of knowing. However, there is always a slippage between groups and individuals as 'knowers' when the term identity is brought into play. Identity can be used to apply to both positions (group and individual) and this has led to confusion over who 'owns' the knowledge that is produced from oppression. From Hill Collins' standpoint it would be the ethnographer's role to understand how structural historically reproduced inequality leads to the formation of particular political understanding of oppression.

It is Nancy Hartsock (1983, 1997, 1998) who offers the most extensive development of standpoint.[18] Translating Marx's (1967) analysis of the 'standpoint of the proletariat' into feminist terms and adapting Lukács' (1971) essay on reification and standpoint she argues that it is the perspective gained from political opposition to power that produces a standpoint. This means that experience has to be translated into a perspective before it can be a standpoint. As Weeks (1996) argues, the project of transforming subject positions into standpoints involves an active intervention, a conscious and concerted effort to reinterpret or restructure lives. A standpoint, Hartsock argues, is a project not an inheritance; it is achieved and not given. The interpretative frameworks of Marxism or feminism offer the potential for producing a standpoint; they are the mechanisms by which experience is translated into a perspective and known as oppositional. Some knowledges offer more scope and explanatory power for understanding oppression than others. Feminist ethnography produces experience viewed through the critical analytical interpretative device of feminism (or of feminism with Marxism, or postcolonialism, etc.). The standpoint advocated by Hartsock is therefore about processes and not about things and this is why her variant is particularly suited to the practice of ethnography which because of its duration and movement within space enables processes to be known. It is not about individual activities but about a subaltern experience across a group which can only be known through praxis, practical activity.

Du Bois (1968) argues that subaltern groups have a 'double consciousness' whereby the understanding of themselves is not compatible with the dominant categories and knowledge available (and produced by dominant groups). My ethnography *Formations* showed how a group of white working-class women – a marked and subaltern group in Gramsci's (1971) terms – continually challenged the categories of class, gender and heterosexuality by which they were positioned, but which were impossible to inhabit, and produced themselves as something more socially valuable, that is 'respectable'. They maintained a critical analysis and distance on the categories that were used to position them whilst putting their energy into showing they were something else. The process of 'becoming respectable' was a continual repeated performance, produced against dominant classificatory systems.[19] Indeed, as Scott (1992) notes, it is not individuals who have experience, but subjects who are *constituted* through experience. Using categories of experience as the basis for knowledge is very much dependent on how experience is used to theorize. Les Back (1996), in a study of young people, race, gender and class in South London, carefully explores the limitations of categories of race when attempting to understand how racism is spatially informed. Ethnography is probably the only methodology that is able to take into account the multifaceted ways in which subjects are produced through the historical categories and context in which they are placed and which they precariously inhabit.

This is why the insights from post-colonial theory (e.g. Minh-ha, 1989; Mohanty, 1992; Spivak, 1988, 1990) and the application of these to the critique of anthropology (Narayan, 1993; Ong, 1995; Visweswaran, 1994) have been particularly important in moving ethnographic analysis from unadulterated experience of culture to exploring how power and structure set limits on what can be known as experience. Spivak (1990), for instance, has shown how subjecthood is denied to those considered not capable of congnizing their lives in the frameworks of anthropologists. Narayan (1993) shows how the category 'native' has been used in order that the white man can know about himself rather than others. Consistently, post-colonial work has pointed to ethnography as a mainstay of global capitalism, imperialism and power, which is able to establish the terms for the categorization of others. Rather than using these categories 'race', 'class', 'gender' they have interrogated for whom they were produced. Rather than focus on individual experience, they have drawn attention to process. Rather than focus on identity they have drawn attention to positioning. Visweswaran (1994) describes her own ethnography:

> Suspicious of feminist and ethnographic desires to 'know' the other, I rendered a subject who resists any single positioning for very long. My attempt was to describe how a woman emerged out of a series of performances and positionings, and not to render the category 'woman' intelligible through recourse to sociological variables as abstract descriptions of reality. (1994: 76)

For those ethnographers who have not had the privilege of not being categorized, positioned and pathologized, it is impossible to ignore the wider relations that reproduce the processes of 'keeping in place' intact.

What is at stake in the translation/interpretation of the experiences of 'others' by ethnographers is made explicit in 'the Bell debate'. This was generated after white feminist ethnographer Diane Bell and her 'collaborator' Aboriginal woman, Topsy Nelson, published an article in *Women's Studies International Forum* (1989) on the rape of Aboriginal women by Aboriginal men. Bell and Klein (1996) later note critiques that were made: ' ... creating divisions within the "Aboriginal community", appropriating Topsy Nelson's voice by citing her as a co-author rather than as an "informant", of exhibiting white imperialism, of exercising middle-class privilege' (1996: 108). Ahmed (2000) argues that what is at stake in this debate is not just a question of who is speaking and who is being spoken for, rather it is about the relations of production that surround the text: how was it that Bell came close enough to Topsy Nelson to enable this debate to be aired in public. The ethical problems of ventriloquism (Visweswaran, 1994), of producing the 'native' as authentic and truth (Narayan, 1993; Spivak, 1990), of spuriously 'giving voice' (Spivak, 1988, asks 'can the subaltern speak?' to which she answers 'no'), of accountability and responsibility and 'sheer arrogance' (Agar, 1980) are all produced through post-colonial critique. It is these ethical-political issues that the next section will discuss.

FEMINIST ETHICS

Feminist researchers often use prescriptive ethics such as reciprocity, honesty, accountability, responsibility, equality, etc., in order to treat participants of ethnography with respect. This enables an acknowledgement that their time is important and establishes the intention of non-exploitation. There were substantive debates in the 1980s, most notably by Carol Gilligan (1982) and Sara Ruddick (1989), about how women were more caring than men. This was translated into feminist research as a prescriptive ethic of care. This, however, created its own problems by reproducing a form of biological and cultural essentialism, which assumed that women were predisposed to care. It also raised questions about how it is possible to be caring towards women who are responsible for political atrocities. Blee (1991) outlines her difficulties and ambiguities when talking with women who were proud of their involvement in the Ku Klux Klan and saw it as: 'just a celebration ... a way of growing up' (1991: 1). She knows how feminist researchers are meant to be respectful and caring but notes:

I was prepared to hate and fear my informants ... I expected no rapport, no shared assumptions, no commonality of thought or experience. What I found was more disturbing. Many of the people I interviewed were interesting, intelligent and well informed. (1991: 6)

Blee's movement between hate, astonishment, empathy and caring provides for a very nuanced and detailed account of the relationship between gender and racism in a specific historical context. Most feminists have learned to be wary of generalizing ethical prescriptions. Christine Griffin (1991), in a study of racism, argues that when the participants in the research are reproducing damaging and racist ideas, enabled and legitimated by years of collusion from other white people, then the 'researcher should talk back', arguing that not to do so (the ethical prescription of care, for instance) would reproduce, legitimate and collude in the racist ideas being articulated. Griffin argues less for caring for the researched and more for caring about wider inequalities.

Maria Meis (1983) argues for studying crisis or ruptures in the pattern of normality, so that the pathology of the normal may be perceived. For her ethics occurs in the disruption of the power and privilege of normalization. Kum-Kum Bhavnani (1994) argues that the crucial question for all (feminist) researchers to ask is 'does the analysis re-inscribe the researched into powerlessness, pathologized, without agency?'. Ethics thus informs throughout the research process: from the choice of topic and participants, to negotiation of access, to relationships, to interpretation, to representation and this is why reflexivity has always been a differentiating motif of feminist ethnography. Sensitivity to power has forced feminist researchers to be constantly vigilant of the relations in which they are inscribed.

One ethical proscription which most feminists begin with is the ideal of reciprocity. To use and objectify others is seen to be a particularly masculine way of conducting research. Valerie Walkerdine (1984) suggests that the power of the researcher to objectify and scrutinize the 'subject' of research engages the researcher in a process similar to that of the male gaze. Another ethical debate taking place across the many different sites of feminism is about responsibility. For instance, Stanley and Wise (1983) argue that it is the responsibility of the researcher to equalize power differences between women, in order, as above, not to reproduce research participants as powerless. However, there is a difference between taking responsibility for not producing powerlessness and being able to equalize power. When we enter ethnography we enter it with all our economic and cultural baggage, our discursive access and the traces of positioning and history that we embody. We cannot easily disinvest of these. In fact we may not even know that much

about ourselves. Moreover, many of the interactions we engage in may be informed by factors beyond our control. Many relationships are generated through such things as projected fears, that is, the researchers may be read as being authoritative and powerful when in fact they are not. However, I do think we have to try to work out how interactions are framed by as many factors as possible (we are after all researchers) and then try to work through these in terms of power. Recognition of the positioning and channels of power may be one way of not engaging in normalizing power relationships. This is an on-going feature of any ethnography as it occurs over time and relationships change. Taking responsibility for the reproduction of power may be more possible than equalizing power (see Bhavnani, 1994; Haraway, 1991).

Linked to this, Stanley and Wise (1983) argue that there is another feminist principle which should be about *relinquishing control* of the research. This means that the researched should control the outcome and analysis of the research. If the researched do not like the explanations given or do not want the research to be published they should have the right to control it. It was after all their lives which formed the basis for the research. But what if they do not agree with something that the researcher thinks is important and can ultimately improve the quality of their lives? What if, as happened in my research, they deny ever having said what they did when they hear themselves on tape or read the transcript (see Skeggs, 1997)? What if the research is about exploring the contradictions that go into producing the murky waters of subjectivity, which when given back to the participants exposes the fragmentation of their lives that they have invested a great deal of time in covering over. I would argue, in this case, that it is about exercising discretion and responsibility. Ultimately it is an argument about representations, which will be discussed in a later section.

One way in which certain ethics may be achieved is through reciprocating knowledge. The researched give us information so the researcher returns the favour to provide them with something that may be useful. Ann Oakley's (1981) study is the classic example where she offers important health and maternal information that assuages the doubts and anxieties of the women she is studying. They know they can approach her for vital information. There are limits to reciprocity, however. Whereas it is now common practice to pay for participation in a focus group which may last a few hours, it is unlikely that an ethnographer could pay for years of contact. For feminist ethnographers this involves finding ways in which to reciprocate the time given by participants; an activity which then itself becomes part of the research process (see Skeggs, 1997).

Another feminist ethical prescription which is hotly contested in feminist research is what Maria Meis (1983) calls *conscientization*, which, she argues, is the means by which feminist researchers should make the researched aware of the feminist explanations and frameworks that can explain the circumstances of their lives. Romero (1992) has argued that this may be both inappropriate and patronizing. In her study of *Maid in the US*, which focuses on Chicana domestic workers, she shows how they already have very clear understandings of the conditions of their exploitation. What they do not have, she argues, is any means to escape it. Mairtin Mac an Ghaill's (1994) study of young Asian men, which deploys feminist analysis, shows how his participants have a far clearer understanding of the workings of class, race, gender and sexuality than many of the theories that purport to explain these intersections.

The deployment of feminist principles such as respect, equality and reciprocity has led Judith Stacey (1988) to argue that the ethnographic approach masks a deeper, more dangerous form of exploitation than had previously been imagined, precisely because it rests on engagement and attachment 'placing the research subjects at a greater risk of manipulation and betrayal by the ethnographer' (1988: 23). Stacey shows how the relationships generated during her ethnography *Brave New Families* (1990) placed her in a position of 'inauthentic dissimilitude' in which 'the inequality and potential treacherousness of this relationship seems inescapable' (1988: 23). However, it is Judith Stacey's partially naturalistic assumptions about authenticity and truth that lead to these pessimistic conclusions. She has since argued that feminist ethnography offers greater explanatory power than other methodologies, if also simultaneously more risk (Stacey, 1994).

Stacey maintains that there cannot be a fully feminist ethnography, there can only be ethnographies that are partially feminist, accounts of culture enhanced by the application of feminist perspectives. In a rejoinder to Stacey's pessimism, Elizabeth Wheatley (1994) argues that the moral dilemmas evoked by Stacey are not necessarily feminist but more generally epistemological and ethical and can be addressed by attention to interpretative and representational practices. Using her ethnographic experience of studying women's rugby teams in the mid-western United States, she notes that Stacey's claim that there cannot be a fully feminist ethnography might be read as suggesting that there cannot be a fully ethical ethnography, as a fully ethical study would mean that all ethical issues are fully resolved. All ethnography involves irreconcilable conflicts. It is how feminists use their knowledge to resolve dilemmas that produce a particular feminist ethnography. Wheatley points out that Stacey's highly critical reflexivity and ethical sensitivity are a case in point. Moreover, it is the epistemological recognition that all knowledge is situated, partial, contingent and interpretative

that enables us to avoid the quagmire of women = experience = truth that has bedevilled many feminist debates.

Yet if we return to the Topsy Nelson/Diane Bell debate we can see how all these ethical issues intervened. Both Nelson and Bell argue that their article was produced as a result of friendship. Yet Bell constantly references her work and her ethnography. Nelson was not passively abused in this situation and argues that she used Bell 'to write it all down for her'. Yet as Ahmed (2000) argues, their friendship was strategically framed; their friendship was a technique of knowledge. She argues that the need to make friends with strangers (the basis of most ethnography) works, in terms of relationality and dialogue, to conceal the operation of an epistemic division within the process of becoming more intimate with one who has already been designated as strange. Centuries of colonialism designates some people as knowers and some as strangers (sometimes with some stories worth telling). To support her argument, Ahmed (2000) draws on Bell's earlier ethnography *Daughters in the Dreaming* (1993a) to show how Bell authorizes her ethnography through reading all the available literature on Aboriginal lifestyles and her ethnography is framed through an academic debate about how traditional anthropology accounts for the reality of Aboriginal women's lives. In other words, Ahmed argues, Aboriginal women are present in the ethnography only insofar as they establish a term in an argument which has its terms of reference in anthropology. It is these sorts of debates that have led to greater attention being paid to the issues of representation and the conditions of possibility which enable ethnographies to be produced at all.

REPRESENTATIONS

The final product of the feminist ethnography, the text, is informed by what is 'writable' and what is 'readable' (Atkinson, 1992). These definitions are formed through locations in disciplines, traditions of prior ethnographies and decisions about style. For feminist ethnographers, this will be informed by the issues listed above: by the 'rules' of the discipline and by the historical positioning of the particular theorists and the demands of publishers. Many feminist ethnographers will still be located in traditional disciplines and will have to conform to their regulations. These factors will all be reflected in the representations that are produced and are being given increased attention. For instance, the 'aesthetics of authenticity' (Lury, 1991), that is, the way in which ethnography uses the juxtaposition of everyday speech with academic styles of writing, is being disputed as a spurious rhetoric of authority. The inclusion of everyday speech is one of the stylistic conventions that define ethnography as a distinctive genre, as a distinctive textual production (Atkinson, 1990) yet this is being challenged by those who pay attention to textual constructions as authorizing practices (Visweswaran, 1994). Attention is also being drawn to the 'fictions of feminist ethnography', otherwise known as a fully reflexive experiential ethnography. Margery Wolf (1990), for instance, has produced three different narrativizations of her ethnography in Taiwan. Deploying different frameworks, rhetorical strategies and authorizing claims, she exposes the different ways in which her ethnography can be told. In a similar gesture she re-writes her 'self' in another series of writing, asking 'which of these constructions is my real self' (1990: 130), hence, what is authority? What is real? What is truth?

Judith Stacey (1988) argues that a major area of contradiction between feminist principles and ethnography is the dissonance between the fieldwork practice and the ethnographic production:

> [The] ethnographic method appears to (and often does) place the researcher and her informants in a collaborative, reciprocal quest for understanding, but the research product is ultimately that of the researcher, however modified or influenced by informants. With very rare exception it is the researcher who narrates, who 'authors' the ethnography. In the last instance an ethnography is a written document structured primarily by a researcher's purposes, offering a researcher's interpretation, registered in a researcher's voice. (1988: 23)

The ethical issues raised, she argues, cannot be overcome by what Strathern (1987b) identifies as 'representational tact'. However, recognizing that all research can only ever be partial forces an engagement in analysis of the power of cultural representations. The halt to the search for truth may make us more aware of our complicity in knowledge production. For feminists it is a means to think about strategy, complicity and our relationship to others. Writing and reading, Wheatley argues, 'are viable sites for engendering ethnography with feminist sensibilities' (1994: 409). She cites Marsha Millman's (1980) work on the social world of fat people as a way in which feminist writers can mobilize people's imaginations in particular ways. Other examples include Kreiger (1983), who uses a multi-voice approach to question the potential for essentializing her lesbian research participants and to disrupt the traditional authoritative researcher position, and Weston (1998), who also plays with analysis and authority in tales of lesbigay life. Griffiths (1984) added drama to her ethnographic repertoire.

Atkinson argues that 'the combination of feminism and postmodernism produces a powerful critique of the complacency of texts that claim a privileged insight into a universe of stable meanings (1990: 149). But Bell (1993b) argues that any combination would be difficult as many postmodern texts produce a distance from the self which is in marked contrast with the attention to the self within feminism. She argues that the male postmodern ethnographers

> are the very authors of the 'new ethnography' who, under the guise of democratizing ethnography through plurivocality, avoid scrutiny of their own power. By reducing ethnographic encounters to texts, the postmodernists have mystified the power of the ethnographer, and their experimentations mask the location, and hence the ability of the author to structure and choose text and voice ... Yet the consequences of tracing a genealogy through women's reflections and experiments would be to position postmodernism not as a withering critique of the 1980s, but rather as a somewhat peevish, peripheral, self-interested and in particular, male construction. (Bell, 1993b: 8)

Moreover, as Rabinow (1986) notes, groups long excluded from positions of institutional power may have less concrete freedom to engage in textual experimentation. And Strathern (1987b) argues that a lot of the ironic re-readings of the 'new ethnographers' look remarkably self-referential. It is the feminist imagination, Wheatley (1994) argues, that makes the difference; it is committed political-ethical investments argues Stacey. For as Wolf (1990) points out, the postmodernist fascination with style and rhetoric may lead not to better ways of doing ethnography, but better ways of writing unethical ones. This is where feminism takes a different direction. It is not just the product but the ethico-political process in which feminist ethnographers are engaged that counts.

Whilst other researchers may, through normalization, privilege and complacency, be able to ignore ethical and political issues in particular, it is the constituency of a very critical feminist readership that keeps feminist ethnographers on their toes. Accountability to participants as well as other feminists is often a strong incentive for rigour. As Weber (1949), not famous for his feminism, would note: 'does it have value relevance, is it worthy of being known?' (1949: 76). We have to ask worthy for whom? Patricia Williams (1991) and Lorraine Code (1995) speak of a 'rhetorics of space' in which the researcher is responsible to the groups whom they claim to represent and should be accountable for any representation produced. This leads to prioritizing obligations and responsibility in any ethnographic account. It leads to an understanding of circuits of distribution and circulation and a keen sense of audience.

CONCLUSION

Feminist ethnography is always informed by feminist ethics. This attention to ethics has produced different types of ethnography which across a range of disciplines have all, over a long historical period, displayed a sensitivity to the power effects of the researcher. This has led to debates on reflexivity and problematizing the objectification of the other. This reflexive attention has produced important interventions into the debates over the authorizing and legitimacy of knowledge production. Questioning the virtues of objectivity, distance and detachment, feminist ethnographers have shown these to be a 'god trick', a belief that knowledge comes from nowhere (Haraway, 1991). So feminist ethnography has not just produced some of the most in-depth material about women's lives but also enabled significant challenges to what comes to be counted as knowledge.

The differences between feminist ethnographers is due to many issues: pragmatics, motivations, autobiography, historical positioning, disciplinary homes and access to frameworks for understanding, perceptions and demands of audience, the area being researched, methods used. It is always a question of location in its widest usage:

> Location is not a listing of adjectives or assigning of labels such as race, sex and class. Location is not the concrete to the abstract of decontextualisation. Location is the always partial, always finite, always fraught play of foreground and background, text and context, that constitutes critical enquiry. Above all, location is not self-evident or transparent ... Location is also partial in the sense of being *for* some worlds and not others. (Haraway, 1997: 37)

The fundamental question that constantly informs feminist research is always 'in whose interests?' (*cui bono?*).

Feminist ethnography will always exceed the limits of the research practices in which it engages through its dialectical relationship with feminist theory and ethics. It is not neat and cannot be contained. Feminism enters the research at many different stages and how it does and how it is used inform the final product. Haraway (1997) argues that 'ethnography is a method of being at risk in the face of the practices and discourses into which one inquires' (1997: 190). Risk, in this sense is understood as a challenge to previous stabilities, convictions, or ways of being of many kinds. It is for this reason that I'd argue for a difference between feminist ethnography and ethnographies of women. This division parallels a debate in women's studies in the 1990s between studies that focus on gender and those that deconstruct gender. The former reproduces gender as a category leaving it intact, the other deconstructs and re-signifies, emphasizing process and focuses on challenges to how we conceive of feminism rather than providing descriptions of women's lives. Both have their uses and values, and demonstrate the range and scale of feminist research. But they are making very different theoretical moves.

The range and depth of the debates in feminist ethnography has led to feminist theorists calling for every researcher to adopt an 'ethnographic attitude'. Haraway (1997) argues that an 'ethnographic attitude' can be adopted within any kind of enquiry, including textual analysis. It is, she argues, a way of remaining mindful and accountable. It is not about taking sides in a predetermined way but is about the risks, purposes and hopes embedded in knowledge projects. It is what Peggy Phelan (1998) calls an ethics of witnessing which is both responsive *to* and responsible *for*. Whether this 'attitude' can do justice to the careful, scholarly, rigorous analysis that has been carried out over long periods of time, with intensity and pain, remains to be seen; but as a recommendation for vigilance it may finally introduce the arguments of feminist ethnographers into the main-male-stream.

NOTES

1 Methods such as questionnaires, historical documentation and statistical analysis can also be used – they often provide a wider socioeconomic context (Skeggs, 1994: 76).

2 See Gupta and Ferguson, 1997 for how the definition of ethnography is contested in anthropology through the use of the figure of the field. Clifford (1997a, 1997b) has tried to challenge the centrality of the definition of ethnography in 'the field' by using metaphors of travel.

3 See Lee, 1995: 31–4 for different accounts of ethnography and espionage. Hutnyk (1998) suggests that this is not just a historical practice but that ethnography has continually been used by imperial global powers as a source of intelligence.

4 But not only women have been excluded from the formation of anthropology: working-class men were used as labourers to collect data. The were often not credited with or had any say in what was done with their material (Kuklick, 1997). Of course, it was unknown in the history of anthropology to have black anthropologists, as it was precisely the non-whites who were turned into strangers and objects for analysis, so that civilizing distance could be drawn from them (McClintock, 1995).

5 Sarah Franklin crosses the boundaries between anthropology and cultural studies making definition and location even more difficult to specify.

6 See also Ann Gray (1992) *Video Playtime* on how women use the technology of videos as well as watching videos; Joke Hermes (1995) *Reading Women's Magazines*; Virginia Nightingale (1996) *Studying Audiences* (Nightingale (1989) also asks 'what is ethnographic about ethnographic audience research?'); Andrea Press (1991)

Women Watching Television; and not feminist but informed by feminism, Moores (1993) *Interpreting Audiences*; Morley (1992) *Television, Audiences and Cultural Studies*; Schlesinger et al. (1992) *Women Viewing Violence*.

7 Within the British Sociological Association Journal a debate occurred between Martyn Hammersley (1992), who claimed to be judging the cogency of feminist methodology, and feminist respondents Ramazanoglou (1992) and Gelsthorpe (1992). He argues that many of the ideas of feminists are also to be found in non-feminist literature and concludes by arguing against the idea of a specifically feminist methodology. As Ramazanoglou and Gelsthorpe point out, feminists are not homogeneous. It is rare, they argue, for feminists to argue for a feminist methodology and if a cross-citational analysis were to occur it is more likely that feminists look outwards, because there is less space for feminist work within the academy and most feminist researchers have to work within traditional disciplines. Moreover, Hammersley positions himself as ungendered, performing what Haraway (1991) describes as a 'god trick'.

8 I wrote *Formations of Class and Gender* as a challenge to the complacency of a great deal of feminist theorizing which assumed a homogenous white bourgeois subject at the centre of feminism. It is not a new argument but the use of ethnography in this way may be.

9 Williams (1993) is a notable exception.

10 CCCS was the Centre for Contemporary Cultural Studies at Birmingham University which represented a disciplinary intersection of literary, historical, sociological and educational analysis produced to more adequately explain the contemporary political situation. It has since been greatly romanticized and mythologized.

11 See Hinds et al. (1992) and the debates in the journal *Feminist Review* on the place of women's studies in the academy to understand the ferocity and ethics of this proscription.

12 See Skeggs, 1992 for a discussion of the historical context, methodology and importance of Willis' *Learning to Labour* (1977).

13 This short explanation does not do justice to the complexity of the arguments presented by Joan Scott (1992), which should be used as a reference point.

14 Oddly the concept of experience belongs to a classical empiricist tradition, the very source of positivist science which feminism was at odds to challenge.

15 These arguments do not just apply to empirical research but any research whose foundation is that women are different because of their experiences. Gynocentric textual analysis was developed on this basis (see Probyn, 1993).

16 The use of the term standpoint has become closely associated with ossified positions in feminism. Its use in labour history had a completely different meaning. It meant taking a standpoint – anyone could do it – and making a connection. It was not tied into experience but to political commitment (see, Popular Memory Group, 1982).

17 See Chapter 7 in Fuss, 1989 and see Brunsdon, 1991 for the implications of these arguments for feminist pedagogy. Parmar (1989) argues that 'identity politics

may be enough to get started but not enough to get finished' (p. 61). (See Adams, 1989; Parmar, 1989; Fuss, 1989 for extensive debates.)

18 As well as Hartsock's extensive works, there is considerable debate in feminist journals: see *Signs*, 1997: 22 (2) and *Women and Politics*, 1997: 18 (3). Hekman (1997) generated considerable debate when she assessed standpoint theory on the basis of whether it has the epistemological potential to justify the truth claims of feminism. See also Ahmed et al. (2000) on the value of asking about the justification of knowledge.

19 And as psychoanalysis has shown, we never do become, it is always a process.

References

Abu-Lughod, L. (1990) 'Can there be a feminist ethnography?', *Women and Performance: A Journal of Feminist Theory*, 5 (1): 7–27.

Adams, M.L. (1989) 'There's no place like home: on the place of identity in feminist politics', *Feminist Review*, 31: 22–34.

Afshar, H. and Maynard, M. (eds) (1994) *The Dynamics of 'Race' and Gender: Some Feminist Interventions*. London: Taylor and Francis.

Agar, M.H. (1980) *The Professional Stranger: An Informal Introduction to Ethnography*. New York: Academic Press.

Ahmed, S. (2000) *Strange Encounters'*. London: Routledge.

Ahmed, S., Kilby, J., Lury, C., McNeil, M. and Skeggs, B. (2000) *Transformations: Thinking Through Feminism*. London: Routledge.

Atkinson, P. (1990) *The Ethnographic Imagination: Textual Constructions of Reality*. London: Routledge.

Atkinson, P. (1992) *Understanding Ethnographic Texts*. London: Sage.

Back, L. (1996) *New Ethnicities and Urban Culture: Racisms and Multiculture in Young Lives*. London: UCL Press.

Bar-On, B.A. (1993) 'Marginality and epistemic privilege', in L. Alcoff and E. Potter (eds), *Feminist Epistemologies*. London: Routledge.

Bell, D. (1993a) *Daughters in the Dreaming*. Sydney: Allen Unwin.

Bell, D. (1993b) 'The context', in D. Bell, C. Caplan and W.J. Karim et al. (eds), *Gendered Fields: Women, Men and Ethnography*. London: Routledge. pp.1–19.

Bell, D. and Klein, R. (eds) (1996) *Radically Speaking Feminism Reclaimed*. North Melbourne, Va: Spinifex.

Bell, D. and Nelson T. (1989) 'Speaking about rape is everybody's business', *Women's Studies International Forum*, 12 (4): 403–47.

Bhavnani, K-K. (1994) 'Tracing the contours: feminist research and feminist objectivity', in H. Afshar and M. Maynard (eds), *The Dynamics of 'Race' and Gender: Some Feminist Interventions*. London: Taylor and Francis. pp. 26–41.

Blee, K.M. (1991) *Women of the Klan: Racism and Gender in the 1920s*. Berkeley, CA: University of California Press.

du Bois, W.E.B. (1968) *The Souls of Black Folk*. New York: Fawcett World Library.

Blumer, H. (1969) *Symbolic Interactionsim*. Englewood Cliffs, NJ: Prentice–Hall.

Brunsdon, C. (1991) 'Pedagogies of the feminine: feminist teaching and women's genres', *Screen*, 32 (4): 364–82.

Brunsdon, C. (1996) 'A thief in the night: stories of feminism in the 1970s at CCCS', in D. Morley and K-H. Chen (eds), *Stuart Hall: Critical Dialogues in Cultural Studies*. London: Routledge. pp. 276–87.

Burawoy, M., Burton, A., Arnett Ferguson, A. et al. (1991) *Ethnography Unbound: Power and Resistance in the Modern Metropolis*. Oxford: University of California Press.

Caplan, P. (1988) 'Engendering knowledge: the politics of ethnography', *Anthropology Today*, 14 (5): 8–12.

Cavendish, R. (1982) *Women on the Line*. London: Routledge and Kegan Paul.

Clifford, J. (1983) 'On ethnographic authority', *Representations*, 1 (2): 118–46.

Clifford, J. (1986) 'Introduction: partial truths', in J. Clifford and G. Marcus (eds), *Writing Culture: The Poetics and Politics of Ethnography*. Berkeley, CA: University of California Press.

Clifford, J. (1997a) 'Spatial practices: fieldwork, travel and the disciplining of anthropology', in A. Gupta and J. Ferguson (eds), *Anthropological Locations: Boundaries and Grounds of a Field Science*. Berkeley, CA: University of California Press.

Clifford, J. (1997b) *Routes: Travel and Translation in the Late Twentieth Century*. Cambridge, MA: Harvard University Press.

Code, L. (1995) *Rhetorical Spaces: Essays on Gendered Locations*. London: Routledge.

Coffey, A. (1999) *The Ethnographic Self: Fieldwork and the Representation of Identity*. London: Sage.

Dickens, L. (1983) 'Is feminist methodology a red herring?', Letter to the editor of *Network* (Newsletter of the British Sociological Association), 26 May.

Finch, L. (1993) *The Classing Gaze: Sexuality, Class and Surveillance*. St Leonards, NSW: Allen and Unwin.

Fish, S. (1980) *Is There a Text in this Class? The Authority of Interpretative Communities*. Cambridge, MA: Harvard University Press.

Franklin, S. (1997) *Embodied Progress: A Cultural Account of Assisted Conception*. London: Routledge.

Franklin, S., Lury, C. and Stacey, J. (eds) (1991) *Off Centre: Feminism and Cultural Studies*. London: Hutchinson.

Fuss, D. (1989) *Essentially Speaking: Feminism, Nature and Difference*. London: Routledge.

Gelsthorpe, L. (1992) 'Response to Martyn Hammersley's paper "On Feminist Methodology"', *Sociology*, 26 (2): 213–19.

Gillespie, M. (1995) *Television, Ethnicity and Cultural Change*. London: Routledge.

Gilligan, C. (1982) *In a Different Voice*. Cambridge, MA: Harvard University Press.

Ginsburg, F. (1989) *Contested Lives: The Abortion Debate in an American Community*. Berkeley, CA: University of California Press.

Glaser, B. and Strauss, A. (1967) *The Discovery of Grounded Theory*. Aldine: Chicago.

Gramsci, A. (1971) *Selections from the Prison Notebooks of Antonio Gramsci* (eds Q. Hoare and G. Nowell-Smith). London: Lawrence and Wishart.

Gray, A. (1992) *Video Playtime: The Gendering of a Leisure Technology*. London: Routledge.

Griffin, C. (1980) *Feminist Ethnography* Birmingham. Stencilled Paper: CCCS.

Griffin, C. (1985) *Typical Girls: Young Women from School to the Job Market*. London: Routledge.

Griffin, C. (1991) 'The researcher talks back: dealing with power relations in studies of young people's entry into the job market', in W.B. Shaffir and R.A. Stebbins (eds), *Experiencing Fiedwork: An Inside View of Qualitative Research*. Newbury Park, CA: Sage. pp. 109–19.

Griffiths, V. (1984) 'Feminist research and the use of drama', *Women's Studies International Forum*, 7 (6): 511–19.

Griffiths, V. (1995) *Adolescent Girls and Their Friends*. Aldershot: Avebury.

Gupta, A. and Ferguson, J. (eds) (1997) *Anthropological Locations: Boundaries and Grounds of a Field Science*. Berkeley, CA: University of California Press.

Hammersley, M. (1992) 'On feminist methodology', *Sociology*, 26 (2): 187–206.

Haraway, D. (1991) *Simians, Cyborgs and Women: The Reinvention of Nature*. London: Routledge.

Haraway, D. (1997) *Modest_Witness@Second_Millennium. FemaleMan © _Meets_OncoMouse* ™: *Feminism and Technoscience*. London: Routledge.

Harding, S. (1991) *Whose Science, Whose Knowledge? Thinking from Women's Lives*. Milton Keynes: Open University Press.

Harstock, N. (1983) 'The feminist standpoint: developing the ground for a specifically feminist historical materialism', in S. Harding and M.B. Hintikka (eds), *Discovering Reality: Feminist Perspectives on Epistemology, Metaphysics, Methodology and Philosophy of Science*. Dordrecht: Reidel.

Hartsock, N. (1997) 'Comment on Hekman's "Truth and Method: Feminist Standpoint Revisited": truth or justice?', *Signs*, 22 (2): 367–73.

Hartsock, N. (1998) *The Feminist Standpoint Revisited and Other Essays*. Boulder, CO: Westview Press.

Harvey, D. (1989) *The Condition of Postmodernity*. Cambridge: Polity Press.

Harvey, P. (1996) *Hybrids of Modernity: Anthropology, the Nation State and the Universal Exhibition*. London: Routledge.

Hay, V. (1997) *The Company She Keeps: An Ethnography of Girls' Friendships*. Buckingham: Open University Press.

Hekman, S. (1997) 'Truth and method: feminist standpoint revisited', *Signs*, 22 (2) : 341–65.

Hennessy, R. (1993) *Materialist Feminism and the Politics of Discourse*. London: Routledge.

Hermes, J. (1995) *Reading Women's Magazines: An Analysis of Everyday Media Use*. Cambridge: Polity Press.

Hill Collins, P. (1990) *Black Feminist Thought*. London: Routledge.

Hill Collins, P. (1997) 'Comment on Heckman's "Truth and Method: Feminist Standpoint Theory Revisited": where's the power', *Signs: Journal of Women in Culture and Society*, 22 (2): 375–81.

Hill Collins, P. (1998) *Fighting Words: Black Women and the Search for Justice*. Minneapolis, MN: University of Minnesota Press.

Hinds, H., Phoenix, A. and Stacey, J. (eds) (1992) *Working Out: New Directions for Women's Studies*. London: The Falmer Press.

hooks, b. (1989) *Talking Back: Thinking Feminist, Thinking Black*. London: South End Press.

Hutnyk, J. (1998) 'Clifford's ethnographica', *Critique of Anthropology*, 18 (4): 339–78.

Kanter, R.M. (1977) *Men and Women of the Corporation*. New York: Basic Books.

Kreiger, S. (1983) *The Mirror Dance: Identity in Women's Community*. Philadelphia: Temple University Press.

Kuklick, H. (1997) 'After Ishmael: the fieldwork tradition and its future', in A. Gupta and J. Ferguson (eds), *Anthropological Locations: Boundaries and Grounds of a Field Science*. Berkeley, CA: University of California Press.

de Lauretis, T. (1990) 'Upping the anti (sic) in feminist theory', in M. Hirsch and E. Fox Keller (eds), *Conflicts in Feminism*. London: Routledge.

Lazreg, M. (1994) 'Women's experience and feminist epistemology', in K. Lennon and M. Whitford (eds), *Knowing the Difference: Feminist Perspectives in Epistemology*. London: Routledge.

Lee, R.M. (1995) *Dangerous Fieldwork*. London: Sage.

Lukács, G. (1971) *History and Class Consciousness*. Boston, MA: Beacon Press.

Lury, C. (1991) 'Reading the self: autobiography, gender and the institution of the literary', in S. Franklin et al. (eds), *Off-Centre: Feminism and Cultural Studies*. London: Hutchinson.

Mac an Ghaill, M. (1988) *Young Gifted and Black: Student Teacher Relations in the Schooling of Black Youth*. Milton Keynes: Open University Press.

Mac an Ghaill, M. (1994) *The Making of Men: Masculinities, Sexualities and Schooling*. Buckingham: Open University Press.

Marcus, G.E. (1986) 'Contemporary problems of ethnography in the modern world system', in J. Clifford and G.E. Marcus (eds), *Writing Culture: The Poetics and Politics of Ethnography*. Berkeley, CA: University of California Press. pp. 105–93.

Marcus, G.E. (1992) 'Past, present and emergent identities: requirements for ethnographies of late twentieth-century modernity world-wide', in S. Lash and J. Friedman (eds), *Modernity and Identity*. Oxford: Blackwell.

Martineau, H. ([1837] 1962) *Society in America* (ed. S.M. Lipset). New York: Anchor Books.

Marx, K. (1967) *Capital*, vol. 1. New York: International Press.

McClintock, A. (1995) *Imperial Leather: Race, Gender and Sexuality in the Colonial Context*. London: Routledge.

McRobbie, A. (1982) 'The politics of feminist research: between talk, text and action', *Feminist Review*, 12: 46–59.

Meis, M. (1983) 'Towards a methodology for feminist research', in G. Bowles and R. Duelli Klein (eds), *Theories of Women's Studies*. London: Routledge and Kegan Paul.

Melia, K. (1987) *Learning and Working: The Occupational Socialisation of Nurses*. London: Tavistock.

Millman, M. (1980) *Such a Pretty Face: Being Fat in America*. New York: Berkeley Books.

Minh-ha, T.T. (1989) *Woman, Native, Other*. Bloomington, IN: Indiana University Press.

Mirza, H.S. (1992) *Young, Female and Black*. London: Routledge.

Mohanty, C. (1992) 'Feminist encounters: locating the politics of experience', in M. Barrett and A. Phillips (eds), *Destabilising Theory*. Cambridge: Polity Press.

Moores, S. (1993) *Interpreting Audiences: The Ethnography of Media Consumption*. London: Sage.

Morley, D. (1992) *Television, Audiences and Cultural Studies*. London: Routledge.

Morris, M. (1988) 'Introduction: feminism, reading, postmodernism', in M. Morris (ed.), *The Pirate's Fiancée: Feminism, Reading, Postmodernism*. London: Verso.

Narayan, K. (1993) 'How native is the "native" anthropologist?', *American Anthropologist*, 95 (3): 19–34.

Nightingale, V. (1989) 'What's ethnographic about ethnographic audience research?', *Australian Journal of Communication*, 16: 50–63.

Nightingale, V. (1996) *Studying Audiences: The Shock of the Real*. London. Routledge.

Oakley, A. (1981) 'Interviewing women: a contradiction in terms', in H. Roberts (ed.), *Doing Feminist Research*. London: Routledge and Kegan Paul.

Ong, A. (1995) 'Women out of China: travelling tales and travelling theories in colonial feminism', in R. Behar and D.A. Gordon (eds), *Women Writing Culture*. Berkeley, CA: University of California Press.

Parmar, P. (1989) 'Other kinds of dreams', *Feminist Review*, 31: 55–66.

Phelan, P. (1998) 'Performance and death: Ronald Regan'. Paper presented to Institute for Cultural Research, Lancaster University, 28 October.

Pilcher, J. and Coffey, A. (eds) (1996) *Gender and Qualitative Research*. Aldershot: Avebury.

Pollert, A. (1981) *Girls, Wives and Factory Lives*. London: Macmillan.

Popular Memory Group (1982) 'Popular memory, theory, politics, method', in R. Johnson, G. McLennan, B. Schwarz and D. Sutton (eds), *Making Histories: Studies in History, Writing and Politics*. London: Hutchinson.

Press, A. (1991) *Women Watching Television*. Philadelphia: University of Pennsylvania Press.

Press, A. (1998) *Imagining Our Lives: Television, Women's Talk and the Political Culture of Abortion*. Chicago: University of Chicago Press.

Probyn, E. (1990) 'Travels in the postmodern: making sense of the local', in L.J. Nicholson (ed.), *Feminism/ Postmodernism*. London: Routledge. pp. 176–90.

Probyn, E. (1993) 'True voices and real people: the "problem" of the autobiographical in cultural studies', in V. Blundell, J. Shepherd and I. Taylor (eds), *Relocating Cultural Studies*. London: Routledge. pp. 105–22.

Purcell, K. (1988) *Gendered Jobs: Factory Gates*. Oxford: Oxford University Press.

Rabinow, P. (1986) 'Representations are social facts: modernity and post-modernity in anthropology', in J. Clifford and G. Marcus (eds), *Writing Culture: The Poetics and Politics of Ethnography*. Berkeley, CA: University of California Press.

Radway, J. (1987) *Reading the Romance*. London: Verso.

Ramazanoglou, C. (1992) 'On feminist methodology: male reason versus female empowerment', *Sociology*, 26 (2): 207–12.

Reinharz, S. (1992) *Feminist Methods in Social Research*. Oxford: Oxford University Press.

Riley, D. (1987) 'Does a sex have a history? "Women" and feminism', *New Formations*, 1: 35–45.

Roberts, H. (ed.) (1981) *Doing Feminst Research*. London: Routledge and Kegan Paul.

Robinson, P. (1952) 'The logical structure of analytic induction', in G. McCall and J. Simmons (eds), *Issues in Participant Observation*. Reading, MA: Addison–Wesley.

Romero, M. (1992) *Maid in the USA*. New York: Routledge.

Ruddick, S. (1989) *Maternal Thinking: Towards a Politics of Peace*. New York: Ballantine Books.

de Saussure, F. (1960) *Course in General Linguistics*. London: P. Owen.

Schlesinger, P. Dobash, R.E., Dobash, R.P. and Weaver, C. Kay (1992) *Women Viewing Violence*. London: British Film Institute.

Schutz, A. (1972) *The Phenomenology of the Social World*. Heinmann: London.

Scott, J.W. (1992) 'Experience', in J. Butler and J.W. Scott (eds), *Feminists Theorise the Political*. London: Routledge.

Seiter, E. (1990) 'Making distinctions in TV audience research: case study of a troubling interview', *Cultural Studies*, 4 (1): 61–85.

Seiter, E. (1995a) *Sold Separately: Parents and Children in Consumer Culture*. New Brunswick, NJ: Rutgers University Press.

Seiter, E. (1995b) 'Mothers watching children watching television', in B. Skeggs (ed.) *Feminist Cultural Theory: Production and Process*. Manchester: Manchester University Press.

Seiter, E. (1999) *Television and New Media Audiences*. Oxford: The Clarendon Press.

Skeggs, B. (1992) 'The cultural production of "Learning to Labour"', in A. Beezer and M. Barker (eds), *Reading into Cultural Studies*. London: Routledge.

Skeggs, B. (1994) 'Situating the production of feminist ethnography', in M. Maynard and J. Purvis (eds), *Researching Women's Lives*. Basingstoke: Taylor and Francis.

Skeggs, B. (ed.) (1995) *Feminist Cultural Theory: Production and Process*. Manchester: Manchester University Press.

Skeggs, B. (1997) *Formations of Class and Gender: Becoming Respectable*. London: Sage.

Smith, D. (1997) 'Comment on Hekman's "Truth and Method: Feminist Standpoint Theory Revisited"', *Signs*, 22 (2): 392–8.

Spender, D. (1981) *Men's Studies Modified*. Oxford: Pergamon Press.

Spivak, G.C. (1988) 'Can the subaltern speak?', in C. Nelson and L. Grossberg (eds), *Marxism and the Interpretation of Culture*. Urbana, IL: University of Illinois Press.

Spivak, G.C. (1990) *The Post-Colonial Critic*. New York: Routldege.

Stacey, Jackie (1994) *Star Gazing: Hollywood Cinema and Female Spectatorship*. London: Routledge.

Stacey, Judith (1988) 'Can there be a feminist ethnography?', in *Women's Studies International Forum*, 11 (1): 21–7.

Stacey, Judith (1990) *Brave New Families: Stories of Domestic Upheaval in Late Twentieth Century America*. New York: Basic Books.

Stacey, Judith (1994) 'Imagining feminist ethnography: a response to Elizabeth E. Wheatley', in *Women's Studies International Forum*, 17 (4): 417–19.

Stafford, A. (1991) *Trying Work: Gender, Youth and Work Experience*. Edinburgh: Edinburgh University Press.

Stanley, L. and Wise, S (1983) *Breaking Out*. London: Routledge and Kegan Paul.

Steier, F. (ed.) (1991) *Research and Reflexivity*. London: Sage.

Strathern, M. (1987a) 'An awkward relationship: the case of feminism and anthropology', *Signs*, 12 (2): 276–92.

Strathern, M. (1987b) 'Out of context: the persuasive fictions of anthropology', *Current Anthropology*, 28 (3): 251–81.

Visweswaran, K. (1994) *Fictions of Feminist Ethnography*. Minneapolis, MN: University of Minnesota Press.

Walkerdine, V. (1981) 'Sex, power and pedagogies', in *Screen Education*, 38: 14–26.

Walkerdine, V. (1984) 'Some day my prince will come', in A. McRobbie and M. Nava (eds), *Gender and Generation*. London: Macmillan. pp. 162–85.

Walkerdine, V. (1986) 'Video replay: families, films and fantasy', in V. Burgin, J. Donald and C. Kaplan (eds), *Formations of Fantasy*. London: Methuen. pp. 167–200.

Weber, M. (1949) *The Methodology of the Social Sciences*. (trans. E.A. Shils and H.A. Finch). New York: The Free Press.

Weeks, K. (1996) 'Subject for a feminist standpoint', in
S. Makdisi, G. Casarino and R. Karl (eds), *Marxism
Beyond Marxism*. London: Routledge.

Weston, K. (1998) *Render Me, Gender Me: Lesbians Talk
Sex, Class, Color, Nation, Studmuffins*. New York:
Columbia University Press.

Westwood, S. (1984) *All Day Everyday: Factory and
Family in the Making of Women's Lives*. London: Pluto
Press.

Wheatley, E. (1994) 'How can we engender ethnography
with a feminist imagination? A rejoinder to Judith
Stacey', in *Women's Studies International Forum*, 17
(4): 403–16.

Williams, A. (1993) 'Diversity and agreement in feminist
ethnograpy', *Sociology*, 27 (4): 575–89.

Williams, P. (1991) *The Alchemy of Race and Rights:
Diary of a Law Professor*. Cambridge, MA: Harvard
University Press.

Willis, P. (1977) *Learning to Labour: Why Working-Class
Kids Get Working Class Jobs*. London: Saxon House.

Wolf, M. (1990) *A Thrice Told Tale*. Stanford, CA:
Stanford University Press.

30

Ethnography After Postmodernism

JONATHAN SPENCER

As a fledgling ethnographer in Sri Lanka in the early 1980s I spent as much time as conscience would allow in the company of other anthropologists, swapping tropical symptoms and intellectual anxieties. One recurring theme in our conversations concerned the way we would eventually try to write about our fieldwork, in doctoral dissertations and, if we were lucky, in monographs and articles. We were clearest about the way we didn't want to write ethnography, but a bit less sure about how we did want to write it. The positive aspiration was summed up in two or three words: we wanted to include 'people' and 'stories', or what, most recently, has been summed up in the single term 'voices'. We also wanted to write ethnography that people actually felt like reading. The analogy here was with writing in history, a discipline in which cutting-edge researchers in the 1960s and 1970s – Natalie Davis, Eric Hobsbawm, Le Roy Ladurie, E.P. Thompson – were able to communicate sophisticated, theoretically astute analyses to enormous general audiences. We were, I now realize much more clearly, reacting against the last wave of grand theory – structuralism and structural Marxism, in particular – which had dominated the anthropology we were taught as undergraduates in the 1970s. In particular, we were reacting against the tendency to abstraction and depersonalization, found in most anthropological writing of the 1950s and 1960s, but raised to a particularly fine art in the 1970s.

There were, of course, exceptions to this broad tendency: mavericks who broke the ethnographic rules, like the young Gregory Bateson ([1936] 1958), or ethnographers apparently obsessed with their own literary effect, like Clifford Geertz (1973). There was also a small, but significant corpus of autobiographical writing by ethnographers like Laura Bohannon (the 'Eleanor Smith Bowen' of *Return to*

Laughter, 1954), recently swelled by the likes of Jean-Paul Dumont (1978) and Paul Rabinow (1977), while a concern with the literary dimension of ethnographic writing can be traced as far back as Malinowski's *Argonauts of the Western Pacific* (1922) or the urban explorations of Robert Park and his associates in Chicago at the same time (Atkinson, 1991). Nevertheless, there was a very strong sense of collective pressure – within British anthropology at least – which blocked off issues of ethnographic writing, and often issues of fieldwork as well, from any public discussion. Yet something had clearly happened to provoke those discussions from the field itself with which I started this chapter. For whatever reason, many ethnographers in the generation of fieldworkers trained in the late 1970s and early 1980s had simply ceased to believe in the models of scientific and textual authority provided by our disciplinary ancestors.

This was the context in which *Writing Culture* (Clifford and Marcus, 1986) was published, to immediate extraordinary effect. In this book, a group of academics concerned with issues of representation in ethnography – mainly male, mainly American, mainly anthropologists – addressed what the subtitle described as 'the politics and poetics of ethnography'. At about the same time, two of the contributors published their own manifesto for the new ethnographic times, *Anthropology as Cultural Critique* (Marcus and Fischer, 1986), followed shortly after by an extremely influential collection of essays by the most prominent non-ethnographer of ethnography, James Clifford's *Predicament of Culture* (Clifford, 1988). For good or ill, the impact of these books was huge: ethnography would never be the same again.

This is a familiar enough story, implicitly or explicitly told in many of the other contributions to this volume. Yet I want to start by giving it an unfamiliar contextual critique. As my opening description of over-heated conversations with my peers in the early 1980s suggested, in many ways *Writing Culture* was an accident waiting to happen. Or, to put it slightly differently, the impact of the book was over-determined by a number of relatively autonomous, yet converging, causes. The models of phlegmatic orthodoxy, which had dominated ethnographic writing in anglophone anthropology, had somehow ceased to carry conviction. Students, as I explain below, had long since queried the lofty generalizations ethnographers made about other people's world-views and modes of thought. Their criticisms of ethnographic generalization (or 'essentialism' as we swiftly learned to call it) were given a political twist by Edward Said's blistering attack on the academic representation of the non-Western world in his *Orientalism* (1978), while the authority of ethnographic representations, written as it were 'from nowhere', had been thoroughly undermined throughout the 1970s by feminist critiques, which pointed out that the view from nowhere was in fact always a view from somewhere in particular – usually a male view, representing the opinions and arguments of male informants (see the chapter by Skeggs in this volume). Finally, in America in particular, the humanities and social sciences were suddenly immersed in what literary critics simply called 'theory' – a body of ideas and arguments, mostly French in origin, usually post-structuralist, often post-Marxist. 'Theory', as it was found in the imitations of Foucault and Derrida which swiftly abounded, combined, among many other things, a highly mannered mode of exposition with a rhetoric of apparent radicalism. It opened up new and exciting areas of enquiry across the human sciences – gender, sexuality, the body – while paradoxically often closing the door to all but the most devoted and academic of readers. Whereas followers of Althusser in the 1970s could write as if one correctly situated problematic, and some careful symptomatic reading of *Capital III*, might yet bring about the collapse of world capitalism, their successors in the 1980s sometimes wrote as if repeated use of words like 'discourse' and 'metanarrative' marked a decisive victory over the whole tainted history of Western rationality.

The publication of *Writing Culture* brought these disparate strands together in one, sometimes internally contradictory yet very powerful, package. In Britain at least, much of the volume's early impact was heavily polarized, along more or less generational lines. Yet, younger ethnographers who had been waiting for something which would provide, as it were, a licence to use their literary imagination, were sometimes almost as dismayed as their more conservative elders by the content and tone of some parts of *Writing Culture*. In a paper written in haste during my first term as a temporary lecturer, I attempted to address the immediate reaction to the book, separating out some of the different strands I have just identified as contributing to its particular appeal. In particular, I attempted to demonstrate that the critique of previously existing ethnographic writing demanded attention, even from those like myself, suspicious of the uncritical theoretical name-dropping and oppositional rhetoric found in parts of *Writing Culture*. That paper was eventually published in *Man* (Spencer, 1989) – a journal since congenially emasculated as the *Journal of the Royal Anthropological Institute* in keeping with the spirit of the times – and I have used parts of its core argument in the next part of this chapter. It quickly took its place alongside a suite of critical articles (Mascia-Lees et al., 1989; Roth, 1989; Sangren, 1988) which appeared about the same time, all of which took a more or less 'yes, but ... ' line on the critique of ethnographic writing: yes, much of the critique is justified and intellectually worthwhile, but we would be wrong to exaggerate the importance of academic literary criticism as a model for (or even a substitute for) other forms of social and political criticism. (Feminist anthropologists were especially bemused by the editors' tortured explanation of why it proved necessary to invite only male anthropologists to the workshop which produced the eventual volume: Clifford, 1986: 20–1; Mascia-Lees et al., 1989: 13–14.)

WRITING AND INTERPRETATION

The thrust of my original argument concerned the relationship between text and context. Up to the 1970s, for various reasons, the context of anthropological representations – the actual work of enquiry and the material on which generalizations are based – had been omitted from much ethnography. This context could be restored in two ways: by re-reading ethnography in terms of some wider historical context we may learn a great deal about the past of our discipline; while the effort to incorporate some self-consciousness about such matters within anthropological writing promises to improve the usefulness of new ethnography. But if we want to effect more significant change in the writing and reading of ethnography, then, I argued, we shall have to reconsider not just anthropological writing – most of which takes place at considerable remove from ethnographic experience – but anthropological practice as a whole.

The florescence of literary self-consciousness in American anthropology in the 1980s can be conveniently traced to an apparently innocuous footnote in Clifford Geertz's 1973 essay 'Thick description':

> Self-consciousness about modes of representation (not to speak of experiments with them) has been very lacking in anthropology. (Geertz, 1973: 19 n.3)

The essay in which this is embedded is a dense and allusive text which is accordingly difficult to summarize. It makes a number of assertions: that anthropology is what anthropologists do; that what they do is ethnography; and that ethnography is (or at least should be) writing of a very particular sort. To characterize this peculiar sort of writing Geertz borrows a term and an example from the philosopher Gilbert Ryle. This is of a boy winking; to describe this as 'a contraction of the eyelid' is what Ryle calls 'thin description'; to unravel the significance of it – the boy may be winking, he may be parodying a friend winking, he may be imitating a friend parodying a third party winking and so on – requires interpretation, what Ryle, and Geertz after him, call 'thick description'. Ethnography is, then, an interpretative exercise in 'thick description'.

Ethnography moreover should not be assessed by the amount of undigested information it contains but rather by the clarification it offers. But one apparent advantage of 'information' as a criterion of ethnographic worth is, of course, that it is relatively tangible. The disadvantage, for many, of Geertz's 'clarity' is that it sounds subjective on the one hand, while, as a final arbiter of ethnographic success, it has its own peculiar dangers – Margaret Mead's account of Samoa (1928) was if nothing else beautifully clear; it seemed to generations of American readers to correspond to Geertz's criterion of interpretative success: ' the power of the scientific imagination to bring us into touch with the lives of strangers' (1973: 16). The problem, of course, was that the strangers themselves disagreed not with the power, or even the imagination, but with the *content* of Mead's representation of their lives.[1]

A further problem occurs when the ethnographer – and this is something that much absorbed me in trying to write about Sri Lanka in the early 1980s, a place which, in many respects, was on the brink of political disintegration – is concerned to represent areas of cultural incoherence and confusion. It is, after all, a recurring aspect of change in the modern world, perhaps especially in those areas of it where anthropologists have been thickest on the ground, that old answers prove inadequate, old cultural cloth no longer stretches to cover uncomfortably new and worrying experience. Yet ethnographers are understandably reluctant to report that some things may not make sense in any particular cultural context. 'If law is anywhere' as Tylor ordained 'it is everywhere', and if you couldn't find it you can't have looked hard enough or in the right places (Lévi-Strauss, 1969: xi).

Geertz, it is true, acknowledges these problems, complaining that 'Nothing has done more ... to discredit cultural analysis than the construction of impeccable depictions of formal order in whose actual existence nobody can quite believe' (1973: 18). But this is precisely what Geertz himself can be accused of doing; it may not *necessarily* be true of

his ethnographic analyses but it is impossible to tell because he so often denies his readers the opportunity to assess for themselves the material from which he has constructed his accounts. His justification for this way of working lies in the distinction between thick description and thin description: one cannot assess an ethnographic interpretation against some sort of raw data, 'radically thinned description' as he puts it, because this is itself already an interpretation, a construction:

> What we inscribe (or try to) is not raw social discourse, to which, because, save very marginally or very specially, we are not actors, we do not have direct access, but only that small part of it which our informants can lead us into understanding. (1973: 20)

The problem is that Geertz ignores two things – that interpretation itself can be situated socially, and that different forms of life vary in the kind and degree of interpretation they can or should receive. Without denying the real methodological problems involved, it is obvious that something like raw figures for paddy ownership or demographic change is less dependent on informants' constructions than, say, the changes in tenancy patterns and justifications for those changes that follow demographic change. As well as interpreting and writing, many ethnographers do a great deal of counting or weighing or surveying, not to mention reading documents in archives and in the writings of their predecessors.

But let me now return to Geertz's first evasion – that interpretation is a socially determined activity. It is surely palpably obvious that, for example, a paddy-farmer's explication of decisions over the hiring of labourers on his field is likely to be different from an anthropologist's; the anthropologist should certainly use the farmer's account, and the labourers' too if it is accessible. A good anthropologist will also allow his or her readers to assess the differences between the two or three versions, differences which we can expect to correspond to the different purposes and positions of the explicators. Indeed, in skilled hands, these differences can become the centre of the whole analysis.[2]

But this is what Geertz refuses us. In his ethnographic writings, especially those from the mid-1960s onward, there is less and less space allowed for readers to agree or disagree or make their own connections. His characteristic strategy is to seize on a metaphor – likening a peasant economy to a style of baroque decoration, describing the pre-colonial Balinese state as a theatre, talking of the Balinese cockfight as a text in which the Balinese can, as it were, read about themselves – and then sustain it through flashes of description, before climaxing in a kind of adjectival blizzard. On the cockfight:

> Any expressive form lives only in its own present – the one it itself creates. But, here, that present is severed

into a string of flashes, some more bright than others, but all of them disconnected, aesthetic quanta. Whatever the cockfight says, it says in spurts. (1973: 445)

You may find such writing either exciting or enervating according to taste or academic inclination; much of the time I incline to the former view. What you will have difficulty doing is sorting out the kind of evidence Geertz could possibly adduce to support it. What, one wonders, is the Balinese for 'aesthetic quanta' and what sort of statements, what informants' explications, what entries in sweaty notebooks, could have been synthesized into the account Geertz presents?

Geertz's answer would fall back on the impossibility of using uninterpreted data in anthropological work: 'what we call our data are really our own constructions of other people's constructions of what they and their compatriots are up to' (1973: 9). This may well be true. But it would seem the merest politeness to acknowledge the source of a particular construction. One may not inscribe raw discourse; one does take down a lot of quotes, explications, constructions and any half-decent fieldworker has some idea of who it is who has provided the quote, explication, or whatever.

The idea that there is no dividing line – because all is interpretation – between the high literary gloss of Geertz's ethnography and what one assumes are the drabber, more mundane jottings in his notebooks may be a useful excuse for the exercise of a particular kind of literary style; but the style in question presupposes a passive readership. In Geertz's world, ethnographic accounts are assessed on a take-it-or-leave-it basis; one study rarely replaces an earlier deficient study, different accounts of the same place tend to run in parallel rather than building directly on each other. The ethnographer provides a finished product and never anything less than a finished product.[3]

James Clifford in his essay 'On ethnographic authority' (1983) glosses this move of Geertz's in terms of Ricoeur's (1971) discussion of text and discourse. Discourse, says Ricoeur (following Benveniste), is to be found in the specific moment of its production, in the I–and–you of its referents; textualization removes discourse from these specific conditions of production so that it can speak to other people at other times. So ethnographers take away from the field texts that are by definition already freed from the conditions of their own production, and the turning of these texts into ethnography further eliminates the specificities of the original context. The losses in such a process – and Clifford's catalogue (1983: 132) of such losses is similar to the one I have already provided – are, it seems, the inevitable result of the process of textualization.

But are they? It seems to me that Clifford (who merely describes but doesn't endorse this position)

is following Geertz in confusing Ricoeur's arguments – a feat easily accomplished as may become apparent. Ricoeur in the paper they both cite ('The model of the text', 1971) is concerned to establish an analogy between the interpretation of a text and the interpretation of what Weber called 'meaningful action'. A given action may be subject to competing interpretations, just as a given text is the subject of competing interpretations; but in both cases some interpretations are more probable than others: 'It is always possible to argue for or against an interpretation, to confront interpretations, arbitrate between them, and to seek for an agreement, even if this agreement remains beyond our reach' (Ricoeur, 1971: 550). These possibilities are greatly reduced with Geertz's work because he insists on filling the dual role of author–producer of the text which is Bali – and interpreter. The text is, in Ricoeur's phrase 'a limited field of possible constructions' (1971: 550); but an assessment of competing interpretations of a given text *presupposes access to the text itself*, not merely another critic's interpretation of it. The 'text' of Geertz's interpretation is the Bali of his experience and his notebooks – this is what he is interpreting. The irony is that this most hermeneutical of anthropologists adopts a literary practice which tries above all to close the hermeneutic circle by limiting his readers' access to that which he wants to interpret for himself. Geertz's argument in 'Thick description' has important implications for the relationship between theory and practice in anthropology. The conventional view is pretty straightforward (which isn't to say that anyone would accede to it when presented as starkly as this): there are facts, found in variable quantities in different ethnographies, and there are theories which attempt to make general statements based on those facts. Facts which don't fit can disprove a theory; odd facts can be used for new theoretical synthesis. Of course it has been long recognized that theoretical preconceptions determine what does or doesn't count as a fact to the ethnographer; Malinowski, for example, used this as the criterion to mark off scientific anthropology from the work of enthusiastic amateurs (1922: 9). But for Geertz anthropological theory is found in specific interpretations in specific ethnographies: 'Theoretical formulations hover so low over the interpretations they govern that they don't make much sense or hold much interest apart from them' (1973: 25).

DESCRIPTION AND INTERPRETATION

Some anthropologists, especially in Britain, may be ready to dismiss Geertz's discussion of anthropology as representation, feeling it to be no more than the personal preoccupation of one of the discipline's foremost literary dandies. But similar points have also been made from the point of view of a would-be generalizing anthropologist, unafraid to use *outré* words such as 'science' and 'epistemology'. Dan Sperber, in his essay 'Interpretive ethnography and theoretical anthropology' (1985), acknowledges the limited nature of anthropological theory but argues that this is because what we call our theory is, by and large, nothing of the sort; it is in fact a rag-bag of vague generalizations that provides a sort of intermediate language that is useful for the task of interpretation and translation, but useless for the real task of a scientific anthropology – the building of generalizations (a task which he disguises behind the construction of an 'epidemiology of cultural representations'). As an example of genuinely scientific anthropological generalization he proffers Berlin and Kay's (1969) celebrated work on colour classification.

Sperber's strictures are, though, of relevance, even for those of his colleagues who are sceptical of his broader project. Ethnographies, he says, deal in representations. Representations can be divided into two kinds: descriptive and non-descriptive. Descriptions are a kind of representation which are 'adequate when they are true'; that is to say, they can be refuted by observation. Truth and falsity are properties of propositions; propositions are utterances; therefore descriptions can only come in the form of utterances. Moreover, they are the kind of utterance which can be used in a logical argument: 'The Nuer are transhumant pastoralists ... ', 'If the Nuer are transhumant pastoralists ... ' 'Therefore the Nuer are transhumant pastoralists ... '.

Unfortunately for Sperber (but not, I suspect, for the rest of us) only a small part of ethnography comes in the form of descriptions. Non-descriptive representations come in two forms: reproductions and interpretations. Interpretations involve a combination of objective and subjective elements – characteristically they are what the interpreter makes of an experience and offers to an interlocutor. For Geertz, remember, ethnography is, from notebook to monograph, a seamless web of interpretation: 'our own constructions of other people's constructions of what they and their compatriots are up to' (1973: 9). Sperber, on the other hand, is concerned to unpick the stitches that hold it all together. Rather than settle for the finished ethnographic product, he wants to ask – indeed his overall project requires him to ask – *whose* construction of *what*?

If we are to use anthropological interpretations as the materials for building empirical generalizations, they need a particular kind of qualification – what he calls a 'descriptive comment':

A descriptive comment identifies the object represented and specifies the type of representation involved. It thereby makes it possible to draw non-empirical inferences from a non-descriptive representation. It

provides, so to speak, the directions for its use. (Sperber, 1985: 12)

Obvious examples of descriptive comments include captions to pictures and keys to maps. Less obvious examples – like, for example, what would count as an adequate descriptive comment in an ethnographic account – are a little harder to come by. Sperber, unfortunately, does not offer his readers an example of what an anthropologically useful ethnographic account might look like.

We can, though, get the general idea, which is not in itself especially wild-eyed or radical. Consider how a historian constructs a historical monograph. The language in such cases is likely to be quite similar to the language of the typical anthropological monograph, and to contain a similar mixture of description and interpretation. Where the two tend to differ is in the way in which the reader is made aware of the raw material upon which the account is based. The raw data of an historical account, apart from the occasional direct quotation, are no more present than the raw material of an anthropological account. They are, however, made explicit through footnotes and documentary citations. Most readers will be content to read the surface of the text and ignore the fine print which details the conditions of production of the main text, but the fine print is there for specialists and the sceptical to scrutinize. Above all, it allows the possibility of empirical challenge to both the description and the interpretation found in the main text.[4] That this leaves us no closer to an impossible contact with 'what really happened' in no way detracts from the importance of this rule of the game of historical discourse. It is still adequate to its purpose of limiting the 'field of possible constructions'.

The scholarly apparatus of footnotes in a work of history is, I suggest, an example of a highly developed system of what Sperber calls 'descriptive comment'. Compare this with Sperber's remarks on an example from Evans-Pritchard's *Nuer Religion* (1956). The chosen passage is an account of an incident when a man had been accused of practising too many sacrifices. Of the account itself Sperber notes that, while it seems 'about as raw a factual statement as you will ever find in most ethnographic works ... not a single statement in it expresses a plain observation' (1985: 14). Of the generalization which the anecdote and its gloss are called forth to support by Evans-Pritchard ('Through the sacrifice man makes a kind of bargain with his God'), Sperber asks the sort of questions that generations of bright undergraduates have asked of standard ethnographies: whose interpretation is this? the anthropologist's? the Nuer's? all Nuers' or just one or two? In fact, he concludes, the interpretation in question seems to be an attempted compromise between Nuer thought and the ethnographer's means of expression (1985: 16). And much of what passes for anthropological theory is, in fact, 'interpretative generalization' of a low and rather uninformative kind, employing terms such as 'sacrifice', 'shaman', 'ritual', which have been long since cut adrift from any original and specific denotation and instead act as intermediaries in the interpretation of ethnographic examples.

Now if I were Evans-Pritchard – to borrow the master's own idiom (cf. Evans-Pritchard, 1965: 24) – my answer to these strictures would, I imagine, be something like this. The task of the anthropologist is the translation of culture; our first priority is to render intelligible the ideas and actions of people in another culture; it is therefore quite reasonable that we should attempt to do so by working *away* from a specific utterance or incident, through various intermediary interpretations, such that the content of the original is rendered as faithfully *and* as coherently as possible. It is true that someone like Sperber, interested in gaining access to a wide range of more-or-less unmediated representations, may be disappointed by this procedure; but his is a minority interest, and an ethnography that would satisfy him would probably frighten off all but the most dedicated of readers. I imagine that a similar argument would be advanced by quite a few other ethnographers, especially those – probably now a majority – with little or no commitment to the building of general models of the variability of human social and cultural existence.

I think, though, that the force of Sperber's critique is not limited to its implications for what he sees as a properly scientific anthropology. Although he approaches ethnography with very different assumptions and intentions he nevertheless, like Geertz, has to concede the problematic status of interpretation in anthropological work. Unlike Geertz, though, he would have us make all possible effort to separate interpretation from description. This can be seen in the second part of his argument where he examines the use of 'free indirect speech'. Free indirect speech is 'the style which allows the author to tell a story "from the point of view of the actors", and the reader to identify with them' (1985: 19). 'Through the sacrifice man makes a kind of bargain with God' is a representation which allows the reader to see things as if he or she were a Nuer. The relationship between this and any utterance provided by a Nuer to Evans-Pritchard is, as Sperber's analysis demonstrates, unclear, as is the relationship of Geertz's 'disconnected, aesthetic quanta' to any real or imagined Balinese representation of a cockfight.

THE PROBLEM OF NATURALISM

In other words, a great deal of ethnographic writing carries little or no explicit reference to the ethnographic work on which it is based. Why should this be so? The most compelling reason would be the uneasy status of ethnographic work itself, in particular the relationship between individual experience and 'scientific', or, if you prefer, 'objective', generalization. Because ethnographic experience is so specific as to be unrepeatable – a fact that in itself removes ethnographic evidence from most understandings of scientific data – generalization is peculiarly problematic. A male ethnographer learns different things from a female ethnographer, and countless contingencies intervene during the time in the field, from world historical eruptions – such as elections and droughts and wars to such apparent trivia as chance meetings, illness and missed buses. Obviously, good ethnographic practice involves the attempt to make methodical what may have been first discovered by chance; but there is no denying the idiosyncrasy of individual ethnographic experience.[5] In addition, the tradition of the lone fieldworker (occasionally supplemented by spouse and children) magnifies the personal anxieties faced by all researchers. The anthropological habit of writing at arm's length is not to be dismissed as an act of simple bad faith; it is as often a tactic of emotional self-defence.

In that crucial period of professional consolidation between, say, 1940 and 1962 – marked in British anthropology by the publication of Evans-Pritchard's *The Nuer* (1940) at one end, and the polemical attacks of Needham (1962) and Leach (1961) at the other – it is possible to discern the growth of a style of ethnographic writing which I shall call 'ethnographic naturalism'.[6] I use 'naturalism' by analogy with dramatic theory, to refer to the creation of a taken-for-granted representation of reality by certain standard devices. My choice of terms comes in particular from Raymond Williams' discussion of Brecht's dramatic theory; this is because Williams' discussion is imbued with a recognition of the power and importance of some kinds of naturalism. The danger of naturalism, though, is 'the exclusion, by particular conventions of verisimilitude, of all direct commentary, alternative consciousness, alternative points of view' (Williams, 1971: 278). For Brecht, the effect of such naturalism was to lull the audience and render it passive; in its place he proposed the use of various techniques which would make the audience aware of the conditions of production of the play itself, and also of the circumstances of the action within the play. For modern anthropology in its period of professional consolidation one effect of naturalistic devices was to deny the particularity of ethnographic experience *by literary means* rather than confront the implications of such particularity. Against this we have to chart the gains of the style, not least the success of classic ethnographies in establishing the potential intelligibility of what had hitherto been dismissed as 'savage', 'primitive', or 'superstitious'.

Free indirect speech – the replacement of 'An old man told me at a sacrifice, "This is a kind of bargain with God"' with 'Man makes a kind of bargain with God' – is but one feature of 'ethnographic naturalism'. The devices of ethnographic naturalism do not serve as one more-or-less adequate way amongst others to represent a chosen object. Rather they serve to constitute a particular sort of object – *homo ethnographicus* – and, in the process, other possible understandings of the ethnographer's material are eliminated. Take for example the way in which this object of discourse is homogenized: 'The Nuer is a product of hard and egalitarian upbringing, is deeply democratic, and is easily roused to violence' (Evans-Pritchard, 1940: 181). We know that some of our neighbours and colleagues are more democratic than others, we know that different kinds of English people are more easily roused to violence than others (men for example); but the Nuer, as represented by Evans-Pritchard, do not appear to vary in this way. 'In the normal course of things, the Balinese are shy to the point of obsessiveness of open conflict' (Geertz, 1973: 446) – except, one presumes, those that are not, or moments when the course of things is palpably abnormal (1965 for example).[7] It may well be the case that Balinese society and Nuer society are culturally homogeneous in a way that Britain and the United States are not; but given that consensus has been taken to be a defining feature of primitive society, at least since Durkheim's mechanical solidarity, while difference is read as the sign of the modern, it seems probable that this feature is as much a product of our stylistic repertoire as it is of any particular observation. Certainly, my own field experience in Sri Lanka was of a cultural setting characterized by argument, scepticism and dispute about all sorts of aspects of everyday culture; yet it is none the less quite possible to read recent ethnographic accounts of a curious homogeneous thing called 'Sinhalese culture'.

Most spectacularly of all, a few writers have performed the same levelling process in the West, for example David Schneider, whose account of American kinship and American culture (1968) eliminates differences of class and ethnicity and presents instead a disturbingly seamless description of key American symbols and their interpretations. It is at this point, in my experience, that students start to give voice to their worries about what it is that they are supposed to be reading about. Ethnographic naturalism, while working with ostensibly unproblematic literary devices, in fact constructs a kind of object – a world robbed of its idiosyncrasies and foibles which is foreign to the experience of its readers; and while the readers can accept such foreignness if the object is said to be from a distant time or place, the use of similar devices in describing a known area of experience provokes considerable resistance. Defenders of Schneider (e.g. Marcus and Fischer, 1986: 149–51) might argue that his true purpose is defamiliarization – the

rendering strange, and thus new, of the commonplace and unquestioned – and there is an element of truth in this. But the most telling lesson of Schneider's work concerns ethnography rather than America – it is anthropological writing that it puts in question as much as American kinship.[8]

Another aspect of ethnographic naturalism is the absence of any tangible point of view. The narrator is invisible and omniscient – an effect much enhanced by the use of free indirect speech. The reason most often put forward for the habit of ethnographic effacement – the removal of the ethnographer from the scene of writing – is that without it ethnography will descend into subjectivity and autobiography. This is indeed a danger, but the alternative, the denial of ethnographic presence and the specificity of ethnographic experience, is equally dangerous: it substitutes an unchallengeable subjectivity for a challengeable subjectivity.

ETHNOGRAPHY AFTER *WRITING CULTURE*

At this point in my 1989 paper, I discussed three American ethnographies of the late 1970s and early 1980s – Paul Rabinow's *Reflections on Fieldwork in Morocco* (1977), Vincent Crapanzano's *Tuhami* (1980) and Kevin Dwyer's *Moroccan Dialogues* (1982) – under the heading 'experimental ethnographies'. A decade later, those three books seem a little less startling (and a great deal less interesting) than they did in the mid-1980s. I also expressed the fear that *Writing Culture* 'will provoke a trend away from doing anthropology, and towards ever more barren criticism and meta-criticism' (1989: 161). A decade later, this looks like one of the least accurate predictions of its times. The market for essays on the minutiae of ethnographic style seems mercifully to have dried up, while the range and quality of ethnographic writing has expanded exponentially. It would be impossible now to compose a short but comprehensive account of 'ethnography after *Writing Culture*', but two important points stand out.

The first is the speed with which the 1980s critique of ethnographic writing has been routinized within mainstream anthropology. When the occasional, old-style, experience-distant ethnography appears from an academic press, even the least trendy of reviewers may now be expected to criticize its lack of reflexivity. The strong objections to any use of the first person, any concern with the position of the fieldworker, any dwelling on the issue of style, have, as it were, melted away, with little trace that, only a few years ago, it was possible to write as if the corrosive effects of postmodern introspection might signify the end of anthropology as we know it.[9] Yet, just as recent generations of anthropologists were trained to find the writings of a once-worshipped figure like James Frazer 'unreadable' (Strathern, 1987), so new generations now seem to find the canonical work of Malinowski and Evans-Pritchard just as hard to read, while the stereotype of the 'colonial ethnographer' has become as familiar a figure as the caricature 'armchair anthropologists' invoked by Malinowski and his successors.

More strikingly, a formularized version of postmodern ethnography, alternating between stock passages of ethnographic self-consciousness and (carefully edited and positioned) 'voices', is in danger of becoming the disciplinary norm, while students have to be constantly warned that sometimes the people they are talking to are more interesting than the people asking the questions.[10] At the same time, genuinely radical experiments with the mode of ethnographic representation remain as rare as ever – despite the apparent possibilities opened up by new and ever cheaper multi-media technologies. All this may just confirm my earlier judgement that *Writing Culture* acted as a kind of catalyst for different criticisms and currents which had been independently building up for years. What was less expected, though, was the way in which some of the concerns of the 1980s have been translated into practical research issues. In 1989 (in an allusion to the fact-obsessed pedagogue of Dickens' *Hard Times*), I expressed scepticism that the policy-driven Gradgrinds who controlled social science research funding in Britain would be much impressed by ethnographic agonizing about self-and-other. Yet, to take an unexpected example, in the field of social development at least, increased concern with issues of 'participation' and 'empowerment' has led to the growth of Participatory Rural Appraisal (PRA) methodologies – methodologies which, at their best, force researchers to think about ways in which the powerless and the excluded can be encouraged to articulate their concerns about policies that directly affect them, but which, at their crudest, might be seen as instant polyphony kits, allowing even the least engaged researcher the opportunity to obtain authentic 'voices' to paste into their otherwise pre-fabricated reports. In this respect, two of the many strands that coalesced in the moment of *Writing Culture* – the reaction against positivism and the populist valorization of the voices of 'ordinary people' – can be seen to resonate with political trends in a wider, non-academic world.

The second, striking feature of the ethnographic universe after *Writing Culture* also owes much to changes in the world outside the university. This is the collapse of confidence in what might have been thought of as the central object of anthropological or ethnographic enquiry: the idea of culture itself. In a remarkably short period of time it has simply become impossible for ethnographers to write as if their subjects lived in sealed, often timeless, bubbles called 'cultures'. Intellectually this may be because the awareness of global movement and communication has rendered the view of cultures as discrete and internally coherent, simply incredible (Gupta and Ferguson, 1997). It also owes much to the achievement of feminist scholars who have revealed the differences and contestation within apparently unitary cultural settings.[11] Finally, it has become politically distasteful for ethnographers to share a model of human difference with extreme nationalists and proponents of ethnic cleansing. By 1988, it was possible for Clifford to talk of culture as 'a fundamentally compromised concept I cannot yet do without' (1988: 10); a few years later, Lila Abu-Lughod (1991) could talk of the need to write '*against* culture'. Within the space of little more than a decade, the notion that we all live in discrete, distinctive 'cultures', and that ethnography's task is the 'interpretation' or 'translation' of culture in this plural sense, has ceased to carry conviction in anthropology.

Although this critique of the notion of culture is less novel than is sometimes claimed – Edmund Leach's (1954) classic *Political Systems of Highland Burma* anticipates much of the empirical case, as does Eric Wolf's *Europe and the People without History* (1982) – its success exemplifies some of the broader concerns that have impinged on the issue of ethnographic writing. At its heart is a strong reflexivity which recognizes that the ethnographer and his or her language are inevitably a part of the phenomenon that is being investigated – we cannot seal off ethnographic representations of culture from, for example, nationalists' use of the same representations and ideas (Handler, 1988; Spencer, 1990).[12] Linked to this reflexivity is a sense of responsibility for the consequences of a particular way of representing the words and practices of other people; in this case a responsibility to recognize complexity and difference, rather than hide them beneath a veil of homogeneity and generalization. Finally, there is the recognition that this sense of responsibility can be a source of liberation, rather than simply an unwelcome burden: it is now possible to write extraordinarily rich, and even sometimes extraordinarily readable, ethnographies which are quite open about their limitations and partiality, and which manage to acknowledge the complexity of the world, and thus the difficulty of rendering it through words on a page, without sacrificing coherence or clarity.

Ackowledgements

Parts of this chapter draw on material first published in *Man*. I am grateful to the Director and General Council of the Royal Anthropological Institute for permission to reproduce this material. The earlier version of the argument in this chapter owed an enormous amount to the influence of Mark Whitaker. Ralph Grillo and Ruth Finnegan encouraged it on its way to first publication. Moira Young provided technical assistance in its revision.

NOTES

1 The furore over Freeman's (1984) attack on Mead was, I suspect, far more traumatic to American anthropology than it was in Britain; the search for alternatives to Mead's 'scientistic' ethnographic epistemology, of which *Writing Culture* is obviously one, can be partly traced to this trauma.

2 The example is in fact based on Scott's (1985) brilliant account of class in everyday peasant life in a Malay village, a text which modestly embodies much that I am recommending. It is all the more ironic that it is the ethnographic contribution of a political scientist rather than an anthropologist.

3 It is interesting to note that Geertz's non-ethnographic writings show a growing irritation with the usual trappings of scholarly attribution, preferring instead the knowing allusion and the buried half-quote, while in *Negara* (1980) and *Islam Observed* (1968), footnotes are replaced by a parallel scholarly commentary, citing references and quibbles of detail, printed at the back of the volume and loosely tagged to the pages of the main text.

4 Public questioning of the empirical content of ethnography is extremely rare, and, tellingly, almost always confined to cases where an ostensibly anthropological text has won a wider public audience – *Coming of Age in Samoa, The Mountain People, The Teachings of Don Juan, Shabono*. Such questioning seems as much a product of the patrolling of disciplinary boundaries as of anything more high-minded. For a consideration of some of the consequences of ethnographic subjects' critiques of ethnographic writing, see the collection edited by Brettell (1993).

5 This is the main thrust of Marilyn Strathern's incisive response to Freeman's (1984) critique of Mead (Strathern, 1983).

6 Marcus and Cushman describe a similar style which they call 'ethnographic realism'; I have problems with their claim that this has been dominant for 'approximately the past 60 years' (1982: 25), i.e. since the publication of Malinowski's *Argonauts*. This is to gloss over the considerable stylistic differences between Malinowski, Mead, Firth, Evans-Pritchard, Fortune and Benedict, let alone the differences between them and recent figures such as Geertz or the ethnoscientists of the 1960s. My choice of the term 'naturalism' allows me to draw on Williams and Brecht and, thus, to remind readers that issues of representation and realism have a longer theoretical genealogy within literary studies.

7 In fairness it should be pointed out that Geertz himself alerts the reader to the danger of this practice in the earlier 'Person, time and conduct in Bali' ([1966] 1973: 368, n. 7), without in any way modifying the main text to take account of possible exceptions and qualifications. By the time of 'Deep Play', seven years later, he seems to have felt no such qualifications necessary (cf. n. 3 above).

8 Nevertheless, the critical spirit of Schneider's work has inspired some extraordinarily creative critical responses (e.g., Strathern, 1992; Yanagisako and Delaney, 1994).

9 This view was most strikingly expressed in Gellner's (1988) suggestion that copies of Geertz's *Works and Lives* (1988) should be kept in a locked cupboard for fear of permanently corrupting the minds of young graduate students. It has never been clear to me just how far Gellner's tongue had inserted itself in his cheek when he made the suggestion.

10 As the apocryphal informant is said to have told the apocryphal postmodern ethnographer 'Okay, enough about you, now let's talk about me' – a joke Newton (1993: 3) attributes to Marshall Sahlins by way of David Schneider.

11 Anyone interested in pursuing these points further should start with Micaela di Leonardo's (1998) bracing survey of recent American anthropology.

12 What I have called a 'strong reflexivity' draws on the theoretical contributions of Bourdieu (Bourdieu et al., 1999; Bourdieu and Wacquant, 1992), Fabian (1983) and Scholte (1969), and can be contrasted with the less sociological, and more personal, 'self-reflexivity' found in some post-*Writing Culture* ethnography.

REFERENCES

Abu-Lughod, L. (1991) 'Writing against culture', in R. Fox (ed.), *Recapturing Anthropology: Working in the Present*. Santa Fé, NM: School of American Research.

Atkinson, P. (1991) *The Ethnographic Imagination: Textual Constructions of Reality*. London: Routledge.

Bateson, G. ([1936] 1958) *Naven. A Study of the Problems Suggested by a Composite Picture of a Culture of a New Guinea Tribe Drawn From Three Points of View*. Stanford, CA: Stanford University Press.

Berlin, B. and P. Kay (1969) *Basic Color Terms*. Berkeley, CA: University of California Press.

Bourdieu, P. (1999) *The Weight of the World: Social Suffering in Contemporary Society*. Cambridge: Polity.

Bourdieu, P. and Wacquant, L. (1992) *Invitation to Reflexive Sociology*. Cambridge: Polity Press.

Bowen, E.S. [Laura Bohannan] (1954) *Return to Laughter*. New York: Harper and Row.

Bretell, C. (ed.) (1993) *When They Read What We Write: The Politics of Ethnography*. Westport, CT: Bergin and Garvey.

Clifford, J. (1983) 'On ethnographic authority', *Representations*, 1: 118–46.

Clifford, J. (1986) 'Introduction: partial truths'. In J. Clifford and G. Marcus (eds) *Writing Culture: The Politics and Poetics of Ethnography*. Berkeley, Los Angeles: University of California Press.

Clifford, J. (1988) *The Predicament of Culture*. Cambridge, MA: Harvard University Press.

Clifford, J. and Marcus, G.E. (eds) (1986) *Writing Culture: The Politics and Poetics of Ethnography*. Berkeley, CA: University of California Press.

Crapanzano, V. (1980) *Tuhami: Portrait of a Moroccan*. Chicago: University of Chicago Press.

Crapanzano, V. (1986) 'Hermes' dilemma: the masking of subversion in ethnographic description', in J. Clifford and G. Marcus (eds), *Writing Culture: The Politics and Poetics of Ethnography*. Berkeley, CA: University of California Press.

Dumont, J.-P. (1978) *The Headman and I*. Austin, TX: University of Texas Press.

Dwyer, K. (1982) *Moroccan Dialogues*. Baltimore, MD: Johns Hopkins University Press.

Evans-Pritchard, E.E. (1940) *The Nuer: A Description of the Modes of Livelihood and Political Institutions of a Nilotic People*. Oxford: Oxford University Press.

Evans-Pritchard, E.E. (1956) *Nuer Religion*. Oxford: Oxford University Press.

Evans-Pritchard, E.E. (1965) *Theories of Primitive Religion*. Oxford: The Clarendon Press.

Fabian, J. (1983) *Time and the Other: How Anthropology Makes Its Object*. New York: Columbia University Press.

Freeman, D. (1984) *Margaret Mead and Samoa: The Making and Unmaking of an Anthropological Myth*. Harmondsworth: Penguin.

Geertz, C. (1968) *Islam Observed*. Chicago: University of Chicago Press.

Geertz, C. ([1966] 1973) *The Interpretation of Cultures*. New York: Basic Books.

Geertz, C. (1980) *Negara: The Theatre State in Nineteenth-Century Bali*. Princeton, NJ: Princeton University Press.

Geertz, C. (1988) *Works and Lives: The Anthropologist as Author*. Palo Alto, CA: Stanford University Press.

Gellner, E. (1988) 'Review of Geertz *Works and Lives'*, *Times Higher Education Supplement*, No. 807, 22 April, p. 26.

Gupta, A. and Ferguson, J. (eds) (1997) *Culture, Power, Place: Explorations in Critical Anthropology*. Durham, NC: Duke University Press.

Handler, R. (1988) *Nationalism and the Politics of Culture in Québec*. Madison, WI: University of Wisconsin Press.

Leach, E.R. (1954) *Political Systems of Highland Burma*. London: Athlone.

Leach, E.R. (1961) *Rethinking Anthropology*. London: Athlone Press.

Leonardo, M. di (1998) *Exotics at Home: Anthropologies, Others, American Modernity*. Chicago: University of Chicago Press.

Lévi-Strauss, C. (1969) *Elementary Structures of Kinship*. London: Tavistock.

Malinowski, B. (1922) *Argonauts of the Western Pacific*. London: Routledge and Kegan Paul.

Marcus, G.E. and Cushman, R. (1982) 'Ethnographies as text', *Annual Review of Anthropology*, 11: 25–69.

Marcus G.E. and Fischer, M. (1986) *Anthropology as Cultural Critique*. Chicago: University of Chicago Press.

Mascia-Lees, F., Frances E. Mascia-Lees, Patricia Sharpe and Colleen Ballerino Cohen (1989) 'The postmodernist turn in anthropology: cautions from a feminist perspective', *Signs: Journal of Women in Culture and Society*, 15 (1): 7–33.

Mead, M. (1928) *Coming of Age in Samoa*. New York: Morrow.

Needham, R. (1962) *Structure and Sentiment*. Chicago: University of Chicago Press.

Newton, E. (1993) 'My best informant's dress: the erotic equation in fieldwork', *Cultural Anthropology*, 8 (1): 3–23.

Rabinow, P. (1977) *Reflections on Fieldwork in Morocco*. Berkeley, CA: University of California Press.

Ricoeur, P. (1971) 'The model of the text: meaningful action considered as a text', *Social Research*, 38: 529–62.

Roth, P. (1989) 'Ethnography without tears', *Current Anthropology*, 30 (5): 555–69.

Said, E. (1978) *Orientalism*. Harmondsworth: Penguin.

Sangren, S. (1988) 'Rhetoric and the authority of ethnography: "postmodernism" and the social reproduction of texts', *Current Anthropology*, 29 (3): 405–35.

Schneider, D.M. (1968) *American Kinship: A Cultural Account*. Englewood Cliffs, NJ: Prentice–Hall.

Scholte, B. (1969) 'Toward a reflexive and critical anthropology', in D. Hymes (ed.), *Reinventing Anthropology*. New York: Pantheon.

Scott, J.C. (1985) *Weapons of the Weak: Everyday Forms of Peasant Resistance*. New Haven, CT: Yale University Press.

Spencer, J. (1989) 'Anthropology as a kind of writing', *Man*, 24 (1): 145–64.

Spencer, J. (1990) 'Writing within: anthropology, nationalism and culture in Sri Lanka', *Current Anthropology*, 31: 283–300.

Sperber, D. (1985) *On Anthropological Knowledge*. Cambridge: Cambridge University Press.

Strathern, M. (1983) 'The punishment of Margaret Mead', *Canberra Anthropology*, 6: 70–9.

Strathern, M. (1987) 'Out of context: the persuasive fictions of anthropology', *Current Anthropology*, 28 (1): 251–81.

Strathern, M. (1992) *After Nature: English Kinship in the Late Twentieth Century*. Cambridge: Cambridge University Press.

Williams, R. (1971) *Drama from Ibsen to Brecht*. London: Chatto and Windus.

Wolf, E. (1982) *Europe and the People without History*. Berkeley, CA: University of California Press.

Yanagisako, S. and Delaney, C. (eds) (1994) *Naturalizing Power: Essays in Feminist Cultural Analysis*. New York: Routledge.

31

Computer Applications in Qualitative Research

NIGEL FIELDING

Ethnography seems unlikely terrain in which to encounter sophisticated information technology. Ethnography's methodological orientation has largely been that of a craft rather than a technique. That it works mainly with text rather than number presents a challenge to computer scientists. It is unsurprising that it was not until the 1980s that experiments with software to support ethnographic research emerged. The rapid uptake and increasing sophistication of the software owes more to the increasing use of qualitative methods than to the enthusiasm of the established community of ethnographers. It is worth noting, then, that quite apart from this chapter's principal topic – computer-assisted qualitative data *analysis* (or CAQDAS) – the computer has become an increasingly familiar part of the ethnographic scene. As Weitzman and Miles (1995) suggest, computers are commonly involved in several stages of ethnographic research, including transcribing, editing and storing fieldnotes, writing reflective commentaries, displaying data and preparing publications.

However, it is one thing to admit of the computer as a useful tool for preparing, storing and displaying text, quite another to concede it a major place in the analytic process. Ethnography has never been entirely explicit about the analytic process. A research funding agency convened a seminar in the 1980s on the advancement of qualitative methods. It was told, in an adamant declaration, that 'the *only* way to learn to *write* ethnography is to *read* the ethnographies'. The speaker had done so for a dozen years before venturing to write a scrap of his own. To those steeped in that tradition the fear was that the computer would somehow 'take over', that text would simply be fed in and an ethnographic analysis (based on hidden assumptions, standardized,

sterile) would 'emerge'. Risible as this was to those who knew what the early software could do, and were preoccupied with the severity of its limits, early discussions emphasized that CAQDAS posed no real threat to the ethnographer's autonomy. Things have moved on. CAQDAS has become more highly developed. Other information technologies show increasingly relevant promise. Some methodologists speak of 'transformative technologies'. Should ethnographers be excited or alarmed?

Fear of the machine is only warranted if ethnographers abdicate to the computer. The craft approach is, after all, just as open to abuse as is the computer-based approach. The approach to craft as mystery affords opportunity to conceal just how superficial analytic work has been, to mask just how little of the data has informed the analysis, and so on. Ethnography is no more perfect a practice than any other discipline. It has characteristic faults and limitations. This chapter suggests that ethnographers can use CAQDAS to help them correct some of those faults and to advance some of ethnography's traditional objectives.

We have noted that ethnography's analytic process is often hidden. CAQDAS offers features to help make it transparent, to facilitate the participation of others in its production. Qualitative research is often lauded as a method of discovery but condemned for its lack of generalizability. CAQDAS supports systematic, formal approaches to analysis which can help here. Ethnography values the voice of the research subject. CAQDAS offers means by which research subjects can participate in producing ethnography. Ethnography adopts a reflexive, recursive perspective on field data. CAQDAS offers means to honour that perspective. But you are not reading a sales pitch. CAQDAS is not the answer to everything. Particular packages have limits and quirks. CAQDAS has generic limits. There is still room for traditional ('manual') approaches to analysis. One may even conclude that CAQDAS is itself no more than a craft skill, a new tool to make an old craft more itself.

A TYPOLOGY OF QUALITATIVE SOFTWARE

'CAQDAS' is a generic term, not the name of one software package. There are more than 20 packages specializing in supporting qualitative data analysis and a number designed for other purposes which include facilities supporting qualitative data analysis. The most comprehensive review is offered by Weitzman and Miles (1995; this is also an excellent source for people starting out in this field; see also Fisher, 1997; Weaver and Atkinson, 1994). But to demonstrate what CAQDAS can and cannot do to assist ethnographic research, we must sketch in its principal characteristics. This chapter does so using examples from several packages, selected for their widespread use and/or distinctive features (there is no particular implication in the sequence in which they are discussed, and it should be noted that, with continual software development, the versions discussed may be superseded). Following Weitzman and Miles, we may identify three basic types of CAQDAS: text retrievers, code-and-retrieve packages and theory-building software (the typology is convenient but not rigid, because theory-building can be done with the help of code-and-retrieve software, which can perform some of the tasks supported by theory-building software, albeit with some extra effort).

Text Retrievers

Coding is a key step in qualitative analysis. Researchers sort data into categories by marking codes on fieldnotes, transcripts or other text so they can see which segments represent each category. Text retrievers recover data pertaining to a category using keywords. If 'social class' is one of the categories, one types in to search for 'social class' and it will list all the occurrences. If the category name is not in the data source one must insert it so it can be retrieved. Most text retrievers are generic, commercially produced packages, including 'Metamorph', 'The Text Collector', 'WordCruncher', 'ZyINDEX' and 'Sonar Professional'.

Text retrievers find all occurrences of words, phrases and combinations of these, in one or a number of files. They can also find words that sound alike, mean the same thing, or have certain patterns (such as the sequences of letters and numbers used in personal identifiers like social security numbers). They can sort retrieved text into new files, and link

annotations to the original data. Some also have content analysis capabilities: counting, creating word lists and 'concordances' (organized lists of words in their contexts; these features derive from the long tradition of quantitative content analysis, one of the earliest social science applications of computers). 'Textbase Managers' do more to organize, sort and make subsets of the text. They may structure text into 'records' (specific cases) and 'fields' (numerical or text information for each case); examples like 'askSam' and 'FolioVIEWS' also have advanced hypertext, annotation and memoing features.

Code-and-retrieve Packages

These are dedicated qualitative data analysis packages, designed by qualitative researchers to help users divide text into segments, attach codes to segments, and find and display segments with a given code or combination of codes. Most can search for character strings as well as codes. Examples include 'HyperQual', 'Kwalitan', 'QUALPRO', 'WinMAX' and 'The ETHNOGRAPH' (although refinements mean later versions of some of these packages could be re-classified, for example, WinMAX could be regarded as a code-based 'theory builder').

Code-and-retrieve software will recover data that relates to a category like 'social class' but in which the words 'social class' do not necessarily appear. Highlighting is used, or symbols are typed in by the analyst, to indicate the beginning and end of the segment relating to 'social class'. All the data pertaining to that code can then be recovered: a 'single sort'. This strategy is important to the 'constant comparative method' of grounded theory (Glaser and Strauss, 1967) which requires that as each new 'incident' is coded, it should be compared 'with the previous incident in the same and different groups coded in the same category'. Most packages will also retrieve data where codes coincide, for example, all instances where data are coded as relating both to 'gender' and 'social class': a 'multiple sort'. Such features are an important step towards conceptualization, hence we should not overemphasize the distinction between 'code-and-retrieve' and 'theory-building' software.

Analytic memos are important in qualitative analysis, especially grounded theory. Glaser and Strauss observed that the process of coding inevitably stimulated exploring the theoretical properties of particular categories. Because delineating categories and their properties reflected emerging conceptual awareness, they made a second rule of constant comparison. Coding should be interrupted in order to record a memo on the present state of theoretical understanding associated with the category. Because sorting memos provides a spur to conceptualization, memos should have a form that facilitates sorting and cross-referencing. Code-and-retrieve packages often support memo-writing, but may not always link memos directly to the text or code(s) they are about. They may also provide hypertext, facilitating navigation of the database. This is particularly relevant to the coding step called 'open coding', which aims to stimulate conceptualization, generate initial formulations as a 'springboard' to more expansive thinking about theoretical implications and guide further fieldwork (Strauss, 1987: 63). Ease and speed of movement around the database are important here. Code-and-retrieve software also addresses a third stipulation of grounded theory, that the analytic importance of any category should always be demonstrated rather than assumed (Strauss, 1987: 32). Software enables the steps of the coding, data saturation and theorizing process to be recovered, documented and displayed.

Because these packages were developed by qualitative researchers rather than software houses their non-commercial origin may be reflected in problems of supply, documentation and support, but these problems are becoming less marked.

Theory-building Software

The software so far examined focuses on analyses of relationships between categories and data. Theory-building software focuses on relationships between the categories themselves. Such packages usually have the same capabilities as code-and-retrieve packages but add features supporting theory-building, including extensive use of hypertext to link parts of a dataset. They help users make connections between codes, develop more abstract, formal classifications and categories, or test propositions that imply a conceptual structure which fits the data. Examples include AQUAD, Ethno, QCA, Atlas/ti for Windows, HyperRESEARCH and NUD*IST version 4.

Some packages enable users to construct semantic networks by displaying code names as 'nodes' (the name for a single point when data are symbolically represented on-screen) in a graphic display and linking them to other nodes by specified relationships. Nodes may be a snatch of text, a code or memo name. Among the things to look for are whether the links are of a single, unspecified type, of multiple types (like 'leads to', 'is a kind of') or can be specified by users. Some theory-builders (notably HyperRESEARCH) let users develop and test 'if → then' propositions or hypotheses while others (like QCA) support 'configurational' analysis across cases, looking for case-specific patterns of predictors associated with an outcome.

Thus the different types of CAQDAS have some common features and characteristics, but also address a variety of analytic traditions. The more specialist the software the more its flexibility is an issue, a factor to bear in mind when choosing software.

SOFTWARE IN THE ANALYTIC PROCESS

Data Management

Qualitative software developers have always aimed to support systematic analytic procedures as well as provide the more straightforward advantages computers offer for data management. But research on software use suggests a tension between these aims (Lee and Fielding, 1996). For many users, the strongest benefit has been the computer's function as a supremely effective electronic filing cabinet. Confronted with the range of CAQDAS software prospective users naturally ask 'what is the best package?'. This is, however, like asking 'what is the best car?'. It depends on one's purposes, competences and requirements. Several user issues should inform choice.

Some packages permit direct *data entry*, others require data to be imported from a word processor. Sometimes users can format data however they like (helpful if data have been typed before choosing a package or a scanner is being used), sometimes there are strict formatting rules, like limiting lines to 59 characters. Among *storage* issues is whether all the information about a particular 'case' (say, a fieldwork site) can be kept in the same place, and the control users have over sorting cases in various orders or groupings.

Virtually all packages now have on-screen *coding*. Researchers attach codes in several ways: one or several to a chunk, or on nested or overlapping chunks. Programs may not support all of these. Many support hierarchical or multi-level coding (for example, 'cat' might have a higher level code of 'mammal'). Look for how easy it is to reorganize codes (for example, by inserting new levels in the hierarchy), rename codes, replace one or several with another, or revise specific applications of codes to segments. Many attach 'source tags' to show where retrieved segments came from. Some will show the complete coding scheme in a list or hierarchical 'tree'.

Memoing/annotation features reflect grounded theory's emphasis on making explicit one's reasoning in assigning a code to a given segment, especially important in team research. Some programs let users write marginal annotations and/or memos. They vary in whether they actually link the memos to the things they are about; ideally one wants to be able to access that memo every time one inspects the segment and the package should tell users it is there. Some packages let users code memos.

When *search and retrieval* finds a segment that matches a search request (a 'hit') it may display the whole source document with the hit highlighted, the hit on its own with no context, or with context. If it cannot display the complete context one may instead be able to jump to where the hit originated.

Programs vary in giving information about the origin of the hit and making a record of searches and retrievals. A search may sometimes be repeated simply by selecting it from the record. Some packages offer statistical facilities.

Many changes to CAQDAS represent developers' responses to users' requests. Innovations include facilities to move CAQDAS projects around via the Internet and lodge projects on web sites for team research or presenting drafts, the inclusion of graphic analytic facilities, more automated coding, full suites of Boolean operators, better-designed interfaces and 'drag and drop' functionality. But this does not exhaust the information technology (IT) developments relevant to ethnographers. 'Direct transcription software' records speech on a CD-ROM and enables the application of codes not to text but to the sound segments themselves. Thus, when a search on a given code results in a 'hit' the researcher can listen to the data rather than read it as text. There is also increasing interest in collecting data over the Internet. Data capture from the Internet, along with electronic archiving, may stimulate secondary analysis in ethnography. Our gaze need not only be directed at CAQDAS in respect of IT developments that may affect ethnography.

ANALYTIC STRATEGIES

There is no one 'analytic process' but a profusion. Similarly, packages vary in the analytic approaches they support (Tesch, 1990). The relatively well documented assumptions of grounded theory are reflected in the design of several packages. Other analytic traditions are less well-served. Several approaches will be considered here, but the coverage is not exhaustive and should not be seen as prescriptive or as an obstacle to creative use.

Code-based Analytic Strategies

Grounded theory represents a systematic, code-based analytic strategy. The ETHNOGRAPH is among the packages explicitly oriented to grounded theory. It is versatile in displaying retrieved segments in context. It can display both overlapping and nested segments. The example in Figure 31.1 shows a fully coded page. Information about the interview appears at the top. On the left margin are code terms applicable to particular segments. In some cases several codes apply and they stretch across the page. In the right margin are symbols showing the extent of the data covered by a given code. Note that a given code does not always have the same symbol, but the program reminds users what symbol refers to what code by the display in the left margin. One way to sort the data is to look

at segments where two particular codes apply. Figure 31.2 shows data segments where the codes PAIN and HISTORY have both been assigned. Note that the symbol for HISTORY runs all the way down the right margin.

While the term 'coding' is controversial (Dey, 1993: 58), the activity is widespread. At one extreme the 'code' may be no more than a convenient place to dump data which is commensurate in only one of its properties. The application of the code is weak and temporary. At the other extreme the code may take its place in a formal hierarchy, with data rigidly assigned to it and a formal relation to other code-terms dictated by theory.

The role of coding is to stimulate the identification of analytic themes, organize the data so that the strength of its support for those themes can be determined, illustrate themes by providing quotable material, and support data reduction by representing its key features and identifying redundant, peripheral or irrelevant data. The coding process can be sub-divided. There is the business of familiarization, where data are inspected, often repeatedly, to generate an initial focus. Software should permit rapid navigation of the database, be able to control the amount of data on-screen and be able to hold multiple sources of data (including sound and vision). Familiarization will often result in a first, tentative set of codes. Procedures for assigning codes to data segments should be straightforward. Software varies in how much it can automate this process (for instance, by allowing a code term to be revised in such a way that all – or only selected – segments are assigned the new coding term in one operation). A frequently encountered problem is knowing how many codes are 'enough' (Fielding and Lee, 1998). Software can help by calculating the proportion of data to which codes have been assigned.

Defining codes is demanding work. The principal software aid is memoing features which specify the definition and appear whenever code lists or segments are displayed. Software permitting memos to be assigned to any entity (for example, not only to data, but lists of code definitions, nodes in a conceptual diagram, or other memos) is advantageous, as is software that displays memos whenever segments to which they apply are retrieved (the less useful alternative is where the program indicates that a memo applies to the segment but the user has to perform a separate operation to retrieve it). There is a particular use for memos where several researchers are working with the database and must share how they have assigned codes.

There are several 'coding pathologies' (Fielding and Lee, 1998). Among these are knowing when to stop (although grounded theory includes a step involving 'saturating' the categories with data, there is no explicit criterion for knowing when a category is indeed saturated), the proliferation of

```
        +PROGRESS STAFFING OF EARL MICHAELS                    1

# – PATIENT  $ – PAT REVIEW
        MD:    Okay. Earl Michaels. Okay, oh,              3   –  #  –  $
               you staffed him last week. Okay –          4   –  #     |
                                                          5               |

# – PROBLEM
               Okay, he's got some musculoskeletal        6   –  #     |
               problems. What are you doing in            7   –  #     |
               physical therapy?                          8            –  $
                                                          9

! TREATMENT
        PT–1:  Relaxation, muscle stretching –           10
                                                         11

# – MOTIVE          # – EVAL          # – PAIN    # – EVIDENCE    # – PROGRESS
        PT–3:  He's well motivated and he's              12   –  #
               ready to get better. I think he's         13      |
               tired of the life style that he's been    14      |
               living. He's shown – (– – –) pain          15      |
               slips steadily decreasing (– –).          16   –  #
                                                         17

# – DIAGNOSIS
        MD:    Are you all clear on what the final        18   –  #
               physical diagnosis was for him. You       19      |
               know, we were questioning the spinal      20      |
               cord tumor. We were questioning           21      |
               multiple sclerosis.                        22   –  #
                                                         23

# – HISTORY
               As you reconstruct the history, when      24    –  #
               he fell – this guy fell off the back      25       |
               of his truck. The first thing that        26       |

$ – SIGNS
               happened he had – he had weakness or      27    | – $
               paralysis and numbness in both his        28    |   |
               legs. Couldn't move for almost an         29    |   |
               hour. And it began to come back. And      30    |   |

% – PAIN
               ever since that time he's had these –     31    |   |  –  %
               these weird sensations and pain –         32    |   |     |
               pain has gone from his legs.  Bladder     33    |   |  –  %
               and bowel disturbance.  Had a GU work–    34    | – $

$ – DIAGNOSIS
               up. They can't document that he has a     35    | – $
               (– – – – – –). I think he does.           36    |   |
               Impotence. And I think he contused        37    |   |
               the spinal cord is what he did.           38  – # – $
                                                         39
```

Figure 31.1 *Printed output for coded version In The ETHNOGRAPH*

(increasingly fine-grained) codes beyond what is needed to support the final analysis, concerns about rigidifying the meaning of segments and/or losing sight of their context, and the extent to which the next step in analysis – retrieval – should be taken account of during coding. These were issues long

```
SORTED OUTPUT FOR FILE CASE42
SC–BIG PICTURE:        + PAIN           + HISTORY
─────────────────────────────────────────────────────────────────

CASE42      MD        + PROGRESS STAFFING OF EARL MICHAELS

SC:     + PAIN      + HISTORY

# – HISTORY
        : As you reconstruct the history, when        24  – #
        : he fell – this guy fell off the back        25    #
        : of his truck. The first thing that          26    #

$ – SIGNS
        : happened he had – he had weakness or        27    # – $
        : paralysis and numbness in both his          28    #   |
        : legs. Couldn't move for almost an           29    #   |
        : hour. And it began to come back. And        30    #   |

% – PAIN
        : ever since that time he's had these –       31    #   |  – %
        : these weird sensations and pain –           32    #   |     |
        : pain has gone from his legs. Bladder        33    #   |  – %
        : and bowel disturbance. Had a GU work–       34    # – $

$ – DIAGNOSIS
        : up. They can't document that he has a       35    # – $
        : (– – – – – –). I think he does.             36    #   |
        : Impotence. And I think he contused          37    #   |
        : the spinal cord is what he did.             38  – # – $
```

Figure 31.2   *Sorted output – The Big picture In The ETHNOGRAPH*

before CAQDAS emerged. 'Computerizing' the process has simply made them more apparent. Statistical features can help researchers decide when inferences are well-grounded in the data, though there are of course issues of meaning which cannot be settled through counts. Code proliferation can be checked by displaying the coding scheme graphically; this helps to spot dead-ends, disparities between the development of different codes, or codes which are only thinly supported by data. The ability to return to the 'raw data', to zoom in and out of context, is valued by ethnographers, who emphasize the importance of 'closeness to data'. Software offers varying degrees of control over context; it is a matter of how much of the surrounding text one may display, and of the ease with which one can move around the database. As to looking ahead to the retrieval stage while one negotiates coding, retrieval features do not, in the main, require that coding be done in a specified way. While researchers may naturally start to ponder what analytic themes will emerge, the fact that software will be used to conduct that work need not intrude on the coding process.

Retrieval strategies include: retrievals of all data in a category, retrievals aimed at supporting numerical counts, hypothesis-testing retrievals evaluating propositional forms, retrievals by respondent characteristics, retrievals aimed at establishing formal relationships (such as the logical elements of a causal explanation), retrievals aimed at exploring substantive relationships (such as the different dimensions of a phenomenon which account for its meaning to respondents), retrievals using Boolean operators and those employing set logic. We have already distinguished between single and multiple 'sorts', where data pertaining to a single code, or to the coincidence of two or more codes, is retrieved. Much useful analytic work can be done using these procedures, but not all analytic concerns are addressed by making lists of segments which have been given the same code. There are so-called 'Boolean' requests, to do with 'and/or/not' relations. For example, if we have two codes, 'power' and 'conflict', Boolean retrieval may recover segments coded power AND conflict, power OR conflict, power NOT conflict. A more sophisticated step is to string these together to formulate precise search requests, perhaps drawing on defined characteristics of research subjects, so that a particular Boolean relation is applied to all male respondents under the age of 40, and so on. Another issue is searches for overlapping or nested chunks. Packages with that ability can find where a segment coded 'power' OVERLAPS with a segment coded 'conflict' or find a segment coded 'power' which is NESTED in a segment coded 'conflict'. Another approach is that of 'set logic', which is like Boolean logic but allows requests like 'find all segments with at least three of the following five terms'.

The face-sheet feature in 'The ETHNOGRAPH' illustrates a retrieval strategy which explores variations in the data through variables. The user creates a list of variables and a face-sheet for each data file. Let us say we are studying union militancy among factory workers, with variables like age, union participation and job title. An example of a selective search would be to retrieve all segments coded 'union participation', with the face-sheet variable for age, and examine to what extent the factory workers' age helps to explain militancy. Note that the retrieval strategy allows researchers to identify and select data relevant to their analytic interest. It does not itself resolve whether age explains militancy. While some packages (for example, WinMAX) allow users to assign numerical values for the strength with which a datum captures the meaning of the code, the onus still rests with researchers to decide whether the relationship being examined is borne out by the data.

Exploring Language and Narrative Structures

In interpretative or hermeneutic approaches analysis involves the interpretation of cultural representations treated as texts. The relationship between text as social construction and its audience-derived meanings is highlighted in discourse analysis, narrative analysis and ethnomethodology. There has been little codification of analytic procedures, and the relative underdevelopment of software to support these approaches reflects this.

Discourse analysis seeks 'insight into the forms and mechanisms of human communication' (van Dijk, 1985: 4) by examining 'the many dimensions of text, talk and their cognitive, social and cultural contexts' (1985: xiii). Code-and-retrieve and theory-building software can be used to classify discursive and rhetorical strategies by assigning codes to selected segments of data. For example, those following the 'accounts critique' of interview data (which emphasizes the variability of accounts according to audiences and purposes; see Scott and Lyman, 1968) may find CAQDAS useful to identify and select particular kinds of accounts and to set up a series of categories that match what the researcher takes to be the different accounts offered by each respondent. These might comprise different nodes in the 'tree structure' of a NUD*IST project or a sequence of conceptual maps in the 'network display' of an Atlas/ti project.

Ethnomethodology is concerned with 'how members of situations assemble reasonable understandings of the things and events of concern to them and, thereby, realize them as objects of everyday life' (Gubrium, 1988: 27). Ethnomethodology,

particularly its 'conversation analysis' branch, is not well served by software. The ethnomethodological stance presents special problems of data entry and coding. While conversation analysts' fine-grained transcripts cannot be readily managed by most software, some packages allow control of data entry formats and macros (short command files) can be written to produce the specialist transcript notation. Although ethnomethodologists regard data as topic rather than as resource, particular segments can be identified as instances of routines that recur in talk. These can certainly be coded using a term for the routine. A CAQDAS user studying talk about dreams performed a selective retrieval based on counts of frequently occurring topics in order to identify three features of talk for a conversation analysis. The steps in elaborating the category system were (i) coding by type of discourse strategy, (ii) counting frequencies of types of discourse within the interviews, (iii) selection of three from the set of types, (iv) check for deviant cases where an identified discourse form was used to another purpose than that observed in other cases, and (v) detailed conversation analysis of the three identified forms. The last step was done off-line.

Formal Analytic Strategies

Ethnographic research has largely resisted formal approaches to analysis. There is long-standing debate over generalization from ethnographic studies and the reliability and validity of ethnographic data. Some believe that ethnography's scope is not exhausted by occupying a niche as the premier 'method of discovery', a source of interesting ideas but proof of none. There is renewed interest in analytic induction, the scope for hypothesis-testing when data are held in the form of words not numbers, and the potential of ethnographic data to support mathematical modelling. Software has undoubtedly boosted these approaches. The effort to stretch the method's limits poses some intriguing methodological and epistemological conundrums (which have been much debated; see Kelle, 1995, 1997; Lee and Fielding, 1991).

These become apparent when we consider the HyperRESEARCH package and its 'hypothesis test feature'. The researcher hypothesizes relationships between the occurrence of a particular kind of statement and the occurrence of another kind of statement. When the two kinds of statements indeed coincide this forms part of another hypothetical relationship. In Figure 31.3 the bottom half of the screen shows some data. Highlighted at the top is the segment coded 'I am making high salary'. The code list is in the top half of the screen. On the right is a list of the code names. On the left are page references of data to which the codes have been assigned. The screen for building a hypothesis (see

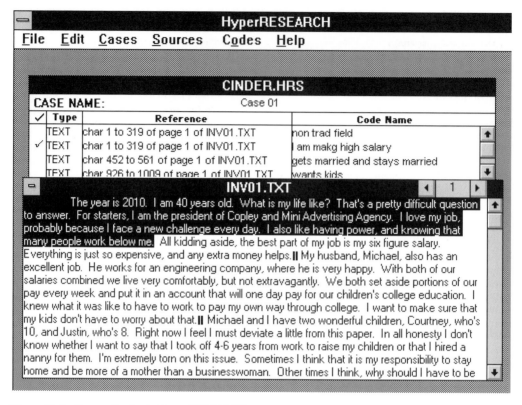

Figure 31.3   *Screen display in HyperRESEARCH*

Figure 31.4) includes a pane for composing 'if→then' propositions, and a pane relating these propositions into the rules of a hypothesis. The hypothesis is entered as a set of 'production rules' and tested against any or all cases available. The production rules have the structure: IF some set of codes is present THEN add a certain conclusion. Creating the production rules means inferring new codes not derived directly from the data.

The example concerns female students' career and family aspirations and the 'Cinderella complex', 'unreasonable' expectations in young women whereby they could combine high career aspirations with fulfilling family lives. The first production rule was: IF the code 'I am making high salary' is present AND the code 'fabulous nontraditional job' is present THEN ADD THE CODE 'high work commitment'. This procedure is itself theory-building since it moves away from codes which are in the data to new codes based on a logic of their relationship.

The second set of proposition rules was: IF 'gets married and stays married' AND 'wants kids' THEN ADD 'high family commitment'. The third set of proposition rules combines the two higher-level codes from the first two proposition rules, high work commitment and high family commitment. If they co-occur then the code 'high potential for work/family conflict' is added. This code relies

on the logic of relationship between two higher-level codes which are not directly present in the data. Finally, if this code is present plus the code 'combine work and family with no problems' OR the code indicating that the person's life is 'successful', then the 'Cinderella complex' is present. The program applies the production rules, reporting the success or failure of each of the rules and if the given hypothesis holds for each case available.

It is necessary for the researcher to assume that the data supporting these hypothetical relationships is comparable. This raises issues to do with the status of field data. It leads us, for instance, to consider what conditions are required for us to be satisfied that assertions based on the particular ways in which people express themselves can be manipulated in accord with the positivist tenets behind hypothesis-testing. The approach remains controversial (Kelle, 1995; see Part III), and its developers themselves caution against its naive application.

Another formal approach, 'event structure analysis', represents series of events as logical structures (elements and their connections) to produce explanatory models (Heise and Lewis, 1988), giving it a strong chronological orientation and preoccupation with causality. Arguing that each situation offers only limited choices, and that certain events cannot precede their prerequisites, abstract logical structures

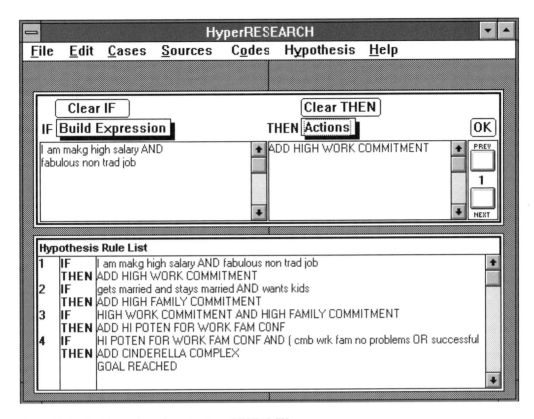

Figure 31.4 *Building a hypothesis in HyperRESEARCH*

of events are compared to actual event sequences. Most CAQDAS programs assume there is no temporal relationship between codes. This is a problem when one wants to know if one activity tends to follow another. Nor does current software allow us to ask questions like 'where did action B follow A with action C happening in between?' However, event structure analysis is supported by a package called Ethno (Heise, 1991), which helps researchers to model narratives of event sequences to produce mathematically based causal accounts. Ethno can both elicit a user-generated model and test for the completeness and implicative correctness of its logical structure. Heise's approach has affinities with Abell's theory of comparative narratives (Abell, 1985) where narrative structures are compared to see whether 'two or more structures ... are sufficiently similar to be regarded as embodying a generalization' (Abell, 1988: 187).

Our third formal approach is a compelling instance of emerging potential, in that it is in practical terms impossible without the computer. Qualitative Comparative Analysis or QCA (Ragin, 1987) uses Boolean algebra to analyse patterns of causation. Let us say that a study of worker resistance to plant closures suggests resistance was linked to certain institutional supports (Rothstein, 1986). A table is constructed which relates the presence or absence of worker resistance to four conditions: (i) early involvement of trade unions, (ii) plant location within a mono-industry region, (iii) local support for leftwing parties, (iv) availability of regional development funds. Each row represents a case. The last column of the row shows the output variable, worker resistance, or its absence.

The *configuration* of causes associated with the outcome is examined for each row. As Ragin points out (1994: 112), focusing on configurations of conditions and outcomes allows for the possibility that different combinations of conditions can generate the same outcome. Also, a particular condition may generate a positive outcome with some variables, with others a negative one. The patterns may show that a particular condition is not essential to the outcome. Proceeding by 'Boolean minimization', software such as QCA or AQUAD (Drass, 1992) systematically compares each configuration in the truth table with all the other configurations, simplifying the truth table by removing configurations through combination: 'Only one condition at a time is allowed to vary (the "experimental" condition)' (Ragin, 1994: 124). This produces a Boolean expression containing only the logically essential 'prime implicants'.

Unlike most qualitative analysis, this approach forces researchers to select cases and variables systematically, reducing the likelihood that inconvenient cases will be ignored. It is, however, subject to criticisms concerning the specification of input conditions (Amenta and Poulsen, 1994), the requirement for dichotomous input variables (necessitating considerable data reduction), problems of sample variability (Coverdill et al., 1994) and difficulties in handling process (Firestone, 1993). As Firestone suggests, 'the definitions of the situation and belief systems of those studied are at best reduced to simplified categories if not entirely ignored in favour of conceptually neat variables developed by the researcher. For highly analytic efforts at theory development, these losses may be minor. Yet they are some of the major reasons why people turn to qualitative research' (1993: 21). The case of QCA makes several points. It shows how software has enabled new approaches to qualitative data analysis. It shows that, at the leading edge, software-based qualitative analysis does indeed challenge the conventional assumptions of qualitative method. It further shows that the challenges it poses are not intrinsic to the software but instead reveal methodological and epistemological issues that have quietly brewed beneath ethnography's surface.

Hypertext and Hypermedia

'Hypertext' facilities provide electronic paths between elements of the text to be analysed, the categories or codes assigned to the text, memos about the categories and/or conceptualization and, possibly, graphical representations of the coding scheme. Once links have been defined packages may allow the links between entities to be labelled, for instance, designating the relationships between linked codes. Users may begin a session by scrolling through primary text to re-acquaint themselves with the data, then identify a new code to be assigned to a segment, check what codes have already been assigned, read a memo explaining a particular code, check the relations between this code and others in a graphical display of the conceptual scheme linking the codes and then move from a code displayed in the conceptual scheme back to the data segments to which that code has been assigned. All these moves can be achieved in moments with hypertext linking; one can move from one object to any other object, by any route. Further, hypertext can support work outwith a coding scheme by enabling one to move from one data segment to another without needing to assign a code to the segments. Hypertext can also provide data display in charts showing links and nodes and the relations between them. The charts can be linked electronically to the data.

The dynamic, associative and non-linear character of hypertext is rather close to the heuristic and iterative processes typical of qualitative research. However, Fischer points out that 'little about hypertext is automatic. Hypertexts are "authored", and the authoring process must be done by someone who is familiar with the material' (1994: 109). Cordingley (1991) suggests that the non-linear features of hypertext can disorientate users. The need to assimilate information about the linkages between material means the very speed which hypertext offers may confuse users unfamiliar with the data. Fortunately, hypertext features generally allow particular operations readily to be undone.

Research suggests users principally employ these features when refining precise meanings of particular codes, using hypertext to read applications of the code to different segments in quick succession and traversing periodically to memos about codes (Fielding and Lee, 1998). Users also apply hypertext to browse through their data. In short, users employ hypertext as a method of discovery relatively early in the analysis. Preliminary browsing produces initial ideas, the identification and recording of which forms a basis for analytic development. Hypertext provides a means to juxtapose data segments, facilitating the comparisons that prompt the designation of categories. It also provides a means of returning to previous steps along the path that the user has followed, an 'audit trail' which can be useful in articulating the conceptualization under development. Hypertext tools allow commentary to be added to data in a way that ensures that the original context is not lost. Data can easily be re-examined and interpretations modified as analysis proceeds.

While some see an affinity between grounded theory and code-and-retrieve procedures, Weaver and Atkinson (1994) argue that hypertext methods fit grounded theory well. Grounded theory combines a reluctance to collect more data than is theoretically necessary with an expansive concern to seek theoretically relevant data wherever it might be. The tools for doing this – memoing, theoretical saturation and theoretical sampling – depend on links, associations and trails which are difficult to maintain. Hypertext provides a means.

Hypertext is multidimensional. One is not confined by the printed page. Textual, graphical, audio and visual material can be juxtaposed, compared and contrasted, if need be at a variety of resolutions. Indeed, the multidimensional character of hypertext can blur traditional distinctions between 'analysis' and 'publication'. According to Weaver and Atkinson (1994: 153), hypertext challenges the ethnographic monograph itself. With hypertext there is no need to achieve the final linear document; one could even argue that producing such a text is to forego the advantages inherent in hypertext, where readers not only consume but interact with ethnography. Readers need not be bound by the ethnographer's interpretation, and can indeed use the material to form a critique of the ethnographer's interpretations. Opening a text to multiple readings increases its 'contestability'. Hypertext thus empowers the reader. Because it maintains a 'sense of complexity, intertextuality and non-linearity' the technology is compatible with approaches drawing their inspiration from postmodernism (Coffey and Atkinson, 1996).

However, there is an issue about what background one needs to produce meaningful interpretations from a hypertext resource. The use of hypertext, and beyond that, hypermedia, makes 'untutored use' possible. Further, it is the ethnographer who chooses items for expansion and reference (by creating 'buttons' in the text) and specifies links. This may subvert the very polyvocality implicit in hypertext. Faced with a resource offering all manner of subsidiary information, the naive user may feel it contains all there is to know about the topic. A resource seen by its creators as encouraging a sophisticated appreciation of the very contingency of social knowledge may instead be regarded as supremely – and ironically – authoritative.

In fact, hypertext cannot wholly circumvent working practices associated with traditional print technologies. Only some kinds of information within a hypertext, the data, for instance, transfer easily to hard copy. Trails between documents or information in 'pop-up' windows are hard to produce in printed form (Weaver and Atkinson, 1994). Cordingley (1991) also notes that users maintain reading strategies from printed forms, so even where no specific structure is implied, they tend to read diagrammatic representations of link structures from left to right and top to bottom.

Research comparing the analysis of the same data using hypertext and a relational database suggests that researchers would gain most by using both (Horney and Healey, 1991). Hypertext encouraged consideration of single pieces of information in larger chunks and multiple contexts. It facilitated browsing and 'fuzzy' connections among ideas where segments could be linked without specifically defining their relationship. Segment size was critical in the way data were interpreted. In the relational database sentence-sized segments predisposed researchers to code with a few distinct categories to characterize the topic unambiguously. The paragraph-size segments used in the hypertext package encouraged placing segments in multiple categories to examine relationships among the categories as well as among data. This resulted in differences between the categories developed in the two packages. For example, in the hypertext package statements were not coded as positive or negative since these categories were ambiguous when applied to longer segments. While subsequent development has seen a convergence which makes these distinctions less significant, this early research helped identify analytic effects of software design.

Hypertext raises intriguing possibilities. How far they are embraced by ethnographers remains to be seen. Hypertext may have less appeal in areas such as applied research, where goals are more narrowly defined than in ethnographic research. Policy-makers may feel that researchers are already too equivocal, and regard the invitation to 'make their own sense of the data' as an abdication of responsibility rather than an opportunity to celebrate the postmodern turn.

Building Theory

For followers of grounded theory, theory emerges as coding proceeds, and iteratively as the researcher moves between data and coding. Code-and-retrieve software may therefore provide all the support such researchers need. But Glaser and Strauss were clear that their approach could be used to produce formal theory, and theory claiming more general application than to the empirical phenomena at hand (1967: 110). Theory-building software focuses on relationships between the categories applied to data as well as relationships between data and category. Such relationships may subsume one category under a more general category, or subdivide one category into several more refined sub-categories. Such an approach can be represented by hierarchical networks. For instance, NUD*IST provides extensive features supporting the construction of hierarchies of code categories. Relationships between categories may not only take hierarchical form but that of a whole network of categories, containing, for example, chains or loops. For instance, Atlas/ti supports the building of non-hierarchical networks.

Some theory-building software offers graphical means to represent data and coding schemes. For instance, Atlas/ti displays code names as nodes in a graphic display and can link them to other nodes by specified relationships such as 'leads to', 'is a kind of' and so on. Its 'network view' helps researchers develop and extend conceptual networks. Theory is represented in the form of a 'semantic network', a graph made up of interconnected nodes and lines. The nodes are labelled with the categories that form the conceptual elements of one's theory. These are (usually) derived from higher-level codes that have emerged during the analysis process.

When users want to make complex retrievals the Query Tool in Atlas/ti (see Figure 31.5) will retrieve coded text passages by combining codes. Boolean, semantic or proximity searches are possible. An example of a Boolean query is 'Give me all segments coded either with any of the codes included in code family BIG FAMILY or with those in code family MAGIC STUFF but not coded with code MAGIC 3' (note that the 'code family' concept is derived from grounded theory). Double-clicking on code family BIG FAMILY produces the result list of hits in the bottom right pane. The procedure is repeated for the MAGIC STUFF code family. The XOR operator is clicked (the 'either' in the query) and the resulting hits appear, creating a

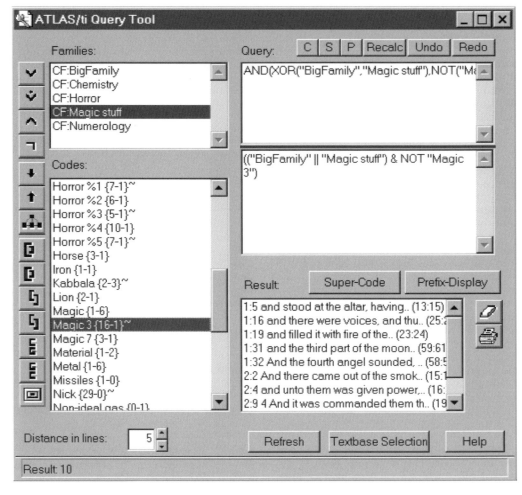

Figure 31.5   *The query tool in Atlas/ti*

single complex operand from the previous two. Double-clicking on code MAGIC 3 and then clicking the NOT operator will display all segments not coded MAGIC 3. There are now two operands in play. The result of ANDing the two operands is displayed in the results list, which gives all the text segments fulfilling the example query.

The most distinctive feature of Atlas/ti is the 'network view'. The Network Editor (Figure 31.6) is used to create, edit and refine visual displays of the conceptualization. Users can 'grab' concepts, text passages and memos, move them around the screen, draw and cut links between them. By clicking on any of the nodes they can go to the text that it represents, whether a code definition, data segment or memo. The symbols between the nodes indicate the nature of the link or relationship between those nodes. The main purposes of the network view are to enable semantic retrievals and construct models. A semantic retrieval uses the

code network, the relationships between codes which have been visualized in the network view. For instance, in Figure 31.6 the nodes for 'Number magic' and 'Magic' are linked by an ISA relationship, the meaning of which is indicated in the box in the bottom middle of the figure.

Theory-building software seeks to facilitate theoretical development by treating codes as building blocks for the production of interrelated conceptual categories. NUD*IST, for example, provides advanced Boolean retrievals and 'system closure' (Richards and Richards, 1994). The results of searches and retrievals do not simply end up on the researcher's desk, they can be incorporated into the emerging set of theoretical categories. Analytic procedures, interpretations and other results can be re-entered as input into the analytic process. For example, a memo written when analysing a primary document can be re-entered, enabling it to become part of the input data to be analysed or creating a

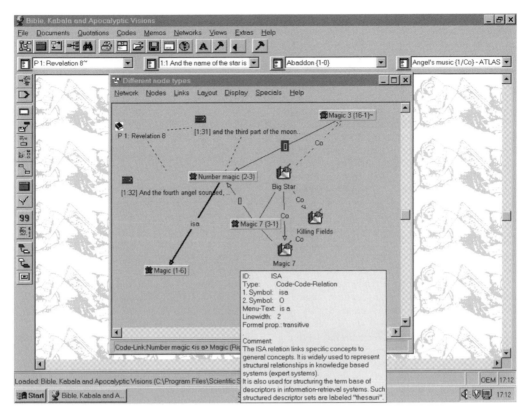

Figure 31.6 *The network editor in Atlas/ti*

'handle' for the result of a code-based retrieval operation allowing it to be re-used. In NUD*IST this is done by creating a new code (or index node) referring to the elements of the result set. However, if a record of the retrieval instructions (or 'query') which produced this result is required, the query has to be added as a comment so that the researcher can later see what was done to produce the result set. System closure is also possible with Atlas/ti, but its system closure facility ('super code') stores the original query. For instance, Supercode C may refer to the query 'A or B'. When code C is later used, the query is processed again. This has the advantage that it will correctly revise the results after the deletion or addition of new data and/or coding.

CHANGE AND STABILITY

Introducing software to the qualitative research process has inspired efforts to more closely specify in what resides the essence of qualitative research. It has exposed weak points in epistemology and methodology. Such matters arise naturally when ethnographers direct attention to what they want from software. An enduring concern is 'closeness to data'. Ethnographers worry that computer methods will discourage intimate acquaintance with the data and lead to superficial analysis (Agar, 1991; Seidel, 1991). However, manual methods do not themselves guarantee a productive closeness to data. Indeed, the volume of paper produced by ethnographic research can be a substantial discouragement to 'closeness'. Where manual methods still score over computer-based methods is in the tactile experience of handling data. For instance, there is no computer equivalent of C.W. Mills' suggestion that one periodically spill files on the floor and re-sort them to gain the stimulus of chance connections. Another obstacle is the number of lines (and hence context) which can be displayed on a computer screen. One may more readily form an impression of the structure of a text by flipping its pages than scrolling it on-screen. Some testify that they get analytic inspiration only by being able to visually scan, write and erase ideas, in Agar's case, the preferred device being a number of adjacent blackboards (Agar, 1991: 193).

It may be that the disciplines of sociology and anthropology read differently the icon called 'closeness to data'. For the sociologist it may lie in organizing and coding the data, as steps towards inferences to be systematically tested. For the anthropologist 'closeness' may mean periodically reviving one's memory of the field experience by handling artefactual material in much the same way as a scrapbook souvenir may elicit memories of some foreign place. It would be hard to argue, against those who testify that all five senses are involved, that the computer can offer such closeness. Indeed, Kelle (1997) holds the commercialization of CAQDAS accountable for a misleading impression of high sophistication. Instead the functions of present software are basic and 'very straightforward'. It remains a tool to mechanize clerical tasks of ordering and archiving text which have been routine in hermeneutics for centuries. Kelle feels that the software should not be typified as being for 'data analysis' but for 'data administration and archiving'. As he whimsically notes, the remarkable thing is that 'for many researchers the idea of software capable of "theory-building" does not sound as absurd as the idea of an index card system performing theory-building' (1997: para. 6.3).

Some of these criticisms are now succumbing to technical solutions in operating system capability and interface design. Simultaneous display on-screen of codes and data is now widely offered, as is the ability to annotate screen displays (giving 'pencil-level richness'; Weitzman and Miles, 1995). Already beckoning is a significant move toward computer-supported 'closeness', using digital video instead of analogue audio tape to record data. One might argue that analytically productive 'closeness' is best achieved by a tightly iterative process which involves cycling between reading, comparing, segmenting, coding and commenting on text, and that this is far easier using a computer than paper. What of our sensually engaged anthropologist? The trite answer is that multimedia technology may yet offer competing richness of experience. But as Pfaffenberger (1988) asserts, the ultimate answer to concerns that the computer will deny inspirational closeness or prefigure analysis in hidden ways lies in maintaining a detached and critical awareness towards the analytic process.

References

Abell, P. (1985) 'Analysing qualitative sequences: the algebra of narrative', in M. Procter and P. Abell (eds), *Sequence Analysis*. Aldershot: Gower.

Abell, P. (1988) 'The "structuration" of action: inference and comparative narratives', in N. Fielding (ed.), *Actions and Structure: Research Methods and Social Theory*. London: Sage.

Agar, M. (1991) 'The right brain strikes back', in N. Fielding and R. Lee (eds), *Using Computers in Qualitative Research*. London: Sage.

Amenta, E. and Poulsen, J. (1994) 'Where to begin; a survey of five approaches to selecting independent variables for Qualitative Comparative Analysis', *Sociological Methods and Research*, 23: 22–53.

Coffey, A. and Atkinson, P. (1996) *Making Sense of Qualitative Data: Complementary Research Strategies*. Thousand Oaks, CA: Sage.

Cordingley, E. (1991) 'The upside and downside of hypertext tools: the KANT example', in N. Fielding and R. Lee (eds), *Using Computers in Qualitative Research*. London: Sage.

Coverdill, J., Finlay, W. and Martin, J. (1994) 'Labor management in the Southern textile industry: comparing qualitative, quantitative and qualitative comparative anlaysis', *Sociological Methods and Research*, 23: 54–85.

Dey, I. (1993) *Qualitative Data Analysis: A User-Friendly Guide for Social Scientists*. London: Routledge.

Drass, K. (1992) *QCA3: Qualitative Comparative Analysis*. Evanston, IL: Center for Urban Affairs and Policy Research.

Fielding, N. and Lee, R. (eds) (1991) *Using Computers in Qualitative Research*. London: Sage.

Fielding, N. and Lee, R. (1998) *Computer Assisted Qualitative Research*. London: Sage.

Firestone, W. (1993) 'Alternative arguments for generalizing from data as applied to qualitative research', *Educational Researcher*, 22: 16–23.

Fischer, M. (1994) *Applications in Computing for Social Anthropologists*. London: Routledge.

Fisher, M. (1997) *Qualitative Computing: Using Software for Qualitative Data Analysis*. Avebury: Aldershot.

Glaser, B. and Strauss, A. (1967) *The Discovery of Grounded Theory*. Chicago: Aldine.

Gubrium, J. (1988) *Analyzing Field Reality*. Beverly Hills, CA: Sage.

Heise, D. (1991) 'Event structure analysis: a qualitative model of quantitative research', in N. Fielding and R. Lee (eds), *Using Computers in Qualitative Research*. London: Sage.

Heise, D. and Lewis, E. (1988) *Introduction to ETHNO*. Raleigh, NC: National Collegiate Software Clearinghouse.

Horney, M. and Healey, D. (1991) 'Hypertext and database tools for qualitative research'. Paper presented at the annual meeting of the American Educational Research Association, Chicago, Illinois, April.

Kelle, U. (1995) *Computer-aided Qualitative Data Analysis*. London: Sage.

Kelle, U. (1997) 'Theory building in qualitative research and computer programs for the management of textual data', *Sociological Research Online*, 2: <http://www.socresonline.org.uk/socresonline/2/2/1.html>

Lee, R. and Fielding, N. (1991) 'Computing for qualitative research: options, problems and potential', in N. Fielding and R. Lee (eds), *Using Computers in Qualitative Research*. London: Sage.

Lee, R. and Fielding, N. (1996) 'Computer-assisted qualitative data analysis: the user's perspective', in F. Faulbaum and W. Bandilla (eds), *SOFTSTAT '95: Advances in Statistical Software 5*. Stuttgart: Lucius.

Pfaffenberger, B. (1988) *Microcomputer Applications in Qualitative Research*. Newbury Park, CA: Sage.

Ragin, C. (1987) *The Comparative Method: Moving Beyond Qualitative and Quantitative Strategies.* Berkeley, CA: University of California Press.

Ragin, C. (1994) *Constructing Social Research.* Thousand Oaks, CA: Pine Forge Press.

Richards, L. and Richards, T. (1994) 'Using computers in qualitative analysis', in N. Denzin and Y. Lincoln (eds), *Handbook of Qualitative Research.* Thousand Oaks, CA: Sage.

Rothstein, L. (1986) *Plant Closings: Power, Politics and Workers.* Dover, MA: Auburn House.

Scott, M. and Lyman, S. (1968) 'Accounts', *American Sociological Review*, 33: 46–62.

Seidel, J. (1991) 'Methods and madness in the application of computer technology to qualitative data analysis', in N. Fielding and R. Lee (eds), *Using Computers in Qualitative Research.* London: Sage.

Strauss, A. (1987) *Qualitative Analysis for Social Scientists.* Cambridge: Cambridge University Press.

Tesch, R. (1990) *Qualitative Research: Analysis Types and Software Tools.* New York: Falmer Press.

van Dijk, T. (ed.) (1985) *Handbook of Discourse Analysis*, vol. 4. London: Academic Press.

Weaver, A. and Atkinson, P. (1994) *Microcomputing and Qualitative Data Analysis.* Aldershot: Avebury.

Weitzman, E. and Miles, M. (1995) *Computer Programs for Qualitative Data Analysis.* Thousand Oaks, CA: Sage.

32

Ethnodrama: Performed Research – Limitations and Potential

JIM MIENCZAKOWSKI

Despite Victor Turner's (1986) initial call for research that also participated in performance, the worlds of theatre and research at that time were too far apart for a viable elision between the aesthetic assumptions of performance and the methodological and theoretical ambitions of research to truly take place. Only recently has the full import and understanding of ethnodramatic research been given sufficient and effective credence by theatre communities and research communities to prompt a coherent and cogent development of theory with practice. Theoretically, these developments are occurring because of (and paradoxically despite) the precedence established by a raft of early documentary style dramas involving oral history techniques (Cheeseman, 1971; Paget, 1987) and *verbatim theatre*. There are numerous possible reasons for this. One might be the differing interpretations of research and its foundations and emphases within recognized *artistic performance processes and qualitative academic traditions*. Whereas the former 'artistic' process is often viewed as a process of self-discovery and self-learning at an aesthetic and emotional level, the latter 'research' conception is often perceived to revolve around understandings of science, theory and methodology.

It is not my intention to enter the debate over the much rehearsed issues distinguishing the research emphasis and critical basis of ethnodrama from earlier verbatim and oral history performance approaches. Suffice it to say that the distinctions between early oral history and verbatim theatre techniques and ethnodrama research are clear. The aforementioned verbatim theatre largely draws upon *verbatim* recordings of interviews or eyewitness accounts of historic events. Proponents of the form consider that it is the *verbatim nature* of the presentations themselves which lends meaningful authority, import and significance to the resulting realizations. As verbatim and documentary style performances are often about cultural reification they frequently ignore the potential of their dramas to explore the present moment. Conversely, ethnodramas and ethnographic performances are about *the present moment* and seek to give the text back to the readers and informants in the recognition that we are all co-performers in each other's lives. In the way that ethnographic semiotics explores and decodes the meaning of culturally symbolic signs of visual and verbal communication, particularly in the realm of film (Worth, 1978), so ethnodrama is explicitly concerned with decoding and rendering accessible the culturally specific signs, symbols, aesthetics, behaviours, language and experiences of health informants using accepted theatrical practices. It seeks to perform research findings in a language and code accessible to its wide audiences. Yet, too often, performed ethnographic narrative is associated by arts practitioners with less articulated verbatim and documentary approaches.

Ethnodramas consensually construct both their scripts and performance scenarios with informants controlling the text and representations made. The performance process is subject to continual processes of validation – including validation by expert audiences (health consumer groups) not involved as informants but otherwise familiar with the health experiences being represented. Typically, ethnodramas utilize trainee nurses and students in their research, construction and depiction of health scenarios and consequently act as pre-professional vicarious learning opportunities for nurses about to enter the work domains being researched and performed. Performances of such researches are opened to audience comment and debate at the close of each performance and through other structured opportunities to inform the production team and cast through fax, telephone, questionnaire or interview. Specific health agencies promote ethnodramas and most performances provide appropriate discrete counselling facilities (that is, representatives of relevant alcohol and drug services; mental health counsellors, psychiatric nurses or sexual assault service counsellors, etc.) to assist in supporting and de-briefing audiences and participants after performances. Ethnodrama performances are constantly updated according to data drawn from audience interactions. Scripts are made available to audiences prior to or at performances so that audience members may seek clarification or revisit the issues represented in the performances. Ethnodramas operate on a set of themes considered central and pertinent to understanding the experience of a particular health or social issue by relevant informants. Verbatim theatre, oral histories and documentary theatres do not articulate their thesis beyond theatrical presentation to their audiences.

Beyond oral history and verbatim approaches, Mulkay (1985) has proposed an ethnographic dramatic narrative that uses parody as a form of social analysis. His application of humour is a deliberate ploy to portray the myriad interactions of society (which might otherwise be inaccessible or of no apparent interest) to audients using traditional comedic devices to instigate perceptual shifts in their response to ethnographic data. Similarly, Laurel Richardson's creation of a dramatized narrative 'The Sea Monster: An Ethnographic Drama' (Richardson and Lockridge, 1991) enabled her to discuss those issues central to the postmodern reconstruction of ethnography through both parody and irony. Performance ethnography should be seen, in a sense, to occupy a space in ethnographic discourse which challenges traditional reporting approaches through the incorporation of genres, practices and techniques used in 'theatre, film, video, ethnography, performance, text' (Denzin, 1997). Incorporated with audience responses this may promote wider understanding for participants. Ethnodramas differ from other forms of performance ethnographic practice because it is their overt intention not just transgressively to blur boundaries but is a form of public voice ethnography that has emancipatory and educational potential. Thus, the extensive validatory processes inherent in the interactionist data-gathering techniques of the ethnodrama methodology and the reflexive nature of its performance processes overcome some of the structural difficulties inevitable in the ethnographic venture.

Of particular significance in ethnodrama is the consensual nature of the validatory processes that seek to create a sense of *vraisemblance* (Todorov, 1968). Atkinson's (1990) more apt description: the creation of *plausible accounts* of the everyday world by project participants and audiences of the report, is one of the major objectives of ethnodrama. This is because both textually and, in the case of ethnodrama, physically, vraisemblance is sought in order to evoke belief by representing *perceived* social realities in terms that mask the cultural influences affecting the constructors of the report. In order to consensually agree that both the written research report and its physical interpretation on stage are in the authentic language of, and therefore recognizable to and interpretable by informants, the ethnodrama processes are extended through Bakhtinian (1984) *dialogic interactions*. These dialogic interactions may thus be interpreted as the informant group's *struggle* to create and share meaning by developing an appreciation for, and understanding of, health patients' and health professionals' experience of order and reality through formally structured group discussions that are extended via forum theatre techniques (Boal, 1979; Mienczakowski, 1994). The product or outcome of these dialogical engagements is the research report: the ethnodramatic script. This script, using the language of the informants in a lyrical, sometimes verbatim but always realistic, portrayal of informants' experiences of health practices, may then be seen as a collective endeavour to demolish or blur the barriers between health care recipients, professionals, policy-makers and the general public.

Denzin (1997) connects the overall and rapidly expanding move towards ethnographic performance as a logical turn for a number of human disciplines in which *culture* is increasingly seen as performance and *performance texts* as being able to concretize experience. In general, the move to academically essentialize and articulate the reflexive aspects of these earlier ways of working has been limited. Denzin (1997) has clearly recognized that many forms of research performance work are bound to aesthetic conventions that need to be set aside for audiences of ethnographic performances. Thus notions of aesthetics and artistry need not subvert the potential of research narratives and their public analysis from meeting the real ethnographic goals of public explanation and cultural critique by allowing an analysis of the representations made through the 'co-participatory' performance nature of postmodern ethnographic researches. Consequently, ethnographic performance texts are about *speaking with* informants and audiences rather than *speaking for* or *about* them. Interactive ethnographic performances often go further still in experimenting with and disturbing the delineation between performers and audiences, texts and authors. Although Denzin (1997) opens the door to this conversation there is still much work to be done in connecting the work of performance ethnography to the natural development of certain forms of professional/fringe theatre, which increasingly involves contesting and blurring the same aesthetic, performance and textual boundaries. For example, the work of the *Triangle Theatre Company*[1] (Coventry, UK) exemplified the performance use of autoethnography, or critical analysis of self through autobiographical reflection, to explore and articulate personal responses to the loss of a child then performed these ethnographic narratives in its productions.

What has been Done

The progression and heritage of ethnodrama has been more serendipitous and pragmatic than most theoretical turns. In 1992 academics involved in theatre, education and health were prompted to construct a performance piece for Australia's 'Mental Health Week'. The brief was to construct a research performance project that sought to represent and then open for debate within the audience and cast certain key themes of schizophrenic experience. Initially the original team of theatre practitioners and academics in psychiatric nurse education and psychology embarked upon uncovering the experience of psychosis through detailed ethnographic and phenomenological research processes which would ensure that all team members might understand the meaning of the health issues involved (Morgan and Mienczakowski, 1993). The aim was to provide accessible data in order to inform and foreground the future theatre performance. The result was the realization that, in a small way, this process had the potential to represent a new theoretical turn through finding limited grounds for Habermas' notion of human communicative consensus/competence (Mienczakowski, 1995, 1996). Furthermore, the process encouraged the development of a public voice form of research (Agger, 1991), provided significant learning opportunities for the health students involved, and importantly reached large, nightly audiences with ethnography.

The explanations, meanings and insights generated by ethnodrama performances are consensually controlled and created by informant groups. As informants validate not only their own data but the scripted and performed scenarios generated by the research, the ethnodrama process represents not only an opportunity to voice informant understandings, explanations, experiences and emotional location within the circumstances of their experiences of health or society but further gives rise to opportunities for student nurses, guidance counsellors, teachers and health professionals to reflect, as participants or audience members, upon their own professional practices (Coffey and Atkinson, 1996).

Specifically, the ethnodrama is concerned with the recontextualization of dialogue and discourse thus providing immediate public access to health participants including audients. This polyphonic voicing of our informants' agenda in a 'public voice' (Agger, 1991) to wide audiences who might otherwise be disadvantaged or inhibited from accessing and interpreting the more traditional academic presentation of research data is not an attempt to return to a metanarrative or to lionize the worth of individual mini-narratives. If, in effect, we view the postmodern fracturing of metanarratives not in Lyotard's (1984) terms of 'shattering' but more in Bernstein's (1996) terms as dislocation, specialization and localization then we might see postmodern stories not as a limiting rupturing of human understanding but as a tenable micro-minutia discourse on what is going on (Mienczakowski et al., 1996). That is, our performance of postmodern stories through the medium of ethnodrama extends Bernstein's theories of giving the power of authorship back to those who live the health phenomena that is being taught or described.

The initial project in experiences of schizophrenia, *Syncing Out Loud* (Mienczakowski, 1992), was presented for a season within a university and also at Wolston Park Hospital, a large psychiatric hospital. The intent of this latter performance was twofold: first as validation of the research report (or script) and secondly as a beneficial event for the clients of the hospital, as viewed from within an emancipatory critical social framework (Mienczakowski, 1995, 1996; Morgan et al., 1993). This work, along with its successor project *Busting* (Mienczakowski and Morgan, 1993), which concerned itself with alcohol detoxification, has been reported fairly widely in a number of journals and disciplines (education, nursing, social sciences and dramatic arts). Whilst this reporting has focused on the relatively innovative combination of health, drama, social research and critical social theory, the team involved in developing the work came to understand that the implications such performances held for audiences were, at times, far from being symbolic. It is this realization that has informed much of the debate presented in this chapter.

ETHNOGRAPHY: CONTEMPORARY TRENDS

The development of ethnographic narratives into a full-scale performance vehicle is clearly an elaboration and enhancement of ongoing, world-wide interest in evolving ethnographic constructions and practices (Ellis and Bochner, 1996). Ethnodrama sits within an extant school of theatre which searches for social change (Epskamp, 1989) but differs from other forms of similar theatre in that it adheres to the principles of a formal and recognizable ethnographic research methodology, above and beyond the artistic demands of aesthetics, in its attempt to produce cultural critique (Denzin, 1997).

This is a route now being further explored by some high school and college practitioners (Diaz, 1997; Fox, 1997).

Contemporary ethnographic research is also written and disseminated in formats that have embraced poetry and biography (Ellis, 1995; Richardson, 1994) and interpretative interactionism (Denzin, 1989, 1997). Such moves are part of developing methodologies that attempt to use ethnographic and social science practices to question the usefulness of boundaries between literature, arts and social science explanations of the world (Ellis and Bochner, 1996). The recognition that explanations of the world made through literature and the arts are closer to understandings gained through anthropology and the social sciences than those made via the physical sciences (Rorty, 1980) is of significance here. Turner (1986) envisaged ethnographic practice in which the *performance* of ethnography could be seen as a means of investigating channels of reception and human understanding. Critical ethnodrama seeks to meld the traditional values of textual, academic presentation and those of performance in its investigation of human understanding.

The proposition is that performed ethnography may provide more accessible and clearer public explanations of research than is frequently the case with traditional, written report texts (Mienczakowski, 1996). The public performance of ethnography in the argot of its informants may be argued to de-academize the report construction process. Significantly, ethnodrama also returns *the ownership*, and therefore the power, of the report to its informants as opposed to *possessing it* on behalf of the academy (Mienczakowski, 1996). The following script extract, largely verbatim transcription, exemplifies the potential power of this mode of research presentation to influence audiences emotionally and intellectually. Sally's monologue in this script is intentionally contrasted with the dialogue/data drawn from serving police officers who are more concerned with the unreliability of victims' testimony in court than the victim's experience of crime. It must be remembered that actors in costume perform these data and are supported with all the trappings of suspended disbelief and staging that *theatre* entails. Reading the data straight from the page might not have the same import.

Baddies, Grubs and the Nitty-Gritty (Mienczakowski and Morgan, 1998b)

Scene 2: Rob, a new recruit to the Sexual Assault Squad, is advised by Col, the Senior Detective Inspector running the unit.

Rob: Will we use a female constable to do the interview?

Col: No. Not one available today. Look, I might as well put you straight on this. I reckon that this woman–woman stuff is all bullshit – I am a professional person and so are you, the lawyer, the doctor even ... I can't guarantee a jury of women only so why start now?

Strewth, if this was a rape-murder and we were looking at the naked body of a deceased female victim nobody would be expressing these sensibilities?

I want to be there when they gather evidence, if I'm allowed, to be able to direct the investigation. To be able to say photograph that bruise, what's made that scar? Take a shot of that.

Her body is a crime scene and I'm gathering evidence – to try and piece the story together and make sure it fits. Anything at all to get enough evidence for a watertight case.

And,

Scene 2 (Audio tape and slides)

Sally: Well, when I was initially sexually assaulted it was around the Christmas period and I couldn't get help. I don't think funding was very good at the time but eventually, I did speak to somebody in Brisbane, um ... I rang as many different organizations as I could – people were either on breaks or no one was available, so in the end I was forced to ring the police.

It was very intimidating, and the police officer I saw, er, whilst he befriended me, um ... he actually eventually crossed the line of his professional role, ah ... Started to come around ... – we eventually had a relationship for a while. I think he found my vulnerability and dependence, all of those things, he found them erotic.

When I went to the police ... I wasn't ... It wasn't offered to me to see a woman, and retelling the whole saga took eight hours. The first four hours ... oh shit ...

Finally I saw him, I think I saw him about a week after it had occurred. He took me into an interview room and ah ... didn't record anything or anything the door was open. I had to come back the next day and make my statement in a public office and you could have heard a pin drop – so it was quite intimidating really. Everyone could hear and there were lots of interruptions. He very kindly came in on his day off, the next day, to take my statement 'cause he saw my genuine distress. Ah, it was still pretty intimidating I would have much preferred to talk to someone ... a woman in an office in a sexual assault clinic.

Look, the first positive thing I did after the assault was to go to the police, well before that the first positive thing was to physically run away and hide from my assailant, the second positive thing was to go to the police. That was a really big step because it was putting all of my eggs in one basket and publicly saying 'its not my fault' ... in front of a lot of uniformed men. So I think it was a big step in the healing process ... and going through with the stalking charges was a big step too, because it meant that I was saying that I count and have rights and the law should protect me.

And,

> Rob: ... OK. That's the baddy, so what about this woman in the interview room? What female support have we got for this woman we are about to interview?
>
> Col: You keep banging on about support don't you? Maybe her mother – if she sits still and shuts up. She can sit there and shut up. Say nothing. Evidence just walks out of the room. Counsellors give them words and language that a decent lawyer would shoot holes through. Give them ideas about dropping charges. And they are so cowardly that most of them won't go anywhere near a courtroom. But some are really good. They know the score. It's the young idealistic feminist types that are the problem. It's hard to deal with contamination of story after support service intervention.
>
> Rob: They probably just want the person healed.
>
> Col: Us too. We are the real bloody therapists in this.
>
> Rob: How come?
>
> Col: Seeing a baddy caught and sent to court to answer publicly is part of the recovery. Most victims need to hear 'Yeah – you are right – he did rape you.'

Transgressive or Progressive?

Peter Woods (1996) interestingly sidelines the postmodern turn in ethnographic practice as symptomatic of deliberations upon methodological trends and modes of representation. Rather than viewing postmodern approaches to qualitative research as part of an alternative or competing paradigm he explains them simply as extensions of interactionist practices. Some may shy away from this recognition, but Woods firmly aligns meaningful and productive research with the apperception that both teaching and research have synergies as forms of art which in turn strongly relate to Mead's (1934) concept of self and self identity. In relation to both the artistry and generalized tenets of research, Woods sees postmodern trends in qualitative approaches as opening spaces in which ethnographic research can, through a form of practitioner artistry, convincingly help the voices of participants to be heard. Some of these newly created spaces include the explanation and interpretation of ethnographic research through poetry, literary narrative and performance.

Denzin (1997) draws clear connections between authentic expression and the transmission of validated, authentic research with the immediacy, contestability and accessibility of performance. In essence, the potential of performance is relegated by Woods to the expression of research, and drama is limited to the status of a useful tool for prompting emotional recognition and connections between the drama's subject, participants and audiences in general. Nevertheless, drama's potential lies in its ability to demonstrate research through the argot, codes and symbols of its informants thus opening research up to public disclosure and informant engagement, in the same manner as research is said to be disseminated through literary and poetic channels.

As they are constructed in both a written and hybrid form of language, it might also be argued that poetic narratives represent culture-bound and inhibitory approaches for the dissemination of research. While Laurel Richardson certainly doesn't claim to produce open, public voiced texts and I emphatically imply no criticism of her lyrical poetic approach on such grounds, I do draw attention to postmodern concerns with informant and peer contestation of the written codes and stilted patriarchy of extant scientific research report writing codes. Such concern, it may be supposed, merits their replacement with more accessible written and explanatory codes. Yet by suggesting a literary, narrative or poetic route to explanation we may be faced with an equally difficult genre for some readers to access. The use of transgressive poetic-literary writing styles undoubtedly evokes deep emotional and intellectual impacts upon those audiences *who are comfortable* with these particular expressive idioms – whilst it may perforce deny access and disenfranchise other audiences.

Denzin's (1994) uncertainty is that the construction of poetic accounts shouldn't be sanctioned simply because they provide an alternative to the many standard written approaches towards dissemination which are often viewed as boring. He effectively insinuates that if the writer is dull their attempts to create poetic interpretations of research may also be less than exciting. The call for contemporary ethnographers to heed is that of intellectual coherence, insight, quality of argument and the *appropriateness of presentation and organization* (Denzin, 1994) as the key elements of any ethnographic construction.

Another criticism of transgressive approaches I would like to include here is that of Snow and Morrill (1995) as referred to by Woods (1996). Snow and Morrill suggest that screenwriters and playwrights may have a better eye and feel for artistry and the possibilities of constructing performance pieces than either ethnographers or academics toying with literary structures. Literature, they posit, is as hard a fought for territory as is any academic discipline and *not everyone who is an ethnographer can also write decent and viable performance scripts*. It is at this point that I am obliged to argue on behalf of an emergent trend. Postmodernism has seemingly taught us to be healthily sceptical of attempts to rigidly name and compartmentalize *the other* within predetermined categories. If we distinguish literature as the domain of *literary* writers and believe that only artists *who live the life of artists* can produce art, then surely it must follow that only ethnographers can construct ethnography and only teachers can teach (Mienczakowski, 1999)?

Essentially, the arena we are in is one in which artists' *works and lives* are perceived as grounded within rigid categories and are often inseparably considered as *art*. Here also the products of the individual (books, scripts, poems or paintings) may be considered creative, aesthetic and 'art' although the group products (scripts, performance researches, ethnodramas, etc.) may not. With the reconstruction of ethnographic research as ethnodrama I believe the boundaries between lived realities, art, theatre, literature and various other eliding genres are abandoned rather than blurred or crossed. I would suggest that such artificially imposed boundaries are symbolic, largely representing the *self-interests of identity* of particular groups. Such identities are embodied within the general conception of artist, writer, poet, etc. Consequently, artists, writers, poets seek to control both their received identities and the public judgement of what counts as an artistic or literary product. I am not for an instant suggesting that researchers, teachers and ethnographers *per se* can all make useful and successful attempts to communicate and explain research through performance, literature and poetry but I consider they should try. Or at the very least, they should not be disheartened or discouraged by the hypothesis that only professional writers, painters, poets and playwrights have the skill, artistry and aesthetic penchant to devise works of artistic worth or quality. It seems likely that such 'validity claims' might functionally constrain or disenfranchise some attempts by researchers and teachers to have their artistic research works viewed on an aesthetic or artistic basis. Comparable arguments are frequently used against collaborative health theatre which in some circumstances is inappropriately branded as purely *therapeutic* or aesthetically, artistically *compromised* as a form of theatre in that it seemingly cannot meet the same aesthetic criteria as theatre derived from a sole professional playwright's deliberations. That may, at times, be the case but logically these suppositions have no credible or challenged theoretical foundation. It is, perhaps, a form of solipsism.

A point I have laboured elsewhere is that of Woods' acknowledgement of the potential of poetics to access audiences previously left unmoved by more traditional research approaches. This understanding is tempered by his calls for a model endorsing the supplementation of poetic-narrative interpretations with an explanatory (academic) text. Woods believes that the inclusion of such text might assist claims of veracity and confirm authority by demonstrating examples of triangulated data whilst simultaneously relating how the literary text was constructed. In his comprehension of the underlying reticence from some quarters, Woods suggests that *validity* claims might be replaced with *quality* checks to aid navigation and rigour within research. The duality of these notions makes me uneasy. On one hand, the ethnographer turned poet/playwright is forced to justify his or her research through secondary traditional academic categories which may be irrelevant to the aesthetic, semantic and emotional construction of artistic interpretations. On the other hand, a subjective, external criterion of quality is applied to the work. Such a criterion must ponder the power of the representations to move audiences and increase understanding. Not an easy task and one that is seldom set for the authors of more traditional ethnographies! In either scenario it seems that the transgressive arts ethnographer must produce double the work to gain the credibility and status afforded to ethnographers who chose more traditional data presentation approaches.

Happily, there are bodies of research and experimentation work that move far beyond Woods' concerns with validity and quality in performance researches. Such works have attempted to seek audience understanding of and responses to ethnographically derived performance pieces and have gone a long way towards exploring the implications of constructed, *staged audience catharsis*, collective audience responses and *emotional enlightenment* (Mienczakowski et al., 1996).

It is also possible that an entirely fictional work may receive higher aesthetic accolades, or construct stronger empathetic connections with audiences, under some criterion, than research based performance ethnographies or transgressive literary approaches. However, Ellis and Bochner's (1992) short performance piece concerning their experience of deciding upon and undergoing an abortion may be an example of a different conception of theatre for a new kind of audience. The performance of this work is reported to have, none the less, still evoked high levels of emotional impact and connection with its audiences despite its non-fictional status. The piece's authoritative effectiveness most likely resided in its foundations in personal account as opposed to fictional construction or the performance abilities of the authors. Ellis and Bochner related to their academic audience by illuminating experience and emotional context in tandem. The opening of research to new and wider audiences via poetic, literary, narrative and performance vehicles needs to be recognized too. With ethnodrama we know that we draw upon audiences specifically interested in the subject matter and intellectual location of the work. This is a new type of audience for whom aesthetics is subordinate to cogency.

Consequentially, a new conception of aesthetic understanding combined with a new consideration of audience may be required for research narratives that are not always rounded or complete in their interpretation into poetic or performance forms. Simply to adhere to and comply with a standard form of performance categorization and expectation through the insertion of dramatic plot devices or by contriving dramatic or poetic impact at the expense of research authenticity may subvert research authenticity to meet dramatic form.

I suspect that what is urgently required is a shift in the understanding and expectations of dramatic and literary form in order to acknowledge and embrace the change in form and genre that transgressive/alternative writing portends. These emergent forms – which demonstrate through performance research basis, validity, aesthetic qualities and emotional connection combined with literary style – represent potentials yet to be realized, fully explored and developed. The future is fraught with possibilities!

PROBLEMS IN POTENTIAL

To accent some of the potentials and problems of ethnodrama, I move on to elaborate upon some of the problems of presentation. A co-author and I have had cause (Mienczakowski, 1997; Mienczakowski and Morgan, 1998a) to divulge how we had unknowingly cast a student actor with unexpressed fundamentalist religious beliefs in a situation of personal vulnerability. Herein the student was confronted by the devil. That is, a student actor who believed schizophrenia to be the manifestation of the devil speaking through possessed persons, was happily cast as a psychiatrist for the run of a play concerning schizophrenic illness. When a group of psychiatric institution patients clambered on stage and confronted the actress as if she were *a real psychiatrist* during a performance we (the production team) viewed the play as being re-written and vitally enhanced through active audience participation and commentary. Simply, the subjects of our research were actively adding data. The fundamentalist actor perceived the situation altogether differently. Her religious belief system forced her towards a disturbing recognition. She believed that the psychotic patient who had confronted her and argued with her was possessed by the devil. *He was, therefore, the devil and he was trying to engage her in conversation.* She responded by taking flight and disappeared off stage and into the night.

A further demonstration of the power of plays to accurately portray events associated with health care caused us to question at what cost this was to the rehabilitative processes of our informants? An actor portraying the needle-related behaviours observed in detoxification units during rehearsals for the project performance *Busting: The Challenge*

of the Drought Spirit simply discarded needles from a sharps box whilst demonstrating the routine use of multivitamin shots in detox treatment. To our special validating audience of informant detoxees from a local halfway house this prompted recognition of 'needle fixation' and associated behaviours. Several informants became agitated and excited and could not resist handling and examining the needles and further professed to be unable to concentrate on the play from that point onwards (Morgan and Mienczakowski, 1999).

Most serious of all, and it is this determination that has prompted me to recant these tales, we became aware of tendencies amongst academic and professional theatre companies in Australia to seek funding from health care sources in the name of health research theatre and health promotion specifically, to promote anti-suicide awareness programmes for young people. Hooray! Hooray! Ooops! In a nation that boasts one of the highest youth suicide rates of the Western world we should be involved in seeking resolution to such an issue. Performed ethnographic research could be an expansive and public voice method through which logical pursuit of these goals might be achieved. Wow, hold those horses – take a rain check and step right back.

From 1996 to 1999 *$AUS 31 million* in Federal government funding was committed to projects specifically related to addressing issues pertaining to youth suicide prevention strategies and programmes, research and evaluation. We (members of our ethnodrama research team) found ourselves involved at a national level in providing some evaluation for a significant aspect of these preventative programmes relating to performances involving suicide issues. It allowed us the opportunity to assess the work of colleagues and kindred approaches and, more importantly, to further research the implications of performances with emancipatory intent (Morgan et al., 1998).

Instead of empowerment we witnessed vulnerable audiences *placed at risk*. Though we can make no incontrovertible association (nor would we wish to do so), we saw health informant performers act out their own therapy to potentially vulnerable audiences. So much so, in fact, that a performed scenario concerning depression and a realistic staged suicide by hanging was echoed by the real life suicide of the cast's musical composer who hanged himself behind stage on the final night of the production. This was one of a number of suicides directly involving members of this health performance group and their health consumer network.

Notions surrounding the very real potential for drama depicting suicide to bring about copy-cat or clusters of suicides in real life may be traced back to similar concerns linked to the works of the writer Goethe (Phillips, 1989). Gould and Shaffer (1989) and Schmidtke and Haffner (1989) have depicted strong links between suicide scenes portrayed on

German and US television to cluster suicides occurring in a 2-week period after the scenes were viewed (Morgan and Mienczakowski, 1999).

I emphatically do not wish to reject the use of research performance, as it is a vital element of health education and promotion. It seems clear, however, that performance research approaches may not suit the issue of suicide. There may be other, as yet unidentified, areas best left unfathomed or treated with caution by this very public mode of research investigation and dissemination.

For some people and under some circumstances exposure to theatre which seeks to redefine a person's relationship to a particular personal, health or social topic may be loosely understood as entering the therapeutic realm. Transformational possibilities can also exist through observation alone, although within the context of deliberately interactive and critical ethnodrama a participatory role for the audience may also be understood. Although substantial work is currently being undertaken in this field by a founding member of the ethnodrama project group, Steve Morgan, it has long been identified from our earlier investigations (Mienczakowski, 1995; Mienczakowski and Morgan, 1998b; Morgan et al., 1999) that research-based health performances attract a mix of health-interested persons and others who may or may not usually be attracted to theatrical presentations. Those audience members who seek a therapeutic encounter through the constructs of ethnodrama seem more likely to be affected by such strong performance themes (suicide, child abuse to name but a few) than those who would more usually visit the theatre for the purposes of entertainment or aesthetic appeasement (Mienczakowski et al., 1996). There are reasonable grounds to explore the audience as existing cohesively as a momentary group unified in their relationship and interest in the health circumstances presented to them. In respect of audiences being in theatres for purposes of professional development and group learning, we may see ethnodrama performances as a mode of critical intervention operating within a variety of interpretative frameworks.

NOTE

1 Triangle Theatre Company, Coventry: *My Sister My Angel* (1997), Carran Waterfield, directed by Ian Cameron.

REFERENCES

Agger, B. (1991) 'Theorising the decline of discourse or the decline of theoretical discourse?', in P. Wexler (ed.), *Critical Theory Now*. New York: Falmer Press. Ch. 5.

Atkinson, P. (1990) *The Ethnographic Imagination: Textual Constructions of Reality*. London: Routledge.

Bakhtin, M. (1984) *Problems of Dostoevsky's Poetics* (ed. and trans. Caryl Emerson). Minneapolis, MN: University of Minnesota Press.

Bernstein, B. (1996) *Official and Local Identities*. Marriot Seminar by Emeritus Professor Basil Bernstein, Griffith Univeristy, Gold Coast, 27–28 May.

Boal, A. (1979) *Theatre of the oppressed* (trans. C.A. and M.L. McBride). New York: Urizen Books.

Cheeseman, P. (1971) 'Production casebook', *New Theatre Quarterly*, 1: 1–6.

Coffey, A. and Atkinson, P. (1996) *Making Sense of Qualitative Data: Complementary Research Strategies*. Thousand Oaks, CA: Sage.

Denzin, N. (1989) *Interpretive Interactionism*. Newbury Park, CA: Sage.

Denzin, N. (1994) 'The art and politics of interpretation', in N.K. Denzin and Y. Lincoln (eds), *The Handbook of Qualitative Research*. London: Sage.

Denzin, N.K. (1997) *Interpretive Ethnography: Ethnographic Practices for the 21st Century*. Thousand Oaks, CA: Sage.

Diaz, G. (1997) *Turned On/Turned Off (a Clarion Call)*. Qualitatives '97 OISE (eds L. Muzzin et al.). Toronto, ON: Desktop Publication. ISBN 0-9682062-0-4.

Ellis, C. (1995) *Final Negotiations: A Story of Love, Loss and Chronic Illness*. Philadelphia: Temple University Press.

Ellis, C. and Bochner, A. (1992) '*Telling and Performing Personal Stories: The Constraints of Choice in Abortion*', in C. Ellis and M.G. Flaherty (eds), *Investigating Subjectivity: Research on Lived Experience*. Newbury Park, CA: Sage. pp. 79–101.

Ellis, C. and Bochner, A. (1996) 'Talking over ethnography', in C. Ellis and A. Bochner (eds), *Composing Ethnography: Alternative Forms of Qualitative Writing*. Walnut Creek, CA: AltaMira. pp. 13–45.

Epskamp, K. (1989) *Theatre in Search of Social Change: The Relative Significance of Different Theatrical Approaches*. The Hague: Centre for the Study of Education in Developing Countries (CESO).

Fox, K. (1997) *First Blood: Rituals of Menarche*. Qualitatives '97 OISE (eds L. Muzzin et al.). Toronto, ON: Desktop Publication. ISBN 0-9682062-0-4.

Gould, Madelyn S. and Shaffer, David (1989) 'The impact of suicide in television movies: evidence of imitation', in Rene F.W. Diekstra and Ronald Maris (eds), *Suicide and Its Prevention: The Role of Attitude and Imitation*. (Advances in Suicidology, vol. 1). Leiden: Brill. pp. 331–40.

Lyotard, J-F. (1984) *The Post Modern Condition: A Report on Knowledge*. Minneapolis, MN: University of Minnesota Press.

Mead, G.H. (1934) *Mind, Self and Society*. Chicago: University of Chicago Press.

Mienczakowski, J. (1992) *Syncing Out Loud: A Journey into Illness*. Griffith University Reprographies, Brisbane.

Mienczakowski, J. (1994) 'Theatrical and theoretical experimentation in ethnography and dramatic form', *ND DRAMA, Journal of National Drama, UK*, 2: 16–23.

Mienczakowski, J. (1995) 'The theatre of ethnography: the reconstruction of ethnography into theatre with emancipatory potential', *Qualitative Inquiry*, 1 (3): 360–75.

Mienczakowski, J. (1996) 'An ethnographic act', in C. Ellis and A. Bochner (eds), *Composing Ethnography: Alternative Forms of Writing*. Walnut Creek, CA: AltaMira Press. Ch. 10.

Mienczakowski, J. (1997) 'An Evening With the Devil: The Archaeology of Emotion.' Society for the Study of Symbolic Interaction, 11–12 August, Colony Hotel, Toronto, ON.

Mienczakowski, J. (1998) 'Reaching wide audiences: reflexive research and performance', *NADIE Journal*, 22 (1): 75–82.

Mienczakowski, J. (1999) 'Ethnography in the hands of participants: tools of discovery', in G. Walford and A. Massey (eds), *Studies in Educational Ethnography*, Volume 2: *Explorations in Methodology*. Oxford: Oxford University Institute of Educational Studies/JAI Press.

Mienczakowski, J. and Morgan, S. (1993) *Busting: The Challenge of the Drought Spirit*. Brisbane: Griffith University, Reprographics.

Mienczakowski, J. and Morgan, S. (1998a) 'Finding closure and moving on', *Drama*, 5: 22–9.

Mienczakowski, J. and Morgan, S. (1998b) 'Stop! In the Name of Love and Baddies, Grubs and the Nitty-Gritty'. Society for the Study of Symbolic Interaction: Couch Stone Symposium, 22–24 February. University of Houston, University Hilton Hotel Complex, Houston, TX.

Mienczakowski, J., Smith, R. and Sinclair, M. (1996) 'On the road to catharsis: a theoretical framework for change', *Qualitative Inquiry*, 2 (4): 439–62.

Morgan, S. and Mienczakowski, J. (1993) *Re-animation of the Research Report. Shaping Nursing Theory and Practice*. Monograph No. 2. La Trobe University Press, Melbourne.

Morgan, S. and Mienczakowski, J. (1999) 'Ethical dilemmas in performance ethnography: examples from ethnodrama and theatre'. Unpublished paper presented at Couch Stone Symposium, SSSI, SSSI conference, Las Vegas, February 1999, pp. 9–15.

Morgan, S., Mienczakowski, J. and King, G. (1999) 'The Dramatic Representation of Suicide: Issues, Concerns and Guidelines'. Suicide Prevention Australia, Melbourne Convention Centre. 25 March.

Morgan, S., Mienczakowski, J. and Rolfe, A. (1993) 'It's funny, I've never heard voices like that before', *Australian Journal of Mental Health Nursing*, 15 (6): 244–9.

Morgan, S., Rolfe, A. and Mienczakowski, J. (1998) 'Exploration! Intervention! Education! Health Promotion!: A Developmental Set of Guidelines for the Presentation of Dramatic Performances in Suicide Prevention'. Mental Health Services Conference and Proceedings, Hobart, October 1998.

Mulkay, M.J. (1985) *The Word and the World: Explorations in the Form of Sociological Analysis*. London: George Allen and Unwin.

Paget, D. (1987) 'Verbatim theatre: oral history and documentary techniques', *New Theatre Quarterly*, 12: 317–36.

Phillips, D. (1989) 'Recent advances in suicidology: the study of imitative suicide', in R. Diekstra (ed.) and the World Health Organization, *Suicide and Its Prevention: The Role of Attitude and Imitation*. Leiden: Brill. pp. 299–312.

Richardson, L. (1994) 'Nine poems. Marriage and the family', *The Journal of Contemporary Ethnography*, 23: 3–13.

Richardson, L. and Lockridge, E. (1991) 'The sea monster: an ethnographic drama', *Symbolic Interaction*, 14: 335–40.

Rorty, R. (1980) *Philosophy and the Mirror of Nature*. Princeton, NJ: Princeton University Press.

Schmidtke, A. and Haffner, H. (1989) 'Public attitudes towards and effects of the mass media on suicidal and self-harm behaviour', in R.F.W. Diekstra (ed.) and the World Health Organization, *Suicide and Its Prevention. Advances in Suicidology*. vol. 1. Leiden: Brill.

Snow, D.A. and Morril, C. (1995) 'New ethnographies: review symposium: a revolutionary handbook or a handbook for revolution?', *Journal of Contemporary Ethnography*, 24 (3): 341–62.

Todorov, T. (1968) 'Introduction: Le Vraisemblable', *Communications*, 11: 1–4.

Turner, V. (1986) *The Anthropology of Performance*. New York: Performing Arts Journal Publications.

Woods, P. (1996) *Researching the Art of Teaching Ethnography for Educational Use*. London: Routledge.

Worth, S. (1978) 'Toward an ethnographic semiotic'. Unfinished paper presented at the 'Utilisation de L'ethnologie par le cinema/Utilisation du Cinema par L'enthologie Conference, UNESCO: Paris URL: http://www.temple.edu/anthro/worth/sethnosem.html

## 33

Postmodernism, Post-structuralism and Post(Critical) Ethnography: of Ruins, Aporias and Angels

PATTI LATHER

[T]he point of *Glas* is to confess the loss of autonomy, the loss of self, of the author, of the subject, of self-creation ... Derrida would never want something purely unreadable ... But it is true up to a point ... which is its point ... to experience unreadability, undecipherability, ... Derrida wants us to get a little lost.

(Caputo, 1993: 164)

Reading the space of the range of discussion concerning the current order of knowledge about postmodernism, post-structuralism and ethnography is a daunting task. The writing culture debates of the 1980s have settled into an historical occasion; postmodernism has become its own containment; ethnography is under duress from a range of critiques, marked and motored (and mired, some would add), by a 'reflexive' turn.[1] In what follows, my sense of task is not to map the complexities of the forces that (re)shape and (re)direct ethnography via a review essay. Rather, I offer more of a philosophical meditation that draws particularly on Walter Benjamin for his ideas on history and culture as ruins and Jacques Derrida for the glimpse he gives of a different logic, a logic of aporia, with some Nietzsche thrown in for good effect.[2] Given post-structural demands for practices of knowing with more to answer to in terms of the complexities of language and the world, my sense of task is to situate ethnography as a ruin in order to work its problematic status as an index of a general crisis of how to proceed in post-foundational times. My particular focus will be critical ethnography, both as a means to make do-able my task by (de)limiting the field and as the sort of ethnography I most read and practice.

I approach this task out of the transdisciplinary travels of ethnography. Such travels go well beyond anthropology, with an inheritance of concern regarding issues of representation and the legitimation of knowledge across the human sciences.[3] Grounded in critical studies of education and cross-disciplinary feminist methodology (Lather, 1991), I work the 'ruins' of postmodernism, science and, finally, ethnography itself. I then introduce the concept of aporia as a fertile site for developing a praxis of stuck places.[4] Three stuck places are approached, loosely marked as ethics, representation and interpretation. I conclude with some thoughts on a postmodern science via Walter Benjamin's (1968) angel of history as a way of thinking the thought of the limit and Michel Serres' ([1993] 1995) 'quasi angel' that evokes the anxieties attendant upon the collapse of foundations and the end of triumphalist versions of science.

My interest is in both the 'new' ethnography, that which comes after the crisis of representation (Marcus and Fischer, 1986), and what Derrida refers to as the 'already coming' (1996: 64), 'the as yet unnameable which is proclaiming itself' (1978: 293). In this, I look for the breaks and jagged edges of methodological practices from which we might draw useful knowledge for shaping present practices of an ethnography in excess of our codes but, still, always already: forces already active in the present. As French philosopher of history Michel de Certeau notes, 'we never write on a blank page, but always on one that has already been written on' (1984: 43). Hence, using a sort of palimpsest approach, what follows carries the weight of previous re-tellings of ethnography and, then, begins again. My aim is to evoke the 'restlessness and rumination' of ethnography, 'its poetics of encounter, sheer action, and intensity, its abjection, its states of exile and dreams of return, its spectacles of impact, and its experimental activities ... ' (Stewart, 1996: 11).[5] Delimiting, re-presenting and proliferating in excess of the space allotted to it, my hope is that the text will work against itself in disavowing prescription, tidy tales and successor regimes of truth as we address how to proceed in such a moment.

RUINS

The object of philosophical criticism is to show that the function of artistic form is as follows: to make historical content ... into a philosophical truth. This transformation of material content into truth content makes the decrease in effectiveness, whereby the attraction of earlier charms diminishes decade by decade, into the basis for a rebirth, in which all ephemeral beauty is stripped off, and the work stands as a ruin.

(Walter Benjamin, *The Origin of German Tragic Drama*, 1977: 182)

As a point of departure for addressing postmodernism, post-structuralism and ethnography, I situate the central concepts of my title as ruins. The failures of ethnography are no news to anthropology. Geertz, for example, writes of the field as 'a task at which no one ever does more than not utterly fail,' particularly in light of decolonization and critiques of representation (1988: 143). My move is something else: to track failure not at the level of method, but of epistemology (Visweswaran, 1994: 98). My claim is that embracing epistemological insufficiency can generate practices of knowing that put the rationalistic and evidentiary structures of science under suspicion in order to address how science betrays our investment in it (Albanese, 1996). The goal is to enable the science which ethnography has wanted to be, a science in another register and time. Derrida calls this other register and time 'messianicity': the experience of response, promise and responsibility where the very order of knowledge is suspended in opening to a different sort of future (1996: 36). To approach such a concept of science which is, perhaps, already in reach, I draw on a 1992 address to the American Historical Association by Judith Butler.

Butler delineates what opens up when economies of victory narratives are interrupted and what is left

is worked for the resources of its ruins toward new practices. Drawing on Benjamin's (1968) 'Theses on the Philosophy of History', Butler gestures toward the value of taking the failure of teleological history, whether Marxist, messianic, or, in its most contemporary formulation, the triumph of Western democracy (e.g., Fukuyama), as the very ground for a different set of social relations. It is the ruins of progressivist history, naive realism and transparent language that allow us to see what beliefs have sustained these concepts; only now, at their end, Butler argues, does their unsustainability become clear. Hiroshima, Auswitz, Mai Lai, AIDS, for example, make belief in history's linear unfolding forwardness unsustainable. None of the usual recourses can save us now: god, the dialectic, reason, science (Haver, 1996).

In such a time and place, terms understood as no longer fulfilling their promise do not become useless. On the contrary, their very failures become provisional grounds, and new uses are derived. The claim of universality, for example, 'will no longer be separable from the antagonism by which it is continually contested' in moving toward a configuration of ethics and sociality that is other to the Hegelian dream of a reconciliation that absorbs difference into the same (Butler, 1993: 6). Butler terms this 'the ethical vitalization' (1993: 7) of the failure of certain kinds of ideals, a Nietzschean transvaluation of working the pathos of the ruins of such ideals as the very ground of the development of new practices.

This move underwrites the new Nietzsche scholarship which positions him as a 'proto-deconstructionist' who works the ruins of hierarchical binaries toward a healthier being and doing against those who read him as a nihilist. In an exemplary way, Judith Butler writes, 'For that sphere [of politics] will be the one in which those very theoretical constructions – those without which we imagine we cannot take a step – are in the very process of being lived as ungrounded, unmoored, in tatters, but also, as recontextualized, reworked, in translation, as the very resources from which a postfoundational politics is wrought' (1995: 131). In this move, the concept of ruins is not about an epistemological skepticism taken to defeatist extremes, but rather a working of repetition and the play of difference as the only ground we have in moving toward new practices.

POSTMODERNISM/POST-STRUCTURALISM

What are we calling postmodernity? I'm not up to date.

(Michel Foucault, 1998: 447)

Whatever postmodern and post-structural mean these days, they are pervasive, elusive and marked by a proliferation of conflicting definitions that refuse to settle into meaning. Indeed, refusing definition is part of the theoretical scene. To help situate my readers, however, I provide a cursory overview of postmodernism and post-structuralism[6] by looking at a case study of its transmission and reception on the part of those who do their work under the sign of 'critical ethnography'.

Critical ethnography, rooted in the sociology of Pierre Bourdieu, the sociolinguistics of Basil Bernstein and the British cultural studies of the Birmingham School[7] has attachments to local knowledges and to illuminating the exercise of power in culturally specific yet socially reproductive processes. Reworking Marx after Gramsci, Althusser and Foucault, as well as a rich profusion of feminisms, post-colonialisms and critical race theories, its focus is the construction of consent and the naturalization of inequities. Objectivism, empiricism and subjectivism are at issue as well as the limits of earlier methodologies of symbolic interactionism and phenomenology (Foley, in press). Breaking with conventional ethnographic practices of detachment, its particular interest is activist collaboration with oppressed groups (Levinson et al., 1996; Quantz, 1992; Thomas, 1993).

Leftist efforts to accommodate/incorporate postmodernism have not been easy. Much mobilized in the reception of postmodernism and its entrance into the discursive networks of leftist intelligentsia are Teresa Ebert's categories of resistance and ludic postmodernism (1991). Within critical ethnography of education, for example, Kincheloe and McLaren urge a 'cautionary stance' toward ludic postmodernism with its focus on hyperreality and the playfulness of the signifier. Other characteristics they warn against include proliferation of differences, textualism, skepticism, quietism, nihilism, localism and the lack of normative ground given radical uncertainty, undecidability and contingency (Kincheloe and McLaren, 1994: 143–4). Using Ebert's categories, they offer, in contrast, 'oppositional' or 'critical' or 'resistance' postmodernism: a praxis of materialist intervention in 'real' social and historical differences based on normative foundations of emancipatory democracy.

Philosopher John Fekete troubles such a formulation in a paper on postmodernism and cultural studies. Intrigued with the recent Anglo-American acceptance of postmodernism, he posits this as due to its recuperation into a politically intelligible place 'in the frame of the already established purposes of the day' (1992: 3). Tracking the earlier dismissal of postmodernism by the left intelligentsia, he notes that the postmodern is now deployed, remarkably, in the service of politics, but in a way that tames 'the wildness, the excess, the interest in whatever would differ from and defer the productivist machinery of Marxism and the interpretative machinery of Freudianism'. 'Put to work' in the Anglo-American context, made useful, 'highly serious and "inescapably political"', postmodernism is 'reduced to political sociology ... modern structural polarities and the liberal-egalitarian rationality of identity politics' (1992: 3).

It is this logic which has been read into the American scene of phenomenology, pragmatics and practical politics to produce a 'politicized postmodernism' that characterizes Anglo-American cultural studies. Fekete terms this sort of postmodernism 'an amalgam of race–class–genderism' that reinscribes the praxis philosophy, oppositional, adversarial logics and cultural alienation of Marxism. The Enlightenment concepts of agency, praxis and critical self-reflexivity are asserted against the excesses of postmodernism.[8] Reinscribing dualisms, searching for some non-complicity, recuperating theory to praxis, this is but one narrow adaptation and selection, Fekete argues. His urging is toward a more 'mixed economy' of the postmodern that avoids the 'too quick re-moralization' that typifies the American scene.[9]

Post-structuralism understands structures as historically and reciprocally affected by practice within contingent conditions of time, particularly conceptual practices and how they define disciplinary knowledges (Prado, 1995: 154). It is about complicating reference, not denying it, through a profound vigilance regarding how language does its work. It is a skepticism not about the 'real', but about 'when a language is taken to be what being itself would say were it given a tongue' (Caputo, 1997b: 17). The key is Derrida's argument in *Specters of Marx* (1994) that 'the trial of undecidability' has to be gone through prior to the work of revaluation and how much must be refused[10] as we move into a post-Enlightenment, post-humanist loss of transcendent universals. In short, whatever the postmodern/post-structural is, it is not about offering a competing ontological frame but about looking at the historical, philosophical and cultural construction of frames, that which invests with patterns of belief and habit, including those that imbue critical ethnography.

What is at issue here is the distinction between deconstruction and ideology critique. The latter is about uncovering hidden forces and material structures and salvaging determinism and conflict theory. It endorses foundational criteria for science and a binary of textual/material in its calls for grounding our knowing in some real assumed knowable outside of the rhetoricity of language. Such reception is symptomatic of the continual hold of Enlightenment frameworks as it works against post-structural claims that it is what seems impossible from the vantage point of our present regimes of meaning that is the between space of any knowing that will make a difference in the expansion in equity and the canons of value toward which we aspire with our research. The deconstructive sense of task is to move to some place interrupted, out of balance, extreme, against the leveling processes of the dialectic and for the excesses, the non-recuperable remainder, the difference, in excess of the logic of non-contradiction. This is another logic to that of dialectical opposition with its binary of a good 'critically resistant postmodern ethnography' that is a 'balance' of postmodernism and critical theory and a bad or 'extreme postmodernism' with its 'irrationalist spontaneity' and 'textuality fetish'.[11]

Post-critical might serve as an interruptive term in such a space.[12] Philosopher John Caputo prefers the term post-critical to postmodern, given the latter's 'opportunistic overuse' (1997b: 119). For Caputo, post-critical means post-Kantian in the sense of a continued commitment to critique and demystification of truth but with a meta layer of being critical of demystification itself. He posits a postmodern modernity that mimes the Enlightenment desire for universals and demystification, a new Enlightenment of testimony and witness that differs from the authoritative voice of verification, proof or demonstration, the kinds of knowledge we are used to: knowledges of demarcation and certitude (1997b: 154). Out of engagement with Derrida's *Specters of Marx*, Caputo sees post-structuralism and postmodernism as a way to continue emancipation but by another means. This postmodern sensibility shakes the assured distinctions of any ontology of the 'real', of presence and absence, life and death, a post-critical logic of haunting and undecidables. Here Walter Benjamin's ([1940] 1968) 'Theses on the Philosophy of History' uses the irreducible resources of theology to break with ossified discourses (Rochlitz, 1996). Benjamin's 'messianic Marxism' or 'secular messianism' argued both the limits of secularized reason and the intertwinement of theology and philosophy. The secularized discourse of post-Kantian modernity is not as different from earlier theological discourses as modernists would like to believe – this was Benjamin's turn to theology, against the devaluation of truth in the name of knowledge. But this is theology present 'as form rather than content', the hunchback who stays out of sight in order to better guide the hand of the puppet of historical materialism (Nagele, 1991).

What I posit is that to understand ethnography under conditions of postmodernity entails a shift from a Kuhnian to a more Benjaminian/messianic sense of crisis (Caputo, 1997b: 74).[13] Calling on the resources of theology as a way through the aporias of modernity, Benjamin's thinking is neither Marxism nor theology but a contesting of both while twisting/queering their resources for practices of living on. Rather than the epistemological concerns that characterize modernity (Greene, 1994), this is about 'the discontinuous, catastrophic, non-rectifiable, and paradoxical' crisis of the self-regulation and purpose of ethnography (Lyotard, 1984: 60). 'Past the post' (Knauft, 1994) of epistemological wrestling with

representation, blurred genres and the ethics of the gaze, such a sense of crisis asks how we come to think of things this way and what would be made possible if we were to think ethnography otherwise, as a space surprised by difference into the performance of practices of not-knowing. Meaning, reference, subjectivity, objectivity, truth, tradition, ethics: what would it mean to say 'yes' to what might come from unlocking such concepts from regularizing and normalizing? A post-secular, post-critical, post-Enlightenment undecidability becomes not the last word, but the first in making room for something else to come about. Motored by a desire to stop confining the other within the same, this is a sort of preparation that is more about not being so sure, about deferral while entire problematics are recast and resituated away from standard logics and procedures (Caputo, 1997b).

Just as Derrida, and before him Benjamin, has called upon Jewish mysticism as a way to think against secular humanism, in this move, angels are of use as a (post-)critical gesture in shattering the sorts of rationalities that have shaped our negotiation of previous crises. Something other to the reductionisms of secularism, rationalism and transformationalism, the angel is not so much about opposition as *perversion*.[14] This takes 'the form of the unacceptable, or even of the intolerable, of the incomprehensible, that is of a certain monstrosity' in delivering us from the certainties of science, just as science delivered us from the certainties of religion (Derrida, quoted in Caputo, 1997b: 74). Welcoming the angel/monster into where we are is to use Derrida's move of repetition forward as a way through aporia, but a disloyal repetition, a risky business that produces what it repeats in order to see this not as loss but as letting something new come. This is more about Benjamin and Derrida's justice to come than Kuhn's theory of normal and revolutionary science. It is about bending the rules with respect for the rules, a certain respectful mimicking in order to twist, queer science to come up with a better story of itself. Hence, my argument is that what Derrida calls the 'investigation, research, knowledge, theory, philosophy' (1997: 38) of most use is that which addresses how such efforts remain possible given the end of the value-free notion of science and the resultant troubling of confidence in the scientific project. Such a move uses post-structuralism to distinguish between a narrow scientificity and a more expanded notion of science.[15]

According to French philosopher of science Michel Serres, in the old system, in order to understand, nothing must move. The new image of knowledge is of turbulence which isn't system so much as confluence, traversing scales of dimension. Here, Serres argues, angelology is key: a turbulent array of messengers, tracking and composing relations outside of defined concepts, producing the grammar of these modes of relating beyond fetishes of consciousness, essence, being, matter. 'We must invent the place of these relations,' Serres writes, as ground for a new science where philosophy no longer has the right to judge everything, but the responsibility to create, to invent, to produce what will foster production, to understand and apply a science in the face of holdovers and exhaustions ([1993] 1995: 137). Formed by science, but not constrained by scientism, more interested in ethics than demarcation issues, the borders between science and not-science fluctuate constantly. Such counter-narratives of science help to situate ethnography with/in the postmodern as a science 'after truth' (Tomlinson, 1989). It is to that I now turn: not ethnography *among* the ruins, but the ruins of ethnography.

ETHNOGRAPHY

The received and familiar story of ethnography is that it studies the production of everyday life by often 'othered' people analysed at the level of meaning, social structure, power relations and history. Its specific disciplinary claim is its ability to situate culture as relative in order to denaturalize via cultural comparison. Perhaps because of both its subject and its process, often despite itself, ethnography has escaped the sort of scientism that haunts other disciplinary methodologies. As a double practice, both science and a wanderer outside of the scientific paradigm it unevenly purports to follow, ethnography exists between travelogue and science, narrative and method, story and data in a space Harry Walcott has termed 'the most humanistic of the sciences and the most scientific of the humanities' (Mehan, 1995: 242). Now at the cultural moment of the decanonization of science, this marginal scientific status situates ethnography well to draw on the vitality of the deviations that elude taxonomies in order to address the question of practice in post-foundational times. Ethnography is, in short, a productive site of doubt if one can manage to avoid the 'too strong, too erect, too stiff' (Caputo, 1993: 161) in working the inside/outside of ethnography. This entails being adept at its practices and moving within its disciplinary habits while disrupting its tendencies to congratulate itself on being the knowledge-producing practice best situated in the contemporary scene to learn from its instructive complications.

Enacted at its best classical moments in such works as Pierre Clastres' *Chronicle of the Guayaki Indians* (1998),[16] ethnography took a 'literary' turn in the 1980s with concerns of 'textuality, disciplinary history, critical modes of reflexivity, and the critique of realist practices of representation' (Marcus, 1997: 410). As the defining practice of anthropology, ethnography is perhaps most notably characterized in the present moment as quite the

traveler (Clifford, 1997). As a method of cultural representation, it has moved across disciplines, creating blurred genres (Geertz, 1980) and troubling the transparent realist narrative. What George Marcus (1994) has termed 'messy texts' announce the new: partial and fluid epistemological and cultural assumptions, fragmented writing styles and troubled notions of ethnographic legitimacy, including the 'ethnographic authority' of fieldwork (Clifford, 1983).

In the present moment, the 'new' ethnography has turned on itself and a sort of 'self-abjection' has come to characterize the field (i.e., Behar, 1996). Full of a sense of failed promises, charged anxieties and mourned history, ethnography is trying to think its self-estrangement as a way out of a mimetic relation to the natural sciences with their mathematized empiricism in the face of the refractory object of its study (Albanese, 1996: 9). If, as Foucault (1998) states, we are freer than we feel, how can we feel freer in this space? How might we think ethnography as 'an art of being in between', of finding ways of using the constraining order, of drawing unexpected results from one's abject situation (de Certeau, 1984: 30), of making the dominant function in another register, of diverting it without leaving it? What does ethnography give us to hear and understand about the force needed to arrive at the change to come, that which is, perhaps, under way?

Here, one might begin to speak of a 'new' new ethnography or a (post-)ethnography,[17] deferred and diffused across disciplines, working borders and wrestling with urgent questions: something good to think with in moving into post-foundational practices. Kathleen Stewart characterizes the 'new' ethnography as too much about 'a discipline of correctives' (1996: 24), too much within assumptions of 'cure', particularly via the 'solution' of experimental writing.[18] More interested in what Visweswaran argues for as ruptured understandings and practices of failure as 'pivotal' (1994: 100),[19] Stewart calls on James Agee's *Let Us Now Praise Famous Men* as instructive in its imperfections. 'Nothing worked,' Stewart notes, and yet his palimpsest of layered evocations still carries force (Quinby, 1991; Rabinowitz, 1992). Hence, textual 'solutions' have their limits and a doubled epistemology is called for where the text becomes a site of the failures of representation. Here textual experiments are not so much about solving the crisis of representation as troubling the very claims to represent. Visweswaran distinguishes this as the difference between a Saidean critique of inadequate representation and a Nietzschean critique of representation itself (1994: 134).

This might, perhaps, be the contemporary problematic of ethnography: 'double, equivocal, unstable ... exquisitely tormented' (Derrida, 1996: 55), an ethnography of ruins and failures that troubles what Visweswaran calls 'the university rescue mission in search of the voiceless' (1994: 69). Moving across levels of the particular and the abstract, trying to avoid a transcendent purchase on the object of study, we set ourselves up for necessary failure in order to learn how to find our way into post-foundational possibilities. The task becomes to throw ourselves against the stubborn materiality of others, willing to risk loss, relishing the power of others to constrain our interpretative 'will to know', saving us from narcissism and its melancholy through the very positivities that cannot be exhausted by us, by the otherness that always exceeds us. Given the demise of master narratives of identification, perspective and linear truth, such ethnography draws close to its objects in the moment of loss where much is refused, including abandoning the project to such a moment (Haver, 1996). It is this drawing close, 'as close as possible' (Dirks et al., 1994: 16), that has long been the seduction of fieldwork, the reason why we will never have done with it. This closeness to the practical ways people enact their lives has been the promise for understanding how the 'everyday' gets assumed. The reflexive turn has broadened such understanding to include the very space of our ethnographic knowing. Hence, to situate ethnography as a ruin/rune is to foreground the limits and necessary misfirings of its project, problematizing the researcher as 'the one who knows'. Placed outside of mastery and victory narratives, ethnography becomes a kind of self-wounding laboratory for discovering the rules by which truth is produced. Attempting to be accountable to complexity, thinking the limit becomes our task and much opens up in terms of ways to proceed for those who know both too much and too little.

Aporias of Practice

> This book ... tells its story through interruptions, amassed densities of description, evocations of voices and the conditions of their possibility, and lyrical, ruminative aporias that give pause.
>
> (Stewart, 1996: 7)

I turn, finally, to methodological practices at the edges of what is currently available in order to work the aporias of ethnography toward an enabling violation of its disciplining effects. Foucault defines aporia as 'difficulty', that which 'stops us in our tracks' (1998: xxiii). Derrida defines it as 'an undecidability, a double bind' (1997: 39). Sarah Kofman (1988) elaborates the semantic richness of poros and aporia as finding a way out of situations from which there is no way out. This, she argues, is necessarily about a 'storm of difficulties' where we are out of our depth and forced to be resourceful, elusive, wily in finding a path that does not exist. Here we must think against technical thought and method

and toward another way that keeps in play the very heterogeneity that is, perhaps, the central resource for getting through the stuck places of contemporary ethnography. This might be termed a 'praxis of stuck places' (Lather, 1998a), a praxis of not being so sure, in excess of binary or dialectical logic that disrupts the horizon of an already prescribed intelligibility. Such a praxis addresses Derrida's question: 'What must now be thought and thought otherwise?' (1994: 59). To situate ethnography as an experience of impossibility in order to work through aporias is what Ellsworth terms 'coming up against stuck place after stuck place' as a way to keep moving in order to produce and learn from ruptures, failures, breaks and refusals (1997: xi).

Within the post-Enlightenment stirrings and strivings of contemporary theory, the philosophy of the subject, reflection and praxis are being rethought. Levinson (1995), for example, formulates a 'post-dialectical praxis' that is quite different from a Kantian or Hegelian analytic. The modernist metaphysics of presence, assured interiority and subject-centered agency, the valorizing of transformative interest in the object, Hegel's affirmative negativity and dialectical overcoming: all are at risk, refused in a way that signals the size and complexity of the changes involved. Such a praxis is about ontological stammering, concepts with a lower ontological weight, a praxis without guaranteed subjects or objects, orientated toward the as yet incompletely thinkable conditions and potentials of given arrangements.

Aporia 1: Ethics

> [Is it possible for anthropology] to be different, that is, to forget itself and to become something else ... [or must it] remain as a partner in domination and hegemony?
>
> (Edward Said, 1989)

Kate McCoy, in a 1998 paper on ethnographic drug research asks, 'Am I just doing spy work?' This is especially so in government-funded drug research, but the point is more broadly applicable to all of the social sciences. McCoy argues that in spite of good intentions, 'all research is to some degree surveillance' (1998: 6). This argument interrupts the romance of empowerment that drives much current ethnography, obscuring the surveilling effects of the best of researcher intentions. This is Foucault (1998), of course, and his insistence that nothing is innocent and everything is dangerous, but that just because something is dangerous does not mean that it is useless. While calls for self-reflexivity usually accompany such recognitions, it is key to recognize the limits as well as possibilities of self-reflexivity, an issue to which I will turn. Here, I want to trouble the romance of empowerment in the face of the invasive stretch of surveillance.

Given the dangers of research to the researched, ethnographic traditions of romantic aspirations about giving voice to the voiceless are much troubled in the face of the manipulation, violation and betrayal inherent in ethnographic representation (Visweswaran, 1997). Linda Tuhiwai Smith, for example, in *De-Colonizing Methodology* (1999), presents a counter-story to Western ideas about the benefits of the pursuit of knowledge. Looking through the eyes of the colonized, cautionary tales are told from an indigenous perspective, tales designed not just to voice the voiceless but to prevent the dying – of people, of culture, of ecosystems. The book is particularly strong in situating the development of counter-practices of research within both Western critiques of Western knowledge and global indigenous movements. Informed by critical and feminist critiques of positivism, Tuhiwai Smith urges 'researching back' and disrupting the rules of the research game toward practices that are 'more respectful, ethical, sympathetic and useful' versus racist practices and attitudes, ethnocentric assumptions and exploitative research. Using Kaupapa Maori, a 'fledgling approach', toward culturally appropriate research protocols and methodologies, the book is designed primarily to develop indigenous peoples as researchers. In short, Tuhiwai Smith begins to articulate research practices that arise out of the specificities of epistemology and methodology rooted in survival struggles, a kind of research that is something other than a 'dirty word' to those on the suffering side of history (see also Tyson, 1998).

Visweswaran raises suspicions of 'the dangerous ground between intimacy and betrayal' that characterizes feminist work intended to 'testify' and 'give voice' (1995: 614). In her ethnography of Indian women in the freedom movement against England, Visweswaran (1994) tells stories of the gaps and fissures, the blind spots of her romance of empowerment. Situating her practice within the loss of innocence of feminist methodology, she engages with the limits of representation and the weight of research as surveillance and normalization. Advising the workings of necessary failure versus the fiction of restoring lost voices, Visweswaran positions the feminist researcher as no longer the hero of her own story. All is not well in feminist research, she argues, and the problems cannot be solved by better 'methods'. To give voice can only be attempted by a 'trickster ethnographer' who knows they cannot 'master' the dialogical hope of speaking with (1994: 100), let alone the colonial hope of speaking for.

Here, the necessary tension between the desire to know and the limits of representation lets us question the authority of the investigating subject without paralysis, transforming conditions of impossibility into possibility where a failed account occasions new kinds of positionings. Such a move is about economies of responsibility within non-innocent space, a 'within/against' location, where research into the lives of others is welcomed as a troubling, as an ethical move outside mastery, heroism and the wish for rescue through some 'more adequate' research methodology (Britzman, 1997). Such a move displaces the idea that the work of methodology is to take us to some non-complicitous place of knowing. Instead, the work of methodology becomes to negotiate the 'field of play'[20] of the instructive complications that knowledge projects engender regarding the politics of knowing and being known. Here method is resituated as a way into the messy doings of science via risky practices that both travel across contexts and are re-made in each situated enquiry.

Aporia II: Representation: Authenticity and Voice

Is the concept of authenticity immovably mired in a view of agency requiring authorship in the sense of a transcendent subject present to itself, proprietor of action and master of causality? Is it a notion that makes sense only in an epistemology rooted in a cogito, representation, and a metaphysics of presence which demands primacy of focus on agency and intentionality?

(Leach, 1993: 3)

In contemporary regimes of disciplinary truth-telling, authenticity and voice are at the heart of claims to the 'real' in ethnography. Indeed, in the 'new' ethnography, that which comes after the loss of faith in received stories and predictable scripts, the authority of voice is often privileged over other analyses. Confessional tales, authorial self-revelation, multivoicedness and personal narrative, all are contemporary practices of representation designed to move ethnography away from scientificity and the appropriation of others (Behar, 1993, 1996; Behar and Gordon, 1995; Foley, 1998; McGee, 1992; Richardson, 1994, 1997; Van Maanen, 1988, 1995). At risk is a romance of the speaking subject and a metaphysics of presence complicated by the identity and experience claims of insider/outsider tensions. From the perspective of the turn to epistemological indeterminism, authenticity and voice are reinscriptions of some unproblematic real. This is a refusal of the sort of realism that is a reverent literalness based on assumptions of truth as adequation of thought to its object and language as a transparent medium of reflection. The move is, rather, to endorse complexity, partial truths and multiple subjectivities. Such tensions surface the uneasy interface between the post of post-colonialism and the post of post-structuralism. The post-colonial wants to retain a referential purchase on oppositional truth-claims while simultaneously drawing on the post-structural suspicion of the referent in order to deconstruct colonial power (Slemon, 1990). The post-structuralist wants to historicize all truth-claims, oppositional or not. How then to think about authenticity and voice?

Henry Louis Gates, in writing of the scandal regarding *The Education of Little Tree*, castigates 'the ideologues of authenticity' (1991: 2).[21] The key, Gates argues, is to see the 'troublesome' role of authenticity as linked to 'imputations of realness' that elide how, while identity indeed matters, 'all writers are "cultural impersonators"' (1991: 3). Whatever it means for a writer to speak as a this or a that, authenticity is much more complicated than singular, transparent, static identity categories assumed to give the writer a particular view.

One way to mediate representational violence without falling into static claims of 'authenticity' is the sort of 'researching back' of Francisco Ibanez-Carrasco's study of those who study HIV/AIDS. As a Person With AIDS (PWA) himself, Ibanez-Carrasco asks what becomes seeable/knowable when one speaks from within the disease about those who study it. He asks such questions out of a diasporic positioning rather than in the name of some restored immediacy of self and voice. Across multiple, shifting positions of gay, Chilean, working-class, healthy and gravely ill, Ibanez-Carrasco offers no cure of positionality, standpoint, or authenticity. Rather, moving away from ontological claims of identity, he entertains Foucault's idea that perhaps we need to refuse what we are, not recover it.[22]

My attempt here is to defamiliarize common sentiments of voice and authenticity in order to break the hegemonies of meaning and presence that recuperate and appropriate the lives of others into consumption, a too-easy, too-familiar eating of the other. Such a move is not so much about the real as it is about a horizon *in* insufficiency (Scott, 1996: 127). Against homogeneous spaces of collective consensus and communication, such work is emotive, figurative, inexact, dispersed and deferred in its presentation of truth-telling toward responsibility within indeterminacy. But the demand for voice also has much to do with subjugated knowledges and multiple fractured subjectivities, the unheard/unhearable voices of Spivak's (1988) 'Can the subaltern speak?'

Hence my attempt is not so much 'against' authenticity and voice as it is a double economy of the text to move toward de-stabilizing practices of 'telling the other' (McGee, 1992) in ways that displace the privileged fixed position from which the researcher interrogates and writes the researched (Robinson, 1994). Arguing that recuperating traditional realism is no answer to the aporias of the left, I am faced with the dual agendas of 'pissed-colonialism' (Pillow, 1996)

and those who try to use post-structural theory to think against the various nostalgias of leftist thought and practice. Such issues can be gestured toward via a process of layering complexity, foregrounding problems, thinking data differently, outside easy intelligibility and the seductions of the mimetic in order to work against consumption and voyeurism. Key is Lyotard's argument regarding the totalitarian dangers of realism: 'We have paid a high enough price for the nostalgia of the whole and the one, for the reconciliation of the concept and the sensible, of the transparent and the communicable experience' (1984: 81–2). By working the limits of intelligibility and foregrounding the inadequacy of thought to its object, a stuttering knowledge is constructed that elicits an experience of the object through its very failures of representation. To explore what this might look like, I turn to some examples of postmodern ethnography with a focus on issues of interpretative responsibility and the limits of self-reflexivity.

Aporia III: Interpretation and its Complicities

We arrive, then, to the third and final aporia that I want to address, the tensions between the weight of members' meaning and the ethnographer's interpretative responsibility. Key here is the limits of reflexivity in negotiating such tensions. What does it mean to critique practices of usurpative relation to people's stories of lived experience while still troubling experience as a 'grand narrative?' (Scott, 1992)

Perhaps the primary interest of deconstruction is 'in awakening us to the demands made by the other' (Caputo, 1997b: 15). Confining the other within the same is a violence of Western thought and to affirm the limits of such thought is to unlearn one's privilege. Yet reflexive gestures, partial understanding, bewilderment and getting lost as methodological stances are rhetorical positions that tend to 'confound refutation' and fragmentation of texts hardly avoids imposing one's interpretation of a fragmented world-view (Hekeman, 1988). Often too clever by far in dizzying involutions and perhaps less counter-hegemonic than hoped/declared, reflexivity can be unproductive in re-centering the angst of the researcher, resulting in what John Van Maanen (1988) has termed 'vanity ethnography'. Yet, too, it does its double work in estranging us from our own culture. What would a 'reflexivity under erasure' look like that both troubled reflexivity as a modernist 'cure' and, yet, worked toward a deconstructive reinscription of reflexivity via subversive repetition?[23]

Doug Foley explores what he terms 'post-modern reflexivity' by using George Marcus' (1994) three categories of reflexivity to look at the influence of postmodernism on critical ethnographers.[24] First presenting two critical ethnography texts as 'not particularly deconstructive' (Foley, in press: 13),[25] he turns to examples of postmodern ethnography, including a 'quasi-ethnography' that I co-authored on women and HIV/AIDS and an ethnography by Katie Stewart of poor whites in Appalachia. Foley characterizes *Troubling the Angels* as written in different linguistic registers that include authorial methodological and ethical reflections, factoid boxes on AIDS, and angel inter-texts that 'evoke' rather than explain the weight of AIDS in individual lives and cultural contexts. Too much 'disjointed jumble' for Foley, he finds ironical the text's intentions to be 'decidedly anti-realist' in its refusal of coherence while, nevertheless, containing 'a powerful residual realist style narrative' due to the documentary style presentation of the (seemingly) unmediated interview transcripts that occupy the top half of the split-text format. Noting my being 'bent on disrupting the realist trope of a heroic, empathic ethnographer on a knowledge quest' and my working to 'maintain a respectful, unsentimental, emotional distance' from the women Chris and I worked with, Foley articulates a kind of deconstructive reflexivity in my refusal to 'play the expert and explain their lives'. In this, my avoidance of the modernist position of the grand theorist and master interpreter 'strikes at the heart' of standard ethnographic practice where the author is 'discovering, explaining, and giving a "deep reading" of her field experience'.

According to Foley, Stewart's narrative style takes a different tack in moving between local dialect and high theory as a 'surreal space of intensification' to break the 'you are there' documentary style of realist ethnographies and the authority of the field that such studies carry. Rather than presenting herself as 'the one who knows', based on fieldwork, her sense of narrative task is to 'evoke the aporia' of her fieldwork (Foley, in press: 16). What Foley terms 'a dazzling carnival of postmodern cultural critics' are brought to bear to make meaning of the local talk Stewart hears. This 'montage' in 'two distinct registers' presents the narrative self-representations of those she has studied as a kind of poetics of everyday life. Foley articulates Stewart's deconstructive practices as much about the indeterminate play of signifiers where 'you can't get it right' and 'It's just talk. It don't mean nothin' at all.' Undermining the knowledge she has worked so hard to create, Stewart both 'downplays/ disavows her own theorizing efforts' and presents a '"deep reading" of folk narrativization'.

In summarizing his efforts to delineate the characteristics of postmodern reflexivity, Foley makes the important point that textual experimentation will not be 'the silver bullet that slays the dragon of misrepresentation'. Misrepresentation is part of telling stories about people's lives, our own included.[26] His larger argument is that the realist tale has its place, particularly in work that intends to

find an audience beyond the academy. Urging that we 'continue to work through familiar narrative forms and everyday language', Foley endorses the new ethnographic practices of reflexive experimentation as long as they 'enhance rather than dilute the practical, political intent of critical ethnography'.

Foley is more confident than I in finding our way into a shared clarity. My interest is more in getting us all lost: reader, writer, written about (Lather, 1996). Somewhere outside easy reading of the spectacle of the displayed reflexive self, my interest is in de-authorizing devices within a recognition of a necessary complicity. *Troubling the Angels* (Lather and Smithies, 1997), for example, uses shifting counter-voices and subtextual under-writing which ruptures the narrative and forces reading in two directions; dialogic openness and variability of meaning that undercut the authors as 'the ones who know'; partiality, chunkiness and deferral rather than depiction to signal that representation is irreducible to the terms of the real; and a refusal of closure that works against ending on the sort of recuperative note typical of 'the religious left' (Gilbert-Rolfe, 1995: 56). Getting both in and out of the way of participants' stories, such textual moves can be situated within and against the historical and normative status of the 'new' ethnography where the aim is not so much more adequate representation as a troubling of authority in the telling of other people's stories. Actively searching for ways to overcome the aporias marked by the loss of innocence of ethnography and the crisis of representation, such efforts work the ruins of ethnography as the very ground from which new practices of ethnographic representation might take shape.[27]

Interested in the tensions of 'holding back analytically' in the midst of efforts to make some interpretative sense, I am looking for places where things begin to shift via practices that exceed the warrants of our present sense of the possible. Rather than a priori templates, my interest is in a disciplining space of returns and reversals, knowings and not-knowings, slippages from and dispersals of the Marxist dream of 'cure, salvation, and redemption' (Felman and Laub, 1992: 177). Deepened in encounter with such complicating of testimony as Blanchot's *The Writing of the Disaster* (1986), Felman and Laub's *Testimony* (1992) and Nobel Peace Prize winner Rigoberta Menchú's *I, Rigoberta Menchú: An Indian Woman in Guatemala* (1984), the danger is to 'risk ethically violating the testimony of the other by subsuming her body or her sentiment to the reductive frames' of our interpretative moves (Mehuron, 1997: 176). Given such complicities, as Derrida notes, the 'authentic' witness is necessarily a 'false' witness, caught in aporias, where to succeed is to fail in making the other part of us. To leave the other alone outside our efforts to master through reading and writing and knowing: this is what it means to tell the story of others in a way that takes testimony seriously enough not to tame its interruptive force into a philosophy of presence and a romance of the speaking subject (Derrida, 1976).

Such a doubled sense of the responsibilities of interpretation requires a shift toward a reflexivity marked by limits as well as possibilities. While Foley sees reflexivity as the very mark of postmodernism on ethnography, it is as much about modernist assumptions of consciousness, intentionality and cure.[28] Visweswaran, for example, distinguishes between interpretative/reflexive and deconstructive ethnography. Reflexive ethnography authorizes itself by confronting its own processes of interpretation as some sort of cure toward better knowing, while deconstruction approaches 'knowing through not knowing' (1994: 80).[29] In delineating reflexivity under erasure, Felman's distinctions between Hegelian, Nietzschean and Freudian philosophies of knowledge are useful. The former *believes it knows all there is to know;* a post-Nietzschean philosophy of knowledge is that 'which *believes it knows it does not know,'* and Freudian is that where authority is given 'to the instruction of a knowledge that does not know its own meaning, to a knowledge ... that is not a mastery of itself' (Felman, 1987: 92; emphasis in original). We often do not know what we are seeing, how much we are missing, what we are not understanding or even how to locate those lacks. This is an effort to trouble the sort of reflexive confession that becomes a narcissistic wound that will not heal and that eats up the world by monumentalizing loss. My interest is, rather, in Derrida's ethos of lack when lack becomes an enabling condition, a limit used (Butler, 1993). Here we cannot fail to note fatal contingencies, deceitful language, the self-deceptions of a consciousness that does not know what it acts towards, the experience of consciousness at its limits. What I am endorsing is work that attests to the possibilities of its time yet, in the very telling, registers the limits of itself as a vehicle for claiming truth in a way that is an 'opening of a relation to the future' (Derrida, 1996: 72). Such a practice is a topology for new tasks toward other places of thinking and putting to work, innovations leading to new forms, negotiation with enabling violence attentive to frame narratives that work within and against the terrain of controllable knowledge (Spivak, 1993).

Conclusion: The Angel to Philosophy of Science

At the conference, the range of presentations was broad ... An interesting phenomenon was the fact that South Africans during the times of isolation had developed their own angel [*sic*] to philosophy of science.

(Newsletter, Centre for Qualitative Research, Psychology Institute, University of Aarhus, Denmark, October, 1995: 4)[30]

When I read the above, I was much taken with the misprint that resulted in the 'angel to philosophy of science'. Somewhat obsessed with angels myself, as a means to trouble familiar categories and logics (Lather, 1997), I end with a meditation on what an 'angel [angle] to philosophy of science' might be made to mean. I do so within the context of all that is involved in examining (post-) ethnography as 'not something that can be set "straight" but it has to be tracked through its moves and versions, its permeabilities and vulnerabilities, its nervous shifts from one thing to another, its moments of self-possession and dispersal' (Stewart, 1996: 9).

Walter Benjamin's 'Theses on the Philosophy of History' is no easy read. Struggling with his backward-facing angel of history suggests what a non-teleological history might look like, a history thought against the consolations of certain meaning and knowing and toward the thought of the limit as a way to make a future. Benjamin's angel of history is a way of both negotiating a relationship to loss and, through its very dangers, steering away from the melodrama and/or easy sentiment attendant upon either a romance of the sublime or a metaphysics of presence. Enacting how language cannot NOT mean and how it leads to identification, subjectivization and narrative, the angel can be used not to recuperate for a familiar model, but to deconstructively stage the angel as a palimpsest, a failure at containing meaning, a means to empty out narrative in advance and make it generate itself over its impossibility.

Ethnography, too, is a much written-on and about palimpsest that has moved from the consolations of mastery to a sort of self-abjection at the limit as a way to live on in the face of the loss of the legitimating metanarratives of science. A failure at containing meaning, it travels across disciplinary sites, generating itself out of its own impossibility, a hybrid sort of monster that evokes the anxieties that follow the collapse of foundations. Always already swept up by language games that constantly undo themselves, we are all a little lost in finding our way toward ethnographic practices that open to the irreducible heterogeneity of the other in the pursuit of a science that tells better stories about itself. This is a science that has 'grown up' in relation to the withering critiques of realism, universalism and individualism that take us into this new millennium, a less comfortable science appropriate to a post-foundational era characterized by the loss of certainties and absolute frames of reference (Borgmann, 1992; Fine, 1986).

In such a space, I think of ethnography under conditions of postmodernity as a kind of local action developed in the face of our unbearable historicity. An unauthorized protocol, it is a sort of stammering relation to its object that exceeds the subjectivity and identity of all concerned. Positioned within the incomplete rupture with philosophies of the subject and consciousness that undergird the continued dream of doing history's work, such an ethnography marks the limit of the saturated humanist logics of knowledge as cure within a philosophy of consciousness that determines the protocols through which we know (Melville, 1986). Here, caught in enabling aporias, we move toward ethnographic practices that are responsible to what is arising out of both becoming and passing away.

NOTES

1 Sacks, for example, speaks of anthropology/ethnography as 'busily eating its own tail' (1995: 103). Geertz (1988) speaks of a 'diary disease'. See also Nash, 1997; Wolf, 1992. Stewart (1996) catalogues critiques from post-colonial and feminist perspectives to correctives from 'invented traditions and imagined communities' and discourse-centered, performance theory and dialogic, reflexive and deconstructive approaches. See notes 6–11 of her first chapter. For post writing culture debates, see James et al., 1997.

2 To scandalous effect might be better said, although this is not as odd a group of background texts for a feminist to draw on as might at first be supposed. For feminist work on Nietzsche, see Burgard, 1994; Oliver, 1995; Oliver and Pearsall, 1998; Patton, 1993. For Derrida, see Cornell, 1991; Feder et al., 1997; Holland, 1997; Spivak, 1993. For Benjamin, see Buck-Morss, 1989; Buci-Glucksmann, 1994; McRobbie, 1994; Wolff, 1995.

3 Long (1997), for example, tracks the travels of ethnography from Chicago School sociology to cultural studies.

4 Poreia means path; aporia means impassable passage (Caputo, 1997b: 14, 38). This concept will be further developed later in the chapter.

5 Stewart (1996) is writing about the social imaginary of the Appalachian community that is the site of her ethnography.

6 I use the terms post-structural, postmodern and, sometimes, even deconstruction interchangeably as the code name for the crisis of confidence in Western conceptual systems. Postmodern generally refers to the material and historical shifts of the global uprising of the marginalized, the revolution in communication technology, and the fissures of global multinational hyper-capitalism. Post-structuralism refers more narrowly to a sense of the limits of Enlightenment rationality, particularly the limits of consciousness and intentionality and the will to power

inscribed in sense-making efforts which aspire to universal, totalizing explanatory frameworks. Deconstruction is both a method to interrupt binary logic through practices of reversal and displacement, and an anti-method that is more an ontological claim. Deconstruction 'happens', Derrida says, as an outcome of the way language undoes itself (Derrida, in Caputo, 1997a: 9). More elaborated definitional fields pertinent to the social sciences are offered in Dickens and Fontana, 1994; Haraway, 1997; Hollinger, 1994; Kreiswirth and Carmichael, 1995; Lather, 1991; Scheurich, 1997; Scott and Usher, 1996; and, less usefully, Roseneau, 1992.

7 See Morley, 1997 for a tracing of the roots of critical ethnography in audience response studies and the question of experience.

8 A recent example is McLaren, 1998. While McLaren's focus is critical pedagogy, his call for a more 'vigorous' Marxism as the antidote to the political impotence of postmodernism parallels the concerns in relation to critical ethnography.

9 For this amassing critique, in addition to Fekete, see Brown, 1993, 1995; Butler, 1993; Caputo, 1993; Spanos, 1993. Political theorist Wendy Brown (1993), for example, uses Nietzsche's concept of *ressentiment* to trouble the limits of oppositional political formations and identity politics.

10 Refusing such a move is tempting in the face of the much that must be rethought: resistance and agency (Pitt, 1998); certainty, praxis, morality and meaning (Leach et al., 1998; Levinson, 1995); the unconscious (Britzman, 1998); empowerment (Orner, 1992); rationalism and dialogue (Ellsworth, 1989; Leach, 1992); empathy, voice and authenticity (Lather, 1998b).

11 This paragraph grows out of conversations and correspondence with Dennis Beach at the University of Goteborg, Sweden, and his unpublished paper, 'Resisting (some) postmodernism with/in critical ethnography of education'.

12 In earlier writing on pedagogy, I delineated postcritical as that which 'foregrounds movement beyond the sedimented discursive configurations of essentialized, romanticized subjects with authentic needs and real identities, who require generalized emancipation from generalized social oppression via the mediations of liberatory pedagogues capable of exposing the "real" to those caught up in the distorting meaning systems of late capitalism. Within (post)critical practices of pedagogy, emancipatory space is problematized via deconstruction of the Enlightenment equation of knowing, naming and emancipation. Especially placed under suspicion are the philosophies of presence, which assume the historical role of self-conscious human agency and the vanguard role of critical intellectuals [via] crusading rhetoric [stuck in a framework that] sees the "other" as the problem for which they are the solution ... [This] may have more to do with the end of some speaking for others than the end of liberatory struggle' (Lather, 1992: 131–2).

13 Caputo elaborates that, in positing a shift from Kuhn to something more messianic, Derrida writes not about a

paradigm shift in understanding but about 'a more Jewish ... ethico-political' grasp of difference that 'shatters understanding, that underlines the saliency of the incomprehensible, something we confess we do not understand'. This is not a new way of seeing but, rather, 'a blindness, a confession that we are up against something ... to which we can only bear witness' (1997b: 74).

14 In *Politics of Friendship*, Derrida writes of the necessity of 'the deliberate perversion of the heritage' so that 'opposites slide into each other' (1997: 61, 64, 80).

15 Stanley Aronowitz defines scientificity as not so much the actual practices of science as 'the permeation of the standard elements of the scientific attitude into all corners of the social world: seeing is believing; the appeal to "hard facts" such as statistical outcomes to settle arguments; the ineluctable faith in the elements of syllogistic reasoning' (1995: 12).

16 Thanks to Deborah Britzman for introducing me to this book.

17 I take this from Marian Hobson's 1998 book on Derrida where she speaks of 'the new new' and George Marcus (1994) who writes of 'the post-post.' It also comes from my growing discomfort with the idea of the 'new' ethnography that has been talked about now since the mid-1980s. This reminds me of the 'new scholarship on women' that was talked about for some twenty years (e.g. Howe, 1981; McIntosh, 1983).

18 Other critiques of the conventions of ethnographic writing birthed by the 'new ethnography' with its interest in voice, discontinuity and situatedness include Britzman, 1998; Foley, 1998; Kirsch, 1997; Lather, 1998b.

19 See also Gordon, 1995; Kondo, 1990; St Pierre, 1997a, 1997b, 1999).

20 Derridean 'play' is like the 'play' in a machine, to move 'freely' within limits that are both cause and effect. For a textual enactment, see Richardson, 1997.

21 *The Education of Little Tree*, selling over 500,000 copies, is used in myriad multicultural courses as 'authentic autobiography'. Its author, 'Forrest Carter', presenting himself as a Cherokee story-teller, was found to be Asa Earl Carter, a Ku Klux Klan sympathizer who wrote segregation speeches for governor George Wallace (see Carter, 1991). Johnston (1997) writes of how an Alberta Canada high school reading list shifted the book from 'autobiography' to 'fiction' in order to keep it in the multicultural curriculum.

22 Francisco Ibanez-Carrasco, 'Qualitative research on AIDS in the social sciences and humanities: a critical view of researchers and research practices under catastrophic circumstances'. Unpublished dissertation, Simon Fraser University, Canada.

23 As delineated by Gayatri Spivak (1976) in her introduction to Derrida's *Of Grammatology*, to work 'under erasure' characterizes the 'doubled' movement of deconstruction: to both use and trouble a concept at the same time. This move of 'within/against' is well captured in Barnett, 1998 in terms of the respect involved, a sense of how what one critiques enables the critique, in this case Hegel after Derrida.

24 Marcus posits three forms of reflexivity in contemporary ethnography: confessional, as practiced by many feminist and native ethnographers; intertextual, where much attention is paid to how disciplinary discourses produce the 'truth' of their object; and theoretical, where basic analytic concepts are troubled in the face of everyday practice.

25 Michelle Fine and Lois Weiss' *The Unknown City* (Boston, MA: Beacon Press, 1998) explores race, class and gender in the lives of the young adult urban poor. Relatively unedited segments of interviews are intermixed with researcher interpretations and reflexive discussion of field relations, textual representation, and political commitment is minimal. Foley's own 1995 ethnography of Indian–White relations in his Iowa hometown is presented as combining post-Marxist concerns with hegemonic discursive regimes and what he terms 'postmodern reflexivity' about one's own practices of knowledge production. Using an autobiographical voice in order to create an accessible text, Foley foregrounds the self–other relationship and his own biases, culminating in an epilogue where those he researched respond to his (mis)representation of their lives. What marks both of these critical ethnographies is realist narration and what might be termed strategic romanticization (Schuman, 1997), the deliberate desire to present portraits of the subaltern that counter negative hegemonic stereotypes.

26 Evans (1999) captures this well in her title: *Missing Persons: The Impossibility of Autobiography*.

27 My thinking in this section is inspired by Malini Johar Schueller's 1992 critique of James Agee's *Let Us Now Praise Famous Men* where she situates Agee as paternalistic and liberal in his idealization of those whose stories he tells but, nevertheless, opening up a space for subverting narrow and consensual definitions of the tenant farmers who people his book.

28 And, as Nash (1997: 18), notes, the first calls for reflexivity in anthropology came in the mid-1960s well before postmodernism appeared on the disciplinary scene.

29 Ironically, deconstructive ethnography courts a situation of being on the whole too convinced of success as an ambivalent failure in a way that recuperates a sense of mastery through the very defense of risky failures.

30 From report on 14th International Human Science Research Conference, Midrand, South Africa 21–25 August 1995, written by Ingunn Hagen, Dan Yngve Jacobsen and Birthe Loa Knizek.

REFERENCES

Albanese, Denise (1996) *New Science, New World*. Durham, NC: Duke University Press.

Aronowitz, Stanley (1995) 'Bringing science and scientificity down to earth', *Cultural Studies Times*, 1 (3): 12, 14.

Barnett, Stuart (ed.) (1998) *Hegel after Derrida*. London: Routledge.

Behar, Ruth (1993) *Translated Woman*. Boston, MA: Beacon.

Behar, Ruth (1996) *The Vulnerable Observer: Anthropology that Breaks the Heart*. Boston, MA: Beacon Press.

Behar, Ruth and Gordon, Deborah (eds) (1995) *Women Writing Culture*. Berkeley, CA: University of California Press.

Benjamin, Walter ([1940] 1968) 'Theses on the philosophy of history', in *Illuminations* (ed. Hannah Arendt). New York: Schocken Books. pp. 253–64.

Benjamin, Walter (1977) *The Origin of German Tragic Drama* (trans. John Osborne). London: Verso.

Blanchot, Maurice (1986) *The Writing of the Disaster* (trans. Ann Smock). Lincoln, NB: University of Nebraska Press.

Borgmann, Albert (1992) *Crossing the Postmodern Divide*. Chicago: University of Chicago Press.

Britzman, Deborah (1997) 'The tangles of implication', *Qualitative Studies in Education*, 10 (1): 31–7.

Britzman, Deborah (1998) *Lost Subjects, Contested Objects: Toward a Psychoanalytic Theory of Learning*. Albany, NY: State University of New York.

Brown, Wendy (1993) 'Wounded attachments: late modern oppositional political formations', *Political Theory*, 390–410.

Brown, Wendy (1995) *States of Injury: Power and Freedom in Late Modernity*. Princeton, NJ: Princeton University Press.

Buck-Morss, Susan (1989) *The Dialectics of Seeing: Walter Benjamin and the Arcades Project*. Cambridge, MA: MIT Press.

Buci-Glucksmann, Christine (1994) *Baroque Reason: The Aesthetics of Modernity*. London: Sage.

Burgard, Peter (ed.) (1994) *Nietzsche and the Feminine*. Charlottesville, VA: University of Virginia Press.

Butler, Judith (1993) 'Poststructuralism and postmarxism', *Diacritics*, 23 (4): 3–11.

Butler, Judith (1995) 'For a careful reading', in S. Benhabib, J. Butler, D. Cornell and N. Fraser, *Feminist Contradictions: A Philosophical Exchange*. New York: Routledge. pp. 127–44.

Caputo, John (1993) 'On not circumventing the quasi-transcendental: the case of Rorty and Derrida', in Gary Madison (ed.), *Working through Derrida*. Evanston, IL: Northwestern University Press. pp. 147–69.

Caputo, John (ed.) (1997a) *Deconstruction in a Nutshell: A Conversation with Jacques Derrida*. New York: Fordham University Press.

Caputo, John (1997b) *The Prayers and Tears of Jacques Derrida: Religion without Religion*. Bloomington, IN: Indiana University Press.

Carter, Dan (1991) 'The transformation of a Klansman', *The New York Times*, 4 October, p. A31.

de Certeau, Michel (1984) *The Practice of Everyday Life*. Berkeley, CA: University of California Press.

Clastres, Pierre (1998) *Chronicle of the Guayaki Indians* (trans. Paul Auster). New York: Zone Books.

Clifford, James (1983) 'On ethnographic authority', *Representations*, 1 (2): 118–46.

Clifford, James (1997) *Routes: Travel and Translation in the Late Twentieth Century*. Cambridge, MA: Harvard University Press.

Cornell, Drucilla (1991) *Beyond Accommodation: Ethical Feminism, Deconstruction, and the Law*. New York: Routledge.

Derrida, Jacques (1976) *On Grammatology* (trans. Gayatri Spivak). Baltimore, MD: Johns Hopkins University Press.

Derrida, Jacques (1978) 'Strucuture, sign and play in the discourse of the human sciences', in *Writing and Difference*. Chicago: University of Chicago Press. pp. 278–93.

Derrida, Jacques (1994) *Specters of Marx* (trans. Peggy Kamuf). New York: Routledge.

Derrida, Jacques (1996) *Archive Fever: A Freudian Impression* (trans. Eric Prenowitz). Chicago: University of Chicago Press.

Derrida, Jacques (1997) *The Politics of Friendship* (trans. George Collins). London: Verso.

Dickens, David and Fontana, Andrea (eds) (1994) *Postmodernism and Social Inquiry*. New York: Guilford.

Dirks, Nicholas, Eley, Geoff and Ortner, Sherry (1994) 'Introduction', *Culture/Power/History: A Contemporary Reader in Social Theory*. Princeton, NJ: Princeton University Press. pp. 3–45.

Ebert, Teresa (1991) 'Political semiosis in/or American cultural studies', *American Journal of Semiotics*, 8: 113–35.

Ellsworth, Elizabeth (1989) 'Why doesn't this feel empowering? Working through the repressive myths of critical pedagogy', *Harvard Educational Review*, 59 (3): 297–324.

Ellsworth, Elizabeth (1997) *Teaching Positions*. New York: Teachers College Press.

Evans, Mary (1999) *Missing Persons: The Impossibility of Autobiography*. New York: Routledge.

Feder, Ellen, Rawlinson, Mary and Zakin, Emily (1997) *Derrida and Feminism: Recasting the Question of Woman*. New York: Routledge.

Fekete, John (1992) 'Postmodernism and cultural studies'. Paper presented at the Theory Culture Society conference, Pennsylvania, August.

Felman, Shoshona (1987) *Jacques Lacan and the Adventure of Insight: Psychoanalysis in Contemporary Culture*. Cambridge, MA: Harvard University Press.

Felman, Shoshona and Laub, Dori (1992) *Testimony: Crises of Witnessing Literature, Psychoanalysis, and History*. New York: Routledge.

Fine, Arthur (1986) *The Shaky Game: Einstein, Realism and the Quantum Theory*. Chicago: University of Chicago Press.

Foley, Doug (1995) *The Heartland Chronicles*. Pennsylvania: University of Pennsylvania Press.

Foley, Doug (1998) 'On writing reflexive realist narratives', in Jeffry Shacklock and John Smyth (eds), *Being Reflexive in Critical Educational and Social Research*. London: Falmer Press. pp. 110–29.

Foley, Doug (in press) Critical ethnography in the postmodern moment. In H. Trueba and Y. Zou (eds), *Advances in ethnographic research: From its theoretical and anthropological roots to postmodern critical ethnography*. New York: Roman and Littlefield.

Foucault, Michel (1998) *Aesthetics, Method, and Epistemology* (ed. James D. Faubion). New York: The New Press.

Gates, Henry Louis (1991) '"Authenticity", or the lesson of Little Tree', *New York Times Book Review*, 24 November, pp. 1–4.

Geertz, Clifford (1980) 'Blurred genres', *The American Scholar*, 49: 165–79.

Geertz, Clifford (1988) *Works and Lives: The Anthropologist as Author*. Stanford, CA: Stanford University Press.

Gilbert-Rolfe, Jeremy (1995) *Beyond Piety: Critical Essays on the Visual Arts, 1986–1993*. Cambridge: Cambridge University Press.

Gordon, Deborah (1995) 'Border work: feminist ethnography and the dissemination of literacy', in R. Behar and D. Gordon (eds), *Women Writing Culture*. Berkeley, CA: University of California Press. pp. 373–89.

Greene, Maxine (1994) 'Epistemology and educational research: the influence of recent approaches to knowledge', in Linda Darling-Hammond (ed.), *Review of Research in Education*, No. 20. Washington, DC: American Educational Research Association. pp. 423–64.

Haraway, Donna (1997) *Modest Witness@second Millennium: Feminism and Technoscience*. New York: Routledge.

Haver, William (1996) *This Body of My Death: AIDS and Historical Consciousness*. Stanford, CA: Stanford University Press.

Hekeman, Susan (1988) 'History, ethnography, myth: some notes on the "Indian-centered" narrative', *Social Text*, Fall/winter: 144–60.

Hobson, Marian (1998) *Jacques Derrida: Opening Lines*. London: Routledge.

Holland, Nancy (ed.) (1997) *Feminist Interpretations of Jacques Derrida*. University Park: Pennsylvania State University Press.

Hollinger, Robert (1994) *Postmodernism and the Social Sciences*. Thousand Oaks, CA: Sage.

Howe, Florence (1981) 'Feminist scholarship – the extent of the revolution', in *Liberal Education and the New Scholarship on Women*. A report of the Wingspread Conference, 22–24 October 1981. Washington, DC: Association of American Colleges. pp. 5–21.

James, Allison, Hockey, Jenny and Dawson, Andrew (eds) (1997) *After Writing Culture: Epistemology and Praxis in Contemporary Anthropology*. New York: Routledge.

Johnston, Ingrid (1997) 'Dilemmas of identity and ideology in cross-cultural literary engagements', *Canadian Ethnic Studies Journal*, XXIX (2): 97–107.

Kincheloe, Joe and McLaren, Peter (1994) 'Rethinking critical theory and qualitative research', in Norman K. Denzin and Yvonna S. Lincoln (eds), *The Handbook of Qualitative Research*. Thousand Oaks, CA: Sage. pp. 138–57.

Kirsch, Gesa (1997) 'Multi-vocal texts and interpretive responsibility', *College English*, 59 (2): 191–202.

Knauft, Bruce (1994) 'Pushing anthropology past the post: critical notes on cultural anthropology and cultural studies as influenced by postmodernism and existentialism', *Critique of Anthropology*, 14 (2): 117–52.

Kofman, Sarah (1988) 'Beyond aporia?', in Andrew Benjamin (ed.), *Post-structuralist Classics*. New York: Routledge. pp. 7–43.

Kondo, Dorrine (1990) *Crafting Selves: Power, Gender, and Discourses of Identity in a Japanese Workplace*. Chicago: University of Chicago Press.

Kreiswirth, Martin and Carmichael, Thomas (eds) (1995) *Constructive Criticism: The Human Sciences in the Age of Theory*. Toronto, ON: University of Toronto Press.

Lather, Patti (1991) *Getting Smart: Feminist Research and Pedagogy with/in the Postmodern*. New York: Routledge.

Lather, Patti (1992) 'Post-critical pedagogies: a feminist reading', in Carmen Luke and Jennifer Gore (eds), *Feminisms and Critical Pedagogy*. New York: Routledge. pp. 120–37.

Lather, Patti (1996) 'Troubling Clarity: The Politics of Accessible Language', *Harvard Educational Review*, 66 (3): 525–45.

Lather, Patti (1997) 'Drawing the line at angels: working the ruins of feminist ethnography', *Qualitative Studies in Education*, 10 (3): 285–304.

Lather, Patti (1998a) 'Critical pedagogy and its complicities', *Educational Theory*, 48 (4): 487–97.

Lather, Patti (1998b) 'Against empathy, voice and authenticity'. Paper presented at the annual conference of the American Educational Research Association, San Diego, April.

Lather, Patti and Smithies, Chris (1997) *Troubling the Angels: Women Living With HIV/AIDS*. Boulder, CO: Westview Press.

Leach, Mary (1992) 'Can we talk? A response to Burbules and Rice', *Harvard Educational Review*, 62 (2): 257–71.

Leach, Mary (1993) 'The problematics of "authenticity"'. Paper presented at American Educational Studies Association, Houston.

Leach, Mary, Lather, Patti, McCoy, Kate and Pillow, Wanda (1998) 'Mourning Marxism? Philosophical explorations in feminism, poststructuralism, and education'. Symposium presented at the annual meeting of the American Educational Research Association, San Diego, April.

Levinson, Bradley, Foley, Doug and Holland, Dorothy (eds) (1996) *The Cultural Production of the Educated Person: Critical Ethnogaphies of Schooling and Local Practice*. Albany, NY: State University of New York Press.

Levinson, Marjori (1995) 'Pre- and post-dialectical materialisms: modeling praxis without subjects and objects', *Cultural Critique*, Fall: 111–27.

Long, Elizabeth (1997) *From Sociology to Cultural Studies*. Oxford: Blackwell.

Lyotard, Jean François (1984) *The Postmodern Condition*. Minneapolis, MN: University of Minnesota Press.

Marcus, George (1994) 'What comes (just) after "post"? The case of ethnography', in Norman K. Denzin and Yvonna S. Lincoln (eds), *The Handbook of Qualitative Research*. Thousand Oaks, CA: Sage. pp. 563–74.

Marcus, George (1997) 'Critical cultural studies as one power/knowledge like, among, and in engagement with others', in Elizabeth Long (ed.), *From Sociology to Cultural Studies*. Oxford: Blackwell. pp. 399–425.

Marcus, George and Fischer, Richard (1986) 'A crisis of representation in the human sciences', in *Anthropology as Cultural Critique: An Experimental Moment in the Human Sciences*. Chicago: University of Chicago Press. Ch. 1.

McCoy, Kate (1998) 'Drug research and the politics of knowing and being known'. Paper presented at the 2nd Harm Reduction Conference, Cleveland, October.

McGee, Patrick (1992) *Telling the Other: The Question of Value in Modern and Postcolonial Writing*. Ithaca, NY: Cornell University Press.

McIntosh, Peggy (1983) 'Transforming the liberal arts curriculum through inclusion of the new scholarship on women: directory of projects', *Women's Studies Quarterly*, 11 (2): 23–9.

McLaren, Peter (1998) 'Revolutionary pedagogy in post-revolutionary times: rethinking the political economy of critical education. *Educational Theory*, 48 (4): 431–62.

McRobbie, Angela (1994) 'The *Passagenwerk* and the place of Walter Benjamin in cultural studies', in *Postmodernism and Popular Culture*. London: Routledge. pp. 96–120.

Mehan, Hugh (1995) 'CAE 1994 Presidential Address: Resisting the politics of despair', *Anthropology and Education Quarterly*, 26: 239–50.

Mehuron, Kate (1997) 'Sentiment recaptured: the performative in women's AIDS-related testimonies', in Nancy Holland (ed.), *Feminist Interpretations of Jacques Derrida*. University Park, PA: Pennsylvania. State University Press. pp. 165–92.

Melville, Steven (1986) *Philosophy Beside Itself: On Deconstruction and Modernism*. Minneapolis, MN: University of Minnesota Press.

Menchú, Rigoberta (1984) *I Rigoberta Menchú: An Indian Woman in Guatemala*. London: Verso.

Morley, David (1997) 'Theoretical orthodoxies: textualism, constructivism and the "new ethnography"', in M. Ferguson and P. Golding (eds), *Cultural Studies in Question*. London: Sage. pp. 121–37.

Nagele, Rainer (1991) *Theatre, Theory, Speculation: Walter Benjamin and the Scenes of Modernity*. Baltimore, MD: Johns Hopkins University Press.

Nash, June (1997) 'When isms become wasms: structural functionalism, Marxism, feminism and postmodernism', *Critique of Anthropology*, 17 (1): 11–32.

Oliver, Kelly (1995) *Womanizing Nietzsche*. New York: Routledge.

Oliver, Kelly and Pearsall, Marilyn (eds) (1998) *Feminist Interpretations of Friedrich Nietzsche*. University Park, PA: Pennsylvania State University Press.

Orner, Mimi (1992) 'Interrupting the call for student voice in "liberatory" education: a feminist poststructural perspective', in C. Luke and J. Gore (eds), *Feminisms and Critical Pedagogy*. New York: Routledge. pp. 74–89.

Patton, Paul (ed.) (1993) *Nietzsche, Feminism and Political Theory*. London: Allen and Unwin.

Pillow, Wanda (1996) 'Embodied analysis: *un*thinking teen pregnancy'. Paper presented at the annual conference of the American Educational Research Association, New York City, April.

Pitt, Alice (1998) 'Qualifying resistance: some comments on methodological dilemmas', *Journal of Qualitative Studies in Education*, 11 (4): 535–53.

Prado, C.G. (1995) *Starting with Foucault: An Introduction to Genealogy*. Boulder, CO: Westview Press.

Quantz, Richard (1992) 'On critical ethnography (with some postmodern considerations)', in Margaret D. LeCompte, Wendy Millroy and Judith Preissle Goetz (eds), *The Handbook of Qualitative Research in Education*. San Diego, CA: Academic Press. pp. 447–506.

Quinby, Lee (1991) *Freedom, Foucault, and the Subject of America*. Boston, MA: Northeastern University Press.

Rabinowitz, Paula (1992) 'Voyeurism and class consciousness: James Agee and Walker Evans, *Let Us Now Praise Famous Men*', *Cultural Critique*, No. 21: 143–70.

Richardson, Laurel (1994) 'Writing: a method of inquiry', in Norman K. Denzin and Yvonna S. Lincoln (eds), *The Handbook of Qualitative Research*. Thousand Oaks, CA: Sage. pp. 516–29.

Richardson, Laurel (1997) *Fields of Play: On Writing an Academic Life*. Brunswick, NJ: Rutgers University Press.

Robinson, Jill (1994) 'White woman researching/representing "others": from antiapartheid to postcolonialism?', in Ann Blunt and Gillian Rose (eds), *Writing Women and Space*. New York: Guilford. pp. 197–226.

Rochlitz, Rainer (1996) *The Disenchantment of Art: The Philosophy of Walter Benjamin*. New York: Guilford.

Rosenau, Pauline (1992) *Post-Modernism and the Social Sciences: Insights, Inroads and Intrusions*. Princeton, NJ: Princeton University Press.

Sacks, Karen (1995) 'Response to Anna Grimshaw and Keith Hart's "Anthropology and the crisis of the intellectuals"', *Critique of Anthropology*, 15 (1): 103–5.

Said, Edward (1989) 'Representing the colonized: anthropology's interlocutors', *Critical Inquiry*, 15: 205–25.

St Pierre, Elizabeth A. (1997a) 'Circling the text: nomadic writing practices', *Qualitative Inquiry*, 10 (3): 403–17.

St Pierre, Elizabeth A. (1997b) 'Methodology in the fold and the irruption of transgressive data', *Journal of Qualitative Studies in Education*, 10 (2): 175–89.

St Pierre, Elizabeth Adams (1999) 'The work of response in ethnography', *Journal of Contemporary Ethnography*, 28 (3): 266–87.

Scheurich, James (1997) *Postmodern Methodology*. London: Falmer.

Schuman, Amy (1997) 'Feminist ethnography and the rhetoric of accomodation'. Paper presented at the

Feminism(s) and Rhetoric(s) Conference, Corvallis, Oregon, August.

Schueller, Malini Johar (1992) *The Politics of Voice: Liberalism and Social Criticism from Franklin to Kingston*. Albany, NY: State University of New York.

Scott, Charles (1996) *On the Advantages and Disadvantages of Ethics and Politics*. Bloomington, IN: Indiana University Press.

Scott, David and Usher, Robin (eds) (1996) *Understanding Educational Research*. London: Routledge.

Scott, Joan (1992) 'Experience', in Joan Scott and Judith Butler (eds), *Feminists Theorize the Political*. London: Routledge. pp. 22–40.

Serres, Michel ([1993] 1995) *Angels: A Modern Myth* (trans. F. Cowper). Paris: Flammarion.

Slemon, Steven (1990) 'Modernisms' last post', in *Past the Last Post: Theorizing Post-colonialism and Post-modernism*. Calgary: University of Calgary Press. pp. 1–12.

Spanos, William (1993) *The End of Education: Toward Posthumanism*. Minneapolis, MN: University of Minnesota Press.

Spivak, Gayatri (1976) Translator's preface to Jacques Derrida, *Of Grammatology*. Baltimore, MD: Johns Hopkins University Press. pp. ix–xc.

Spivak, Gayatri (1988) 'Can the subaltern speak?', in Cary Nelson and L. Grossberg (eds), *Marxism and the Interpretation of Culture*. Urbana, IL: University of Illinois Press. pp. 271–313.

Spivak, Gayatri (1993) 'Responsibility', *Boundary 2*, 21 (3): 19–64.

Stewart, Kathleen (1996) *A Space on the Side of the Road: Cultural Poetics in an 'Other' America*. Princeton, NJ: Princeton University Press.

Thomas, Jim (1993) *Doing Critical Ethnography*. Newbury Park, CA: Sage.

Tomlinson, Hugh (1989) '"After truth": post-modernism and the rhetoric of science', in Hilary Lawson and L. Appignanesi (eds), *Dismantling Truth: Reality in a Post-modern World*. New York: St Martin's Press. pp. 43–57.

Tuhiwai Smith, Linda (1999) *De-Colonizing Methodology: Research and Indigenous Peoples*. London: Zed Books.

Tyson, Cynthia (1998) 'A response to "Coloring Epistemologies: are our qualitative research epistemologies racially biased?"', *Educational Researcher*, 27 (9): 21–2.

Van Maanen, John (1988) *Tales of the Field: On Writing Ethnography*. Chicago: University of Chicago Press.

Van Maanen, John (1995) 'An end to innocence: the ethnography of ethnography', in J. Van Maanen (ed.), *Representation in Ethnography*. Thousand Oaks, CA: Sage. pp. 1–35.

Visweswaran, Kamala (1994) *Fictions of Feminist Ethnography*. Minneapolis, MN: University of Minnesota Press.

Visweswaran, Kamala (1997) 'Histories of feminist ethnography', *Annual Review of Anthropology*, 26: 591–621.

Wolf, Margery (1992) *A Thrice-Told Tale*. Stanford, CA: Stanford University Press.

Wolff, Janet (1995) *Resident Alien*. New Haven, CT: Yale University Press.

Index